Wings over Wiltshire

Alistair
Lofthouse
DESIGN
&
PRINT

Rod Priddle

This book is dedicated to
Ossie Priddle dfc

Copyright © 2003

First published in Great Britain by
ALD Design & Print
(0114) 267 9402

ISBN 1-901-587-34-7

Also by Rod Priddle

GWR to Devizes (with D. Hyde)
Wings of the Brave
Bombers' Moon
On a Wing and a Prayer
One Step to Heaven
Flying without Wings
Shades of Blue

Front cover: *Early Morning Arrival* a painting by renowned aviation artist Robert Taylor, is reproduced by kind permission of the Military Gallery, Bath. The scene is of Lancaster KB726 VR-A, No.419 (Moose) Sqn RCAF, making a landing approach to Colerne on the morning of 6th June 1944. Following an operation, it was diverted there due to bad weather at its Middleton St. George base. The crew included mid-upper gunner Plt Off Andrew Mynarski, who on 12th June 1944 lost his life on operations when the aircraft was shot down. For his bravery in the lead-up to the crash he was posthumously awarded the Victoria Cross.

THE LAST RETURN

We last met when both were young,
A time of war but a time of fun.
You I remember oh so well,
I, one of many, scared and pale.
We joined together and became a team,
Afraid of the night and of tomorrow to dream.
Down your runways with the engine's roar,
Into the darkness and away to war.
Those who were lucky would return,
To that welcoming light and your arms so firm.

Your reason for being has now gone,
Nature has returned with a different song.
I came back to see you, my old friend,
Together with the shadows of those other men.
I came with concern, with sadness and fears,
For the last time I'm sure, in my fading years.
You'll excuse me I know for the mist in my eyes,
As I leave you to rest and cry my good-byes.

Rod Priddle

Contents

Acknowledgements

The support I have received in preparing this book has been immense. I have experienced nothing less than 100% co-operation, whether my approach has been to serving or former RAF personnel, from AC1s to ACMs, to those working for the military in a civilian capacity, to relatives of those who lost their lives serving in the forces, to fellow historians, museums and record offices. The contributions have come in the form of recognised historical detail, photographs, personal recollections, facts previously unpublished, advice and occasionally material felt unsuitable for repeating in these pages. To all I express my sincere appreciation and whilst there are some to whom I must record particular praise, the contribution by ever one has been of equal value in its own way.

In respect of Alton Barnes, I am indebted to David Carson for making available to me the farm correspondence which passed between the Air Ministry and his grandfather between 1935 and the outbreak of war, when part of the farm was requisitioned. Although the Carson family traditionally are associated with service in the Army, David is enthusiastic in his support for maintaining the village's historical links with the RAF.

Whilst my own research has been of benefit to local historical groups, the contribution they have made towards this book has been far greater. I thank therefore David & Annette Hitch of the Colerne History Group, Alan Thomsett and Ray Ward of The Keevil Society, Alan served with No.192 Sqn as a captain flying Wellingtons during World War 2, Danny Hicks of the Wroughton History Group and Peter Marshall of the Cricklade Historical Society. Peter has been instrumental in introducing me to contacts serving at Blakehill Farm during its operational years.

Much appreciation is expressed to those two men of Amesbury, Terry Heffernan M.R.Ae.S and Norman Parker, between them what they don't know about the history of flying in the Salisbury Plain area, is not worth knowing. Terry has written numerous features in flying magazines, and with Brian Johnson was co-author of *A Most Secret Place Boscombe Down 1939-45*. Many visits were made to the home of Norman Parker who kindly answered my many questions, spent hours proof reading 90% of the book and advised on improvements where necessary. Norman has first hand knowledge of a number of Wiltshire airfields having done his basic RAF recruit training at Yatesbury at the end of the war and subsequently worked as a fitter for Vickers at Colerne and High Post, and as an aircraft technician at Boscombe Down. On visits to Norman I was always amazed that what ever topic I discussed with him, he would delve into his archives and find additional material or photographs of the subject matter. Mrs Parker also keeps a marvellous assortment of biscuits.

No amount of words can express the debt I owe to Chris Green who, as a former RAF officer and pilot on Hastings based at Colerne and Lyneham, has fed me with material, opinion and advice, not only in respect of these stations but Boscombe Down and Upavon, where he also served. In addition, he has allowed me the benefit of his knowledge of military flying and military history in general. There have not been many weeks during the past four years since our first meeting, that we have not discussed some aspect relating to the book. Chris has accommodated all of my queries and patiently proof read the Upavon and long Colerne chapter.

I greatly appreciate the generous help and inspiration of my fellow Air Force historian and author, Martyn Ford-Jones of Swindon. He kindly introduced me to some of his own contacts who have experienced service in Wiltshire, aided me with facts and figures from his considerable reference library, accompanied me on visits to some of our wet and windy former airfields, and allowed me the use of photographs from his collection.

Netheravon airfield has a history stretching back to the earliest days of military flying in the county and continues in the hands of the Army Air Corps. RSM Kevin Spink No.7 Regiment Army Air Corps, who recently retired from the Corps and emigrated to Australia, thoroughly researched the history of the airfield during the time he served there. Prior to his retirement, he gave me a detailed tour of the site and very generously provided me with copies of his entire research material. To Kevin, I owe considerable gratitude.

To Ralph Godden, who served with the RAF at Netheravon in the early years of World War 2, I am also indebted, not only for giving me a detailed day by day account of what life and duties were like at the time, but also for the use of his photographs and for proof-reading another of the long chapters of the book.

Overton Heath was an airfield for which I found considerable difficulty in locating previously unpublished material. I did however receive 100% support from Martin Pitt, who was farming the site at the time of my research. He allowed me unrestricted access over several days, at which time I was able to photograph surviving structures. Albert Dean, who as a young man lived alongside the airfield during the war, I also thank for his recollections, for showing me where incidents occurred on the landing ground and for providing me with a list of the aircraft types he recorded there.

No.16 Sqn Association has been incredibly helpful. Frank Jewell, their eldest member, provided a wealth of detail relating to the years he served as ground staff with the RAF prior to World War 2, this covering a period when the squadron was based at Old Sarum. Jimmy Taylor, Secretary of the Association, added to this with factual details of some of the flying personnel.

Dr Hugh Thomas of Salisbury flooded me with photographs taken at Old Sarum, mainly during the years between the wars. So many in fact, it has been a problem deciding which to use in the book and which to leave out. Many of them relate to No.16 Sqn and the School of Army Co-operation. Another who supplied me with a valuable collection of photographs was Gordon Goodier. These were taken by his father who was a pilot at Netheravon with the RFC in 1918. Tony West in Vancouver, Canada was a further source of Netheravon and Stonehenge photographs from the same period. Again there were so many he made available to me, I was spoilt for choice. A further collection of interesting early Netheravon and Upavon photographs were loaned by Tony Mellor-Ellis. To all these good men, I thank you, and I am only sorry that the content of all of your collections can not be used.

Some to whom I owe thanks have regrettably died during recent years. Ann Welch OBE, the well known ATA pilot, who kindly extracted from her log book, every one of the flights she made to and from Wiltshire airfields. Des Blake, whom I visited on a number of occasions at his home near Salisbury, and who generously loaned me some of his RAF records. Des flew from Clyffe Pypard during World War 2, from Wroughton when during the late 1960s early1970s he was CO of the MU and then later from Boscombe Down, during his years as RAF Liaison Officer at Porton Down. Wg Cdr D.R. Collier Webb RAF - Directorate of Flying, Boscombe Down, who provided facts in respect of Boscombe Down aircraft accidents. Fellow Air Force historian and writer Don Neate of Devizes, and Eddie Brown from Malmesbury, both made significant contributions. Together the three of us spent many hours carrying out research in our respective subjects at the PRO in Kew. Eddie and his son Paul were instrumental in forming the Yatesbury Association which, despite the death of Eddie, has a developing membership and goes from strength to strength.

In landlocked Wiltshire, Royal Navy deployments were minimal but Clyffe Pypard was one of the locations where personnel of the *Andrew* were prominent. Ray Steel was one of these and I appreciate his input of detail for the senior service, of which I was not familiar.

My grateful thanks to historian and author Terry Crawford, who has continuously fed me material which he has come across when carrying out his own research into the military history of Salisbury Plain.

My family have had to endure long periods of my absence during the research and writing of this book over the past six years. For this I apologise and thank them for their considerable patience.

I wish to sincerely thank the publisher for having taken the decision to promote this historical account of military flying in Wiltshire.

Finally to all the others whose contributions are valued equally and with apologies to any who I may have overlooked:

A&AEE Boscombe Down
Barry Abraham Airfield Research Group
Air Historical Branch (RAF) MoD
Peter Amos Airfield Research Group
S, Anson
Kathleen Anstie
Jack Archer
Michael Armstrong
Chris Ashworth
Graham Aymes - Apsley Engineering
Katie Ball
Wilson Baird
Sqn Ldr Chris Bartell RAF
Bath & North East Somerset Archives and Records Officer
Sqn Ldr David Berry RAF
Harry Billett
Graham Birt
Adrian Bishop - Castle Combe & District Historical Society
Ken Border
Glenn Boulton
Des Bowles
Chaz Bowyer
Brian Bradfield - Science Museum, Wroughton
Bert Brothers
Dennis Brown
Paul Brown
Steve Brown
Jack Bruce
Lord Charles Brudenell-Bruce
Jean Buckbury RAF College Cranwell
George Buckland
Albert Bull
George Bullough
John Bulmer
Bundesarchiv-Militararchiv
Bob Burgess
Pat Burke
Major Bynes Canadian Forces Photographic Unit
Calne Town Council
Lord David Cardigan
Air Cdre David Bywater RAF
John Cackett
Graydon Carter
Bruce Chivers
Leonard Cheshire Archive Centre
Chrysalis Books
Bill Chorley
Peter Clark
Dave Clarke
Don Clarke
Eddie Clarke
Susan Cole
Wg Cdr Derek Collier Webb
Chris Collins
Commonwealth War Graves Commission
R.A. Cooke
Eric Coombs
G.H.F. Cousins
Bill Crosbie-Hill
Commander R.M. 'Mike' Crosley DSC*, RN
David Cunningham
John Dalley
Alf Daltry
Peter Daniels
The Rev Canon F.H. Davey

John Davey
Bob Davidge
Roger Day
Tony Day - PRO - DERA Boscombe Down
Ken Delve - *FlyPast*
Roderick De Normann
Flt Lt E. Denmark RAF
A.M. Dew
Andrew Deytrickh
Phil Diamond
Colin Dixon
Frank Druce
Peter Elliott RAF Museum
Ken Ellis - *FlyPast*
Jonathan Falconer
Derek Farr
Peter Fahy
Don Fennell
Jack Field - Curator, Warminster Museum
Fleet Air Arm Museum - Jerry Shore, Records & Research
Frank Foster
Roger A. Freeman
Harold Fudge
Craig Fuller Aviation Archaeological Investigation &
    Research
Jim Gatehouse
Roy Goddard
Cpl Neil Good - RAF Fire Section Upavon
Eddie Gordon
F.J. Gosling - Old Dauntseian
Lt Col Grant - Trenchard Lines - Upavon
A.J. Gray
Fred Gray - McAlpine Museum
Geoff Green
James J. Halley MBE - Air-Britain
Haycombe Crematorium, Bath-Reg Greenall, Mike Ryall,
    Lorraine Horton, Rosemary Tiley, Maureen Hicks.
Ken Harper
Ken Head
Arie-Jan Van Hees
Bill Higgs
John Hill
Cyril Hine
Jim Hodges - Dauntsey's School Head of English (rtd)
Ken Hodges
Terry Holloway The Marshall Group of Companies
Harry Howard
Revd. Philip Hughes
Geoff Hunt
Capt. John Hunter 8th Parachute Battalion
Donald Hutchins
Don Hutchinson
Joan Hutchinson WAAF
David Hyde
Imperial War Museum - Dept. of Printed Books
Gordon Inness
Gordon Jackson
Gwyneth F. Jackson
Roger Jackson
Terence Jones
Garth Kenderdine-Davies
Les & Marion Kent
Bill King
Will Knight
Sir Albert 'Archie' Thomas Lamb KBE, CMG, DFC, RAF

Dick Lardin
Colin Latham
Paul Leaman Cross & Cockade
Flt Lt B.J. Leech - RAFRO Bristol University Air Sqn
  Colerne
Gareth R. Lewis
Bill Leyland
Sqn Ldr M. Llewellyn-Thomas RAF
John Loader RAFA Wimborne Branch
Dr. Longbourne - Mere Museum Curator
Donald Lovelock
Harry Loxton
Alex Lugg
Major Andrew Lyell DFC
Flt Lt J. Makinson-Sanders BA (Hons) RAF
Marillyn Maklouf
Jeff Malton
Sir Arthur Marshall
Elisabeth McDougall
Lt Col E. McLaughlin Royal School of Artillery
Glenda Martin
McMurdo Ltd., Mary Creese - PRO
Kenny May
Jack Meaden
Ken Mills
Jack Milne
Ministry of Defence - Air Historical Branch (RAF)
Glen Moreman
Edna Morris
David Mosdall
Revd. David Moss
Mrs Murray - Dauntsey's School Librarian
Joan & Dave Nash
National Monument Record Centre
Sqn Ldr A.C. Neve MBE, RAF
New College, Oxford
Bob Newman
John Nicholls - Airfield Research Group
J.I.M. Oates - GCHQ Cheltenham
Lt Col O' Sullivan Royal Logistics Corps, Hullavington
  Barracks
Eric Palmer RAF Amateur Radio Society
Gerry Parkins
Richard Pearce
Air Marshal Sir Ian Pedder, KCB, OBE, DFC, RAF
John Perry
Alan Phelps
Photographic Section - DERA, Boscombe Down
Mr Pickford - Long Newnton Airfield
Bernard H. Pike
Oliver Pike
Stan Pollard
Dr Ian B. Porteous
Public Record Office, Kew
Flt Lt J.F. Querzani - CRO RAF Lyneham
Tom Ramsden-Binks - Cricklade Museum Curator
Joanne Ratcliffe Royal Air Force Museum (Hendon)
Laurie Rawson
D.A. Read
Dave Reeves
Rex Reynolds
P.A. Robbins
Eric Rock
Dr Terry Rogers - Honorary Archivist Marlborough College
Wg Cdr Jack Rose, CMG, MBE, DFC, RAF

Royal British Legion Salisbury
Royal New Zealand Air Force Museum
William Rumbold
C.R. Russell
Francis Rynn
The Dean & Chapter - Salisbury Cathedral
Wg Cdr J.G. Sanders DFC
Wg Cdr Jeff Scholefield RAF
Gerry Scott
Harry Scott
Mark Snell
Phil Sellens
Roger Seward - The Spread Eagle Inn at Stourhead
Sqn Ldr John H. Sharpe MBE, MIMgt RAF
Len Sharpe
Bob Shimmell RCAF
Karl Shuttleworth Trenchard Lines, Upavon
Joe Smee
Brian Smith - CSOS Blakehill Farm
Mary Smith
Peter Smith - RAF Ibsley Historical Group
Sqn Ldr Ernest Sandford Smith RAF
Yvonne Smith
John Snook
Patrick Soper
Howard Strawford - Castle Combe Circuit Ltd.
Neil Stevens Wilts & Berks E.T.O. Research Group
Ray Sturtivant Air Britain
Bonar Sykes
Graham Tanner
Dr. John W.R. Taylor OBE
The Daily Telegraph
Andy Thomas
Les Thorpe
Charles Tull - Tull Properties Ltd
Bob Underwood
Stan Vigor
Rex Wagstaff
Ken Wakefield
Major S.P. Wallis - 21 Signal Regiment (Air Support) Colerne
Wg Cdr Alan B. Walker RAF - Old Dauntseian
Major H.B. Warburton
Ray Ward
Francis Warneford
Greg Webb
Laurie Weeden
Tony West
Rev. Paul Wilkinson
David Williams
W.A. Williams - Bridge Books
AlfieWiltshire
Wiltshire County Library & Museum Service - Devizes &
  Local Studies Trowbridge
Wiltshire County Record Office
Alfie Wort
Fred Youngs

*Every effort has been made to trace copyright holders of
quoted material and illustrations reproduced in this book.
In some cases, and after considerable research, this has
not in all cases been successful. I apologise if any
copyright has been accidentally infringed.*

Authors Notes

1) I am aware that there are recognised ways of identifying airfields locations with Ordnance Survey map references, namely using the centre point of a runway intersection. In this book however, I have chosen to use the OS six figure map reference location point for the main entrance point of the site. Most of the airfields are no longer clearly recognisable as such, and any runways that there were have been removed. What generally remains however, are the former main entry points and visitors should be able to locate them without too much difficulty. Visitors must remember that permission will be necessary to enter most sites.

2) Map references found in many of the World War 2 RAF records are based on the War Office Cassini Grid system. In this book, these have been substituted for the current OS map references.

3) Some of the photographs used are not of the highest quality but are felt worthy of inclusion for their interest value.

4) Photographs with out a credit underneath are either from the authors collection or from a collection of a person who requires no recognition.

5) In the majority of chapters I have tried to record events in date order, as a general practice. This however has not always been possible as in the case of Colerne, which had a large number of squadrons deployed there during World War 2. Some of these where rotated every few months and others remained for long periods. Considerable fragmentation occurred when trying to record the operations of squadrons which were based on site at the same time. In the Colerne chapter therefore, each squadron record is detailed individually, as is the case in other chapters such as Lyneham, where deployment covered several years.

6) Where aircraft allocated to squadrons/units are known, their serial numbers appear in brackets within the text. In some cases only one or two numbers may be shown and in others a considerable list.

INTRODUCTION

I have lived in Wiltshire for 30 years and, during that time, have become aware of the many aviation-related memorials in the county. I developed an interest in these memorials and the reasons for their origin, and so decided to explore the story behind each one. David Smith further sparked my interest with his excellent book *Britain's Aviation Memorials & Mementoes* published in 1992 by Patrick Stephens Ltd (PSL), now Haynes Publishing of Sparkford, Somerset. Since then additional memorials have appeared in Wiltshire with, undoubtedly, more to follow. I set out to photograph them all and record their wording for, as time passes, the inscriptions on the stone made ones tend to erode as was the case with the well-known *'Airman's Cross'* near Stonehenge. In 1997, however, this particular memorial was renovated and rededicated by the Army Air Corps. There are differing views on what constitutes a memorial but, in this book, I have included items that are covered in general by the Concise Oxford Dictionary definition which quotes 'an object or custom, established in memory of an event or person(s)'. While individual gravestones would meet the criteria, the sheer numbers involved prevent inclusion. I have visited most of the churches close to airfield sites, and the larger cemeteries in this county and in a good many of them can be seen aviation head stones erected privately or by the Commonwealth War Graves Commission. Some graves of interest are mentioned in the book as are the churches and cemeteries where, in particular, Commonwealth airmen rest, having been killed while serving in this country.

During the course of my research and in discussions with local people and former Air Force personnel, it occurred to me that both disused and active airfields are in themselves a form of memorial to past service, and certainly a 'memory of an event'. With most of the airfields built for war now returned to agriculture, it leaves in the county only Lyneham, Boscombe Down, Colerne, plus Upavon and Hullavington to a certain extent, having an RAF presence and Netheravon used by the Army Air Corps. It seemed appropriate,

therefore, that I should include the history of all 35 airfield sites in this book, as in many cases they are closely linked with nearby memorial stones and plaques. Two of the airfields which survive in Army occupation, Upavon and Netheravon, have a long history, with the former being considered the birthplace of the Royal Flying Corps in 1912. Both of them however, were preceded by Larkhill, which was the site of the first aerodrome founded in 1910 for the Army.

The deployment of squadrons or units, which have been active from Wiltshire airfields during their operational use, has been fully covered by the well-known *'Action Stations'* series of books also published by PSL. These deployments are included in this book with additions such as enemy engagement, aircraft accident detail and facts collated by research and discussion with people who served at, or were familiar with, the sites when they were operational. Personal recollections have been included, also anecdotes which, it is felt, will help to create the kind of human detail generally not recorded in the official archives. My aim has been to set down material in the book, which is worthy of recording for future reference and to prevent it from fading into the mists of time. Much of the research has been carried out at the Public Record Office in Kew with information extracted from Squadron and Station Operations Record Books. The accuracy and content of these documents varies considerably, depending on the diligence of those compiling them at the time. This accounts for the discrepancies seen in different publications, especially in relation to squadron formation, movement and disbandment. Even the much respected Commonwealth War Graves Commission, perhaps understandable in times of war, have not always quite got their facts right. During my research I discovered the headstone of a Canadian pilot, who was buried in a French Cemetery, was indicating his death in May 1944. From his squadron records I found he was still flying from Blakehill Farm after this date but was subsequently killed during the D-Day landings of June 1944. As would be expected of the CWGC, they are correcting the mistake.

The airfields listed in the book are those which are generally recognised

as having been in use on a more than temporary basis. Many were, of course, temporary in so far as they were built for the duration of hostilities only and reverted, in the main to farming, on cessation. There have been numerous other places in Wiltshire used in the 20th century as aircraft landing grounds. These have been for training exercises, storage, ceremonial reviews, personal use and have been by aircraft of all the three main services. One example is the landing strip at Conock, beside the main A342 Devizes to Upavon road. The landing ground was used by Robert Smith-Barry who had been a pupil on the first course held at the Central Flying School at Upavon in 1912 and subsequently served as a World War 1 RFC pilot and instructor. On occasions he was known to fly to the aerodrome at Upavon from his home at Conock Manor in a private Puss Moth and it was to this Station he reported when rejoining the RAF in 1940. Perham Down, over looking Ludgershall, is another site where pictures survive of large formations of aircraft assembled to take part in military reviews prior to World War 1. During World War 2, the U.S Army used numerous landing strips which they termed 'Cub Strips', such as those at Breamore, Codford, Chitterne, Trowbridge, Warminster, Wylye and the polo field at Perham Down. The latter was one of the first U.S. Army strips in the UK and was also one of the largest. Today helicopters of the British Army are continually landing on and taking off from the Plain and from the camps at Larkhill, Bulford and Tidworth.

During World War 2, many airfields had their own decoy sites constructed close by. The intention was that these would be mistaken for the real thing and attacked by the enemy aircraft. These areas were referred to as 'Q' Sites for night decoys and 'K' Sites for day decoys. One of the former, in the village of All Cannings, was a decoy for RAF Upavon. 'Q' Sites were basically open fields over which were strung lengths of electric wiring and lamps attached to poles, which would be operated at night. Some sites used only Gooseneck flares. Generally three men would be the custodians of sites operating with electrical apparatus, and a party of 6/7 men where flares were used. The type of land taken over for this purpose was not important and did not even need to be flat because the only necessity was to reproduce the lighting effect of a nearby primary airfield. 'K' Sites required a certain amount of reality and were often equipped with dummy aircraft and buildings.

There are, and have been, many RAF establishments in the county which were not landing grounds. Some examples are Rudloe Manor at Corsham, the Sector Headquarters of No.10 Group during World War 2 and, until the 1998 Defence Cuts, the Headquarters of the RAF Provost & Security Services and Nos.1 & 1001 Signal Units. Nearby the underground stores of RAF Spring Quarry, whose original construction was as a factory for the production of Bristol aircraft but was used instead for the assembly of aero engines. In later years the underground site had the capability for use as the Seat of Government in nuclear war. RAF Compton Bassett near Calne where radio and radar training took place during and after the war. The RAF Princess Alexandra Hospital at Wroughton near Swindon, and RAF Melksham, which was a School of Technical Training, were establishments without airfields. Despite the main station entrance, the domestic buildings and most of the runway being within the Wiltshire border, Kemble airfield is recognised as coming within Gloucestershire. It has, therefore, been omitted from this record.

Today the airfields of Wiltshire are few but the skies above are rarely empty. Hercules from Lyneham are an every day sight, Tornadoes, Harriers and a great variety of aircraft operate from Boscombe Down. From Odiham, Chinooks appear frequently, often with military vehicles slung beneath. The army helicopters from Netheravon and from Middle Wallop on the Hampshire/Wiltshire border, hover in the sky or creep out from behind a clump of trees. The ever-busy Air Ambulance helicopter based at Police Headquarters in Devizes, even the high-flying jet liners leaving their contrails over Wiltshire, all reflect the great development which has taken place in a short period of time, and reminds us that Wiltshire has a rich aviation heritage. It could well be said of the county that it is the cradle of military flying.

The book has been prepared with the intention of being *In Memoriam* and so the emphasis placed on the demise of airmen and their aircraft is deliberate but respectful. It is hoped the reader will consider that the book honours those who paid the ultimate price.

(1) 174/SU266757 8 miles South East of Swindon

In the Memorial Hall on the C189 road to Baydon off of the A419. On the north/east wall, a brass plaque with the inscription: -

> IN MEMORY OF THE
> GALLANT MEN OF
> THE U.S. 436th
> TROOP CARRIER GROUP
> WHO OPERATED FROM
> MEMBURY AIR BASE
> DURING W.W.11

The plaque was presented by Tony Cox who, as a young boy in 1944, made visits to American Air Force Station 466 Membury in Berkshire, where personnel of the 436th TCG befriended him. Wishing to recognise and record their service at Membury Airfield, he had the plaque made.

(2) Another black faced aluminium plaque on the wall of the Memorial Hall has the inscription: -

> UNITED STATES ARMY
> Commemorating the
> 101st Airborne Division 506th Parachute Infantry Regiment
> stationed in this Village
> prior to taking part in the D-Day landings
> for the Liberation of Europe
> 6th June 1944
> "For Peace and Freedom"

The plaque was presented by former American paratrooper Joe Beyrle and unveiled at a ceremony on 5th August 1999. This band of GIs were the famed 'E' Easy Company who left Aldbourne for USAAF Station 462 Upottery in Devon, from where they were flown to Normandy on 5th June 1944.

The two plaques in the Village Hall, displayed between the Union Jack and the Stars and Stripes. Photo: Bill King.

ALTON BARNES RLG

Location (173/SU104617 - 6 miles East of Devizes)

The site of the former RAF Station in the centre of the village is bordered on the north side by the C8 Devizes to Pewsey road and on the east side by the C38 Woodborough to Lockeridge road. The Kennet & Avon Canal is located 400 yards to the south.

Airfield Development

The majority of land used for the aerodrome belonged to New College, Oxford and was leased to local farmer Guy Stratton of Manor Farm. It was first inspected in June 1935 by two RAF officers, one of whom was Flt Lt Barwell, to determine its suitability as a practice forced landing ground for use by the Central Flying School at Upavon. Guy Stratton was then asked to keep his fields clear of stock on 13th August so that an aircraft could make a test landing. The landing and take-off was successfully carried out and the Air Ministry informed the farmer that the RAF would start using the field for this purpose. A rent of £50 per year was paid on the understanding that one field would be clear of stock throughout the year, between the hours of 5.30am and 4.30pm every day except Saturdays and Sundays. RAF Upavon provided a large white painted wooden cross to be positioned in the field. The only other facility was a windsock. It was also agreed that on occasions when the Central Flying School (CFS) wished to use the fields on a Saturday, RAF Upavon would ring the farmer to warn him. The Air Ministry agreed to pay for damage caused to fences but would not pay for damages to stock straying into the field.

In early 1939, with war clouds looming, the Air Ministry looked at the country around the Pewsey Vale with a view to providing five relief landing grounds (RLGs) to serve the needs of three important aerodromes, Upavon, Netheravon and Boscombe Down. The RLGs were to be used to relieve congestion, which possibly could have led to an added risk of flying accidents, on these parent aerodromes. Upavon and Netheravon were both Flying Training Schools with the former training all of the country's flying instructors. Alton Barnes was an obvious choice as an RLG much

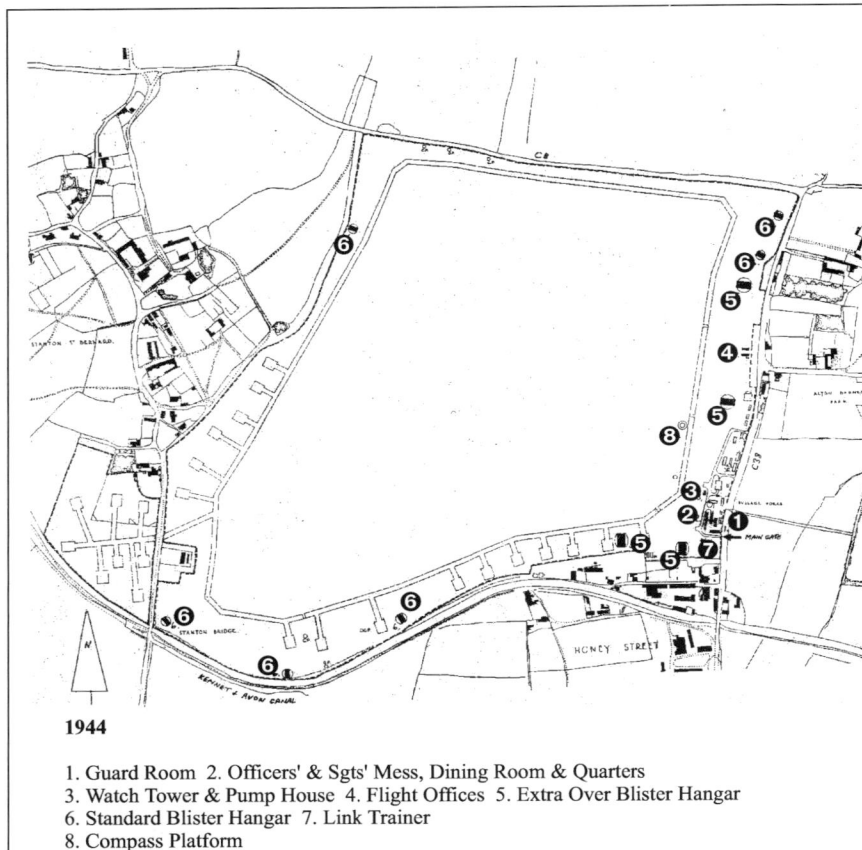

1944

1. Guard Room 2. Officers' & Sgts' Mess, Dining Room & Quarters
3. Watch Tower & Pump House 4. Flight Offices 5. Extra Over Blister Hangar
6. Standard Blister Hangar 7. Link Trainer
8. Compass Platform

against the wishes of the farmer who wrote to the local MP Sir Percy Hurd protesting that the proposal was likely to involve risk to those living in the neighbourhood. Guy Stratton even wrote to the Air Ministry suggesting two alternative sites in the Pewsey Vale but was advised that they were unsuitable. On 31st August 1939 the Air Ministry informed him that his fields were being requisitioned under the Defence Regulations 1939. An additional area of land between the existing landing ground and the canal to the south was requisitioned from Robbins, Lane & Pinnigar, the local coal and timber merchant. This provided a site of 3000yds x 2550yds.

By the end 1941 the landing ground was temporarily closed when work commenced to upgrade it to RLG standard. Local man Roy Goddard recalls civilian construction workers having to carry out a considerable amount of levelling work at the west end of the site. Most of the buildings were erected along the edge of the east side of the landing ground close to the

road and village. Timber barrack huts were built to accommodate 130 personnel. The Dining Room, Sgts' Mess, Officers' Mess and Quarters were all in one single storey block, also of timber construction. The Watch Tower with Pump House and the Link Trainer building were brick built. The two Flight Offices and the store buildings were Nissen huts. Ten Blister hangars were provided consisting of three Extra Over and two Standard types on the eastern boundary, an Extra Over and three Standard backed onto the canal on the south side and a single Standard towards the NW corner. The Extra Over on the east side nearest the canal was used for aircraft maintenance and repair. Take-off and landings were made on four grass strips, NE/SW 1,100yds, N/S 820yds, E/W 870yds and SE/NW 870yds. These were encircled with a 31' 6" wide perimeter track of Sommerfeld tracking. The same material was used for the dispersals of which there were 10 on the south side and 14 on the west. The tracking was laid during the 1943/44 winter to combat the water

4

logging caused by a considerable amount of rain during that period.

Inter War Years

The CFS commenced its use of the landing ground as of Monday 15th September 1935. Two forced landings on 25th October and 25th November caused damage to fencing around the field and the sum of 15 shillings for each incident was paid to Guy Stratton. The use made of the landing ground in the early days was by the trainee instructors of Upavon carrying out landings and take-offs in a less busy sky than at their home aerodrome. The aircraft were Avro 504Ns, superseded from March 1936 by Tutor biplanes. These continued in use until June 1941 when Masters and Oxfords became the principal aircraft for flying instructor training at Upavon. Before World War 2 just one RAF man, Roy Richards, carried out duties at the landing ground.

World War 2 Years

To combat the probable invasion by German forces during 1940, three gun posts were positioned to the south of the landing ground near the canal and three alongside the road to the north. North of the airfield are the steep hills that mark the edge of the Marlborough Downs running east/west through the Pewsey Vale. The Alton Barnes White Horse is cut into the chalk, next to Milk Hill, which is almost opposite the landing ground. Whilst this made the location of the landing ground easy for the pilots from Upavon to find, it would do the same for the Germany pilots. The Camouflage Branch of the Ministry of Home Security therefore wrote to farmer Guy Stratton on 18th June 1940, directing him to obscure the white horse and to secure the speedy carrying out of the work which would be paid for from Government funds. It was not long after this that three bombs were dropped by an enemy aircraft during the night of 14th September but no damage was sustained. An Anti-aircraft gun was positioned on Milk Hill with accommodation buildings for the gunners close by. The Germans photographed Alton Barnes landing ground as can be seen below. The first flying accident at Alton Barnes occurred when Tutor[I] K3406 crashed whilst making its approach to the aerodrome on 25th September 1940.

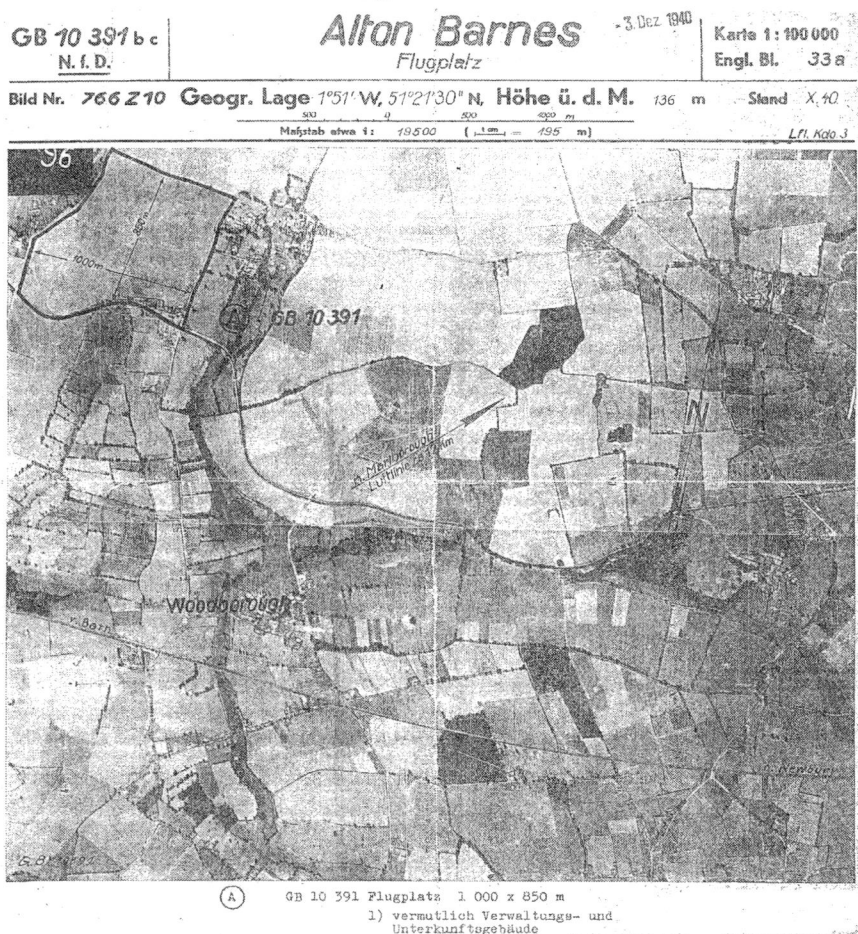

German photograph of Alton Barnes dated 3rd December 1940, showing the aerodrome outlined in the top left hand corner. This was one of the aero-photographs found in the map room at Lubeck Airfield in Germany five weeks after VE Day by RAF officer Herbert Bowell, of No.504 Sqn, who was a Devizes man.   Photo: Ray Pope

By this time there was an ever-increasing need for trained flying instructors and these were passing through Upavon on courses with a reduced duration. As a consequence of the increase Alton Barnes was in constant use. On 4th February 1941, a CFS Oxford II P1081 crashed on approach to the aerodrome without injuries to the crew. The same occurred with Tutor I K3236 on 23rd May, Master III W8438 on 21st June and Tutor I K4828 two days later. Two fatal accidents did occur during this time. The first on Wednesday 18th June involved a collision between Miles Master III W8477 and Oxford I N6365. It appears the Master was landing into the sun and was unaware of the stationary Oxford. Trainee instructor Plt Off Kenneth J. Holmes DFC, in the Master, was killed. Nurse Mary Smith, who witnessed the crash and was first on the scene, rescued the instructor Fg Off Phillip C. Price. The rescued airman was taken to Yatesbury Hospital with facial burns and bruising. In the Oxford both the

instructor Plt Off Arthur Gibbons and the trainee Sgt Kenneth Oswald Bate were killed. Plt Off K.J. Holmes DFC was buried at Chippenham Cemetery and Plt Off Gibbons at Upavon Cemetery.

Plt Off Holmes had been awarded the DFC for his actions on the night of 14th/15th April 1941 when piloting a No.217 Sqn Coastal Command Beaufort I Torpedo Bomber. He was involved in the attack against the two German cruisers Scharnhorst and Gneisenau in the harbour at Brest.

The second crash occurred on 4th September when a CFS Master III W8472 stalled off a turn on approach to the field and dived into the ground. The two men killed were Sqn Ldr Wilfred Bennet Beale and Plt Off George Henry Brown.

In December 1941, Alton Barnes was transferred to No.29 EFTS Clyffe Pypard and was in use from early in the month for day-time flying only. The

The wedding of Kenneth Holmes and his wife Mary at St Andrew Church, Chippenham in 1939. The Best Man was Phillip Price the only survivor of the accident. Both men were Sergeants at this time. The bride's parents are on her left. The church entrance where the picture was taken faces the town war memorial on which the name of Plt Off Kenneth Holmes DFC now appears. Photo: John Bulmer

'B' Flt instructors and pupils with a Tiger Moth at Alton Barnes in the summer of 1942. The young girl in the front row was the time-keeper. Her duties were to clock the aircraft out and back in. Photo: Audrey Hampshire

site closed towards the end on the month when work began on upgrading the landing ground.

Alton Barnes officially re-opened as from 3rd June 1942 which coincided with Clyffe Pypard's Flights being increased to six, two of which 'A' & 'B' Flts operated from Alton Barnes. 'A' Flt occupied buildings on the south end of the station backing on to the canal and 'B' Flt in huts alongside the road. Each Flt had a Flt Cdr and six instructors with four pupils to an instructor.

Courses for Army pre-glider pilot training had started at Clyffe Pypard on 20th May and following its re-opening they operated from Alton Barnes, flying Tiger Moths. Residents of the village recall meeting airmen from many of the Commonwealth countries and men who had escaped to Britain from the European countries over-run by Germany. On 30th November the personnel of the Anti-aircraft Flt were withdrawn to Clyffe Pypard and the anti-aircraft defences at Alton Barnes were manned by flying personnel. Station security at night was maintained by personnel under training and by the RAF Regiment. Army pilot training ceased at the end of the year and RAF trainees returned to use the airfield.

The Glider Pilot Exercise Unit based at Thruxton, disbanded into an Operational and Refresher Training Unit on 9th December 1943 and used Alton Barnes for one of its light glider flights until the end of February 1944.

Marshal's of Cambridge employed civilian ground staff to work on the aerodrome and they carried out a wide range of duties. Some of the staff travelled to Alton Barnes from Clyffe Pypard to work, whilst others were employed locally. Richard Pearce, John Flippance and Bill Pinchin were prop swingers and refuellers. Their wages were paid at 1/1d per hour. Richard Pearce recalls driving a three-wheeled petrol bowser along the twisting lanes to the parent station at Clyffe Pypard on the day Alton Barnes closed to flying on 9th July 1945.

Ivy Muddle was the Mess Room cook between 1942-44, having transferred from RAF Compton Bassett. She lived close by in Woodborough and was pleased to be able to work closer to her home from where she could cycle to work each day. Audrey Goddard started work at the aerodrome as a waitress/cleaner in 1941. Nora Keepance and Gwen Top were employed on similar duties. Their wages were 18 shillings a week. Another locally employed young girl carried out the station administration. George Marshall was a Storeman and he recalls a day in 1944 when a USAAF P-38 Lightening landed at Alton Barnes. The American pilot wanted to visit his colleague who was in the American military hospital in Devizes. Alton Barnes was the nearest airfield. The pilot asked George Marshall if he could use his telephone but was told that use of the phone was forbidden. It is thought that he wanted to arrange transport to reach the hospital 6 miles away. He went off to seek permission from higher authority at the airfield.

The P-38 was not the only un-expected aircraft to visit Alton Barnes. Local man LAC George Buckland, serving at Upavon, remembers the day when an OTU Wellington which was lost, probably whilst on a cross-country training flight, landed and took off again, after re-fuelling. On Tuesday 28th September 1943, Wellington IC W5724 from No.11 OTU Westcott was on a cross-country flight when the port engine caught fire. The pilot skillfully crash-landed the aircraft at 1350hrs in a field on Harepath Farm, 3 miles west of Alton Barnes. Flt Sgt R. F. Hall RNZAF (pilot) suffered multiple injuries, Sgt Glover (1st Nav), had severe burns to his hands and Sgt Scott

A 500 gallon capacity petrol bowser and civilian operators at Alton Barnes.
Photo: George Marshall

(2nd Nav.), minor bruising. They were conveyed to the RAF Hospital at Yatesbury by the RAF Alton Barnes ambulance. The three other crew suffered serious injuries with Sgt John M. Underwood RNZAF (BA) dying shortly after the crash and Sgt William H. Evans RCAF (AG) the following day. They were buried in Haycombe Cemetery, Bath. Sgt W. J. Southern RAFVR (WOP/AG) also succumbed to his injuries on 29th September.

Clyffe Pypard started training Naval Cadet Pilots from 13th October 1944 and like the Army pilots before them they carried out much of their training flying Tiger Moths at Alton Barnes. The Naval cadets were bussed in from Clyffe Pypard on a daily basis.

Local man Jessie Bailey tells of the occasion when one of the instructors who, after leaving the nearby Barge Inn, flew his Tiger Moth through one of the Extra Over blister hangars. The span and height of this type of hangar was 69' and 20' 4" respectively and that of a Tiger Moth 29' 4" and 8' 9½". It seems that he had space to play with but, depending on his consumption at the Inn, it would still appear to be skilful flying on his part. He was however carpeted by the CO.

Flt Lt Alister Renvoise was another one of the instructors at Alton Barnes during 1944 and has fond memories of his service there. At the time he was living close by in Pewsey with his wife and travelled the short distance to Alton Barnes each day. On days when the weather appeared unsuitable for flying, he would ring Clyffe Pypard to ask if he was needed and, if hearing he wasn't, was able to stay at home until he was contacted when the weather cleared and flying could resume. As with other instructors, he flew his pupils to the Manningford Landing Ground where mushrooms grew in season. Hare chasing in the Tiger Moth at Alton Barnes was another good pastime.

A fatal accident occurred on 25th October 1944 when an Albemarle II V1755 of No.22 HGCU at Keevil crashed in a field just a short distance east of the airfield. It was carrying out a training flight with a Horsa glider in tow when the crash occurred killing the crew of two in the tug. The glider landed safely on the airfield where it remained for several weeks before being towed out by a Whitley.

After the war in Europe ended Alton Barnes was no longer required for RAF use and on 7th July 1945 all aircraft were returned to Clyffe Pypard. Ancillary transport, stores and equipment was also returned over the next few days and from the 9th July the station was officially closed and placed on C&M.

Post War Years

The site had a brief respite when the Army carried out some building modifications and used it for weapons research.

Closure

During 1947, the then former airfield was de-requisitioned and was returned to agricultural use. The farmers wasted little time in removing the majority of the airfield infrastructure although one of the Extra Over Blister hangars was used for hay/straw storage and remained beside the road into the 1960s. After its removal the concrete base was used as a farm manure storage area. Although the land returned to farming in 1947, it remained in the ownership of the Air Ministry until 1959 when New College Oxford bought 70 acres. It was not until 1968 that the College was able to buy two small remaining pieces of land from the MoD. One of these on the west side of the village fronted the road and was the location of the airfield domestic buildings.

Now in the third year of the 21st Century, very little remains to remind us of RAF Alton Barnes. At the former

Tiger Moth No.39, the mount of Instructor Flt Lt 'Jonney' Fielding, outside the Extra Over blister hangar between the dispersals on the south side of the field. The 19 gallon tank giving 3 hours flying duration can be seen on the plane above the front cockpit.
Photo: Richard Pearce

main gate, the original concrete road is discernible as it winds its way past the Link Trainer building on the left. The building is the food store for the sheep grazing in the field. Immediately inside the gate on the right is an underground air-raid shelter in remarkably good condition and close to it the base of the Officers' latrine. On the northern boundary alongside the road to Devizes, two of the gun posts can clearly be seen.

Memorials

The former Link Trainer building and the concrete road leading from the main gate.

(1) 173/SU108613 - quarter of a mile east of Honey Street

In Conigre Meadow alongside the tow path of the Kennet & Avon Canal. Taking the tow path from the road bridge over the canal on the C38 at Honey Street, access to the field is via a stile immediately before the next canal bridge. A direction sign provided by British Waterways stands by the stile pointing the way to the memorial.

Plt Off Arthur Gibbons RAFVR

On the north side of Conigre Meadow, with the canal immediately to the rear, stands a memorial cairn of Sarcen Stone into which is set a plaque of Nabresina Stone, inscribed with the

Aerial view of the former RAF Alton Barnes photographed from a Benson based Mosquito XXXIV of No.540 Sqn on 12th July 1946. The domestic buildings can be seen in the centre standing beside the road, and most of the blister hangers around the landing area are evident. Photo: NMRO

An immediate post war view looking north from Honey Street Bridge, crossing the Kennet & Avon Canal. On the left side of the lane, white flag stones are seen at the main entrance to the airfield. To the rear of this are barrack huts and one of the Extra Over Blister hangars. The white horse on the hill has been released from its wartime covering. Photo: Chris Gibson

following words beneath the RAF Crest: -

An Albemarle in relief view is inscribed here.

This memorial is dedicated to Flt. Sgt. Thomas C. Newton R.A.F.V.R. - Pilot Sgt. John A.C. Wilson R.A.F.V.R. - W.Op. /Air Gunner who lost their lives when their Albemarle Bomber V1755 of No. 22 H.G.C.U. RAF Keevil crashed near here on the 25th October 1944.

At the going down of the sun and in the morning we will remember them

The Memorial to Flt Sgt Newton & Sgt Wilson.

Flt Sgt Tom Newton RAFVR Pilot
December 1943

Sgt John Wilson RAFVR
WOP/AG
possibly at RAF Keevil 1944

The memorial was provided by David Carson (Grandson of Guy Stratton) on whose family farm it stands, and the author. Conigre Meadow has only ever been used for grazing and because no cultivation has taken place, the impact area remains visible. The memorial on the edge of the field stands in a direct line with the indentation at a distance of 20 yards.

When the crash occurred in 1944, Albemarle V1755 had taken off from nearby RAF Keevil on a training flight towing a Horsa Glider. The Accident Report indicates the glider overtaking the tug aircraft and raising its tail to a 70 degree angle, at which point the tow rope broke (witnesses indicate it was released) and the now out of control tug dived into the ground. The aircraft burst into flames on impact and the two-man crew, recovered from the canal, were both killed. The glider was able to make a landing at Alton Barnes airfield. The Report also indicates that the two pilots were unable to communicate with each other, as there was 'no R/T kit available on new unit'.

A dedication and unveiling ceremony was staged at the memorial on 25th October 1997 and was attended by relations and friends of the two crewmen, the MP for Devizes, the Rt.Honorable Michael Ancram QC, Wg Cdr Paul Morris OC No.70 Sqn and other officers from RAF Lyneham, representatives from RAFA and the Royal British Legion together with local residents. The brother of Sgt Wilson and a close friend of Flt Sgt Newton carried out the unveiling. The service was conducted by The Rev. Wg Cdr Robert Bailey, the Padre of RAF Lyneham and the service concluding with the playing of the Last Post followed by a low-level fly past from Lyneham's No.70 Sqn Hercules C130K, Mk.1 XV218 piloted by Sqn Ldr Ian Hartley.

(2) 173/SU104617 - on the former airfield off of the C38

The former Link Trainer building stands in a field 30 yards from a gate on the roadside. This was the original main gate and Guardroom location. Immediately inside the gate, on the right hand side, is a grass sided air raid shelter. Access to the field is now from the next gate to the north where a sign indicates 'To the Airfield Memorial'.

Set over the steps leading into the air raid shelter is a plaque of Crown Stone inscribed with the following words beneath the RAF Crest: -

This memorial on the only remaining air raid shelter marks the site of RAF Alton Barnes, which was used as an airfield for flying training between 1935-45. C.F.S. Upavon operated here until 1941 when the site transferred to No. 29 E.F.T.S. Clyffe Pypard.

The memorial is dedicated to those who lost their lives whilst training here:

P/O K.J. Holmes, DFC. RAF 18th June 1941
P/O A. Gibbons RAFVR 18th June 1941
Sgt. K.O. Bate RAFVR 18th June 1941
Sq. Ldr. W.B. Beale RAF
4th September 1941
P/O G.H. Brown RAFVR
4th September 1941

"Sunward I've climbed, and joined the tumbling mirth ...
... Put out my hand and touched the face of God"
W.H.M.S.

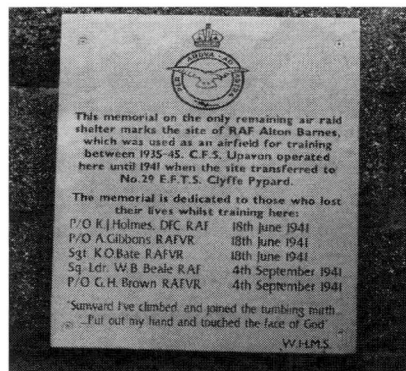

The Memorial plaque above the doorway leading into the air-raid shelter at the former RAF Alton Barnes.

The provision of the memorial plaque was undertaken by the Wiltshire Historical Military Society. A dedication and unveiling ceremony was held on Saturday 18th September 1999, attended by a relative of Plt Off Kenneth Holmes, who flew in from Saudi Arabia for the ceremony. Former personnel serving at the airfield during the war and local residents were also represented. The memorial plaque was unveiled by Gp Capt Mark Stevens RAF, Head of Combat Aircraft at Boscombe Down and the service was conducted by The Rev. Wg Cdr Tony Fletcher RAF, Padre of RAF Lyneham.

AMESBURY

In Amesbury CE Aided Junior School off the A345 at the junction of Kitchener Road/School Lane, is kept a brass altar cross with the following inscription on the base: -

IN MEMORIUM
LIEUTENANT HAROLD HUGH-WALLIS RAF
KILLED JULY 2ND 1916 AGED 22

The brass altar cross was used in the former RAF church at Boscombe Down Airfield until its demolition in 1994 when it was presented, initially to the Church of St Mary & St Melor and then to the local school.

The brass alter cross previously used in the RAF church at Boscombe Down.

In the car park of the Red Lion public house on the C6 Marlborough to Ramsbury road, a memorial stone dedicated on 28th May 1994 with the following inscription beneath a coloured 437th Group emblem and a C-47 Dakota towing a Horsa Glider in relief: -

Dedicated to honor the members of the
437th Troop Carrier Group
United States Army Ninth Air Force
World War 11
who were stationed at Ramsbury Airfield
and participated in the campaigns of
Normandy, Ardennes, Northern France,
Rome, Arno, Southern France,
Rhineland and Central Europe.

Where the River Kennet flows over
the small weir below this spot,
Major Donald E. Bradley
and 1st Lt. Gayford Strong
members of the 83rd Squadron
437th Troop Carrier Group,
died in the crash of a
Douglas Dakota C47 aircraft on
March 11th 1944.
They were attempting to retrieve a
Horsa glider that had broken free
in a practice mission and landed in the
field above this spot.
Captain Lee Gillette, 83rd Squadron
Flight Surgeon, although seriously injured,
survived the accident and returned to duty
after 5 weeks in the US Army Hospital at
Burderop Park, Wroughton, Wilts.

The memorial stone in the car park of the
Red Lion Public House.

The Purbeck Stone memorial was erected in Axford on 14th/15th August 1993. It was instigated by Neil Stevens of Marlborough who had previously formed the 'Wilts & Berks E.T.O. Research Group' to explore the role of the American GIs in Wiltshire during World War 2. As a result of his research he became aware of the crash of the C-47 at Axford in March 1944 in which two crew members died.

The C-47 Dakota, serial No.42-100877, piloted by Major Donald Bradley, Squadron Commander of the 83rd Troop Carrier Squadron, came from the US 9th Air Force's 437th Troop Carrier Group based at Ramsbury Airfield. In this particular incident an attempt was being made to recover a Horsa glider. On the morning of 11th March 1944, during a training exercise, it broke free from its tow aircraft and landed in a field. In the recovery attempt that afternoon, on board were Major Bradley, his co-pilot Lt Gayford Strong and Capt Lee Gillette 83rd Flt. Surgeon, who had volunteered to act as observer for the flight. Just as the C-47 and the glider became airborne the tug struck power lines at the end of the field and crashed. Bob Frank and Ken Weber the pilots in the glider, seeing the plane veer off after contact with the power lines, quickly released the towrope and landed safely. Major Bradley sustained serious head injuries and died an hour later. Lt Strong had numerous fractures and a head injury and died two days later. Capt Gillette received several broken ribs and a torn lung but, after a stay in hospital, was able to return to his duties. The next day an announcement was made asking for blood so that the two men could receive blood transfusions. Within half an hour around 500 men volunteered. The crash occurred during the intensive training which took place prior to the 437th's participation in the D-Day Invasion of 6th June 1944, robbing the 83rd Squadron as it did, of an already combat experienced Squadron CO.

Capt Lee Gillette, the sole survivor, together with other members of the 437th Veterans' Association came back to Ramsbury to attend the dedication of the memorial stone on 28th May 1994.

The Rev. R. K. Hyatt, Vicar of Ramsbury conducted the service of dedication, with prayers led by Chaplain Goff 437th AW USAF. Doctor Lee Gillette and Neil Stevens unveiled the memorial stone. The ceremony culminated in a flypast by a C141 Starlifter of the 437th Airlift Wing USAF, a C130 Hercules from RAF Lyneham, a 1944 L4 Piper Cub privately owner by Ken Wakefield and a RAF C-47 Dakota from the Battle of Britain Memorial Flight.

BLAKEHILL FARM AIRFIELD
Location (173/SU078919 - 7 miles North West of Swindon)

The former airfield is located east of the B4040 Malmesbury Road, near Chelworth, between Cricklade and Minety. The site was purchased by the Secretary of State for Air and its construction late in the war was in preparation for the reoccupation of north west Europe (Operation *Overlord*). The airfield took its name from the farm where building work commenced in 1943.

Airfield Development

Three hard surface runways were constructed - 24/06 NE/SW 2000 x 50yds, 13/31 NW/SE 1410 x 50yds and 19/01 N/S 1410 x 50yds. The NE/SW runway had an area of PSP at either end. The airfield at a later date received the Blind Approach landing system. The technical, domestic and communal accommodation was constructed on the north side of the field. Although the threat from air raids was considerably reduced by this time in the war, the dispersal of the Sites away from the airfield was in keeping with the lessons learned during the Battle of Britain. The larger than normal NAAFI building occupied a complete block of large Nissen huts, but was not completed until 8th March 1944, a month after the official opening. The billets consisted of 8 Sites of which Sites 1 and 2 were the WAAF quarters. With the formation of No.437 Sqn RCAF in September 1944, Sites 5 & 6 were assigned to them for sleeping quarters. Each morning at 0815 hrs one of the squadron lorries called at Site No.6 to collect personnel. Those who missed the transport had a mile walk or cycle ride to the mess. The Technical Site on the edge of the perimeter track housed the Operations Block, M.T. Section, station offices, post office, stores and crew rooms. The Canadians named their recreation lounge 'Canada House'. They were pleased with its spaciousness, which gave crews a good locker room and ample lounging area, with plenty of easy chairs, writing and card tables, two table-tennis tables and a radio. The facilities were in almost constant daytime use by the aircrews. An Education Centre was set up where anyone could study subjects such as French language. These sessions would be held in 'Canada House'.

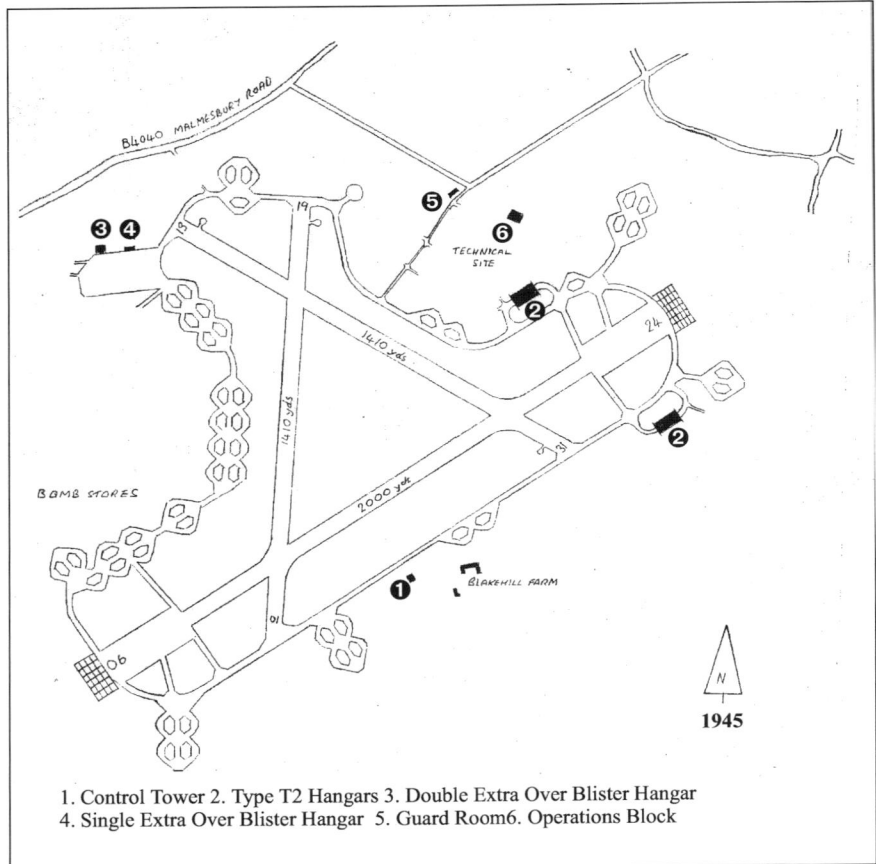

1. Control Tower 2. Type T2 Hangars 3. Double Extra Over Blister Hangar
4. Single Extra Over Blister Hangar 5. Guard Room 6. Operations Block

Outside 'Canada House', No. 437 Sqn's Adjutant, Flt Lt Ed Joynt 2nd from left and the CO, Wg Cdr Jack Sproule, talking to other squadron personnel.

The Headquarters building of No. 437 Sqn at Blakehill Farm

Cpl Robert O. Shimmell of No. 437 'Husky' Sqn RCAF together with 'Brevet' the squadron mascot outside one of the Blakehill Farm blister huts. 'Brevet' was a Samoyed belonging to the CO, and apparently it was afraid of cats. Photo: Bob Shimmell.

The Flight Huts were on the south side of the airfield about half a mile from the crew rooms and were reached by lorry. The Canadians found this a strange mode of transport, being more used to the comfort of buses. Two Type T2 hangars were built off of the perimeter track on either side of the NE end of the main runway. One of the hangars was used by R & I (Repairs & Inspections), for carrying out major aircraft servicing and repairs. The control tower was sited off the perimeter track on the south side of the field in a midway position. The two-letter station identification code was XF. The BF code was already in use at nearby Babdown Farm in Gloucestershire and had been in operation since 1940. As Blakehill Farm was built late in the war it was one of a number of airfields having a code which was not in keeping with its name. At the NW end of runway 13/31 there was a single and a double extra over blister hanger and the sheds of the Air Dispatch & Reception Unit, which handled outgoing freight. These buildings stood alongside a large hard-standing area where the Dakotas were assembled for loading.

The main runway with the TypeT2 hangars at the N/E end. The control tower is seen on the right in the middle and, at the rear of it, the original Blakehill Farm buildings. The airfield was in use as a RLG when the photo was taken in C.1949.

World War 2 Years

Initially the Station came under No.70 Group A.D.G.B. but from 6th February 1944 was transferred into Transport Command in No.46 Group, newly formed on 17th January with HQ at Harrow Weald. Its primary function on opening was to receive and operate squadrons, which would engage in Air Support operations, in what was to be the forthcoming invasion of Europe. The station opening was planned for the week ending Friday 9th February 1944. The Station Commander was to be Gp Capt W.M.C. Kennedy. The opening up party under the command of Sqn Ldr A.W. Bennett arrived the following day to find suitable accommodation had not been completed so they had to use billets at nearby Down Ampney. The contractors still had considerable work to do and the 300-400 Irish labourers were camped on what was intended as the two WAAF Sites. It was considered unsuitable for the ladies to take up their accommodation under these circumstances so they were temporarily accommodated on another Site. A detachment of Royal Engineers was billeted on the station whilst engaged in planning and operating the Airborne Transit Camp. The lack of motor transport for ferrying, communication and general run-around duties added to the difficulties in the early days.

The first major unit to take up its post at Blakehill Farm was No.233 Sqn which had returned from Gibraltar, where it had been in Coastal Command, equipped with Hudson IIIAs and had carried out U-boat patrols. In early 1944 many experienced crews were being drafted back to the U.K. from overseas to form the nucleus of the rapidly expanding Dakota squadrons forming in No.46 Group. The main squadron party arrived on 5th March 1944 followed the next day by the aircrews and 12 C-47 Douglas Dakota IIIs, flown in for conversion and training purposes. Also on 5th March No.11 Horsa Glider Servicing Echelon formed on the station. On 24th March HQ No.2 Wing Glider Pilot Regiment arrived, followed two days later by the 13th Parachute Battalion and on the 30th by the 1st Canadian Parachute Battalion. The latter did not stay long and moved to a base of its own on 6th April.

13

No.233 Sqn Dakota III FZ692.

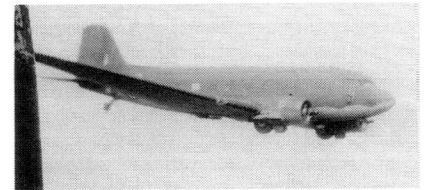

A No.233 Sqn Dakota on formation drop over Netheravon.   Photo: Joe Smee

Some 30 Staff Sergeants and Officers of the Glider Pilot Regiment were posted to Blakehill Farm at the end of March. These 1st Pilots were followed shortly afterwards by about the same number of Sergeants having completed their 2nd Pilot training. They were paired with the 1st Pilots so making-up the full complement of No.14 Flt. 'F' Sqn under the command of Lt Aubrey E. Pickwoad.

In the early stages of forming the glider-borne forces, there had been disagreement over who should fly the various types of glider which would be used. The Army was prepared to provide pilots but the Air Ministry was of the opinion that ordinary soldiers could not be given the appropriate training required to land a large un-powered personnel carrying aircraft. It was resolved that the Army would appoint the pilots but the RAF would train them. The pilots would be attached to the Glider Regiment which became the Glider Pilot Regiment when formed on 24th February 1942.

Two (Forward) Staging Post (FSP) units were based at Blakehill Farm, No.92 arriving from Broadwell on 16th March and No.93 from Lyneham on 1st June. They were there to train in casevac and freight loading duties. No.91 based a few miles along the road at Down Ampney also carried out training there. During March 21 Horsa gliders arrived on station from Swanton Morley and North Luffenham. As Horsa numbers increased, No.16 Glider Servicing Echelons joined No.11 to handle maintenance. No.14 Flt. GPR assisted with glider ferrying duties. At the end of March WAAF Air Nursing Orderlies arrived for attachment to No.233 Sqn. They became known as the "Flying Nightingales". One of these was LACW Edna Birbeck who took her first training flight in a Dakota on 20th April, and a year later married the WOP of the crew that day, Sgt Glyn 'Taffy' Morris. Personnel of No.233

Sqn were now fully engaged in training for the D-Day operation. On 21st April a Corps Exercise was staged, Operation *Mush*, as a dress rehearsal for the airdrop phase of the forthcoming invasion. This took place over an area between the Wiltshire and Oxfordshire borders and the Severn estuary. 22 aircraft of No.233 Sqn formed part of the 700 exercised. An operation was undertaken on the 25th and 26th April when each night 6 Dakotas carried out 'Nickelling' operations and leaflet drops in the Caen and Alencon areas. These drops which each crew flew, gave them experience of cross-Channel operating. With the D-Day operation getting nearer the station was now becoming established and during April and May it was heavily involved in training exercises which involved glider towing, formation flying, paratroop and container drops. The dropping zones used for the 6th Airborne Division

paratroop and container drops, were those at Netheravon and Kelmscott although longer range sorties with large formations of transport aircraft were also undertaken. Some of the training flights were night exercises.

Recreation was not forgotten during the busy training period. Glider pilot S/Sgt Laurie L. Weeden recalls that it included horse riding on some 'past their sell by date' nags from a local stables, swimming in the local gravel pits at South Cerney and visits to Stroud. There they could meet with a number of attractive young ladies, who had been evacuated from London and were working for a local business.

Early in May six glider crews from 'F' Sqn were chosen for an unspecified operation. Training for it involved night landings without flare paths in fully loaded Horsa gliders. Steel bars were used in place of troops or equipment. The operation was to be on

Horsa Glider landing at Blakehill Farm after exercise.   Photo: Joe Smee

Dakota preparing to take off from Blakehill Farm with Horsa glider in tow.   Photo: Joe Smee

the night before D-Day and would involve the carrying of ammunition and equipment to France for the 8th (Midland Counties) Parachute Battalion.

The policy to add Air Ambulance Orderlies to each aircrew was confirmed at this time. All Dakota aircraft were modified in the fuselage areas and fitted with stretchers in readiness for Blakehill Farm to become the hospital unit for the Group. The hospital, Casualty Air Evacuation Centre (CAEC), was large and under canvas. Following treatment, casualties would be moved by ambulance to other hospitals. There were other CAECs at Down Ampney and Broadwell where casualties were returned in Dakotas. Burn cases would be taken directly on landing to Odstock Hospital, Salisbury where specialist treatment was available. By early May the number of Horsa gliders on the station had increased to 50. The 5th May brought a station visit from ACM Sir Trafford Leigh Mallory KCB, DSO, and Major General F.A.M. (Boy) Browning CB, DSO, G.O.C. Airborne Forces. They addressed all aircrew assembled in the briefing room. No.92 FSP left for Watchfield on 25th May. Off station squadrons were sending personnel to Blakehill Farm for training and operations, as on 31st May when ground and aircrews from both No.271 Sqn Down Ampney and a detachment from No.575 Sqn Broadwell arrived. Personnel of the 8th

(Midland Counties) Parachute Battalion, 3 Parachute Brigade arrived from Tilshead on 27th May, camping on the airfield in tents.

Two units, Nos.18 and 19 Terminal Staging Post (TSP), nucleus formed at Blakehill Farm on 22nd May. No.18 was not officially formed until 2nd August 1944 and then from ex No.93 FSP at B14 Amblie. No.93 FSP arrived at Blakehill Farm from Lyneham on 1st June. No.19 TSP officially formed on 8th August from a nucleus of No.91 FSP at Down Ampney and left the next day for B.14 Amblie.

Dakotas of No.233 Sqn line up on the perimeter track at Blakehill Farm in preparation for D-Day. Photo: Don Neate Coll.

On 1st June the station was brought to a state of readiness with 'A' State manning in force, this being for Operation *Tonga*, the first phase of the airdrop of Operation *Overlord*. Two days later the station was completely sealed with no one allowed off base and no one on to it. The activities of the civilian farmers living and working within the confines of the base were curtailed at this time. Returning from a non-duty spell on the 4th, L.A.C. Jim Leaman a Flight Mechanic Engineer with No.233 Sqn, unaware of the restriction, left the Station to meet his girlfriend (later to be his wife) at a dance in Ashton Keynes. His departure was by way of a hole in the fence. He was surprised to find no other air force personnel at the dance when he arrived but was soon told of the airfield closure by the local girls already there. John made a rapid return to base through the hole in the fence and quickly changed into uniform before joining his

colleagues. Orders were received from Group on the 4th June to commence briefing of the 30 crews who would be participating in Operation *Tonga*. One of No.233 Sqn's pilots, Fg Off Phil Diamond recalls that, on D-Day -1, because of a 24 hour delay, it was necessary for the paratroops to be entertained or distracted from the task ahead. A number of pianos were wheeled onto the runway for singing sessions.

On the evening of 5th June 1944, the final briefing of all personnel was attended by Maj.Gen. Browning commanding the British Airborne Corps, Air Cdre Fiddament AOC No.46 Group, AVM. A. Collier Deputy Commander-in-Chief of Transport Command, and AVM C.H.K. Edmunds ADGB. Personnel were addressed by ACM Sir Trafford Leigh Mallory and the AOC No.46 Group. It was made clear to the No.233 Sqn crews that the LZ they were expected to locate was the furthest inland and achieving it was of vital importance. Navigation from base was by *'Gee'* until homing on the LZ using a Eureka beacon and holophane lights which had been positioned, shortly before the landings, by the pathfinders of 22 Independent Parachute Brigade. At 2250 hrs 6 Dakotas of No.233 Sqn lifted off from Blakehill Farm, towing 6 Horsa gliders of 'F' Sqn carrying the 8th (Midland Counties) Parachute Battalion jeeps (6), trailers (6), motor cycles (8), bicycles (12) and T.N.T. for use of paratroops at LZ 'K' near Toufreville. 6

LtoR Fg Off Russ Downes (Canadian), Fg Off Joe Proctor and Fg Off Bill Greenwood of No.233 Sqn with Venetia Rickards the Landlady of the Plough Inn at Ashton Keynes, village close to the airfield. Photo: Joe Smee

Sappers and a few other army personnel accompanied the gliders. The primary object of the 8th Parachute Battalion together with the 3rd. Parachute Sqn RE, was to destroy two bridges one at Bures and one at Troarn so delaying any armour attempting to force the eastern flank of the Allied armies.

Glider, Chalk No.218, was piloted by Lt Pickwoad and Sgt Watts with Wg Cdr Morrison as tug pilot. Chalk No.219 was piloted by S/Sgt Ridgeway and Sgt Foster with WO Bailey as tug pilot. Chalk No.220 was piloted by S/Sgt Banks and Sgt Hebblethwaite with Fg Off Wood as tug pilot. Chalk No.221 was piloted by S/Sgt England and Sgt Graham with Flt Lt Barley as tug pilot. Chalk No.222 was piloted by S/Sgt Heron and Sgt Davidson with Fg Off Fram as tug pilot. Chalk No.223 was piloted by S/Sgt Weeden and Sgt Griffiths with Fg Off Hardimand as tug pilot.

On arrival in the area of LZ 'K' the 6 'F' Sqn gliders found it obscured by low cloud and the smoke of war and only the two gliders flown by Lt Pickwoad and Sgt Banks managed to land on the correct LZ. This was primarily because the Eureka beacon had been incorrectly placed on LZ 'N'. Three gliders flown by S/Sgts England, Heron and Weeden put down at LZ 'N', 3 miles from LZ 'K', and one, piloted by S/Sgt Bill Ridgeway and Sgt Foster, landed in the marshes at Vimont which was too far inland. Both of these glider pilots were taken prisoner and whilst Sgt Foster successfully escaped and joined the Free French Forces, he was killed on Sunday 18th June attempting to cross over to the British lines. He is buried at La Delivrande War Cemetery, Douvres, Calvados, France. For this operation two of the glider pilots, S/Sgt Dickie 'Admiral' Banks and Lt Aubrey Pickwoad were awarded the DFM and DFC respectively.

24 aircraft with 406 paratroops, 89 containers and 109 kit bags followed the initial flight. Crossing the Channel, troops in the back of the Dakotas thought they were coming under fire when they heard a rattle on the fuselage but this was just hailstones.

No.233 Sqn Dakota III KG420 was one of the 24 aircraft carrying paratroopers. Flown by New Zealander Flt Lt R. McIlraith with Flt Sgt Phil Diamond (2nd pilot), Flt Sgt Don Phillips (nav) and Fg Off Joe Smee (WOP), they successfully dropped a stick of 17 paratroops of the 6th Airborne Division on the DZ near Caen at 0058 hrs. Twelve 20lb fragmentation bombs were dropped on the beach and the aircraft landed back at base at 0311 hrs. The No.2 Dakota in their 'vic' of three was KG356 piloted by Captain Fg Off Harvey E. Jones RCAF. This aircraft was attacked and set on fire on the approach to the DZ but refusing his parachute Jones managed to keep it airborne until all the troops had jumped. The aircraft crashed at Bassenville, east of Caen at approximately 0010hrs on 6th June. Two of the crew, Flt Sgt John A. Daldorph RAF (2nd pilot) and Fg Off Lewis N. Williams RAF (nav.) baled out. They remained with the paratroops and linked up with the seaborne forces before returning to England on 12th June. WO Corby Engleberg RCAF (WOP/AG), who had been unable to bale out in time, was rescued from the crashed aircraft and returned to hospital in England on the same day as his colleagues. Fg Off Jones of Niagara Falls, who sacrificed his own life for the paratroops and his crew, was initially buried in an isolated field at Bassenville, but was later consecrated in the Ranville British Military Cemetery, Calvaldos, France.

Another No.233 Sqn Dakota lost that night was KG429 with its crew of WO Munro M. McCannell RAFVR, Flt Sgt Alexander R. Porter RAFVR, WO Albert T. Downing RAFVR and WO Nathan L. Berger RCAF. All four were killed and are also buried at Ranville Cemetery. Operation 'Tonga' was carried out successfully, although not all went according to plan.

On the following night 21 aircraft on Operation 'Rob Roy One', set off on the first re-supply run to drop 371 panniers on DZ 'N' in the Caen area, for the 6th Airborne Division. The panniers contained ammunition, fuel, radio sets and provisions. Approaching the French coast at the mouth of the River Orne, intense light flak from Allied naval vessels damaged two of the aircraft which were forced to return to base. The two lead aircraft went down in flames. One of these was KG424 crewed by Sqn Ldr C. Wright AFC, RAF (pilot), Fg Off E.Q. Sample RCAF (2nd pilot), Fg Off B. Cowie RNZAF (nav) and Fg Off C. J.

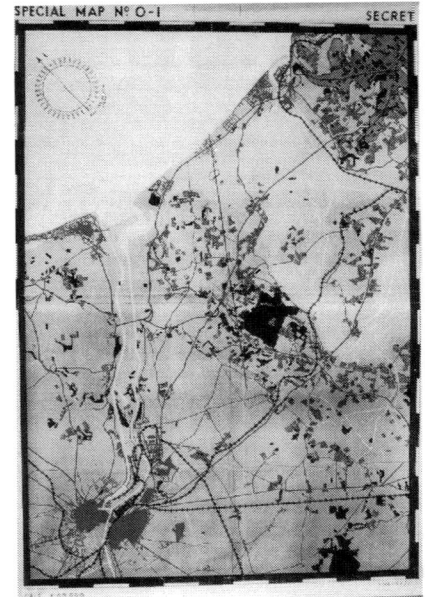

SPECIAL MAP Nº O-1   SECRET

The D-Day navigation map used by the crew of Dakota KG420 showing the flight path from the French coast to the Drop Zone near Caen. Copy: Phil Diamond

Williams RAF (WOP). The aircraft turned to starboard and went down in a controlled dive with smoke coming from the engines. The Captain and Navigator became PoW but the 2nd Pilot and WOP escaped and returned to their squadron on 3rd July. The second aircraft was KG329 with Fg Off E. E. Wood RAF, Flt Sgt A.S. Illingworth RAF, Plt Off D.W.B. Carr RAF and Sgt. L. Thomas RAF. Fg Off Wood was killed in the crash and his crew became PoW. There was damage to other aircraft KG433 and FZ688 but they were still able to drop supplies at the DZ.

The laying of temporary runways in France had begun following the landings and lasted for ten days. Hedges were bulldozed and metal strips were laid across cornfields. Each of the strips was given a 'B' number. Some of them later became Advanced Landing Grounds. On completion re-supply missions were flown in, with casualties being brought out. LAC Ken Mills was a Wireless Operator (Directional Finding Section) with an Air Transportable Signals Unit (ATSU) at Blakehill Farm. With the completion of the Landing Grounds, these units were flown in to set up radios and transmitters and begun linking up with Hospital Staging Posts for the repatriation of the wounded. Ken Mills recalls that their transmissions attracted attention from the enemy so it was necessary to ensure that their tents were dug into the ground to give some form of protection from the anti personnel bombs dropped. The ATSUs would move forward as the Army advanced. After a few weeks, Ken Mills and his unit were returned to Blakehill Farm in preparation for the Arnhem operation. Circumstances changed however and the unit eventually left Blakehill Farm for occupational duties in Norway during 1945.

On Friday 13th June two Dakotas IIIs of No.233 Sqn escorted by Spitfires, landed at B2 Bazenville, a refuelling and rearming strip. They carried 4 tons of screw pickets and returned from there with 20 casualties consisting of 14 stretcher cases and 6 walking wounded. These were the first aircraft of Transport Command to land in France after the D-Day invasion and the first to evacuate casualties by air. The aircraft taking off at 0506 hrs were KG427- Fg Off C.D. Hamilton, Fg Off W. Menzies, WO F.B. Knight and Flt Sgt Jimmy Firth. The two Australians, Hamilton and Firth were later killed at Arnhem. FZ686- WO R.F Holliday, Flt Sgt E.J. James, WO G.A. Cozens and Flt Sgt H.J. Richardson. The two aircraft touched down at Blakehill Farm at 1922 and 1905 hrs respectively, where they were met on arrival by 42 Press War Correspondents representing the British, Canadian and American newspapers.

On the same day two other No.233 Sqn Dakotas were detailed to transport Air HQ personnel of No.83 Wing from Thorney Island to B.2. They took off at 1300 hrs escorted by 6 Spitfires out and back. The aircraft were KG440- Sqn Ldr G.D. Lane (later Lord Chief Justice), WO M.W. Lee, Fg Off H.A. Wallace and Fg Off J.F. Sweeney. FZ678-Flt Lt H.J. Barley DFC, Fg Off W.I. Greenwood, Flt Lt G.N. Taylor and Flt Lt C. Ingleby DFC. Sqn Ldr Lane returned with 3 stretcher cases in his aircraft. The two Dakotas landed at Blakehill Farm at 2147 and 2150 hrs respectively.

On these flights, three Air Nursing Orderlies (WAAF) were carried for the first time on casevac duties, LACW Myra Roberts, Cpl. Lydia Alford and LACW Edna Birbeck.

No.93 FSP left Blakehill Farm for B8 Sommervieu on 29th June.

LtoR Flt Lt H.J. Barley DFC (New Zealand) with his WOP Flt Lt C. Ingleby DFC at Blakehill Farm where they served with No.233 Sqn. Both had previously completed tours with Bomber Command, Barley on Lancasters and Ingleby on Wellingtons. Barley was serving with No.44 Sqn when he received his DFC on 12.10.43 and Ingleby served with No.11 OTU when his DFC was gazetted on 29.12.42. Photo: Joe Smee.

LACW Edna Birbeck on board a No.233 Sqn Dakota having returned with the first flight of wounded from Normandy on Friday 13th June 1944, D-Day +7. Photo: Edna Morris

During June and July the pattern of operations was fairly routine with re-supply deliveries of equipment being made to the army in France and personnel brought back from the Advanced Landing Grounds. On outward flights the Air Nursing Orderlies accompanied the supply mission and quite often landed in hostile areas before returning to their home bases with casualties. Fg Off Diamond who was newly married would cycle from the airfield to see his wife at the White Hart Hotel in Cricklade and later in Swindon. He remembers the lanes around the airfield being stacked on either side with containers of war supplies awaiting delivery by the aircraft as and when required.

The detachment of No.271 Sqn returned to Down Ampney on the 12th August having operated from Blakehill Farm to relieve pressure at their home base. On 18th August additional pilots for No.14 Flight 'F' Sqn of No.2 Wing Glider Pilot Regiment arrived for forthcoming operations and the following day a detachment of No.168 Sqn arrived. On the Continent, Allied forces who had fought their way from

WAAF Air Nursing Orderlies outside their quarters at Blakehill Farm. LACW Edna Birbeck (left) displaying some of the German souvenirs obtained when she was in France to repatriate Allied troops. Photo: Edna Morris

A No.233 Sqn crew at Blakehill Farm before take-off for Landing Strip B3 at the Normandy Bridgehead on 16th June 1944. The cargo on this re-supply flight was bombs, returning with 25 casualties: - Flt Sgt Phil Diamond (2nd Pilot), Flt Lt 'Mac' McIlraith (Pilot), Flt Sgt Don Phillips (Nav), Fg Off Joe Smee (WOP) and unknown Nursing Orderly. Photo: Phil Diamond

Normandy, were in pursuit of the retreating German armies, which were now falling back towards Germany. Ahead of the Allies was the formidable Siegfried Line, a chain of static defences, which on reaching, the Germans armies were planning to hold and re-group. Blakehill Farm, as in the preceding two months, continued to support the Allies with routine freight carrying and casualty evacuation. No.233 Sqn at this time was heavily involved in flying food supplies to Orleans/Bricy for the relief of the people of Paris. On the 28th August, HQ No.2 Wing Glider Pilot Regiment left

for a new base at RAF Broadwell.

In August No.14 Flt. 'F' Sqn GPR took part in a massed night landing exercise at Netheravon airfield. Fog covered Netheravon and this resulted in gliders landing in all directions and some in surrounding fields. Out of 30 gliders only 10 were serviceable the following day. Fortunately the only casualties were two passengers who sustained back injuries.

No.14 Flt 'F' Sqn GPR under the command of Capt Pickwoad, remained at Blakehill Farm following their

participation in the June D-Day landings. The main element was based at Broadwell. For the Arnhem operation a temporary detachment was that of No.5 Flt 'D' Sqn GPR No.1 Wing based at Keevil with Capt John M. Morrisson as CO. The glider pilots for the Blakehill Farm serials, were however, mainly supplied from No.14 Flt.

No.437 (T) 'Husky' Sqn (RCAF), No.46 Group, was formed at Blakehill Farm on 14th September with the first contingent arriving four days prior to this. It was the first Canadian Transport Sqn to operate from the UK. It consisted of three Flights 'A', 'B' and 'C' and No.4437 Servicing Echelon. No.233 Sqn had a number of RCAF crews who were posted to make up No.437 Sqn. The first CO was Wg Cdr John A. Sproule DFC who appropriately was the first squadron member to arrive at Blakehill Farm together with the Adjutant Flt Lt Ed Joynt on 4th September. The squadron, as with No.233 Sqn, was equipped with 30 Dakotas plus 5 reserves. As of the 15th September, two days prior to Operation Market, No.437 Sqn had nine crews fully operational.

No.123 (Major) Staging Post in No.46 Group, formed at Blakehill Farm on 5th September and 75 C-47s of the USAAF landed on the same day en-route to the seat of fighting in France. They were loaded with urgently needed petrol in Jerry cans for US General George S. Patton and his tanks of the 3rd Army, who were spearheading a rapid drive east, and General Miles Dempsey's British 2nd Army advancing east through Belgium. Both armies were desperate for fuel supplies having outrun their chain of supply, which stretched back some 200 miles. On 13th September, No.575 Sqn detachment returned to its home base at Broadwell.

On 17th September 1944, Operation 'Market', the air landing of the British 1st Airborne Division at Arnhem, commenced. For this operation General Browning was designated commander of the airborne forces and US General Paul L. Williams as air commander of the glider, troop and supply aircraft. From Blakehill Farm 22 Dakotas of No.233 Sqn with 22 'F' Sqn Horsa gliders took-off at 0956hrs carrying troops of the 7th Kings Own Scottish Borderers, handcarts, jeeps, trailers, blitz buggies, wireless sets,

Wg Cdr Jack Sproule DFC & Sqn Ldr Charles 'Mac' McVeigh No. 437 Sqn RCAF wit 'Brevet' the squadron mascot.   Photo: National Defence

motor cycles, 1 anti-tank gun, bicycles and cars. Despite difficulties with cloud and slipstream during the three hour flight, all of the contingent bar one, arrived safely on LZ 'S' near Wolfheze, around 6 miles NW of Arnhem, between 1311-1320 hrs. 21 Dakotas returned to base between 1518-1547hrs. One No.233 Sqn Dakota KG427 piloted by Fg Off Hamilton aborted and returned to base when its towrope broke. The Horsa (Chalk No.185) it was towing, landed near the USAAF base at Andrews Field, with no injuries to those on board. The glider pilots were RSM 'Mick' Briody, the Regimental Sgt Maj of No.2 Wing GPR and S/Sgt Marshall. They and the 28 troops on board were flown back to Blakehill Farm and the following day took off again and landed successfully at Arnhem.

On its first operation, 12 Dakotas of No.437 Sqn with 12 No.14 Flt 'F' Sqn Horsa III gliders took-off for LZ 'S' at 1003 hrs. The gliders carried 146 troops of the 1st Battalion, Border Regiment, handcarts, jeeps, trailers, blitz buggies, wireless sets and motorcycles. The 12 DC IIIs and gliders reached the Arnhem LZ between 1311-1320 hrs and all the squadron Dakotas arrived safely back at Blakehill Farm.

The following day 17 No.233 Sqn aircraft with 17 No.5 Flt 'D' Sqn Horsa gliders started take-off on the 2nd Lift for LZ 'X' at 1043 hrs. They carried 84 troops of the 2nd Air Landing Anti-Tank

Horsa gliders on LZ 'S' on 17th September, some gliders are seen burning. On the left, the light strip running from top to bottom, is the sandy base of an unfinished autobahn. Out of picture to the right is the Arnhem to Utrecht railway line with LZ 'Z', where the gliders from Keevil landed.
Photo: The Keevil Society

Battery, 15 jeeps, 7 trailers, 6-pounder Anti-Tank and machine guns, handcarts and motor cycles. Dakota KG448, Flt Lt Lew Cody DFC, DFM (pilot), aborted when the towrope broke from Horsa (Chalk No.773) with pilots S/Sgt Browne and Sgt Auty. Both aircraft landed safely at Andrew's Field where the load was transferred to the tug, which then returned to base. Two other Dakotas were slightly damaged by enemy action.

Six No.437 Sqn Dakotas towing 'D' Sqn Horsa gliders took-off with the No.233 Sqn aircraft with 21 troops and similar equipment for LZ 'X'. All the tugs returned to base between 1628-1642 hrs, one having sustained damage from enemy action.

Only one flight operated on the 19th September for the 3rd Lift. No.233 Sqn provided one Dakota KG448, flown by Flt Lt Cody and towing Horsa (Chalk No.773) with pilots S/Sgt Browne and Sgt Auty of 'D' Sqn. This was the aborted combination from the previous day and it was tasked to land on the LZ as originally briefed. It was therefore the only glider landing in this area west of Wolfheze. Take-off was at 1138 hrs, carrying 6 troops of the 2nd Air Landing Anti-Tank Battery RA, jeep and trailer. The Horsa safely reached LZ 'X', although damaged by flak which killed one of the soldiers and injured another. The Dakota also suffered flak damage and, on landing back at Blakehill Farm at 1752hrs, it was discovered that the wing tanks had been perforated like a colander.

On 20th September, 18 No.233 Sqn aircraft took-off at 1311 hrs for supply dropping on a DZ west of Arnhem. 14 aircraft returned to base, 3 were shot down by enemy fighters and one landed at B.56 Evere, Brussels after suffering severe damage over the DZ. This had been the lead aircraft and had Blakehill Farm's Station Commander Gp Capt Kennedy flying as co-pilot to the No.233 Sqn Commander, Wg Cdr W.E. Coles DFC, AFC. Fg Off Sharp (WOP) was injured by flak and the dispatcher, L/Cpl Clements was dragged out of the aircraft when the containers were released. Despite its severe damage, the aircraft landed safely at Brussels but was written off. The Stn Cdr and crew returned to base later as passengers in another No.233 Sqn Dakota. 10 No.437 Sqn aircraft took-off at 1311 hrs on a supply drop to the same DZ. Five returned safely to base at 1828 hrs, 1 aircraft landed at B.56 with its port engine damaged by flak and 4 failed to return. On 23rd September, 17 No.233 Sqn aircraft took-off between 1317-1323 hrs on a re-supply mission to a DZ near Arnhem. 210 panniers were dropped on or near the DZ but some of these jammed and were brought back. All aircraft returned safely to base.

No.109 (Transport) OTU detached 3 aircraft from Crosby-on-Eden to Blakehill Farm between 22nd-28th September to augment losses during Operation *'Market'*. A detachment from No.168 Sqn visited Blakehill Farm during the month.

As had happened during the D-Day landings, the intention was that the glider pilots used at Arnhem would endeavour to return across the Channel following the landings. As it turned out, with the relieving forces many miles to the south, a prompt return was not possible. The very heavy casualties suffered by the parachute battalions and the 1st Air Landing Brigade in the early stages of the battle resulted in No.14 Flt 'F' Sqn being used in an infantry capacity from the third day onwards. Initially near Osterbeek church and then in the north west corner of the perimeter in the Sonnenberg area. During the ensuing fighting 11 members of the Flt were killed. On the evening of the 9th day the Flt joined the general withdrawal and by Friday 29th September, 33 personnel of the 66 who landed at Arnhem on 17th had returned to Blakehill Farm. 20 had been wounded and taken prisoner. S/Sgt Banks, who received the DFM for the D-Day operations, was one of the glider pilots killed in a Luftwaffe attack at Arnhem on the third day. The 10 other glider pilots who died were S/Sgts Moorcock, Mathews, McLaren, Drurey, Sgts Graham, Mogg, Marriot, Howes, Parkinson and Hebblethwaite.

From October 1944 through to February 1945 the squadrons at Blakehill Farm were mainly involved in passenger/troops and casualty transportation and re-supply runs to Belgium and Holland with ammunition, petrol, drop tanks, mail and newspapers. On 1st October 1944, four No.437 Sqn aircraft shipped 26 barrels of *'Special Fluid'*, under armed guard, on a return flight to Blakehill Farm. This was in fact, water taken from the River Rhein and was required for testing to see if it had possibly been used for cooling purposes in an atomic reactor. This would give the Allies an indication that the Germans had developed a nuclear bomb. When the barrels left the care of No.437 Sqn for the testing laboratories, they were accompanied by a quantity of French wine with a label requesting 'Please Test'. Later a report was received to the effect that 'Testing of river water

Horsa gliders lined up for an exercise on an over-cast day. The 'T' Type Hangar is in the distance behind the Dakotas of No.233 Sqn. The No.437 Sqn personnel are (l to r) Fg Off Wally Hughes, Sgt Jack Chambers, Fg Off Earl Simpson, Flt Lt Dick Souter, Fg Off Doc Wynn, unknown, Fg Off *'Sinbad'* Phillips and Fg Off *'Blackie'* Burns.

proved negative - tests on wine interesting, please send more samples'.

No.233 and 437 Sqns were accompanied by aircraft of No.168 and 512 Sqns on some of the missions. On Tuesday 24th October 1944, 9 No.437 Sqn Dakotas took-off from Blakehill Farm at 1000 hrs for B.70 Deurne, Antwerp, where they arrived at 1230 hrs approximately. The task was the delivery of 27,856lbs of ammunition and 19,570lbs of Army freight. Take-off for the return flight commenced at 1415 hrs and during the flight Dakota FZ655 went missing. The crew were Flt Sgt D.C. Schnelder (pilot), Flt Sgt J.W. Lockwood (co-pilot), Sgt Sidney A. Gumbrell RCAF (nav/bomber), WO John H. Soper RCAF (WOP/AG) and a Scottish WAAF Nursing Orderly LACW Margaret Campbell. She together with Sgt Gumbrell and WO Soper were buried in Calais Canadian War Cemetery.

In between its operational commitments, training was not overlooked by No.437 Sqn. Each month, two half days as a minimum, were spent in practising glider towing and pannier drops with half a day spent on each. A Dakota was set aside exclusively for this training.

No.123 (Major) Staging Post left for Perranporth on 5th December 1944.

On 9th January 1945, No.233 Sqn's Flt Lt Cody, still flying KG448, took off from Eindhoven and, in the climb in poor visibility, his aircraft struck another Dakota. A large section of the port outer wing was lost but, with considerable effort by himself and the co-pilot, he was able to make a successful emergency landing. His actions on this day were mentioned in the citation of the award of the AFC he received in February, adding to his DFC and DFM.

In this group of WAAF Nursing Orderlies at Blakehill Farm, LACW Margaret Campbell is pictured 4th from the right in the back row.   Photo: Edna Morris

No.437 Sqn's Dakota Mk.III KG425 Z2 'M'. The two letters OM in the diamond on the nose indicate the code given to the squadron and the individual aircraft. 'O' relates to the Sqn No. and 'M' the aircraft identification letter. This form of identification was adopted by Transport Command during the latter stages of the war. KG425 later suffered considerable damage when force landing in Holland. The inscription beneath the cockpit is *Fort Rae*, in keeping with the naming of the squadron aircraft after forts established in Canada by the Hudson's Bay Company.
Photo: National Defence

On 3rd February 1945, 'B' Flt No.233 Sqn proceeded to, and operated from, B.75 Nivelles in Belgium taking over the commitments undertaken by a detachment of No.575 Sqn.

On 24th March 1945, 24 aircraft of No.233 Sqn and 24 of No.437 Sqn were sent to Birch. With 12 Dakotas of No.48 Sqn, which was on detachment there, they took part in airborne Operation *'Varsity'* in support of the US 9th & 2nd British Armies Rhine crossings. They towed 60 Horsas to LZs 'O' & 'U' north/west of Wesel on the east bank of the Rhine. 33 aircraft with Horsa Mk IIs took off with troops of the 2nd Oxfordshire & Buckinghamshire Light Infantry and 27 with troops of the Royal Ulster Rifles. The load included jeeps, trailers, artillery, motorcycles and bicycles. The aircraft were escorted by Spitfires and Mustangs. 4 Dakotas of No.437 Sqn suffered minor flak damage whilst releasing gliders on to the DZs. Over 5000 aircraft of all types took part in what was, at the time, the largest Allied airborne force in history. The operation was a complete success.

There were a considerable number of sorties flown during April and May 1945. These were mainly re-supply drops, the transportation of passengers, and the return of PoW and casualties. No.437 Sqn moved to Nivelles in Belguim on 7th May. On the same day a Dakota III KG585 of No.233 Sqn, captained by Fg Off Ernest 'Smudge' Smith, with WO E 'Inky' Stephens and

Fg Off Alec 'Jack' Payne, was ordered from B156 Luneburg to Flensburg for a special mission. At the Gp Capt's briefing, his opening comment to Fg Off Smith was "Young man, you are going to make history". After spending the night at Flensburg the crew were given the task of taking the German Chiefs of Staff to Berlin calling on route at R34 Stendal. The Germans were to attend the official ceremony for the signing of the Instrument of Unconditional Surrender of the German Armed Forces to the Allied Forces. The passengers were Generalfeldmarschall Wilhelm Keitel (Chief of the High Commander of the Armed Forces), Generaladmiral Hans Georg von Friedeburg (Supreme

Rations being unloaded at B75 Nivelles by Fg Off Jack Wells and Fg Off Pete Porter.
Photo: National Defence

Commander of the German Navy) together with Vizeadmiral Burkner and Generaloberst Hans-Juergen Stumpff of the Luftwaffe. In addition there were 4 German Staff Officers (Aides), Oberstleutnant Bochm Tettelbach, Hauptmann Salman, Major Stangl, Ministerialrat Bottger with 2 DAPMs (RCAF) escorting them. They were met unexpectedly at Stendal by ACM Arthur Tedder, who wanted to know why they were two hours late. Apparently there had been a party on the previous evening where a considerable amount of drinking had taken place. Tedder directed Fg Off Smith to take-off last and fly in formation with two other aircraft which were already at Stendal, and would be carrying the Allied Leaders. With a fighter escort provided, the three aircraft took-off and flew to Templehof. On arrival the passengers were taken to the Russian HQ building where the final act of surrender was signed. Fg Off Smith and his crew were lavishly entertained by the Russian Army. They were grateful to the Russians for the very friendly and warm feelings expressed towards the British and Americans. After a short night's rest, the aircraft took off at 0747 hrs on 9th May to return the surrender party to Flensburg. Generalfeldmarschall Keitel thanked Fg Off Smith and his crew for a safe journey. The next day the crew recorded an interview with Chester Wilmot of the BBC for inclusion in the Victory Parade broadcast. Unfortunately the recording was lost in transit to the UK. The crew was debriefed on their return to Blakehill Farm.

Aircraft having delivered supplies rarely returned empty to the UK. Here wounded soldiers are transferred from ambulances to a No.437 Sqn Dakota by personnel of a Canadian Field Hospital. Photo: National Defence

French and Belgian PoW having just been released are about to board a *Husky* Sqn Dakota on their journey home. The RCAF crew are (l to r) Fg Off Louis Botari, Sqn Ldr Robert Joyce, Fg Off Harry McKinley, Fg. Off John Rehenuc. Photo: National Defence

The Dakotas were loaded with spares and ground crew when No.437 Sqn moved from Blakehill Farm to B75 Nivelles. Here in a cramped fuselage during the transfer are (l to r) Bill Hanson, W.E. Madrill, Fred LaMontagne, Pat Kearney, Lloyd Mills, C.E. Eady, Leo Dandurand, (centre) Vern Hanson, (standing) Frank Royce, Joseph McGhee, Jack Paull, Osborne McClure and Forbes McGill. Photo: National Defence

No.233 Sqn left for Odiham on 8th June 1945. The Canadian No.437 Sqn had been adopted by the Hudson's Bay Company and their Dakota aircraft carried the names of forts established by the Company. In April 1945 whilst still based at Blakehill, the squadron crest was granted Royal Assent by King George VI. The crest, designed by Flt Lt A.A. Baker, was formed with the head of a Husky and the motto *"Omnia Passim"*, meaning Anything Anywhere. As a Canadian Transport Sqn it was symbolic that it was given *"Husky"* as a title.

No.22 Heavy Glider Conversion Unit/Operational Refresher Training Unit arrived from Keevil on 15th June 1945 with Albemarles and Waco Hadrian gliders. The unit was using Fairford as a satellite. With its arrival at Blakehill Farm, Horsa training had ended and the Unit was engaged in conversion training of Hadrian pilots for the Far East. The period ending 30th June was used for Refresher & Advanced Training of Operational Glider pilots with a total of 209 crews receiving instruction. Five Albemarle VIs and five Hadrian Is were struck off charge during the month.

Post War Years

Training for glider pilots continued through September 1945. Unit training of staff pilots was also being carried out. An accident occurred on 21st September when a tug aircraft towing a WACO glider No.56532 got into difficulties on take-off. The glider was released but collided with trees on landing and was written off. The second pilot, Sgt M. Smith of the Glider Pilot regiment, suffered injuries. No.22 HGCU/ORTU ceased operating at Blakehill Farm on 21st October and formally disbanded on 15th November 1945. Large numbers of Albemarle VIs, Hadrian IIs, 9 Oxfords and a Proctor were SOC and the remaining unit aircraft were flown to Fairford pending disposal. This allowed Blakehill Farm to receive No.575 Sqn, which arrived at 2230 hrs the following day. The squadron flew from Melbourne, Yorkshire with Dakota IIIs. No.2 Wing HQ Glider Pilot Regiment with 'A' & 'C' Sqns moved to RAF Finmere the same day.

No.22 HGCU personnel grouped in front of an Albemarle in the summer of 1945.
Photo: Derek Farr

Over the next few weeks flying consisted mainly of air testing and removal of aircraft to MUs but also, from the 27th November, day and night flying by No.3 (P) AFU, South Cerney. During December HQ Training Command Aircrew Examination Unit arrived with the task of assessing the performance of aircrew and No.1528 Radio Aids Training Flt arrived from Valley with their Oxfords on 17th December 1945.

On 14th January 1946, Dakota C.4 KK154 of No.575 Sqn crashed following take-off on a categorisation flight. Both engines were feathered in error and the aircraft came down on the Cricklade to Wootton Bassett road. Residents scattered as the aircraft approached them before it came to rest with one wing on the wall surrounding a row of thatched cottages. The aircraft caught fire and was attended by Swindon NFS, Swindon Army Fire Service and the crash tender from Blakehill Farm. All of the Dakota crew escaped, with the pilot Flt Lt Trought being admitted to SSQ suffering from concussion. As a result of this incident, an unfortunate accident occurred when the fire tender responding from Blakehill Farm knocked down a local 8 year old boy David Hicks, inflicting serious injuries.

Incoming flights to Blakehill Farm were now being made by the Dakotas of No.512 Sqn based at Bari in Italy. The Dakotas of No.575 Sqn started moving to Bari on 11th January with the final five leaving on 29th January.

No.1528 Radio Aids Training Flt (RATF) moved to Fairford on 1st February 1946 and disbanded there on 4th March. Personnel and 7 Oxfords from the disbanded Flight were taken over by No.1555 RATF which moved to Blakehill Farm on 30th April but regressed to Fairford in July 1946. The unit continued to use Blakehill Farm's Blind Approach Beam System landing aid. This facility was not then available at Fairford. Tiger Moth N6866, serving with the Station Flt, was flown to No.9 MU Cosford for storage and eventual disposal. It was sold in March 1947 and registered as G-AJHS. It continues to fly today in Holland.

Blakehill Farm closed on 5th November and was placed on C&M from 1st December 1946. The station passed to Flying Training Command on 21st January 1947, which held it as an unmanned RLG for South Cerney. No.2 Flying Training School (FTS) based at South Cerney from 6th April 1948 used Blakehill Farm as a satellite. The runways were often preferable to their own grass ones. One of their aircraft, a Harvard T.2B, KF454 was written-off on 9th January 1951 when it flew into the ground two miles from the airfield, during a night take-off from Blakehill Farm. No.2 FTS was re-designated Central Flying School (Basic) on 1st May 1952 and its Percival Provost trainers continued to use Blakehill Farm with its landing aid equipment, as a RLG.

Closure

When CFS (Basic) and (Advanced) elements amalgamated at Little Rissington on 1st June 1957, the special radio apparatus at Blakehill Farm was removed and flying finally ceased.

The airfield was handed over to Government Communication Headquarters (GCHQ) by the MoD in 1963, whereupon it was operated as an 'experimental' radio station until its final closure in early 1997. The sign at the main entrance of the former airfield indicated 'Government Communication Headquarters, Experimental Radio Station'. This then was one of GCHQ Cheltenham's Radio Listening stations with a large aerial mast towering over the site. When the author was given a conducted tour of the establishment in 1996, it was anticipated that its use by GCHQ would cease in the following year. When it was closed the site was declared surplus to requirements and a decision was taken to dispose of it. Former owners were contacted under the Crichel Down Rules. This is a procedure whereby the land is offered for return to the former owners or their successors in title, thus enabling them to purchase the land conveyed. From this exercise at Blakehill Farm, two former owners have purchased their land and the remainder has been purchased by the Wiltshire Wildlife Trust.

The original runways were torn up in 1971 to provide hard-core for the construction of the nearby M4 Motorway. A few of the original wartime buildings remain but in poor condition. The fire and ambulance stations are recognisable, as are parts of the perimeter track and some dispersals. The base of the control tower is still evident as are the ruins of Blakehill Farm House and its out-buildings. On the north east side, some of the former support buildings are now used for farming. The Chelworth Industrial Estate occupies a further section and parts of the airfield have been returned to farming. The Operations Block survived into the 21st century but was demolished to extend the industrial estate.

Two familiar names serving at Blakehill Farm during the war years were Len Harvey the boxer whose duties were those of Station Sports Officer, and No.233 Sqn had Flt Lt Rank who was a relation of J. Arthur Rank the cinema magnate.

Memorial

173/SU079919 - On the road junction close to the main entrance gate of the Station. A memorial stone dedicated to the Canadian squadron serving at Blakehill Farm during World War 2. The metal plaque on the stone is inscribed: -

WHEN YOU PAUSE TO SEE THE TIME OF THE DAY REMEMBER THE CANADIANS WHO FLEW FROM THIS AIRFIELD BRAVE AND COURAGEOUS, SOME NEVER RETURNED, OTHERS RETURNED WITH LIFETIME MEMORIES.

DEDICATED BY THE MEMBERS OF 437 (T) HUSKY SQUADRON WITH THE GRACIOUS HELP OF THE PEOPLE OF CRICKLADE ON 25TH SEPTEMBER 1994 NO.437 SQUADRON ROYAL CANADIAN AIRFORCE R.A.F. BLAKEHILL FARM 14TH SEPT 1944 - 7TH MAY 1945

The memorial stone was dedicated on 25th September 1994 to mark the 50th Anniversary of the Canadians serving at Blakehill Farm with No.437 (T) *'Husky'* Sqn. Following the dedication, Canadians attending made presentations to the people of Cricklade and these items form part of a Blakehill Farm Airfield presentation on display in the local museum. They in turn received a presentation made from the original flagpole which had stood by the airfield control tower.

No.437 Sqn RCAF memorial at Blakehill Farm.

The former fire and ambulance station site with the ruins of the Blakehill Farm buildings in the background.

BOSCOMBE DOWN AERODROME

Location (184/SU172407 1½ miles East of Amesbury).

Positioned below Beacon Hill on the A303 and off of the C32, lies the airfield of Boscombe Down, one of the most renowned in the country. Its reputation stretches world wide, from North and South America, Canada, China, Australia, New Zealand, to the Middle and Far East and to various European countries whose pilots have attended the Empire Test Pilots' School (ETPS) for training over a period of almost 60 years. The school is one of five throughout the world but the reputation of the ETPS at Boscombe stands alone. The exchange of tutors with the U.S. Navy Test Pilots'School at Patuxent River has been a regular feature bringing benefits to both establishments.

Boscombe Down's fame has been further enhanced by the testing and development role carried out on aircraft of all types but primarily on those used by the Air Force, Army and Navy. Boscombe Down is the major military test-flying airfield in the United Kingdom with some 10,000 sorties flown annually. At any given time there can be as many as 60 aircraft, of more than 20 different types, on trial for the MoD.

Aerodrome Development

Red House Farm with 964 acres of land, on part of which the aerodrome was built, was sold by the Antrobus Estate in 1915 to Messrs. Wort & Way a Salisbury based farming and building company, for £5,600. 333 acres of this farm land was later requisitioned from the company by the War Office for an aerodrome. The site was first established in 1917, one of five to be adopted on Salisbury Plain in that year. It was controlled by 33rd (Training) Wing, Royal Flying Corps (RFC) which formed on 30th August 1917 at 2A Winchester Street, Salisbury in Southern Training Command with its Headquarters in Waine-a-Long Road.

In 1917/18, the aerodrome covered an area of 333 acres, of which 80 acres were occupied by the station buildings. Boscombe Down was not at that time added to the Ministry's permanent list of stations.

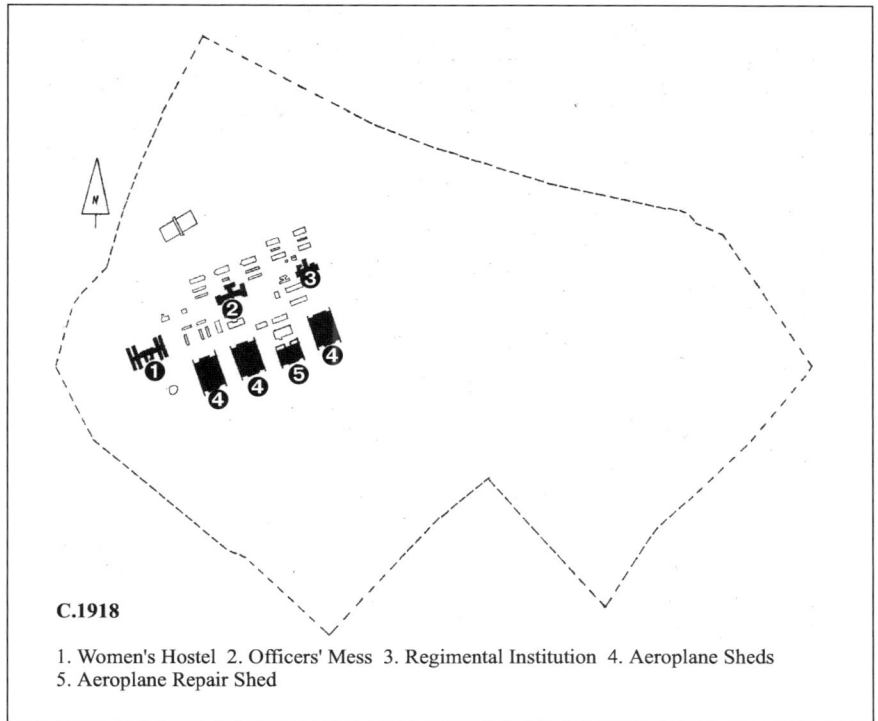

C.1918

1. Women's Hostel 2. Officers' Mess 3. Regimental Institution 4. Aeroplane Sheds
5. Aeroplane Repair Shed

The aerodrome buildings C.1918
Four large General Storage Sheds and an Aeroplane Repair Shed (each 180' x 100') are seen in the centre, with the grass landing area to the right. The sheds were still being built at this time and some of the Belfast Trussing is laying on the ground awaiting installation. The large permanent building north of the service road is the Officers' Mess. A railway siding can be seen at the top of the photograph leading from the Amesbury branch line. A considerable number of Bell tents are in use for accommodation purposes and a baseball diamond has been laid out to the left of the aeroplane hangars, evidence of use by the Americans of the US Aero Squadrons who were on detachment during the war.

The airfield infrastructure had developed by 1918 as can be seen in the photograph. The Technical and Domestic Sites were separated by a service road and by the spring of 1918 many permanent buildings were in position on both sites. The Domestic buildings included the Officers' Mess, 4 Officers' Quarters for staff and 3 for pupils, Sergeants' Mess, 4 Men's billets, Women's Hostel and numerous service huts, stores and offices. 218 of the 858 staff employed were women, a third carrying out 'house-keeping' duties. On the Technical site the Aeroplane Sheds under construction would replace the 13 Bessonau type and the original BE tents. 6 coupled Aeroplane Sheds were built each 180' x 100', 1 Aeroplane Repair Shed (ARS) (with 2 Plane Stores) 180' x 100', 1 salvage Shed, 2 MT Sheds, 2 Workshops (Wood & Metal), various stores, instructional huts and offices. Plans and the photograph of the time show no indication of a Watch Office.

The Amesbury & Military Camp Light Railway skirted the aerodrome and during the 1917 building works a 530 yards branch line was built from the Military Camp line into the aerodrome. This allowed building materials to be brought direct to the site by the contractors train using a 0-6-0 tank engine named 'Lively'. A temporary signal box was provided at the junction with the single track branch. This line entered the airfield and ran parallel to the present main road through the site. In front of the officer's mess a passing loop was formed. The track was lifted and the signal box removed when the airfield closed in 1919. The aerodrome construction work was the responsibility of the Royal Engineers (RE) but using civilian labour and German prisoners of war (PoW).

When the war ended on 11th November 1918, elements of the construction work remained incomplete.

World War 1 Years

No.6 Training Depot Station formed on the 12th October 1917 at Red House Farm, controlled by 36th (Training) Wing, which had formed four days before at Thruxton. The aerodrome was known as Red House Farm but this was only for a matter of days as on the 17th October 1917 it was re-named

Boscombe Down. This was probably about the time when Lt A.V. Hurley arrived on site with some 100 personnel and 6 BE tents to take over the site. Initially their over-night accommodation was in a barn at nearby Stockport Bottom Farm but Lt Hurley was soon to establish a temporary Officers' Mess in the George Hotel in Amesbury and was joined there soon after by 5 instructors and four pupils. Gradually the numbers increased to 25 officers. This facility was used until a permanent Officers' Mess was established at the airfield site. During 1918 a pane of glass from one of the hotel window, on which the officers had etched their names, was removed and for a number of years, before being damaged, was retained by Lt Hurley. He gave this to Boscombe Down during the 1960s. With the tented hangars erected the first BE2 arrived. Unfortunately on landing it turned over onto its back after running into a rabbit mound. A replacement BE2B was sent from Farnborough and the initial 4 pupils had to share use of it. This machine was given the name *Virgo Intacta* as it was the first aeroplane to arrive safely.

The role of No.6 Training Depot Station was one of Day Bombing with three Flights being formed: - 'A' Flight from No.82 Sqn (Waddington), 'B' Flt from No.83 Sqn (Spittlegate) and 'C' Flt from No.59 Training Sqn (Yatesbury). It was formed to give advanced training to pilots of the RFC, some of whom were from the Empire countries. They were joined on the station by Americans of the 119th Aero Park and the 188th Aero Sqn when they entered the war. During 1918 there were further detachments from the 216th, 247th, 306th, 310th, 315th, 337th and 823rd Aero Sqns. Ground crews unused to aeroplanes also received training.

As the station developed, Lt Hurley was superseded by Maj. B.F. Vernon-Harcourt as the first recognised CO. Additional aircraft used for training at that time were DH4s, DH6s, DH9s and the AW.FK8s.

Inter War Years

Coinciding with the end of World War 1, No.11 Training Depot Station at Old Sarum transferred the few miles to Boscombe Down as did No.14 TDS as a cadre from Lake Down. The latter returned to Lake Down in March 1919.

Closure

The use of the Station for advanced training ceased on 15th May 1919 when the cut backs following the end of the war brought closure. The site, then on Care & Maintenance, was used as an aircraft storage unit until 1st April 1920 when it was returned to Wort & Way who must have been very pleased with the many substantial buildings they inherited for farming and storage purposes at a cost of £1000. No longer were the sheep and cows subjected to the elements that swept over Salisbury Plain as they were living the good life in the enclosed hangars. Farm machinery was stored and maintained in the dry and even hayricks were built in the ample space of the hangars.

Boscombe Down c.1922 showing dereliction in front of the Aeroplane Sheds

Aerodrome Redevelopment

In 1926, 500 acres of land and buildings were purchased by the Air Ministry for £15,000 and the renovation and construction commenced of a permanent RAF Station, suitable for use by two bomber squadrons under the administration of Wessex Bombing Area. A new Officers' and Sergeants' Mess were erected together with a NAAFI and married quarters. The original Officers' Mess became the main stores and a gymnasium. The timber billets were replaced by brick ones, and an additional large Type 'A' aircraft hangar was erected on the west end of the original Aeroplane Sheds. A Watch Office and searchlight enclosure was added in front of the centre Shed. Construction work was incomplete when the station reopened on 1st September 1930 and was still on going in 1932.

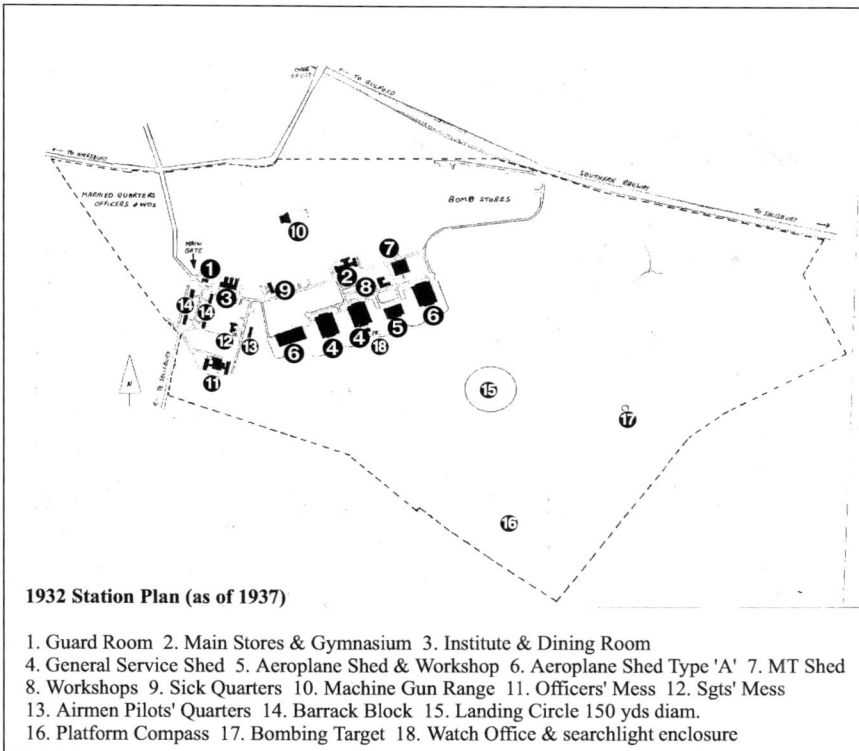

1932 Station Plan (as of 1937)

1. Guard Room 2. Main Stores & Gymnasium 3. Institute & Dining Room
4. General Service Shed 5. Aeroplane Shed & Workshop 6. Aeroplane Shed Type 'A' 7. MT Shed
8. Workshops 9. Sick Quarters 10. Machine Gun Range 11. Officers' Mess 12. Sgts' Mess
13. Airmen Pilots' Quarters 14. Barrack Block 15. Landing Circle 150 yds diam.
16. Platform Compass 17. Bombing Target 18. Watch Office & searchlight enclosure

Improvements to hangar accommodation commenced during 1937. A Type 'C', larger than the Type 'A' built ten years earlier, was erected on the site of the M.T. Sheds at the rear of the east-end World War 1 hangar.

The airfield was equipped with Mk.II landing lights prior to World War 2. The Lorenze approach equipment was operating from July 1939 and was used by the Blind Approach Training and Development Unit which formed in September 1939.

When World War 2 broke out there were still no hard runways at Boscombe Down, no stop butts until 1940 and range facilities relied on the co-operation of the Army in utilising some of the areas of Salisbury Plain which it used. Take-off and landings were carried out from four grass strips with a NE/SW being the longest in use at 1400yds. Land had to be requisitioned to extend the existing grass runways and to provide dispersals. The winter of 1939/40 was one of the severest on record. During the last week of January 1940 a heavy snowfall on top of the already icy conditions prevented flying for that week but despite this, construction work went ahead.

Flying Control was equipped with HF radio and manual direction finding equipment. An underground operations room was formed in 1940 to duplicate the equipment operated by Flying Control and the station telephone system. At the end of 1939 work on a new Watch Office commenced at the west end of the hangars. The two-letter station identification code was now BD. A decoy site was established south west of the aerodrome at South Newton, a village on the A36 between Wilton and Warminster. A second 'Starfish' site was built at West Winterslow in 1940.

With the increase in aircraft, 12 69' Extra Over blister hangars were erected in various on site locations from January 1942.

The accommodation for the Empire Test Pilots' School when it began as an experiment in May 1943, was situated on the south side of the airfield separate from that of A&AEE. It comprised two Seco wooden student's classrooms, four Nissen huts, brick built ablutions and an air raid shelter.

Boscombe Down had to make do with grass runways throughout World War 2. These ran N/S 1300yds, NE/SW 1900yds, E/W 1660yds and SE/NW 1300yds. A 10' wide Macadam and concrete perimeter track was also in use. Even an early jet aircraft, a DH E6/41 Spidercrab, the forerunner of the Vampire, which arrived on 18th April 1944, took-off from grass when it was taken on its initial test flight by Gp Capt Purvis on 22nd April. Scorched grass marks from the jet pipe regularly appear on photographs of the period.

It was not until January 1944 that a contract for £822,000 was commenced by the civil contractor Robert McAlpine Co. to construct a hard surface runway suitable for faster and heavier aircraft coming into service. To accommodate the new runway, the airfield was enlarged by cutting down part of Porton Firs and by the closure of the Porton Road. A railway siding was installed on the airfield, for materials to be brought in for the runway construction. The track was laid to form a junction at Allington with the Amesbury (SR) line, where a temporary signal box was installed. This was east of the position from where the 1917 junction had been sited when the airfield was originally built. Locomotives used on the contractors siding were all Huswell Clarke 0-6-0 STs with No.31 operating from 23rd March to 20th December 1944. This particular engine is preserved at the McAlpine Museum in Fawley. Other engines used within the duration of the contract were Nos.55, 79, 82 and 85. In June 1944 when the new runway was still incomplete, a USAAF Liberator from Middle Wallop was severely damaged when landing on it and written off. The crew was uninjured. The main concrete runway 24/06 NE/SW opened in October 1945. It was initially constructed to 3000yds x 100yds and later extended to 3500yds x 150yds. The railway siding installed for the construction work was retained after the runway opened.

There had not been a satisfactory Mess building at Boscombe for the civilian workers since the influx from Martlesham in 1939. It took until April 1945 to resolve, when a purpose built restaurant and hostel was provided. Two A1 hangars were built for the ETPS and for the Intensive Flying Development Flight in 1944 and 1945 respectively. These were positioned on the south side of the runway 24/06.

During July 1948 two Type B1 hangars, which had become redundant at High Post Airfield, were taken down and re-erected at Boscombe Down for use by 'A' Sqn and Repair & Inspection Flt (Light). During November 1948 work commenced on the additional runways, 17/35 N/S

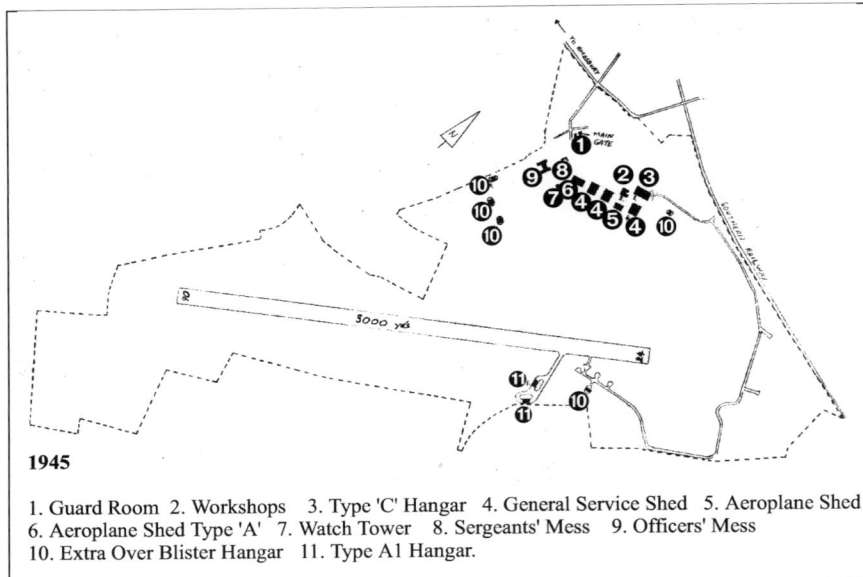

1945

1. Guard Room 2. Workshops 3. Type 'C' Hangar 4. General Service Shed 5. Aeroplane Shed
6. Aeroplane Shed Type 'A' 7. Watch Tower 8. Sergeants' Mess 9. Officers' Mess
10. Extra Over Blister Hangar 11. Type A1 Hangar.

2100 x 100 yards and 28/10 E/W 1400 x 50 yards and comprehensive connecting taxiways. When work commenced to build the hardened aircraft shelters in 1979, this small runway was closed.

With the completion of the runways airfield aids were then improved to include a new radar and approach lighting system. An explosives store, bulk fuel installation of 192,000 gallon capacity and new domestic, technical and administrative accommodation were provided in 1950. The domestic buildings replacing the early facilities provided for nine new barrack blocks, each able to accommodate 100 airmen, an Airman's Mess and an enlarged Sergeants' Mess. The original Station Headquarters building was converted to additional Sgts' Mess accommodation with the absorption by A&AEE of the Airborne Forces Experimental Establishment (AFEE).

A new Air Traffic Control building was completed during 1952. The same year, building of the imposing Weighbridge Hangar was started. It was anticipated this would accommodate large aircraft being designed such as the Bristol Brabazon. Although this huge aircraft from the Filton Works took to the skies, it never did put down at Boscombe but the hangar, completed in March 1954, was no 'white elephant' unlike the Brabazon. Its size enabled work on future large aircraft to be carried out under cover and it provided an accurate weighing facility. It was capable of providing the weight plus vertical and horizontal centre of gravity of aircraft weighing anything

up to 250,000lbs. During 1953 the pre-war workshops were progressively replaced with suitable facilities for modern aircraft. Other provisions included a new MT section, fire and police stations, stores, navigation and radio section and a photographic section. A new armament building opened on the 28th May 1954. In March of the following year work started on a new T2 Type hangar for use by 'C' Sqn. This was positioned on the south side of the 'C' Type and replaced three of the originals from 1918.

A new building was constructed on the airfield for airborne radio trials and was in operation by 1972.

The general appearance of Boscombe did not change significantly until 1979 when work started to build a number of hardened aircraft shelters (HAS) when the Station became a designated NATO dispersal base. This layout included a Wing Operations Centre (WOC) and two Squadron Operations Centres (SOC). From the former, all flying and scheduling was done together with maintenance control. The latter provided facilities for mission planning. The (SOC) worked in conjunction with the (WOC) but differed in that it had decontamination capabilities. These NATO funded structures have outer walls two feet thick and inner walls of one foot. The drab green coloured buildings had the provision of being fully self-supporting in the event of needing to be totally isolated in an emergency situation. The numerous aircraft hangar re-vetments are painted in the same camouflage pattern as the (WOC) and (SOC). These hardened structures are built of reinforced concrete and steel in the shape of a Quonset hut. The massive steel doors, some 70 tons each in weight, can be closed within a minute. The doors close at one speed up to a certain stopping point and then close all the way by use of an over-ride button. This avoids impacting at speed and provides a built in safety feature. At the rear is a jet blast port/deflector for engine run-ups and testing. The aircraft would taxi up to the building before turning around. A steel cable

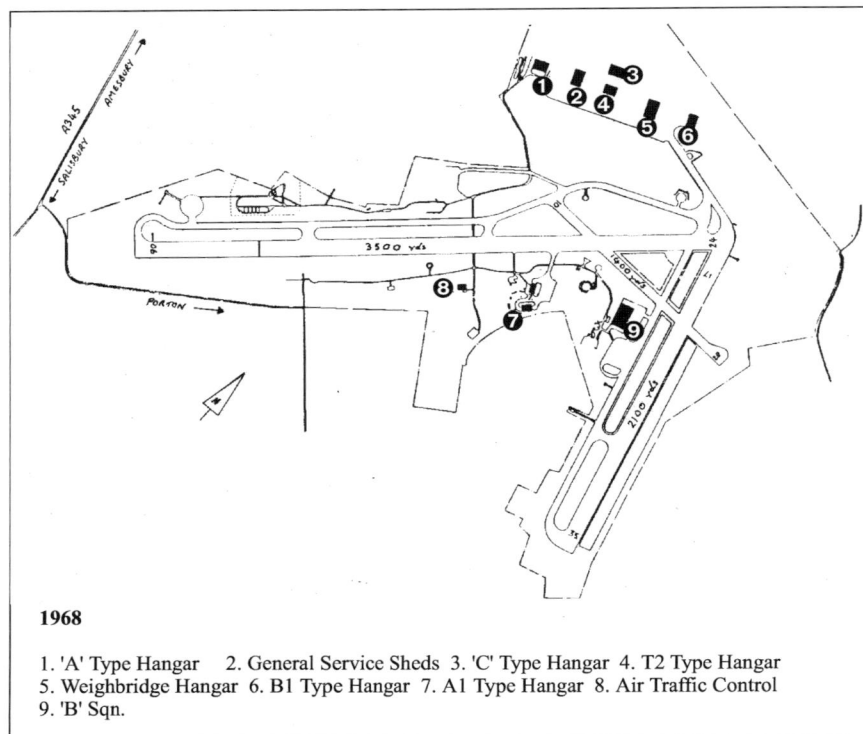

1968

1. 'A' Type Hangar 2. General Service Sheds 3. 'C' Type Hangar 4. T2 Type Hangar
5. Weighbridge Hangar 6. B1 Type Hangar 7. A1 Type Hangar 8. Air Traffic Control
9. 'B' Sqn.

This aerial photograph shows the 'A' Type hangar in the foreground, behind are two 1918 ARSs with reclad roofing but original doors, the T2 hangar and the 'C' Type. At the rear of these the Weighbridge Hangar and then the pair of B1s from Highpost.

would then be attached to the aircraft so that it could be towed in backwards. The main runway was being resurfaced at this time, when an unexploded German bomb was found and made safe.

One of the HAS received a £2 million conversion to provide DERA with a unique testing chamber. The 100' long building was unveiled on 18th October 2000. The building is lined with carbon impregnated foam which will eliminate radio frequencies. This will allow electronic and other high-tech equipment on anything from aircraft to railway rolling stock to be tested without outside interference. Usually the electromagnetic compatibility and performance of large systems are tested in an open environment where they are subject to various types of potential interference from radio/radar transmissions. The "Anechoic Test Facility" at Boscombe Down will ensure future tests can be undertaken without affecting, or being affected by, interference from such sources.

The appearance of the airfield changed significantly with the construction of the large 'DERA Hangar' in 1992. It is in use for maintenance and stands between the ETPS Hangar 45 and the Weighbridge Hangar.

With the turn of the new century, there are still some signs of Boscombe Down's past. The 1918 built Hanger 45, re-roofed with a steel trussed roof, the 1927 Type 'A' hangar and a number of World War 2 structures which includes a Control Tower and a large number of Pill Boxes, remain intact as do a series of underground tunnels constructed during the war. It is doubtful that these signs of the past can be maintained for many more years as their usefulness expires and condition deteriorates. It is probable that the same fate, during the latter part of the next century, will await the hardened aircraft shelters that already serve for storage purposes, their original use no longer appropriate.

Until October 1994 a very pleasant RAF Church stood close to the main entrance but this was found to contain a considerable amount of asbestos and was hastily demolished. This Church of England purpose built structure was originally dedicated on 10th October 1931 by the Right Rev. the Bishop of Salisbury together with the RAF Chaplain. The premises were not large enough to accommodate its own bells so loud speakers were installed from which a peal would be played. Some of the contents of the RAF church were passed to the church of St. Mary & St. Melor in nearby Amesbury and a brass altar cross is in use at Amesbury CE Aided Junior School (refer to) **Amesbury.**

Re-opening

The RAF Expansion Scheme of May 1935 brought new aerodromes and additional squadrons but by then Boscombe Down had been operational since its re-opening on 1st September 1930 when 2 officers with 35 men arrived from RAF Andover to take over the new station.

Following the re-opening, No.9 (B) Sqn commanded by Wg Cdr W.Strugnell MC and equipped with the Vickers Virginia (K2664) arrived from Manston on 26th November. The Sqn engaged in exercises and displays. The Meteorological Station also moved in from Manston at the same time.

On 2nd February 1931 the Porton Flight consisting of 1 Hawker Horsley and 1 Fairey Fox for experimental duties with Porton Gas School, transferred from Netheravon. The RAF records of the day indicate that the Flt used a Relief Landing Ground (RLG) at Sway in the New Forest.

F-111D of the 27th Tactical Fighter Wing outside a HAS in September 1983.

Boscombe Down's RAF Church.

No.9 (B) Sqn was joined on 1st April 1931 by No10 (B) Sqn commanded by Wg Cdr P.C. Sherren MC arriving by air, road and rail from Upper Heyford. This Sqn arrived equipped with the Hyderabad and during the month collected from Handley Page, Hinaidi K1915 to K1923. In September 1932 the adoption of the Virginia X commenced with the collection from Vickers Ltd of J7430, K2331 and K2332. From HAD Henlow J8907 was collected but this was a IX.

Wg Cdr W. Sowrey DFC, AFC was appointed CO of No.9 (B) Sqn. on 22nd November 1932. From 1st October 1933 Wessex Bombing Area ceased and became Western Area. Wg Cdr H. K. Thorold DSC, DFC, AFC was appointed as No.10 (B) Sqn CO on 4th February 1933. He was superceded by Wg Cdr G. B. Dalison AFC on 20th February 1934 and he was followed by Wg Cdr M. B. Frew DSO, MC, AFC on 14th August 1934.

On 8th February 1933 three No.9 (B) Sqn 'B' Flt machines endeavoured to carry out a camera obscura exercise at Bicester in adverse weather conditions. The first to take-off from Boscombe Down was Vickers Vimy J7129 crewed by Sgt R.A. Allen (pilot), Fg Off T.P. Pilcher (nav), Cpl C. Smith (WOP), AC2 E.C. Sholl (WOP u/t) and LAC Hipwell (Rear-gunner). This machine, negotiating the high ground just north of Tidworth, struck a tree, crashed and caught fire. Those in the front cockpit were trapped in the wreckage and died in the fire. LAC Hipwell in the tail cockpit was thrown into the flames but escaped with superficial burns. The other two machines returned to base. The squadron had a change of CO on 27 February with the appointment of Wg Cdr A.W. Milne. On 22nd March another fatality occurred when an Atlas of the Cambridge University Air Squadron crashed at Boscombe Down killing Plt Off Sikes.

Since its arrival at Boscombe Down No.10 (B) Sqn had engaged in co-operation with the Air Defence Brigade, attended No.1 Armament Training Camp at Catfoss, No.2 Armament Training Camp at North Coates Fitties, and night co-operation with the RAF Balloon Centre at nearby Rollestone Camp. In May 1933 a Fairey Hendon B 19/27 with Kestrel III engine was allocated from A&AEE

Martlesham Heath for evaluation purposes but it crashed when striking a wall on landing.

Wg Cdr M. B. Frew DSO, MC, AFC assumed command of No.10 (B) Sqn on 15th August 1934 and from November 1934 the squadron started to re-equip with 10+2 Handley Page Heyford 1As (K4030), (K4031). These had replaced the Virginia Xs by January 1935.

Gp Capt A. Corbett-Wilson assumed command of Boscombe Down on 26th January 1935.

In April 1935 No.10 (B) Sqn was awarded the 'Sassoon Cup' for Long Distance Night Flying which had been won in the 1933/34 Competition. In July the Sqn left Boscombe Down by air and rail for Mildenhall for an appearance at the George V Jubilee Review. On return it took part in a bombing attack exercise on various vulnerable targets around Portsmouth and Southampton.

On 16th September 1935, as part of the RAF Expansion Scheme, No.214 (B) Sqn reformed on a single Flight basis from 'B' Flight of No.9 (B) Sqn equipped with 5 Virginia X (all Initial and no Reserve). Three days later Sqn Ldr D.F. Lucking was posted to command the new squadron. In addition No.97 (B) Sqn reformed at Catfoss from 'B' Flight of No.10 (B) Sqn which was detached there on exercise. The new squadron was equipped with the Heyford 2A. Both squadrons came under the command of Wg Cdr Frew and returned to Boscombe Down on completion of the exercise period. Nos.9 (B) and 214

(B) Sqns moved to Andover on 15th October. On 12th November 1935 No.10 (B) Sqn collected 6 Heyford Mk.IIIs with Kestrel VI (Fully rated) engines from Radlett and these equipped the new 'B' Flt. The Heyford was the last biplane bomber to come into service with the RAF.

At this time experiments were being undertaken at Farnborough to improve bomber interception by night fighters. One experiment was set up where by four square miles of the sky was illuminated from ground lights. Nos.10 and 97 Sqn Heyfords were flown to Farnborough each night from Boscombe Down to act as targets for the Demons of Nos.23 and 74 Sqns, and the Gauntlets of No.111 Sqn were used as interceptors. Farnborough at this stage had no night landing facilities so all aircraft were required to return to their home bases on conclusion of the night's work. This was one of many experiments where further development was overtaken by success in other areas such as Radio Direction Finding.

A double disaster occurred on 19th February 1936 when Nos. 10 (B) and 97 (B) Sqns both lost aircraft in

Heyford K4023 (K) of No.10 Sqn at Boscombe Down.
Photo: Don Neate Coll.

crashes. During its return flight to Boscombe Down following an air exercise attack on the Queen Mary Reservoir Pumping Station at Laleham in Surrey, Heyford K4024 of 10 (B) Sqn crashed into the side of Beacon Hill, Treyford near Midhurst at 0100 hrs. Sgt Pilot C.A. Deakin suffered minor injuries, Sgt Pilot E.K. McDermott died of his injuries at the scene, LAC C. J. Westlake (WOP) and LAC C. J. Adams (AG) were killed. This was the first squadron fatality since its formation on 3rd January 1928. Heyford K4034 of 97 (B) Sqn, a former 10 (B) Sqn aircraft, also on a night exercise, force landed in the sea off the coast of Le Havre at 0405 hrs having run out of fuel. Flying Officer R.H. Page (pilot) swam towards the shore and was rescued by a French canoeist. Sgt Pilot W. Jole (nav), A.C.1s C.A.T. Bickham (WOP) and W. Watkin (AG) of No.10 (B) Sqn drowned. All the men who died that night were buried together in Amesbury Cemetery.

As of 1st May 1936 Western Area ceased to exist and Boscombe Down came under the administration of No.3 (Bomber) Group, which was formed and had its Headquarters at Andover. This continued for a short period until Bomber Command, Fighter Command, Coastal Command and Training Commands were formed on 14th July 1936, when Boscombe Down came under the former at its Uxbridge Headquarters.

Boscombe Down was one of the airfields to hold the first of the Empire Air Days on 30th June 1934. This allowed the general public to have their first chance of seeing the inner workings of the RAF. The station threw open its gates from 2pm to 7pm with an admission charge of 1 shilling charged for adult admission, 6 pence for children and 3 pence a head for organised parties. Proceeds were donated to the RAF Benevolent Fund. Handley Page Heyfords gave a bombing display and an aerobatics performance was given by three Gloster Gauntlets. A visiting Avro Rota Autogiro also performed and was probably one of those based at nearby Old Sarum.

Under the RAF Expansion Scheme No.166 (B) Sqn reformed on 1st November 1936 from 'A' Flight of No.97 (B) Sqn on a single Flight basis and was affiliated to the parent squadron for all purposes. Its CO was Flt Lt C.D.C. Boyce. On the same date No.78 (B) Sqn re-formed on a single Flight basis from 'B' Flt. of No.10 (B) Sqn. Wg Cdr Frew was the CO for these squadrons. Both the new squadrons were equipped with the Heyford 222 with Kestrel 2V engines.

On 1st February 1937 RAF Boscombe Down transferred into No.16 Reconnaissance Group, Coastal Command with HQ at Lee-on-Solent. Nos.97 (B) and 166 (B) Sqns moved to Leaconfield on 7th and 20th January 1937 respectively. The latter squadron was commanded by Sqn Ldr J.H.C. Wake as of 2nd January. Nos. 78 (B) and 10 (B) Sqns moved to Dishforth on 1st and 25th February respectively.

Boscombe Down briefly hosted Coastal Commands No.224 G.R.Sqn in No.16 Group arriving from Manston on 15th February 1937 with no machines and No.217 G.R.Sqn which reformed at Boscombe on 15th March 1937. No.224 Sqn collected 11 Anson Is from the manufacturer at Woodford towards the end of February. Sqn Ldr R.N. Waite was appointed as squadron CO on 19th March. No.217 Sqn was also equipped with the Anson I and the CO Sqn Ldr D. d'H. Humphreys was appointed on 19th March. In April No.224 Sqn received an order

On 24th March 1937 No.58 (B) Sqn with Wg Cdr J. Potter as CO and No.51 (B) Sqn moved temporarily from Driffield to Boscombe, pending completion of their new station at Linton-upon-Ouse. They arrived equipped with 14 Anson És and 8 Virginia Xs between the two squadrons. The squadrons were brought up to strength each with an 'A' Flt. of 6 + 1 Ansons and a 'B' Flt. of 4 + 1 Virginias. The squadrons were in No.3 (B) Group Bomber Command until transferring to No.4 (B) Group on 1st July 1937. Eight days later RAF Boscombe Down transferred back to Bomber Command but in No.4 Group.

Serving with 'A' Flight of No.51 Sqn at this time was Wiltshire born LAC Thomas Gray. Later in 1940 he was killed, when as a Sgt Observer, his Fairey Battle was shot down during an attack on a heavily defended bridge over the Albert Canal. As a result of

A Hinaidi of No.10 Sqn crossing the track to Beacon Hill and one of the squadron Virginia Xs seen in the hangar at a Boscombe Down Empire Air Day on 24th May 1934.

indicating it was to lead the 200 aeroplane formation at the Hendon Air Display. 5 Ansons from both squadrons made up a strike force on 6th May for a fleet exercise off of St Alban's Head and Dungeness, carrying out bomb drops on ships of the 2nd Battle Sqn HMS Nelson and HMS Rodney. On 25th May the squadrons exercised with the Home Fleet, which was on course from Spithead to Portland, with the exercise comprising ship recognition, course and speed judging. No.217 Sqn moved to Tangmere on 7th June and No.224 Sqn moved to Thornaby on 9th July 1937.

their actions, he and the pilot Fg Off Donald Edward Garland were awarded the Victoria Cross. The airgunner, who was also killed, received no recognition. It was considered Garland and Gray were engaged in offensive action whilst the gunner was only defensive.

The following squadrons were temporarily accommodated for a coastal defence exercise during the summer of 1937: -

No.42 TB Sqn - equipped with Vildebeeste - 12th June - 17th July
No.99 (B) " - " " Heyford - 8th July - 16th July
No.149 (B) " - " " " IA - 10th July - 16th July
No.220 GR " - " " Anson I - 14th June - 28th June
No.269 GR " - " " " - 10th July - 17th July

No.88 (B) Sqn moved in from Waddington on 17th July 1937 under the command of Sq Ldr E.C. Lewis. It was equipped with 6 Hawker Hind as initial allocation. 2 immediate reserve was received in August. The Sqn re-equipped with 12 + 0 Fairey Battles on 31st December and the 8 Hinds were transferred to No.609 Sqn at Yeadon.

On 15th October 1937 No.58 Sqn started to re-equip with the Whitley with K4210 the first to arrive. The squadron took delivery of 6 of the type for each Flt. In 'A' Flt 4 were Mk.22s and the remainder in each Flt were Mk.Is. By the end of the year all of the squadron's Virginias and Ansons had been transferred to No.51 (B) Sqn pending its own re-equipment with Whitley Mk.IIs in February 1938.

No.51 (B) Sqn were still flying Ansons when on 24th January 1938 K6272 crashed near Basingstoke whilst on a night flying exercise. Serious injuries were suffered by Sgt. Mansbridge (pilot), Plt Off C.W. Poulter and A.C.2 Price (WOP). Plt Off D.L.L. Morris (nav) was killed. This squadron together with No.58 (B) Sqn moved to the completed airfield at Linton-on-Ouse on 20th April 1937.

No.218 (B) Sqn moved in from Upper Heyford on 22nd April 1938 equipped with Fairey Battles (K9356). On this same date Boscombe Down transferred from No.4 Group to No.1 Group.

No.88 (B) Sqn lost Fairey Battle K7680 on 7th August 1938 when it crashed at Norton Heath, Ingatestone while on a Home Defence exercise. Flt Lt Gardener ordered his crew to abandon the aircraft at 1500ft but remained at the controls. Cpl W.E. Wheeler (Air Observer) was killed when parachuting too low but A.C.2 W.T. Cable (WOP) landed safely. The pilot, who at the subsequent enquiry was praised for his actions in

remaining at the controls, suffered severe burn injuries.

No 150 (B) Sqn re-formed at Boscombe Down on 8th August 1938 as a medium bomber squadron and equipped with 12+4 Fairey Battle Is with Merlin II engines.

The following month these were exchanged for Merlin I Battles from No.12 (B) Sqn at Andover. During November and December No.150 (B) Sqn received 16+5 Merlin II Battles with the Merlin Is transferred to other units. Initially Fg Off J.E. Innes-Crump was posted in from No.218 (B) Sqn as Acting Sqn CO, and CO 'A' Flt Sqn Ldr W.M.L. MacDonald was appointed Sqn CO on 1st October 1938. He was succeeded by Wg Cdr A. Hesketh DFC on 3rd March 1939, a month before the squadron moved to Benson on 3rd April.

From August 1938 No.4 Group Experimental Flt operated from Boscombe Down having transferred from Porton Down. Known aircraft attached to the Flt were Battle K7574 and Hind L7217.

Between 6th-12th October 1938 No.88 (B) Sqn exchanged its Battle Mk.I aircraft for the Mk.II from No.101 (B) Sqn Thornaby. No.218 (B) Sqn collected 5 Battle Mk.Is, with Merlin engine IIs from Fairey Aviation, which gave a 16+5 establishment. By 12th December No.88 (B) Sqn was likewise equipped, and the two squadron CO ranks were upgraded to Wg Cdr. On 6th December No.218 (B) Sqn had its squadron crest presented by AVM Playfair CB, CVO, MC, at the AOCs Annual Inspection.

The last Empire Air Day was staged at Boscombe Down on 20th May 1939. This was attended by 14,000 visitors who were joined in the afternoon by ACM Sir Edgar Ludlow Hewitt KCB, CMG, DSO, A.O.C in C Bomber Command and AVM P.H.L. Playfair who both arrived by air on a visit of inspection.

Wg Cdr K.H.R. Elliott DSO was

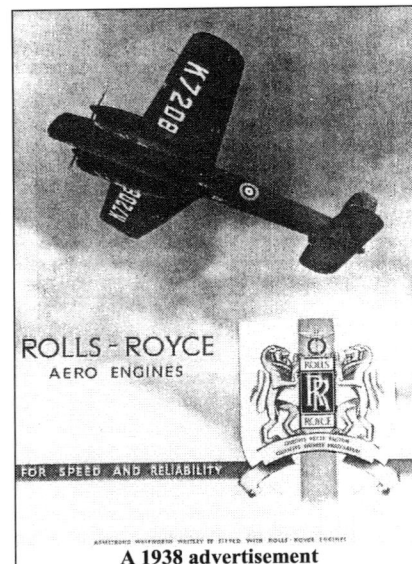

appointed as CO of No.88 (B) Sqn on 16th March 1939. The squadron lost Fairey Battle K9249 on 26th June when it caught fire in the air and crashed at Netherhampton near Salisbury. It was returning from Portland Bill at 2,600 ft. having flown a night cross-country exercise. Plt Off D.A.J. Foster (pilot) baled out at 300ft and landed safely as did A.C.2 E.G. Williams (WOP) but Sgt. H.G. Ing

(observer) was killed.

Aeroplanes making night landings at Boscombe Down in 1938 were aided by a red flashing beacon displaying Morse letter 'D'. The Lorenz Blind Approach equipment (Transmitters T1122 & T1123) was in full operation on the aerodrome by July 1939.

No.88 (B) and 218 (B) Sqns, which from June 1939 had their Flts increased to 3, both collected 11 new Battles from the Austin Works during July for the extra Flts.

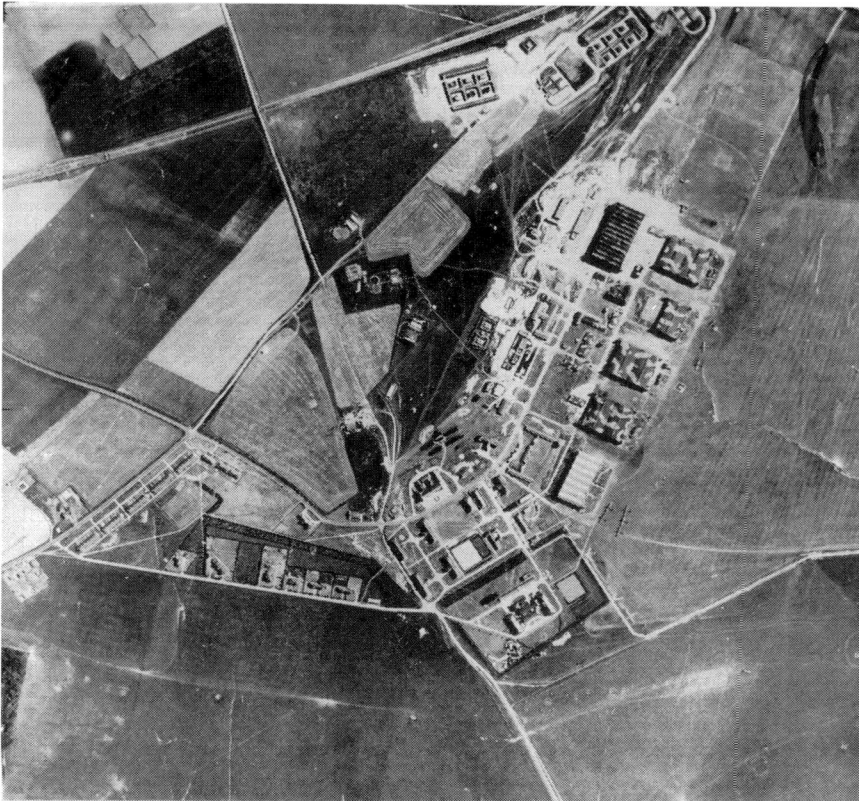

An aerial view of Boscombe Down on 19th August 1939 in which Fairey Battles can be seen outside the freshly camouflaged hangars and outside the Type 'A' hangar which appears not to be camouflaged at that stage. The relatively new Type 'C' hangar is seen at the rear of the top most hangar.

No. 218 (B) Sqn lost Fairey Battle K9328 on 11th August 1939 when it struck an electric pylon near Carlton in Bedfordshire while carrying out a low-level raid in a Home Defence exercise. The pilot, Acting Flt Lt W. Kinane and the observer, Sgt Allan were killed instantly and the WOP A.C.1 Roberts died at Cranfield sick quarters two days later.

On 28th August 1939 Air Commodore A.A.B. Thomson MC, AFC, A.O.C. No.3 (Bomber) Group landed at Boscombe Down in Wellington L4325 of No.115 Sqn RAF Marham. He was the pilot and was engaged in testing a special type of bomb on Larkhill Ranges. The bomb failed to release so he landed at Boscombe with the intention of finding out why it had malfunctioned. During the inspection beneath the bomb bay, the bomb released itself onto the ground and in haste the Air Commodore stepped back into the aircraft's still revolving propellers. He received severe head injuries and died in the ambulance taking him to Tidworth Hospital.

No.75 Wing, part of the Advanced Air Striking Force, No.1 Group Bomber Command, formed at Boscombe on 24th August 1939 in preparation for

mobilisation overseas should war be declared. Wiltshire has not been renowned for the deployment of operational bomber units in the same way that counties on the east side of the country have been. This brief association ended at Boscombe Down on 2nd September 1939 when No.75 (B) Wing left for France with the forward air and sea contingent of the AASF. No.218 (B) Sqn under Wg Cdr L.B. Duggen, with two Flts, each with 8 Battles, one was from No.88 (B) Sqn, were despatched to Auberives-sur-Suippes. Boscombe Down's other RAF personnel boarded 10 civilian aircraft for the same destination. Airmen with brooms hastily applied camouflage paint to some aircraft before departure from Boscombe Down. Other personnel left in a fleet of buses for onward passage across the Channel. When war was declared the following day, additional personnel and stores were flown out by civilian aircraft and others left by train from Amesbury (SR) Station. The Air Party of No. 88 (B) Sqn with 16 Battles and crews led by Sqn Ldr T.C. Dickens moved to Mourmelon-le-Grande on 12th September. The remainder of the squadron left by road from Boscombe Down.

The balance of No.75 Wing comprising 12 officers and 150 men, commanded by Sqn Ldr E.J. Routh left

No. 88 (B) Sqn Battles in 1939 with K9348 in the foreground.
Photo: Don Neate Coll.

Amesbury by train for Southampton Docks on 16th September.

World War 2 Years

The Aeroplane and Armament Experimental Establishment at Martlesham Heath in Suffolk was vulnerable to attack because of its Channel Coast location. In accordance with a pre-arranged war plan A&AEE commenced a move to Boscombe Down in No.23 Group on 3rd/4th September bringing with it, over the two days some 70 aircraft of varying types. Not all of these remained some returning to Martlesham Heath. A&AEE aircraft flying from Boscombe Down during the first two months were: -

Oxford N4720, Battle K9231, Hampden P1149, Hampden P1169, Blackburn Skua L2867, Gladiator K7919, Gladiator K7964, Blenheim K7044, Blenheim L8662, Wellington L4213, Harvard N7001 Hawker Hardy K5919, Fairey Gordon 1 K2749.

The main group of staff and all their equipment arrived by road and rail from Martlesham Heath on 8th and 14th September 1939. At this time the transfer to Boscombe Down was made only on a temporary basis and for the duration of the war. A Committee set up to look at the future of Experimental Establishments had considered using other airfields for prototype aircraft testing should war be declared, including Lyneham and Hullavington. A proposal was also made that the Armament Development Unit formerly at Martlesham Heath should be permanently moved to Shrewton. This was rejected as it was thought that Larkhill Ranges were unlikely to be made available by the War Office other than for the requirements of the Bomber Development Unit. Consideration was also given to enlarging the Porton bombing range so that this Unit could be based at Shrewton. It was decided to use Boscombe Down for the war emergency move even though Bomber Command had ear-marked its use for some of their non-mobilisable group pool squadrons in East Anglia and as a result had to make alternative arrangements. With the move complete A&AEE took over Boscombe Down on 20th September under the command of Gp Capt B. McEntegart.

With the arrival of A&AEE from Martlesham in 1939, it absorbed the Special Duties Flight (SDF) with 2 Lysander IIs L4737 and L4738, Wellington I R2703 and Battle K7574.

The function of the A&AEE was to clear prototype military and civil aircraft for operational use following tests carried out by the manufacturers own test teams and to liaise with them regarding any necessary design and safety features. The evaluation of armament and other equipment was a further function. As of September 1939 the trials were carried out by five Flights - 'A', 'B' and 'C' Flights Performance Testing Section with 'A' and 'B' Flights Armament Testing Sections.

Boscombe Down was one of the few stations to have a Standard and Lorenz Beam Approach System installed before the outbreak of war. The Blind Approach Training & Development Unit (BATDU) was formed on 18th September 1939 at Boscombe Down to train pilots for bad weather approaches using the then new Lorenz equipment. For the two-week training courses, 2 Anson Is, L7967 & L9155 initially equipped the unit. Two Link Trainers were installed in the 'C' Type hangar during September and November. The CO of the Unit was Sqn Ldr R. S. Blucke AFC who was appointed on 1st September. He had a landing accident in Anson L9155 at Boscombe Down on 7th December 1939. He escaped without any injury and was promoted to Wg Cdr on 1st January 1940. This particular Anson must have had a jinx as it was crash-landed again on 5th February 1940 by Sgt A. Reece, once more with no injuries. The two initial Ansons were supplemented in January and March when N9938, N9945 and N9998 were received from the manufacturers. Fg Off Guy Gibson

was an early student of the BATDU, attending a course between 27th March and 5th April 1940. The BATDU was closed down on 6th June 1940 but reopened seven days later as the Beam Approach Development Unit (BADU). The training element was dropped and the function was to carry out investigation into enemy wireless signals, to which the code name 'Headache' was allocated.

The 5 existing Ansons were equipped to conform to specific requirements of the new unit. The establishment was increased to 8 Ansons, 3 of which were N9945, L7967, R3313 and 3 Whitleys P5019, P4943, P4944 plus crews. These last two aircraft were returned to No.2 MU Aston Down on 5th July and replaced by Whitleys P5047 and P5057. The establishment increased during July and August with the arrival from the manufacturers A.V. Roe of Ansons R9812, R9814, R9815, N9534.

The two Link Trainers installed for the BATDU and not used by the BADU, were transferred during October to No.1 FTS Netheravon and No.3 FTS South Cerney. This coincided with the formation of the Wireless Intelligence Development Unit by re-designation of the BADU on 14th October 1940. The role of the WIDU was to combat the method used by Germany whereby radio beams were used to guide their bomber aircraft to a target. Coventry was one such city which was heavily bombed on the night of Thursday 14th November 1940 using this form of navigation. The Germans switched on their transmitters with the main one, on the Cherbourg peninsula code-named *Weser*, directing its beam directly at Coventry. The beam crossed the English coast at Christchurch before passing just east of Salisbury and Swindon. Three transmitters in Boulogne codenamed *Rhein*, *Elbe* and *Oder* directed their beams close to London and these crossed the main beam at three separate points south of Coventry. The German aircraft had no difficulty locating Coventry and virtually unopposed carried out a concentrated and protracted bombing raid. In this single raid England suffered one of its heaviest losses to life and property of the war.

WIDU used the Anson for beam identification. Like the BADU before it, WIDU operated with a detachment

at Wyton as well as from Boscombe Down. Flying from Wyton on Friday 8th November Anson N9945 crashed at Stechford, Birmingham during a night special duty flight. Plt Off George E. Goldsmith RAF (pilot), Plt Off G. P. Fry (nav), Sgt H. McGeoch (AG), Sgt John E. Murphy RAF (WOP) and LAC Donald N. Biggs RAFVR (Special W/T Op) were killed. Anson W1891 was allocated as the replacement aircraft.

A further re-designation came when the unit reformed in Technical Training Command as No.109 Sqn at Boscombe on 10th December 1940. The CO Wg Cdr W. S. Hebden was appointed 10 days later. The squadron formed into 'A' Flt (Wireless Reconnaissance), 'B' Flt (Wireless Investigation), 'C' Flt (Wireless Development) and HQ Flt. The initial aircraft allocation was 4 Wellington Is, 3 Whitley Vs, and 8 Anson Is. During the twelve months the squadron was at Boscombe additional Wellingtons and Ansons were allocated plus Leopard Moth AX858. The Wellingtons T2513, T2552, T2556 and T2884 were used on bombing operations against radio transmitters in France.

On 19th January 1942 HQ and 'C' Flt moved to Tempsford. 'A' Flt with the exception of the Wyton detachment left for Upper Heyford, with 'B' Flt remaining at Boscombe Down until 23rd March when it commenced a move to Stradishall.

On 30th September 1939, No.58 (B) Sqn No. 4 Group Bomber Command, on temporary transfer to Coastal Command, returned to Boscombe from Linton-on-Ouse with their 16 Whitley Mk.IIIs. They had been in action since the first day of war when, together with No.51 Sqn, they had carried out leaflet drops over Germany. From Boscombe the squadron carried out anti-submarine patrols and convoy escort duties over the English Channel. On two occasions U-boat attacks were made. The squadron moved back to Linton-on-Ouse on 14th February 1940.

Whitley Mk.III aircraft used by the squadron for these duties during its period at Boscombe Dow: - K8934, K8962, K8964, K8967, K8971, K8973, K8974, K8975, K8990, K8999, K9000, K9001, K9003, K9004, K9005, K9006, K9007, K9009, K9013, K9973.

The Lysander Flt formed at Boscombe Down on 20th November 1939 as a Special Duty Flt for France.

From November 1939 Boscombe Down came under the umbrella of No.24 Group Training Command, with HQ at Halton and from 3rd July 1940 No.23 Group in Flying Training Command with HQ at South Cerney. The staff of A&AEE from Martlesham who were both RAF and civilian were not impressed with the conditions they found on arrival in September 1939. Boscombe Down at that time did not have the facilities, accommodation and general comfort of their previous home.

Plt Off Paul Rivington based at St. Eval with No.6 Coastal Patrol Flight was given leave over the Christmas of

A 1939 advertisement

1939 and living in Devizes, hitched himself a flight home to Boscombe Down in the front turret of a Whitley I. There was a Flt of Whitleys based at St. Eval at the time which were able to give longer-range convoy cover than the Ansons of No.217 (G.R.) Sqn which were also based there. On landing he observed a number of aircraft, some of which he had only heard about. Two he picked out were a Beaufighter and a radial-engined single seat fighter, the Gloster F5/34, K5604. The latter was at Boscombe for five months with the Performance Testing Sqn but never went into production, being superseded by the Hurricane and Spitfire.

During World War 2 every type of aircraft that entered squadron service

with the RAF and FAA was evaluated at Boscombe Down. Some of the aircraft proved a success and became 'famous' such as the Lancaster, Halifax, Hurricane and Spitfire. There were other types passing through the Establishment that were not a success, such as the Handley Page Hereford (L6002), Westland Whirlwind (L6845) and the Armstrong Whitworth Albemarle (V1743), the latter type being designed as a medium bomber/reconnaissance aircraft but was used in RAF service mainly for transport and glider-tug duties.

The RAF's first four-engined bomber of World War 2 was the Stirling and on 22nd April 1940, L7605 the second prototype was delivered to Boscombe Down for trials which continued until 19th August. This aircraft was joined on 21st May by the first production model N3635 arriving for performance trials and on the 30th by N3637 for the preparation of pilots' notes.

From spring 1940 until the end of the year the Demons and Hurricanes of the Armament Testing Squadron's 'A' Flight moved to Exeter.

The Wellington Flight was formed in April 1940, for the purpose of testing Wellington V pressurisation cabin aircraft. The intention was to use these for high altitude Pathfinder duties. The Flight was absorbed into the High Altitude Flight (HAF) when it formed on 30th December 1940 to investigate flying problems above a ceiling of 30,000'. Amongst other tests, the HAF was used for meteorological research

and for high altitude trials using Spitfires applied with different types of camouflage paint. Other aircraft used by the HAF were the Hurricane, Mosquito, Boston, Hudson and Welkin (DX333). Although two of the Wellington type subsequently went into service with No.109 Sqn., they were never operational as they were found to have no practical use. In September 1944, the HAF was incorporated into 'A' Sqn.

Italy entered the war on 10th June 1940 and with Malta being so close it was decided to reinforce the Island's defences by deploying 12 Hurricane Is. These aircraft had been modified to carry 88gallon fuel tanks and flew out of Boscombe, together with a Blenheim for navigation purposes, transiting through France where it was intended they would refuel. The French however attempted to prevent them landing by obstructing the airfield with vehicles. By this time, low on fuel, the pilots had no choice and began to put down as best they could. The obstructive actions by the French led to eight of the Hurricanes and the Blenheim crash landing. The four undamaged Hurricanes reached Malta and were used to good effect during Italian raids.

There was no damage done when four 50kg German bombs were dropped around the airfield perimeter on 26th June 1940. Whether this determined in someone's mind that aerodrome defences needed to be increased, is not known but during the following three months over 100 ground gunners with Bofors guns arrived. Vickers 'K' and Lewis guns were also in use. In the latter part of 1941 the gunners became established as No.786 (Defence Sqn) which became No.2786 Light Anti-Aircraft Sqn and on 7th June 1943 when moving to Netheravon, was replaced by No.2837 LAA Sqn. In August 1939 the Wiltshire Yeomanry had been posted in to provide aerodrome defence.

Operational Squadrons were using Boscombe Down aerodrome in the summer of 1940 with Fighter Command's No.249 Sqn in No.13 Group arriving from Church Fenton on 14th August with twenty Hurricane Is. ACM Sir Hugh Dowding the Air Officer Commander-in-Chief, Fighter Command had chosen this date to rest some of the squadrons which had become battle weary and No.249 Sqn was brought in as support for the No.10 and 11 Group squadrons. They were scrambled shortly after arrival but failed to locate three Ju 87s, which attacked the aerodrome and swiftly climbed back into cloud cover. Boscombe Down suffered no damage from this raid but three cows were killed in an adjoining field.

One of the pilots of No.249 Sqn was Flt Lt James Nicolson who on Friday 16th August 1940, despite severe injuries to himself, stayed with his burning aircraft whilst continuing a diving attack on a Messerschmitt Bf 110, before baling out over Southampton. For this action he was awarded the Victoria Cross, the sole recipient of Fighter Command to do so during World War 2. He was to die on 2nd May 1945 when the Liberator he was being flown in, came down in the Bay of Bengal. A memorial stone was unveiled at Boscombe Down on 16th August 1990, the 50th Anniversary of the action for which his VC was awarded.

HRH the Duke of Kent visited Boscombe Down and met with No.249 Sqn personnel during their 18 day stay at the base. He was accompanied on the tour by Gp Capt Ralph Sorley the Station Commander and Sqn Ldr John Grandy CO of No.249 Sqn.

No. 249 Sqn exchanged bases and aircraft with another Hurricane I Squadron, No.56 (Punjab) Sqn from North Weald on 1st September 1940. No.56 Sqn had been in the thick of the fighting during the August raids and arrived at Boscombe with just seven aircraft and minus a CO. The aircraft exchange was necessary because No.56 Sqn aircraft were equipped with VHF and Boscombe Down only had HF. The Sqn spent the first two weeks training but on Saturday 14th September claimed its first success, whilst flying from Boscombe Down, when Flt Sgt F. W. Higginson shot down a Dornier Do 17 forty miles off the coast of Bournemouth. The following day Sgt Thomas R. Tweed RAF was killed when his Hurricane P3660 spun into the ground one mile NW of High Post during a training flight. The crash site was on the proofing ground operated by Wessex Aircraft Engineering Company (WAECO) and in the wreckage was found a landing flare manufactured by

the company. Sgt Tweed was buried at Amesbury Cemetery. Another local flying accident on Friday 20th September claimed the life of Sgt Charles V. Meeson. The pilots were probably getting used to the respite from North Weald when on 27th they carried out various interceptions in the Bristol area where the raid was concentrated on the Parnall aircraft works at nearby Yate. This resulted in Fg Off K.T. Marston destroying a Me 110 and damaging another, Plt Off W.H. Constable-Maxwell destroying a Do 17, the now commissioned Plt Off Higginson damaging a Me 110 and Plt Off D.C. Mackenzie damaging a Do 17.

On Monday 30th September the squadron was scrambled morning and afternoon to meet incoming raids and during the course of the fighting 7 of the squadron's Hurricanes were shot down, 5 of which were Cat.3. There were injuries to three of the pilots but the four others escaped safely. In the morning the enemy aircraft were intercepted near Warmwell and Plt Off Higginson damaged a Me 110. Fg Off Marston in Hurricane P2866 and Sgt Ray were both shot down in their aircraft near Warmwell by Me 110s. The afternoon raid was directed at the Westland Aircraft Factory at Yeovil. Some forty Heinkel and Dornier bombers escorted by Me 110s crossed the coast near Weymouth around 1630 hours and were engaged south of Portland by the Boscombe Hurricanes and by Spitfires of No.152 Sqn from Warmwell. The German bombers scattered before reaching their target but a number of bomb loads were jettisoned on Sherbourne. The German Me 110s on this raid shot down five No.56 Sqn Hurricanes and five Spitfires of No.152 Sqn. All of the pilots survived with the exception of Sgt Leslie A.E. Reddington RAFVR No.152 Sqn who was killed flying L1072 at 1645 hrs. His name appears on the Runnymede Memorial. Flt Lt H.M. Pinfold of No.56 Sqn shot down a Do 215 and Plt Off Higginson shared the destruction of a Me 110 with a No.152 Sqn Spitfire. Flt Lt R.E.P. Brooker and Sgt P.E.M. Robinson each damaged a Do 215. The Germans repeated this raid on the afternoon of 7th October inflicting light damage to the Yeovil factory. No.56 Sqn Hurricanes were scrambled from Warmwell where they were on detachment from Boscombe Down.

Sgt Dennis H. Nichols was heading for his first experience of the enemy. The formation took off led by Flt Lt Brooker. Sgt Nichols heard no warnings and suddenly found they were engaging the enemy when he saw tracer from his leader's guns. Still in formation he opened fire at a Ju 88 before breaking off to avoid colliding with his leader. He consequently found himself alone but noticed some Me 110s above him in a defensive spiral. Seeing a Spitfire attacking from above, Nichols intercepted the enemy from below but head-on. He opened fire but his aircraft was hit by the heavier forward firing guns of the enemy aircraft. With his engine on fire and a blackened windscreen he broke away and inverted his aircraft at 25,000', to roll out and take to his parachute. The lanyards on one side of his parachute were twisted and he tried unsuccessfully to untangle them. Despite this he felt he was making a controlled descent but on hitting the ground he broke his back. Sgt Nichols short experience of the Battle of Britain was over. Sgt Jaroslav Hlavac a Czech pilot joined No.56 Sqn on Tuesday 8th October but was killed in action two days later when his Hurricane P3421 was shot down by Me 109s over Wareham at 1220 hrs.

On 26th October, 3 HE bombs and 1 oil bomb were dropped from a German aircraft, impacting in the Porton road close to Boscombe Down aerodrome.

The Battle of Britain drew to a close at the end of October. No.35 (B) Sqn reformed at Boscombe Down on 7th November 1940 in No.1 Group. It received its first Halifax on 13th November but seven days later the squadron moved out to Leeming. No.56 Sqn left Boscombe for neighbouring Middle Wallop on 29th November.

Two units under the auspices of A&AEE were established during November 1940. The Handling Flight on detachment from Upavon on the 8th November and the formation of the Bomber Development Unit (BDU) on the 21st November. The Handling Flt would be allocated aircraft for which it would have the responsibility for assessing handling capabilities and for producing from the findings, the necessary Pilot's Notes. From 11th June 1941, the Flt became a Sqn.

The Bomber Development Unit formed under the control of No.6 (Bomber) Group as a lodger unit at Boscombe Down. Its role was to undertake trials of bombing equipment having an operational capacity and evaluating bombing problems experienced in the Command. The unit was equipped with 3 Wellingtons, 2 Hampdens and 2 Blenheims. Blenheim ²V L4893 arrived at Boscombe in October 1940 to be used for bombing trials but crashed at Filton the following month. The BDU disbanded on 1ˢᵗ May 1941.

Airacobra P.39c DS173, the first to arrive in the UK from America, seen here at Boscombe Down. The 4 machine guns in the nose and no wing guns distinguish it from the British built version. Photo: Don Neate Coll.

Under the Lend/Lease agreement with the U.S., aircraft brought over from America started arriving for evaluation at Boscombe Down during 1941. The French Navy had ordered a batch of 81 American Grumman Martlets which with the fall of France in June 1940 resulted in them being transferred to the Fleet Air Arm. Two of these, Mk.I, AX826 and AX 828 arrived at Boscombe Down for handling and armament trials respectively in September 1940. They had 1,240 hp

AR703, was in fact attacked by British Hurricanes while flying from Boscombe Down during January 1941. Tests had to be suspended as over stressing was caused to the aircraft, by the pilot taking evasive action. Captured German aircraft were also evaluated at the Establishment. Fg Off M.H. Brown of No.1 Sqn who when in France during the first half of 1940, captured a Bf 109E which he flew in a "dogfight" with six of his squadron's Hurricanes before flying it over to

Boscombe Down on 3rd May 1940 for the 'boffins' to evaluate. A Junkers 88A-5, Me109, Me110 and a Heinkel He111H of the Enemy Aircraft Flt arrived for testing in mid 1942. The tests involved flame damping in the Blower Tunnel.

On 19th February 1941 the prototype Mosquito W4050 was flown but tests were halted by a fuselage failure which necessitated a rebuild.

A No.44 Sqn Hampden X3137 crash-landed in fog at Boscombe Down at 0110 hrs. on 21st March 1941. It had taken off from its base in Waddington at 1835 hrs on 20th March on a 'Gardening' operation near St Laurier. The crew was Plt Off Hedley G 'Hazel' Hazelden (pilot) who later as a Sqn Ldr became a student of the first Test Pilots' School, Plt Off Bell, Sgt Horner and Sgt Melton. There were no serious injuries but the Hampden was Category 'B' damaged. The number of operational aircraft of Bomber Command landing at Boscombe Down was starting to increase considerably having been diverted due to bad

Fortress II FK187 at Boscombe Down. A Stirling is visible in the distance.

Wright Cyclone G-205A engines and an armament of four machine-guns. As with the British built types there were successes such as the B-25 Mitchell, B-17 Fortress, although not in the hands of Bomber Command, and the Mustang. The first of the latter, Mustang I AG351, with its Allison V-1710 engine, arrived at Boscombe Down in January 1942 for performance trials. As is now well known, this excellent airframe really came into its own later in the war after it was re-engined with the Rolls-Royce Merlin. The American aircraft industry also had its fair share of failures with the likes of the Bermuda, Chesapeake and Martin Maryland. One of the latter

Corsair IV KD903 built by Goodyear at Akron, Ohio but seen here at A&AEE on bomb-rack trials. The FAA began to receive the type under Lend-Lease in June 1943. Photo: Don Neate Coll.

weather at their home bases. Other damaged aircraft returning from raids were landing wherever they could, having managed to reach the English coast-line safely. Casualties from these were treated in local hospitals.

In March and three times in a 10 day period during April 1941, Boscombe Down received some early morning raids in which two Blenheim Is L1173 and L1407 of the SDF were destroyed and some 40 aircraft damaged. There was also structural damage to a number of buildings and two hangars but no injuries to personnel.

Boscombe Down received some royal visitors when Queen Mary arrived on 29th September followed by King George VI and Queen Elizabeth on 23rd October 1941.

ATA pilots were frequently used for delivery of the various types of aircraft to and from Boscombe Down as on 24th October 1941 when Ann Welch flew Swordfish V4444 to Lee-on-Solent.

The Intensive Flying Development Unit was formed on 15th November 1941 so that aircraft could be subjected to a short term heavy flying programme to gauge long term reliability. By June 1942 it had been redesignated as a Flt.

The Aircraft Gun Mounting Establishment moved from Duxford to Boscombe Down on 23rd November 1941, becoming the Gunnery Development Section on 3rd January 1942 and was absorbed into A&AEE on 29th January. By May of that year the unit had undergone another name change to become the Gunnery Proofing Flt. One of the first trials carried out by the Flt was of the 40mm Vickers 'S' guns fitted to Hurricanes.

In 1942 a team of specialised meteorologists were deployed to the High Altitude Flt to investigate contrail formation. Initially equipped with two Spitfires and a Boston into which the scientists themselves installed the testing apparatus which they operated at the limits of the aircraft's ceiling. A Mosquito was issued in 1943 and also a B-17 FK192 which arrived on 8th June. The improved performance of these aircraft led to the first accurate forecasting of contrail formation.

After the war meteorological research was transferred to Farnborough where a larger and better funded Meteorological Research Flight was formed on 1st September 1946. In March 1994 the MRF transferred to Boscombe Down and two of the unit's aircraft became familiar in the skies over Wiltshire. These were Canberra B2 (WJ582) and the Hercules W2 XV208 (*Snoopy*). The latter was subsequently sold to DERA and operated by crews from the Heavy Aircraft Test Sqn.

From April 1942 Boscombe Down became a station in No.23 Group with the Headquarters at South Cerney.

The first production Stirling III R9309 arrived for tests on 14th July 1942. This aircraft proved to have a very poor rate of climb and was the subject of a number of test performances. It crashed on one of these on 6th September 1942.

Warwick I, BV214 arrived for handling trials on 12th August 1942 but crashed two weeks later. The Handling Sqn left Boscombe Down for Hullavington on 22nd August 1942 as part of ECFS.

The first rocket launching tests were carried out from August 1942 using Beaufighter V^2 EL329/G. Four rocket projectiles were carried under each wing for carriage and firing trials. The aircraft and crew were lost the following month when it crashed on a trial's flight.

By this stage in the war, Bomber Command had become increasingly alarmed at the poor performance of some aircraft being received by squadrons from the factories. Halifax bombers in particular were causing alarm with the number crashing for reasons unknown. It was determined that Boscombe Down would become responsible for evaluating every 100th four-engined aircraft to come off the production line. The testing started in January 1943. Each flight of three hours plus, was carried out at maximum weight and with a full crew of RAF personnel. Of the aircraft tested, most were satisfactory and the scheme ended on 18th April 1944.

A landing accident occurred on 10th March 1943, involving Halifax II DT772 of No.408 RCAF (Goose) Sqn.

The aircraft had been on a raid to Stuttgart and on return was diverted to Boscombe because of bad weather at its base at Leeming. It had been the first operation of his tour for the pilot Sgt E.B. Dungey RCAF. He made his night time approach to Boscombe too fast, overshot and collided with Boston IIIA BZ201, which was at dispersal.

Mosquito B. Mk.IV Series II DK290/G commenced extensive handling and range trials in April 1943. Flights were made with and without two dummy *Highballs* in the bomb bay. The stores were rotating mines similar to those carried by No.617 Sqn for breaching the German dams. Although *Highball* Mosquitoes later equipped No.618 Sqn, they never were used operationally. DK290 first arrived at Boscombe on 9th June 1942 for handling trials. The 'G' suffix would have been added for the *Highball* role and it denoted that a permanent guard had to be posted to the aircraft when not in the air.

The famous Empire Test Pilots' School within A&AEE was initiated in May 1943 although it was not so named until 28th July 1944. From 15th January 1944 it became a separate unit and was known as the Test Pilot Training Flight. It was commanded by Wg Cdr C. E. Slee MVO, AFC. The School which was set up to provide specialist pilots for test flying duties at aeronautical research and development establishments, transferred to Cranfield in October 1945 following Course No.3, but returned again on 29th January 1968 from Farnborough where it had been since 1947. It has been resident at Boscombe ever since. Course No.1 commenced on 10th June 1943, ending on 28th February 1944.

The cost of putting students through the course even in those early days was in the region of £10,000 per man. Halifax L9520 arrived for use by the school on 26th May 1943 followed by Miles Master III, W8573 on 29th May and Hurricane I L2006 on 3rd June. Further aircraft arrived after the course started, these being a Beaufort AW343, Proctor XV451, two Oxfords HN782 and HN581, two Hurricanes Z2399 and HD264 together with Mitchell FL215. Five students of Course No.1 were later to lose their lives while flying as test pilots. From the commencement of course No.2 in 1944, the duration became 12 months.

Gp Capt John Francis Xavier 'Sam' McKenna was appointed Commandant of the School on 19th February 1944 but was killed at 1620 hrs on 19th January 1945 when flying a Performance Testing Squadron Mustang IV KH648.

After D-Day Boscombe Down was used as a Reception Centre where wounded troops were returned by Dakotas on direct flights from Europe. This was a convenient airfield for the hospitals in Salisbury, in particular Odstock Hospital.

In September 1944 the Testing Flts were redesignated as follows: -

```
'A' Sqn No.1 Flt Performance Testing
'A'  "    " 2  "  Armament      "
'B'  "    " 1  "  Performance   "
'B'  "    " 2  "  Armament      "
'C'  "         Naval Aircraft   "
```

Communications & Special Duties Flt 'D' Sqn No.1 Flt Performance Testing 'D' " 2 " Armament " Intensive Flying Development Flight (IFDF)

'A' Sqn at Boscombe had as its responsibility, the evaluation and testing of fighter aircraft, 'B' Sqn dealt with bomber aircraft, 'C' Sqn with naval fixed wing aircraft and 'D' Sqn the testing for example, of aircraft general modifications.

Although the American Mustang played a major part in the air war, in particular after receiving the Merlin engine, the rear vision for the pilots was a problem. Boscombe therefore received a Mustang III in which to carry out tests with a rear view canopy. It was similar to the one-piece canopy of the Spitfire. The tests and canopy proved successful and the Malcolm hoods, named after the designer, were soon being fitted to production models.

Boscombe Down needed to find an extra 110 meals on 8th March 1945, when 16 Lancasters of Bomber Command landed off 'ops' at 0030hrs, having been diverted there.

Ashley Walk in the New Forest was the site of a bombing range opened in 1940 and used by A&AEE. A test drop of a live 22,000lb 'Grand Slam' bomb was made there on 13th March 1945. It was released from a modified Lancaster

bomber which the Establishment had earlier tested. The bomb drop proved a success and later that day a message giving clearance for use of 'Grand Slam' was taken by despatch rider from Boscombe Down to the Ministry of Aircraft Production in London. The following day Sqn Ldr C.C. Calder in a Lancaster of No.617 Sqn attacked the Bielefeld railway viaduct and 100yds of the structure collapsed due to the 'earthquake effect' of dropping this large bomb.

There were 176 aircraft on charge at Boscombe Down on 2nd August 1945. After VJ-Day, Boscombe was left with a considerable number of military aircraft, not all of British construction, many of which no longer had a function and it took time to dispose of these.

Post War Years

With the end of the war a decision was taken to adopt Boscombe Down as the permanent home of A&AEE. Numerous organisational changes then took place. In early 1946 'D' Sqn together with the Communications and Special Duties Sqn disbanded.

Civil aviation had been growing through the 1930s and having been of low priority during the war, was now set to take off in a big way. The Civil Aircraft Test Section (CATS) was implemented on 1st November 1946 to continue the pre-war function of A&AEE when all civil aircraft received their Certificate of Airworthiness via A&AEE. Many of the early aircraft tested were converted wartime bombers such as the Lancaster, Halifax, Liberator and Stirling. Types such as the Apollo, Avro Tudor, Hermes and York appeared later for evaluation and Certificate of Airworthiness testing. A Dakota was flown by CATS to establish testing techniques, particularly engine cuts on take-off. The Section was manned by civilian personnel with former RAF experience. The CATS functioned at Boscombe Down until responsibility for testing civil aircraft was taken over with the formation of the Air Registration Board Flight Testing Unit in early 1951. CATS however continued at Boscombe Down in the same name but with different areas of trials testing. As the only civilian servicing section on the establishment

they had built up a reputation for reliability that was worth retaining. They assumed responsibility for aircraft on the establishment not involved directly in type testing. They subsequently became the core of civilian serving personnel when civilian servicing began in 1957.

Neville Duke was one of the RAFs most successful pilots of World War 2, having accounted for 28 enemy aircraft. He joined 'A' Sqn in 1947 on a three-year secondment at the end of which he resigned his Sqn Ldrs' commission for a civilian contract as experimental test pilot with Hawkers.

The functions of the Airborne Forces Experimental Establishment (AFEE) was absorbed by A&AEE on 14th September 1950 and its aircraft ferried from Beaulieu. The unit was redesignated as the Airborne Forces & Rotary Wing Flt. This later became 'E' Sqn and progressed to the testing of civil versions of military aircraft and rotary types.

In January 1952 Boscombe Down was hosting a detachment from the 8th USAF Strategic Air Command (SAC). Having by then retired their war-time B-17s and B-24s, the 8th Air Force was equipped with the mighty 10 engined (6 piston/4 turbojet) Convair B-36D Peacemaker strategic bomber. The visit to Boscombe was being undertaken as a non-stop reinforcement flight from Texas to the U.K. as part of SACs round the clock deterrent policy. In the early hours of Sunday 27th January, with Salisbury Plain covered in snow, B-36D 44-92042 of the 7th Bombardment Wing based at Carswell AFB Texas, made its approach to Boscombe Down's main runway from the south-west end but it touched down outside the confines of the airfield. Boscombe Down at the time was not equipped with precision radar or a proper system of approach landing lights. The lighting provided was the Drem Mk.II, consisting of an arc of lead-in lights in the fields some 2000 yards distant from the airfield perimeter. This indicated to pilots the rate of turn necessary to line up with the runway. These were followed by three sets of 'funnel' shaped light indicators set in pairs on either side of the extended runway centre-line, forming a 'V' narrowing with the approach towards the runway threshold. This gave the pilot flying within the 'V' a continuous indication of the direction to the runway. The outer funnel lights were set 1,500 yards from the threshold with the intermediate and inner lights at 500yard intervals. The Americans did not use off-airfield lighting and so not being aware of the system, the pilot thought that Boscombe Down's approach lighting, was in fact the runway lighting. The approach brought him in over High Post airfield then touching down in the adjoining fields from where the aircraft continued on across the main A345 Salisbury-Amesbury road at a point known locally as 'Low Flying Corner'. The pilot passed a message to Boscombe Control that the runway was a bit bumpy, and received a reply that he was not on the runway. The B-36D came to rest outside of the crash gate in the airfield perimeter fence and just a short distance from the end of the runway. Later that day the Americans, acting promptly to overcome the embarrassment, removed the fencing and the grass between it and the runway and by Tuesday had towed the aircraft inside. Remarkably there were no injuries to the crew and very little damage sustained by the aircraft as a result of the rough landing, most damage being to American pride and the pilot's reputation. Over the next week the B-36 received minor repairs, was checked and test-run on the runway before being flown back to Fort Worth by a different pilot on Friday 1st February. The original pilot travelled as a passenger.

On VE-Day A. E. 'Ben' Gunn, who had flown Spitfires and Tempests during the war, took up a post as a test pilot at Boscombe Down. In 1952 he was chosen to fly the Boulton Paul P.120 delta wing jet research plane nicknamed the Black Widow. Flying at 5,000 ft. over the south coast, he heard a loud bang and the aircraft started to roll. 'Ben' decided to eject over Salisbury Plain, but just as he prepared to do this the aircraft flipped over and he fell out upside down. He managed to release himself from the seat and his parachute inflated sufficiently to arrest his fall before crashing into some trees. This was the first ejection from a delta wing aircraft and 'Ben' Gunn was the first pilot to eject from an inverted position and to survive.

The outward appearance of the airfield was changing during the 1950s but

B-36D 44-92042 displaying the war time *Triangle-J* with its 'six turnin' and 'four burnin' engines idle as it awaits the ignominy of being towed on to the airfield at Boscombe Down.
Photo: T. Heffernan Coll.

also the internal structure changed to accommodate the increasingly sophisticated aircraft equipment and armament. A Photographic Trials Section was modernised in 1950 to cover tests on new cameras for reconnaissance and high altitude survey work. A&AEE had responsibility for Units based abroad as with the Tropical Experimental Unit which relocated from Khartoum to Idris in 1954 and the sub-Artic aircraft trials held at Namao in Canada the same year. To support the increasing overseas commitment an Air Transport Flight was formed in June 1955 equipped with a Bristol Freighter XJ470, Hastings TG500, Valetta WD171 and York MW234. The Navigation and Radio Division was formed in 1956, responsible for testing instruments, radar equipment and dealing with the radio reference.

The Handling Squadron, which had left Boscombe Down for Hullavington in 1942 returned from Manby on 12th April 1954 as a lodger unit in No.41 Group.

On 4th August 1954 the prototype English Electric Lightning WG760, which had been assembled at Boscombe Down, made its first test flight. This became the first supersonic aircraft of the RAF. At this time also the new supersonic research aircraft the Fairey Delta 2 made its first flight at Boscombe Down on Wednesday 6th October 1954. It was flown by Peter Twiss, Fairey Aviation Co. Ltd's own test pilot. During a later trial flight on 17th November, it almost came to grief when following a fuel system problem

and engine failure, which caused hydraulic power for the controls to be lost, it left the runway when gliding in to land. It recovered to set a closed course world speed record of 1,132 miles per hour on 10th March 1956.

Runway 24 was installed with a 'HILO' mirror sight c.1959. It was in use by aircraft of the Royal Navy's 'C' Squadron to evaluate the day and night effectiveness of the mirror. It was an early version of the mirror landing light. A single source light was shone at a mirror 50 yards up-wind. Its reflection was directed at the pilot's eye, showing above a horizontal line when the aircraft was too high and below the horizontal line reflection when too low. When the spot reflection was kept on the horizontal line, the aircraft could be landed and on a carrier the arrester wire would be caught.

The RAF's V-Bombers were periodically found dispersed at Boscombe in the late 1950s/early60s, ready at 4 minutes notice to head for Russia with their deadly Atomic bombs. In 1963 No.XV Sqn were re-allocated to Boscombe Down having been dispersed at St Mawgan. Air Cdre David Bywater RAF (Retd), served with the squadron as a co-pilot and a captain between October 1958 and January 1964. His log book records him landing at Boscombe Down on 13th November 1963 in Victor B Mk.1 XA936 at the start of a *"Micky Finn"* dispersal exercise. Earlier that year he had visited Boscombe Down as the ground operations crew. Air Cdre Bywater recalls the V-bomber dispersal being on the south side of the airfield, in the 'D' (Helicopter) Sqn area, using the standard Bomber Command five man sleeping caravans and a number of dispersal buildings for operations, messing and ablutions. The squadron Victors were parked on the helicopter parking apron adjacent to runway 17/35 parallel taxiway. Boscombe Down remained No.XV Sqn's dispersal airfield until their disbandment on 1st October 1964. Air Cdre Bywater was posted to 'B' Sqn at Boscombe Down in January 1965 for the first of his test pilot tours. He believes by that time the V-bomber dispersal was no longer in use. He served at A&AEE for a total of sixteen years spread over four tours of duty and completed his time as a serving officer, as Commandant of the Establishment.

During the 1950s, visiting VIPs provided an excuse for flying displays to be laid on at the airfield. Three pilots of 'C' Sqn in particular had party pieces. One would fly a Sea Fury inverted with the top of the rudder brushing the grass beside the runway. One would provide an aerobatic display in a Seahawk and would end it by doing a low-level loop, put his under-carriage down when at the top and then land off it. Another would beat up the field in a Hornet with both engines feathered. These impromptu displays tailed off in later years when financial accountability became the norm.

With the start of the 60s decade, the RAF of 'A' Sqn at Boscombe Down were concentrating on the testing and evaluation of the Lightning and the Hawker P1127 VTO whose successor was the Harrier. 'B' Sqn were carrying out tests on the V-bombers and military transport aircraft such as the Blackburn Beverley and 'C' Sqn of the Royal Navy, the Buccaneer, Sea Vixen and Scimitar. 'D' Sqn was now concentrating entirely on helicopters with anti-submarine sonar trials underway, using the successful Wessex Mk.3. In November 1960 the Air Transport Flight amalgamated with 'A' Flight of 'D' Sqn to form Support Sqn which in turn was made up of three Flights -Transport, Trials and Meteor. 'D' Sqn with their former CATS personnel hived off their fixed wing responsibility to the Support Sqn and with this the CATS name finally disappeared from Boscombe Down.

On 1st January 1964 'E' Sqn was formed to conduct flight trials of transport and communications aircraft such as the Andover, Basset, Belfast, Dominie, VC.10 and the Hercules which arrived in 1967. Support Sqn, which embraced the Airborne Forces Development and the A&AEE air transport, communications and continuation training aircraft fleet, was absorbed with the formation of the new squadron. 'E' Sqn was formed into two Flts, the Air Transport Flight and a Trials Flight.

In 1961 the Trials Management Division was formed as Weapons Systems Division to co-ordinate the more advanced and complex projects being handled by A&AEE.

No.13 Joint Services Trials Unit arrived from Upavon for 'Red Top' AAM evaluation on 1st February 1962. The aircraft used was the Sea Vixon FAW.1. (XN684). The Unit was disbanded on 14th July 1967.

Boscombe Down was home to another legend of British aviation history when on the 27th September 1964 the first pre-production model of the English Electric TSR-2 took-off over Wiltshire. This aircraft was one of the most advanced of its type in the world and looked as if it would provide the RAF with a machine, which would be the envy of all others. Its performance was exceptional and it had fantastic potential with the capability of both attack and reconnaissance roles. Unfortunately it became a political pawn and was tragically cancelled by the Labour Government of the day who prior to election had claimed its cost to be exorbitant.

No.22 Joint Services Trials Unit formed at Boscombe Down on 1st January 1966. It was equipped with the Sea Vixen FAW.1 (XJ488) which was painted black overall. The Unit disbanded on 31st December 1974.

The ETPS returned to Boscombe Down in 1968 with No.27 Fixed Wing Course and No.6 Rotary Wing Course.

During the 1970s the practice of allocating aircraft to the Handling Sqn for assessment changed. The aircraft were no longer made available and the Pilot's Notes which became the Aircrew Manual were written up by the manufacturers and sent to the

Handling Sqn to be checked, together with Flight Reference Cards, and any amendments made. The Squadron continues to maintain this role and the provision of normal and emergency handling advice for the aircraft of all three Services.

By 1971 the Establishment work had developed to such an extent that it was necessary to re-organise it into eight divisions and these were: Armament, Engineering, Flying, Navigation and Radio, Performance, Photographic, Technical Services and Trials Management. This coincided with the fifty years of aeroplane and armament testing which was celebrated on 19th March when Boscombe opened its gates to families and invited quests. The quest of honour that day was Princess Anne, deputising for the Queen who was unwell. A memorial recognising the fifty years of A&AEE was erected to coincide with the visit by the Princess. This is located, together with the memorial to Flt Lt James Nicolson VC, next to the former World War 2 Control Tower now used as the HQ Flying Dept. It also serves as the offices of the Chief Test Pilots and the Meteorological Offices. The building is now clad with narrow plastic horizontal sheets presumably enhancing the internal temperatures.

An exhibition was laid out in two hangers and a large static park of aircraft was assembled on the apron outside. Some of these can be seen in the photograph.

Despite atrocious weather conditions a reduced flying display took place and the audience witnessed some remarkable flying and a considerable number of aircraft types. Some of the participating aircraft were: - Gloster Gladiator 1 K8032 from the Shuttleworth Trust, Gloster Meteor NF.13 WM367, the FAAs Fairey Swordfish 11 LS326, Blackburn B.2 G-AEBJ, Blackburn Beverley C.1 XB261, De Havilland D.H.98 Mosquito T.3 RR299, one of Boscombe Down's yellow North American Harvards T.2B KF183, Avro 698 Vulcan B.2A XH539, Handley Page Hastings C.2 WD496, Hawker Hurricane 11C G-AMAU/PZ865, Hawker Hunter F.6. XE601. E.E. Canberra B.2 WJ638 gave a low level demonstration with seat ejection and the spray rake Canberra B (1) 8 WV787 (*The Rainmaker*) in all black

On display in the Aircraft Park (front to rear) Jaquar S.1 XW560, Harrier GR.1 XV740, Hunter F.6 XE601, Lightning T.4 XL629, Buccaneer S.2B XW529, Nimrod MR.1 XV148 (left side) Argosy C.1 XN817 and Hercules C.1 XV178. Other aircraft displayed in the distance include a Beverley, Britannia, Hastings, Hellcat, Meteor, Phantom, Sea Fury, Sea Hawk, Sea Vixen and Vulcan. Photo: Don Neate Coll.

livery flew past with Hawker Siddeley Nimrod MR.1 XV148 being sprayed from its icing rig. Hawker Siddeley Argosy C.1 XN817 flew alongside as chase plane.

The large Weighbridge Hangar was one of the two used for an exhibition depicting the scope of work undertaken by A&AEE and showing the effects on aviation over the years since its inception at Martlesham Heath in 1921. Displays were grouped under the various Divisions. The Armament Division showed a development Harrier XV 281 displaying temporary U.S. insignia. The Flying Division used a Supermarine S.6B S1596. The Performance Division a Gloster Javelin FAW.9 XH897 with red and white stripe trim. No.22 Joint Services Trials Unit a Hawker Siddeley Buccaneer S.2A XV352 and the ETPS a Hawker Hunter T.7. XL579. In the second hangar the Engineering, Photographic, Technical Services, Navigation & Radio Divisions were represented. Displays consisted of another Hunter T.7. XL564, a North American Harvard T.2B FT375, weapons, aircraft parts etc.

It was at this time that 'C' Sqn, which had been concerned with naval aircraft, was disbanded and absorbed by 'A' and 'B' Sqns. It stemmed from the reduction of fixed- wing flying by the Navy and the retirement of HMS Ark Royal.

The Grant of Arms was made to A&AEE as part of the 1971 celebrations.

The Arms incorporate features representing the history of the Establishment and perpetuate the central feature and motto of the unit badge authorised by King George V[2] in 1939. The background to the shield is of green and white bars from the Arms of the County of Wiltshire, to reflect its origin as part of the Central Flying School at Upavon in 1914, and the location at Boscombe Down since 1939. The central motif is from the unit badge and shows an arrow, representing true flight, between an

form. They recall the Establishment's time at Martlesham Heath (Martlets Village) in Suffolk from 1917 to 1939. The dominant feature of the Crest is the great bustard, once Britain's largest native bird, which last roamed wild on Salisbury Plain towards the end of the nineteenth century. It is also present on the Arms of the County of Wiltshire

A&AEE Coat of Arms

but is shown in a different stance. The Arms also incorporate a heraldic pun. The device on the wing is the *boss* from a horse's bit and the bird is standing in a valley or *combe* in a *down*, the name given to the chalk uplands above or between river valleys. The bearings are completed by the motto *Probe Probare* meaning 'Properly to Test'.

The structure of the ETPS courses altered in 1974 when No.1 Flight Test Engineer Course was added to No.33 Fixed Wing and No.12 Rotary Wing Course. As Flight Test Engineers

Harvard FT375 on 21/9/85. In the background can be seen the hangars originally at High Post Aerodrome.

Mosquito RR 298 on 21/9/85.

airman's glove and a mailed gauntlet representing aeroplanes and armament. The birds in the quarters are martlets, or swallows, in heraldic

worked closely with Test Pilots, it was thought that training them together as a team would create improved efficiency and working relations.

During 1975 a project was under-taken by airframe fitters, technicians and various other volunteers to restore a Bolingbroke for the RAF Museum Collection. The rebuild was done to a very high standard and when complete the aircraft was transported to Hendon in sections. There it was reassembled by Boscombe Down personnel and placed on display in the Battle of Britain exhibition.

The norm of having a gate guardian at an RAF station was not introduced at Boscombe Down until 1979 when English Electric Lightning T4 XL629 was allocated and mounted outside of the NAAFI shop close to the main gate of the airfield. This aircraft had been the second prototype T4 and had been in service with the ETPS.

On 1st May 1980 No.29 Joint Services Trials Unit arrived from Yeovilton where it had formed to evaluate the Sea Skua missile system. It was equipped with the Lynx HAS.2. (XZ228). The Unit left for Aberporth on 15th September 1980.

A squadron of 15 USAF F-111Ds deployed to Boscombe in May 1980 as part of a training programme for European augmentation forces. This was code named exercise 'Coronet Hammer'.

The Argentinean invasion of the Falkland Islands on 2nd April 1982 provided A&AEE with a programme of priority testing at short notice. Trials were carried out with Sidewinders fitted to Harrier GR3s of No.1 Sqn and even the Nimrod was cleared to carry these missiles to protect their vulnerability in the war zone. The aged Vulcan was modified to carry Shrike anti-radiation missiles and set up to ensure the success of the 'Black Buck' raids on Port Stanley. With the long haul down to the South Atlantic much work was done on the re-fuelling capabilities of aircraft. The Establishment's contribution to the Falklands War maintained its previous high standards in times of conflict.

A second detachment to exercise the co-located operating base (COB) at Boscombe Down, took place in September 1983 code named exercise 'Coronet Archer'. On this occasion the deployment was 8 F-111Ds belonging to the 27th Tactical Fighter Wing (TFW) 522 Tactical Fighter Squadron (TFS) based at Cannon Air Force Base, New Mexico. They were known as the 'Fighting Fire Balls' following their practice of dumping fuel then cutting their engines to pass through the fuel cloud and obtaining re-ignition. The exercises were planned by HQ USAF Tactical Air Command (TAC), and 20 (TFW) Upper Heyford was the sponsor unit for the deployment. The 8 F-111Ds arrived at Boscombe Down on 8th September all touching down between 1727-1758 hours, the airfield continuing to operate outside of its normal close down time of 1730 hours. C-5 and C-141 transport aircraft were used for stores and equipment back-up and the detachment included personnel of the National Guard as well as regular USAF staff. Building 104 (ETPS) was used as a passenger terminal and by the USAF Maintenance Control as a

15 F-111Ds on the apron in front of the Weighbridge Hanger.

One of Boscombe Down's Technical Officers, Norman Parker, receiving the Bolingbroke for renovation.   Photo: Norman Parker

freight reception and stores area. Half of the hangar area was shared with the Royal Navy Fleet Requirements Air Direction Unit (FRADU) which at this time in1983 was deployed at Boscombe Down with Hunter and Canberra aircraft while the runways at Yeovilton were being resurfaced. The hangarage was used in the event of essential aircraft engine changes. Three of the USAFs own aircraft refuelling bowsers and operators supported the F-111Ds and for Exercise 'Coronet Archer', used the bowser (HAS) for the first time. During what was deemed to be a successful operation, 290 sorties, which incorporated exercises 'Cold Fire' and 'Brown Falcon' were flown by the American aircraft before their return to Cannon AFB on 5th October. The visit to Boscombe Down attracted the attention of members for the Campaign against Nuclear Cruise Missiles, an off-shute of CND, who demonstrated outside the main entrance gate but without causing any major disruption. A subsequent exercise *'Coronet Comanche Papago'* was held in 1986 this time adding EF111 Raven electronic warfare aircraft to those being exercised.

Parented by Strike Command, the Tornado Operational Evaluation Unit was lodged at Boscombe Down on 1st September 1983 to evaluate the Tornado GR1. The benefits evolved from its liaison with the Establishment led to the Unit's expansion on 5th October 1987 with the addition of the Harrier GR5 and a title change with the formation of the Strike Attack Operational Evaluation Unit (SAOEU). Harrier GR7 ZG860 T was operating with the unit in 1994.

In January 1988 the Fixed Wing Test Sqn was formed from an amalgamation of 'A' and 'B' Sqns. The opinion at the time was that test flying would reduce, so this merger was advantageous to the aircrews who, had up until then specialised in either the fast jets of 'A' Sqn or the transport aircraft of 'B' Sqn. The merger enabled crews to gain experience of the two types. 'D' Sqn became the Rotary Wing.

As with the Falklands War, Boscombe Down found itself fully involved in trials of weapons and equipment in use during *'Operation Desert Storm'* following Iraq's invasion of Kuwait in 1990. Clearances were hurried through on the Thermal Imaging and Laser Designated pod which was in use with the Gulf deployed Tornado squadrons, on missile approach warning systems, flare dispensers and a revision undertaken of the Sidewinder missiles and Air to Air Refuelling needs. Once again the Establishment played its part in the subsequent successful outcome of the war.

From 1st April 1995 Boscombe Down lost its title as A&AEE and became D.T.E.O. (Defence Test Evaluation Organisation) and subsequently D.E.R.A. (Defence Evaluation & Research Agency). These functions continue on all types of aircraft and equipment, carried out by the Establishment's scientists and test engineers. Civilian and RAF personnel

fly the various aircraft. Studies into the development of pilot-less aircraft for a wide range of military missions including maritime patrol, naval airborne early warning and transport missions is just one of the projects evaluated. Another has been trials with airships to decide if they could offer a cost effective means of performing a range of military tasks. A Skyship 600 was a familiar sight in the skies of South Wiltshire during the mid 90s and with its quiet approach and hovering capabilities, its use for counter-terrorist surveillance duties was one of the considerations by an Army assessment team. Another was its possible use by field surgical units as stable floating hospitals. The absence of engine vibration makes airships ideal as airborne surveillance platforms and also has medical benefits for personnel with burns or spinal injuries. The airship was found capable of carrying personnel or around 30 tons of equipment, which is four times the capability of the Chinook helicopter and only a third less than the Hercules transport aircraft. It might also provide an advanced communication function, similar to those of the airborne warning aircraft. The DERA boffins have also hailed the success of a unique airship-based system used in Kosovo to detect mines. The airship called *Mineseeker* carries a new form of radar allowing it to penetrate foliage and the ground. The radar developed over a decade and trialed at Boscombe, achieves an exceptional resolution, allowing detection even of small, plastic anti-personnel landmines. The radar was tested in Kosovo against surface-laid, foliage-obscured and buried mines and unexploded ordnance with the trials team deployed over a live mine site used for training explosive detection dogs. The success of the equipment should in future make mine detection safer and quicker than it has been in the past.

The new Eurofighter will be tested before it enters service with the RAF. Much of the work at Boscombe Down must of course by necessity remain classified. Within the Test and Evaluation structure is the Fast Jet Test Sqn being the equivalent of the former 'A' Sqn, and the Heavy Aircraft Test Sqn, the equivalent to 'B' Sqn. In addition is the Rotary Wing Test Sqn sited on the east- side of the airfield

through which helicopter types of all three services pass, including Air Sea Rescue. The first of the new Army Apache AH.I helicopters arrived for trails at Boscombe Down during the summer of 2000. The Army's order for 67 of the type, comprise of the first 8 being supplied by Boeing with American General Electric engines and 59 supplied by Westland's of Yeovil, with Rolls-Royce RTM turbo-charged engines. This 'flying tank' is probably the most sophisticated piece of flying equipment the British Army has ever had. The trials Apache is equipped with an instrumentation package that will record a vast amount of data, most of which will be relayed in real time to telemetry stations at the airfield. The 230mph machine boasts 16 Hellfire missiles capable of destroying a small village from a distance of five miles, and a 30mm Gatling-type gun capable of unleashing 625 rounds per minute. Unfortunately during trials it was found that debris ejected on launching the Hellfire missiles could cause catastrophic damage to the main or tail rotors, causing the helicopter to crash. The American Forces had to restrict the Apache to firing missiles only from the right hand side of the aircraft which limited its effectiveness in Afghanistan where it was in use against al-Qaeda terrorists during Operation *Anaconda*.

With the arrival from America of the new Hercules C130J, trials are being carried out at Boscombe Down that include paratroop and load dropping. The C130Js with head-up displays, computerised screens and avionics, and operating with a three man crew, are replacing the C130Ks which have been in use since 1967, crewed by five personnel.

With the turn of the century the RAF have two units at Boscombe Down: S.A.O.E.U. flying Harriers, Jaguars and Tornadoes plus the Southampton University Air Squadron (SUAS) including No.2 Air Experience Flight flying 6 Grob G.115Es which replaced Bulldog T.1s in May 2001. The SUAS has been at Boscombe Down since its arrival from Lee-on-Solent on 2nd April 1993 and No.2 AEF since its arrival from Hurn on 1st April 1996 when it was parented by SUAS.

The Empire Test Pilot's School operates with both RAF and civilian personnel as did *'Snoopy'* the Hercules WMk2 XV208, probably the most

Hercules WMk.2 XV208 *'Snoopy'* outside an HAS.

sophisticated flying weather laboratory in the world. It belonged to DERA but was contracted to the Meteorological Research Flight. The nickname, from the cartoon character, derived from the 20' 6" long probe on the nose of the aircraft which would measure accurate air movements clear of aircraft induced turbulence. The Met Office contract expired at the end of March 2001 and the Government decided future funding had to be civilian-contracted. So *'Snoopy'* which had been in service since 1973 and at Boscombe Down since March 1994, was made redundant and is to be replaced by a BAE Systems-owned BAe 146-300.

The aircraft in use by the ETPS are the Andover C.1. , BAC 111, Hawk T.1, Hunter T.7, Jaguar T.2, Tucano T.1, Lynx AH.7, 2 Gazelles and a Squirrel. The School of Aviation Medicine operates with 2 Hawk T.1s, XX162 and XX327. In addition the base also operates a number of 'Lodger Units'.

At the rear of the Fire Section on the south side of the airfield is the site of the HAS used to house the aircraft of the private Bustard Flying Club which moved in from Old Sarum in 1989 and commenced flying training in 1990. The Bustard Club was formed by staff at A&AEE in 1957 when, with the help of the Kemsley trust and the RAF unit, two ex-Ministry Tiger Moths were acquired, later replaced by a Jodel DR1050-M1. This still operates together with a Beagle Pup 100, a Cessna 172 and the member's private aircraft. The Club celebrated its 40th Anniversary by holding an aviation day on 10th August 1997.

Boscombe Down hosted one of its rare 'Open Days' when over the weekend of 9th/10th June 1990 it staged a Battle of Britain Air Show to commemorate the 50th anniversary. The air show was very successful and was repeated in 1992.

Some Large visitors

Vulcan XH558

Boeing AWAC

B-52

Photos: Donald Lovelock

Another first for Boscombe Down was in fact a last - on Friday 14th March 1997 the world's last airworthy DH 106 Comet 4C XS235 made her final official flight from Boscombe's main runway. Named *'Canopus'* after the brightest star in the Southern Hemisphere it made its maiden flight on 27th July 1949 with World War 2 ace and, at that time de Havilland test pilot, Gp Capt John *'Cats Eyes'* Cunningham at the controls. Boscombe Down took delivery of the aircraft in December 1963 and since then it had been in constant service as a flying laboratory, testing navigation equipment and radios for all three Services. This particular Comet became the first jet aircraft to cross Antarctica in 1969. It's final flight ended a flying career totalling 8,620 hours and was made with a group of VIPs on board who included 78 year old Gp Capt Cunningham. The Comet was the World's first jet airliner and this one was due to be sold by auction on the 8th May 1997 but was withdrawn by the MoD to allow a consortium the opportunity of raising sufficient cash to keep it in this country. Subsequent to this it was sold to the de Havilland Aircraft Museum Trust Limited at Hatfield Airfield but plans to take the aircraft to BAe Hatfield could not be realised. Alternative locations were considered and *Canopus* slipped quietly out of Boscombe on 30th October for its final home with the British Aviation Heritage Collection at the former

Comet XS235 leaving Boscombe for the last time on its journey to retirement at Bruntingthorpe.

The wheels of Concorde retracting as it crosses the airfield boundary of Boscombe Down en route for New York.

World War 2 bomber airfield at Bruntingthorpe. It is the intention to keep the veteran airliner in 'working' order so that it can participate in the various 'taxi days' held at the airfield during the summer months. The personnel of Boscombe Down were sorry to lose the use of this fine aircraft to which they had become very much attached during its lengthy and reliable service at the base.

DERA has another elderly aircraft which is a favourite amongst its pilots and this is North American Harvard KF183. It was originally built in Canada in 1944 and was used by the RAF for training followed by the Torpedo Development Unit at Gosport. It arrived at Boscombe Down in 1947 and currently its primary use is as a photo-chase aircraft for parachute trials. It provides a very stable photographic platform from which a photographer in the rear seat can take good quality shots for example, of drops involving heavy equipment and paratroops.

On Wednesday 12th August 1998, the MoD allowed a commercial holiday flight to operate when a British Airways Concorde took off at 1100 hrs for New York. The aircraft was on charter to the Bournemouth based Bath Travel and Boscombe Down had the only runway long enough in the South to allow Concorde to take-off with a full fuel load to reach its destination in America. Passengers paid £2,895 for the 11- day package, which included a 6-day return cruise to Southampton on the QE2. They were collected by coach and taken to The Inn at High Post to

check in and then transferred to Boscombe Down. The check in of course was at the former High Post Hotel being part of the former High Post airfield.

The Control Tower stands on the south side of the main runway. Boscombe Down is the busiest military airfield in the country in terms of movements handled by the RAF Air Traffic Control operators.

Boscombe Down is very conscious of its valuable heritage and to this end the Support Unit of the RAF, along with a number of enthusiasts, are actively engaged in putting together a collection of artefacts which are being displayed in one of the HAS structures. Understandably visits by enthusiasts and other interested organisations can only be accommodated on a prior permission basis. A major aim is to develop a range of 'hands-on' exhibits to encourage children's interest in aviation that might inspire some to take it up as a career. The historical side of the collection, it is hoped will create an awareness of the birth of aviation, its rapid development and the human sacrifices made. Volunteers are encouraged to undertake a large number of restoration projects.

Consideration was given to Boscombe Down becoming the home of the RAF's fleet of tanker aircraft. The 24 VC10s and 9 Tri-Stars currently based at Brize Norton are coming to the end of their working lives. If the Future Strategic Tanker Aircraft (FSTA) programme had become installed at Boscombe Down, a further 500 jobs

would have been added to those already carried out by the 1,200 persons employed there. There would also have been a need for a hotel, 300 homes and a passenger terminal building. In 2001 QinetiQ, the privatised part of DERA, sought planning permission for new buildings to provide offices, light industry and research facilities, as well as changes to the runway, taxi-ways and the airfield layout. However in August 2001 an announcement was made that the scheme was to be withdrawn and that Brize Norton would remain the base for the new generation of tanker aircraft.

On 20th July 2001 Hawker Hunter WB188 (GA.11 WV256, G-BZPB) belonging to Classic Jets and flown by AVM 'Boz' Robinson, recreated the first flight of the Hunter prototype from Boscombe, 50 years to the day. The last Hunter in British military service, T.7 XL612 made its final operational flight from Boscombe Down on 10th August 2001. It was piloted by ETPS Fixed Wing Flying Tutor Sqn Ldr Rhys Williams, who was accompanied by a pupil of the school, Lt Laura Herath, a US Navy helicopter test-pilot on a fixed-wing familiarisation flight.

Aircraft Accidents involving aircraft at Boscombe Down from WW2 to date

1) Whitley V P5019 of the Beam Approach Training & Development Unit, flown by Flt Lt J.S. Kendrick, crashed at Boscombe Down on 12th July 1940. The pilot, who was inexperienced on type, misread the windsock, landed downwind and ran through the aerodrome boundary into the bomb dump, but with no injuries to those on board. The BATDU received a replacement aircraft, Whitley P5053.

2) On Thursday 5th September 1940, Anson I R9815 of the BATDU, which had previously crashed in December 1939 and February 1940, crashed again at Boscombe Down whilst on a Blind Approach landing in fog at night. On its approach the aircraft banked but struck the ground with collapse of the undercarriage and a wing digging in. The Anson caught fire and burnt out. The crash claimed the lives of four of the five men on board. Fg Off Kenneth Munro RAF (pilot) and Sgt Francis W. K. Wood RAF (obs) were killed. Both were buried at Amesbury Cemetery. Flt Lt E. J. Always (W/T Obs.) died on the way to hospital and Sgt Charles K. Hames RAF (WOP/AG) died in Tidworth Hospital. Sgt A. D. F. Allen (AG) suffered minor injuries but was able to extract his colleagues from the wreckage. For his actions he was awarded the George Medal.

3) On 22nd October 1940, photo chase Hampden I P4354 collided with Buffalo I AS430 and crashed at Bower Chalke near Salisbury. The pilot of the Hampden, Fg Off W.J. Carr and the pilot of the Buffalo Flt Lt S. *Sammy* Wroath, parachuted to safety but the two photographers in the Hampden, Mr F. L. Oxley and J.W. Parsons, were both killed. Fg Off Carr had fought with No.235 Sqn during the Battle of Britain.

4) On Saturday 16th November 1940, Bristol Blenheim IV L4893 of the Bomber Development Unit, when making its final approach to the Bristol Aircraft Company aerodrome at Filton, stalled and spun in killing pilot Plt Off George E. Stansbury RAF. He was buried at Devizes Road Cemetery, Salisbury.

5) Albemarle (P) I P1360 was carrying out speed trials on 4th February 1941 but on completion suffered a structural failure, causing a wing to drop and a loss of height. The order was given to abandon the aircraft. Mr J.D. Hayhurst (FTO) made a successful parachute landing but the parachute of Mr N. Sharp (FTO), caught on the tailplane and streamed out behind, with him suspended. He managed to haul himself up the shrouds and to cling onto the tailplane. The aircraft passed through a high hedge before hitting the ground, at which point Flt Lt B.O. Huxtable (pilot) was thrown clear with minor injuries. Mr Sharp was dislodged by the hedge and rolled down a steep snow-covered ravine and suffered serious injuries. The incident occurred near Crewkerne in Somerset and the aircraft was burnt out.

6) On Friday 21st February 1941, Hurricane II Z2398 of the HAF, piloted by Fg Off Lionel G.H. Kells RAF, disappeared without trace. The pilot had served with No.29 Sqn during the Battle of Britain, and his name is commemorated on the Runnymede Memorial.

7) On 1st March 1941, Mohawk I BK877, engaged in gun heating tests, crashed at Hanging Langford following an engine failure. The pilot Sqn Ldr John E. Dutton AFC was killed.

8) On 1st March 1941, No.109 Sqn Wellington T2556 flown by Fg Off Summerville was written off after crashing on landing at Boscombe Down. Its replacement was T2565. No injuries were sustained by the crew.

9) On 3rd July 1941, Flt Lt Samuel A. Ellaby was killed carrying out unauthorised low level aerobatics in Spitfire II P8273 of the HAF, when it crashed 1 mile north of Over Wallop.

10) On 24th July 1941, Anson I R9813 of No.109 Sqn crash landed on the aerodrome and collided with A&AEE Spitfire II P8036 and Spitfire VB R7337. There were no injuries to personnel.

11) On Monday 3rd November 1941, Blenheim IV V5797 crashed when its bomb load prematurely detonated during a low-level trial over Crichel Down Bombing Range. Fg Off Francis N. Heapey and LAC Alfred V. Hinks (No.78 Sqn) were killed. Fg Off G.F. Betts was injured.

12) On Friday 21st November 1941, a fatal accident occurred, involving No.109 Sqn Wellington T2552. This aircraft crashed at Oakington killing Flt Lt Brendan P. Hennesey RAFVR (pilot), Fg Off R. M. Lewin (nav), Flt Sgt Thomas A. Bates RAF (obs), Sgt James W. Cornforth RAF (WOP/AG), Sgt Thomas D. Snape RAFVR (AG) and Sgt Hackey.

13) On 11th February 1942, Wg Cdr William S. Jenkins was killed when Airacobra I AH573 crashed on the east boundary of the airfield. The pilot taking off tried to turn back after an engine failure at 600'.

14) On 28th February 1942, Albemarle I P1368, carrying out intensive flying trials, crashed and burnt out at Shalbourne near Hungerford. It was being flown by an operational crew attached to the Establishment. The three crewmen killed were Plt Off Thomas W.Caston RCAF, Plt Off John C. Fisher RCAF and Flt Sgt David L. Mullins.

15) On 24th March 1942, Liberator II AL546 crashed at Race Farm, Lytchett Minster in Dorset killing the pilot Wg Cdr John W. McGuire AFC. The others in the crew who parachuted to safety were WO F.J. Robinson, who was injured, Cpl R. M. Leach (1st Eng), AC1 Brian G. Hibbs (Fitter) and Mr J.J. Unwin (Flt Test Obs). The aircraft suffered failure of the instruments, followed by the starboard outer engine over-speeding and catching fire. When this could not be extinguished, the pilot gave the order to bale out. The body of Wg Cdr McGuire was recovered from the wreckage and as a result of his actions he was later awarded a posthumous bar to his AFC.

16) On 18th April 1942, a Handling Sqn Lancaster I R5539 carrying out a high-speed dive to test recovery without the use of elevator trim, crashed at Charlton near Malmesbury. It only made a partial recovery from a dive and struck the ground. The investigation determined that wing rivets had progressively failed causing the skin to separate. Wg Cdr Peter S. Salter (pilot), Sqn Ldr Jack D. Harris DFC, Flt Lt Norman G. Wilson, Fg Off Percy F. Wakelin and Sgt Kenneth J. Jones were killed in the accident.

17) On 6th May 1942, Master I T8852 suffered a port wing failure during a

series of dives. It crashed just outside of the aerodrome killing the passenger AC2 Frank E. Bartlett. The pilot Fg Off G.C. Brunner parachuted to safety. The wing was discovered to have failed due to defective gluing of the plywood skin.

18) On 12th July 1942, a pressurised Wellington VI W5795 of the High Altitude Flt broke up during a dive and crashed near Derby. Sqn Ldr Cyril Lancelot Fellowes Colmore (pilot), Plt Off Kenneth Radford (AG), Sgt Arthur James Smith (obs), Sgt Ronald Potts Gillott (WOP/AG) and Mr C.V. Abbott (Flt Test Obs) were killed.

19) On Wednesday 26th August 1942 Warwick I BV214 crashed 2 miles south-west of Shrewton following separation of the fabric covered port wing. The four-man crew killed was Sqn Ldr William J. Carr AFC (pilot), Cpl Raymond Leigh (Fitter), Cpl Frederick W. Shenton (AG) and Mr E. R. Staniland (Flt Test Obs).

20) On 6th September 1942, Stirling III R9309, whilst carrying out a test performance with an AUW of 70,000 lbs., fire broke out in the starboard outer engine due to a fracture of the No.8 cylinder which severed the carburettor inlet pipe. The crew, Plt Off R. Jarvie, Sgt D. Tucker, Cpl P. Taylor plus FTOs Mr Middleton and Mr Lofts of 'B' Flt. Performance Test Sqn, took to their parachutes while the pilot Flt Lt S.F. Reiss (Polish Forces), attempted to recover the aircraft to Boscombe aerodrome. He found that the feathering equipment, bomb doors, bomb jettison gear and flaps were inoperative. Unable to jettison the bomb load and forced to throttle back the port outer engine to maintain lateral trim, the aircraft was unable to maintain height on the inner engines and crashed into trees on Porton Down. The pilot survived the crash as he had another the previous month, when on 17th August the nose-wheel of a B-24 Liberator AL505 collapsed on landing.

21) On 24th September 1942, after the trial firing of a rocket at a height of 50' over Compton Range, the port engine of Beaufighter VIC EL329/G seized and the aircraft crashed onto Bulford Camp parade ground killing Sqn Ldr Vernon M. Bright and LAC Robert F. Brown (Armourer).

22) On 23rd October 1942, Hurricane I

Z4993/G on bomb carrying trials at Lyme Bay Range, crashed at Ridgeway Hill, Upwey, between Dorchester and Weymouth, killing Wg Cdr Horace R. Allen.

23) On 23rd December 1942, Spitfire IX BS139 engaged in fuel system and spinning trials, crashed following an engine failure at Cadbury Farm, Mottisfont in Hampshire, killing Flt Lt Gillian L. Campbell DFC. The pilot had served with No.236 Sqn during the Battle of Britain and later with No.272 Sqn.

24) Compared with the previous year, Boscombe Down's fatality rate for 1943 was considerably less. One of the two accidents involved Halifax II W7917 which crashed on 4th February, 2 miles east of Sutton Scotney in Hampshire. This aircraft on loan from No.4 Group's No.102 Sqn was being used on tests to try and determine the reason for some of the mysterious crashes. The pilot lost control when part of a rudder became detached. It was seen to dive and pull out in a shallow turn, which terminated in a flat spin and struck the ground. The aircraft broke into three with the wings catching fire. The three crew killed were, Flt Lt Stanislaw F. Reiss, (pilot) Polish Forces, Sgt James Fielding (Flt Eng) and Mr Joseph J. Unwin MBE (Flt Test Obs). The pilot had already survived two crashes the previous year.

25) The other accident occurred in the circuit when a No.617 Sqn. Lancaster III JA894 collided with Oxford II EB 981 of No.7 FIS Upavon at 1000 hrs on 10th September 1943. The Lancaster had a crew of Flt Lt Frank James Robinson (pilot), Flt Sgt Joseph William Bamber (Flt. Eng), of 'B' Flight Performance Test Sqn and 17 year old Mr R. Stevenson a Ministry of Aircraft Production Laboratory Assistant. The Oxford crew was Flt Lt David de Bower Banham (Instructor) and Sgt Howard John Burkhard (pupil) of No.7 FIS with RN Cadet John Naunton Bates of Pangbourne School. The Lancaster was carrying out Position Error Trials at a loading of 55,000lb. It had completed its third PE run over Boscombe airfield at 50ft and 160 mph and had started to turn for the fourth PE run when it collided with the Oxford at 150' just short of High Post Airfield, where the Oxford was about to land. The starboard wing and

engine of the Oxford struck the Lancaster starboard outer engine and wing. The Oxford then spun round, striking its fuselage on the Lancaster wing, which broke off. The Lancaster caught fire before hitting the ground a mile east of High Post. There were no survivors from the crash and as a result of the accident on the over-lapping circuits, training at High Post was discontinued not long afterwards, following the recommendation by Boscombe Down's Station Commander.

26) 1944 was another bad year for fatal accidents with Mosquito B.IX LR495 being the first casualty of the year when it crashed at nearby Larkhill on 29th January killing Sqn Ldr Eric M. Metcalf, and Flt Lt Rowland H.A. Williams escaping with serious injuries. The crew, with the Special Duties Flt, was engaged in carrying out smoke canister tests at the time of the accident.

27) The Establishment suffered three fatal accidents in March 1944. On Tuesday 1st March Firefly I Z1839, flying at 420 mph, had a starboard wing failure and crashed in a field at Bury Hill Camp, Goodworth Clatford near Andover killing Wg Cdr Peter F. Webster DSO, DFC*. This was his first day with the Performance Testing Squadron at Boscombe Down, having completed Test Pilot Training Flt's Course No.1 the previous day. He took off to carry out rapid rolling trials in the Firefly, which had been fitted with modified ailerons.

28) On 24th March 1944, Typhoon IB JR448 crashed one mile south west of Grateley, killing Fg Off Denis Grundy of the Special Duties Flt. The pilot lost control when carrying out practice attacks against a Boston of the SDF.

29) On 26th March 1944, Typhoon IB JR307 broke up when recovering from a dive bombing trial and crashed at Crichel Down bombing range, 3 miles north of Tarrant Rushton airfield. Sqn Ldr Hedley N. Fowler MC was thrown from the cockpit but his parachute failed to fully deploy and he was killed. In September 1943 he had escaped from Colditz.

30) On 4th July 1944, the Test Pilot Training Flt lost Wellington Mk.III X3549 when, carrying out longitudinal stability tests, it crashed at Chilmark

killing Flt Lt Norman J. Bonnar AFC and Flt Lt Laurence R. Brady.

31) On 9th August 1944, Mosquito BXX KB209 of the High Altitude Flt crashed 3 miles west of Blandford in Dorset, killing Flt Lt Hubert J. Camps and Fg Off Thomas G. Thomas. The cause was unknown.

32) On 24th August 1944, Hurricane IIC HW187 and Hurricane IID KX176 collided and crashed at Downton, when returning to Boscombe following gunnery test flights on the firing range. Flying in formation, HW187 suddenly turned to starboard, striking KX176. The pilot of the IID, Fg Off John D. Baker suffered injuries when he forced landed in a field and the aircraft turned over. In the collision the wing tip of the IIC broke away and the aircraft spun into the ground killing Sqn Ldr John F. Pettigrew, OC Gun Proofing Flt.

33) On 19th January 1945, just after taking off from Boscombe Down, Mustang IV attached to the Performance Testing Sqn, was seen to lose a wing after an ammunition panel detached and the Mustang crashed close to Old Sarum airfield. The pilot Gp Capt John F. X. 'Sam' McKenna AFC, RAF, Commandant of the Empire Test Pilots' School was killed. His widow was later to present a cup to the School in his memory. Known as the McKenna Trophy, this is awarded at the conclusion of each course to the top Fixed Wing student.

34) Air Commodore David J. Waghorn AFC, CBE was killed in a No.106 Group Spitfire XIX PS831, when it crashed at Boscombe Down on 1st April 1945. The Air Commodore had joined the Group on promotion.

35) Prototype Mosquito PR32 NS586 arrived at Boscombe on 13th September 1944 for performance testing. It was fitted with experimental Merlin engines, had extended wings and was of a lighter structure. It had four-bladed de Havilland hydromatic propellers and on 12th April 1945 was carrying out diving tests from 35,000' to monitor possible over-speeding. During a dive one of its wings came off and it crashed close to the airfield at Weston Zoyland in Somerset, killing Flt Lt John R. Smith and Mr Gordon Douglas (FTO).

36) The Test Pilot's School lost Oxford T.I NM247 on 19th July 1945 when it crashed at Rowlands Farm, Haven Street, Isle of Wight killing Major Everett W. Leach, USAAF. The pilot had been carrying out steep gliding turns prior to the crash. It was determined that parts of the aircraft separated and fire had developed in the port auxiliary fuel tank bay, prior to impact.

37) On 25th July 1945, Tempest F.V NV946 crashed on Enford Ranges. It stalled when climbing out of a dive having fired its rockets. The pilot Sqn Ldr Lynn Gregory was killed.

38) On Friday 31st August 1945, Miles Monitor TT.II NP409 crashed into the sea half a mile west of Yarmouth, Isle of Wight killing Sub Lt Kenneth W.A. Fehler RNVR and Sub Lt Leonard R.J. Habgood RNVR of HMS Daedalus. The Monitor was an aircraft designed as a high-speed target tug.

39) Auster AOP 5 NJ630 and crew were lost on Christmas Day 1945 when the small aircraft hit buildings while low flying and crashed inverted at RAF Kingston Bagpuize near Oxford. This A&AEE aircraft had forced landed at RAF Kingston Bagpuize during bad weather. Whilst left unattended, the Auster was taken without authority by a pilot based at the station, Sgt G.F. Wykes and accompanied by LAC D. A. Garvin. The aircraft was flown around the station recklessly and at low-level. During a dive the port wing struck a Nissen hut and the Auster dived into the ground and burst into flames. Both occupants were killed.

40) On 2nd July 1946, Meteor F.III EE312 crashed on Porton Range during a spinning trial killing pilot Sqn Ldr Antoni R. Majcherczyk DFC, Polish Air Force.

41) On 19th July 1946, one of Boscombe's naval pilots, Lt Cdr R.B. Pearson, was tragically killed when having landed at Calshot in Sea Otter ASR.II RD869, in error he exited through the cockpit window and his head was struck by the propeller.

42) Flt Lt Thomas W.G. Morren (pilot) and Flt Lt Ian J. Hartley DFC (nav) were both killed on 19th July 1947 when Brigand TF.I RH752 crashed in Lyme Bay during firing trials.

43) On 28th May 1948, during a climb the tail assembly came off Miles Marathon (P) G-AGPD and it crashed at Quarley, between Amesbury and Andover killing Mr Brian Bastable and Miss Beryl R. Edmunds. Brian Bastable was a civilian test pilot for CATS who had served in the RAF and had been awarded the DFC when as a Fg Off and captain of a Catalina, he attacked and sunk U-boat U241 on 18th May 1944. Miss Edmunds, who was 20 years of age, was the first female FTO to lose her life at Boscombe Down.

44) On 22nd June 1948, Attacker (P) TS413 crashed near Bulford village killing naval pilot Lt Cdr T.J.A. King-Joyce. The cause of the accident could not be determined but the long-range tank, which had just been fitted by Supermarine, had been jettisoned immediately before the crash, and a spanner was found in the wreckage. Possibly the spanner had jammed the controls.

45) On 2nd July 1948, Lincoln BII RF560 crashed 1½ miles north of Wylye with the loss of Sqn Ldr Albert Tooth DFC (pilot), Flt Lt Arthur G. Bradfield (Air Signaller), Flt Lt Glyndwr W. Williams (Flt Eng) and Mr P.W. Howes (Flt Test Observer). The aircraft was being used to test the handling characteristics of low speed flight with the No.1 engine feathered and the No.2 engine throttled back but with its propeller windmilling. The pilot lost control of the Lincoln at 3500' and flying at insufficient height to recover. It spun into the hillside. Whilst the test pilot was well qualified, he had little experience of the handling characteristics of four-engined aircraft in unusual configurations and the tests should have been carried out by a pilot who was familiar with these.

46) On 5th March 1949, Meteor F.4 RA382 crashed at Figsbury Ring, four miles NE of Salisbury killing Gp Capt Thomas B. Cooper OBE, DFC, Superintendent of Flying. The aircraft dived into the ground out of cloud, probably due to instrument failure, whilst on a test flight.

47) On 26th September 1949, Hastings C.1 TG499 crashed 1 mile east of Boscombe Down at Beacon Hill with the loss of Sqn Ldr Philip G. Evans DFC, Flt Lt Ian P. Bishop DFC and Fg Off Raymond Hodge. An underslung

large detachable container for dropping parachutists as a group, known as a 'Paratechnicon', broke away and wrecked the tailplane.

48) On 8th June 1951, Wyvern TF.2 VW869 was seen to break up during a shallow dive and crash at Seven Barrows, 1 mile west of Amesbury during an air test, killing Lt Cdr D.K. Hanson RN. The investigation determined that the cockpit canopy detached involuntarily and struck the fin causing it to break up. This started a chain of events leading to the crash.

49) On 5th February 1952, Attacker F.1 WA485, carrying out trials to test a new flat sided elevator, crashed near Leckford when operating from Chilbolton airfield. The pilot, Lt Cdr Malcombe R. Orr-Ewing RN, was killed (See South Marston for further detail).

50) On 12th June 1952, Harvard T.2B FX371 stalled and spun in on Figheldean Drop Zone, 2 miles north of Amesbury killing Flt Lt Ivor K. Johnson and, a photographer, Mr R. J. Whatley.

51) On 2nd July 1952, Brigand B.1 RH753 crashed at Bemerton Heath, Salisbury killing Flt Lt Gordon Wood-Smith DFC and photographer Mr D. Purse of the Ministry of Supply. The aircraft had the port engine cut on take-off and losing height it struck trees before crashing into some houses. There were injuries to 9 civilians and a fireman attending the incident.

52) On 25th November 1952, Venom FB.1 WE258, lost its starboard wing following a collision with Valetta C.1 VW203. The Venom crashed 2 miles west of Boscombe Down killing Sqn Ldr Christopher G. Clark DFC. The Valetta rapidly lost height, fell to the ground at the end of the runway and broke up but without loss of life to Sgt J. J. Campbell, his crew and 9 Army passengers.

53) On 27th June 1953, Sea Hawk F.1 WF149 crashed at the rear of the Officers' Mess when its port wing folded after take-off. The pilot Sqn Ldr David W. Colquhoun was killed. On the ground ACW1 Beryl Lodge was slightly injured.

54) On 10th November 1953, Swift 1(P)2 WJ965 crashed on Breamore Down, 3 miles NNW of Fordingbridge, killing Sqn Ldr Noel E.D.'Ned' Lewis. The Swift had an engine cut during stalling tests and spun into the ground.

55) Hastings C.2 WD484 took off from Boscombe on 2nd March 1955 to carry out Radar trials over the ranges at Larkhill. It took off with the elevator control locks engaged and at 200ft, in an almost vertical plane, it rolled over and crashed onto the airfield. Flt Lts E.H. Edmunds (nav) and F.W.W. Seaman (Signaller) were killed. Flt Lt K.J. Chase (pilot) and Flt Lt A.J. Mills (Flt Eng) were seriously injured but the two FTOs, Mr J.W.B. Wright and Mr L.H. Philpotts escaped without injury.

56) On 6th July 1955, Supermarine 525 VX138 crashed at Idmiston, south of Boscombe, during slow speed handling trials. Following a spin and stall the pilot was unable to release the canopy and eject. Ejection was achieved at 200', too low to allow the parachute to fully deploy. The pilot, Lt Cdr T.A. Rickell RN, struck the ground with force and died later from his injuries.

57) On 27th November 1955, Canberra B(1)8 (P) WT326 crashed east of Harnham Bridge, Salisbury killing Sqn Ldr Frank C. Cook DFC* and Flt Lt Philip Hyden. Carrying out a handling exercise, it stalled when flying with its undercarriage down and spun into the ground.

58) On 30th April 1956, Whirlwind HAR.3 XJ395 crashed 2 miles NE of Lyndhurst railway station, after a rotor failure at 9000', killing (FTOs) Mr Michael Booth, Mr John W. Lowman and Miss Gwenda M. Warman. The pilot, Flt Lt M.H. Beeching, gave the order to bale out. He and two others did so but only he survived with his parachute opening when close to the ground. The body of the other FTO was found in the wreckage.

59) On 7th May 1956, Canberra B8 WT328 flew into the sea 2½ miles south of Shoreham on 7th May 1956, when carrying out low-altitude altimeter trials 50'above sea level. Sqn Ldr Michael R. Alston and Flt Lt Victor D. Hall were killed in the crash.

60) On 26th February 1958, Javelin FAW.7 XH714 crashed in the New Forest at Sandford near Ringwood, killing the pilot, Flt Lt Richard S. May and the navigator, Fg Off John V. Coates (No.23 Sqn). The aircraft was being test flown after major servicing, when the pilot was ejected because the seat was not properly secured. The pilot remained in the seat, connected by a lap strap and his personal equipment connector. The parachute was unable to deploy and the pilot was killed hitting the ground. The navigator ejected but his parachute equipment snagged on the aircraft and did not fully deploy before he hit the ground and was killed.

61) On 5th June 1958, Saro SR.53 (P) XD151 crashed at Idmiston, killing Sqn Ldr John S. Booth DFC. The pilot taking off from Boscombe tried to abort by cutting the engine but the aircraft then over-ran the runway, striking the post of a runway approach light. The aircraft broke up and caught fire and the pilot was killed when attached to his ejector seat, it was thrown clear of the aircraft.

62) On 15th October 1958, Gnat F.1 XK767 on a test flight, dived into the ground at Stapleford, 4 miles north of Wilton. The aircraft appeared to be in difficulties during a steep climb shortly after take off. Sqn Ldr Ernest J. Roberts AFC* successfully ejected but the automatic seat separation failed and he was killed when, still strapped to the seat, it hit the ground.

63) A 'B' Sqn Victor B.2 (P) XH668, the first proto type Mk.2 crashed at St. Brides Bay off Milford Haven, Pembrokeshire at 0935 hrs. on Wednesday 20th August 1959 with the loss of all 5 crew members, Sqn Ldr Raymond J. Morgan, Sqn Ldr Gerald B. Stockman (pilots), Flt Lt Lewis N. Williams (nav), Flt Lt Ronald J. Hannaford (AEO), and Mr R. Williams of Handley Page Ltd. The aircraft was on a high-speed manoeuvrability trials flight. The analysis of the accident was only achieved after a 14 month sea search which ended on 19th March 1960, during which time 46 ships had been involved, 11,069 deep sea trawls made and 592,610 pieces of wreckage recovered amounting to 70% of the aircraft. The co-pilot's wristwatch was one of the items recovered. Expert opinion was that the watch had been stopped at 11.30 hrs. 46secs. by a single violent blow, which was most likely the Victor hitting the sea. The

damaged aircraft parts dredged from the sea and re-assembled determined a fatigue fracture induced the loss of the starboard wing tip pressure head, which led to loss of control. The aircraft progressed into a high-speed dive from 54,000 ft, did not recover and crashed into the sea at .855 mach.

64) On 12th October 1959, a Naval Test Squadron Buccaneer (P) 5 XK490 flown by Test Pilot William Lewis Alford USN on detachment from NASA and his English observer John Joyce, a FTO of Blackburns, crashed near Lyndhurst in the New Forest while carrying out single engine stalls. The aircraft was fitted with a NASA invention called Boundary Layer Control (BLC) which had the effect of lowering the stalling speed by 15 knots in the landing and take-off configuration which its high wing loading made essential if it was to be safely operated from an aircraft-carrier. (BLC) failed to maintain its pressure due to a malfunction of a non-return valve in the 'blow' circuit when on one engine only. This led to a stall at 10,000', too low to make a recovery, and from an inverted position, to successfully eject, resulting in the deaths of both men.

65) Flt Lt J.S. Duncan AFC took off from Boscombe on 11th November 1960 in Meteor T.7 WF766 and 17 minutes later the aircraft disintegrated. The wreckage struck the ground 3 miles NW of Lyme Regis and the pilot was killed.

66) On 31st August 1961, Buccaneer S.1 XK529 crashed into Lyme Bay killing Lt Cdr O. Brown RN and Mr T.D. Dunn (FTO). Trials of hands off launchings were being carried out from HMS *Hermes*. The aircraft pitched up and stalled after a catapult launch and fell into the sea ahead of the ship. The canopy was jettisoned but the crew did not escape before the aircraft sank.

67) An accident involving Buccaneer S.1 XN922 on 5th July 1962, seriously injured Lt W.A. Newton RN (pilot) and killed Lt G.W.N. Jones RN (obs). When taking-off the aircraft crashed into 'D' Sqn hangar offices on the south side of the runway killing Mr P.G. Wright 'D' Sqn Engineer Officer and seriously injuring Mr C. Froggatt 'D' Sqn Foreman.

68) On 11th May 1964, Avro Vulcan B.2. XH535 of 'B' Sqn, crewed by Mr

O. J. Hawkins (Avro Test Pilot), Flt Lt Robert L. Beeson AFC (pilot), Flt Lt Jack Dingley (nav), Fg Off Peter Chilton (AEO), Master Signaller Laurence Christian AFM (Signaller) and Flt Lt Frank A. Young (Eng), was on trials involving initial firing of rapid blooming window and other aircraft checks, when loss of control was experienced at 19K ft during a low speed/high rate descent. The aircraft spun with the pilots being unable to regain control. They both ejected at around 2K ft but the rear crew members remained in the aircraft. It impacted at Chute Causeway near Ludgershall, 9 miles NE of Boscombe Down, The two pilots suffered major injuries and the other 4 crewmen were killed.

69) On 14th May 1968, Hawker Hunter T.7A XL611 dived into the ground when on GCA approach training. It crashed at Milton Farm, East Knoyle killing Flt Lt Robert L. Beeson AFC (pilot) and Sqn Ldr Michael John Profit Hallahan Mercer, an Engineering Officer of the Armament Division. Although a spanner was found in the wreckage, it was not thought to have contributed to the crash and no real cause was established for the accident.

70) On 1st October 1968, Capt. Jean G. Depui, a French Air Force ETPS student, was killed when he ejected too late from Canberra B.2 WH715, and struck the ground still attached to the seat. The aircraft dived into the ground out of cloud, at Crewkerne in Somerset, after the pilot lost control during an asymmetric assessment exercise.

From the period after World War 2 when A&AEE became permanent at Boscombe Down until the end of the 1960's, the Establishment lost 45 aircraft and 42 aircrew. Most of the aircraft came to grief on the airfield of within the county generally. A smaller number were lost further a field.

71) On 1st May 1970, Canberra TT.18 WJ632 crashed into Lyme Bay at 5041N 0242W. All 3 crew ejected but Major James R. Weaver USAF (pilot) and Flt Lt George W.E. Foster AFM (obs) died. Flt Lt J. Nichol (nav) was injured but rescued by RN helicopter. The Canberra was on target towing trials at the time and the cause of its failure is unknown.

72) Although the incident did not involve an aircraft crash, on 17th December 1970 Sgt Leslie D. Hicks of the Parachute Test Team was killed in a fall from Argosy C.1 XN817, when his chute malfunctioned over Fox Covert on Salisbury Plain, 3 miles north west of Shrewton.

73) On 22nd November 1974, a Jaguar 2 of 'A' Sqn crashed between Wimborne St. Giles and Gussage St. Michael near Blandford Forum in Dorset with Wg Cdr Clive C. Rustin of ETPS and Flt Lt Colin J. Cruickshanks ejecting to safety. The latter went on to become Director Air Operations of the DERA Boscombe Down in the rank of Air Commodore, retiring from there in 1999.

74) The ETPS had been free of accidents for eight years when, on 22nd January 1976, Hawker Hunter T.7 XL579 crewed by exchange student Lt Cdr W. Honour USN and Cdr D. Kemp USN, on a aircraft type familiarisation flight, crashed between High Post and Winterbourne Dauntsey. Following a total engine failure whilst downwind, the crew ejected successfully at low level but suffered back injuries.

75) On 19th March 1976, Wessex HC.2 XS678 was written off in a heavy landing on the airfield but with no loss of lives.

76) On 27th April 1976 an ETPS Argosy C.1 XR105, engaged on a two-engine out overshoot and approaching runway 06, dropped a wing before striking a building and crashing on the airfield. An Italian Air Force student pilot Capt Giuseppe Puglisi and the ETPS Engineer Flt Lt T. Colgan were killed. Sqn Ldr Mike Vickers the QFI was rescued from the wreckage but suffered a number of fractures. Incredibly this had not been the first aircraft crash from which he had escaped with his life. The author who attended the crash and witnessed the complete devastation of the Argosy, was amazed not only that he had survived but that just a few weeks later, saw the Sqn Ldr at Boscombe Down in uniform, having returned to duty on crutches.

77) On 12th June 1979, a BAe prototype Tornado XX950, based at Boscombe Down, crashed into the sea in mist 44 miles west of Blackpool during loft bombing trials, having

ETPS Argosy XR105 seen here at Lyneham in November 1972. Photo: Adrian Balch

taken off from Warton. Mr Russ Pengelly BAe Chief Test Pilot and Sqn Ldr L. Gray (nav) were killed.

78) On 24th July 1981, ETPS Jaguar T.2 XX916 was lost as a result of a bird strike over the Bristol Channel. It came down in the sea 12 miles off Hartland Point. Sqn Ldr Barnett (pilot) was rescued but Flt Lt Shean Sparks (nav) drowned.

79) On 22nd February 1982, Harvard T.2B KF314 was lost when it crashed 2½ milesNE of Chilmark. Sqn Ldr Thomas E.B. Chambers (pilot) and Flt Lt Raymond C. H. Beyer were both killed when the aircraft dived into the ground during spinning practice.

80) Although not involving a Boscombe based aircraft, on 22nd October 1987, amysterious tragedy occurred when contact was lost with Taylor Scott, a pilot of a BAe Harrier GR.5 XZ325, which was on a test flight over Salisbury Plain from the maker's airfield at Dunsfold. The pilot sent a routine message but shortly after this, contact by Boscombe Down Control was lost. All aircraft flying the area were immediately alerted and eventually a USAF C-5 Galaxy was vectored towards the Harrier which was apparently flying in a normal attitude 140nm west of the southern tip of Ireland. On closer observation the American crew could see that it was minus its canopy and pilot but with ejector seat still in position. They followed the Harrier for a further 260nm until out of fuel, it spiralled down and disappeared beneath the

Atlantic Ocean. The RAF instigated a search for the pilot. His body was eventually discovered by a gamekeeper in a field at Winterbourne Stoke near Boscombe Down on 23rd October. He was attached to a badly damaged parachute and dinghy. The parachute having deployed within the cockpit was damaged. Because of this it failed to arrest his fall and he was killed on impact with the ground. With the ejector seat having been seen in the aircraft, the mystery remains as to how and why he came to be separated from it. There were a number of possibilities, the most probable being that a foreign object lodged under the ejector seat Manual Override sear. This may have caused it to dislodge and fire the cartridge, perhaps when the pilot lowered his seat. An extensive search by the RAF failed to locate the wreck of XZ325.

81) On Thursday 24th August 2000, Harrier T.10 ZH654 came to grief on the runway having returned from exercise. It made a standard landing as opposed to a hovering manoeuvre but the nose was seen to pitch downwards when it was about 50' off the ground. The pilot and navigator both ejected safely but were admitted to hospital with injuries that were not serious. The £20 million aircraft smashed into the ground, caught fire and was a write-off.

Memorials

(1) 184/SU172404 - North side of former Control Tower.

Standing on open ground, a rough

quarry-cut stone memorial with plaque and beneath cut into the stone, a Hurricane I. The plaque at the head of the memorial stone has the inscription:

IN MEMORY OF
JAMES NICOLSON VC
1917 - 1945
On the 16th of August 1940 Flight Lieutenant James B. Nicolson was leading Red Section of No. 249 Squadron from RAF Boscombe Down. An Attack by enemy aircraft whilst over Southampton left Nicolson wounded and his Hurricane on fire. When about to bail out he sighted and shot down one of the attacking aircraft, only then did heabandon his own aircraft. For this deed of gallantry Nicolson was awarded the Victoria Cross, the only member of Fighter Command to be so honoured during the war.

James Brindley Eric Nicolson was born in Hampstead, London on 29th April 1917. On leaving Tonbridge School in 1934 he joined the firm of Ricardo Engines at Shoreham-on-Sea as an experimental engineer. Having harboured an interest in aviation he decided two years later to volunteer for the Royal Air Force and as a result was granted a four year Short Service Commission with the rank of Acting Pilot Officer in the General Duties Branch commencing 12th October 1936. He was trained at the de Havilland School of Flying at White Waltham where he obtained his flying certificate on 16th November 1936. From his time of joining the RAF he was known by his colleagues as 'Nick'. After gaining his certificate he was posted to No.10 FTS Ternhill, as from

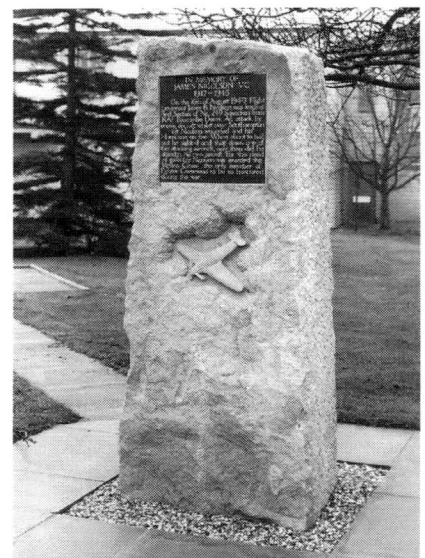

The memorial was unveiled by Wg Cdr T.F. Neil DFC, AFC, AE, RAF on 16th August 1990 to coincide with the 50th Anniversary of Flt Lt Nicolson's action for which he was awarded the Victory Cross.

16th January 1937, where he flew Hawker Hart and Audax biplanes. In July he received specialised gunnery training at No.3 Armament Training Camp at Sutton Bridge in Lincolnshire. His first operational posting was with No.72 (Fighter) Sqn at Church Fenton in North Yorkshire on 7th August. This was a Fighter Command squadron in No.11 Group equipped with Gloster Gladiators. 'Nick' was confirmed in the substantive rank of Plt Off on 12th October. Over the next two years he developed into a very capable pilot and marksman. In April 1939 the squadron re-equipped with the new Spitfire Mk.I Taking advantage of the lull before the storm, 'Nick' married his fiancee Muriel Kendal in July.

No.249 Sqn was re-formed at Church Fenton on 16th May 1940 equipped with Spitfire Is which in June they lost to the depleted squadrons in the south of the country. These were replaced with Hurricane Is. 'Nick' was transferred to this squadron on 15th May and on 1st June was appointed Flight Commander with the rank of Acting Flt Lt.

On 14th August No.249 Sqn. was transferred to Boscombe Down as support for the hard-pressed squadrons of the South. Two days later at 1305 hours, 'A' Flight commanded by Flt Lt R. A. 'Butch' Barton was scrambled to patrol the Poole - Southampton area at 18,000 feet. Red Section was led by Flt Lt Nicolson as Red One, in GN-A (P3576), Plt Off Martyn A. King was Red Two, in GN-F (P.3616) and Sqn Ldr Eric 'Whizzy' King, Red Three, in (P.3870). 'Nick' was the first to spot a formation of three Ju. 88s and his section were detailed to engage. On approach he noticed twelve Spitfires already in pursuit so he broke away and climbed to rejoin 'A' Flight. During this manoeuvre his Section were bounced by Messerschmitts Bf.110s and 'Nick' was injured in the face and foot by cannon shell and his petrol tank was struck and set on fire. About to abandon his aircraft he noticed a Bf.110 diving and converging with him so he decided to remain and give chase. The enemy aircraft flew hard in trying to shake him off but diving at around 400 mph 'Nick' drew within range, raking it with gunfire. The cockpit of the Hurricane was now a mass of flames and 'Nick' could see the skin peeling from his throttle hand. Confident that he had dealt sufficiently with the Bf.110 he set

about saving himself. He slid back the canopy, at the second attempt removed his harness straps, pushed himself out of the aircraft and took to his parachute. He then noticed an enemy aircraft approaching him so he played dead, expecting at any moment to be shot at. This did not happen although the plane made a second pass. During his descent he became aware of the burns to his hands, the blood seeping from his shoe, he had lost an eye-lid and his uniform was in shreds. His oxygen mask still covered his face but he was unable to remove it because of the state of his hands. As he dropped lower he could see he was heading for the sea and knowing he would not be able to swim in his condition he managed to direct himself over land and was fortunate in clearing a high tension cable. His troubles were not yet over as he was then to be shot in the buttocks by an over enthusiastic member of the LDV. 'Nick' landed in a field at Millbrook near Southampton, from where he was transported to the Royal Southampton Hospital. In the mean time Red Two had been shot down with Plt Off King losing his life when his parachute collapsed and he plunged to the ground. Sqn Ldr King managed to return to base with his severely damaged aircraft.

'Nick's' Hurricane came down in an open field at Lee near Romsey, between the Salisbury - Southampton railway line and the A3057 road. The Messerschmitt he attacked was seen to dive into the sea.

Acting Flt Lt Nicolson was experiencing combat for the first time on this day and as it transpired, he was Fighter Command's first and only recipient during World War 2 of this nation's highest military decoration, the Victoria Cross which was Gazetted on 15th November 1940. As of 3rd September he had been confirmed as a substantive Flt Lt.

His strength and resolve enabled him to survive his injuries but he spent many months receiving treatment. He was transferred to the hospital at RAF Halton and later to the Palace Hotel in Torquay which was in use as a RAF hospital. Whilst at home on sick leave he attended with his family, the Investiture of his medal by King George VI at Buckingham Palace on 25th November 1940.

'Nick' was discharged by the medical board as fit for non-operational duties in February 1941. He was posted to No.54 OTU Church Fenton on 24th February as Chief Ground Instructor (Operational Training). As of the 13th March, he held the rank of Acting Sqn Ldr. He was pleased to be involved again although desperate to be flying against the enemy, a role for which he had trained so long. It was the disablement of his hand which was preventing this but repeated pleas to his senior officers eventually brought him a transfer on 22nd September, to Hibaldstowe where a revolutionary system known as Turbinlite was being researched to combat night time raids by German bombers. Basically this involved a large searchlight being fitted to a suitable aircraft which would fly alongside the incoming bombers and illuminate them, so enabling the accompanying British fighters to direct an attack. While at Hibaldstowe 'Nick' became an Acting Wg Cdr serving as the CO of the operational No.1459 Flt, the duties still being of an administrative nature. The Turbinite experiment however proved ineffectual and so the Flights involved were disbanded in January 1942.

His next posting was as Administrative Officer at the Headquarters of No. 293 Wing at Alipore, India on 15th May 1942. With the departure of Wg Cdr Harry Daish the CO of No.27 Sqn, 'Nick' took over from him at Agartala, East Bengal on 4th August 1943. He soon made himself familiar with the squadron's Beaufighter aircraft which was in use against Japanese targets. He had taken over a well organised and efficient squadron and these standards were maintained and built upon. Wg Cdr Nicolson was liked and respected by his personnel. He led by example and was in his element when leading his crews on operations. He flew hard and he played hard the latter being a trait that had endeared him to his colleagues throughout his time with the RAF.

In April 1943 the squadron had received some Mosquito IIs for evaluation purposes and in December Mk.VIs were taken on charge. As could be expected and following conversion, 'Nick' led the first operation with their new aircraft against Japanese rail and river craft in Southern Burma. No.27 Sqn were moved a short distance to Parashuram on 8th February 1944. The

Mosquito's had to be withdrawn in March when it was found they were not suited to this particular theatre of war. Being of timber construction the glue joints were prone to separation due to the humid climate in Burma. No.27 Sqn reverted to an entirely equipped Beaufighter unit before moving again on 7th March to Cholavarum as part of No.225 Group. Here they were joined by No.47 Sqn and together were deployed in attacking shipping in the Bay of Bengal.

'Nick' was relieved of his No.27 Sqn command on 6th May to take up a posting as Wg Cdr (Training & Tactics) at the 3rd Tactical Air Force Headquarters, Allied Command South East Asia. For his leadership and command of his squadron, he was awarded the DFC Gazetted 11th August 1944. His next move was on 4th December when he was posted to Headquarters, Royal Air Force, Bengal/Burma in a training/supernumerary role.

'Nick' was later the following year, seconded to No.355 Sqn at Salbani with the task amongst others, of developing safe methods of flying in monsoon weather conditions. The squadron was detailed on 1st May 1945 during the monsoon, to attack Rangoon in preparation for the Allied invasion. The Liberator VI KH 210 'R' Robert in which 'Nick' was being flown, took off at 0050hrs on 2nd May. Two hours into the flight the starboard outer engine burst into flames followed shortly after by the starboard inner. The fires could not be extinguished so the bomb load was jettisoned and the aircraft ditched. It sank almost immediately on striking the sea. Two of the crew survived the ditching but 'Nick' was killed on what transpired to be the last day of the War in Europe. Wg Cdr James Brindley Nicolson is commemorated on the Singapore War Memorial at Kranji War Cemetery.

The following are his decorations: -
Victoria Cross
Distinguished Flying Cross
1939-45 Star
Battle of Britain Clasp
Aircrew Europe Star
Burma Star
Defence Medal
War Medal 1939-45

(2) 184/ SU172404 - North side of the former Control Tower.

Positioned next to the 'Nicolson' memorial, a concrete plinth supporting a glass lantern shaped case incorporating inside a shield depicting the A&AEE Coat-of-Arms together with a Harrier and a Bristol Bulldog mounted on a support. The two aircraft are made of bronze-sprayed brass and together with the glass lantern were designed by A.H. (Tony) Richardson in the Mechanical Design Office. A plastic kit was assembled initially to obtain the correct scale for the Bristol Bulldog. Construction was carried out by the Mechanical Workshops at Boscombe Down with the exception of the concrete plinth which was made by an outside contractor. The art work was painted by Alan Woods and refurbished by him in the late 1990s. The plaque on the concrete plinth has the inscription: -

> 1921 - 1971
> TO COMMEMORATE THE VISIT OF
> HER ROYAL HIGHNESS
> THE PRINCESS ANNE
> TO
> A & A.E.E.
> BOSCOMBE DOWN
> 19TH MARCH 1971

3) Empire Test Pilot's School

To perpetuate the memory of Gp Capt J.F.X.'Sam' McKenna, AFC the second Commandant of the ETPS during 1944/45, killed in a flying accident whilst in post, his wife presented the school with a silver cup known as the McKenna Trophy. This is presented to the best all round student at the end of each course. The presentation is made by the current Commandant at the McKenna Dinner, which is held in the Officers' Mess and is given to 'dine out' the Course. One of the traditions at this dinner is for the Commandant to don the "titfer" before making his speech and the presentations. The "titfer" is a battered academic's mortar-board presented to the school for use on such occasions by Air Marshal Sir Ralph Sorley in 1944. He was a distinguished test pilot during the 1920s/30s and a previous Commandant of the A&AEE. The inscription on the McKenna Trophy reads: -

The A&AEE Memorial.

McKenna Trophy
Empire Test Pilots
School 1945
Winners

(List of Course Nos. Ranks, Names & Awards engraved)

Gp Capt J.F.X. McKenna is buried at Durrington Cemetery on the A345 immediately north of Amesbury.

(4) In the church collection of the new Boscombe Down Museum is displayed a brass wall plaque mounted with the RAF Wings and Crown.

IN MEMORY OF
SQUADRON LEADER
K. L. ASHFOLD. R.A.F.
ASSISTANT AIR FORCE EXPERIMENTAL OFFICER   JULY 1938 TO MAY 1940.
O.C. SPECIAL DUTY FLIGHT BOSCOMBE DOWN.   MAY 1940 TO JUNE 1941.
SQUADRON LEADER (FLYING) FIELD EXPERIMENTAL STATION, SUFFIELD, ALBERTA. JUNE 1941 TO SEPTEMBER 1941.
WHO WAS KILLED IN A FLYING ACCIDENT AT MEDICINE HAT, ALBERTA. CANADA.
22ND SEPTEMBER 1941.
AGED 26 YEARS.
"PER ARDUA AD ASTRA."

The brass memorial plaque to Sqn Ldr K.L. Ashford RAF. Photo: Norman Parker

Sqn Ldr Ashford was flying a Canadian Lysander No.471 when it crashed and he was killed. He was buried at Ottawa (Beechwood) Cemetery, Ontario, Canada. The plaque was originally displayed in the former RAF church at Boscombe Down Church until its demolition.

Next to the War Memorial near the bridge over the River Avon on the A363. On the outside face of the former Town Council Offices at Westbury House Annex, a brass plaque with the inscription: -

TO COMMEMORATE THE CREW OF
THE HANDLEY PAGE HALIFAX BOMBER
'V' FOR VICTOR
OF No 425 SQUADRON ROYAL
CANADIAN AIR FORCE
WHO DIED IN THE CRASH AT
BRADFORD ON AVON, WILTSHIRE
ON 26TH MARCH 1944

PILOT OFFICER BRIAN HALL
R.C.A.F. AGED 22
PILOT OFFICER DON GROVER
R.C.A.F. AGED 23
PILOT OFFICER ROY PORTER
R.C.A.F. AGED 21
SERGEANT HARRY NEWTON
R.A.F.V.R. AGED 22
SERGEANT NORMAN SIMPSON
R.A.F.V.R. AGED 20
SERGEANT GRAHAM EVANS
R.A.F.V.R. AGED 21

The Brass Memorial Plaque.

Aviation author Jonathan Falconer, with the help of public subscriptions, brought about the erection of this plaque which was dedicated on the 25th March 1994, fifty years after the crash at Bradford-on-Avon of Halifax Mk.III LW693 of No.425 (Alouette) Sqn in No.6 (RCAF) Group based at Tholthorpe in Yorkshire. The aircraft with, on this occasion a crew of eight, was on a night cross-country exercise. The extra man was Cpl Craig Reid RCAF, a groundcrew radar technician whose reference was to monitor the functions of the aircraft's electronic and radar aids, Gee, H2S and 'Monica.'

The Halifax 'V' Victor had been taken on charge on the 4th March. It had not been used in an operational capacity and its flying time was just 25 hrs 5mins. It took off from Tholthorpe at 1630 hrs piloted by Plt Off Brian Hall who set a course south. Some 4 hrs later, having skirted the English coastline, the aircraft made landfall near Weymouth heading north. It was shortly after this that the aircraft started to shudder violently. At a height of around 10,000 ft and several miles south of Warminster, the pilot lost control of the plane which went into a dive. He gave his crew the order to abandon the aircraft. Sgt Bill Cameron the Mid-Upper Gunner, Sgt Norman Simpson the Flight Engineer and Cpl

Reid baled out. Bill Cameron landed safely in a field near Westbury and Craig Reid at Clivey near Dilton Marsh. Norman Simpson was in the habit of flying with his parachute harness loosely secured to him and on dropping through the rear escape hatch, the slipstream tore his chute from him. Two farmers in a field at Rudge found his body next morning. Bill Cameron was killed a few months later when in July his aircraft was lost on a raid over the Ruhr.

Control of the aircraft was apparently regained but lost again over Bradford-on-Avon where it was seen to be losing height, with engines surging and one on fire, in a tight spiralling, uncontrolled dive. Three more of the crew baled out over the town, Plt Off Don Hernando Grover (nav), Plt Off Roy Porter (B/A) and Sgt Harry Newton (WOP). The aircraft was too low when they baled out and all three were killed. Two were struck by the falling plane. The aircraft came down just before 2100 hours, high above the town in Priory Field close to Christ Church, the only piece of open ground in the area (173/ST825613). Sgt Graham Evans the rear-gunner was pulled from the wreckage but died shortly afterwards and the body of Brian Hall the pilot was removed from the cockpit section. Fire and explosions from the ammunition, fuel tanks and oxygen bottles destroyed the aircraft.

The burial places for the crew members who lost their lives are: -
Haycombe Cemetery, Bath - Brian Hall, Don Grover, Roy Porter,
St Matthew's Church, Stretton, Cheshire - Norman Simpson,

Greenacres Cemetery, Oldham, Lancs. - Harry Newton,
Holy Trinity Church, Ystrad Mynach, Mid Glamorgan - Graham Evans.

The Accident Record Card (RAF Form 1180) states that the pilot lost control between 10,000 and 5000ft and probably let the air speed drop too low, consistent with panicking or dizziness. The pilot was considered to be competent and it is unlikely that below 10,000ft, dizziness would have occurred. The result of the Court of Enquiry held on 29th March 1944 proved inconclusive. It is probable that the cause was due to a combination of circumstances evolving from a technical malfunction leading to an engine fire with the pilot being unable to deal with the results of this.

Friday 25th March 1994 was chosen as the day for the dedication and unveiling of the memorial plaque. A Hercules of No.57 (Reserve) Sqn RAF Lyneham carried out a flypast over the town. The Rev. Bill Matthews of Holy Trinity Church conducted an act of remembrance and the blessing of the plaque. Sole survivor of the crash, Craig Reid flew from his home in Calgary to attend the ceremony and he performed the unveiling by releasing the ensign of the Royal Canadian Air Force. The Hercules then flew slowly over the town dipping its wings in salute.

Note: The above detail is reproduced by the kind permission of Jonathan Falconer with extracts from his unpublished typescript "Seven Bomber Boys" (1986 revised 1994).

BROMHAM

In the Parish Church of St. Nicholas on the C250, west of the A342. On the north wall a stone plaque, mounted beneath St.George and the Dragon, the inscription: -

IN GRATEFUL MEMORY OF
FLIGHT SERGEANT PILOT
ROY BARTON FENNELL R.A.F.V.R.
WHO WITH HIS CREW DID NOT
RETURN FROM OPERATIONS
OVER ENEMY COUNTRY, MARCH
30TH/31ST 1944, AGED 22 YEARS
"THE NOBLEST GIFT A HERO
LEAVES
HIS RACE, IS TO HAVE BEEN A
HERO."

The stone memorial plaque in St Nicholas Church, Bromham.

Flt Sgt Roy Barton Fennell RAF (VR) No.1318683 served with No.166 Sqn in No.1 Group Bomber Command based at Kirmington in Lincolnshire from November 1943 to March 1944. The Squadron was equipped with the Lancaster Mk.I and III. He was born in Bromham on the 19th March 1922 and joined the Air Force in 1942. He trained as a pilot in Canada under the auspices of the British Commonwealth Air Training Plan. Having gained his wings he returned to England and crewed up before joining No.166 Sqn. He flew his first operation as a familiarisation sortie with another crew on 18th November 1943 to Berlin. His first trip

as Captain with his own crew took place on 26th November and was again to Berlin. Take-off was at 1723hrs and en route over France, Roy's Lancaster DV365, received a head on attack from an enemy aircraft which caused damage to the Lancaster, wounds to the rear gunner and put the mid-upper turret temporarily out of action. Immediately afterwards a further attack took place in which a cannon shell burst in the front cockpit and also damaged the elevators, resulting in the aircraft becoming uncontrollable. Roy Fennell gave the order to jettison the bomb load and for the crew to abandon the plane. Shortly afterwards, he managed to regain control so cancelled the last order but by then Sgt Ron Moodey the bomb aimer had already baled out. Unfortunately his parachute failed to open and he was killed. The aircraft turned for home and was continuously attacked another 10-12 times before finally escaping the attention of the fighters. During this time George Meadows RCAF the rear-gunner, who had received wounds from a bullet which entered his back and exited from his groin, continued firing from his turret. The badly damaged aircraft touched down at Ford at 23.30hrs with a severely wounded rear-gunner and slightly wounded WOP, Navigator and Mid-Upper gunner. For his actions that night Sgt Meadows was awarded the CGM. By the time he had recovered from his injuries, the crew had carried out too many operations for him to catch up so he joined another crew serving with the Pathfinder force and completed his tour. Flt Sgt W.J.C. Keigwin who was ultimately to be the only member of the crew to survive the war replaced Sgt Moodey.

Flt Sgt Roy Fennell and his crew carried out further operations to Berlin (2.1.44), Stettin (5.1.44), Berlin (28.1.44), Berlin (30.1.44), Leipzig (19.2.44), Schweinfurt (24.2.44), Stuttgart (15.3.44), Frankfurt (18.3.44), Frankfurt (22.3.44) and Essen (26.3.44). What was to be their thirteenth and final operation took place on 30th March 1944 when the crew took off at 2200hrs in Lancaster ME624 'X' for a raid on Nuremberg. Roy Fennell's aircraft, which had

flown 83hrs from new, was shot down by a nightfighter over Geissen Airfield in Southern Germany, the 42nd to be lost. Flt Sgt Keigwin was the only survivor and became a prisoner of war. This raid was one of the major disasters of the war for Bomber Command. No.166 Sqn lost 4 of their 20 Lancasters detailed that night together with 30 crew (two aircraft were carrying 2nd pilots on familiarisation trips), and over 90 aircraft were lost in total.

Flt Sgt Roy Barton Fennell RAFVR - Pilot age 22 was buried in Hanover War Cemetery in Germany together with his crew: -

Sgt. William George Sydney Pettis
RAFVR No.1851255 -
Flight Engineer age 20
Flt Sgt James Smyth RAFVR
No.1504638 - Navigator age 29
Flt Sgt Albert Patrick Jones
RAFVR No.929021 -
Mid Upper Gunner age 21
Sgt William James Allan RAAF
No.409130 - Rear Gunner age 22.

Flt Sgt Douglas Venning Harvey RAAF No. 420835 - Wireless Operator age 27 was reported missing and his name appears on the Runnymede Memorial to airmen who have no known grave.

Roy Fennell whilst training for his wings in Canada.   Photo: Don Fennell

(2) 173/ST958658 - 4 miles East of Melksham

Westbrook House on the A3102 was the home until his death in 1973 of Air Chief Marshal Sir Edgar Ludlow-Hewitt GCB, GBE, CMG, DSO, MC, DL, RAF.

In the Garrison Church of St. George at Bulford Camp on the C11, north of the A303. On the north wall, a brass plaque depicting the badge of the Royal Engineers with beneath the inscription: -

TO THE GLORY OF GOD, AND IN MEMORY OF
WALTER JOHN VEZEY, LIEUTENANT, R.E.
WHO WAS KILLED ON DUTY IN A FLYING ACCIDENT
AT ARAWALI, N.W.F.P., INDIA, ON APRIL 4TH 1926,
AGED 25 YEARS.

ERECTED BY THOSE OF HIS BROTHER OFFICERS WHO WERE
STATIONED WITH HIM IN THIS GARRISON 1922 -1924.

The brass memorial plaque in the Garrison Church at Bulford Camp.

In the Council Chamber of Calne Town Council Offices, The Strand, on the A4 and in the centre of town: -

(1) A wooden presentation shield depicts the unit badge of No.3 Radio School, Compton Bassett with its motto ' Ex Terrenis Ad Aetheria'. The brass plate beneath the badge is inscribed: -

> PRESENTED TO
> THE BOROUGH OF CALNE
> FROM ROYAL AIR FORCE
> COMPTON BASSETT
> 27TH NOVEMBER 1954

(2) A wooden presentation shield depicts the badge of the Royal Air Forces Association.

(3) A wooden presentation shield depicts the badge of RAF Lyneham with its motto 'Save, Support, Supply'.

(4) A wooden presentation plaque depicts the badge of the Boy Entrants Association, Royal Air Force with its motto 'We Trained To Serve'. A silver plate below the badge is inscribed: -

> Presented By Members Of
> 2nd Entry Boy Entrants,
> On 18-10-97 At The
> 50th Anniversary Re-Union
> To Commemorate Their Arrival At
> R.A.F. Compton Bassett
> In October 1947

(5) A gavel and block presented to the Mayor of Calne on 3rd May 1960 by RAF Compton Bassett. The block is of old English oak, encased in mahogany. It was constructed at the Station by Cpl R. Ormion and LAC D. Oliver in co-operation with Wg Cdr J.E.S. Salter (O/I/C Administration) and Sqn Ldr N.W.G. Collins (Civil Liaison Officer). A contingent from RAF Compton Bassett marched past Calne Town Hall following the presentation.The gavel and block is in regular use at meetings of the Council.

A silver plate on the block is inscribed:

> A TIME TO KEEP SILENT AND A TIME TO SPEAK
>
> Presented to the Mayor and Aldermen
> and Burgesses of CALNE in
> the County of Wiltshire.
>
> By the Commanding Officer, Officers,
> Non Commissioned Officers, Airmen and
> Airwomen of Royal Air Force Station
> COMPTON BASSETT.
>
> As a tangible symbol of mutual esteem
> and respect and in witness of the close
> bonds of friendship which unite us.
>
> This Third Day of May in the Year
> of Our Lord 1960.
>
> Group Captain   Councillor
> G.F. GORDEN   C.R. SYMS
> Commanding Officer   Mayor

Gavel and block.

CASTLE COMBE RLG

Location (173/ST848772 5 miles North West of Chippenham)

Close to the picture postcard National Trust Village of Castle Combe on the B4039. The former airfield is now used as a motor racing circuit.

Airfield Development

The site was originally established as a satellite landing ground (SLG) for No.9 Flying Training School (No.9 FTS), Hullavington.

During 1940 work commenced on up-grading Castle Combe to that of a Relief Landing Ground (RLG).

Water-logging at Castle Combe had been a real problem over the winter of 1942/43 but during 1942 work began to develop the airfield and its necessary facilities. On completion the site was fully useable again. The airfield had two Sommerfeld Track runways NE/SW 1,085yds x 50yds and NW/SE 930yds x 50yds. A 50ft wide concrete perimeter track circled the field. Five hangars were positioned on the east and southeast side of the field, 2 Over Blister, 2 Extra Over Blister and a T1 type. On the western edge were 3 Over Blister hangars. The Technical Site was on the north west side behind the control tower. The two-letter station identification code was CJ. The off-airfield sites were all to the northwest, Technical and Instructional Site (Site No.2), Communal (Site No.3), WAAF (Site No.4), Officers, Sergeants and Airmen's Quarters (Site Nos. 5-8), Sick Quarters (Site No.9) and the Sewage Disposal Works (Site No.10). In the village, the RAF used the Manor House as a hospital from 1941-45. Its tenant Mrs Mills continued to live there during the military occupancy.

Castle Combe Manor during its use as an RAF Hospital.   Photo: Adrian Bishop

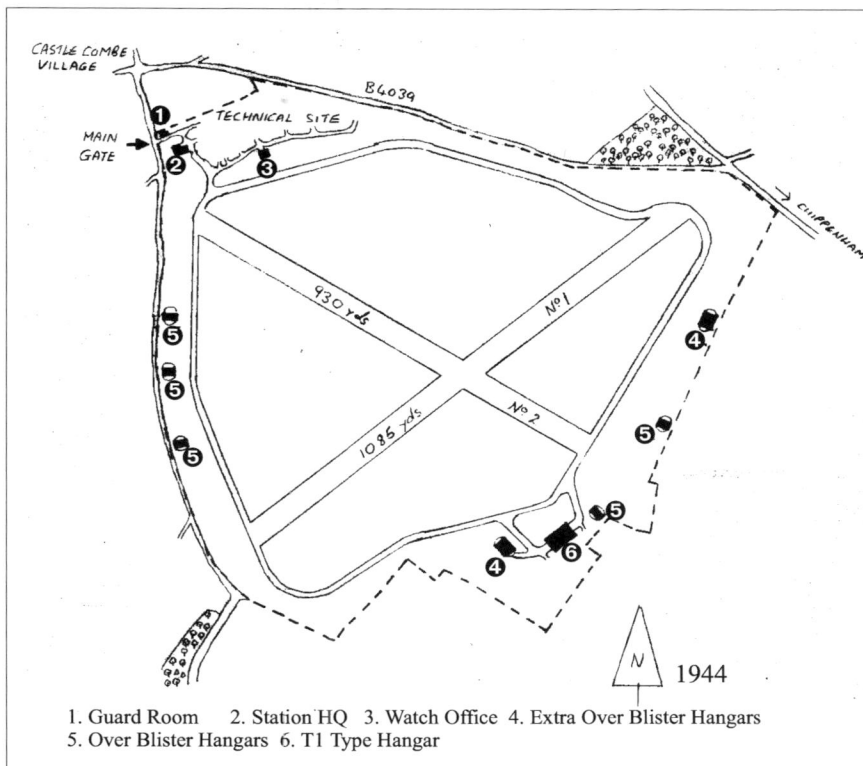

1. Guard Room   2. Station HQ   3. Watch Office 4. Extra Over Blister Hangars
5. Over Blister Hangars 6. T1 Type Hangar

Inter War Years

No.9 FTS operated there before the war with Hart, Audax, Oxford, Fury and Battle type aircraft.

World War 2 Years

Castle Combe was a No.23 Group station with HQ at South Cerney. Babdown Farm was its Parent Station. With the outbreak of war No.9 FTS was redesignated No.9 Service Flying Training School (No.9 SFTS) and it re-equipped with Harvards and Ansons, although some of the latter already formed part of the establishment. From July 1940, No.9 SFTS had ceased twin-engine training and from September was equipped with Masters and Harts.

On completion of the RLG up-grading, the SFTS started using Castle Combe from May 1941, for day and night time circuit training with Masters and Hurricanes. Master I T8483 crashed there on a night time approach on 9th June, N7774 crashed on landing four days later, T8838 crashed on approach the next day and T8676 crashed on take off on 24th June.

It appears however that the landing ground was used in the interim, as Hart (T) K5846 crashed on approach on 8th February 1941. Another crash there on 16th April 1941, involved Stirling I N6002 of No.10 MU Hullavington.

In addition to using Shrewton, No.1 SFTS Netheravon also used Castle Combe for night flying from 23rd May 1941.

No.9 SFTS Hullavington was redesignated No.9 (Pilot) Advanced Flying Unit (No.9 (P)AFU) as from 14th February 1942, and in addition to training RAF pilots it trained Torpedo Spotter Reconnaissance (TSR) pilots for the Navy. The unit was equipped with the Master, Hurricane, Albacore and Swordfish. It utilised Castle Combe as a RLG for the short period up until 1st August before moving to Errol.

No.3 Flying Instructors School (Advanced) No.3 FIS(A), formed at Hullavington from this date, using temporary accommodation and pending a move to Castle Combe on 8th August. Flying training commenced using Master IIIs and Oxford IIs. The

Castle Combe airfield from the south side on 15th April 1943.

Chief Flying Instructor was Wg Cdr R. J. Gosnell DFC. One of the Masters was involved in a fatality on Thursday 27th August when it crashed killing the instructor Flt Lt Maurice H. Holder and his pupil Plt Off Belc (Polish). Flt Lt Holder was buried at Tetbury (St. Saviour) Churchyard, Gloucestershire.

Two German aircraft landed at the airfield on 31st October. These were a Ju 88A and Me 110C with British markings flown by No.1426 (Enemy Aircraft) Circus Flt, known as the *RAFWAFFE*. This was a specialist RAF unit that operated captured enemy aircraft during the war. Tours were made to different areas of the country to provide flying and ground familiarisation training for aircrew, aerodrome defence personnel and ground staff. The enemy aircraft were also used for fighter affiliation trials and aircraft recognition training.

On the days when water-logging prevented training at Castle Combe, as in the winter months of 1942/43, flying training would continue using Hullavington, Babdown Farm, Colerne or Charmy Down. No aircraft maintenance was carried out at Castle Combe, it was always done at Hullavington.

No.1532 Beam Approach Training Flt, which was affiliated to No.3 (P)AFU, was at Babdown Farm to provide training on a newly installed Beam Approach in June 1943, and at the same time had a detachment at Castle Combe.

Oxford[2] X6858 of No.3 FIS(A) crashed one mile south of Wickwar in Gloucestershire on 1st July 1943 in which Flt Lt Kenneth Munro DFC*, RAAF and Flt Lt William W. Colledge DFC, RCAF were killed. The Canadian was awarded his DFC as a result of his actions in 1942 when he and his crew ditched in the North Sea in a No.10 OTU Whitley which had taken off from Abingdon. Both men from the Oxford crash were buried at Haycombe Cemetery, Bath. No.3 FIS (A) moved to Lulsgate Bottom on 1st October 1943. A Flt of No.15 (P) AFU was the next unit to arrive on 4th November. It moved in from Ramsbury equipped with twin-engined Oxfords. Another Flt arrived from Long Newnton in January 1944 where the weather conditions had made the airfield a quagmire. The qualified pilots were under instruction for multi-engine aircraft. Pupils with the AFU had their training interrupted on 14th March at 0040hrs when a No.75 Sqn Stirling III EF236 AA-J forced landed on the short NW/SE runway. It had taken off at 2300 hrs from Mepal, a No.3 Group station in Cambridgeshire. It was on a *Gardening* operation to lay mines off the coast of Brest. However on route, the pilot, Plt Off C. Baker RNZAF, experienced the breakage of an aileron control rod necessitating the emergency landing at Castle Combe. The aircraft ran out of runway at the NW end and came to rest with its undercarriage broken. All but the tail-wheel was outside of the airfield boundary. The Stirling was carrying five magnetic sea mines, two of which exploded causing considerable damage to housing and to the RAF buildings on the nearby No.2 Instructional Site. Despite this there were no injuries to the seven man Stirling crew or to Castle Combe personnel. Temporary accommodation was necessary before training could be resumed three days later.

The Castle Combe runways continued to suffer from wet weather and on occasions between March and June 1944, Bath Racecourse was used to maintain daytime flying training. No.15 (P) AFU at Babdown Farm continued its role until it was disbanded there on 19th June 1945. Sqn Ldr Ted Cowling who had been an instructor with the AFU at Castle Combe for about a year, flew the last Oxford out of the base. Whilst carrying out his flying duties during that period of time, he heard a new and delightful voice over the R/T. On landing he went direct to Flying Control to find the girl with the voice and eventually he married her.

On 14th August 1944, a No.12 OTU Wellington X HE754 took-off from Chipping Warden at 2209hrs for a *Flashlight* sortie. While flying at 15,000ft in the Bristol area, the port engine failed. Flt Sgt A. C. Lockyer RNZAF (pilot) ordered the five crewmen to bale out as he headed for Castle Combe where he crash-landed at 2325hrs. The aircraft ended up in the overshoot area where it caught fire.

Post War Years/Closure

When the war ended the airfield came under Care & Maintenance and was unoccupied until July 1946 when No.27 Group at Southrop moved in No.2 (Polish) Resettlement Unit. The Unit stayed until June 1948 after which the airfield was not used again and was disposed of on 18th October 1948.

The only significant original structure remaining on the airfield site is the control tower.

60

The original World War 2 Control Tower with additions,
but still in use as a control for the race circuit.

Memorial

173/ST853773 Eastside of the former
Control Tower

A memorial to the personnel who
served at this training airfield. The
obelisk made of locally quarried
Cotswold stone, was provided by the
race track owner Howard Strawford
and was constructed by his staff.
Following a two-minute silence at 1100
hrs on 11th November 1996, wartime
Sqn Ldr Michael Shekleton who served
at the Station and lives locally, together
with Wg Cdr Peter Williams from
nearby RAF Lyneham, unveiled the
memorial. A Hercules from Lyneham
carried out a flypast. The plaque on the
memorial has the inscription: -

The memorial stone at Castle Combe race
circuit.

RAF CASTLE COMBE
1940 - 1946
TO COMMEMORATE
ALL THOSE WHO
TRAINED AND SERVED HERE
UNVEILED BY
MICHAEL SHEKLETON
11th NOVEMBER 1996

184/ST970328 - 11 miles West of Salisbury

In the Parish Church of St. Margaret of Antioch on the C276, south of the B3089.

Close to the main isle leading towards the altar: -

(1) Royal Air Force Ensign and Staff

(2) Wooden plaque with badge of No.11 Maintenance Unit

(3) Kneeler with embroidered badge of No.11 Maintenance Unit

The kneeler embroidered with the badge of No.11 MU.

Until its closure on 31st March 1995 RAF Chilmark was an underground ammunition depot. It was set up in March 1937 as one of the Expansion Scheme Air Ammunition Parks formed when the RAF was rebuilding to combat the threat from Germany. By January 1939 it was fully operational as No.11 Maintenance Unit, under the command of Wg Cdr A.W. Smith and was to provide one of the largest stock grounds in the United Kingdom for high-powered explosives and other military equipment. Chilmark was the supply and engineering maintenance depot which received, inspected, serviced and issued ammunition and POL (packed oil and greases). The site was a former limestone mine and quarries which the Air Ministry purchased. Its advantages, in addition to the storage capacity, was its location in a quiet part of Wiltshire, the natural camouflage in a wooded area which could not be seen from the air and the fact that it was close to the main London to Exeter railway line. Stone from this site was used for the building of Salisbury Cathedral and later in its renovation. Because of the wooded location of the ammunition stores, they could not be served by road transport. A narrow gauge railway was therefore used above and below ground. A four-mile spur connected with the British Rail exchange sidings at Dinton, utilising part of the former double track main line from Exeter to Salisbury. Although closed before Chilmark, the RAF also had stores at Dinton and nearby Baverstock, both with rail connections.

It was decided to close Chilmark when the RAF's needs for large amounts of ammunition had diminished and it was proposed that future storage could be accommodated with the other armed services. The run down of RAF Chilmark started in 1994 and at the time Wg Cdr Mike Woolridge was Officer Commanding. Most of the ammunition was taken by rail to the NATO depot at Glen Ross in Scotland. Empty cases went to the MoD Procurement Depot at Aston Down in Gloucestershire and the POL to a RAF Maintenance Unit at Carlisle.

In the village church of St John the Baptist on the C51 road north of the A342. On the south wall, a marble memorial plaque mounted with the coat of arms of the Sykes family with beneath the inscription: -

REMEMBER
MAJOR GENERAL
THE RIGHT HONOURABLE
SIR FREDERICK HUGH SYKES
PRIVY COUNSELLOR
G.C.S.I: G.C.I.E: G.B.E: K.C.B: C.M.G.
OF CONOCK MANOR
FIRST COMMANDER OF THE
ROYAL FLYING CORPS.
MILITARY WING
CHIEF OF THE AIR STAFF
CONTROLLER GENERAL
OF CIVIL AVIATION
MEMBER OF PARLAMENT
GOVERNOR OF BOMBAY
CHAIRMAN
OF THE MINERS WELFARE
COMMISSION
1877   1954
*Whatsoever thy hand
findeth to do, do it
with thy might*

The memorial plaque was dedicated in October 1957. On the base and positioned centrally is the badge of the 15th Hussars.

The marble memorial in the church at Chirton.

As is seen from the wording on his memorial, Sir Frederick Sykes led a full life in which the range of his appointments was worthy of more than one life span. His first connection with the military was in 1900 when he took a passage to South Africa and on arrival joined the Imperial Yeomanry Scouts on 26th March as Trooper No.6060, fighting the Boers. Following capture and release he was offered a commission with Lord Robert's Bodyguard and later was shot and injured, resulting in repatriation to England. Following convalescence, a commission in the regular army was offered and on 2nd October 1901 he became a Second Lieutenant with the 15th Hussars serving in India and on secondment in Sierra Leone. He was promoted to Lt on 29th July 1903. Returning to England in 1904, he attended a number of courses to correct the lack of theoretical training he had missed by not having passed through Sandhurst. One of these was a ballooning course, which was his introduction to flight, a subject which had interested him from boy-hood. He spent some time attached to a Balloon Camp at Bulford on Salisbury Plain and attended an artillery practice camp in Wales before completing theoretical instruction and examination at the Farnborough Balloon Factory.

On 1st October 1908 he was promoted to Captain and in October 1910 was appointed to the General Staff at the War Office. During this time he learnt to fly with the Bristol Company flying school at Brooklands. He was among one of the first hundred to gain a pilot's certificate (No.95) on 20th June 1911.

An aeronautical service for naval and military purposes, to be known as the Royal Flying Corps, was established by Royal Warrant in May 1912. This consisted of a joint service of Naval and Military Wings, plus a Central Flying School, a Reserve and a Royal Aircraft Factory. With the formal inauguration on 13th May 1912, promotion and command of the Military Wing was given to Major Sykes. Commander Sampson RN was in charge of the Naval Wing and Captain Paine RN commanded the Central Flying School, which would be established at Upavon. In January 1913, Major Sykes was further promoted to the rank of temporary Lieutenant Colonel.

There was an assortment of uniforms being worn by personnel of the Royal Flying Corps in the early days and Lt Col Sykes decided for the sake of efficiency and *esprit de corps* that they should have a distinctive one of their own. This was a double-breasted khaki uniform with folding cap, which the War Office approved. Early in 1918 this was changed to a light blue uniform, being a compromise between the Army and the Navy. Together with Brigadier-General David Henderson, Director of Military Training, they sketched the 'Wings' to form the RFC badge. Lt Col Sykes then asked his officers to make suggestions for a suitable motto and J.N. Fletcher proposed *Per Ardua Ad Astra* 'Through Struggle to the Stars' which in turn had been suggested to him by J.S. Yule a fellow former officer of the Royal Engineers. The badge and motto were later adopted by the RAF, the letters replacing RFC in the centre. Henderson and Sykes also designed the pilot's brevet.

These first two senior officers of the RFC travelled to Salisbury Plain in the spring of 1912 and selected Upavon Down as a suitable site for the Central Flying School which opened in June 1912.

In June 1914 Lt Col Sykes assembled the whole of the Military Wing at Netheravon for training under his command. The Wing comprised the Aircraft Park together with Nos. 2,3,4,5 and 6 Squadrons. Personnel were subjected to a concentrated training course which lasted for two months. Its timing could not have been better planned as World War 1 broke out on the 3rd August. It was determined that Lt Col Sykes was too junior to command the RFC in action abroad so command was given to Brigadier-General Henderson, previously Director-General of Military Aeronautics with Lt Col Sykes acting as his Chief of Staff. On

13th August they left Dover with four squadrons for Amiens in France. The RFC equitted itself well in support of the army and rightfully received the recognition its service deserved. Major Hugh Trenchard succeeded Lt Col Sykes as Commander of the Military Wing. The two men were deeply antipathetic and a bitter argument during the take over resulted in continuous friction. Trenchard's hostility was apparent when on 22nd November 1914, Sykes was appointed to command the RFC as Wing Commander, in place of Henderson who had been promoted to command the 1st Infantry Division. Trenchard had been posted to France to take charge of one of the new operational wings into which the RFC had been divided. On finding that he was to be under the command of Sykes he requested to be transferred to his original regiment. Lord Kitchener intervened with the result that Henderson and Sykes reverted to their previous posts. Henderson went sick in December, and so with a temporary rank, Colonel Sykes commanded the RFC in France at a time of rapid expansion. Henderson returned to command in May 1915. A few days later Sykes was instructed to proceed to the Dardanelles to report on aircraft requirements in the Eastern Mediterranean. He completed this report, returning to England on July 12th and on the 24th was appointed to command the air services in that area of the Mediterranean. As his command would take in the services of the Royal Marines, R.N.A.S. units and the Royal Navy it was necessary for him to be given ranks to avoid the technical difficulties this would present by virtue of his army rank. He was at one and the same time a Captain in the 15th Hussars, Brevet Lieutenant Colonel and Temporary Colonel in the Army, Wing Commander RFC, Wing-Captain R.N.A.S. and Colonel Commandant of Royal Marines with the seniority of a Royal Navy Captain. For the next 8 months he directed the operations of the Air Service units against the Turks, as required by the Navy and Army. He dealt with the organisation of air raids, of counter attack, defence against enemy aircraft and carried out the duties associated with the headquarters type organisation which he had established following his appointment.

By the early months of 1916 the changing conditions in the Dardanelles made the Air Services no longer

Major-General Sykes Chief of the Air Staff (1918-19).
Photo: Bonar Sykes

necessary, resulting in the commission of Wing-Captain Sykes being terminated by the Lords Commissioners of the Admiralty. As an expression of their high appreciation of the services he had rendered, the Lords recommended to the King, who in turn approved the appointment of Companion of the Order of St Michael and St George in recognition of those services.

During the following two years Colonel Sykes served in the War Office where he organised the Machine Gun Corps and the start of the Tank Corps. On 8th February 1917 he was promoted Temporary Brigadier-General and Deputy Director of Organisation at the War Office. At the end of the year followed a period on the Inter-Allied Staff of the Supreme War Council at Versailles. The Royal Air Force was officially launched on the 1st April 1918 and Major-General Sykes accepted the appointment of Chief of the Air Staff on 12th April. Around this time there had been acute disagreements amongst members of the Air Council, which necessitated a reshuffling of portfolios. The first Chief of the Air Staff, Hugh Trenchard, following some disagreement with Lord Rothermere, the Secretary of State for Air, had tendered his resignation on 19th March. Other members left for different appointments. Following family bereavements and because he felt unsuited to carry out the duties, Lord Rothermere himself resigned on the

25th April 1918. In his resignation letter he paid a high tribute to Major General Sykes stating ' this brilliant officer with his singularly luminous mind...an ideal Chief of Staff of the Royal Air Force.' On taking office Major-General Sykes met with considerable opposition in the Air Ministry from supporters of the previous regime. His promotion on appointment should have been in the rank of Lieutenant General conforming to the usual practice in the Army and Navy, of having the Chief of Staff holding the senior Service rank in the Council. However objections to this were made and upheld.

One of the objectives during his term as Chief of the Air Staff was the concept of an Imperial Air Force. In this he was supported by Lord Weir the Secretary of State for Air but with Weir's decision to leave the Air Ministry voluntarily on 14th January 1919, not only were these plans for expansion dropped but the Government drastically reduced the Air Force. Winston Churchill, who took on the dual roll of Secretary of State for War and Air, succeeded Lord Weir. With the war having just ended the nation was preoccupied with demobilisation and the return to pre-war conditions. Little thought seemed to be given to future needs of the Air Force. Had the plans for an Imperial Air Force been implemented, in part involving deployment in areas of the British Commonwealth, it may well have prevented the loss of so many lives in later years amongst those called upon to fight again.

Soon after taking office Winston Churchill informed General Sykes that William Weir had left behind him a recommendation that the Air Ministry should be divided into Service and Civil Departments. The Cabinet had accepted the proposal and Trenchard had been selected to take charge of the Service Department. Sykes was chosen to run the Civil Department. Churchill considered Sykes's plans as too grandiose and preferred those of Trenchard whom he was consulting behind Sykes's back. The initial impulse of General Sykes was to reject the offer from Churchill to become the first Controller-General of Civil Aviation but he came to the view that with the Governments backing, he would be able to promote and build up civil aviation on a lasting basis. He considered that this would be better achieved if a civilian administered it. He therefore resigned his commission so severing his ties with the military, sections of which he had largely been instrumental in creating and which he had served with distinction. Trenchard regained his position as Chief of Air Staff as from 31st March 1919.

Sykes served in this new post from April 1919 to April 1922 and during that time promoted and opened up many air routes around the world in particular to countries of the Empire. In 1919 he received the insignia of Knight Grand Cross of the Order of the British Empire from King George V. When his three year term of office was due to terminate, he was asked to continue for a further year but decided against this because of the frustrations he was experiencing in the lack of funding.

Sir Frederick Sykes married the daughter of the Right Honourable Andrew Bonar Law on 3rd June 1920. Two years later, Law became the first Conservative Prime Minister since 1906. Sir Frederick himself stood as Unionist Member for the Hallam Division of Sheffield at the same election of 1922 and was returned with a majority of 4232. In his time at the House of Commons he concerned himself primarily with debating matters of defence and the Air Force.

In December 1928 Sir Frederick was appointed to the Governorship of Bombay but before leaving England with his wife and six-year old son Bonar for this new appointment, King George V invested him with the insignia of Knight Grand Commander of the Order of the Indian Empire. During his five years in India he implemented schemes for social, industrial and agricultural reform but his plans suffered considerably from unprecedented financial difficulties coupled with an outbreak of Civil Disobedience. From 1932 however, when emergency powers had been granted he was able to implement some of his plans and when his period in office terminated, he had the satisfaction of knowing he was leaving the country in a better state than when he had arrived five years earlier. Following his return from India in December 1933 King George V invested him with the Knight Grand Commander of the Order of the Star of India at Sandringham.

With the outbreak of the Second World War in September 1939, Sir Frederick decided to return to Parliament where he considered his experience would best benefit the war effort. In July 1940 he was returned unopposed as Member for Central Nottingham.

Sir Frederick Sykes purchased Conock Manor, near Devizes where he lived with his family from 1945. During the war the Manor had been used as a hostel by the Land Army. Until 1941 the Manor had been the home of Lt Col Robert Smith-Barry, himself an officer of the RFC and one of the first pupils at the Central Flying School, Upavon. He vacated Conock Manor in 1941 on the death of his wife whose grave is in the church of St John the Baptist at Chirton. Sir Frederick Sykes died in London on 30th September 1954.

While Marshal of the Royal Air Force Lord Trenchard is referred to as the 'Father of the RAF', I doubt whether today it is appreciated the truly significant contribution Sir Frederick Sykes gave to the development of the RFC, RAF and Civil Aviation. The reality of this is apparent in his autobiography *"From Many Angles"* published in 1942. He was a person of high intelligence and much charm, although he did not thaw very easily. He was clearly a most capable administrator but his contribution to the formative period of the Air Force as an independent arm, has been obscured by the hostility between him and some of his brother officers. One of these was Trenchard whose opinions subsequently became gospel in the Royal Air Force, thereby conditioning much of the Services's historiography.

The following are foreign decorations conferred on Sykes by grateful countries: -

Order of St. Vladimir of Russia, American Distinguished Service Medal, Croix de Commander de l'Ordre de Leopold, Legion of Honneur, Order of the Rising Sun of Japan and the Grand Cross of the Order of the Lion of Persia.

CLYFFE PYPARD AERODROME

West of the B4011 Wootton Bassett to Broad Hinton road lies the village of Clyffe Pypard. On a hill above and to the south of the village, on an un-classified lane, is the site of the former Clyffe Pypard airfield, now Nebo Farm.

Airfield Development

Unusually the Technical and Domestic buildings were not on separate sites. At this Station the four large Bellman hangars, stores, M.T. Section, the timber built barrack blocks and mess buildings were positioned together in the N/E corner of the site. This included accommodation for the civilian work force. The No.4 Bellman hangar was used primarily as a gymnasium. 15 Standard Blister hangars were grouped in areas around the perimeter track with 3 in the north west corner, positioned outside of the perimeter, on the opposite side of the lane. Some of the original farm buildings remained as part of the camp and were utilised. The Station had a theatre but it was not opened until Christmas Eve 1942.

The training establishment, which was built on farmland, used only grass runways throughout its service. Initially these had lengths of N/S 1,100yds., NE/SW 830yds., E/W 1,050yds and NW/SE 1,100yds. Sometime before December 1944, the lengths of three of these had changed to NE/SW 1,116yds., E/W 1,333yds., and NW/SE 1,050 yds. A 10' wide concrete perimeter track ran from the N/W boundary and around the southern boundary with turning points every 600yds. Each runway, with its own control hut at one end, was used during daylight hours depending on wind direction. At night the NE/SW facility, which was the runway nearest to the Watch Office, was generally used. During night flying a mobile electric 'Chance' light powered by a petrol-fed generator was used to floodlight the landing area. A number of lights along the runway, which formed an electric flare-path of CFS pattern, were generator powered. Paraffin fuelled gooseneck flares were used in emergencies. A series of coloured lights under the control of the Night Sergeant was used to assist pilots with

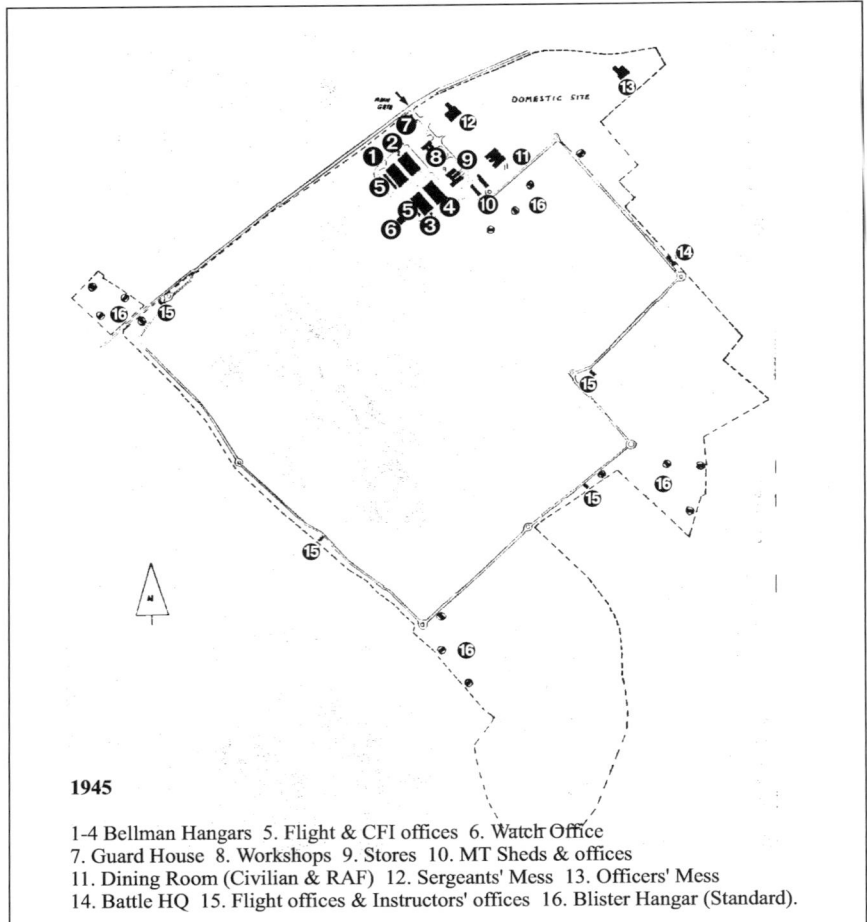

1945

1-4 Bellman Hangars 5. Flight & CFI offices 6. Watch Office
7. Guard House 8. Workshops 9. Stores 10. MT Sheds & offices
11. Dining Room (Civilian & RAF) 12. Sergeants' Mess 13. Officers' Mess
14. Battle HQ 15. Flight offices & Instructors' offices 16. Blister Hangar (Standard).

An aerial view of the airfield camp at Clyffe Pypard shortly after construction.
Photo: Marion Kent

This scene in 1947 shows the barracks and ablutions occupied through the war years by the civilian personnel working on the station. Two blister hangars can be seen to the rear.
Photo: Terry Crawford Coll.

their landings. This was known as a Glide Path/Angle of Approach Indicator. The first AAI was designed for use with the 1941 Drem Mk.1 lighting system. The unit was manufactured by Messrs R. E. Beard Ltd., and was a self-contained box 1ft sq. x 2ft long, containing a 230 volt, 250 watt optical projector lamp, spherical reflector, condensers and a 6" focal length lens assembly. With suitable adjustment, a 500watt lamp could be used. The angle from the horizontal was set so that the pilot of an approaching aircraft on the correct angle of glide, nominally 5 degrees, would follow a constant green light, with red seen when too low and amber when too high. Clyffe Pypard with Drem Mk.2 used an AAI unit placed on both sides of the runway, angled at 4.5 and 5.5 degrees to the horizontal. This gave an improved resolution to the pilot, and only a glide angle between these settings would allow two greens to be seen. With this system each unit provided a flashing light, following modification with the addition of a rotating shutter.

Having landed, aircraft were guided to the dispersal by 1' high 'Glim' lamps operating from 2volt acid batteries. A marshalling post illuminated with blue lights operated from a 12 volt car battery indicated the night-time re-fuelling point.

In June 1941 the Air Ministry approached Marshall's of Cambridge and asked them to accept responsibility for the formation of No.29 EFTS at Clyffe Pypard. During the First World War this Company had maintained and

repaired military vehicles including Rolls Royce armoured cars and ambulances which were used to collect wounded soldiers returning from France. Marshall's Flying School Limited was established in 1930 as an independent company with its own airfield on the outskirts of Cambridge. Pilot training for air minded civilians commenced soon after and continued throughout the 1930s until the outbreak of war in September 1939 when the flying school was impressed by the Air Ministry for RAF pilot training. Arthur Marshall, the managing director, remained in charge and in the second year of the war was directed by the Ministry to undertake the development of Clyffe Pypard as a flying training school second only in size to Cambridge. Yet he was disinclined to proceed with the Wiltshire hilltop project because of anticipated difficulties arising especially in respect of civilian staff recruitment and problems in catering for the establishment. Marshall brought his fears to the attention of the Ministry when he asked to be relieved of the Clyffe Pypard managership but his request was brushed aside with an assurance by the Ministry that it would undertake to arrange the provision of civilian catering staff.

World War 2 Years

On 8th September 1941 No.29 EFTS was formed at Clyffe Pypard to carry out initial flying training for pupil pilots of the RAF under No.50 (T) Group of Flying Training Command. Sqn Ldr A.D. Bennett, then Chief Instructor of the newly established

No.4 Supplementary Flying Instructor School at Cambridge, was appointed CO of Clyffe Pypard and Marshall's manager, with the rank of Acting Wg Cdr. Sqn Ldr Tribe was appointed as Chief Instructor. From August 1941 until the end of the war, Arthur Marshall would visit Clyffe Pypard every other Sunday. He flew himself there from Cambridge in a camouflaged Miles Falcon G-ADLI.

The camp was new when No.29 EFTS took up occupancy and had provision for 40 officers, 30 Sgts, 440 airmen and 208 civilians with Marshalls undertaking the contract for operating the school. The Ministry appointed caterers arrived on the first day with just 12 of the 40 staff necessary and as fast as they engaged more over the preceding days, others left. The catering manager, an Italian, was in the habit of strutting around the camp in highly polished riding boots, adopting a very arrogant attitude towards the flying instructors, and visiting the dispersal Flights in his car, for which he had obtained a petrol ration. As a result of the confusion, the Ministry caterers were dismissed and Marshalls arranged their own. Some of the other civilian duties included aircraft maintenance, laundry, general station maintenance, barbers, tailors, shoemakers, and stores. A Home Guard unit was used to patrol the station perimeter fence but was sometimes relieved by civilian workers. Fred Youngs, whose home was in Southend, was one of them and recalls having to patrol alone at night with a rifle and one round. Station defence duties were also shared with personnel under training and the RAF Regiment. Fred Youngs married Jean Harris, the daughter of the replacement-catering manager. He later moved to London where tragically his wife was killed by a flying bomb dropped on Westminter during a visit she was making there in 1944.

The initial aircraft allocation comprised 72 Tiger Moths of which 24 were immediate reserves, and 36 Magisters. Two Tiger Moths were written-off before the first training course officially commenced when on 13th September 1941 they collided over the airfield. Sgts Weller-Poley and Love with their pupils Cpl Smith and LAC Bateman were admitted to the RAF Hospital at Wroughton.

No.1 Training Course commenced on

One of Clyffe Pypard's Tiger Moth trainers, possibly T6297 displaying its individual identity No.14. Photo: Ray Steele

15th September 1941 with 70 pupil pilots. All except one arrived from No.7 ITW Newquay. Construction of the perimeter track was completed on 31st September. No.2 Pupil Pilots Pool was formed at Clyffe Pypard on 3rd November flying aircraft of No.29 EFTS. Night flying training commenced on 11th November and to relieve the congestion at Clyffe Pypard, a Landing Ground at Alton Barnes in the Pewsey Vale was made available in December for daytime training only. Later work commenced to upgrade it to RLG status. Acting Wg Cdr Donald Bennett relinquished command of Clyffe Pypard on 27th December, returning to Cambridge. He was replaced as CO by Acting Wg Cdr C.E. Goldsmith AFC, who later became substantive in the rank, and remained in post until July 1947.

Pilots such as those from No.21 EFTS Booker used Clyffe Pypard for cross-country flights. Pilots would land their Tiger Moths and check in at Flying Control where the Duty Controller would submit a report on the standard of landings made by the visiting trainee pilot.

The Station was cut off by heavy falls of snow in January 1942 and very little flying took place. The poor weather continued throughout most of the following month. However flying was possible on Sunday 8th February when a further mid air collision occurred between two Tiger Moths. One was piloted by Sgt Will L.B. Wright RAFVR with LAC. John W.G. Johnson RAFVR as pupil, and the other had as pilot LAC Ray E.C. Pollard RAF. Both pilots were killed and LAC Johnson was admitted to the RAF Hospital at Wroughton with serious injuries from which he died two days later. On 16th

April the night flying 'Rendezvous Lights' at White Horse Hill were bombed by a friendly aircraft, believed to be a Wellington. There was a similar occurrence the following night with six bombs dropped 60 yds from the goose-neck flares.

Glider pilot training for the Army commenced on 20th May with pupils from the 1st Glider Regiment attending No.1 Glider Course. Glider pilots were under instruction for 12 weeks with elementary flying instruction undertaken in Tiger Moths. Marshalls gave a challenge cup and medal to the best non-commissioned pupil of each course which the Army recognised by automatically promoting the winner to the rank of sergeant.

With the RLG at Alton Barnes about to be fully operational, a meeting with Upavon's CFI was held to discuss co-operation and medical arrangements in the case of accidents occurring there. It was determined that a Medical Orderly from Clyffe Pypard would accompany the pupils, departing at 0800 hrs and returning at 1300 hrs. A second Orderly would leave with the afternoon group and return when flying for the day was completed. A Medical Officer would be flown to Alton Barnes in an emergency.

The School at Clyffe Pypard was up-graded to six Flts on 3rd June 1942. Four Flts, 'C', 'D', 'E' and 'F' operated from Clyffe Pypard with 'A' and 'B' from Alton Barnes, which was officially opened as a RLG from this date.

At 1400 hrs on 16th June, Tiger Moth T.7454 piloted by Cpl F.H. Palmer of No.1 Pre-Glider Training Course got into a spin 1 mile N/W of the airfield

and crashed. He suffered spinal injuries and was taken to the RAF Hospital at Wroughton.

A fatal accident occurred at Purton on Wednesday 30th September when Magister V1026 stalled during its final turn when carrying out a forced landing approach which may have been a practice or intentional one. Plt Off Peter J. Graves RAF was killed and his pupil Cpl A.J. Bowerman died later from his injuries. Plt Off graves was buried at St. Peter churchyard, Clyffe Pypard.

At 1835hrs. on 18th October a Liberator II AL538 on a ferry flight from Prestwick to Lyneham crashed when attempting to land on the aerodrome. Cloud base was 200' and visibility poor. The aircraft had been homed into Lyneham by radio but the pilot made his landing attempt at Clyffe Pypard by mistake. He approached at excessive speed down-wind, overshot and crashed through the eastern boundary fence. The aircraft caught fire as it came to rest. The port main plane of Tiger Moth T7392, picketed by the boundary fence, was wrecked when struck by the Liberator. The crew and passengers who escaped uninjured were Sgt K.W. Jones (pilot), Sgt J.L. O'Sullivan (2nd pilot), Sgt G. McDonnell (observer), Sgt B. Westermark (WOP) of No.1445 Flt, Lt Gough RN, 781 RN Sqn and Sub Lt Tolstoy RNVR, 772 RN Sqn. The aircraft fire was extinguished by the station fire picket but the Liberator was written off.

As of 21st November, the ELG at Manningford, previously in use by CFS Upavon, was transferred to No.29 EFTS. From January 1943 the aircraft allocation of No.29 EFTS was increased to 108 Tiger Moths but the Magisters were withdrawn.

Two instructors, Fg Off Angus Gerald Williams RNZAF (pilot) and Fg Off Alfred Gifford Moss RAFVR (passenger), took-off for Alton Barnes in Tiger Moth T6641 on 2nd March 1943. In low cloud and bad visibility the aircraft crashed at Hill Covert, Roundway Hill, Devizes, six miles from their destination. Both men died trapped in the wreckage of the over-turned aircraft, which was destroyed by fire. US Army personnel mounted guard at the crash site until the bodies were recovered. Both of the airmen were later buried in the village churchyard of St. Peter at Clyffe Pypard. On 8th March 1943 No.2 Pupil Pilots Pool was disbanded.

A second large visitor arrived on 22nd March 1943 when at 2210 hrs a Stirling III, BK667 LS-'H' of No.XV Sqn, No.3 Group, based at Bourn, crash landed at Clyffe Pypard with engine trouble. It overshot the flarepath, passing through the boundary on the N/E side of the field before crashing into trees. The incendiary bombs, which were still on board, ignited and wrecked the aircraft. It was returning from St. Nazaire after suffering a starboard outer engine failure followed by the port inner. Flt Sgt James L. Sheills (pilot) and Sgt Leslie A. James (B/A) escaped uninjured, but Sgt J. K. Compson (2nd pilot) was trapped in the cockpit and suffered leg injuries. Five of the crew parachuted out on approach to Clyffe Pypard. The two gunners, Sgt Donald J.A. Hyde and Sgt Bertie J.A. Bessette RCAF walked into camp at Yatesbury airfield. Three others came down at Clyffe Pypard. Sgt B. Taaffe (Flt.Eng.) was found unconscious by the perimeter fence with Sgt Clive B. Perring (nav) and Sgt John Gould (WOP/AG) found hanging from some trees. The Stirlings of No.XV Sqn had been recalled before reaching St. Nazaire but one crew presumably did not receive this message and carried on to bomb the primary target. Flt Sgt James Sheills was later awarded a DFM and was promoted to Plt Off. Having escaped this crash landing in Wiltshire, with the exception of Sgts Compson and Taaffe, all of the crew were killed on 16th/17th April during an operation to Mannheim in replacement Stirling [222] BF474 LS-H. Tiger Moth N9198 flew into HT electricity cables near Steeple Langford on 19th May 1943. Sgt R.F. Gavin (pilot) was injured and taken to the 1st American Field Hospital in Salisbury but Sgt R.M. Kemsley (nav) was killed.

Another unexpected visitor was a Wellington of No.301 FTU Lyneham at 2330hrs on 23rd May. Plt Off S.J. Green was carrying out circuits and bumps at nearby Lyneham when he mistook Clyffe Pypard's flarepath and landed before over-shooting the flarepath and passing through the boundary fence. The aircraft suffered damage but the crew were uninjured.

Marshalls continued their exceptional output of trained pilots through

'F' Flight Instructors and office staff of
No. 29 EFTS in 1943.
Photo: Mrs Pat Walker

1943/44. Preliminary Pilot Advanced Flying Unit Courses were being undertaken at this time and Plt Off Des Blake, later to be CO at Wroughton, recalls attending one of the courses and flying the camouflaged Tiger Moths to and from Alton Barnes. Unfortunately success

multiple injuries. Both were taken to the sick quarters at RAF Upavon where Sgt Harrison was pronounced dead on arrival. On the afternoon of Tuesday 25th July Tiger Moth T7643, with pilot instructor Sgt Stanley C. Slade RAFVR in the front cockpit and his pupil Plt Off J.M. Paton in the rear, struck a tree in the low flying area. The aircraft caught fire and crashed N/E of Braydon Pond near Wootton Bassett. Sgt Slade was killed and his pupil suffered 2nd degree burns to his face and a fractured skull. He was taken to the sick quarters at RAF Long Newnton from where he was admitted to 120th American Army Hospital at Charlton. On Friday 25th August Typhoon MM407 from No.3 T.E.U. Aston Down, in attempting a forced landing at Clyffe Pypard following engine failure, stalled and crashed on the cliff face 150 yds N/W of the Station. The aircraft caught fire and was declared Category 'E' damaged. The pilot Flt Sgt Colin S. Cameron RAFVR No.165 Sqn was killed. Thick fog conditions on 13th September forced Dakota KG423 to land on the airfield. It was returning from France with 13 stretcher cases and 5 walking wounded. They were all taken off the aircraft, which was parked outside the watch office, and transported by road to the RAF Hospital at Wroughton.

The Flying Instructors with Royal Navy pupils in 1944.
Front row: 2nd left Flt Lt Rothwell, 3rd left Flt Lt Phillips, 5th left CO Wg Cdr C. E. Goldsmith,
1st row: 1st left Flt Lt Robertson, 3rd & 4th right Flt Lts Tom Sawyer and Alister Renvoise.
Photo: Alister Renvoise

was often punctuated by disaster. In the late afternoon of Saturday 20th May 1944 a mid air collision occurred near West Wick Farm, Oare between Tiger Moth T.6744, piloted by Sgt S.F.P. Stanley, and Tiger Moth DE246, piloted by Sgt Percy A. Harrison RAF, both P.R.C. Pilots. Stanley parachuted to safety but Harrison's parachute caught on the aircraft mainplane and he sustained

On 13th October 1944 the training of naval cadet pilots commenced with 245 pupils attending No.1 Naval Grading Course. This course lasted for four weeks terminating on 9th November. Pilots who reached a satisfactory standard would then proceed, after a period of leave, to HMS St. Vincent at Gosport for further flying training. As each course which comprised 6 Flights ended, a new intake commenced.

Despite the large numbers of naval pupils under instruction, the RAF courses continued in tandem. A dual Station accident occurred on Tuesday 31st October when Tiger Moth N9408 from Clyffe Pypard and Proctor III LZ629 from Yatesbury collided and crashed at Manor Farm, Wedhampton. The crew of the Tiger Moth, instructor Flt Sgt John R. Dunford (pilot) and N.A.2. Kevin Davies RNVR (FAA) HMS Daedalus (pupil), were killed as were the two-man crew of the Proctor. All of the six Flts were accommodated at Clyffe Pypard, with 'A' and 'B' Flts operating from Alton Barnes and bussed there daily for flying training.

poor visibility all combining to reduce the amount of flying. On 31st May Mr S.N. Jordan the High Commissioner for New Zealand and Mr Skinner the New Zealand Naval Affairs Officer arrived by air to examine pilot selection methods for naval candidates.

On 7th July 1945, all the aircraft at Alton Barnes were flown back to Clyffe Pypard. Two days later the RLG was closed down and placed on Care & Maintenance. Clyffe Pypard was then reduced to a 4 Flt status with each Flt having a 15 aircraft allocation instead of the previous 18.

Pilots of No. 6 Naval Grading Course, which became the 77th Pilot's Course, seen at Clyffe Pypard in March 1945:
LtoR *in windows*- NA.2s Farmer & Bowskill, *standing*-NA.2s Plaskett, Paku (New Zealand), Young, Williams, Swift, Steele, *sitting*- N.A.2s Britten & Cooper. Photo: Ray Steele

For the Naval course each Flt was divided into Port and Starboard. The days training would be separated into half a day on flying duties and half as Ground School. If Port flew in the morning, they were Ground School in the afternoon and this was reversed the following day. N.A.2 Ray Steele was a pupil learning to fly Tiger Moths on the 6th Naval Grading Course during March/April 1945. His instructors were Flt Sgt Newell, WO Jarvie and Knape, Flt Lt Wood and Fg Off Muraille. Ray's instruction was not confined to one particular Tiger Moth but was carried out on ten different aircraft.

The last few days of January 1945 found Clyffe Pypard unserviceable, first due to heavy snow and then water logging from a rapid thaw. February was no better with more snow falls, strong winds, low cloud, thick haze and

Post War Years

Between July and November 1945, 240 naval pilot trainees attended courses at Clyffe Pypard. These included Royal Navy Officer's Pilot Selection Courses and a 20 hour RN Ratings Refresher Course. On the second of the 20-hour courses, the 77th Pilots Course, which operated from 17th August to 15th September 1945, was A/LA Ray Steele. He had returned to Clyffe Pypard having undergone initial flying training there earlier in the year. Unlike his previous course, on which he learnt to fly receiving tuition from a number of instructors and flying numerous Tiger Moths, this time he had one instructor and a particular aircraft allocated to him. The instructor used Tiger Moth DF191 with an aircraft individual identity No.52. When he was on morning flying duties,

Ray was responsible for getting the instructor's aircraft out of the hangar and taking it to the Flight before the instructor arrived from his home in Swindon. On one occasion, it ran out of fuel immediately outside of the Flight Office, which resulted in a reprimand for the trainee pilot. No.52 always flew left wing low but on odd occasions the instructor was issued with Tiger Moth N9205 No.63, which Ray Steele found easier to handle as it flew in the correct plane. All of the Tiger Moths at Clyffe Pypard were camouflaged with the exception of the CFIs, which was yellow. Pilots who wished to carry out unauthorised flying moves ensured that the yellow aircraft was not in the area before attempting to do so. When pupils were sufficiently proficient to go solo, they were instructed to look for the Paddington to Bristol railway line or the Kennet & Avon Canal should they become lost. A frequent training flight made by pilots from Clyffe Pypard was to the Giant at Cerne Abbas. As the crow flies this was a 104 mile round trip. A cross-country, Clyffe Pypard Colerne Upavon Clyffe Pypard would have legs of 16, 24 and 14 miles respectively. Instructor John Snook serving at Clyffe Pypard from October 1945, would teach cross-country flight map reading using the 'England South' map of the Geographical Section, General Staff No.3957 (AIR) Published by the War Office 1943. Every pilot and navigator learning to fly received instruction on altitudes and altitude variations wind factors in relation to escarpments rain shadow areas river valleys afforestation henge stones and monoliths barrows and tumuli etc.

John Snook had served with the RAF on the Island of Malta from 1941 to 1944 and then in North Africa. He returned to England and prior to arriving at Clyffe Pypard, had instructed Free Dutch personnel at Wolverhampton Civil Airport and Army personnel at Shellingford. His immediate superior at the Wiltshire airfield was Flt Lt Phillips who then was in his early sixties and in peacetime had been a senior lecturer at Southampton University. With the end of the War, John found Clyffe Pypard beginning to run down and life there very casual. Flt Lt Phillips who was good at delegating, made a point of going home every weekend and left John Snook to carry out Saturday morning classes with one specific order to "Keep 'em occupied". Having instructed Free Dutch personnel at Wolverhampton Civil Airport and the Army at Shellingford prior to arriving at Clyffe Pypard, he had found no problem with such an order. Here, however, he was confronted with an intake of Naval officers who were two and two and a half ringers with a considerable number of medal ribbons on their uniforms. Some were ex-submariners and all had exceptional service records. John Snook sensed that almost every man in the elite body of trainees felt the best opportunity for promoting his career lay in Navy flying. In one class were the sons of three Admirals, one of whom, Boyd, had a new 500 hp 16 H model Norton motor-cycle which he would race around the perimeter track. This was more than John Snook dare do with his own motorcycle, which ran on a cocktail of 90 Octane aircraft fuel mixed with paraffin courtesy of the A.S.T. civilian personnel. The young Senior Service men tended to be a law unto themselves and on Saturday mornings when they wanted to go 'up town' for the weekend, half the class would disappear through the ground floor classroom windows. Those who were left agreed that should questions be asked, they would provide suitable reasons for the absence of their colleagues. John Snook accepted this behaviour and was happy to continue his duties as instructor at Clyffe Pypard until he was demobilised in June 1946. In general, with the exception of flying training, John Snook considered Clyffe Pypard to be unique because instructing was carried out in 'Phillips' style. On a heraldic crest it could have been emblazoned as 'Efficiency and in a civilised manner without any suggestion of hassle'. On the campus (as Flt Lt Phillips always referred to the station) at mid morning break on most days, instructors and trainees headed for the Clyffe Pypard NAFFI which was no ordinary airmen's canteen. The trainees, regardless of rank, used the airmen's canteen and the instructors occupied the Corporal's Club section of the building. John Snook remembers it having the atmosphere, as well as the furnishings and décor, of a 1930s provincial hotel. There the, most excellent manageress, Miss Zella Bamsey personally made a point of ensuring everything was to the satisfaction of Phillips and his small staff. The good lady's life for the rest of the day must have been tedious because

the number of other ranks at Clyffe Pypard could have been counted on one hand and this meant she had very few customers to serve after mid morning break. Indeed, there was only a lad in the Orderly Room, the CO's batman and a grey haired old chap known as the station barber. It was rumoured he shaved Wg Cdr Goldsmith every morning to justify his existence on the camp. The batman meanwhile also served as the station postman but spent most of his day exercising the pedigree dogs which the CO bred.

By October 1946 Royal Navy training at the Station had ended but RAF and Army Pre-Glider Pilot Courses were still being carried out. Training of RAF personnel had ceased by February 1947, but the Army added A.O.P. Courses to those of Glider Pilot training. The courses continued until No.29 EFTS was closed to flying on 31st October 1947 and it disbanded into to No.21 EFTS RAF Booker on 5th November. Following the withdrawal, some of the hutted accommodation remained in use for passenger and troop transporting flights necessitated by the lack of facilities at RAF Lyneham. At that time Clyffe Pypard had a staff of 4 officers and 50 men. Garth Kenderdine-Davis, who was then serving in the RAF, recalls being accommodated overnight at the transit camp in February 1950 before flying from Lyneham the following day. In November 1953 Mike Holmes recalls a long cold night spent huddled in front of the mess room fire with 5 fellow pilots. It was with some relief that they flew out next morning in a Hastings from Lyneham to Nairobi. From there they were to join No.1340 Flt tasked with supporting the Army in the ground attack role against the Mau Mau. During 1956 Phil Sellens who had joined the RAF the previous year as a three year regular Nursing Attendant (medic), was sent to Lyneham on courses for aviation medicine and air ambulance training. Whilst there he was billeted at Clyffe Pypard. He recalls the transit camp as being in a very run down and dilapidated condition with a general air of neglect. The billeting consisted of typical 18 to 20 bed timber huts on brick piers. There were still a number remaining but only three or four habitable. Two cast iron combustion stoves heated each occupied billet. Occupants were required to collect coke in a wheelbarrow from the coke dump but

generally used coal from the coalfired cookhouse which was much nearer. Large pieces of coal were collected and broken up inside the billets. Authority was presumably lax owing to the impending closure. The dining hall and adjoining cookhouse were timber built and the latter was quite primitive. Although there were resident cooks, the students prepared their own breakfasts before the staff arrived. This involved stoking up an iron range before cooking bacon, eggs and triangular soya sausages, which came in large tins. A meal was prepared by the resident cooks for when the students returned from Lyneham at 1700 hrs. Phil Sellens felt the NAAFI building, also of timber construction, to be somewhat large for the nature of the station and having an air of faded grandeur. The worn out but good quality furniture, such as leather armchairs, reminded him of an officers mess. One of the hangars contained a large quantity of aeroplane engines, airframe components (wings, parts of fuselages etc) and mobile starter units. In April 1958 the Station was given a further two years life span but by then the standard of the accommodation had further declined. In June the Station accommodated large numbers of troops waiting to be airlifted to Cyprus to help stabilise the expected riots. It was to Clyffe Pypard that the troops later returned from Cyprus. New trooping facilities were eventually provided at Lyneham and Clyffe Pypard's RAF association ended in June 1961.

Closure

Following closure the site was returned to agricultural use and commercial use. Today over 40 years later a considerable amount of the airfield infrastructure remains and is used for farming. The most noticeable building on the site is one of the three Bellman hangars and to the S/W side are the former Flight and CFI offices. The tall wall forming the butts of the machine gun range stands to the west of the offices. On the N/E side of the hangar are the main stores and M.T. Shed. Three Mk.II Mushroom Pillboxes in excellent condition can be seen, one beside the perimeter track on the N/E boundary, one on the S/W boundary and the other by the hedge bordering the road on the north side. The underground Battle Headquarters in the trees close to the first of the pillboxes can be entered by way of the original vertical raking ladder at one end and the external staircase at the opposite end. The complete perimeter track continues in use by the farm vehicles.

The remaining Bellman hangar, Flight and CFI Offices.

The main stores on a day when the Army were exercising.

The underground Battle HQ and raking ladder exit.

The MT Shed now used as a hay barn.

An inside and outside view of a Mk.II Mushroom Pillbox.

Until the 1987 storms blew it down, this 'F' Flight Instructor's Office stood on the south side of the field.

Close to the village of Colerne and immediately east of the Fosse Way, with the main entrance off the unclassified Doncombe Lane, is the former RAF Colerne. This was one of the sites stemming from the 1934 Government decision to expand the Air Force. It was planned as a 'permanent station' and as one that would provide aircraft maintenance and storage facilities. The 880 acre site was surveyed by a three man team from the Air Ministry in 1936. As with many other Aircraft Storage Units (ASUs) it would eventually have its Sites 1-4 at separate locations around the perimeter of the aerodrome. The land forming a triangle had a number of occupiers, but in the main comprised three farms and of these the two with the most land to lose were Doncombe Farm with 400 acres and Vineyards Farm with 102 acres. On the land was a Roman Villa which had first been discovered by ploughmen in 1834 and fully excavated in 1854 before being covered over again. The villa had been of a good size with around a dozen rooms, and it is thought the stone for its construction came from a Roman quarry at Ashwicke near Chippenham. One of the runways now covers the villa.

Aerodrome Development

A Wing Commander and two Squadron Leaders from the Aerodrome Improvement Board visited Colerne on 2nd February 1938. They were tasked with determining the suitability of the proposed site, for the installation of a Lorenz Blind Landing System. It was over a year before the actual aerodrome construction started during the first week of June 1939. The Air Ministry gave the contract for demolition of the farm buildings to Sunley & Co. of London who also cleared and levelled the ground. A fleet of D8 Caterpillar tractors towing large scrapers, carried out the groundwork. Following the declaration of war on 3rd September, there was increased pressure for completion of the station, but the long working days were hampered by the restrictions imposed by black-out lighting, and by one of the worst winters in living memory. Two 'L' Type hangars were constructed but before all the ties were in place, they blew down

Colerne's 07/25 runway in 1993, viewed from a Cessena 152 heading southwest.
Photo: Glen Boulton

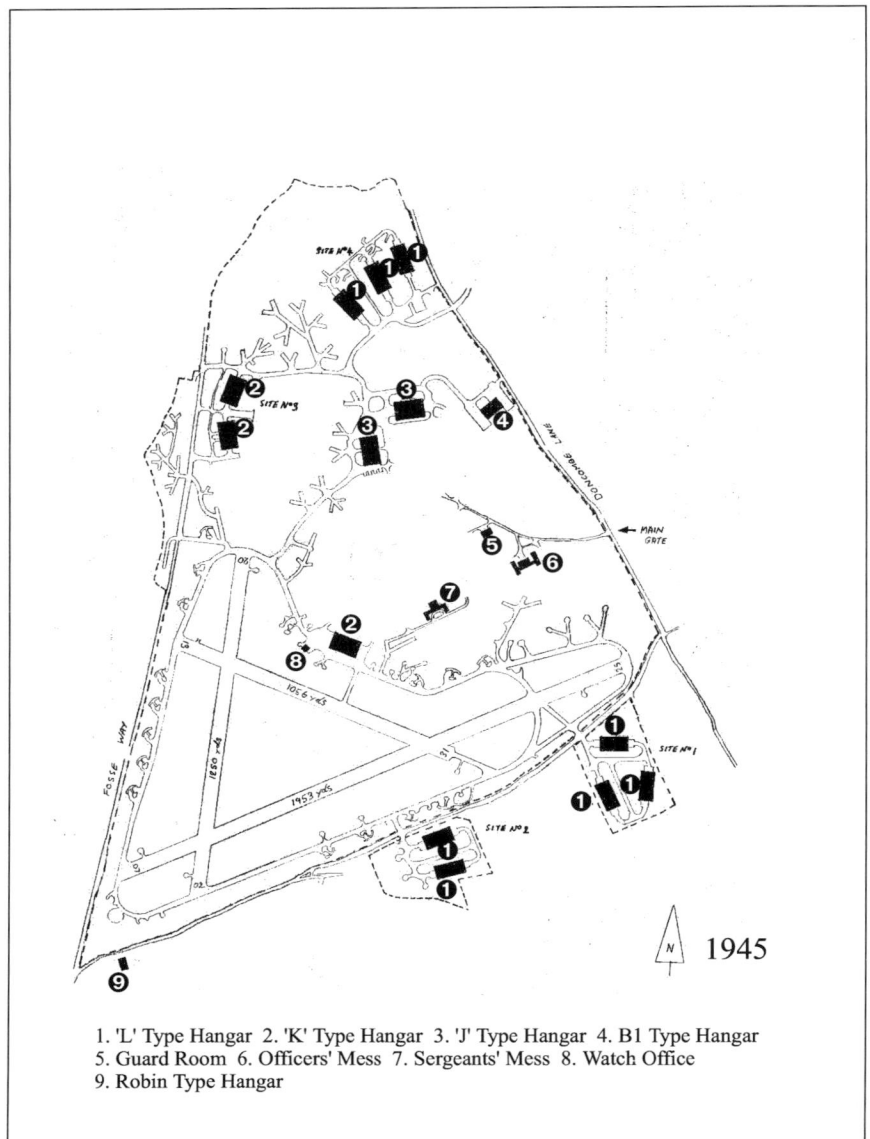

1. 'L' Type Hangar 2. 'K' Type Hangar 3. 'J' Type Hangar 4. B1 Type Hangar
5. Guard Room 6. Officers' Mess 7. Sergeants' Mess 8. Watch Office
9. Robin Type Hangar

during high winds. They looked as if they had been bombed. The main administrative and domestic buildings initially proposed, were a Station Headquarters, Officers' Mess, Sgts' Mess, Institute/Airmen's Mess, Guard Room and 6 H- type barrack blocks. These were later added to with the change in the role of the Station, and its' further development.

Some of the construction workers were living with families locally, and until the accommodation on the aerodrome improved, so were some of the airmen. In addition to the extreme weather conditions experienced during January and February 1940, other factors adding to the construction problems at Colerne were the lack of skilled labour and the difficulty in obtaining sufficient transport, the latter affected the quantities of material that could be delivered. The situation was bad enough to warrant the rare step of ministerial intervention. Sir Archibald Sinclair, Secretary of State for Air, wrote to his opposite number Ernest Bevin Minister of Labour, explaining the problems in completing the building of RAF Colerne and asking for his help. The reply basically acknowledged the circumstances without the guarantee of any assured assistance. The unfinished building work with its lack of facilities was responsible for the first fatality on the station when on Tuesday 22nd October 1940 LAC William R. L. Coombes was found dead early one morning at the bottom of the stairs in barrack block 'B'. It is thought he had fallen down the stairs in the blackout whilst carrying out the duties of Station Orderly.

Initially aircraft were required to operate from a grass strip to the north of the domestic site and well away from the construction work. The station sports field later occupied the position of the grass strip. A small brick building with an external staircase was in use as a Flying Control near to the grass strip. The two-letter station identification code was CQ, changed post war to CN. On its hill above the city of Bath, the elevation of the airfield is 595 ft AMSL. Fields and trees along the Fosse Way were used for aircraft dispersal, with an area of the road being widened to allow aircraft to be towed there from the aerodrome. Other dispersals were located on the east side of Doncombe Lane in Lucknam Park, one opposite Site No.4 and another opposite the main entrance to the

The Watch Office built at Colerne in 1940 and sadly demolished in 2002, until then one of the few remaining of the type.

Station. A decoy site was established north west of the aerodrome, at West Littleton, and three searchlight batteries were placed around Colerne during the early months of the war. One of their uses was to form a path of light over the aerodrome to guide in aircraft returning from operations. They were only used briefly for this purpose and were quickly extinguished once the aircraft had identified the station. At the end of October 1940 two 3" A.A. guns and one 13lb field gun had been installed.

The decision to construct three hard surface runways and a perimeter track was approved on 3rd July 1940. The runways were: - No.1 N/S 950yds x 50yds, No.2 NE/SW 1375yds x 50yds and No.3 NW/SE 1375yds x 50yds. Airfield lighting was Drem Mk.II. The runway numbering system was changed by late 1942 and runways were known, and still are, by their magnetic headings. No.1 became 02/20, No.2 07/25 and No.3 13/31.

No.2 runway was the first to be completed in September, but by the second week of October 1940, owing to bad weather, No.1 and No.3 runways together with the perimeter track, still required considerable work before completion. The Officers' Mess was half built, the Sgts' Mess with Quarters was built but only one wing had windows fitted and there was no water or cooking facilities. The Institute and Airmen's Mess were habitable, and of the 6 barrack blocks required to accommodate 150 men in each, only one could be used. The Station HQ, Stores and Workshops were incomplete, and the Medical Block and WAAF Quarters had not been started. No.39 Maintenance Unit (MU) and No.4 Aircraft Assembly Unit (AAU) had the use of 2 'J' Type and 1 'K' Type hangars but no hangars were available for use of the fighter

squadrons. Building of the Watch Office, north of runway No.3, to type 2328/39 was also completed in September 1940.

There was no heating on site because the boiler room was not finished, and there was only partial lighting and sewerage, so personnel were taken weekly to the public baths in Bath. Later the aerodrome would have an emergency water supply stored in a number of large tanks, positioned one above the other, set into the hill north of the airfield. These were located in woodland where also a small asbestos building housed the diesel-powered water pumps. The pumps were maintained and serviced by Air Ministry Works Department (AMWD) fitters. Two steel tanks elevated on steel frames provided the main water supply. These were positioned near the southern boundary of the airfield and were superseded by a pre-cast concrete tank during the 1990s.

Although Colerne was planned as an ASU/MU station, attacks in the SW of England by German aircraft confirmed the need for fighter cover to be provided in the area. To combat the threat, a decision was taken to use this aerodrome near Bath to provide cover, and to be the No.10 Group Sector HQ in Fighter Command.

On 24th April 1941 the Operations Room became fully operational. Queen Mary, then living at nearby Badminton, was able to see the completed facilities on a station visit she made that day. Construction of all runways, and most of the perimeter track, had been completed. Most of the hangars were built with the allocation of: - 'J' Type (2), 'O' Blister (1), 'K' Type (3), 'L' Type (8), Robin Type (1). The distribution was: - Site No.1. 'L' Type (3), Site No.2. 'L' Type (2), Site No.3. 'K' Type (2), Site No.4 'L' Type (3). North of the main

'J', 'K' & 'L' Type hangars at Colerne.

station buildings were 'J' Type (2) and on the west side midway along runway No.3 was a 'K' Type.

The position of the 'O' Blister hangar is believed to have been on the north side of the perimeter track at the east end of runway No.2. On the east side of the station a Ministry of Aircraft Production (MAP) hangar was built and was commonly referred to as the 'Black' hangar. This was a B1 Type which at one time was used for glider storage. A Robin Type hangar was located in a field by the Fosse Way at the south end of runway No.1, this was also an MAP hangar. On the road to Ford and at Thickwood, hutted living accommodation was under construction at this time. Between the two was a communal site which included a cookhouse and well equipped dance hall. The station sick quarters was two and half miles south of the airfield at Middle Hill House. The emergency operations room was also off station at Ditteridge, north of Box.

During May 1941 two Bofors guns arrived to supplement the existing defences. At the same time the public roads on the west and east sides of the aerodrome were closed to other than military traffic. A flatbed lorry carrying a Lewis gun known as an armadillo, was also being used for aerodrome defence.

Camouflaging of Colerne's runways began during July 1941, and Ashwicke House was requisitioned from Major Pope to provide accommodation for crews primarily engaged in night flying operations. The house was situated west of the airfield in a quiet position. In 1970, over 20 years after the RAF stopped using the property, it was discovered that the water rates were still being paid by the MoD! Air Force buildings were erected in the grounds of Ashwicke House, these included Barrack Huts and it is believed, a Dome Trainer used for teaching ground to air anti-aircraft gunnery. On 23rd July 1941 Colerne's officers were at long last able to

celebrate the opening of their own mess, and organised a dance there in the September to mark the occasion. The WAAF officers also had their own mess from 12th September 1941, when it opened using the Air Ministry Warden's cottages on Site No.4. The same day the station church was formally dedicated by the Bishop of Bristol.

The west end of No.2 runway was extended to join the perimeter track, and as a result it was necessary to remove some of the trees which lay on the flight path in Ashwicke Park. It is probable that No.1 runway was also extended at this time, as an aerial photograph dated June 1942, shows the runway to be at its maximum and final length of 1250yds. Post war No.2 runway was further extended at the east end to provide its present length of 1953 yds. A 1945 Air Ministry drawing shows the length of No.3 runway as 1056 yds, 323 yds less than when constructed. Possibly the measurement was taken only as far as its inter-section with No.2 runway.

The building programme had almost been completed at Colerne by November 1941 although there was still a strain on facilities because of the lack of accommodation at its satellite, Charmy Down. Throughout the rest of the war, and for several years after, the domestic and airfield sites changed little. In the late 1950s/early 1960s, many new married quarters were built in the NE corner of the site.

During June 1952 two grass landing strips, each approximately 200yds in length were established north of the 02/20 runway in the area of the sports field, for use by aircraft of No.622 (AOP) Sqn. A VHF/DF Tender (Type No.105) was sited on the airfield as an approach aid. Another approach aid in the form of an A.1 beacon (coded CQ) was also installed on the airfield. Also c.1960 an Airfield Control Radar (ACR7) was sited on a small tower at the SW corner of the airfield.

The building of a replacement A.T.C. Tower commenced during 1962, with a position alongside the perimeter track and on the west side of Site No.2. When the new A.T.C came into operation in the spring of the following year, the former WW2 Control Tower, which incorporated the Met. Office, also became Flying Wing HQ.

In early 1965 the main part of the Officers' Mess was refurbished. Part of the refurbishment was to remove a very large Cotswold Stone fireplace from an ante-room, and replace it with an 'occasional use' bar. Two civilian contract workmen were removing the fireplace and it appears they did not have the necessary props in place to provide support. A couple of tons of stone collapsed on them, one of the men unfortunately was killed and the other seriously injured.

Many of the original Nissen and Seco huts were still in evidence at the end of the 1960s with the Officer's Mess utilising 6 of the latter. All new arrivals (unless Sqn Ldr or above) had to spend several months in the Secos with the coke stoves, before a room became available in the main Mess. In early 1966 however these huts were refurbished to include central heating. Other major works were undertaken in the late 1960s to accommodate the forthcoming arrival of the Hercules C130. Taxiways were widened and resurfacing carried out in the areas of the ASF Hangars. The 5 'J' and 'K' Type hangars had radiant water heating installed in the roof areas which were also insulated, and the doors at both ends modified with sections cut out to accommodate the C130 tails. The door modifications were done at a total cost of £77,000.

World War 2 Years

No.39 Maintenance Unit (MU)
With the station nowhere near completion, it opened on 1st January 1940 in No.41 Group, Maintenance Command. The first unit at Colerne was No.39 Maintenance Unit, formed there on this date, but not opening as an aircraft storage unit until 18th May 1940. The MU had in fact been resident at Colerne since early September 1939, but without receiving aircraft. The task of the service manned MU was:

- To prepare aircraft received from the factories for operational use.
- The modification of aircraft to the latest operational standard and preparation for their issue to squadrons/units.
- The servicing of aircraft kept in storage.
- The servicing of all ancillary equipment belonging to the aircraft held in stock, and the modification of this equipment to the latest standards.

Regular examination of the aircraft and equipment was carried out during the period in storage, and the stringent inspection and tests by the unit Test Pilot ensured that flying characteristics and performance under all conditions were satisfactory.

During the course of the war the MU would supply aircraft to the North African, Middle Eastern and Far Eastern theatres of war. Hundreds of aircraft operating in those areas were initially ferried out from Colerne. One of the first tasks of the MU was the fitting of 'Identification, Friend or Foe' (IFF) to newly arrived Spitfires. Impressed civil aircraft, mainly Hornet Moths, were overhauled and issued to the service. Sqn Ldr Chalmers was appointed as the first Stn Cdr in May, but was replaced in July by Wg Cdr R.B. Harrison.

On 30th May 1940 a No.236 Sqn Blenheim IF L8717, based at Filton, crashed a little over a mile south of the aerodrome whilst making an approach to land.

Aircraft types with the MU by 15th August 1940 were the Anson, Blenheim, Hertfordshire, Lysander, Spitfire, Wellington, Whirlwind, Fulmar, Tiger Moth and Queen Wasp.

When Colerne became a Fighter Command station in September 1940, No.39 MU became a lodger unit. From 1st December the MU had the use of a Satellite Landing Ground (SLG) at Slade Farm in Oxfordshire, where they could disperse aircraft awaiting delivery. Air Transport Auxiliary (ATA) pilots, who were often women, were frequent visitors to the MU at Colerne in their aircraft ferrying role. The famous Amy Johnson was one of them, sadly she was to lose her life carrying out ATA duties on 5th January 1941 when she was killed piloting an Airspeed Oxford, which came down in the Thames Estuary. It is believed she may have taken to her parachute when the aircraft ran out of fuel. Another view is her aircraft was shot down by what today is called 'friendly fire'!

Sgt A.J. (Jack) Jackson served with No.39 MU from August 1941 to June 1945. He was responsible for a number of working parties each headed by a Cpl (Cpls Llewellyn, Baldwin, Terry and Brierly). Sgt Jackson listed the various types of civil aircraft arriving

at the MU during his time there and these comprised: - AW.27 Ensign, GAL Cygnet, DH.95 Flamingo, GAL Monospar ST-25, AW.38 Whitley, Piper J.4A Cub Coupe, Miles M.17 Monarch, Dakota, Liberator, Mosquito, Warwick and York, most of these were registered to B.O.A.C. No 39 MU started using SLG No.2 Starveall Farm in Oxfordshire from 14th June 1941.

The following are some of the military aircraft types in storage with No.39 MU at Colerne on 2nd September 1941: - Blenheim, Hertfordshire, Kittyhawk, Liberator, Lightning, Lysander, Mohawk, B-25 Mitchell, Spitfire, Tomahawk, Whirlwind, Fulmar, Tiger Moth and Hotspur. September was not a good month for Tomahawks landing at Colerne. On the 18th AH819 ground-looped on landing with the undercarriage collapsing, and on the 27th AH804 and AH 837 both swung on landing with undercarriages collapsing.

From 30th September 1941, No.39 MU started using a further SLG at Barton Abbey in Oxfordshire. The facility was used by Colerne until February 1943.

The weather during January 1942 had not been good for flying, with much rain, low cloud and poor visibility. The first few days of February were no better with snow now covering the ground as well. It was at this time that No.39 MU was urgently awaiting the arrival of Spitfires in desert camouflage, destined for the beleaguered island of Malta. These had to be fitted out and flown north in April to meet the aircraft carrier USS *Wasp* which was to ship them towards the Island. When about 250nm from Malta, the Spitfires would be flown off to the Island.

The Spitfires were at Chattis Hill near Stockbridge with ATA pilots of No.15 Ferry Pool tasked for delivery with Priority 1 Wait. This meant that pilots had to remain with their aircraft until conditions allowed immediate take-off. The importance placed on these aircraft was sufficient for a question to be raised in Parliament regarding the delay. On the afternoon of 2nd February, two of the Spitfires flown by ATA pilots Ann Welch and Mabel Glass managed to get away during a brief improvement in the visibility.

No.39 MU Test Flight commanded by Wg Cdr Wooliams in front row with his dog
Photo: Glen Boulton Cty of D. Thompson

Ann Welch was flying AB339 and both aircraft made the 50mile flight to Colerne safely. ATA pilots were conscious that in their case the aircraft they were flying were more valuable than the pilot, this was in contrast with operational status when the fighter pilot was considered more valuable than the aircraft. As weather conditions improved, Chattis Hill gave up, over the next few days, its remaining Malta bound Spitfires for preparation by the MU.

During May 1942, No.39 MU and No.218 MU were busy preparing numerous Tomahawk, Airacobra and Typhoon aircraft. The staccato rattle of machine-gun and cannon fire coming from the stop-butts until the last hours of daylight. No.218 MU assembled 50 aircraft during the month, 61 during the following and 82 in July, No.39 MU were also preparing Spitfire Vs for tropical use. At SLG Starveall Farm, Lancasters and Manchesters were arriving.

From the middle to late 40s, No.39 MU was continuing to supply various Mks. of Spitfire in considerable numbers for the RAF, and Seafires for the Royal Navy. Other types handled during the year included Masters, Martinets and Wellingtons.

No.4 Aircraft Assembly Unit (AAU)
The setting up of this unit had been promulgated on 29th July 1940 and was operating at Colerne within weeks. It was under the control of Lord Beaverbrook's Ministry of Aircraft Production and was concerned with the assembly of Curtiss aircraft shipped in crates from America. On arrival at the port of Avonmouth, the crated aircraft travelled by train to Box railway

station, and from there to Colerne by 'Queen Mary' aircraft transport lorries. With the fall of France the aircraft started arriving in this country from late June 1940 when they were diverted from a contract for the French Air Force. The first batch comprised 227 Hawk 75A-4s, given the name Mohawk by the RAF, and Colerne received 14 of these. Following assembly they were fitted with six 0.303 inch Browning machine guns, British throttle movements, gun sight, instrumentation and radio. The completed aircraft were held at MUs, including Colerne and Wroughton, where they were stored pending possible issue. By the spring of 1941 a substantial number of them were being dismantled and crated for shipment to No.4 Sqn SAAF, others went to Portugal and India.

The AAU initially occupied the 'K' Type hangars close to the Fosse Way, a section of which was used as an access track to the dispersal area on its west side. Later the unit was allocated Site No.4 where it occupied 3 'L' Type hangars following their completion. In 1941 BOAC provided a repair facility together with staff from Whitchurch aerodrome in Bristol. Alex Sleap was one of these aircraft engineers who worked alongside the AAU personnel. American test pilots and aircraft engineers from Curtiss and Bell aircraft corporations were also seconded to Colerne well before America entered the war. Two of the American officers were Major George Price and 1st Lt H. Zenck.

During March 1941 No.4 AAU received Tomahawk aircraft from America for assembly, followed later by Kittyhawks.

In April 1941 No.4 AAU became a lodger unit.

On 3rd and 4th July 1941 three Bell Airacobra P-39Cs DS173, 174 & 175, supplied under the terms of the Lend-Lease Act, arrived crated at Colerne. They were shipped to England because the air delivery route via Newfoundland, Greenland and Iceland, which thousands of American warplanes would use in the next few years en route to the European Theatre of Operations, called for longer stages than the Airacobra was capable of flying. The original plan was for assembly by Scottish Aviation at Prestwick, but this was changed, with the task allocated to B.O.A.C. at Colerne. Bell assigned three field engineers to support the British Airacobra programme, and the USAAF provided two officers and five NCOs. They wasted no time in assembling the first aircraft (DS173), which was test flown by Major Price, five days after arriving. This was then sent to A&AEE Boscombe Down for handling and armament trials. The trials, staged between the 9th July and 26th September, proved a disappointment to the RAF when it was found that claims by the manufacturer of a top speed of 392 mph was in fact only 359 mph.

Further Airacobras arrived at Colerne towards the end of July and were assembled over the following weeks. The first and only Fighter Command squadron to equip with the type was No.601 (County of London) Sqn based at Duxford under the command of Sqn Ldr E.J. Gracie DFC. Nineteen squadron pilots were checked out on the type by 1st Lt. Melvin F. McNickle USAAF. The squadron had received eleven aircraft from Colerne by the end of September 1941 and four were used on *Rhubarbs* flying from Manston along the French coast, over a three-day period in October. They were then withdrawn from operations owing to compass problems. That was the extent of their service with the RAF who took the opportunity of off loading the type, when a decision was made to divert the bulk of the British contract to Russia as part of a British aid package. This was following Germany's attack on Russia on 22nd June 1941. Some Airacobras were also sent to the RAAF.

No.4 AAU became No.218 MU on 1st March 1942.

No.10 Group Communications Flight

No.10 Group Communications Flt arrived on 1st July 1940 having formed at Hullavington the previous month and operating the Anson, Proctor and Dominie.

No.2 Aircraft Delivery Flight (ADF)

On 18th March 1941, No.2 Aircraft Delivery Flt (ADF) formed in No.10 Group at Colerne, initially equipped with a single Dominie É R5922.

No.2 Supplementary School of Technical Training

The 10th British Airacobra AH579 following assembly at Colerne. The 20mm Hispano cannon has yet to be fitted in the nose cone.

No.2 Supplementary School of Technical Training reformed on 31st March 1941 in No.20 Group at Colerne, for instruction in assembly and maintenance of the American aircraft. The school operated at Colerne until closure on 5th May 1941.

No.218 Maintenance Unit

On the 1st March 1942 No.218 M.U. was formed at Colerne and staffed by RAF personnel. It replaced No.4 Aircraft Assembly Unit and took over the work being done on the assembly of Airacobras by BOAC. From the 25th August 1942, when this assembly work came to an end, the Unit re-formed to become a Secret Installation Fitting Unit in No.43 Group. Initially this was confined to the installation of airborne radar but later involved aircraft modifications to numerous types.

The order to form Colerne as a Fighter Sector Station was issued by HQ Fighter Command on 1st September 1940. As the building of the station was incomplete, Fighter Command formed the No.10 Group Sector HQ at Filton on 16th September. This was short term

as it moved to Colerne on 22nd September 1940 temporarily occupying barrack block 'A'.

Sqn Ldr C.E. St. J. Beamish DFC was posted from HQ No.25 Group to Colerne as Stn Cdr with the acting rank of Wg Cdr on 14th September 1940. The only flying during the month apart from ferrying to and from No.39 MU and No.4 AAU was by the Comms Flt using the original grass runways by day and the new Tarmac runway at night.

OPERATIONAL SQUADRONS 1940-1945

The initial intention of Fighter Command was to move in two Hurricane squadrons, No.56 Sqn from Boscombe Down and No.87 Sqn from Exeter, to provide air defence for Bristol, Bath and South-West England. This had to be cancelled because by the second week of October 1940, the domestic facilities were still incomplete, and water logging of the ground surrounding the one completed runway prevented aircraft taxiing.

The station defence at the time came under the jurisdiction of No.39 MU CO and was provided by a section from the Staffordshire Regiment who were quartered in Ashwicke Park. A section of two three-inch anti-aircraft guns and one thirteen-pounder field gun were positioned on the aerodrome. Other Army regiments followed these until station security was taken over by the RAF Regiment following its formation in 1942. Aerodrome defence responsibility passed from the CO of No.39 MU to the Colerne Station Commander in December 1940.

Incessant rain during the first two

weeks of November 1940 further delayed construction work. The officers at this time had to share accommodation in the Sergeants' Mess, and also had to use two small houses close by the airfield.

No.87 Sqn

On 28th November the Hurricanes and groundcrew of No.87 Sqn with Sqn Ldr R.S. Mills as CO, arrived from Exeter by road and air, to provide permanent night fighter cover. It had the distinction of being Colerne's first fighter squadron but because of the unfinished state and the thick mud, it was not a popular move amongst the squadron personnel. In fact the same day 'B' Flt moved with their black night fighter Hurricanes to Colerne's satellite station at nearby Charmy Down which at least had three good runways but also plenty of mud. 'A' Flight which was on detachment from Exeter to Bibury, remained there until joining 'B' Flt at Charmy Down on 11th December 1940. The squadron remained at Charmy Down as a permanent posting until returning to Colerne in August 1941.

From Charmy Down, two of the squadron's Belgian pilots found themselves posted to No.56 Sqn because the language difficulty over the R/T was too great an obstacle for efficient night operation.

No.256 Sqn

The next unit to arrive at Colerne was No.256 Sqn with Sqn Ldr G.H. Gatherall as CO. The squadron, equipped with Boulton Paul Defiant I night fighters, completed a move from Pembrey on 6th February 1941. The first of several royal visits took place the next day when HRH The Duke of Kent carried out a Welfare visit to Colerne and Charmy Down. The squadron lost a Defiant on Thursday 20th February when it crashed killing the pilot Sgt David K. Rees RAFVR who was buried at Bath Haycombe Cemetery. Six days later a second loss occurred, the pilot Flt Lt Sidney F.F. Johnson RAuxAF was killed when his Defiant crashed at Collingbourne after running out of fuel whilst engaged on night operations, Sgt C. S. Lewis the gunner baled out safely. Sqn Ldr Robert A.E. Traill RAF and Sgt Hockwell were killed on Wednesday 12th March when their Defiant I

N3451 crashed at Imber when returning to Colerne from Exeter. The pilot was buried at Box General Cemetery, which lies in the valley below Colerne. On 26th March the squadron moved to Squires Gate in an exchange with No.307 (Polish) Sqn.

No.307 (Polish) Sqn

The CO of this squadron was Sqn Ldr Grodzicki, it also was equipped with the Defiant I night fighter. With its two-man crew, the Defiant was the first fighter in the world to incorporate a power-driven gun turret instead of conventional forward-firing guns. The gun turret, positioned to the rear of the pilot's cockpit, had four .303 Browning guns. The vulnerability of the Defiant to attack from beneath by German aircraft, experienced during the Battle of Britain, resulted in its relegation to the night fighter role.

Squadron personnel arriving by train and air on 26th March 1941 were: - Officers 12, Senior NCOs 34 and airmen 132. Seven additional personnel arrived the following day. The main party travelled by train from Crewe to Box Station located on the main Bath to London GWR line. On the journey south and whilst stopped at Gloucester Station, an enemy aircraft dropped two anti-personnel bombs close to the train and attacked it with machine gun fire but no one from the squadron was injured. Having settled in, the squadron were soon carrying out Sector reconnaissance familiarisation flights during the daytime followed by night flying training when the weather conditions allowed. At the end of the first week in April, operational patrols commenced. The first engagement took place on the 8th April when Defiant N1809 on Patrol Milk 'D' at 16,000', attacked a Dornier which escaped into cloud. Two days later N3391 attacked a Heinkel 111 but the crew were unable to claim it. The same day N3390 crashed at Rocks Marshfield on the west side of the airfield, stalling on approaching to land having carried out an R/T test. Sgt Maksymilyan Frychel RAF (pilot) and Sgt Jan Dziubek (pilot/passenger) were killed. Both were buried at Haycombe Cemetery, Bath on 14th April. The first real success flying from Colerne came on 12th April 1941 when Sgt Jankowiak (pilot) and Sgt Lipinski (AG) in Defiant N3315, engaged a Heinkel 111. The AG fired one short and one long burst into the nose of the enemy aircraft from 40

Pilots of No.501 Sqn with Spitfire I X4381 at Colerne on 23rd May 1941.
Photo: Glen Boulton Coll.

yards. Small explosions were observed with parts of the aircraft thrown off. It dived steeply into cloud and disappeared. The Observer Corps reported its crashing, and the squadron were credited with their first enemy aircraft destroyed. Flt Lt Jakszewicz and Sgt Starosta intercepted and attacked another Heinkel 111 in the vicinity of Boscombe Down. Four times they were vectored onto it and opened fire with return fire being made during one of the engagements. It finally disappeared and no claims were made. On 15th April Fg Off Lewandowski and Sgt Zakrocki in Defiant N3390 attacked a Heinkel 111. Firing continuously at it, the aircraft lost height rapidly. At 5000' the Defiant ran out of ammunition when the enemy was still losing height with smoke coming from its port engine. It was claimed as a probable. N3391 was lost on 24th April when it suffered an engine failure whilst on an operational patrol. The pilot Sgt Dukazto and the airgunner Sgt Banys parachuted to safety with minor injuries. Two days later the squadron moved to Exeter.

The Defiants arriving at Colerne with the squadron were: -

N1641	N1675
N1769	N1772
N1809	N1812
N3315	N3336
N3390	N3391
N3404	N3432
N3437	N3439
N3925	

Wg Cdr A. V. Harvey was appointed as Stn Cdr with the acting rank of Gp Capt as from 3rd April 1941.

No.118 Sqn

On 5th April 1941, No.118 Sqn with Sqn Ldr F.J. Howell DFC as CO, arrived from Filton with Spitfire Is. The squadron spent four days at the station re-equipping with the Spitfire IIA before departing for Warmwell.

No.501 (County of Gloucester) Sqn

On 9th April, No.501 Sqn with Sqn Ldr E. Holden DFC as CO, arrived from Filton with Hurricane Is. At Colerne the squadron initially re-equipped with Spitfire Is, and in May/June with Spitfire IIAs.

No.501 Sqn had a change of CO from 3rd June 1941 when Sqn Ldr Boyd DFC replaced Sqn Ldr Holden. On 10th June Sgt C. J. Barton struck a balloon cable and survived a crash in Spitfire IIa P8143 at Bleadon near Weston-Super-Mare. The aircraft, which had only been taken on charge by No.501 Sqn the previous month, was destroyed by fire. The squadron left Colerne for Chilbolton on 25th June 1941.

A lone German bomber got through to the aerodrome on 10th April 1941 and dropped three 50kg bombs which damaging the 'Black' hangar by Duncombe Lane on the east boundary and the NAAFI Canteen. The latter had been full with personnel eating just before the attack and a little later would have been in use for a concert. Of the two men rehearsing when the bomb dropped, one was killed and one lost an eye. Other occupants received slight injuries, two of whom, Mrs Flossie Sheppard and Miss Aggie Ham who worked there, returned the following day despite their ordeal.

No.600 (City of London) Sqn

Over the two days of 27th and 28th April 1941 No.600 Sqn moved in with Wg Cdr G.H. Stainforth AFC as CO. He had been a member of the Schneider Trophy team and also the first pilot to

Sgt Pilot C. J. Barton of No.501 Sqn seen on the right of a squadron colleague at Colerne in 1941. Photo: Glen Boulton Coll.

exceed the 400m.p.h. speed barrier. He gained a reputation at Colerne for driving his car at speed, and flying aircraft in a similar fashion. The squadron arrived from Drem with Beaufighter I & IIF night fighters plus Blenheim IFs.

No.600 Sqn was the first operational squadron at Colerne with aircraft fitted with Airborne Interception Radar (AI). The Beaufighters were among the first really successful night fighters. AI equipped aircraft could only work effectively at night, with guidance from Ground Radar (GCI), and by early 1941 great strides had been made in the performance and accuracy of both ground GCIs and airborne AI. The GCI would direct the fighter to a position and range, at which the enemy aircraft could be engaged.

The squadron personnel had been excited when they learnt of their move south as they anticipated an improved opportunity to engage the enemy, but they were not impressed with the conditions they found on arrival. An entry in the Squadron Records indicates 'we arrived at an aerodrome which is a mass of unfinished buildings, unfinished roads, unfinished everything.' The squadron's flying personnel had their wish however and were soon in action. On the night of 3rd/4th May 1941, Fg Off R. S. Woodward (pilot) and Sgt A.J. Lipscombe (nav/rad), in Beaufighter T4632, shot down a Ju 88 near Shepton Mallet. Its crew baled out before the Beaufighter crew saw the enemy

aircraft explode on the ground. On returning to Colerne, the pilot attributed the success to the skill of his Sgt in operating the AI set. On the same day a number of incendiary bombs were dropped on the western side of the aerodrome with no damage done. Two 250kg bombs fell near the south west corner but failed to explode.

No.600 Sqn was experiencing a number of technical problems with its new Beaufighters and AI at this time and even the longer serving Blenheims were developing faults. Plt Off Calvert carrying out dusk landings on 6th May in Blenheim L2693, found the under-carriage would not function and coinciding with this, the port engine

cut out. On landing, this resulted in the aircraft careering across the aerodrome, crashing into a new Merlin engined Beaufighter and writing off both aircraft. Fortunately neither Plt Off Calvert nor Sgt McDonald were injured. A further success was claimed on this day when Sqn Ldr Pritchard and Sgt Gledhill in Beaufighter T4640, were vectored onto a He 111 near base when on a G. L. Carpet and shot it down near Sherborne. The squadron shot down two more enemy aircraft the next day. Fg Off Howden and Sgt Fielding in Beaufighter R2188 destroyed one near Weston-Super-Mare. Fg Off Woodward and Sgt Lipscombe despatched the other after a chase from Bristol to The Needles, Isle of Wight, where it crashed on Tennyson Down.

On 9th May the squadron lost one of its own aircraft when it was shot down at 0355 hrs by a British fighter. This occurred when Fg Off Woodward and Sgt Lipscombe were on G.C.I. patrol over Plymouth in Beaufighter IF T4641. The attacking aircraft was a Beaufighter of No.604 Sqn from Middle Wallop. Both of the crew baled out successfully. Flt Lt Boyd and Fg Off Clegg in Beaufughter R2184

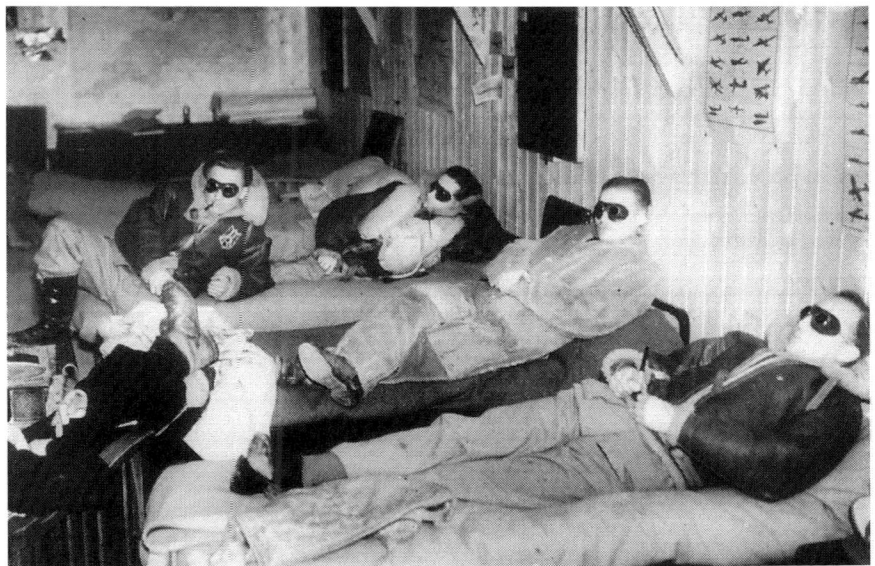

No.600 Sqn pilots and navigators prior to night flying duties. The dark goggles worn, were to accustom their eyes to night flying. Photo: Glen Boulton Coll.

destroyed a Ju 88 near Honiton on 16th May. Another unfortunate incident occurred the next day. Sqn Ldr C.A. Pritchard and Sgt Gledhill were vectored onto an enemy aircraft south of Gloucester. They followed it close to Coventry but their Beaufighter I X7544 was twice illuminated by searchlights. On the second occasion they were in visual contact and only 100yds away from the enemy aircraft which they identified as a Ju 88. The Beaufighter crew was blinded by the searchlights and their aircraft became an easy target for the German gunner who blew in the starboard side of the cockpit, setting fire to the petrol feed. The resulting flames engulfed the pilot, and Sgt Gledhill was shot in the leg. Both men were able to bale out and on landing were admitted to hospital. 'B' Flt. of No.600 Sqn moved to Predannack on 16th June and 'A' Flt to Fairwood Common near Cardiff on 17th June 1941.

No.125 (Newfoundland) Sqn
The first fighter squadron to re-form at Colerne during the war was No.125 Sqn on 16th June 1941 with Sqn Ldr H.M. Mitchell DFC as CO. The squadron worked up with Defiant Is before moving to Charmy Down on 7th August to continue this training.

No.316 (City of Warsaw) Sqn
On 18th June 1941, the second Polish squadron to serve at Colerne arrived. This was No.316 (City of Warsaw) Sqn with Sqn Ldr C. J. Donovan as CO. The squadron arrived from Pembrey where it had been working up on Hurricane Is since formation in February. While at Colerne it was equipped additionally with the Hurricane IIa and IIb. There were also two squadron 'hacks' attached, these were Battle R7410 and Magister T9871. The Battle seemed to be popular with the squadron personnel and was flown regularly from Colerne to other airfields around the country. The squadron's role at Colerne, was one of convoy protection, and commenced four days after arriving.

Ten Hurricanes flew to Friston from where they assisted on a sweep over Brest and Lorient on 10th July 1941. All aircraft returned safely to base although one of them landed at Alton Barnes having lost oil pressure. Fg Off Klawe attacked a He 111 flying at 16,000/17,000' 1½ miles north west of Lynton on 14th July. He delivered 6 bursts in 4 attacks at ranges of 150 yards closing to 50 yards. With smoke pouring from both engines the enemy aircraft dived into clouds at 9000'. Out of ammunition and low on fuel, Fg Off Klawe returned to base without knowing the fate of his quarry. On 24th July the squadron escorted Hampden bombers on Operation *Sunrise*. This was an attack on the German cruisers

Scharnhorst moored at La Pallice and *Gneisenau* at Brest, 17 British aircraft were lost on this mission with very little damage sustained by *Gneisenau* and despite five direct hits on the *Scharnhorst*, it also failed to suffer major damage. While covering the withdrawal of the Hampdens, a Me 109E was seen flying below two Spitfires, 20 miles north of Ushant near Brest. Sqn Ldr J. Frey attacked from astern and above while Fg Off Gabszewicz made a beam attack. The German aircraft climbed then dived steeply with smoke pouring from it and the pilot baling out. Five minutes later Fg Off Gabszewicz saw another Me 109E on the tail of a Hurricane, he attacked the enemy but it dived away. Sqn Ldr Frey had become CO before the squadron left Colerne on 2nd August, moving to Culmhead to join the newly formed No.2 Polish Fighter Wing.

No.317 (Polish) Sqn
On 26th June 1941 No.317 Sqn with Sqn Ldr A. Brzezina as CO, arrived from Ouston with Hurricane Is, stayed one day and before having time to unpack its equipment, was moved out the following day to Fairwood Common.

No.600 (City of London) Sqn
On 27th June 1941 No.600 Sqn 'B' Flt returned having spent 10 days at Fairwood and Wg Cdr H.M. Pearson having replaced Wg Cdr Stainforth as CO. The squadron remained until 6th October 1941 when it left for Predannack.

No.1454 (Fighter) Flt
No.1454 (Fighter) Flt. formed on 27th June 1941 at Colerne. This night fighter unit was equipped with 8 + 1 reserve Havocs with Turbinlite searchlights fitted in the nose. It was used to illuminate enemy aircraft which would then be attacked by an accompanying fighter aircraft. In this case the fighter aircraft would be one of No.87 Sqn's Hurricanes IICs from Charmy Down. No.1454 Flt itself, moved to Charmy Down on 26th January 1942.

No.87 (United Provinces) Sqn
Having carried out an attack against Maupertus aerodrome the previous day, No.87 Sqn with Sqn Ldr Ian R. Gleed DFC as CO moved from Charmy Down to Colerne on 7th August 1941, equipped with the

Hurricane I & IIC. The squadron exchanged bases with No.125 Sqn.

Six months before this, on 6th February, Ian Gleed in his Hurricane P2798, on which he had painted the Walt Disney cat *Figaro*, flew a demonstration dog-fight against a US Curtiss P-40 Tomahawk. The P-40 was flown by Wg Cdr Victor Beamish DSO, DFC, AFC. The press had been invited to Colerne to witness the demonstration between the two aircraft, which resulted in the Hurricane having slightly the upper edge. Ian Gleed had flown P2798 from its delivery, as new, to the squadron in France on 18th May 1940. Built by the Gloster Aircraft Company it survived its many operations and was struck off charge on 1st November 1941. The cockpit door was retained by Ian Gleed and kept by his family after his death in combat on 16th April 1943.

At Colerne the squadron continued its night interception role, providing area protection. It also carried out detachments to St Mary's in the Isles of Scilly. Within a couple of days of arriving at Colerne, searchlight and Havoc co-operation exercises commenced in conjunction with No.1454 Flt. These were the flights where in theory the Havoc operated its searchlight to illuminate the enemy aircraft, which would then be attacked by the accompanying Hurricane. No. 87 Sqn had no more success with the method than other units operating it. On the night of the 12th/13th August, enemy aircraft were plotted in the area but weather conditions were too bad for the squadron to take-off in pursuit.

Late in the afternoon of 16th August, after a long chase, Fg Off Forsyth flying V7011 shot down a Ju 88 30 miles south of the Scilly Isles. He fired a few short bursts from the Hurricane's guns and watched the port wing of the enemy aircraft break off before the whole thing blew up and hit the sea. On an evening flight ten days later, and also off the Scilly Isles, Plt Off Musgrave flying Hurricane I W9139 shot down a Ju 88 after It had dropped its bombs on the Island, killing two young women.

No.87 Sqn Hurricane IIC Z3576, was involved in a fatal crash on Tuesday 2nd September 1941, spinning in from 500' when Sgt Joseph M. Loughridge

RAFVR made a violent turn to prevent a head on collision with another Hurricane over the aerodrome beacon. Another fatality occurred on Friday 26th September when Sgt Percy Edwards RAFVR was killed carrying out a practice "beat up" of gun positions at Doddington. The previous evening, the squadron carried out practice attacks on a glider towed up to 10,000' by a Hector.

A number of enemy aircraft entered the Sector soon after dark on 7th October 1941. Two No.87 Sqn Hurricanes and a Havoc were sent off and tried to intercept but without success. On the evening of the 20th October, Sgt Thomson flying W9139 attacked a Me110 off the Scilly Isles and claimed it as a 'probable'. The following morning the same pilot flying W9196 together with Plt Off Musgrave flying W9139 shared in the destruction of a Me110.

On 18th November, Sqn Ldr Gleed was promoted to Wg Cdr and left the squadron the following day for Middle Wallop, where he was to lead a fighter wing.

The squadron suffered a loss on Saturday 13th December 1941, when Sgt Harold J. Robinson RCAF was killed when his Hurricane crashed after it spun in cloud and he was unable to regain control. He was buried at Bristol (Canford) Cemetery. Another crash claimed the life of Sgt William F. Horsham RAFVR on Sunday 4th January 1942 when his aircraft was in collision with an Oxford. The crew of the Oxford also died.

On 26th January 1942, No.87 Sqn, whose CO Sqn Ldr D.G. Smallwood had replaced Ian Gleed on 19th November 1941, exchanged bases with No.263 (Fellowship of the Bellows) Sqn and No.417 (City of Windsor) Sqn from Charmy Down.

No.89 Sqn
No.89 Sqn. re-formed at Colerne on 25th September with Wg Cdr G.H. Stainforth as CO, he was formerly CO of No.600 Sqn. The night-fighter squadron was fully equipped with the Beaufighter 1F by October 1941, and personnel were issued with tropical kit. The squadron left Colerne for the Middle East on 24th November 1941.

No.1457 (Fighter) Flt
No.1457 (Fighter) Flt formed at Colerne with 8 Havocs on 15th September. As with No.1454 Flt, this was a night fighter unit which had Havocs fitted with Turbinlite searchlights in the nose to illuminate enemy aircraft. The attack aircraft flying in to co-operate with No.1457 Flt were the Hurricanes of No.247 Sqn from Exeter. The Flt's stay at Colerne was short and they moved to Predannack on 17th November 1941. These Air Target Illumination Units later became squadrons in their own right. The Turbinlite experiment turned out to be a failure however, and the various squadrons involved were disbanded on 25th January 1943.

During October 1941 Air Marshal Sir W. Sholto Douglas KCB, MC, DFC, A.O.C in C Fighter Command flew in from Hendon. He inspected No.87 and No.89 Sqns before leaving for Salisbury Plain to witness a demonstration of fighter aircraft attacks on infantry tanks and lorries by squadrons of Spitfires, Hurricanes and Whirlwinds. This involved No.87 Sqn and No.263 Sqn from Charmy Down.

Colerne and Charmy Down lost one of their most popular officers on Tuesday 28th October 1941 when Sqn Ldr John Sample DFC was killed in a mid-air collision. He served originally with No.607 Sqn and after service in France, commanded No.504 Sqn during the Battle of Britain. He later served at Colerne as Sector Controller in the Operations Room before appointment as CO of No.137 Sqn when it re-formed at Charmy Down in February 1941, equipped with the Whirlwind I. On the day of the accident Sqn Ldr Sample with Sgt. M. J. Peskett took off from Charmy Down in their respective aircraft at 1745 hrs to undertake formation practice with attacks carried out by Sgt J.F. Luing flying another Whirlwind I. The three aircraft initially flew turns at about 1000' before Sgt Luing broke away to carry out the first attack on John Sample's orders. This was commenced from about 1000 yards closing to 70/80 yards. When Sgt Luing again broke away and approached for a second attack, he saw the Sqn Ldr's aircraft going down out of control with part of the tail unit falling off. The aircraft was in a spin and when close to the ground

Sgt Luing saw his leader leave the stricken aircraft and his parachute operate. His aircraft P7053 crashed onto a farm building at Manor Farm in Englishcombe Village near Bath and burst into flames. Sqn Ldr Sample's parachute did not deploy fully and he fell onto the roof of the farmhouse and was killed.

On return to base Sgt Peskett reported his aircraft had been struck in the air but he was able to maintain control. The damage to his aircraft was repaired. As evidence of the respect in which Sqn Ldr Sample was held, wreaths were sent by officers and men of his squadron, Colerne, Charmy Down and Operations Room personnel, tenants of the Manor House and residents of Englishcombe Village. He was returned to his home of Bothal in Northumberland for burial.

No.286 (Anti-aircraft Co-operation) Sqn
No.286 (AAC) Sqn with Sqn Ldr H.R. Allen as CO arrived on 30th December 1941 from Filton, where it had formed from No.10 Group AAC Flt. in November. The squadron arrived with an assortment of aircraft types comprising the Defiant I & III target tugs, Hurricane I, Master III and the Oxford. The squadron participated in Army co-operation courses before moving to Lulsgate Bottom on 24th January 1942.

1st January 1942 saw Colerne fully established as a major station in No.10 Group of Fighter Command, as well as a busy maintenance and aircraft storage unit. As a Sector Station it now had a fully manned Operations room close by the 'K' Type hangar, north of the 13/31 runway. All major building work was complete, and the station was soon to get a second Beaufighter IIF squadron, with improved AI.

No.125 Sqn
On 25th January 1942, Sqn Ldr E. G. Barwell brought back to Colerne the HQ and 'B' Flt. of No.125 Sqn from Fairwood Common, still equipped with Defiant I & IIs. From 8th February, the Flt was non-operational during re-equipping and training with the Beaufighter IIF. Until then, convoy, and dawn and dusk operational patrols were undertaken but without making contact with the enemy. In the mean

time 'A' Flt remained at Fairwood Common to re-equip and start training with Beaufighter IIFs, before returning to Colerne on 10th February 1942. As well as the Beaufighters, 'A' Flt had a Blenheim I, L6710 from No.456 Sqn at Valley, and an Oxford. As a squadron 'hack', they had a Magister, P6465 supplied from a No.43 Gp MU.

Some of No.125 Sqns obsolete Defiant Is: - T3428, T3944, T4073, T4076, N3403 and N3459 were despatched to Messrs. Reid & Sigrist at Desford. The squadron continued to work-up during March and April and on 21st April, was declared operational. Although No.125 Sqn would move out for good after only four more weeks, further night fighter squadrons, with ever improving AI, would keep Colerne in the forefront of Air Defence in the South West.

The lull which Colerne had experienced in the early part of 1942 was interrupted on the nights of the 25th/26th April when Bath took a pounding in the first of the 'Baedeker' bombing raids. The name was taken from a book published in 1842 - *German Handbook for Travellers to Britain* by Karl Baedeker which listed 'notable and historic cities worthy of a visit'. Although the Colerne and Charmy Down squadrons were scrambled to intercept, success was limited. On the first night the enemy tactics in a moonlit sky over a small target area, resulted in no engagements. On the following night, in view of the previous night's experience, 'Fighter Night' tactics were employed with improved results and Defiant and Hurricane aircraft borrowed for the occasion were used to patrol directly over the target area. Plt Off White (pilot) and Plt Off Gavegan (AG) of No.125 Sqn. in Defiant I N3370, closed on a He111 to 50'. The AG gave it a two-second burst and pieces of the aircraft were seen to fly off. A further two and a half second burst saw more damage and fire spreading from the wing root to the tail. This was claimed as a 'Probable'. The new squadron CO, Wg Cdr D.V. Ivins in a Hurricane I, shot down a Do.17 after a difficult chase. Sgt Gruchy (pilot) and Plt Off Langley (AG) in Defiant I N1730 were attacked by a He 111. Plt Off Langley held his fire until the enemy aircraft was close enough to ensure a strike, but at this point the guns failed to operate. It was later discovered the fault was due to hurried servicing. No.125 Sqn

continued operational patrols but had no further contact with the enemy before moving to Fairwood Common on 14th May 1942.

No.263 (Fellowship of the Bellows) Sqn
On 26th January 1942, No.263 Sqn moved in from Charmy Down. The CO was Sqn Ldr T.P. Pugh DFC and the squadron was equipped with the Whirlwind I of which P7116 was the CO's aircraft.

The Whirlwind had been used for a number of different roles such as anti-shipping patrols, bomber escort duties and low-level straffing. At Colerne No.263 Sqn tried it as a night fighter but unsuccessfully, and as a result the squadron moved out to Fairwood Common on 11th February.

No.417 (City of Windsor) Sqn
On 26th January 1942 No.417 Sqn moved in from Charmy Down. The CO was Sqn Ldr C.E. Malfroy and the squadron was equipped with the Spitfire IIA which it exchanged for the Mk.VB in February 1942. The squadron then became operational but saw no action before moving to Tain on 24th February.

One of the all too common tragedies of war occurred on Tuesday 24th February 1942 when Flt Lt Geoffrey L. Roscue, a Flt Cdr with No.87 Sqn was killed. The squadron had moved over to Charmy Down from Colerne on 29th January and seventeen days before that, he was married in Colerne Parish Church. His bride was Section Officer Barbara Anne Brock a Senior Cypher Officer at RAF Colerne and the daughter of Air Commodore Brock DSO. Sqn Ldr Smallwood the CO of No.87 Sqn was best man at the wedding. Flt Lt Roscoe at 25 years of age was one of the oldest members of the squadron and a valued Flt Cdr. He was killed when his Hurricane flew into H.T. cables whilst strafing positions during an army co-operation exercise.

In March 1942 Colerne had a change as Stn Cdr when Gp Capt A.V. Harvey transferred to Gp HQ and was replaced by Gp Capt H.M. Pearson previously in command of No.600 Sqn when it was at Colerne the previous year.

No.286 Sqn
No.286 Sqn returned from Lulsgate Bottom on 2nd March 1942.

No.402 (Winnipeg Bear) Sqn RCAF
No.402 Sqn with Sqn Ldr R.E. Morrow DFC as CO arrived on 4th March 1942. The squadron came from Warmwell where the Hurricane IIB was being flown in a fighter/bomber role. At Colerne it re-equipped with the Spitfire VB before moving to Fairwood Common on 17th March 1942.

Marshal of the RAF Viscount Trenchard KCB, GCVO, DSO, DCL, LL.D, visited the station on 29th March.

The following month, 5 acres of the aerodrome were ploughed to grow vegetable crops and so make the Command in the area self-supporting. Three months later Colerne was judged to have the best garden in the Group following the Unit Garden Competition!

No.286 Sqn
No.286 Sqn. having carried out Army co-operation courses returned to Lulsgate Bottom on 30th April 1942. In addition to its existing aircraft types, it was now equipped with the Hurricane IIC.

No.264 (Madras Presidency) Sqn
The air party of No.264 Sqn with Sqn Ldr C.A. Cook as CO flew in from West Malling on 1st May 1942 with Defiant IIs. The ground party of 202 airmen plus 2 officers arrived at Box Railway Station. The squadron duties commencing on 3rd May were searchlight 'stooge' flying and providing aircraft availability for any night flying work. The squadron had come to Colerne to re-equip with the Mosquito NFII, which had a further improved Mark of AI, and later the same day the first one W4086 arrived on station. The following day squadron personnel started working up on type, and by early June the Mosquito had replaced the Defiants. On completion of familiarisation the squadron became operational, when on 8th June Sqn Ldr Chisholm carried out the first night patrol. Coinciding with the new aircraft, the squadron received a new CO, Wg Cdr H.M. Kerr DFC, who together with some of the squadron officers were introduced to HRH The Duke of Kent when he visited the Station on 16th July.

On the night of 30th/31st July No.264

Sqn gained their first victory since becoming operational with the Mosquito when Sqn Ldr C.A. Cook and Plt Off R.E. McPherson in DD639 were vectored onto a Ju 88 whilst on patrol at 0130 hrs. A chase followed, during which the Ju 88 took evasive action and Sqn Ldr Cook obtained a visual, then manoeuvring into position fired two or three cannon bursts at the enemy aircraft. It immediately burst into a huge sheet of flame and spiralled down breaking up in the air. It finally crashed near Malvern, the four crew baling out to become PoW.

Sqn Ldr MacLannahan claiming a 'probable' on 18th August 1942 when the squadron was sent to intercept, and engaged enemy aircraft attacking shipping in Southampton waters.

The squadron achieved its next kill the following day, when Sqn Ldr G.G. McLannahan and Fg Off R.C. Wright, took-off on patrol at 1750hrs in DD634. They were vectored onto, attacked and shot down a Ju 88 5 miles south of The Needles, returning to base at 1940hrs.

On Friday 2nd October 1942, Sqn Ldr Philip T. Parsons and Plt Off Paul A. Harding of No.264 Sqn, were both killed when, during a single engine landing on No.1 runway, their Mosquito DD369 swung and crashed into the doors on the west end of a hangar containing fighter aircraft. Fire broke out instantly and the aircraft in the hangar had to be moved out rapidly. Sqn Ldr Parsons, the son of a Sqn Ldr, was buried in the Church of St. John the Baptist in Colerne.

The squadron had experienced some night flying success but with the reduction of enemy activity, concentrated on daytime patrols over the Bay of Biscay. It also undertook a few night *Rangers* over occupied Europe. The appalling weather being experienced at the end of the year had a detrimental effect on the wooden construction of the Colerne based Mosquito aircraft. At one time there were 12 sodden frames under renovation.

No.264 Sqn had a bad start to the New Year when on Friday 22nd January 1943 one of their Mosquitos on a weather test lost the port engine and crashed 1 mile NW of the aerodrome. The pilot Flt Lt William L. King and his navigator Plt Off Hugh B. Bell were killed.

For the second time in two weeks the squadron suffered another fatality when on Tuesday 2nd February two Mosquitos collided over Southampton and crashed at 2315 hrs. This happened during G.C.I. practice, Plt Off D.S. Corser and Fg Off R.G. Clark baled out successfully from DZ785 and so did Fg Off F. Mountain from DD665 but the body of Plt Off Sydney B. Fuller DFM was found in the wreckage near RAF Thorney Island.

The squadron was now carrying out both day and night *Ranger* operations, shooting up railway locomotives, buildings, a power station and merchant shipping. Two crews went missing on the night of Thursday 11th/Friday 12th March 1943 and a search failed to locate any wreckage. The crews were Fg Off Arthur W. J. Piers and Flt Sgt Thomas B. Hill on night *Ranger 14* and Fg Off Anthony H. Stanley and Plt Off Charles R. Lawrence on night *Ranger 15*. All but the last of these are commemorated on the Runnymede Memorial and all died on 12th March 1943.

The Sqn's Mosquitos now went on detachment to Portreath for *Ranger, Instep* and *Intruder* operations. A change of CO occurred during the month with Wg Cdr W.J. Alington DFC. AFC replacing Wg Cdr H.M. Kerr.

On 22nd March WO D. McKenzie and Plt Off J.M. Simpson shot down a Ju 88 in the Bay of Biscay. Another was shared by the two crews of Flt Lt W.F. Gibb with Plt Off K.F. Mills in DD727 and Fg Off R.M. Muir with Fg Off F. Mountain in DD737.

Mosquito DD727 crashed 1 mile south of Oakhill near Shepton Mallet on Monday 12th April. It occurred shortly after take-off from Colerne at 0815 hrs, on a *Ranger* operation. Fg Off Arthur L. Barge and Fg Off Arthur J. Matthews were both killed.

No.264 Sqn left Colerne for Predannack with 22 aircraft on 30th April 1943 but would return for a few days in late 1944.

No.19 Sqn

For the moon period between 24th and 31st July 1942, Colerne was reinforced by a detached Flight of cannon equipped Spitfire VBs from No.19 Sqn at Perranporth, commanded by Sqn Ldr P.R.G. Davies. They had little trade in the period.

Mosquito NF IIs of No.264 Sqn at Colerne prior to a night time sortie in early 1943. Photo: New York Times

No.263 Sqn

No.263 Sqn with Sqn Ldr R.S. Woodward DFC as CO arrived from Angle on 16th August 1942. The squadron was equipped with 22 Whirlwind Is and was brought to readiness two days later when a number of raids on shipping in Southampton water were reported.

The Whirlwinds of Blue Section were scrambled at 0920 hrs on 28th August to intercept an incoming raid on Bristol but they were unable to gain sufficient height in time. Again at 1415 hrs they were sent off to intercept two enemy aircraft at 38,000' over Cardiff but the height prevented contact.

No.263 Sqn moved to Warmwell on 7th September 1942, to undertake armament training on completion of conversion to a fighter/bomber role.

No.286 Sqn

No.286 Sqn with Sqn Ldr H.J. Boddington DFM as CO arrived from Zeals on 21st August 1942 equipped with the Hurricane IIC, Oxford, Master III, Defiant I and III. and was allocated a hangar used by No.218 MU. The HQ was in a house originally meant for an Airmen's Married Quarters. The officers quarters were at Ashwicke Hall and the airmen's in Barrack Block 'B'. The CO was posted super-numerary, and was replaced by Sqn Ldr D.G. Smallwood DFC from No.87 Sqn on 11th September 1942. The squadron carried out Army co-operation and night flying until moving to Weston-Super-Mare on 10th October.

Fire broke out in one of the 'J' Type hangars on 24th August 1942 resulting in one complete Lancaster being destroyed and two others damaged.

Plt Off Pat Taylor and Flt Lt 'Sammy' Sampson RAAF, No.16 Sqn under canvas at Colerne during a night flying detachment in September 1942. Pat Taylor was killed in action two months later. Photo: Eric Martin/H.J.S. Taylor Coll

Gp Capt H. Eeles arrived from Catterick on 4th September 1942 to replace Gp Capt Pearson as Stn Cdr.

No.421 Sqn

On the 8th September 1942, three Spitfires VBs of No.421 Sqn arrived from Fairwood Common to be briefly based at Colerne for interception of high flying hostiles.

No.16 Sqn

No.16 Sqn, based at Weston Zoyland, carried out a night flying detachment at Colerne with their Mustangs during September 1942.

27th Fighter Sqn, USAAF

On 15th September the 27th Fighter Sqn, 1st Fighter Group, XIIth AF, USAAF arrived from High Ercall with 23 twin-tailed Lockheed P-38F Lightnings. The period at Colerne was for training prior to Operation *Torch*, the invasion of North Africa. Personnel of this American 'Pursuit' Sqn expressed their pleasure with the comfortable accommodation made available and for the British messing arrangements. These were probably the first USAAF aircraft to operate from the West Country in World War 2, Colerne was United States Army Air Force Station 353 to the Americans.

Also on 15th September, personnel at Colerne were able to view a captured Ju 88A, He 111H and Me 110C flown in by No.1426 (Enemy Aircraft) Circus Flt. This was a specialist RAF unit, which operated captured enemy aircraft for exhibition purposes to operational personnel in this country. The enemy aircraft were also used in fighter liaison and aircraft recognition duties. The aircraft had dark green and dark earth top and side surfaces with yellow under-surfaces.

A few more American airmen found their way to Colerne on 26th September 1942 when they landed in B-17E No.41-2628 of the 92nd BG based at Bovingdon in Hertfordshire. The pilot was 1st Lt Chorak with an eight-man crew, and the aircraft put down with one engine out on returning from an operation over France.

Since the beginning of the year there had been a steady build up of visiting aircraft at Colerne, and this increased over the next two years. The reasons varied but were generally because aircraft were lost, damaged or diverted. Not all were coming off operations as many were OTU crews on X-Country practice flights.

On 25th September 1942, ACM Sir William Sholto Douglas again visited Colerne, flying himself from Zeals in a Proctor. He carried out a station inspection including the Mosquitos of No.264 Sqn and the P-38Fs of the 27th Fighter Sqn, 1st Fighter Group,

USAAF. The P-38Fs carried out an offensive operation from Colerne on 9th October in conjunction with USAAF aircraft based at Ibsley. The Americans left Colerne for Chivenor en route to Tafaraoui in Algeria on 6th November 1942.

A Fortress Flt, which had formed at Colerne earlier in the year, disbanded on 13th October 1942.

Amongst the many aircraft worthy of note arriving at Colerne on return from 'Ops', was a No.35 Sqn Halifax DT488 TL-S on 19th November 1942, landing with just one man on board. This was the pilot Wg Cdr Basil V. Robinson DSO, DFC who was also the squadron CO. With his crew, he had taken off from their home base at Graveley at 1812 hrs, as a Pathfinder, on an operation to bomb Turin. Having dropped flares and bombed the target with 3 x 1000lb.G.P bombs, whilst over the Alps on return, a bundle of flares which had hung-up, caused a fire in the bomb bay. The pilot gave the order to bale out, which all the crew did. When, as the last man to leave the aircraft, he was preparing to bale out himself, the fire subsided so he returned to the cockpit. He flew the damaged Halifax back to Wiltshire and when orbiting Bradford-on-Avon, noted the Colerne searchlight canopy. The aircraft was safely landed at 0150 hrs with the aid of pyrotechnics and R/T. The 6 crew who baled out over the Alps became Italian PoW. Two later managed to escape, Flt Sgt E.F. Butler and Flt Sgt N. McHalliday. Basil Robinson was awarded a bar to his DFC for his tenacity, and the aircraft was repaired and used again.

No.52 OTU Chedworth sent some of its Spitfires to Colerne on 1st December 1942, to be considered as 'Operational'. They were available for scrambles on approach of hostile aircraft, practice interceptions, ground-controlled interceptions and searchlight co-operation.

No.184 Sqn

On 1st December 1942, No.184 Sqn was formed at Colerne and worked up with Hurricane IID 'tank-busters', which arrived on 21st December. The CO was Sqn Ldr Jack Rose DFC.

On 1st January 1943, Colerne now had two squadrons based, as well as the two MUs, No.39 and No.218. The squadrons were No.264 with

Mosquitos and No.184 with Hurricanes. These, together with more powerful and efficient GCI Stations along the South coast, gave No.10 Group more punch in defence of the South West. The tide of war was slowly turning in the Allies' favour. Throughout the coming year Colerne would see five more squadrons pass through some to stay others to re-equip or re-organise. Most of the moves were a prelude to Operation *Overlord*, the invasion of Europe in 1944.

No.1487 (Target Towing) Flt.
No.1487 Flt arrived from Warmwell and spent a month at the Station from 3rd January 1943 providing air gunnery refresher training using Lysanders.

On 26th January 1943 a rehearsal was held for a tactical exercise being staged for 50 MPs. The exercise took place two days later, in co-operation with the Army, with the venue at Silk Hill near Bulford. An Airborne Division from Netheravon took part with No.184 Sqn's Hurricanes from Colerne and No.263 Sqn's Whirlwinds from Warmwell, providing close air support. The exercise involved ground strafing, the laying of smoke screens to cover paratroop landings, and landing of glider troops and transport.

There was a fatal accident on Saturday 27th February 1943, but not involving a Colerne aircraft. A Wellington III X3985 of No.16 OTU Upper Heyford, with one engine out and losing height rapidly, made its approach but overshot the aerodrome in a southerly direction and hit some trees near Hazelbury House Farm, Box. In the resulting crash all five crew were killed and the aircraft burnt out. Fg Off Graham Brayshaw RAFVR (pilot), Plt Off Charles H. Nicholls RAFVR (nav), Plt Off Dennis O. Moss RAFVR (BA) and Sgt. Barry C. Burton RAFVR (WOP/AG) had private burials but Sgt. Cecil E. Vyse RCAF (AG) was buried at Haycombe Cemetery in Bath with full military honours provided from Colerne.

No.184 Sqn with its 14 Hurricane IIDs moved on attachment to Chilbolton on 1st March 1943 for Exercise 'Spartan'. Sqn Ldr Rose felt it was aptly named, as they were required to live in tents. It was not known at the time but the exercise was an early rehearsal for the D-Day invasion in 1944. No.184's role was to make camera gun attacks on armoured fighting vehicles, and the squadron received an intake of new pilots from OTUs on 9th March. They arrived at Colerne whilst the squadron were away on exercise. Sgt Len Thorpe who was one of them, recalls that the CO and the Flt Cdrs on learning of the new arrivals, returned to the Station to welcome them to the squadron. This was done by beating up the airfield at zero feet and making the newcomers wonder what in earth they were in for. Exercises were now becoming quite frequent with the most common being those known as *Bullseyes*. These involved interceptions of mass mock attacks on large towns and cities in the Group area. In addition to the aircraft and crews, it also exercised the ground crews, ground control, radar and defence systems.

No.456 (RAAF) Sqn
On 16th March a 3 aircraft detachment and ground crews of No.456 (RAAF) Sqn with Wg Cdr M.H. Dwyer as CO arrived from Valley. Equipped with the Mk II Mosquito, they spent two weeks at Colerne for deep penetration *Ranger* operations in Europe. These were directed against railway installations in France with two aircraft deployed on 21st and three on 29th March. Bad weather on both occasions prevented any claims of success. The complete squadron from Valley and Colerne moved to Middle Wallop on 29th March 1943.

Colerne had a change of Stn Cdr with the arrival on 19th March of Acting Gp Capt M.B. Hamilton from No.10 Group HQ, he replaced Gp Capt Eeles.

No.183 Sqn
No.183 Sqn. with Sqn Ldr A.V. Gowers as CO arrived from Church Fenton on 25th March. The squadron had been working-up since forming in November 1942 and was now equipped with 12 Typhoon IB fighter-bombers. When they left Colerne for Gatwick on 8th April 1943, they went with 4 additional Typhoons and a Hurricane.

No.175 Sqn
The same day No.175 Sqn with Sqn Ldr J.R. Pennington-Leigh DFC as CO, arrived from Stoney Cross with 13 Hurricane IIBs. Its deployment was to re-equip with the Typhoon IB at Colerne and when this was complete they moved to Lasham on 29th May.

On the 17th April 1943 Queen Mary with her equerry toured the station.

In early 1943 it was decided to fly a Lancaster bomber to Australia to show the people of the nation the type of aircraft their countrymen were going to war in. It would also act as a means of raising money for the war effort. The aircraft chosen was ED930 *Queenie VI*, which was a Mk.III fresh off the production line at the Avro factory in Woodford. It was collected from there on 9th May by Flt Lt Peter Isaacson DFC, DFM, RAAF and his crew of Australians, all veterans of No.156 (Pathfinder) Sqn. They flew it to Colerne where No.39 MU modified it by removing the mid-upper turret, fitting long-range fuel tanks and loading life rafts and aircraft spares. On completion they flew the short distance to Lyneham before leaving on the first stage of the their journey across the Atlantic and Pacific Oceans on 21st May 1943. The aircraft was flown all around Australia and to New Zealand, and raised thousands of pounds. Towards the end of the war it was used for training Lincoln crews, followed by a period in storage before sadly being scrapped in 1948.

No.124 Sqn
A detachment of No.124 Sqn with Sqn Ldr J.C. Nelson (United States) as CO, arrived by air and road from North Weald with three Spitfire VIIs on 28th April 1943 to form a Sub Stratosphere Flt. The detachment carried out a number of patrols, remaining until 14th May when it moved to Exeter. The S.S. Flt. was formed to destroy the high-altitude reconnaissance Ju 86Ps.

No.151 Sqn
On 30th April 1943, No.151 Sqn with Wg Cdr Donald V. Ivins as CO arrived from Wittering with 24 Mosquito IIs and an Oxford as the 'hack', to fly night time *Intruder* and daytime *Ranger* operations over France. The first *Ranger* carried out after the squadron's arrival at Colerne, was operated by the CO with his regular mount, DZ712. He had to return to base on finding cover over France was unsuitable. He went again the next day but at dusk and accompanied on this sortie by Sqn Ldr Bodien DFC flying DZ750. The CO carried out an attack on a transformer station. Flt Sgt Lucas returning from an aborted day *Ranger* on 6th May 1943, was hit by flak in the starboard wing while crossing the French coast. With

an undercarriage that would not operate, he made a successful belly landing at Hurn with no crew injuries. The squadron lost their CO when Wg Cdr Ivins and Flt Sgt N.P. Daly flying DZ712 failed to return from a *Ranger* patrol on Tuesday 18th May 1943. Wg Cdr Ivins is buried at Dinard English Cemetery, Ille-et-Vilaine in France. Wg Cdr S. P. Richards AFC from No.456 Sqn was appointed as replacement CO for No.151 Sqn.

At 0200hrs on 19th May 1943, 30 hostile aircraft crossed the south coast making for targets in the south west and South Wales. Flt Sgt Kemp with Sgt Maidment flying HJ642 destroyed a Ju 88 near Minehead. Fg Off Morris and Plt Off Fisher had a lucky escape the following week when carrying out a night flying test in Mosquito DD749, the port engine caught fire and they had to make a forced landing. When it was obvious to the pilot that he would over-shoot, he retracted the undercarriage to make a belly landing, the two man crew managed to scramble from the aircraft as it burnt out on the Colerne runway. On Monday 31st May 1943, DZ245 on a daytime G.C.I. exercise, crashed at Brixworthy in Cornwall. Severe icing was experienced and the aircraft went into a spin, one wing and engine broke off the aircraft in the air. Plt Off Bushen fell out and parachuted to safety but Sgt Charles J.A. Ferguson could not get out and was killed. Throughout the month of May, No.151 Sqn had operated dusk, night and daytime *Rangers* gaining some success with strikes against trains, shipping, convoys and aircraft on airfields.

During June 1943 the squadron carried out dawn patrols, *Bullseye* operations by night and *Instep* operations out of Predannock. Fg Off James D. Humphreys and Fg Off Harold J. Lumb, whilst carrying out one of the latter operations from Cornwall, were killed in an accident on Wednesday 23rd June. Both men are commemorated on the Runnymede Memorial. Sqn Ldr Bodien AFC managed to return to base and make a safe landing in his aircraft, despite having his large dinghy wrapped around the rudder. With the arrival of the Beau Circus at Colerne on 30th June, the squadron was expecting a busy period. This was a Fighter Command Unit, with Beaufighters, and a mobile ground trainer, all used to train crews to use the new AI Mk VIII. Over the next two months, until its move from Colerne, the squadron was

involved in searchlight and bomber co-operation exercises, *Intruder* patrols, night *Rangers* and *Bullseyes*.

It was at this time that an Alsatian dog bit the squadron mascot, 'Harold' the goat, but the MO carried out the necessary repairs. A far more serious but unfortunate incident occurred on the night of 15th/16th August 1943 when Sgt O'Connor with Sgt Webb mistook a No.21 OTU Wellington IC R1152 for a He177 and shot it down with the loss of two lives. Coincidentally the Colerne crew had taken off in Mosquito HK177, to intercept a reported enemy aircraft. The Wellington was returning to Moreton-in Marsh from France where it had been on a *Nickel* Operation and was shot down at 0052hrs into the Deer Park at Wimborne St. Giles, Dorset. Three of the crew baled out but the skipper Flt Sgt F. M. Gilkeson RAAF, who made a valiant effort to save his aircraft, and Sgt E. Causer were killed. Having converted to Mosquito NF XIIs in July, No.151 Sqn accompanied by No.3068 Servicing Echelon moved on posting to Middle Wallop on 16th August.

Wellington DV444 from No.28 OTU Ossington put down on the 17th June 1943. It was assisted in this by the use of Pyrotechnics and Sandra Lights (cones of searchlights). Some other notable visitors arrived on 28th June by way of 11 B-17s, 91st Bomb Group USAAF. They landed off operations at St. Nazaire owing to bad weather at their own base. One of the aircraft was damaged but landed safely with the aid of '*Darky*'. A Blenheim IV V5890 of No.2 ADF crashed 3 minutes after take off, 2 miles NE of the aerodrome on Monday 12th July. The aircraft was on a delivery flight to Cardiff and the pilot WO Jaroslav Dohnal (Czech) was killed. He was buried at Haycombe Cemetery, Bath. Just over a week later on the 23rd July, No.2 ADF moved to Cranfield in No.9 Group.

No.1498 Flt (Target Towing) with Fg Off B.W. Cooke as CO, moved in from Hurn on 14th August 1943, where equipped with the Lysander, it had formed to provide air gunnery refresher training for units in No.10 Group. With its arrival at Colerne it assumed these duties for both the Colerne and Fairwood Common Sectors. It moved on to the latter station from 13th September 1943.

No.456 Sqn

On 17th August 1943, No.456 Sqn with Wg Cdr. G. Howden as CO, returning for their second spell at Colerne, with the Mosquito VI in addition to Mk IIs. The squadron was accompanied by No.3064 Servicing Echelon.

On Wednesday 29th September 1943 Mosquito DZ690 piloted by Flt Lt Ernest H. Griffiths (RAAF) and with Cpl William H. Blakeley (RAAF) as passenger, took off in the early morning on an air test. At 0755 hrs the aircraft flying at around 800-1000ft above the aerodrome, was seen entering a shallow dive. It banked steeply to port, spun and several pieces fell away from it, before it crashed 100 yards from the aerodrome boundary. It was thought that the cause of the accident was a spin at low altitude. Both the crew were killed and are buried at Haycombe Cemetry, Bath.

No.456 Sqn moved on posting to Fairwood Common, accompanied by No.3064 Servicing Echelon on 17th November 1943.

The Rt.Hon. Harold H. Balfour MC*. MP. Parliamentary Under-Secretary of State for Air, arrived from Hullavington on 27th August in a prototype Miles M.38. He was visiting HQ No.10 Group at nearby Rudloe Manor. Harold Balfour had himself served with No.60 Sqn in France during 1916 after transferred to the RFC from the King's Royal Rifle Company. He was a test pilot at Martlesham Heath before going back to France in 1917 as a Flt Cdr with No.43 Sqn. In this role he destroyed 3 enemy aircraft plus 1 shared, and damaged 5 more. He retired from the RAF in 1926 and entered politics, but kept in flying practice. He was Minister of Aviation, before becoming Under-Secretary of State for Air in 1938.

One Flt of the 357th Sqn, No.355 Fighter Group, 8th AF, USAAF from Steeple Morden arrived on 26th October 1943. Equipped with P-47 Thunderbolts, they came on attachment for defensive training over a two week period. The Flt comprised 9 aircraft, 10 officers and 24 men. This was to be the first of a number of attachments at Colerne by different American Fighter Sqns from Steeple Morden.

No.151 Sqn

No.151 Sqn returned for its second tour of duty at Colerne now with Wg Cdr G.H. Goodman DSO, DFC as CO. The Sqn moved in from Middle Wallop on 18th November equipped with the Mosquito NF XIII and accompanied by its Servicing Echelon. Soon after this return to Colerne, Flt Sgt J. Playford with Flt Sgt B.O. Kelsey, flying HK177, were scrambled at 2005 hrs on 20th November. They shot down a Me 410 and claimed a Fw190 as a probable. The squadron lost HK183 on 24th November when, with one engine defective, it crashed one mile NE of the airfield. Sqn Ldr N.W. Scott and his navigator escaped with injuries. Another No.151 Sqn aircraft and crew were lost on Boxing Day when HK190 crashed on a hill, obscured by cloud, at Furze Knoll (173/SU031668) by the North Wilts Golf Club near Devizes. The crew were Sub Lt Silas J.R. Madeley RN and Sub Lt Thomas A.M. Hooley RN. They were returning to Colerne having been at readiness at Ibsley. Visibility at the time of the crash was poor.

The squadron was scrambled at 2100 hrs on 21st January 1944, again at midnight and at 0400 hrs the following day. On the first of these WO H.K. Kemp (NZ) with Flt Sgt Maidment shot down a He177 near Haslemere. When the first contact was made, the crew of the enemy aircraft were obviously aware of the Mosquito presence and took marked evasive action. At 11,000' this ceased and the He177 resumed straight and level flight on a north east heading. Closing astern and below the enemy, a visual was obtained at 800'. WO Kemp then closed to 50' and maintained this position for two minutes to confirm identification. This achieved he dropped back and made an approach dead astern and 5 degrees below from where he opened fire with a short burst. Bombs had been noted between the port engine and fuselage and the short burst produced immediate effect with a violent explosion observed on the port wing. No return fire came from the He177. The white Swastika was noted on the rudder as the aircraft skidded violently to port and went down in a spiral dive, too steep to follow, and crashed near Haslemere. The crew returned to Colerne at 2235 hrs.

The He177 which was seldom seen over Britain was one of Germany's failures. It was initially produced as a four-engined strategic bomber. Its engines were mounted in pairs, side by side, each pair coupled by means of a clutch arrangement and driving a single four-bladed propeller. At face value it looked like a twin-engine aircraft. The coupled engine system caused problems during development, and when used operationally, it was prone to sudden engine fires throughout its service life. The Germans called it the 'Luftwaffe's cigarette lighter'. German pilots had no faith in it and regarded it as one of the 'RAFs finest aircraft', many crashing with fatalities. It was used mainly on long-range patrols spotting Allied shipping.

On Friday 18th February 1944 HK223, returning from a GCI practice, crashed 5½ miles from Colerne. Technical Sgt R.A. Smith USAAF and Sgt Derek E. Jacques were killed.

No.151 Sqn's Mosquito aircraft had considerable success on the night of 1st/2nd March 1944 when six aircraft were scrambled for hostile raids approaching Beachy Head. HK377, call sign "Limber 63", with Wg Cdr G.H. Goodman and Fg Off W.F.E. Thomas, took off at 0145 hrs and destroyed 2 Ju 88s and 1 Ju 188. The Wg Cdr then had to make an emergency landing at Ford at 0325 hrs as his aircraft had been damaged by debris from the exploding enemy aircraft and Fg Off Thomas had injuries to his eye, ear and head. HK448, call sign "Limber 16", with Sqn Ldr R.H Harrison and Fg Off E.P. Horrocks took off at 0205 hrs and destroyed a Ju 88 before landing again at 0400 hrs. HK232, call sign "Limber 21", with Flt Lt A.J. Stevens and Fg Off A.C. Aldridge took off at 0115 hrs. They destroyed a Ju 88 and landing back at Colerne at 0425 hrs. The squadron flew standing patrols from dusk to dawn on 6th March. Four Beaufighter VIFs from Fairwood Common reinforced the squadron during the period of the patrols.

No.137 Sqn

The New Year would see even more intense activity in the build-up to *Overlord*. This started for Colerne on 2nd January 1944 with the arrival of No.137 Sqn, under Sqn Ldr J.R. Dennehey DFC, together with No.3054 Servicing Echelon. It moved in from Lympne with the rocket-carrying Hurricane IV to re-equip with the Typhoon IB. The stay at Colerne was short, and following conversion the squadron returned to Lympne on 4th February. No.137 Sqn had re-formed at Charmy Down in February 1941 as the RAFs second Whirlwind unit. When the Sqn re-equipped with the Hurricane IV, at the end of June 1943, its aircraft passed to No.263 Sqn which was then based at Zeals.

No.131 Sqn & No.165 Sqn

Two squadrons moved in on posting from Culmhead on 10th February 1944, as a Spitfire Wing under the command of Wg Cdr Denis G. Smallwood DFC. No.131 Sqn was equipped with the Spitfire IX and its CO was Sqn Ldr J.J. O'Meara DFC*, and No.165 Sqn had the Spitfire IXB and Sqn Ldr M.E. Blackstone was its CO. On arrival the squadron took charge of an Oxford for training all pilots on twin engines. Why this was done is not known.

Both squadrons moved to Predannock on 19th February to take part in *Instep* patrols, as it had been reported that a damaged U-boat was working its way back to the Bay of Biscay from the Atlantic protected by Ju 88s. An *Instep* patrol was to intercept the enemy aircraft, and 9 Spitfires of the two squadrons led by Wg Cdr Smallwood set course at sea level and arrived south-east of Ushant at 1547 hrs. They patrolled for 30 minutes without making contact and returned to the forward base where they were relieved by a further patrol. A convoy was spotted by a No.165 Sqn patrol but because of heavy fire from two flak ships, the leader decided not to attack owing to the aircraft's comparatively ineffective armament.

No.131 Sqn left Colerne for Fairwood Common on 23rd February, where for the next five days they participated in a Air Firing & Bombing Course. The squadron went with 17 Spitfires and a Tiger Moth. During this period 10 Spitfire VIIs arrived at Colerne for the squadron to re-equip with on their return.

No.165 Sqn proceeded to Martlesham Heath on 24th February to fly fighter cover for Marauders on a No.11 Group *Ramrod*. The Wing was completed by No.616 Sqn from Exeter with Spitfire VIIs and led by Wg Cdr Smallwood. Penetration was made near Gravelines with the patrol in the area between

Guines and Abbeville. All aircraft returned safely to Kenley for the night. The next day the same two squadrons flew close escort to Marauders on another No.11 Group *Ramrod*. The target was the airfield at St. Trond where strikes were recorded on runways and dispersal buildings. A large fire was apparent from one building. No flak came from the target but inaccurate flak was experienced on the approach and withdrawal. All aircraft returned safely from this operation which was carried out from Manston.

15 No.165 Sqn pilots with their Spitfires were sent to Fairwood Common during the first week of March 1944 where they took a bombing and gunnery course. The two days following the course the squadron were engaged on shipping protection flights in the Start Point to Plymouth area. On 11th March, standing patrols were operated to cover U.S. Army exercises on Slapton Sands. The following day 'B' Flt came to readiness at 1430 hrs and was scrambled almost immediately. Four enemy aircraft were reported south of Portland Bill but the Flight was unable to make contact with these. On 20th March, six aircraft operating from Bolt Head made a low-level penetration of the Brest Peninsula. They penetrated to the Kerlin Bastard/Vannes area and when 15 miles north of the latter, a Ju 88 was sighted. It was promptly shot down near Loriens by Plt Off J.M. Haslops RAAF with Fg Off D.C. Eva flying Spitfire MH601 'D'. On the same type of operation four days later, the squadron aircraft observed six pillboxes on the French coast near Provan. Machine gun fire from one of these struck the aircraft flown by Plt Off E.R. Lewis RAAF. It streamed black smoke and glycol. He was told to bale out but being unable to do so, crash-landed 8 miles south east of Quimper. The following day eight aircraft in two sections of four put up patrols from south of Portland to south of Lyme Regis where they covered an exercise involving 300 tugs and gliders. No.165 Sqn moved to Predannack on 2nd April.

Aircraft of No.131 Sqn were at this stage carrying out cross-country trips, low-level shipping reconnaissance and defensive channel patrols from Predannack. On 4th March, together with No.165 Sqn they operated as a Wing on a No.11 Group *Ramrod 623*

from Manston acting as withdrawal support for USAAF B-17s and B-24s returning from a bombing mission. 10/10th snow cloud prevented contact and the fighters returned to Manston.

No.131 Sqn carried out convoy escort duties on 7th March between Cardigan Bay and Portsmouth for 15 American ships. Two days later the squadron left for Harrowbeer from where they gave cover to exercises *Fox* and *Frank*, two amphibious combined operational exercises taking place in the Slapton Sands and Studland Bay areas. It was in the early hours of 28th April 1944, during exercise *Tiger* at Slapton Sands, that a terrible loss of life occurred. Due to a combination of circumstances, not least loss of radio contact with Navy escorts, a convoy of eight American Tank Landing Ships (LSTs) were attacked at will by German E-boats in Lyme Bay. Two LSTs were sunk, one badly damaged and 946 American servicemen were killed. In a tragic irony, when the same units landed on Omaha and Utah beaches on 6th June, they lost just 200 men.

18 Spitfire VIIs had been delivered to Colerne by 14th March, this being the official day No.131 Sqn re-equipped with the type. The squadron sent eight Spitfires to Warmwell on the 18th March for a No.11 Group *Ramrod 667*, providing escort to Mosquito bombers. On 24th March the squadron left Colerne for Harrowbeer on a ten-day detachment to provide standing patrols off Start Point and to cover the American amphibious exercises in the Slapton Sands area. On the last day of the month, No.131 Sqn personnel learnt that they were to remain at Harrowbeer. No.165 Sqn with its Servicing Echelon moved to Predannack on 2nd April 1944.

No.219 Sqn
On 26th March 1944 No.219 Sqn with Wg Cdr A.D. McNeill Boyd DSO. DFC as CO. arrived from Honiley equipped with the Mosquito NF XVII and accompanied by No.3136 Servicing Echelon. It was soon in action when, the following evening, 5 crews were scrambled (4 from the mess bar) to intercept a reported 100 hostile aircraft approaching Start Bay and Lyme Bay. Flying HK260, Sqn Ldr Ellis and Flt Lt Craig obtained contact on a Ju 88 which was held in spite of considerable 'Window' being dropped by the Germans on this raid. The crew shot down this aircraft of 3/KG 54 near

Yeovil. This was the first 'kill' since the squadron had returned to England from North Africa. On 4th May No.219 Sqn with its Servicing Echelon moved to Bradwell Bay.

On 28th March No.6203 Bomb Disposal Flt arrived at Colerne from Northern Ireland.

No.488 (New Zealand) Sqn
On the evening of 4th May 1944, 'B' Flt of No.488 Sqn with Wg Cdr R.C. Haine DFC as CO, flew in from Zeals with Mosquito XIII and maintained a state of readiness for the night. 'A' Flt continued at Bradwell Bay joining 'B' Flt at Colerne two days later. Lack of facilities prevented occupation of Zeals at the time. This was the first Tactical Air Force squadron to be based at Colerne and the complete mobility of the unit and personnel was noticeable. During its brief stop-over at Colerne, the squadron carried out patrols and flying training. 'A' Flt moved to Zeals with most of the ground personnel on 11th May and 'B' Flt maintained a state of readiness at Colerne until moving south to Zeals the following day.

Air Commodore Reginald Pyne DFC, Senior Air Officer of HQ No.10 Group was killed on Wednesday 17th May 1944 when his Hurricane of No.10 Gp Comms Flt collided with a balloon cable when flying to Colerne from Bolt Head.

No.286 Sqn
No.286 Sqn (AAC) returned to Colerne on 20th May 1944, this time from Culmhead and with Sqn Ldr F.P. Joyce as CO. By this time it was equipped with 1 Tiger Moth, 1 Defiant I, 15 Oxfords, 7 Hurricane IICs, 2 Hurricane IVs and 3 Martinets. Three days later a detachment of five No.587 Sqn (AAC) aircraft followed from Culmhead. This squadron had a similar aircraft allocation, and both units provided training targets for Army Anti-aircraft guns. No.286 Sqn moved out to Zeals on 28th July 1944.

By May 1944, Colerne had become responsible for a practice bombing range at Hilmarton, 8 miles south west of Swindon, the range had previously been allocated to the US Army as a mortar range.

Nos 29, 85, 151, 410 and 604 Sqns
During the afternoon of 5th June 1944 it was announced that all personnel

were confined to camp, off station communications were barred and nobody was allowed to enter. This preparation for the D-Day landings was accompanied by the arrival of 12 Mosquito night fighters of No.85 Sqn, 4 of No.151 Sqn, 3 of No.604 Sqn, 3 of No.29 Sqn and 4 of No.410 Sqn. The operations they were to undertake were directed by No.11 Group's Head of Night Operations, Gp Capt John 'Cat's Eyes' Cunningham DSO, DFC who arrived the same day. Earlier in the war he had become celebrated, as with his then NCO radar operator, C.F. Rawnsley, his tally of night kills mounted. He ended the war with a total of 20 victories, 19 at night.

In late 1940, in an effort to conceal the then highly secret airborne interception radar (AI), propaganda was put out that John Cunningham had been born with remarkable night vision, 'like a cat', and this was enhanced by eating a lot of carrots. It is not known if the Germans were fooled by any of this. What is known, is that John Cunningham was saddled with a nickname he loathed all his life, and many night-fighter aircrew were fed up, in more ways than one, with the amount of carrots they had to eat to support the myth.

Together with Wg Cdr Constable-Maxwell of No.125 Sqn who was based at Hurn, Gp Capt Cunningham briefed the crews for that night. The visiting squadrons were tasked to carry out patrols in relays south of the Cherbourg peninsular. The specific objective was preventing any interference by the Luftwaffe during the various troop landings. Other Mosquito squadrons of the 2nd TAF were given the role of destroying German surface transport during the night, once the invasion was under way. They were assisted in this by flare-dropping Mitchells.

In the early hours of the following day, massed formations of troop-carrying aircraft and glider formations, both British and American, passed over the station. The Mosquitos carried out their sorties over France where the Luftwaffe was noticeable by its absence. Everyone arrived back safely, and later that morning they were allowed to return to their home bases.

On the night before the dawn landings commenced, Bomber Command was tasked with the bombing in Normandy of German troop and gun positions,

ammunition and oil dumps and to continue attacking the road and rail communications to the German battle front. Lancaster KB726 VR-A of No.419 (Moose) Sqn RCAF based at Middleton St.George bombed the heavy coastal guns at Longues, five miles west of Arromaches. The bombs were dropped through a low layer of cloud from 1,500 feet at 0400 hours, just before the landings began. Because of bad weather on the return flight to its home base, this mainly Canadian crewed aircraft diverted to Colerne. The brand new Lancaster was being used operationally for the first time that night, having only 25 hours flying time. One of the crew was Plt Off Andrew C. Mynarski, the mid-upper gunner who, three operations later on 12th June, was to lose his life and be awarded a posthumous VC for his selfless bravery.

On 21st June Mosquito F.B.VI HX866, detached to Colerne from No.13 OTU Bicester and piloted by Fg Off J. Walker, suffered a port engine failure. It overshot and crashed through a stone wall at the end of the runway. The pilot was not injured but the aircraft was a write-off.

No.604 Sqn
No.604 Sqn arrived from Hurn on 13th July 1944 with Wg Cdr D.F. Hughes DFC** as CO and equipped with the Mosquito XIII. The squadron provided night defence over the Normandy invasion beaches. On 7th July one of the squadron pilots Flt Lt John Surman, whilst carrying out a defensive patrol over the Cherbourg peninsula, shot down a Me 110, killing Hauptmann Helmut Bergmann and his crew. The German pilot had been known for shooting down 7 Allied aircraft in 46 minutes in the early hours of 11th April 1944 and 6 more on the 4th May 1944.

At Colerne the squadron had some success four days after their arrival. Flt Lt G.A. Hayhurst and WO D. Gosling took off at 2210 hrs in HK527 and destroyed a Ju 88 near Coutances in Normandy, landing back at 0110 hrs. This was their first kill as a team. Mobile GCI convoys had been landed in Normandy by late June 1944, these gave radar cover and direction to Allied fighters, both day and night. On 24th July six aircraft and crews left for A15 Maupertus, in Normandy, with stores and support going over in 2 Dakota aircraft. This was the first

Allied night fighter unit to operate from French soil. No.604 Sqn moved from Colerne to Zeals the next day, but with No.149 Wing commanded by Wg Cdr R.C. Wilkinson OBE, DFM, the squadron returned to Colerne three days later together with No.488 (RNZAF) Sqn and No.410 (RCAF) Sqn both equipped with Mosquito XIII night fighters.

On the first day back at Colerne No.604 Sqn flew 4 aircraft on defensive patrols. Flt Lt J.P. Meadows and Fg Off R. McIlvenny took off at 2205 hrs in MM500 and destroyed a Ju 88 between Lisieux and Bernay landing back at 0300 hrs. The same number of aircraft were on patrol 2 days later with Sqn Ldr B. Maitland-Thompson and WO G.F. Pash taking off at 2200 hrs in MM621. They obtained their first kill when destroying a Ju 88 30 miles south of Cherbourg before returning at 0200 hrs. On 1st August, 3 aircraft were sent on patrol. Flt Lt F.C. Ellis and Fg Off P.C. Williams took off at 2325 hrs in MM496 and destroyed a Ju 88 SE of Caen, landing back at 0325 hrs. On 6th August 1944, No.604 Sqn moved to A8 Picauville in France. The squadron was airlifted from Colerne by Dakota aircraft from Blakehill Farm, and on arrival, the whole squadron was under the administrative control of No.142 Wing.

No.410 Sqn
No.410 Sqn had arrived at Colerne with their Mosquito XIIIs from Zeals on 28th July 1944, the CO was Wg Cdr G. A. Hiltz. The squadron had an early success when on 29th July Flt L Dexter and Lt Richardson, on a night patrol in HK430, destroyed a Ju 88. Taking off at 0001 hrs they were vectored onto the target which was taking violent evasive action. They closed in and identified the enemy aircraft before opening fire from dead astern with a short burst. The starboard engine blew up and pieces of the aircraft were seen to fall away, and the aircraft dived into the ground with a violent explosion. The following night nine aircraft were despatched at 0245 hrs on a beachhead patrol. During the course of this operation another Ju 88 was destroyed by Plt Off MacKenzie and Plt Off Bodard in MM501. Following the encounter they had to land in France owing to lack of fuel.

At 2200 hrs on 31st July 1944, Fg Off J. Maday and Fg Off J. R. Walsh took off in HK430 on a patrol and the navigator reported a contact, range 5 miles, 10 o'clock, 20 degrees. The pilot requested permission to investigate whilst closing to 6000', the enemy aircraft up to then had only been taking mild evasive action, it began issuing *Window* in very large quantities and this continued throughout the remainder of the interception. A visual was obtained at 2000', 12 o'clock, 10 degrees above. The pilot closed to 400' below and to starboard where the enemy aircraft was identified as a Ju 88, the navigator confirmed identification using Ross night glasses. The pilot dropped behind dead astern and 10 degrees below before opening fire with a short burst. Strikes were observed around the port engine together with flames which died down. The enemy dived steeply to starboard followed by the Mosquito which opened fire again with two short bursts allowing a two ring deflection. Strikes were observed on the starboard engine which exploded with large orange flames. The Ju 88 dived vertically into the ground and exploded.

Sqn Ldr Somerville and Fg Off Robinson were sent off on a patrol in ML477 at 2310 hrs on 1st August 1944. The GCI turned them onto a vector of 320 degrees then a constant was obtained on an aircraft weaving 30 degrees contrary to 320 degrees and at a range of 3 miles. Sqn Ldr Somerville closed to 2000' and obtained a visual. As the range dropped to 600', the target was identified as a Ju 188. The enemy saw the Mosquito at the same time and peeled off violently to starboard, but luckily for Sqn Ldr Somerville it peeled off directly into the chandelier flares and visual was maintained during the dive. The Ju 188 pulled up into a steep climbing turn. Somerville closed to 900' where he opened fire allowing a 1 ring deflection. The port wing of the German aircraft disintegrated outward of the engine nacelle. The aircraft flipped over into a steep half turn to starboard and dived into ground 10 miles NE of Tessy-sur-Vire in France.

'A' Flt of No.410 Sqn were effectively placed as non-operational on 1st August in order to convert to the Mosquito XXX with Mk.X AI with which the squadron was being re-equipped. Four aircraft remained in use for night patrols. Mk.X AI was the final, and most effective AI produced in World War 2, and remained in use for some years after the war.

Sqn Ldr Somerville and Fg Off Robinson took off at 2150 hrs on 2nd August and during their patrol destroyed a Do 217. They closed in to 1000' and identified the enemy aircraft by pulling off to starboard and getting a silhouette against the bright northern sky. The pilot pulled the Mosquito into line astern and opened fire at 800'. It appeared the enemy saw the Mosquito, and started a hard starboard turn as Sqn Ldr Somerville opened fire. On the first burst, half the enemy aircraft's port tail plane and port rudder flew off, and an oil tank must have been holed, as Somerville's windscreen was smothered in oil. The German then lost height rapidly. The combat developed into a dogfight as return fire was experienced from the dorsal and ventral guns. Whenever Sqn Ldr Somerville could see through the oil on the windscreen he would open fire. Just as he exhausted all his ammunition the enemy aircraft dived into the ground 6 miles NW of Pontorson. Throughout the engagement flak had been experienced, and on return to base at 2345 hrs it was discovered the aircraft had 13mm shell damage inboard of the port engine.

At 2320 hrs on the same date Flt Lt Plummer and Fg Off Evans took off on patrol in HK465 and obtained a contact at a range of two and a half miles, crossing from starboard to port. The target was taking mild evasive action but no *Window* was being released. Flt Lt Plumber closed to 3000' and closed further before obtaining visual confirmation of a Ju188 carrying a large bomb externally on either side, inboard of the engines. He then dropped back to 600', gave the enemy aircraft a short burst, and saw the port engine explode. The aircraft fell over to port, went down burning fiercely and hit the ground with a violent explosion. The crew completed their patrol and landed at base at 0130 hrs.

On the evening of the 3rd August Flt Lt Dinsdale and Fg Off Dunn took off at 2320 hrs in MM449 and obtained a contact below and head-on at a range of 5000' with a height of 7000'. They turned to starboard on a reciprocal and regained contact on the bogey at a range of one mile. They closed to 800' where the enemy aircraft was identified as a Me 110 carrying one external bomb outboard of each engine. The target was taking only mild evasive action. Flt Lt Dinsdale pulled

up the nose of his Mosquito and opened fire with a fairly long burst but no results were seen. He fell back to 400' dead astern and opened fire again. Strikes were observed on the starboard engine which caught fire. The Me 110 took violent evasive action and a short wild burst of fire came from the rear gunner. The enemy aircraft then peeled off to port followed by the Mosquito. Navigator Fg Off Dunn reported to his pilot that they were approaching the ground rapidly and Yardley control (GCI) called with the same detail. The Mosquito pulled out of the dive at 800'. The enemy aircraft was last seen going down with the starboard engine on fire. The Mosquito returned to Colerne at 0245 hrs and claimed a 'probable' with the possibility of upgrading to 'destroyed' following receipt of further information.

The sequence of success continued later that day for the same crew. They took off at 2150 hrs in MM449 and made contact at a range of 5000', slightly below and to port. They closed rapidly and overshot the target but a brief visual was obtained on the aircraft outlined in the moonlight. Fg Off Dinsdale made a more cautious approach with flaps down, airspeed reduced to 130mph. Great difficulty was experienced in identifying the target which was carrying a long range tank between the undercarriage. They followed the enemy aircraft for 25 miles on a vector of 140 degrees, finally identifying it as an Hs126. It appeared not to be displaying any national identification marks. They opened fire at 400' with two short bursts striking the fuselage. The Hs126 exploded and went down in flames south of Tours in France. The crew returned to base at 0240 hrs. On some Beachhead Patrols, the Mosquitos of No.410 Sqn were accompanied by those of No.488 Sqn.

A couple of days passed before No.410 Sqn added to their tally. On 7th August Fg Off Bayliss and WO Broderick took off at 2305 hrs in HK430. They were patrolling south of St. Malo when they were given a vector of 060 degrees and after several heading changes, a contact was obtained at a range of 2 miles. The Mosquito was at 4000' when the navigator advised the pilot to climb hard as the enemy aircraft was considerably higher. Although their starboard engine was missing badly they reached 5,500' where a visual was obtained at 1000' above and dead ahead. Flak opened up ahead of the enemy aircraft so he did a port turn and started to let down. The Mosquito closed to 900' and slightly below where a visual confirmed the aircraft to be a Ju 88. It was carrying 2 large bombs externally inboard of its engines. Fg Off Bayliss pulled up the nose of the Mosquito and opened fire at 700' with strikes seen on starboard engine that caught fire. The enemy aircraft struck the ground in the St. Hilaire-du-Harcouet area with a violent explosion.

On the same date Flt Lt Currie and Fg Off Rose of No.410 Sqn took off from Colerne at 2140 hrs in MM571. They were vectored on 190 degrees and almost immediately a contact was obtained through heavy *Window* at a range of 6000'. The pilot closed to 1,500' where a visual was obtained on an enemy aircraft still dropping *Window* but taking only mild evasive action. The Mosquito closed to 500' below where the aircraft was identified as a Ju 88. Flt Lt Currie closed to 200' dead astern and opened fire with 2 short bursts but no strikes were observed. He dropped back to 400' and below. Then as the enemy aircraft began a rate 1 turn to port, Flt Lt Currie closed again, pulled up the nose and fired a fairly long burst. Strikes were observed on the port engine, wing, wing route and fuselage. The enemy aircraft exploded in a mass of white flames and plunged into the ground SW of Rennes at 2315 hrs. The Mosquito was down at base at 0300 hrs.

On 9ᵗʰ August 'B' Flt began converting to the Mosquito XXX, also equipped with Mk.X AI.

The following day Wg Cdr Hiltz and Fg Off Walsh took off at 2140 hrs in HK465. During their patrol they obtained a contact at a range of 3½ miles. They closed to 4000' then the enemy aircraft started dropping *Window* but this ceased after they closed to 1000'. A visual was then obtained from a position dead astern and slightly above. Wg Cdr Hiltz closed to 400' with the enemy aircraft to starboard and slightly above. He was now able to identify it as a Ju 88 and this was confirmed by the navigator using Ross night glasses. The Mosquito dropped back to 1000' and closed again to 750/800' and opened fire from dead astern with no deflection. Strikes were seen on the starboard wing and an explosion followed which appeared to

be the bomb it was carrying. The Ju 88 hit the ground with a large explosion north of Points et Pas de la Porsea. The crew was given more trade by the GCI but with an oil-covered windscreen permission was obtained from Control to return to base. Owing to bad weather at Colerne they landed at Middle Wallop at 0050 hrs. The squadron received notification from Group later in the day, to reduce operational requirements to 3 aircraft for night patrols and 2 on standby.

On 14ᵗʰ August Sqn Ldr Somerville and Fg Off Robinson of No.410 Sqn took off on a patrol at 2130 hrs in MM477. They made contact with an enemy aircraft at a range of 1½ miles and started to close on it. The enemy aircraft commenced a climb and did a rate half turn to starboard. The Mosquito crew maintained contact on AI and closed on the target, which levelled off at approximately 10,500' after making a 360 degree turn. Although well below the German, a visual was obtained at about 1,800', this was lost but regained at 800'. Pulling up to 600', the target was identified as a Ju 88 and this was confirmed by Fg Off Robinson using the Ross night glasses. It was also seen to be carrying 2 bombs inboard of the engines. Sqn Ldr Somerville dropped back to 450', pulled up dead astern and opened fire. The fuselage of the Ju 88 burst with a violent explosion and disintegrated in the air. A fix was given by Control as 15 miles due west of Le Harve. The crew landed at Colerne at 0040 hrs. This was their 4ᵗʰ aircraft 'destroyed' in 2 weeks. During the same patrol Flt Lt Dexter and Sgt Richardson made contact with a bogey at 0030 hrs and gave chase but had to break off twice when it entered heavy flak areas. Contact was not regained.

By 15ᵗʰ August conversion of crews to Mk.X AI was proceeding well. All of 'A' Flt with the exception of one navigator and half of 'B' Flt. had been checked out. However a Form 'D' was received from No.85 Group HQ stating No.410 Sqn was to be placed as non-operational for the next 14 days and that No.125 Sqn was to take over. No.410 Sqn personnel were not impressed with the directive, bearing in mind the success they were achieving against the enemy and the fact that it was expected the whole squadron would be checked out on Mk.X AI within a few days. On this

basis an effort was made to have the order cancelled. The following day the squadron became non-operational and both Flts completed training on the *Circus* training aircraft of Wellingtons and Hurricanes. Crew training also continued on the Mosquito XXX. On 17ᵗʰ August a Form 'D' was received from Group stating the squadron was to carry out 3 patrols nightly using the new Mosquitos with the improved AI.

The 19ᵗʰ August saw No.410 Sqn back in business. Fg Off Fullerton and Fg Off Gallagher took off at 2215 hrs in Mosquito XXX MM744 and during their patrol destroyed 2 enemy aircraft. The crew received a message from Control that a raid was coming in from the east and they were given a vector of 350 degrees. The pilot saw flares from the raid and turned into them on 170 degrees. Through *Window* being dropped they picked up a contact well above them and at a range of 3 miles. They closed to 800' and identified a Do 217 that immediately carried out a violent peel-off to port. They followed it down from 7000' to 2000' where contact and visual were lost. The navigator searched and picked up more *Window*. The pilot turned into this and picked up a contact at 3 miles range and above at 4000'/5000'. The Mosquito closed to 700'/800', when a Ju 88 was identified and confirmed by the navigator with night glasses. They closed to 600' and gave a short burst. Strikes were seen on the port engine, with clouds of sparks passing back over the port wing of the Mosquito. The German turned to starboard and then to port and as he levelled off another burst of fire struck his starboard engine which caught fire. The enemy aircraft did a violent peel-off to starboard and was seen diving hard with starboard engine burning fiercely. The Ju 88 hit the ground and exploded. Fg Off Fullerton asked Control for further information and was told the raiders were returning so he turned onto a vector of 120 degrees, height 4000' and picked up a free-lance contact at range 3 miles and above. The target was taking fairly violent evasive action and throwing out *Window*. The pilot closed to 400' and identified a Ju 88 this was confirmed by the navigator. The violent evasive action initially prevented Fg Off Fullerton opening fire so he waited until it steadied down. He then gave a short burst from 500' dead astern. No strikes were observed as he was blinded by his ring sight and gun flashes. The enemy aircraft peeled off to port followed by the Mosquito diving after it, the enemy aircraft was seen to hit the ground and explode. The starboard engine of MM744 then failed and the aircraft was forced to land at B5 in France. The crew returned to Colerne on the evening of 20th August where Fg Off Gallagher confirmed the new AI was an improvement on the previous Mk.VIII in that contacts were not lost so easily in *Window*.

A Form 'D' from Group on 25th August notified No.410 Sqn that patrols were to be increased to 6 aircraft. As the month drew to a close, patrols had become uneventful and the squadron was keen to increase their 'bag' of 47 aircraft destroyed to 50. August had brought them 11 'destroyed' and 1 'probable'.

The squadron officers moved from the camp into Ashwicke Hall on 1st September 1944, where they were to stay until the squadron moved overseas to Vannes. On the same day Flt Lt MacTavish and Fg Off Grant destroyed a Fw 190. This was 'Macs' first kill and the first Fw 190 bagged by the squadron. They took off in MM743 at 2100 hrs and patrolled inland south of Le Havre. They were taken out to sea off the beachhead where the GCI informed them of trade in that area. The pilot observed a bomb flash amongst shipping off the coast west of Le Havre and turned into it, picking up a contact at 2322 hrs at range 4 miles, height 7000'. The enemy aircraft was carrying out mild evasive action and gradually losing height. 'Mac' closed and obtained a visual at a range of 2,200' over Le Havre, identifying it as an Fw 190 and confirmed by the navigator. 'Mac' dropped back to 800' and fired a short burst, the enemy aircraft exploded and was timed at 2335 hrs, violent evasive action was needed to avoid flaming debris. The crew saw the aircraft hit the ground, and this was confirmed by an aircraft of No.488 Sqn whose crew saw it going down in flames. 'Mac' landed back at Colerne at 0045 hrs. This same crew on a patrol five days later reported that they spent the entire patrol evading 'Black Widows' instead of chasing 'Jerries'. 'Mac' felt the 'Yanks' were very keen but he wished they were keener on their aircraft recognition. On 9th September No.410 Sqn moved out to Hunsdon.

No.488 Sqn

After arriving from Zeals on 28th July 1944 with their Mosquito XIIIs, together with No.410 Sqn, No.488 Sqn was soon in action. Flt Lt P. Hall RNZAF and Fg Off R. Marriott took off at 2200 hrs in MM513 and under GCI control, intercepted and destroyed a Ju 88 that crashed 10 miles NW of Vire in Normandy. They then picked up a free-lance contact that they identified as a Ju 88. 3 short bursts were delivered and they saw it explode on the ground. Both of the enemy aircraft were despatched within 7 minutes of one another. The crew landed back at Colerne at 0035 hrs.

Also on the first evening Fg Off Doug Robinson RNZAF and Flt Lt W. Clarke DFM took off at 2325 hrs in MM439 and whilst on patrol under GCI control, identified a Ju 88. They were engaged by the enemy aircraft but without result. On closing they gave it 2 short bursts and it exploded in front of them. The aircraft hit the ground 10/15 miles north of Mayenne. The Mosquito landed back at Colerne at 0250 hrs. Flt Lt Clarke was in fact visiting his former squadron at this time. Fg Off Robinson had previously been his pilot and he flew with him again on this patrol because Robinson's regular navigator was on sick leave. Later in the day Flt Lt Clarke rejoined his unit at North Weald.

A crew was lost on the night of 29th/30th July. Sqn Ldr Edward N. Bunting DFC* and Fg Off Edward Spedding took off in MM476 at 2330 hrs. Engaged in chasing a Fw 190 at a low altitude over France, they ran into flak. Sqn Ldr Bunting reported he had been hit and 15 seconds later at 0045 hrs an explosion was seen on the ground. Both men are buried in a joint grave at St. Remy Churchyard, Calvados in France.

No.488 Sqn achieved its greatest success on the night of Sunday 30th July 1944. A glorious page in its history was written by the remarkable performance of Flt Lt George Jameson DFC, RNZAF and Fg Off A.N. Crookes DFC when carrying out a patrol between Caen and Lisieux. They took off at 0255 hrs in MM466 and flying under GCI control were given an enemy aircraft contact, this was intercepted and identified as a Ju 88 and shot down 5/6 miles south of Caen. Immediately another contact was

obtained and the crew gave chase, and another German came out of the clouds in front of them, they attacked it and last saw it disappear into clouds well alight. Unable to claim it as 'destroyed', they were off after two more contacts. These turned out to be friendly but another contact was obtained soon after. This they identified as a Ju 88 and shot it down 5 miles south of Lisieux. They then headed for some flak bursts where they intercepted and identified a Do 217, after delivering a short burst they saw it crash in flames. In despatching these 4 enemy aircraft only ninety rounds were used from each cannon and the four attacks occurred in a twenty-minute spell. Arrival back at Colerne was at 0640 hrs.

August 1944 was a very busy month, with more mobile GCIs now well established in Normandy. On 2nd August Flt Lt P. Hall RNZAF and Fg Off R. Marriott took off on a patrol at 0001 hrs in Mosquito MM498. Under GCI Yardley call sign they intercepted and destroyed a Ju88 which crashed 10 miles east of St. Lo. The Mosquito landed at base at 0230 hrs.

Flt Lt A. Brown RNZAF and WO T. Taylor took off at 2205 hrs on 3rd August in Mosquito HK532. Carrying out a beachhead patrol they engaged a Do 217 which returned fire but crashed in flames after a second attack, on the shore 4 miles east of Avranches in Normandy. The Mosquito landed at Colerne at 0150 hrs. On the same patrol WO T. Mackay RNZAF and Flt Sgt A Thompson RNZAF took off at 2335 hrs in MM459 and were free-lancing when they contacted a Ju188 which they shot down 5/10 miles south of Avranches. They landed back at 0140 hrs. This was the first success for each crew. Another crew shooting down their first German aircraft were WO G. Patrick RNZAF and Flt Sgt J. Concannon, both almost tour expired. They took off for a patrol at 2155 hrs on 4th August in HK532. Although subjected to heavy flak during the whole of the chase, they shot down a Ju 88 2 miles west of Avranches. The combat was under the control of GCI and arrival back at base was at 0135 hrs. On the same patrol Flt Lt Jameson DFC and Fg Off Crookes DFC in MM466 despatched a Ju 88 which crashed 8 miles north of a position between St. Lo and Bayeux.

Wg Cdr R. Haine DFC and Flt Lt A.

Bowman took off at 2325 hrs on 5th August in HK504 and shot down a Ju 88 8 miles ENE of Vire. Fg Off A. Shaw RNZAF and Flt Sgt L. Wyman took off at 2330 hrs in MM439. During the patrol and under GCI control, they intercepted and destroyed a Ju 88 which crashed 10 miles NE of St. Lo. They then engaged another Ju 88 which they damaged but had to break off when their AI failed. They landed at Colerne at 0220 hrs. WO J. Moore, taking off on the same patrol force, landed at Hullavington and after inspection he took off again. 10 minutes later he crash landed after engine failure at Castle Combe and without injury.

The same night Flt Lt P. Hall DFC and Fg Off R. Marriott DFC took off at 0130 hrs in MM513 and destroyed a Do217 NW of Rennes before returning at 0425 hrs. Flt Sgt T. Maclean and Fg Off B. Grant took off at 0315 hrs in MM502 and shot down a Do 217 10 miles west of Angers in the Anjou region of France. They returned at 0605 hrs. The following evening Flt Lt Jameson DFC and Fg Off Crookes took off at 2150 hrs in MM466 and added to their score by destroying a Ju 88 east of Avranches before returning at 0135 hrs. Flt Lt A. Browne and WO T. Taylor took off at 0130 hrs in HK420. During the course of their patrol they claimed 3 victims. Two of the aircraft were unidentified but flew into the ground SW of Rennes while trying to evade the Mosquito. The third aircraft was a Ju 88 shot down SW of Avranches. Return to Colerne was at 0435 hrs.

Flt Lt J. Hall DFC and Flt Lt J. Caine DFC took off at 0310 hrs on 15th August in MM466. They shot down a Ju88 20/30 miles south of Caen and returned at 0650 hrs. This had been the squadron's 50th victim. The following evening Plt Off O. McCabe RNZAF and WO F. Newman took off at 2130 hrs in HK377. While free-lancing they contacted a Ju88 which they shot down 6 miles south of Caen. They were back at Colerne at 2335 hrs.
Fg Off H. Jeffs RNZAF and Fg Off A. Crookes DFC* took off at 2155 hrs on 19th August in MM622. They intercepted and destroyed a Do 217 which crashed around 10/15 miles south of Rouen. The Mosquito landed back at Colerne at 0045 hrs. Later the same day Fg Off Doug Robinson RNZAF and WO Nat Addison DFC, DFM took off at 2120 hrs in MM439. They were patrolling south of Caen in

France and were vectored by GCI Radox call sign, to a 'bogey' east of the town. The nav/radar operator gained a contact on his AI Mk.VI radar set and directed the pilot until he was able to make visual contact at 300 yds. The aircraft was identified by the pilot as a Ju 188 and it was using 'window' in an attempt to jam the fighter's radar. Fg Off Robinson opened fire with bursts from his 20mm cannon, setting fire to the port engine of the enemy bomber. It was then seen to bank before diving into the ground and exploding 15 miles east of Caen. The Colerne crew returned to base at 0115 hrs.

During a patrol on 26th August, the Mosquito of Wg Cdr R.C. Haine DFC and Flt Lt A.P. Bowman, was attacked by an unidentified fighter, believed to be a 'Black Widow' of 422 Fighter Sqn USAAF. The aircraft received some damage to the fuselage but out manoeuvred the attacker and returned to base.

August had been a successful month for No.488 Sqn with 17 enemy aircraft destroyed and 4 damaged.

September 1944 opened with 7 operational sorties flown during the night. The squadron CO Wg Cdr R.C. Haine and Flt Lt A.P. Bowman took off at 2055 hrs in MM566 and were vectored onto an enemy aircraft which they successfully intercepted and identified as a Ju188. The enemy aircraft was followed in a turn; the Wg Cdr firing short bursts with his gun-sight partly u/s. Strikes were observed resulting in a small explosion. The Mosquito was pulled up to avoid debris but turning quickly contact was regained. Opening fire from astern more strikes were apparent and the enemy aircraft was seen to dive vertically before hitting the sea 10/15 miles west of Le Havre. The crew landed back at Colerne at 0035 hrs.

Sorties continued and on the 11th September the squadron began converting to the Mosquito NF XXX with the new improved AI Mk.X.

No.149 Wing with Wg Cdr N. Hayes DFC as CO moved to Vannes airfield in France on 3rd September. No.410 and No.488 Sqns with their respective Service Echelons remained at Colerne until moving to France on 9th September and 9th October respectively. Both left Colerne for Hunsden together with radar specialist

personnel, where they prepared for deployment to the continent as part of the 2nd Tactical Air Force. No.488 Sqn completed re-equipping with the Mosquito NF XXX in October 1944.

No.406 (Lynx) Sqn RCAF

No.406 Sqn moved in on Sunday 17th September 1944 with Wg Cdr D. J. Williams DSO, DFC as CO, arriving from Winkleigh in Devon equipped with 19 Mosquito XXXs and accompanied by No.6406 Servicing Echelon. The squadron's Oxford brought passengers and the main body of men arrived by rail. The officers were quartered in Ashwicke Hall together with officers of No.488 Sqn, which made for very cramped conditions. Things were no better on the base where the barracks were likewise overcrowded, with 5000 personnel resident at that time.

The following day the squadron was welcomed by the Station Commander, Gp Capt M.B. Hamilton, before commencing its duties. Its main role was to carry out offensive patrols in the Lorient area against supply carrying enemy aircraft. In between operations the squadron carried out familiarisation and cross-country flying, N.F.Ts, air to ground and air to air firing, AI practice and GCI exercises at night. On Tuesday 10th October the squadron suffered its first fatality for a year when Flt Sgt R.S. Walker RCAF and Plt Off Donald K.I. MacNicol RCAF crashed at Lymington when testing an MU Mosquito. An eye witness saw an engine on fire before the aircraft blew up in the air. The pilot, Flt Sgt Walker, reported being blown out of the aircraft before deploying his parachute. He was admitted to hospital with a dislocated shoulder and severe shock. The body of the navigator was found near the aircraft with his open parachute close by. He was buried in Brookwood Military Cemetery.

The following month the fortune of the squadron improved with the arrival of 50,000 cigarettes donated by their adopted City of Saskatoon. A few days later, on 21st November, Wg Cdr Bennock DFC* arrived to replace Wg Cdr Williams as squadron CO. The squadron moved to Manston on 27th November 1944. During the short stay at Colerne some of the squadron had been allowed to vote in the Saskatchewan General Election.

On 18th September 1944, Wellington X LP625 of No.12 OTU Chipping

Warden, experienced an engine fire whilst carrying out a night cross-country, so Flt Sgt Crabtree RAAF (pilot) called Colerne's Flying Control for an emergency 'Mayday' homing on '*Darky*' frequency. On landing at 2139hrs the aircraft swung off the runway to port and crossed the peri-track. The pilot tried to take off again but unsuccessfully. The Wellington struck a No.409 Sqn Beaufighter VIF MM882 before crashing onto a stationary No.488 Sqn Mosquito NF30 MT456, destroying both aircraft, and then crashing into the 'B' Flt dispersal hut occupied by LAC H. Pinnock and LAC J.C. Dixon of No.6488 Echelon. Both suffered serious injuries and were admitted to hospital. Two of the Wellington crew died of their injuries, Sgt Leslie H. Kilby (nav) and Flt Sgt Robert D. Jones RAAF (WOP). The funeral arrangements were carried out by Colerne with Flt Sgt Jones being buried at Haycombe Cemetery in Bath. Early in November 1944 this cemetery, where so many Air Force personnel were laid to rest, was visited by ACM Sir Arthur M. Longmore GCB, DSO, who was the Air Ministry representative on the Imperial War Graves Commission.

30 USAAF B-17s and various other aircraft were diverted to Colerne on 16th November 1944, it being almost the only airfield open because of bad weather. The mess rooms that evening had standing room only.

The 'Q' Sites at Monkton Farleigh and West Littleton were closed down on 12th October 1944, there being no purpose in maintaining decoy sites with the Luftwaffe retreating from France. 29 USAAF B-17s diverted to Colerne when returning from a raid in support of the American 1st and 9th Armies in an area between Aachen and the Rhine. They were part of a force of 1,239 US heavy bombers and 1,188 RAF bombers attacking targets at Duren, Julich and Heinsburg. Colerne provided accommodation and rations for 116 aircrew in the Officers' Mess and 135 in the Sergeants' Mess. The B-17s flew out two days later except for two damaged by flak and one damaged in a taxiing accident.

On 25th November 1944 a No.22 OTU Wellington X LP579, took-off at 2220hrs from Stratford-upon-Avon for a night cross-country. While cruising at 19,000', Fg Off E.G. Paquette RCAF (pilot) noticed that his engine revolutions were fluctuating and this was followed by sustained rough running. During an attempt to land at Colerne at 2345hrs, the aircraft crashed through the wall on the edge of the airfield. No injuries to the crew were reported.

No.264 Sqn

On 30th November No.264 Sqn moved in with Wg Cdr E.S. Smith AFC as CO. It arrived from Predannack equipped with 6 Mosquito XIIIs and 1 Oxford, accompanied by No.6264 Servicing Echelon. The squadron carried out day and night practice interception and shipping reconnaissance over the western approaches. The need for fighter aircraft in the West Country had by then diminished, so the stay was short lived and the squadron left for Odiham on 21st December 1944.

The previous day another mass visit had taken place, with the arrival of 46 USAAF B-17s diverted owing to bad weather conditions at their bases.

During December some 2,300 U.S. Army personnel of IX Troop Carrier Command moved into tented accommodation at Colerne using the aircraft dispersal sites by Northwood Farm. They were accompanied by 97 USAAF C-47s under the command of Lt Col Pate, all with the intention of staging an 'exercise' of U.S. Airborne Forces. The Air Force personnel were accommodated at Ashwicke Hall, and Barrack Block 'G' was handed over for officer's accommodation and administrative offices. The weather was so bad each day that the 'exercise' (if in fact that is what it was, it might well have been a reinforcement for Bastogne, where the enemy had made a sharp advance) had to be cancelled and most of the Americans returned to A.41 Druex in France. The final contingent did not leave until almost the end of January 1945 at which time a Marching-Out Inspection took place.

The station had a change of Stn Cdr on 23rd December 1944 when Gp Capt E. M. Donaldson DSO, AFC took over from Gp Capt Hamilton.

No.616 (South Yorkshire) Sqn

The final year of war began with the arrival on 17th January 1945, of the first jet aircraft to use Colerne. No.616 Sqn with No.6616 Servicing Echelon moved in from Manston equipped with Meteor IIIs and under the command of Wg Cdr Andrew McDowall DSO, DFM*. He was a former Battle of Britain pilot with No.602 Sqn. No.616 Sqn was the first jet fighter squadron in the RAF when it equipped with the Meteor I in July 1944. It was also the only operational RAF jet squadron of the war. Three days after arriving at Colerne the squadron commenced training and on 28th February 1945 moved out to Andrews Field in Essex, in preparation for operations over Europe.

No.29 Sqn

On 22nd February 1945 No.29 Sqn arrived from Hunsdon with Wg Cdr J.W. Allen DSO, DFC as CO. It arrived with 12 Mosquito Mk.XIIIs but to re-equip with the Mk.XXX. No.6219 Servicing Echelon accompanied the move. Having worked-up on type, the squadron moved out to Manston over the two-day period of 11th/12th April 1945. No.29 Sqn was the last night fighter squadron to leave Colerne and the departure coincided with the closure of the Operations Room. The station held its first Air Display at this time and it included a demonstration given by a helicopter.

Colerne was selected as the RAF's first jet conversion unit and on 8th March No.1335 (Meteor) Conversion Unit was formed there in No.10 Group, tasked with converting pilots to jet fighters. The CO was Wg Cdr Allan S. Dredge DSO, DFC, and the Unit was initially equipped with 8 Meteor Is, 6 Meteor IIIs, 4 Oxfords and 4 Martinets.

No.10 Fighter Command Servicing Unit formed at Colerne on 27th March.

No.504 Auxilary Air Force Sqn

On 28th March 1945, No.504 Auxiliary Air Force Sqn with Wg Cdr M. Kellett as CO together with No.6504 Servicing Echelon moved in from Hawkinge. It arrived for conversion during April, from the Spitfire IX to the Meteor III and under the training of the C.U., but it was too late in the war for them to see action.

Through May and June the squadron took part in a number of practice *Ramrods* with their Meteors. The squadron lost Meteor 3, EE288 on Friday 8th June 1945 when it spun into the ground at West Kington when carrying out aerobatics. It claimed the life of its pilot, Flt Sgt Raymond E. G. Chase RAFVR.

On 1st July 1945 No.504 Sqn together with its Service Echelon No.6504, left Colerne for Lubeck on detachment. It returned on 10th August, was disbanded and reformed as No.245 Sqn. The Servicing Echelon then became No.6245. With the change of squadron number, came a change of CO when Sqn Ldr T. D. Williams took over.

In May Colerne transferred to No.11 Group. There was no operational flying from the station during the month. With Victory in Europe declared on 8th May, it was a signal for the station to celebrate. An all ranks dance with free beer and refreshments was held in the station dance hall, and the officers held a dance in their mess on another day. The CO reported his pleasure, that throughout the few days of celebrations, the behaviour of station personnel was of an exemplary manner worthy of the highest traditions of the RAF.

No.74 Sqn

No.74 Sqn moved in from the continent on 11th May to convert to the Meteor F3 and for training by the CU. Sqn Ldr A.J. Reeves was CO and the squadron arrived with 19 Spitfire XVIEs. Together with No.504 Sqn it formed the first jet fighter Wing in the RAF. They had a new CO with the appointment on 28th May of Wg Cdr H.C. Kennard DFC.

On 24th July the squadron lost Meteor EE308 with Flt Sgt James T. Rees killed. During a low run over the airfield when rehearsing for a press demonstration, it struck trees on the airfield's southern boundary and crashed at 1520 hrs in Black Cross Wood, half a mile south of the airfield (173/ST805702).

Victory Sunday on 13th May was marked by RAF Colerne providing two contingents attending church parades with march-pasts in the village of Colerne and the city of Bath.

Wg Cdr A.S. Dredge, Wing Commander Flying and CO of No.1335 CU was killed at Farnborough on Friday 18th May while carrying out a low aerobatics demonstration in a Meteor. It struck the ground at over 300 mph and the cause was determined as an error of judgement on his part. The replacement CO of the Unit was Wg Cdr Harold A. C. Bird-Wilson DSO, DFC*, who had previously served in Wiltshire as CO of No.66 Sqn at Zeals.

The Meteor Conversion Unit which had transferred from No.10 to No.11 Group on 2nd May, left Colerne for Molesworth on 27th July 1945 where it was re-designated as No.226 Operational Conversion Unit.

Post War Years

The Second World war finally ended at midnight on 14th August 1945 with the announcement of the Japanese surrender and so the following day an all ranks Victory Dance was held in the Dance Hall at the Station.

Colerne soon started to receive some of the many surplus aircraft that were no longer required by the RAF. Lancaster bombers in particular arrived in vast numbers, to be lined up nose to tail on the area which became the sports pitches at the north end of Runway No.1. Their undercarriages were collapsed and they were cut up for scrap where they fell.

Another Meteor and pilot were lost on 23rd August 1945, on this occasion from No.245 Sqn, with Sqn Ldr Brees losing his life when his aircraft crashed into the sea off Weston-Super-Mare. The Wing provided eight aircraft, four from each of the two squadrons, led by Sqn Ldr Williams, to escort S.S. Queen Elizabeth when she sailed for America on 26th August carrying U.S. troops. In September they also took part in a flypast over London to commemorate the Battle of Britain. For the rest of the year, the operational activity of No.245 and No.74 Sqns as a Wing, concentrated on practice *Ramrods* and *Balbos*.

On the last day of August 1945, Colerne welcomed the celebrated Battle of Britain Ace, Gp Capt Douglas Bader who arrived from North Weald in Spitfire RK917. He paid a second visit in October, on this occasion flying a Proctor.

Colerne had a change of Stn Cdr on 3rd September with the appointment of Gp Capt R.W. Stewart OBE, AFC. He only stayed for five months and was succeeded by Gp Capt Sampson OBE on 5th February 1946.

No.39 MU no longer had need for the SLGs at Starveall Farm and Slade Farm and these were vacated respectively on 29th September and during December 1945. Some of the

aircraft in storage at these sites were flown back to Colerne for disposal or in most cases, for breaking up. Among these was Spitfire P7350 flown out of Slade Farm by ferry pilot Sgt Jeff Malton on 1st November. This was one aircraft which was saved for preservation. Jeff reports that during his time as a test and ferry pilot during the war, all flights were undertaken without radio assistance.

No.245 Sqn lost another pilot and Meteor when on 8th October 1945 Fg Off Lamont was killed when his F.3 EE302 spun in from 10,000' near Frome, during formation flying practice.

On Wednesday 2nd January 1946, Flt Lt Leonard Miller RNZAF of No.74 Sqn was killed in a Meteor F.3 EE335, which dived into the ground after a low run and upward roll at Warmwell. Flt Lt Miller had flown Whitley Vs with No.102 Sqn, survived a crash near Eindhoven on 19th May 1940 and was a PoW for the rest of the war. Following repatriation he joined No.74 Sqn at Colerne on 8th August 1945. He was buried at Haycombe Cemetery, Bath. No.74 Sqn also lost an aircraft and pilot killed on 8th March 1946. The pilot had been briefed for practice dummy attacks over Salisbury Plain in Meteor F.3 EE344. He was carrying out an attack on a goods train travelling on the GWR Bristol to Swindon line. The train driver, who stopped his train, witnessed the aircraft in trouble before it crashed in Sutton Lane, Langley Burrell. Debris was spread over a large area including adjoining farmland, Chippenham NFS dealing with parts of the wreckage that were on fire. The pilot was Fg Off Bamjee of the Royal Indian Air Force. A scarf he wore when flying was found in a hedge some distance from the main wreckage.

A week earlier on 1st March, Lancaster B.3 RF326 of No.218 MU, piloted by WO Hatton, was leaving Colerne on a flight to St. Eval. The undercarriage was retracted by the pilot, to abort the take-off, as the ASI was not working. The aircraft slid off the end of runway 07/25 and crossed the Fosse Way into the field on the other side. Fortunately there were no injuries to passers-by or to the crew. The Lancaster was written off. Another No.245 Sqn Meteor F.3 EE293 crashed on 23rd April 1946 when landing in a cross-wind on one engine, it stalled and spun in killing the pilot Fg Off Crawshaw. A Mr Lithgow in Spiteful RB518, probably the first seen at Colerne, made an emergency landing there one day in May 1946 with engine trouble during a test flight from the factory at Highpost.

The accident rate continued when on 10th July Flt Lt Davies of No.74 Sqn was killed when his Meteor F.3 EE334 crashed 4/5 miles north east of the airfield at Burton after colliding with EE309 in formation. Before the crash, Davies (Bagpipe Red 2) had requested an emergency landing but control was lost and it dived into the ground. Nine days later Flt Lt Freeman DFC also of No.74 Sqn in Meteor F.3 EE346 (Bagpipe 38), was forced to make a single engine approach. The starboard engine had failed, as had the flaps and nose wheel, which would not lock down. It would then not retract, and on going around again, the aircraft would not maintain height. A forced landing was made across the A350 Chippenham to Lacock road at Showell Farm 1½ miles SSW of Chippenham. The pilot was uninjured but the Meteor was a write-off.

No.74 Sqn moved out to Horsham St Faith on 14th August, followed two days later by No.245 Sqn. This left Nos.39 and 218 MUs operating at Colerne the latter having been engaged in fitting out Yorks and Lancastrians with radio and radar aids, until the last one was delivered out on 3rd July. The main occupation of the Station during September and October seems to have been a heavy involvement in sporting activities. Soccer, rugby and hockey matches were played against local clubs and other service establishments.

At the end of October Colerne ceased to be in Fighter Command and on 1st November 1946 came under Maintenance Command. The new Stn Cdr appointed at that stage was Wg Cdr W.G. Wooliams. The next five years were a quiet period for Colerne in comparison with the previous five, the station being primarily used for ferrying and test flying. However, No.62 Group Communication Flight moved in from Middle Wallop on 7th January 1948, No.92 Gliding School arrived on 20th February and No.218 MU was disbanded on 29th February 1948. The Unit was replaced by No.49 Maintenance Unit moving in from Lasham on 4th May 1948 and occupying the three 'L' type hangars on Site No.4.

Its official title was a Repair and Salvage Unit, and initially its area of operations covered all of Southern England and France. No.49 MU would receive notification of any seriously damaged or crashed aircraft in these areas. An officer would be dispatched to determine the necessary action to be taken. A No.49 MU repair party would then be mobilised to carry out repairs which could take anything up to eight weeks to complete. Anything beyond repair was returned to Site No.4 which soon became a mass of bent and broken aircraft parts awaiting disposal as scrap, a veritable aircraft 'graveyard'. Meanwhile No.39 MU were servicing Meteors and Vampires and preparing Hurricanes for the Turkish Air Force.

Colerne trained Army pilots for the AOP Sqns, these were Artillery Observation Posts, capable of obtaining a better view of the 'front line' than an observer on the ground, their functions were to report information, to observe and direct fire and to take photographs. No.1956 Reserve AOP Flight formed on 1st February 1949 as Type 'A' within No.622 Aux (AOP) Sqn, RAuxAF in No.62 Group. It was affiliated to the Divisional Artillery, 43rd (Wessex) Infantry Division (TA) and was equipped with two Auster 5s and three Auster 6s. These two-seater aircraft were supplied and maintained by the RAF but flown by Royal Artillery pilots. VF 543 was one of the aircraft. No.1963 Reserve AOP Flight was formed at the same time but affiliated to No.91 AGRA (TA) and equipped with two Auster 4/5s and three Auster 6s.

On 15th September 1949, the Headquarters of No.27 Group, Technical Training Command, moved to Colerne from Debden where it had been for the previous two years. It controlled four large schools of technical training, specialising in radio and radar instruction. Two of these Yatesbury and Compton Bassett were in Wiltshire.

A series of Stn Cdrs were appointed during this time: -

Wg Cdr H. H. Hillier CBE November 1946
"   "   G.L. Lister January 1948
"   "   W.W. Loxton AFC May 1948
"   "   J.M. Tome October 1950
"   "   M. McClelland OBE July 1951

No.62 Group Communications Flt had Anson C.12, PH620 written off on 15th March 1950 when it crashed on a single engine overshoot. On 31st August the Flt had a further write-off when Tiger Moth T.2, N9160 swung on take-off and hit a grass bank.

No.81 Group Communication Flt re-formed at Colerne on 1st January 1952. On Sunday 20th April 1952, Colerne provided an RAF Guard of Honour at a ceremony held at Haycombe Cemetery in Bath, where a Cross of Sacrifice was unveiled by the High Commissioner for Australia, Gp Capt the Honourable Sir Thomas White. The simple white cross was erected by the Imperial War Graves Commission and dedicated by the Bishop of Bath and Wells. It serves as a memorial to the 200 members of the RAF and the Air Forces of Canada, Australia, South Africa and New Zealand together with 100 members of the British Army whose graves are at Haycombe. With the official dignitaries, around 5000 people attended the ceremony many of them were relatives from home and abroad. LAC Bob Burgess, a National Serviceman at Colerne from 1951-53, recalls with pride his part in the ceremony as a member of the RAF Guard of Honour and its inspection by the High Commissioner and the Mayor of Bath, Cllr. R.W. Pearson.

Colerne was transferred from No.41 Group Maintenance Command back to Fighter Command in No.81 Group on 15th May 1952 with Gp Capt C.M. Wight-Boycott DSO appointed as CO. This was a period that will be remembered for increasing tension in the 'Cold War'. The CO must have had little doubt of the seriousness of the situation, when in the programme notes for a Colerne Battle of Britain Open Day he extended

"... a welcome to all and sundry, who would like to see for themselves the life and work of the Service which will in the next war, as in the last, be your principle defence against attack from the air"!

No.39 and No.49 MUs, the AOP Flts and HQ No.27 Group all remained as lodger units. A new No.39 MU M.T. Section was formed during July 1952, occupying the M.T. Bays on the HQ Maintenance Site.

The Airborne Interception School moved in from Leeming on 12th June

Personnel from the Vickers Service Dept, Boas Hill, Oxfordshire, at Colerne in the summer of 1946. Lancasters are seen behind the port wing of the Spitfire.   Photo: Norman Parker

1952 and was re-designated No.238 Operational Conversion Unit (OCU) on 15th June, with the first course commencing the following day. The Unit was allocated to Site No.1 for its Headquarters. It used the 3 'L' type hangars on the site for aircraft storage and the 'K' Type hangar near the ATC building. Because of a shortage of barrack blocks and offices the students were accommodated in aluminium tents, eighteen of which were situated behind the Officers' Mess. Aircraft allocation was 3 Buckmasters and 17 AI equipped Bristol Brigands, and used Balliols from No.288 Sqn Middle Wallop as targets. By July the twin-engined, three-seater Brigands on strength had increased to 24. The type was originally developed as a long-range attack aircraft, intended mainly as a torpedo carrier or minelayer. The unit was responsible for basic training of Fighter Command night and all-weather radar operators/navigators, in locating and tracking hostile aircraft. There were not only RAF personnel under training, but students from all over the world, many from the NATO Alliance. They would arrive at the OCU from Air Navigation Schools as substantive or Acting Pilot Officers. The latter were confirmed in their commissions and awarded their Flying Badges after successfully completing the course.

The RAF Colerne Communication Sqn formed on 1st August 1952 with the disbanding of No.62 Group Comms Flt. It flew Air Officers Commanding and Staff Officers of Nos.27, 62 and 81 Groups, Southern Sector and Nos.2 and 3 Radio Schools at nearby Yatesbury

and Compton Bassett, to venues for important staff visits. It was also used to maintain flying currency for these officers and provided flying for Apprentices and Boy Entrants, and for cadets of the ATC and Combined Cadet Force. In a war situation the role of the Squadron would have been in maintaining communications between bases and front-line squadrons.

In peacetime it tended to be a 'maid of all work', ready at all hours and in all weathers to carry out a wide variety of tasks. The Flt used Site No.2 and was equipped with the Meteor, Vampire, Anson, Oxford, Proctor, Tiger Moth, Chipmunk, Varsity and Spitfire VB. John Dalley who served with the Sqn from 1953-60 recalls the squadron pilots being mostly ex WW2 veterans, British, Polish and Czechoslovakian. They were both officers and NCOs, and could be 'twitchy' at times, but great to be with as long as you didn't mention fire or make loud noises. This could be difficult as the Ansons were prone to intake fires on start-up and the Meteors to jet pipe fires.

A fatal accident occurred on Monday 23rd February 1953 at 1510 hrs when a Brigand T.4 RH760 of No.238 OCU, crashed two miles south of the airfield, at Cheney Court Farm, Ditteridge. On approaching to make a single engine landing, the under-carriage failed to lower completely. The pilot over-shot and on the second approach the aircraft lost height and speed, and stalled on turning. It was seen to flip over on to its back before nose diving into a ploughed field and bursting into flames. Fire appliances from RAF

Colerne, Bath, Corsham and Chippenham attended the scene. The four bodies that were taken from the wreckage after the fire had been controlled, were those of Flt Lt Archibald A.J. Symington (pilot), Flt Sgt Walter E. Cox (nav), and two student navigators, Plt Offs William B. Parker and David Wilmot. All died of multiple injuries. The navigator and the two students were buried in St. John the Baptist Church, Colerne. Flt Lt Symington was a popular figure with all personnel at Colerne where he captained the station rugby team.

Harry Billet a civilian charge hand with the MT Section from 1952-76 recalls the 07/25 main runway being resurfaced during October 1963. The runway already had an extension to the eastern end before Harry started work at the airfield.

It is probable that these notes were written with a National Service man in mind: -

KINDLY ADVICE TO A VERY YOUNG AIRMAN COMPILED BY MEMBERS OF RAF COLERNE TO ASSIST HIM IN HIS FIRST DAYS ON THE STATION.

If there is no one at the guardroom when you arrive, ring the bell outside.

If you see a service car with a flag flying, it means you may thumb a lift.

Be tactful towards any airman wearing their stripes upside down: they are in mourning for a close relative.

If you have any problems of a delicate or intimate nature, you should consult the Station Welfare Officer. Just go to SHQ and ask for the SWO.

Never lift a parachute except by the silver handle provided.

If you have a pet you would like to keep on the station, do not hesitate to place it in the accommodation provided at the back of the Fire Section.

Corporals with white caps and belts are members of the Station Band: if you call out to them "Go and blow your bugle" as you pass by, they will enjoy the joke.

The first unit at Colerne when it opened, No.39 MU, was disbanded on 1st October 1953. During the early 1950s the MU had in storage Valetta C.1, Lincoln B.2, Tiger Moth aircraft

LtoR John Dalley, unknown, Bryan (Ingrid) Bergham and the Flt Cdr in front of a Comms Sqn Anson on Site No.2 at Colerne in 1955. Note the trolley acc. in front of the group.
Photo: John Dalley

No. 39 MU still held a considerable number of Lincoln bombers in the early 1950s. From LtoR AC1 Tom Wynn, LAC Bob Burgess and unknown AC1, behind the rear turret of one of these aircraft at Site No. 3. The MU was able to store 3 Lincolns in each of its 'K' Type hangars.   Photo: Bob Burgess

Gp Capt L. Fox DSO, DFC was appointed as Stn Cdr in April 1954 replacing Gp Capt Wight-Boycott who had been in post for two years. From this period until closure of RAF Colerne, the appointment of the station CO would be for a two, or three-year tenure of office, which was the peacetime norm.

On 17th September 1954 a No.238 OCU Brigand T.4 RH807 was written off after overshooting on landing and hitting a wall. A Brigand T.5 RH831 also from the Unit crashed on 8th March 1956 after both engines cut in the circuit and it hit trees whilst attempting a forced landing on the airfield. The aircraft had been on a routine training flight and crashed on the Rocks Estate 200yds short of runway 07/25. A police constable who arrived at the scene immediately after the crash was surprised to see two RAF men walking away from the wreckage. Both were the pupils under instruction and only one had minor burn injuries. One of the flying crew was rescued by firemen, but died shortly afterwards and the body of the other was not retrieved until the severe fire had been extinguished. The two who died were Sgt David W.H. Hanson (pilot), who was married to a WAAF Sgt at Compton Bassett, and Fg Off R.J. Crocker (nav). By a sad coincidence Colerne had experienced an aircraft fatality exactly ten years before, to the day.

Gp Capt E. G. Watkins CBE, AFC, assumed command of the station in April 1956, with major changes for the station imminent. On 1st January 1957,

and various Mks of Anson. All stock aircraft were despatched from the Unit by the 28th September, in preparation for closure. No.49 MU remained and continued the repair and salvage of damaged and crashed aircraft from such remote parts of the world as Morocco, Aden and Christmas Island. The unit was reinforced in September 1953 by the Special Installation Sqn, which carried out prototype installations of special signals and aircraft equipment. This involved the design and manufacture of a great variety of fittings, some of which were very intricate, for many different types of RAF aircraft. No.238 MU Calshot used Colerne as a sub-site for the storage of airborne lifeboats and ancillary handling trolleys from 1st April 1956-1st July 1958.

Civilian Charge Hand (MT Section) Harry Billett and National Service man stood by Leyland 32-AD-36 in September 1953. This was the first pressure fuel tanker in use at Colerne. It had a 2,500 gallon capacity and carried AVTAG for supplying jet aircraft.
Photo: Harry Billett

No.238 OCU which had converted to Meteor NF12s during 1956, moved out to North Luffenham, and a detachment of Valettas from No.228 OCU Leeming, moved in for 5 months only for AI training. Also on 1st January, Colerne came under the control of No.38 Group Transport Command, which needed an airfield in South West England.

No.24 (Commonwealth) Sqn moved in from Abingdon on 1st January 1957 with the Hastings C1A, C2 (WJ340) and C4. The squadron occupied the 'K' Type hangar next to the disused 13/31 runway, and would stay at Colerne until the Hastings was retired as a Transport aircraft, eleven years later. The disused runway was initially used for aircraft parking, but by the early 1960s an area of PSP had been laid up to the north edge of the runway, to provide dispersal parking. The area of this was about 150yds x 40yds and Flt Lt Chris Green a No.24 Sqn pilot, recalls the solid surface being ideal for parking/taxiing aircraft and ground equipment, but hazardous to walk on when icy or wet.

Before and during the war, No.24 Sqn carried VIPs and mail, and in 1943, it became a part of the newly formed Transport Command. During the siege of Malta the squadron carried out 323 shuttle flights in unarmed Hudson aircraft and delivered to the Island the George Cross awarded by King George VI. In 1947 authority was given by the Air Ministry for the squadron to be recognised on a Commonwealth basis and to be renamed No.24 (Commonwealth) Sqn. A number of Australian, Canadian and South Africans served on the squadron, and by 1948 it was operating Yorks and Dakotas, which were flown on the Berlin Airlift helping to break the blockade. In 1956, 1957 and 1958 the squadron was presented with the Berlin Airlift Gold Cup, Transport Command's coveted efficiency award.

No.24 Sqn was followed to Colerne on 1st May 1957 by No.511 Sqn from Lyneham also with the Hastings C1A and C2. The squadron was allocated one of the three 'L' Type hangars on Site No.1 with offices in a Seco building alongside. This hangar was the one nearest to the runway 25 threshold. It was used for storage of ground equipment, not being large enough to accommodate the Hastings. When

work on one of these was required to be done under cover, the ASF hangar, or that of No.24 Sqn, would be used. The squadron used the dispersal bays vacated by No.238 OCU at the SE end of the disused runway. One of No.511 Sqn's C1A Hastings TG615 was written off on 21st October 1957 when it undershot during an asymmetric landing. It bounced and yawed on an attempted overshoot and flew into a hill 1 mile SSW of Colerne where it caught fire, all the 5 crew luckily survived. It is probable that the concrete apron by the perimeter track, between Site No.1 and 2, was constructed pending the arrival of the Hastings squadrons.

Flt Sgt John 'Cliff' Hill who was posted to No.511 Sqn in February 1958 as a Signaller, recalls being on the last flight through Habbaniya, Iraq in June of that year and departing during a

When the squadron was renumbering in 1958 its CO was Wg Cdr Green. The squadron was then involved with the Atom Bomb tests at Christmas Island in the Pacific. Flt Sgt 'Cliff' Hill was one of the double crew on Hastings C2 WD481 which left Lyneham on 5th September 1958 with Captains Flt Lt Collyer and Flt Lt Glover. The reason for the double crew was because of the 'hot load' being carried by the Hastings. The aircraft with its bomb arrived at Christmas Island on the 10th September and the test drop was carried out there at first light the following day, from a Valiant flown by Sqn Ldr Flavell AFC. The Hastings crews remained on the Island during the test and departed later in the day for Honolulu. With similar tests continuing, this No.36 Sqn crew was on Christmas Island from November for a three-month detachment, to keep the island in fresh fruit and vegetables. These were

Buckmaster RP201 of No.238 OCU in all silver finish at Colerne in September 1956.

coup in which King Faisal was assassinated. He had a similar experience a year later in Karachi, from where he and the rest of the crew made a rapid departure as tanks rumbled through the streets.

No.511 Sqn was disbanded on 1st September 1958 and renumbered as No.36 Sqn in order to retain the identity and tradition of an older squadron. During the war the majority of the squadron were killed or captured with the fall of Singapore to the Japanese in February 1942. Re-formed in India with the Wellington 1C in October 1942, it subsequently moved to North Africa in an anti-submarine and convoy escort role. It continued then in Coastal Command but was disbanded and re-formed twice in the 1940s and '50s.

collected from Honolulu by flying three return trips a week. During one such flight the aircraft was turned round at Christmas Island to take a severely injured Warrant Officer to the USAF Hospital at Hickham AFB. The Hastings crew managed to knock 20 minutes off of the usual six-hour flight time to Honolulu in an attempt to save his life, but they never heard whether or not they were successful in this.

No.114 Sqn was reformed at Colerne on 13th April 1959 equipped with the Hastings C1A and C2. The three squadrons now operated as a Wing, carrying personnel and freight between the U.K. and the main RAF Bases overseas. Also to various countries such as the U.S.A., Canada, Fiji, Japan and South Africa and along the well established trunk routes to Australia through the Mediterranean, the Persian Gulf and the Indian Ocean. With the A-Tests involvement on Christmas Island, routes were flown East-about and West-about. With the many former Colonies gaining independence, aircraft frequently made diplomatic trips to unlikely places such as Peshawar. Add to this commitment, participation in NATO exercises, and we can see just how busy the Hastings squadrons were in the late 1950s and early 1960s. The squadrons, with their counterparts at Lyneham, were continually on call to ensure the rapid movement of the nation's air-transported forces to any part of the world where they might be a needed. They were also tasked with supplying these deployments and evacuating any casualties. The Colerne aircraft were required to position to Lyneham the day before scheduled or special flights. There freight would be loaded, and passengers boarded prior to the flight. On return from a long 7 or 8 hour flight, aircraft would land at Lyneham, take an hour or two to off-load and clear customs before a final 5 minute hop to Colerne.

In addition to all normal tasking, the most vital role of all for Colerne Hastings Sqns from 1960 to the close of Hastings transport force, was support for and dispersal of 'V' Force. Known as Exercise *Kinsman*, call out came about 2 or 3 times a year and 2 aircraft had to be airborne within 1½ hours of the exercise being called. To do this each squadron had to have a crew, a reserve crew, 2 aircraft -1 main and 1 reserve, available 365 days a year. The task was to get to 'V' Force stations as quickly as possible, to pick-up 'V' Force aircrew, spares, groundcrew and take them to whichever dispersal airfield was needed. There were several of these such as Honington, Scampton, Cottesmore, Manston, Boscombe Down, St Mawgan and Yeovilton.

To the aircrews on the squadrons at Colerne in those days, the station could be compared to a garage; continuation flying (circuits and bumps and practice instrument approaches) was undertaken, with the engineers and technicians maintaining the aircraft. Crews were often away from their base for long periods at a time and were unable to involve themselves in station activities to the extent they may have wished. Flt Lt Chris Green, a pilot with No.24 Sqn at Colerne from 1963-68

found that most RAF stations, flying and ground, had their own character. He remembers Colerne having a most pleasant atmosphere. It was a neat and compact airfield with most things where they needed to be. On landing back there, he invariably felt the warmth and friendliness of being 'home'. Not all stations fell into this category.

One of the last official duties to be carried out by Gp Capt Watkins in his position as CO of RAF Colerne, was to accept the 'Freedom of Entry into the City of Bath'. This was conferred by the Mayor of Bath at an official ceremony held at the Royal Crescent in Bath on 4th April 1959. The ceremony was attended by a number of Air Force and City of Bath dignitaries and by the Under-Secretary of State for Air and Vice President of the Air Council Airey Neave DSO, OBE, MC, TD, MP. Following the presentation there was a fly-past of nine Hastings aircraft from Colerne, led by Wg Cdr D.W. Hutchings AFC, RAAF, OC No.24 Sqn. This coincided with the Parade, headed by the Central Band of the RAF, exercising the right conferred upon RAF Station Colerne, to march through the streets of the City with swords drawn, bayonets fixed, colours flying, drums beating and bands playing. The Freedom was exercised every following year with a parade through the City. From April 1959, all Colerne Hastings carried the City of Bath coat of arms either side of the nose.

One of No.36 Sqn's Hastings TG522, crashed at Wadi Seidna, Khartoum, on 29th May 1959, on route to the U.K from a Christmas Island detachment. No.2 engine failed after take-off and was shut down, and the prop feathered. The Captain Flt Lt Alan B. Eyre, after jettisoning fuel, obtained clearance to land on Runway 18, but as the Hastings was incorrectly positioned for it, he was given permission to land on Runway 36. On the final turn onto the runway heading, the port wing-centre section stalled. The Captain mistook this for vibration of No.1 engine and feathered this one as well so that there was now no power on the port side. The low level and low speed of the aircraft forced the Captain to make a crash landing one mile south of Runway 36 threshold, and the aircraft caught fire on impact. All the crew were killed except for the AQM, and four of the 26

passengers were seriously injured. The AQM was later decorated for saving his passengers. In addition to the Captain, the crew who died were Fg Off Anthony L. Millard (co-pilot), Flt Sgt Frank M. Jones (nav), MEng. Mansel Atyeo (Flt Eng) and Flt Sgt Arthur Dobson (air signaller). At the end of the runway there was a wood-yard containing large stacks of timber. TG522 crashed into the stacks of timber.

The No.2 engine had failed owing to cylinder seizure, and the Accident Investigators concluded that the primary cause of the accident was the Captain's error in flying his circuit on assymetric power at too low an altitude and airspeed, the low airspeed causing a pre-stall judder. A contributory cause being his mistaking this for No.1 engine vibration and feathering it thus aggravating the stall. News of this crash soon spread to Colerne crews around the world with the story that the Captain in conversation the previous night had said "that damn place Khartoum will be the death of me". Crews never relished mid-day departures out of Khartoum with temperatures of 40 degrees C and used to say that they would not fancy their chances if they lost an engine on take-off. Aircraft performance at high weight and high temperature is significantly reduced under these circumstances.

In July 1959 Gp Capt P. Fleming OBE took over as Stn Cdr. At this time criticism was being directed at the base because of the noise and disturbance caused by the Hastings aircraft. In October he replied to some of the criticism in a local paper. A resident of Corsham claimed the aircraft were flying at night "at little more than roof top height". The Stn Cdr pointed out that RAF Colerne was some 300' higher than the highest point in Corsham and to land at the base, a heavy four-engine transport aircraft would have to climb around 400' in just over three miles to make a landing. This not being practical, presumably disproved this particular claim.

The Colerne Communication Flt was transferred from Transport Command to Technical Training Command on 1st January 1960 when it re-formed at Colerne as No.24 Group Communication Flt. It was equipped with various Mks of Ansons of which the following are known and are all Mk C19 Series 2: VL288, VL348, VM333, VM351, VM377, VP520, VP533.

The three Hastings squadrons each had their complement of aircraft reduced to an establishment of eight on 1st January 1960, but continued to provide sterling service. During the autumn, detachments were maintained in Ghana and Nigeria, in support of the Ghanaian and Nigerian Forces that formed part of the United Nations Forces deployed in the Congo. Colerne's aircraft provided the only link between the troops of the two forces and their homelands.

Gp Capt G. B. Johns DSO, DFC, AFC, was appointed Stn Cdr in February 1962. No.49 MU was disbanded on 1st March having spent its last years carrying out modifications on aircraft which included the Shackleton, and with the closure, the Special Installation Sqn was absorbed into No.60 MU at Dishforth. No.114 Sqn was disbanded on 30th September reforming the following day at Benson where it was to be equipped with the Argosy. Its Hastings aircraft were divided between the two remaining squadrons, and by the end of the year, each had thirty on strength.

In addition to the freight and troop transport roles, the aircraft were being used for paratroop and supply-dropping exercises at home and abroad. Colerne worked closely with the Strategic Reserve of the British Army and the 16th Parachute Brigade Group of the Regular Army. The 44th Independent Parachute Brigade Group of the Territorial Army, frequently jumped from Colerne's Hastings aircraft.

In 1962 a new era began when No.2 (Field) Sqn RAF Regiment arrived at Colerne. The squadron was unique in that it was the only parachute trained RAF Regiment unit and therefore it worked in close co-operation with the flying squadrons. It was frequently on 24 hour standby to go anywhere in the world. Its origins were with No.2 Armoured Car Company, formed at Heliopolis in April 1922. During World War 2 it operated during the first offensive in the Western Desert, with General Wavell's ground forces and saw action at Ramadi, Fallujah and against the Vichy French Forces at Homs. At the opening of the 'Crusader' offensive the Company was re-

Anson T.21 VS569 of No.24 Gp Comms Flt making its approach to land at Colerne on 17th June 1960. One of the Hastings at dispersal is a No.36 Sqn aircraft. Photo: M. Metcalf

equipped in Jordan. It fought in the Western Desert until the end of the North African Campaign, when it returned through Egypt to Transjordan and Palestine. Here it was employed in internal security and training until the end of the war. On 3rd October 1946, it was incorporated into the RAF Regiment as No.2 Armoured Car Sqn and in November 1953 was renamed No.2 (Field) Sqn. In April 1955 the Squadron moved to Cyprus to assist in anti-terrorist operations and in 1960 was posted to the U.K. for the first time since its formation. The Squadron converted to a parachute unit as part of No.38 Group in 1962. On arrival at Colerne, the Sqn moved into hangars vacated by No.49 MU. In November 1967, the Sqn covered the withdrawal of our Forces in Aden.

A Canberra B.2 arrived at Colerne on 19th December 1962 to be used for ground instructional purposes by students bussed in from RAF Melksham and Yatesbury. During its period at the airfield it was maintained by No.24 Group Comms Flt.

In 1963 the first Army Unit was stationed at the base, this was No.47 (Air Despatch) Sqn Royal Corps of Transport, which later moved the few miles to Lyneham. On 1st April 1964 No.24 Group Comms Flt. was disbanded and its vacated 'L' Type hangar on Site No.2 near the perimeter track came into use as a museum for Colerne's aircraft preservation collection. It was administered by Fg Off Bob Osborne, a co-pilot of No.36 Sqn, (details of the collection appear later in this chapter). At this time, of the two 'K' Type hangars by the Fosse Way,

one was used for storage and the other by a Handley Page working party. The Aircraft Servicing Flight (ASF) used the two 'J' Type hangars by the Headquarters Site. 1st and 2nd line aircraft servicing was carried out by the squadrons own Engineering Officers and ground crews, with 3rd and 4th line servicing done by the ASF. Major overhauls were done by Handley Page at Radlett where the aircraft were ferried to and from by the squadron crews. In July Gp Capt A.C.L. Mackie DFC became the Stn Cdr and in October Wg Cdr R.T. Saunders replaced Wg Cdr R.B. Sillars as No.24 Sqn CO.

A tragedy occurred on Tuesday 6th July 1965, when a No.36 Sqn Hastings C1A, TG577, crashed killing all 41 on board. This was Colerne's worst accident during the operational life of the station. The aircraft with Flt Lt John Akin and his crew had flown from Colerne to Abingdon to carry out parachute dropping sorties for the Parachute Training School over several days. The aircraft took off from Abingdon at 1605 hours on its final sortie of the day to Weston-on-The Green DZ. The weather at the time was good, but immediately after take-off a message was transmitted to the effect that trimming problems were being experienced. This was followed by another message indicating that the controls were sloppy and a request for priority landing was made. The pilot was advised of the runway to use and this was acknowledged. When flying downwind, the Hastings was seen to suddenly rear up and climb to around 2000', before stall-turning to port, spinning and diving vertically into the ground at Little Balden, five miles ESE of Abingdon. The investigation placed no blame on the pilot but found the cause to be fatigue fracture of two upper bolts attaching the starboard outboard elevator outrigger to the tailplane drag member. With the failure of the bolts, the outer half of the starboard elevator became unstable, causing the problems experienced immediately following take-off. As a result of this accident all the RAF's remaining Hastings aircraft were grounded for 6 weeks for modifications to be carried out. Nearly all the station personnel of Colerne attended the military funeral for the crew at Colerne Village Church. All Hastings were flying again by late September, although 2 or 3 were scrapped because of corrosion problems.

RAF Colerne celebrated its 25th Anniversary on 18th September 1965 with around 20,000 people attending an 'At Home' day. The station was still a good employer then, with nearly 400 local civilians working there. Around 6000 military personnel and their families lived on the base.

It came as a relief to all Colerne-aircrew, groundcrew, administrators and Air Traffic-when in October 1965 the ground floor of the old Control Tower was converted into a neat passenger arrival/departure lounge, and a Customs area. This ended the tedious positioning at Lyneham before overseas trips, and on return, the wearisome wait for the crew to clear Customs, before starting up again to fly 5 or 10 minutes (depending on weather) back home to Colerne.
In November Wg Cdr G. Moss AFC replaced Wg Cdr Saunders as No.24 Sqn CO and about the same time Wg Cdr J.D. Payling became CO of No.36 Sqn in place of Wg Cdr D.J. Dodimead. An interesting facet of CO appointments with the two squadrons was that No.36 Sqn alternated between a pilot and navigator, but the CO of No.24 Sqn was always pilots.

In early December 1965, 6 aircraft and about 12 crews, together with about 20 groundcrew, all from both squadrons, under the command of OC No.36 Sqn Wg Cdr J.D. Payling, were detached to RAF Khormaksar, Aden.

Ian Smith, Prime Minister of the (then) Southern Rhodesia, had declared the country independent (UDI) and

Zambia was cut off from supplies of many vital materials. The UK Government decided to supply Zambia with oil by air from Kenya, and a large detachment of Britannias from Lyneham was based at the International airport (then known as Embakasi) at Nairobi. They would fly many daily sorties to N'dola and Lusaka, each aircraft carrying about 20,000lbs of oil in 40 gallon drums.

The Hastings at Khormaksar flew one sortie per day, via Nairobi/Eastleigh to N'dola, with a small amount of oil or kerosene, but also much varied freight including food, medicine, vehicle spares and so on. At the end of January 1966, the whole detachment, now commanded by OC No.24 Sqn Wg Cdr Geoff Moss AFC, moved to and operated from, the former RAF Station at Nairobi/Eastleigh. Daily supply runs to N'dola and sometimes Lusaka, continued until the end of February. By early March 1966, the whole detachment had returned to Colerne.

Hastings aircraft known to have flown on the 'mini oil-lift' included: - TG528, TG551, TG557, TG605 and TG607.

Gp Capt F.O. Barrett DFC was appointed Stn Cdr in May 1966. Towards the end of 1966 a number of the more experienced Hastings Captains, Navigators and Engineers were sent to Sewart Air Force Base in Tennessee to attend the Hercules C130 conversion course.

During January/February 1967, 'bits' of No.36 Sqn started moving to Lyneham (furniture and fittings) and more of their aircrew were converting to the C130 at No.242 OCU, Thorney Island. In April Colerne became the major engineering base for the RAFs new fleet of 66 C130K Hercules. Eventually there would be 6 squadrons, 4 in the UK and 2 overseas, plus the OCU at Thorney Island. For the next eight years all major servicing and overhaul, would be done at Colerne.

The last Colerne aircraft to be lost was Hastings C2 WD491. On 9th June 1967, Flt Lt Robin Cane and his 5 crew from No.24 Sqn were returning to RAF West Raynham in Norfolk with an empty aircraft to pick up a further load of Army exercise freight

for Germany. On the landing roll, a fatigue failure in the starboard mainwheel hub caused the tyre to deflate, and the wheel to lock solid. The aircraft swung uncontrollably off the runway at 30 to 40 knots, and the locked wheel dug into the ground, tipping WD491 onto the nose.

The 5 flight deck crew climbed out through the port escape hatch, and dropped to the ground. The AQM, who had been correctly seated at the rear of the aircraft, slid down the escape rope from the port door. The rope can be seen hanging down in the photograph. All 6 were shaken but unhurt, and although the aircraft was repairable, as the Hastings had only 6 months to run, it was scrapped at West Raynham.

On 1st July No.36 Sqn moved to Lyneham to re-equip and become operational with the new Hercules transport aircraft. With this departure, No.24 Sqn acquired additional Hastings aircraft to add to its own. The surplus Captains, co-pilots, navigators, engineers and AQMs, were also inherited by the squadron. Many surplus signallers were not required at Colerne, and they received postings to Coastal Command squadrons operating Shackletons or as console operators for Flight Simulators at various RAF stations.

On 1st August 1967 Transport Command was renamed Air Support Command. At this time some of the ex-Colerne crews, together with others from former Beverley Sqns, who had completed C130 conversion courses at Thorney Island, returned to Colerne with new C130s which were parked on the former No.36 Sqn dispersal. This was the fledgling new No.48 Sqn which was re-formed in October. They carried out circuit and 'shakedown' flying before moving from Colerne to Changi, about the second week in October.

In late 1967 there were indications that No.24 Sqn was to be disbanded and later re-formed but this never came about much to the relief of all squadron personnel. The CO of the squadron during these uncertain times was Wg Cdr Geoff Moss, and it was mainly thanks to him, that the squadron continued.

On 5th January 1968, a ceremony was held on the Station and subsequently a farewell fly-past by 4 Hastings of No.24 Sqn (planned for that day but postponed because of bad weather). It signalled the retirement of the famous RAF transport after nearly 20 years operating in all parts of the world. Although several T Mk.5 Hastings, modified as radar trainers for Bomber Command, together with 2 C1As, would continue flying at Windholme and Scampton until 1977. The prototype, TE580, first flew on 7th May 1946 and the type entered service with No.47 Sqn in September 1948. No.24 Sqn received the type in November 1950 and flew it longer than any other unit. The Squadron officially moved over to Lyneham following the ceremony, where it also re-equipped with the Hercules. A detachment of the squadron did continue at Colerne for a short period with the very last operational transport Hastings landing there in February on returning from the Far East. The last Hastings at Colerne was towed from the No.24 Sqn hangar to the fire dump on or around the 10th February 1968. Others had been flown to stations such as Manby, Lindholme, Wildenrath and Laarbruch, where they also ended their days (still usefully) as ground crash/fire trainers.

Gp Capt C. J. Turner MBE, assumed command of the station in January 68, and oversaw the change from a flying station, to one of mainly engineering. Colerne would now be receiving the new Hercules from Marshalls of Cambridge, who had installed much of the equipment and painted the bare metal aircraft. At Colerne, final checks would be done before the brand new, and in later years, refurbished aircraft were issued to squadrons.

Gp Capt Turner remained for only 13 months and was succeeded in February 1969 by Gp Capt G. Young OBE who was followed in September 1971 by Gp Capt D.W. Richardson. The early 1970s witnessed the full build up of the Hercules maintenance programme with aircraft from the RAFs 66 strong fleet, constantly passing through the station. From 1st September 1972 Air Support Command was absorbed into No.46 Group Strike Command, but the station role remained the same.

A year later on 10th September 1973 disaster affected the Station when Hercules C1 XV198 of No.48 Sqn, based at Lyneham, crashed into the woods on the edge of the Lucknam

Hastings C1A TG527 displaying the No.36 Sqn badge. In the background are Hastings C1A TG528 and Hastings C2 WD494. They are lined up at Colerne on bays 4, 3 and 2 (former No.36 Sqn dispersal) respectively in late September 1967. TG527 sadly was scrapped at Abingdon in 1968, despite being ear-marked for preservation, TG528 survives with the IWM Duxford and WD494 was also scrapped. Photo: Chris Green

Park estate. The aircraft was in use for co-pilot training and was carrying out circuits/rollers on r/w 07. No.1 engine had been closed down on take-off, which was a normal procedure, but the other engine on the same side, No.2, flamed out. On crashing the aircraft caught fire and the crew of five were killed. Flt Sgt Peter R. Coate (Engineer) and Walter C. Nutt

In January 1974 Gp Capt G.M.G. Cooper was appointed Stn Cdr, and was holding the post when in 1975 Colerne was listed in a Defence White Paper, as one of the five major RAF bases 'no longer required'. In October 1975 an announcement was made that the Station would be modified for occupation by the Army, and Hercules major servicing moved to

Hastings C2 WD491 on its nose at West Raynham on 9th June 1967. The escape rope is seen hanging from the open port door. Photo: Chris Green

(Master Air Load Master) are buried at St Michael's Church, Lyneham. Sqn Ldr A.V. Tony Barrett (Capt/Instructor) who died was the nephew of the former Colerne Stn Cdr, Gp Capt F.O. Barrett DFC. Investigation revealed that the extremely rare failure of an aneroid capsule, in No.2 engine fuel control unit, had caused No.2 to run down. With take-off power on No.3 and 4 engines, had the crew realised the problem, their only action would have been to close all the throttles and crash straight a head, and hopefully without loss of life.

Lyneham. The Hercules aircraft started leaving as did the many preserved aircraft in the museum, which finally closed in February 1976 with the sale of the last five, a Javelin, Hunter, Anson, Meteor and Provost. Fortunately most of the aircraft found homes with other collections.

Closure

The last RAF Stn Cdr appointed in January 1976, was Wg Cdr R.T. Johnson. RAF personnel remained, as the task of closing down continued until finally on 31st March 1976 RAF Colerne became Azimghur Barracks.

Bannerdown Gliding Club belonging to the RAF Gliding and Soaring Association now had to relocate to Hullavington. The club had formed at Colerne in 1960 taking its name from the ridge of Bannerdown which extends from Colerne towards Bath. Initially the club was equipped with a Slingsby T31 and a Cadet Mk.1.

The MoD held a sale of Colerne's furniture and fittings in February 1977 at which ten RAF blankets could be bought for £24. The Station was initially retained on reserve but received hardly any use by aircraft. Hercules aircraft did return in September 1987 as part of a 5 Airborne Brigade exercise. Chinook and Puma helicopters were also involved in the non-stop flying role of the exercise.

Hercules C130 taking-off from Colerne.   Photo: Donald Lovelock

A complex, housing a ground station for the MoD Skynet 4 Communications Satellite System was built on the airfield in 1989. The station comprised a static 46' (14m) Antenna, and a mobile 23' (7m) Antenna with a Telemetry and Control Station. The station was controlled by the RAF, No.1001 Signals Unit, whose HQ was at Oakhanger in Hampshire.

Re-occupation

RAF flying returned to Colerne in August 1993, when No.3 Air Experience Flt (AEF) with 6 Chipmunk T10s, moved in from Hullavington and occupied the old No.24 Sqn hangar by the disused runway. However, asbestos was found in the hangar, and whilst it was cleared the AEF moved to St Athan in South Wales, from February to September 1994. There was then a further delay,

while a security fence was built round both the hangar and the adjacent Satellite Communication complex. No.3 AEF finally moved back into the hangar in October 1994.

In November 1994, Bristol University Air Sqn (UAS) relocated from Hullavington with Bulldog T1s. They shared the hangar occupied by No.3 AEF the previous month. In January 1996 the AEF began to convert to the Bulldog, and by March 1996 the last Chipmunk had gone, the UAS and AEF then shared the Bulldogs and later the Tutors.

The new basic trainer, the Grob 115E 'Tutor', replaced the Bulldog when Colerne's allocation of 8 began to arrive in September 2000. The Bulldog had been phased out, it was the end of an era, the RAFs last British built piston-engined aircraft had gone.

Until the late summer of 2002, visitors to Colerne looking over the hedge from the Fosse Way, would have seen a station that remained much as it had been when completed in 1940. Unlike many even older stations, very little had been demolished, as is often the case when different Services or Formations take over. The two 'J' Type hangars, and the Control Tower with the Met. Office next to runway No.3, were demolished after 62 years service. In need of serious maintenance, it was determined to be less costly to remove the structures than to renovate them. The cinema, night flying shed, parachute store and ration store were other buildings removed at this time. The other hangars, the runways and new

Control Towers are still evident. Most of the domestic buildings and all the messes survive, the latter still used as intended, but now by the Army. The Central Heating Station, with the prominent tower is clearly seen, and close to the main entrance the church survives, but in poor condition. Other structures, amongst them the Decontamination Centre, the 'Black' hangar and Blister hangar have disappeared, the latter in fact soon after the war. In March 2003, the three 'L' Type hangars on the north side of the airfield were put on the market to rent at £2.50p per sq ft.

The only runway now used, 07/25, is as it was when the last Hercules took off, although large aircraft can no longer land because of runway loading restrictions. As the traffic lights on the Fosse Way and Doncombe Lane are long gone, the touch-down markings at each end of the runway have been moved in by about 100 yards, so that the Tutors can cross both roads safely on their landing approach. Now in the 21st Century, the former RAF Colerne has lasted well. Built in haste, but soundly, it still serves the Country.

The Colerne Collection of Historic Aircraft

When we look back and see how the collection developed over the years, it is probable that its roots began shortly after the war when John Dale (Foundries) Ltd, a salvage company from London Colney, Hertfordshire, bought a quantity of war surplus aircraft from the Air Ministry on 5th July 1948. The company had mobile furnaces and one was sent for use at Colerne where several hundred Spitfires of various Mks were parked wing to wing around the edge of the airfield awaiting disposal. Using the furnace the aircraft were converted into scrap metal. It appears that some of Colerne's officers made an approach to Peter Wood, the John Dale site manager at Colerne, asking if one of the Spitfires that had a good war time record, could be saved. The Directors of John Dale agreed, and presented one of the Spitfires to Colerne. The aircraft was Spitfire IIa P7350 and it was probably the pioneer of the Colerne Collection. A plaque was attached to the aircraft commemorating its presentation by John Dale (Foundaries) Ltd. P7350 survived at Colerne in good condition, so presumably it was kept under cover and was not abused for spares.

When Gp Capt T.G. (Hamish) MaHaddie was scouring the world for aircraft to be used in the making of the 1969 Battle of Britain film, P7350 was a prime candidate and was returned to flying condition by the film makers. After its' role in the film it was presented on 8th November 1968, to the Battle of Britain Flight with which it is still flying and exciting the air display crowds, over half a century after it was built at Castle Bromwich. It is in fact the oldest flying example of its type and the oldest aircraft currently operated by the RAF. It first entered service on 6th September 1940 with No.266 Sqn at Wittering, and in time to see action in the Battle of Britain. It went on to serve with Nos.603 Sqn, 616 Sqn, and 64 Sqn. It was flown by the Central Gunnery School and No.57 OTU before being put into storage at Colerne in July 1944.

Another sequence of events leading to the acquisition of display aircraft commenced with the programme of evaluation carried out on captured enemy aircraft during and immediately following the war. These aircraft were also flown to the operational stations for familiarisation purposes by the Enemy Aircraft Flt, Colerne having been one of the places visited by the Circus. Some of these enemy aircraft were later distributed to bases throughout the country. In 1956, the Officer Commanding Engineering Wing at Colerne, Wg Cdr W.R. Owens, a veteran from RAF Halton's 3rd Apprentice entry, visited nearby RAF Melksham. On the salvage dump he saw a German Heinkel 162 'Salamander' and a Messerschmitt 163 'Komet'. He arranged for these to be transported back to Colerne and after some renovation they were displayed at that year's Battle of Britain Air Day.

From these humble beginnings the collection was added to whenever the opportunity arose. Its development was solely as a result of the efforts of many individuals. The Colerne Aircraft Museum eventually housed much of the RAF Museum, Hendon's reserve collection. As it grew, so did its accommodation, using hangars No.19, 24 and 25. As well as the aircraft, the collection at Colerne comprised an extensive range of propulsion displays, missiles, models, aviation memorabilia and information, providing an

Jeff Malton who flew Spitfire P7350 from Slade Farm to Colerne at the end of the war. He is seen here with the aircraft at its Battle of Britain Memorial Flight base at RAF Coningsby.
Photo: Jeff Malton

evocative and tangible history of powered flight. The following are just a few of the aircraft of interest that made up the collection:

Spitfire Mk.5b BL614

It served with Nos.611 Sqn, 242 Sqn, 222 Sqn, 64 Sqn. and 118 Sqn, during 1942/43. When with No.222 Sqn, it flew in support of the Dieppe raid on 19th August 1942. It was a 'Gate Guard' at RAF Hereford before being used for taxi scenes in the Battle of Britain film. It then went to RAF Wattisham before arriving at Colerne in October 1972.

Meteor Mk.8 (Prone-Position) WK935

This aircraft was the only one built in this form. Armstrong Whitworth Ltd was responsible for its conversion from a standard Mk.8 to its form as a prone pilot test bed. The object of the conversion was to investigate the effects of 'G' loadings on pilots and the feasibility of the arrangement for the Bristol 185 rocket interceptor project. The extra cockpit in the nose enabled pilots to lie face down on a couch and this had the effect of minimising 'G' loadings and thus the strain on the heart. These experiments were a success but pilots reported severe disorientation while flying on instruments. The escape system for the nose pilot was a rather primitive escape capsule. A safety pilot always flew in the rear cockpit in case of an emergency, when he would be required to take control from the nose pilot. WK935 first flew on 10th February 1954 and its last flight was in July 1955.

Hawker Hunter Mk.3 (P 1067) WB188

This was a prototype Hunter Mk.1 which first flew in 1951. It was converted in 1953 to become the one and only Mk.3. With pilot Sqn Ldr Neville Duke it became the holder of the World Speed Record at 727.6 mph. Its other Wiltshire connection was as a static display item at RAF Melksham.

Bleriot Monoplane Type X1 No.225

From the early 1900's, this was a rare and genuine aircraft of its type and in airworthy condition. It had miraculously survived a number of accidents in the hands of a number of owners. It was in the private ownership of Commander L.D. Goldsmith during its display by the Colerne Aircraft Museum.

Hastings Mk.1 TG536

This particular aircraft was presented to the Museum following its retirement from RAF service. It flew into Colerne on 19th February 1974 and was back where it was based from 1958 to 1968. The first Mk.1 Hastings flew on 7th May 1946 and TG536 was one of the many which took part in the Berlin Airlift.

Liberator Mk.6 KN751

The aircraft was presented by the Indian Air Force following its retirement. It had previously served in India with No.99 Sqn until disbanded there in November 1945. Its journey to the U.K. commenced on Saturday 6th July 1974 when it took off from Almaza, Cairo on the first leg to Rome.

The pilot was Wg Cdr Chopra. The second leg on the following day was Ciampino, Rome to Lyneham. A low run over Lyneham was executed for the benefit of the guests awaiting the arrival, before taxiing in past a line of Hercules. On the Monday the aircraft made its final flight of 15 minutes to Colerne. When later it moved on to the Aerospace Museum at Cosford, it was transported there on a low-loader.

Handley Page 115

The aircraft was built at Radlett in 1960 for experiments in the slow flying characteristics of slender delta wing aircraft. Most of its 490 hours of flying was carried out from RAE Bedford. This forerunner to Concorde with its Bristol Siddeley Viper engine was flown into Colerne by Flt Lt John Rudin on 30th January 1974 and handed over to the Museum. To commemorate the occasion, a Concorde flew over the base following the arrival of the Handley Page 115.

Spitfire Mk. 5b BL614 Photo: Donald Lovelock

Armed with four 20mm Hispano cannons, the Mk.3 was used in fighter and ground attack roles.

Photo-call (next page)

The display design for the photo-call was controlled by Flt Lt John Frapwell and the aircraft movements were supervised by Chief Technician Geoff Richardson. It took three days to position them with the lightweight

Messerschmitt 163 'Komet'. Photo: Donald Lovelock

Dakota KG374

This aircraft had been restored to the war time livery of No.271 Sqn. It was with this squadron based at Down Ampney, just over the Wiltshire border, and with detachments at Blakehill Farm, that Flt Lt David Lord won the VC. The post war comedian Flt Lt Jimmy Edwards DFC also served with the squadron. KG374 was originally KG645 used after the war by Field Marshal Viscount Montgomery for VIP flights.

Vampire Mk.3 VT812

This aircraft served with No.601 (County of London) Sqn and arrived at the Museum from Cardington in 1964.

ones being wheeled out at the last moment. The series of photographs were taken by Senior Aircraftsmen Trevor Olner and Ronald Phillips positioned on a mobile gantry.

Victoria Cross Recipients

Lancaster KB726 VR-A of No.419 (Moose) Sqn RCAF which had landed at Colerne from operations on the morning of 6th June 1944, took-off with the same crew from its base at Middleton St. George at 2144 hours on 12th June 1944 to bomb the rail yards at Cambrai. On the approach, the aircraft was attacked by a Ju 88 night-fighter, its cannon fire destroying both port engines and setting fire to the hydraulic supply

lines in the rear fuselage. The Captain Fg Off Arthur De Breyne gave the order to bale out. The mid-upper gunner Plt Off Andrew C. Mynarski left his turret and made his way to the rear escape hatch. He opened the door and was about to jump when he noticed the rear-gunner Fg Off Pat Brophy trapped in his turret. This became immovable when the hydraulics were put out of action by the damage, additionally Brophy had broken the manual rotating gear handle in his desperation to get out. The mid-upper gunner turned away from the safety of the hatch and on hands and knees crawled through the blazing hydraulic oil towards his trapped colleague. His uniform and parachute were well alight and the rear-gunner shouted for him to go back and tried to wave him away. Mynarski ignored this and attacked the turret with a fire axe. He tore at the doors with his bare hands but all was to no avail. By now he was a mass of flames below the waist and Pat Brophy again shouted for him to get out. Mynarski realised he could do no more to help the trapped gunner. He reluctantly made his way back through the flames to the escape hatch and standing up, came to attention and saluted Fg Off Brophy and mouthed the words "Good Night Sir" before jumping. The aircraft crashed against a tree and miraculously the rear-gunner in his turret survived. The remainder of the crew also survived with the exception of Andrew Mynarski who was seen by French people on the ground, making a rapid burning descent and was found mortally burned. For his selfless courage he was posthumously awarded the Victoria Cross.

Liberator Mk. 6 KN751.   Photo: Donald Lovelock

The 33 aircraft of the RAF Colerne Aircraft Museum take a photo-call on Thursday 19th June 1975 prior to dispersal and sale by auction. Hastings C Mk.1, Heinkel HE162, Liberator B24L, Valetta C Mk.1, Campbell Gyrocopter, Dakota, Dragonfly, Meteor Mk.4, Canberra B2, Vampire Mk.6, Flying Flea, Chilton, Javelin F(AW) 4/9, Hunter Mk.2, Canberra B(I) 8, Catalina, Mosquito B34, Vampire T11, Anson Mk.19, Lightning 18, Supermarine 510, Meteor NF Mk.14, Meteor Mk.8 (Prone Position), Spitfire Mk.24, Provest T1, Sea Fury FB11, Hawker P1052, Hunter Mk.3 P1067, ME163 (Komet), Vampire Mk.3, Spitfire Mk.5B, Bleriot X1, Handley Page 115.   Photo: Bob Burgess.

MEMORIALS

173/ST821712 - 5 miles North East of Bath

Inside the church of St. John the Baptist, on the unclassified road passing through the village: -

Somerset and Gloucester. As a result elements from the arms of each have been taken to form Colerne's crest. The design was approved by George V1 in 1944. The motto beneath the badge is "Age pro Viribus". The official translation is "Do your Utmost" and carries the connotation of St Paul's message "Quit yourself like a man. Be Strong." The Station had their badge presented to them by the AOC No.10 Group Air Commodore A.V. Harvey CBE at a ceremony on 8th March 1945.

The crest of RAF Colerne depicted on a lead wall mounted shield.

(2) Close by on the same wall is a brass plaque displaying the names of local men killed during World War 2: -

1939 - 1945
PETER BEDFORD CDM. GDS.
DENNIS I. BRAIN R.A.F.
ARTHUR FIELD R.E.M.E.
GEOFFREY GRANT R.A.F.
MAURICE LITTLEWOOD R.A.F.
PETER LITTLEWOOD R.A.F.
DAVID F. POWELL R.A.F.
FRANK C. ROBSON R.N.
ALBERT T. SHEPPARD R.E.
WILLIAM TILEY M.B.E., R.A.F.
FREDERICK W. WALE R.A.F.

(3) A Kneeler in one of the pews is embroidered with the badges of the RAF and RAF Colerne 1940 - 1976.

In the churchyard there are 38 RAF, 3 RCAF, 1 RNZAF and 1 WAAF grave.

(1) On the north wall a large round lead shield on a wood backing displaying the badge of RAF Colerne beside a standard of the RAF. In formal language RAF Colerne's crest is described as 'In front of a horseshoe a dragon rampant'. The airfield's location in Wiltshire is very close to

COMPTON BASSETT

Memorial 173/SU022705 - 2 miles East of Calne

On the C15 road leading to the village of Compton Bassett, set into the original brick pillar of the Station's main gate, is a stainless steel plaque inscribed with a plan of the Station. Prepared by Paul A. Brown the words read: -

RAF Compton Bassett circa 1946
1940 - 1964

The plaque, manufactured and supplied by Hanman Split Ltd., Gloucester, was erected by the Yatesbury Association and was donated by D.S. Engineering (Tetbury) and Mr W. Brister the son of Gp Capt Arthur John Brister OBE a former Chief Instructor at RAF Yatesbury and Stn Cdr at Compton Bassett. It was unveiled on Saturday 16th August 1997 by a former WAAF Olga Mawer (nee Porter).

The station was initially known as RAF Calne when it opened with the formation of No.3 Electrical & Wireless School on 10th June 1940. It was redesignated RAF Compton Bassett on 26th June 1940. The station was administered by No.26 Group Technical Training Command and was intended for the training of wireless operators. It had the capacity for 4000 personnel with a weekly intake of 200. Within weeks the School was disbanded and reformed on 26th August 1940 as No.3 Signals School to train ground operators. During the summer of 1941 WAAFs started arriving on station following a new policy of substituting them for RAF personnel in certain wireless trades. In November 1942 WAAF recruit courses were introduced with a straight through element for wireless operators. On 1st January 1943 this School was redesignated No.3 Radio School in No.27 Group and engaged in training telegraphists. No.5 Radio School also formed on the same date at Compton Bassett, ex No.5 Signals School, Oxford, carrying out code and cypher training. No.15 Recruits Centre formed on 8th October 1945 as a lodger unit, remaining until May 1947.

The commemorative plaque set into the original gatepost at the main entrance of the former RAF Compton Bassett. Photo: R. Priddle

It carried out the training of wireless and teleprinter operators, code and cypher operators, telephonists plus boy entrants. No.5 Radio School disbanded on 30th January 1946.

The Station was transferred to No.24 Group on 15th September 1958 when No.27 Group disbanded. In July 1959 No.3 Radio School was re-organised from a four to a three squadron training unit and in May 1961 was further reduced to two squadrons. The School was disbanded on 30th November 1964, the station reduced to Care & Maintenance and transferred to Transport Command, parented by RAF Lyneham.

Demolition of the training buildings commenced on 31st March 1970 but the married quarters remain in use for housing and the roads are named Dowding Drive, Boyle Avenue, Atcherley Road, Speckly Road, Beamish Close, Whittle Avenue and Trenchard Avenue.

In January 1952 Calne Borough Council presented the station with an illuminated certificate signifying its affiliation to the Borough under the Municipal Affiliation Scheme. In November 1954 the Mayor of Calne was presented with a replica of the unit badge of No.3 Radio School. On 3rd May 1960, the Station presented the Mayor of Calne with a gavel and block on a base bearing an inscribed silver plate (see **CALNE**).

On the south side of the A342, beside a copse and 150 yards west of the Conock village road junction, stands a small aircraft hangar built for Lt Robert Raymond Smith-Barry one of the original pupils at the Central Flying School at Upavon. He was later to be recognised as an instructor of considerable notoriety, famous for his 'Flying Notes' which formed the basis adhered to by pilots for decades afterwards. It is considered that these ground rules saved the lives of many a pilot. This metal framed, galvanised hangar with wooden sliding doors, and fan-lights in the roof, was used to house his private De Havilland Puss Moth 'Annabelle' which as with military aircraft, he flew to the limit. Hubert Hibbard, the farmer in whose field the hanger stood, maintained two grass airstrips for Smith-Barry. These ran east/west and north west/south east and the landing ground was indicated by a wind-sock. Smith-Barry lived at Conock Manor from 1920 until a year after the death of his first wife Kitty on 18th May 1941. She is buried at the church in the adjacent village of Chirton.

Smith-Barry's Aircraft Hanger at Conock.

In today's society Smith-Barry would be recognised as a 'character' and it was probably his non-conformity which prevented the kind of progress in the Service his abilities doubtless warranted. When attending the first CFS course at Upavon, Major John Salmond, one of his instructors, referred to him as 'independent-minded'. Father of the RAF, Lord Trenchard wrote "The great Smith-Barry...the man who taught the Air Forces of the world how to fly."

Robert Smith-Barry was born in 1886 and descended on his father's side from the fourth Earl of Barrymore, of County Cork while his mother, Lady Charlotte, was a daughter of the third Earl of Enniskillen. He was educated at Eton until dismissed because he did not put enough effort into his studies. As a result he was coached in Norfolk for a university place at Cambridge. When it was discovered that he was teaching the other pupils agnosticism, his father was asked to remove him. His ambition was to make a name for himself in music and until joining the Consular Service in 1909, he studied the piano in London. The appeal of his posting to Constantinople as an honorary attache did not last and he returned to continue his music in London and to the warmth of family life at Stowell Park near Pewsey in Wiltshire. In 1911 he learnt to fly at the Bristol School of Aviation at Larkhill, passing the tests for his flying certificate (No.161) on 28th November. In the latter part of that year and in early 1912 he did some instructing at the School before being commissioned as a Second Lieutenant into the RFC Special Reserve on 10th August 1912. On 17th August he attended the first CFS course at Upavon as one of seventeen pupils. On the course with him were Major H.M. Trenchard and Lt F.F. Waldron. The pupils of this first course qualified for their flying badges when they were awarded a RFC Flying Certificate, dated 5th December 1912.

Smith-Barry was confirmed in his rank of Second Lieutenant and gazetted as a Flying Officer in April 1913. He was transferred from the Special Reserve to the RFC in July. This same year he married Kitty Colburn, a daughter of an Indian Army Officer. In 1914 Smith-Barry was attached to No.5 Sqn as a pilot and was serving at Netheravon in May when Lt Col Sykes assembled the complete Military Wing for training under his command. On 6th July the Squadron moved to Fort Grange Aerodrome at Gosport where training and working up for war duty continued.

The possibility of war in Ireland was building in the early summer of 1914 and one of Smith-Barry's reasons for learning to fly was in preparation for this. However it was all over shadowed by the developing European crisis and his efforts were directed accordingly. On 14th August 1914, with the outbreak of World War 1, he left with his squadron for staging to Maubeuge in France as part of the Air Contingent accompanying the British Expeditionary Force. The aircraft flown by his squadron at the time were Henry Farmans, Avro 504s and BE8s. It was whilst flying a BE8, nicknamed 'Bloaters', from Amiens to Maubeuge on the 18th, that a control fault developed and the aircraft crashed from a height of 60'. Cpl F.Gerard the observer-mechanic was killed and Smith-Barry taken to hospital in Peronne with two broken legs and a smashed kneecap. On 20th August he received a letter from Major J.F.A. Higgins his Squadron Commander telling him not to worry about the smash as it was not his fault and it was lucky that it was not worse. These comments would seem to have been a little insensitive although Smith-Barry was not then aware of the observer's death. Although he was able to return to service flying, he afterwards walked with a bad limp and often resorted to using a walking stick. The British retreat began following the Battle of Mons on 24th August and soon enemy forces entered the outskirts of Peronne so Smith-Barry got the nursing staff to lift him on to a stretcher and into a horse-drawn cab which took him to St. Quentin. From there he escaped to Rouen by boarding the guard's van of a train. He reached the coast and next day was ferried across the Channel. That evening he was admitted to a nursing home in London where he remained until November. On 24th December his name appeared in the *London Gazette* on his promotion to Flying Officer.

Early in 1915 he was passed fit for home flying duties and was posted to Northolt where he instructed pilots on 50h.p. Gnome Avros. On 22nd January he was promoted to Lieutenant. He was still suffering from his injuries at this time and hobbling with sticks was a pathetic sight. He had received offers of a staff job and an A.D.C. appointment but turned them down. His courage and resolve kept him going and he gradually recovered from his injuries. Whilst instructing by day, he took on the duties of flying anti Zeppeline patrols by night. On 5th November he was gazetted as a Flight Commander with a temporary rank of Captain.

In April 1916 he was again serving at Gosport in a scout instructional squadron. This became the nucleus of No.60 Sqn, and was sent to France commanded by 'Ferdy' Waldron who had been at Upavon with Smith-Barry. He together with Harold H. Balfour later Parliamentary Under Secretary of State for Air and Charles Portal, later appointed as Marshal of the Royal Air Force, was chosen by 'Ferdy' as his Flight Commanders. On 28th May, No.60 Sqn's Morane H aircraft were flown to St. Omer and on the 31st to nearby Boisdinghem. They moved again on 16th June to the farm of Vert Galand. During combat with Fokkers over Cambrai on 3rd July, the Commanding Officer was killed. Smith-Barry had also been engaged in this combat and during a fight with two Fokkers his aircraft suffered considerable damage. One bullet entered the tail and passed along the fuselage and if it had not been deflected by the final cross member, it would have struck him in the back.

With the loss of the CO, Smith-Barry was promoted to Temporary Major and given Command. He was of the opinion that the replacement pilots being sent to him were poorly trained and this proved to be the case with heavy casualties occurring. One seasoned campaigner referred to these replacements as 'Fokker-fodder'. It was not long before No.60 Sqn was withdrawn from operations and re-equipped with fifteen Nieuport biplanes, two Moranes and a Spad. New young pilots joined the squadron following its return to operations, one of these being Second Lieutenant Albert Ball soon to be recognised as the first great ace of the RFC. The number of pilots lost continued to mount and replacements were arriving with only seven hours flying time. Smith-Barry refused to send them over enemy lines and told General Trenchard, the Commander of the RFC in France, his reasons. He also took the opportunity

of writing to him setting out his ideas on how pupil pilots should be taught. In those days instructors tended to look upon their reference as a second rate appointment and they had a lackadaisical approach to teaching their pupils. He pointed out that apathetic instructors bred second rate

L to R Capt Moore, Smith-Barry, Capt Parker and Kitty Smith-Barry. They are on the lawn at *Alverbank*, a house rented by Smith-Barry at Gosport for use as an Officers' Mess.
Photo: A.J. Jackson Coll.

pupils. In his letter Smith-Barry stated that the right men to teach flying with 'dash and confidence' were experienced scout pilots and he proposed that a proper school for turning qualified pilots into instructors should be founded. He wanted more positive teaching and aircraft with dual-control to be used. He emphasised that the pupil should always fly the aircraft from the seat in which he would fly it solo. By using experienced scout instructors and giving them a status and a system on which to work, he thought it would improve the complete instructional format and produce pilots with a higher morale than previously. Trenchard, who was under pressure because of the losses the RFC was experiencing in France at the time, welcomed Smith-Barry's views and told him to go to England and try out his ideas but not to let himself or Trenchard down. He handed over command of No.60 Sqn to Major Graves on Christmas Eve 1916 and left for England where he was given No.1 (Reserve) Sqn at Gosport. In January 1917 he formed his staff and gave them specific and detailed instructions as to how he required pupil pilots to be trained. The instructional aircraft used for this new revolutionary method of training were Sopwith Pups and

Camels, Avro 504s, S.E.5s and Bristol Scouts. The students were given 12 hours instruction on dual-control with exercises and lessons providing a complete understanding of every necessary manoeuvre and the correct method for its implementation. They were given confidence building so that by the time they were ready to go solo they were sure of their own abilities. In May 1917 Smith-Barry issued his "Notes on Teaching Flying for the Instructors' Courses" at what by then was known as No.1 Training Squadron, Gosport. Something he was keen to achieve was a facility for communication between pupil and instructor in a dual-control aircraft. After some failed experimentation at his own cost, a satisfactory system was developed which became known as the 'Gosport Tube' and this was in continuous use by Air Forces all over the world for over thirty years.

From the 23rd August Smith-Barry was appointed Commandant of the School (graded as Wing Commander) with the rank of temporary Lieutenant Colonel. By October his "Notes" had been reproduced in pamphlet form and distributed by the War office throughout the RFC under the title "General Methods of Teaching Scout Pilots". As Commandant Smith-Barry had use of two 'private' aircraft, which were a Sopwith one and a half Strutter B8912 and a 504J Mono-Avro B4221. The latter in which he had the instrument moved to the front cockpit and the resulting space in the rear filled with a small chest of drawers in which he could pack his 'smalls' when staying away from base for the night. The disability in his leg made no difference to his popularity with the ladies and was probably the cause of much friction with his wife, who on one occasion was seen driving their Rolls Royce towards Upavon and shaking her fist at Smith-Barry flying above the road in his aircraft. His flying exploits were matched by his love of fast cars, which he drove at great speeds on the roads and on Salisbury Plain. His friend Douglas Lang wrote that he was as wild as a hawk and utterly fearless. When racing through Burbage near Marlborough on one occasion in 1910, Douglas was shot through the windscreen, over a hedge and into a pond. Smith-Barry even had a Rolls Royce built to accommodate his dogs at the rear. He also owned an open top Lagonda and a brown coloured Napier, which like his private dark blue Puss Moth was well cared for and always in immaculate condition.

On 9th November 1917 he left England on a tour of French flying schools. On 1st January 1918 he was promoted to Brevet Major and on 27th January to the temporary rank of Brigadier-General to command the Northern Training Brigade at York. During this appointment, he made himself very unpopular with some of the high ranking RFC officers and with Trenchard in particular for whom he held little regard. One of his habits was the tendency to 'go over their heads' in his efforts to achieve his aims and this was in contravention of King's Regulations. His ally was Lord Rothermere who had been appointed as the first Air Minister. It was his decision to install Smith-Barry in the London office of Ludlow-Hewitt the Inspector of Training whilst he was away on a tour of inspection. When Ludlow-Hewitt returned and found out about this, he made representation to Trenchard who ordered Smith-Barry to return to Gosport. In a rage Trenchard told the Air Minister that such underhanded behaviour must cease and that there must be better ways of conducting affairs than stimulating the restless brain of a young man who, though a genius among pilots, was an eccentric among administrators. Smith-Barry sent a personal signal to Trenchard which read "Brigadier-General Smith-Barry left London 4.30pm. Major Smith-Barry arrived Gosport 6pm." Officially it was

reported that from 23rd February 1918, he had relinquished the temporary rank of Brigadier-General and taken up the appointment of Commandant in the temporary rank of Lieutenant-Colonel. This did not, however, put an end to his association with Rothermere who, following the formation of the Royal Air Force in April of that year, circulated to the Government a paper on future RAF policy. It is quite probable that much of the paper included submissions from Smith-Barry. He was promoted Temporary Colonel on 17th April.

With his fall from grace amongst the senior Air Force officers, they decided to post him out of harms way. As America was showing signs of interest in the Gosport training methods, it was to New York that he was shipped with a small detachment of staff and twelve crated aircraft. Before departure, however, it was announced, on 18th June, that he was awarded the Air Force Cross.

The course run by Smith-Barry in America, using the Avros taken with him, was run in parallel with a Curtiss Aviation Company course using their own aircraft. On completion the Americans were so impressed with the results of Smith-Barry's School of Special Flying that they endorsed his methods and the Avro aircraft, over that of their own Curtiss built. The Americans proceeded to send both army and navy pilots for the same training.

After the end of the war, the Royal Air Force began to be reduced in size and complement in 1919. As a result Smith-Barry joined the unemployed list on 4th February with the rank of Lieutenant-Colonel. He stayed in America dabbling in stocks and shares until returning to England in 1920, living in Somerset for a short period before moving to Conock Manor, near Devizes in Wiltshire. During this civilian period he had shown little interest in flying but in 1931 he was taken for a flight from Hamble and this re-kindled his enthusiasm so he bought himself a Puss Moth with the registration letters GABLP.

On 9th July 1938 Smith-Barry flew to Brooklands for a re-union of those who had pioneered the early days of flying training in Britain and during this function he was presented with a model

A 1935 advertisement

of the Avro B3157 by the Brooklands Club. This aircraft was the first to be given an engine conversion by Smith-Barry in 1917. The model he was presented with survives in the ownership of Richard Newman, who lives locally, and whose Grand-mother was housekeeper, and his aunt May was cook to the Smith-Barrys.

With the clouds of war looming again, he enrolled on an instructor's course at Brooklands. He felt that it was in this capacity that his services would be directed.

He was fifty-five years old when, on 23rd May 1940, he was appointed to the General Duties branch of the RAFVR in the rank of Pilot Officer. He reported to the Central Flying School Upavon to attend a Flying Refresher Course. He made over eighty flights both dual and solo, flying Masters, Oxfords, Tutors, Harvards, Beauforts, Blenheims and a Hurricane. On 19th August he was posted to No.4 Ferry Pilots' Pool at Kemble from where he proceeded to ferry various types of aircraft between storage depots in Britain. On 16th October, a not very fine day, he was delivering a much needed Blenheim (Z5964) from Woodford to Charmy Down, Bath, when lost and surrounded by cloud covered hills, he crash landed, coincidentally, on the estate of Guy Smith-Barry, a relative living at Holt in Wiltshire. He released his harness prior to the crash on the basis that in two previous crashes it had resulted in him being thrown clear and so saved his life. The aircraft was ripped apart when it hit a large tree, and an engine and wing caught fire. Smith-Barry was

The Brooklands Club model Avro B3157.

The following are his decorations shown in the photograph of the Avro B3157 which he was presented with by the Brooklands Club:-

Air Force Cross
1914 Star
British War Medal
Victory Medal 1914-18
Defence Medal
Commander de l'Ordre de Leopold
Medal of American Aero Club

thrown out and suffered serious facial injuries which included a broken jaw. He picked himself up, located his walking stick and inspected the damage before being taken to hospital in Bath. He was transferred from there to the Queen Victoria Hospital in East Grinstead where his smashed jaw was worked on by the eminent surgeon Archie McIndoe. The injury however was to leave him with a twisted mouth.

Following convalescence Smith-Barry went to the Air Ministry on 15th February 1941 where he carried out duties with the Director of Flying Training. On 22nd May he was passed fit to fly again and appointed as a substantive RAFVR Flying Officer but given the acting rank of Sqn Ldr, for a posting to command RAF Gravesend, a Fighter Command airfield. On 15th June he was transferred to command Croydon and on 22nd July was further promoted to war substantive Flt Lt. Command of Stapleford Tawney followed on 5th October. All three of these airfields were satellites. Three weeks later on 27th October he was posted to No.3 Service Flying Training School, South Cerney as Chief Ground Instructor.

Smith-Barry left Conock Manor in mid 1942 after asking for a posting to India. He took up his appointment with Air Headquarters Delhi on 19th June 1942 and went to No.151 OTU at Risalpur on the North West Frontier on 9th September. His appointment and rank were the same as at South Cerney. The Unit was engaged in training Indian pilots on Hurricanes prior to joining front line squadrons. The younger instructors and pupils alike were apprehensive on his arrival, noting his age, limp and battered face but they were soon won over by his character, unique flying ability and his sportsmanship. He paid little heed to regulations and applied his own standards as he saw fit. He would never fly with a parachute but instead always had with him a cushion with his initials embroidered on. He also took the various drugs which were available in India at that time. This was just another experience he had to try. Such behaviour was the source of much amusement to his colleagues but he also held their greatest respect.

The Chief Flying Instructor of No.151 OTU, Wing Commander C.W. Stone put Smith-Barry's name forward to command the Initial Flying Training School which at the time, was turning out pilots of an inferior calibre. He was the obvious person for the post but the recommendation was viewed as controversial and, although he was summoned to Delhi for interview, he was not awarded the position. It was obvious that he continued to be of considerable embarrassment to the Air Ministry. In June 1943 Smith-Barry resigned his commission. He continued to live in India on a houseboat on the Dahl Lake in Kashmir until September 1945 when he returned to England to marry Anne Garnier. They returned to India after the wedding to live in Natal. Two years later they bought a house in Durban and went there to live. By this time Smith-Barry was in considerable pain from his damaged leg and walking was becoming ever more difficult. In 1949 he had an operation to relieve the pain but suffered a sudden relapse the day afterwards and died on 23rd May. He was laid to rest in a Zulu burial ground.

EVERLEIGH SATELLITE LANDING GROUND

Location -173/SU195562 - 2 miles East of former Upavon Airfield

The landing strip at Everleigh was on an area of West Everleigh Down known as Round Down off of the C53 Pewsey to Everleigh road and NW of the Village of Everleigh.

Airfield Development

The name given to the airfield was Everleigh Ashes. Its use as a Satellite for aircraft dispersal was ideal with the natural camouflage afforded by the surrounding Everleigh Ashes woods. The main grass runway running NW/SE, 1600yds x 150yds had been prepared by December 1941. There was already a certain amount of accommodation at this stage, namely the HQ building and a guard room hut. Two Lewis gun emplacements provided defence for the site. These were manned by a RAF Defence Flt accommodated initially at nearby Upavon airfield and later on site in army type Nissen huts. Further improvements such as hard standings and approach roads continued through 1942. In May 1942 an additional NE/SW runway 1050yds x 150yds was prepared. A 200yd rifle range was also provided.

Official figures for only one of the runways has been found (1050yds) and the longer of the two at Everleigh was reached, by surveying the ground, having pegged it out from a 1945 aerial photograph, so the length given should not be taken as accurate.

During the summer of 1943 a Super Robin Type hangar was built by G.M. Carter north of the landing ground and on the opposite side of the C53 Pewsey to Everleigh road. Catering accommodation and an armoury were also added at this time.

World War 2 Years

Everleigh was in use as a practice forced landing ground and for circuit training in 1940/41 by Master aircraft from the CFS at Upavon based 1 mile away. Master I N7426 of the CFS crashed on landing at Everleigh on 13th May 1941. On 22nd November 1941 the landing ground became No.31 SLG in No.52 Wing and used by No.15 MU

Wroughton, from where aircraft arrived in considerable numbers during the first few months of 1942.

Winston Churchill visited Everleigh in April 1942 to witness an airborne exercise in which paratroops were dropped and landed by Whitleys towing Hotspur gliders. Unfortunately the paratroops were dropped late and found themselves in the landing path of the Hotspurs. Two soldier were killed and some of the gliders got into difficulties trying to land clear of the men on the ground. The exercise was a failure and an obvious embarrassment to the army officers in the presence of the Prime Minister.

By the spring and of 1942 aircraft numbers at Everleigh were increasing. Hurricanes and Wellingtons were prominent but in addition there were Spitfires, Lysanders, Oxfords and Hotspur gliders. AVM Laing of No.41 Group inspected the Satellite on 1st September 1942 in preparation for its transfer to Lyneham. He was shown the dispersal areas, camouflage and defence arrangements and the new rifle range. He also discussed the welfare needs of the civilian staff employed on site.

Exercise *Eve* was staged on 11th September 1942, with 91 troops of 1st Air Landing Brigade being given air experience in 13 Hotspur gliders towed

from Hurn to Everleigh by Whitleys of No.296 and No.297 Sqn. Five of the gliders were damaged on landing and three were recovered by Hectors the following day. A repeat of the exercise coded *Mars*, was staged on 14th September but bad weather prevented landings at Everleigh. Three of the gliders landed at Netheravon and one crashed at Maiden Bradley near Zeals. These glider exercises would have been staged on the nearby ranges at Everleigh and not on the site of the SLG.

On 17th September 1942 the SLG was transferred to No.33 MU Lyneham although the first three aircraft had already arrived for dispersal on the 7th September and a further six the following day. Concern was expressed that some of the chalk access ways to the dispersals were clearly visible from the air and camouflaging was required. Everleigh remained under the control of Lyneham for the rest of the war but was still used on occasion when required by No.15 MU Wroughton. Both No.39 MU Colerne and No.10 MU Hullavington also used the facility. Being one of the largest SLGs, this was possible because of its capacity to hold 105 aircraft.

Stirlings from No.10 MU started arriving in December 1943 and continued to build up to a total of 87 by the summer of 1944. At this time US

**Civilian Ground Staff with Harvard training aircraft at Everleigh SLG C.1944/45.
Standing 2nd from left - Richard Pearce, 3rd from right - John Flippance
Photo: Richard Pearce**

tanks, equipment and fuel stocks were arriving at Woodborough railway station from where they were transported to the landing ground at Everleigh on route to the Normandy landings. Part of the route from the railway station was via the narrow lanes and past the butcher's shop of Vigor & Son in Woodborough. During one of these convoys the shop lost its verandah when it was demolished by a tracked vehicle which in turn ended up in the garden.

The airfield was guarded at night by dogs, which were kept in kennels in the woods during the day. The dogs would be released by their handlers after the last of the civilian ground staff finished work for the day. They were allowed to run free around the dispersed aircraft during the night and would be re-kennelled again, first thing in the morning.

Harvards began replacing the Stirlings of No.10 MU in the latter part of 1944 and were the principle type in storage, with the exception of one Stirling, when the war ended in 1945.

It is recalled locally that most of the take-off and landings were carried out using the NW/SE landing strip. The Stirling was the largest aircraft at Everleigh and if necessary it could have taken-off on the shorter NE/SW strip. In mid 1940 A&AEE Boscombe Down, which at the time only had grass strips, tested a Stirling and, at 57,000lbs, it unstuck at 640 yards.

The two grass runways with Harvards in storage on the opposite side of the road on 11th October 1945.

Photo of Super Robins type hangar at Everleigh.

Harvards in storage at a dispersal slightly west of the landing ground but on the opposite side of the road on 27th July 1945.   Photos: NMRO.

Aerial views showing: A Stirling at the west end of the main runway on 22nd July 1945.

Closure

The site was closed after the war and returned to agriculture. It remains as Crown property and the Army's helicopters on exercise can still be seen on occasion, emerging from behind the trees of Everleigh Ashes.

The Robins type hangar was re-skinned in the 1990s and is used for agricultural purposes. The access track from the road and the apron is the original concrete laid during the war. In Everleigh Ashes at the rear of the hangar, two Maycrete storage buildings remain in good condition together with signs of derelict buildings. Two identical buildings remain in the woods at the SE end of the main runway.

1) 174/SU278647 - 6 miles South East of Marlborough

Close to the centre of the village of Great Bedwyn on the C74. In the Memorial Field on the east side are planted 9 oak trees, one for each of the servicemen from the village who gave their lives during World War 2. Set amongst the trees is a memorial stone surrounded by a white wooden fence. The stone which was dedicated on Sunday 16th May 1993, is inset with a plaque displaying the names of those killed, each beneath an oak tree and headed with the following inscription: -

These trees, planted in the Memorial Field of Great Bedwyn, are a living memorial to those who gave their lives in the 1939-45 War								
Acting P.O. RF Burgess RN	Troop Baker FJ Cambridge MN	Stoker P.O. WTG Cope RN	C.S.M. JA Collier Wilts Reg	Corpl. RE Fruen Royal Berks Rgt	Private WG Grace RE	P/O D McLeod Craik RAF	Sergt AG PAD Lawrence RAF VR	W/O DC Trench RAF

The Bedwyn Memorial Stone and Plaque.
Photo: R. Priddle.

The following are service details of one of these RAF men: -

Sgt Percy A.D. Lawrence RAFVR - joined the air force in 1943 and commenced his training as an airgunner on 9th November completing the course on 10th December. No.626 Sqn (No.1 Group) had formed at Wickenby on 7th November equipped with Lancaster Is & IIIs. He joined this new squadron as a mid-upper gunner, commencing operations in 1944. Sgt Lawrence was one of the crew of Lancaster I LM102 UM-Z2 which was shot down over the village of Belloy 26 miles ENE of Beauvais, France on 22nd/23rd June 1944. The crew had taken off at 2222 hrs for their twelfth operation, a raid on the railway yards at Rheims. The squadron had put up 20 aircraft for this operation. Very little flak was encountered and fighter opposition was moderate. Nothing however was heard of 'Z2' following take-off. All seven airmen were buried in the local churchyard at Belloy on 24th June. These were Flt Sgt R. A. Woolley (pilot), Sgt A. D. Hawkins (Flt Eng), Sgt F. Goddard (nav), Sgt H.E. Brown (WOP), E.G. Lewis (B/A), Sgt P.A.D. Lawrence (mid-upper gunner) and Sgt E.R.S. Kirby (rear gunner), all were RAFVR. At this stage of the war, it was quite unusual to find an all sergeant crew in the RAF.

Note: While this is a multi-service memorial, it has been included by the author because of its RAF content and the pleasant format of the display. Stone memorials displaying the names of the nine Bedwyn men can also be seen in the churchyard and another on the north wall of St. Mary the Virgin Church, Church Street, Great Bedwyn.

2) 174/SU278645 6 miles SE of Marlborough

In Church Street, next to the post office, can be found a firm of stonemasons, Lloyds of Bedwyn. At the entrance is a memorial in the form of a stone aeroplane. The memorial is dedicated to Captain The Honourable Eric Fox Pitt Lubbock MC, RFC, 45th Sqn RFC, son of Lord and Lady Avebury. The family had the memorial made, and positioned on their estate in Kent, after Capt Lubbock was killed during World War 1. He was buried in Lijssenthoek Military Cemetery, Poperinge, West Vlaanderen, Belguim. The memorial, which was later moved to its present location, has the following inscription: -

CAPT ERIC FOX PITT LVBBOCK RFC MC SON OF JOHN BARON AVEBURY AND ALICE HIS WIFE BORN 16 MAY 1893 KILLED IN ACTION 11 MAR. 1917 BURIED AT POPERINGHE BELGIVM

The aeroplane memorial to Capt Lubbock.

HIGH POST AERODROME
Location - 184/SU150365 - 4 miles North of Salisbury

This former airfield is located at the junction of the A345 and C292 road to Upper Woodford and at the rear of The Inn at High Post which was originally the High Post Hotel.

Aerodrome Development

The aerodrome was opened in May 1931 for the private use of the Wiltshire Light Aeroplane & Country Club, which subsequently became The Wiltshire School of Flying Ltd (Telephone No. Middle Woodford 23). Initially there were no buildings and facilities on site. Later however, provision was made for a clubhouse and two aircraft hangars, one of which was obtained from Stonehenge Aerodrome where it had been used by the Handley-Page Flying School. This was one section of a corrugated iron multi-bay hangar and a suitable size for housing the Club's private aeroplanes. The height however, was reduced to half its original dimensions. The clubhouse later had a watch-tower added on one end and beside it, what looked like a water tank on top of a tower but was in fact a fuel storage tank.

The cost of club membership was: -

Entrance Fee	£1 : 1s : 0d
Annual Subscription - Flying	£3 : 3s : 0d
- Associate	£2 : 2s : 0d

In 1935 The Wiltshire School of Flying Ltd took the decision to construct new aerodrome buildings on the site consisting of offices, observation tower, wireless room and a fully licensed hotel with a public restaurant. One of the requirements of the main complex was that it should have no recognisable back elevation to it. One side was to face the aerodrome and the other the main Salisbury to Amesbury road from which entry would be gained. Therefore both elevations had to look attractive. The appointed architects, Bothams & Browns of Salisbury provided a satisfactory solution. Their drawings show the aerodrome fascia (top) and the Salisbury to Amesbury main road fascia (bottom).

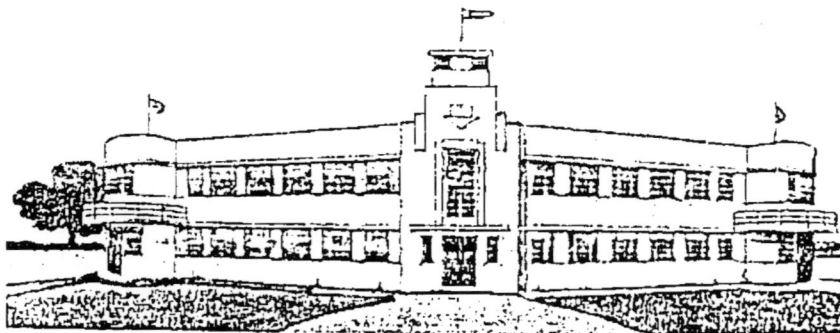

High Post Hotel sketches

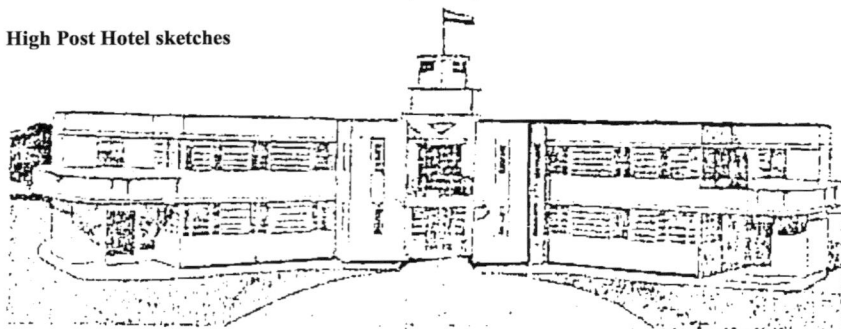

High Post Aerodrome Hotel and observation tower seen shortly after building work had been completed.   Photo: Norman Parker Coll.

In 1941 Vickers Armstrong Supermarine operated from the airfield using both of the Flying School hangars for Spitfire assembly. The second hangar was purpose built adjacent to the hotel and petrol filling station. The two small buildings were used until June 1944 when a double Type B1 hangar was built for aircraft assembly, south of the junction of the A345 and the C292. This land has now been developed and is occupied by Mahle Tennex Filter Systems Ltd.

The original club house belonging to the Wiltshire School of Flying was used as a canteen by Vickers staff who were not too impressed with its location on the opposite side of the airfield, reached after a considerable walk along the road to Upper Woodford. The same could be said of the accommodation provided, which consisted of a number of railway carriages sited near the farm buildings, south of the Woodford Valley road.

A 1939 advertisement.

When High Post was taken over for military use in World War 2 it was a relatively small aerodrome. As the weight and performance increased it was expanded and grass runways were prepared. This necessitated the removal of the clubhouse and the Flying School hangar. The latter was rebuilt inside the WAECO compound for the use of their transport section.

In June 1944, when the new manufacturing and assembly works came on line close to High Post, the C292 road was closed to provide for a 1760 yd N/S runway leading from the works across the road and passing the rear of the hotel. The barriers on the road were in the temporary form of 4 Hawker Tomtit aircraft fuselages easily removed with the end of hostilities and aircraft production. High Post's three runways were on grass with the main one NE/SW 2000yds also crossing the same road on to farm land at a point just east of the WAECO site. This terminated on the N/E end, close to the A345 Salisbury to Amesbury road. The third E/W 1500yds ran from the side of the hotel to the Upper Woodford road. It went directly through the WAECO proofing site. Permission was obtained from the control tower on occasions when tests were staged. It was also essential that smoke from any tests did not obstruct any of the runways in use.

Inter War Years

The School's early aircraft were two Robinson Redwing G-ABMF and G-ABLA. The latter crashed at nearby Great Durnford on 12th October 1932.

de Havilland Gipsy Moths at High Post C.1937. Photo: Ken Sholto, Cty. Dr. H.F. Thomas

The Club founder and managing director was former RAF pilot Mr J.E. (Jimmy) Doran-Webb. His brother R.F. (Frank) Doran-Webb formed the Wessex Aircraft Engineering Co. Ltd (WAECO) in March 1933, leasing an acre of land adjacent to the road to Upper Woodford. In the early days the company was formed to manufacture smoke generators which, when dropped by the pilots of private light aircraft, would indicate wind direction for landing. However restrictions imposed by the Air Ministry resulted in the failure of this product and the business for a few years struggled to survive. The Wiltshire School of Flying Ltd, on the other hand, developed into a prosperous concern and during the last quarter of 1935 the Company increased its capital from £4000 to £10,000 with Mr C.G. Lumsden, late of Imperial Airways Ltd., among the new directors.

During the mid 1930s High Post was one of five aerodromes operating in Wiltshire. It quickly gained an impressive reputation which was greatly enhanced by the building of the High Post Hotel, petrol filling station, and the golf course on the opposite side of the A345. The aerodrome at High Post was the only civilian operated one to be open to the general public for the first 'Empire Air Day' held on 24th May 1934.

World War 2 Years

This private aerodrome was closed in September 1939 when war broke out and was taken over for military use. The first unit to use it was 'D' Flight, who had formed at Old Sarum on 1st February 1940, and was at High Post for equipping during that month. It was followed on 6th June by an advance party of No.112 (AC) Sqn RCAF from

Post card picture showing the completed aerodrome buildings/hotel in 1937 with High Post Golf Course in the foreground. The aeroplane hangar in the top right of the picture is believed to be the one used by the former Handley Page Flying School at Stonehenge Aerodrome which was moved to High Post in 1931. This was later in use by the Wessex Aircraft Co. (WAECO) which gave its name to the pyrotechnic factory on the same site. Later still it became the Pains Wessex factory Photo: Rex Reynolds

The camouflaged High Post Hotel and Control Tower. The 'Pundit' code for night-time airfield identification was 'HP' with the beacon flashing green when in civilian use and red in military.
Photo: Rex Reynolds

Old Sarum. They set up a tented camp and were engaged in providing air raid shelters, airfield defences and camouflaging the buildings in preparation for the expected invasion.

The hotel was taken over as the Officers' Mess and the main party of Canadians moved in from Old Sarum on 14th June 1940. Their Lysanders began to arrive ten days later and flying commenced in July. The artillery observation training and live shoots were staged on the ranges at Larkhill. On 3rd August two gliders from the Special Duty Flight at Christchurch were in use for towing trials at High Post. A Scott Viking crashed after its wing touched the ground whilst avoiding one of them. On 3rd September 1940 Tiger Moth II R4970, in use by the Canadian squadron, crashed outside of the airfield perimeter. No.112 Sqn moved to more permanent accommodation at RAF Halton on 13th November 1940 with its two remaining Tiger Moths and seven Lysanders.

With the enforced cessation of private flying at High Post the aircraft, which in the main were Piper Cubs, were stored in the hangars. In November 1940 they were taken to Old Sarum for preparation prior to joining 'D' Flight at Larkhill.

A Botha I L6254 piloted by Sqn Ldr R.G. Slade, suffered a double engine failure on take-off from Boscombe Down on 11th December, and made a wheels-up landing at High Post. The main fuel cocks had not been turned on before take-off, and whilst there was sufficient fuel in the system to allow take-off, both engines cut soon after.

The fuel cocks could not be reached from the pilot's seat.

From 29th November 1940, No.1 SFTS Netheravon and CFS Upavon started using High Post for circuit training with Masters, Battles and Oxfords. No.1 SFTS wanted to extend the site to allow night flying training but this was refused. Some night flying was tried in March 1941 but the restricted length of the aerodrome landing area and the close proximity of the munitions factory made it impractical. A detachment of No.41 OTU Old Sarum was at Highpost from 1st-15th November 1942 prior to moving to Hawarden.

Use of Highpost as a Relief Landing Ground (RLG) ended shortly after an accident on 10th September 1943. A No.617 Sqn Lancaster JA894, which was in the Boscombe Down circuit, collided with Oxford MK.II EB981. At the time the Oxford, a No.7 FIS (A)

A 1939 advertisement

aircraft from Upavon, was carrying out a routine landing approach at High Post. There were no survivors. The two airfields were so close to each other that their circuits overlapped in the vicinity of the collision. Another A&AEE aircraft was involved in a serious accident at High Post on 4th January 1943. This was Mosquito PR VIII DK324. It was not written off however, and continued in squadron service until SOC on 1st November 1946.

Supermarine's main factory for Spitfire production in Southampton was damaged beyond use in the raids of September 1940 and considerable disruption was caused to the various production units in the area. Because of this vulnerability, a decision was taken to disperse production and assembly to safer locations away from the coast. Trowbridge and Salisbury were two Wiltshire locations chosen for this work. The overall plan was to develop each area into a self contained Spitfire production unit with its own airfield. In Trowbridge this was not achieved until later in the war, but in Salisbury, production commenced in various premises in the city. When the aircraft had been assembled at High Post and Chattis Hill in Dorset, they were flown out from the airfields. The first Spitfire assembled and flown from High Post was a Mk.I X4497 on 12th January 1941. It was subsequently converted to PR Type C in April 1941.

Production of wings and fuselage installation work, which included the engine installation, was carried out in the requisitioned Wilts & Dorset Bus Garage in Castle Street and Leading Edge assemblies were built opposite, in the garage of Anna Valley Motors. Fuselages were built in the Wessex Garage, New Street, in the shadow of Salisbury Cathedral. A new factory was built in Castle Road near Old Sarum for final fuselage and engine assembly with a No.2 factory added later. These completed aircraft would be moved on Queen Mary aircraft transport vehicles to High Post or Chattis Hill for final assembly, weighing and compass calibration. Use of the premises in Salisbury continued until the end of the war with the Castle Road Works No.2 factory remaining in production until the 1950s.

An aerial view of the High Post site on 29th October 1946. The two Type B1 hangars are seen by the row of trees, and the grass runway to the right passes over the closed lane to Upper Woodford, ending close to the Winterbourne Gunner turning.Photo: NMRO

Cyril Russell an employee of Vickers was at High Post in 1942/43 and part of his work involved the reception of the equipped fuselages and wings prior to assembly. When the Queen Marys arrived, strops were placed under the leading edges of the wings and lifted off vertically and stored vertically until required. When assembled to the fuselage, men would be summoned by a shout "All under the Wings". Eight to ten men would take the weight of the wing onto their backs on its under surface and shuffle their way into the assembly shed until the alignment with the fuselage wing spar had been made and the wing bolts driven home. The building had a large set of double doors on the western airfield side, wide enough to allow the assembled aircraft to pass through. On the east-side facing the A345, there was a smaller set of double doors suitable for receipt of the aircraft parts. These however were rarely used as the Queen Marys invariably drove to the doors on the airfield side.

Once the wings had been secured, control wires, hydraulics to under-carriage, pneumatics to gun bays and electrics would be installed. With the undercarriage functioning, the wheels would be locked down and the Spitfire would rest on them. All the other various fitments would be carried out by both the male and female fitters. Machine guns and, or cannon, would be released from the adjoining armoury

room for installation in the wings dependent on the Mark of the Spitfire. The bay for the camera gun would be prepared, camouflage would be touched up where the joints of the wings to the fuselage had been made. Stencils would be applied to spray on

before the engine was run-up by a Rolls Royce representative. The compass would then be 'swung' and a final inspection carried out by an Air Ministry representative, who would authorise it for flight-testing. A test pilot would be detailed to carry out the test. Jeffrey Quill, Vickers' Chief Test Pilot had a team of pilots to assist with production testing, often they were experienced service pilots seconded between operational postings.

When the pilot signed the aircraft as being satisfactory the Air Ministry representative would complete a form indicating the aircraft as being taken 'on charge' and arrangements would be made for an ATA pilot to fly it to a Maintenance Unit after testing. Many of the High Post Spitfires were collected by No.15 Ferry Pilots Pool at Hamble. For example on 13th February 1942 ATA pilot Ann Welch flew from there the short distance to 39 MU Colerne with Spitfire AB413 and on the following day to 6 MU at Brize Norton with Spitfire AB459.

The initial assembly shed at High Post was only capable of accommodating three Spitfires at a time. Work on them was continual, with two shifts working night and day, month and month about.

In the foreground a Seafire 47 with, on top Arthur Edridge a Vickers' Inspector and standing left to right aircraft mechanics Tony Dean and Maurice Henderson. In the backround, outside the assembly shed, is the 2nd prototype Spiteful NN664.   Photo: George Harris

the serial number allocated to that aircraft. One of the last fitments would be the propeller before the aircraft was pushed outside and the fuel tanks filled. Various checks were then made

The output was generally six completed aircraft per week. The aircraft assembled at High Post through the war years were the Spitfires Mks I, V, VIII, IX, XII, Seafires, and the

Spiteful which was developed as a Fighter/Bomber. The first production flight of the latter was by Spiteful NN660 on 30th June 1944 in the hands of Jeffrey Quill. This aircraft crashed in the Woodford Valley near Campdown Hill in September when it was being flown by the Vicker's test pilot and former horse-race jockey Frank Furlong, who was killed. Seafire 47s came into service after the war and served with success in Korea.

On Friday 31st August 1945, Westland built Seafire F.XVII SW987, flown by Flt Lt Francis S. Banner DFC*, RAFVR, crashed at High Post. The aircraft stalled on approach whilst practising airfield dummy deck landings. The pilot later died from his injuries.

From June 1944 Supermarine's Experimental Flight Test Department transferred to High Post from Worthy Down. A number of Sea Otters were delivered there during 1944/45 and taken on charge by the Royal Navy.

Post War Years

High Post continued as a test centre for the Company during the immediate post war years. The prototype of the first jet aircraft to enter service with the Royal Navy, Supermarine's Type 398 Attacker F1 TS409, was assembled and made its first flight from Boscombe Down on the opposite side of the A345 on 27th July 1946, landing back at High Post for future testing. Trial flights by the Attacker continued from the grass runways of High Post until the airfield closed in 1947.

The Wiltshire School of Flying returned to High Post on 16th April 1946, now with Magisters and Austers (British Taylorcraft Plus D), and was re-joined by the Royal Artillery Flying Club. The airfield, however, did not return to its 1930s affluence and the glory years of private flying because, with the decision to retain and develop A&AEE at Boscombe Down, flying from High Post was impractical. The flight path of the new runway at Boscombe Down was directly over the club airfield.

Known Austers at High Post during 1946/47 G-AHKO (LB381), G-AHAF (T9120), G-AHUG. These were painted metallic silver-blue with red noses.

Closure

The airfield closed in February 1947 with Vickers Armstong Ltd transferring their Flight Test Centre to the vacated airfield at Chilbolton, and both flying clubs moving east to Thruxton just over the county boundary in Hampshire.

In July 1948 the obsolete double Type B1 hangars were taken down and re-erected at Boscombe Down. These appear under **Boscombe Down** when photographed in 1985 behind Harvard FT375.

The original Flying School hangar from Stonehenge is still used by Pains Wessex Ltd, who are recognised producers of marine and military pyrotechnics. The hotel has been considerably extended, but the control tower is no longer recognisable, following external work to the premises. The building used as a Spitfire assembly shed is in use, appropriately enough, for precision and production engineering by Apsley Engineering, and has a new office block built onto the southern end.

The airfield itself is now used by farmer Wilson Baird, who also uses a Robin type hangar as a grain dryer beside the road to Upper Woodford. This, however, was erected after military use of the airfield ceased and originally housed a cigarette and cigar manufacturer.

Robin type hangar in use for farming.

The Spitfire assembly shed prior to occupation by Apsley Engineering.   Photo: Graham Aymes

In St. Michael's Church on the A361. In the Warneford family chapel, a marble memorial plaque mounted with the coat of arms of the Warneford family, which is inscribed: -

THIS TABLET WAS PLACED HERE BY MEMBERS OF THE WARNEFORD FAMILY THROUGHOUT THE WORLD IN MEMORY OF FLIGHT SUB LIEUTENANT REGINALD ALEXANDER JOHN WARNEFORD V C R N CHEVALIER OF THE LEGION OF HONOUR AGED 23 YEARS SON OF THE LATE REGINALD WILLIAM HENRY WARNEFORD Grandson of the late Rev. T L J Warneford Chaplain to the forces in India Gt. Nephew of the late Rev. Canon Warneford of Warneford Place. He was honoured by his King with the Victoria Cross & by the French Nation with the Medal of the Legion of Honour for pursuing & destroying single-handed a Zeppelin Airship nr Ghent in Belgium on 7th June 1915. He was killed 10 days later when flying in Paris on 17th June 1915 & lies buried in Brompton Cemetery where the Nation has shown its gratitude & recognition of his great achievement in the erection of a Memorial by Public Subscription+

To God only wise
be glory.

The marble memorial plaque to Sub Lt Warneford.

Flight Sub Lieutenant R.A.J. Warneford VC, RN was born in Darjeeling, India on 15th October 1891. Reginald, known as Rex, returned to this country in 1902 to be educated at King Edward VI School, Stratford-upon-Avon. His education was cut short for financial reasons and at the age of thirteen he was back in India as an apprentice with the British India Steam Navigation Company. In 1914, at the age of twenty-three, having served with various shipping lines, he was first officer on an oil tanker outward bound from Cardiff to San Francisco via the Panama Canal. On the return trip, which was around Cape Horn, the ship went aground and was badly holed. She was re-floated and managed to reach a dry dock at Talcahuano where the full extent of the damage was discovered. As the repairs were going to take a long time, Rex was sent back to England on the first available ship to give the owners a full report. This was to be his final voyage

and on the 8th January 1915 he enlisted with the 2nd Sportman's Battalion. The following month he transferred to the Royal Naval Air Service for training as a pilot. He attended the civilian school at Hendon and in a very short time obtained his wings. He was granted his Royal Aero Club Certificate No.1098 on the 25th February 1915 and then attended at CFS Upavon for further training. On leaving Upavon he was posted to 2 Sqn RNAS at Eastchurch where he spent a short time before flying an Avro 504 to join 1 Squadron RNAS at St Pol close to Dunkirk on the 7th May 1915.

At this time Zeppelin airships were being used to carry out bombing raids over England and neither attack from the ground or air defences had succeeded in bringing any down. On the night of the 6/7th June, Zeppelins LZ37/38 & 39 were launched from their bases in Belgium for an attack on London. Due to bad weather and in the case of LZ38, an engine fault, all three turned back but their radio signals had been picked up. Flight Sub Lieutenants Warneford and Rose were ordered to

Rex Warneford in front of a Maurice Farman 11 at Hendon.
Photo: Elizabeth McDougall/FAAM

intercept the airships in the vicinity of Ghent but, failing contact, to bomb the airship sheds at Berchem St Agathe, to the west of Brussels. The two pilots took off from the Belgian aerodrome of Furnes which was used by the RNAS as an ALG. Soon after take-off Rose suffered an instrument light failure. He made an emergency landing in which his Morane turned over but he escaped injury. Warneford continued the interception and the details of his engagement appeared in his official report of the 8th June as follows: -

I left Furnes at 1.00am on June 7th on Morane No 3253 under orders to proceed to look for Zeppelins and attack the Berchem St Agathe Airship Shed with six 20lb bombs.

On arrival at Dixmude at 1.15am, I observed a Zeppelin apparently over Ostend and proceeded in chase of the same.

I arrived at close quarters a few miles past Bruges at 1.50am and the Airship opened heavy maxim fire, so I retreated to gain height and the Airship turned and followed me.

At 2.15am he seemed to stop firing and at 2.25am I came behind, but well above the Zeppelin; height then 11,000 feet, and switched off my engine to descend on top of him.

When close above him (at 7000 feet altitude) I dropped my bombs, and, whilst releasing the last, there was an explosion which lifted my machine and turned it over. The aeroplane was out of control for a short period, but went into a nose dive, and the control was regained.

I then saw that the Zeppelin was on the ground in flames and also that there were pieces of something burning in the air all the way down.

The joint on my petrol pipe and pump from the back tank was broken, and at about 2.40am I was forced to land and repair my pump. I landed at the back of a forest close to a farmhouse, the district is unknown on account of the fog and the continuous changing of course.

I made preparations to set the machine on fire, but apparently was not observed, so was enabled to effect a repair, and continued at 3.15am in a South Westerly direction after considerable difficulty in starting my engine single handed.

I tried several times to find my whereabouts by descending through the clouds, but was unable to do so. So

eventually I landed and found that it was Cape Gris Nez, and took in some petrol. When the weather cleared I was able to proceed and arrived at the Aerodrome about 10.30am.

As far as could be seen the colour of the Airship was green on top and yellow below and there was no machine gun or platform on top.

Zeppelin LZ37 unfortunately fell onto the convent of St. Elisabeth in the Mont St Amand district of Ghent, part of which was destroyed by fire and resulted in the deaths of two nuns and a child. When the war was over, despite these losses the nuns erected a commemorative plaque in the convent, inscribed in French and Flemish, with the head and shoulders of Flt Sub Lt Warneford in flying helmet shown in relief. In addition, a street near to the convent has been named after him. There were 28 persons on the Zeppelin and all perished with the exception of the *Steuermann* (coxwain) Alfred Muhler, who was able to return to flying after recovering from his injuries.

On the 8th June, King George V, without precedent, sent a telegram to Sub Lt Warneford informing him that he had conferred upon him the Victoria Cross. The following day General Joffre recommended that he be awarded the Knight's Cross of the Legion of Honour. Warneford also went to Paris where the Minister of War, Alexandre Millerand, presented him with his own insignia, saying "I shall be proud to wear the one destined for you in its stead".

His orders while in Paris were to attend any functions the French had arranged in his honour and afterwards to collect and test a new Henri Farman Biplane at Buc Aerodrome. He was then to fly it back to St. Pol. On 17th June 1915, even though the new plane was minus some fittings such as the body straps in the cockpit, Warneford took off on a test flight with a journalist named Henry Beach Needham but the plane went into a spin on its landing approach and broke up in the air. As neither of the men were strapped in, they both fell to the ground. Needham was killed instantly and Flt Sub Lt Warneford died shortly afterwards at the British Military Hospital in Versailles.

On Monday 21st June his body was

brought back across the Channel from Dieppe and borne by train to Victoria Station for burial the following day at Brompton Cemetery. The people of the nation were considerably moved by this particular death, as it had occurred so soon after the celebrations of his act of heroism. Crowds of people had gathered outside the railway station and several hundred followed the cortege on its journey to the cemetery. Warneford's body lay that night in the annexe of the cemetery chapel. Although the interment was at 4pm, crowds were forming at the cemetery in the morning. By 4pm the police and service men were struggling to hold back the vast numbers of people. After the service of remembrance in the chapel attended by the family and officers only, the coffin was placed on the gun-carriage by eight men of the Royal Naval Division and escorted to the grave-side by 150 men of the Division. A salute from a firing party of 50 men was given and the last post was played. A memorial service was held the following day at the British Embassy in Paris.

His mother received the following telegram from King George V: -

It is a matter of sincere regret to me that the death of Flight Sub-Lieutenant Reginald Alexander John Warneford deprived me of the pride of personally conferring upon him the Victoria Cross, the greatest of all naval distinctions.

Not everybody was enamoured with the awarding of the VC for this particular deed and in the light of later acts of valour, the reasons for this are perhaps understandable. Possibly with its occurrence early in the war, it was also the first Zeppelin brought down, and having no precedent in that campaign to match it against, the award was hastily made and promulgated. It still, however, took an act of supreme courage to drop six bombs onto an envelope of gas from just 70' above it. Presumably had he been killed in the act of destroying the Zeppelin that afternoon, it may have been looked upon differently by the critics. Having said this however, the following year a VC was awarded in similar circumstances. This was to Lt William Leefe-Robinson who was awarded his VC for the destruction of the German Schutte Lanz type Airship SL.11 on the night of 3rd September 1916. This was the first one to be brought down over England when it crashed in flames at Cuffley, Hertfordshire when attacked by Leefe-Robinson in his BE2c. Whenever war is waged there will always be some controversial awards bestowed and in the eyes of some there will be acts of apparent heroism for which awards are not made but are considered justified. Whatever people's views are or were in relation to the award made to Sub Lt Warneford, at the end of the day, like so many others he gave his life for his country in a time of war.

A few days after his death an unpleasant rumour was circulating that Sub Lt Warneford had been drinking prior to his last fatal flight. This, fortunately, could be disproved by Lt Cdr Robert Francis Lee-Dillon RN, who not only travelled in a car with him to Buc Aerodrome from the Ritz Hotel in Paris but flew with him minutes before the last fatal flight. He was also present when the crash occurred, picked him up from the ground afterwards and had the task of officially identifying his body at Versailles Hospital. The rumour is thought to have started when earlier that morning he entered the Chatham bar on the rue Daunou. A bar tender announced that Warneford was in attendance and made him a 'free member of the premises' which meant for the rest of his life, his drinks were to be given free. The truth is that he lost his life when flying a machine which was not airworthy.

The memorial in St. Michael's Church, Highworth was unveiled and dedicated on 21st August 1917 by Mrs Maude Nightingale. Other family members attending included the Rev. Harry Launcelot Warneford, Rector of Foxley near Malmesbury, Lt John Warneford, RFC of Australia and Miss Margaret Warneford Nightingale. The service was conducted by the Rev. D.S. Gilmore, curate of Highworth and the words of dedication were read by the Rev. H.L. Warneford. The memorial was subscribed to by 68 members of the Warneford family throughout the world and all belonging to the main branch of the family who occupied Warneford Place, Wiltshire for 700 years.

Hush! For his heart, that knew not any fear
Is stilled for ever, and our praises fall
Upon deaf ears. He is no longer there
To spend himself, a splendid prodigal,
As the two crosses that the Nations gave
Will shine, not on his breast, but on his grave.

(Anon)

In October 1987 the Victoria Cross awarded to Sub Lt Warneford was purchased by the Fleet Air Arm Museum at Yeovilton for £55,000. It now forms part of a display in memory of one of the Navy's most famous pilots.

HULLAVINGTON AERODROME

Location - 173/ST915807 - 4 miles South of Chippenham.

On the A429 Chippenham to Malmesbury road, three quarters of a mile north of the M4 is the former RAF Hullavington, now used by the Army, and called Buckley Barracks. It is occupied by 9 Supply Regiment, Royal Logistic Corps.

Aerodrome Development

In a debate at the House of Commons on 13th March 1934, Stanley Baldwin gave an assurance that, should the round of talks at the Disarmament Conference fail, the RAF would be expanded to equal the strength of any other Air Force within range of our shores. The Conference did fail and Germany left the League of Nations. With the signs of war looming, moves were made to re-arm Britain. This was slow at first, but ended up as a race against time. The first phase of the expansion commenced in 1934 with a plan to train an additional 2,500 pilots and 27,000 airmen over a two year period. It became apparent there were insufficient aircraft, materials to build them, mechanics to maintain them and airfields to accommodate them. In 1936, therefore, a more rapid expansion and reorganisation of the RAF was authorised by the Government and, as a result of this, construction of many new aerodromes was started, and work on those already begun was accelerated.

Over a two-year period Air Ministry surveyors, had been looking at land which would be suitable for aerodrome development. One of these was Bell Farm near the village of Hullavington. The land, owned by the Duke of Beaufort, was flat. There was a railway station in the village and road access to the site was good. The building of RAF Hullavington commenced in 1936 with permanent buildings constructed in a classical style, using local Bath stone and brown tiles. At that time most military camps were built using breeze blocks and corrugated iron. Hullavington was designed to accommodate a major Flying Training School and an Aircraft Storage Unit with a capacity for 400 aircraft. Together the two would have an allocation of over 500 aircraft of

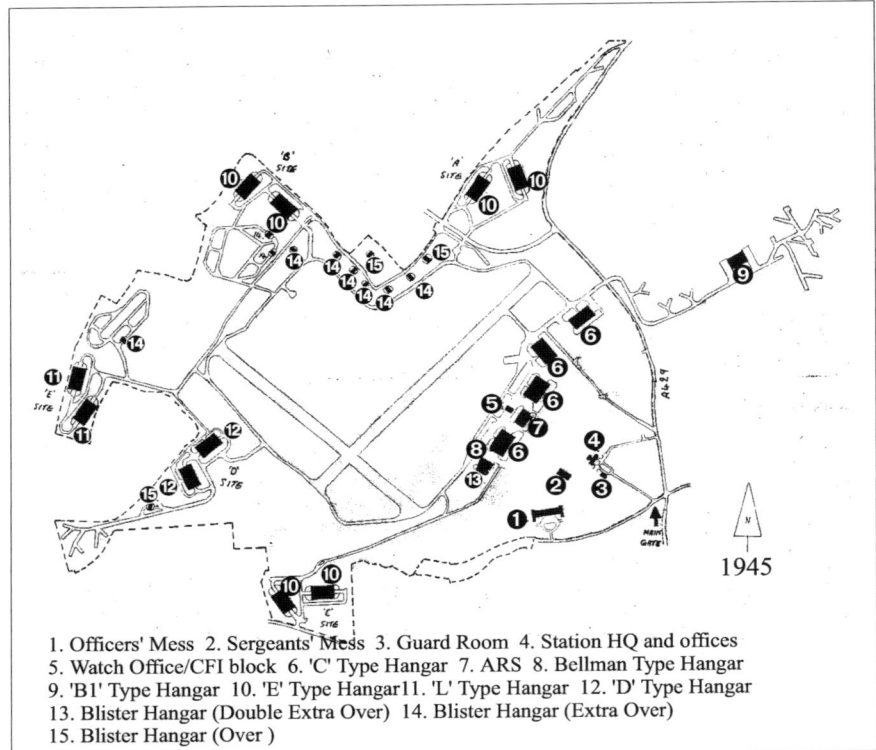

1. Officers' Mess 2. Sergeants' Mess 3. Guard Room 4. Station HQ and offices
5. Watch Office/CFI block 6. 'C' Type Hangar 7. ARS 8. Bellman Type Hangar
9. 'B1' Type Hangar 10. 'E' Type Hangar 11. 'L' Type Hangar 12. 'D' Type Hangar
13. Blister Hangar (Double Extra Over) 14. Blister Hangar (Extra Over)
15. Blister Hangar (Over)

The RAF flag flying over the main entrance to the Headquarters building with the guard room on the left.   Photo: George Bullough

varying types. As the station developed during the late 1930s and early 1940s, it provided in addition to the Station HQ and the No.10 MU Site, five Sites A-E, around the perimeter of the field. On the opposite side of the A429, a Ministry of Aircraft Production (MAP) Dispersal Area was established.

The main buildings consisted of the Officers' Mess and Quarters, which was an attractive structure of three

storeys, Sgts' Mess and Quarters, Station Headquarters and offices, General Instruction Block, stores and workshops plus a Watch Office/Chief Instructors Office 53'4" x 39'. This was a two-storey structure with a central three-storey tower. The tower included the watch office, rest room and observation room. Clocks were installed at the top of the tower on each face. A control room on a tall metal gantry was added later to provide an

The watch office with the aircraft repair shed to the rear.

improved view of the runways and approaches. When war was declared in 1939, the tower was far superior to that at other RAF Stations or civil aerodromes because it had a range of the most modern safety and traffic control aids installed. Aerodrome lights, flare-path lights, obstruction lights and wind indicator were fully controlled from within. With the development of radar facilities, the Senior Control Officer was supplied with information about all movements in and out of Hullavington and within the area.

The 4 'C' Type hangars, three on the HQ Site and 1 on the MU Site HQ, were the first to be completed. This was used for aircraft assembly and was referred to as the 'Erection Shop'. The latter two hangars were stone-faced. A single ARS was sited at the rear of the Watch Office and a Bellman completed the line on the south end. This hangar was to help cater for the needs of No.9 FTS. Each of the five Sites A-E had a pair of aircraft storage hangars for use by the MU. A-C Sites had the 'E' Type, 'D' Site had the 'D' Type for storage and maintenance of large aircraft and 'E' Site had 'L' Types. At the MAP Dispersal Area a 'B1' Type was built in 1943 for the assembly of gliders. This became 'F' Site. 12 Blister hangars were erected, mainly close to the storage sites, but one double blister was sited next to the Bellman. The 'E' and 'L' Type hangars were earth and grass covered.

In the early stages of the war Mk VIII Vickers guns were used for the station air defence. In May 1941 they were replaced by Lewis guns, and later the same month, 4 Bofors guns were installed.

In 1954 100 single airmen's prefabricated quarters were constructed by Chivers Bros. of Devizes, probably in response to the Korean situation.

Initially runways were grass, the preferred surface at FTSs at that time as it allowed take-offs and landings in any direction. The designated strips were N/S 1000 yds, NE/SW 1300yds, E/W 1200yds and SE/NW 1200yds. These were fine at Hullavington until, with the advent of war, the larger aircraft coming and going from the MU soon cut up the grass landing areas. The construction of two concrete and tarmac covered runways commenced in October 1941 by Landing Grounds Corporation Ltd. These were 23/05 NE/SW 1350yds x 50yds and 14/32 NW/SE 1130 yds x 50yds. Whilst the work was still in progress, it was decided to further extend 23/05 to 1433yds with completion in May 1942. The runway lighting was initially goose-neck flares and the airfield identification code was HV. A Standard Beam Approach System had been installed by 1942. All five Sites had a generous provision of dispersals with that of 'A' Site extending north as far as the boundary with the Paddington to South Wales railway line. A Decoy Site was located at Allington south of the aerodrome.

Inter War Years

Hullavington opened as a RAF station on 14th June 1937 under the command of Gp Capt C.H. Elliott-Smith AFC, RAF. The Station was occupied by No.9 FTS on its arrival from Thornaby

A 'E' Type hangar under construction by Kier & Co. of London, at Hullavington in 1938.   Photo: V.G. Smith via Glen Moreman

One of the grass covered 'E' Type hangars on 'A' Site on 4th September 1996.

on 29th June. It was equipped with the Hart (K5808), (K6490), Audax (K5169), (K5173), (K5252), (K7431) and Fury (K8218), (K8222), (K8254), (K8264), (K8285), (K8289), (K8290), (K8303), (K8305). Initially the task of the school was to train forty pilots per course on these single engine aircraft. The following year pupils were also trained to fly multi-engine aircraft. Twin engine Ansons (N9254), (N9650) were used for this training and the first of the type arrived on 7th March 1938.

churchyard at the nearby village of Stanton St. Quinton. Methods of instruction were constantly revised and it was decided to train pilots directly on multi-engine aircraft. The direct training commenced on 7th March 1938 using the Avro Anson.

The total strength of No.9 FTS as of May 1938 was 100 officers, 70 of whom were under training, and 600 men.

gas masks and demonstrating how casualties were dealt with and decontamination carried out. The Station building work was not yet complete but the public was allowed to inspect the barrack blocks, sick quarters, NAAFI, Airmans cookhouse, Ration store, gas chamber, aeroplane engine repair sheds, photographic, educational, armoury, camera obscura and parachute sections. In addition the most modern aircraft were on static display in the aircraft park.

As part of their instruction, pupils were sent to the Bombing and Gunnery School at Warmwell in Dorset. Flying their own No.9 FTS machines, they

Before Hullavington opened this No.15 Sqn Hawker Hind K5436 came to grief c. Sept/Oct 1936. At the time the squadron was based at Abingdon from where cross-country training flights were made. It is thought this machine was carrying out such training when it suffered the landing accident.   Photo: Martyn Ford-Jones

No.9 FTS was at this time one of the few units giving training in twin-engined aircraft. The Ansons had been in storage at Manston since May 1937, awaiting issue to the school, which later had Oxfords, Battles and Hurricanes added to the establishment.

There were three squadrons for flying training, Basic, Intermediate and Advanced. The majority of those under training were Reservists, of whom a number were fairly mature, and embraced a cross-section of careers such as solicitors, barristers, company directors, publicans etc. The Instructors who in the past had been used to training young and humble Plt Offs and NCO pilots, found a certain amount of difficulty in dealing with these students whose behaviour was alien to them. However a degree of mutual respect soon developed on both sides and it was not unknown for a student with a Rolls Royce to drive one of the Instructors to the flight line. Training proceeded in a relaxed atmosphere but inevitably flying accidents occurred. Plt Off J. R. Vincent RAF and Plt Off R. B. La Pointe RAF were two students who were killed on 7th April 1938. They were the first airmen from Hullavington to be buried in St. Giles

The Station hosted an Empire Air Day on Saturday 28th May 1938 to which the public were invited for a nominal entry fee. The proceeds donated to various RAF charities. Cameras were not allowed however. A flying display

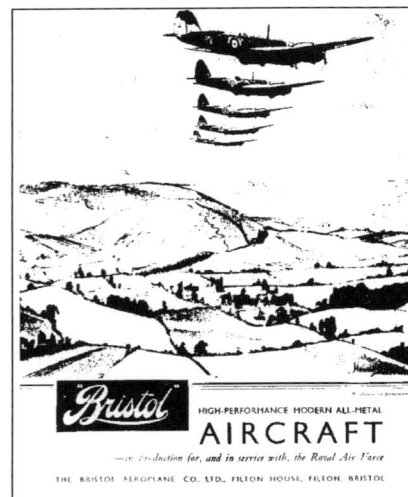

A BAC advert of the time, for their Blenheim aircraft.

Anson 1 L7067 of No.9 FTS at Hullavington in June 1939.
Photo: Sqn Ldr M. Llewellyn-Thomas

consisted of aerobatics, inverted flying, picking-up messages by aircraft, formation flying and attacks on target towed aircraft. Forty aircraft of eleven different types took part. These were the Anson, Audax, Avro Tutor, Battle, Blenheim, Fury, Gladiator, Hart, Heyford, Oxford and Wallace. An assimilated gas attack on the aerodrome was staged. The Air Raids Precaution personnel donned

carried out live gunnery firing, and practise bombing along the shoreline of Chesil Beach. Cpl Daniel was killed there on 10th December 1938, when diving at the ground his aircraft struck a bank and crashed into the sea. Another fatality occurred 10 days later when A/Plt Off N.A. Bagnald was also killed there when he was struck by an airscrew.

Starting a No.9 FTS Hawker Audax in the rain at Hullavington in June 1939.
K7431 crashed on approach to the aerodrome on 10th September 1939.
Photo: Sqn Ldr M. Llewellyn-Thomas

No.9 MU had formed at Hullavington on 8th July 1938 initially for MT storage. On 1st February 1939 it was redesignated No.10 MU to avoid confusion with No.9 FTS. By this time it was receiving various aircraft types such as the Battle, Blenheim and Wellington (Wimpy N3640 arrived on 8th July). Many, including a number of Harrows, had to be stored in the open fields close to the station because of insufficient hangar space. The dispersed storage resulted in a certain amount of possible sabotage. The final Site 'E' was not completed until August 1940. The Unit's first Stirling was now on 'D' Site and this was first test flown on 8th July 1940. Stirling aircraft became a regular feature at Hullavington. The civilian manned MU was also responsible for the fitting of any modifications and preparation for operational service. As of 3rd April 1939 No.10 MU was administered by No.41 (Maintenance) Group in the newly formed Maintenance Command. Lysander II N1303 of No.10 MU crashed on approach on 11th September 1939. The MU used Yatesbury for aircraft storage in 1940 and then Townsend from October 1940 to September 1941.

In his early days with the RAF Plt Off M 'Tom' Llewellyn-Thomas attended a course with No.9FTS between January and August 1939. He recalls with some clarity a night take-off in a Hawker Audax for a routine triangular cross-country to Bath-Bristol with return to Hullavington. Whilst on the Bath-Bristol leg, the heavens opened with him and the open cockpit soon engulfed in water. Lightning was apparent and he quickly took the decision to forget Bristol and to return to base. This proved difficult as in low cloud, flying blind and drifting at 1,400' he was conscious that going up could leave him marooned in space above the 'clag' but going down an impact with high ground was a possibility. He was the second pilot to fly the aircraft that night which left it low on fuel. He started a square search by the watch with no success so he let down another 200' but all he could see was water and darkness. With fuel for five minutes flying his thought was to climb and bale out and then a voice in his head warned him of his aircraft hitting an orphanage. He thought he saw a red aerodrome light and kept orbiting but received no green light from the tower. He decided on two more minutes then to hell with the orphans, he would climb and jump. Then from out of the gloom two car headlights appeared lighting a path onto a grass strip. Without formality he put the Audax down for a safe but not textbook landing. He had arrived at Tern Hill in Shropshire. The Adjutant, who was leaving the Station for home, had heard the aircraft circling and realising it was in trouble had driven to the aerodrome boundary where he illuminated the field with the car headlights. Overdue at Hullavington, bets had been taken as to his fate. Plt Off Llewellyn-Thomas in later years achieved Sqn Ldr rank. The OC Advanced Training at No.9FTS was Sqn Ldr A. King-Lewis and Flt Lt Paul Ruston was Plt Off Llewellyn-Thomas's Flight Commander.

A fellow pupil on the same course was Plt Off Adrian Warburton, who was awarded his wings in May 1939 but was assessed as 'below average'. There was no lower rating than this and, anything less, he would have been 'wiped out'. At this time pupils were introduced to the Hawker Hart trainer and the similar but better performing Hawker Fury. For night flying the Hawker Audax was used. Plt Off Llewellyn-Thomas recalls that Warburton, like himself, was slated for single engine types only. He remembers watching Warburton hold off far too high on coming in to land and spreading the undercarriage of his biplane all over the grass. Despite this 'Warby' went on to become one of the RAFs most revered pilots. He was posted to Malta with No.431 Flt in September 1940, to carry out armed photo-reconnaissance, flying the American Maryland. Despite the intended role he actively engaged the enemy at every opportunity and is credited with destroying 9 enemy aircraft. In August 1942 he was a Sqn Ldr and CO of No.69 Sqn flying Spitfire Vs modified as PR Mk.IIs and in November was promoted to Wg Cdr. In 1943 he became the first CO of No.683 Sqn. He was a legend in his own lifetime on the Island. He was, unfortunately, killed over Europe in 1944 flying an American P-38F, which was shot down by German flak. In his short service, along the way he had collected the DSO and Bar, DFC and two Bars and DFC (USA).

A/Plt Off M.W. Stanton-Hope in the Advanced Training Sqn was killed on 21st February 1939, when his aircraft crashed whilst night-flying. Another fatal flying accident occurred on 20th June involving Hawker Fury II K8222 which had been delivered to No.9 FTS in July 1936. The Fury was flown by the Canadian, Acting Plt Off E. R. McGovern. He was practising front-gun air/ground camera shots when the aeroplane stalled turning into the target and spun into the ground.

From a course of 20, which commenced in August 1939, three of the pupils would become well known RAF names. Leonard Cheshire, later to be awarded the Victoria Cross for his actions as a Bomber Command pilot, also Denis Crowley-Milling and Christopher Foxley-Norris both of whom served on fighter squadrons during the Battle of Britain and went on to become Air Marshals in the post-war RAF. On leaving Hullavington Fg Off Foxley-Norris was initially posted to Army Co-operation duties at Old Sarum.

World War 2 Years

After the months of tension, war was finally declared on Sunday 3rd September 1939 and the School became No.9 Service Flying Training School in No.23 (Training) Group with HQ at South Cerney. Harvards and Oxfords were then allocated for training except that the former type never materialised. One of the Oxford Is L4571 was destroyed on Monday 18th September when it dived into the ground killing the pilot, Plt Off Richard Bowyer RAF.

The pace of training was now increasing, with 36 Reserve Sgt Pilots joining the FTS in October 1939. There were then four simultaneous courses being run in an effort to produce the 40 trained pilots a month. A shortage of accommodation now meant that 90 RAF personnel had to live in tents. This would have been an uncomfortable existence in the severe winter of 1939/40.

Audax K7334 crashed on Saturday 7th October 1939 and claimed the life of Sgt Kenneth G. Sherman RAFVR of

No.10 MU was mainly manned by civilians and of all the resident units on the airfield, it was responsible for the largest number of aircraft on the station at any one time. In the spring of 1940 the few remaining airworthy Furys in storage were shipped out to South Africa for use by training units there.

By May 1940 No.9 SFTS was equipped with 63 Ansons, 45 Harvards, and various Harts and Audax trainers. In the summer of 1940 a decision was taken that SFTSs should specialise in either single or twin engine training and not both as had been the current practice. Hullavington was designated for single engine instruction by way of a 12 week course and had its twin engine aircraft withdrawn. The school now received Miles Masters which were built up to an establishment of 72 + 36 reserves by 24th November 1940. However Audax and Hart trainers continued in service.

No.10 Group Communications Flt formed on 1st June 1940 but moved out to Colerne on 1st July. Aerodrome defence measures were improved with the arrival of rapid firing 20mm Hispano cannons, the construction of Pill Boxes, digging of trenches and the drawing up of plans for the destruction of the aerodrome in case of invasion. On 25th June a lone enemy aircraft dropped 12 H.E and incendiary bombs. All of the bombs missed the aerodrome but destroyed a barn in the nearby village. Shortly after the bombing attempt, the aerodrome was camouflaged and additional anti-aircraft guns were set up. In addition three Hurricanes were supplied and crewed by No.9 SFTS instructors for station defence duties.

A No.9 FTS line-up at Hullavington on 17th July 1939 with Fury 1 K8222 and Audax K7431 in the foreground.   Photo: Sqn Ldr M. Llewellyn-Thomas

No.9 FTS Audax K7319 with an Anson Mk.I in front of it at Hullavington on 17th July 1939. The two large aircraft in the background are Handley-Page Harrows Mk.II, of No.10 MU. Photo: Sqn Ldr M. Llewellyn-Thomas.

Hullavington was prepared to receive Bomber Command aircraft which were being dispersed from the airfields close to the east coast. On 1st September 10 Blenheims of No.114 Sqn arrived from Wyton followed six days later by 7 from No.139 Sqn at Wyton. Rotation of aircraft from these squadrons continued for just a couple of weeks, until it was realised that the expected attacks on their own base were not imminent. Also at this time No.4 Section of the 448/664 Searchlight Regiment arrived for aerodrome defence duties.

On 23rd September H.M. Queen Mary visited the station with the Duchess of Beaufort. Her Majesty showed a keen interest in the Link Trainer.

Bristol. He was buried at Canford Cemetery, Bristol. Training suffered due to the terrible weather conditions, with engines unable to start, pipes of the petrol installations cracking and petrol freezing. Petrol had to be brought in by tankers from Avonmouth and the courses extended by two and a half weeks to make up for flying time lost. By April 1940 things had returned to normal but on orders from No.23 Group HQ South Cerney, the length of courses was reduced from ten to eight weeks. Bombing and gunnery training was carried out on detachment to Penrhos, Porthcawl or Warmwell. No.6 SFTS Little Rissington used Hullavington as a RLG for a short period from December 1939 to January 1940.

No.10 (Fighter)Group formed at Rudloe Manor, Box on 1st June 1940 for the defence of South West England, with Plymouth, the Royal Navy dockyards, ports, airfields, aircraft factories, and Channel convoys likely to be prime targets. The number of squadrons and aerodromes available to the Group at the time was small. It was realised that the cities of Bath, and Bristol with its docks, would be targeted by the enemy, probably with night raids. Hullavington was used to provide cover, first with a section of Spitfires of No.92 Sqn from Pembury detached each night between 1st-9th July. They carried out patrols during this time but with no contacts. This squadron was followed by 'B' Flt. of

No.87 Sqn on detachment from Exeter. They brought with them Hurricane Is P2881, P3389, P3394, P3404, P3593 and P3596. Whilst on patrol at 2325 hrs on 26th July, the pilot of Hurricane P3394 picked out a He 111 in searchlights south of Bristol. He opened fire, observing strikes on the enemy but lost contact with it east of Portishead Point. These night patrols meant that Hullavington had to operate night landing lights for returning flights and it was decided that this was placing the aerodrome, with its other primary tasks, at too much of a risk from enemy attacks. An order to form Colerne as a Fighter Sector station was issued by HQ Fighter Command on 1st September 1940. From there defensive cover would be provided for Bristol and Bath. No.87 Sqn's Hurricanes moved out of Hullavington to a RLG at Bibury until Colerne became operational towards the end of November. No enemy aircraft were shot down by Hullavington based fighters.

When No.10 Group HQ Rudloe Manor near Box became operational, personnel visiting the HQ often flew into Hullavington and continued their journey to Box by road.

In July 1940 the station's first permanent RLG was opened at Babdown Farm. Night flying was then transferred. On 14th August Hullavington was attacked by a lone He 111 dropping 16 H.E. bombs from between 3000'/4000'. The bombs killed 4 airmen, with 1 officer, 5 airmen, 4 soldiers and a civilian injured. A 'C' Type hangar in use by No.9 SFTS was extensively damaged and a petrol bowser exploded and burnt out. Various degrees of damage was caused to Ansons K8734, N9561, N5365, Audax K5173, K7434, K3082, K5133, K3711, K5125, K6463, Hart K4753, K6487, K6486, K7430 and two of the station defence Hurricanes which had just landed off patrol and were being re-fuelled. Two nights later another raid took place but the bombs missed the aerodrome and no damage was done. This was a period when the Luftwaffe was attempting to destroy the RAF both on the ground and in the air.

The SFTS also used Long Newnton as a RLG between September and November 1940. ATA pilot Ann Douglas (better known as AnnWelch after re-marriage in 1953) flew D.H.

Hornet Moths from Halton to Hullavington in December 1940/March 1941. These were G-ADKP and X9445 respectively.

In the closing months of 1940 a number of pilots under training (U/T) lost their lives in flying accidents. Hart K6537 crashed on Tuesday 29th October 1940, killing pilot (U/T) LAC Wilfred D. Shaw RAFVR. He was buried at St. Giles churchyard, Stanton St. Quinton. Hart K4769 was lost on Thursday 14th November killing LAC Norman D. Steele RAFVR. His name appears on the Runnymede Memorial. Hart K5802 crashed on Tuesday 3rd December killing LAC Thomas I.R.H. Harris RAFVR and LAC Frank E. Whittaker RAFVR who was buried at Stanton St. Quinton. Audax K7413 crashed on Saturday 7th December killing LAC Donald J. P. MacDonald RAFVR. Hart K4297 crashed the next day killing LAC Daniel W.D. Britto RAFVR and instructor Sgt William V. Knight RAFVR. Audax K7445 crashed on Thursday 12th December killing LAC Stanley R. Phillips RAFVR. Fg Off Bernard Walker RAFO was killed when the aircraft he was piloting crashed on Tuesday 17th December 1940.

Training accidents in December resulted in ten aircraft being written-off and seven deaths. During the year there had been in excess of 20 No.9 FTS aircraft crashes involving mainly Harts but also Audax and Oxford aircraft. Not all of the accidents appear in the Station Operational Record Book (ORB).

No.8 (Service) Ferry Pilots Pool formed on 5th November 1940. This was a pool of RAF pilots who were used to ferry aircraft from factory to MUs and squadrons, prior to the growth of the ATA. One of these, Blenheim IV T2327, flown by an unknown pilot from No.8 FPP, flew into high ground near Colerne on 11th February 1941. With the arrival in Britain of Polish pilots who had escaped from their own country, those considered unsuited to join operational squadrons were often used as ferry pilots and this freed-up RAF personnel in Ferry Pools. On 27th March 1941 No.8 (S) FPP was superseded by No.10 (Polish) Ferry Flt. The Polish unit had their base at Steinbrook House, Kington Langley and flew from Hullavington. The Poles worked-up on

Hurricanes and Spitfires. No.10 (P) FF was in turn absorbed into HQ Service Ferry Sqn based at Kemble in July 1941.

The No.9 SFTS training courses were extended by two weeks in January 1941 because pilots arriving on operational squadrons were considered to need more training before they could be used. The courses were further extended by a week in June. The School was now equipped with 56 Masters and on 6th February eight Hurricane Is were taken on charge for advanced training. They were also used for airfield defence.

The aerodrome was bombed and strafed again at 1500 hrs on 27th February 1941 by a low flying He 111. It was engaged by the station defences which claimed three strikes. A No.10 MU hangar, the AMQs, 11 Audax, 1 Hampden, 15 Harts, 1 Hurricane and 1 Master sustained damage from the attack.

Canadian, Dutch, Polish and Indian pilots arrived for training during March 1941 as well as British pilots who had completed basic flying training in the Dominions. Plt Off G. Singh, who arrived on 21st March, was killed on 12th April when Master I N7959 flew into the ground at Corsham. These pilots from the Empire Air Training Schools overseas, who had gained their flying prowess in blue and sunny skies, required additional training in navigating in the clouds and 'clag' which they would experience over Europe. Their attendance at a SFTS was to take an 'Advanced Flying' course in preparation for their further training at an OTU.

Twelve-year old Ian Porteous witnessed the crash of Hawker Hart K3146 on Wednesday 16th April 1941. He and two daughters of the Rev. Hudson were in the garden of the vicarage at Charlton, a village 6 miles northeast of Hullavington. He recalls seeing the trainer in a vertical dive before it crashed in a field nearby (173/ST975893). The three children set off to locate the site but missed it by one field. The following day Ian was interviewed by an air force officer but was only able to tell of seeing the last few seconds of the dive. The following Monday Ian visited the crash site and saw a large hole in the ground, a flying boot and a Rolls Royce engine which had been recovered. The U/T pilot of the No.9 SFTS Hart, LAC Douglas St John Shipway-Fowler RAFVR was killed together with fellow U/T pilot LAC Louis Raphael RAFVR. The enquiry determined that the pilot flew at 800' and dived at 45 degrees until he was almost down to the tops of the trees. Then having climbed to about 500' losing speed in the process, dived into the ground. The manoeuvres, which caused the crash, contravened the pilot's flying orders. LAC Shipway-Fowler was buried at Stanton St. Quinton (St. Giles) churchyard extension, immediately south of the airfield. A flying accident on Tuesday 22nd April claimed the lives of pilot Instructor, Flt Lt Eric E. Noddings RAF and his U/T pupil pilot LAC James A.B. Day RAFVR. On Saturday 17th May U/T pilot Sgt Hugh A. Hounam RAF was killed in Master I T8638 when it spun into the ground at Grittleton, 2 miles WSW of the aerodrome. Plt Off Michael F.S. Laughton RAF (Instructor), Plt Off Douglas R. Parker RAF (pupil) and Plt Off John F. Saward RAF (pupil) were killed on Sunday 29th June in a mid-air collision between Master I T8445 and T8448 Plt Offs Laughton and Parker were buried in Chippenham Cemetery.

Many more flying accidents during the year claimed the lives of Instructors and pupils. On Tuesday 12th August Sgt Frant Seda RAFVR (Czech Instructor) and LAC Antonin Mikolas RAFVR (Czech pupil) were killed, both buried in Chippenham Cemetery. LAC Reginald Howard RAFVR was killed on 18th August and on Friday 29th, so was Sgt Jan Klos RAFVR (Czech pupil), who also was buried in Chippenham Cemetery. During August, 7 Masters and 1 Hurricane were destroyed and 16 aircraft seriously damaged.

The following month, 6 Masters and 1 Hurricane were destroyed and 12 aircraft seriously damaged. Dutchman LAC V.D.J. Janson (pupil) was killed on 1st September when Master I N8064 spun into the ground. LAC John V.W. Shand-Kydd RAF (pilot u/t) was killed on Wednesday 10th and the following Monday LAC Trevor Audsley RAFVR (pupil) died from injuries suffered in a crash. On Friday 19th, Fg Off Martin F. Scragg RAF (Instructor) and Sgt Joseph Fyvie RNZAF (pupil) were killed, with the latter buried in Chippenham Cemetery. Not all deaths

in flying accidents were air force personnel, as on Thursday 25th September when 2nd Lt Arthur H. Barlow (pupil) of the Green Howards (Yorkshire Regiment) was killed.

No.10 MU had the use from April 1941 of No.14 SLG Overley and from 15th May 1941 No.23 SLG Down Farm, Westonbirt. Both were in Gloucestershire, the latter provided a large storage facility where nearly 250 aircraft were on site at the end of the war. Castle Combe, already used by Hullavington, was upgraded to a RLG from May 1941. At this stage of the war the MU at Hullavington was preparing Wellingtons for despatch overseas, and Hudsons and Spitfires for operational squadrons.

14 aircraft received superficial damage in a raid on the night of 8th/9th July 1941.

During 1941 there were visits to the station by a number of dignitaries including The Duchess of Gloucester and later Prince Bernhard of the Netherlands who was there to meet the Dutch pilots. 750 pilots were trained during 1941.

In January 1942 the first American servicemen arrived for training. So did an element of the RN, training torpedo spotter reconnaissance pilots who brought with them their own Fairey Swordfish torpedo bombers. On 14th February No.9 SFTS was renamed No.9 (Pilot) Advanced Flying Unit with the role of short course training. Its establishment was 3 Albacore, 3 Swordfish, 6 Hurricane and 24 Master Is.

With the needs of the proposed Empire Central Flying School being paramount, No.9 (P) AFU moved its aircraft to Castle Combe in February 1942, maintaining its HQ at Hullavington until the unit moved to Errol in Scotland on 31st July 1942.

On 1st April 1942 the Empire Central Flying School formed at Hullavington from the nucleus of CFS Upavon. It was commanded by Gp Capt H.H. Down AFC on transfer from CFS Upavon. Later in the year he was succeeded by Air Commodore G.S. Oddie DFC, AFC. The other staff members were Gp Capt A.D. Selway as CFI and 14 flying instructors of Sqn Ldr rank. Although the School took over many of the secondary

responsibilities of the CFS, it was never intended as a Flying Instructor's School. Its remit was to standardise training procedures for the RAF and Dominion Air Forces and to pool knowledge and experience of the attending students. The School was staffed with experienced, ex-operational pilots from Commonwealth countries. It developed with four categories: -

- The school with courses of a 13 week duration for around 40 student pilots of not less than Flt Lt rank, from the RAF and Dominions who were given an introduction to a wide variety of flying detail.
- A Research Flight which investigated new training aircraft and equipment, together with flying techniques. The results of these studies formed the basis of future training methods.
- A Handling Squadron, which received new aircraft types from the manufacturers on which test pilots gained the knowledge to produce 'Pilot's Notes'. The squadron moved from Boscombe Down on 22nd August 1942.
- The Examination Flt tasked with ensuring that required standards of training were maintained at the various RAF training establishments.

The first course included officers from the RAF, RN, US Navy, RAAF, RCAF, RNZAF, SAAF, USAAF and RRAF. Students were not, however, restricted to being from the 'Empire' as Rumanians and even Chinese students attended.

Most of the flying was done on the then standard Harvard and Oxford trainers but a wide variety of other aircraft types were available to initiate students. The School was equipped with 2 Anson Is, 4 Blenheim Vs, 4 Hurricane Is, 10 Oxford, 10 Master IIIs and 10 Magister aircraft. Hudsons and Wellingtons joined the establishment the following year. One of the latter, Mk.X NA928 converted to T10 status, and went to Boscombe Down with the Handling Sqn before returning to Hullavington with No.1 Air Navigation School. One of the last 'Wimpys' in RAF service, it was SOC on 30th December 1953. In addition, specific types of aircraft were loaned to the ECFS by squadrons to allow students to gain experience in them. The students were not restricted to

A scene at Hullavington C.1943/44. Some of the aircraft lined up for use of ECFS students. Back row LtoR-Stirling, Miles Master, Mitchell, Boston, Wellington, Magister, Lancaster, Tiger Moth, Oxford. Front row LtoR-Tarpon (Avenger), Proctor, Spitfire, Typhoon and Mosquito V I **HJ665**. In tow on the hardstanding is a Hotspur glider. Photo: Oliver Pike Coll.

flying from Hullavington. There were occasions when a research project needed to be carried out under operational conditions and the student would join a crew carrying out an operational sortie.

No.1427 (Ferry Training) Flt arrived from Thruxton on 18th May 1942 and attached to No.10 MU. Its function was to convert ATA pilots and No.41 Group test pilots on to four-engined aircraft. It was in residence for just over three months before moving to Marham on 5th September. It was equipped with the Stirling. No.1 Ferry Pool at White Waltham was responsible for clearing aircraft from No.10 MU.

In 1942, Hotspur gliders were being assembled at No.10 MU, having arrived in sections from the various furniture manufacturers. In June, Horsa gliders were also being assembled with the first completion being towed away by glider tug on 2nd August. Hamilcars started arriving for storage in October. Glider work was conducted at 'B' Site until completion of the purpose built M.A.P. hangar in June 1943. This was positioned alongside the taxiway to 'F' Site, east of the main airfield site. The obsolete Albemarle bombers arrived for conversion to troop carriers and later in 1942 Venturas appeared, accompanied by a servicing party from No.22 MU Silloth. A number of Albemarles, Masters and Wellingtons were delayed in preparation due to a shortage of propellers.

On 27th July 1942 a Do 217 dropped four 500kg bombs from 300'. These fell between two hangars on No.10 MU

Main Site and caused considerable blast damage to buildings and 3 Horsa gliders. There were no human casualties.

No.3 Flying Instructors School (Advanced) formed on 1st August 1942 equipped with 36 + 18 reserve Oxfords, also 7 + 3 Masters, which were transferred from No.7 FIS (A) Upavon. The School was formed to train instructors to teach at OTUs. It was outbased at Castle Combe seven days later but servicing and maintenance of its aircraft remained at Hullavington, which it also used for night flying on occasions when the grass runway at Castle Combe was too waterlogged for flying.

No.1532 Beam Approach Training Flt formed on 15th October 1942 in No.23 Group equipped with 4 Oxfords. The Flt was formed to provide beam approach training for ECFS and No.3 FIS students. It was affiliated to No.15 (P) AFU, and, because of the congestion at Hullavington, used the beam facilities at Babdown Farm. The entire Flt moved there on 13th May 1943 when sufficient accommodation became available.

No.1426 (Enemy Aircraft) Flt with a German Ju 88A and Me 110C aircraft arrived for demonstration purposes on 31st November 1942.

The Commandant of ECFS changed in 1943 with the appointment of Air Commodore Claude McClean Vincent CB, DFC*, AFC. In 1944 he was succeeded by Air Commodore E.D. Barnes DFC, who remained until 1946

when the ECFS was redesignated Empire Flying School.

Young boys living in the Hullavington area at this time must have been in their element if they were interested in aircraft types. The ECFS added many different aircraft to its initial establishment and the Handling Squadron had all the latest types passing through. There were so many in fact, that most were parked in the open air on the west side of the airfield. Hullavington was a far from ideal location for this squadron, which was not only restricted for space but found the short runways unsuited to testing fully loaded heavy bombers and high performance fighters, when for example, carrying out flapless landings. Flt Lt R.W. 'Bobby' Pearson who had won his 'wings' at Hullavington in 1941 was back again from 1st July to 10th September 1943, on detachment from No.140 Sqn. He evaluated for Handling Sqn the Oxford, Hudson, Ventura, Spitfire IX and the Mosquito for day and night PR.

Another pilot on a 12 month attachment with the Sqn from the summer of 1942 was Peter Parrot DfC.\ He had fought in France with No.607 Sqn and in the Battle of Britain with No.145 Sqn. He was posted to No.605 Sqn in September 1940 and was officially credited with 6 'kills'. His dashing looks saw him appear on an RAF recruiting poster with the caption *"Volunteer For Flying Duties."* From 1948-50 he served as a Wg Cdr at Boscombe Down, test flying the early Meteors and Vampire jets.

Defiant I N1671 arrived at No.10 MU on 16th May 1943 after been used for anti-aircraft co-operation duties by No.285 Sqn at Wrexham. The Defiant left Hullavington for No.52 MU Pengam Moors, Cardiff on 8th September 1944. This was an Overseas Packing Unit. N1671 was subsequently preserved and is currently displayed in the RAF Museum, Hendon.

In May 1943, as part of a general rationalisation within No.41 Group, the MU work concentrated exclusively on operational Mosquito and Stirling aircraft. Non operational aircraft continued to be processed, such as the Defiant, Hart variant, Harvard and Martinet. Sites 'A', 'B' and part of 'E' were used for the Mosquito work and 'F' Site for Stirlings. With the Lancaster and Halifax aircraft now primarily equipping Bomber Command, there were many surplus Stirlings in storage. Parking of these was a problem at Hullavington and 110 of them were sent to Down Farm. Even this was insufficient so in December Everleigh SLG was taken over for Stirling storage with the numbers building up there during the first half of 1944.

In preparation for D-Day, the Horsa glider was prominent at No.10 MU during the lead up to the invasion.

By the third week in June 1944, the ECFS was equipped with 15 Harvards, 3 Havoc, 2 Hotspur Is, 9 Hudsons, 5 Hurricanes, 1 Lancaster, 8 Magisters, 2 Masters, 2 Mosquitos, 12 Oxfords, 2 Proctors, 5 Spitfire IIs and 3 Wellington IIIs. Later in the year 1 Halifax, 3 Mitchells and 2 Baltimores were added. One of the Baltimore aircraft crashed on take-off on 16th September 1944. Venturas were also used in small numbers.

In 1945 and up until the war ended, the Mosquito was the primary aircraft handled by No.10 MU.

Post War Years

At the end of the war the various airfield Sites and surrounding fields were a mass of aircraft, some on long term storage, but many for scrapping. Those who drove along the A429 past the airfield, recall lines of four-engined aircraft, mainly Lancasters, on both sides of the road, towering above them like trees in a forest. Lancaster Mk.I W4963 was one of these. It arrived in July 1945 from Boscombe Down where it had served as a test aircraft and was scrapped in November 1946. Two other Lancaster Is SW244 and HK541, which were used at Boscombe Down for high temperature and long range trials, also fell to the scrap man at No.10 MU. The former was scrapped in November 1946 and the latter was SOC in January 1947.

Hornets were used by ECFS immediately after the war with Lincolns joining the fleet at the School and operating between August 1945 and March 1946. On 28th January 1946 Reliant C1 FB649 dropped a wing during take off, swung and caught fire.

On 1st February Mosquito T3 LR542, with port propeller feathered, banked steeply to port on approach and crashed killing the pilot Flt Lt Alfred E. Lomas DFC. On 5th June 1946 No.10 MU experienced a similar accident when Mosquito FB26 KA265 lost power on its approach to the airfield. The port wing dropped and the aircraft struck the ground killing Flt Lt Charles R. Dwight DFC and injuring a civilian fitter who was on the test flight.

No.23 SLG Down Farm closed on 25th February 1946.

The ECFS was redesignated the Empire Flying School on 7th May 1946 and was tasked with introducing training for all weather flying. It continued at Hullavington for three years until disbanded into the RAF Flying College at Manby on 31st July 1949. The EFS, during the three year period, acquired additional types of aircraft such as the Auster AOP.6, Dakota C4, Buckmaster T1 (RP246 FCV-E), Spitfire LF.9e (BS348 FCW-C), Lancastrian C2, Meteor F3/F4, Mosquitos various, Prentice T1 and Hastings C1. On 1st April 1948 the School lost Spitfire LF Mk.9 MA709 which had been airborne for about 40 minutes in all weather flying detail. During an overshoot following a normal approach, the aircraft was climbing away when the engine was enveloped in smoke and flame which resulted in an explosion. The aircraft dived into the ground at Kingston St. Michael, two and a half miles north of Chippenham, killing the pilot Flt Lt Leonard T. Taylor.

Coinciding with the disbanding EFS, the Handling Sqn moved to Manby on 31st July 1949 and the Examining Sqn to CFS Little Rissington.

No.88 Gliding School arrived from Wroughton on 28th September 1947 equipped with the Cadet 1 and 2. The School was disbanded in May the following year.

Oliver Pike, an airman at Hullavington, recalls the M.A.P. hangar on 'F' Site being full of Hotspur gliders during his period of service between 1947-49. An aircraft fire in a No.10 MU hangar on 24th May 1950, involving Hornet F3 PX331 resulted in two Tiger Moth T2s T7439 and T7473 being damaged beyond repair and written-off.

Unit Inspection Dept staff in 1944.   Photo: Oliver Pike

Staff of the Unit Inspection Dept. with Wellington RP588 at Hullavington C.1944/45.
LtoR: (unknown) Reggie Gearing Bill Dickinson Raymond Gearing.   Photo: George Bullough

Various single, two and four engine aircraft awaiting their fate on 'B', 'C', 'D' & 'E' Sites on 14th April 1946.   Photo: Dan Gurney Coll.

An aerial view of the station and runways on 14th April 1946.   Photo: Dan Gurney Coll.

No.10 MU civilian staff outside hangar D2. The group in front of a Prentice aircraft includes the Foreman Max Sleighterhouse (back row, centre with tie) and Jim Outlaw (2nd from left, standing).   Photo: Jim Outlaw

.No.1 Air Navigation School (ANS) in No.21 Group arrived from Topcliffe on 7th July 1949 equipped with 17 Anson T21s (WB453) (EG353), 21 Wellington T10s (JA532), (LA819), (MF628), (NA781), (NA846), (NA928), (PG265), (RP319), (RP382), (RP524) and Tiger Moth T2 T5684. No.1 ANS was responsible for the training of Air Navigators, many of who were two-year National Service men.

The Wellingtons were used mainly for advanced navigation training on night flights. The Ansons were used for initial training by students using *Rebecca* radar during day flights. The rear guns were removed from the former bombers and the nose faired over. Both aircraft types had silver coloured fuselages with a yellow band denoting them to be a training aircraft. Each Wellington had two Mk.2 *Gee* radar sets and a *Rebecca* Mk.4. For its operation the *Gee* system relied on receiving radio signals from three ground stations approximately 100 miles apart. These were referred to as the master and two slaves. The *Rebecca* system enabled an accurate homing on a ground radar beacon known as *Eureka*. In the Wellington the two student navigators sat side by side on a bench in front of their *Gee* sets. The remainder of the crew was made up of the Pilot, Co-pilot, WOP and the Navigator Instructor.

The course included a long-haul navigation exercise generally flown to RAF Luqa in Malta. The crews much appreciated these deployments in the sunshine and blue skies of the Mediterranean. A radar/wireless mechanic was added to the crew on these flights to deal with any problems. Take-off from Hullavington was at 0600 hrs with generally five aircraft in the flight. A refuelling stop was scheduled in the South of France before completing the final leg to Malta. On arrival the Wimpys, some having been refurbished, would generally require a certain amount of maintenance to make them air-worthy for the return journey. The length of time spent on Malta depended on the degree of maintenance, but crews could generally expect to have two to three days of leisure time.

The School suffered a number of aircraft mishaps during its time at Hullavington. This was possibly

Vampire XE919 on fuel level checks at No.10 MU.   Photo: Jim Outlaw

because the Wellingtons were then nearing the end of their serviceable life. Most of the accidents, however, did not result in serious injury or loss of life. An early casualty on 22nd February 1950 was Wellington T10 JA532, which overshot on night landing, hitting trees and then undershot its next approach resulting in a collapsed undercarriage. Flt Lt H.W. Howell, Fg Off R. Thomson and 4 other crew members were injured. On 29th March 1950 Wellington T10 LN819 had a power loss during a turn, following a night take-off. It spun into the ground a mile from the airfield killing the four-man crew, Pilot II Charles R. Barrow, Sgt Thomas Miller, Aircrew Cadets Trevor D. Simpson and Roy Henderson. Five months later on 31st August, Wellington T10 NA781 lost a propeller, overshot on landing and tore off its undercarriage. Both JA532 and NA781 were write-offs. Anson T21 VS580 was written off when it lost power on take-off and crashed on 1st January 1951 and Wellington T10 RP382 flew into the ground between the village of Grittleton and the airfield during a night approach on 29th May 1951. Two of the crew were killed. On arrival of the crash crew, LAC Jarrett who was in charge, rescued one of the Wellington crew and attempted a further rescue. For his bravery he was awarded the George Medal. Both aircraft were write-offs. Wellington T10 MF628 FFK-B suffered a Category 4 flying accident in December 1951 and had to be returned by road to Vickers at Brooklands for repair. The aircraft went on to greater fame by featuring in the epic film *The Dam Busters*, and on 26th October 1971, took up its current position at the RAF Museum in Hendon. Another crash occurred on 15th October 1952, involved Wellington T10 RP319, which swung during an instrument take-off in fog, from runway 23/05. Failing to gain height because of heavy icing, the aircraft struck one of the

hangars on 'D' Site, crashed and caught fire. The four-man crew were killed, Sgt Norman L. Paine (pilot) from Trowbridge, Flt Sgt Leonard B. Hodges (Air Sig), Plt Off John P. Phillips (nav) and Plt Off Anthony J. Saunders (nav).

After aircraft accidents, the crash sites had to be guarded. Flt Sgt Gordon Harker was often given the task of forming the guard party and he recalls that his entry into the mess following a crash was a sure-fire way of clearing the building in no time flat, as no one wanted the guard duty.

The Wellingtons were replaced by the Vickers Varsity and Vickers Valetta T3s, the first of the former type arriving at the end of 1951. Varsity T1 WF391 flew into the ground at night on a BABS approach on 20th January 1954. When the wreckage was found near the airfield, the position of the undercarriage and flaps suggested the aircraft had been set up for an overshoot and the pilot had lost control and probably stalled. The four-man crew who were killed were Flt Lt Aubrey H. Fernihough DFC, AFC (pilot), Flt Lt Kenneth W. Grice (nav), Flt Sgt John Wright DFC (Air Sig) and A/Plt Off Ronald A. Moore (student nav). No.1 ANS disbanded on 1st May 1954, when navigator training transferred to Canada under a NATO agreement.

No.2 Flying Training School (FTS) arrived from Northern Ireland on 1st June 1954 equipped with Provost T1s and Chipmunk T1s for elementary training. The School had reformed on 22nd September 1953 in response to the increased need of pilots for the Korean War. As on previous occasions at Hullavington, much of the flying training was carried out away from the busy base and for this purpose the airfield at Keevil was used as a RLG from 17th January 1955 to 18th

November 1957, the date when the School moved to Syerston. In September 1955 the School became the first unit to successfully introduce the revolutionary concept of 'all through' pilot training in jet powered equipment, utilising Jet Provost T1 aircraft. The first such course passed-out on 2nd July 1956.

Flt Lt Harry Loxton served as a flying instructor with No.2 FTS from 1954-57 and has fond memories of flying from Hullavington and Keevil. One of the benefits of Keevil was having plenty of room in the circuit. He recalls one pleasant summer when the pupil pilots spent a fortnight there under canvas. They ran everything on site themselves, including their own bar. The instructors flew the Provosts to Keevil each morning, returning to Hullavington in the evening. Harry thought it a very enjoyable way to spend a tour as a flying instructor.

Not all of his memories are good ones. For an FTS, he feels there were remarkably few incidents, probably due to the improving airmanship and training standards after the urgency of war. One incident he did witness c.1955, concerned a visiting Sqn Ldr from Group. On his arrival he had parked his Provost in front of the ATC. When the time came to leave, instead of taxiing around to the end of the runway in use, he took off at about a right angle to it, and had reached about 30' when he crossed over it. At that point he flew into a 3 aircraft formation of Provosts that had just become airborne from the runway. He collided with the left-hand aircraft of the vic, bringing it and himself down. The other two aircraft took violent avoiding action and escaped. Remarkably there were no serious injuries. Harry thinks the two Provosts were probably written off and that the Sqn Ldr perhaps received a similar fate.

An accident with far more serious consequences did occur on 24th October 1955 when two Provost T1s WV627 and WV631 collided in the Hullavington circuit at night. Both aircraft came down at nearby Yatton Keynall and both pilots were killed. These were respectively Flt Lt Humphrey A. Stenner and Fg Off Peter J. B. Tucker.

Harry recalls on one occasion being one of those unfortunate instructors who, trying too hard to enable a pupil very close to washout to go solo, allowed things to go too far. They were very close to landing off a short field approach, which, if successful, would have enabled the pupil to go solo. With full flap, a very low airspeed and about 30' of height, the pupil closed the throttle and wouldn't let go. Harry forced the throttle open again but it was too late and they stalled onto the runway. The combination of bounce and full power dragged the Provost back into the air again. The only alternative left to Harry was to try and go round again. The main spar was damaged and both wings badly buckled where the undercarriage was forced upwards. It took all the power the Leonide engines had to keep the aircraft in the air and they eventually staggered around the circuit to land on two burst tyres.

Flying Training Command Modification Centre formed on 16th August 1954 in No.23 Group disbanding on 31st July 1956.

No.1 Air Electronics School arrived on 23rd December 1957 initially equipped with 18 Anson T22s and later with Varsity T1s (WJ907 'Q'). It became The Air Electronics School c. January 1960 and moved to Topcliffe on 14th January 1962.

No.114 Sqn reformed at Hullavington on 20th November 1958. The squadron was equipped with the Chipmunk T10 and on 15th December was deployed to Nicosia, Cyprus on internal security duties.

No.33 MU, which formed at Lyneham in 1940, used Hullavington as a SLG/sub-site but this facility ceased on 1st December 1959 pending the disbanding of No.10 MU on 31st December 1959.

No.2 Air Navigation School moved in from Thorney Island on 15th January 1962 equipped with the Varsity and Valetta. It arrived in time for the ceremony on 3rd April when the Freedom of the Borough of Chippenham was granted to RAF Hullavington.

The School lost an aircraft and crew on 28th August 1962 when Valetta T3 WJ480 crashed 5 miles west north west of Chippenham. The pilot was carrying out a normal asymmetric overshoot with

Valetta T4 WJ487 'Q' in the markings of The Air Electronics School. The aircraft is seen in the Wiltshire area of Kemble Airfield outside of the main MU Site, prior to its departure for the fire dump at RAF Valley in 1962. When the School left Hullavington, many of its aircraft were taken into storage at Kemble awaiting disposal. Photo: Ray Deacon via Glen Moreman

the starboard propeller feathered. The aircraft proceeded westerly with both propellers turning and with the undercarriage retracted. It turned north and in a flatish turn, before crashing into the ground and cart-wheeling. The main cause was that the starboard engine master fuel cock was left shut off and hence the engine could not be restarted and speed decayed. The crew, who were killed, were Flt Lt David R. Kenward (Captain) and Flt Lt Donald H. Blundy (pilot). Sgt Ivor P. Mew (Air Signaller) died from his injuries on 5th September. The School moved to Gaydon on 1st September 1965.

From 26th July 1965 Hullavington was used for a RLG by a Primary Flying Training Sqn based at South Cerney.

During early 1966 Hullavington entered the computer age when the Defence Codification Data Centre (DCDC) was established. It was responsible for allocating every line on the RAF Inventory with a NATO Identification Code. The Centre moved to Glasgow in May 1986.

When the Airborne Forces formed during World War 2 the responsibility

for parachute training and packing was allocated to the RAF. The Parachute Collection & Display Unit, the Transport Command Parachute Servicing Unit and the Balloon Unit moved to Hullavington between October 1966 and January 1967. They combined to form on 1st July 1967, the Parachute Support Unit, later known as the Parachute Servicing Flt (PSF), and the Balloon Operations Sqn (BOS). The balloon and support units were in Training Command. From February 1971 until it disbanded in September 1976, RAF parachuting activities were complemented by the presence of No.16 Parachute Heavy Drop Unit, RAOC, an element of 16 Parachute Brigade. It was responsible for the rigging of parachutable platforms on which were loaded vehicles, equipment and stores required for airborne assault operations. Practice loads were dropped on the airfield. Parachute load dropping by Hercules aircraft from Lyneham commenced on 1st March 1971 and continued until Station closure in 1993. Following the handing over of most of the parachute packing to civilian contractors, the PSF disbanded at the end of 1992. The residual elements were relocated in

Hullavington based Valetta T3 V564 'M' originally built as a VIP Mk.C1 and later converted to be the prototype T3. It ended its service with No.2 Air Navigation School. The aircraft is seen here on Wiltshire ground at Kemble Airfield having been temporarily removed from its storage hangar to accommodate other aircraft movements. Photo: Ray Deacon via Glen Moreman

early 1993. The Balloon Operations Squadron continued in situ after the closure of the Station but was disbanded on Friday 31st March 1995, with personnel transferring to motor transport duties. Sqn CO Chris Pickthall said that one reason for its disbanding was that the Swiss made Egyptian cotton used for the balloon fabrics was out of production. It was cheaper for the RAF to contract out the parachute training than to obtain new non-synthetic fabrics capable of holding highly flammable hydrogen. So the training was civilianised with trainee soldiers and airmen making their parachute jumps from privately run Short Skyvan aircraft. The last RAF balloon flew over Hullavington on 29th March 1995.

RAF Hullavington was honoured again on 30th April 1970 when it received the Freedom of the Borough of Malmesbury. The privileges which were conferred by two local Boroughs were exercised regularly until the final parades on 26th March 1992.

The 6th World Aerobatic Championships were staged at Hullavington between 13th-24th July 1970 followed on 26th July by the 1st World Festival of Aerobatics. The organisation was by the Royal Aero Club of the United Kingdom, founded in 1901. The RAF displayed an Avro Lancaster and a BAC Lightning amongst other types. The Navy displayed a Swordfish, DH Sea Vixon and some Westland Helicopters.

In 1976 The Bannerdown Gliding Club of the RAF Gliding & Soaring Association, moved in from Colerne, where it had formed in 1960. It remained until October 1992 when, with the announcement of the Station closure, it moved to Keevil.

Proposals made in a 1976 White Paper on Defence to transfer the Station to the Army were withdrawn in 1980, spare capacity being filled by an influx of new units. Consequently, Hullavington commenced its association with the RAF Regiment when in August 1980 No.11 Sqn moved in. In October 1982 HQ No.5 Wing RAF Regiment formed and No.15 Sqn arrived in mid 1983. Their activities were complemented by the presence of No.3 Sqn in 1987/88. In August 1990 HQ No.5 Wing and No.15 Sqn were disbanded. The Station links with the Regiment ended with the departure of No.11 Sqn in March 1992.

No.621 VGS at Hullavington on 20th April 1997. One of the two 'D' Type hangars on 'D' Site seen to the rear.

From 1977 onwards, Hullavington hosted University Air Sqn summer camps with their aircraft, the Bulldog. This was a rekindling of a long tradition. Harriers of No.1 Sqn were also annual visitors for exercise purposes. Chinook and Puma helicopters regularly used the field.

In 1980 No.1 Administrative Support Unit (ASU), who were responsible for the storage and distribution of specialist hot and cold weather clothing equipment for the RAF, arrived; the ASU was subsumed within the Station supply organisation.

From 1980 to 1993 Hullavington was the home of the Mobile Catering Support Unit (MCSU), who were responsible for training all RAF catering personnel in the art of field catering. During this time MCSU personnel provided an estimated 13 million meals to Service personnel and allied forces at home and throughout the world, both on exercise and on active service.

Following the invasion of the Falkland Islands by Argentina on 2nd April 1982, preparations were made by the RAF to attack the captured airfield of Port Stanley. Hullavington was used as the pattern airfield for Port Stanley which was attacked in Operation *Blackbuck* by No. 44 Sqn's Vulcan B2 XM607 on 1st May 1982.

In 1986 No.4626 (County of Wiltshire) Aeromedical Evacuation Sqn. RAuxAF took up residence. Called to full time service, they served with distinction in the 1990-1991 Gulf War and relocated immediately prior to the Station closure in April 1993.

No.3 Air Experience Flt (AEF) arrived from Filton on 6th July 1989. Its Chipmunk aircraft were used to provide flights for hundreds of cadets. The Flt moved to Colerne in August 1993. Bristol University Air Sqn (BUAS) arrived on 6th March1992,

relocating to Colerne in November 1993.

No.625 (Volunteer) Gliding School arrived in late 1992 from South Cerney followed on 30th June 1993 by No.621 VGS from Locking. This further extended the tradition of cadet flying which can be traced back to Hullavington's earliest days. These two glider schools continue to fly from Hullavington.

Closure

On 1st April 1993 the RAF Ensign at Hullavington was lowered for the last time, and the Station handed over to the Army by the Station's 31st CO Wg Cdr M.W.P. Chapple AFC, RAF. For 56 years the unit had truly justified its motto *Service to Many*.

Many people were saddened that this grand station with a marvellous pedigree was no longer of use to the RAF. One of its most famous students, Gp Capt Sir Leonard Cheshire VC, DFC, DSO** was moved to write this letter:

Cavendish
Suffolk

To: Officer Commanding,
RAF Hullavington   14th February 1992

Dear Wing Commander Chapple,

It came as a considerable shock when some months ago I read through the list of RAF Stations to be closed and found that Hullavington was one of them. Now I understand from Greathouse that the end is approaching, and I feel that I can't let another day pass without sending you a brief line.

As you may perhaps know, No.9 FTS, Hullavington was my first RAF posting, after two years or so with the Oxford University Air Squadron. I did my first flight on 10th October 1939 with F/Sgt Boyd as instructor and my last on 1st April 1940 on a 'Road Race' with 'Dinghy' Young, who was later killed while flying with 617. Not many of those on that course survived the war, but I know that I speak for all when I say that we could hardly have been given a better start to our wartime operational careers. The instructors stood out for their professionalism and also for the genuine care that they showed to each one of us, with the result that, though we were mostly posted to different Commands, certainly different Groups, we felt a common bond and used to keep in touch with each other whenever possible.

I have a feeling that the Station over the years has maintained the high standard for which it was so well known during the war, and my one regret is that I have had so few opportunities of coming back to revisit you; though in thought and in spirit I have often done so. As the successor of those who trained and formed me in 1939/40, perhaps you would allow me to express my gratitude for the grounding I was given 52 years ago, without which my operational fortunes might well have been different.

May I also thank you warmly for the outstanding and consistent support that the Station has given in so many ways to Greathouse since its opening in 1958. That, I assure you, has meant a great deal to me.

Yours sincerely,
Cheshire

Copy of Cheshire's letter to the Hullavington CO. Leonard Cheshire Archive Centre.

The infrastructure of the former RAF Hullavington remains much as it did in its early days. The original stone barn of Bell Farm is a listed building, one of the hangars on 'E' Site is used for storage by the Royal Navy and one on 'A' Site for 'Go-Kart' racing. In an arson attack, fire destroyed one of the HQ 'C' Type hangars used for parachute packing. Wiltshire Fire Brigade received a 999 call at 0234 hrs on 3rd January 1992 and despite a large attendance including appliances from surrounding brigades, the contents in a large undivided area contributed to the destruction of the building.

Neither runway is any longer structurally maintained and all lighting has been removed, although some taxiway lighting points are still evident. Only the main runway remains usable. In addition to the parachute drops from Lyneham's Hercules and Chinook landings during exercises, small private civilian aircraft bring people on business trips to Bath and Bristol and the BBC helicopter uses the facility during the annual Badminton Horse Trials. The control tower is used on these occasions.

With the HQ of the Brigade of Gurkhas resident at Netheravon Airfield, it is intended that around 100 men of the newly formed Queen's Own Gurkha Logistic Regiment will be stationed at Hullavington during 2003.

Memorials

Three memorials stand as reminders of the Air Force occupation: -

1) 173/ST909811

On the grass opposite the former RAF Fire Section, now a workshop, stands a rough stone post and plinth with a copper plaque inscribed: -

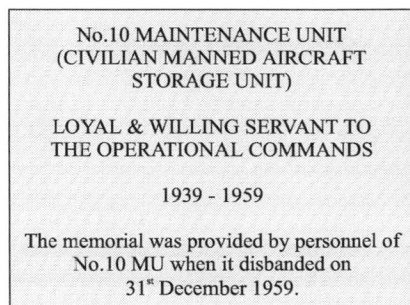

No.10 MAINTENANCE UNIT
(CIVILIAN MANNED AIRCRAFT
STORAGE UNIT)

LOYAL & WILLING SERVANT TO
THE OPERATIONAL COMMANDS

1939 - 1959

The memorial was provided by personnel of
No.10 MU when it disbanded on
31st December 1959.

No.10 MU memorial stone.

2) 173/ST913808

On the grass, immediately inside the main entrance gate and next to the Guard Room, a Gloucester Brown brick memorial inset with a Portland stone block carved with a Wessex Dragon and torch. The memorial is topped with a Portland stone slab carved on the face with the inscription:-

RAF HULLAVINGTON 1937 - 1993

At the rear of the memorial, a metal gantry supports three plaques of cast metal depicting the history and units of the RAF serving at the Station over the 56 year period. The memorial was the idea of Sqn Ldr Tony Neve MBE, RAF who previously served at the Station. He carved the stone and built the memorial which was dedicated and unveiled on 1st April 1993, at a ceremony to mark the closure of Hullavington as an RAF base.

The three plaques at the rear of the memorial,
inscribed with the RAF units serving at
Hullavington from 1937 - 1993.

SASO Air Commodore Anthony James
Stables CBE, unveiling the memorial with
Chaplain-in-Chief RAF The Venerable
B.H. Lucas, CB, QHC, BA and the
Hullavington Station Commander,
Wg Cdr M.W.P. Chapple OBE, AFC.
Photo: Sqn Ldr Tony Neve

3) 173/ST911806

In the dining hall of the Officers' Mess, on the balcony facia of the "Minstrels' Gallery", there is a row of painted wooden Air Force badges of those countries whose pilots trained at Hullavington during its period of use by the Empire Central Flying School. The centre badge is that of the ECFS. The badges were carved and painted by a Canadian at the School.

The Air Force badges displayed in the
Officers' Mess.

KEEVIL AERODROME
Location - 173/ST920565 - 4 miles East of Trowbridge

Keevil airfield is located west of the village of the same name and east of Steeple Ashton. Access to the airfield is from an unclassified road leading east from the C19 on the south side of Steeple Ashton. The airfield remains under the control of RAF Lyneham as a parachute dropping area and on occasion, landings and take-offs by its Hercules. The airfield is also used by Bannerdown Gliding Club.

Airfield Development

Keevil was originally scheduled as a fighter OTU, but during construction, priorities changed and it was built as a bomber OTU. It was never used as such and was allocated instead to the USAAF as a troop carrier base. The land needed for the aerodrome was requisitioned in 1941 and was allocated to Army Co-operation Command when, on 13th July 1942, the RAF advance party arrived with a skeleton crew on Care & Maintenance duties. During the time the airfield was being constructed, a Whitley bomber became the first aircraft to land. On rolling to a stop the pilot, whose name was Parfitt, was met by an Irish construction manager who told him to take-off as he was not allowed there. There was no choice, however, as the Whitley was out of fuel.

The domestic and technical sites and two T2 Type hangars were located on the south-west side of the field, with a number of the domestic buildings on off airfield sites. Altogether around 400 buildings were provided catering for staffing levels of 165 officers, 523 SNCOs and 1854 other ranks. Nine Extra Over Blister hangars were scattered around the site. The three concrete runways were (07/25) NE/SW 2000 x 50 yds, (13/31) NW/SE 1400 x 50yds and (02/20) N/S 1400 x 50yds. The 50 feet wide perimeter track served 51 dispersal pans and the nine blister hangars. Some of the dispersal pans were later increased in size to accommodate the large, mainly Stirling, aircraft. The pans totalled 9 x 150' diam., 41 x 125' diam. and 1 x 75' diam. The Control Tower was built to Type 12779/41 with small windows Type 343/43. The station identification

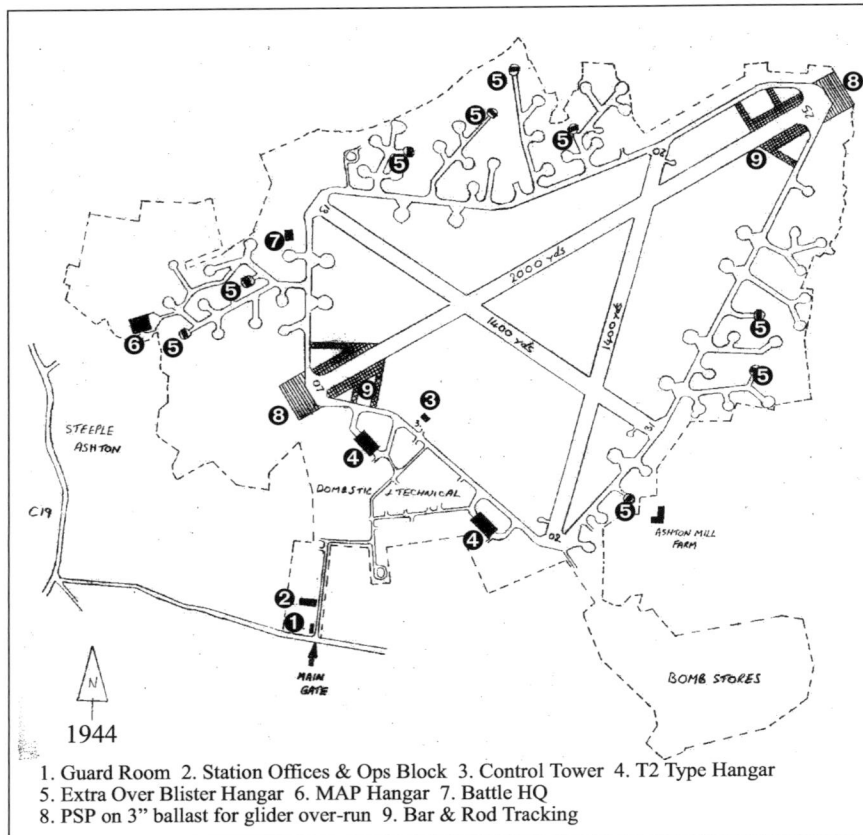

1. Guard Room 2. Station Offices & Ops Block 3. Control Tower 4. T2 Type Hangar
5. Extra Over Blister Hangar 6. MAP Hangar 7. Battle HQ
8. PSP on 3" ballast for glider over-run 9. Bar & Rod Tracking

A Lyneham Hercules parachute dropping over Keevil airfield.   **Photo: Donald Lovelock**

code letters were KV and standard Mk.II Drem runway, perimeter and circuit lighting was installed. It is probable that the main NE/SW runway operated a Standard Beam Approach System.

By August 1943 a Ministry of Aircraft Production (MAP) Type B1 hangar and offices had been constructed on land requisitioned on the western boundary Accessed from Steeple

Ashton, a taxiway connected the site with the dispersals, and runways of the airfield.

In July 1947 some of the airfield buildings were released to the Ministry of Health and Ministry of Works. The following year the airfield boundaries were reduced. In 1952, 38 huts were sold to the Warminster and Westbury Rural District Council for housing.

140

Keevil's Control Tower and surviving 'T' Type hangar in present day condition.

After 1947, when the airfield was placed on C&M, no maintenance was undertaken on the airfield infrastructure until the winter of 1971/72 when the main runway 07/25 was completely resurfaced and drainage improved. The control tower, which had been left open to the elements, was renovated and improved communications installed. Further improvements to the main runway and perimeter track took place in 1990.

One of the two T2 type hangars which had deteriorated was demolished under MoD contract in September 1987. It was re-erected, following renovation, at Popham and subsequently moved to the Yorkshire Air Museum at Elvington. From 1955 to 1965 the Americans had used the hangar to store hospital equipment. The other T2 type hangar was re-clad with aluminium.

At the end of the war the Spitfire assembly hangar was given to the farmer on whose land it had been built and continues to be used for agricultural purposes. The MoD retains use of the control tower, and it is manned by air traffic control personnel whenever military operations are undertaken at the airfield. Some of the Maycrete buildings on the dispersed sites are used for agriculture.

World War 2 Years

The initial airfield construction was incomplete when on 25th September 1942 it became American Air Force (AAF) Station 471 and the four squadrons (4th, 7th, 8th and 51st) of the 62nd Troop Carrier Group USAAF 12th Air Force, 'staging' to North Africa, started to move in. The fourth and last arrived on 10th October and all were concentrated in training with the paratroops which they would transport between the 11th and 18th November on Operation 'Torch', the British and American landings in Algeria and Morocco. The Group was under the command of Col Samuel J. Davis. Its aircraft allocation was 52 C-47 Skytrains and C-53 Skytroopers.

On 28th November 1942, following the departure of the 62nd TCG, the airfield passed into the hands of the RAF's No.70 Group Care & Maintenance. A Royal Air Force detachment continued to be based at Keevil and was, in fact, increased on 8th February 1943 to 5 officers and 210 other ranks. On 30th May 1943, an American pilot flying a Spitfire from an unknown airfield, lost control and with it upside down just above ground level, the aircraft flew through the

M.T. workshops killing three mechanics who were servicing a Commer van. One of those killed was Cpl Stanley Kingham RAF who is buried in Steeple Ashton churchyard. Two other MT Section personnel who were not in the building at the time were Sgt Massey, who was in charge, and LAC Laurie Rawson, who had gone to see his girlfriend serving with the National Fire Service (NFS) at Trowbridge. The two-bay M.T. workshop was rebuilt. Laurie Rawson recalls another occasion when the M.T. Section was called out to Capps Lane near Bratton. A German bomber had been brought down not far from the main London to West of England railway line and in which the four-man crew had been killed.

From 1st June 1943 the station was again allocated to the USAAF, which began deploying personnel there over the next two months. The non operational status continued until 8th August 1943 when it became a supply base for the 67th Observation Group US 8th Air Force at Membury, taking over Keevil as a Satellite for its 153rd Observation Sqn. It was equipped with a number of different aircraft. These were Piper L-4B Cubs (officially named Grasshoppers), ex-RAF Spitfire MkVBs and Bostons (Douglas DB-7 Havoc Mk.Is). The 67th Observation Group later became the 67th Reconnaissance Group.

From 8th August 1943, Major Allen, the USAAF Commanding Officer, agreed with the RAF to allow Vickers Armstrong Ltd to use the hard-standing immediately outside of their assembly hangar for dispersal of the Spitfires as they came off the assembly line and were awaiting allocation.

From August 1943 Spitfires, which were being constructed for Vickers Ltd in various dispersed locations in and around Trowbridge, were assembled and test flown at Keevil from the new MAP hangar. Prior to the facility being available at Keevil, the constructed Spitfire sections were delivered to the assembly works at High Post, where Vickers were assembling and despatching Spitfires. The major sub assemblies were transported on 'Queen Mary' trailers, leaving in convoys at night to avoid possible attack from enemy aircraft. Most of the production sites were in Trowbridge with several commercial garages being used. Premises in Southwick and Westbury

Queen Mary with female production staff at the Vickers Works in Bradley Road, Trowbridge in 1943.   Photo: The Keevil Society

were also requisitioned. The opening of the airfield at Keevil with its MAP hangar presented the opportunity to assemble, test and deliver aircraft which had been produced within a 10 mile radius. Following completion of assembly, the aircraft engines were test run and prepared for the maiden flight. The flights were generally undertaken by company or military pilots. When accepted as satisfactory, the aircraft were flown out of Keevil by pilots of the ATA to MUs, squadrons or units. Keevil's Spitfires comprised Mks VII/VIII/IX/XIV/XVIII/XIX and Photographic Reconnaissance X/XI/XII. Some of these were export variants. With the post war closure of the Castle Bromwich works, the orders for Mk.22s and Mk.24s, some already part built, were diverted to South Marston but actually assembled at Keevil. Other Mk.24s were sent to Keevil for modifications and maintenance. During its time as an assembly shop, almost 600 Merlin and Griffon engined variants passed through the Keevil hangar.

The second wave of Americans soon settled in at Keevil. The RAF personnel noticed a vast improvement in the catering although one LAC Rawson didn't much like having his pudding on the same plate as his main course. The children of the villages of Steeple Ashton and Keevil appreciated the candy which they were given and the organised parties which they were invited to attend on the station. Steve Brown, later to become a RAF navigator, recalls being taken for a flight from Keevil in an American crewed Boston. Some familiar

American names came to entertain their countrymen such as Ben Lyon and Bebe Daniels. Joe Louis gave boxing exhibitions.

RAF personnel were frequently required to escort American Officers off the base and on such occasions were required to draw side arms from the armoury to accompany these duties. Presumably it was felt that personal protection was compromised when off base. A large number of American military personnel arrived on troop trains at Seend Station. Provisions and hardware also arrived at this small village station. Convoys would wind their way from there, around the country lanes, to the airfield at Keevil.

The Americans began to standardise with the Boston A-20Bs which started to arrive. At this time, a decision was taken back in the States, to re-designate the 153rd as a Liaison Squadron. This order failed to reach Keevil until later in the year by which time the Bostons had been equipped with cameras and the squadron was carrying out photographic sorties along the French coast. One of three Bostons, after landing on fire following an operation, blew up on the runway seconds after the crew had sprinted to safety. On 10th September 1943 four A-20Bs flew from Keevil to AAF Station 470 Wattisham. Aircraft No.13387 flown by 2nd Lt Van S. Walker landed by mistake on the short runway. Noticing a 'gas truck' and a number of men directly ahead of him on the perimeter track and being unable to stop in time, the pilot attempted by use of brakes and

engine to ground loop the aircraft. He successfully achieved this but owing to the wet surface he slid into a ditch beside the perimeter track causing damage to the landing gear and propeller blades of No.2 engine. The subsequent enquiry determined that pilot error was 75% to blame, as he had not thoroughly checked the landing conditions. 25% was attributed to poor visibility and the fact that the control tower operators did not use a red flare to send him around again.

On 12th October 1943 the 153rd lost its photo-reconnaissance status and was re-identified a Liaison Squadron. Keevil was re-allocated to the Ninth Air Force on 16th October. The 153rd. moved back to its parent station at Membury on 3rd October but returned to Keevil on 28th November having re-equipped with L-4s. With the move the courier role terminated and numerous sergeant pilots were posted in to replace the officer pilots and crews who were transferred to a newly formed 2911th Bomb Squadron equipped with Boston A-20s. This unit was soon deactivated and its personnel returned to the 153rd, which most had never left anyway. This resulted in the squadron having an exceedingly large establishment of liaison pilots, 15 A-20Bs, 2 L-4Bs and an ex-RAF Oxford. On the 12th December 1943, the 153rd were assigned to IX Fighter Command of the U.S 9th Air Force which had a role providing close air/ground support to the army. On 23rd December the Unit was joined by the 363rd Fighter Group, 70th Fighter Wing, 9th AF. The 363rd FG worked up to operations using the 67th Tactical Reconnaissance Group's Spitfires until the delayed allocation of its North American P-51B Mustangs which arrived in January 1944. The Group had been chosen as the third in the ETO to be equipped with the type. The Unit, commanded by Col John R. Ulricson, remained at Keevil until leaving for its operational base at Rivenhall (AAF Station 168) on 22nd January 1944. It commenced operations the next month escorting bombers and fighter bombers to targets in France, Germany and the Low Countries. In August the Group had a role change from fighter to tactical reconnaissance when its Mustangs were fitted with cameras and were designated as P-51B/F-6s.

On 25th December 1943 the 153rd was formally declared a Tow Target Flight

Pilots of the 153rd Liaison Sqn studying a map on the airfield at Keevil in February 1944. The two aircraft are L-4s.   Photo: L.E. Shrum

No.299 Sqn at Keevil in 1944.   Photo: The Keevil Society

RAAF personnel of No.196 Sqn at Keevil in 1944.   Photo: The Keevil Society

but the necessary modified Douglas DB-7s or A20Bs were slow in being issued. This resulted in the squadron reverting to its original liaison role. Surplus personnel were then moved to other units and L-4s became the standardised aircraft on charge. On 13th March 1944 the 153rd Liaison Sqn left for nearby New Zealand Farm, but not before they had undergone yet another administrative change on 4th February with attachment to the First U.S. Army. With the departure of the 153rd, Keevil's war-time association with the Americans ended. The official handing over of the station by the USAAF to the RAF was held on 10th March 1944. At 1200 hrs a parade was held involving the RAF Holding Party, USAAF personnel and the Glider Pilot Regiment. 'Old Glory' was struck and the RAF Ensign hoisted on the mast in front of the Station Headquarters building. Gp Capt C.D. Troop arrived from Netheravon to take up the post of Station Commander. At a later date Prime Minister Winston Churchill paid a visit to Erlestoke Camp, landing at Keevil in his York.

Six Stirlings and gliders of No.299 Sqn arrived at Keevil from Stoney Cross on

14th March 1944. They were followed the next day by the main air and road parties and with Wg Cdr P.B.N. Davis DSO as CO. No.196 Sqn moved in the same day from Tarrant Rushton with Wg Cdr N. Alexander as CO. Because of bad weather only 10 Stirlings towing loaded Horsa gliders left Tarrant Rushton the first day and it was four days before the move to Keevil was completed. Both these No.38 Group squadrons were equipped with the Stirling III and IV. Some Mk. IIIs were converted to Mk. IV specification shortly after arrival, and others were ferried out to Tilstock. No.1 and 2 (Horsa) Glider Servicing Echelon also arrived at this time from No.1 Heavy Glider Servicing Unit at Netheravon. No.196 Sqn's move to Keevil was achieved over two days by shuttling back and forth with Horsas loaded with equipment and stores. The change of location did not prevent the squadrons from starting to train straight away. This involved cross-country, circuits and bumps and light Horsa towing. On the 18th March, 25 Stirling Mk IIIs & IVs from both squadrons towed 25 Horsa gliders on an exercise to Brize Norton. A Group Exercise *Bizz 1* was staged on 20th March for which No.196

Sqn provided 13 aircraft, although 2 failed to take-off when they developed magneto drops just before departure time. No.299 Sqn contributed 13 aircraft. A glider on tow broke loose from its tug over the sea because of excessive slipstream disturbance. It ditched approximately 4 miles from the coast. Two of the occupants were lost but the rest were saved by Air Sea Rescue launches and a Walrus seaplane. Five days later Exercise *Bizz 2* was held and this time No.196 Sqn provided 10 Stirlings and No.299 Sqn 15 Stirlings. A glider in which No.299 Sqn CO Wg Cdr P.B.N. Davis was flying as a passenger again broke loose from its tug whilst over the sea and ditched. On this occasion all were rescued.

On Sunday 26th March 1944, aircraft from both squadrons went to Brize Norton for the retrieval of gliders. A No.299 Sqn aircraft piloted by Fg Off Duncan J. Cameron RCAF crashed after take-off at Brize Norton due to an engine fire. The Stirling was wrecked and the pilot and navigator sustained injuries. These were so severe in the case of the pilot that he died three days later at the RAF hospital in Wroughton, and was buried at Bath (Haycombe) Cemetery.

The Horsa glider allocation at Keevil started building up to 100 during the month.

Prior to their invasion operations of June and September 1944, both the squadrons carried out Special Air Service and Special Operations Executive duties in support of the French Resistance, occasional bombing sorties and glider towing training. The Stirling crews comprised RAF, RAAF, RCAF, RNZAF and SAAF personnel. Little detail is shown of all the clandestine operations of the SAS and SOE in the Station/Squadron records but during their time at the station, No.196 and No.299 Sqns

Staff Sgt Bill Higgs at Keevil before D-Day.
Photo: Bill Higgs

Stirlings at Keevil, assembled in preparation for Operation *Tonga*.
Photo: The Keevil Society.

Contemporary sketch of Stirlings and Horsa gliders leaving Keevil on the evening of 5th June,
as witnessed by A. B. Walker, a pupil of nearby Dauntsey's School.   Photo: A. B. Walker

contributed too many such trips, No.196 Sqn carrying out 14 S.O.E. sorties in March alone. Most of these were to France and were anything but 'milk runs'. They were generally made on clear nights, flown at low level to avoid radar detection, required accurate navigation and map reading, the ability to maintain a close watch on hazards such as HT cables and the need to arrive at the predetermined time. Crews from Keevil were frequently despatched to Tarrant Rushton during the daytime to await the signal that an operation was authorised and would commence from that Station. The ground reception party would be at the dropping site in preparation for the aircraft's arrival. Aircrews were ordered to drop their supplies only if they could accurately identify the site, which on occasions would be briefly illuminated, and the correct code was received from the ground. After the drop the risks of a lone aircraft returning were considerable. Enemy flak and night fighters together with a warm welcome from British defences could be expected and was frequently experienced. Both squadrons carried out SAS and SOE drops throughout their period of deployment at Keevil.

Sir Stafford Cripps arrived by air at Keevil on 31st March 1944 to visit Vickers Ltd. He was able to watch demonstrations of the Spitfire Mks XIV and the Seafire. The aircraft were flown by pilots attached to the M.A.P.

Through April 1944 the two Stirling squadrons continued their build up to D-Day. Staff Sgt Bill Higgs, piloting Horsa glider 114 over Keevil on 25th April, created a height record when after casting off from a Stirling 'K' King, he reached an altitude of 15,000'.

Stirling EF269 of No.299 Sqn, carrying out a fighter affiliation exercise, came

down at Rowde near Devizes on 25th April, when with the aircraft at 3000', the dinghy wrapped around the rudder, jamming it hard to port. The aircraft, piloted by Fg Off J.H. Clark RCAF, was abandoned with the crew taking to their parachutes. 6 RAF crew and 2 men of the Glider Pilot regiment were lost in another Stirling crash.

On 19th May 1944, 12 No.196 and 13 No.299 Sqn Stirlings took part in Exercise *Exeter*, in which 25 gliders were successfully released over Netheravon Airfield. The exercise was witnessed from Netheravon's control tower by the King, Queen and Princess Elizabeth.

As Francis Drake took time to play bowls before doing battle with the Spanish, so Keevil's personnel found time in May 1944 to play three cricket

matches and a game of football against the Trowbridge NFS before engaging in battle against the Germans. All the games were played away from the station with results unrecorded.

An Avro York I 4999, ex MW107, of SAAF (Field Marshal Smut's personal aircraft) piloted by Lt Col Nell, with 3 Staff Officers of Field Marshal Smuts' Personal Staff, forced landed at Keevil on 1st June 1944. They were on route from Gibraltar to Northolt.

On 3rd June Flt Cdrs of the RAF and GPR at Keevil were summoned to Netheravon for a confidential briefing prior to Operation *Neptune*, the airborne assault on Normandy, and the D-Day invasion.

On Monday 5th June, the eve of D-Day, 46 aircraft of the two squadrons at

No. 196 Sqn and Australian Glider Pilot crews with Horsa glider *Shy Tot* at Keevil.
Top: Unknown Glider Pilot, 3rd Row: Plt Off Henry *Chuck* Hoystead & Flt Sgt C.E. Light,
2nd Row: Flt Sgt C. Campbell, Unknown GP, Plt Off Wally Marshall, WO George R. Oliver,
Unknown GP, Plt Off Jack James, 1st Row: Flt Sgt Mann, WO H. J. Kilday,
Fg Off Ron Minchin.   Photo: The Keevil Society.

Keevil took part in Operation *Tonga*. They were part of a larger airlift charged with dropping paratroops of the 12th Battalion 6th Airborne Division in Normandy. Their role was to secure the Allied left flank in the opening of the invasion of France. The aircraft were lined up in sequence at the end of the runway. The troops arrived at Keevil throughout the day, which was one of poor weather conditions. In the late evening, assisted by the airmen and WAAF ground crews, parachutes were attached and the paratroops boarded the aircraft for take-off. This commenced at 2319 hours. The aircraft were waved off by a large number of ground service and civilian personnel. The troops on the aircraft comprised the 13th Parachute (Lancashire) Battalion and 225th Parachute Field Ambulance, RAMC. 46 aircraft took-off and successfully dropped 806 paratroops of the 5th Parachute Brigade in total darkness on a 2½ square mile DZ'N' near Caen on the eastern side of the River Orne. No.299 Sqn lost Stirling LJ819 'H' piloted by Flt Sgt Leslie J. Gilbert DFM, RAAF. He is commemorated on the Runneymede Memorial. No.196 Sqn lost Stirling IV LJ841 flown by Flt Lt Fred Gribble. His aircraft was thought to have been the one seen by most crews to be on fire east of the DZ. This pilot is buried at Cagny Communal Cemetery, Calvados, France. Both

aircraft were lost on 6th June. Flt Sgt Keith Prowd, the pilot of Stirling IV EF276, experienced problems after making his drop when he found difficulty in getting the strops back into the aircraft. Fg Off W. Baker, pilot of Stirling IV LJ440, had two engines out after receiving flak damage over the DZ. Two of his crew baled out, Fg Off James K. Anderson RCAF (nav) and Flt Lt Richard N.P. Luff DFM (BA) and were not heard of again. This aircraft re-crossed the Channel and force landed at Ford Airfield. An Oxford from Keevil flew to Ford the following day to collect Fg Off Baker

and the remaining crewmen. Fg Off Anderson is buried in the Calais Canadian War Cemetery and Flt Lt Luff who lived at Maiden Bradley, not far from Keevil, is commemorated on the Runnymede Memorial. The No.299 Sqn aircraft of Fg Off Gib Goucher, Stirling EF243 received considerable flak damage over the DZ. This resulted in a leg wound to WO Leonard Brock the Flt Eng. The paratroops were, however, successfully dropped and the Stirling returned to Keevil where it crash-landed. The Keevil ground crews worked extremely hard repairing, servicing and preparing the returning Stirlings, which were lined up at the east end of the main runway in preparation for towing the Horsa Gliders on that evening's operation to transport more troops.

A No.1 Group Lancaster, returning from operations over Orleans, landed at Keevil. The bomb-aimer Sgt West had been killed by flak when over the target.

Tuesday 6th June saw the arrival of D-Day and Operation *Mallard*, the second phase of the opening up of the second front. This was the main airborne landing of glider-borne troops and heavy equipment. The contribution of Keevil to Operation *Mallard* commenced between 1903 and 1930 hours with 33 aircraft from the two squadrons towing Horsa gliders carrying Divisional troops of the 2nd Ox & Bucks Light Infantry to LZ 'W', west of the River Orne. The objective was to reinforce the troops dropped on Operation *Tonga*.

Horsa glider under tow over Ghent. The photograph was taken by rear gunner
'Bunny' Mason from the turret of his Stirling tug aircraft from Keevil.
Photo: 'Bunny' Mason/Cty. The Keevil Society.

Landings in France began at 1930 hrs and casualties were relatively light. One of No.299 Sqn's Stirlings failed to return, having been struck by flak after releasing its Horsa. The Stirling 'K' piloted by Fg Off James H.Clark RCAF crashed into the sea with no survivors after releasing its Horsa glider piloted by Sgt Richardson, Glider Pilot Regiment (GPR). It was Fg Off Clark and his crew who had survived the Stirling crash at Rowde on 25th April. His body was recovered after his aircraft crashed into the sea on 7th June, he was buried at Hermanville War Cemetery, Calvados, France. Lt Eric Martin, GPR, pilot of a glider towed to the LZ by Sqn Ldr D.W. Triptree in Stirling 'G', was killed when it crashed on landing with its cargo of troops and equipment. He lies in Ranville War Cemetery, Calvados, France. The 17 No.196 Sqn aircraft that took-off, all returned safely.

Staff Sgt Bill Higgs was one of the glider pilots from Keevil who landed in France on 6th June. His glider took-off from Tarrant Rushden towed by a Halifax. On the approach to the LZ there was considerable flak and much smoke from the bombing which had taken place. He lost sight of his tug and became disorientated. Having passed through the smoke he discovered that not only was he now above instead of behind his tug but also the starboard yoke rope was hitched around his starboard wheel. In addition he had overshot the LZ. After reforming behind the tug, its pilot Sqn Ldr Rymills informed him they would go round the circuit again. Communication between the two aircraft was by way of an intercom which ran along the tow-rope. They passed through the flak again without serious problems and Staff Sgt Higgs pulled off from the Halifax. Fortunately the rope around the wheel of the Horsa fell away and a successful landing was made despite the aircraft wing being ripped off. Bill and his second pilot cut the central wire running through the glider and unshackled the bolts which held the tail plane on. The tail end fell away, the metal ramps were laid to the ground and the gun and jeep on board were removed from their stowage. The team then moved off to the designated position for setting up. Bill was involved in fighting during the next few days but his instructions were to return to the UK as soon as circumstances

RAF and RAAF Stirling aircrew with glider pilots in front of a Horsa glider at Keevil on 16th September 1944, immediately prior to Operation *Market*, the air assault on Arnhem: - (Rear) Fg Off Tovell RAAF, unknown GP, Fg Off Charlesworth, unknown, unknown, Flt Lt George Copeman RAAF, Fg Off Rowbotham. (Front) Plt Off Lance Coates, unknown GP, unknown, unknown, unknown GP.   Photo: The Keevil Society

permitted. To aid his return to the coast, he was issued with a folding bicycle. Glider pilots were in short supply and needed for later landings. He made his way to the beachhead, hitched a lift from the RN and arrived back at Keevil with his bike. As an Acting Sqn Sgt Major, he later took part in the Arnhem landings, on this occasion flying a Horsa from Keevil. Severely wounded from rifle fire after landing his glider, he was taken prisoner. Following eventual repatriation he spent two years in hospital. The 2nd Ox & Bucks Regiment remained in France until returning to their base at Bulford Camp on 3rd September 1944.

On 8th June 1944, 7 No.196 Sqn aircraft took-off on a re-supply operation to drop containers on DZ'N'. This was Operation *Rob-Roy*. The aircraft were recalled on-route, although one failed to receive the message before dropping its load successfully. All aircraft returned safely. For the remainder of the month crews were engaged in training, mainly glider towing and cross-countries. A number of re-supply operations were undertaken, although some were cancelled prior to take-off. During the month Lord Trenchard visited the station.

Through July, August and early September, operations, of which a number were SOE supply drops, and

training exercises continued. Many of the Stirlings on operations received damage from heavy flak which prevented a return landing at Keevil after crossing the Channel. LJ919 of No.299 Sqn piloted by Fg Off Gib Goucher RCAF was one such case. Having taken 24 containers and a pannier for a night drop over France on 2nd August, the starboard elevator was damaged by flak and it landed at Weston Zoyland. The crew were taken back to Keevil but returned two days later to collect the repaired aircraft. It was found that the fuel tanks had been fully fuelled and whilst they were able to take-off, they had to fly over Salisbury Plain to dump around 1000 gallons before being allowed to land at their home airfield.

On occasions Keevil received training flights from other stations as on 8th July 1944 when 10 Whitleys landed from Netheravon towing gliders. On the night of 13th/14th August a No.10 OTU Whitley V BD221 on a cross-country flight from Abingdon force-landed at 0210hrs on its approach to Keevil. The aircraft came down close to West Ashton cross roads near Trowbridge. It followed a loss of power caused by the flame traps burning out. Sgt M. Kinsella (pilot) lost sight of Keevil's flare path while trying to set the altimeter. The six-man crew were all injured.

No.196 Sqn had a change of CO in August 1944, with the appointment of Wg Cdr M.W.L. Baker.

As with all stations involved, the personnel of Keevil had been confined to camp during the build up to the biggest landing operations ever carried out. The operation was in two parts, a ground assault and an air assault. The airborne part was called *Market* and the ground part, conducted by the Army, was *Garden*. Commencing on Sunday 17th September 1944, the brief for the airborne troops was to secure the bridges over the Lower Rhine and River Waal. The crews from Keevil had the allotted task of transporting part of the 1st Airborne Division, comprising the 9th (Airborne) Field Company Royal Engineers, 1st Parachute Brigade and 1st Airlanding Light Regiment RA to LZ 'Z' two miles west of Oosterbeek and close to Arnhem. The subsequent task was to re-supply the troops as required. At this time Keevil was holding 130 Horsa gliders, more than any other station engaged on the Arnhem operations. Many of the gliders had been towed into the station by Halifaxes. One of these, when landing on runway 13/31 with the trailing tow rope still attached after release of its glider, cut a haystack in two and sliced through the telephone wires of Ashton Mill Farm, which was very near to the end of the runway. Various fields around the airfield were recognised rope drop zones but some pilots chose to drop on the airfield itself. On occasions this proved disastrous as when a Dakota, dropping its rope, cut the wing off a Hadrian glider which had just landed.

For Operation *Market*, 'D' Sqn of the Glider Pilot Regiment, commanded by Maj J.F. Lyne, operated from Keevil with the following Flights and Commanders: -

No.8 Flt	Capt G. Murdoch
No.13 Flt	Capt S.G. Cairns
No.21 Flt	Capt F.M. Barclay
No.22 Flt	Capt I.C. Muir
No.5 Flt	Capt J.M. Morrisson

(deployed and operated from Blakehill Farm)

The two Stirling squadrons at this time, No.196 and No.299, were commanded by Wg Cdr W.M.L. Baker and Wg Cdr P.B.N. Davis DSO respectively.

On the first lift the total number of troops transported was around 290. The airborne hardware comprised 66 jeeps, 20 trailers, 25 motor-cycles, 116 folding cycles, 4 x 75mm Pack-Howitzers and 3 compressor trailers.

On 17th September 25 Stirling tugs from each of the two squadrons, towing 50 Horsa gliders, flown by pilots of No.13 Flt and No.21 Flt, began taking off from Keevil at one minute intervals from 1015 hours. The lead aircraft was flown by Wg Cdr Davis. Disaster struck early when, over Paulton, Somerset, the tail assembly was seen to separate from Horsa RJ113, Chalk No.389, towed by No.299 Sqn Stirling LJ868. It was witnessed by Sgt Wally Simpson, the rear gunner. The glider immediately began to drop and the tow rope broke which was fortunate for the crew of the Stirling, as it could easily have been brought down had this not have occurred. The glider crashed at Double Hills killing the two pilots of the Glider Regiment, S/Sgt Leonard J. Gardner and Sgt Robert A. Fraser together with the 5 NCOs and 16 sappers of No.1 Platoon, 9th (Airborne) Field Company R.E. The Stirling dropped out of the formation, circled the crash site and sent a message to Keevil before returning. On landing at 1125 hours, Fg Off Geoff Liggins RAAF and his crew boarded a jeep and drove to the scene. They were confronted by utter carnage. The glider had caught fire from the ammunition explosions and the fuel in the tanks of the miniature motor cycles being carried. The bodies had remained in the fuselage. They were later all buried at Weston-Super-Mare and a memorial stone now stands on the crash site at Double Hills, where a memorial service is held each year. Two other No.299 Sqn tugs on route to Arnhem lost their gliders over England. These were Stirling LJ919 Fg Off Gib Gougher RCAF (pilot) towing glider Chalk No.385 with pilots S/Sgt Smith and Sgt Morgan and Stirling LK544 with WO Brown (pilot), towing glider Chalk No.399 piloted S/Sgt Ted Legge and Sgt Pinnock.

No.196 Sqn had five aircraft aborted. Fg Off Powell in EF234 failed to take off because of severe damage to glider,

Chalk No.457. During marshalling before taking off the tow -rope of the Horsa caught around a runway light. This swung the glider into the revolving propellers of another Stirling. The pilots of the glider Lt Norman Adams and Sgt Waterman plus 6 troops of No.1 Forward Observation Unit R.A. with their jeep and trailer, took-off the following day as part of the second lift. Flt Sgt Fordham in LJ954 lost his glider Chalk No.474, with S/Sgt Ramsbottom and Sgt Harvey over England. Flt Lt Meredith in LK566 lost his glider HG930, Chalk No.462, with pilots S/Sgt Ken Beard and Sgt Geoff Tapping, when the tow-rope broke and it ditched in the North Sea, off the Dutch coast, near the island of Walcheren. The two pilots and three men of the 1st Para Brigade were rescued from their dinghy shortly afterwards, when an Air Sea Rescue launch arrived on the scene. Glider Chalk No.468, piloted by S/Sgt Edwards and Sgt Oram, towed by LJ848 with Sqn Ldr Brown (pilot), and glider Chalk No.478, piloted by S/Sgt Cram and Sgt Whitehead and towed by LJ843 with Flt Sgt Green (pilot), landed prematurely in Holland because of broken tow-ropes. All of the Stirlings taking part returned without loss. Most crews, on arrival back at Keevil, reported that the trip had been 'a piece of cake'. A total of 42 gliders reached LZ'Z'.

Fighter cover was provided by Air Defence of Great Britain (A.D.G.B.) and squadrons of the US 8th Air Force. The aircraft used for this cover consisted of 19 Spitfire, 5 Tempest and 3 Mustang squadrons. As well as for fighter interception, they were used for attacking flak positions.

For the 2nd Lift on 18th September, Operation *Market* D +1, 22 aircraft from each of the two Keevil squadrons towed 44 Horsas flown by pilots of No.8 Flt and No.22 Flt to LZ 'Z'. These carried about 120 troops, 55 jeeps, 45 trailers and 9 motorcycles as part of the 2nd Lift. Wg Cdr Davis of No.299 Sqn in Stirling LK135, with Horsa Chalk No.950, was first to take-off from Keevil at 1125 hours. The same route was followed as on the previous day. 39 of the gliders reached the LZ but 5 landed prematurely. No.196 Sqn had three aborted. Stirling LJ843 piloted by Flt Sgt Green lost glider Chalk No.1026 with pilots S/Sgt Stocker and

No.299 Sqn Stirlings returning to Keevil following the re-supply mission to Arhem on 18th September. The lead aircraft is that of Wg Cdr Davis who was killed the following day. At the rear is the aircraft of Sqn Ldr Dale OC 'B' Flt. The photograph was taken by Flt Sgt Les Ede RAAF, navigator in the Stirling of Fg Off Farrell. The 'vic' formation provided tail and beam protection from fighters, with the combined fire power of twelve Brownings from the rear turrets. The disadvantage was a larger target offered to the anti-aircraft guns, but returning empty at maximum altitude reduced the risk.   Photo: Les Ede/Cty. The Keevil Society.

Sgt Allen. It was forced to cast off because it had been 'badly loaded'. The glider landed safely on the airfield at Martlesham Heath and took part in the 3rd Lift. WO Prowd in EF234 lost glider Chalk No.457, with pilots Lt Norman V.M. Adams and Sgt Ken Waterman. Over the Channel the glider overshot the tug and had to pull off, landing in the sea 50 kilometres east of Ipswich. Its load was 1 jeep and trailer plus 6 troops of a Forward Observation Unit attached to the 1st Air Landing Light Regiment RA. All personnel were picked up by a RAF Air Sea Rescue launch except for Lt Adams, who remained in the fuselage trying to operate the gas terminal to inflate the dinghy. It is thought that he drowned when the fuselage sank and dragged him down. This was the same glider which had aborted from the 1st Lift when its tow-rope caught on the runway light at Keevil. Fg Off James in LJ810 lost Horsa LH175, Chalk No.1011, with pilots S/Sgt Stevenson and Lt Moorwood when the tow-rope broke and it landed prematurely in Holland 10 miles from the LZ.

No.299 Sqn had two gliders which failed to make the LZ. Fg Off Gig Gougher in LJ919 lost glider Chalk No.956, with pilots S/Sgt Bernard Black and Sgt Philip Hudson, when the tow-rope broke and it landed safely on the island of Schouwen-Duiveland. The two glider pilots were captured by German troops on 7th December. Flt Lt Berridge in LK130 lost glider Chalk No.964, with pilots S/Sgt Coombs and Sgt Knowles, when it was forced to cast off due to problems caused by the slipstream of a previous combination. The Stirling and the Horsa landed at Martlesham Heath where they hitched-

up and took off again. By now they were late but joined a stream of US C-47s. The result was that Chalk No.964 was the sole British glider to land on LZ 'W' with 450 American Waco gliders and troops of the US 101st Airborne Division. All the Stirlings from the Keevil squadrons, engaged on the 2nd Lift, returned safely to base.

For the 3rd Lift of Operation *Market* on D + 2, Tuesday 19th September, the two squadrons despatched 16 Stirling/Horsa combinations between them. On this occasion the Horsa pilot pairings were made up of various squadrons of the GPR. The gliders carried 35 troops of the glider element of the 1st Independent Polish Parachute Brigade, 22 jeeps and 11 trailers to LZ 'L'. No.196 Sqn took-off first at 1210 hrs contributing 9 tugs, and followed by No.299 Sqn with 7 tugs. Only 11 of the combinations made it to the operational area and the gliders arrived on LZ 'L' in the midst of a fierce battle between the 7th Battalion King's Own Scottish Borderers and enemy troops. No.196 Sqn experienced three abortive sorties. Fg Off McComie in LJ846 experienced an engine seizure that forced the glider, Chalk No.1026 with pilots S/Sgt Stocker and Sgt Allen, to land prematurely at Manston. This same glider had landed prematurely the day before at Martlesham Heath. Fg Off Jones in LK146 experienced engine problems en route to Holland and had to return to base with glider, Chalk No.154 piloted by S/Sgt Roy Howard DFM and Sgt Davy. Flt Sgt Green in LJ505 also developed engine trouble and the glider, Chalk No.152 with pilots S/Sgt Aldridge and Sgt Wright, was forced to release between Penn and High Wycombe. The glider

pilots did not have enough time to select a suitable place to land and on its approach the glider struck a telegraph pole and a lorry on a road. It then crashed near the village of Little Marlow resulting in two broken legs for one of the pilots. The other pilot and three soldiers were uninjured. The Stirling tug landed safely at Benson. Flt Sgt Hill in LK505 lost its tow when the rope broke 35 kilometres west of Ostende and the glider, Chalk No.149 with pilots S/Sgt Fred Baacke and Sgt Garratt, ditched in the North Sea. Both pilots and the three Polish Medical Company personnel on board were rescued by the RAF Air Sea Rescue launch H.S.L.140. No.299 Sqn suffered just the one abortive sortie. Plt Off Rowell in LJ893 ran into thick cloud after reaching the Belgian coast. Visual contact between the glider and tug was lost and then the tow-rope

Stirlings flying through flak to drop supplies to troops near Arnhem on 19th September. Photo: The Keevil Society

148

**Possibly Fg Off J.A.Norton and crew of No.196 Sqn Stirling LK147 at Keevil in 1944.
Photo: The Keevil Society.**

broke. The glider, Chalk No.144 with pilots S/Sgt Henry Blake and Sgt Lee, just managed to cross the coast before hitting a roof top and crashing to the ground five kilometres south east of Ostend. The area had recently being taken by the 2nd Canadian Infantry Division, so the two pilots of the GPR and the three Polish soldiers fell into Allied hands. Cadet Sgt Edward Holub was injured. None of the Stirlings of No.196 and No.299 Sqns had been lost to enemy action.

As part of the 3rd Lift, 33 aircraft then took-off for re-supply purposes, starting at 1200 hrs and dropped containers and panniers on SDP 'V'. This intended drop zone was in enemy hands and desperate efforts were made by the troops already on the ground to make this known to the incoming aircraft, but without success. The aircraft came under heavy enemy fire, suffering damage and loss. Although supplies were dropped as intended, most fell into the hands of the Germans. No.299 Sqn lost 3 aircraft, and their CO Wg Cdr Peter B. N. Davis DSO, RAFVR was killed together with his crew, Sqn Ldr Cecil A.G. Wingfield RAF from Group, and an army man. The CO was flying Stirling EF319 which was seen to be on fire but continued dropping its load before crashing in flames onto the LZ. The other two aircraft lost were EF267 piloted by Plt Off Bayne and LJ868 piloted by Fg Off Geoff Liggins RAAF. The first of these bellylanded and the crew were taken prisoners. The second force landed south of the River Rhine

with four of the crew injured. One of the injured was the co-pilot, who had to have his leg amputated by a British Medical Officer, before becoming a PoW. Two days before this, Fg Off Liggins had been piloting the aircraft towing the glider which broke up in the air over Somerset. No.196 Sqn lost Stirling EF248 when it crashed at Warnsborn N/W of Arnhem having been hit by anti-aircraft fire as it approached the supply dropping point at Lichtenbeek. WO K. Prowd and two of his crew survived the crash as did Fg Off Reginald C. Gibbs RCAF (nav). However he died from his injuries two days later. Sgt Dennis A. Matthews RAF (Flt Eng) and Fg Off George H. Powderhill RAFVR (nav) were killed together with Fg Off Frank D. Chalkey and Air Mechanic Leonard A. Hooker RN, who were both travelling as passengers on the flight. The Navy man was serving with HMS Daedalus, a shore based station and at the time was following a technical course at Keevil. Two Army Air Despatchers from 63 (Airborne) Composite Company (Royal Army Service Corps) died in or as a result of the crash. These were Driver William J. Chaplin and Driver S.G. Smith. The aircrew and the naval man are buried at the Airborne Cemetery in Oosterbeek and the soldiers at Rheinberg Cemetery, Kamp Lintfort, Nordrhein-Westfal, Germany. Of the 16 gliders which left Keevil, only 11 were successfully landed. With the loss of Wg Cdr Davis, Wg Cdr P.N. Jennings was appointed temporary CO until the appointment of Wg Cdr C.B.R. Colenso DFC on 1st November 1944.

On D+3, Wednesday 20th September 1944, the two squadrons were again over Arnhem on a re-supply sortie. Between them they put up 33 aircraft and, despite bad weather it was reported that all of the supplies reached the troops who were desperate by that time. Flak and fighters took their toll with 6 aircraft lost and others returning badly damaged. Plt Off Karl B. Ketcheson RCAF (Nav/BA) of No.299 Sqn was killed instantly when a lone bullet passed through the Perspex nose of Stirling LK118. He was buried at Brookwood Cemetery. These types of re-supply drops continued until the end of the month although there were days when no operations were flown from Keevil. Both squadrons suffered losses and heavy damage to their aircraft during the last few days. One such was LK545 of No.299 Sqn, piloted by Flt Lt R.T.F. Turner, which crash landed west of Nijmegen in Holland after flak damage on D+4. In February 2003 the fuselage of this Sterling was discovered in good condition on a farm, having been used initially to keep pigs. It now resides at Deelen Airfield Museum north of Arnhem. No.196 & No.299 Sqns left Keevil on 9th October 1944 and moved to Wethersfield. The station had been vacated by the 416th Bomber Group USAAF which had crossed the channel to France.

In spite of wartime security, it appears that two old ladies in an Austin 10 somehow managed to stray on to the perimeter track at Keevil while night flying was in progress, thinking that they were on the road to Devizes. Their mistake became obvious when a rather large rotating aircraft propeller cut into the car. Luck was obviously with them that night and they escaped serious injury.

The role of Keevil now changed to one of training when No.22 HGCU/ORTU was formed there on 15th October 1944, with Fairford as its satellite. Both stations were transferred from No.38 to No.23 Group. The station opened with a commitment to five courses, each of 14 days duration, comprising 35 1st pilots and 35 2nd pilots for conversion to Horsa and Waco Hadrian gliders and to carry out practice glider assaults. In addition to conversion courses the syllabus included ground training for glider crews. The 1st pilots came from No.3 GTS and the 2nd pilots from No.21 EFTS. They crewed up after

A wrecked Albemarle of No.22 HGCU at Keevil in 1945.   Photo: Derek Farr

flying together on the course. The opening up party of the Unit arrived on 14th October and the main party 2 days later. The CO was Gp Capt W.D. Ferris DFC. The aircraft allocation was initially 29 Albemarles and 23 Horsa gliders which built up to 58 Albemarles and 46 Horsa/Waco gliders.

The unit's first fatality occurred on 25th October 1944, when, on exercise over the Pewsey Vale, Albemarle V1755 crashed in a field beside the Kennet & Avon Canal at Alton Barnes. Flt Sgt Thomas C. Newton RAFVR (pilot) and Sgt. John A. C. Wilson RAFVR (WOP/AG) were killed. The glider under tow at the time landed safely at Alton Barnes Airfield. A memorial stone now stands on the crash site - refer to **ALTON BARNES**.

Accidents to unit aircraft were happening on a monthly basis. Albemarle VI V2027 crashed with Cat. E damage during November and another came down while glider towing between Bratton and Westbury at 1430 hours on Friday 22nd December. Fg Off Vernon J. Bouchard DFC, RCAF (pilot) and WO Arthur W. Bannier RAFVR (nav) were killed. Later in the month a Horsa glider crashed on take-off coming down on the road between the Station HQ and Officers' Mess. The glider was severely damaged but the crew escaped unharmed. The beginning of 1945 was no better when on Friday 5th January 19 year old AC2 Walter G. Furze RAFVR, a member of one of the rope crews, was killed when struck by a glider landing on the flarepath. At the time of the accident he was laying out ropes and because it was cold had a balaclava on his head. Because of this he did not hear the glider's approach and the landing flaps caught him on the back of the head. Frank Foster, who was in another rope

crew, recalls the delivery of a new Albemarle by a woman pilot of the ATA. The undercarriage would not lower and she had to make a forced landing on the grass. The aircraft was badly damaged but the pilot survived.

On Saturday 20th January 1945 at 2000 hours Albemarle VI V1848 crashed on Salisbury Plain and burnt out with Cat.E.2 damage. Fg Off Tom U. Williamson RAFVR and Flt Sgt Dennis O. Wheatley RAFVR were

killed. Both were buried at Bath (Haycombe) Cemetery. Flt Lt Derek Farr, a pilot with the HGCU serving at Keevil and Blakehill Farm between 24th January and 28th August 1945, recalls his own crash landing at Keevil in an Albemarle. It was caused by a wheel failure at the point of touch down and he indicates this to have been a not un-common occurrence with this type of aircraft.

In mid January runway repairs were begun by A.M.W.D. Each runway in turn was closed to allow concrete defects to be repaired. This work was not completed until March 1945.

The Americans made a brief return to Keevil on 12th December 1944 when 45 C-47s of USAAF 50th Troop Carrier Wing arrived for a 17th Airborne Division exercise. It was later cancelled and the aircraft left again after six days.

On 22nd February 1945 the 1st Sqn Glider Pilot Regiment arrived from Mushroom Farm for Refresher Glider Training. Keevil was transferred to

Stood in front of a No.22 HGCU Albemarle at Keevil in 1945 are
LtoR LAC A. Wyatt, LAC Frank Foster, AC.1 H.Cane, AC.1 J.Marriott, LAC L.Stone, AC.2
J. Griffiths.   Photo: Frank Foster

Flt Sgt Derek Farr of No.22 HGCU with an Albemarle he piloted at Keevil in 1945.
Photo: Derek Farr

BOXING PROGRAMME

R.A.F. KEEVIL

R.A.F. MELKSHAM

WEDNESDAY, FEB. 21st, 1945,

STATION GYMNASIUM

(by kind permission of G/Capt. W. D. Ferris, D.F.C.)

Commencing 2000 Hrs.

OFFICIALS :

Referee : F/L. E. Rengart.
Judges : Sub./Lt. T. A. Guthrie.
F/O. A. E. Roberts.
Timekeeper : S/L. Rev. J. E. Preece.
M.O. : S/L. C. K. Cole.
M.C. : F/Sgt. Ellison, J.
Whips : F/Sgt. Sherman, P.
Cpl. Godfrey, W.
Cpl. Parnham, J.

"Wiltshire Times' Press, Trowbridge.

PROGRAMME

BOUT	WEIGHT	R.A.F. Keevil (Red)	R.A.F. Melksham (Blue)	BOUT	WEIGHT	R.A.F. Keevil (Red)	R.A.F. Melksham (Blue)
I	Welter	L/A/C. Gane v.	L/A/C. Brown WON	6	Bantam	A/C. Foster v. WON	A/C. Freer BOWEN (Keevil)
2	Feather	A/C. Orridge v.	A/C. Middleton WON	7	Welter	Cpl. Brown v. WON	Cpl. Whittaker
3	Welter	A/C. Batty v.	A/C. Moir WON.	8	Welter	Cpl. Davis v. WON	Sgt. Hoskins (Keevil)
4	Welter	Sgt. Butt v.	A/C. Short WON	9	Welter	Cpl. Myers v. WON	L/A/C. Jenkins
5	Bantam	A/C. Davies v.	A/C. Bowen HEWITT. WON	10	Middle	Sgt. Gilchrist v.	A/C. Miller WON

PRESENTATION OF PRIZES.

THE KING.

In a 1945 Boxing Tournament at Keevil, the programme shows that the home team won 6 of the 10 bouts.

Christmas Festivities

Sunday, December 24th
Carol Singing
23.30 Hours Carols followed by Holy Communion in Station Chapel
Monday, December 25th
0.800 " Holy Communion, Steeple Ashton Church
10.00 " Morning Service in the Station Chapel
11.00 " Sergeants visit Officers' Mess
11.30 " Officers visit Sergeants' Mess
12.00 " Officers and Senior N.C.O's. serve Christmas Dinner in Airmens' Mess   Music by Station Band
15.00 " Football Match
17.00 " Tea in Airmens' Mess
18.00 " Sergeants Mess Christmas Dinner   Music by Station Band
20.30 " All ranks Dance in Airmens' Institute
Tuesday, December 26th
15.00 " Mixed Hockey Match
20.00 " Officers Mess Christmas Dinner   Sergeants Mess Dance
Wednesday, December 27th
19.30 " W.A.A.F. Dance in W.A.A.F. Institute
Sunday, December 31st
20.00 " Officers' Mess Dance
Monday, January 1st, 1945
20.30 " All ranks Dance Airmens' Institute

Cinema Programme all the week including Christmas Night

ROYAL AIR FORCE KEEVIL

Christmas Day

→ 1944 ←

SOUP
CREAM OF TOMATO

JOINT
ROAST TURKEY
ROAST PORK
APPLE SAUCE   STUFFING

VEGETABLES
ROAST AND CREAMED POTATOES
BRUSSEL SPROUTS

SWEET
CHRISTMAS PUDDING
RUM SAUCE

CHEESE
APPLES   ORANGES   NUTS
TEA   COFFEE
BEER AND MINERALS

Keevil's 1944 Christmas Menu and Programme of events.

Fighter Command on 17th March but three months later on 1st June was transferred to Transport Command. From early May 1945 the Horsa gliders of No.22 HGCU started being replaced by the Waco, designated the Hadrian by Britain. On 15th and 16th June No.22 HGCU left Keevil for Blakehill Farm and the Rear Party were left to hand over the station to No.12 Group by 20th June.

No.61 OTU Fighter Command arrived from Rednal and its satellite Mountford Bridge on 21st June 1945. The unit had absorbed the Fighter Reconnaissance Wing of No.41 OTU. The task of the unit was to provide courses to convert newly qualified pilots on to Mustangs IIIs and Spitfires Vs, also to stage courses in Fighter Reconnaissance. The OTU consisted of three fighter squadrons (squadron letters HX, KR and UU) and one fighter reconnaissance unit. Other aircraft types on charge were the Hurricane, Harvard T.2b, Martinet T.1 and Master T.2 (DM350). Students had to demonstrate that they could land a Harvard safely from the rear seat (with no forward view) before they went solo on the Mustang and Spitfire (also with no forward view). Many of the groundcrews maintaining and servicing the aircraft were WAAFs.

Two days before the OTU arrival, a Mustang was being delivered to Keevil by Flt Lt McLurg of No.437 'Husky' Sqn RCAF and he landed with the under-carriage partially retracted. The 12 week training courses were soon underway and the fatalities from aircraft crashes were as prevalent as they had been with the previous Unit at Keevil. An early case was that of Mustang FZ181 which broke up in a dive at Marston, two miles east of the airfield, on 6th July. The pilot Flt Sgt Geoffrey J. Clifton RAFVR was killed and was buried at Haycombe military cemetery in Bath. On 27th July Gp Capt Fleming arrived to assume command of the station. The same day a further fatality occurred when Mustang III FZ115, observed flying straight and level, suddenly nose dived into the ground near the village of Imber, which was occupied by the military. The pilot who died was Fg Off Ronald H. E. Dunsford RAF, who was also buried at Bath's Haycombe cemetery.

A line up of Albemarles and Waco gliders of No.22 HGCU at Keevil in May/June 1945.
Photo: Derek Farr

Photographed at the rear of a Waco glider LtoR Flt Sgt D.Farr, unknown, Flt Lt Harland, unknown.
Photo: Derek Farr

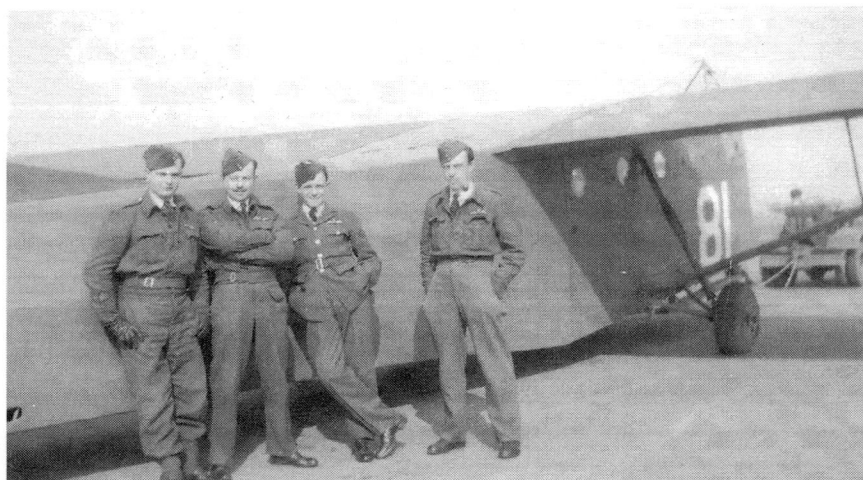

2nd left is Flt Lt Harland No.22 HGCU 'A' Flt. CO with colleagues beside a Waco glider being
prepared for moving by a tow-tug.   Photo: Derek Farr

The Inspector of Prisoners of War from the War Office visited Keevil on 9th August 1945 to inspect the station accommodation which he passed as suitable for housing PoW.

Post War Years

A No.61 OTU Spitfire LF.5 W3207 collided with a truck whilst taxiing on 20th September 1945 and was written off. Four days later an OTU Mustang FB.3 HB876, which was believed to have stalled during a climbing turn on an aerobatics exercise, crashed killing pilot WO Ronald H. Bolland RAFVR. During October Mk.XIV and XVI Spitfires started arriving to equip the OTU.

An early present arrived just before Christmas Day in the shape of a new Dominic from No.13 OTU. This was for use as the station hack and probably replaced the Anson.

The OTU Master T.2 AZ619 suffered an undercarriage leg collapse when it stalled on landing at Keevil on 24th January 1946. On 5th February a unit Hurricane F.2 LF337 suffered an engine failure during a tactical reconnaissance training flight and bellylanded in a field at Wilsford. During the month nine new Spitfire XVIs with the Packard built Merlin 266 engines in place of the British Merlin 66 of the Mk.IX, arrived for the OTU. Four additional new Spitfire LF.XVIs arrived at Keevil during March. Over the next few months, the Spitfire XVI would replace the Mustangs and Spitfire Vs at Keevil. The fighter reconnaissance unit was allocated the Spitfire IV with the Rolls-Royce Griffon engine. A month after delivery the first fatalities involving Spitfires occurred when, on the Thursday 14th March 1946, the cockpit hood of LF.XVI TE310 detached in flight probably as a result of a malfunction of the jettison release and not from pilot error. The aircraft stalled and crashed on its landing approach killing Plt Off Keith G. Chapman RAF. Spitfire LF.XVI TE183 stalled in the circuit, crashed and caught fire half a mile from the SSE airfield boundary on 22nd March. The pilot Sgt Albert T. Paramanathan RAFVR was killed and buried at Bath Haycombe cemetery. He was one of 17 pilots on No.65 Course, which also had as a pupil a man who later became well known as the Governor of the Falkland Islands during the Argentinean Invasion, Sir Rex Hunt. Air Marshal Sir Ian Pedder KCB, OBE, DFC was a Plt Off on the same course. He recalls that his 20th birthday occurred whilst on the course and on that day he flew an armed- reconnaissance training flight over Salisbury Plain at low level in Spitfire XVI UU-G, an experience which he feels was hard to beat in his subsequent 45 years.

Some of the flying instructors at the OTU were Wg Cdr Johnny Shaw, Wg Cdr R.T. Thomas, Sqn Ldr J.V. Marshall, Sqn Ldr Garrard-Cole, Sqn Ldr Berry, Sqn Ldr Dieu (Belgian Air Force), Flt Lt Peter Fahy, Flt Lt Gerry Percival, Flt Lt Dickie de Burgh and Flt Lt Ken MacKenzie DFC, AFC who had been a Battle of Britain pilot with No.501 Sqn. Ground instructors were Sqn Ldr Page DFC and from the Army,

An unknown Sgt of No.22 HGCU sat on an Albemarle engine cowling at Keevil with Waco gliders in the background.   Photo: Derek Farr

One of No. 61 OTUs Mustang IIIs at Keevil in 1945.

No.61 OTU Spitfire LF. XVI SL688 taxies out for take-off from Keevil.
Photo: AM Sir Ian Pedder

No.61 OTU, No.65 Course March - June 1946.
Photo: AM Sir Ian Pedder

Plt Off Rex Hunt, later Sir Rex Hunt, Governor of the Falkland Islands during the period of the Argentine Invasion, seen here in a No.61 OTU Spitfire at Keevil in March 1946.
Photo: The Keevil Society

Pilots of No.65 Course and a Mk XVI Spitfire with the Packard built Merlin 266 engine. Plt Off Ian Pedder stands on the wheel chock in this 1946 scene.   Photo: AM Sir Ian Pedder

Capt Darlington. Peter Fahy having finished a tour with No.16 Sqn flying the Spitfire IX, was posted as an instructor with No.57 OTU at Eshott in November 1944. When it disbanded in June 1945, a number of instructors were posted to No.61 OTU at Keevil. Peter was a tactical reconnaissance instructor and later OC of the Tactical Reconnaissance Flight. He remained at Keevil until the end of April 1947 before moving to CFS Little Rissington.

As a result of the inspection carried out by the Inspector of Prisoners of War the previous year, Keevil received 21 German PoW who were collected from RAF Kingscliffe on 1st April 1946.

Three more new Spitfire LF.XVIs arrived during the month, SL720 and SL 552 from No.29 MU High Ercall, and TD143 from No.33 MU Lyneham. During April and May 1946 the Mustangs began leaving for MUs as by then these aircraft were surplus to establishment. They had all disappeared from the skies over Keevil by September 1946. No.61 OTU had

153

two Hurricanes on charge and these were disposed of in September when they were flown to No.22 MU Silloth which, at that time was engaged in aircraft scraping. Unit Harvard T.2b KF208 came to grief on 27th June 1946 when it crashed into a ditch near Wootton Bassett, when believed to be making an approach into Lyneham.

The VISTRE Flight was formed on 1st August 1946 under the control of Keevil but based at nearby Erlestoke Camp. Its use was by the RAF Wing, Visual Inter-Service Training & Research Establishment at Netheravon where it moved to on 16th November 1947. The Flt was equipped with an Anson I. The role of the Flt was the establishment of decoys including aircraft and army tanks.

Keevil, as with many other RAF stations immediately after the War, had personnel attached who had joined the service with the intention of qualifying as pilots or on other forms of flying duty. There was already, however, a surplus and many new entrants found themselves being rejected for flying duties and having to re-muster in other trades. One of the frustrated fighter pilots at Keevil was AC.1 Monty Britton from Bristol who, instead of training with the OTU, was attached to flying control duties. He recalls the occasion in 1946 when, confined to the station for a minor misdemeanour, he found himself too late to catch the RAF transport taking personnel on weekend pass to Trowbridge railway station. Desperate to get back to Bristol to spend a leave period with his girlfriend Jeanie, who later became his wife, he 'borrowed' a service bicycle and raced off to catch a train. Unfortunately in Keevil village he smashed into the back of a stationary post office van, wrecking the bicycle and sustaining cuts and bruises to himself. The postman was most sympathetic and agreed to give him a lift to the rail station providing he lay flat on the floor between the mailbags in the back of the van, as it was against regulations to carry passengers in a post van. On returning to duty after the weekend, Monty found questions being asked as to the whereabouts of a missing RAF bicycle.

Keevil suffered from the bad winter of 1947, with heavy snow and frost preventing much training during January and February. The last Fighter

Gliders over Keevil. Photo: The Keevil Society

Command OTU disappeared when No.61 OTU became re-designated No.203 Advanced Flying School in No.12 Group on 1st July 1947. Tasked with training fighter and reconnaissance pilots, it was equipped with 46 Spitfire XVIs, 3 Spitfire XIXs, 9 Harvards and 5 Martinets. The School moved to Chivenor on 15th October 1947. From then Keevil was placed on C&M and although it was to remain in use, would no longer be as a fully staffed and equipped operational airfield.

Keevil became an RLG for No.2 FTS Hullavington between 17th January 1955 and 18th November 1957. It was used for pilot training on Provost T1s. The aircraft would be flown over each day but on occasions pupils camped on the airfield in tents. Additionally, in December 1955, the USAF occupied the airfield when it became a stand-by base for the 3rd Air Force. In April 1958 the USAF set up a portable navigation radio beacon (VOR Annexe) near the southern perimeter track. This was manned by a small team of American radio operators of Sgt rank, and remained in use until March 1965. The operators included Thomas Spence, William McVey, Walter Pelkey and George Batchelor. All lived in the nearby village of Steeple Ashton during their tours of duty. Two low flying B-47s were observed 'beating up the airfield' over the beacon on one occasion. The Americans occupied a small hut near the beacon and also used one of the hangars to store a large amount of military hospital equipment. When

need for the use of the hangar ceased, many local families acquired new blankets.

After the war and before the airfield was regularly in use for RAF training purposes, it was used for limited private flying. A private Mosquito, purchased at a knock down price when the war ended, flew for a period of time until it became unserviceable. It was parked under the trees near the airfield boundary but the wooden structure of the aircraft deteriorated from exposure to the elements. Another private owner was a Steeple Ashton resident, who would fly himself to work each day. The Bath & Wilts Gliding Club was based on the airfield for almost 30 years until 1992 when it moved to The Park at Longbridge Deverill. The Service based Bannerdown Gliding Club is now resident having moved in from Hullavington in October 1992 as the station was too close. The club took over premises previously used by the Bath & Wilts Club. The new occupant at Keevil was fortunate to receive support from RAF Lyneham who 'adopted' it under the chairmanship of a RAF Wing Commander. The club has been renamed RAFGSA, Lyneham Regional to attract additional membership from Lyneham based personnel. The last remaining T2 type hangar, which has been reclad, and the rewired Nissen huts, are used by the club.

From 1964 until the present day, Keevil has been used by Transport Command for various training/exercise functions and these would appear to be on the increase. The exercises often involve the Army Air Corps with their Lynx and Gazelle helicopters plus the RAF Chinooks from Odiham. During exercise periods, the RAF Fire Appliances garaged at the former RAF Upavon, are mobilised to Keevil on stand-by duties to provide the required fire cover. An exercise during the early part of the 60s involved Blackburn Beverleys carrying out day and night time flying. A series of approach lights were strung out on poles in the fields of Pinkney Farm at the north east end of the main runway. Hastings carried out supply drops on the airfield in the mid 60s and it was used also by the Ghurka Regiment for training. Hercules have been seen frequently at Keevil since their initial allocation to Lyneham in 1968. Then they were often accompanied by Andovers and Argosys carrying out supply drop training. The facilities at Keevil are also used for jump training by the Parachute Regiment.

The Royal Navy used the airfield for two weeks in September 1989 during an exercise of Sea King helicopters from the RNAS Yeovilton. During the Spring of 1981 the U.S. Army used Keevil for ten days, when they flew in their Cobra gunships from Germany, via RAF Manston. Exercises on Salisbury Plain have brought aircraft from the NATO Alliance to the airfield. Harrier jump jets were in evidence in the summer of 1987 for Exercise 'Roaring Lion'. They were despersed in camouflaged hides close to the former Spitfire assembly hangar. During the week commencing 13th September 1999, the Oxford based Formula 1 Benetton grand prix racing team used Keevil's main runway for testing and analysis of two of their cars to be used during the Millennium season.

On Friday 20th July 2001, 15 Hercules aircraft from Lyneham deployed to Kemble where at 30 second intervals they took off to launch a mock night parachute assault on Keevil airfield. On other days during the same week troops and equipment were dropped on Keevil by Hercules aircraft. This was all part of Exercise 'Eagles Strike', involving the Army's No.16 Air Assault Brigade. It also served to test the ability to mount a major operation away from the main base at Lyneham.

Bob Underwood who lived in Ashton Mill Farm on the southern boundary of RAF Keevil from July 1944, saw a number of interesting incidents which occurred on and around the airfield: -

Approaching the southern end of runway 13/31 during 1944, a Stirling of either No.196 Sqn or No.299 Sqn landed short of the airfield and ended up straddling the hedge. It remained in situ for some time and provided the opportunity for Bob to explore the inside.

A Horsa glider detached from its Albemarle tug on 4th May 1945 during take-off. The glider bounced heavily in a field, with the rubber shock absorbers from the under-carriage legs punching out through the top of the wings. The glider rose again, first striking an oak tree and then an elm, before crashing into netting spread over a bomb dispersal area. The nose of the aircraft disintegrated and of the six men on board, Sgt Hunt and four others were killed.

Two Spitfires collided whilst taking-off and crashed outside the eastern boundary. One ended up with its nose into the ground and tail in the air. The other shed its wings, tail and propeller before crashing through the boundary fence on its side. Bob Underwood and a farm worker were first at the scene and rescued the pilot from the cockpit. The canopy was in the open position and the cockpit was full of mud which had covered the pilot.

A Spitfire landed short of runway 13/31 and its propeller blade detached and went through the Dutch barn of Ashton Mill Farm as Bob was passing it. He picked the blade up and took it to the crash site where the RAF personnel gave him a severe talking to for removing evidence.

Another Spitfire crashed short of runway 13/31 in Elliots Field, where it broke in half. The engine trapped the American pilot in his cockpit and he died from the resulting fire. The Coles rescue crane sent to release the pilot got bogged down in the wet field and a Sherman tank was sent to extricate it. Parts of the aircraft were man-handled back to the airfield.

A Spitfire engaged in aerobatics crashed into trees near the airfield killing the pilot, Sgt Ronald S. Norris RAFVR, on 25th June 1943. His parents, who were hay making in Hinton saw it happen. Sgt Norris is buried in the Church of St. Mary, Steeple Ashton.

The first jet aircraft to visit Keevil were two Meteors, which landed in 1947. These created considerable local interest and amongst the spectators there were those of the opinion that the two aircraft would not get airborne again. They were to be disappointed, although one during take-off did strike the wire perimeter fence causing a huge flash of blue sparks.

From at least the latter part of 1944 until a few years after the war had ended, the Blister hangar beside Ashton Mill Farm was occupied by a unit of the FAA, carrying out work on Fairey Barracudas. One fine summer morning a Typhoon beat up the airfield and, on its second run, laid a smoke screen which not only ruined Mrs Underwood's washing on the line in the farm but also filled the blister hangar in which the naval personnel were carrying out maintenance on an aircraft. It appears from the language heard, that the men from the *Andrew* were not impressed. Sometime during 1948 a Petty Officer called Bob over and asked him to assist in pushing one of the two Barracudas out of the hangar. It apparently had an engine fault. The engine was fired up out in the open, and the Petty Officer used a steel bar held to his ear to detect a broken pump shaft.

On one occasion a USAAF P-61 'Black Widow' twin-boom fighter landed. This was possibly from Station 487 Charmy Down, home of the first P-61 unit assigned to the European Theatre of Operations. The 422nd Night Fighter Sqn. arrived there in March 1944 moving to Scorton on 9th May. A second P-61 Sqn replaced them, the 425th NFS, which also moved to Scorton in June. Six aircraft from these two squadrons were attached to a RAF night fighter squadron at Hurn from 29th June 1944, from where the first operations were carried out on the evening of 3rd July.

Memorial

173/ST921580 - 4 miles East of Trowbridge

In the centre of Keevil village on the C218 at the junction of Main Street and Martins Road, on a stone wall by the small grass island. A Cumbrian green slate plaque unveiled on Saturday 24th September 1994 to commemorate the 50th Anniversary of D-Day and the Arnhem Operations. The plaque was unveiled by former Army Air Corps S/Sgt Bill Higgs, once resident of Trowbridge, who flew from Keevil Airfield and was wounded at Arnhem. The village played host to a large number of veterans, many returning for the first time since they flew from Keevil 50 years ago. A number attending were former No.196 and 299 Sqn aircrew, some from Australia and Canada. There were also former glider pilots, airborne troops and Air Force ground crews. Wg Cdr K.R.C. Greaves OC No.47 Sqn Lyneham and the Chaplain The Rev. Sqn Ldr D. McKavanagh from the station, represented the present day RAF. The Bishop of Ramsbury, The Right Rev. Peter St. G. Vaughan MA was in attendance. With the unveiling, a No.47 Sqn Hercules from Lyneham flew over the village dipping its wing in salute. It

The 50th Anniversary commemorative plaque on the village green at Keevil.

then landed on the airfield at Keevil where guests were invited to view it, together with a Piper Cub in D-Day markings and a Miles Messenger. These were later joined by a second Hercules which gave a fast descent and take off display. The commemorative weekend and plaque was arranged by The Keevil Society and former World War 2 RAF pilot, Alan Thomsett, a local resident. The plaque displays the badge of the RAF and is inscribed: -

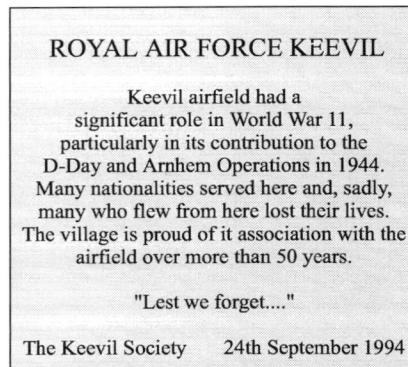

ROYAL AIR FORCE KEEVIL

Keevil airfield had a significant role in World War 11, particularly in its contribution to the D-Day and Arnhem Operations in 1944. Many nationalities served here and, sadly, many who flew from here lost their lives. The village is proud of it association with the airfield over more than 50 years.

"Lest we forget...."

The Keevil Society   24th September 1994

LAKE DOWN AERODROME
Location - 184/SU099390 - 2 miles South West of Stonehenge

The aerodrome was situated on the A360 opposite Druid's Lodge, a private country house.

Aerodrome Development

The domestic buildings stood approximately a quarter of a mile north of the house and on the same side of the road. They were built close to the road and east of Horse Down. The War Office requisitioned an area of 160 acres of loam on chalk pastureland in early 1917, of which 30 acres would contain the Technical Site positioned directly alongside the A360. Air force establishments normally took their identifying names from the nearest town, village or farm to where they were formed and in this case Lake Down was the name given to the area of land which was a mile and a half west of the village of Lake. The architecture of the buildings was very much in keeping with the other aerodromes under construction in the area at the time such as Stonehenge and Boscombe Down. The sizes of some of the Technical buildings such as the Aeroplane Sheds did however differ. Lake Down had 6 of these, each 170' x 80', forming 3 pairs, an A.R.S. of the same size, 2 M.T. Sheds, 2 workshops and various other stores, huts and offices. An unknown number of Bessonneau hangars were used for various purposes. The name of the aerodrome was marked out in large chalk letters.

Two of Lake Down's Bessonneau hangars one of which is camouflaged.
Photo: Daughters of Horace Bathe/Cty. Martyn Ford-Jones

The Domestic Site consisted of an Officers' Mess, 4 Officers' Quarters for staff and 3 for pupils, a Sergeants' Mess, 4 Men's Barracks, Women's Hostel, Reception Station, Regimental Institute and numerous other small service buildings. Druid's Lodge was requisitioned as the Wing HQ building. Lake Down was serviced by the

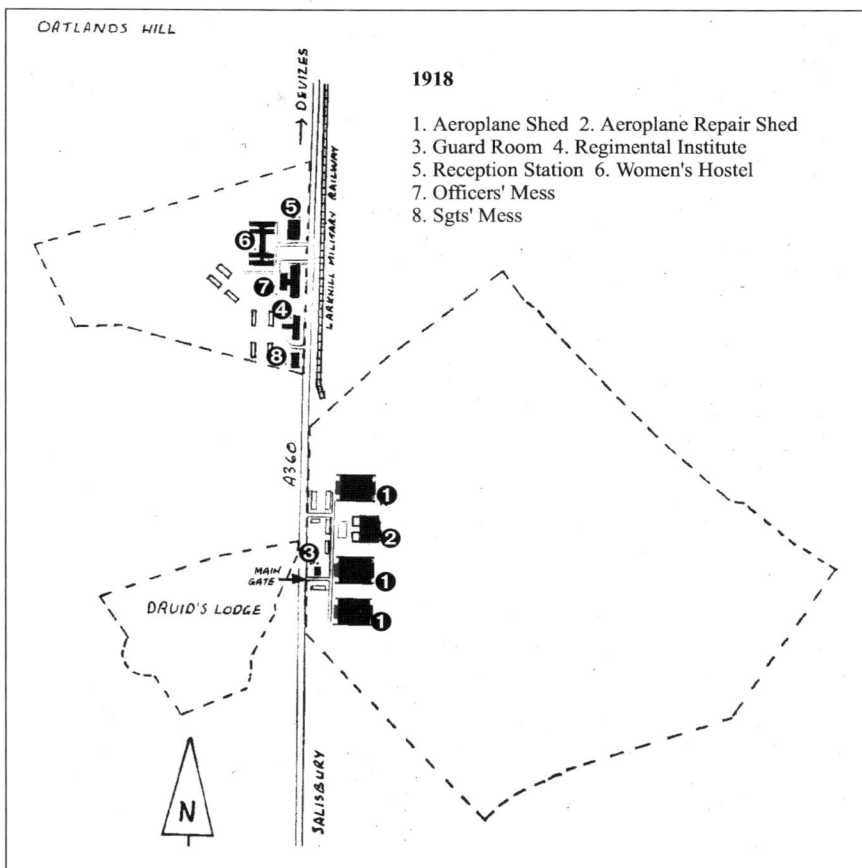

1918

1. Aeroplane Shed 2. Aeroplane Repair Shed
3. Guard Room 4. Regimental Institute
5. Reception Station 6. Women's Hostel
7. Officers' Mess
8. Sgts' Mess

Larkhill Military Railway, which terminated just past the Domestic Site on the opposite side of the A360. En route to the terminus at Lake Down, the railway line, which formed a junction with the Amesbury & Military Camp Light Railway near the A303 at Amesbury, serviced the Army camps at Larkhill, Rollestone Camp, Fargo Military Hospital, the Handley Page hangars and Stonehenge aerodrome. Construction work at Lake Down continued well into the summer of 1918.

World War 1 Years

The station opened on 15th August 1917 with No.2 TDS forming for training British and American Expeditionary Force pilots in day bombing. Machines in use were the DH4 (B5527), BE2c (B6195), RE8 and FK8 (B5808). On 30th August the 33rd (Training) Wing RFC formed at 2 Winchester Street, Salisbury in Southern Training Brigade to control Lake Down, Stonehenge and Boscombe Down aerodromes. No.2

TDS moved the short distance to Stonehenge aerodrome on 2nd December exchanging places with No.107 Sqn which had been at Stonehenge since 18th October 1917 and No.108 Sqn and No.109 Sqn which had been there since 12th November 1917. These three day bomber squadrons were equipped with Airco DH9s, five of which were (B2150), (D515), (D593), (D693), (D3221).

Lake Down was home to four day bomber squadrons when No.136 Sqn formed there on 1st April 1918. DH9s were delivered to the squadrons during May, June and July. No.14 TDS (SW Area, No.7 Group, 33rd Wing) assumed control of the squadrons when it formed at Lake Down on 6th June 1918, with the day bombing training continuing. The Wing HQ was located in Druid's Lodge. No.14 TDS was equipped with 36 DH4/9s and 36 Avro 504Ks (C700), (D7579), (E1842), (E3313), (E3320), (E3321) On 5th June No.107 Sqn left for Le Quesnoy in France equipped with DH9s, No.108

157

The main road south to Salisbury separates the Domestic Site in the foreground and the Technical Site to the rear in September 1918. A row of Bessonneau hangars are seen at the rear of the Aeroplane Sheds and the nearest of the sheds still awaits the completion of its roof.
Photo: P.Liddle/Cty. G. S. Leslie

Druid's Lodge on 28th September 1918 when used as the 33rd Wing HQ. The temporary hangars at the southern end of the aerodrome are seen on the opposite side of the Salisbury road. Druid's Lodge was occupied during World War 2 by RAF Instructors from Oatlands Hill airfield located half a mile to the north.   Photo: P.Liddle/Cty. G. S. Leslie

Airco DH4 B5527 coded 6 built by The Vulcan Motor & Engineering Co. Ltd, came to grief by nosing into construction works still in progress at Lake Down. The white disc on the fuselage indicates the machine as having been with No. 99 Sqn which was at Ford Farm (Old Sarum).
Photo: Daughters of Horace Bathe/Cty. Martyn Ford-Jones

BE2 c/e B6195 built by British Caudron Co. at Alloa seen lying on its side at Lake Down.
Photo: Daughters of Horace Bathe/Cty. Martyn Ford-Jones

Sqn left for Kenley on 14th June, No.136 Sqn disbanded at Lake Down on 4th July and No.109 Sqn disbanded there on 18th August 1918. No.14 TDS built up to an establishment of 858 personnel and had a M.T. allocation of 42 vehicles. The station's training role continued unabated until the Armistice on 11th November 1918 when a run-down commenced and No.14 TDS moved to Boscombe Down as a cadre.

Inter War Years

On 17th February 1919 No.201 Sqn arrived at Lake Down which had been reduced to a cadre, staying until 2nd September when it left for Eastleigh. Two Handley Page 0/400s arrived from Hendon on 14th March 1919. D8331 was re-allocated from No.2 Aircraft Acceptance Park where it had been delivered for use by the Expeditionary Force and D8335 by No.1 Communication Sqn.

No.14 TDS returned from Boscombe Down during March 1919. It was redesignated No.14 Training School in June but was disbanded in September 1919. The 33rd Wing was disbanded at Lake Down on 15th May 1919.

Closure

In October 1919 a decision was taken to close the aerodrome at Lake Down. Major Jack Slesser the Assistant

A crash landing at Lake Down by A.W. FK8 B5808 built by A.W. at Gosforth. This machine served with No. 99 Sqn when working up at Ford Farm (Old Sarum). The mechanic on the left was with the United States Air Service.
Photo: Daughters of Horace Bathe/Cty. Martyn Ford-Jones

A.M.2 Horace Bathe RFC at Lake Down where he served as a photographer attached to the 33RD Wing. Photo: Daughters of Horace Bathe/Cty. Martyn Ford-Jones

Airco DH9 D593 built by Cubitt Ltd, Croyden being prepared for flight by the groundcrew, one of whom turns the propeller, whilst the other turns the starting handle. The pilot is seen in the cockpit. Beyond this machine are two other DH9s, the centre one is D693 which was sold to Estonia after the war ended. Photo: Daughters of Horace Bathe/Cty. Martyn Ford-Jones

Unidentified member of the United States Air Service at Lake Down
Photo: Daughters of Horace Bathe/Cty. Martyn Ford-Jones

Ground crews by the damaged remains of two machines outside hangars at Lake Down. The nearest machine is a DH9. Photo: Daughters of Horace Bathe/Cty. Martyn Ford-Jones

Commandant of CFS Upavon, who with the war having ended reverted to the rank of Flt Lt, arrived to oversee the closure. By 1920 the majority of buildings on both sites had been removed. After the closure of the aerodrome the section of railway line that ran south to Lake Down beside the A360 remained unused and the track had been lifted by 1923.

World War 2 Period

The large chalk letters identifying the name of the aerodrome during World War 1 survived until World War 2. These were then removed during ploughing of the fields to prevent identification of the area from the air.

Although no building work took place, Lake Down was briefly re-united with flying during World War 2 when it was used as a DZ. One user was No.295 Sqn operating from Netheravon in Exercise *Snoop* on 23rd December 1942. Four Whitley V aircraft carried 10 paratroops and 2 containers, which were dropped on the former World War 1 site. Three separate drops were made on this day.

The fuselage of an unidentified machine, in two sections with fabric removed, undergoing repairs outside a Lake Down hangar.   Photo: Daughters of Horace Bathe/Cty. Martyn Ford-Jones

Avro 504K B3320 built by Parnall & Son being prepared for recovery following a landing accident at Lake Down.Photo: Daughters of Horace Bathe/Cty. Martyn Ford-Jones

An unidentified RFC Corporal in the evening sunshine at Lake Down. In the background are the unloading platforms forming the terminus of the Larkhill Military Railway. Photo: Daughters of Horace Bathe/Cty. Martyn Ford-Jones

A group of RFC groundcrew pose at the rear of a solid tyre RFC vehicle. On the left is thought to be a blacksmith and sitting on the step next to him is A.M.2 Horace Bathe. Photo: Daughters of Horace Bathe/Cty. Martyn Ford-Jones

A working party thought to be German PoW, (their jackets had discs on the back) move earth in an effort to level the surface of the railway platform at Lake Down. The Stars & Stripes fly from the flagpole.   Photo: Daughters of Horace Bathe/Cty. Martyn Ford-Jones

The flags of Great Britain, France and USA being paraded on what was possibly a Victory Day celebration at Lake Down.   Photo: Daughters of Horace Bathe/Cty. Martyn Ford-Jones

A workshop on the north side of the water tower at Lake Down.

Another user on 22nd July 1943 was No.653 (AOP) Sqn which arrived from Penhurst for Exercise *Fortesque*. The SHQ was established at Springbottom Farm, the Corps HQ at Lake and 'A' Flt. at Urchfont. During the week of the exercise, the squadron Austers took off from Druid's Lodge to participate in day and night observation exercises. Night-time sorties were used to test illumination of targets using flares. The Unit returned to Penhurst on 30th July.

Lake Down has returned to agricultural use and the only structures to survive from this World War 1 aerodrome are the Water Tower and Engine Shed standing opposite Druid's Lodge, and a Workshop on the north side of the Tower.

The water tower and engine shed on the site of the former Lake Down aerodrome.

The site of the original aerodrome lies on the south side of the unclassified road known as the Packway and west of Tombs Road. It comprised a large uneven rectangular grass field of 2,284 acres with a number of hangars on the eastern side.

Aerodrome Development/Early Use

Tests were carried out on Larkhill Ranges during May 1909 to establish whether observation balloons intended for use by the Army could be shot down by artillery. Two months later an event took place at Larkhill which could be claimed to be the first step towards the subsequent formation of the Royal Air Force. Horatio C. Barber, an early flying enthusiast, rented a piece of land 50 x 25 yds on Durrington Down, known locally as Hill of Larks, in order to carry out aeronautical experiments and he had a tin shed erected in which he kept a Valkyrie aeroplane of his own design. He taught himself to fly in the Valkyrie and later it became the first British machine to carry a passenger. Shortly afterwards the War Office built an additional shed next to Barber's which was intended for use by the Hon. C. S. Rolls so that he could instruct army pilots. However he died before this could happen. Towards the end of 1909, G.B. Cockburn, a civilian aviator, arrived and erected another shed for his Henri Farman biplane. G.B. Cockburn was described as 'a philanthropic private aviator' who at his own expense taught the first four Royal Navy pilots to fly and obtain their Royal Aero Club Certificates. They achieved this by averaging only three solo flights each before taking their certificates. The four who took the course at Eastchurch were Lt C.R. Sampson RN, Lt A.M. Longmore RN, Lt R. Gregory RN and Lt E.L. Gerrard RMLI.

Capt. J.D.B. Fulton of the 8th (Howitzer) Brigade RFA, who was stationed at Bulford, initially tried to build his own machine but found progress slow going. When C. S. Rolls was killed on 11th July 1910, the second day of the Bournemouth air meeting, Fulton bought his 25 h.p

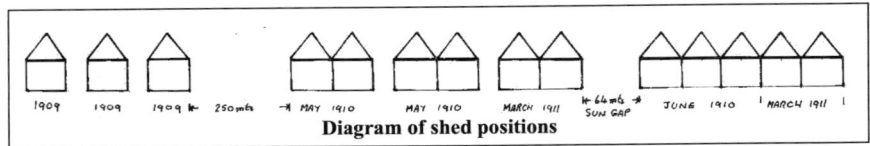
Diagram of shed positions

Anzani-engined Bleriot monoplane, using money received from the War Office for patents of field gun improvements he had invented. The aeroplane shed intended for use by C. S. Rolls was rented by the Army for housing the Bleriot. Fulton was to be recognised as one of the leading aviators at that time.

Although the Royal Engineers at Woolwich Arsenal began experimenting with balloons for reconnaissance purposes in 1878, the War Office was now attaching greater importance to the use of aeroplanes for such purposes. Because of this new emphasis, in May 1910 two double sheds were built for the Army at Larkhill by Messrs. Harbrow of South Bermondsey in London. These were positioned some 250 metres south of the Barber and Cockburn sheds. The following month the same building company erected a three-bay shed further to the south for the British and Colonial Aeroplane Company Ltd.

In March 1911 W.E. Chivers & Sons of Devizes constructed two additional double sheds for The Bristol Flying School. One immediately to the south of the three-bay shed and one south of the Army's two sheds. The positioning of this shed was important because of what was known as the 'sun gap'. This is an approximate 64 metre wide 'path' along which, on the morning of the Summer Solstice, the sun could be seen from Stonehenge rising over the horizon. Building was not permitted on the line of the 'path' in a position that would obstruct the natural horizon above which the sun rose.

The British & Colonial Aeroplane Company kept in their sheds aircraft for the flying school which they were forming and for carrying out testing and development, for their factory at Filton, Bristol. The sheds were metal framed with corrugated iron sheeting, gabled sloping roofs and with doors at one end opening onto the landing

ground. The size of each shed was 48' x 38' x 12'. The British and Colonial Aeroplane Company had been formed with a capital of £25,000 by Sir George White on 19th February 1910 together with three other companies which included the Bristol Aeroplane Company. The offices of the companies were at 2 Clare Street, Bristol and at the Aeroplane Works at Filton, a former tramway depot. The company gained a licence to build six Zodiacs. These proved to be failures so instead the Bristol Boxkite was developed. The first flight of a prototype Bristol designed and built Boxkite biplane No.7 was made from Larkhill on 30th July 1910. It was stripped down at Filton and taken by road to Larkhill where it was reassembled and flown by Pierre Edmund to a height of 150'. In flight it had a speed of 40mph.

In setting up the Flying School at Larkhill, the Bristol Company could see the opportunity to attract Army officers from the nearby camps at Bulford and Tidworth. The chief instructor of the Bristol School of Aviation was Henri Jullerot whose assistants were Mr E. C. Gordon England, Mr H.R. Fleming and Harry R. Busteed, an Australian. They worked long days instructing 17 pupil pilots simultaneously. Between 1910 and 1914 over 400 pupils were taught to fly in Bristol Boxkites. One of the pupils who was to become famous in the annals of RAF was Robert Smith-Barry. He was taught to fly at Larkhill in early 1911 and by June of that year was instructing there.

In October 1911 the War office decided to expand army flying by reorganising the Balloon School so that it would incorporate aeroplanes, airships, kites and balloons. Horatio Barber's shed was taken over by the Flying School during September when he left for Hendon. The first Army experiments in aerial reconnaissance using an aeroplane were carried out at Larkhill

The Aeroplane Sheds of the British & Colonial Aeroplane Company at Larkhill C.1912.
Photo: T.L.Fuller © J.T.Fuller.

A Bleriot monoplane at Larkhill C.1910
Photo: T.L.Fuller © J.T.Fuller.

Personnel of the Royal Engineers, Col Cody and the local constabulary from Amesbury at
Larkhill C.1912. The monoplane is a Hanriot. Photo: T.L.Fuller © J.T.Fuller.

in September 1910. Involved in this were Capt. Bertram Dickson of the Air Battalion RE, and Robert Loraine the actor-pilot both of whom flew Bristol Boxkites loaned to the Army by the Bristol Aeroplane Company, which had agreed to co-operate with the War Office in the experiments. Lt L.D.L. Gibbs also participated, flying his own clipped-wing racing Farman. One of the successes of the trials was Loraine who sent details of the army manoeuvres using Morse wireless messages from the air over a quarter mile to Larkhill. The Boxkite flown by Dickson was No.8, which had been constructed at Filton as a prototype at the same time as No.7.

The War Office decided that the Balloon School should be reformed as the Air Battalion Royal Engineers and the following Army Order was issued on 28th February 1911: -
With a view to meeting Army requirements consequent on recent developments in aerial science it has been decided to form an Air Battalion to which will be entrusted the duty of creating a body of expert airman. The training and instruction of men in handling kites, balloons and aeroplanes, and other forms of aircraft, will also dissolve on this Battalion. The establishment of this Battalion will be organised into Headquarters and two Companies. The officers will be

selected from any regular arm or branch of the Service on the Active List. A selected candidate will, on joining the Air Battalion, go through six months' probationary course. An officer who satisfactorily completes the probationary period will be appointed to the Air Battalion for a period of four years.

Battalion HQ and No.1 (Airship) Company responsible for airships, kites and balloons was established at Farnborough. In addition No.2 (Aeroplane) Company, responsible for aeroplanes, was based at Larkhill under the command of Capt. J.D.B. Fulton RFA. This was implemented on 1st April 1911. It was also at this time that the Balloon Factory was re-named the Aircraft Factory. The first officers appointed to No.2 Company were Capt C. J. Burke, Royal Irish Reg., Capt E.M. Maitland, Essex Reg, later to command No.1 Airship, Balloon & Kite Company, Lt R.A. Cammell, R.E, Lt B.H. Barrington-Kennett, Grenadier Guards, and Lt D.G. Conner, R.A, who were soon joined by Capt Eustace Loraine, S.D. Massy, Lt H.R.P. Reynolds, R.E, G.B. Hynes, R.A. and A.G. Fox. All were true pioneers of early military flying. The officers and men of No.2 (Aeroplane) Company were provided with accommodation in the mess at Bulford Barracks, where they were paying guests of the R.A. They were taken daily to Larkhill aerodrome and back in horse-drawn wagons. When later forming as No.3 Sqn, the officers used the Bustard Inn at Rollestone as their mess until improved facilities were made available at the Cavalry Barracks, Netheravon. Machines that were flown at the time were the Bleriot, Bristol Boxkite, Howard Wright biplane and a Paulhan Biplane. Later that year 2 Farmans, 1 Nieuport Monoplane and 1 Breguet biplane were added to the strength. One of the Bleriots was owned by a Lt Cammell.

In June 1911, Pierre Prier joined the Bristol Company as an instructor for the two flying schools at Larkhill and Brooklands. He had been at the Bleriot flying school at Hendon as Chief Instructor, when in April 1911 he made the first non-stop flight from London to Paris. In addition to being a competent pilot he was a qualified engineer who designed the Bristol-Prier P1, a single-seater monoplane with a 50hp Gnome engine. A number of these were built, No.56 was used at the Larkhill flying school. Some of the type were converted by using low powered Anzani engines of 35hp for use as advanced trainers at the Larkhill flying school. A two-seater version followed, and later still a modification by Prier and Capt. Bertram Dickson produced the Prier-Dickson monoplane for which orders were received from the RFC, Spain, Italy, Turkey and Germany. The first of these, No.82 was at Larkhill in 1912 before being sent to Spain as a replacement for No.83 that had crashed. Henri Coanda succeeded Pierre Prier at the Bristol Company in 1912.

The amount of flying from Larkhill aerodrome during 1911 was considerable, both military and civilian. NCOs were taught to fly by the commissioned officers. The light mornings of the summer months often saw operations at Larkhill commencing at 0300 hrs. The still air of early morning was beneficial to the flying machines of the day. Henri Jullerot was known to fly to Rollestone and take breakfast with the officers at the Bustard Inn before taking off again to continue instructing. The personnel of No.2 (Aeroplane) Company had a summer befitting the reputation now associated with that period of history. Cross-country flights were made by officers, wearing suitable civilian clothes, to country houses where they indulged in weekend parties, returning to Larkhill for Monday duties. Mishaps occurred while flying but many ended without serious injury to the fliers. In Cambrideshire army manoeuvres were being staged and the pilots of Larkhill were detached there for the duration. On the first day, Brooke-Popham and Burke flew in a Farman to Wantage, continuing to Oxford the next day. There they were diverted to Burford, using the Company's only car, where they assisted Barrington-Kennett to take-off again, after he had forced landed. Massey's engine cut out whilst in the air and the machine was severely damaged during landing but he was not injured. Conner crashed on high ground when flying in fog but escaped injury. Brooke-Popham and Burke, whilst continuing their flight towards Cambridge, damaged the tail-skid of their Farman. Reynolds, flying the other Farman, ran into a thunderstorm and a strong gust of wind turned it over and into a dive. He fell out but managed to hold onto a side strut whilst lying on the underside of the lower wing. He

The upside-down Bristol Tractor biplane after running into the crowd when landing at Larkhill on 19th May 1912.   Photo: © J.T.Fuller./Terry Crawford Coll.

stood up while the machine continued downwards swaying from side to side in long swoops. When it was about ten feet from the ground, Reynolds jumped off and survived. Only two serviceable aeroplanes arrived at Cambridge, which were the ones flown by Lt Cammell and Lt Barrington-Kennett. On arrival both of the officers were shown considerable hospitality by the University members. Between the 9th-13th September 1911, the various officers returned to Larkhill from Cambridge. Those arriving in the evenings were welcomed back by beacons which had been lit to guide them in. Within days of their return, cavalry manoeuvres were being staged on Salisbury Plain and Barrington-Kennett took aerial photographs whilst other pilots practised dropping despatches and bombing. Lt Cammell was killed shortly after this when he crashed a Valkyrie at Hendon.

Snow storms, fog and high winds restricted flying in January 1912 but a number of flights were possible. The following month Lt Barrington-Kennett of the Grenadier Guards with Corporal Ridd of the Royal Engineers flew 250 miles in 5 hours at a height of 250' creating a world record for a passenger flight and so winning the RFC element of the Mortimer Singer Prize.

Pupils attending the Bristol School of Flying were accommodated at the George Hotel in Amesbury. One morning in March Henri Jullerot flew low over the building to awaken his pupils. He then raced them in their cars back to Larkhill aerodrome and record has it that the outcome was a draw.

An unfortunate accident occurred on the airfield on Sunday 19th May 1912 when 15 year old Leonard Williams, the son of George Williams, a fishmonger of Amesbury, was struck and killed by a Bristol Tractor biplane when it was landing. It was being flown by Lt A.E. Burchardt-Ashton of the 4th Dragoon Guards. Also in the crowd of about 300 spectators was Albert Wotton who escaped without injury when the aeroplane wheels ran over him. Another Amesbury boy, who was not so lucky, was Harry Maggs. He was hit by the aeroplane and was taken to Bulford Military Hospital with internal injuries and ruptured back muscles. The funeral in Amesbury of Leonard Williams was well attended by family and friends as well as many pilots from Larkhill. Lt Burchardt-Ashton was unable to attend because of his military duties but those who did were the Italians, Lt Rinaldi and Eroole and a German, Herr Gutt. The inquiry into the accident found:

• the aviator was not to blame
• the accident was caused by the spectators being on the landing ground which they had encroached owing to the absence of proper control
• the accident might not have occurred had the aviator's view ahead not been obstructed by the radiator.

The development of flying generally resulted in the Committee of Imperial Defence being asked to consider the whole question of military aviation with the view to the formation of an Air Force. Two sub committees were set up to progress the introduction and their findings were accepted by the Imperial Defence Committee. Consequently the

Hangars, Flying Station, Salisbury Plain.

The Aeroplane Sheds of the British & Colonial Aeroplane Company at Larkhill. In the foreground can be seen an Henri Farman and behind it BE.3 No.203 *The Goldfish*. The mechanic with his hand on the nose of the Farman appears to be smoking a pipe, presumably not concerned with any possible petrol vapours from the engine. Photo: Terry Crawford Coll.

A Bristol Prier School Monoplane, possibly No.98, at Larkhill after its delivery there in September 1912. Seven of the single seat advanced trainers were built and most of them were used at Larkhill. The gentleman in the Homburg is possibly Pierre Prier, instructor/designer for the British & Colonial Aeroplane Company. Photo: T.L.Fuller © J.T.Fuller.

A Bristol Prier of No.3 Sqn. delivered originally to the Bristol Aeroplane Company at Larkhill in 1912. Photo: Rex Reynolds Collection.

Royal Flying Corps was formed on 13th April 1912. One of the principles agreed was that within the Corps would be the inclusion of a Military Wing, Naval Wing, Central Flying School, a Reserve and the Aircraft Factory at Farnborough. This resulted in the abolition of the Air Battalion with No.1 (Airship) Company becoming the RFC's No.1 Sqn still based at Farnborough and No.2 (Aeroplane) Company forming as No.3 Sqn at Larkhill on 13th May 1912. This squadron had a mixture of aeroplanes at the time of formation which included

the Henri Farman III, Avro Type 'E', Bristol Boxkite, Nieuport, Deperdussin, Bristol Prier monoplanes and the BE.3. History recognises No.3 Sqn as being the oldest in the RAF having been the first to fly aircraft within the formation of the service. It has the motto *Tertius Primus Erit* meaning 'The Third shall be First'. No.2 Sqn was formed at Farnborough from the reserve of pilots from No.2 (Aeroplane) Company and with Capt Charles James Burke of the Royal Irish regiment as CO. On 18th May 1912,

Major H.R.M. Brooke-Popham was appointed CO of No.3 Sqn, replacing Capt J.B. Fulton who transferred to the CFS at Upavon as an instructor.

It was from Larkhill that Capt E.B. Loraine and Staff Sgt R.H.V. Wilson of No.3 Sqn were flying when, during a sharp turn, their Nieuport monoplane side-slipped and crashed near the road to Shrewton on 5th July 1912 killing both men. These were the first casualties of the newly formed RFC. The details of the accident and the memorial raised at the crash site are covered under **WINTERBOURNE STOKE**.

Considerable activity took place at Larkhill throughout the summer months of 1912 with the build up to the British Military Aeroplane Trials from 1st - 25th August. These were an attempt by the War Office to establish a specification for an aircraft best suited to the needs of the military. The trials were open to anybody who wished to enter but the aeroplanes had to meet certain criteria. The winning aeroplane was required to carry a crew of two, have a speed of 55mph, fuel capacity for 4hrs 30mins, fly for 3hrs fully loaded and to attain an altitude of 4,500'. The rate of climb had to average not less than 200' per minute for the first 1000'. It was to maintain a height of 1,500' for 1hr, be able to rise in a short distance from long grass or harrowed ground, and to land on rough ploughed land without damage. It had to be readily adaptable to travel by road in tow on its own wheels, or on a lorry. There was also a quick assembly test and one of the conditions was that after the assembly, the aeroplane should display its flying capacity by making a circuit of the complete course. It was this quick assembly device which later would fail in flight causing a crash which would result in a ban on the use of monoplanes.

At the end of July the Bristol Company was temporarily moved from Larkhill to Brooklands to enable their hangars to be used for the Bristol entries. During this period of involvement, No.3 Sqn was likewise temporarily moved to Upavon, returning to Larkhill at the end of August.

Twenty temporary hangars were erected east of what is now Tombs Road for the duration of the trials, in which the participating aeroplanes were housed. These were also Harbrow built and measured 60' x 25' deep with back projection of 15' x 20' deep. After the trials these were taken down and re-erected at Farnborough.

The different entries were put through their paces with varying degrees of success. The British & Colonial Aeroplane Company entered two BE.2 biplanes and two Coanda monoplanes. One of the latter, No.105 was awarded a runner-up prize of £500 for pilot Harry Busteed.

The outstanding BE.2 (Bleriot Experimental) tractor biplane with its 70 hp Renault engine was flown by Geoffrey de Havilland who was chief designer at the Royal Aircraft Factory at Farnborough. He and Maj Frederick Sykes set up the British altitude record of 10,560'. During the competitions it was used to fly the officials around the area. It was allowed to perform the climbing, gliding and speed tests as a means of forming comparative data and proved a very capable entry. In the climb test it beat all other competition aircraft, reaching 1000' at 365 ft/min. British and foreign aircraft constructors were eligible to enter the trials but this did not include de Havilland's BE.2 because it had been designed and built in the Government Royal Aircraft Factory.

On 25th August 1912 Lt Wilfred Parke RN and his observer Lt Le Breton RFC flew in an Avro biplane with an enclosed cabin. They were lucky not to have had a serious accident because the Avro went into a steep dive from which Parke could not recover. He tried everything he could to do so, and in desperation finally jammed on full opposite rudder and let go of the control stick. The Avro swooped out of the dive in front of the hangars about 50' from the ground. Considerably shaken he completed a circuit and managed to land it. A full report of his experience was made for the benefit of other pilots who might have a similar experience. This particular facet of flying became known as 'Parke's Dive'. A fatality did occur on Tuesday 13th August when Mr Robert C. Fenwick (R.Ae.C. No.35), took-off on a trial flight in the all-British Mersey pusher monoplane which he had designed and built himself in Liverpool. His machine had the engine in the normal position in the nose but the propeller was behind the wing, driven by a shaft passing between the two seats in the cockpit position. Mr Fenwick was doubtful as to the aircraft's stability and on reaching a point some one and a half miles from Larkhill Aerodrome, it was seen to dive, recover briefly and then dive into the ground. Mr Fenwick was killed on impact.

The four judges of the trials were Brig.Gen. David Henderson, Director of Military Training, Capt Godfrey M. Paine RN, Commandant of the CFS, Maj F.H. Sykes, OC Military Wing RFC and Mr Mervyn O'Gorman, Superintendant of the Royal Aircraft Factory. The overall winner of the trials was judged to be 52 year old Colonel Samuel Franklin Cody with his self built 'Flying Cathedral' biplane. This was equipped with an Austro-Daimler engine. It had a span of 43' and was 37' 9" in length. It won for him both the Open and British sections of the competition for which he received £4000 and £1000 respectively. Col Cody, an American by birth, was one of the great pioneers of military flying. He was believed to be the first man to fly in this country in 1908. Cody was one of the most flamboyant and innovative of the early pioneers of flight, hence his title of Colonel, which appears to have stemmed from his meeting with King Edward VII. On his introduction the King said "I have heard of you Colonel Cody" but was confusing him with Buffalo Bill. Cody then claimed the title of Colonel which the King had 'bestowed'. Cody initiated a flying school of sorts at which he taught the rudiments of aviation to some of the early members of the RFC. Just prior to these first military trials he built a high wing monoplane which he intended entering. It was fitted with a Beardmore engine and had a two to one reduction in the airscrew, which was chain driven. Owing to the exceptionally low centre of gravity the craft performed a kind of flat turn instead of the necessary bank turn. It was written off before the competition when it crashed onto a cow.

Weather conditions frequently interrupted the trials and on such occasions the flamboyant Cody organised entertainment for the participants which, unusually for an American, included games of cricket. Although his aircraft was judged the winning entry and earned Cody the £5000 prize money, it did not prove afterwards to be a success. A condition of the trials was that the War Office had the right to purchase the winning aeroplane and runner-up, plus another example of each. Cody's trial biplane subsequently crashed and Cody himself was killed on 7th August 1913 when a new hydroplane he had built collapsed at a height of 200' above Laffan's Plain before crashing on to trees. Neither Cody or his passenger Mr W.H.B. Evans were strapped in and both were thrown out when the machine turned over. He had built the new plane with the intention of entering a competition to race around the coast of Britain for a prize of £5000 and another where the first airman to cross the Atlantic would receive £10,000. Due to the great charisma of this cowboy from Iowa, the coffin was borne on an open gun-carriage and escorted by pipers of the Black Watch at his funeral in Aldershot on 11th August. He was buried with full military honours and massive crowds turned out to pay their respects. Cody was held in such high regard by the nation and by royalty, that King George V sent a personal telegram to his widow, expressing his own grief.

The runner-up to Cody's 'Cathedral' in both sections of the Trials was the Bristol monoplane. It was one of the type which later suffered from a wing failure. This resulted in a twenty-year ban on monoplanes.

The Military decided that, of the various aeroplanes taking part in the trials, the BE.2 was best suited for their purposes. Other versions such as the BE.2c and BE2d were developed from it and used successfully by the RFC during World War 1. After the Trials, the importance of Larkhill began to diminish. This coincided with the CFS operating from June 1912 at Upavon and the opening of the aerodrome at Netheravon in 1913.

Immediately after the conclusion of the Military Trials, the RFC was called upon to take part in the First Army Manoeuvres which were held in Cambridgeshire. No.3 Sqn was attached to the force commanded by Sir Douglas Haig. Four aircraft were despatched under the command of Maj. Brooke-Popham.

Lionel Wilmot Brabazon Rees, who was commissioned in the Royal Garrison Artillery, transferred to the RFC in August 1910. He attended the

Col Sam Cody with his winning biplane at Larkhill in August 1912.
Photo: Rex Reynolds Collection

Bristol School of Flying at Larkhill at his own expense and in his own time and gained his flying certificate in January 1913. He later served a brief spell at CFS Upavon from November 1915 before an appointment as CO of No.32 Sqn with the rank of Major. This squadron was formed at Netheravon in January 1916. The squadron went to France on 28th May 1916, where later he was awarded the Victoria Cross for a single-handed attack on ten enemy aircraft (see **NETHERAVON**).

On 5th March 1913, Geoffrey England, who designed Bristol aeroplanes and who was the brother of Bristol's instructor E.C. Gordon England, was killed when the military-type two-seat Bristol Coanda monoplane he was flying crashed. He had volunteered to carry out a flight in excess of one hour's duration, as an acceptance test of the aircraft prior to its delivery to the Romanian Government. He took off in a wind of 30 mph and flew around Larkhill aerodrome for thirty-two minutes at a height of 3000 ft. The machine was seen then to be descending in a steep glide with the pilot switching his 80 hp Gnome engine on and off, as was the accepted practise. At around 600 ft all the ribs for about 6ft from the left side wing tip, fell off the steel spars and the machine dived into the ground. On 16th April 1913 Lt R. Cholmondeley of No.3 Sqn carried out some experimental night flying when by the light of the moon he flew a return flight from Larkhill to Upavon in a Maurice Farman. It proved satisfactory until he came in to land and found that below 100' it was much darker, with the moon not illuminating

the aerodrome sufficiently. He was the first officer of the Military Wing RFC to make a night flight. He later tried landing by the light of opened aeroplane shed doors.

On 9th May 1913, No.3 Sqn flew to Farnborough as a unit. Maj Brook-

Popham the Squadron Commander first tested the air before giving orders for nine aircraft to take off at five-minute intervals. 'A' Flt with BE.2 tractor biplanes were first away followed by 'B' Flt's Henri Farman pusher biplanes with 'C' Flt bringing up the rear with Maurice Farman pusher biplanes. Sgt Frank Ridd of the latter Flt was the only one not to complete the course as he force landed near Andover with a serious engine fault. The War Office decided that the use of Larkhill as an airfield was no longer suitable after Upavon opened in June 1912 and Netheravon the following year. No.3 Sqn left for Netheravon on 16th June 1913 equipped at that stage with the BE.2A, 3 & 4, Longhorn, Bleriot XI, Henry Farman F.20 and Avro Type Es. The day before the move James McCudden joined the squadron at Larkhill. This mechanic would later achieve fame as one of the country's top pilots and was awarded the VC (see **NETHERAVON**).

Another fatal accident occurred just over a year after Capt Loraine's crash.

A Bristol monoplane and a balloon at Larkhill C.1912.
Photos: T.L.Fuller © J.T.Fuller.

The wreckage of the Bristol Prier-Dickson at Larkhill Aerodrome in which Major Hewetson was killed on 17th July 1913. The aeroplane hangars, with the sun-gap between, can be seen in the distance. A blade of the propeller survives in a local private collection.
Photo: T.L.Fuller © J.T.Fuller.

On 17th July 1913, Maj A.W. Hewetson, RFA died when his Bristol Prier-Dickson monoplane, modified by Coanda to carry two pilots side-by-side and known as *The Sociable*, crashed on the airfield during a test for his aviator's certificate. The site of the crash is marked by a stone memorial slab surrounded by posts and railings.

1914 commenced with another fatality at Larkhill. Warren Merriam, a well known and most capable instructor, was transferred from Brooklands to the Bristol School at Larkhill for a short period of time. On 26th January he took off in a Bristol Coanda monoplane, modified with side-by-side seating and accompanied by G. L. Gipps, one of the more advanced pupils. The purpose of the flight was to give the pupil some dual instruction. The machine was not equipped with an air speed indicator, rev. counter or bank indicator and neither of the pilots was strapped in or wearing head protection. After completing a circuit at a height of around 80 ft. the aircraft performed a violent flat turn, stalled and dived into the ground. Warren Merriam was severely injured but G. L. Gipps was killed. It appears that the latter ignored his instructor's initial application of rudder and then suddenly relaxed his leg, with the result that Warren Merriam jerked on full rudder and the machine stalled before he could counteract its effect.

At this time Henri Coanda started to build a single seat monoplane, the SB5, but work stopped and he left the British & Colonial. Frank S. Barnwell became chief designer, developing it as a single-seat biplane No.206 and it was test flown at Larkhill in February 1914. The following month it was exhibited at Olympia as the Bristol Baby Tractor biplane. From this was developed the famous Bristol Scout which acquitted itself so well in France during World War 1 and was popular with the RFC pilots.

Closure

The Bristol Company and its Flying School continued to use the aerodrome at Larkhill until it moved to Brooklands on 2nd June 1914 becoming No.1 Reserve Sqn with the declaration of war. Turkish Officers were some of the last pilots taught at the Bristol School at Larkhill. It then closed as an aerodrome but soon had a series of railway lines laid as an extension of the Bulford branch. The extension was built by Sir William Jackson and was known as the Larkhill Military Railway. It was used initially to bring in building materials for the hundreds of timber framed, corrugated iron huts that formed a sprawling army camp on the aerodrome site for the many troops preparing for war. It was operated by the RE from their base known as 'Countess Crossing' where the railway crossed Countess Road. The railway was extended to serve Stonehenge and Lake Down airfields, remaining in operation until 1928.

Among the troops at Larkhill in 1918 was the 154th US Army Aero Sqn from 9th - 19th March when they left for Stockbridge. The Australian Flying Corps also had personnel at Larkhill and one of them died on Tuesday 15th October 1918 following a car crash two days previously. The car driven, by Sgt A.O Weeks of an American Aero Sqn, was returning from Chattis Hill following an inspection of wireless telephony equipment. In London Road, Salisbury the car struck the kerb, skidded and overturned. Passengers,

2nd Lt C. J. French RAF, Lt Francis and Lt Hector Nicol of the Australian Flying Corps, were thrown out. Lt French and Nicol were injured, the latter suffering head injuries when trapped under the overturned car. He died and was buried at Stratford-sub-Castle (St. Lawrence) Churchyard, Salisbury.

A fatality involving the Air Force occurred on Thursday 13th February 1919 when the aircraft flown by 2nd Lt W.S. Featherstonhaugh at 100' above No.5 Camp, suffered a mechanical failure resulting in a forced landing. In carrying this out the wing struck Private Joseph Tairue, New Zealand Maori (Pioneer) Battalion NZEF on the head and killed him. He was buried at Tidworth Military Cemetery.

Memorials

1) 184/SU144435 - Wood Road off of the Packway

Most of the aeroplane sheds have been removed over the years but five survive and are used as stores by the MoD. Modifications have taken place, including the replacement of the doors facing the landing ground by brick and concrete block walls and small doors. The sheds are situated at the south end of Wood Road and it is believed that they are the oldest former flight sheds in existence in this country.

2) 184/SU144436 - Wood Road off of the Packway

20 yards north of the former aeroplane sheds on the same side of the road, in the centre of what was known as the 'Sungap', stands a stone pedestal displaying a metal plaque with the inscription: -

> ON THIS SITE THE FIRST
> AERODROME FOR THE ARMY
> WAS FOUNDED IN 1910 BY
> CAPT. J.D.B. FULTON RFA
> AND MR G.B. COCKBURN
>
> THIS LATER BECAME
> 2 COY AIR BN RE
>
> THE BRITISH AND COLONIAL
> AEROPLANE COMPANY
> FORERUNNERS OF THE
> BRISTOL AEROPLANE COMPANY
> ESTABLISHED THEIR FLYING
> SCHOOL HERE IN 1910
>
> THE FIRST MILITARY AIR TRIALS
> WERE HELD HERE IN 1912

Five aeroplane sheds built in 1910 and 1911 for the Bristol Flying School. These stand on the site of the former Larkhill Aerodrome and are arguably the oldest buildings designed for military flying surviving in the UK.

Stone memorial slab to Maj Hewetson at the crash site on Larkhill Aerodrome.

The memorial was unveiled by Brigadier R. S. Streatfield MC on 12th February 1968. Also attending were AM Sir Ralph Sorley KCB, OBE, DSC, DFC and Cyril Uwins the Chief Test Pilot and Director of British Aircraft Corporation.

Some of the wording on the memorial is not strictly accurate and it is believed that the reverse side of the metal plaque displays wording which is even more inaccurate.

3) 184/SU139439 - On the former airfield south of the Packway

A stone slab surrounded by 6 wooden posts and railings with a gated entry marks the site on which Maj. Alexander William Hewetson was killed when he crashed at Larkhill aerodrome on 17th July 1913. This was the first fatality involving a pupil carrying out tests for an aviator's certificate at Larkhill. He had been under instruction at the Bristol School for some two months. The machine he was flying was a Bristol Prier-Dickson monoplane, modified by Coanda as a two seat side-by-side cockpit, known as the Sociable Model. While performing a figure-of-eight test he over-banked the machine and side-slipped into the ground from 100'. Maj. Hewetson was forty-four years old when he was killed and at the inquest his instructor Henri Jullerot stated that he considered it inadvisable for men of the Major's age to take up flying.

The words on the stone slab became eroded over the years but renovation was arranged by the Royal School of Artillery, Larkhill in 1997. The original posts and railings surrounding the site

The unveiling of the commemorative pedestal and plaque on the site of the original 1910 Larkhill Aerodrome. Photo: Norman Parker Coll.

were also renewed with the complete works costing £1000. A re-dedication ceremony was held on Monday 6th October 1997. The inscription again clearly reads: -

IN MEMORY
... OF ...
MAJOR ALEXANDER WILLIAM HEWETSON
66TH BATTERY ROYAL FIELD ARTILLERY
WHO WAS KILLED WHILST FLYING
ON THE 17TH JULY 1913 NEAR THIS SPOT

The inscription is incorrect in that the memorial stands on the precise spot where the aeroplane crashed.

A further memorial to this officer, who was one of the first members of the Royal Aero Club, was erected at Fargo Plantation near Stonehenge, 2 miles south west of the crash site (see **STONEHENGE**).

The re-dedication of the memorial to Maj Hewetson at Larkhill conducted by the Garrison Chaplain, the Rev. Mark Jones, School of Artillery on Monday 6th October 1997. LtoR - Lt Col E. McLaughlin - Garrison Adjutant, Maj. R.S Jackson MBE, RA - Chief of Staff, Royal School of Artillery, Brigadier M.G. Douglas-Withers CBE, ADC - Director Royal Artillery, Col J.C Longfield MBE - Commandant Royal School of Artillery, Lt Col D.W Lewthwaite RA - CO 14 Reg. Royal School of Artillery, WO1 (Master Gunner) Moyse. Photo: Royal School of Artillery

LARKHILL (Knighton Down) AERODROME

<u>Location</u> - 184/SU127453 - 2 miles North of Stonehenge

North of the unclassified Larkhill to Shrewton road, known as The Packway, lies Knighton Down and this was the site of a second Larkhill airfield which first came in to use in the late 1920s during army exercises.

Aerodrome Development

From January 1936 it was recognised as an RAF airfield used by Nos.2, 4, 13, and 16 (Army Co-operation) Sqns. A No.16 AC Sqn Audax crash landed on the site in June 1937. Take-off and landings were from rough grass-land with facilities even in the Spring of 1941, consisting only of a wooden hut, a tent for a 'Watch Office' and a windsock. An aircraft hangar was built, it is believed, in December 1941 and this was probably not of new construction as it was given a replacement roof on 15th April 1942. Capt Andrew Lyell, one of the instructors at Larkhill, recalls the hangar being occupied by a rarely flown Lysander and in use for all aircraft servicing and repairs.

World War 2 Years

The first unit posted to Larkhill after war was declared was 'D' Flight, formed there on 1st February 1940 under No.1 S of AC. The Flt assembled at Old Sarum before moving to Hawkinge on 17th April and to France two days later, where it was to carry out AOP duties with its Taylorcraft and Stinson. 'D' Flt. returned to Old Sarum in May 1940 as a result of the Expeditionary Force evacuation and on 3rd June 'D' Flight was back at Larkhill. It was then involved in a number of Area Army Command exercises during the remainder of the year and the first few months of 1941. Aircraft allocation at that stage was Taylorcraft 3, Lysanders 2, Stinson 105s 2, and 3 J-4A Piper Cubs (BT440), (BT 441) and (BT442), these three were impressed from the Wiltshire School of Flying during November 1940. The following month Army Co-operation Command was formed from No.22 Group at Farnborough to control Nos. 70 and 71

Groups. At that stage 'D' Flt came under No.70 Group.

AOP courses were held at Larkhill where Army Officers, who had already learnt to fly at an EFTS, attended for conversion to operational duties. Accommodation for instructors and pupils was close by at the School of Artillery. This consisted of Nissen huts for sleeping in and a hut where lectures were held. The CO had a small office in the same building. Instruction was primarily concerned with teaching the art of carrying out Air OP shoots and short landings. Each course would consist of 5/6 pupils with 2/3 instructors. The CO during 1941 was Charles Bazeley, an army officer who wore the blue uniform and wings of the RAF, and was paid by the RAF and carried the rank of a Sqn Ldr.

On 20th September 1941, No.1424 (AOP) Flight was formed at Larkhill from 'D' (AC) Flight. In addition to its allocation of Taylorcraft light aircraft, Piper Cubs were received. One of these (HL530) arrived on 5th December. A Proctor landing to collect the ATA pilot came down outside the perimeter of the aerodrome and in doing so damaged the under-carriage, airscrew and engine bearers.

By the end of December 1941 a number of Vigilants had arrived. A Spitfire landed at the aerodrome on Christmas Eve. The pilot Fg Off Brannigan had become lost and dropped in for directions. Early in 1942 several Tiger Moths fitted with Type 21 wireless sets had arrived for use on artillery shoots.

On 24th January 1942, a Blenheim with pilot Fg Off Redmond and two Sgts forced landed with a seized engine. They were on a flight from South Wales to Odiham.

Capt. Andrew Lyell who had been one of the students on the first series of AOP courses in 1941 returned to Larkhill as an instructor in April 1942. The CO had by then been replaced by Sqn Ldr Roddy Davenport. Other instructors were Capts Evelyn Prendergast, Norman Lane, John Ingram, 'Moke' Murray and H.B.(Warby) Warburton. The Station Adjutant was Flt Lt 'Pop' Manning. In May when instructing on No.7 AOP Course, Capt Lyall was flying in a DH82 with a student pilot who inexplicably cut the throttle at around 100' and the aircraft plunged to the ground. Neither was injured but the DH82 was written off and the student was sent back to his regiment, as it was decided that he was not pilot material. Another DH82 was written off during the same course when Capt Pat Henderson crashed. He was making a simulated attack on a regiment in the Wylye Valley. When making a concealed approach between two woods he collided with three HT cables which he had not seen, as the wooden pylons were hidden by the trees at the extremities of the woods. One of the cables sliced through the fuel tank, which in a DH82 is above the pilot's head. The petrol in the tank ignited and the aircraft crashed in flames alongside an ammunition dump. Capt. Henderson received third degree burns to his face.

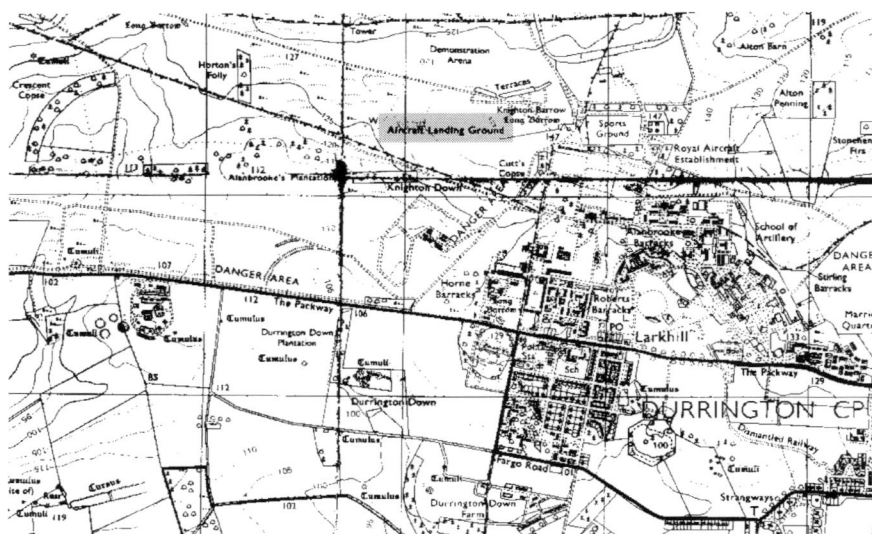

The Knighton Down aerodrome at Larkhill, 1½ miles NW of the first site.

Sqn Ldr Davenport left Larkhill on promotion to Wg Cdr in June 1942 and was succeeded by Sqn Ldr Donald Walker.

From 18th September 1942 the establishment was expanded and extra aircraft allocated including Auster 1s. The Flight was redesignated No. 43 OTU in 70 Group ACC from 1st October. Its function was to train Auster air observation post pilots and observers. The Unit re-organised into 'A', 'B' & 'C' (Exercise) Flts. Fifteen officers were allotted to 'B' Flight which detached to Shrewton between 15th-19th November 1942. From the latter date the whole of No.43 OTU, with the exception of the Rear Party, moved from Larkhill to Old Sarum taking with it an establishment of 36 aircraft of 5 types. Detachments did return briefly in April 1943 and August 1944. This ended the RAF's association with Larkhill airfield and its use as such.

Larkhill is believed to have also been used by the L-4 Piper Cubs of the US Army 9th Air Force Liaison Squadrons during 1944, when engaged on exercises on the nearby firing range.

Post War Years

The landing strip remained in evidence for many years after the war with both Beverley and Hercules aircraft known to have used it for exercise purposes.

Various other areas of Larkhill and its ranges have been used since the war for landing both fixed and rotary wing aircraft but there is no longer a designated airfield. In 1967 a Vulcan B.2 of No.12 Sqn dropped, what was then, the RAF's new 1,000lb parachute-retarded bombs during a fire power demonstration aimed at static vehicles dispersed on Larkhill Ranges during 'Unison '67'. The area used was just west of the World War 2 RAF Larkhill site and close to Rollestone. Today helicopters occasionally fly into the School of Artillery at Larkhill where a landing pad is provided.

LONG NEWNTON AERODROME

Location - 163/ST923920 - 2 miles South East of Tetbury

The former Fighter Training Command aerodrome is located about 1 mile east of the village of Long Newnton on the C80 off the B4014. It lies on the eastern side of the Fosse Way along which the county boundary runs. Long Newnton village is in Gloucestershire whilst the aerodrome and the majority of its technical buildings were in Wiltshire.

Airfield Development

The first buildings were built early in World War 2, for storage by No.11 Maintenance Unit (MU).

The airfield was developed as a satellite in early 1942. Two Sommerfeld Track runways were laid, 22/04 NE/SW and 28/10 E/W, both 1335yds x 50yds. These were encircled by a concrete perimeter track. Four 65ft. span Over Blister Hangars were assembled on the west side of the Fosse Way. The Technical Site buildings were established parallel with and between the Roman Road and the perimeter track. The Watch Office (13726/41) stood inside the perimeter track, also on the western side of the field. The two-letter station identification code was LN. An attempt was made to camouflage the area within the perimeter track by painting simulated hedgerows but with the bright new concrete of the encircling perimeter track, it is unlikely to have confused the German Air Force. Seven Domestic Sites were established north west of the aerodrome off of Crudwell Lane.

Additional hangars were provided after the station was redeveloped in May 1942, with six 69 ft. span Extra Over Blister Hangars erected around the perimeter track, five were on the south elevation. A T1 Type hangar was also provided, next to the Roman Road, on the Technical Site.

World War 1 Years

From August 1918, Long Newnton was used as an aerial gunnery range by squadrons of the Australian Flying Corps based in Gloucestershire. Nos. 5 and 6 Training Sqns were based at Minchinhampton and Nos. 7 and 8 Training Sqns at Leighterton. The

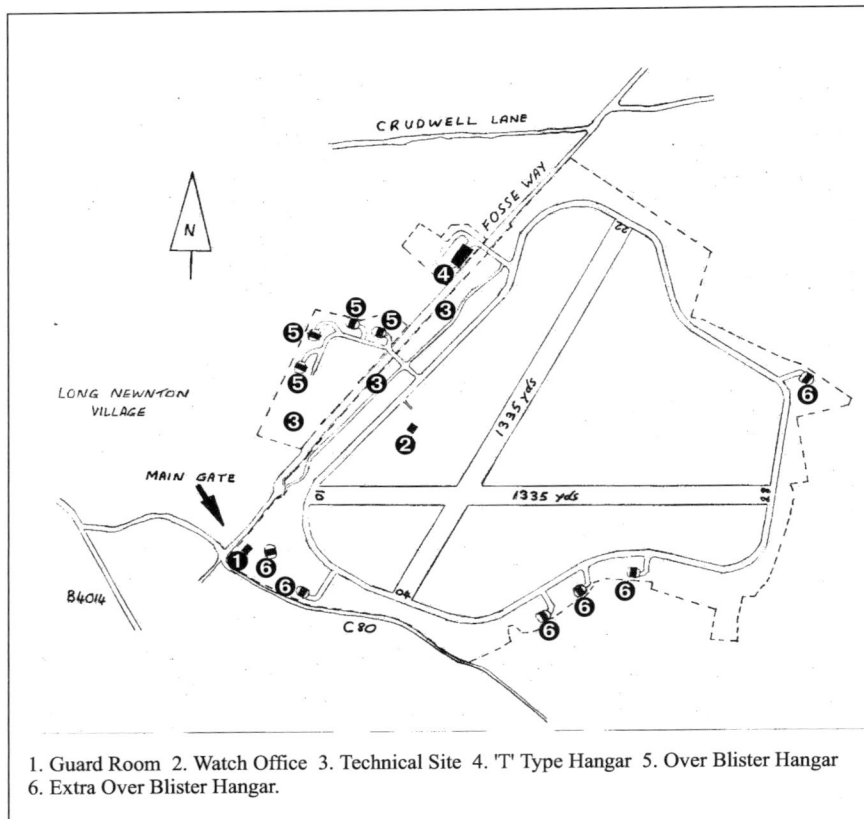

1. Guard Room 2. Watch Office 3. Technical Site 4. 'T' Type Hangar 5. Over Blister Hangar 6. Extra Over Blister Hangar.

crews flew from these bases and landed at Long Newnton, where they received gunnery instruction on the ground, before taking off and putting into practice what they had been taught.

World War 2 Years

During the Second World War, Long Newnton was in use by October 1939 as a sub-site of No.11 MU for ammunition storage purposes. In 1940 Long Newnton formed as a Q Site for Kemble aerodrome, which straddles the same county boundary approximately three miles to the north. From September to November 1940, No.9 SFTS Hullavington (No.23 Group) used Long Newnton as a RLG for single engine training with their Harvards. By February 1941 No.3 SFTS South Cerney (No.23 Group) were using the field as a RLG for twin engine training with Oxfords. No.14 SFTS Lyneham (No.23 Group) then took it over as a RLG from 16th August 1941 to relieve pressure at the home base, and used it for twin engine training with Oxfords. One of these, N4589, crashed when it overshot

during a landing on 18th August 1941. The School vacated the site on 26th January 1942 and the site was closed for redevelopment as a satellite.

Long Newnton came back into use for No.3 (P) AFU South Cerney (No.23 Group) on 29th May 1942 and was used by their Oxfords. This Unit moved out on 30th September 1943 to be immediately replaced by No.15 (P) AFU, which moved Flights in, which were detached at Greenham Common, for advanced pilot training with Oxfords. This was necessary because of the occupation of Greenham Common by the USAAF. Another Flt arrived from Ramsbury on 4th November. Persistent rain during the winter of 1943/44 caused water-logging of the airfield, therefore in January 1944 a Flight of the AFU was dispatched to Castle Combe for training.

A No.320 Sqn Mitchell II based at Dunsfold crashed at Long Newnton on 31st August 1944 when it overshot on landing.

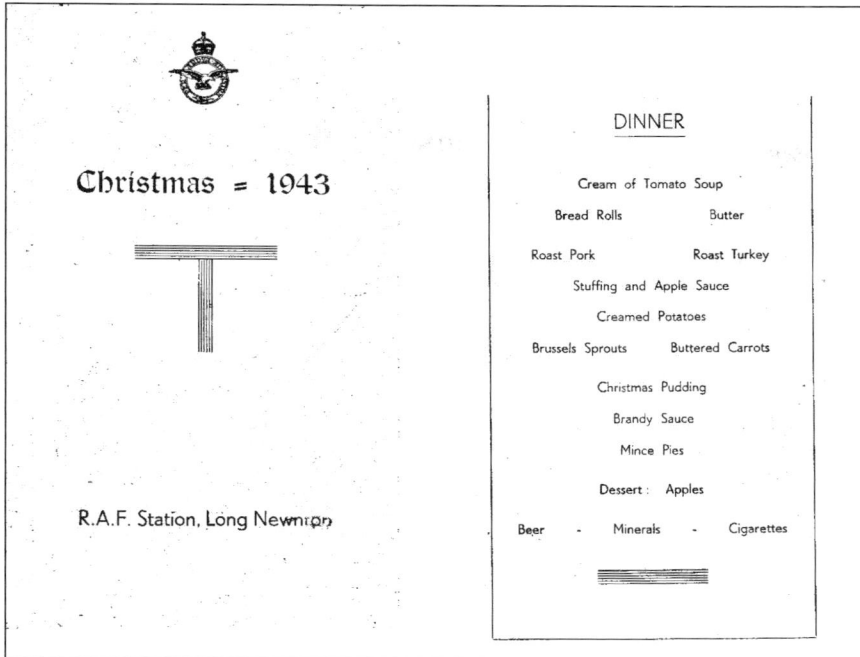

DINNER

Cream of Tomato Soup

Bread Rolls   Butter

Roast Pork   Roast Turkey

Stuffing and Apple Sauce

Creamed Potatoes

Brussels Sprouts   Buttered Carrots

Christmas Pudding

Brandy Sauce

Mince Pies

Dessert : Apples

Beer   -   Minerals   -   Cigarettes

Christmas = 1943

R.A.F. Station, Long Newnton

The 1943 Christmas Menu as sampled by No.15 (P) AFU.

The site returned to agriculture when the RAF moved out, but many of the wartime structures remain. These include the Watch Tower, Operations Room, Fire Tender Shed, T1 Hangar, numerous Maycrete huts and much of the perimeter track. The Decontamination Centre is evident, as are other buildings on dispersed sites.

Whilst aviation enthusiasts would appreciate viewing this former airfield and its buildings, visits are not encouraged.

No.15 (P) AFU remained until 15th May 1945 when it moved out in preparation for disbanding on 19th June 1945. Long Newnton was placed on C&M from the date the Unit left but on 31st July, once again became a sub-site of the Explosive Storage Unit of No.11 MU Chilmark.

Post War Years

No.11 MU continued to occupy the Station until 15th January 1950. It appears from reports in the local paper that there were occasions after closure when country walkers discovered the odd item of ordnance.

The surviving watch tower at Long Newnton with the Operations Room at the rear and the Fire Tender Shed on the far right.

LYNEHAM AERODROME

Location - 173/SU023785 - 5 miles North East of Calne.

In the village of Lyneham on the A3102 is unique airfield of RAF Lyneham, covering an area in excess of 2500 acres, this is the last truly operational RAF airfield in the county

Aerodrome Development

RAF Lyneham is unique for the varying roles it undertakes, and that in its construction, it does not conform to the standard RAF base. The older buildings are not in keeping with the usual design of the Second World War period and the station layout is likewise non uniform. Lyneham was intended for use as an Aircraft Storage Unit with building work starting in 1937. This involved the demolition of Lyneham Court and Cranley Farm buildings, levelling and drainage of the land. The Unit commenced forming in December 1939 as No.41 Maintenance Unit in No.41 Group.

The aerodrome had a grass landing area and mainly 'J' type hangars, four of which were positioned together in a convex semi-circle on the north side of the flying area. One of the hangars was smaller than the other three. The landing area provided for two grass runways with the main NW/SE of 1200 yards and the NE/SW of 450 yards. Like many grass runways in this country they proved unsatisfactory, in the wet climate, for the heavy use to which they were subjected. The hangars were provided for use by a Service Flying Training School with the Maintenance Unit having two 'K' and eight earth topped 'L' type hangars around the perimeter track for aircraft storage. Official records at the end of 1944 indicate that 30 blister and 10 Robin Type hangars were provided, the latter remaining in use until the late 1940s. An Air Ministry Drawing of 1945 only shows 13 blister hangars on the dispersal pans, all appearing to be of the standard type. The Control Tower was positioned west of the four hangars, facing the NW/SE runway.

In the early days there was no suitable accommodation for pupils under training but sufficient wooden huts had been erected to provide for this by the

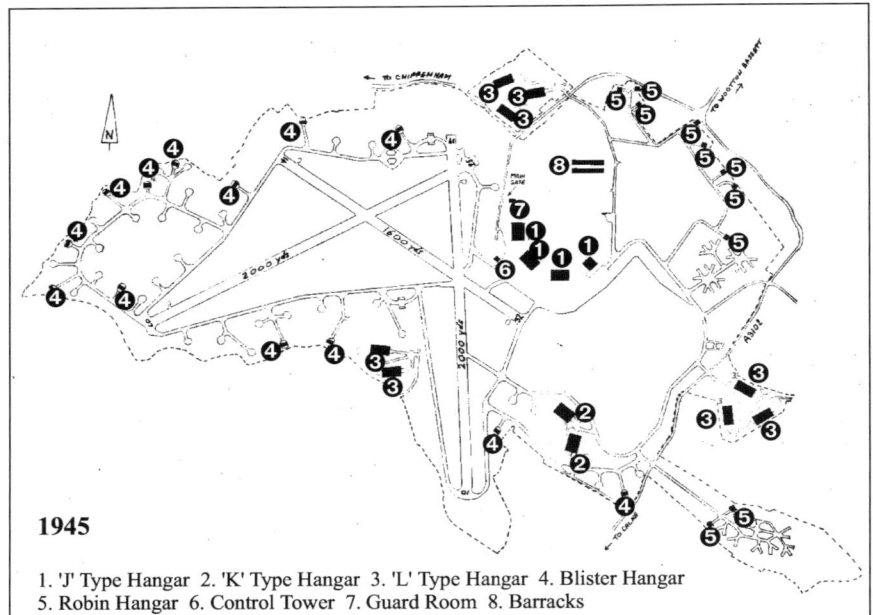

1945

1. 'J' Type Hangar 2. 'K' Type Hangar 3. 'L' Type Hangar 4. Blister Hangar
5. Robin Hangar 6. Control Tower 7. Guard Room 8. Barracks

As appearing in a copy of the Transport Command Route Book No.12 for May 1945.
Cty: The Rev Canon F.H. Davey RAF (Retd)

summer of 1941. W.E. Chivers & Sons of Devizes was awarded the contract for the building work. WAAF accommodation was in Lyneham village. The building construction coincided with work commencing on two new hard surface tarmac runways west of the existing landing ground. These were laid out NE/SW-2000 x 50 yds (07/25), extended, for the arrival of the Comet in June 1956, to 2600 yds, and NW/SE-1600 x 50 yds (14/32). They were completed in February 1942 and that summer work commenced on a third with a heading

N/S- 2000 x 50 yds (19/01). This runway has a slight bend in the centre caused possibly by construction having been started at both ends. During the war airfield lighting was Drem Mk.II with sodium light approaches and Standard Beam Approach was operating. The two-letter station identification code was YM, this was later changed to LA.

On 1st May 1949, additional barrack blocks with single rooms had been provided. These replaced some of the earlier 'Z' blocks, of which the first of

174

the type had been built at Lyneham. The first married quarters were also completed at about the same time. Possibly to coincide with the runway extension in 1956, a new Air Traffic Control was built, and next to it a new fire section. The end of the newly extended runway would not have been visible from the original control tower.

The war-time accommodation in use as a terminal building was replaced with a purpose built premises. Building work started in 1960 at a cost of £135,000. The terminal accommodated Operations, Customs and passenger handling. Unusually the Station Commander's Office was on the top floor, overlooking the aircraft apron. The building was officially opened on 5th April 1967 by the Chief of the Air Staff, ACM Sir Thomas Pike KCB, CBE, DFC. A new Officers' Mess and Airman's Restaurant had also been completed. A new Sgts' Mess, Medical Centre and Passenger Hotel followed. Possibly the T2 Type cargo hangar, next to the terminal building, was also built at this time.

The runway surfaces are tarmac on concrete. The two main ones were provided with the Instrument Landing System (ILS) at the same time as the new terminal building was constructed. The shorter 13/31 is no longer used for take-offs and landings.

With the 1956 extension of the main (07/25) runway, it was necessary to demolish two of the three original 'L' Type hangars close to the NE end. Whilst not directly in the path of the extension, they were close enough to form an operational hazard. Prior to construction of the runway extension, the main entrance to the station and the guardroom had been from a lane on the western side of the field. This then changed to the eastern side in Lyneham village where the entrance is in use today.

In 1958 some of the original dispersal pans were removed on the south side of runway 07/25, for the construction a larger dispersal, suitable for 4 Victor or Vulcan aircraft. Lyneham became one of the 18 stations, Boscombe Down was another in Wiltshire, designated as a dispersal airfield for the nuclear 'V' Force of the RAF. A number of huts were built at the dispersal so that the visitors would be self-contained and able to maintain a degree of isolation.

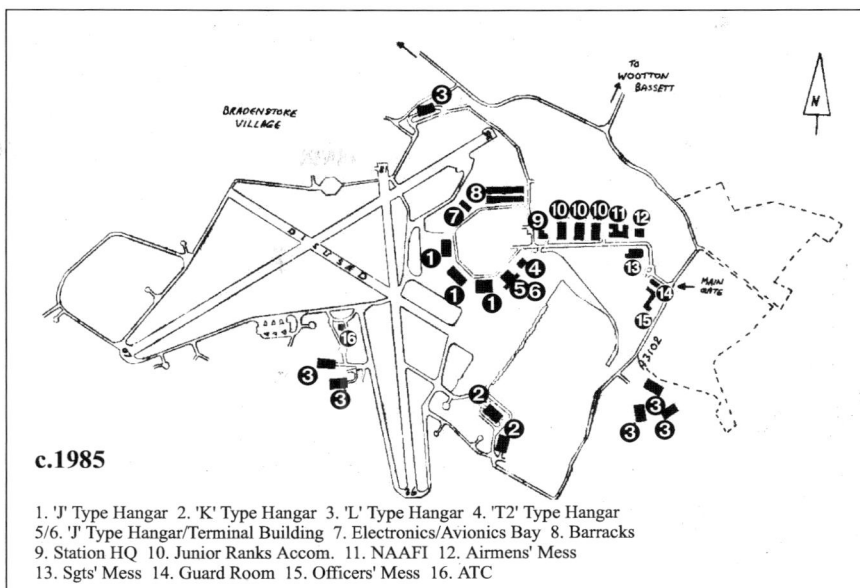

c.1985

1. 'J' Type Hangar 2. 'K' Type Hangar 3. 'L' Type Hangar 4. 'T2' Type Hangar
5/6. 'J' Type Hangar/Terminal Building 7. Electronics/Avionics Bay 8. Barracks
9. Station HQ 10. Junior Ranks Accom. 11. NAAFI 12. Airmens' Mess
13. Sgts' Mess 14. Guard Room 15. Officers' Mess 16. ATC

To accommodate Britannia training, a purpose built building was erected in which a simulator was installed. This came on line on the 21st March 1959, two days after the delivery of the first aircraft. Before receipt of the first Britannias, Lyneham's 'J' Type hangars required modification to facilitate the 37½ ft high tail. Basically this involved cutting the hangar door supporting structure and fitting additional doors that were closed after entry by the aircraft. The same arrangement was later needed for the C130 Hercules.

With the arrival of the Hercules fleet in 1967, new aprons were built to accommodate them on the south side of the 'J' Type hangars.

World War 2 Years

No.41 MU was redesignated No.33 Maintenance Unit in No.41 Group on 6th March 1940. Manned by service personnel, No.33 MU was renumbered because of the confusion the number was liable to cause in being used for both the MU and its parent Group. No.33 MU was officially formed on 18th May 1940 having an establishment of 4 officers, one other rank and 15 civilians. A number of essential vehicles were allocated. The role of the MU was for storing various types of new aircraft which at the time were not required for service use. The first aircraft, a Tiger Moth and an Albacore, arrived in June and by the end of that month the unit had 10 Proctor Is, 10 Tiger Moths, 10 Blenheim IVs, 6 Wellingtons and 2 Lysander IIs. Besides storing aircraft it had the task

of fitting them out with guns, radio etc prior to delivery. By September there were 150 aircraft of varying types at the MU which included the Glen-Martin (Maryland), Albecore, Queen Wasp and Masters but come the end of the year it was handling mainly Beaufighters, Bothas, Lysanders, Masters, Spitfires, Tiger Moths and Wellingtons.

The airfield attracted the attention of an enemy aircraft and in a raid on the 19th September 1940, four civilian workers were killed and the MU hangar they were building was damaged when two HE bombs were dropped. Incendiaries were also released and a machine gun attack made.

The increased number of aircraft at Lyneham generated the need to construct additional hardstandings. As with all airfields the vulnerability to enemy attack made it prudent to disperse some of the MU aircraft away from the main airfield site and three fields on the east side of the A3102 road were designated as Dispersal Areas for this purpose. No.33 MU also utilised for dispersals at various times, the nearby aerodrome at Yatesbury and the adjoining No.45 SLG Townsend, together with the larger No.31 SLG Everleigh, 2 miles east of RAF Upavon. From 21st May 1941, No.33 MU was one of the units controlled by No.52 (Maintenance) Wing, Southern Region in No.41 Group at Gatcombe Park near Stroud.

With the near completion of the wooden huts at Lyneham, No.14 Service Flying Training School specialising in twin engine training for prospective RAF and Commonwealth Bomber pilots, arrived with their fleet of 108 Airspeed Oxford trainers on 16th August 1941 from Cranfield in No.23 Group. Three days later, No.41 Group, Maintenance Command relinquished control of Lyneham to No.23 Group, Flying Training Command, although No.33 MU continued to operate at Lyneham. The day and night time flying activity now intensified considerably with four 10½ week courses running at the same time. There was a never ending procession of Oxfords in the circuit. The SFTS stayed for 6 months and during that time used the RLGs at Long Newnton and Wanborough to relieve the congestion at Lyneham. The inevitable crop of accidents occurred especially when pupils were low flying. On 17th September Oxford II N4774 flew into trees on the boundary of the airfield during an overshoot and was written off. There was fatalities on 7th October when two Oxfords, V3145 and V3947, collided in flight, crashed and were destroyed. On Wednesday 10th December Oxford I L4630 struck HT cables at Potterne near Devizes and crashed at Larborough Farm killing pilot instructor Sgt Arthur W. Jack RAFVR and his pupil, LAC Ronald C. Summerell RAFVR. Sgt Jack is buried at St Michael Churchyard, Lyneham and LAC Summerell at Holy Trinity New Churchyard in his home town of Nailsea, Somerset.

No.14 SFTS left for Ossington on 20th January 1942 to form No.14 (P)AFU, with Lyneham transferring to the control of No.44 Group, Ferry Command on 14th February 1942. From this date Lyneham was under the command of Gp Capt G.H. Cock. At that stage the station was set to become the centre for the training of aircrew engaged on ferry duties to overseas destinations and for the preparation and despatch of aircraft from MUs for overseas service.

On 27th February 1942 No.1445 Flt was formed at Lyneham for the preparation and despatch to the Middle East of 32 Liberator IIs for Nos.159 and 160 Sqns. Operating as the Liberator handling unit, it was also known as No.2 Flt, with a monthly output of 10 aircraft. Later on the Flt also despatched Halifaxes and Fortresses.

A logical step was taken at Lyneham to

site a Ferry Unit with the MU and so No.1 Flt Ferry Training Unit was formed on 12th March 1942, to undertake air despatch. An Air Despatch & Reception Unit formed in April 1942, remaining until disbanded there on 19th June 1944.

On 25th June 1942 No.1444 (Ferry Training) Flt arrived from Horsham St. Faith where it had been training crews for ferrying Hudsons overseas. It continued its training role at Lyneham.

No.1425 (Communications) Flt arriving from Honeybourne on 7th April 1942 with its 2 + 1 Liberator Is AM911, AM913 and AM922. These provided the first RAF air transport service to Cairo. The unit went on to specialise in providing a long distance military transport service. In June two additional Liberators from BOAC were added, and becoming, in the process, the route from which Transport Command developed.
Early flights were made from Honeybourne until suitable facilities were established at Lyneham in July 1944.

No.1425 (Communications) Flt with its Liberators, was used to transport VIPs to various parts of the globe, one of these being Prime Minister Winston Churchill. He was flown from Lyneham in a specially converted Liberator AL504 *Commando* to Moscow on 2nd August 1942 where he held talks on the 'second front' with Stalin. The pilot of *Commando* was William J. Vanderkloot, a 26 year old American who was in the RAF before America joined in the war. The route flown, took them between Portugal and the Azores and east to Gibraltar. Flying by friendly aircraft in the vicinity of the route was banned so that any flying observed by the pilot would be taken as being hostile. A day was spent in Gibraltar before taking-off with a fighter escort, flying south-east over North Africa, crossing the Sahara Desert and north into Cairo. The next few days were spent in Egypt discussing the campaign in North Africa and on 10th August special US envoy W. Averell Harriman, representing President Roosevelt, joined the Prime Minister. The flight was continued north-east across Jordan and Iraq to Tehran where a Soviet adviser joined the group for the last leg, north over the Caspian Sea to Moscow. Winston Churchill arrived back at

Lyneham on 24th August 1942. Churchill asked for the same pilot on other flights he made during the war and so the following year Vanderkloot found himself piloting *Commando* to Casablanca, Middle East, Turkey, Cyprus and Tripoli.

No. 511 Sqn

This squadron had one of the longest periods of service of any squadron at Lyneham. It covered a period of 32 years over three terms, the first of which are covered over the next few pages.

On 10th October 1942, No.511 Sqn formed at Lyneham from No.1425 (Communication) Flt which had been considerably expanded. The squadron, commanded by Wg Cdr W. J. Pickard, was engaged in the carriage of passengers and freight to and from Gibraltar, Malta and the Middle East and often returned with ferry crews no longer required out there. No.511 Sqn was equipped with the Liberator I and II and with 3 Albemarle Is P1449, P1451 and P1453 from November 1942. The crews for these were drawn from RAF Lyneham. The Albemarles and crews were detached to Gibraltar from where they were used for mail services to Libya and Algeria. On Saturday 21st November P1451 left empty from Gibraltar en route for the UK and crashed into the sea shortly after a night take-off. Flt Lt Gordon W. Thorougood RAF (Capt), Flt Sgt Leo C. Webster RNZAF (2nd pilot), Flt Sgt Denison C. Henderson RNZAF (nav) and Sgt Henney (WOP) were killed. The name of the Captain appears on the Gibraltar Memorial and those of the New Zealanders on the Malta Memorial. Flt Sgt Webster had only just joined the squadron, having served with A&AEE Handling Sqn at Boscombe Down.

Two weeks prior to this, on Friday 6th November, another crash claimed the lives of a squadron crew. Liberator AL595 crashed ½ mile SE of Lyneham during a night training flight. The crew were Flt Lt George J. Le Mar RAF (Capt), Fg Off Samuel A. B. Gordon RAF (2nd pilot), Fg Off John H. Fuller RAFVR (nav), Fg Off Deiniol Davies RAFVR (WOP/AG) and Sgt Gilbert H. Gregg RAFVR (WOP/AG). Both of the pilots were buried at St Michael's Church, Lyneham.

On 17th October 1942, No.511 Sqn Detachment (Gibraltar) was formed at Lyneham and was carried by air to RAF Station North Front, Gibraltar. The function of the detachment, commanded by Flt Lt A. A. J. Sanders DFC, was to carry all freight from the west to Malta. The preliminary target was 80,000lbs per month. The unit was equipped with 2 Liberator IIs AL516 and AL561. The heavy long-range bombers were adapted for the carriage of freight but retained their defensive armament of a tail turret mounted with 4 light machine guns. On 31st October, one of the two Liberators, AL516, crashed into the sea on its approach to Gibraltar from Malta. Of the 34 passengers on board 14 were killed, but the rest of them, together with Capt Flt Lt R. Walton and his crew, were rescued by personnel on the airfield, although all on board suffered injuries. Some of the aircraft's cargo was salvaged before the Liberator was taken to deep water and sunk.

Due to the early losses, Halifaxes DT542, DT543 and W1229 were seconded for six months from No.138 Sqn and these arrived at Lyneham on 2nd December 1942. They were used principally on the supply operation to the Mediterranean. The aircraft attachments were for specific flights and in between would be returned to their own squadron until required again. DT542 NF-Q was lost at Malta on 17th December 1942. It took-off from Luqa, having staged through Malta from Cairo, and crashed at 0230 hrs just beyond the runway at Zeitun. All on the aircraft were killed and buried at Capuccini Naval Cemetery. They were Fg Off K.L. Dobromirski PAF (pilot), Fg Off S. Pankiewicz PAF, Fg Off Z.A. Idzikowski PAF, Flt Sgt O. F. Zielinski PAF, Flt Sgt A. E. Kleniewski PAF, Sgt R. Wysocki PAF, Sgt D. Spibey, Sgt A. C. Watt, Cpl D. S. Hounslow, LAC R. Clegg, Sqn Ldr J.H. Wedgwood, Flt Lt F.G. T. P. Earle, Flt Lt L. A. Vaughan, LAC C. D. Brown, Maj Lord A. A. B. Apsley DSO, RAC and Maj A. D. C. Millar, Indian Army.

No.161 Sqn also provided Halifaxes DG244 and DG245 and these operated to the Middle East on 6th December 1942.

During 1943 the Liberators and Albemarles of No.511 Sqn were to be used for the evacuation of civilians

Winston Churchill with ACM Sir Charles Portal at Lyneham, on return from Operation *Static*, visiting Casablanca, Middle East, Turkey, Cyprus and Tripoli.
Photo: Imperial War Museum (CH8550)

from Malta but on 13th January 1943, 3 Liberators were required to transport some very important VIPs on Operation *Static*. AL504 flown by Capt Van Der Kloot took-off for Casablanca from Stanton Harcourt and AM919 piloted by Sqn Ldr J. F. Sach DFC, AFC and AM922 piloted by Flt Lt R. Walton MC, took-off from Lyneham. The passengers carried were PM Winston Churchill, ACM Sir Charles Portal; Admiral Sir Dudley Pound, 1st Sea Lord; General Sir Alan Brooke, Chief of the Imperial General Staff; Lord Louis Mountbatten, Air Marshal J. O. Slessor, C-in-C Coastal Command and Lord Leathers, Minister for War Transport. AL504 and AM919 returned to Lyneham on 1st February.

Liberator AM913 crashed at Talbenny on Friday 29th January 1943 when returning from Mediouna via Gibraltar. The No.4 engine caught fire and fell out over the sea. The No.3 cut out on approach to land. The result was that the aircraft ran up the side of a hill and broke up as it crossed a sunken dyke. A passenger, Brigadier Vivian Dykes CBE, RE was killed and two others on board, Brigadier Guy M. Stewart RE and a supernumerary pilot Fg Off Kenneth C. R. Maskell RAFVR, died from their injuries.

On 16th February 1943, No.511 Sqn was expanded with the formation of 'C' Flt. Sqn Ldr Pascall DFC was appointed CO and 6 Albemarles were allocated P1475, P1510, P1520, P1556, P1561 and P1564. The role of

the Flt was to maintain regular mail services between UK-Gibraltar-UK. Three days later the squadron aircraft establishment changed from 10+0 Liberators and 6+0 Albemarles, to include 20+5 Yorks.

The squadron was now to experience a number of losses over the sea, the first was Liberator AL587 which went missing between Gibraltar and the UK on Tuesday 23rd March 1943. It was carrying freight and 13 passengers including AVM Robert P.M. Witham CB, OBE, MC. The crew were Flt Lt Geoffrey T. R. Francis RAFVR, Flt Sgt Carlo E. Ferro RCAF, Fg Off John S. Renouf RCAF, Sgt Richard P. Marvin RAFVR, Sgt Lloyd G. Burry RAFVR and Fg Off Ronald S. Tedder RAFVR. The names of the crew and the AVM are commemorated on the Runnymede Memorial.

Albemarle P1556 with Plt Off Thurston, Sgt R.V. Jones (co-pilot) and two other crew crashed into the sea, following an engine failure, after taking off from Gibraltar on 30th April. All were injured, but with no fatalities. The Albemarle gained a reputation in various theatres of the war, for suddenly dropping out of the sky, the cause usually associated with an engine malfunction.

On 24th May 1943, General Sikorski head of the Polish Government in exile, together with his daughter Chief of the Polish Women's Auxiliary and other mainly Polish officials, left Lyneham for a tour of the Middle East, visiting Polish troops. They flew in Liberator II AL523 of No.511 Sqn, the Captain was Flt Lt Edward M. Prchal Czechoslovakian Air Force. The tour lasted for six weeks and the party with the same aircraft and crew left Cairo West on 3rd July, staging through Gibraltar where they were overnight guests of the Governor. Three additional passengers had boarded at Cairo, Brigadier J.P. Whitley RA and two civilians, Mr Pinder and Walter H. Lock, both thought to have been agents with the Secret Service.

At 2310hrs on Sunday 4th July Liberator II AL523, with 11 passengers and 6 crew took off from Gibraltar for return to the UK. The aircraft cleared the end of the runway but then crashed into the sea. The only survivor was the Captain. He was quickly rescued along with the bodies of General Sikorski and his Chief-of-Staff. Some bodies were never found. The crew who died were Sqn Ldr Wilfred S. Herring DSO, DFM, RAF (2nd pilot, attached from No.104 OTU), WO Lewis Zalsberg RAFVR (nav), Sgt Francis S. Kelly RAF (Flt Eng), Flt Sgt G.B.R. Gerry RAF (WOP/AG), Flt Sgt Dobson Hunter RAFVR (WOP/AG). The navigator was buried at Gibraltar (North Front) Jewish Cemetery and the names of Sgt Kelly and Flt Sgt Gerry appear on the Gibraltar Memorial. Their bodies were recovered and buried at sea. The names of the other two appear on the Runnymede Memorial. The Court of Inquiry set up to establish the cause, opened at Air HQ in Gibraltar. The Court heard from Flt Lt Prchal that after take off and at about 150ft, he levelled off to gain speed but when he then tried to climb, the control column was locked. The aircraft then hit the water. Various theories have been raised about this inexplicable incident including sabotage but the official reason was put down to human error.

On Tuesday 10th August 1943, Albemarle P1433 also went missing over the sea after taking off from Gibraltar. The crew lost were Fg Off D.G.W. Clarke (pilot), Flt Lt Kiddmay, Fg Off Albert W. Little RCAF, Fg Off Jack C. Valder RAAF, Cpl Keith T. Alexander RAF. The names of Fg Off Little, Fg Off Valder and Cpl Alexander appear on the Malta Memorial.

On 3rd July 1943 Wg Cdr C.E. Slee MVO, AFC was posted in from A&AEE Boscombe Down to command the squadron.

In October the squadron received 4 Douglas Dakotas from No.512 Sqn. On 30th November FL515, with Capt WO John H. Gillies RAFVR, Plt Off J. Bennet RAFVR (co-pilot), 2 other crew and 8 passengers, crashed into the sea after taking off from Portreath, resulting in the deaths of all on board. The names of both officers appear on the Runnymede Memorial. The loading of the aircraft may have been a factor in the crash.

In November additional Avro York Is started to arrive, the first of which MW100 and MW 101 were VIP versions. They were flown on special VIP flights to the Middle East until February 1944 when they were allocated to Northolt. Two passenger versions, MW104 and MW106 and a freighter MW105 replaced them. These were used for flights to North Africa, the Far East and the Mediterranean.

Between December 1943 and February 1944 the Sqn's Albemarles were replaced by additional Dakotas, giving an allocation at that time of 19 Dakotas and 2 Albemarles. Dakotas FL586 and FL597 were allocated for training purposes on 30th March 1944, this coinciding with the last Albemarle P1561 being struck off squadron strength.

Liberator AL545 caught fire in J3 hangar on 7th May 1944. Although the aircraft was completely burnt out the hangar was not severely damaged.

On 3rd June a ceremonial parade was held on the station to mark the occasion of the presentation of the No.511 Sqn crest. The presentation was made to the squadron CO, Wg Cdr C.E. Slee, by ACM Sir Frederick Bowhill GBE, KCB, CMG, DSO. This was one of Wg Cdr Slee's final squadron duties before a posting on 26th June to No.229 (Transport) Group at New Delhi in India. His replacement was Wg Cdr E. W. Whitaker DFC, AFC on posting from No.282 Wing.

By mid July 1944 the squadron aircraft strength comprised 'A' Flt. 13 Yorks and 'B' Flt. 12 Liberator VIIs (C-87s). The Dakotas were now surplus to

requirements but continued to be held pending delivery of the Liberator allocation. 7 more arrived together with 5 Yorks during August and further Yorks in November. The squadron lost its first York when it was written off following a crash landing at Gibraltar on 26th July. This was MW119 en route from Northolt with senior officers of Transport Command. The captain, Flt Lt C. Halse AFC, with most of his crew and the passengers suffered injuries.

In October 9 Liberators were transferred to No.246 Sqn which was reforming at Lyneham from a nucleus from No.511 Sqn.

ACM Sir Trafford Leigh-Mallory, KCB, CB, DSO was appointed Air Commander for South East Asia in August 1944. No.511 Sqn supplied the aircraft which was to take him and his wife to Kandy, Ceylon where he was to take-up his new appointment. The aircraft, York I MW126, was practically new, having made only one flight abroad before allocation to Leigh-Mallory. He selected his own crew for the flight which included as Flt Eng, Fg Off Alfred J. Enser RAFVR, of No.511 Sqn. The Captain, from No.228 Sqn equipped with Sunderlands, was Sqn Ldr Charles G.D. Lancaster DFC*, RAF, who flew the York from Lyneham to Northolt on 3rd November. Other crew members were Flt Lt Peter Chinn RAFVR (2nd pilot), Flt Lt Keith A. Mooring RAFVR (nav), Flt Lt John A. Casey RAAF (WOP) and Sgt. Harold J. Chandler RAFVR (steward). Two fitters also flew, Cpl John Ellis RAF and LAC John C. Burnett RAFVR.

The York with Leigh-Mallory, his wife and crew took-off at 0907hrs on Tuesday 14th November and with an escort of 7 Spitfires of No.313 Sqn headed for the English Channel on a 1,120 nautical mile journey. At 0925hrs the escort broke off and returned to base. There was soon a rapid deterioration in the weather with heavy snow and thick cloud. It was so bad that the pilot of a No.24 Sqn Dakota, flying from Lyneham to Naples, turned back. This pilot reported seeing a York flying south at 1000hrs and this almost certainly was MW126. This was the last official sighting of Leigh-Mallory's aircraft which crashed into the Le Ferrouillet mountains, 12 miles east of Grenoble and 130 miles north of the intended flight path. All ten on board were killed. Despite numerous searches the crash site was not discovered until Monday 4th June 1945, following the thaw in the region. The bodies were recovered and buried at Allemont (Le Rivier) Communal Cemetery, Isere in France. At the Court of Inquiry convened on 23rd November 1944 there was insufficient evidence to determine the primary cause of the aircraft's disappearance but contributory factors were the extreme weather conditions and the pilot's inexperience on type.

On Wednesday 5th December 1944 York MW116 caught fire on the tarmac whilst being defuelled. In their efforts to limit the fire spread Sgt Alexander J. Crammond and Sgt Patinson suffered severe burns from which the former died from his injuries the following day in the RAF hospital at Wroughton. Only the aircraft cowling was slightly damaged by fire.

On Thursday 1st February 1945 this same aircraft ditched, owing to a fuel shortage, off Isola Di Lampedusa, an island midway between Malta and Tunisia. The Captain Flt Lt A. Eaton-Clarke, Fg Off A.V.J. Veonieux (2nd pilot), Flt Lt J.W. Holloway (nav) and Cpl H.J. Burge (Steward) were injured. WO William Wright RAF (WOP), Flt Sgt Alfred C.J. Walker RAFVR (Flt Eng), Fg Off Arthur Appleby RAFVR (AG) and 14 passengers were killed. Some of these were the Prime Minister's staff travelling to the Yalta Conference. WO Wright was buried at Medjez-el-Bab War Cemetery in Tunisia and Flt Sgt Walker at Imtarfar Military Cemetery in Malta. The name of Fg Off Appleby apears on the Runnymede Memorial.

The squadron aircrew expressed genuine concern with the characteristics of the York during take-off in hot climatic conditions. It was a subject raised during squadron briefings over a number of months from June 1945. Another 'gripe' at the time was the poor conditions experienced by crews staging through Karachi. If there was no room for the crews in the No.2 Mess, they had to use tents. The billets, food and transport facilities for passengers were likewise of an inferior standard. Karachi was felt to be the 'blackest' of staging posts by squadron personnel.

Lancaster BI PP780 was allocated to

the squadron from No.41 Gp and arrived at Lyneham on 19th July 1945. The squadron was allocated a Lancastrian C2 in October 1945 and it remained on the squadron strength until April 1946.

The squadron experienced another aircraft lost at sea when York I MW125 was forced down over the Bay of Bengal, about 100 miles west of Penang, en route from Lyneham to Singapore on Sunday 6th October 1946. The aircraft was carrying squadron ground support personnel, and contact was lost when it was about 30 minutes flying time from Penang. An initial search was called off when no trace of the York was found but later a Sunderland flying boat landed within the search area and found wreckage. The crew who were lost were former No.635 Sqn Lancaster bomber pilot Flt Lt Donald H. Courtenay DFC, RAFVR (Capt), Fg Off David J. Johns RAFVR (co-pilot) and Fg Off Wilfred W. Armstrong RNZAF (nav). Other squadron members who died were Flt Lt Clifford J. McPherson DFC, RAFVR who was awarded his DFC serving on Lancasters with No.582 Sqn, WO Leonard Sawkins RAFVR, WO Raymond J. N. Bowerman RAFVR, Flt Sgt Ivan Kendrick RAFVR, Flt Sgt John J. Leitch RAF, Sgt Timothy C. Murphy RAFVR, Cpl Ronald Kirk RAFVR, LACs Tom Bone, Donald Cowell, Maldwin W. Davies, Roy L. M. Stilwell, James F. Latham, Granville R. Pritchard, AC1s Francis N. Beckett, Ronald C. Clarke, Francis Flood, AC2s George A. Griffiths and William N. Westbury, all RAFVR. Their names are displayed on the Runnymede Memorial. The cause of accident was unknown but as a result of the loss, a recommendation was made that an air sea rescue launch unit of at least two large speed sea-going launches be based in the Penang/Phuket Island area.

No.511 Sqn disbanded on 7th October 1946.

From 3rd November 1942, a re-structuring took place with No.1 Flt Ferry Training Unit, Nos.1444 and 1445 Flts amalgamating to form No.301 FTU at Lyneham. The Unit comprising three Flts 'A' Flt. (ex No.1 Flt) with Blenheim Vs, Beaufighters, Beauforts and Wellingtons, 'B' Flt. (ex No.1444 Flt) with Hudsons and 'C' Flt (ex No.1445 Flt) with Halifaxes and

Liberators. One of these aircraft, Hudson FK673, was lost on 24th February 1943 when it was destroyed by fire inside one of the hangers. Gp Capt G.N.J. Stanley Turner was CO of the unit and was later succeeded by Gp Capt W.J. Pickard. The duties of this unit were the preparation of aircraft and training of ferry crews for despatch to the Middle and Far East. During February 1943, 8 Halifaxes and 9 Hudsons were despatched to North Africa, 2 Liberators, 2 Mosquitos, 6 Wellingtons and 27 Blenheim Vs to India, 26 Beauforts to the Middle East with 51 Beaufighters to North Africa and the Middle East. These aircraft from Lyneham staged through Portreath before crossing the Bay of Biscay on route to Gibraltar. A number of such aircraft were lost during these crossings, some falling to attacks from German fighters and others ditching because of mechanical defects. A number in trouble did manage to divert to neutral countries, as did Halifax BB322 on 10th April when it landed at San Fernando near Cadiz in Southern Spain. Operations and training by the FTU continued to develop during 1943. As a result of its early ferrying role, the station was becoming established as a terminal airfield for international flights.

Other aircraft at Lyneham at this time including the Whitley, Maryland, and smaller single engined aircraft such as the Lysander, Tiger Moth, Proctor and Miles Master.

On 25th March 1943 Transport Command was formed under the command of ACM Sir Frederick Bowhill, the new Command absorbing Ferry Command.

The fledgling BOAC operated from Lyneham between 1942 and 1944, flying VIPs and civilian services to various world-wide destinations. The BOAC operations were under the control of the RAF who made available for the airline's use one of the 'K' type hangers. As with Ferry Command, BOAC were using three Liberator Is, one of which was accidentally shot down by a RAF night fighter when flying back from Cairo on 15th February 1942. Another of the airline's Liberators was used on 10th June 1943 for the inaugural Lyneham to Moscow service. Other long haul operations soon followed with Lyneham to Karachi becoming a regular scheduled service. For urgent missions BOAC used the fast unarmed DH Mosquito's and for less urgent trips, unarmed and unescorted DC3s were flown. From November 1943 the company were provided with a BI Lancaster DV379 and this was often seen at Lyneham in use as a test bed and registered as G-AGJI. BOAC received the first of its Yorks G-AGJA (MW103) on 21st February 1944 and in April a second G-AGJB (MW108) was used on the inaugural Lyneham-Morocco-Cairo service. The aircraft of BOAC were painted in military camouflage but carried civil registration markings.

In the mean time, No.33 MU had been the subject of a policy change in 1943, with the unit playing an important role as a Spitfire holding unit from which supplies were made to the Fighter Command squadrons. On 3rd June 1943 a stock of 240 Spitfires of various Mks was held, together with a number of Seafires. In August 1943, Parent Preparation Units were evolved, these being responsible for the preparation of specific aircraft types. Allocated to No.33 MU, in addition to its Spitfire role, was the storage of the US built Beech C-43 Traveller, a utility and communications biplane, and the assembly of the Hamilcar glider of the General Aircraft Ltd. The Company constructed the first 22 gliders but then bulk orders were manufactured as sub-assembly parts by the Co-operative Wholesale Society, the Birmingham Railway Carriage and Wagon Company and AC Motors Ltd. At Lyneham, these largest of tank carrying gliders were assembled in two 'J' and 'K' type hangers. By the end of 1944, 179 had been prepared with most being used in the major airborne operations. In the early part of 1945 a special flight of three Halifax aircraft was formed to carry out test flying of these heavy gliders. No.33 MU's association with the type did not cease with the end of the war and converting Hamilcars to the powered Mk 10s continued until the end of 1951.

The MU used nearby Calne Railway Station for despatching some of their damaged aircraft, and aircraft engines were sent out weekly, some crated for shipment abroad. Air Movements

One of the Spitfire fuselages from Lyneham loaded on to a Parrot 20 ton wagon in Calne Station goods yard. The wagon for transporting aircraft was the railway version of the RAF Queen Mary road transporter. Photo: Donald Lovelock

Section baggage arrived at Lyneham by air from overseas and was sent out again by rail from Calne to various RAF establishments. Coffins of those killed in service were dispatched by rail to the home towns of the deceased. They were carried with great respect in cleaned out parcel vans with whitened windows. In-coming freight for Lyneham included aircraft-towing tractors, buses, jeeps, coal, coke, goods for the NAAFI and for the married quarters. The weekends were a busy time for the railway staff at Calne with RAF personnel leaving on weekend pass and returning again for Monday duty. Bank Holidays likewise would provide for a mass exodus. At the end of the war there was an occasion when a complete train of Spitfires for disposal was sent out by rail.

No.1 Ferry Crew Pool in No.44 Group formed at Lyneham on 1st August 1943 from a Ferry Crew Pool formerly at Filton. It arrived with 70 crews and was immediately expanded to 150 crews. The Pool was equipped with three Wellington IIIs. It moved to Melton Mowbray on 14th January 1944.

No.1577 Flt was formed at Llandow on 9th August 1943 as a Trials and Transport Flight, to carry out special tests with Halifax Vs and Lancaster IIIs under Indian conditions. The unit operated under the control of No.221 (Bomber) Group. The Flight moved to Lyneham on 1st September and consisted of four crews. The pilots were Sqn Ldr J.H. Leyland DFC* as CO, Flt Lt Middleton, Fg Off Stewart RCAF and Fg Off Richardson RAAF. Two days later the first aircraft arrived for the Flt, this was Halifax DK524. Due to the lack of facilities at Lyneham, the Flt moved back to

Llandow on 4th September 1943.

The USAAF used Lyneham at various times during 1944 for airlifting the massive supplies necessary to equip the Allied Forces in Europe. On 3rd September, 30 8th Air Force B-24s and 20 B-17s arrived and together with a force of C-47s they airlifted vast quantities of fuel in cans to the continent. The fuel which had been stock-piled in a store near Swindon was necessary because of a failure with the Pluto pipeline system. The airlift continued through the month and at its peak 358 flights left Lyneham on one day. In November and December around 70 C-47 flights a day were leaving with PSP tracking for use as runway material on forward airstrips as the Allies progressed towards Germany.

An unnecessary accident with loss of life occurred to a Lyneham Beaufighter on Thursday 7th October 1943 when it crashed near Combe Down in Bath during a deliberate low flying 'beat-up' of a girlfriend's home. Sgt Derrick Hunt (pilot) and his navigator were both killed.

Four (Forward) Staging Posts in No.44 Group were resident at Lyneham in early 1944. No.91 formed there on 10th January and departed for Broadwell on 23rd February. No.92 arrived from Doncaster on 26th January and also left for Broadwell the same day as No.91. On 15th January Nos. 93 and 94 FSPs formed at Lyneham. No.93 left for Blakehill Farm on 1st June and No.94 to Broadwell on 19th February.

On 5th February 1944 the Transport Command Base Unit arrived from Weston Zoyland where the previous year it had formed as a static administration party for Transport squadrons based there from time to time. It disbanded at Lyneham two days after its arrival.

No.525 Sqn flying Warwick Is, later Dakotas, the Stirling III and Warwick IIIs, moved in from Weston Zoyland to join No.511 Sqn on 6th February 1944. The squadron was commanded by Wg Cdr D. R. Miller. The Warwicks were used on scheduled services to Istres, Elmas, Maison Blanche and Rabat

Sale, calling also at St. Mawgan and Gibraltar. On 17th April Warwick HG247 crashed into the sea on take off from St. Mawgan resulting in the deaths of the crew and twelve passengers. Because of this accident it was decided to cease using the type so conversion to Dakotas took place in June. The following were allocated to the squadron Dakota I FD944, FD945, Dakota III FL517, FL546, FL547, FL562, FL563, FL649, KG731, KG733, KG735, KG737, KG741, KG744, KG751, KG774, KJ966, KJ970, KJ971, KJ970, KJ972 and KK156.

A Stirling III LJ312 arrived on 24th May for evaluation by No.525 Sqn, departing on 27th July. Stirling IIIs were part of the squadron establishment in July as were Warwick IIIs the following month. The Squadron was at Lyneham until 15th July 1945 before moving to Membury, east of Swindon.

On 16th March 1944 No.301 FTU moved to Pershore where it amalgamated with No.1 Ferry Crew Pool.

With the formation of Transport Command on 25th March 1943, Lyneham became part of its structure on 24th July 1944. This was following the formation of No.116 (Transport) Wing on 1st January 1944, to take over scheduled services to India from No.44 Group.

No.246 Sqn reformed from a nucleus of No.511 Sqn at Lyneham on 11th October 1944. Seven crews were posted to the squadron which was commanded by Sqn Ldr P. H. L. Barclay pending the appointment of Wg Cdr Lombard seven days later. Nine C-87 Consolidated Liberator VIIs were allocated intended for operating the U.1 Air Route to India. The aircraft were EW612, EW613, EW617, EW624, EW626, EW627, EW630, EW631 and EW633.

The first flight to India using EW627 with Capt Fg Off J. J. Vaughan, took-off on 19th October but two days later it crashed at Karachi while being flown by a slip crew of No.511 Sqn. The aircraft overshot on landing, caught fire and burnt out. Flt Lt D.R. Bagnell and his crew survived but four passengers were killed.

An Avro York with passenger arrivals in 1945
Photo: Imperial War Museum (CH16268).

Arrivals boarding a bus to London in 1945
Photo: Imperial War Museum (CH16271)

In November the squadron received 4 Halifax IIIs. These were titled the Halifax Development Flt and became 'C' Flt. The task of the HDF was to evaluate the conditions under which passengers could be carried in this type of aircraft. No.246 Sqn moved to Holmsley South on 1st December 1944. Regular passenger carrying flights to India commenced on 17th January 1945 with Halifax NA683 leaving Lyneham on the UK-Istres-Cairo service. A second flight was made on 21st January by Halifax NA769.

BOAC moved its operations to Hurn when their new terminal came on line there on 1st November 1944 but they continued to use Lyneham for maintenance of Liberator and York aircraft.

Lyneham had hosted diversionary aircraft at various times, occasionally returning from raids over enemy territory. This was the case on 19th December when 38 B-17s and 8 B-24s landed after a bombing operation. On 24th December 8 Stirling IVs of

No.161 Sqn in No.3 Group based at Tempsford put down following a spoof raid to cause confusion to the Germans in their offensive opened up in the Ardenns Salient.

No.150 Staging Post in No.47 Group formed at Lyneham on 12th January 1945 for despatch by sea and air to Sechi, Crimea in connection with the Yalta Conference. The unit was disbanded the following month. On 22nd January, 7 Dakotas of No.525 Sqn took off conveying supplies to the Crimea so that No.150 Staging Post could be implemented for the Yalta Conference. Other flights in connection with the conference were flown later by Nos. 24, 246, 511 and 525 Sqns.

On 19th February, the VVIP Skymaster EW999 with York LV633 'Ascalon', brought the Prime Minister and other dignitaries back from the Yalta Conference. They landed at Lyneham having diverted from Northolt.

Bowood House near Calne on the A4, the home of Lord Shalbourne, was being used at this stage of the war as an RAF Transport Command guesthouse, which must have been very popular with both civilian and service personnel flying in and out of Lyneham.

Post War Years

With the termination of hostilities in Europe in 1945, Lyneham became very busy with flights leaving to bring home troops and equipment. The number of aircraft held by No.33 MU increased rapidly and by the end of 1946, 700 plus were being stored, the majority of which were Spitfires.

On 10th October 1945 a long range Meteorological Reconnaissance Flight No.1409 equipped with 7 Mosquito XVIs arrived from Upwood where it had been with No.139 Sqn in No.8 (PFF) Group. Its role was to gather weather data on the emerging civilian air routes. It partially re-equipped with Liberators before being disbanded on 13th May 1946.

A No.46 Sqn Stirling C.5 PJ904 from Stoney Cross, piloted by Flt Lt Gray making a GCA landing in the late afternoon of 23rd November 1945, was involved in a serious accident. In poor visibility it failed to touch down on the runway but came down beside it, from where it crashed into some wooden buildings, the canteen, the Operations Block and destroyed the Operations & Briefing Room. The Duty Operations Officer and a female canteen worker were killed and three others injured. The aircraft was a write off but none of the crew was injured.

On 1st December 1945, No.1359 Transport Command VIP Flight formed at Lyneham, equipped mainly with Lancastrians and Yorks. As of January 1946 it was equipped with four of each. The Flight staying until 25th February 1946 when it moved to Bassingbourn.

No.6 (Mobile) Radio Aids Training Flt

Stirling PJ904 close to the Watch Tower, having crashed on landing.
Photo: Norman Parker

moved in from Waterbeach in July 1946 equipped with the Oxford and left for Full Sutton on 24th October.

A re-organisation resulted on 16th October 1946, with No.246 Sqn disbanding into No.511 Sqn. The No.511 Sqn CO at the time, Wg Cdr W.S.R. Hughes, was posted on 11th October and replaced by Wg Cdr R.J. Burrough DFC.

During 1946 between 500 and 700 passengers per month were being flown from Lyneham to the Far East by Transport Command.

Lyneham Station Flt with code N7 had two Avro Ansons allocated for use as 'hacks'. They arrived in November 1947 and remained until September 1954.

On 17th November 1947 Nos.99 and 206 Sqns were reformed at Lyneham equipped with the four-engined Avro York CIs which were able to carry 20 passengers or 8000lb of freight. These together with No.511 Sqn, also equipped with Yorks, would be used on supply runs in Germany the following year, from their detached base at Wunstorf in the British sector.

No.206 Sqn carried out trunk route services, transporting freight, mail and passengers to Fayid, Tengah, Palam, Mauripur, Istres and Habbaniyah. 'Specials' were flown, on occasions, with passengers and freight to Gibraltar and Ballykelly.

No.99 Sqn likewise operated trunk route services to similar destinations. On 4th July 1948, the squadron lost the six-man crew of York C.1 MW248 when it collided with a civilian SAS DC-6, SE-BDA on approach to Northolt and crashed at Shrubs Corner, Harefield in Middlesex. The aircraft was on a flight from Tengah, staging through Malta, to Lyneham. The York was diverted to Northolt but having descended in bad weather near Reading and flying in thick cloud, it collided with the DC-6 which had failed to land because of the weather conditions over London and was returning to Amsterdam. The Lyneham crew who died were Flt Lt George R. Coates DFC, Flt Lt John K. Nowrie DFC, Flt Lt Cyril Ingleby DFC, Flt Lt William T. Trotman DFC, Signaller Harold G. Lewis and Engineer John I. Rees. A passenger on the aircraft was Sir Gerald E. J. Gent H.M. High

Commissioner for Malaya who was also killed. The death toll on the DC-6 was 32.

From 24th June 1948, Russia imposed a blockade on surface communications between Germany's western zone and its old capital in an attempt to prevent the British, Americans and French from unifying the western part of Germany. It was necessary for the Allied Air Forces to use every available aircraft to ferry vital supplies into the besieged city. The British and Americans was the two Major Powers sustaining the airlift, the French government dissociated itself from all responsibility. Although there was no practical input from the French they did support all decisions made by the British and American governments.

The Berlin Airlift as it became known, was a massive operation code named *Plainfare* by the British, which from 1st July and over the following twelve months kept Lyneham aircraft fully involved assisting the delivery of 400,000 tons of supplies. On occasions refugees were brought out of Berlin on the return flights. The airlift was given top priority over all Transport Command's other duties. The majority of the world wide scheduled services were cancelled and all routine training ceased. Training of aircrew for the Berlin run was undertaken at Lyneham which was also one of the three UK bases used as an aircraft pool from where they were issued as required to German airfields. In addition to the three Lyneham squadrons, some of the others from the RAF participating were Nos. 24, 51 and 242 Sqns, also with Avro Yorks, Nos.47 and 297 Sqns with Handley Page Hastings C.1s, Nos.30, 46, 53, 77, 238 Sqns and No.240 O.C.U. flying Dakotas. The Hastings squadrons operated from Schleswigland and the Dakota squadrons initially from Wunstorf before being transferred to Fassberg and later still to Lubeck. Coastal Command's flying-boats of Nos. 201 and 230 Sqns supplemented the land based units by flying in and out of Lake Havel which lay on the edge of Berlin. The corrosion proof hulls of the Short Sunderland GR V flying boats were ideal for the task of carrying salt of which many tons were flown from a depot at Finkenwerder on Hamburg's Elbe River to Havel Lake, Berlin. This supply route was only halted on 15th December 1948 when the river froze. Colerne was almost a ghost station during this period of its history, although the Yorks were returned for servicing, and personnel on detachment were rotated for leave purposes.

Aircraft were required to adhere strictly to a designated flight-corridor and this was often hazardous with some aircraft pilots reporting aggressive action by aircraft such as the cannon firing Yak-9 fighters of the Russians. Other harassing tactics employed by the Russian aircraft was dazzling the pilots of aircraft making their landing approach, by shining searchlights on them. In addition flares were directed at the aircraft, radios jammed and on occasions they were met by ground fire. By a 1945 agreement, all non Russian air traffic between Berlin and the West had to use 3 x 20 mile wide, 10,000 ft. high corridors. These led directly from Berlin to Hamburg (Northern Corridor), Berlin to Hanover (Central Corridor) and Berlin to Frankfurt (Southern Corridor). The Anglo/American airlift used 7 West German bases, from Schleswig up near the Danish border to Rheine/Main (Frankfurt) in the south. The North and South Corridors were used for all flights into Berlin and the Central Corridor for all return trips, except that Hamburg and Schleswig aircraft used the Northern Corridor both ways. Wunstorf aircraft flew into Berlin via the Northern and returned along the Central Corridor, which led almost directly to base. The complexity of the operation can easily be appreciated. Celle and Fassberg were two busy bases on the central corridor used by both the RAF and the USAF whose code name for the airlift was Operation *Vittles*. Many civilian companies were utilised on this supply operation and while the military included fuel stocks of coal and petrol in their delivery programme, it was Flight Refuelling Ltd based at Tarrant Rushton who was engaged in delivering bulk petrol supplies to the beleaguered city. This company had been the sole tanker aircraft business prior to the airlift, having evolved immediately post war, in-flight refuelling with BOAC's Empire Flying Boats on the North Atlantic route and before the war had experimented with a Bombay tanker. One of Flight Refuelling's pilots was Wiltshire born Peter Rivington a former World War 2 RAF Sqn Ldr who together with the company's Lancasters and Lancastrians was detached to Wunstorf which was an ex-Luffwaffe base. He reports that

there were 7 Lancastrian and 2 Lancaster tankers there plus 13 Haltons (civil registered Halifaxes) which were mainly of Lancashire Aircraft Corporation and 3 Avro Tudors of Airflight Ltd. These aircraft in 1949, were responsible for delivering vast quantities of the liquid fuel requirements of Berlin. Some of the aircraft in use were ex-BOAC and the 2 Lancasters were still fitted with the in-flight refuelling equipment and were without the faired in nose and tail sections that characterised the Lancastrian. These aircraft were turned into tankers by simple fitting a large fuel tank in the bomb bay and connecting this to the two outer fuel tanks in the wings. The aircraft used the inner wing tanks in flight and to dump the cargo fuel it was necessary to open a single valve in the cabin after a fuel line had been connected to the refuelling outlet protruding from the bomb bay. 1500 gallons of fuel was capable of being delivered on each trip. Peter Rivington whilst flying Lancasters over the bomb damaged ruins of Berlin, was conscious of the irony that these aircraft had through the war years aided this destruction but were now providing the Berlin people with a life line.

A number of civilian aircraft were lost whilst engaged on the embargo and by the time it was lifted by the Russians at one minute past midnight on 12th May 1949 the RAF had lost eight aircraft. One of the civilian aircraft was lost when it crashed at Chute in Wiltshire on 23rd November 1948. This was Lancaster G-AHJW, one of Sir Alan Cobham's Flight Refuelling Ltd tanker aircraft. It was returning to Tarrant Rushton from Germany when it came down at the rear of Conholt Manor House. The Lancaster was carrying personnel who were returning on leave, which is why there was such a heavy loss of life. The only survivor was the (WOP) B. Stanley and those killed were Capt Reginald M.W. Heath (pilot), Alan J. Burton (nav), Kenneth A. Seaborne (Flt Eng), Capt William Cusak, Capt Cyril Taylor, Dornford W. Robertson (radio officer) and Michael E. Casey (nav).

From Lyneham No.206 Sqn lost York C1 MW288 and its crew when an engine cut on night take-off from Wunstorf and it dived into the ground on 19th September 1948. The crew was Flt Lt H.W. Thomson (pilot), Flt Lt G.

Kell (co-pilot), Nav.II L.E.H. Gilbert (nav), Sig.II S.M.L. Towersey (signaller) and Eng.II E.W. Watson (Flt.Eng.). On 10th November, MW270 of No.206 Sqn was written off when the take-off run was abandoned with the under-carriage being raised to halt its progress. This was because of an ASI failure. The crew survived. No.99 Sqn lost York C.1 MW305 on 10th October when it overshot landing at Gatow, again with the crew surviving.

Operation *Plainfare* resulted in the RAF making 49,733 flights and moving 281,727 tons of supplies into Berlin by the time the embargo was lifted. Relief flights continued until October 1949 by which time the carriage of supplies had increased to some 400,000 tons. The 12 Yorks of No.206 Sqn returned to Lyneham on 15th August 1949 and the Yorks of No.99 Sqn the same month. 10 Yorks of No.511 Sqn returned on 5th September.

This same month the crews of No.511 Sqn started converting to the Hastings aircraft. A Tiger Moth, on which pilots were checked out, was on strength at this time.

The squadron continued to operate on long and medium range scheduled services to countries such as Australia, Japan, Singapore, Fayid, Habbaniyah and Aden.

With the crisis over, the West felt a need to demonstrate to Russia its determination to maintain the air corridors into Berlin and use them on a continual basis. The most obvious way to achieve this was by the use of civil airlines. It was felt however that civilian crews should not be involved in the circumstance of further military threat or action. A decision was therefore taken to train RAF crews to fly civilian aircraft should the need arise and so it was that crews of Nos.99 and 511 Sqns took on the responsibility, receiving training and route experience with BEA. This commitment continued for many years with RAF pilots taking the controls of aircraft such as the Viscount and Vanguard.

No.33 MU was still storing Spitfires with many being prepared for sale to foreign air forces. Vampire jets were also held and issued to squadrons in this country and in Germany.

Spitfires awaiting their fate at No.33 MU dispersal in March 1948. One of the Robin hangars can be seen, and a Lincoln appears in the circuit. Photo: Norman Parker

No.242 Sqn arrived at Lyneham on 25th June 1949 and with the other station squadrons, had re-equipped with Hastings C1 and C2s by October. The one exception, No.206 Sqn, disbanded at Lyneham on 31st August 1949.

These would be the long-range transport aircraft in use until the arrival of the Britannias in 1960. The Hastings had a carrying capacity of around 40 passengers or 12,000lb of freight. During the Korean War from 1950 to 1953, these aircraft flew large numbers of long-range transport flights, including medical evacuations of British troops back to the United Kingdom.

No.242 Sqn had provided 17 crews for *Plainfare* so with the crews on leave following their return from Germany, the squadron was on stand-down until the end of July 1949. On return they commenced conversion training to the Hastings. Route flying commenced in September to places such as Fayid, Mauriput, Takoradi, Luqa and Shallufa.

Five squadron personnel attended a ceremony at Buckingham Palace on 7th December 1949 to commemorate the part the squadron played in the Berlin airlift. The parade was inspected by King George VI.

In addition to its route flying, this squadron also assisted in moving other squadrons between bases. During 1950 it moved No.82 (PR) Sqn from Takoradi to Nairobi and No.56 Sqn from Thorney Island to Aclington and back again. 'Specials' were flown to Tengah in Singapore, which from 15th March 1950 was replaced by Changi as the terminal airfield. The end for No.242 Sqn came quickly when it was learned on 6th April that it was to be

disbanded. It was withdrawn from route flying on 20th April and disbanded on 1st May 1950.

No.99 Sqn crews converted onto the Hastings in September/October 1949 and continued the route flying role they performed prior to the Berlin airlift. Scheduled passenger flights to Singapore were flown and, following outbreak of the Korean War in June 1950, trooping 'specials' to Japan. In the latter months of 1951, with tension building in the Middle East, 'specials' were flown to Castel Benito.

No.24 Sqn, equipped with the York C1, moved in from Oakington on 27th November 1950 to operate scheduled passenger and VIP Flts. Prior to the move the squadron's Dakota and Valetta aircraft and their crews were transferred to No.30 Sqn at Abingdon. On its arrival at Lyneham, No.24 Sqn, 'B' Flt was re-equipped with the Hastings C1. Three Australian crews already at Lyneham joined the squadron, which was made up with crews from No.297 Sqn, which had disbanded at Topcliffe on 15th November. These crews were soon back at Topcliffe, as No.24 Sqn moved there on 9th February 1951 in an exchange with No.53 Sqn operating the Hastings C1 and C2.

No.53 Sqn was route flying on the 'Singapore Slip' until these flights were suspended on 25th May 1951, when the Sqn started flying troops from Lyneham to Suez and assisting with the evacuation of British nationals. In October, the 16th Airborne Brigade was carried from Cyprus to the Canal Zone. Route flying continued after the conflict and in June 1952 Hastings C2s were added to the establishment. The Sqn continued its duties at Lyneham until 1st January 1957 when it moved to Abingdon.

In 1953 the Lyneham squadrons flew troops and equipment to Kenya for operations against the Mau Mau Terrorists.

In the mid 1950s the RAF were operating Beverleys, a four-engined tactical transport aircraft designed to use relatively primitive airfields where usually short take-offs and landings were required for freighter and troop deployment. The Beverley also had the capability of parachute dropping both stores and troops. It was however a slow aircraft with a low operating ceiling. The Beverley was later joined by the VIP - variant of the de Havilland Comet 2 jet liner and the Bristol Britannia *"Whispering Giant"* which was the first operational turbo-prop to serve with the RAF. Both were strategic transport aircraft operating over long distances and delivering their payloads to the larger type airfields from where redistribution could take place over land or if necessary by aircraft of the Beverley, Argosy, Andover type.

No.216 Sqn, with Sqn Ldr W. J. Swift as CO, arrived at Lyneham with eight Valetta C1s on 10th November 1955 following a four and a half-year detachment at Fayid in Egypt. On 17th June 1956 the squadron became the first jet transport unit in the world when it equipped with the Comet 2 series. Together with the other Lyneham squadrons, these were soon in action flying troops to Malta and Cyprus in support of the Suez Crisis. The Comet 2 was powered by Rolls-Royce Avon engines, replacing the de Havilland Ghost of the early Comet 1 civil version. The Comet 1 suffered from metal fatigue, causing a series of disasters. The Comet 2 had a carrying capacity of 44 passengers. The squadron operated two T2s and eight C2s which they flew successfully on world-wide routes. An example of this aircraft stands today as Lyneham's gate guardian.

At a ceremony on Friday 24th May 1957 held on the airfield at Lyneham, No.216 Sqn was presented with its standard by Air Chief Marshal Sir Donald Hardman KCB, OBE, DFC. In June 1957 the squadron started operating a high-speed passenger service to the Far East and Australia.

The Casualty Air Evacuation Sqn formed in August 1952 as a temporary unit at the RAF Medical Research Unit at Chessington. Its role was for participation in casualty air evacuation exercises. It moved to Lyneham the day after its formation but returned to Chessington and disbanded the following month.

No.160 Wing which had reformed in March 1956 at Hornchurch in No.61 Group was at Lyneham in November in preparation for transfer the following month to Christmas Island for Atom Bomb tests. The two Hastings squadrons at Lyneham at this time, No.99 and No.511, started flying to Christmas Island for Operation *"Grapple"* in support of the Atom Bomb tests carried out in that Pacific location. The flights 'westabout', staged through some very attractive places. Consequently these duties were popular with the crews and with the handling party personnel who were deployed at each of the staging posts. Accommodation and catering arrangements on American and Canadian bases were of a very high standard. Aircraft leaving Lyneham flew via Aldergrove, RCAF Goose Bay in Labrador, Namao in Alberta, USAF Travis AFB San Francisco and Hickham AFB in Honolulu.

The Hastings aircraft were loaded at Lyneham with large steel drums containing the radioactive nuclear material. This was done under armed guard and aircraft likewise were guarded whilst on the ground at each of the staging posts en route. On arrival at Travis AFB with the 'hot loads', crews would hand over the aircraft to a slip crew who would have flown out the same cargo a few days earlier. The crew then had a few days to enjoy San Francisco whilst they awaited the arrival of the next flight from Lyneham. The last leg of the journey from Honolulu to Christmas Island was a flight of about 6 hours. The crews would spend the night there under canvas before commencing their return to Lyneham the following morning.

Sqn Ldr R.E. Dyson was No.511 Sqn CO from January to June 1955, when Sqn Ldr G.W. Turner was appointed. On 1st May 1957 No.511 Sqn was re-deployed and moved to Colerne. On 1st September 1958 it was renumbered No.36 Sqn.

In May 1959 No.41 Group Test Pilots' Pool arrived from Wroughton with Meteor T7s and attached to No.33 MU. It was absorbed into Maintenance Command Communications and Ferry Squadron on 1st November 1960.

The Ministry of Supply placed an order with BAC for twenty Britannia Series 253s designated C1s for RAF Transport Command. This series introduced the 4,400 e.h.p. Proteus 255 engine, a strengthened metal floor with tie-down points and a large cargo door. The type was capable of carrying a full freight load with conversion to full passenger carrying capability. Five of the type: - XM498, XM517-XM520 were built in the Bristol Factory at Filton with the remaining fifteen at Short Brothers & Harland in Belfast. One of these, XM496 *Regulus*, delivered to Lyneham on 17th September 1960 was destined to make the worlds last Britannia flight when on 16th October 1997 it put down for the last time at Kemble Airfield to be

cumbersome and there were limitations on the floor loading. The 252s were used almost exclusively for training and VIP work. They did come into their own however in October 1964 when they took on the responsibility for the trooping flights to Cyprus and Malta. This involved flights three times a week flying families on postings to and from the Eastern Mediterranean. The rest of the Britannia years were taken up by this continuous commitment. Britannias were operating at Lyneham from the 19th March 1959, when the first one XN398 touched down at 1752 hours, until 16th June 1970 when they moved to Brize Norton to collate with the VC.10 fleet. The first of the 253 Series, C1, XL636 flew into Lyneham on 4th June 1959. Between 9th June and 20th December the Hastings of No.99 Sqn were replaced by Britannia C1s and C2s. They also equipped No.511 Sqn when it reformed at Lyneham on 15th

During the early days of Britannia operations, XM 520 *Arcturus* is seen outside of the Terminal Building. The aircraft is being loaded for the daily route departure to Changi in Singapore.
Photo: Peter Hicks/Rolls Royce Heritage Trust (Bristol Branch)

preserved in 'working order' by the Britannia Aircraft Preservation Trust. Three Series 252s designated C2s, XN392, XN398 and XN404 were also built in Belfast. These were a cargo-passenger version with Durestos cabin floors. The heavy-duty stressed flooring was capable of transporting large loads in the forward section of the fuselage. A moveable bulkhead allowed separation between the cargo and passenger areas. The type however saw little use in cargo hauling as the change between the two modes was

December 1959. The log books for the squadron's first Britannia XM157 was presented to Wg Cdr A.W.G. Le Hardy OBE by Peter Masefield the Managing Director of Bristol Aircraft Company.

The replaced Hastings aircraft were relocated to nearby Colerne. Nos.99 and 511 Sqns operated the 23 Britannias and together with the Comets of No.216 Sqn, covered the RAF's long-range needs. The major routine task for the Britannia fleet was to support British garrisons in the

Middle and Far East and to this end, an aircraft was flown daily to Singapore. This was the 'Changi Slip', Changi being the terminal airfield in Singapore and 'Slip' referring to the aircraft being kept on the move towards its destination by changing or 'slipping' the crews along its route. No.511 Sqn carried out its first 'Slip' schedules to the Far East and Australia in July 1960. The crews were slipped at Khormaksar and Changi outbound and inbound.

The Britannia aircraft were used in a variety of different roles. These included oil deliveries to Zambia in 1966, the transportation of various VIPs and members of the Royal Family, airborne surveillance during the 'Cod War' with Iceland in 1973, assisting with the UN repatriation scheme of PoW and refugees between Pakistan and Bangladesh in both directions during 1973/74 and numerous flights to bring back injured personnel for medical treatment in the UK. When the Britannia was retired by the RAF in 1976, many of the aircraft continued to provide sterling service in civilian use.

No.216 Sqn took charge of the up-rated Comet C4 in February 1962, this being a stretched version of the C2 with a carrying capacity of 94 passengers. This version was also faster and had a longer range. The older C2s continued in service with the squadron until May 1967 when they were withdrawn. During the 1960s Lyneham became the hub of the RAFs long-range freighting, trooping and VIP operations.

Gloster Meteor NF.14s WS806 'O' and WS844 'P' with No.33 MU in 1961. Photo: Don Neate Coll.

An unusual incident occurred in July 1964 involving No.33 MUs engineering officer, Wg Cdr Walter 'Taffy' Holden. During test flights carried out by Flt Lt J. Reynolds from A&AEE Boscombe Down on Lightning F1 XM135 the previous month, a fault developed when the standby inverter operated. A decision was taken to isolate the two parts of the inverter and to ground test them independently by operating the engines on the brakes. Flt Lt Reynolds was unavailable to carry out the test but briefed Wg Cdr Holden accordingly. The Lightning was positioned at the north end of runway 18/36. The cockpit checks were carried out, and three engine test runs made. On the fourth run the 40 year-old Wg Cdr inadvertently pushed the throttles too far forward and locked them into reheat. The speed of the aircraft built up rapidly and as his mistake dawned on him, he realised the end of the runway and the village of Bradenstoke was getting nearer. The only course open to

him was to take off. This he achieved albeit he had never flown a jet before having soloed on a Harvard many years before. The aircraft had no canopy, he was not wearing a helmet and the radio was not turned on, so he had no communication with the tower. He was partially strapped into the ejector seat but this was not 'live' and he was unable to extract the pins to make it so. He now realised he would have to try and land it as he could not bale out. Having got the aircraft out of reheat he made three attempts to land from the south-west end of runway 07/25 but none were anywhere near successful. He decided to try from the other direction where a head wind and the uphill gradient would aid him. On the second attempt he got it down at considerable speed, nose high and with the tail impacting with the ground. Braking heavily the aircraft eventually came to rest near the end of the runway with a much relieved Wg Cdr completing a 12 minute flight.

From December 1965 to October 1966, Nos 99 and 511 Sqns were deployed airlifting oil into Zambia, when the oil pipeline through Southern Rhodesia was shut off because of UDI.

The Lockheed C.130 Hercules made its maiden flight in America on 23rd August 1954. The first C.130K Hercules C.1 destined for squadron service with RAF Transport Command was delivered to Lyneham during July 1967 to begin re-equipping No.36 Sqn which moved in from Colerne on the 1st July under the command of Wg Cdr J.D. Payling. Sixty-six of the type had been ordered for the RAF, twenty having been delivered from the Lockheed factory, for modification and camouflaging by Marshall's of Cambridge, by the end of July. Of these Lyneham had received five of their allocated nine, with the balance being delivered by the end of September. The

No.216 Sqn Comet 2 XK716 at Lyneham on 25th March 1967, just a few weeks prior to being withdrawn. Photo: Adrian Balch

5 Hercules C.1s of No.36 Sqn on a rain swept dispersal having arrived from the Lockheed factory in America in September 1967.
Photo: J.D.R. Rawlings/Cty Don Neate Coll.

C-130K was based on the C-130H model but was fitted with British navaids, radios, autopilot, a roller conveyor and other British airframe components. The payload capacity of this aircraft being 45,000lb over 2,500 miles or 20,000lb over 4,600 miles at a cruising speed of 345 m.p.h. The Hercules over the next three decades was to prove a most flexible aircraft, capable of carrying out a multitude of roles. In addition to its payload capacity it was capable of accommodating 92 troops. It could despatch 62 paratroops from both side doors simultaneously, or forty jumping from the large rear exit ramp which under reduced speed could be lowered in flight. Small army vehicles or a Puma type helicopter could be carried, also a variety of equipment, either on pallets for paradropping or for ground delivery. The Hercules would receive modifications, but they would maintain their flexible capabilities being used for stretcher cases, famine relief drops, evacuation of civilians, in-flight re-fuelling, weather surveys and many other roles. The RAF was destined to be the largest operator of Hercules outside of America.

No.36 Sqn with its full complement of aircraft was integrated into No.38 Group's role and became fully involved in building up the operational experience from which the rapidly ensuing squadrons would benefit. Crews of No.48 Sqn F.E.A.F. which was based at Changi, Singapore, took delivery of their Hercules at Lyneham and deployed to the Far East in October 1967. The squadron had been at Changi during the 1940/50s, in the latter years equipped with the Hastings C1 and C2. These were used for troop delivers to places such as Pusan on the Southern tip of the Korean peninsula.

On 1st August 1967, "Transport Command" was renamed "Air Support Command" retaining its HQ at RAF Upavon.

No.33 MU disbanded on 31st December 1967. The aircraft held in storage in its final years had been primarily Canberras and Lightnings.

No.24 Sqn was the second of the two Hercules squadrons to be formed at Lyneham when it moved in from Colerne on 5th January 1968 where it had been equipped with the Hastings.

The 47th Air Despatch Sqn of the Royal Corps of Transport arrived at Lyneham in 1968, with the responsibility for the loading and despatch of airdropped stores

A major rationalisation of Services air transport based policy began in 1970 with the move to Brize Norton on 16th June of No.99 and No.511 Sqns with their Britannias. This became the base for long-range transportation with Lyneham, the following year, becoming the sole base for Hercules in this country. On 1st February 1971, Nos. 30 & 47 Sqns moved in from Fairford to be joined on 1st September by No.48 Sqn on its withdrawal from Changi in the Far East. Thus Lyneham was home to five of the six Hercules squadrons in being during the early 1970s, the other was LXX Sqn serving in Cyprus. No.48 Sqn suffered a loss in September 1973 when Hercules C1 XV198 crashed on the edge of Colerne airfield. Details of this accident appear in the **COLERNE** section.

Further rationalisation taking place over the following years saw the deep servicing organisation move in from Colerne and No.70 Sqn returning from Akrotiri, on 15th January 1975. No.216 Sqn flying the Comet C4 disbanded on 30th June 1975. As a result of the 1974 Defence Review No.242 OCU moved in from RAF Thorney Island on 31st October 1975 to be badged as No.57 (R) Sqn on 1st July 1992. The role for this squadron was Hercules initial training. No.36 Sqn disbanded on 3rd November 1975 and No.48 Sqn on 9th January 1976.

In 1974 the UK Mobile Air Movements Sqn moved from Abingdon to Lyneham. They were responsible for all aspects of passenger and freight loading of Lyneham aircraft in the UK and abroad.

Since entering service the Hercules of the various squadrons have undertaken a varying number of roles such as the support of military operations of UN and NATO activities, evacuation of British subjects and troops, refuelling, humanitarian relief and on the home front, search and rescue, maritime reconnaissance and assisting essential services in times of need. Soon after delivery in 1967, the aircraft carried out 52 evacuation sorties from Bahrain. During the 1970s relief support was provided to Jordan, Turkey, Peru, West and North Africa, St. Helena, Nicaragua, Phnom Penh and Bangkok. Service families and international tourists were evacuated following the Turkish invasion of Cyprus in 1974 and the year after, a similar duty in bringing home British Embassy Staff from Saigon immediately prior to the fall of that city. In 1979 British and other Western nationals were brought out of Teheran following the over-throw of the Shah.

On 18th September 1978 a luncheon was held at Lyneham to mark the first half million flying hours accumulated by Hercules of the RAF. Vice President of Lockheed-Georgia, David Crockett made a presentation to RAF Lyneham as did Sir Arthur Marshall on behalf of Marshall's of Cambridge, who from 1966 were appointed UK Technical Centre for RAF Lockheed Hercules aircraft.

The Hercules C.3 came on line with the RAF in 1980. This was a stretched version of the Mk.1 converted by adding an extra 15ft to the fuselage. With this introduction the three maintenance hangars at Lyneham required a stretched capability to allow the usual three aircraft at a time to be dealt with and this was achieved with the provision of a rolling front to the bay doors. Hercules maintenance is no longer an entirely in-house function with the private company Hunting Aviation awarded a multi-activity contract to carry out some of the tasks previously the domain of the Engineering Wing.

With the invasion of the Falkland Islands by the Argentinians on 2nd April 1982, Lyneham's first support Hercules was within 24 hours en route to Wideawake Airfield on Ascension Island. Some 163 sorties were flown by the Lyneham aircraft during the first three weeks of the conflict, conveying

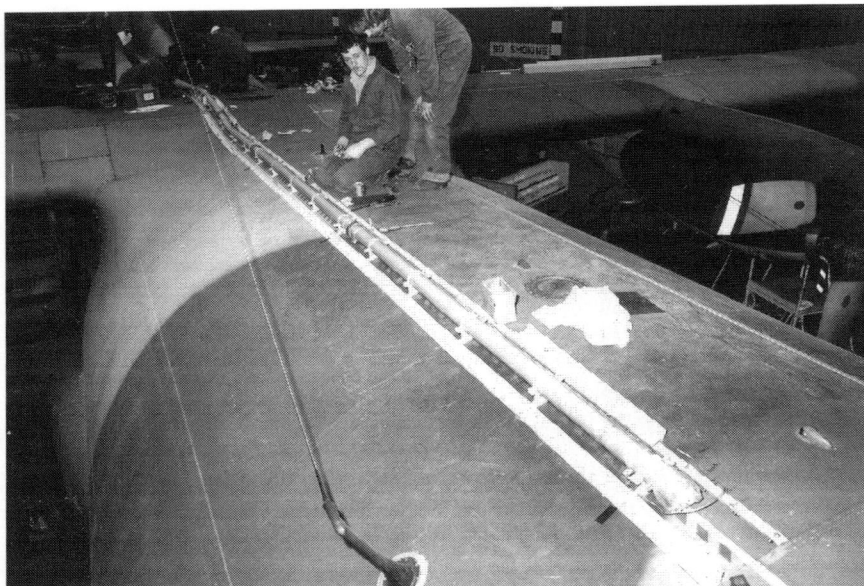

The fuel supply line being installed on the fuselage of a Hercules by the staff at Marshall's of Cambridge.   Photo: Marshall of Cambridge Aerospace Ltd.

Hercules XV200 on the running pan at Cambridge following modification to provide an air-to-air refuelling capability.   Photo: Marshall of Cambridge Aerospace Ltd.

over three million pounds of supplies. To enable supply and personnel back-up to rapidly reach the Task Force on the Falklands, there was an urgent need for the Hercules transport aircraft to have an extended flight time capability. Marshall's of Cambridge were given the task of providing the Hercules with an air-to-air refuelling capability so allowing a round trip from Ascension to the Falklands to be made.

Within 14 days of modification work commencing, the first aircraft completed flight trials at Cambridge and was delivered to Boscombe Down on 29th April for final flight trials which included day and night transfer of fuel from a tanker aircraft. Lyneham received its first aircraft on 5th May 1982. Three further aircraft were delivered on 13th, 25th and 31st May with the fifth and six on 3rd and 6th June. Eventually the complete

Hercules fleet was converted. The first long range AAR sortie to drop parachutists and stores to the Task Force within the Total Exclusion Zone was completed on 16th May with a flight time of 24hrs 5mins. This time was surpassed on 18th June, four days after the Argentinian surrender, when Flt Lt Terry Locke on a drop to Mt. Kent, established a world endurance record for the Hercules of 28hrs 3mins. He experienced a strong head wind on the outward journey that was repeated on the return trip to Ascension Island.

Initial refuelling trials had shown that the speed of the Victor tanker aircraft could not be matched by the Hercules. It was necessary therefore to use a tobogganing procedure that entailed commencing the transfer of fuel at altitude and adopting a shallow descent. It was decided the conversion of a Hercules to a tanker role would be far more efficient and Marshalls

received the first trials aircraft XV296 on 1st May. Four ex-Hawker Siddeley Andover auxiliary fuel tanks, each having an 875 imperial gallon capacity, were installed in the fuselage. On completion of modifications, A&AEE Boscombe Down carried out a series of trials resulting in Lynehams first Hercules Mk 1KP being delivered on 15th July. A total of four aircraft were modified to a tanker role, the others arriving on 19th, 21st and 26th July 1982. These were established at Stanley to provide around the clock support to the F4 Phantoms and F3 Tornados providing Air Defence (AD) for the Islands. Four Hercules squadrons were involved post war in and around the Falklands and in addition to their fuelling and supply role, they carried out a surveillance commitment.

A night scene at Lyneham sees Hercules C.1 XV188 with XV206 in the background.
Photo: Donald Lovelock

No.1312 Flt reformed at Mount Pleasant on 20th August 1983 with the Hercules air-to-air refuelling duties in the Falkland Islands. Aircrew who joined the Flight came from Nos. 24 and 30 Sqns. The Hercules tankers continued to operate until they were withdrawn on 31st March 1996. They were replaced by the VC-10 K4 of No.101 Sqn. The Flt continues to operate one Hercules 'K' type in the Falklands where its duties comprise search and rescue together with supply drops to South Georgia.

The humanitarian aid operation, code named *Bushel*, resulting from the drought of Ethiopia, commenced in November 1984. This involved dropping from low level, food and medical supplies over vast areas of in-accessible country but in some areas being able to land with their relief loads. By the time the crisis was over in November 1985 and the *Fat Alberts* had come home, 52,000 tons of supplies had been delivered from the air. The residents of Wiltshire who complain about the low flying of the Hercules should perhaps consider the

Wiltshire Fire Brigade's Bedford fire appliance being loaded into Hercules XV 181 during a snow storm at Lyneham before its flight to the heat of Gambia.
Photo: John Lakey

Hercules C130J ZH889 and ZH887 at Lyneham 17th August 2001. The main notable difference between the 'J' and 'K' type is that the former has six bladed propellers, and is minus the wing fuel tanks visible on the latter. Its superior fuel efficiency obviates the need for these.

wider implications of this training requirement.

A different type of humanitarian service was accommodated when an obsolete fire engine of the Wiltshire Fire Brigade was delivered by Hercules to Banjul in the Republic of Gambia in the early part of 1987. There it became Gambia Fire Brigade's most modern appliance, with the gift providing service for many years.

In 1989 the Hercules was used for rescue operations in the aftermath of Hurricane *Hugo* in the Caribbean.

Lyneham and the Hercules of Nos. 24 and 30 Sqns went to war again when Saddam Hussein's Iraq invaded Kuwait on 2nd August 1990. Operation *Granby* was mounted on the 6th with a Hercules leaving Lyneham within 24hrs to be the first RAF aircraft into the Gulf. A total of 12 Hercules were sent to Saudi Arabia staging through Akrotiri, these were supplemented by a number of Boeing 707 civilian freighters. Station personnel and aircrew worked night and day to ensure the success of many hundreds of missions flown with troops, support units and the armoured brigades. This was the transportation service which the unit had been formed for 40 years previously. Over 40,000 hours were flown over 7 months; twice the normal schedule.

In 1991 airdrops were made to the Kurdish refugees in the harsh mountainous regions of Iran and then to the safe havens set up by the UN in protected camps close to the Iraq border.

1991 also saw the return to this country, of three hostages from Lebanon. They were all brought back to RAF Lyneham where a VIP suite had been provided in which they stayed for a period of medical checks, counselling and de-briefing. The journalist John McCarthy was the first to return early in August and six weeks later former Battle of Britain pilot Jackie Mann, landing in an RAF VC10, was welcomed back with a Spitfire flypast. In November Terry Waite the Arch Bishop of Canterbury's Special Envoy also returned to Lyneham in a VC10.

Operation *Cheshire* commenced in July 1992 when in excess of 50,000,000 pounds of food, medicines, clothing, fuel and general goods were airlifted into the besieged city of Sarajevo in the former Yugoslavia, on behalf of the UN. The Hercules aircraft involved were provided with defence against heat seeking missiles and crews were issued with personal arms. Because of their vulnerability from shellfire when on the tarmac, it was essential that the Hercules were turned around as quickly as possible and 4mins 50secs was the fastest time recorded during the period of operation. There were occasions when aircraft were the subject of small arms fire and when the tarmac was targeted by mortar fire. Operation *Cheshire* turned out to be a larger supply mission than the renowned 'Berlin Airlift'. The fighting in Bosnia resulted in many badly injured children needing urgent medical attention. Operation *Irma* saw medical teams from the RAF Hospital at Wroughton flown out by the Lyneham crews to treat and accompany the worst cases back to England for treatment.

No.38 Group reformed at High Wycombe on 1st November 1992, taking over from No.1 Group, responsibilities for air transport and air-to-air refuelling.

Deployment of operation *Vigor* took place on 10th December 1992 and involved support for the American Marines and the airlift of relief supplies into Mogadishu and the hinterland of Somalia. The 90 strong detachment from RAF Lyneham was based with the American forces in Mombasa.

RAF Lyneham became a No.2 Group station in Strike Command when the Group formed on 1st April 1993.

In 1996 the Hercules Conversion Flt and the Hercules Training Flt, both of which operated as part of No.242 OCU and later No.57 (R) Sqn, combined as one unit. The Hercules Operational Evaluation Unit was formed.

During the first three months of 1998 the Hercules of Lyneham were involved in support of the Government's stand over weapons inspections in Iraq. They flew from this country and from Germany to Kuwait and bases in the Gulf with aircraft spares and equipment, vehicles, domestic supplies and military personnel.

Through the 90s and into the new century, the Hercules of Lyneham continued their many roles and are rightly proud of their reputation for being 'first in - last out'. The In-flight C.130 tankers however, ceased operating as from 1st April 1996. Many of the C130Ks were coming to the end of their service and 1998/99 should have seen the introduction of the modern improved Hercules C.130J of which the MoD ordered 25 at a cost of £1 billion. The first of these arrived at Boscombe Down for the UK phase of the trials and evaluation on Wednesday 26th August 1998 some two years behind schedule and at a cost of around

£30 million in compensation payments to the MoD. It was nineteen months later that the order was completed. The first fifteen C.130J.30s, designated Hercules C4, are the stretched versions being 15 feet longer with a 33% greater volume carrying capacity. These were followed by ten standard length C.130Js, designated Hercules C5. Representatives of Lockheed Martin handed over the first aircraft to the MoD Procurement Executive and DERA for tests which comprised performance and flying qualities in its strategic and tactical roles; air to air refuelling and air drop capabilities of personnel and equipment. With the turn of the century the 25 Hercules C.1s and 29 C.3s of Lyneham were operated by Nos.24 Sqn, 30 Sqn, 47 Sqn, LXX Sqn and 57 (Res) Sqn.

The 'J' Conversion Flight of No.57 (Reserve) Sqn received the first C.130J ZH875 at a station ceremony on 23rd November 1999. The log book for this first aircraft was handed over to AVM Philip O. Sturley MBE, BSc, FRAeS, AOC No.38 Group, by Tom Burbage the president of Lockheed Martin Aerospace Systems. The new aircraft then flew in formation over Lyneham with one of the older 'K' type. The second of the new aircraft arrived two weeks later flying non-stop from America to Lyneham. By the spring of 2001 16 C130Js were in operation by No.24 Sqn flying mainly to the Middle East re-supplying bases in Saudi Arabia and Turkey, used by the RAF fighters policing the no-fly zones in Iraq for the UN. By the summer 2001, 12 crews had converted to the 'J' type and all 25 aircraft had been supplied. Both No.24 and No.30 Sqns have been re-equipped with the new aircraft, crewed by just 2 pilots and 1 Air Loadmaster. 12 of the old C130Ks were returned to Lockheed Martin in the States as part of the replacement deal and 29 have been refurbished and will continue in service until 2007. These equip Nos. 47 and LXX Sqns.

The Hercules of Lyneham have had a good safety record during their long service although inevitably there have been accidents as with the exercise in Italy where one flew into the ocean at night while carrying paratroopers. One crashed when carrying out circuits and bumps at Colerne and another during take-off in Albania. Also there was a crash in Scotland and this is detailed later.

Photograph of Hercules C.1 XV192 over Lyneham with the wing fuel tanks clearly visible.   Photo: Donald Lovelock

Another branch of the RAF is the Princess Mary's Royal Air Force Nursing Service. This is a responsibility of the Director General of Medical Services RAF and includes No.4626 (County of Wiltshire) Royal Auxiliary Air Force Aeromedical Evacuation Squadron. Its members are all volunteers who carry out part-time service in support of the RAF, while continuing their civilian occupations. They are committed to regular training and the units are formed when an operational situation is identified. During the first Gulf War, Lyneham's Aeromedical Evacuation Sqn was mobilised for Operation *Desert Storm* deploying field hospitals at four locations in Bahrain and Saudi Arabia. The Sqn forms part of the Tactical Medical Wing (TMW).

A further auxiliary unit based at Lyneham is the Royal Auxiliary Air Force Defence Force whose role is to support parent units by supplementing regular personnel as and when necessary. They work as clerks, chefs, gunners, suppliers and aircraft loaders.

The Army's No.47 Air Despatch Sqn provide the facilities and personnel required when the Hercules are operating supply drops. The squadron occupies two of the three 'L' type hangars to the east of the B3102.

Lyneham is a Military Emergency Diversion Airfield being available at any time to accept other aircraft that may be in difficulties. It is also visited on a non-emergency basis by VC10s from Brize Norton and Nimrods from their base in Scotland.

Four times the station has been awarded the Wilkinson Sword of Peace for its work over the years. In 1973 came the first sword for the humanitarian and famine relief work in

Nepal and Mali. In 1984, the year-long Ethiopian Famine operation brought the second award and in 1992 the third sword was awarded for work both with local charities and involvement in UN operations. In 2001 Lyneham received a fourth award for enhancing and promoting the good name of the RAF in the field of humanitarian activities.

Most of Lyneham's humanitarian aid work is carried out in countries far from these shores but on 13th/14th February 1998 they were able to provide a service on their own doorstep. A number of Second World War German bombs were located on a construction site in a built up area of Chippenham. The army bomb disposal unit worked on these over a four-day period and decided during this time that the surrounding area needed to be evacuated. Over 1,100 inhabitants had to be found alternative accommodation and it was to RAF Lyneham that many of them were taken. The largest of the bombs, a 1,000lb 'Fat Boy' had to be detonated on site and this was achieved on the 16th after which residents were allowed home.

December 1998 saw Britain and America involved in Operation *Desert Fox* in which attacks were carried out against Iraq's chemical arsenal and military installations. The Hercules was used for re-supply missions to Kuwait. The first flights operated on Sunday 20th December when three aircraft called at stations around this country to pick-up Tornado fuel tanks, bombs etc., before departing on 24 hour round trips. Further flights were made during the week but the attacks ended before Christmas resulting in a short involvement by the Lyneham crews on this occasion.

The crisis in the Balkans saw Lyneham swing into action by carrying a variety of loads to British Forces supporting the NATO campaign in Yugoslavia. In addition to their weapons re-supply tasking, the Hercules had the additional task of carrying humanitarian aid to the Kosovo Albanians fleeing into Macedonia and Albania. The first Hercules left with supplies for the refugees on 31st March 1999. On one of these missions, No.47 Sqn lost Hercules C.1 XV298. On 11th June when taking off at night from an airstrip in Kukes, Northern Albania, the load being carried shifted. The aircraft failed to get off the ground and

Hercules C130K XV206 being prepared on Friday 17th August 2001 for a flight that weekend to Macedonia.

overshot the landing strip before crashing and catching fire a quarter of a mile from the refugee camp they had been delivering aid to. The five crew and seven passengers escaped without serious injury.

In its 60th Anniversary year, Lyneham was again doing what it is good at. With troops and equipment urgently needed in the former British colony of Sierra Leone to stabilise the fragile political situation there, the Hercules were mobilised for the transportation. Flights commenced in early May 2000 to bases at Dakar, Senegal and to the capital Freetown. Over half of Lyneham's fleet of 54 Hercules were used in this operation.

The above operation coincided with RAF Lyneham receiving the Freedom of Swindon and a visit from Honorary Air Commodore Princess Anne.

A visit by her brother Prince Charles was made to Lyneham on Monday 14th May 2001 to inspect a gathering of units of the Royal Auxiliary Air Force. Personnel from Lyneham's own Hercules Reserve Aircrew Flt and No.4626 Aeromedical Evacuation Sqn were amongst those the Prince spoke to. He also witnessed demonstrations by the various units.

On Friday 17th August 2001 a Hercules from Lyneham transported an advance party of troops and equipment to Macedonia as part of a NATO force. 41 soldiers from 16 Air Assault Brigade flew into the capital Skopia, on a flight from Wattisham. The immediate task, code name Operation *Essential Harvest*, was to

implement a lasting cease-fire and the assessment of conditions for collecting weapons from the rebel Albanian National Liberation Army. Ten sorties were flown out of Lyneham the following day, seven on the Sunday and four more on Monday. On following days Lyneham despatched 5 or 6 aircraft most days. Loads comprised mainly army vehicles, drivers and freight.

Following the terrorist attacks on the twin towers of the World Trade Centre in New York on 11th September 2001, and the subsequent initiative to flush out the perpetrators, Lyneham engaged in troop and supply missions to and from Oman, Afghanistan and Parkistan. Initially the Hercules C130Ks were used for this task but from 5th June 2002 No.30 Sqn became the first squadron to operate the C130J to supply troops in combat. Until this time the aircraft had not been fitted with electronic defence equipment to protect them from ground to air missiles. Bullet-proof Kevlar was also fitted to protect the crews from small arms fire. The C130Ks had infra-red flares fitted.

News broke in November 2001 that a new Ministry of Defence review might decide to place 25 new A400M cargo planes at Brize Norton instead of Lyneham. A statement confirming this was made by Armed Force Minister Adam Ingram on Friday 16th August 2002. The decision put a huge question mark over the future of Lyneham, where 2,700 military personnel work alongside 700 civilian staff. It was anticipated that the fleet of Hercules would be transferred to Brize Norton

when and if the A400M's enter service. However in a Parliamentary reply to local MP James Gray, at the conclusion of the second Gulf War in early May 2003, the Prime Minister indicated that he was sure Lyneham would play a key role in future times of necessity. This proved to be a hollow statement when on 4th July 2003, the Government annouced that RAF Lyneham would close in 2012.

On Thursday 14th March 2002 No.57 (R) Sqn was disbanded. The squadron's role of training aircrew to fly the C130K in a variety of situations to meet the Air Forces's tactical and transportation needs had become obsolete with the introduction into service of the newer C130J. The policy now was to streamline training at the base with the four remaining squadrons having this responsibility. A ceremony attended by past and present members of the squadron was held which involved a service at the base church followed by a fly-past and formal lunch. Among the past members attending was 81 year old AM Sir Ivor Broom, who served with the squadron during World War 2. Also in attendance was C-in-C Strike Command, AM Sir John Day. The No.57 (R) Sqn Standard was taken to the RAF College at Cranwell where it will be kept in the college rotunda. The squadron emblem is the Phoenix and possibly at a future date the squadron will rise again from the ashes as it has on three previous occasions.

The second Gulf War which started on 20th March 2003 saw elements of Nos 24, 30, 47 and LXX Sqns posted to the region. They were accompanied by the Tactical Medical Wing and by No.4626 Aeromedical Evacuation Sqn, for use in bringing out and repatriating the wounded. Personnel of the UK Mobile Air Movements Sqn were deployed for the loading and unloading of stores and equipment from Lyneham's Hercules transport aircraft. In subsequent days the Hercules flew daily missions to the Gulf carrying rations, military equipment and post for the troops.

MEMORIALS

A number of memorials are apparent on and around the airfield site with some of the street names of the married quarters displaying well known names in memory of former RAF personnel such as Trenchard, Tedder etc.

Comet C.2 XK699 & Stone Plaque.

plaque has a pale 'ensign' blue background with lettering in white. The Britannia aircraft and badges are in full colour. The memorial was unveiled by the then President of The Britannia Association Joy McArthur who at the time was the RAF's senior female Warrant Officer serving with No.10 Sqn. A similar memorial was unveiled the following day at RAF Brize Norton by Air Chief Marshal Sir Thomas Kennedy GCB, AFC.

Photograph of Britannia Wall & Plaque (below).

BRISTOL BRITANNIA LONG RANGE TRANSPORT AIRCRAFT OPERATED FROM ROYAL AIR FORCE LYNEHAM FROM 19 MARCH 1959 TO 1 JUNE 1970							
BRITANNIA C MARK 1							
XM 489	DENEBOLA	XM 490	ALDEBARAN	XM 491	PROCYON	XM 496	REGULUS
XM 497	SCHEDAR	XM 498	HADAR	XM 517	AVIOR	XM 518	SPICA
XM 519	CAPELLA	XM 520	ARCTURUS	XL 635	BELLATRIX	XL 636	ARGO
XL 637	VEGA	XL 638	SIRIUS	XL 639	ATRIA	XL 640	ANTARES
XL 657	RIGEL	XL 658	ADHARA	XL 659	POLARIS	XL 660	ALPHARD
BRITANNIA C MARK 2							
XN 392	CRUX	XN 398	ALTAIR	XN 404	CANOPUS		

Badge of 99 Sqn	Badge of RAF Lyneham	Badge of 511 Sqn

TO ALL WHO CONTRIBUTED TO THE SUCCESSFUL OPERATION OF THE BRITANNIA
PRESENTED BY THE BRITANNIA ASSOCIATION 30 APRIL 1994

1) 173/SU023786 - Inside of the Station Main Gate

Set back on a grassed area facing the main entrance gates stands as Gate Guardian, Comet C.2 XK699 *Sagittarius* formerly of No.216 Sqn. Positioned close to the nose of the aircraft is a circular stone plaque on a stone base displaying the following inscription: -

COMET C Mk2 XK699
'SAGITTARIUS'

GATE GUARDIAN
OF RAF LYNEHAM
UNVEILED ON THE
22ND JUNE 1987
BY THE HONORARY
AIR COMMODORE
HER ROYAL HIGHNESS
THE PRINCESS ANNE

The unveiling by Princess Anne took place shortly after her appointment as The Princess Royal.

2) 173/SU023786 - Inside of the Station Main Gate

On the grass in front of the Comet gate guardian there stands a brick built memorial into which is set a plaque mounted by a Britannia in relief and at the base the badges of No.99 Sqn., No.511 Sqn. and between them, that of RAF Lyneham.

The wall of the memorial has been constructed of Blue Brick with special bullnosed shaped finishing bricks. The

3) 173/SU022779 -At HQ No.47 (Air Despatch) Sqn.

Douglas Dakota G-AMPO was moved by road from Coventry to Lyneham on 22nd September 2001 to serve there as a memorial to the men and women of Air Despatch who lost their lives in service around the world. The aircraft, which as KN566, was used in the Berlin Airlift, had become surplus to the requirements of the Air Atlantique Group. The move was carried out by

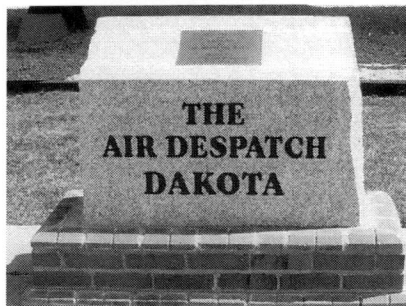

Dakota FZ626 and memorial stone at the HQ No.47 (Air Despatch) Sqn.

the RAF's Aircraft Recovery and Transportation Flight. After personnel of 47th (Air Despatch) Sqn refurbished and repainted the aircraft as FZ626, which on 19th September 1944 flew from Down Ampney on Operation *Market Garden*, the Dakota was installed as the gate guardian at the HQ of No.47 (Air Despatch) Sqn Royal Logistics Corp. The aircraft was unveiled at a ceremony conducted by Maj Gen White on Friday 21st June 2002. Attending the event were survivors of the squadron and relatives of those killed. In front of the Dakota stands a granite/marble memorial stone on a brick base displaying a brass plate with the inscription: -

THE AIR DESPATCH DAKOTA

WAS INAUGURATED

BY

Major General MS White

CB CBE DL

ON 21st June 2002

In honour of those Air Despatchers

Who made the ultimate sacrifice.

4) 173/SU022779 At HQ No.47 (Air Despatch) Sqn.

Outside the HQ building a bench with brass plaque displaying: -

IN MEMORY OF
PRIVATE CHRIS GAME ROYAL
LOGISTICS CORPS,
AN AIR DESPATCHER FROM JATE,
WHO LOST HIS LIFE AT SOUTH CERNEY
DZ
4 AUGUST 1994

Memorial bench.

5) 173/SU022779 -At HQ No.47 (Air Despatch) Sqn.

Outside the HQ building beneath the flag pole: -

A number of plaques set into the stone base, displaying the names of personnel killed whilst serving with the squadron.

6) 173/SU022785 -Inside of the Station Main Gate to the north of the Officers' Mess: -

Positioned on the grass and set back from the roadway leading to the mess is a small brick built memorial into which is set a metal plaque with an inscription which reads:-

THESE 3 LIME TREES WERE
GENEROUSLY PRESENTED
TO RAF LYNEHAM BY THE SENATE
OF THE CITY OF
BERLIN TO MARK THE 40TH
ANNIVERSARY OF THE
INVOLVEMENT OF 24, 30 AND 47
SQUADRONS IN
THE BERLIN AIRLIFT 1948

Photograph of Berlin Memorial with one of the trees behind.

Photograph of Hercules Memorial Seat.

7) 173/SU022785 - Inside of the Station Main Gate and north of the Officers' Mess: -

Positioned on the grass close to the 'Berlin Memorial' is an English oak seat made by Paul Winter a wood worker from Shropshire. It is set in a semi-circle of nine trees that flower in May. No.70 Sqn's Hercules C.3P XV193 *Startrek 3* crashed in the Grampian Mountains, 30 miles north of Perth, on 27th May 1993 while on a routine low level flying exercise with the loss of life of all on board. The aircraft stalled after a cargo drop before crashing and catching fire. All nine on board were killed of which three were army personnel. A memorial service was held for them at Lyneham on 23rd June. The seat was provided by colleagues of No.70 Sqn as a mark of respect. Four propellers are engraved into the back rest of the seat which also displays the names of the crew and an inscribed plaque: -

IN MEMORY OF THE CREW OF
"STARTREK 3"
HERCULES XV 193.
27TH MAY 1993

Squadron Leader
G.P.Young. AFC RAF
Squadron Leader S.D. Muir. RAF
Flight Lieutenant G.R.J. Southard.
BSc RAF
Flight Lieutenant S.P. McNally RAF
Flying Officer J.H. Owen RAF
Master Engineer T.J.W. Gilmore
Sergeant C.T. Hillard
Sergeant A.K. King
Lance Corporal G.R. Manning

8) 173SU/024787 - 5 miles North East of Calne

In the Parish and Royal Air Force Church of St. Michael & All Angels on the A3102 a quarter of a mile north of RAF Lyneham's main gate. In the north wall is set the Memorial Window to commemorate the 50th Anniversary of RAF Lyneham.

Henry Haig A.R.C.A. was asked to create a window which would combine the themes of St Michael and All Angels and the 50th Anniversary of RAF Lyneham. The window in essence, is designed to lift the eye from the busyness of life on the Station to things spiritual.

The background of the lower panels are the maps used by the aircrew, in distinctive blues and greens. Superimposed but scattered throughout the panels are the names of the Squadrons who have served at Lyneham and representative parts of the aircraf tbased at the station. Medieval techniques have been used here, transposing animals and plants for squadrons and aircraft, the object being to avoid complete pictures of aircraft which appear flat in this medium. The Station Crest is set in the hanger roof.

Photograph of Memorial Window.

The hangers have changed little and their shape forms an element of continuity. In the centre of the window, the outline of the airfield is depicted as seen by crews landing at night. Above this is one of the runways appearing as the sword of St Michael. Above the central motif are the scales of St Michael, normally depicting the weighing of souls in the balance. The RAF eagle has been taken as the fulcrum balancing on the left side with hands and an empty bowl and also the sacks of the Berlin airlift. This theme gives a clear indication of the Stations relief operations. On the right side of the scale is a loaded pallet ready for stowing on the Hercules. In the top of each of the main panels is a circle. The left and right panels contain radar scopes from the Air Traffic Control Tower and the centre one is the RAF roundel. Taking up the colours of the roundel, two bars run through the right hand side of the centre window. These intersect with a rainbow in the top panels to form a cross. In the top centre is a depiction of St Michael the Patron Saint of the Parish Church. The window as a whole is very complex and by searching the panels in it, there can be found a wealth of detail such as the rank badges, weather maps, navigational aids etc. The window was unveiled by Her Majesty The Queen in May 1990.

9) A number of RAF Standards are displayed within the church.

10) In the churchyard, positioned close to the service graves is a wooden seat displaying the inscription: -

Presented by
2491 (Lyneham) Sqd. ATC
In commemoration of
50 years of the Air Training Corps
1941 - 1991

As can be expected, the churchyard holds the graves of numerous service personnel mainly of the RAF but also the RAAF, Polish Forces, Royal Logistic Corps and a Sgt Aviateur Mort Pour La Belgique. Three of the crew from Hercules "STARTREK 3" and two from the Hercules crash at Colerne are among those of the RAF.

MALMESBURY

Memorial 173/ST933874- Town Centre

In Malmesbury Abbey on the B4040. A stained glass window depicting an early attempt at flight by Elmer, an 11th century Anglo-Saxon Benedictine monk. He leapt from the Abbey tower with a pair of wings strapped to his hands and feet. He was carried almost 200 yards before crash-landing and breaking his legs. This left him lame for the rest of his life but he lived until his eighties. He blamed the cause of his failure to fly successfully on forgetting to attach a tail to his back. Elmer was thought to have been born in about 981 AD, for it was recorded that twice in his lifetime he saw Halley's Comet which appeared in 989 AD and 1066 AD. He made his attempt at flight as a young man, probably between 1000 and 1010 AD.

A re-enactment of the flight by Elmer, the early aviator, was staged at the Abbey in 1962 by the RAF Royal Tournament Display Team. A 23 year-old RAF Junior Technician, Bernard Collins, dressed as a monk with wings attached to his arms, descended on a wire from the Abbey roof. The same display was repeated again in 1976 using a stuntman.

Stained glass window at Malmesbury Abbey.

195

MANNINGFORD RELIEF LANDING GROUND

Location - 173/SU122590 - 7 miles East of Devizes.

Manningford Bohune Common is located off an unclassified road between the villages of Woodborough and Manningford Bruce and close to the main Paddington to Westbury railway line.

World War 2 Years

Manningford was in use as a Relief Landing Ground (RLG) from September 1939 by the Central Flying School (CFS) at Upavon in No.23 Group Training Command. It was three and a half miles NW of Upavon Airfield and two miles SE of the RLG at Alton Barnes. The site, although part of Manningford Bohune Common, was in fact agricultural land forming part of Mullen's Farm. There were no airfield buildings and not even a windsock to identify it as a landing ground, although a white cross was marked out on the grass. Initially Avro Tutors Is were seen at Manningford, and flown by students attending courses at the CFS. One of these K3290, crashed on making its approach to land on 11th September 1940. Tutor I K3254 crashed in forced landing on 6th August 1941.

On 9th February 1943 a Mustang 2 AG647 of No.4 (AC) Sqn based at Clifton near York, crashed at Hilcott, ¾ mile SW of Manningford ELG. Whilst flying in low cloud, the aircraft struck the roof of 2 Hardings Terrace before crashing into a field at the rear and off Gores Lane (SU173/105589). The pilot, Plt Off W. T. Richardson RAFVR, was killed and buried at Upavon Cemetery. Ted Giddings, who lived with his parents in the terraced house which was struck by the aircraft, arrived home for lunch to find his bedroom wrecked and the tail-plane of the Mustang protruding through the roof.

When the CFS Upavon was disbanding on 1st April 1942, Manningford was retained as an ELG by its replacement, No.7 Flying Instructors' School (FIS) which, six days later was redesignated No.7 FIS (A). Miles Masters and Oxfords were in use but were replaced with Miles Magisters from 1st August 1942. On 7th December 1943 No.7 FIS (A), carrying out 8 weekly Flying Instructor courses, stopped using Manningford.

Manningford was also used by No.29 EFTS Clyffe Pypard as an RLG from 21st November 1942. This training establishment, 1 mile north of Yatesbury was in No.50 Group Flying Training Command. No.29 EFTS was flying Tiger Moths at this time. Fleet Air Arm pupil pilot Ray Steele landed a Tiger Moth at Manningford on more than one occasion. Part of his pilot training involved creating forced landings. His instructor would cut the engine and at the same time call for him to "find a field". As pupil pilot Ray Steele's flying progressed, the instructor changed the routine and, on cutting the engine, showed him a field in which to land. The field chosen was inevitably Manningford and, on landing, the instructor jumped out and picked mushrooms, with Ray Steele following behind in the Tiger Moth.

There was an occasion during the war when the Mullens family heard a low flying aircraft circling their land at night. The farmer's son raced out to the landing area waving a paraffin lamp. The aircraft, which was a Boston, landed safely although damaging a wing on a hedge. This was repaired the following morning by fitters from Upavon and the aircraft was able to take off again.

Post War Years

In May 1946 Manningford was transferred to No.2 EFTS Yatesbury in No.50 Group, for use as a satellite airfield for its Tiger Moths. One of these, DE531, hit a hedge on approach to Manningford during a practice forced landing and turned over on 28th May 1946.

Closure

Manningford RLG closed and reverted to its original agricultural use when Yatesbury transferred into No.23 Group on 21st April 1947 and No.50 Group disbanded on 31st May.

Mullen's Farm is currently operated by Vitacress Salads Ltd, suppliers of vegetables to supermarket chains. Vegetables are grown on the former landing ground and at the south end a large reservoir has been constucted for irrigation purposes.

West of the A346 Marlborough to Salisbury road, and Savernake Forest.

Airfield Development

The landing ground on Brown's Farm was originally set out by the Earl of Cardigan around 1932. The field was 'L' shaped, running N/S and E/W, approximately 1,500 ft/1,800 ft respectively. Part of the ground was on top of Marlborough Tunnel carrying the GWR Marlborough to Savernake Low and High Level railway lines. The farmer agreed to maintain the landing ground for permanent pasture and to allow the Earl a section of a barn on the field in which he could keep his aeroplane.

A Romney Hut was provided on the Landing Ground at an unknown date but presumably early in World War 2. It probably had a combined use for storage, workshop and for crew messing arrangements.

Inter War Years

The Earl flew his private Gipsy Moth G-AALJ (*Liza Jane*), which he purchased second-hand for somewhere between £400 and £500. Other private owners were also allowed use of the airstrip. The Earl later acquired an Avro 504N G-ACZC. He navigated his way around the area with the use of a flying map issued by the AA. The map indicated the bearings of all the various places where he liked to fly, all worked out from a point one mile south-west of the town.

In the early days of flying from Marlborough, the Earl admitted to some concern on days when he found cattle grazing, and he wanted to take-off or land. As he became more experienced this troubled him less as he realised that they never moved particularly fast, and, by selecting a line between them providing a margin of 20/30yds, he could execute his move safely. His flying soon took him to other parts of the country and later to Europe where on one occasion in 1938, having landed at Orly on return from Switzerland, the Earl, looking for the

Lord Cardigan and his aircraft on the Landing Ground at Marlborough, Gypsy Moth G-AALJ, Avro 504 G-ACZC and Auster G-AFWM.
Photo: Lord Charles Brudenell-Bruce

reason why his aircraft had been giving a poor performance, was shocked when a 9" section of the propeller broke away in his hand. On another occasion he flew all the way to Czecho-Slovakia with his friend Bill Herbert occupying the rear cockpit, making numerous refuelling stops en-route. The Earl would quite often land in any field of suitable size. He would frequently meet friends in Oxford at the Trout Inn, landing close by in Port Meadow. In these carefree days he also found most RAF aerodromes would allow him to land.

From January 1936, the CFS Upavon had use of the landing ground for forced landing training on weekdays by personnel on Flying Instructor courses. This was initially for a one-month trial period as there was concern locally that disruption would be caused to Marlborough College. This presumably was found not to be the case. (The liaison between the CFS and the Air Section of Marlborough College was good). Aircraft using the facility were, initially, in the main Tutors, and from 1938 Ansons and Furies. One of the latter crashed there in May 1939.

World War 2 Years

With the outbreak of war in September 1939, private flying ceased with the needs of the CFS taking precedent.

A number of flying accidents occurred during the early part of the war, not all confined to CFS aircraft training there. One was Blenheim IV L9033 from the School of Army Co-operation at Andover, it crashed in a forced landing on 11th December 1939. A CFS Tutor I K3410 crashed on approach on 25th May 1940, K3293 did the same on an overshoot on 16th October 1940 and likewise K3356 on 13th March 1941. In the early afternoon of Wednesday 19th June 1940, Fairey Battle I K9468 of No.12 OTU Benson, also overshot when attempting to land. After going through a fence, it fell over the embankment completely blocking the Marlborough to Savernake High Level railway line and obstructing the Low Level line. It appears that the pilot, Plt Off Sievers, was overcome by fumes during bombing and gunnery practice. Tutor I K3344 from CFS crashed on landing on 18th June 1941. On the morning of Saturday 7th February 1942 Bristol Blenheim IV V5817 crashed and burnt out, also on the same stretch of railway line. The crash was discovered by the crew of a passing gravel train, who reported it as they passed through Marlborough Station. Ganger Trotman of the GWR boarded the engine of another goods train travelling in the direction of the crash and on arrival at the scene found most of the aircraft fuselage burning on the line and also the body of one airman under some smouldering wreckage. Plt Off Peter Mackenzie Stobie RAF, Sgt Allan Bennett RAFVR and Sgt Thomas Jack RAFVR (WOP/AG) were killed. RAF Yatesbury responded

with a lorry and a hired tractor to clear the debris from the line. This failed when the cable broke so an additional lorry and cable were supplied but still without success. An RAF crane was eventually used to recover the aircraft remains, and as soon as the line was clear a delayed troop train and two Cheltenham to Andover passenger trains were allowed to pass.

An RLG at Overton Heath on Clench Common two miles to the south west was opened in 1941 and the CFS started using this in preference to Marlborough.

Post War Years

The landing ground returned to agricultural use after the war. The Earl however continued to use it for private flying and by 1948 was making flights in his Auster G-AFWM.

The surviving Romney Hut.

The Romney Hut has been moved from the landing ground and is now in the main area of the farm buildings.

Memorial

173/SU184687 - 10 miles South of Swindon

Marlborough College stands on the A4 west of the town centre. Set back off the road at the rear of a large square is the College Memorial Hall constructed at the end of World War 1 to the memory of the large number of former students who gave their lives. Inside the hall and at the rear of the auditorium the names of military personnel from all branches of the armed services span the stone wall. On the walls of a wing off the auditorium are the names of those who were killed during World War 2. A total of 42 airmen lost their lives during the First World War and 123 during the Second. When the College Council agreed to the provision of the Memorial Hall, Old Marlburians were invited to submit designs. The design by Lt Col

Marlborough College Memorial Hall in which the names of former students who died in two World Wars are listed on the walls.

W.G. Newton was chosen. His proposal was a semi-circular hall of Greek type, with wooden seating for 1,516 and with the names of the fallen inscribed on the walls.

The following are service details of some of these former College students who served with the RFC and RAF: -

Captain Sidney Edward Cowan MC**, RFC was serving with No.24 Sqn as a 2nd Lt when it was formed at Hounslow on 1st September 1915. He moved with the unit to France on 7th February 1916 and claimed his first victory on 4th May when, flying a DH2 5966, he destroyed an unidentified two-seater aircraft. His second claim was made on the 1st July when, in a DH2 5964, he strafed an unidentified two-seater on the ground, killing both of the crew. He then suffered an engine failure and forced landed close to his victims and behind enemy lines. He was able to re-start the engine and returned to his base at Bertangles. He claimed 4 further victims whilst serving with No.24 Sqn and became one of the first aces of the RFC. His seventh and final victim was claimed when serving as 'C' Flight Commander with No.29 Sqn at Le Hameau. Capt Cowan was killed on 17th November 1916 when his aircraft collided with another British one. He was awarded the MC in May 1916, a Bar in October and second Bar on 14th November.

2nd Lt Edmund Llewelyn Lewis RFC was Commissioned in the 7th Essex Regiment and seconded to the RFC in February 1916. He attended CFS Upavon for flying instruction from 16th April and received his Graduation Certificate on 21st June. He was posted to France and, on 1st July 1916, joined his brother Gwilym Hugh Lewis (also a former Marlborough College student) serving with No.32 Sqn at Treizennes. On 28th July Edmund Lewis, whilst flying a DH2, 6002, was wounded during combat with, it was thought, half a dozen enemy aircraft. He was admitted to No.7 Stationary Hospital Boulogne on 30th July with a gunshot wound to the heel. He was brought back to the Eastern General Hospital at Brighton. He returned to France in September 1916 where after a couple of weeks at No.2 Aircraft Depot waiting for a posting, he joined 'B' Flt. of No.24 Sqn. He engaged the enemy on numerous occasions leading up to Christmas but was killed in aerial combat on an offensive patrol over the German lines on 26th December 1916. Edmund became separated during the patrol and after a single-handed fight with five enemy aircraft of which he accounted for one, his DH2 7885 crashed at Beaulen Court. He was shot down by Leutnant Dieter Collin of Jasta Boelcke. Edmund was 21 years old and on the day following his death was gazetted Lieutenant.

2nd Lt Edmund Lewis of No.32 Sqn.
Photo: Marillyn Maklouf

Captain Philip Scott Burge MM, MC, RFC served with the 10th Royal Fusileers from September 1914 and was awarded the Military Medal at the Somme in July 1914 before joining the RFC in September 1916. Commissioned a 2nd Lt, he qualified as a pilot on 24th May 1917, joining No.64 Sqn on 14th October and leaving for France where the squadron was based at Le Hameau. He claimed his first victim on 23rd March 1918, when flying a SE 5A B125 he destroyed a Fokker Dr1. He became a Flight Commander in April and was awarded the Military Cross for his actions

during May 1918, when he claimed 5 enemy aircraft destroyed. During a dogfight on 24th July 1918, he was killed when his aircraft SE 5A D6900 was hit by enemy fire and crashed in flames west of Seclin. He is thought to have been shot down by Unteroffizier Marat Schumm of Jasta 52. Capt Burge's total of aircraft claims was 11 with 2 shared.

Flying Officer Hugh Alastair Yuille Barkley RAFVR served with No.640 Sqn in No.4 Group based at Leaconfield. He was piloting Halifax III LW585 C8-H when it took off at 1747 hrs on 15th February 1944. The target was Berlin where the 891 aircraft despatched inflicted heavy bomb damage. This was one of the last raids during the 'Battle of Berlin'. On returning from the operation, Fg Off Barkley's aircraft crossed the English coast but crashed at 0130 hrs onto a 300' hillside at Cloughton, 4 miles NNW of Scarborough in Yorkshire. All of the crew were killed and Hugh Barkley, a Cambridge University Bachelor of Arts graduate, was buried at Harrogate (Stonefall) Cemetery.

Sqn Ldr Humphrey William Albert Chesterman AFC, RAF first served with the RAF during the 1920s and was recalled to service during World War 2. He then served with No.7 Sqn in No.3 Group based at Oakington. He was the pilot of a Stirling III BK760 MG-X which took off at 2331 hrs on 10th April 1943 for an operation to Frankfurt. His aircraft was shot down at 0345 hrs by a night-fighter (Hauptmann Walter Ehle, 11/NJG1) and crashed at Tongerio (Limburg), 5 km ESE of Bree in Belgium. This was the first Stirling III lost by No.7 Sqn. Two of the crew evaded capture but Sqn Ldr Chesterman and the remainder were killed in the crash and are buried in Heverlee War Cemetery.

Sqn Ldr Edward Nigel Bunting DFC*, RAFVR joined the RAF in October 1939. He was serving with No.488 Sqn based at Zeals when flying a Mosquitoe XIII he shot down his eighth and ninth German aircraft whilst operating over the Normandy beaches in June 1944. He was killed on Sunday 30th July 1944 when, operating from Colerne. His Mosquito MM476 was hit by anti-aircraft fire when chasing an Fw190 at low level over France. He was buried at St. Remy Churchyard, Calvados, France.

Sqn Ldr David John Hatfield Maltby DSO, DFC, RAFVR joined the RAFVR in 1940 and following pilot training was posted as a Plt Off to No.106 Sqn at Coningsby on 4th June 1941, flying Hampdens. He was promoted to Fg Off on 12th January 1942 and joined No.97 Sqn at Woodhall Spa on 26th June 1942. This squadron was equipped with the Lancaster I & III. He received the DFC following completion of twenty-seven operations in July 1942. On 12th January 1943 he was promoted to Flt Lt joining No.617 Sqn on 25th March 1943. He flew on probably the most famous raid carried out by Bomber Command during World War 2, Operation *Chastise*, attacking the dams in Western Germany. No.617 Sqn was formed at Scampton on the 23rd March 1943 with the top men from other squadrons selected to form the crews. These were all under the command of Wg Cdr Guy Gibson DSO*, DFC*. The raid took place on 16th May 1943 with Flt Lt David Maltby DFC piloting one of the three Lancaster III (Specials), in the second flight behind Gibson. Maltby took-off from Scampton at 2147 hrs flying ED906/G AJ-J and followed the same route as the first flight of three aircraft. The initial target was the Mohne Dam which the special bouncing bombs carried by the first four Lancasters failed to breach. Gibson called up Maltby to make his run at the dam. His bomb was dropped at 0049 hrs and successfully completed the breach in the dam wall. The remaining aircraft went on to attack other dams with Maltby returning to base and landing at 0311 hrs. It was as a result of this raid that he was awarded the DSO.

David Maltby was promoted to Sqn Ldr but four months later was to lose his life on an operation to the Dortmund-Ems Canal near Ladbergen. Still with No.617 Sqn he took-off from Coningsby at 2350hrs on 14th September 1943 in Lancaster III JA981 KC-J carrying a 12,000lb HC bomb. Before reaching the target, his aircraft was recalled but for reasons unknown it crashed into the sea at 0040hrs, 8 miles NE of Cromer. Sqn Ldr Maltby is buried at Wickhambreaux in Kent and his crew who were with him on the Dams raid are commemorated on the Runnymede Memorial.

In the pivotal Battle of Britain of 1940, Marlborough College supplied a total of 16 participants. This total was bettered by only two other schools in the country, namely Eton with 22 from its much higher enrolment, and Harrow with 17. The following are names of Marlborough students who were pilots that fought and died in the campaign or subsequently: -

Flt Lt Norman Whitmore Burnett	No.266/46 Sqns	k. 11.6.41
Sqn Ldr Peter Edward Drew	No.236 Sqn	k. 1.8.41
Plt Off John Vinter Gurteen	No.504 Sqn	k. 15.9.40
Plt Off James Hammond Hoare-Scott	No.601 Sqn	k. 20.11.40
Plt Off David Nicholas Owen Jenkins	No.253 Sqn	k. 30.8.40
Plt Off Peter Litchfield	No.610 Sqn	k. 18.7.40
Fg Off Derrick Charles MacCaw	No.238 Sqn	k. 8.8.40
Plt Off Donald Kennedy MacDonald	No.603 Sqn	k. 28.8.40
Plt Off William Alan Ponting	No.264 Sqn	k. 24.8.40

A Portland Stone memorial stands outside the original gymnasium of RAF Melksham. It is positioned near the main entrance of what is now the Christie-Miller Sports Centre in Lancaster Road. The badge of RAF Melksham is depicted with the following inscription:-

COMMEMORATING
THE SITE OF
RAF MELKSHAM
1940 - 1964

On Saturday 18th June 1994 a dedication ceremony took place and the stone unveiled. Some 200 people including former personnel who had served at the station together with their families attended the event. A kilted piper played and there was a flypast of Jaguar, Tornado and Nimrod aircraft.

V.E. Day at RAF Hospital Melksham, 8th May 1945
Matron Mansell is sat in the centre of the front row with Wg Cdr Smith, Sqn Ldr Appley, Sqn Ldr Gordon and Fg Off Troy to her left and with Sqn Ldr Grant, Sister R. Hale and Sqn Ldr Edwards to her right. Photo: Kathleen Ball

The Melksham Memorial.

RAF Melksham opened on 12th June 1940 as No.12 School of Technical Training. It had 8 hangars, a hospital, and an infrastructure similar to that of an airfield. Various types of aircraft were used for instructional purposes. These included the Whitley, Wellington, Manchester, Lancaster, Lincoln, Hampden, Battle, Bristol Bulldog, Tomahawk, Spitfire, Anson, Boulton Paul Overstand, Defiant, Typhoon, Boston, Beaufighter, Supermarine Swift and Tiger Moth. Melksham was never in use as an aerodrome although it is sometimes referred to as such. The exception being a short period when one of the COs, Gp Capt S.B. Lynch flew a Tiger Moth trainer which had been struck off charge and issued to Melksham for instructional purposes. The CO had Fg Off Anderson, who controlled the Instrument Repair School, arrange to reinstate the Moth 2400M to airworthy condition. An engine was acquired, instrument panel constructed and various instruments fitted. The Gp Capt made a number of flights in this non standard aircraft, with 2400M emblazoned across the wings and fuselage, until it attracted the attention of the Royal Observer Corps who reported it, resulting in the flights being stopped by higher authority.

Some of the many courses undertaken at Melksham were the training of Instrument Repairers, Armourers, Cooks, Bomb Disposal, Sparking Plug Testers, WAAF Parachute Packers, Electricians, Air Mechanic Naval Ratings, Dinghy Packers, recruits and numerous others. RAF Melksham in No.24 Group closed on 26th February 1965.

With the turn of the century, the hangars remain in use for commercial purposes and the gymnasium as a sports centre. Most of the buildings have disappeared and the officers' married quarters have been sold off. The site is known today as the as Bowerhill Industrial Estate. Much of the site is absorbed by commercial units and estates of private housing. On 21st May 1977 the Ludlow-Hewitt Residential Home was opened in Halifax Road. Most of the road names have an Air Force connotation - Lysander Road, Merlin Way, Wellington Drive etc. A new public house originally opened as *The Harrier*, was subsequently changed to one of the ignominious modern names *The Pickled Pilot*, to some local annoyance, but it has now settled as *The Pilot*.

The Harrier public house before its renaming.

In the village church of All Saints on the C42, east of the A360. On the north wall set beneath a commemoration plaque to the servicemen of World War 1 who gave their lives, is a brass plaque bearing the inscription: -

> ALSO OF THOSE WHO FELL
> 1939 - 1945
> FLT. SGT. NAV. H.G. HARDING RAF
> CPL. R.F. WILKINS 1st SURREY REGT.

Flt Sgt Henry George Harding RAFVR. No.160968 served with No.61 Sqn, No. 5 Group, based at Skellingthorpe. He was navigator of Lancaster I NG182 which took off at 1642 hrs on 6th December 1944 for a raid on Giessen. The operation comprised 255 Lancasters and 10 Mosquitoes. There were two intended targets, with 168 aircraft directed to attack the town centre and 87 the railway yards. The crew of NG182 was Fg Off J. Bain (pilot), Sgt P.G.Gee (Flt.Eng), Flt Sgt H.G. Harding (nav), Flt Sgt T.E. Morgan (B/A), Sgt J.H. Hodgkins (A/G) and Sgt J. Casey (A/G). Flt Sgt Harding was killed when the aircraft was attacked by a German fighter over the target. The rest of the crew survived and the Lancaster landing at Woodbridge at 2256 hrs. Flt Sgt Henry Harding is buried in Middle Woodford (All Saints) churchyard.

There is one other World War 2 airman's grave in the churchyard and it is that of Sgt Cyril R. Hallet RAF (obs). He was based at Scampton with No.83 Sqn and was killed on 8th July 1940 when Hampden I L4066 crashed on an operation to Frankfurt.

Why this airman's name does not appear on the memorial plaque is unknown.

East of the A345, off the C32 between Bulford and Netheravon, set back from the road, stands a Georgian house in its own grounds close to the River Avon. This is Syrencot House, which during World War 2 had the codename *Broadmoor*. It was used as the Headquarters of the Airborne Forces and was where the formation took place of the 1st and 6th Airborne Divisions. Positioned on the wall to the right of the front entrance door is a silver coloured plaque depicting a Pegasus emblem with the inscription: -

> SYRENCOT HOUSE
> THIS HOUSE WAS USED BETWEEN NOVEMBER 1941 AND
> MAY 1943 AS THE HEADQUARTERS OF MAJOR GENERAL, LATER
> LIEUTENANT GENERAL F. M. (BOY) BROWNING, CB, DSO, THE FOUNDER OF
> AIRBORNE FORCES. MUCH OF THE PLANNING WHICH LEAD TO THE
> FORMATION OF THE 1ST AND 6TH AIRBORNE DIVISIONS WAS DONE IN THIS HOUSE.
> IN MAY 1943, IT BECAME THE HEADQUARTERS OF THE
> SIXTH AIRBORNE DIVISION COMMANDED BY MAJOR GENERAL R.N. GALE, OBE, MC
> THE AIRBORNE ASSAULT BY THE 6TH AIRBORNE DIVISION ON THE NIGHT OF
> 5/6 JUNE 1944, TO SECURE THE LEFT FLANK OF THE ALLIED INVASION OF
> EUROPE - OPERATION OVERLORD WAS PLANNED AND MOUNTED FROM THIS HOUSE.
> AD UNUM OMNES

The 6th Airborne Division was formed at Syrencot House on 3rd May 1943. It was prefixed the 6th to mislead the Germans into believing that there were six British airborne divisions, when in fact there were only two. The building remained in the ownership of the MoD after the war and was used as offices by a local building company through the 1970s/90s. After the company left, Syrencot House stood empty and boarded up for a number of years and was subjected to considerable vandalism. Fortunately someone had the good sense to remove the commemorative plaque before this occurred. The house which stands in its own secluded grounds is currently privately occupied and is being returned to its former glory.

The new occupiers are not averse to visits from persons who may wish to see the reinstated plaque. Visitors should appreciate that the house is private property, and prior permission to view/photograph the plaque should be obtained.

The plaque at Syrencot House

NETHERAVON AERODROME

Location - 184/SU155488 4 miles North of Amesbury

In the village of Netheravon on the C260 road off the A345 Salisbury to Marlborough road. Now Airfield Camp with the Army Air Corps the main occupier. The aerodrome at nearby Upavon was being used slightly earlier than Netheravon but the latter is the oldest military airfield in this country that is still operational. It has been in almost continuous use since June 1913. Flying takes place 365 days of the year with the role of No.7 Regiment AAC supporting Army requirements when and where needed.

Aerodrome Development

On 28th February 1911, aviation affairs in the British Army expanded to battalion strength with the establishment of the Air Battalion, RE, with No.1 Coy responsible for lighter-than-air machines and No.2 Coy the revolutionary new aeroplanes.

On 13th April 1912, a Royal Warrant created the Royal Flying Corps. A month later Army Order 13/1912 decreed that the headquarters of the Corps would be placed at Netheravon. In addition to establishing a Central Flying School at nearby Upavon, a decision was taken to form another aerodrome in place of the landing ground at Larkhill. By the autumn of 1912 Netheravon had been chosen. The land chosen for this RFC station was already owned by the War Department which, on 31st March 1898, acquired the Netheravon Estate from Sir Michael Hicks Beach, Bt, the then Chancellor of the Exchequer. In the summer of 1904, the Army Cavalry School was established at Netheravon House. The newly-formed Air Battalion of the Army took over some of the Cavalry School buildings which were unused in 1912. The horse gallops there were suitable as an aeroplane-landing area. It was good grazing land and the original agricultural use is discernible by the original farm buildings at the rear of the current Parachute Centre, which are referred to as Choulston Ox Barn. It was beside the gallops that work commenced to erect aeroplane sheds and camp buildings during the winter of 1912/13.

The War Office specification was to develop Netheravon and Farnborough on similar lines, although the former was to be a two-squadron station and the latter a one squadron. Firstly, the common type of structure at each station represented a move towards standardisation; secondly, they were intended for the RFC's first regular squadrons, rather than for the experimentation role of Larkhill, or the training role intended for Upavon.

Six types of building were required in the January 1913 roster, namely aeroplane sheds, vehicle sheds, workshops, petrol stores, latrines and a vehicle-washing platform. These buildings were known collectively as 'Group B' structures. The combination of buildings reflected the Military Wing's demand for a large complement of mechanical transport to accompany the Expeditionary Force.

The specifications circulated to contractors in January 1913 by the War Office Directorate of Fortifications and Works (DFW), detailed the accommodation required for each function and the construction method and materials to be used. The structures would be soundly but cheaply built. All buildings were to be timber-framed, with top and bottom plates, braces, horizontal rails and intermediate uprights, the main uprights set into concrete bases with sole-plates and spurs. Roofs were to be supported on trusses with timber compression members and wrought-iron or steel tension rods, the large span trusses, such as those of the hangars, requiring additional bracing at right angles against wind pressure. Timbering was to be of 'good, sound, well-seasoned yellow deal', linings were to be of asbestos sheeting and all buildings clad in corrugated iron, coated with Silesian spelter. Unusually for military buildings, the external design consisted of white panels bordered by vertical and horizontal timber bonding strips. These were painted black, giving a Tudor appearance. The specification stated that the responsibility for determining the 'arrangement of buildings on the site' lay with the Commanding Royal Engineer.

It was a busy time for the local building company of W.E. Chivers & Sons of Devizes who were contracted for building work at CFS Upavon, and at Netheravon were constructing the water and drainage systems for the new accommodation.

The aerodrome was formed with two main sites comprising an Upper (eastern) and Lower (western) Aerodrome Camp. The Lower Camp contained the domestic and administrative areas with accommodation, classrooms and offices. Some of the original 1913/14 single-storey buildings on the Lower Camp were the Officers' Mess, Sgts' Mess, Regimental Institute, Airmens' Dining Room, Single and Married Officers' accommodation, Single Airmens' accommodation, Senior NCOs' Accommodation, NAAFI Stores and Shop, Classrooms, Mortuary and Fire Station. It is unlikely that construction of these buildings was very far advanced by the summer of 1913 as the first squadrons to arrive were without sleeping quarters. New barracks for the airmen were not completed until October 1913.

An access road runs approximately east to west the whole length of the complex with the linear nature of the Upper and Lower Camp buildings on both sides of it. The Upper Camp at the east end was the main area for flying activities and contained most of the hangars, Motor Transport (MT) sheds and workshops.

The first 15 aeroplane sheds were built on the Upper Camp in 1913 to accommodate two squadrons. The sheds were all the same pattern and constituted 6 double sheds and 1 triple. They were timber-framed and were required to provide a clear internal space 65' wide, 70' deep and 15' high, with the entrance spanning the full width and clear height of the buildings. The sheds had 10' wide sliding doors held in place by removable posts. The doors were only on the landing-ground end, and the sheds were of a size sufficient to house up to 3 BE type aircraft. Internally each building required a dressing room, 60sq.ft in area, with a dwarf partition wall rising

This 1925 photograph shows the early layout of the Aeroplane Sheds on the Upper Camp at Netheravon.   Photo: Tony Mellor- Ellis Coll.

DH6 C7352 stands in front of the original Watch Tower in 1918.
Photo: S. Bradley/Cty. Tony West

7' from the floor, which was of 1inch yellow deal boards. A skylight with an area of around 300sq.ft was required, together with glazed windows in the back wall and over the main door. Each of the sheds was completed in time for the opening of the Station in June 1913. A subsequent timber framed/coupled aeroplane shed with a gabled front and side-opening doors was built to the 1913 pattern, on the west end of the original 15 sheds. This appears in a photograph of spring 1918 but it was almost certainly in place a lot earlier than this and probably just before or after the outbreak of war.

As with the coupled aeroplane sheds, the MT sheds were also positioned together in sets. The specification at Netheravon called for four groups of sheds each with ten bays, one shed of twelve bays and one of thirteen, so providing garaging for 65 vehicles. Each bay was 10' wide, internally each shed was 30' deep with a clear opening, and 13' high. Bays were partitioned one from the other with 11' steel angle framing, lined on one side with corrugated iron, which was also used for both external and internal cladding of the main walls. Skylights similar to those in the aeroplane sheds lit the buildings. Apart from their much

smaller span, the main structural differences between the aeroplane and vehicle sheds lay in the doors, which in the latter were made from a similar angle-frame and corrugated iron arrangement to that used for the partitions, and the floor, which was of Portland cement concrete. Four of the bays were provided with a concrete-lined vehicle-inspection pit, 12' x 3' 6" x 3' deep, with a sump at the base. The associated vehicle washing platforms, to avoid the area turning to mud, were 25' x 16' standings of 6" concrete on hardcore.

The carpenters' and fitters' workshops were 40' x 30' internally, with a clear height to the working space of 10'. Skylight areas for these buildings were set at a ratio of the internal area, not less than 10% of the floor space, whilst a lean-to annex to each, 8' high and 150sq.ft in area, contained the forge. Interior forge walls were lined with corrugated iron, with asbestos sheeting for the internal walls of the main building. Floors of the main workshops were mainly of deal boarding, although 25% of the floor area in each was formed from hardwood block paving. The forge floor was of rammed broken chalk covered with 3" of smiths' ashes, and doors throughout were of deal framing.

The petrol stores comprised a pair of buildings 20' x 6' internally and 6' high at the eaves. The framework for these comparatively small structures was fashioned from steel angle members similar to that used for the partitions in the MT sheds, with corrugated iron used to clad both the walls and the segmental roof. The doors at the front were 4' 6" wide by 6' high, reaching eaves level, with a 2' 3" door at the rear. A large concrete lined central pit was provided in each store 18' 6" x 4' 6" x 3' deep, with its tops projecting 4" above floor level.

The remaining item in the 'Group B' schedule was a pair of latrines. These were constructed with light timber framing and clad with corrugated iron. They contained urinals and earth closets.

A number of timber and asbestos built offices and service buildings soon followed. One of these was used as a wireless station. A watch tower was positioned at the end of the line of sheds. This appeared to be two platforms suspended on scaffolding poles.

By mid 1915, the aerodrome site developed to the size of a small village. There were permanent aeroplane sheds, permanent accommodation for officers and airmen and numerous other service buildings. The inhabitants were very pleased with the standard afforded and happy to have a good mess and recreation room with a billiard table. No sleeping accommodation was provided in the main mess.

There were quite comfortable conditions for the many who attended the Concentration Camp in June 1914 although, in the month leading up to the start of the training, these facilities were augmented by tents for personnel and for aeroplanes. Some of the tents were of unusual shapes. The tents used for the aeroplanes are thought to have been designed by the Royal Aircraft Factory the previous year. The tents were 53' x 43' x 19' 6" high at the centres.

Another coupled aeroplane shed was built to the east of the original 1913 hangar line. The shed was in place by the summer of 1918 and was still there during 1944. Possibly these sheds were those under construction when the gale

The tents as supplied for the Concentration Camp and the machines of Nos. 2, 3, 4 and 5 Squadrons in July 1914. Photo: Cty. Army Air Corps

The five span and two span Handley Page hangars

Handley Page hangars were constructed, however, to house the HP 0/400s on the aerodrome. Hangars of this type were designed to store these bomber aircraft with wings folded, hence their span of only 70'. The hangars were constructed in multiple spans according to needs. Immediately on the east side of the Lower Camp is the first of the two Handley Page hangars, built with a five-span gabled roof. The hangar was in place by February 1920 and was probably completed in 1919 but had not been started in the summer of 1918. Post Second World War, it was sub-divided and used variously as an M.T.R.S. and Driving School. On the extreme end of the Upper Camp, the second Handley Page hangar of two spans was provided, and believed to have been built in two stages with final completion by the summer of 1920. Air Ministry drawings issued in February 1920 are shown by their titles to be associated with the completion of this shed, and show the Bath stone walls of the structure resting on purpose built brick foundations already in place. These points suggest that the two Handley Page hangars were originally conceived as a single project, but that whilst the five-span shed on the Lower Camp was completed as intended, construction of the Upper Camp shed was begun, then interrupted. It is possible the hiatus was associated with a change in materials. Handley Page hangars are rare buildings, and this Bath stone example is unique.

These coupled, single-end-opening aeroplane sheds were used at Netheravon during the Second World War for parachute drying and, in later years, as a MT and Fire Section. The Handley Page hangars are known as 'Cathedral' types because of their dignified ecclesiastical appearance.

Other major building of the immediate post World War 1 years are the second Officers' Mess to the north of the original 1913 building, and its associated accommodation blocks. Construction was believed to have been accomplished in 1919 and is first seen on a plan of 1921. The plan also shows similar overspill officers' hutting to the south of the original 1913 built mess, together with temporary officers' married quarters in the area now occupied by the later permanent structures.

force wind blew them down on 27th December 1915. Two more non-coupled sheds, each 210' x 65', were positioned half way between the Upper and Lower Camps and close to the road. It is not known when these were removed but it was before 1944. By the summer of 1918, Netheravon had 21 aeroplane sheds.

On the north side of the road and close to the camp entrance, the Quarter-master's Office and stores were built in 1919. This has since been enlarged. The camp had a Church of England as well as a Roman Catholic church.

At the end of World War 1, plans had been drawn up to use Netheravon as a base for the RAF's heavy bombers. The intention was to construct an additional camp, which would have been known as the Handley Page aerodrome. The project was never developed. Two

The 1927 and possibly late 1930's watch offices seen in 2001 when occupied by the Fire Section.

Two aerial views of the Upper Camp on 3rd November 1927, taken from a No.11 Sqn aeroplane based at Netheravon.

1) Looking west from a height of 200', the new 'A' Type hangar is seen in the centre and the new watch tower is under construction in front of it. This would replace the tower which is seen in the right foreground at the end of the apron. By this time the early built tower appears to have been upgraded from its original scaffolding with two platforms. The original Choulston Ox Barn is the first building on the left side of the road.   Photo: Tony Mellor-Ellis

2) Looking east from a height of 1000', the framework for the second new 'A' Type hangar under construction is apparent between the end of the timber aeroplane sheds and in front of the Handley Page hangars. Photo: Tony Mellor-Ellis

By the early 1920s, the aerodrome had its own golf course.

'Netheravon' was marked out on the aerodrome in chalk letters following Air Ministry Order No.197 of 1921. The idea was to aid pilots in locating their correct destinations.

A new standard type of hangar (Type 'A') was developed from early prototypes at Upper Heyford (one of the reacquired stations), together with a number of other standard building types. The programme at Netheravon was represented chiefly by two Type 'A' hangars and a new two-storey watch office with a slate covered pitched roof. A date stone indicates it was built in 1927, to a 1926 specification 2072/26.

Two of the original 1913 built double aeroplane sheds on the Upper camp were demolished in 1925/26 with an 'A' Type hangar in use on the site by 1927. This same year the building of a second 'A' Type hangar commenced at the extreme end of the 1913 hangar line. The new watch office lay directly in front of the first of these two hangars and not many yards away from that of the original pre- World War 1 type.

The expansion period of the late 1930s produced a Medical Centre in the brick style of the period and was in use as such until the RAF left Netheravon. It was possibly at this time that another watch office was built alongside the 1927 provision. Its format in keeping with those recognised as being of World War 2 specification. It was two-storey, flat-roofed but had no balcony on the frontage at first floor level. The building was 20ft sq and of a similar height.

As of 1942/43, the grass runways were N/S 900yds, NE/SW 1,180yds, E/W 1550yds and SE/NW 1000yds. By December 1944, the runways were NE/SW 1400yds, E/W 2000yds and SE/NW 1,500yds. A 12' wide concrete perimeter track surrounded the landing areas. A flarepath provided night landing facilities. Hangars were 'A' Type (2) 250' x 120', Bellman (1), Handley Page (2), 1913 built Aeroplane Sheds (3 doubles, 1 triple), 1913 pattern Aeroplane Shed (1), and the pre-summer 1918 coupled Aeroplane Sheds adjacent to the Handley Page (2). At least one Blister hangar was built during the war. A 1927 Watch Office without a balcony

The 1913 pattern Aeroplane Shed used currently as the Joint Service Parachute Centre. The tower stands on the site of the original Watch Tower.

This recent view of the Upper Camp looking east shows the two-span Handley Page hangar in the foreground, the modern ATC at the end of the service road, the two 'A' Type hangars, the 1913 pattern Aeroplane Shed at the east end of the apron and the five-span Handley Page hangar by the Lower Camp.

remained in use as a Contol Tower. The two-letter station identification code was NE. A cinema/lecture theatre built of concrete slabs was added in the early 1940s as was a new dining room and cookhouse which was built to a 1940 design. In 1944, during the period leading up to the invasion of Europe, about 17 temporary accommodation buildings, forming a completely separate living area, were built in the fold of the ground to the north of the main aircraft hangars. These buildings were removed soon after the war ended. New WAAF accommodation was completed on the Lower Camp in September 1945. Post war a new Control Tower was built opposite the second 'A' Type hangar. The Bellman hangar was, for a time, used by the M.T Driving School.

More generally, in common with all RAF stations extant at the beginning of World War 2, Netheravon was provided with ground defences against air-landing attack. Built in 1940/41, these works everywhere generally consisted of pillboxes, weapon pits and infantry defences, from where the aim was to repel attempts at capture by parachutists and troops landed from aircraft and gliders. From September 1940

airfield defences were governed by a national scale according to each site's proximity to ports and other key invasion targets, on the reasoning that the airfields would be used by the invaders largely as springboards to other objectives. Lying neither near a port nor one of the key vulnerable points, Netheravon was in the lowest defence category Class 3, and was expected to be provided with only 10-16 genuine pillboxes, half-a-dozen dummies and however many earthwork weapon pits the local defence commander determined suitable. Netheravon's modest collection of pillboxes and other

features conformed to these scales.

Much of the post World War 2 structural history at Netheravon has been impossible to trace although from 1977 there has been little major structural development. Major replanning did take place at both the Upper and Lower Camps during the 1940s and 50s, the Lower Camp to a greater extent. On the Upper Camp, by 1959 only one of the original 15 Aeroplane Sheds survived and this had gone by 1977. Many of the World War 2 huts had gone by 1959 and all of them by the end of the 1970s.

Nothing appears to have survived on the Upper Camp from the early-1913 built structures although the 1913 pattern side-opening aeroplane shed has, and is used as the Joint Service Parachute Centre. The sequence of buildings east of this are the two 1920s built 'A' Type hangars with the 1927 Watch Tower and the Handley Page hangar, the latter now unused due to falling masonry. Part of this 'Cathedral' hangar was occupied by the Army Fire Service until 1998 when it moved to the pre-war Watch Tower.

On the domestic site, the area to the north of the original 1913 barrack layout was entirely remodelled in the early 1950s when a new Airmans' Institute for 1000 personnel in Uni-Seco hutting (1951 design) replaced the original block of World War 1 accommodation. An extensive layout of Seco hutting to the north of this complex was built to a drawing issued in 1951. The original married mens' quarters were built in Choulston Close but were demolished, with replacements built behind the original in 1952. New officers' married quarters, which have been built at various times since 1925 including in the 1950s, are in Kerby Close.

Through all the changes on the Lower Camp, the original layout of Officers' Mess, Sergeants' Mess and barracks has remained in continuous use since its construction between the summer of 1913 and the following spring. The survival of these buildings is quite remarkable when one considers the development and demolition that has gone on around them. The five-span Handley Page hangar survives and is in use as vehicle sheds and vehicle servicing.

The Cavalry School (Netheravon House) is still in existence but, as was the case in 1912, it is presently unused. The 1930s Medical Centre building currently houses the HQ of No.2 Military Intelligence Battalion.

Pre World War 1 Years

The completion of only the aeroplane sheds and technical buildings at Netheravon by the summer did not prevent the commissioning of the aerodrome on 16th June 1913 and No.3 Sqn with Major H.R.M. Brooke-Popham as Commanding Officer (CO), moving in from Larkhill. The squadron arrived with a considerable selection of aircraft types, namely the BE2a, 3 and 4, Longhorn, Bleriot X1, Henry Farman F.20 and Avro Type E. Two days later No.4 Sqn, which had formed on 16th September 1912 and was commanded by Major G.H. Rayleigh, arrived from Farnborough also with an assortment of aircraft. They comprised the Breguet Biplane, Longhorn, Caudron G11 and Shorthorn.

On 28th July 1913, a No.3 Sqn Flt proceeded to South Farnborough for the purpose of organising the fifth of the eight squadrons authorised for the Military Wing of the RFC. This arrangement resulted in No.5 Sqn forming on 26th July with Major J.F.A. 'Josh' Higgins DSO, RA as CO. The squadron was equipped with 4 Maurice Farmans with 70 hp Renault engines and 7 or 8 two-seater Avros with 50 hp Gnome engines. No.5 Sqn consisted of a HQ and only one Flt, when it was called to take part in the Army manoeuvres of 1913. However, a composite Flt of machines drawn from the Royal Aircraft Factory and elsewhere, plus a Flight of Naval aeroplanes lent by the Admiralty, enabled it to take to the field as a complete unit.

No.2 Sqn had formed at Farnborough on 13th May 1912 from No.2 (Aeroplane) Coy and was equipped with the Bristol Boxkite, Breguet, BE1 and Longhorn. No.1 Sqn had also formed there on 13th April 1912 from No.1 (Airship) Coy but was still equipped with balloons and airships. It was not until May 1914 that these were transferred to the Royal Navy and No.1 Sqn reconstituted itself as an aeroplane unit commanded by Charles Longcroft.

During the summer of 1913, No.3 Sqn

Officers of the RFC (Military Wing) at the Concentration Camp in 1914. Those marked with an asterisk were members of No.5 Sqn.   Photo: B. Sykes

Front row: Capts. Beatty & Dawes, Majors Hon. C. Brabazon, Musgrave, Raleigh & Higgins*, Lt Col Sykes, Lt Barrington-Kennett, Capts. Conner*, Cholmondeley, Herbert, Charlton & Carmichael*.
2nd row: Capts. Holt, Shephard, Grey*, Stopford, Beor, Todd, Waldron, Lts Hynes, Mills, Joubert de la Ferte & Fuller.
3rd row: Lts Smith, Christie, Stodart*, Rodwell, James, Spence, Mansfield, Humphreys, Gould, Mitchell, Cogan, R.G.D. Small, Allen & Pryce.
4th row: Lts Penn-Gaskell*, Dawes, Martyn, Vaughan*, Birch, Read, Adams*, Borton*, Corballis & Mapplebeck.
5th row: Lts Harvey-Kelly, Freeman, McNeece, Glanville*, Noel, Wadham, Porter, Playfair, Hubbard, Lewis, Morgan & F.G. Small.
6th row: Lts Mansergh, Carpenter, Shekleton, Atkinson, Hartree, Moore, Hoskins, Waterfall*, Lywood & Hordern.

with 'A', 'B' and 'C' Flts, was carrying out experiments using aircraft in co-operation with artillery. This was staged near Knighton Down using Henri Farmans flown by Capt. Stopford, Capt. P.L.W. Herbert, Lt Roupell and Lt A. Shekleton. Lt Wadham, one summer evening, took off in Avro 500 No.290 and managed to attain a height of 10,300'. The flight was considered an excellent achievement at the time. During August 1913, a BE4 and two Bleriots of 'C' Flt were sent to Ford in the Vale of Evesham. This movement was for an exercise to see how the aircraft could be maintained under 'field' conditions. The pilots involved were Capt. Allen, Lt Wadham and Lt Conran. The NCOs and mechanics in the party travelled by road in Mercedes and Daimler light tenders.

No.3 Sqn now started receiving the Bleriot XI with the 80h.p. Gnome engine. The first to arrive was No.292. The type had the passenger seat set well to the rear of the pilot.
As with the 1912 army manoeuvres, No.3 Sqn was used again in those exercises of September 1913. This operation covered a three-week period

in which the squadron operated from Hungerford, Wantage, Oxford, Bicester and Towcester before returning to Netheravon. The squadron was used for reconnaissance and attacks against 'hostile' aircraft.

By 1914, No.3 Sqn was experimenting in aerial photography with officers using personal cameras. The officers evolved a type that enabled them to develop negatives during the flight that were ready to print on landing. Using this method, a photographic survey of the defences on the Isle of Wight and the Solent was made in a single day. During the spring, the squadron experimented with different forms of lighting used for landing at Netheravon.

The squadron lost two of its experienced pilots who were killed when BE4 No.204 crashed on Wednesday 11th March 1914. These fatalities were Capt. C.R.W. Allen, Welsh Regiment, and a passenger Lt J.E.G. Burroughes, Wiltshire Regiment. Take-off was in favourable conditions, and at a height of 300/350' the pilot made a half turn in the direction of Upavon. Suddenly the

Military observers at the Concentration Camp on 29th June 1914.
Photo: Terry Crawford Coll.

A gathering in front of the water tower on the Upper Camp at Netheravon during the summer of 1914 includes Lord Kitchener, in uniform on the left with Mr Asquith approaching the camera. In uniform on the right are General David Henderson and Lt Col Frederick Sykes.

RFC Officers of the Military Wing inspecting Maurice Farman S.11 Shorthorn 343 at the Concentration Camp.

last training camp before the outbreak of war. The programme of concentrated training commenced on 2nd June. At no time during the training of the whole strength of the RFC was it possible to put more than 30 aircraft into the air at the same time. This gives some idea of the strength of the five squadrons which comprised the RFC at that time. The compliment was about 50 pilots and 800 NCOs and airmen. An aerial review was staged at Netheravon on 29th June to which foreign military attaches were invited, including the German and Austrian attaches who were particularly interested in seeing as much as possible. The aircraft types flying in the review were the Avros, Bleriots, BEs, Henri Farmans, Maurice Farmans, Shorthorns, Sopwiths and an RE.5. A 'Grand Review' was also staged at Perham Down on Monday 22nd June 1914, to celebrate the birthday of the King.

The Military Wing attending the training camp at Netheravon comprised the Aircraft Park under Major A.D. Carden, No.2 Sqn commanded by Major C.J. Burke which flew in from Montrose on the 30th June, No.3 Sqn which was already resident at Netheravon under Major Brooke-Popham, No.4 Sqn, also resident at Netheravon, under Major Raleigh and No.5 Sqn under Major Higgins which moved in from Farnborough on 28th May 1914. No.5 Sqn was equipped with one Flt of Sopwiths (No.319) and two Flts of Henri Farman F.20s. No.6 Sqn, under Major Beck, was in the process of formation at South Farnborough, so arrived later.

The object of the 'Camp' was to train personnel, both in the air and on the ground, and in the handling of aircraft and motor transport, both by day and night. Experimental night flying across country, observation, signalling, air fighting, bomb dropping, speed, climb and short landing (over a tape) tests, photography, wireless and the rapid packing up and moving of transport by night were some of the subjects covered. On the ground, the training addressed meteorology, stores and equipment, systems of maintenance and repair, supply and transport, changing camps, construction of temporary aerodromes and mobilisation. Morning sessions were given to exercises and experiments and

rudder bar snapped and the machine flicked into a spin, pitched nose downwards and dived into the ground. Capt. Allen was thrown clear of the aeroplane but struck the ground head first, killing him instantly. The body of Lt Burroughes was found in the wreckage. Both were removed to Bulford Military Hospital.

No.3 Sqn included amongst its personnel, James T.B. McCudden who had been posted to the squadron as a air mechanic at the age of 18. McCudden was responsible for maintenance of Bleriot 80 h.p. No.389 during the period leading up to the departure of the squadron from Netheravon to

France. The ambition of the mechanic was to fly like his elder brother and he took every opportunity whilst at Netheravon to do so, accompanying squadron pilots such as Lt Vivian H.N. Wadham and Capt. R. Cholmondeley. Both pilots were killed in the war.

In June 1914, Lt Col Frederick Sykes, OC the Military Wing of the RFC, concentrated the whole of the Military Wing at Netheravon for training. The Wing of five squadrons was in the process of being built up to seven aeroplane squadrons, one airship and kite squadron, and an aircraft park with its own Corps headquarters. This would be the Military Wing's first and

RFC Lorries parked during the Concentration Camp. All appear to have solid tyres.
Photo: Army Air Corps

A Henri Farman of No.5 Sqn carrying out a 'short landing' across a tape during training
at the Concentration Camp.

DH BE2A 336 with 70hp Renault engine built by Vickers, seen at Netheravon in June 1914.
It was issued to No.4 Sqn. on 31st July 1914 and was sent to France with the squadron the
following month. Photo: T. L. Fuller © J. T. Fuller.

World War 1 Years

War had been declared on Monday 3rd August 1914. At Netheravon, armed personnel were posted to each of the aeroplane sheds to guard the machines. Everybody was issued with live ammunition. The aircraft were prepared for war and this involved fitting cockpits with racks to hold rifles, sacks to hold ammunition and issuing maps for navigation.

No.3 Sqn was next to depart when it left on Wednesday 12th August for Swingate Down en route to Amiens the following day. Lorries and tenders left with the stores, spares and equipment. Most of the NCOs and airmen travelled by road. Some however, flew in two-seater aircraft. The day before leaving Netheravon, a single-seat Bleriot Parasol No.616 had been collected from Farnborough by Lt Conran. Netheravon experienced a fatal flying accident when a Bleriot crashed on the day No.3 Sqn moved out. The machines had started leaving Netheravon at 0430 hrs. 'A' and 'B' Flts were first off, 'A' Flt with Bleriots and BE4s and 'B' Flt with Henri Farmans. 'C' Flt was last off with its Bleriots. Lt Joubert de la Ferte with Air Mechanic Gardiner were followed by Lt Conran in his single seat Parasol, then Lt Pretyman with Cpl. Robins and lastly 2nd Lt R.R. Skene with Air Mechanic Keith Barlow. Air Mechanic James McCudden started up the engine of the last machine and then waved the chocks away. Having taken off, the machine was seen to be flying with the tail down at about 80'. The machine was lost to sight behind one of the sheds when the engine failed and shortly afterwards the noise of a crash was heard. James McCudden ran the half-mile to the scene and found the machine in a small copse of fir trees. Climbing over a fence, he pulled the wreckage away from the crew but found them both dead. Lt Skene was renowned as the first Englishman to have looped the loop. The squadron personnel sailed from Southampton on the tramp steamer *Dee* at 1800 hrs that evening.

No.4.Sqn assisted the Royal Navy in coastal patrols before departing Netheravon equipped with the BE2a (240) the day after No.3 Sqn and followed the same route. At the outbreak of war, Great Britain had four squadrons and an Aircraft Park ready

afternoons to lectures and discussions.

Experiments were also made with wireless telegraphy, and a major advance in this field was recognised when Lts D.S. Lewis and B.J. James, flying from Netheravon to Bournemouth, succeeded in communicating with each other in the air over a distance of 10 miles. These practical experiments, at the time of the Concentration Camp, were to be of major significance in shaping the initial use of aircraft and their associated tactics during the early months of World War 1.

The Concentration Camp commenced breaking-up on 4th July 1914 when the Aircraft Park left for Farnborough early in the morning. No.6 Sqn should have followed later in the day but were prevented by deterioration in the weather. No.5 Sqn did not return to Farnborough but left 2 days later for a new air station at Fort Grange, Portsmouth. No.2 Sqn, whose personnel had largely been recruited in the south, were allowed to take leave and, on return, the squadron left on 5th August 1914, not for Montrose but for Farnborough, the first part of its journey to France.

for active service. The aircraft were an assortment of about 130 machines comprising BEs SEs, REs, Horace and Maurice Farmans, Avros and Sopwiths. Pilots numbered around 150. On the naval side, there were about 100 seaplanes, plus 2 first class and 2 second class airships.

During the first few months of the war, Netheravon became a temporary annex of the Central Flying School at Upavon in order to train officers who had not yet obtained their aviator's certificate. The annex was closed in October 1914 and reopened as an instructional establishment by No.3 Reserve Aeroplane Company. On 21st January 1915, this training was transferred to Shoreham. Netheravon then became a base for the formation of new squadrons under the command of No.4 Wing. The arrangement continued until December 1916.

No.6 Sqn moved in from Farnborough on 21st September 1914, equipped with the BE2a, BE8 and Henry Farman F.20. The squadron, commanded by Major G.H. Raleigh, had a training school role but its stay was short since it returned to Farnborough on 4th October en route to Bruges in Belgium. The replacement was No.7 Sqn on 24th October, arriving from Farnborough with Capt. John Salmond as CO and equipped with the Avro Type E, Vickers FB 'Gun Carrier' and RE5. The squadron stayed until 8th April 1915 when it left for St. Omer where its operations were artillery observation, reconnaissance, bombing and photography. Capt. John Aidan Liddell MC joined the squadron's 'A' Flt. on 23rd July 1915 and his actions seven days later earned him the VC. Flying RE5 2457 over Bruges, the aircraft was attacked and damaged and Liddell seriously injured. He lost consciousness as the RE5 dropped 3,000' but he recovered to hand his observer, 2nd Lt R.H. Peck, a written note indicating his intention to reach the Allied lines. This he somehow managed to do, so saving his machine and observer. Liddell's injuries were so serious that he died in hospital on 31st August, eight days after hearing of his award. His aircraft, RE5 2457, was repaired and returned to England where it was allocated to No.7 Reserve Sqn at Netheravon for flying instruction.

From October 1914 to mid-summer 1916, the station trained squadrons for combat duties.

No.1 Sqn arrived on 14th November 1914, equipped with the Longhorn. The squadron was also in a training-school capacity and carried out these duties until it left for St. Omer on 17th March 1915 with Major C.G. Honce as CO. By that time, the squadron had re-equipped with the Avro 504, BE8 and Caudron G111. No.1 Sqn took to France 8 Avro 504s and 4 BE8s which were used in artillery-spotting, bomber and fighter roles.

No.4 Wing formed on 29th November 1914 as 4th Wing RFC at Netheravon initially with Nos. 1 and 7 Sqns and commanded by Lt Col J.F.A. Higgins. He was known as *Colonel Bum & Eyeglass*, so-called because of his jutting backside and monocle. No.4 Wing was renamed CFS and Netheravon Wing on 23rd August 1916 and became the responsibility of the newly constituted Training Brigade that had formed in July.

Netheravon continued with the build-up and training of new squadrons. No.XI Sqn was sanctioned and formed from the nucleus of No.7 Sqn on 28th November 1914. The squadron became a separate Unit on 14th February 1915 with Major G.W.P. Dawes, Berkshire Regiment, RFC as CO. The three Flt Cdrs, Lionel W.B. Rees, P.H.L. 'Pip' Playfair and C.C. Darley, were already veterans of the Western Front. In 1916 when commanding No.32 Sqn, Rees was awarded a VC. No.XI Sqn was equipped with the Henry Farman F.20, Vickers FB 'Gun Carrier' and, from June, the Vickers FB5 'Gun Bus'. This squadron, which was the first to be organised primarily for two-seater air fighting, left for St. Omer on 25th July 1915. One of the pilots joining the squadron nine days earlier was Lt G. S.M. Insall who later that year was awarded the VC.

No.12 Sqn formed on 14th February 1915 from the nucleus of No.1 Sqn and equipped from May with the Avro 504 and from June with the BE2c. The squadron CO was Maj. C.L.N. Newall. After working-up the squadron left for St. Omer on 6th September 1915, the BE2cs taking off at ten-minute intervals.

No.10 Sqn moved in from Hounslow on 7th April 1915 equipped with the BE2c with a 70 hp Renault engine. The CO was Major U.D.J. Bourke.

Instruction of pilots commenced immediately. The squadron moved to St. Omer on 23rd July 1915.

It was realised that the rapidly expanding RFC would require uniform training at established training schools. Netheravon was one of 17 of these set up by the end of 1915 and operating a number of Reserve Aeroplane Sqns. Two of these, Nos.7 and 8 Reserve Sqns formed on 28th July 1915 as part of 4th Wing at Netheravon. The squadrons were equipped with Maurice Farman Shorthorns and Henri Farmans respectively.

Flying training was claiming many lives at this time and Netheravon was no exception. On Friday 2nd June 1916, a machine, possibly Maurice Farman MF11 Shorthorn L5059, started up in one of the hangars, taxied out and took-off. The machine banked steeply to the left before side-slipping into the ground and bursting into flame. The pilot, Lt William A. Buchanan, 1st Connaught Rangers, RFC, from New Zealand, was admitted to Tidworth Military Hospital where he died of his injuries five days later. He was buried at Tidworth Military Cemetery. The Observer, Capt. Lancelot Prickett, 71st Heavy Artillery attached to the RFC, was trapped in the wreckage and died before he could be released.

A No.7 Reserve Sqn pilot, 2nd Lt Victor S.H. Abbott RFC, was killed on Friday 15th September 1916 when his Maurice Farman S.7 Shorthorn approached Netheravon to land but nose-dived into the ground. He was buried at Upavon Cemetery.

O.B.W. Wills in a letter wrote *'I am feeling rotten just now as I've seen the sixth fatal accident in three days...so we've had two more killed and one terribly burnt today. I rushed up with several more to extricate the men from the ruined aeroplane, but we could only get one out and the other was burnt stiff and black in a kneeling attitude, trying to get out.'*

In a title change in May 1917, Reserve Sqns became Training Sqns and most amalgamated in 1918 to become Training Depot Stations. These particular squadrons left Netheravon for Witney in April 1918 where they disbanded into No.33 Training Depot Station (TDS).

No.21 Sqn formed at Netheravon on 23rd July 1915 from the nucleus of No.8 Reserve Aeroplane Squadron (RAS) and were equipped with the RE7. The CO was Major F.W. Richey. The squadron left for Boisdinghem in France on Saturday 22nd/ Sunday 23rd January 1916. In July 1915, a Canadian joined the squadron at Netheravon for training as an observer. He was Lt William Avery Bishop who, in June 1917, was awarded the VC.

Lt Harold W. Butterworth from Auckland, New Zealand was posted from Brooklands to Netheravon on 11th August 1915 for 'higher instruction in aviation'. He arrived by train at Pewsey from where a light tender conveyed him, with his boxes, to Netheravon. He flew a Henri Farman for the first time the following day and soloed on it two days later. The same day he was Squadron Orderly Officer and his duties were to inspect the men on parade and send them to their work places. The barracks had to be inspected and, at the end of the day, he had to dismiss the men and ensure the sheds were all locked. Butterworth's Flight was equipped with two Henri Farmans for four pilots but one man smashed up both machines in as many days, so for a few days in August there was no flying for the Flight. The third weekend of the month, Butterworth had weekend leave and travelled to visit a friend near Weston-Super-Mare. Flying Corps officers were not allowed to wear uniform when taking leave so he travelled in *mufti*. On Saturdays, many officers travelled to Paddington by train departing from Pewsey at 0930 hours, so Butterworth joined them in the light tender but took the train in the opposite direction, travelling via Trowbridge, Bath and Bristol. On his return from Somerset the following day, he left the seaside town at 1130 hours and arrived back in Pewsey at 6.20pm, having waited 2 hours at both Bath and Trowbridge stations for connecting trains. He went to church in Pewsey and then awaited the 8.45pm train from Paddington and, with his fellow officers, arrived back in Netheravon at 9.30pm. After such a journey he must have been relieved that next day the Flight had nothing to do.

A week later Butterworth was given the duties of Wing Orderly. He was required to hoist the correct flag for flying in the morning and see that it

was kept flying throughout the day. He had to visit personnel breakfasting at 0700 and 0745 hours, attend working parade at 0845 hours, inspect all the barracks, inspect rations and sign the ration book. He had to visit the Institute, visit personnel dining at 1230 and 1.15pm, inspect the fire engine and appliances, test the ambulance, attend fire parade and see it was properly carried out. At 6pm he had to mount the guard, collect the absentee reports and see lights out at 10pm. Afterwards he turned out the guard, and then visited the aeroplane sheds and workshops. At some point in the day he also had to go to the bank in Amesbury. The following day he flew a cross country to Salisbury, circling the spire of the cathedral at 4000' before returning to Netheravon. Salisbury was the place where many of the Netheravon airmen headed for an evening when off-duty. In his diary, Harold Butterworth records going there to see a film one evening in September 1915. He walked the four miles from Netheravon to the railway station in the village of Bulford and, after the show, caught the only train back, arriving at 1245 am. He was lucky in catching a RPC 3-ton lorry at the railway station but not so lucky in that it got lost and did not arrive at the aerodrome until 1.40am. This was Butterworth's one and only trip to the Salisbury cinema, which is hardly surprising bearing in mind the journey time, and his view that he never wanted to see such a 'dud' show again as long as he lived.

Lt Butterworth flew a BE8a on a cross country for his 'wings' on 1st October 1915. He had to fly to Warminster, Frome, Malmesbury, Swindon and back to Netheravon. All was well until he left Malmesbury, when the engine stopped and he glided down to a landing in a field. On examination, he discovered the cover had come off the make-and-break in the magneto and it had filled with oil. He found a post office and sent a telegram to Netheravon, explaining his position. He had tea and supper with the farmer before returning to spend the night with his machine as he was not allowed to leave it unguarded. The next day he returned to the farmhouse for breakfast, and later, a tender arrived from Netheravon with Capt. Windham and 3 mechanics. The machine was made good but, because of low cloud, it could not be flown. A local gentleman took all the airmen to lunch. The clouds

had cleared by 3pm and Capt. Windham was able to take-off and return to Netheravon, the remainder travelling in the tender. On 4th October 1915, Lt Butterworth carried out landings for his 'wings' in front of the Colonel. These were good with each landing close to the mark. The following day was spent at Central Flying School (CFS) Upavon on examinations with very high marks achieved for engine, wireless and rigging. For wireless, 95% was awarded and for his cross country, 90% was obtained. He received news the next day that his 'wings' had been awarded.

On 25th October 1915, Lt Butterworth joined No.8 Reserve Sqn as an instructor. The aircraft he had flown were the Avro, Vickers Gun Bus, Armstrong Whitworth, BE8 (Blaster), Curtiss and Martinside. He now found himself instructing on the Henri Farman and in December took the opportunity of flying a Voisin. This was a very large machine with a 140hp Canton Unne engine. The Voisin was able to carry three persons.

Gale-force winds swept through Netheravon two days after Christmas, demolishing a new aeroplane shed that was being built to house 20 machines and a canvas hangar for an RE7. By the 29th December 1915 the weather conditions had improved sufficiently to allow flying to continue and Butterworth took the opportunity of flying a Vickers Fighter with the 100hp Monosoupape Gnome engine.

No.8 Reserve Sqn took delivery of some Avros on 14th January 1916 and these were put to good use three days later, when several Army battalions with motor transport and horses arrived uninvited and started exercising on the airfield. The pilots of No.8 Reserve Sqn, which included Lt Butterworth, were invited by their Colonel to see off the intruders. The Avros took off and swooped down on the Army personnel at about 70 mph and around 10' above their heads. This created a stampede of both horses and men and in no time at all they had all left the aerodrome.

Lt Harold Butterworth left for France shortly after this where, as a Flight Commander, he was engaged in night flying and bomb dropping over the enemy lines. On the night of Saturday 15th July 1916 he and his observer were shot down in their machine by infantry. Lt Harold W. Butterworth RFC is buried at Cabaret-Rouge British Cemetery, Souchez, Pas de Calais.

No.20 Sqn formed at Netheravon on 1st September 1915 from the nucleus of No.7 RAS equipped with the Curtis JN3, BE2c and, from October, the Martinsyde G100. Major C.W. Wilson was the CO. The squadron left for Filton on 15th December.

No.26 (South African) Sqn formed at Netheravon on 8th October from personnel of the South African Aviation Corps. The squadron moved out on 23rd December and embarked on a voyage to Mombasa in East Africa where it served with the East African British Expeditionary Force.

No.32 Sqn formed at Netheravon on 12th January 1916 from the nucleus of No.21 Sqn equipped with the Henry Farman F20 (transferred from No.8 Sqn), Vickers FB5, in February the DH2 and in May the Vickers ES1. The CO was Welshman Major Lionel W.B. Rees MC who, for his actions on the 1st July 1916, was awarded the VC. The squadron was the last to depart Netheravon before the Battle of the Somme. Fourteen machines left for St. Omer via Folkstone on 28th May. One crashed with engine problems near Farnborough but with no injuries, and another landed safely with engine trouble.

No.19 Sqn arrived from Castle Bromwich on 31st January 1916 and re-equipped in February with the Avro 504, Caudron G111, Bristol Scout, Martinsyde S1, BE2c and BE12, FE2b, RE5 and RE7. The squadron moved to Filton on 26th March 1916.

No.42 Sqn formed at Netheravon on 26th February 1916 from the nucleus of No.19 Sqn and left for Filton on 1st April under the command of Major J.L. Kinnear. The squadron subsequently went to France.

No.48 Sqn formed at Netheravon on 15th April 1916 from the nucleus of No.7 RAS. Various aircraft were used by the squadron, which moved to Rendcomb on 8th June. In 1944, this squadron was in Transport Command and, with Dakota aircraft, played a significant part in the major airborne operations.

No.24 Reserve Sqn formed in 4th Wing on 25th May 1916 at Netheravon from the nucleus of No.32 Sqn which, three days later, left for France. Having become No. 24 Training Sqn in May 1917, the unit moved to Witney on 30th March 1918. The CO was Maj Frank.W.Smith and the Sqn was equipped with the Shorthorn.

No.62 Sqn formed at Netheravon on 28th July 1916 from the nucleus of No.42 Sqn and No.7 RAS. The squadron moved to Filton on 8th August 1916.

The former No.4 Wing was revived when it reformed on 10th January 1917 as 4th (Reserve) Wing at Netheravon to control locally-based units, initially with Nos.7, 8 and 24 Reserve Sqns for elementary training, an Aeroplane Reserve Section and a School of Fitters. With the formation of the RAF on 1st April 1918, the Wing came within No.7 Group which also formed on the same date at 'Rokeby', Waine-a-Long Road, Salisbury. Netheravon was controlled by the General Officer Commanding at the Salisbury HQ. The Wing then comprised 1 Training Section, 2 Training Depot Stations, an Artillery Co-operation Section and 2 Naval Sqns. These units remained at Netheravon until the Armistice, after which a reduction in scale took place.

On 13th January 1917, an Artillery Co-operation Sqn formed from the Artillery Co-operation Flights at CFS Upavon and from Lydd, with a HQ at 61 New Street, Salisbury. 'A' Flt was attached to Netheravon, equipped with the Pup, F2b, RE8, BE2d and FK8. The squadron suffered a double fatality on the morning of Monday 4th February 1918 when Lt Ashton Morgan (pilot) and Flt Sgt Lester W. Rowan were killed in a flying accident. Flying from Bristol the previous day, bad weather was experienced so the pilot decided to land at Hindon and spent the night there. Air Mechanic A. Harris was sent from Netheravon to guard the machine, arriving in Hindon around 2300hrs. The following morning Harris spent two hours examining the machine and it appeared to be in flying condition. He witnessed the pilot starting up and watched the machine until it was out of sight. 700 yards from the aerodrome at Netheravon and at a height of about 250', the wing of the machine was seen to have doubled up before it fell to the ground. The crash was witnessed by

A Mess bill issued to Lt J.B.H. Wyman while he was training at Netheravon in June 1917. He qualified as a pilot, joined No.70 Sqn and was shot down while flying Camel B6250 on an offensive patrol over Houthulst Wood near Menin on 15th September 1917. He was wounded in the action and became a POW. He later escaped and crossed the border into Holland where he was interned on 7th May 1918. Some time later he was repatriated.

Capt. C.E.W. Foster RFC, from his position by the Regimental Institute. At the inquest held at the Military Hospital Netheravon, he stated that 'some machines would stand bad weather and some would not'. Air Mechanic Harris confirmed the detail of his examination and added that he 'took a pride in the machine and considered it a good one'. A verdict of accidental death was returned and the two men were buried at Netheravon Cemetery, Figheldean. The squadron remained at Netheravon until disbanded on 29th October 1919.

No.92 Canadian Reserve Sqn formed at Netheravon on 15th March 1917 out of No.7 Reserve Sqn personnel prior to embarking for Canada the following month.

No.72 Sqn arrived from Upavon on 8th July 1917 and during the month, was equipped with 3 Avro 504s and a Sopwith Pup. The role of the squadron initially was to train pilots prior to posting to squadrons. 30 pilots had been trained by 1st November 1917 when the squadron left for Sedgeford where it mobilised to full squadron status prior to departure for the Persian Gulf. No.74 Training Sqn (TS) formed out of No.8 TS at Netheravon in 4th

A HP 0/400 in front of some Bessoneau hangars at Netheravon in 1918.
Photo: S. Bradley/Cty. Tony West

A No.8 TDS Maurice Farman SE.11 Shorthorn at Netheravon during the summer of 1918.
The Unit identification on the nose shows a triangle, which is thought to have been red,
on a white disc.   Photo: S. Bradley/Cty. Tony West

A No.8 TDS HP 0/400 D4576 having its engine removed for overhaul at Netheravon. The Unit
number '5' appears to have been painted by somebody with an artistic touch.
Photo: S. Bradley/Cty. Tony West

Wing on 21st October 1917 and moved to Castle Bromwich on 1st December. No.59 TS arrived from Beaulieu on 20th November and left for Lilbourne on 6th December. No.71 TS formed out of No.7 TS at Netheravon in 4th Wing on 28th November and also left for Lilbourne on 10th December 1917. No.71 TS returned to Netheravon in February of the following year. No.70 TS formed out of No.24 TS at Netheravon in 4th Wing on 20th December 1917, moving immediately to Gosport.

In January 1918, a plan was devised by Air Chief Marshal Hugh Trenchard, Chief of the Air Staff, whereby the training of British and American bomber crews would be combined to form an Allied bombing force.

Netheravon was one of the stations where it was proposed to carry out the training using the HP 0/400. The scheme was not developed before the Armistice was signed and, consequently, was scrapped.

A fatal accident occurred at Netheravon on Monday 21st January 1918 when a FE2b crashed because the pilot lost control in a spinning nosedive. Lt H.P. Freeman RFC and 2nd Lt Claude Eugene Rooke RFC & King's Own Scottish Borderers were killed. The pilot had completed a mere 3½ hours of solo flying at the time of the accident.

No.97 Sqn arrived from Stonehenge on 31st March 1918 and was equipped with the HP 0/400 bomber in June. The squadron remained until 3rd August

1918 when it moved to Xaffevilers in France. No.116 Sqn arrived at Netheravon on the same day as No.97 Sqn, having formed at Andover the previous December. This squadron left for Kenley on 27th July 1918.

On the formation of the RAF on 1st April 1918, Netheravon became home to two newly created Training Depot Stations. No.8 and No.12 Training Depot Stations (TDS) were formed at Netheravon in 4th Wing, No.7 Group, Training Division. The former was equipped with the Avro 504 A & J, Camel, Maurice Farman SE 11 Shorthorn, HP 0/400, FE2b and Airco DH6. By the autumn of 1918, its establishment was 10 HP 0/400s, 30 Avros and 10 FE2bs. The HP 0/400 night-bombers were central to the RAFs developing role in long-range strategic bombing.

Known No.8 TDS machines Sopwith Camel F2197; Maurice Farman S.11 Shorthorn A2185, A2496, A7084, B1971, B2021, B2025, B4674, B4690, B4779, B7084, B9999; HP 0/400 C3495, C9693, C9696, C9703, C9704, C9706, C9707, C9710, C9735, C9755, D4576, D4604; FE2b A5537, A5747, A6537, A6591, B1861, B1866, D3797, D9107, D9153, D9769, F3499, F3501; Airco DH6 B2692, B3043, B3046, B3055, C2002, C2126, C2130, C2133, C2147, C2150, C5467, C5476, C5478, C5479, C5488, C6577, C6518, C6583, C7299, C7352, C7355, C7356, C7357, C7358, C7377, C7675, C9356.

The CO of No.8 TDS was Major B. McEwen with instructors Captains Aitken, Brooks, Gilmore, Hanning, Kelly, McKenzie, Richardson, Satchell, Ward; Lts Asserman, Brodie, Cates, Coutts, Francis, Hankinson, Hopcroft, Humphries, Kempster, Kylie, Palmer, Porritt, Pynne, Thompson, Wallace, Walsh, Wood, Wright and Chief Petty Officer Prickett.

No.12 TDS was equipped with the Avro 504K, RE8, HP 0/400, FE2b and Airco DH6. The two TDSs were responsible for basic and advanced training. No.8 TDS experienced its first fatality in the month of forming when, on Friday 24th May 1918, 2nd Lt Joseph J. Daly RAF (pilot) of New York, and his passenger Major Benjamin S. Jordan, Canterbury Regiment New Zealand Expeditionary Force (NZEF) were killed when their DH6 C6518,

No.8 TDS FE2b D3797 overturned as a result of a bad landing at Netheravon.
Photo: S. Bradley/Cty. Tony West

A No.12 TDS RE8 at Netheravon in 1918.
Photo: S. Bradley/Cty. Tony West

A not unusual occurrence with, on this occasion, a No.8TDS Airco DH6 C7299 resting on the roof of one of Netheravon's aerodrome buildings. Photo: S. Bradley/Cty. Tony West

crashed at Codford. Having completed a loop and a dive to 1000', the machine, on pulling out, began to break up. Damage included the collapse of the port outer wings. Before the crash site could be secured, parts of the wreckage disappeared so that, when the accident investigators arrived, they were unable

to conduct a conclusive examination and determine a cause. Lt Daly was buried at Figheldean (St Michael) cemetery and Maj. Jordan, from New Zealand, at the Church of St. Mary New Churchyard, Codford St. Mary. The Major was the second in command of the New Zealand Command Depot at Codford. No.12 TDS experienced a fatality on Sunday 11th August 1918 when 2nd Lt Ira W. Hathaway crashed whilst making a turn when the engine failed. Lt Hathaway, from Toronto, was buried at Figheldean (St Michael) cemetery.

An early recruit with No.8 TDS was a Canadian, 2nd Lt Stewart F. Bradley. He had enlisted in the 21st Canadian Reserve Infantry and was accepted for RFC training on 22nd October 1917. He spent six months as a cadet at Denham before being posted to No.97 Sqn at Netheravon on 20th April 1918. The initial entry in his log book indicates his first 'air experience' flight was in a Maurice Farman Shorthorn B2021 on 21st April 1918, with Capt. Gilmore at the controls. Some of the flying was carried out from Netheravon and some from Stonehenge. Lt Bradley was

officially posted to No.8 TDS for flight training on 11th May 1918. His regular instructor for most of the period up to then, was Capt. Hanning.

Lt Bradley went solo in DH6 B2692 after eight weeks. Strangely, it was not until the 28th July that he soloed again, this time in a Maurice Farman F2185. After receiving instruction on the FE2b, he flew D9769 solo on 20th August and D9107 on his first night solo on 18th October. Lt Bradley progressed to the HP 0/400, with his first flight in C9704 with CPO Prickett instructing. Bradley went solo in HP 0/400 C3495 on 25th September and in C9755 he night soloed on 22nd November. Lt Bradley next moved to Stonehenge on 27th December 1918 where he attended No.1 School of Navigation and Bomb Dropping. With the war ended, a variety of postings followed until he was repatriated to Canada on 1st September 1919.

No.118 Sqn arrived from Catterick on 13th April 1918, equipped with the HP 0/400. The Sqn remained until 7th August when it moved to Bicester where it disbanded the following month.

No.115 Sqn arrived from Catterick on 15th April 1918, equipped with Sopwith Pups. The CO was Capt. J.W. James. The squadron re-equipped with the HP 0/400 in July before moving to Castle Bromwich on 17th, with Maj. W.E. Gardiner DSO who became the new CO two days before the move.

On 22nd April 1918, No.64 Wing arrived at Netheravon in No.5 Group with Nos. 207 and 215 Sqns. Prior to 1st April, these had both been squadrons of the RNAS. On arrival they began to re-equip with the Handley Page 0/400. The Wing disbanded and both squadrons left for Andover on 13th May 1918.

'A' Flt of the Artillery Co-operation Sqn was at Netheravon towards the end of 1918 and is thought to be the Flight using the Landing Ground (LG) at Tilshead in October/November 1918.

A No.12 TDS Avro 504K E1848 outside the Sheds at Netheravon in 1918.
Photo: S. Bradley/Cty. Tony West

This FE2b side-slipped in after an engine failure during a practice night flight at Netheravon in 1918.   Photo: S. Bradley/Cty. Tony West

Airco DH9 D5806 at Netheravon in 1918 with an HP 0/400 behind it.
Photo: S. Bradley/Cty. Tony West

Inside one of Netheravon's Aeroplane Sheds in 1918 is SE5a F5540.
Photo: S. Bradley/Cty. Tony West

A Beardmore engine on a mobile cradle at Netheravon probably during an engine change.
Photo: S. Bradley/Cty. Tony West

Lt Stewart F. Bradley with his No.8 TDS DH6 at Netheravon in 1918.
Photo: S. Bradley/Cty. Tony West

LtoR: Lts Graham, Williamson, Bradley and Tapping at Tidworth railway station in 1918.
Photo: S. Bradley/Cty. Tony West

Inter War Years

With the end of the 'War to end all Wars' and the signing of the Armistice in November 1918, the Government quickly set about getting rid of as much military hardware and personnel as it could. The Government were assisted in this at Netheravon when, during the night of 4th November 1918, a ferocious gale blew up and completely destroyed 2 Bessoneau hangars, 12 Avro 504Ks, 2 Bristol Fighters, 1 Martinsyde and 2 Handley Page 0/400s. The last two machines became airborne and landed up half a mile from their original locations.

As with Yatesbury, Netheravon was used as a station for disbanding operational units. On 18th February 1919, Nos.42 and 52 Sqns arrived as cadres from Abscon and Aulnoy respectively. No.42 Sqn disbanded on 26th June 1919 and No.52 Sqn left two days later for Lopcombe Corner but didn't disband until October 1919. No.35 Sqn arrived as a cadre on 3rd March 1919 from Ste-Marie-Cappel and disbanded on 26th June. No.208 Sqn arrived as a cardre from Eil on 9th September 1919, to be disbanded on 7th November 1919.

The 15th May 1919 was a significant date for Netheravon with the 4th (Reserve) Wing and No.12 TDS disbanding. No.8 TDS was redesignated as No.8 Training School until the 29th July when it briefly became the Netheravon Flying School and on 23rd December 1919, No.1 Flying Training School in No.7 Group. The School was equipped with the F2b, DH9a, Sopwith 7F.1 Snipe (E6150), Avro 504K and N. Until June 1924, the Unit was engaged in the training of abinitio pupil officer and airman pilots. The two courses overlapped and each had around 36 pupils each year.

Activity in the early 1920s at Netheravon had all but ceased but the years of 1924-28 were a period of steady expansion. The role of the school from June 1924 included the training of naval officers for service with the embryo Fleet Air Arm. Each course was of 6 months duration with 50 officers attending the first course. Although maintaining their ranks and uniforms, the naval officers were granted temporary RAF Commission. The aircraft used was the Bristol Fighter, DH9a and Avros.

The mess buggy and its attendants at Netheravon in 1918.
Photo: S. Bradley/Cty. Tony West

The morning after the storm leaves some clearing up to be done. In the pile of wreckage are
three new Avro 504Ks D9077, D9080 and F9697.   Photo: S. Bradley/Cty. Tony West

Carried across the aerodrome during the storm was HP 0/400 C9706.
Photo: S. Bradley/Cty. Tony West

In September 1922, Fg Off Ashton was injured in the crash at Netheravon of this Avro 504 of
No.1 FTS.   Photo: Rex Reynolds Coll.

The CO from March 1924 until the end of the year was Wg Cdr W.G. S. (Ginger) Mitchell CBE, DSO, MC, AFC. His colourful language was well understood by the pupils. He was promoted to Gp Capt on 1st July. Wg Cdr Mitchell had succeeded Wg Cdr J.A. Fletcher AFC as CO who, in turn, had replaced Wg Cdr P.H.L. Playfair in 1922. As of January 1925, Wg Cdr R.F.S. Morton held the office.

Flying accidents claimed the lives of two naval men attached to the RAF at Netheravon in 1925. Lt David B. Morgan RN was killed on 15th May and Fg Off John Ryan RN was killed on 14th July. Both were buried at Netheravon (All Saints) Church.

By 1927, the establishment had developed to consist of 2 Avro Flts, 2 DH9A Flts and 1 Snipe Flt. On 6th June 1927, the Chief Flying Instructor (CFI), Sqn Ldr Walter H. Longton DFC, AFC, was killed in the air races staged at Bournemouth. (Details under **UPAVON**). Longton was succeeded as CFI later in the month by Sqn Ldr Frew DSO, MC, AFC.

Wg Cdr R.G.D. Small was appointed CO at the end of 1927, and on 29th February 1928 the school was reduced to 4 Flts when 1 Flt left for Leuchers where naval officer flying training was transferred. The school was then equipped with 2 Flts of 8 Avros and 2 Flts of 7 DH9As. The latter began to be replaced in December 1928, when the school staff commenced collecting Atlas aircraft from Coventry.

The school, during 1929 experienced a number of fatalities. On 10th May, Plt Off M. Menzies-Jackson (No.14 Course) was killed in a crash whilst on a solo flight in an Avro trainer. He is buried at All Saints Church in Netheravon. On 2nd July Plt Off R.Y Bootes, also on a solo flight, was killed at Netheravon when his Atlas aircraft crashed. Plt Off R.D. Primrose was seriously injured and LAC Kelly killed on 10th October when their respective Atlas aircraft collided in the air. Both aircraft crashed and were destroyed by fire.

On 2nd September 1929, Wg Cdr J.F. Barton became CO and was promoted to Gp Capt on 1st January 1930. He retired at the end of the year and was succeeded by Wg Cdr E.B. Beauman. He held the post until No.1 FTS was disbanded on 1st February 1931. The FTS reformed four years later at

Leuchars. Sqn Ldr A.H. Stradling OBE commanded the school from 21st February until the 17th April 1931 when the hand- over to No.13 (AC) Sqn was completed.

During the period the school disbanded, the FAA units used Netheravon as a shore base while their aircraft carriers were in harbour. Various squadrons arrived and departed.

On 1st April 1924, No.99 Sqn reformed at Netheravon as a bomber unit equipped with the Vickers Vimy. On 31st May 1924 the squadron exchanged bases with No. XI Sqn when its 'A', 'B' and 'C' Flts arrived from Bircham Newton equipped with the Fairey Fawn. The CO was Sqn Ldr E.A.B. Rice MC. The arrival of these squadrons formed part of Trenchard's Home Defence Expansion Scheme, which was begun in 1923 with the aim of achieving air parity with the French Air Force. The scheme called for the deployment of bomber units at stations in central southern England and East Anglia, some of them reacquired bases of World War 1 vintage.

No.XI Sqn occupied the 5-bay 'Cathedral' hangar. On 31st July 1924, a No.XI Sqn Fairey Fawn J6990 crashed on the aerodrome, injuring the pilot Sgt Grey and killing LAC Maskell. The pilot was making his landing approach when he noticed another machine taking off. In making a climbing turn to avoid it, the engine of the Fawn lost power and it dived into the ground.

Another flying accident involving No.XI Sqn occurred on 10th November 1924 when Fairey Fawn J7202 was in collision with Snipe E6978 which was probably a No.1 FTS machine. Both pilots were killed. One was Sgt George Taylor RAF who was buried at Netheravon (All Saints) Church.

From November 1926, the squadron started re-equipping with the Hawker Horsley. One of them was lost on 18th March 1927 when, during a practice formation by 'A' Flt to Hawkinge, fog was encountered and the aeroplane flew into the ground killing Plt Off Priestman and passenger Pickering. The duties of the squadron at Netheravon involved flying training, exercise raids and display work. A different responsibility was experienced when five Horsleys were

The wreckage of Snipe E6978 on the aerodrome following a collision with Fairey Fawn J7202. Photo: Tony Mellor-Ellis Coll.

despatched to Gosport on 24th June. Two days later the Horsleys escorted HMS *Renown* from St Catherines Point to Portsmouth with the Duke and Duchess of York on board.

Sqn Ldr P.H. Cummings became the new squadron CO in January 1928 and, later in the year, a change of aeroplane took place with the arrival of two Wapiti in October. All the squadron pilots completed solo flying in these during November. Seven Horsleys were collected by No.100 (B) Sqn on 2nd November 1928. Squadron personnel left Netheravon on overseas leave on 16th November and the squadron sailed from Southampton on 29th December 1928, en route for Risalpur in India.

The Special Duties Flt (SDF), which had formed two years earlier at Old Sarum for a role with the Experimental Gas School at Porton Down, arrived at Netheravon on 12th September 1928. The SDF was staffed by three personnel. The O/i/C was Fg Off Florence with 1 rigger and 1 fitter AE. The SDF later became the Porton Flight and its aircraft were a F2b, Horsley and Dart. The Porton Flt left for Boscombe Down on 2nd February 1931 with a Hawker Horsley and a Fairey Fox.

HQ and 1 Flt of No.33 (B) Sqn reformed at Netheravon on 1st March 1929, equipped with 5 Horsley allocated from No.XI (B) Sqn. The CO was Sqn Ldr F.P. Don appointed on 10th April. The squadron was enlarged by 2 Flts on 29th June with Sqn Ldr Don receiving promotion to Wg Cdr on 1st July. 3 additional Horsleys arrived on

9th August and the squadron moved to Eastchurch on 14th September 1929.

No.13 (AC) Sqn arrived from Andover between 23rd/28th September 1929 with Sqn Ldr H.M. Fraser as CO and equipped with the Atlas. The squadron remained at Netheravon for 6 years. There was a change to the CO on 12th November 1929 with the appointment of Sqn Ldr J.B. Cole-Hamilton.

During the summer of 1930, the squadron engaged in a large-scale exercise with mobilisation at full war strength including transport to Odiham, Northolt, Henlow, Bicester and with finalisation at Odiham. During this period, 'A' & 'B' Flts operated on exercise from Tilshead Advanced Landing Ground (ALG).

Sqn Ldr J. Whitworth-Jones was appointed squadron CO in 1931 followed by Sqn Ldr H.L. Rough on 1st April 1933, Sqn Ldr P. Warburton MBE on 21st May 1934 and Sqn Ldr G.O. Venn on 25th April 1935.

Two Atlas machines were returning to Netheravon from Sutton Bridge in Lincolnshire in early May 1931 when one of them dropped out of formation to make its approach to land. As Fg Off Reginald G. Weighill began to lose height from 1000', the engine fell out. He and AC1 Alexander B. Merriman took to their parachutes. The pilot was fortunate that his opened fully just prior to him landing safely but Merriman's parachute failed to fully open and he was killed on impact with the ground.

During the summers of 1932 and 1933, the squadron was again mobilised to

A group of RAF and Naval Officers at Netheravon. Fairey Gordons form an impressive backdrop. These are possibly of No.40 Sqn which was equipped with the type until 1935 and was based at Abingdon from 1932 until war was declared in 1939.　　Photo: Tony Mellor-Ellis Coll.

Cambridge University Air Sqn (1st Attachment) at Netheravon for summer camp in July 1932. 3rd from left seated is Fg Off Joe Cox and stood immediately behind him is Plt Off Sikes who was killed in an Atlax crash at Boscombe Down on 22nd March 1933.
Photo: Joe Cox/Cty. Martyn Ford-Jones.

G.D. Watson of the Cambridge University Air Sqn was killed when Atlas J9562 crashed at Netheravon on 17th June 1932.　　Photo: Joe Cox/Cty. Martyn Ford-Jones.

Fg Off Joe Cox used this photograph on his 1933 Christmas cards. He was the pilot flying Avro 504N K1049 upside down over Netheravon aerodrome. The 1913 pattern Aeroplane Shed is just visible above his wings with the 1926 'C' Type on the right.
Photo: Joe Cox/Cty. Martyn Ford-Jones.

various aerodromes for Army co-operation exercises.

No.13 Sqn moved to Old Sarum on 3rd May 1935.

No.57 (B) Sqn. reformed at Netheravon in Wessex Bombing Area for operations and training on 20th October 1931. The unit was a single engine bomber squadron using the Hawker Hart with Rolls Royce Kestral 1.B engines of 480 hp. The Hart was the standard British light bomber of the early 1930s. The allocation was 12 initial equipment aircraft + 6 immediate reserve. The CO was Sqn Ldr H.G. Bowen with 11 Officers and 87 airmen including 6 airman-pilots. The aircraft started arriving the following month when, on 4th November 1931, 4 'K' Type Harts, including 1 dual-controlled, was received from No.12 (B) Sqn at Andover. The squadron spent a week in April 1932 taking part in Wessex Bombing Area camera obscura exercises, with raids on Polegate, Waddington, Highbridge and Avonmouth. In July, the squadron went to North Coates Fitties, the summer armament practice camp for bomber squadrons. No.57 Sqn stayed at Netheravon until 5th September 1932 when the unit moved to Upper Heyford. Another bomber squadron took its place with the reforming of No.142 Sqn at Netheravon on 1st June 1934, equipped with the Hawker Hart light bomber. The squadron moved to Andover on 3rd January 1935.

509 (FAA) Flight was formed at Netheravon in October 1932 and remained until it joined HMS *Glorious* in January 1933.

RAF Netheravon was open to the public for 'Empire Air Day' between 2pm-7pm on 30th June 1934. Admission charges were 1s for adults, 6d for children and 3d for organised parties. Proceeds were donated to RAF charities. The Fleet Air Arm and Army Co-operation Squadrons gave a display of message-picking-up with the Hawker Audax.

802 (FAA) Sqn arrived on 27th July 1935 and departed for embarkation in HMS *Glorious* on 21st August 1935.

Netheravon again had a training role when No.6 Flying Training School reformed there on 1st April 1935 in

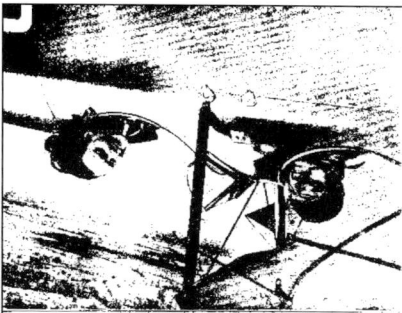

Advertisements of 1933

A mixed course of Naval and RAF personnel inside a hangar.
Photo: Tony Mellor-Ellis Coll.

No.23 Group. Initially the school flew the Hart, Audax and Fury, receiving the Anson in November 1936. The reforming was under the new re-armament expansion scheme to meet the accelerating rearmament of Germany. The function of the school, commanded by Gp Capt Augustine apEllis, was to introduce pilots to service-type aircraft and to provide preliminary training in the arts of formation, cross-country and night-flying plus air-firing. The school operated for three years and, in that time, had its share of accidents. On 1st January 1937, LAC F.W. Barrett died at Tidworth Military Hospital following a crash in Hart (T) K4952 whilst receiving dual instruction from Sgt N. Pickard. Cpl. W.K. Jackson, a pupil on No.4 Course was killed in a flying accident at Porthmadog, North Wales on 23rd April 1937. A/Plt Offs Philip Herbert Baily and D.L.P. Bagot-Gray, pupils of No.5 Course, were killed in a flying accident at Sutton Bridge on 4th August 1937. Bailey is buried at All Saints Church, Netheravon. Ground staff as well as flying personnel were prone to losing their lives as was the case with AC2 Stacey. He was hit by a machine whilst carrying out flare-path duties during night flying on 4th October 1937. Plt Off Guy Gibson, later of Dam Buster fame, was a pupil of the School between February and September 1937.

No. 6 FTS moved to Little Rissington on 11th August 1938 and was replaced on 26th August by No.1 FTS returning from Leuchars equipped with 32 Harts

(K4423). The CO of the station and the school was Gp Capt L.F. Forbes MC. He was replaced by Gp Capt W.B. Farington DSO on 24th November 1938.

On 1st May 1939, No.1 FTS started to re-equip with the North American Harvard and its allocation of 32 (N7062, N7073 and N7078) had been completed by 4th September.

World War 2 Years

During September 1939 and following the outbreak of war, a number of different squadrons arrived at Netheravon under the 'Scatter Scheme'. The squadrons would arrive one day and leave the next. One of these was No.82 Sqn, equipped with the Blenheim which arrived on 10th September 1939. The same day, Blenheim IV P4853 UX took-off from Netheravon for gun practice off the North Devon coast and crashed at Cleeve, 5 miles SE of Clevedon in Somerset. No.516867 Sgt James MacLaughlin RAF (pilot), and AC1 George H. Butler (Flt Mech) RAF were fatally injured and AC2 John Dorman and AC1 Ronald P.A. Dougan were injured. Interestingly the Commonwealth War Graves Commission records indicate that pilot Sgt James Pratt of No.82 Sqn was killed on 10th September 1939. The records also state that Sgt Pratt 'Served as McLaughin [sic], James', furthermore, the service number for Sgt Pratt is 516867, the same as for Sgt MacLaughlin. The RAF has no record of a Sgt James Pratt being killed or injured on this date. It does appear however that Sgt MacLaughin and Sgt Pratt were actually one and the same.

A Harvard trainer outside the timber 1913 pattern Aeroplane Repair Shed in 1941.
Photo: Ralph Godden

221

A two seat Battle Trainer at Netheravon early in the war.
Photo: Ralph Godden

The pilot is buried at the Church of Annunciation, Woodchester in Gloucestershire.

No.1 FTS became No.1 Service Flying Training School on 1ˢᵗ September 1939 and was the only SFTS handling advanced training exclusively for FAA pilots. The school, in No.23 (Training) Group, had its HQ at South Cerney.

Fatalities from flying accidents were all too frequent. Midshipman James V. Reed RN was killed in a flying accident on 15ᵗʰ June 1939. Fg Off Douglas Genders RAF was killed in a flying accident when piloting Harvard N7074. The aircraft spun into the ground at Oare Hill near Marlborough on Monday 11ᵗʰ September 1939. Leading Seaman Ronald E. Heyburn RN, of HMS *Pembroke* was killed in Harvard N7179 crash on Wednesday 20ᵗʰ September and was buried at Netheravon All Saints Churchyard. On Saturday 23ʳᵈ September 1939, two of the school's Harvard 1s P5791 and P5792, collided during flight. Both caught fire and crashed at Collingbourne Kingston. Three men were killed of which two were FAA pilots, Midshipman (A) Roger M.B. Kettle RN and Midshipman (A) John C. Casey RN, both serving with HMS *Pembroke*. The latter was the first New Zealand member of the FAA to be killed in the war. Both men were buried at Netheravon (All Saints) Church. The third man killed was AC1 William R.W. Phillips RAF. Flt Lt Wilson I. Hammond and Acting Sub Lt Donald Copsey RN of HMS *Daedalus* were killed when Harvard N7043 dived into the ground near Netheravon on Monday 13ᵗʰ November 1939. It was at this time that flying students expressed concern that they were experiencing difficulty in taking-off during the 'black out'. This disquiet resulted in the introduction of 'Leading Lights'. The following February the Advanced Training Sqn of the SFTS started to practice night dummy-deck landings.

Ralph Godden arrived at Netheravon in January 1940 as an AC2 Flt Mech. He was later attached to 'F' Flt and left as a LAC in June 1941. His first task, with other personnel, was to get his back under the starboard mainplane of a Battle and to manoeuvre it into position for attachment to the fuselage. At that time personnel referred to aircraft only as 'kites' and the shout commonly heard was 'Two six on the kite' whenever a machine needed pushing in or out of a hangar. 'Two six on the doors' was the call for hangar doors to be opened and closed. Ralph recalls the severe winter of 1939/40 when snow and sleet froze on contact with the ground. At times the atrocious weather prevented flying, and some ground crew were sent home on a week's grant. Ralph went to his home in Southampton. When the time came for him to return to the aerodrome, he recalls his bus was late arriving back at Salisbury because of the treacherous road conditions and he missed his connection to Netheravon. Unable to find a bed, he was given a police cell for the night in which, he feels, the previous occupant must have been a drunk who had left the contents of his stomach all over the cell.

When there was a break in the extreme weather conditions and flying was programmed, one of the problems experienced by the ground crews was starting the engines, particularly in the case of the Battle. The normal routine was to insert the plug of the 'trolley acc' (trolley accumulator) into the starter socket on the aircraft. When the pilot was ready and personnel were clear of the propeller, the pilot would shout 'Contact'. This was repeated by the ground crew member who then pressed the starter button. If this procedure was unsuccessful, a ground-crew member stood on a pair of steps and turned the starting handle. Finally, if the engine still would not start, the propeller was turned until the blade was at the 12 o'clock position. A canvas pouch, with a rope attached, was placed over the tip of an adjacent blade. When all was ready, the ground crew pulled on the rope for all they were worth.

Each day started with *Revellie* at 0600 hours and between then and roll-call on the parade ground at 0700 hours, washing, breakfast, and billet cleaning took place. When parade was dismissed, personnel marched to their places of work. Transport between hangars and the Domestic Site was provided, and it consisted of a Fordson tractor towing three flat-top trolleys to which some ex-cinema seats had been bolted. Travel on the rear trolley was quite hazardous as it swung from side to side when maximum speed was reached on the downhill approach to the Domestic Site. Ground crews worked alternatively, one day until 1700 hours, the next day until the end of flying. Weekend leave was one in three.

One of Ralph's duties was 'Airman of the Watch'. The duty lasted for one week at a time. This involved climbing a vertical ladder at one end of the 'A' Type hangar near the Watch Office, and occupying a small 'office' which commanded a view over most of the aerodrome. The 'office' had a telephone with a direct line to the Watch Office below. The duty involved watching the flying activity, particularly the take-off and landing phases. Any accidents observed were reported to the Duty Pilot. Ralph only ever reported one such incident involving what he believes was a Hawker Osprey of the FTS, which tipped onto its nose during a landing with two other machines in 'V' formation.

'F' Flight was equipped with the Hawker Hind aircraft and Ralph remembers them flown by 18 year old FAA pilots under training. When flying finished at the end of the day, aircraft were refuelled and checked over whilst the armourers fitted explosive bombs. This was at the time when it was

Battle K7613 flown by Cpl Beeston which crash landed after its collision during formation practice on 11ᵗʰ March 1940. Photo: Ralph Godden.

considered by Authority that these aircraft, piloted by trainees, might have to be used against the Germans.

Pupil pilots gained some of their night-flying experience at Shrewton. On return to Netheravon they landed on the flare-path marked by goose-neck flares. A mobile 'Chance' light was sometimes positioned at the touch-down end of the flare-path at Shrewton. Ralph recalls the night he was on the flare-path party and an incoming aircraft demolished the red obstruction light on top of the Chance light. Hinds were fitted with a camera near the leading edge of one of the lower main-planes. The camera recorded the pilots' performance when he was diving at targets on Salisbury Plain. For two weeks the unit moved to Stormy Down in South Wales where live ammunition firing practice at targets in the sea were held.

Gordon Inness was another AC2 Flt Mech who was posted to Netheravon in January 1940 and attached to 'E' Flt. He soon found himself assigned to night flying duties with other 'erks' who, one by one, were dropped off by lorry at various points around the airfield. Gordon was left on the vehicle, and as it continued the airfield got further away, until eventually the lorry stopped and he was told to look after the distant flare. Two 5 gallon drums of paraffin, a large ball of cotton waste and a metal container were off-loaded with Gordon instructed to soak the waste, fill the metal container with paraffin, place the waste in the container, set light to it and not to let it go out. He was to remain with the flare until relieved. Time passed but no relief appeared and to make matters worse the paraffin in the container was going down. It soon became necessary to remove the flare and replenish the fuel. Using the hook provided he removed the lighted waste from the

container and placed it on the grass clear of the paraffin drums. The paraffin was used to top-up the container but on turning to pick up the lighted flare, to his horror, the dry grass of Salisbury Plain was on fire. With no water, blanket or beater, Gordon's only option was to perform a fire dance until eventually he managed to stamp out the fire.

Gordon later joined 'F' Flt where he was paired with a young Irish airframe mechanic. They looked after a Fairey Battle and a number of Hawker Hinds, carrying out daily inspections, small repairs, filling with petrol and oil, starting them up and seeing them out and back. The Irishman decided they should name a plane and *The Red Devil* was painted in red on the yellow engine cowling. There it remained until it was seen by the Flt Cdr.

With the passing of winter and the longer flying hours this allowed, Gordon made his first flight in a Harvard. 'Practice Camps' also commenced which gave him the opportunity of going to Porthcawl where they were held. He went there three times, by train, using his motorcycle and flying by Hawker Hind. At the end of his last detachment, and when the time came to return to Netheravon, the Flt Mechs were given the opportunity of returning in the aircraft they had been responsible for maintaining. His pilot was anxious to return to Netheravon and although they took off in a Hind, visibility was so bad they had to return to Porthcawl. Conditions were the same the next day but the pilot decided to try again. Gordon recalls them flying over the Bristol Channel before returning over the Welsh coast only then to find themselves amongst the barrage balloons of Newport. Dodging the cables they eventually crossed the Channel at wave-top height before

climbing to clear a cliff on the Bristol side of the water. Gordon was surprised and somewhat relieved when the pilot found Netheravon and landed safely. Later the same day a Flt Sgt Instructor returning from Porthcawl, flying solo in a Fairey Battle, crashed into the cliff near Weston-Super-Mare and was killed. Gordon was in the funeral party for this pilot and was conscious of perhaps how fortunate he had been to return safely in the bad flying conditions which had prevailed. Gordon left Netheravon as a LAC in the summer of 1941.

Acting Sub Lt Graham A. Skinner RN, of HMS *Daedalus*, was killed in a flying accident on 23ʳᵈ February 1940. It is thought he became lost in cloud and his Hart K5806 crashed at Lower Clatford near Andover. Leading Airman (LA) C.H. Wines RN and Cpl D. Beeston RM, pupils in Battles, collided on 11ᵗʰ March during formation practice. LA Wines forced landed on the aerodrome with damage to the airscrew. Cpl Beeston, with rudder torn away and elevators partially inoperative, piloted his aircraft back by aileron turns and, when landing on the edge of the aerodrome, severely damaged the undercarriage and airscrew. Both pilots escaped without injury. The same day another Battle from the School crashed at Upavon which was fogbound at the time.

Approval of the official Unit badge by the King was granted on 1ˢᵗ April 1940. The design was representative of the three Services. The naval sword, military sword and 'Winged Crown' were chosen to show the training of naval and military officers entering the RAF for service with the FAA and Army Co-operation squadrons.

LA Herbert E. Cook RN of HMS *Daedalus* and AC2 Alfred C. Lucas RAF were killed on Tuesday 9ᵗʰ April 1940 in Battle K7609 which crashed at Collingbourne Kingston, when it is believed to have been low flying. AC2 Lucas was buried at Netheravon All Saints Churchyard on 12ᵗʰ April and AC1 Ralph Godden attended as a member of the burial party.

During April 1940, Battle Ts replaced Harvards. The Battle T Flight had the purpose of training fighter pilots required by the FAA. The establishment of aeroplanes for the

Intermediate Training Sqn was 28 Harts and 14 Battles. As of May 1940, the aircraft establishment for No.1 SFTS was 54 Harts, 54 Battles and an unknown number of Audax and Hinds. In early May 1940 a directive was received instructing that fuselage roundels had to be encircled with a yellow band. Vertical strips of red, white and blue were to be painted on fins. This was followed two weeks later with an order that Bren guns of the Army detachment had to be mounted on lorries for aerodrome defence against paratroop drops. Additionally, the aerodrome perimeter had to be patrolled every morning.

Five French aircraft, comprising 4 Bloch and a Caudron, landed on 19th June 1940. They were flown over from France by five Polish officer pilots with one WO as a passenger. The airmen were sent to the Polish Legation in London three days later. A week later, 22 Polish airmen arrived to work as Flight Mechanics and Riggers. They had escaped to England when the Germans invaded their country.

Flying accidents remained a regular occurrence and some of the following must have involved fatalities but details are not always possible to trace. AC1 Walter D. Moses RAF, a Flight Rigger, was found dead by the flare-path on Saturday 4th May 1940 and was thought to have been hit by an aircraft taking-off. Hart.T. K3757 and K5820 crashed on landing on 1st May and 1st July 1940 respectively. A more unfortunate incident occurred on 21st July when Hart.T K6485 was shot down by a German fighter at Winterbourne Dauntsey, killing the two-man crew. On 19th November 1940, Hart.T. K4934 flew into the ground 3 miles N of Tidworth and, three days later, K4939 crashed in a forced landing 1 mile W of Amesbury. Two Hind Ts L7233 and K5503, crashed in forced landings on 10th May and 17th July 1940 respectively. Another Hind, K6751, dived into the ground 3 miles ENE of the aerodrome near the air/ground firing range on Wednesday 29th May 1940. The pilot, Lt Raymond J. Hyland RN of HMS *Daedalus*, a pupil of the Advanced Training Sqn, was killed. Acting Leading Airman Ian G. Farquhar RN, of HMS *Daedalus*, was killed in a flying accident at Pylle near Shepton Mallet on 14th July 1940 and is buried at Netheravon All Saints Churchyard.

A Fairey Battle on the aerodrome during the severe winter of 1940.
Photo: Ralph Godden

Acting LAC Pennington was killed on 30th September 1940 when his Hart T. K5038 collided with a Blenheim near Bulford. The Blenheim forced landed with no injuries to the crew.

Two miles north of the aerodome, on 9th July 1940, the Germans dropped two bombs, one of which failed to explode.

No.4 Ferry Pilots' Pool, which had formed at Filton to ferry replacement aircraft to the Continent, had a detached Flt at Netheravon from 28th October 1940.

About November 1940, the school had a shortage of transport as two buses were hired from the Wilts & Dorset Motor Services Ltd, at £3 per day. The buses were used to transport personnel to the RLGs, to the billets and to requisitioned accommodation outside the camp.

On the 14th November 1940, an emergency landing ground was allocated at Winterbourne Stoke but the location of this, and whether or not it was ever used, is unknown. The School used RLGs at Highpost and Shrewton during 1940/41. The RLG at Highpost, taken over from Old Sarum on 29th November 1940, included the offices of the former flying club, civilian garage and hotel. The 'L' shaped aerodrome was not suitable for night flying so the School made an application to extend the site but this was rejected.

Flt Lt Thomas P. de la Rue, a Flight Commander with the Advanced Training Squadron, was killed on Saturday 25th January 1941 at Town Quarry, Weston-Super-Mare. He was en route from Cardiff to Netheravon

when he flew into the ground in bad weather. He was buried at Weston-Super-Mare Cemetery. Hind 1 L7219 dived into the ground at Collingbourne Ducis on 6th February 1941. Acting LA Peter F. Beane RN, of HMS *Daedalus*, a pupil of the Intermediate Training Sqn, was killed on Thursday 20th March. He was in the cockpit of an Audax waiting to take-off when it was struck by an aircraft that was landing. The Audax pilot suffered a fractured skull and died shortly after the collision. Plt Off Henry J. Craig RAFVR and Acting LA George J.B. Kendall RN, of HMS *Daedalus*, instructor and pupil respectively in Advanced Training Sqn, were killed on Thursday 27th March. Fog developed suddenly immediately after a night-time take-off and the Battle flew into the ground. Both men were buried at Netheravon All Saints Churchyard.

No.1 SFTS had use of a new bombing range, which opened on Saturday 17th May 1941 at Pepperbox Hill on the A36 Salisbury to Southampton road. Unfortunately on this first day of use it was the scene of a fatality. Lt Harold G. Hunt RN, of HMS *Cleaner*, a pupil with the Advanced Training Sqn, was killed carrying out a high dive bombing in Battle K7651. The Range Officer reported that the Battle flew straight into the ground.

No.1 SFTS used Castle Combe for night flying, in addition to Shrewton, from 23rd May 1941. Gp Capt F.E. Bond took up his appointment as Station CO during June and was superceded in December 1941 by Gp Capt J. Noakes AFC, MM. On the last day of July, No.1 SFTS started re-equipping with the Master III.

Acting LA Ewen S.F. Ingle RNZN and Acting LA George R.F. Watson RN, both of HMS *Daedalus*, were killed during unauthorised low flying on Tuesday 19th August 1941. The Hart crashed and burnt out after flying into H.T. cables near Bath. LA Watson was buried in Netheravon All Saints Churchyard. Acting LA David W. Dorey RN and Acting LA William E.G. Chaplain RN, with the Advanced Training Sqn and both of HMS *Daedalus*, were killed on Sunday 28th September 1941 when their Master III struck a tree and crashed during unauthorised low flying near Porton. Plt Off Basil A.H. Newton RAF, 'A' Flt Instructor, and Acting LA Edward C. Crouch RN of HMS *Daedalus*, were killed on Saturday 11th October 1941 when parts of their Master III were seen to fall off and the aircraft plunged into the ground. Acting LA Donald Stewart RN, of HMS *Daedalus*, was killed at Pepperbox Hill Bombing Range near Salisbury on Tuesday 28th October 1941 when he failed to pull out of a dive and his aircraft crashed into the ground. Lt Leslie T. Hazeldine RNR, of HMS *Daedalus*, and his passenger Sgt David B. Hancock RAFVR were killed on Saturday 7th February 1942 when, on a cross-country in Master W8770, it struck high ground near Malvern. Acting LA Charles A. Gallagher RNZN was killed on Wednesday 25th February 1942 when his Master W8798 crashed near Reading due to engine failure.

No.1 SFTS disbanded on 7th March 1942 as arrangements had been made to train some of the FAA pilots in the United States. Control of Netheravon passed from Flying Training Command to Army Co-operation Command and, on 21st March 1942 Gp Capt C Noakes AFC, MM, relinquished command of the Station to Wg Cdr Oakey.

With the departure of No.1 SFTS, the airfield was fully utilised by No.38 Wing of Army Co-operation Command, which had reformed with HQ at Netheravon under Air Commodore Sir Nigel Norman on 19th January 1942. The Wing was formed to control No.296 (Glider) Sqn and No.297 (Parachute) Sqn, and to provide the necessary air requirements for the Airborne Division. The HQ for the 6th Airborne Division was established at Syrencote House (see **MILSTON**), a mile and three quarters to the south of Netheravon airfield.

Command passed to Air Commodore W.H. Primrose in May 1943. Because of its considerable expansion, No.38 Wing was redesignated No.38 (Airborne Forces) Group on 11th October 1943 in Tactical Air Force, Fighter Command. The Group was commanded by AVM L.N. Hollinghurst and together with the 6th Airborne Division, worked on planning for the invasion of France. The Group was absorbed into HQ Allied Expeditionary Force on 15th November 1943, and transferred to Marks Hall on 12th October 1944. The Group was taken over by Transport Command on 1st June 1945.

Netheravon's function radically changed and a unique phase in its history began with the arrival of the Parachute Exercise Sqn which moved in from Ringway on 22nd December 1941, having formed there on 15th December 1941. The CO was Sqn Ldr B.A. Oakey who became an Acting Wing Commander on 22nd January 1942. The squadron was redesignated No.297 Sqn as of the same date. Over the next two months it was equipped with the Whitley V and the Tiger Moth II.

During March and April 1942, the squadron carried out a considerable amount of flying training involving cross-country, exercises, container and dummy drops. A Flt of No.296 and No.297 Sqn Whitleys, modified for bomb carrying, left Netheravon on 27th May 1942 for operations with Bomber Command. This was to be the first 1000 bomber raid to Cologne. As reserve aircraft, however, it was determined they were of an unacceptable standard and six disappointed crews returned three days later.

On Sunday 31st May 1942, No.297 Sqn Whitley BD371 crashed at Porton Down during a night flight. The crew of Plt Off Brierly, Sgt Robb, Sgt Pipe and Sgt Donald G. Green RAFVR (WOP/AG), were hospitalised with serious injuries. Sgt Green died from his injuries later in the day. A further accident with fatalities occurred on Thursday 4th June 1942 when Whitley Z9431 crashed at Irthlingborough. Sgt Quintin S. Moore, Sgt Herbert Johns and Sgt Tom L. Jacobs were killed. Fg Off Stott, Flt Sgt Leach and AC Bravery suffered injuries. The following day the squadron moved to Hurn.

No.297 Sqn aircraft at Netheravon
Whitley Vs AD670, BD211, BD371, P9470, Z9189, Z9218, Z9313, Z9318, Z9319, Z9430, Z9431, Z9436, Z9443, Z9476,
Tiger Moth IIs DE157, DE158, DE160, DE167, DE171, DE249, DE251, DE274, DE302, DE303, N5445, T5608, T5974, T7348, T8192,

No.296 Sqn, with Sqn Ldr Davis as CO, started arriving from Ringway on 1st February 1942 where it had been redesignated from the Glider Exercise Sqn in December 1941. Hampered by heavy snow, the move was not completed until 12th February 1942. No flying took place for the next eleven days but, in that time, 10 new Hotspur gliders were received and assembled. On 24th February, the first glider was flown from Netheravon by Plt Off Briggs with Sqn Ldr Davis as tug pilot. The rest of the month was spent test-flying the new equipment. The squadron was equipped with the Hector and Hart as glider tugs, and also with Tiger Moths for training purposes. From early in March 1942, new tug pilots joining the squadron were given experience in flying these aircraft. Cross-country tows, formation flying and Hotspur air tests continued. During April, training with Hotspurs and live troops commenced, as did night-flying training.

A Blenheim 1 L1454 from No.42 OTU, flew into the ground while laying a smoke screen at Netheravon on 27th March 1942. Crew details were not recorded.

A rehearsal for Exercise *Magnum* was staged on 14th April 1942. 8 Hectors towing 9 Hotspur gliders with 63 troops, successfully rendezvoused with their fighter escort over Chippenham at 7000' and proceeded to Everleigh where most landed correctly on the LZ. Two days later, Exercise *Magnum* was held in the presence of Winston Churchill and General Marshall. All the gliders arrived on the Everleigh LZ but one hit a bush in the boundary hedge on approach and overturned. This resulted in two fatalities and serious injuries to the pilot, Sgt. Smith. The following day the exercise was repeated for the Chief of Combined Operations and was a success.

During May and June 1942, No.296 Sqn carried troops on air experience flights, took part in night exercises and trained in low-flying glider towing. Whitley Vs started arriving for the squadron during May. These aircraft were soon in use as tugs to provide towing practice for glider pilots. Both the Netheravon-based Whitley squadrons were, by this time, equipped with 24 aircraft each. Defects and servicing allowed the squadrons to operate about 20 each on a daily basis with two set aside for new crew training or special functions.

On 5th June 1942, 6 Hotspur gliders with full live loads were towed to the airfield at Oatlands Hill where they made night-landings in total darkness. One glider crashed on landing but with only minor injuries to the pilot Sgt Hutchison and one passenger.

The first 6 Horsa gliders arrived on 6th July 1942 and were used to test lashings and the balancing of loads. Taxi trials commenced on 11th August when it was found that the Whitleys had insufficient power to tow a fully laden Horsa. The RAE carried out trials during the following few weeks but was unable to find a solution. The need for the Horsa was paramount, which left the option of reducing the load and keeping the Whitleys or using a four-engined bomber.

Training during July and August 1942 involved cross-countries, local flying with the Whitley, glider towing and night flying with Hectors. Air Experience flights with troops, dive approaches and skid landings were also undertaken. Hotspur glider BT799 crashed during take-off on 6th August 1942. Five troops were injured and conveyed to Tidworth Military Hospital and Sgt John E. Smith (pilot) of the 1st GPR (AAC) died from his injuries the following day.

No.296 Sqn formed into 'A' and 'B' Flts during July 1942 with 'A' Flt following its sister No.297 Sqn to Hurn on 25th July 1942. 'B' Flt remained with the Hectors to form the Glider Pilot Exercise Unit (GPEU) on 12th August 1942. Air Experience flights continued to be flown by the new unit during the remainder of the year. Shrewton was used as a satellite between 8th October and 16th December 1942 and Chilbolton between 18th December 1942 and 8th January 1943. From this date, the unit was based at Chilbolton until 11th May 1943. It then moved back to Netheravon with its Tiger Moths and

with the gliders ferried in by the Masters. Army pilot-training on Tiger Moths and troop-lifting with Hotspurs continued until the GPEU moved to Thruxton satellite on 29th September 1943. This move was short-lived with the unit returning to Netheravon on 14th October 1943 but only for a month as it moved back to Thruxton on 14th November 1943.

On 21st May 1942, King George V² and Queen Elizabeth visited Netheravon where they inspected detachments from the Airborne Division, No.296 and No.297 Sqns. After lunch, Exercise *Jackdaw* was staged for the Royal guests at nearby Brigmerston in which No.296 Sqn demonstrated glider towing. Parachute troops of the Airborne Division were carried by the Whitleys of No.297 Sqn. Smoke screens were laid by Blenheims of No.13 Sqn.

19 Blenheim crews arrived on 16th June 1942 from No.42 OTU at Andover. This move was in preparation for the forming of a Heavy-Glider Conversion Unit at Shrewton on 1st July 1942.

The Germans paid Netheravon a visit on 27th July 1942 when they attacked the airfield by machine gunning the Officers and WAAFs quarters. Minimal damage was inflicted and there were no casualties.

No.295 Sqn formed at Netheravon in No.38 Wing Army Co-operation Command on 3rd August 1942 from the nucleus of captains and other aircrews of No.296 Sqn. The squadron role was for operations with parachute drops and glider towing. Some former bomber crews were trained to tow the Horsa glider without load. 8 Whitley Vs were taken over from the GPEU to equip 3 Flts. The 2nd Flt was formed on 10th August 1942 and the 3rd Flt on 8th September 1942. Acting Sqn Ldr A.B. Wilkinson arrived on 7th August on transfer from No.296 Sqn, and was appointed as the Squadron CO pending the arrival of Wg Cdr G. P. Marvin on 29th August 1942.

The assembly of Horsa gliders now commenced in earnest with the target of 30 achieved in September 1942. No.295 Sqn used Horsas and a number of Hotspurs.

From August to November 1942, the squadron was engaged in dummy and

live paratroop-dropping exercises and with night-flying. The squadron engaged in a number of *Nickel* raids over France during November 1942. Take-offs were all from Netheravon but landing back at Thruxton:

6th Nov - 2 a/c to Rouen, 2 a/c to Caen and 1 a/c to Amiens
Whitley V BD538   Wg Cdr Marvin
"   " EB290   Flt Lt Briggs
"   " EB302   Flt Lt J.N.W. Kerr
"   " EB303   Plt Off J.G. Curtiss
"   " EB311   Fg Off J.K. Matthews

7th Nov 3 a/c to Caen
Whitley V BD303   Sqn Ldr L.C. Bartram
"   " BD437   Fg Off C.V. Wood
"   " EB290   Sgt W. R. Erasmus

13th Nov 1 a/c to Paris
Whitley V EB290   Plt Off W.G. Cooil

14th Nov 2 a/c to Paris
Whitley V BD497   Plt Off R.A. Charter
"   " EB301   Plt Off B.L. Tomkins

23rd Nov 1 a/c to Rouen
Whitley V   EB288   Fg Off D.H. Upsher

24th Nov 1 a/c to Paris
Whitley V BD497   Plt Off R.A. Charter

26th Nov 2 a/c to Paris
Whitley V EB290   Plt Off W.G. Cooil
"   " EB301   Plt Off B.L. Tomkins

30th Nov 3 a/c to Paris
Whitley V BD437   Fg Off C.V. Wood
"   " BD497   Plt Off Charter
"   " BD538   Plt Off Muirhead

On Tuesday 17th November 1942, 7 Whitleys took-off each with 10 paratroops and 2 or 3 containers. Six of the aircraft discharged their loads on a DZ south of Salisbury. One of the aircraft swung on take off, struck a hangar and caught fire. Fg Off John K. Matthews (pilot), Sgt Frederick E. Hewitt (nav/bomber) and Sgt James M. Sutcliffe (WOP/AG) were killed plus five Army paratroops. Five other paratroops and the RAF rear-gunner escaped. Fg Off Matthews and Sgt Hewitt were buried at Netheravon Cemetery, Figheldean.

During December 1942, the squadron continued with day and night paratroop and container dropping exercises plus the following *Nickel* operations:

5th Dec 2 a/c to Lille
Whitley V BD500   Fg Off M.C. Hayes
"   " BD501   Flt Lt G.H. Briggs

1 a/c to Nantes
Whitley V EB289   Sqn Ldr B.A. Wilkinson

2 a/c to Paris
Whitley V EB298   Plt Off J.A.G. Sizmur
"   " EB299   Plt Off E.B. Blackburn

12th Dec 1 a/c to Tours
Whitley V EB289   Sqn Ldr B.A. Wilkinson

1 a/c to Rheims
Whitley V BD501   Flt Lt G.H. Briggs

1 a/c to Orleans
Whitley V BD500   Fg Off M.C. Hayes

1 a/c to Tourcoing
Whitley V EB290   Plt Off W.G. Cooil

1 a/c to Roubaix
Whitley V BD437   Fg Off C. Wood

1 a/c to Lille
Whitley V BD494   Sgt W. R. Eramus

3 a/c to Paris
Whitley V BD435   Plt Off S. Hilton
"   " EB298   Plt Off D.J. Smith
"   " EB302   lt Lt J.N.W. Kerr

The squadron suffered its first operational loss on this night (12th December), when Whitley V BD437 failed to return. The crew was Fg Off Clifford Wood (pilot), Fg Off William A Hinselwood (obs), Fg Off D'Arcy C. M. Ducker RNZAF (WOP/AG), Flt Sgt Douglas L. Grant (A/G) and Sgt Cecil G.G. Hobson (A/G). All five are buried at Abbeville Communal Cemetery, Somme in France.

10 aircraft of No.295 Sqn and 12 of No.297 Sqn took part in Exercise *Eagle* on 15th December 1942. The aircraft flew in 'V' formation of 3 aircraft each, in line astern and at one-minute intervals with the odd aircraft bringing up the rear of the formation. Each aircraft carried 10 paratroops and 2 containers. These were despatched onto the DZ one and a half miles NE of Chitterne (184/ST999455). All aircraft returned to Netheravon after the drop, were reloaded with paratroops and containers and, within 40 minutes, were taking off again for the same DZ.

Four of the aircraft of No.295 Sqn operated from Netheravon in Exercise *Snoop* on 23rd December 1942. Each aircraft carried 10 paratroops and 2 containers, which were dropped on a DZ, 3 miles SW of Amesbury (184/SU115395). The DZ was at Lake Down, the former World War 1 training aerodrome. Three separate drops were made at 1000, 1400 and 1600 hours. The following day, 2 Whitleys carried out container drops on the Divisional DZ, 1 mile south of Netheravon airfield and this function was repeated by 3 of No.295 Sqn's aircraft on 28th December 1942.

The year ended with a further series of *Nickel* operations and these were the first in which the squadron aircraft took-off and landed back at Netheravon:

30th Dec 1 a/c to Nantes
Whitley V BD501   Flt Lt Briggs - Forced landed at Tangmere with engine overheat.

1 a/c to Rouen
Whitley V BD494   Sgt W. R. Erasmus

2 a/c to Rennes
Whitley V BD498   Sqn Ldr Wilkinson - Heavy flak near Cherbourg. Failed to reach target. Dropped leaflets at St. Lo.
Whitley V EB289   Fg Off D.H. Upsher

1 a/c to Caen
Whitley V BD499   Fg Off Wood

31st Dec 1 a/c to Le Mans
Whitley V BD499   Fg Off Wood

1 a/c to Nantes
Whitley V BD500   Sqn Ldr Wilkinson

1 a/c to Caen
Whitley V EB298   Fg Off D.H. Upsher

1 a/c to Angers
Whitley V BD497 - Sgt W. R. Erasmus

1 a/c to Tours
Whitley V BD498   Plt Off Muirhead - Owing to intercom failure, target not reached - drop made at Caen.

The New Year started off with another loss when circuits and landings were flown from Netheravon on Saturday 9th January 1943. A Whitley stalled during an overshoot and crashed on the airfield at Upavon killing Plt Off John C. Curtis (pilot), Sgt James O'Donnell (nav) and Sgt Ronald R. Phillips (WOP/AG). Sgt Knee (AG) survived with injuries. It was this crew's first experience of night flying from Netheravon.

More *Nickel* raids were operated into the spring when the squadron moved out:

9th Jan 1 a/c to Orleans
Whitley V EB288   Fg Off D.H.Upsher- Due to bad weather, dropped on Caen and Bayeux.

26th Jan 1 a/c to Poitiers
Whitley V BD499   Fg Off Wood

1 a/c to Chateauroux
Whitley V BD500   Fg Off Tomkins

1 a/c to Angers
Whitley V BD455   Fg Off Charter

1 a/c to Tours
Whitley V BD598   Fg Off J. H.C. McIlwrick

1 a/c to Orleans
Whitley V EB290   Fg Off Cooil- Returned with leaflets Failed to release.

9th Feb 1 a/c to Poitiers
Whitley V BD498   Fg Off Cooil

1 a/c to Chateauraux.
Whitley V BD494 - Sgt William R. Erasmus RAFVR (pilot), Sgt Sidney A. G. Wraight RAFVR (obs), Sgt Jack H. Beebe RNZAF (WOP), Flt Sgt Edward Froggart RAFVR (AG). This aircraft failed to return.

The names of the pilot, WOP & AG appear on the Runnymede Memorial. The body of the observer was washed ashore at Quend-Plage les Pin and was buried at Abbeville Communal Cemetery, Somme, France.

13th Mar 1 a/c to Bordeaux
Whitley V EB290   Fg Off Wood - Auto-pilot u/s. Leaflets dropped on Angers.

1 a/c to Limoges
Whitley V BD 501   Flt Lt Briggs

1 a/c to Tours
Whitley V BD499   Fg Off Charter

1 a/c to Mantes Gassicourt
Whitley V BD500   Flt Lt Kerr
(landed back at Middle Wallop)

1 a/c to Amiens
Whitley V LA793   Fg Off M.W. Collins

4th April - 1 a/c to Poitiers
Whitley V BD455   Fg Off Tomkins

1 a/c to Nantes
Whitley V EB292   Flt Lt Kerr

1 a/c to Nr. Lun
Whitley V LA790   Fg Off Blackburn

1 a/c to Abbeville
Whitley V LA793   Plt Off D. J. Smith

1 a/c to Paris
Whitley V EB301   Fg Off Cooil

Paratroop and container-dropping exercises continued through January, February and March 1943. On 28th January 1943, No.295, 296 and 297 Sqns took part in Exercise *Chance*, which was a demonstration arranged for a party of M.Ps. No.295 Sqn supplied 2 towing aircraft, one of which took-off from Netheravon with a Horsa glider prior to the exercise, as a routine take-off demonstration. The second aircraft towed a Horsa in which many of the party were passengers. The glider was released onto a DZ two miles to the south of the airfield but crashed on landing. No injuries or fatalities are recorded.

During February 1943, 'A' Flt of No.295 Sqn began re-equipping with the Halifax V and this was completed by 22nd April 1943. On 19th February, 12 Whitley Vs and 2 Halifax Vs were detailed for bombing operations on an electrical installation at Distre near Saumur in France. The Whitley aircraft were BD 538 Sqn Ldr Lysaught, BD790 Sqn Ldr Bartram, BD501 Flt Lt Briggs, EB302 Flt Lt Kerr, EB303 Fg Off Hilton, KB290 Fg Off Cooil, BD499 Fg Off Wood, EB311 Fg Off Sizmure, BD445 Fg Off Charter, EB298 Fg Off Collins, BD498 Fg Off Muirhead and BD793 Fg Off Blackburn. The Halifax aircraft were DK122 Sqn Ldr Wilkinson and DK123 Fg Off Hayes. Two crews failed to return from this operation. In Whitley BD538, Sqn Ldr Philip M.V. Lysaught (pilot), Fg Off James H.C. McIlwrick (2nd pilot), Sgt Ivor W. Arnold (nav), Sgt Joseph E.S. Sasseville RCAF (WOP), Sgt J. Bailey (AG). In Halifax DK123 Fg Off Malcolm C. Hayes (pilot), Fg Off David H. Upsher (2nd pilot), Sgt Walter Mather (nav), Flt Sgt Thomas W. Holland (AG), Flt Lt Michael E. J. Croker (AG) and Sqn Ldr Crighton-Miller (Pass). Both crews are buried at Saumar Communal Cemetery, Maine-et-Loire in France.

Operating from Hurn on 29th March 1943, seven No.295 Sqn Whitley Vs with paratroops, containers and gliders dropped on a DZ at Normanton Down south of Stonehenge and a LZ on the airfield at Oatlands Hill. Later the same day, a further 8 Whitleys towed 8 loaded gliders to Oatlands Hill.
During April, the squadron exercised in night flying, dummy and paratroop drops, cross-country glider tows and operations over the sea by the Halifax aircraft.

On 17th April 1943, eight of the squadron's Whitleys, operating from Hurn, were sent on a raid to bomb a transformer station at Courville :-

Whitley V BD498 Plt Off Muirhead - Primary target not located. Railway track at Le Merlerault bombed successfully as alternative target. Tailplane and fin damaged by A.A fire.

Whitley V BD499 Sqn Ldr Wilkinson - Constant speed unit went u/s after take-off. Returned to Hurn and replaced by a No.296 Sqn Albemarle.

Whitley V BD500 Fg Off S. Hilton - Enemy a/c encountered near Cabourg. Evasive action taken and enemy a/c lost with no action.

Whitley V EB288 Plt Off Blackburn

"   " EB302 Flt Lt Kerr - Damage to starboard wing by A.A. fire.

Whitley V LA793 Wg Cdr B.R. MacNamara

"   " LA883 Fg Off J.W. Bewick - Damage to starboard wing by A.A. fire.

Whitley V ?   Fg Off Tomkins - Observer taken ill after take-off. Sortie abandoned. The raid was a success and aircraft landed back at Hurn.

Towards the end of April 1943, No.295 Sqn was tasked with ferrying 40 empty Horsa gliders to North Africa in preparation for Operation *Beggar*, the invasion of Sicily. The squadron's 'A' Flt. with 13 of their Halifax aircraft moved to Holmesley South on 1st May 1943 where crews were to train and prepare for the task. Wg Cdr MacNamara the squadron CO, and Sqn Ldr A. M. B. Wilkinson, the Flt. CO and most of the personnel travelled in Horsa gliders. Portreath was the departure airfield for the ferry to North Africa. The Halifax aircraft flew from Holmesley South to Cornwall where, in preparation for the operation, the squadron's aircraft had towed the gliders from Hurn. The ferrying operation commenced on 1st June 1943.

The Glider Pilot Exercise Unit formed from 'B' Flt of No.296 Sqn on 12th August 1942 at Netheravon in No.38 Group. The role of the unit was to provide periodical refresher and flying training for pilots of the Army Glider Pilot Regiment. The aircraft allocation was 10 Tiger Moth, 12 Hector and 24 Hotspur gliders. The unit used satellites at Shrewton and Chilbolton.

Exercise *Omega* was staged in August/September 1942. On 1st September 1942, it was operated by the 1st Air Landing Brigade with 126 troops carried in 8 Hotspur gliders towed from Netheravon by the Whitleys of No.297 Sqn. 10 Hotspurs towed by Whitleys of No.296 Sqn also operated from Hurn. 17 gliders landed on Andover airfield and one at Worthy Down.

The GPEU was now carrying out regular training tows in conjunction with the glider pilots from Shrewton. The unit moved to Chilbolton on 8th January 1943 and by April was equipped with 20+10 Tiger Moth, 24+6 Master and 60 Hotspur. The GPEU moved back to Netheravon on 8th May 1943. The CO at this time was

Wg Cdr E.C. Foreman. Another move took place over the 2nd/3rd October when the unit Master Flt and Hotspurs left for Thruxton in Hampshire. The unit returned again to Netheravon on 14th October and the Tiger Moth Flt moved to Shrewton the following day. The GPEU carried out a final move back to Thruxton on 14th November 1943. During the Unit's spell at Netheravon in the summer of 1943, a fatality occurred on Thursday 19th August when Tiger Moth DE217 crashed and burnt out near Mere, killing Sgts Frederick M. Shambrook and Victor P. Elms of the 2nd Wing GPR, AAC. Sgt Elms is buried at Mere Cemetery. Other flying accidents had occurred in the county the previous month during glider-towing training but without serious injuries to personnel. Operating from Thruxton, another fatal crash occurred on Tuesday 7th December 1943 when Hotspur BT822 came down at Collingbourne Ducis. This accident resulted in the deaths of the two pilots S/Sgt Eric A. Jeffs and Sgt Phillip D. Taylor of the 2nd Wing GPR, AAC, together with 6 men of the 6th Air Landing Brigade. It was thought that a premature cast off by the pilot and a restricted view of the ground because of low cloud was the cause of the accident.

Two days after the crash of 7th December, the GPEU disbanded into Operational and Refresher Training Unit.

Halifax crews from No.138 and No.161 Sqns were detached from Tempsford to Netheravon in September 1942, together with experienced glider pilots. The task was Horsa long-tow familiarisation training with the emphasis on night landings and was conducted in great secrecy. The Sqns were to participate in Operation *Freshman*, an attack by specialist troops on the Norsk Hydro Electric Company's 'heavy water' plant at Vermok in Norway. This was one of the most audacious and covert operations of the war. Gp Capt T.B. Cooper was in charge of the operation. Two Halifax aircraft towing two Horsa gliders, each carrying 15 sappers and equipment, took off from Skitten, Wick, for a flight of 800 miles on Thursday 19th November 1942. Sqn Ldr Wilkinson, the Halifax pilot of the first combination, took off at 1750 hrs followed 20 minutes later by Flt Lt

Arthur R. Parkinson, RCAF pilot of the second Halifax combination. The paratroops were from the 9th Field Company (Airborne) and the 261st Field Park Company (Airborne). This was the first British glider-borne operation of the Second World War but turned out to be a failure with a heavy loss of life. Flt Lt Parkinson and his crew were killed when their Halifax crashed into mountains. The glider it was towing also crash-landed in mountains, resulting in three soldiers killed. The others were captured and executed by the Germans. Sqn Ldr Wilkinson, whilst searching for the target in heavy cloud, was forced to lose height due to severe icing. The icing caused the towrope to break, and the glider crashed into the snow-covered mountains at Fylesdalen. Eight men were killed, including the two pilots of the Glider Pilot Regiment. Four others were seriously injured. The four injured survivors were soon captured and were executed by a doctor. The others became P.O.Ws until they were executed by the Gestapo on 18th January 1943. Flt Lt Parkinson was buried at Helleland Churchyard, Norway. Sqn Ldr Wilkinson and his crew returned to Skitten with his Halifax very low on fuel.

No.1426 (Enemy Aircraft) Flt paid a visit to Netheravon on 27th November 1942. The aircraft on show for familiarisation training were He 111H-1 W/Nr 6853 (AW177), Ju 88A 5 W/Nr 6073 (HM509) and Bf 110C-5 W/Nr 2177 (AX772).

Chilbolton became a satellite for Netheravon on 16th December 1942 and was used until 26th May 1943 when all personnel returned to Netheravon.

No.235 Maintenance Unit (MU) formed at Netheravon in No.43 Group Maintenance Command on 14th January 1943 as Mobile Repair & Salvage Unit for 1st line aircraft, crashed gliders and MT. The CO of this Lodger Unit was Flt Lt G.L. O'Hanlon MBE. No.1 Heavy Glider Maintenance Unit, which had formed at Hurn to maintain, repair and modify all heavy gliders attached to 3 tug squadrons in No.38 Wing, arrived at Netheravon on 2nd May 1943 with Flt Lt B.D. Austen as CO. The two units amalgamated on 25th March 1944 to form No.1 Heavy Glider Servicing Unit (HGSU) in No.38 Group at

Repairs being made to the tail unit of Airspeed Horsa 1 glider DP314.
Photo: Army Air Corps

Netheravon. The unit's duties covered the Horsa and Hamilcar- equipped units in the Group. Marshalling and recovery of gliders used for training was also part of the Unit's responsibility. This role was carried out at Rollestone in September 1944 for the Thruxton-based Operational and Refresher Training Unit. No.1 HGSU had a Reserve Pool of 140 Horsa and 10 Hamilcar gliders with 13 servicing crews at Netheravon. Early in September 1944, a Tug Flt. of 6 Dakotas from the Unit began the task of ferrying repaired gliders back from Normandy. The Glider Pick-up method of recovery was in use by the Tug Flt. at this time. A load of serviceable glider components had arrived at Netheravon by road from France the previous month. No.1 HGSU disbanded on the last day of 1946 although its Echelon remained until February 1947.

Thruxton was taken over by Netheravon from Andover as a satellite on 8th March 1943.
King George VI paid a second visit to Netheravon on 1st April 1943 when he inspected No.38 Wings Nos.295, 296 and 297 Sqns, the Glider Pilot Exercise Unit and the Station Flight.

No.403 Repair & Salvage Unit formed on 25th April 1943 out of No.235 MU at Netheravon, moving to Dunsfold in July 1943.

Gp Capt J.W. Homer replaced Wg Cdr

B.A. Oakley as Station CO on 20th May 1943.

An 8th Air Force USAAF B-17G 42-5822 of the 525th Bomb Sqn/379th Bombardment Group (FR-G) based at Kimbolton, with Lt Brown and crew, landed at Netheravon on 29th May 1943 following a raid on U-Boat pens at St. Nazaire. The aircraft was refuelled before taking off for its home base.

A Hotspur glider HH369 crashed on 31st May 1943 and struck the CO's office in the Glider Pilot Exercise Unit's hangar. Both Glider Pilots were injured and conveyed to Tidworth Military Hospital. This was also the date when Army Co-operation Command was disbanded. On the fusion into Fighter Command of Army Co-operation Command on 1st June 1943, Netheravon was transferred to No.10 Group but remained in No.38 Wing. The Tactical Air Force was also formed this day and charged under Fighter Command with the duty of controlling the training and operations of all units which were to be allocated for tactical co-operation with the Army. This brought under their control the GPEU, HGMU, Parachute Maintenance Unit and the lodger unit of Maintenance Command No.235 MU.

No.2786 Light Anti-aircraft Sqn, with Sqn Ldr B. Warner as CO, arrived from Boscombe Down on 7th June 1943 to provide airfield defence against low-flying enemy aircraft attacks. The guns operated by the squadron were 4 Bofors and 32 Brownings.

A Boeing B-17 No.42-30006 (NV-A), with pilot Lt. Hamilton USAAF, on experimental operations from Boscombe Down, diverted to Netheravon on 29th June 1943 with a gas bomb load. The aircraft was placed under armed guard and unloaded the following day under the supervision of Wg Cdr H.J. Black from RAF Porton. The B-17 had been detached from the 325th Bomb Sqn 92nd Bomb Group based at Alconbury.

No.38 Group Communications Flight formed on 26th November 1943 ex Station Flight at Netheravon and moved to Earls Colne on 12th October 1944.

18 year old Pte James Lawrence of 22nd Independent Parachute Corps, Parachute Regiment AAC, was killed on the airfield on Wednesday 15th December 1943, when his parachute failed to open during a dropping exercise.

The Airborne Forces Tactical Development Unit, formed on 1st December 1943 in No.38 Group at Tarrant Rushton, arrived on 14th January 1944 where, as a Transport Command Lodger Unit, it was re-designated Air Transport Tactical Development Unit. For its role in trials work it was equipped with 4 Halifax IIIs, 2 Halifax Vs, 1 Albemarle, 1 Stirling A.IV, 1 Harrow, 1 York (LV626), 2 Oxfords, 2 Horsas, 1 Hamilcar and 2 Hadrians. On 31st August 1945, the unit was redesignated Transport Command Development Unit and moved to Harwell between 13th and 20th September 1945.

There was a dramatic ending to the year. On 31st December 1943, four USAAF B-17 Flying Fortresses, returning from an operation, two suffering from damage, made an emergency landing on the airfield.

Gp Capt C. L. Troop was appointed Station CO as from 31st January 1944. His stay was short as he was posted as CO at Keevil on 15th March when he was replaced by Sqn Ldr R.W.G. West who, himself, was replaced by Gp Capt W.L. Stedman on 3rd April 1944.

An RAF instructor explains the principles of glider towing to pilots of the Glider Pilot Regiment stood at the rear of an Albemarle at Netheravon. The original 1913 Aeroplane Sheds form the backdrop in this wartime scene. Photo: Army Air Corps.

No.46 (Transport) Group in Transport Command which formed at Stanmore in January 1944, had an advanced HQ at Netheravon as of the following month. The Group, under the command of Air Commodore L. Darvall MC, was equipped with the Dakota. The advance HQ remained until July when it disbanded.

No.1677 (Target Towing) Flt formed on 1st March 1944 in No.38 Group at Netheravon equipped with 3 Miles Matinets. The CO was Flt Lt Ravenhill. The role of the Flt was to train air gunners required to crew four-engined aircraft for glider towing. The gunners took part in glider formation and landing exercises on the airfield as part of their training. The Flt left for Rivenhall on 12th October 1944.

Glider pilots and tug crews on occasions were required to ferry gliders to various parts of the country. S/Sgt Laurie Weeden recalls a delivery flight in a Waco glider from Netheravon to Ayr on 31st March 1944. Showers were heavy and, over the River Dee, sight of the Dakota tug was completely lost. The towrope indicated that the glider was nearly abreast of the tug. To prevent a crash, the towrope was released. The glider made a heavy landing on a Welsh hillside.

During the spring of 1944, a number of training exercises were held during the day and night. Exercise *Dingo* was staged on the night of 6th/7th May. 90 Horsa gliders from all operational squadrons in No.38 Group were landed on the two airfields of Netheravon, 30 on the north and 60 on the south. A 'T' of 7 green holoplane lights was laid out on each airfield with gliders using landing lights. The positioning of the 'T' was important as it indicated to the pilots the wind direction. Unfortunately, just before the gliders arrived, the wind changed to the opposite direction. Some pilots realised this whilst others didn't. Gliders were landing in both directions and although there was no mid-air collisions, there were a number on the ground. No fatalities occurred but there was considerable damage to some of the Horsas. On the night of 8th/9th May Exercise *Dingo II* was held and this was a repeat of *Dingo* but without the use of lighting.

The night-time exercises were not always a success and a number of injuries occurred in aircraft accidents. During one such exercise, the aircraft and gliders mistakenly circled the airfield at Upavon before it was realised they were not over Netheravon. It was not just the airfield at Netheravon that was used for glider landings but also some small fields around the perimeter. These were used even for night landings with no markers for illumination. Ground crews retrieved the gliders the following morning and towed them back on to the airfield. Exercises also involved paratroop drops on the airfield and the Divisional DZ.

The King and Queen, accompanied by Princess Elizabeth, visited Netheravon on 19th May 1944 to witness the day-time Exercise *Exeter*. This was a demonstration of the lead-up to the invasion of Europe in June. Squadrons of No.38 and No.46 Groups dropped 300 paratroops of the Canadian Parachute Training Company, and Halifax aircraft cast off Hamilcars carrying tanks onto the north airfield. 100 Horsa gliders made landings on the south airfield. High-ranking officers attending were AM Sir Trafford Leigh-Mallory KCB, DSO, Air Officer Commandering-in-Chief of the Allied Expeditionary Air Force, AVM L.N. Hollinghurst CB, OBE, DFC Air Officer Commanding No.38 Group, Major-General Frederick A.M. Browning commanding the British Airborne Corps and Major-General Richard N. Gale commanding the 6th British Airborne Division. A similar Exercise *Consternation* was staged two days after the visit by the Royal Family involving 75 Horsa gliders towed from Broadwell, Blakehill Farm and Down Ampney and landing on the south airfield.

During the weeks leading up to the D-Day invasion, Netheravon was engaged with the preparation of the gliders that would be involved. This achieved, the invasion and aftermath passed Netheravon by. During the following month however, a demonstration of the glider pick-up technique was given to some of the RAF and Army top brass. Glider pilots arrived from the camp at Fargo near Stonehenge and initially snatched from a standing position using the American Waco glider. This was followed by Col Chatterton and a GPR pilot being snatched in the larger Horsa type. Everybody was impressed with the demonstration. In August some damaged gliders, recovered from Normandy, were returned for refurbishment, as were undamaged ones.

On 3rd June 1944, senior officers of the RAF and GPR were summoned from

The King, Queen and Princess Elizabeth observing the exercise from the open windows of Netheravon Control Tower on 19th May 1944.

The Royal Family inspecting RAF crews and personnel of the Airborne Forces prior to viewing the airborne troop movements at Netheravon on 19th May 1944. Horsa gliders line up behind the Stirling, Halifax and Albemarle.   Photo: Army Air Corps.

Horsa gliders tied down, and with their cockpits covered, stand at Netheravon in readiness for the D-Day invasion. A Blister hangar can be seen at the rear. Photo: Army Air Corps.

their bases in the area to attend a special briefing at Netheravon. All these individuals were security cleared before being conducted to a building containing a large model showing, in fine detail, the beachhead at Normandy with all of the various buildings and other features. It left no doubt in the minds of those making the invasion landings exactly what they would see

on the approach flight to their landing zone. An Operations Officer addressed those in the room and explained the tasks and objectives of the invasion landings. A No.38 Group-produced film, taken with an overhead camera giving a picture of what the pilots would see when they crossed the French coast, was then shown. Before dismissal, everybody was warned of the need for complete security. All personnel were confined to their respective stations with no outside communication.

Netheravon witnessed Operation *Bigot* on 5th June when 9 No.297 Sqn Albemarles from Brize Norton were despatched with a heavy tow to Caen. One of these, V1769 was crewed by Flt Sgt G.W. Cunningham (pilot), Fg Off A. Roddan (nav), Sgt W.M. Forbes (WOP), Sgt T.A.W. Cowden (AG) and Fg Off T.E. Reilly (BA). The crew returned to Caen with another heavy tow on 6th June, this time from their home base at Brize Norton as part of Operation *Mallard*.

A fatal crash occurred on Tuesday 4th July 1944 when a Hadrian glider, being towed from Netheravon, crashed immediately after take-off, killing S/Sgt Dennis Shaw and Sgt Frederick W. Simpson of the 1st GPR (AAC).

Prior to D-Day, eleven glider-pilot crews were taken off training for the invasion and formed a Flight for 'Special Operations'. It was named 'X' Flt with Lt 'Peggy' Clark as CO. The 1st Pilots of the crews chosen had all taken part in the Sicily landings and were familiar with the American Waco gliders. A number of the type was collected from US bases and flown to Netheravon where a further familiarisation and training programme was staged. 'X'Flt was first used on 5th August 1944 for Operation *Dingson 35A*. 10 Waco gliders transported 10 jeeps and 35 French SAS troops, 275 kilometres behind the German lines to Vannes in southern Brittany, where they joined up with the French Resistance in their rear-guard action against the Germans. The SAS actions were a great success and, due to the speed of the Allied advance in France, the 20 glider pilots returned to Netheravon by Dakota eleven days after flying out.

Mass glider exercises by No.46 Group were reintroduced at Netheravon between D-Day and the Arnhem operation. Exercise *Consternation II* was staged on 6th August 1944 when 49 gliders were landed on the south airfield by day. Exercise *Mole* was another one held on 8th/9th August 1944. It involved a night landing of 29 gliders on the south airfield without flares. Fog descended shortly before the arrival of

the tugs and gliders and, as a result there was utter chaos, with gliders landing in all directions and some missing the airfield altogether. Nine Horsa gliders crashed on, and adjacent to, the airfield. A number of personnel received injuries but there were no fatalities, which was probably due to the forgiving nature of the Horsa glider. S/Sgt Laurie Weeden was a passenger in a Horsa from Blakehill Farm. They had arrived late at Netheravon and, in letting down through the 'clag,' made a heavy landing that resulted in the glider breaking into three pieces. In addition, an Albemarle from Harwell crashed while taking off with a Horsa.

A detachment from No.107 OTU, Leicester East, operated from Netheravon for two weeks commencing about 9th September 1944. They flew Dakotas to a landing strip near Ouistreham in Normandy. Here Horsa gliders used in the D-Day landings and which had been repaired and made serviceable, were brought back to England for the Arnhem operation. Fg Off Terence Jones, who was part of the detachment, indicated that the crews were accommodated in barrack huts at Netheravon but were under canvas whilst in France.

During October 1944, US C-47s towing Waco gliders from USAAF Station 469 Ramsbury, used the airfield at Netheravon for landing exercises.

The RAF School of Air Transport formed on 4th November 1944 in No.38 Group at Netheravon equipped with the Oxford. The school disbanded on 5th March 1946.

Gp Capt E.J. George was appointed Station CO as from 4th December 1944. He, in turn, was succeeded by Wg Cdr J.W. White MBE on 13th March 1945. Gp Capt H.A. Purvis DFC, AFC, followed him as CO on 23rd April 1945.

In February 1945, 800 troops were returned from the continent to Netheravon in 40 Dakotas.

During early March 1945, 150 gliders were despatched from Netheravon to the various No.38 Group stations in readiness for the Rhine crossing, Operation *Varsity*. On 8th March, 12 C-47s from Spanhoe were detached at

Netheravon ufrom the 2X US Troop Carrier Command for paratroop drops. Over a five-day period, carrying out six drops a day, they dropped 8,000 paratroops on the Divisional DZ one mile south of Netheravon. There were injuries during this exercise but probably the luckiest man to survive was L/Cpl Phillips of the 6th Airborne Division. On Monday 12th March he jumped from C-47A 42-92736 and was caught up on the aircraft tail wheel. Whilst he dangled there, Sgt Beamish, the instructor, tied together several nylon strops with a kit bag on the end. This was paid-out to the corporal who was able to cling on to it whilst he was hauled in by his colleagues still in the aircraft. This was a successful rescue against all the odds and probably it was the only time it had been achieved.

Following the Rhine crossing operation, Transport Command Dakotas returned 3000 troops of the 6th Airborne Division to Netheravon between 17th and 21st May 1945.

Between 19th and 30th June 1945, Netheravon again witnessed mass landings of Horsa gliders, towed the short distance from Thruxton airfield on the Hampshire/Wiltshire border.

On 24th August 1945, another change of Station CO took place with the arrival of Gp Capt R.G. Harman DFC.

Post War Years

Netheravon staged its first Battle of Britain open day on 15th September 1945 but, unfortunately, it was not well attended by the general public probably because the choice of other venues were more accessible to them. Some of the aircraft on display included a Dakota, Halifax, Liberator, Master, Mosquito, Stirling and York. These were all courtesy of the Transport Command Development Unit which was leaving Netheravon.

With the war now over, it was presumably decided that identification of the airfield from the air needed to be improved and so the entire boundary was outlined by chalk for which there was no shortage in the area.

After the war, a gradual reduction in strength took place but Netheravon continued to be used for training by the

GPR, Parachute Regiment and the Royal Army Service Corps Air Despatch Company. As of April 1946, the Units attached at Netheravon were No.1 HGSU, No.38 GPMU and the School of Mechanical Support. Aircraft on the station strength were 2 Dakotas IVs (KN641) and (KN661), 1 Magister, 3 Wellingtons, 1 Proctor, Hadrian and Horsa gliders. The Magister left for Lichfield in the September. During May 1946, Netheravon assumed parent station responsibilities for the C&M party at Rollestone. During November, the two Dakota aircraft had their camouflage removed.

Personnel, stores and equipment of No.187 Sqn arrived from Membury between 3rd and 7th October 1946 and the main party four days later. The squadron was accommodated as a Lodger unit at Netheravon within No.38 Group. The CO was Wg Cdr P. Fleming and the squadron aircraft were 20 Dakota IVs. 38 new pilots, navigators and WOPs were posted to the squadron between 15th-21st October. The squadron disbanded on 1st December 1946 and was re-formed as No.53 Sqn, using the same aircraft. Although the airfield was unserviceable for 7 days that month, No.53 Sqn carried out 93 operational trips.

The first three months of 1947 saw little flying by the squadron owing to extremely bad weather and the state of the grass airfield. During April some 'Specials' were flown. Dakota IV (KN381) Flt Lt G.D. Cremer to East Africa, (KN590) Fg Off R.E. Troth to Catania in Sicily and (KN608) Flt Lt F.W. Wincott to Athens. In addition 15 crews commenced glider towing and formation-flying continuation training. During May, the squadron was route flying with scheduled services to the Continent as follows:- Northolt - Berlin - Warsaw - Berlin - Northolt - Abingdon - Buckeburg - Abingdon

Wg Cdr G. H. Gatherall took up the appointment of squadron CO on 8th July.

On 6th September 1947, 13 Dakotas, crews and groundstaff left for Abingdon to train for Exercise *Longstop*. The object of the exercise was to demonstrate the use of aircraft in close-support roles. The airfield at Netheravon was assumed to be in enemy hands. An airborne landing had

to be undertaken to secure the airstrip and, once achieved, reinforcements would be poured in. On 22nd September, the first phase of Exercise *Longstop* was launched. 12 Dakotas with paratroops took-off from Abingdon but, high winds prevented a successful drop. Instead they were transported to Netheravon by road ready for the next day's phase. For the next phase, twelve No.53 Sqn Dakotas made two trips between Abingdon and Netheravon, dropping paratroops on each occasion. A total of fifty No.46 Group Dakotas dropped troops. 10 No.38 Group Halifaxes dropped guns, jeeps and gun teams. 12 Horsas and 9 Hamilcars were used. 6 Dakotas landed heavy equipment. The airstrip was successfully secured. The exercise was witnessed by senior military staff from around the world including Field Marshal Montgomery who arrived in a bullet-proof Rolls Royce.

On 11th December 1947, No.53 Sqn left for Waterbeach and a role in the Berlin Air Lift. The move was completed over a five-day period.

Netheravon had a Light Anti-Aircraft Gunnery School which had formed there by 1946 and had No.1353 Flt working with it until the latter moved to Turnhouse on 11th February 1946. The LAA Gunnery School moved to Watchet in Somerset on 15th July 1947.

The Transport Support Practice Camp formed at Netheravon on 1st April 1947 equipped with 11 Horsa Mk.2 gliders, and was disbanded on 5th January 1948.

The VISTRE Flt arrived from Keevil on 16th November 1947 in connection with Netheravons Visual Inter-Service Training & Research Establishment. The Flt was equipped with the Anson and moved to Old Sarum on 18th November 1950. From the VISTRE Flt, on 15th January 1952, was formed the Joint Concealment Centre (RAF Component) in No.28 Group at Netheravon. Equipped with the Anson and Auster, its role was the provision of dummy aircraft and 'Q' Site lighting arrangements. The unit was moved into No.22 Group on 28th July 1958 before disbanding on 31st October 1958.

During September 1947, Gp Capt H.M.A. Day DSO, OBE, AM, took over as Station CO.

No.1333 Transport Support Training

Unit from Syerston had a detachment at Netheravon from 29th December 1947 under the command of Wg Cdr K.J.D. Dickson MBE, AFC. The Unit staged training courses in glider towing, supply and paratroop dropping for RAF crews. The first course commenced on 8th January 1948.

January 1948 saw the start of continuation training courses for Army glider pilots, flying the Tiger Moth. An Air Traffic Control System was installed at Netheravon during the month. Towards the end of June 1948, all available staff crews at Netheravon were despatched to Wunsdorf to assist in Operation *Carter Patterson*, the supply of Berlin by air. Also during the year, the Station had two new COs in quick succession. Gp Capt R.H. Carter was appointed in October and was succeeded by Gp Capt G. Francis in December 1948.

The aircraft types deployed at Netheravon as of May 1949 were the Dakota Mk.4, Tiger Moth Mk.2, Anson Mk.12 and Horsa Mk.2 gliders. One of the Dakota Mk.4s KJ865 of No.240 OCU North Luffenham, towing a Horsa, crash landed on the north side of the airfield immediately after take-off on 13th September 1949. The only injury was to Signaller 2 Bolton, one of the aircrew. During the month, Gp Capt H.M.A. Day DSO, OBE, AM became Station CO. He retired on 3rd June 1950 and was replaced by Wg Cdr D.M. Cross who, in turn was replaced in November 1950 by Sqn Ldr W.F. McIlgrew. He became the CO of the Station and of the RAF Police Dog Centre.

No.27 (Airborne Forces) Sqn was formed and based at Abingdon from 1st March 1950. The Sqn was equipped with 8 Dakotas and had 13 aircrews of pilots, navigators and signallers. These were detached to Netheravon under the command of Sqn Ldr D. J. Penman DSO, DFC. A Development Flt with 1 Hastings and 1 Valetta plus crews remained at Abingdon. The Dakotas and crews were drawn mainly from the disbanded No.1333 Transport Support Training Unit at Netheravon whose role was taken over by No.240 CU North Luffenham. As there was no dropping zone there or trained Transport Support instructors, it was arranged that pupil crews would fly aircraft to Netheravon each day. No.27 Sqn would supply instructors for supply dropping exercises on Netheravon's dropping zone. This activity continued until North Luffenham had its own facilities. No.27 Sqn's role was (a) continuation flying, (b) Army continuation flying and (c) route flying (mainly to Gibraltar). On 20th April 1950 when taking-off on a glider-towing exercise, the starboard engine of Dakota KN250 caught fire. Pupil pilot A. Welvear cast off the glider before crash landing. The aircraft was severely damaged but the crew escaped without injury. The glider landed safely. The damaged Dakota was later replaced by KN641, which was the only aircraft in the Command capable of use for glider-snatches. It was intended to use No.27 Sqn for future glider-snatch demonstrations. The squadron officially moved to Netheravon on 10th June 1950. An accident occurred on the first supply drop of the day on 13th September 1950. An R.A.S.C dispatcher became hooked up in a pannier and was pulled out of the aircraft. His safety harness eventually snapped and he fell to his death. No.27 Sqn disbanded on 10th November.

From the beginning of June 1950, the Parachute Service Section ceased operating and on 20th November the station was transferred to No.62 Group Home Command. The aircraft ferried out during the month were:

On 1st December 1950, Netheravon became the home of the RAF Police Training Centre and Dog School. On their arrival from Staverton the previous day, the dogs were kennelled in the Lower Camp 'Cathedral' hangar. The RAF Police Driving School arrived from Pershore as a Lodger Unit

Horsa Gliders TL261, TL466, TL130 to No.9 MU Cosford
    "   "   TK981, TL353, TK956 " No.15 MU Wroughton
    "   "   TL332, TL527, TL614 " No.48 MU Hawarden
                   (the first two forced landed on route)

Tiger Moth   NM174 to RAF Topcliffe
    "   "   PG701 "   "   Hucknall
    "   "   N9495 "   "   Waterbeach

Dakota Mk.4   KN356, KP279, KN361 to No.8 MU Little Rissington
    "   "   "   KN274, KN629, KN605 to No.12 MU Kirkbride
    "   "   "   KN462, KN129 to No.22 MU Silloth

on 28th February 1951 with Sqn Ldr H.M. Sheperd as CO. In September 1960 the majority of the Police Depot which was by then in four Wings, moved out to Debden. It was not until 1963 that the No.3 (Police Dog Training) Sqn also left for Debden.

During June and July 1951, Flts of Nos. 662, 663 and 664 Auxiliary Air OP Sqns visited Netheravon.

Closure

On the 31st July 1963, RAF Netheravon closed and the camp was transferred to the Army.

The Lower Airfield Camp became an Army transit camp but the Upper Camp was allowed to fall into a state of disrepair which was made worse by vandalism. However, during 1963, the Army Free-Fall Parachute Association took over part of the Upper Airfield Camp and this subsequently became the Joint Services Parachute Centre. The Association used two DH Rapides, one was (G-AHJO), for their free fall jumps. In C.1974 one of the two overshot the end of the grass runway, passed through a hedge and onto the Netheravon to Everleigh road. There were no injuries. A Southern Command Gliding Club and the Royal Artillery Aero Club took up residence, using some of the available hangars.

The Army Air Corps (AAC) was formally constituted in 1957 and became responsible for operating light aircraft and helicopters in direct support of the Army. Previously this had been a function of the RAF's AOP squadrons.

During 1964, a considerable

development took place in Army Aviation which had implications for Netheravon. During August, the HQ of No.651 Sqn moved in from Middle Wallop where it was divided to form two Army Aviation HQs.

Airfield Redevelopment

In 1966, No.2 Wing HQ, responsible for UK and Mediterranean Army Aviation, moved in using the former control tower as a HQ building. Netheravon subsequently became HQ Army Aviation Strategic Command and took over the whole of Netheravon Airfield and commenced its refurbishment. Some new buildings on the Lower Camp were also provided.

Army Air Corps Period

By the end of 1978, No.658 Sqn of 8 Field Force and No.7 Regiment with 6 and 8 Flts were in residence at Netheravon. No.656 Sqn arrived from Farnborough on 31st March 1982 and went to the Falklands during the war against Argentina. There the squadron flew the Scout helicopter and gained two DFCs. On 1st April 1986, No.666 Sqn reformed at Netheravon. This was the first TA squadron to reform flying Scouts and the first reserve flying unit since the disbanding of the RAAF squadrons in 1957. No.666 Sqn supports the UKLF and consists of Sqn HQ and originally 2 Flts of Scouts. These were replaced by the Gazelle (XW904). No.7 Regiment disbanded as a regular unit in April 1994 but reformed as a volunteer unit and, at the same time, No.658 Sqn disbanded as a regular squadron but reformed as a volunteer squadron.

During July 2000, Netheravon Camp became the HQ of the Brigade of Gurkhas which moved from Church Crookham in Hampshire, its home for 29 years. The new prefabricated HQ building has been set amongst the original 1913 offices and accommodation on the Lower Camp and is painted in the same black and white format.

On 29th August 2000, some of the veterans of Arnhem were at Netheravon where they received training at the Joint Services Parachute Centre for a parachute jump they were making at Arnhem to mark the 56th anniversary of the September 1944 assault.

The airfield landing areas are in use mainly for helicopters with some fixed-wing communication aircraft. As of 2003, No.7 Regiment AAC, with the Gazelle, continues to operate at Netheravon.

Victoria Cross Recipients

1) Major James McCudden

Having joined the RE as a bugler in 1910, James McCudden transferred to the RFC in 1913 as a mechanic. He moved with No.3 Sqn from Larkhill to Netheravon and eventually to France in August 1914. By the summer of the following year, he was making unofficial flights as an observer and trainee pilot. By the end of the year he was in combat as an observer. He returned to England as a Flt Sgt in January 1916 and trained as a pilot. By August he was back in France with No.20 Sqn flying FE2s. The next month he was with No.29 Sqn flying DH2s. In July 1917 he was attached to No.66 Sqn flying a Pup and subsequently joined No.56 Sqn as a Flt Cdr in August. His score of enemy aircraft up was seven. By the time he shot down his last enemy machine, on 26th February 1918, five years after his entry into the RFC, Major James McCudden had become famous for destroying 57 enemy aircraft and having been awarded the VC, DSO, MC, MM and Croix de Guerre. He returned to England to instruct and then to command No.60 Sqn. Whilst flying to take over this new appointment, he crashed and was killed in July 1918.

2) Lt G.S.M. Insall

On 7th November 1915, he took off from Bertangles flying Vickers FB5 5074 with Air Mechanic T.H. Donald as gunner. They attacked and forced down an enemy machine the crew of which, after landing, prepared to fire their gun at the British machine. Insall dived at the Germans enabling his gunner to concentrate his fire. This drove the enemy airmen away. By now German infantry had arrived and put up a barrage of rifle and machine-gun fire. Undeterred, Insall dived again and destroyed the enemy aircraft with an incendiary bomb. Passing over the German trenches on their return to the British lines, Insall dived on the enemy and Donald strafed the troops. In this attack, the petrol tank of the Vickers was holed by returning gun-fire and the crew had to land short of the British lines and in shooting distance of the enemy. When darkness came, Insall and Donald were able to repair the Vickers and, at first light, made a hair-raising take-off and returned to Bertangles. For their actions, Lt Insall was awarded the VC and Air Mechanic Donald the DCM.

3) Lt Col William A. Bishop

Whilst serving with No.21 Sqn as an observer in France he was injured in a crash and, after leaving hospital, trained as a pilot at CFS Upavon. He was then posted to No.60 Sqn flying the Nieuport 17 and later the SE5a. He was promoted to Captain in April 1917, awarded the MC and DSO in May and a VC in June. He received the Victoria Cross after returning in his badly damaged machine, having shot down three of the enemy who were taking off from an airfield to attack him. He was then promoted to Major and awarded a Bar to the DSO. By the time he returned to England, in August 1917, he had claimed 45 enemy machines and two balloons destroyed. He returned to France in May 1918 as CO of No.85 Sqn and by 19th June his score totalled 72. During World War 2, he served in Canada as an Air Marshal in charge of training. He died on 11th September 1956.

4) Major Lionel W.B. Rees

Major Rees MC was flying alone in DH2 6015 on 1st July 1916 from Treizennes, the squadron's French base, when he sighted a formation, which he believed to be British bombers, returning from a sortie. He made towards them to provide escort, only to discover they were ten enemy machines. He decided to attack and sent one diving out of control from the formation. Rees attacked another German until it also was damaged and dived away. He then opened fire on five machines at the centre of the formation, causing them to break away. Rees then concentrated on the leader and was about to finish him off when he was attacked from below. Fire from the enemy struck Rees in the leg, which prevented him using the rudder-bar. Despite the injury, he continued firing at the enemy machine until his ammunition was exhausted. Even then he chased the fleeing enemy whilst drawing his service revolver but this he unfortunately dropped. He returned to his base and was admitted to hospital where a serious leg wound was tended. For this action, his VC was gazetted on 5th August 1916.

Memorial

184/SU155488

Within the airfield camp, close to the main gate is the original 1913-built Royal Flying Corps Officers' Mess, now an Army Air Corps Mess. Displayed over the main entrance doors is a large pair of RFC wings carved in wood and painted in the appropriate colours.

The Royal Flying Corps wings above the entrance to the Officers' Mess at Netheravon Airfield.

NEW ZEALAND FARM RELIEF LANDING GROUND
Location - 184/ST974508 - 8 miles South West of Devizes

New Zealand Farm Camp is situated on the high ground of Cheverell Down on Salisbury Plain, 2 miles SW of the village of West Lavington and a mile north of the village of Imber. Imber lost its inhabitants when they were evacuated on 17th December 1943 because of the expansion of Warminster Ranges for military use. Access to New Zealand Farm Camp is via an unclassified road from the A360 at St Joan & Gores Cross.

Airfield Development

The RAF initially set up a Relief Landing Ground (RLG) on Market Lavington Hill on the east side of the A360 but found that the numerous air pockets were not conducive to safe flying. They transferred their operation to New Zealand Farm, which was established as an RLG from 9th October 1940, mainly for night flying training by CFS Upavon. Prior to the RAF occupancy it was an active dairy and oat growing farm. The farmhouse was demolished to make way for the Nissen hutted camp but before this could be built RAF groundcrew used the barn and aircraft packing cases for accommodation. The hutted camp was encircled by trees except at the main entrance on the north side and at the south exit to the landing ground. One Over Blister hangar and two Standard Blister hangars were in use, immediately along side one end of the N/S Landing area. Two grass runways were in use for flying, one E/W and the other N/S. Aircraft movements were controlled from a small timber built watch tower. This had a windowed top section with access via an external wooden staircase. The two-letter station identification code was NZ. Around the perimeter of the site, tank traps and Pill boxes were constructed

When night training took place the runways were lit by gooseneck flares. From mid 1942 additional buildings were added to the camp and Beam approach equipment was installed with the provision of a sodium flare path.

A Fitting Party from West Drayton arrived on 3rd August 1943 to install a Bomber Command 'Darky' transmitter and receiver.

Improvements to the camp accommodation were made after the war, when A&AEE Boscombe Down started using the site for trials. Semi-submerged observation galleries were also built, from where the boffins could observe or photograph the trials.

The control tower was removed in the early 1980s when use of the runways ceased for other than light aircraft.

World War 2 Years

Oxfords and Miles Masters from the CFS Upavon were used for 'day/night' circuit training. Night training was also simulated during the daytime with the pilots using thick filter goggles, opaque to all but pure yellow light of the instruments. Aircraft used for this form of training were identified by red painted cowlings. During 1940 several pilots doing night take-offs in Masters flew into the ground for no apparent reason, when making their first turn. During night flying the groundcrews were on standby to extinguish the flare path should they receive a warning of imminent enemy aircraft. Such a situation arose on 14th April 1941 during night flying practice when a single bomber, attracted by the lighting, made an attack and dropped ten bombs. Only one landed on the airfield and no damage was recorded. The other 9 bombs fell in an adjoining field. A Miles Master T8678 crashed when taking off on the night of Wednesday 30th April 1941, killing the instructor Flt Lt John E. Robins RAF and the student, Plt Off John F. Raw RAFVR who was attending (No.21 War) Course. Plt Off Raw was buried at Upavon cemetery. The accident was repeated on 16th September when an Oxford V3502 crashed at 2345hrs and Sgt Gordon McDonald Jackson RCAF was killed and Sgt G.D. Norton RCAF suffered injuries. Sgt Jackson was buried at Upavon cemetery.

New Zealand Farm was used on 17th January 1942 for demonstrating the Stinson 0.49 to senior officers. Personnel arrived from RAF Larkhill and the demonstration was carried out by No.36 Wing Army Co-operation. The CFS was disbanded on 1st April

1942 and was redesignated in part as No.7 Flying Instructors School (FIS), which continued to use New Zealand Farm. The instructional staff and aircraft were accordingly transferred to the school. On 7th April it was redesignated No.7 FIS (Advanced) and on 1st August, gave up its Masters and Oxfords to No.3 FIS with these being replaced by Miles Magisters.

On the Ranges south-west of New Zealand Farm, the tragic 'Imber Incident' occurred on Monday 13th April 1942. This involved a tactical air demonstration of fighter aircraft making low-level attacks on dummy soldiers and a number of stationary vehicles, including two tanks. The demonstration was in front of an invited audience of military personnel viewing from a spectator's stand. The weather over the target was fine but hazy, making visibility poor when looking into the sun. The demonstration started at 1400hrs with Spitfires from No.234 Sqn making a pass at the targets without firing. This was followed by Hurricanes of No.175 Sqn firing at the targets. Visibility was poor but despite this, from the first five pilots there were two good attacks, two fired too late and one didn't fire at all. Unfortunately the pilot of the sixth Hurricane mistook the spectators stand for the target area and opened fire on his approach. The carnage resulted in the deaths of 25 Army personnel and 71 with various degrees of injury. Brigadier Grant Taylor was one of the officers killed. He was standing next to General Sir Gerald Templar in the position that would have been occupied by Winston Churchill had he not have cancelled a proposed visit. Instead Churchill attended the following day's demonstration.

On 15th and 26th January 1943, two Wellington bombers returning from 'Ops'. forced landed with no injuries to crews in either case but with slight damage to the first aircraft. Sgt Douglas Campbell RAF was killed on 2nd February 1943, when flying from New Zealand Farm, his Oxford crashed at Berwick St. James. He was buried at Upavon cemetery. In March four Oxfords crashed on or near the airfield during training, with injuries in one case. On the night of 16th/17th April 1943 a Halifax bomber returning from a raid on the Skoda Works forced landed. It eventually took off having taken on enough fuel to reach its base but aiming to remain as light as possible. This was followed on 17th June 1943 by a Whitley crash landing.

Another Oxford trainer incident occurred on 17th September 1943 when, in trying to avoid a second aircraft on the flare path during a night flying practice, it crashed and caught fire. The two pilots, Sgts Hanson and Jackson, scrambled clear with minor injuries.

The residents of nearby Imber village recall a German aircraft flying low over-head one night and crashing at New Zealand Farm. This was shortly before they were required by the Army to move out of their homes when the area was requisitioned for training purposes. It was for this same reason that No.7 FIS (A) ceased flying from New Zealand Farm in November and all aircraft and personnel returning to Upavon.

Closure

New Zealand Farm as a RLG closed and transferred to the War Department as from 17th December 1943.

Airfield Re-occupation

It was not however the end of flying at the airfield, as from the 13th March 1944 the 153rd Liaison Sqn, IX Tactical Air Command Unit, First US Army left Keevil for the village of Erlestoke 2 miles NW of New Zealand Farm airfield. The American personnel were quartered at Erlestoke Manor to which they gave the name 'The Castle' but officially AAF Station 435. The Unit's L-4 Cubs were based at New Zealand Farm. The squadron comprised four Flights plus a Headquarters Flight. It had 13 officers and 120 enlisted men, commanded by Captain James R. Cooper. The 153rd LS were involved in flying daily courier runs, communication flights and priority mail runs for the 1st Army. 'A' Flt. served V Corps HQ at Norton Manor Camp, Taunton, 'B' Flt. served VII Corps at Breamore House south of Salisbury, 'C' Flt. served XIX Corps at Knook Camp near Warminster and 'D' Flt. plus HQ Flt. served the First Army HQ in Bristol, using Bristol

An aerial view of New Zealand Farm taken by the Americans on 25th March 1944. The camp buildings nestle within the ring of trees and the blister hangars are clearly seen. A concrete track with turning circle runs parallel to the E/W landing strip.
Photo: NMRO

(Whitchurch) Airport and an airstrip at Beggar Bush Lane, Westbury, Bristol. Shortly after arriving at New Zealand Farm the 153rd LS were equipped with the improved Stinson L-5 Sentinel and by the end of the month these were out-numbering the Piper L-4 Cubs. Compared with the 70mph cruise speed of the L-4, the L-5 was more suited for cross country duties, having an increased cruise speed of 115 mph. By the following month, in addition to their courier and mail service flights, numerous training flights and photographic reconnaissance missions were being undertaken. One of the training exercises carried out on the airfield site was the dropping of 'Window', the strips of silver paper used to confuse enemy radar. It was dropped in quantities reminiscent of a snow-storm and much of it was evident in the area for months afterwards. With the daylight hours lengthening, the pilots of the 153rd LS were flying long hours and often not returning until the late evening. A jeep was used to ferry them the short distance to and from Erlestoke Manor.

Several of the 153rd LS aircraft were involved in crashes and forced-landings. Of these one on 16th April 1944 was a crash resulting from an engine failure and occurred near Warminster when Staff Sergeant Wayne L. White of 'C' Flt. was killed

but his passenger survived. Bad weather caused Staff Sergeant Thomas M. Wood of 'B' Flt. to crash-land and, although injured, he continued his mission on foot for which he received a Commendation. A few days prior to D-Day the aircraft of all Flights were painted with their black and white invasion stripes and were assembled at New Zealand Farm from where all 32 L-5s flew together to Middle Wallop in transit for France. The 153rd LS returned to Wiltshire shortly after D-Day and on 18th June one of its L-5s was involved in a fatal accident when Staff Sergeant Marvin R. Miller was killed when he flew into high tension electricity cables at Ludlow's Farm, Cannimore near Warminster. The same day 23 L-5s left for Normandy and at 1300 hrs the following day the Unit's ground echelon of four officers and 74 enlisted men under the command of Captain Lund, departed Erlestoke in convoy for the Marshalling Area in Winchester. From there they went to Southampton and on the 25th June crossed the Channel for Omaha Beach. The following day the ground crews were reunited with the aircrews at Vouilly and the 153rd LS were again operationally available to support the First Army.

On 6th June 1944 the 112th and 125th Liaison Sqns arrived at Liverpool by ship from New York. The following

237

The camp buildings immediately after the war when used by A&AEE

The E/W landing strip looking west with marker cones and the concrete turning circle surrounding the wind-sock.

Beverley transport aircraft carried out circuits and bumps and parachute drops. In the terrible winter of 1962/63 one of these aircraft was isolated on the airfield for several weeks. The army carried out hovercraft trials but found the site unsuitable because the craft were unable to cross the tank traps without losing their air cushions. During the 1970s Rapide aircraft were flown from Netheravon to New Zealand Farm for parachute drops. Exercises conducted by the Army during 1971/72 were supported by Andovers and Hercules landing on the airfield.

Today the camp accommodation can be seen basically as it was when first constructed and in good condition. The site remains in use by the Army.

New Zealand Farm Camp seen from the main entrance gate looking south. The former main E/W runway was on the ridge of the high ground with the N/S off picture to the right.

day both squadrons were assigned to the 9th Air Force. The 125th travelled by train from Liverpool to Cheltenham where it was supplied with equipment and stores. On 19th June the squadron transferred the short distance to the airfield at Chedworth where it received its L-5s for pilot training which included navigation and familiarisation of UK flying procedures. On 9th July a further move was undertaken to the recently vacated New Zealand Farm and with personnel billeted at Erlestoke Manor. On 29th July the Unit had a change of role when it was attached to the HQ 9th US Army. 'A', 'B' and 'D' Flts. of the 125th LS left for France from 23rd August with the Squadron's ground crews leaving Erlestoke on 1st September 1944, transiting through Southampton Docks.

Post War Years

When the war ended New Zealand Farm became an out-station of A&AEE Boscombe Down, who used it for experimental flying and weapons trials.

In the early1950s a large gantry was constructed at one end of the main runway into which ordinance was directed from a Lancaster bomber. Local farmers recall that later still old steam engines, aircraft and vehicles were dispersed around the site and used as targets by rocket firing aircraft. The airfield was used for trials involving ejector seats fitted with dummies fired from a Canberra bomber.

From the early 1960s the Army Air Corps had use of New Zealand Farm.

OATLANDS HILL AERODROME

Location - 184/SU096404 - 4 miles West of Amesbury

This satellite of Old Sarum was situated on Oatlands Hill, one mile east of Winterbourne Stoke, and at the junction of the A303/A360.

Airfield Development

The airfield, Site No.1, had three grass strips and these were NE/SW 1,600yds, E/W 1,200yds and N/S 1,400yds. Four Extra Over Blister hangars (69' span) were erected, three for aircraft storage and one for maintenance. An Observation Tower was positioned on the western end of the field. This consisted of a small timber cabin elevated on four legs. Night take-off and landings were controlled by a Chance Light and gooseneck flares. The main domestic buildings were dispersed along the western edge of the field and included the NAAFI, Officers' Mess, Sgts' Mess, Dining Room/Cookhouse and Sick Quarters. Barrack huts were spread along the south elevation next to a line of trees, which provided good concealment. Site No.2 in the SW corner of the field also had a line of barrack huts and a Blister hangar used for maintenance. The lack of suitable and sufficient accommodation throughout its period of occupation, coupled with its exposed location, was reason enough for most units deployed to move elsewhere as soon as they possibly could.

World War 2 Years

Oatlands Hill opened in June 1941 and its prime use was the training of pilots for Army Co-operation Command tactical reconnaissance squadrons. Low flying and night flying forming an element of the training. An early casualty on 17th June was Tomahawk IIA AH890 of No.1 School of Army Co-operation, Old Sarum, which suffered a collapsed undercarriage on landing.

No.239 Sqn, with its Tomahawk I & IIs, used the airfield in the summer of 1941. No.1 SofAC Tomahawk IIA AH943 undershot and hit the trees near the landing area on 12th July. Aircraft accidents were to be a feature of this site and on 26th December 1941, Tomahawk AH770 of No.26 Sqn, based at Gatwick, also crashed on

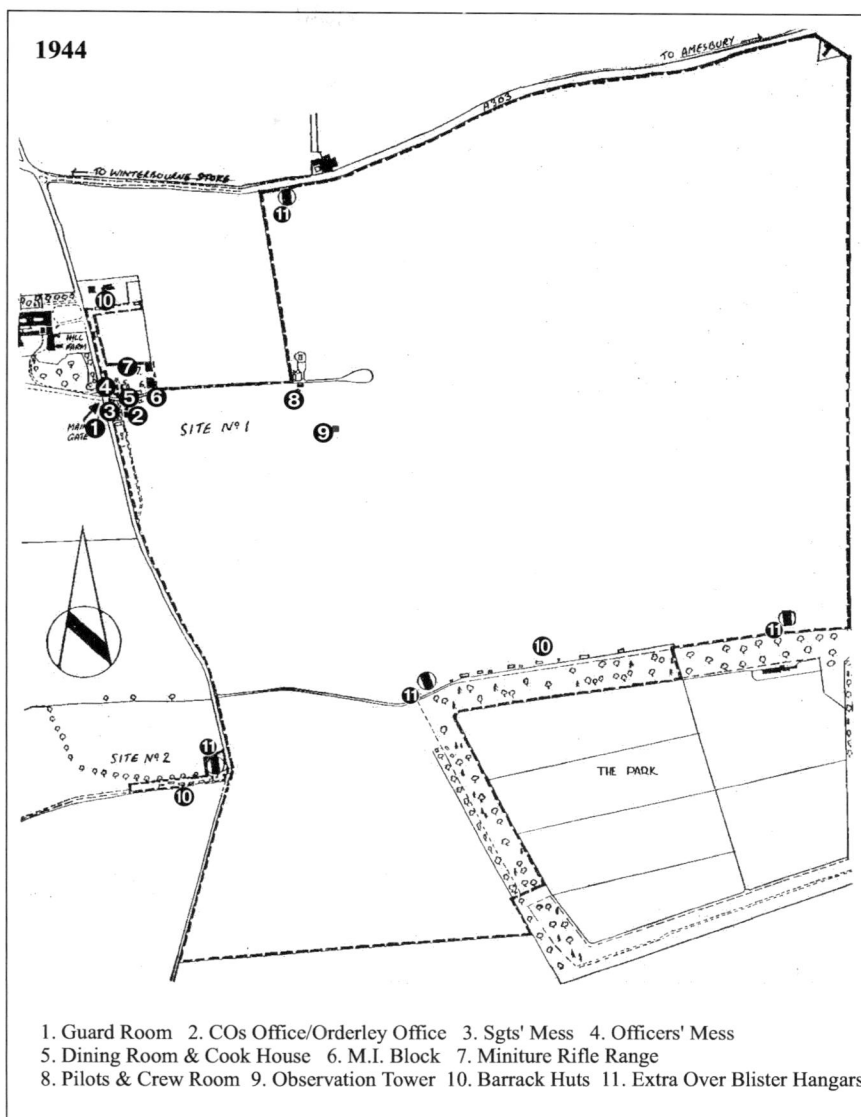

1. Guard Room 2. COs Office/Orderley Office 3. Sgts' Mess 4. Officers' Mess
5. Dining Room & Cook House 6. M.I. Block 7. Miniture Rifle Range
8. Pilots & Crew Room 9. Observation Tower 10. Barrack Huts 11. Extra Over Blister Hangars

landing.

With the formation of No.41 OTU (No.70 Group) at Old Sarum on 20th September 1941, training of Army Co-operation pilots on Lysanders and Tomahawks commenced at Oatlands Hill.

One of the instructors in early 1942 was Bobby Pearson. He had been a Lt in the Green Howards and was evacuated from Dunkirk in May 1940. His ship was torpedoed in the Channel and he had to be rescued from the sea. Later in 1940 he transferred to the RAF. He gained his wings with No.9 SFTS Hullavington on 2nd May 1941 and was then posted to No.1 S of AC at Old Sarum, flying Lysanders. By early

1942 he was at Oatlands Hill as a Flying Officer, instructing pilots on aerobatics in Tutors and Gladiators, and converting pilots onto Tomahawks. In March 1942 he joined No.140 Sqn at Benson, the squadron joining No.34 Wing of 2nd Tactical Air Force when it formed on 1st June 1943. No.140 Sqn was a sister squadron of No.16 Sqn which until February 1940 had spent 16 years at Old Sarum. Bobby Pearson later became a Sqn Ldr DSO, DFC.

Training of Lysander pilots by No.41 OTU ceased at Oatlands Hill from 22nd March 1942. The Unit was then reorganised with 'A' Flt at Old Sarum equipped with Harvards and at Oatlands Hill, 'B' Flt with Tomahawks

Mustang Is of No.16 Sqn at Oatlands Hill in September 1942. One Mustang can be seen taking off and it would appear the tractor is about to tow another.
Photo: Eric Martin/H.J.S. Taylor collection

Mustang AG350 after coming to rest on top of Tomahawk AH771.
Photo: RAF Museum P3186

and 'C' Flt with Mustangs, which arrived in April. A ground accident occurred on 30th May when Mustang AG350 collided with Tomahawk AH771.

During a take-off, Mustang AG396 did the same with a stationary Tomahawk IIB AK159 on 27th June and Plt Off Alfred G. (Bill) Clark RNZAF, the pilot of the Tomahawk was killed. He was buried with full service honours in London Road Cemetery, Salisbury.

On 5th June 1942 the airfield was used as a LZ by Hotspur gliders towed from Netheravon by tugs of No.296 Sqn. This was a night exercise with landings made in complete darkness. One glider crashed resulting in slight injuries to the pilot and one of the soldiers. All of the remaining loaded gliders landed successfully.

A No.16 Sqn detachment of Mustang Is arrived from Weston Zoyland on exercise in September 1942. They had converted to the type from Lysanders in July having changed roles from Army Co-operation to that of Photo Reconnaissance.
Two bombs were dropped close to the

west side of the airfield during a daylight raid on 29th September 1942 and about the same period, staff on the airfield witnessed a Me 110 flying low over the airfield, coming under fire from a chasing Beaufighter.

Corporal David (Bill) Williams, an engine fitter recalls that the favourite antic of Flt Lt Burrough-Robinson, one of the instructors, was to fly his aircraft at personnel to make them dive to the ground. It appears he was a colourful character who had Royal connections.

'B' and 'C' Flights moved out on 15th November 1942 when No.41 OTU left Old Sarum for Hawarden.

Oatlands Hill was used on 29th March 1943 as a LZ for gliders towed from Hurn by the Whitleys of No.295 Sqn based at Netheravon.

A&AEE Typhoon IB R8809, flown by Gp Capt H.A. Purvis DFC, AFC, glided in for a wheels-up landing on 17th May, when his engine failed due to fuel starvation.

Following the departure of No.41

OTU, Oatlands Hill was used for AOP courses of which No.17 Course trained there from the end of April. No.658 Sqn AOP moved in on 6th August 1943. On returning from a route march to Stonehenge on 28th August 1943, the squadron personnel were instructed to leave immediately for a new posting to York.

No.43 OTU (No.70 Group), an AOP training unit, was the next significant unit at Oatlands Hill when it moved in from Old Sarum with its Auster Is, IIIs, Lysander III and a Tiger Moth on 17th February 1944. Wg Cdr P. Legge was appointed OC with Capt H.B.(Warby) Warburton as an instructor. He had previously been instructing at Larkhill with No.1424 Flt RAF. Accommodation remained inadequate for what by the end of May would be a 30 plus Auster complement. The Instructing Officers were therefore billeted in a number of large houses in nearby Winterbourne Stoke, Berwick St James and at Druid's Lodge, the latter was used as the HQ of 33rd Wing when Lake Down aerodrome was operating during World War 1. Officers attending No.31 (AOP) Course were billeted in huts on the camp and other ranks at nearby Rollestone Camp. Future Courses were also billeted at Rollestone following complaints from personnel attending the initial course. The build up continued in March with the arrival of two Auster IVs MS934 and MT163 from No.20 MU Aston Down, and from Taylorcraft Ltd, Mk.IV MT185. Tiger Moth N6784 was received on loan by the Station Flt for use by the Station Commander. Vehicles allocated to Oatlands Hill were a Fordson Fire Tender, Morris Light Ambulance and a 30 cwt lorry. An Oxford I EB812 also arrived at the end of the month from No.60 MU Shipton but this had been sent in error. A number of Auster IIIs arrived from No.20 MU in April, MT442, NJ798, NX541, NJ972, NJ976, MZ214 and MZ110. On 26th April 1944 a fatality occurred when Lt M.R. Kitchen crashed in Auster III MZ186 at nearby Wylye. He had been authorised to carry out pilot navigation and concealed landings when he hit a 70' poplar tree. The aircraft came down 100 yards away and was completely wrecked. Lt Kitchen suffered serious injuries and was taken to the Red Cross Hospital at Bathampton House before being transferred to the 5th American General Hospital at Odstock,

Salisbury. He was visited there by his mother who then returned home as it was considered he would survive his injuries but he died the following day and was buried later at Haywards Heath, his home town. On 29th May 1944 Lt R.H. Symes-Thompson crashed whilst doing air shoots in Auster III NJ976 but escaped without injury. The aircraft was wrecked with damage classified as (Cat.E).The total aircraft on charge as of this date were: - Auster Is (3), Auster IIIs (31), Auster IVs (3), Stinson 105 (1) and Tiger Moths (2).

Carrying out low flying on 26th June 1944 near High Post, Capt L.V. Selva crashed Auster III NJ810, which was badly damaged, but he was uninjured. Capt R.M. Kennedy-Minaros was not so fortunate when on 3rd August 1944 he was killed as a result of his Auster III MZ242 hitting HT cables and crashing at Wilton. A replacement Auster III MZ232 was delivered the following day from No.49 MU Tangmere.

From 30th May 1944, No.43 OTU was required to share Oatlands Hill with a detachment of the 47th Liaison Squadron (LS) of the US Ninth Air Force. This squadron with its six L-5s, had been placed on detached duties with Headquarters Southern Base Section, Communication Zone ETOUSA, for the purpose of flying operational priority mail. The small detachment consisted of Master Sergeant Twain Crabb with eight pilots and a mechanic. The duties were not confined solely to mail deliveries but also to transporting passengers, cargo and to photographic missions. The poor domestic facilities at Oatlands Hill, the bad weather during June and the colds caught by the pilots did not prevent them carrying out the tasks required of them. The six L-5s working with the 3113th Signals Battalion, Southern Base Section, and the Photographic Interpretation Detachment of FUSAG, flew a creditable 365 missions during the month, amounting to 270 hours flying time. Time was also found to experiment with the L-5, with a view to increasing its versatility. L-5, 42-99066 was fitted with two large Venturis and additional flight instruments, whilst another was provided with bomb racks. A Republic P-47D-RE Thunderbolt 42-8686 arrived from the 88th Service Sqn for use as the new high-speed mail carrier. The American pilots at Oatlands Hill wasted no time in testing

A Curved Asbestos Hut used originally as a miniature rifle-range and next to it the former Station Sick Quarters.

The remaining Blister Hangar at Oatlands Hill. The one that collapsed C.1990 was positioned at the far end of the trees.

and accepting it and putting it into operational service.

During the third week of July the 47th LS received orders to proceed to Europe and the detachment at Oatlands Hill moved out in preparation for this, having first received commendations from Brigadier General C.O. Thrasher for efficiency and devotion to duty which had 'greatly contributed to the successful mission of Southern Base Section in mounting cross Channel operations'.

No.43 OTU moved out to Andover on 10th August 1944. After its departure Oatlands Hill was reduced to Care & Maintenance but was occasionally used by the AOP squadrons from Old Sarum, No.655 Sqn locating there for a month in early 1945. On the 10th July 1945 the airfield was transferred to No.11 Group.

Closure

Oatlands Hill closed on 13th May 1946 when it was returned to agriculture. Today it is part of the Druid's Lodge Farm with the airfield site used for dairy farming. Two of the original blister hangars survived into the early 90s when one succumbed to the

ravages of Salisbury Plain's weather and collapsed. The other nearest to the A360 continues to be used for the storage of baled straw. A metal plate inside indicates the hangar was produced in 1942 by Crittall of Braintree, Essex to an Air Ministry contract. Two other blister hangars on the airfield burnt down during the 1950s/60s, one in an arson attack. The water tower was demolished in the mid 1990s. Some of the brick built domestic buildings amongst the trees on the south side of the field were recognisable through the 80s but now only the odd unsupporting wall is evident. Other surviving structures are a Curved Asbestos hut and the Station Sick Quarters on the western side of the field, the latter in use for living accommodation. The underground fuel storage tank is still being used for this purpose by the farm.

OLD SARUM AERODROME
Location - 184/SU152333 - 2 miles North of Salisbury

When the aerodrome was originally constructed it was known as Ford Farm and it occupied a site between the road from Castle Hill to Ford on the Old Roman road to Silchester. Today this is the C56 Portway, from Old Sarum to Winterbourne Gunner. It was one of five aerodromes opened on Salisbury Plain during 1917 and is one of the oldest operating in the U.K. although currently only for private aircraft.

Aerodrome Development

In June 1917 2nd Lt Charles Carrington Gardner, who was stationed at Yatesbury, received a posting as Acting Adjutant to the Nucleus Flight of No.99 Sqn which formed at Yatesbury on 15th August. Shortly afterwards, together with Sgt Maj Deeley and 25 men, they were sent in a lorry to take over the land from a Mr Edwards which was to become the aerodrome at Ford Farm. Immediately inside the gate leading to the field stood an open corrugated iron shed and in the centre of the field, a small thatched barn and windmill, which later led to some problems with take-off and landings.

The day the party arrived at Ford Farm from Yatesbury, it was wet and blowing a gale. Later in the day 7 Bell tents arrived but, as the 25 men were all raw recruits, none knew how to erect them. Lt Charles Gardner did fortunately know how, having become familiar with the practice during his service with the Queen's Westminster Rifles from 1910-13. The tents provided accommodation for the 25 men, with Sgt Maj Deeley billeted at the Castle Inn, near the aerodrome, on the Salisbury to Amesbury road, and the Adjutant, billeted in Salisbury. Bishop Jocelyn of St. Mark's Church, Salisbury was duly appointed as the station padre. Personnel from the station regularly attended church parades in Salisbury Cathedral. Over the following weeks the station took shape with the provision of marquees and canvas Bessoneaux Hangers for aeroplane storage. These were, of course, in temporary use while the permanent buildings were being completed. As the station developed additional officers joining No.99 Sqn

The thatched barn and windmill at Old Sarum c.1918 appears to have obstructed either the landing or take-off of this particular DH6 Trainer.   Photo: Cty. Dr. H. F. Thomas

were Major Douglas Hill, Major L.A. Pattinson, Capt Stanley Graham Gilmore, Capt A.M. Swyny, Lt Minter and 2nd Lt R.W. Atchley as Equipment

2nd Lt Charles Gardner at Ford Farm c.1917.
Photo: Cty. Dr H.F. Thomas

Officer.

The land requistioned by the War Department was 1000 x 900yds, an area of 182 acres of which 29 acres were occupied by the station buildings. The Technical Site comprised 6 coupled Aeroplane Sheds 170' x 80', 1 ARS (with 2 Plane Stores) 170' x 80', 1 Salvage Shed, 2 MT Sheds, workshops for carpenters, sail-makers, coppersmiths, doping, engines and smiths. The Domestic Site immediately to the east consisted of an Officers' Mess, 4 Officers' Quarters for staff and 3 for pupils, Sergeants' Mess, Men's Barracks, Women's Hostel plus various stores and service buildings. These were all formed alongside the Portway on the northern side of the field. Not all were completed when the station officially opened in August 1917 but most of them were by the end of the following year. As with other airfields forming on Salisbury Plain, German PoW were used in aspects of the construction work, as was Chinese labour. In August 1918 a court dismissed a case against Lam Foi, who was accused of stabbing Hop Yow in a dispute over the ownership of a bird in the Chinese quarters on Old Sarum aerodrome.

The function of Ford Farm was that of a

three unit Training Depot Station (No.11 TDS) for Day Bombing. The Establishment eventually built up to a strength of 643 uniformed personnel and 215 civilians. A number of the uniformed staff were from the Royal Naval Air Service. In 1917 Ford Farm was not included on the list of permanent stations. The landing area with its grass landing strips was on the south side of the station buildings. With the formation of the RAF on 1st April 1918, and because of the similarity in name with Ford in Sussex, Ford Farm was renamed Old Sarum. The title was then displayed on the aerodrome in large white chalk letters, and in later days was enclosed with a circle.

Old Sarum was an aerodrome on which the infrastructure did not change very much over the years although some rebuilding occurred during the 1920s. Between the wars the aerodrome was available for civilian flying by prior arrangement. Landing areas then were N/S 1350', NE/SW 2100', E/W 1800' and SE/NW 1800'. The surfaces were good with a slight down slope to the south east and west, requiring central landings in front of the aeroplane sheds. Two artillery practice targets were positioned 600' inside the west and east aerodrome boundaries. Each target had three dummy gun pits, a dug-out and an aerial mast. A watch tower, built of brick on brick pillars, was constructed during the 1930s. This was positioned proud of the two sets of aeroplane sheds on the west end.

During World War 2 the grass runway used was NE/SW 1,200yds with Drem Mk.I lighting available for use on this runway only. Sommerfeld Tracking provided hardstandings and 2 Blister hangars were built on the western side of the site and 1 on the southern side. The two-letter station identification was OM.

During the 1960s a brick built control tower replaced the previous one and was positioned slightly south of the original. The new tower, which continues to be used today for private flying, is of similar pattern to the 1961 built tower at Upavon.

World War 1 Years

The first squadrons of the RFC to move in on 30th August 1917 were Nos. 98 and 99 Sqns, both had formed on the 15th August, No.98 Sqn at Harlaxton

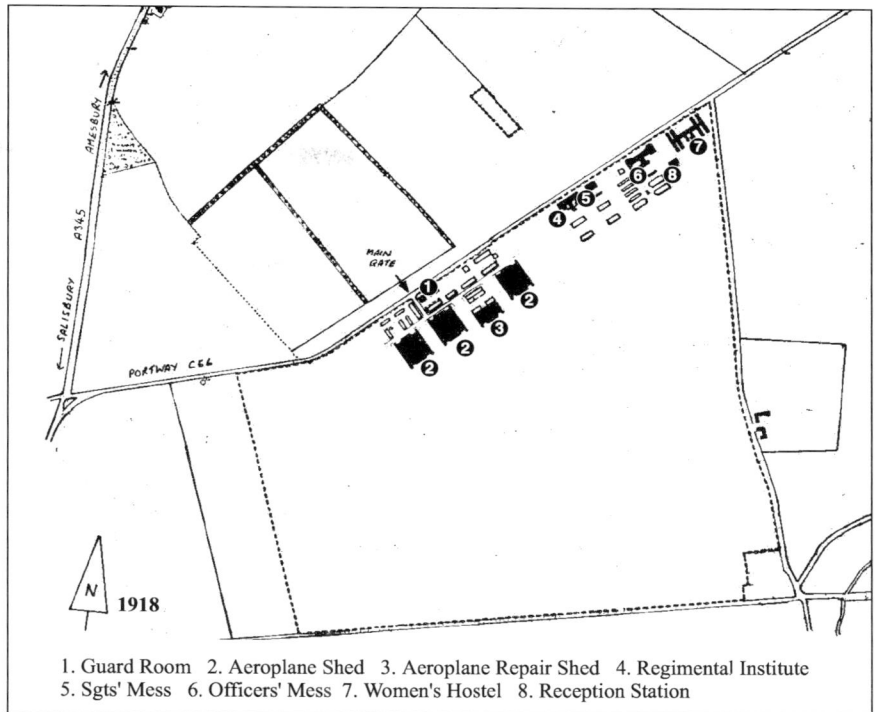

1. Guard Room 2. Aeroplane Shed 3. Aeroplane Repair Shed 4. Regimental Institute
5. Sgts' Mess 6. Officers' Mess 7. Women's Hostel 8. Reception Station

A west to east view of No.11 TDS Old Sarum in 1918. A large number of tents are seen on the east side of the Aeroplane Sheds. Photo: Mrs D.J. Locke

A view of Old Sarum from west to east C.1931. The two nearest hangars were lost to fire on 16th January 1987. Photo: E.A. Shipman/Cty. Dr. H. F. Thomas.

An Avro 504K in the hangar at Old Sarum in 1918.
Photo: F. Bryant/Cty. Dr. H.F. Thomas.

Gerald Swanborough, a fitter with the Royal Naval Air Service at Old Sarum, stands at the front of a DH4 in c.1917/18.   Photo: Mrs D.J. Locke

and No.99 Sqn at Yatesbury. On 8th September they were joined by No.103 Sqn which had formed at Beaulieu on the 1st September. The Station CO at the time was Maj W.A.S. Rough. The squadrons were equipped with DH4s, DH6s, DH9s, and the Armstrong Whitworth F.K.8 with the 160hp Beardmore engine, sometimes referred to as the Big Ack-W. Personnel from the Australian Flying Corps also served at the aerodrome c.1917/18 and the grave of one of these men, Lt Hector Nicol can be seen in St. Lawrence Church, Stratford-sub-Castle. He died on 16th October 1918 in a Salisbury hospital, having sustained accidental injuries while training at Old Sarum.

Nos.124, 125 and 126 Sqns formed at Ford Farm on 1st February 1918 equipped with DH4s and DH9s. Training commenced at Ford Farm but the three squadrons moved to Fowlmere, and No.98 Sqn moved to Lympne on 1st March. No.99 Sqn moved to St-Omar on 25th April and No.103 Sqn to Serny on 12th May 1918.

No.11 Training Depot Station (S.W. Area; No.7 Group, 33rd Wing) formed at Old Sarum on 1st April 1918. The aircraft in use then were DH4s, DH6s and Avro 504Ks. After World War 1 ended, this unit moved to Boscombe Down in November 1918.

The Log Book of Lt Richards shows him on an Instructors Course at Old Sarum during Feb-May 1918 flying dual and solo flights in aircraft types DH6, BE2e and RE8. Use of the other new aerodromes in the county seems to have been the practice for cross-country flights. Lake Down, Yatesbury, Netheravon and Upavon appear on many pages of his Log.

Inter War Years

While the Government clipped the wings of the RAF after the war with the reduction in the number of aerodromes, aircraft and personnel, Old Sarum was retained at the expense of Stonehenge. No.53 Sqn with its RE8s arrived on 15th March 1919. Lts Paul and Goodier delivered two Bristol Fighter F2Bs from Biggin Hill on 3rd April, these were 2362 and 2585 respectively. The pilots left from there at 1620 hrs and flying at 4500', arrived at Old Sarum at 1750 hrs. These two aircraft were possibly for No.34 Sqn which arrived on 3rd May equipped with the type. Both squadrons came as a cadre but were disbanded on 25th October 1919.

On 8th March 1920 the School of Army Co-operation was re-formed at Stonehenge but with the closure of the aerodrome there, transferred to Old Sarum in January 1921. Training courses were held for Army and RAF pilot/observers, concentrating on artillery spotting, tactical reconnaissance and air photography. Live bombing was carried out on Larkhill or Porton Ranges. The principle of all Army Co-operation reconnaissance involved the pilot during a flight recording what he visually observed on the ground on to a message pad which was strapped to his knee. The observations were then transmitted by WT back to the ground where it was received in a RAF WT Lorry. The School operated with Avro 504Ks and Bristol Fighters and still had them on charge in the early 1930s, long after they had become obsolete. These types had a maximum duration of around 2 hrs 45mins and a radius of action of about 100-150 miles. Tactics and flying procedures were still based on lessons learnt in the First World War. Officers attending the school had already learnt to fly and they generally arrived at Old Sarum direct from Cranwell, Uxbridge or a Flying Training School (FTS). All pilots in the Army Co-operation Squadrons were officers. The basic course was of 12 weeks duration with 20 pupils to a course. Three courses a year were held with a syllabus of ground instruction and flying. Flying time was generally Monday afternoons, all day Tuesday plus Thursday and Friday afternoons. The course subject covered - Air Reconnaissance, including map reading and writing reports in the air,

The page from Lt Goodier's Log Book showing the entry when he and Lt Paul delivered a Bristol F2b to Old Sarum on 3rd April 1919, together with the receipt issued on arrival. Photo: Cty. Dr. H.F. Thomas

Artillery Reconnaissance, Photography, which involved operating the air camera whilst flying to get the accurate results, Signals, namely wireless telegraphy and radio telephony, Military Organisation and Tactics. One of the well known exercises carried out by pilots on the course was that of 'puff shoots'. This involved the pilot flying at around 4000' from where he had to locate the target area on the ground at Old Sarum and then correct simulated artillery fire by using the clock code. The drop of shells was represented by puffs of smoke which an operator on the ground would actuate according to the signals which were received by WT from the pilot. Courses for officers of higher command in the army were also staged at Old Sarum. These were generally of one and two week duration and were aimed at giving them a sound working

knowledge of the possibilities and limitations of aircraft uses in conjunction with tactics on the ground. There was also a three-week course held for artillery, cavalry and infantry officers who on passing-out would be attached to Army Co-operation squadrons as Intelligence Liaison Officers or Sqn Artillery Officers. Each squadron had one of each attached to maintain liaison with the Army commands.

No.16 Sqn reformed at Old Sarum on 1st April 1924 attending to the needs of the School of Army Co-operation until the outbreak of war in 1939. No.16 Sqn was equipped with the Bristol F2b Mk.II fighter, known as the 'Biff', with Rolls-Royce 275 hp Falcon engines. The aircraft were marked with a black band on the fuselage by the roundel. Of the type there were (13) Initial and (6)

Immediate Reserve. The squadron consisted of three Flts, a Wireless Section and an Armament Section. The Sqn was commanded by Sqn Ldr J.O. Archer CBE. He was replaced by Sqn Ldr W.A. Coryton MVO, DFC on 30th September 1925. No.16 Sqn was responsible for co-operation with Southern Command. Exercises were carried out with different army units not only locally but in other areas of the country. All of the local operations were under-taken from Advanced Landing Grounds (ALG) such as Imber and Tilshead. Every summer a detachment was sent to one of several small landing grounds near Oakhampton to spot for Yeomanry doing their annual gunnery training. Despite being under canvas, this was a popular detachment. Another annual detachment was to North Coates during the last two weeks of March. This was not so popular because of the cold conditions both on the ground and in the air. The exercise was to carry out bombing and gunnery practice. The gunnery aspect was not very successful due to the stoppages in the rarefied atmosphere but the bombing, using a 'High Altitude Drifting Sight' attached to the side of fuselage, was enjoyed by most with good results recorded.

Another annual event for Old Sarum was the visit of the Cambridge University Air Sqn for their two week summer camp, flying Avro 504Ns. The squadron together with Oxford University Air Sqn formed on 1st and 11th October 1925 respectively with other squadrons such as London University following in later years.

The School of Army Co-operation was parented by No.22 Group from 12th April 1926 and re-equipped with the Armstrong Whitworth Atlas in September 1929.

A Special Duties Flight was formed and operating from Old Sarum in 1926, having duties with the Experimental Gas School at Porton. The Flight, using a Bristol F2b (F4745), Horsley (J7229) and a Dart (N9542), transferred to Netheravon on 12th September 1928 and to Boscombe Down in 1931.

No.16 Sqn was carrying out experimental procedures for artillery observation with the School of Artillery and was testing new aeroplanes for evaluation as Army Co-operation machines. On one occasion

Bristol F2b H1506 of the School of Army Co-operation having stalled and side slipped on 28.4.1924. Photo: Mrs Hayman/Cty. Dr. H.F. Thomas

DH9A J7088 in front of the Aeroplane Repair Shed at Old Sarum C.1924. A Log Book of a Sqn Ldr Probyn records him as having flown this type in October 1926 whilst with the School of Army Co-operation at Old Sarum. Photo: Mrs Hayman/Cty. Dr. H.F. Thomas.

Hawker Woodcock Mk.II J7515 with the civil registration G-EBMA at Old Sarum. This aircraft participated in the 1925 King's Cup Race, but was damaged in a forced landing. Following repair it served with Nos. 3 & 17 Sqns. Photo: Cty. Dr. H.F. Thomas

DH53 'Humming Bird' J7271 coded 2, visiting Old Sarum from Netheravon where it was based in June1924. It became G-EBXN on 25.5.28 and was destroyed in a hangar fire at Hooton Park on 8th July 1940. Photo: Mrs Hayman/Cty. Dr. H.F. Thomas

four were delivered to the squadron and the AW Atlas was chosen as the most suitable. As it would not be available for a few more years, the 'Biffs' were upgraded and in the spring of 1928 the squadron received Mk IIIs. They were designed to carry heavier loads and were much more robust but suffered from an inferior performance as a result of the increased weights.

On 25th September 1928 No.16 Sqn had a change of CO with the appointment of Sqn Ldr D.O. Mulholland AFC.

Throughout the early 1930s No.16 Sqn was training in aerial photography, the use of radio, carrying out Army co-operation duties and evaluation of new aircraft. One of these, arriving in July 1930, was the Hawker Hart Light Bomber which out-performed all the current aeroplanes and had a far more comfortable rear cockpit.

In January 1931 No.16 (AC) Sqn started to re-equip with the Armstrong Whitworth Atlas fitted with a 420 hp Armstrong-Siddeley Jaguar IV engine, although a few Bristol F2bs remained until the squadron completely converted in April. The Atlas had been designed for Army Co-operation work. During May and June the squadron was detached to Tilshead for a Southern Command R.A. exercise. Sqn Ldr Alan R. Churchman DFC was appointed CO of No.16 Sqn on 1st August 1931. Unusually the award of his DFC was gazetted twice on 2nd July and 3rd August 1918. It was given for his considerable skill in directing artillery fire onto enemy positions on many occasions, resulting in great damage. At the time his rank was that of Lt/Temp Capt.

It was back to Tilshead for No.16 Sqn's 'A' Flt in the summer months of 1932 for co-operation with the 1st Medical Brigade R.A.

Flt Lt J. R. I. Scrambler AFC became No.16 Sqn's CO on 10th October 1933. He was later promoted to Sqn Ldr before being replaced on 2nd June 1934 by Sqn Ldr Robert Parker Musgrave Whitham OBE, MC.

The Hawker Audax, fitted with the 525 hp Rolls-Royce Kestral 1b engine, replaced the Atlases of No.16 Sqn in December 1933. This was the Army Co-operation version of the Hawker

Hart. The S of AC, with Sqn Ldr W.A. Coryton MVO, DFC as CO and CFI, was also re-equipped with the Audax from November 1932. He had previously been CO with No.16 Sqn. The Station Commander at the time was Wg Cdr R.E. Saul DFC.

Ted Shipman, who served at Old Sarum as an MT Driver from early 1931-33, recalls the pool of vehicles mainly for army co-operation purposes as being 35 Morris 6 wheeler troop carriers, Morris ambulances and fire tenders. In addition there was a Crossley ambulance, Model T Ford Hucks Starter, Leyland 3/5ton solid tyre lorry and Trojan solid tyre vans for mail and general use. The Morris six wheelers were used for taking children from Bulford Camp to school in Salisbury and for taking pigs to market. The Station maintained its own piggery in the south-east corner of the airfield just below the 25 yard range.

Old Sarum opened to the general public for the first Empire Air Day on 30th June 1934. No.16 Army Co-operation Sqn and the School of Army Co-operation gave demonstrations of supply dropping to ground forces and artillery spotting 'puff shooting' using the Hawker Audax. Aircraft of this type known to be on charge with No.16 Sqn were: - K2025, K3693, K3694, K3695, K3696, K3697 and K3699. 1934 was the year in which No.16 Sqn left the School of Army Co-operation but remained as one of the Army Co-operation Sqns.

Trials with the Avro Type 671 Rota 1 (Cierva C.30A Autogyro K4328, a forerunner of rotating wing designs) were held on the airfield in 1934 but proved unsuccessful. Six of the type was allocated for trial with No.16 Sqn whose pilots learnt to fly it. Ten of the type were built for the RAFs School of Army Co-operation. One of these, K4234 crashed near Salisbury on 21st January 1935. Earlier in the month this aircraft had been flown to the RAE Farnborough by Fg Off Wills-Sanford where it underwent airworthiness trials. It was followed there in February by K4775 and K4235. Officers of the five Army Co-operation squadrons in the country were sent to Old Sarum for instruction on the type. It was hoped, had the trials been successful, to use it as an air support/reconnaissance role.

Gloster Grebe II J.7361 of No.32 Sqn on a visit to Old Sarum from its base at Kenley in 1925. Photo: Mrs Hayman/Cty. Dr. H.F. Thomas

A Bristol F2b outside of the Aeroplane Sheds c.1925. The black band on the fuselage denoting a No.16 Sqn machine. Photo: Capt Neish/Cty Dr H.F. Thomas

Bristol F2b F4542 of Cambridge University Air Sqn at Old Sarum. Photo: Cty. Dr H.F. Thomas

An Avro 504N of Cambridge University Air Sqn based at Duxford, attending summer camp at Old Sarum in 1929. Photo: Cty. Dr. H.F. Thomas

Armstrong Whitworth Atlas J.9531, with a Armstrong Siddeley Jaguar engine, of No.16 Army Co-operation Sqn flying over Old Sarum Castle in 1931.
Photo: E.A. Shipman/Cty. Dr. H.F. Thomas.

1932 advertisements.

A different form of trial was commenced by personnel of No.16 Sqn in January 1935, when, for a six month period, the unit was supplied with a 'Forage Cap'and blue shirts. The trial was to gauge reaction to the proposed new uniform. The results are not recorded.

No.13 Sqn moved in from Netheravon with the Audax on 3rd May 1935 and left for Odiham on 16th February 1937. It was replaced by No.107 Sqn equipped with the Hind, and after a short stay left for Harwell on 15th June. No.59 Sqn reformed at Old Sarum on 28th June with the Hawker Hector of which K9700 was one of the type on charge. These were all Army Co-operation squadrons. No.59 Sqn was flying Blenheims when it left for Andover on 11th May 1939.

No.16 Sqn had a change of CO again from 1st January 1936 with the appointment of Sqn Ldr T. Humble. On 26th June 1936 the first Lysander for Army Co-operation work was tested on No.16 Sqn. As a result of the tests it was considered unsuitable for a war situation but was selected by higher authority anyway.

Frank Jewell signed on with the RAF at Victoria Road, Bristol in 1937. He passed entry tests in essay writing, long division and passed his medical. Basic training followed at West Drayton, Henlow and Cardington whereupon he was posted to the School of Technical Training at Manston. Training was to qualify as a Flt. Mechanic/ Flt. Rigger and he passed out as an AC2 Fitter's Mate in November 1937. At this point

A two seat Army Co-operation Armstrong Whitworth Atlas trainer conversion which was struck by an early Avro 504N J850 at Old Sarum C.1930. This was one of two ordered incorporating all of the features of the 504N. This aeroplane had a 180hp Armstrong Siddeley Lynx engine fitted. Photo: Cty. Dr. H.F. Thomas.

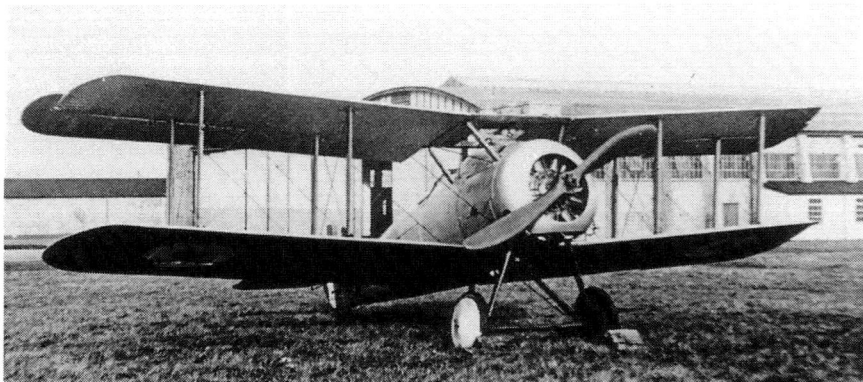

This Sopwith Snipe at Old Sarum was one of the relatively few that were converted into two-seat trainers to allow familiarisation training before progressing to the true single seat fighter form.
Photo: Mrs Hayman/Cty Dr H.F. Thomas

A 1934 advertisement

he joined No.16 Army Co-operation Sqn at Old Sarum. Here he was placed with the Fitters and Riggers in the Aircraft Repair Shop where they boxed main-planes, carried out maintenance on fuselages, wheels, tail-skids and did undercarriage checks. This was mainly on the squadron's Audax aircraft which had Kestrel 10 engines. Frank Jewell indicates by that time they had gone about 100 hours over their limited life.

'Boxed main-planes' was the term given to jacking up the fuselage and removing the wings, which remained as a pair with Jury Struts replacing the fuselage attachments. The wings would be placed on trolleys and serviced. The importance of this was to check for distortion and wear. The aircraft would be air tested following the service and re-assembly and in those days the pilots would often take a ground crew member with them. Hawker Hectors were also serviced in the ARS and the first act by the fitters was to place rigging boards on the fuselage to check for distortion. The Napier Dagger engines fitted to the Hector were so powerful that the fuselage around the engines invariably became twisted. If this was detected the aircraft was written-off as it was impossible to repair the damage.

Many of the officers at Old Sarum kept their own private aircraft in a spare hangar and used them at weekends. Most also had sports cars and Maseratis were not uncommon. Prince Bira Wason was one such officer.

No.16 Sqn Hawker Audax K3697 at Old Sarum in 1935.
Photo: Don Neate Coll.

Hawker Audax 1 K3704 at Old Sarum in 1938 (SOC 31.10.43).
Photo: K. Sholto/Cty Dr H.F. Thomas

Mainly Morris 6 Wheeled Troop Carriers in Old Sarum MT Section c.1933.
Photo: E.A. Shipman/Cty. Dr. H.F. Thomas

A Morris 6 Wheeled Station Ambulance in Old Sarum MT Section c.1933.
Photo: E.A. Shipman/Cty. Dr. H.F. Thomas

249

Cierra Autogiro/Avro Rota K4230 at Old Sarum C.1934/35. 10 Avro Rotas were delivered from June 1934-May 1935. Photo: Don Neate Coll.

Discipline on the station was very strict. As a Fitter's Mate, Frank Jewell wouldn't dream of asking the corporal a question. The corporal was 'God' and questions were asked of him only by a Rigger or Fitter. The Flt Sgt was even less approachable and the WO Engineer only appeared on the workshop floor half a dozen times in the years Frank was there.

The School of Army Co-operation was in the adjoining hangar which Frank and his colleagues kept well away from unless detailed to report for flying duties. This would be to fly camera with trainee pilots attending a course. On receiving instruction via the Gosport tube, the camera would be operated in vertical or oblique mode. Frank got to see plenty of Salisbury Plain but was grateful he never received an order to 'release message hook'. This was difficult to operate and involved looking out for the trailing aerial. On other occasions the tradesmen were used to lay out white canvas markers on Salisbury Plain. These would be in the shape of an 'X' or in horizontal line and were photographed from the aircraft flying over.

There were other duties that all ranks were required to carry out. These included Fire Picket, Guard Duty and Duty Crew. For Guard Duty, Frank recalls being issued with a 1914 rifle with a broken firing pin and marching up and down in front of the hangars. Duty Crew responsibility involved waiting in a small wooden hut on the airfield and if the siren actuated the duty crew would be called out to assist with whatever emergency had arisen. Refuelling visiting aircraft was another duty. When war broke, whilst duty crews were still formed, these particular duties were abolished for those involved in aircraft maintenance. As at school, P.T. was routinely programmed. There was the inevitable 'Bull' at Old Sarum with the white washing of the pebbles outside the Flight Hut. Hangar floors were scrubbed by a line of men who would be granted a 48 hour leave pass, only if the floors were judged to be clean enough on completion.

Anyone returning late from a 48 hour pass (after midnight on Sunday) would spend the night in the Guard Room. The punishment they could expect was confinement to camp, receiving 3 days from the Flt Cdr, 7 days from the Adjutant and 14 days from the CO. Frank Jewell recalls the only occasion during his service when he was placed on a charge. This was for falling asleep during a gas lecture. He appeared before a major in the Tank Corps, pleaded guilty and was given 3 days and 7 days privs. This constituted 3 days full pack drill and fatigues and 7 days confined to camp (loss of privileges).

The airmen had to be on the station for one year and be of good conduct before they were allowed out in civilian clothes with what was known as a PP (Permanent Pass) granted until 0100 hours. Personnel were required to present themselves at the Guard Room and show the PP to the policeman on duty. He would then inspect the airman's dress and, if deemed acceptable, he would allow the man to leave camp. On return personnel booked in at the Guard Room.

One of the things Frank remembers well from his time at Old Sarum was the quality of his billet. It was brick built with Parquet flooring, central heating and was kept in pristine condition.

Frank Jewell of No.16 Sqn prior to a Hector
air test at Old Sarum in 1938.
Photo: Frank Jewell

No.16 Sqn started to receive Westland Lysander Is with the 890 hp Bristol Mercury XII radial engine in May 1938, the first unit to do so. The first of the type to arrive was L4675 and built up to an establishment of 9 + 5 in reserve. The Lysander Is replaced the Audax aircraft and were in turn replaced by the Lysander IIs (L6866) with the 905hp sleeve-valve Bristol Perseus XII engines in April 1939.

The FAA had been visitors at Old Sarum for a month during 1938 when 810 Sqn arrived on 17th September with Fairey Swordfish IIIs, leaving for Southampton on 27th October.

Frank Jewell recalls the visit of the German aircraft designer Heir Heinkel to Old Sarum. He walked through the ARS, where some of the aircraft had been covered with sheets. This could only have been to hopefully persuade him that the RAF had better aircraft than they really did. On 12th September 1938 Sqn Ldr G. P. Charles took up his appointment as CO of No.16 Sqn. That month all personnel were advised that a state of emergency existed following the Munich Crisis and the dismantling of Czechoslovakia. Aircraft were camouflaged according

Personnel of No.16 (AC) Sqn assembled in front of Lysander L4686 and L4679 at Old Sarum in
September 1938. L4686 was shot down by a CR42 near Maktila on 16th October 1940.
Photo: C. Sanderson/Cty. Dr. H. F. Thomas

A No.16 Sqn Audax 'prang' following a night time landing accident at Old Sarum when it ran
into the flare-path party, killing one of the airmen and injuring others. The Audax was piloted
by Sqn Ldr Musgrave-Williams and the ground crew were attending to the goose-neck flares.
Photo: Frank Jewell

The burial party from Old Sarum attending the funeral of Sgt John Tompkins at St. George
Church, West Grimstead near Salisbury in May 1939.   Photo: Frank Jewell

The headstone for Sgt John Tompkins RAF is
of Portland Stone and made to the same
specification as provided by the
Commonwealth War Graves Commission for
military personnel killed in war.

to a new scheme of war markings. All leave was stopped and personnel recalled. Officers were not allowed more than five miles from the station and were required to be on a telephone contact. The hangars and station buildings were darkened, with blue lamps used at night.

In March 1939 No.16 Sqn was ordered to prepare itself as a Fighter Squadron and a detachment of eight Lysanders went to North Weald for two weeks to evolve tactics with the Fighters based there.

In May 1939 Frank Jewell was called upon to make up one of the funeral party attending a burial at nearby St. George Church in West Grimstead. This was for Sgt John F. Tompkins (Observer), No.35 Sqn who had been brought to his home village for burial having been killed when his Battle I

K9489 crashed at Oakham in Rutland on 5th May 1939.

The grave of Sgt Tompkins was not marked with a headstone at the time of his death. Sixty years later when the Wiltshire Historical Military Society learned of this, funds were raised to provide a headstone for this airman who was killed whilst training for war. On 5th May 2001 a dedication ceremony was conducted at the graveside by Canon Michael Ward, when the headstone, draped with the RAF flag, was unveiled by the sister and daughter of Sgt Tompkins.

During the winter of 1939/40, No.16 Sqn WOPs were detached to the Army for exercises with the Artillery. These personnel had to spend nights on wind-swept Salisbury Plain using a small bivouac tent for sleeping and sharing it with the wireless equipment. The 'Lizzies' would fly around spotting 'enemy' targets, transmitting the locations to the WOPs on the ground who passed it on to the gun positions which in turn blasted off their ordnance.

World War 2 Years

Hundreds of reservists flowed into Old Sarum when war was declared on 3rd. September 1939. There was no accommodation available for them and so they all slept on straw palliasses supported by three planks of wood on two trestles in one of the hangars. Flt Lt R.E.S. Skelton (Capt R.T.R.) was appointed CO of No.16 Sqn with its establishment of 16 Lysander IIs. There were only eight RAF pilots on the squadron at the time so its ranks were soon swelled by an influx of Army Officers to maintain pilot strength. Nine days later an Oxford trainer was placed on charge for the use of re-seconded Army officers.

An Army Co-operation Pool formed at Old Sarum on 25th September 1939 from officers attending the S of AC. The Pool provided for the needs of Army Co-operation units and was equipped with 12 + 3 reserve Ansons, 15 + 4 Blenheims, 12 + 3 Hectors and 12 + 3 Lysanders.

The School of Army Co-operation became the No.1 School of Army Co-operation on 20th October 1939 although this was not made official until 20th December. It came under

Hawker Audax K3679 at Old Sarum 1937. Photo: K. Sholto/Cty. Dr. H.F. Thomas

Hawker Hector K9700 flying over the London & South Western Railway near Salisbury prior to World War 2. K9700 was built by the Westland Aircraft Co. Photo: Cty. Dr. H.F. Thomas

No.22 (Army Co-operation) Group with its HQ at Farnborough. The School had received Blenheims in September to train night reconnaissance crews. It is believed that the School absorbed the Army Co-operation Pool.

The two-letter station identification code for Old Sarum through the war years was OM, the two letters taken from its name. A decoy site was established at Pitton to the east of the aerodrome.

With the outbreak of war, War Courses were held by No.1 School of Army Co-operation. These were to train personnel in various aspects of Army Co-operation duties. Plt Off Gerry Scott attended No.2 War Course arriving at Old Sarum on 29th September 1939. He had just completed flying training at No.8 FTS Montrose and was disappointed with his posting having hoped for Fighter Command. On arrival at Old Sarum he was booked in at the Officers' Mess, which he describes as a magnificent

brick building of standard design and a complete contrast to the wooden huts of Montrose. He was greeted in the foyer by the chief batman and was told that, because of shortage of accommodation, pilots would be two to a room. Plt Off Scott was surprised by the number of army officers in the mess, some of who were instructors and some seconded to the RAF as pilots. There were quite a number in Army Co-operation squadrons, often retaining their regimental uniforms but changing to RAF blue early in 1940. It was also a surprise to find women on the aerodrome. Montrose had been a purely male environment but at Old Sarum, WAAFs were employed in numerous roles. Many were still in civilian clothes awaiting their uniform issue. None were batwomen however. The course commenced the next day comprising lectures on Army formations, Army tactics, artillery, map reading, Morse code. This was all reluctantly sat through by officers who, after all were in the RAF. The worst aspect was the exercises on a bitterly cold Salisbury Plain, where they had to observe troop manoeuvres.

In addition the RAF pilots were confronted with the Lysander for the first time. Compared with the Harts and Furys Plt Off Scott had been flying at Montrose, the Lysander seemed a big aeroplane. There were no dual controls or intercom and initiation was a ride in the back for a circuit and landing while trying to look over the shoulder of the instructor. This was a form of tuition which was not very satisfactory. It was then into the cockpit for a quick run through the controls and off they went. It was important however to set the tail trim before taking off because with a fully flying tail-plane, if the trim was left in the landing position, the nose could not be held down and the aircraft would enter a steep climb and stall. One unfortunate pilot did this with fatal results when the course started night flying. Another innovation was the two-speed propeller. There was a red knob on the instrument panel which was pushed in for fine pitch and left out for course pitch. This was new to the pupils of the course and in the case of Plt Off Scott, was not taken in during the somewhat primitive conversion. He assumed it to be the fire extinguisher. It was only after two sorties that a casual discussion in the mess put him right. He had been flying in fine pitch all the time. The training continued with reconnaissance and sending observations to base with the Morse keys on the side of the cockpit. In addition there were artillery shoots, message dropping and receiving, and photography with a vertical F24 camera.

A recruiting poster for the WAAF.

Taylorcraft 'D' W5741, W5740 and T9120 of 'D' Flight at Old Sarum on 16th April 1940, prior to departing for France.   Photo: Cty. Dr. H.F. Thomas

There was little spare time for those on the courses, due to evening lectures, so visits to nearby Salisbury were only possible at weekends. Plt Off Scott thought Salisbury was a lovely city but the blackout was so good that finding ones way around in the dark was difficult and sometimes dangerous. He recalls the occasion when he walked into a lamp-post and nearly broke his nose. With the course completed he went on to serve with No.4 and No.16 Sqns, grew to enjoy Army Co-operation duties and returned to Old Sarum later.

Fg Off Foxley-Norris arrived at Old Sarum following his attendance on an Advanced Flying Course at Hullavington. He remembers his Army Co-operation practical flying training as practising spotting the fall of shot, prolonged visual reconnaissance, flying 'line-overlap' photographic sorties at varying heights and Message Picking Up (MPU) by means of a hook suspended from the fuselage of a Hector, which caught a rope elevated between two poles. In ground school training, one of the amusing recollections was the use by instructors of a 'sand table' to represent the countryside. The table had a curtain around the legs, which concealed an NCO. His role was to blow cigarette smoke up through the surface at appointed times and places. This represented artillery fire and other military explosions and conflagrations. It appears the NCO's cigarette allocation was free because of its use as a training aid. The period of instruction whilst at Old Sarum included conversion to the Lysander.

The Air Ministry approved a trial establishment of a 'Flying Observation Post' Unit to be known as 'D' Flt. It was formed at Larkhill on 1st February 1940 as part of No.1 School of Army Co-operation within No.22 Army Co-operation Group. Practical training commenced immediately with the Flt equipped with 3 Taylorcraft Ds and a Stinson 105 Voyager X1050.

The Army introduced the new Taylorcraft light aircraft to replace the Lysander as a spotting plane. The latter had suffered badly in combat situations in France and was withdrawn from that theatre of operations. The Taylorcraft was renamed the Auster and became the workhorse of the British Army until the 1960s. 'D' Flight was the first army unit equipped with this aircraft and it worked up at Old Sarum under Capt Charles Bazeley R.A., who was promoted on secondment to Sqn Ldr rank. The unit left for the French Army Artillery Practice Camp at Mailly-Le-Camp on 19th April 1940 with three British built Taylorcraft and the Stinson 105 Voyager. The Flt engaged in range work with British and French artillery but had no chance to prove itself before the fall of France. The now Major Bazeley, who had discarded his Sq Ldr rank, and 'D' Flt, returned on 20th May prior to the evacuation of the British Expeditionary Force at Dunkirk. It was intended that the AOP Flt would be based at Old Sarum but Major Bazeley had other ideas. He felt the first thing was to get away from the eyes of the RAF and to this end the Flt left Old Sarum for Larkhill on 3rd June 1940. Major Bazeley also used the aerodrome at High Post to evaluate different types of aircraft for Army Co-operation duties.

No.16 Sqn had been at Old Sarum for 16 years when it moved to Hawkinge on 17th February 1940 with 16 Westland Lysanders IIs. There the squadron prepared and set off for Bertangles near Amiens in France on 13th April as part of the Air Component of the Allied Expeditionary Force. One of the squadron pilots was Plt Off Douglas 'Sammy' Sampson. In the six weeks leading up to D-Day in June 1944, by then a Flt Lt, he was given the task of photographing the Normandy beaches and was one of the select few who knew where the invasion of Europe would be launched. From his No.16 Sqn PR Mustang he photographed all of the beaches from

Drawing of Plt Off Douglas W. 'Sammy' Sampson RAAF No.16 Sqn at Old Sarum. The sketch by 'Hoyo' who is thought to have been a Czechoslovakian airman, hence the 'CZ'. Photo: Eric Martin/H.J.S. Taylor Collection.

north to south so as not to pinpoint for the German intelligence the intended beaches.

The first Canadian squadron in Britain, No.110 (AC) (City of Toronto) Sqn, arrived at Old Sarum on 25th February 1940. It had landed at Liverpool earlier that day having sailed from Halifax on the *Duchess of Bedford*. After a brief, but warm reception, the squadron travelled by train to Salisbury. Once settled in at Old Sarum, the squadron continued their conversion to Canadian built Lysanders, anticipating a move to the Continent in June. With the fall of Holland, Belgium and Luxembourg, and the rapid advance by Germany into France, however, the squadron's move to the Continent was cancelled.

No 110 Sqn came under the control of Army Air Corps Wing, and because of overcrowding at Old Sarum it moved to Odiham when No.225 Sqn arrived from there on 9th June 1940 equipped with Lysander IIs. These were in use for anti-invasion patrols along the South Coast but their stay was short, moving to nearby Tilshead on 1st July.

The Canadians of No.110 (AC) Sqn, under the command of Sqn Ldr W.D. Van Vliet, were referred to as 'Weekend Airmen'. Before the war they had worked in civilian occupations during the week and spent their weekends flying. The quality of training received and their dedication to the cause ensured that they were on a par with

their regular counterparts and under the forceful leadership of their CO, they very soon had been moulded into one of the most efficient Army Co-operation squadrons anywhere. That is not to say they were enamoured with their role in Army Co-operation. Having arrived during the time when the Battle of Britain was at its height, the Canadians wanted to be involved in the action as opposed to the monotony of training. Some of the training included locating and reporting six figure co-ordinates of a hay-stack or a cross-roads; or sitting in a lecture room memorising the number of three-ton lorries in an army engineering company. The thought which kept them motivated was the hope that eventually they would see action.

No.112 Auxiliary (Army Co-operation) Sqn RCAF, commanded by Sqn Ldr W.F. Hanna, also equipped with Lysanders, joined No.110 Sqn at Old Sarum on 29th May 1940, having disembarked at Liverpool earlier that day and travelled by train to Salisbury. They were also engaged in army co-operation training. At the time of the Canadians' stay, a local resident recalls that the field in Ford Lane by the windsock was full of Lysanders. No.112 Sqn moved the short distance down the A345 to Highpost on 14th June 1940.

The RAF posted newly trained Sgt Air-Gunners to the No.1 School of Army Co-operation, where they crewed-up with Army Officers who had volunteered for flying duties as pilots. These teams of two trained together for 6 months in which time the Lysander became very familiar to them. It was used for a variety of roles which included low flying over troops on Salisbury Plain and spraying them with simulated mustard gas contained in 50 gallon tanks attached outboard from the undercarriage.

A number of pilots who fought in the Battle of Britain attended the School of Army Co-operation. Men such as Plt Offs Richard G. A. Barclay, David J. C. Pinckney, Arthur P. Pease, Peter Howes, Noel Le Chevalier Agazarian an Armenian, and of course Richard H. Hillary. These last three arrived together in May 1940 to attend a six-week course and were at Old Sarum when the British Expeditionary Force retreated from France. There were 20 pilots on the course for which the pre-

war syllabus had been modified to map reading, air-to-ground Morse code, aerial photography, long distance reconnaissance and artillery shoots. During the course Plt Off Agazarian turned a Hector onto its back when the propeller dug into the turf during a take-off run, but he was not injured. He was involved in another accident not long afterwards when, together with Richard Hillary and Peter Howes, he was returning by car to Old Sarum late at night somewhat the worse for drink. Driving too fast around a bend, he turned the car over. They managed to extricate themselves from the wreckage and none were seriously injured. Howes commented that maybe their eventual fate was to be a more exciting death and these words turned out to be prophetic. George Barclay's Log Book from 3rd - 9th June shows that he had flown in several different Westland Lysanders, and Hawker Hectors K9726, K9740 and K9762 whilst on No.8 (Army Co-operation) War Course.

With the Army returning from France an invasion scare developed and the Armoury at Old Sarum was busy issuing side arms and ordnance to the officers on the station and all leave was cancelled. On completion of the six week course and owing to the sudden collapse of France, the Air Ministry instructed that 16 of the 20 pilots on Richard Hillary's course who were destined for Army Co-operation duties were to join fighter squadrons. Four names were drawn to join AAC leaving the remainder to be told to which Fighter Command squadrons they were posted. Richard Hillary and George Barclay left Old Sarum for fighter conversion at No.5 OTU, Aston Down. He joined No.249 Sqn on 30th June, flying Hurricanes. George Barclay was to return to Wiltshire on 14th August 1940 when the squadron was posted to Boscombe Down. He completed a year's war service on the 12th November and was made a flying officer. This coincided with his award of the DFC. On Friday 17th July 1942 Sqn Ldr George Barclay DFC, RAFVR was shot down and killed at El Alamein whilst Commanding No.238 Sqn in North Africa. Colin Pinckney RAFVR joined No.603 (City of Edinburgh) Sqn on 6th July 1940 flying Spitfires and was a Flt Lt with No.67 Sqn when he was killed on Friday 21st January 1942. Fg Off Peter Pease RAFVR joined No.603 Sqn on

Flt Lt George Barclay DFC, RAF (VR) who
went to No.5 OTU Aston Down
from the School of Army Co-operation at
Old Sarum in June 1940.
Photo: Cty. Dr H.F. Thomas

6th July and was killed on Sunday 15th September 1940 when his Spitfire X4324 was shot down by Bf 109s over Kent. Plt Off Peter Howes RAFVR joined No.54 Sqn on 8th July flying Spitfires, was posted to No.234 Sqn and then to No.603 Sqn on 11th September 1940. He was killed seven days later when his Spitfire X4327 was shot down by Bf 109s near Ashford. Noel Agazarian RAFVR joined No.609 Sqn on 8th July 1940, flying Spitfires and was a Fg Off with No.274 Sqn when he was killed on Friday 16th May 1941. Richard Hillary joined No.603 Sqn on 6th July 1940. He suffered severe burns when he was shot down in his Spitfire X4277 on 3rd September 1940. He recovered and returned to operational duties, but was killed on Friday 8th January 1943.

With the fall of France, Old Sarum started to attract the attention of German aircraft. On Sunday 21st July 1940 at approximately 1000 hours a No.1 FTS Hawker Hart (T) K.6485 from Netheravon was attacked in the Old Sarum circuit by a Messerschmitt Bf 110C of 4. (F)/14. The two-man crew of the Hart, which was on a cross-country flight, were killed when it crashed close to the Officers' Mess. The German aircraft, which was on a reconnaissance flight, was intercepted 10 miles south of Middle Wallop by the Hurricanes Is of Red Section of No.238 Sqn. The enemy aircraft was attacked by Flt Lt Donald Turner, Fg Off C. T. Davies and Plt Off J. S. Wigglesworth and shot down at Goodwood at 1030

hours. Old Sarum aerodrome was attacked on Monday 21st October 1940 by a lone Junkers 88A-5 of I/KG51. Its intended target had been the Gloster Aircraft Company at Brocksworth but it ended up strafing Old Sarum aerodrome. The enemy aircraft was pursued by Spitfires of No.609 Sqn from Middle Wallop and shot down by Plt Off S. J. Hill and Flt Lt H. J. Howell near Lymington. On the same day that the Junkers 88 attacked Old Sarum a No.225 Sqn Lysander III R9128, based at Tilshead, crashed on take-off from Old Sarum killing the pilot and WOP/AG. On 10th February 1941 Sgt Trevor N. Bassett RNZAF (WOP/AG) was one of the crew of a Lysander which, during a training flight, crashed into a train at Tisbury during a mock attack. Sgt Bassett sustained injuries from which he died the same day in Tower House Emergency Hospital, Salisbury. Sgt Bassett had been posted to Old Sarum on 11th January 1941. He was buried at London Road Cemetery, Salisbury. The pilot, Plt Off Eric Lunoe, RAFVR died in the crash.

No.8 Anti- Aircraft Co-operation Unit arrived from Weston Zoyland on 6th October 1940. The parent unit moved to Cardiff on 9th November, with a detachment remaining at Old Sarum until September 1942, and with a further spell from November 1942 until March 1943. One of the unit aircraft, Dragonfly X9337 crashed taking off from Old Sarum on 24th June 1941.

Hawker Hurricane L1592 from the Special Duty Flight (SDF) at Christchurch, was flown on a 35 minute return flight to Old Sarum, by Plt Off Clifford Wright on 28th October 1940. This unique machine survived the war and is currently displayed at the Science Museum in South Kensington. It is the world's oldest surviving Hurricane and the only known example having fabric-covered wings. It was a Battle of Britain veteran which served also with Nos. 56, 17, 87, 43, 152 and 615 Sqns between 1938 and 1940. It had also been at No.10 MU Hullavington during this period and later, from August 1941 to April 1942 was stored at No.15 MU Wroughton.

No.1 School of Army Co-operation passed to No.70 Group on 1st December 1940.

As of 16th June 1941 the School aircraft allocation was: -

"A" Flt
4 Harvards,
10 Tomahawks,
2 Hurricanes,
1 Tiger Moth

"B" Flt
12 Lysanders,
1 Tutor

"C" Flt
12 Lysanders,
1 Tutor,
1 Gladiator

12 Lysanders were on Care & Maintenance (C&M).

On 3rd December 1940, 32 of Britain's first paratroopers took-off from Old Sarum in two Whitley bombers and were dropped on Salisbury Plain. 'B' Troop carried out a surprise attack on the village of Shrewton, which was defended by troops of Southern Command. It appears the 'fired up' paratroopers with their guerrilla tactics, during the storming of the village, seized a car which turned out to belong to Prince Olav, Crown Prince of the Netherlands. There were no hard feelings however, and on completion of the exercise, the Prince and C-in-C Home Forces retired to the pub where His Royal Highness bought the beer for the troops outside.

The airfield attracted the attention of a German aircraft again on the night of 11/12th May 1941 dropping HE and incendiary bombs and resulting in a fire in one of the hangers. The Signals Section building, Sergeants' Mess and two aircraft were also damaged.

'A' & 'B' Flights of No.239 Sqn commanded by Sqn Ldr York and based at Gatwick, arrived at Old Sarum on 16th May 1941 for the purpose of air firing the rear guns of their Lysanders at Coombe Bissett Range. The following month some of these personnel were back again to collect the Tomahawk aircraft with which the squadron was re-equipping.

The most successful 'spotter' aircraft was the Taylorcraft Auster which was operated by the nine Air Observation Post Sqns, Nos. 651-655, 658, 660-662. The first of these, No.651 Sqn, was formed on 1st August 1941, and evolved from the original 'D' Flight, with the last No.662 Sqn, formed in 1943. These squadrons served with distinction in Europe, Africa (Operation *Torch*) and the Middle and Far East. Although RAF units, they were fully integrated into the RA and were under the command of a RA major. The army also provided the ground crews. The remainder of the squadrons were made up of an adjutant, equipment officer and aircraft mechanics from the RAF. Most of the pilots were RAF trained RA captains but some were RAF. The integration seemed to work to the satisfaction of both services. No.651 Sqn had the standard three flights 'A', 'B' and 'C' and received its first aircraft, a Taylorcraft Model C ES958 on 27th August 1941, with further additions arriving later.

Other aircraft arriving at Old Sarum were those of No.36 (Army Co-operation) Wing Communication Flt. The Wing was attached to Southern Command HQ at nearby Wilton.

No.41 Operational Training Unit (OTU) was formed on 20th September 1941 in 70 Group ACC at Old Sarum from the Training Sqn of No.1 School of Army Co-operation. It used Oatlands Hill as a satellite until 15th November 1942. The primary task of No.41 OTU was initially to train pilots for tactical reconnaissance squadrons on Tomahawks and Lysanders. A further primary flying element taught by the Unit was that of low-flying, below tree-top height. The flat terrain of Salisbury Plain was ideal for this. It was important that pilots learnt to know their way around the cockpit instrumentation by touch. This was imperative with an aircraft travelling at 400 mph just above the ground. All of the pilot's concentration was directed at what was happening outside his cockpit. He could not afford to divert his gaze to the control panel. In the early days of a course some pilots found low-level flying a terrifying experience, especially when they thought that they were low enough and the instructor told them to go lower. Many a pilot was grateful for this disciplined training, when they were carrying out *Rhubarbs* over Europe later in their service.

No.110 Sqn which had left for Odiham in June 1940, was re-numbered as No.400 Sqn on 1st March 1941. On 19th October, Plt Off George Rogers flew a

Preserved Lysander G-BCWL (Great Britain's Canadian Westland Lysander) formally V9281 of No. 41 OTU taking off from Old Sarum. This aircraft was transferred to the RCAF on 25.4.42. It is now in America as part of the Kermit Weeks collection.   Photo: Cty. Dr. H.F. Thomas

reconnaissance from Odiham to Old Sarum. On the return flight his plan was to fly under a road bridge near Winchester, a stunt which two of his squadron colleagues had already successfully attempted. George Rogers was not so fortunate as his Tomahawk AH851 struck the bridge losing a wing tip and pitot head. He recovered to reach Odiham but had to land at a high speed to keep the wing up. On braking, the airscrew dug into the ground and the Tomahawk turned over onto its back. George Rogers received facial injuries but returned to duty after a week to receive a severe reprimand. The bridge in Hampshire was from then until its demolition in 1983, referred to as Spitfire Bridge, presumably on the basis that eye-witnesses at the time were unfamiliar with the Tomahawk.

As of January 1942, No.41 OTU was equipped with 21 + 7 reserve Tomahawks, 7 + 2 Masters, 4 + 2 Magisters and 2 + 1 Tutors. One of the Magisters crashed whilst carrying out a flying exercise on 23rd February 1942, and the two man crew were killed. The pilot was Plt Off Ernest W. Bright RNZAF and the 2nd pilot was Plt Off David G. West RNZAF. Both were buried at London Road Cemetery, Salisbury. Fellow countryman Plt Off Frederick C. Hackett RNZAF was killed on Wednesday 12th November 1941 when flying a Lysander. Making a landing approach at Old Sarum the aircraft swerved to the left and straightened out. The pilot opened up the engine and carried out a climbing turn to port but the aircraft struck the rifle butts and crashed. Plt Off Hackett was buried at Devizes Road Cemetery, Salisbury.

No.41 OTU ceased its Lysander training role on 22nd March 1942. It was reorganised with 'A' Flt remained at Old Sarum flying Harvards and two Defiants while 'B' and 'C' Flts moved to Oatlands Hill with Tomahawks and Mustangs respectively. The Mustangs started to arrive in April and soon Hurricanes began replacing the Tomahawks. As of July the establishment was 32 + 11 Mustangs, 9 + 3 Harvards, 3 + 1 Tutors and an unknown number of Hurricanes. From 1st to 15th November, High Post was used by a detachment, possibly 'A' Flt. On 15th November 1942 No.41 OTU moved to Hawarden

No.1471 (Anti-Aircraft Co-operation) Flight in No.70 Group formed at Old Sarum on 1st April 1942 with three Tomahawks to provide co-operation for the School of Artillery in the development and teaching of methods of artillery reconnaissance. The Flt. later received the Mustang and used a Proctor III. The Flight was disbanded on 10th October 1942.

No.1426 (Enemy Aircraft) Circus Flt, carrying out Tour No.6, arrived on 10th September 1942 with an He 111H, Ju 88A and an Me 110C. The following day a flying demonstration took place at which the Ju 88 was flown hard and dived steeply. The other two aircraft were flown sedately making a number of low passes. The Messerschmitt is the one that was shot down at Goodwood on 21st July 1940, having earlier accounted for the No.1 FTS Hart over Old Sarum.

From 18th November 1942 to March 1943, six Fairey Fulmar Is of 879 Sqn. FAA were resident on army support training. 879 Sqn was a Fleet Fighter unit.

No.41 OTU was replaced at Old Sarum by No.43 OTU which arrived on 19th November 1942 from Larkhill. The unit was commanded by Wg Cdr Donald Walker and equipped with the Taylorcraft, Auster Is, a Piper Cub, Vigilant and Tiger Moth. There was also a DH Dominie at Old Sarum then which gave the AOP Instructors an opportunity of experiencing dual-engine flying. Larkhill was frequently used for practical flying by AOP pilots under instruction. It was known for Wg Cdr Walker to fly with his pet dog to an area of Salisbury Plain where he would land to exercise the animal. In December 1942, one of the pilots, Llewellyn, was the first to be killed on any Air OP Course when he flew into overhead power cables. Under a setting sun, his ashes were scattered over Salisbury Plain from the air by Maj Andrew Lyell the Chief Ground Instructor (CGI). The unit remained until 17th February 1944 when it moved to Oatlands Hill.

No.658 Sqn commanded by Maj Andrew Lyell, formed at Old Sarum on 30th April 1943 equipped with Auster IIIs. This was a Tactical Reconniassance/A.O.P. Sqn, temporarily allocated to Fighter Command (No.10 Group) prior to the forming of 2nd T.A.F. which absorbed the Army Co-operation Command on 1st June 1943. Two pilots Captains Gordon C. Sandeman RA and Philip M. Bogod RA, were lost shortly after the squadron formed. They were killed on Wednesday 19th May when they crashed on their return to Old Sarum after delivering an aircraft to Speke. Their aircraft struck a tree near the River Avon in Durrington. No.658 Sqn moved to Oatlands Hill on 6th August.

No.1 School of Army Co-operation reformed on 1st June 1943 as The School of Army Co-operation in No.70 Group and was renamed RAF School of Army Co-operation in August.

No.3505 Servicing Unit was formed at Old Sarum on 1st December 1943 to centralise maintenance of aircraft used by the various AAC squadrons with southern bases. On 21st February 1944 it moved to Weston Zoyland.

Capt B.G.H. Camp flying an Auster from the RAF School of Army Co-

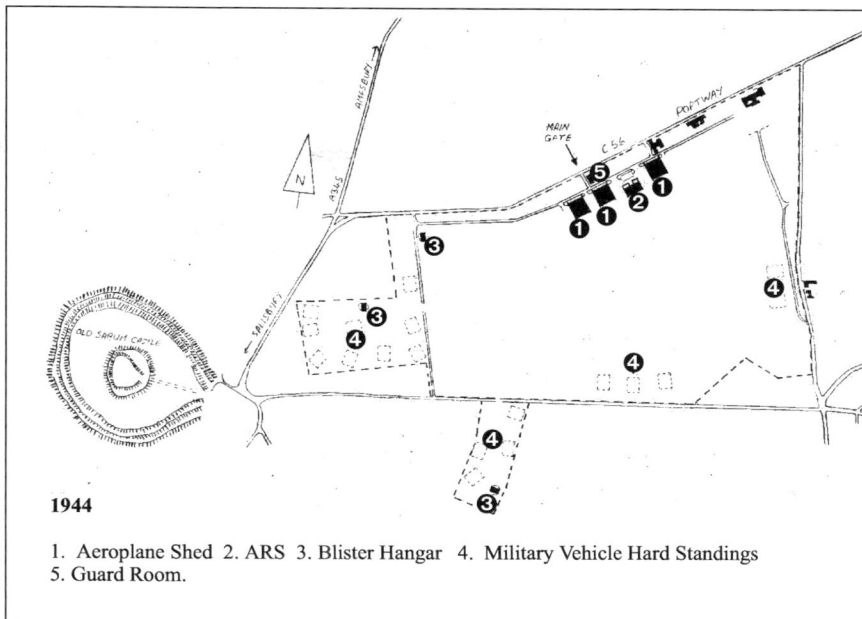

1944

1. Aeroplane Shed 2. ARS 3. Blister Hangar 4. Military Vehicle Hard Standings
5. Guard Room.

**Staff Officers of No.43 OTU in front of an Auster at Old Sarum in December 1943.
Photo: Cty. Dr. H.F. Thomas**

operation on 11th December, witnessed a wheels-up force landing of a Welkin F.1 DX280 at Yarnbury Castle near Winterbourne Stoke on the A303. The Welkin from A&AEE Boscombe Down was being flown by Sqn Ldr J.E. Lydall when the port engine burst into flames. Not having fire suppression installed, he had to make a rapid landing. Capt Camp landed the Auster close to the accident site and ferried the pilot to Boscombe Down for medical treatment. The Welkin was completely burnt out.

Capt J.W.R. Chadwick, one of the instructors, made a heavy landing in Auster III ME188 when flying into Old Sarum on 29th February, breaking the port undercarriage. Little damage resulted from this but whilst being

towed in to Old Sarum, the aircraft was struck by a US armoured car and written off.

The reason for the move to Weston Zoyland by No.3505 Servicing Unit and to Oatlands Hill by No.43 OTU, was to allow the hangars at Old Sarum to be used to modify hundreds of army vehicles in preparation for D-Day. This was known as the SNUG process. The work included water-proofing (this presumably made them snug) and fitting exhaust extensions to enable them to be driven ashore from LSTs and LCTs for the beach landings. Motor Transport Fitter Albert Jones was one of numerous RAF men involved in carrying out this conversion work. He was also one of many such Fitters/Mechanics who were suddenly posted to Middle Wallop from the 8th to 12th October 1943 to receive a crash course on water-proofing vehicles and an introduction to Asbestos Water-proofing Compound (AWC). This was similar to plasticine, was grey in colour and used for pressing around electrical devices such as starter motors, dynamos, cut-outs etc. A red coloured AWC was needed to fix around distributors and spark plugs, which received direct heat from the engine block. Instruction was also given on the fitting of breather pipes and tubes from a fuel tank, engine block and carburettor, so that they terminated at cab top height. Following this instruction, all of the men returned to their various units. On 16th March 1944 they were all seconded to Old Sarum, where their work on the invasion vehicles continued solidly until 21st May 1944. They then moved to a tented camp 'Somewhere in the New Forest', to carry out final checks before the vehicles left for the docks. Albert Jones returned to Old Sarum on 5th July to prepare more vehicles before returning to his unit on 20th July.

The entire airfield and surrounding fields were used to store and prepare vehicles. Sommerfeld Tracking 150' x 125' was laid down to provide hard standings (see 1944 plan). The airfield was divided in half lengthways, leaving a space wide enough for aircraft landings. A USAAF P-47 Thunderbolt attempting an emergency landing at the time, ran out of airfield, crashed through the hedge near the gun-butts and killed a couple of cows in the process. The station also took on a major co-ordinating role for the medical care of invasion personnel and temporary medical units were established around Salisbury. In September, under the direct control of the 2nd Tactical Air Force, 317 Supply & Transport Column was formed at Old Sarum under the command of Sqn Ldr Silcock. The unit referred to themselves as 'Silcock's Travelling Circus'. It's principal task was to equip and supply the Allied Forces from D-Day onwards. In the run-up to the end of the war in Europe this Unit carried hundreds of thousands of tons of equipment, and covered millions of miles, sometimes operating in areas of considerable danger.

No.39 Wing and No.15 Sector were briefly at Old Sarum in June 1944 in transit to France, as was No.72 Wing and an element of No.511 Forward Repair Unit in September 1944.

A No.405 Sqn RCAF Halifax bomber which was attacked when returning from a raid in Europe, crash-landed at Old Sarum. It was flown by Salisbury born Granville Silby who when he realised that he was unable to reach his squadron airfield at Pocklington in Yorkshire, changed course. He decided that if he had to crash-land, he would do so in his own backyard. The grass runway at Old Sarum was obviously far too short for the Halifax which tore through two hedges before coming safely to rest. After the war Silby became well known locally as the leader of his own dance band and continued to live in the city until his death in January 1997 at the age of 83.

Nos. 402/404 Air Stores Park of No.7 MU Quedgeley was at Old Sarum from 5th August and 22nd June 1944 respectively. No.408 (Polish) Air Stores Park of No.206 MU Hillingdon arrived on 18th August and No.418 Air Stores Park on 12th August. All four stayed for only a few days. These Parks were formed to store aircraft equipment and spares for front line squadrons. A Flt of the Airfield Construction Flight was also detached there in 1944.

No.84 Group Communication Flt arrived from Westhampnett on 20th August 1944, becoming a squadron on 9th November, and leaving for France on 1st December 1944.

On 5th November 1944 the RAF School of Army Co-operation became the School of Air Support, with a strong naval presence. The S of A.S. concentrated more on theoretical training for senior officers rather than flying training, but communications aircraft included Dominies, Magisters and Ansons. During 1945/46 the School was using, in addition, Proctors, Seafires and Spitfires.

Post War Years

On 17th August 1945, two days after the War ended, Battle of Britain pilot, Wg Cdr Anthony D. J. Lovell DSO*, DFC*, DFC (US), an instructor with the Ground Support Wing at the School of Air Support, took off from Old Sarum in a Communications Flt Spitfire XII EN234 just after 11.30am.

This was a Salisbury built aircraft. He performed a slow roll to the right from which he exited flying level at approximately 100'. Starting to climb, he carried out a further slow roll to the right but the Spitfire stalled, struck telephone wires, knocked the Union Jack from the flag pole at Old Sarum Farm, swept low past Old Castle Farm, striking a hedge with the starboard wing and crashed on the slopes of Old Sarum Castle. Residents of the Old Castle Inn raced out to assist but farmer Fiennes Gallop, the first on the scene, had already pulled the pilot's body from the wreckage. The official cause of the accident was given as 'an error of judgement on the part of the pilot whilst performing aerobatics at low altitude in contravention of King's Regulations'. There were other views however, especially from some of the distinguished Spitfire pilots who had flown and served with him. They considered him too experienced and professional to carry out such a manouvre and felt that a mechanical failure was a more logical explanation for the tragedy.

Wg Cdr Tony Lovell was no stranger to Wiltshire having trained at No.6 FTS Netheravon together with Al Deere, who as a Flt Lt went on to serve with distinction during the Battle of Britain with No.54 Sqn and reached Air Commodore rank in the post war RAF. Tony served with No.41 Sqn during the Battle of Britain flying Spitfires and with No.87 Sqn on Hurricanes. During 1944 he led a ground attack wing in Italy. He was renowned as a spectacular aerobatic pilot, a meticulous flyer and a dedicated instructor. He was also credited with 23 victories during his wartime exploits. WO J.S. Pollard, who had flown with Wg Cdr Lovell from Old Sarum to Biggin Hill in Proctor DX196 five days before his death, accompanied his body on the flight to his home in Ireland. The flight was made on 19th August 1945 in Dominie NR733 piloted by Wg Cdr Minifie. The aircraft, staging through Squires Gate, flew to Limavady for the funeral service, which was held in Londonderry. On returning to base on 21st August an overnight stop was made at Wolverhampton as Old Sarum at the time had no night landing facilities. The journey was completed the next day.

On 1st May 1947 the name of the S of A.S. changed to School of Land/Air Warfare in No.11 Group with the 4-week officers' courses continuing. Proctors, Ansons, and Oxfords were the aircraft used by the School. Marshal of the RAF Lord Tedder GCB (Chief of the Air Staff) conducted Exercise *Pandora* at the School from 3rd to 7th May 1948. Approximately 255 officers of the three services attended, these included some civilians from the Science Branches. The Prime Minister The Rt.Hon. C.R. Atlee, PC, CH, MP, also attended for the first two days. The three phases addressed by the exercise were:

- operations without the use of weapons of mass destruction
- operations with weapons of mass destruction in use
- future problems (beyond 1955).

A School Anson NL248 was involved in a mid-air collision on 31st May 1948. This happened at Bulford and involved a Royal Navy Dominie C1 NR753 flown by Fg Off Ashley J. Greer with two passengers, Naval Air Mechanics Peter J. Bartlett and Peter C. Damon (RN). The Dominie was leading a small formation of aircraft but the pilot, who didn't have many flying-hours on twin-engines, flew an unsteady course which caused his aircraft to collide with Anson NL248. The propeller of this aircraft struck the tailplane of the Dominie causing it to dive into the ground, killing the pilot and two navy passengers.

A Hillar HTE-2 XB523 helicopter from the School crashed in the Castle at Old Sarum on 26th May 1955. People on a picnic reported seeing the pilot waving to them, followed by the aircraft sliding sideways into the ground. A possible cause was the pilot not being strapped in on the bench seat, sliding sideways and pulling the cydic control with him, causing the aircraft to bank over and hit the ground. The pilot was killed in the crash.

The School of Land/Air Warfare merged into the Joint Warfare Establishment on 31st March 1963.

The VISTRE Flt moved in from Netheravon on 18th November 1950 and was renamed Joint Concealment Centre (RAF Component) when it returned on 15th January 1952.

During the 1950s the Royal Navy

WO Pollard on the right of his navigator at Old Sarum in 1945. The Dominie is possibly NR733
Photo: Stan Pollard

The navigator of WO Pollard with a Proctor at Old Sarum in 1945.
Photo: Stan Pollard

maintained a Hiller HT.1 for use at the School. This was replaced by a Dragonfly Mk.3 in the 1960s. Neil Cameron, later Marshal of the Royal Air Force, was stationed at Old Sarum and his Log Book records him as flying Seafires there during 1950. Sea Fury F.10 TF945 was on charge until February when it was replaced with a type FB11 VW229 which was in use for the following two years. In addition Firefly FR.1 MB738 was attached from June 1949 to January 1954.

The Freedom of the City of Salisbury was conferred on the station on 29th June 1956. This was immediately prior to the Suez War for which the entire military control was conducted from the twin Operations Rooms at Old Sarum.

The Army Air Transport Training & Development Centre was based at Old Sarum during the later part of the 1950s and became the Army Air Transport Development Unit.

The RAF Helicopter Development Unit (HDU) was formed on 1st June 1961 in No.12 Group equipped with Sycamores, but on 1st April 1963 became part of the re-designated Joint Warfare Establishment (JWE) in Fighter Command when the School of Land/Air Warfare amalgamated with the Amphibious Warfare School. It disbanded into the Joint Helicopter Development Unit (JHDU) on 1st February 1965. From 1st June 1963 the JWE came under Transport Command. The RN element came under the parentage of RNAS Yeovilton. The RAF HDU was equipped with a Whirlwind HAR10 whereas the JWE had Chipmunks and Ansons. Major-General Richard Keith-Jones the Commandant from 1966-68 described the post as requiring great patience, discernment and impartiality. The JHDU, along with the Army Air Transport Development Unit, became part of the Joint Air Transport Establishment from January 1968 until its move to Abingdon in April 1971.

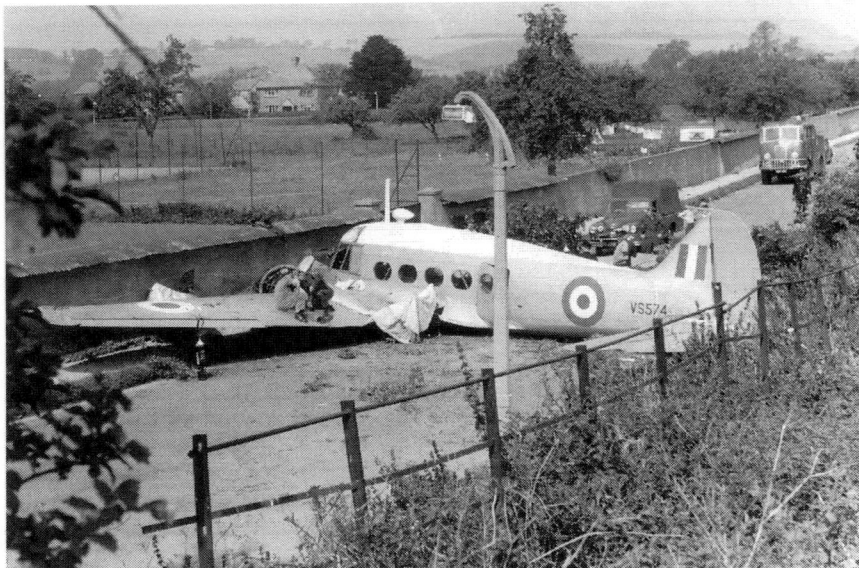

Avro Anson C.21 VS574 of Bomber Command Communication Flt, mistook Hudson's field for Old Sarum when landing on 31st July 1957. It went through the hedge and came to rest in Stratford Road with its nose against the wall of New Sarum Tennis Club. The pilot, navigator and passenger all escaped uninjured.   Photo: Salisbury Journal

Blackburn Beverley XH122 of No. 30 Sqn Transport Command at Old Sarum in December 1959. It was required to stay for a month because the grass runway was too soft for it to take off. The Unit markings consisted of the squadron number in white superimposed on a red diamond on the tail fin. At the rear of the fire engine, the inter-war years built watch office, on brick pillars can be seen close to the hangars. Photo: Cty. Dr. H.F. Thomas.

Chipmunks of East Midlands UAS based at Newton, attending their Annual Camp at Old Sarum C.1970. Photo: Cty. Dr. H.F. Thomas

A detachment of the Royal Navy's 846 Sqn from Culdrose with Wessex HU.5s was based at Old Sarum during Nov/Dec.1968.

A Harvard, Chipmunk and Twin Pioneer, which had been in the flypast to honour Princess Anne on her visit to the A&AEE on 19th March 1971, made landings at Old Sarum when there was bad weather and a low cloud base which prevented them from returning to Boscombe Down. Later that year on 15th December, the RAF's long association with Old Sarum came to an end when it was transferred to the Army. The Joint Helicopter and Trials Development Unit was based at Old Sarum and operated various types of helicopter, most notably being a Westland Whirlwind HAS.7, XN299 758 named the 'Iron Chicken'. The Unit disbanded on 22nd July 1976 and the JWE in 1979 when the station closed as a military establishment.

Closure

Two years after military closure, Edgley Aircraft Ltd arrived in 1981 and began to manufacture the Edgley Optica, an innovative 'spotter' aircraft. Having purchased two of the original 1918 built hangars from the MoD in which to carry out the aircraft construction, a target was set to build an initial batch of 200 aircraft at £55,000 each. The business seemed to be developing well with orders not only from the United Kingdom but Australia and South Africa. An Optica Scout entered service with the Hampshire Police who flew it using their own pilot. Tragically it crashed near Ringwood in 1986 killing both the crew on board. The subsequent enquiry cleared the aircraft of blame, but the Force had sufficient faith in the model to order a second which entered service in December 1987. Production of the Optica at Old Sarum was halted when fire broke out at 2240 hours on 16th January 1987. The fire destroying two Belfast hangars and two Opticas, which had had the drain plugs removed from their fuel tanks and, from which the contents fuelled the fire in what was suspected as a case of arson. Production was to continue under the name of the Brooklands Aerospace Group for a few more years but it failed to develop into a success story and in 1990 the company went into liquidation.

Tiger Moth G-ALND belonging to The Bustard Flying Club.

Each of the students on the ETPS course at Boscombe Down are required to carry out a Pilot Assessment exercise on a particular aircraft towards the end of their secondment and from the 1985 Course a *Luftwaffe* pilot, Harry Fehl, tested the Optica at Old Sarum. This was carried out on a prototype shortly after one had been involved in a fatal accident. The German was a Phantom F4 pilot who had not flown the Optica before or previously taken off from a grass runway. The Company Chief Test Pilot Chris Chadwick, himself a former ETPS graduate and ex-naval test pilot, accompanied Harry Fehl on the Assessment Flight. In his later report the ETPS student indicated that he found the Opticas' sharp loss of airspeed in a climb and the stall characteristics, unacceptable.

In 1984 World War 2 fighter pilot Neville Duke, a successful post war test pilot worked as company test pilot on the Lovaux (nee Brooklands, nee Edgley) Optica, demonstrating the aircraft at Farnborough Air Show in 1992.

Private aircraft have been hangared at Old Sarum (except in wartime) since the 1920s and have been flown by military and civilian owners. The most recent flying clubs have been the Wiltshire Aero Club (1986-1991), The Bustard Flying Club (1957-1989) and since 1992, the Old Sarum Flying Club. Microlight and helicopter training have also been available. Gliding has taken place for many years with No.622 (Volunteer) Gliding School using it from July 1963 until November 1978 when it left for Upavon, and the Dorset Gliding Club until 1992. The Bustard Flying Club limited its membership to 50 who were all civil servants working at Boscombe Down or Old Sarum. Initially the club had one Tiger Moth on which all maintenance was carried out by the membership.

Most of the original hangars remain as do some of the permanent buildings. The Guard Room (pattern 166), by the main entrance gates, survived until demolition, except for the facia, in October 2002. The facia disappeared in early 2003. The one grass runway SW/NE 06/24 is 2562' x 164'. The Air Training Corps 1010 (Salisbury) Sqn is based at the airfield and Grob aircraft from the various University Air Sqns make frequent visits. Privately owned Tiger Moths, Austers, a Taylorcraft, Cubs and Chipmunks can on occasions be seen at Old Sarum, acting as a reminder of the types flown there previously in military guise. A Russian Yak 52, owned by local enthusiasts, visited over the weekend of 19/20th April 1997. The Russian Air Attache in London and his daughter were there to present papers granting permission for the aircraft to display the Soviet Red Stars. Of the twin Belfast hangars, No.3 is shared by the Flying Club and Old Sarum Engineering. During 1997 this firm carried out restoration work on Auster 5 J/1 Autocraft G-AHSP, which took to the air again in mid May. A 'Great Vintage Flying Weekend' was held over the weekend of 31st May/1st June 1997 and amongst the visiting aircraft, Tiger Moths, Austers and Hornet Moths could be seen. A DC3 Dakota touched down on Wednesday 5th August 1998 having been forced to divert from Boscombe Down because a Hawker Hunter had crashed on the runway. Sections of the land have been sold off and are used as a Business Park

and the home of Salisbury Football Club.

There is considerable resentment about the amount of private flying from Old Sarum from many people living in the immediate area. It appears however that the freehold of the airfield contains a covenant that it must remain open as an airfield. The freeholders are associated with Old Sarum Flying Club, and the Local Authority view the airfield and its facilities as a desirable public amenity. There was concern at one stage that the land might be used for housing or commercial purposes. It now looks as if this will not happen and result in the loss of another of Wiltshire's World War 1 airfields.

Memorial

184/SU153335 - North-side of airfield by No.3 Hangar and the Flying Club.

A memorial cairn mounted with a stone bust of an airman and set into the face of the cairn a metal plaque with the inscription: -

THIS MEMORIAL IS DEDICATED TO THE FOLLOWING A.O.P. SQUADRONS THAT
WERE FORMED AT OLD SARUM DURING THE SECOND WORLD WAR, AND
WHOSE GALLANTRY AND TENACITY WERE TO PLAY A VITAL ROLE IN
THE FINAL VICTORY. THEY FLEW LIGHT UNARMED AIRCRAFT OVER ENEMY LINES
AND MANY PAID THE ULTIMATE PRICE.

D Flight 1940 1941 - The Battle Of France
651 A.O.P. Squadron 1941 - North Africa, Sicily, Italy, Austria.
652 A.O.P. Squadron 1942 - Normandy, Belgium.
653 A.O.P. Squadron 1942 - Normandy, Belgium, Holland, Germany.
654 A.O.P. Squadron 1942 - North Africa, Sicily, Italy.
655 A.O.P. Squadron 1942 - North Africa, Italy.
658 A.O.P. Squadron 1943 - Normandy, Belgium, Holland, Germany.
660 A.O.P. Squadron 1943 - Normandy, Belgium, Germany.
661 A.O.P. Squadron 1943 - Normandy, Belgium, Holland, Germany.
662 A.O.P. Squadron 1943 - Normandy, Belgium, Holland, Germany.

No.43 OPERATIONAL TRAINING UNIT R.A.F.
THEIR SACRIFICE WAS NOT IN VAIN
This plaque was donated by members of
the A.O.P. Veterans Association
and unveiled on 6th June 1993 by
General Sir Martin Farndale K.C.B.
The Master Gunner

On the base of the plaque a Taylorcraft Auster is shown in plan view.

The A.O.P. Memorial outside the clubhouse of the Old Sarum Flying Club.

OVERTON HEATH RLG

Location - 173/SU178652 - 2 miles South West of Marlborough

On the hill above the village of Oare on the A345 at Clench Common. The landing ground is located on the north east side of the C265 road, crossing Clench Common to Wootton Rivers.

Aerodrome Development

During the same period of 1939 when the Air Ministry selected Alton Barnes as a Relief Landing Ground (RLG) for use by the expanding CFS Upavon, they determined that nearby Clench Common was another suitable site which could be used for training purposes. The land was then owned by the Marquis of Aylesbury and part of it was common land. An area was in use as a farm with stables and racehorses. Mrs Laye who lived in the farmhouse, was allowed to remain when the landing ground was established because she had cows whose milk yield contributed to the war rations.

The initial work in preparing the site as an RLG was carried out by civilian workers. They undertook a considerable amount of drainage work at the early stage but this proved unsuccessful, as water problems were a feature there throughout the period that it was in operation. The intention was to open the landing ground in October 1940 but the wet conditions prevented this happening until April 1941.

Redevelopment of the site as a permanent station commenced in early 1942. On 13th February Flt Lt Howard and 130 other ranks from No.5 Works Sqn reported to lay Sommerfeld tracking at Upavon and at Overton Heath. The two runways at the latter airfield were laid SW/NE 1750yds and NW/SE 1500yds. LAC Len Brewster serving with the Works Sqn at Overton Heath, recalls spending a considerable amount of time trying to improve the drainage problems. The intersection of the two runways was a particularly bad area where aircraft often became stuck in the boggy conditions. A vast quantity of stone was delivered to the site and was used as ballast. On completion, Sommerfeld tracking was laid and pinned down on top and along the complete length of the two runways. At the intersection, tarred gravel was laid over the metal surface.

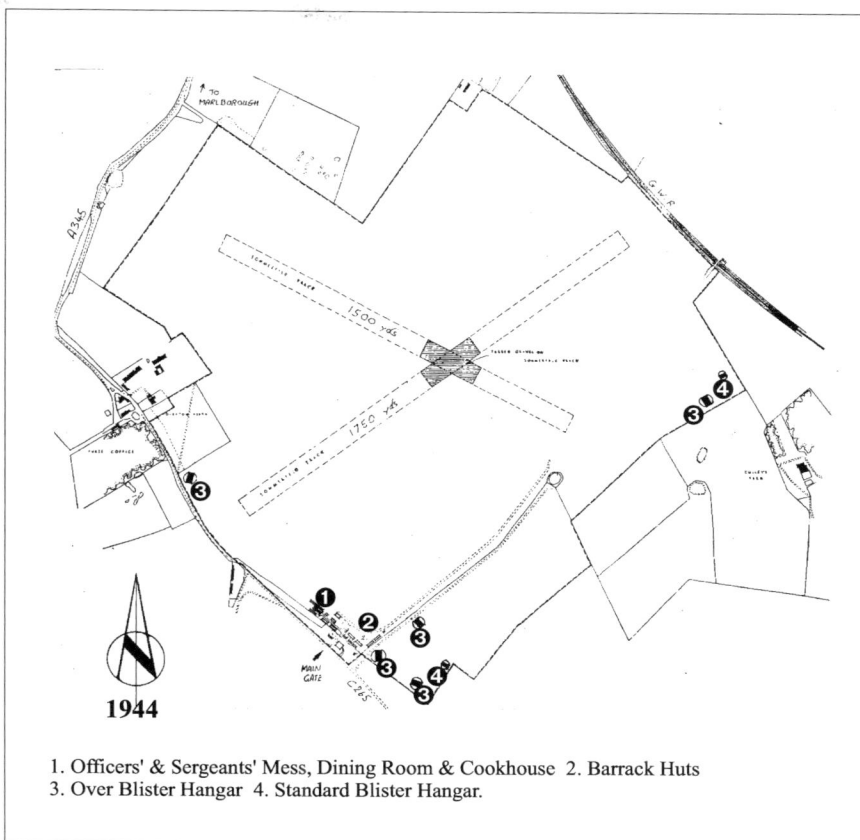

1. Officers' & Sergeants' Mess, Dining Room & Cookhouse 2. Barrack Huts
3. Over Blister Hangar 4. Standard Blister Hangar.

With the exception of the 7 blister hangars, all of the airfield buildings were located in the south corner alongside the C265 road. They consisted of a brick built Officers' Mess/Sgts' Mess/Dining Room and cookhouse in three inter-linked buildings, a Medical Inspection (M.I) Nissen hut, 5 brick built barrack huts, 4 various stores, a bulk petrol compound and washrooms/ablutions. The blister hangars consisted 5 x 65' Over and 2 x 45' Standard. Two of these were on the east-side of the airfield, four were grouped together close to the accommodation site and one close to the farm buildings, this one was used for maintenance. The two-letter station identification code was OV. The station catered for an establishment of approximately 80 personnel, which at one stage included a number of WAAFs.

Airfield defence was provided by an anti-aircraft gun post close to the group of four hangars and the RAF Regiment barrack hut on the southern boundary of the field. Air traffic movement was directed from a mobile control vehicle.

Runway lighting was in the form of lights with batteries stowed in yellow boxes, all mounted on small wheeled trailers, which were towed out to the runway by a Ford tractor. It was probably in use from 1943 when, in November, night flying training ceased at New Zealand Farm resulting in an increased use of Overton Heath.

World War 2 Years

The planned opening as an RLG in October 1940 had to be postponed when it was pronounced out of action for the winter. During a visit to Upavon in April 1941, the Air Officer Commanding carried out an inspection of Overton Heath and following this it did open. Aircraft types using the facility at this time were in the main, Oxfords, Masters and Magisters. In October 1941, consideration was given to using the airfield as a flying training/research and development unit, to be commanded by the famous local airman Sqn Ldr Robert Smith-Barry who had rejoined the Air Force following the outbreak of World War 2. He had served, and built up a reputation during the First World War, with the RFC and RAF. However nothing came of this, for him or for the proposed unit.

During the 1942 redevelopment period, Lord Haw Haw broadcast the enemy's knowledge of the building work at Overton Heath. Soon afterwards the aerodrome came under attack with one bomb creating a massive crater close to the end of the runway on the eastern side of the field. Boys of Marlborough College invaded the site the following day to pick up shrapnel. A number of incendiaries had been dropped prior to this raid but they came down close to the Marlborough to Savernake railway line and the Wernham Farm buildings just north of the landing area.

Overton Heath was a satellite of No.7 Flying Instructors' School (FIS) (No.23 Group) Flying Training Command when the School formed at Upavon on 1st April 1942 from personnel of the CFS. No.7 FIS used Overton Heath until at least February 1943.

Various aircraft types were recorded on the airfield by Albert Dean who lived in one of the houses on the edge of the field. In addition to those already mentioned other types noted were the Hampden, Whitley, Spitfire, Tiger Moth, Anson, Lysander, Boston, Beaufighter and Wellington.

On 26th October 1942 a No.21 OTU Wellington IC Z8967 took-off from Moreton-in Marsh for a cross-country flight. At 1130hrs the aircraft forced landed, with the undercarriage retracted, in a field next to the A345 on the north side of Overton Heath. Both engines had failed to give the requisite power for the aircraft to maintain height. The only injury was to Sgt K.L. Jeffries (AG). The other crew members were Sgt H. B. R. Venning (pilot), Plt Off Churchouse, Sgt Hargreaves and Sgt Hearwood.

On 1st January 1944, Albert Dean witnessed the forced landing of a USAAF B-17. On its approach to the runway from the south west, it took out the hedge as it crossed the Wootton Rivers road but landed without injury to the crew or too much serious damage to the aircraft itself. The damage was sufficient however for it to remain on the airfield for a number of weeks undergoing repairs. As always, the

local children benefitted from the Americans' stay and were sorry when the time came for the B-17 to be flown out.

With the build up to D-Day, the area in and around the airfield was used for storage. Stacks of ordnance lined both sides of the roadway on the edge of the airfield.

On the night of 13th/14th January 1945 a No.17 OTU Wellington X HE856 took-off at 1820hrs from Silverstone for a night cross-country flight. During the flight a message was received that poor visibility at the airfield would prevent a return landing. Believing he was low on fuel, the pilot was looking for an airfield on which to land when it struck the treetops of West Woods and the oak trees in the Wansdyke, before crashing and catching fire in a field at Bayardo Farm, two miles west of Overton Heath. Five of the crew perished, Flt Sgt Alfred G. Humphrey RAFVR (pilot), Sgt Gordon C. Edwards RAFVR (nav), Sgt Reynold Davies RAFVR (B/A), Sgt Victor L. Goddard RAFVR (WOP/AG), Sgt Wilfred R. Askew RAFVR (AG). The one survivor was the rear gunner Sgt James Done RAFVR whose turret was found a short distance from the main wreckage. P.C Furze was first at the scene, followed by the Head Forester

Sgt James Done at No.17 OTU Silverstone prior to the crash. Photo: J. Done

for West Woods, Mr Read, and the RAF crash units. Sgt Done was taken to Bayardo Farm House where he was looked after by the farmer Reg Bull and his family until the ambulance arrived and took him to the 347th Station Hospital United States Army based on Marlborough Common. He was later admitted to the RAF hospital at Wroughton. Sgt Goddard was buried in Upavon Cemetery.

In June 2000 James Done returned to Bayardo Farm where he stayed with Albert Bull. They had not met since the night of the crash when Albert, the son of the farmer, was 15 years old. Also attending the reunion was the brother of the pilot and the sister of the WOP/AG. The tracing of James Done, and the visit to Bayardo Farm, was organised by the Wiltshire Historical Military Society.

No.1537 Beam Approach Training Flight affiliated to No.7 FIS (A) at Upavon used Overton Heath with their Oxfords. This unit, formed in May 1943, was the last to use the airfield for flying, before departing in August 1945.

Closure

After the RAF stopped using the site in 1945, it was placed on C&M until 1948 when it was used by the Ministry of Agriculture, Fisheries and Food until 1951. It then passed to the Crown and was farmed by their agent Tom Ellis until 1959. Martin Pitt, himself an ex RAF man, then took over the site which was known as Levetts Farm. In recent years visits have been made by RAF personnel who served at the base during the war. It appears one pilot flew Lysanders on missions to Europe. He found it difficult to recognise any of the station features because he was driven to the airfield at Overton Heath during the night for an operation, returned before dawn and was driven away. In this way, should he have been captured, he was not in a position to pass any details to the enemy. The chances of his capture were high. Two WAAFs also returned in the 1990s and found their barrack block occupied by livestock.

The airfield is still under the ownership of the Crown and continues to be farmed. Many of the original wartime buildings remain, although some are now derelict. Two underground air raid shelters at either end of the domestic

An aerial view of Overton Heath on 12th July 1946. The Blister hangar which has survived can be seen in the centre and the Domestic Site and three other Blister hangars in the bottom right hand corner. The two runways are just about visible.   Photo: NMRO

The surviving Blister hangar and the contractors plate on an inside column.

site and running parallel with the road, remain in reasonable condition. The blister hangar used for aircraft maintenance is still used by the farmer. It has been reclad and the ends filled in. During its operational use this hanger, as with all hangars of the type, had timber staging internally along its sides on which offices, stores and a restroom was constructed. The thick canvas sheets at each end allowed the facility to be used to carry out work on two aircraft within the building at the same time.

The Transformer House remains with its doors still attached.

Close to the villages of Porton and Idmiston on the C288 alongside the Waterloo to Salisbury railway line, is located the Defence Science & Technology Laboratory (DSTL), Porton Down. When opening in 1916, the site was known as the Royal Engineers Experimental Station and was established to allow the War Office to investigate methods of using and combating the use of gas as an arsenal of war. This resulted from a first gas attack made by the German Army on 22nd April 1915, which caused heavy casualties amongst unprepared Allied troops.

Aerodrome Development

Porton Down's involvement with flying began in 1920 when the ranges there were used for live bomb dropping exercises by the S of AC at Old Sarum.

Preparation of the landing ground was completed in 1928 but aircraft hangars or dedicated buildings were not constructed at Porton Down for the flying element.

During World War 2, Porton Landing Ground was allocated the two-letter identification code PT.

Inter War Years

In 1922 the first RAF Experimental Officer (AFEO) was appointed at Porton, tasked to arrange aircraft as and when required for the dispersal of any substances capable of delivery by aerial means. Initially static balloons were used to study the patterns of smoke when emitted and dispersed by the wind. In 1926 a 'Special Duties Flight' was formed and operated from Old Sarum, carrying out spraying tests for the Porton Gas School. Its allocated aircraft were a Bristol F2b F4675, Hawker Horsley S1236 and a Blackburn Dart. The unit moved to Netheravon on 12th September1928 where it became the 'Porton Flight'. The aircraft were suitably modified to carry the chemical tanks and spray nozzles required to produce smoke curtains. The apparatus fitted to a standard aircraft was known as a Smoke Curtain Installation (SCI). All Wellington

A smoke canister installation beneath a Wellington of the Special Duties Flt at Boscombe Down on 15th May 1940. The aircraft is almost certainly R2703 which left the Flt on 25th May 1940. Photo: © Crown Copyright 1940

bombers carried two large SCI tanks in the bomb bay with a discharge pipe protruding through the bomb doors.

An Avro 504K H7421 was the first aircraft to arrive at Porton Down in 1928, following completion of the landing ground. In 1929 the station was re-titled Chemical Warfare Experimental Station (CWES) and the following year Chemical Defence Experimental Station (CDES). The Porton Flight, comprising 1 Hawker Horsley II J8606 and 1 Fairey Fox I J9025, moved from Netheravon to Boscombe Down on 2nd February 1931, where it again became a 'Special Duty Flight'.

The landing ground at Porton was

increasingly used by Army Co-operation aircraft in the 1930s. A Hawker Audax K3080 of the SDF was one of a number in regular use. It was still with the Flt in November 1937 when it was flown to Farnborough by Fg Off Robinson accompanied by a Mr Bateman, probably one of Porton's civilian boffins. One of Andovers No.12 Sqn Hart Is, K2426 flew into Porton via Boscombe Down on 13th February 1935.

No.4 Group Experimental Flt had formed at Porton by September 1937 and remained until the summer of 1938 when it moved to Boscombe Down. The Flt was allocated Battle K7574 and Hind L7217.

Left to right : Hawker Audax K3695, K3711, K3696 and K3697 of No.16 (AC) Sqn Old Sarum, at Porton in 1937. SCI tanks can be seen on each aircraft, beneath the mainplane. K3697 was later to serve with the South African Air Force. Photo: Cty Graydon Carter

266

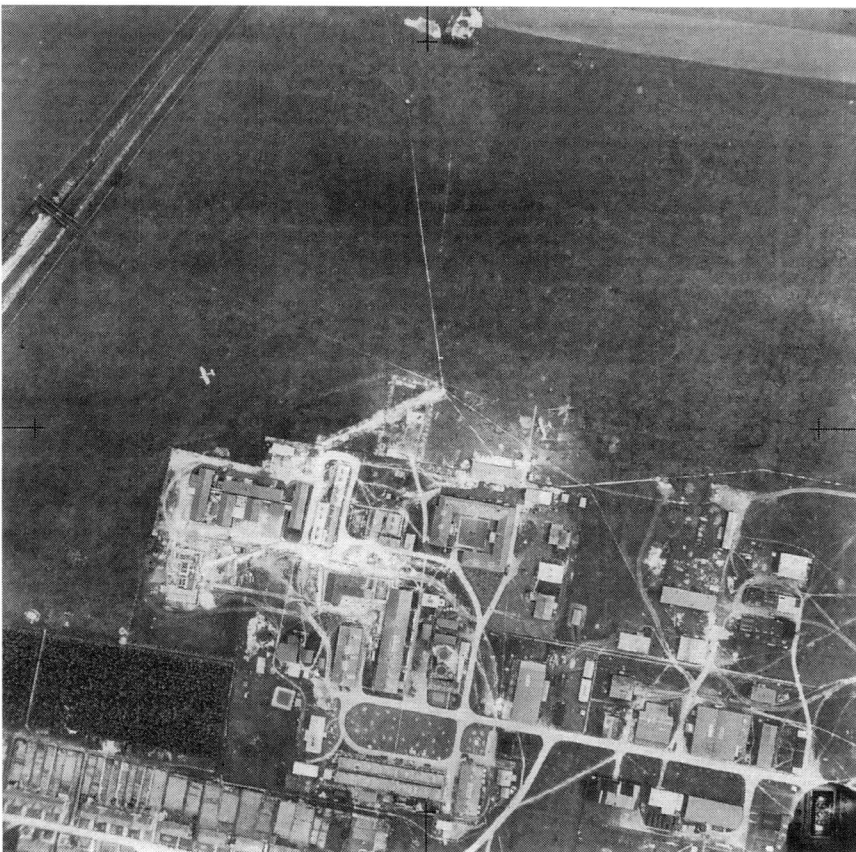

A pre-war aerial view showing an unidentified aircraft on the Porton landing area and another close to the buildings. The Southern Railway London to Salisbury line is seen in the top left hand corner. Photo: Cty Graydon Carter

Aircraft used by the SDF during 1938 were:- Lysander L4737, Hart (Special) K1999, Hart K1994, Hart K1995, Hind K6717, Hind L7217, Fury I K2904, Wellington L4226, Battle K7574, Whitley K4587 and K7216.

The RAF Anti-Gas School moved to nearby Rollestone from Uxbridge on 13th June 1939 and each of the courses culminated with the students being subjected to a series of low level bombing and spray attacks by aircraft using (SCI). Initially the aircraft were from the SDF at Boscombe Down. These were supplemented by aircraft from No.1 FTS Netheravon for a period, after the outbreak of war.

World War 2 Years

The SDF was absorbed by A&AEE at Boscombe Down following its move there from Martlesham Heath in September 1939. During the early months of the war, activity at Porton clearly increased in pace and intensity. It was in use by A&AEE for weapons trials until suitable ranges elsewhere in the area had been prepared for this purpose. Ashley Walk bombing range in the New Forest was one such site which came into use. A number of aircraft were allocated to the SDF when war broke out including Battles K7574, L5280, Wellingtons L4226, R2703 and 2 Lysanders L4737 and L4738. The latter served with the SDF for all of its life until struck off charge in July 1944. Lysander III T1501 was an SDF allocation when it stalled on landing at Porton and the undercarriage collapsed on 11th June 1941. It was being flown at the time by Wg Cdr C.V.J. Pratt who, 18 months later, was killed when mine-laying with a Wellington, in Tripoli Harbour.

On 18th January 1940, SDF Battle I K7574, was being flown from Boscombe Down by Flt Lt K.L. Ashford, on an exercise to attack a convoy of Army vehicles at Sherborne in Dorset. During the exercise the spraying container fell onto a truck and killed 3 soldiers. Flt Lt Ashford, by then a Sqn Ldr, was killed in a flying accident in Canada on 22nd September 1941. (Refer to **Boscombe Down Memorials**).

The CDES was responsible for various aspects of chemical warfare and smoke screen development in preparation for large-scale troop landings. It was demonstrated at Porton on 10th September 1941 for an audience of military personnel. A section for biological warfare was formed at Porton in 1940 and had the title Biological Dept, Porton (BDP), this became the Microbiological Research Dept (MRD) in 1946 and the Microbiological Research Establishment (MRE) in 1957.

Due to the close proximity to Boscombe Down, it was not surprising that Porton should receive unscheduled visitors. One such unfortunate occurrence took place on 21st April 1942 involving a Whitley V Z9158 NF-V of No.138 (Special Operations) Sqn based at Tempsford. It was returning from a leaflet drop in the St-Etienne region and was heading for a landing at Tangmere. A very thick mist developed and the pilot was

Wellington IA L4226 flying over Porton Down in 1939. The discharge pipe from the SCI mounted internally, is seen protruding from the fuselage.
Photo: © Crown Copyright 1939.

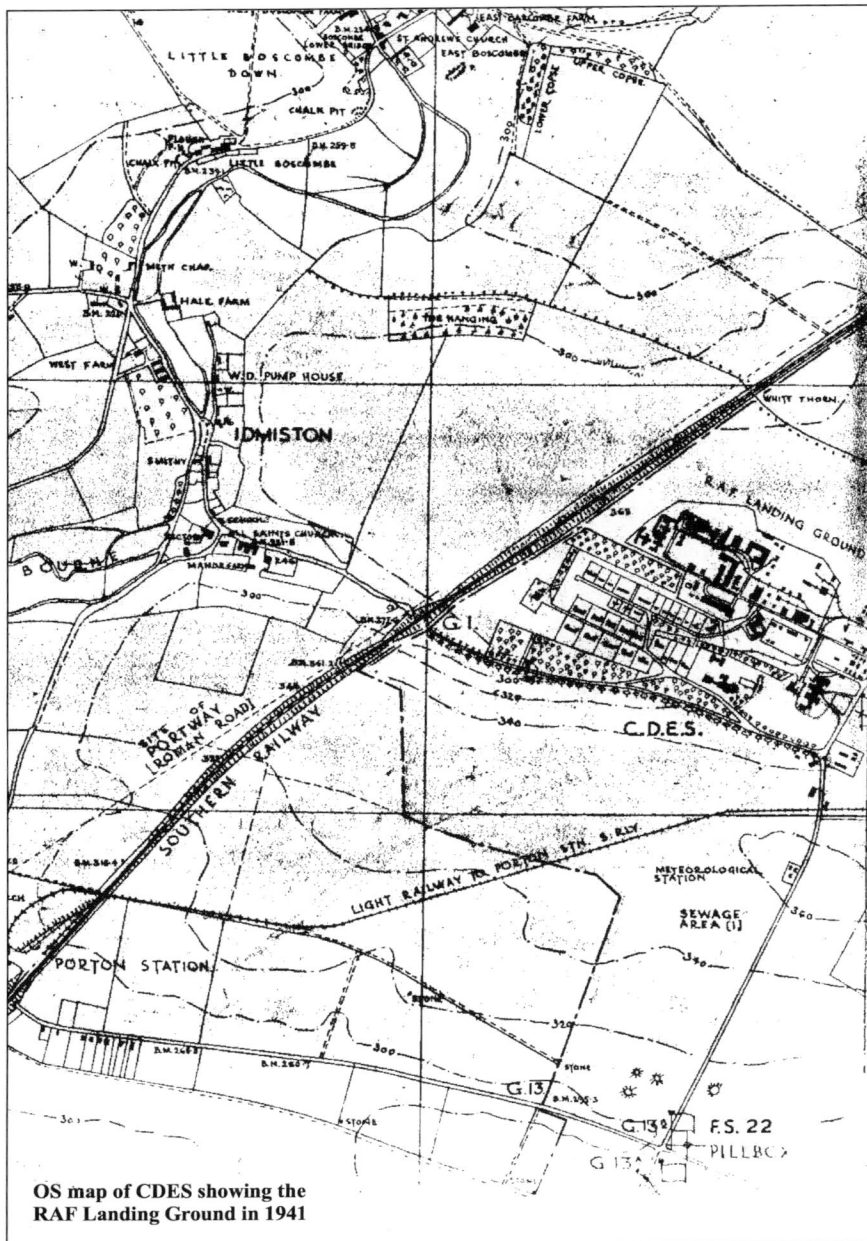

OS map of CDES showing the
RAF Landing Ground in 1941

On Friday 24th March 1944, Fg Off Denis Grundy RAFVR of the SDF carried out a smoke laying demonstration at Porton Range with Typhoon IB JR448. On completion the pilot commenced practice air attacks on a Boston of the same Flt. During one of the attacks, the Typhoon was seen to roll onto its back before diving into the ground, killing the pilot, 1 mile SW of Grateley village near Andover. No aircraft defects were discovered.

Post War Years

The SDF was disbanded in 1946 and thereafter aircraft for Porton were operated on an ad hoc basis by Boscombe Down.

1948 brought another title change with Porton becoming the Chemical Defence Experimental Establishment (CDEE).

Closure

The landing ground was no longer used to the extent that it had been but was retained until 1949. Aircraft, however, continued to land at the Establishment after the closure of the landing strip. During the 1950's, germ warfare scientists preparing for a possible Cold War attack on Britain by the Russians, carried out tests involving the release of zinc cadmium sulphate by aircraft flying over areas of the West Country. This was intended to simulate the spread of lethal nerve gases which it was thought the Russians were ready to use. The trials involved low concentrations of the compound used as an air movement tracer in meteorology. The experiments were aimed at seeing how vulnerable Britain was to biological attack and finding

ordered to land at Boscombe Down instead. On its approach it flew into the side of Battery Hill on Porton Down and caught fire. Four of the crew were killed, Plt Off Ivan A. Miller RCAF, Sgt Raymond F. Shaddick RAFVR (pilot), Flt Sgt Walter E.J. Lines RCAF (observer) and Sgt Sydney W.F. Leigh RAFVR (WOP/AG). Sgt K. Hubbard survived with injuries. On Sunday 31st May a No.297 Sqn Whitley V from Netheravon crashed at Porton and on 6th September a Stirling III R9309 from Boscombe Down, piloted by Flt Lt S. Reiss crashed on Porton Ridge following an uncontrollable engine fire. These last two incidents are detailed respectively, in the Netheravon and Boscombe Down sections of this book.

Wg Cdr H.J. Black was known to be the RAF Experimental Officer at Porton during 1943.

Auster J/5G Autocar G-ANVN/XJ941 seen here at Porton with apparatus fitted for insecticide research. The aircraft was attached to Boscombe Down from 14th February 1955 to 17th June 1957. Photo: Norman Parker Coll.

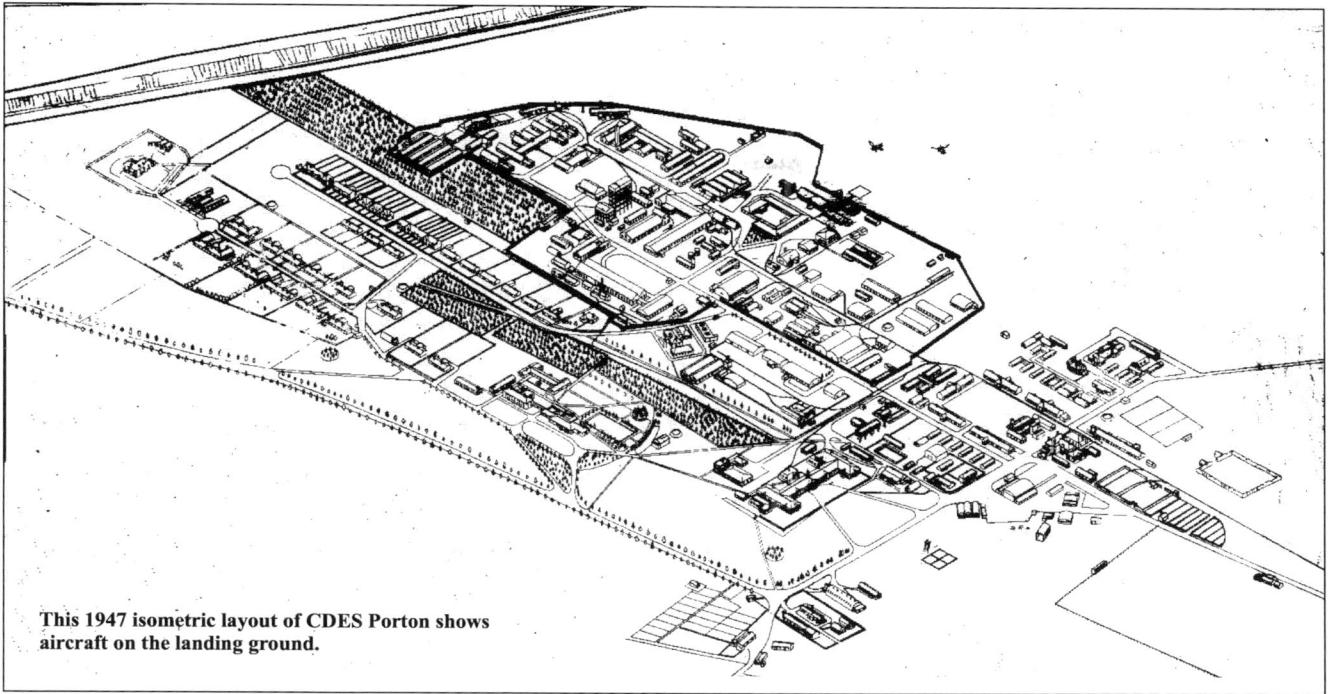

This 1947 isometric layout of CDES Porton shows aircraft on the landing ground.

ways to protect the country. A number of these trials were held, the first was in November 1953 when the chemical was sprayed from the airfield at Beaulieu. It was repeated there again in March 1954 and a month later at Porton. In May 1954, Yatesbury airfield was used and subsequently RAF Hullavington. In 1956 the Colonial Insecticide Research Unit tested chemical spray attachments using Auster Autocar G-ANVN/XJ941, prior to departing for defoliation trials in Malaya in 1956.

In 1964 Whirlwind 7 XG589 was attached to the CDEE and based at Boscombe Down, from whence it operated until it was withdrawn in 1971. The previous year Porton's title was shortened to that of the Chemical Defence Establishment (CDE).

During the 1960s Pat Barlow, a civilian employed at Porton, flew to work each day in his own private aircraft which he landed on Battery Hill.

All three of the armed forces had liaison officers attached to Porton Down where they had offices in the main HQ building. The RAF's serving officer from 1972 until retirement in 1978 was Wg Cdr Des Blake. He arrived from Wroughton following its closure as an RAF unit. He was supported by a 'Crewman' who initially was of WO rank, later reduced to the rank of Sgt. Des Blake had two aircraft at his disposal, both based at Boscombe Down. The Hawker Hunter he flew was attached to 'A' Sqn and the

Whirlwind helicopter with 'D' Sqn. The helicopter later changed to a Naval Wessex.

In March 1979, when the MRE closed, the then CDE became responsible for both chemical and biological defence. It was shortly after this that the RAF ceased to have a presence at Porton Down. Its title in 1991 became the Chemical and Biological Defence Establishment (CBDE) and from 1995 the Chemical and Biological Defence (CBD) Sector of the Defence Evaluation and Research Agency (DERA). In 2001 DERA split into two organisations: QinetiQ, a private company, and DSTL (Defence Science & Technology Laboratory), continuing as a MoD agency.

Porton Down remains in the minds of many, a place of some intrigue and mystery. As the 21st Century dawned, it again became the subject of some controversy. This involves the immediate post war use of National Servicemen for chemical trials. A police investigation is currently taking place.

Wg Cdr Des Blake flying Hunter XE601 whilst laying a water spray (to simulate a chemical discharge) over the ranges at CDE Porton Down in 1974.   Photo: Wg Cdr Des Blake

RAMSBURY AERODROME

Location - 174/SU278705 5 miles East of Marlborough

On the top of Spring Hill south of Ramsbury Village on the C194.

Aerodrome Development

The aerodrome at Ramsbury was initially developed for use as a satellite of Membury which was sited 3 miles to the north-east. The airfield was intended as a Bomber Command OTU and on completion came under the auspices of No.92 Group. Construction began in June 1941 when heavy earth moving equipment arrived to level the ground and remove trees. A number of roads were closed off in part, prior to this.

The Class 'A' aerodrome had three concrete and tarmac runways and a complete perimeter track. The runways were 08/26 NE/SW 3000 yds x 50 yds, 14/32 NW/SE 1100 yds x 50 yds and 02/20 N/S 1100 yds x 50 yds. Pan type hard standings were laid down, the majority of which were concrete and some of PSP. All were on the south side of the field leading from the perimeter track. The pan numbers had been extended before completion of the aerodrome, providing a total of 35 and 18 loop types. In early 1943 four additional loop type pans were constructed. Two T2 Type hangars were provided. The Control Tower was positioned between the Technical Site and the 02/20 runway. The station two-letter identification code was RY and the runway lighting was Drem Mk.II and gooseneck flares. The dispersed domestic accommodation was on the eastern side of the aerodrome and comprised 16 Sites. Locally the station was known as Rudge Airfield and still is by some local people in the area today. The name originates from the area in which Ramsbury airfield was situated.

World War 2 Years

By 1942 circumstances dictated that the site would not after all be required as an OTU and was allocated instead to the USAAF on 11th June 1942 for use by transport and observation squadrons. Not all the facilities had been completed by the time of occupation, but eventually 470 officers and 1,898

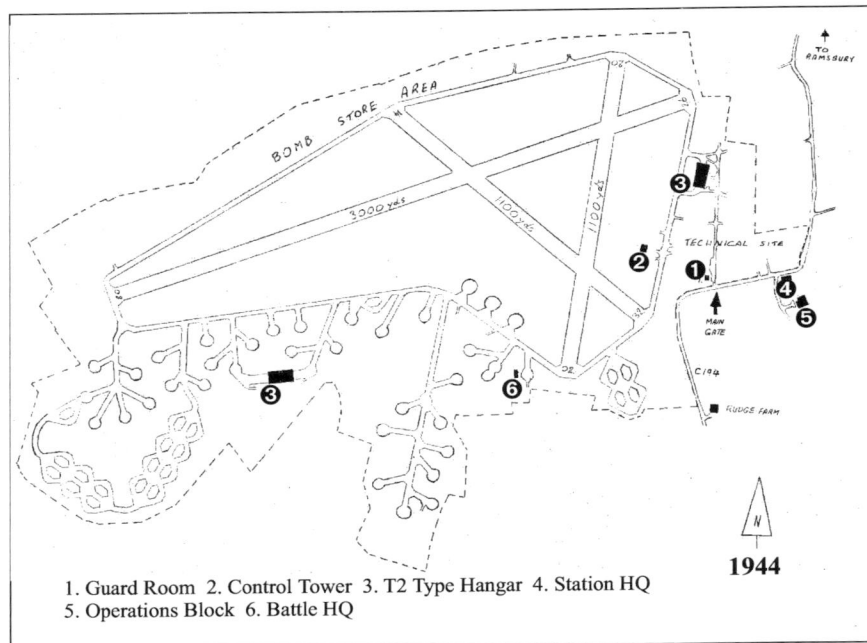

1. Guard Room 2. Control Tower 3. T2 Type Hangar 4. Station HQ
5. Operations Block 6. Battle HQ

1944

Oxford Is of No.15 (P) AFU Ramsbury dispersed at the west end of the airfield c. May/June 1943.
Photo: E. Berry/ Cty Andy Thomas

enlisted men were accommodated. The Americans began arriving on 18th August and consisted of elements of the 64th Troop Carrier Group of the 8th Air Force, commanded by Col Tracey K. Dorsett. The 16th, 17th, 18th and 35th Troop Carrier Sqns were equipped with C-47s and C-53s. The flightpath of the aircraft over the Atlantic Ocean was via the northern ferry route with Prestwick the initial destination. The aircraft left Prestwick for Ramsbury on 23rd August and on take off, one of the aircraft crashed into a Scottish hill with loss of lives.

Shortly after the arrival of the Americans, enemy bombs were dropped on the airfield without causing serious damage or injury.

The following three months were given over to a rigorous training detail leading up to the North African

invasion in November 1942. The 64th TCG became part of the 12th AF on 14th September. Their aircraft carrying paratroops, left for Gibraltar on 9th November. The 64th TCG flew its first mission two days later, landing paratroops at Maison Blanche. The American's role at Ramsbury mirrored that at Keevil where the 62nd TCG were based and were also preparing for Operation *Torch*. Both Groups came under the control of the 51st Troop Carrier Wing. The HQ was established in Bowdown House, a requisitioned mansion on the north east side of Greenham Common aerodrome.

With this, the first departure of the Americans from Ramsbury, the airfield was transferred to the RAF and used as a satellite of Andover in No.70 Group. No.15 (Pilots) Advanced Flying Unit moved into Andover on 15th December 1942 with one Flt arriving at Ramsbury

270

No.15 (P) AFU Oxford I N5946 with pilot Flt Sgt Noel Davis RAAF on an exercise flying from Ramsbury. 'Bill' Berry, who took this shot, and Noel Davis often took off in different aircraft and carried out unauthorised formation and low flying through the Thames Valley. Noel Davis was killed in 1954 when flying a RAAF Canberra which crashed near Brisbane.
Photo: E. Berry/Cty Roger Day

with its twin engine Oxford Is. The first batch of 25 pupil pilots for advanced training arrived on 5th January 1943. The instruction was for pilots who had recently qualified under the British Commonwealth Air Training Plan and who would progress to multi-engine aircraft.

The inevitable training accidents occurred with the first fatality on Tuesday 2nd March when Sgt Roy C.M. Webster RAAF, on a night solo flight in Oxford I V3335, struck trees when in the circuit and crashed. He was buried at Andover Cemetery.

Instructor WO Jack R.T. Hazelton DFM, RAFVR and his pupil Sgt Bryan G.G. Francis RAAF were killed near Standlake in Oxfordshire when their Oxford II AB725 crashed there on Sunday 21st March. Sgt Francis who was from Gooburrum in Queensland was buried at Ramsbury (Holy Cross) Church.

AC Bert Brothers who served with the unit M.T. Section at Ramsbury from April 1943 recalls two Anson Is being used as unit 'Hacks' for communication flights. One of these was N5262. He also remembers crashes involving the

Oxfords whilst they were being flown by the newly qualified pilots. A number of these pilots were killed and at one crash he attended when the aircraft had come down in a bog, it took two days to recover the bodies of the pilot and instructor. He recalls Oxfords colliding on the runway and in flight plus aircraft crashes in nearby Savernake Forest. On Thursday 27th May Sgt Peter R. S. Miller RNZAF was killed when his Oxford I V3949 collided with Oxford II ED136, and crashed close to the perimeter. He was buried at Andover Cemetery.

Sgt Kenneth W. Deacon RAAF (pilot) was killed on Monday 7th June when Oxford R6388 dived into the ground near Ramsbury. He was buried at Andover Cemetery. A mid-air collision occurred near Bishopstone, Salisbury on 25th June, between two Oxford Is V3955 and LX168, in which the crews were killed. A similar accident occurred on 20th July when two Oxford Is BG236 and HN721 collided in flight and crashed with three crew killed and one man injured. On Wednesday 25th August Sgt Leslie G. Leatherland RAFVR was killed when his Oxford crashed after taking off on a night solo and on Sunday 19th September Flt Sgt Rex Frith RAAF was killed in Oxford? HM907 which stalled on take-off. Flt Sgt Frith was buried at Brookwood Military Cemetery.

The airfield became busier after 26th July 1943 when other Flights of the Unit moved in from Grove. The number of WAAFs increased with some working in the M.T. Section. The public houses of nearby Ramsbury were popular with the RAF personnel and whilst the walk down the steep hill was no problem, the climb back up at the end of the evening was often a struggle. Bert recalls that one of the airmen on the station had been a cinema pianist before the war. On one occasion he was allowed to play on the organ in Ramsbury church. The organ had an air pump. The kind of music which he played required much pumping and this was not at all appreciated by the vicar at that time. The rumpus resulting from this impromptu performance by a 'boogie boy' had the RAF banned from the church.

On the night of 3rd/4th August 1943 a No.16 OTU Wellington III BJ585 crashed close to the airfield. It had

Ground crew including WAAFs outside the crew room in the summer of 1943. Those identified are:- back row 2nd from left, Sammy Fenton, 3rd from left *Swede* Barker, centre row far left, LAC 'Jimmy' James, 3rd from left, Norman Eighteen, 4th from left Penny Spencer.
Photo: Ivan Cooke/Cty. Roger Day.

Prior to the arrival at Ramsbury of the 437th TCG, the airfield was used for training by the 434th TCG Aldermaston and the 435th TCG Welford. This exercise with the 101st Airborne Division on 1st January 1944 had the C-47s releasing Horsa gliders onto the south side of the airfield
Photo: Don Neate Coll..

Excluding the crew chief T/Sgt George Montgomery, the crew of C-47 42-100806
L to R - Lt Floyd Kelly (pilot), Lt M.P. Brigance (co-pilot), Lt Joe Salisbury (nav), Sgt Don Bolce (Radio Op). Photo: Don Bolce/Cty Neil Stevens Wilts & Berks ETO Research Group.

taken off from Upper Heyford at 2206hrs on a night navigation flight. Almost three hours into the flight the starboard engine lost its oil and a priority landing at Ramsbury was requested. The pilot lost control during the approach and the aircraft crashed at 0106hrs onto nearby farmland. Sgt George Wilson RAFVR (pilot), Sgt Peter J. Charlier RAFVR (nav) and Plt Off Roderic W. Papineau RAFVR (B/A) were killed. Sgts L. Phillips (WOP) and S. J. Angus (AG) sustained injuries.

In September elements of the American 101st Airborne Division started arriving in the area in preparation for the invasion of Europe the following year. In October the airfield was transferred to the US 9th AF becoming USAAF Station No.469. On 4th November No.15 (P) AFU's Flts moved to Long Newnton, Babdown Farm and Castle Combe. AC Bert Brothers was one of five RAF men, commanded by a Flt Lt, who were left at Ramsbury to form the handing over party. A USAAF Station Complement Sqn arrived at the airfield on 1st November. Bert took the RAF transport to Hungerford railway station to collect the first contingent arriving from Southampton Docks. For the

RAF party the quality of the catering was much improved under the Americans and they were disappointed that they only had a few days to enjoy it before having to rejoin their unit.

Early American arrivals at Ramsbury were the 21st and 22nd Mobile Reclamation and Repair Sqns commanded respectively by Capt William J. Sweeney and Maj Myrle F. Lee. The function of a MR&RS was to recover and repair crashed aircraft. They were also capable of assembling, dismantling and servicing as necessary. The units stay at Ramsbury was brief but in this time they assembled a number of Waco gliders. Both the squadron's convoy of trucks, jeeps and trailers left for USAAF Station 803 Filton on 28th and 29th November 1943.

The air echelons of the 434th and 435th Troop Carrier Groups were based at USAAF Station 469 Ramsbury from December 1943 and in January 1944, taking part in exercises with the 101st Airborne Division.

The 437th TCG was formed at Donnelon in Florida on 1st May 1943 under the command of Col Cedric E. Hudgens a veteran of the North African Campaign. The Group, equipped with some 72 C-47s, comprised the 83rd, 84th, 85th and 86th Troop Carrier Sqns. These had identification markings respectively T2, Z8, 9O and 5K. The Group was part of the 53rd Troop Carrier Wing (TCW) of the 9th USAAF with HQ at Greenham Common.

Balderton airfield near Newark on Trent in Nottinghamshire was used as a reception centre for Skytrain (Dakota) TCGs arriving from America. The air echelon of the 437th TCG arrived with 64 C-47 Skytrains on 20th January 1944. Their arrival in the UK was via Central and South America, Ascension Island and North Africa. The crews remained at Balderton for a week before flying down to Ramsbury.

The sea echelon of the 437th TCG sailed from New York on the *Mauritania* and during the voyage were fortunate to be entertained by Jimmy Cagney the movie star, who was to tour England with a show. The ship berthed at Liverpool on 30th January 1944 after a ten-day passage. The troop train waiting at the dockside transported the men overnight to Hungerford, the closest railhead for Ramsbury. They were met at the railway station by the members of the air echelon, which had arrived in Ramsbury a few days earlier.

On arrival at the airfield in the early hours of the morning the men wasted no time in 'hitting the sack' after their tiring journey. The cold light of the following day brought with it something of a culture shock for the G.Is. They awoke to the barren interior of their sleeping accommodation and made their way to the unheated Mess Hall. Here they were given a breakfast of powdered eggs, salty bacon and coffee so bitter, it was thought that the medics had added something to it. The poor quality of the meal was only a temporary blip however as it was explained that the Quartermaster's Depot had been bombed two nights previously. The base had two Mess Halls, one for the enlisted men and one for the officers. The same food, however, was served in both places.

The next thing the Americans found lacking was adequate sanitary and bathing facilities. Some Nissen huts had an inside W.C. but generally it was necessary to use the strategically placed communal ones. These of course were unheated and had hard Government issue paper which most Yanks substituted with copies of *Stars and Stripes*. The lack of bath houses and especially hot water was the Americans greatest discomfort. They were used to using plenty of water and the arrival in England of so many Americans brought about a water shortage crisis. There was a period in the spring of 1944 when the use of water on the station at Ramsbury had to be curtailed. A concrete bathhouse had been built on the WAAF Site at Ramsbury. This had baths and showers but no heat or light and the glass in the windows had been broken before the arrival of the Americans. There were no duck-boards on the cold floors but despite all these discomforts the Americans used the facility without prolonging their ablutions. A boiler in a shed at the rear of the bathhouse heated the water. The boiler used coke but there was never enough allocated by the British for American needs. The men soon had a system in place for night raids on the coke store. This continued successfully for two months until British protests forced Colonel Hudgens into placing an armed guard on the fuel stock.

The group are all 85th Sqn Staff Sgt Radio Operators outside their Quonset hut No.19 at Ramsbury in 1944, with the sign they made for it "Ye Olde Station Attic".
rear LtoR - James L. Lyons, Lawrence Gordon, Lewis J. Shank, Ray Wisniewski, Don Bolce
front LtoR - Robert Oestreicher, Edward Goldstein, Edward J. Whalen, Robert Carter.
Photo: Don Bolce/Cty Neil Stevens Wilts & Berks ETO Research Group

The Red Cross hotels in London, Reading and Swindon were popular venues for the Americans for their hot water and baths, when they were off duty. Passes from the camp were available in the lead up to D-Day, subject to exigencies. Liberty runs were made down the hill to Ramsbury village, or to Swindon but London of course was their mecca. Each evening a convoy of trucks was assembled outside the Mess Hall for the enlisted men and would leave for Swindon following the evening meal. In Swindon the trucks from the various US bases in the area would form up at a park in the lower town area. The trucks were often from perhaps seven different locations. In the blackout conditions, and often the worse for drink, much confusion reigned when the convoys departed at 2300hrs. Many a G.I. found to his dismay that he arrived back at another unit's base instead of his own. G.Is failing to return to the park for departure time might, if they were lucky, find a taxi with sufficient fuel to get them back to Ramsbury. The fare could be anything from £2 upwards.

Dinner at the airfield was served to the Americans at 1730 hours. This meant there was then no food available until breakfast the next day. The Group soon overcame the problem by opening up an unused building near the four Squadron Operations huts and creating a Pilot's Lounge for the officers. This became known as Duffy's Tavern. It was furnished with easy chairs, tables, radio etc and in the entrance hall a snack bar was installed providing hot coffee and doughnuts. The Tavern was open around the clock and was particularly beneficial to crews on night flying. Pin-up pictures decorated the walls of the lounge. The Red Cross Club near the Mess Hall provided the enlisted men with the same night time facility.

Ramsbury village enjoyed the friendship and hospitality of the Americans who likewise were encouraged by the welcome they received. The public houses were frequently visited. The landlords' only regrets were that, because of rationing, they were unable to obtain sufficient quantities of 'warm' beer and spirits to supply the demand. Many of the Americans used the barber's shop in Ramsbury, where the owner's daughter as well as her father, cut the men's hair. Dances in the Memorial Hall were very popular, especially with the girls of the village. The children also found their friends could provide a constant source of exciting things to eat and to play with. The sick also benefitted from American drugs. One Unit on leaving Ramsbury, left behind a large supply of drugs for the use of the village, which were unobtainable in this country during the war. Whilst the Americans in this country were well equipped and their provisions considerably better than those of our own servicemen, they still experienced hardships. Jim Skidmore, who piloted his C-47 from Ramsbury on many of the missions to Europe, remembers well the experience of spending the coldest British winter in fifty years in unheated tin huts on the bleak hill-top site above Ramsbury.

The Group were soon engaged in concentrated training exercises involving glider towing and parachute drops. Formation flying at night was given priority as were pre-dawn take-offs and dawn glider landings. No actual night glider landings were staged at Ramsbury. Prior to some exercises it was necessary to send a weather aircraft up to find out if conditions were suitable. This was a duty not always appreciated as it was possible for conditions to deteriorate to such an extent during the flight that the aircraft could not land back at Ramsbury. It would then be directed to a base which might be many miles away. This happened on one occasion to Roy Sousley and his crew who then spent the next four days at Ford, West Sussex.

An element of the US 82nd Airborne Division trained with the Group. The objective was the forthcoming D-Day landings in Normandy. On some occasions the exercises would be simulated glider personnel towing. Sand bags in place of paratroops would be carried on board the gliders. The gliders in use were the British built Horsa and the American Waco CG-4A. The duration of training flights was generally around two hours. 50 or so C-47s would fly back over the airfield where between fifty to one hundred gliders would be released before almost silently making their landing. The landings would be followed by the return of the tugs still dragging the heavy nylon towing ropes. These were generally released on an area of grass near the Control Tower. When the drop was complete the glider mechanics would drive over in weapon carriers to collect up the ropes.

On Saturday 4th March 1944, the 437th TCG 84th Sqn lost a ship and crew at the end of a night time formation-flying exercises. This was C-47A 42-100586 with five men on board consisting of 1st Lt Lloyd L. Sloan (pilot), 2nd Lt Richard E. Clark (2nd pilot), Sgt Harold J. Pope (radio op), Pvt Harry S. Scott and Pfc Lawrence H. Ward (paratroopers). The aircraft was participating in a 49 aircraft formation carrying out a simulated paratroop mission. The formation was required to break up into 3 aircraft elements due to very bad weather conditions. The smaller elements were then dispersed to prevent casualties. Lt Sloan's element returned to the home aerodrome and entered the traffic pattern. His aircraft in the left wing position, when attempting to land passed over the field flying in a general south-westerly direction at an altitude of 950' indicated, 350' above the terrain. The element then broke formation to enter the landing pattern. It appears Lt Sloan continued on the same heading for around one minute past the boundaries of the regular traffic pattern. He then made a timed turn, which would normally bring him on the heading, which would approximate that of the runway then in use. He then descended hoping to pick up the lights of the field but due to the fact that he had swung wide on the traffic pattern, his final approach was south of the field. The swathe in the woods cut by the C-47 when it crashed indicated that the pilot was flying a south-westerly heading (that of the runway in use) and from the evidence in the wreckage it appeared that the landing gear was extended. Just prior to the crash the course of the aircraft had crossed open fields for a considerable distance, which as a result of the heavy snow squalls that evening were white with several inches of snow. This made judgement of height above ground difficult. The pilot, probably thinking that he was on his final approach leg, let down hoping to make contact with the ground, but was unable to judge his altitude in the bad visibility. The aircraft crashed into the trees at the end of the field. The crash occurred at 2130 hrs, 3 miles south of the airfield at Horsehall Hill Farm. The cause was determined as pilot error but with the bad weather conditions as an underlying cause. The other aircraft landed safely at Ramsbury, Membury and Welford.

A week later on Saturday 11th March

another C-47 crash claimed the lives of two 83rd TCS personnel, one of whom was the Sqn Cdr. This accident occurred when trying to retrieve a Horsa glider (LG891) from a field in nearby Axford. Details of this incident appear earlier in this book. Refer to **AXFORD**.

No.1426 (Enemy Aircraft) Flt served a five weeks attachment at Thorney Island, from 9th May to 15th June 1944, where it carried out recognition exercises over the invasion fleet off the South Coast. On 24th May, two of the aircraft in the Flt, an Fw 190 A-4/U8 and a Bf 110 were demonstrated at Ramsbury. The latter was the aircraft which shot down a Hart trainer in Old Sarum's circuit in July 1940 before being intercepted by Middle Wallop based No.238 Sqn Hurricanes and forced down at Goodwood. Following repair and evaluation at Farnborough, the Bf 110 joined the Enemy Aircraft Flt.

Although D-Day was obviously a well kept secret, the Americans at Ramsbury were well aware towards the end of May 1944 that the big day was close. On Monday 29th May the 85th TCS were sent to Membury on detached duty with the 436th TCG. It was from there that the Squadron operated on D-Day. The troops of the 82nd Airborne Division, who were to ride the gliders into France, moved up to Ramsbury on 1st June. They were under canvas in a field by the WAAF Site. They were self sufficient, providing their own field kitchens. Also from this date the airfield and off-field accommodation was sealed up and the perimeter patrolled by the Mobile Guard Unit and the Military Police. In addition an anti-aircraft unit arrived and was set up at various points around the airfield. It had been envisaged that the enemy would attack the aircraft on the ground if they learned of the imminent invasion.

A number of precise and very detailed briefings were held at which nothing was left to chance. Everybody heard and understood each others role in the great master plan and knew exactly the function they were given. The 82nd Airborne Division commanded by General James Gavin would drop and land on LZ 'O' near Ste Mere Eglise on the Cherbourg Peninsula. This was slightly inland from the beach code named *Utah* on which sea-borne landings would be made. The primary task was to take and hold the town and to secure bridgeheads over the River Merderet west of the town. On 3rd June the combat crews were marched from the secured WAAF Site to the airfield where they began the task of painting the black and white identification stripes on the tugs and the gliders.

With the mission cancelled the previous day because of unsuitable weather conditions, the Tannoy announcement at Ramsbury finally came at 2300 hrs on 5th June ordering all combat personnel to the flight line.

The invasion landings on 6th June were the first operational involvement for the 437th and the 82nd Airborne Division. Coded Operation 'Detroit', 52 C-47s towing the same number of Waco gliders, took off from runway 026 at Ramsbury between 0159 and 0223 hrs. On board the aircraft were 220 troops, 22 jeeps, 16 57mm Anti-tank guns, 5 trailers and 10 tons of supplies. The lead ship 42-20870 Feeble Eagle, had Col Hudgens and Lt Tom Rataiczak at the controls towing glider 42-46521 with Capt Will Evans and Flight Officer Ralph Toms (most of the glider pilots had the rank of Flight Officer). Following take-off from Ramsbury one of the tug aircraft lost its glider and returned to the airfield to take-off again with a reserve. Weather conditions on the approach to LZ 'O' were poor with impaired visibility. Dropping through the clouds seven gliders became detached from their tugs. Seven more gliders released prematurely and seeing this, a number of others followed suit. Despite this some 23 gliders landed on or close to the LZ. Thirty-four gliders were either badly damaged or destroyed, three of the paratroops were killed and some injured. Most of the cargo of howitzer guns and jeeps survived but there were some lost or damaged. Glider pilot Jim Larkin of the 84th TCS was over France when his tug aircraft dived violently to the right. The rope snapped and the C-47 piloted by Jack Lawson crashed, killing all on board. The operation was far from a success.

On return to Ramsbury, 26 of the C-47s were turned around in preparation for a follow-up mission to supply reinforcements. This was coded Operation Elmira. Owing to the number of gliders involved the operation had to be divided into two

M/Sgt Doyle Corley, a flight line chief with 85th Sqn, standing outside a hut in the 85th Sqn Enlisted Men's area. The trophies of war returned to Ramsbury from Europe are displayed.
Photo: Corley Family/Cty Neil Stevens Wilts & Berks ETO Research Group.

waves each of two serials. The 437th TCG's 18 Horsa and 8 Waco gliders from Ramsbury formed the first serial of the first wave. The second serial of the first wave was from Greenham Common with the 438th TCG. Take-off from Ramsbury commenced at 1907 hrs and all were airborne by 1921 hrs. The destination was LZ 'W' located one mile south of Ste Mere Eglise. Between the two serials 437 troops, 13 anti-tank guns, 64 vehicles and twenty-four and a half tons of supplies were carried. The formations were escorted over the Channel by American Mustang and Thunderbolt fighter aircraft, crossing the French coast over Utah beach. The northern section of LZ 'W' was still under German fire and, unknown to the incoming pilots, the LZ markers were placed two miles north-west of the zone. When the 437th TCG released the gliders only two landed on the LZ with twelve within one mile and the remainder within two. The operation was deemed a success although most of the gliders were destroyed or severely damaged and lives were lost, including those of glider pilots. Most of the vehicles, guns and equipment survived the heavy landings. The C-47 flown by Lt Emerson and Lt Gilbo and their crew was hit by flak and forced down. Four of the five-man crew suffered injuries but were back at Ramsbury a couple of days later.

The 437th operated again on D+1, code named Operation Galveston. It was

divided into two serials providing reinforcements for the 82nd Airborne Div. The first serial involved 32 Waco and 18 Horsa gliders towed by 50 tugs from Ramsbury where take-off commenced at 0439 hrs. The gliders held 717 troops of the 1st Battalion, 325th Glider Infantry Regiment, 17 vehicles, 9 guns and 20tons of equipment. The destination on this occasion was LZ 'E' a mile east of Marie-du-Mont. The second serial of 50 Waco gliders took-off from Aldermaston with the 434th TCG.

The weather conditions at the time of the dawn take-off were pretty foul. This affected one overloaded Horsa at Ramsbury which was unable to get off the ground. One of the Waco gliders also aborted over Dorset when its towrope broke. Despite encountering German fire over the coast of France the remainder arrived over the LZ. Most gliders cast off too early and didn't make the zone. During the landings ten Horsa gliders were destroyed and seven severely damaged as were many of the Waco type. This resulted in the deaths of 17 soldiers with 63 injured. Most of the troops, vehicles and equipment landed safely for what was then the most successful of the glider missions. Radio Operator Donald Bolce recalls his crew operating on each of the first three 437th TCG missions. The aircraft from this mission returned in formation and, led by Col Hudgens, 'beat up' the airfield at Ramsbury at around a height of 50' before landing. At a later date the 437th TCG were awarded a Distinguished Unit Citation (DUC) for its efforts during the D-Day period. Col Donald J. French took command of the unit from 12th June following the sudden death of Col Hudgens at Ramsbury.

There was one post D-Day mission embarked upon by the 437th TCG and that was to retrieve some of the Waco gliders dropped in Normandy. Capt Roy Sousley was sent to an LG at Ste Mere Eglise on 21st June to take charge of this glider pick-up operation. This was the method whereby the retrieving aircraft flew low over the glider, which was snatched from the ground using a hook under the aircraft fuselage, a winch, and a rope attached to the glider. It was found that most of the gliders had suffered too much damage and only 13 were successfully recovered for further use. On 25th June one of the 84th TCS C-47s crashed on a hill near Portland Bill en route to Ste Mere Eglise. Lt William Jenn an 84th Flight Leader and the winch operator were killed but the remainder of the crew on board survived.

A large detachment of the 437th TCG was sent to Italy on 16th July 1944 in preparation for Operation *Dragoon*, the August invasion of Southern France by the US 7th Army. The C-47s took off from Ramsbury around 1900 hrs, staging through Marrakech. The glider pilots remained at Ramsbury for a few extra days before half were sent to RAF St. Mawgan and the remainder split between Greenham Common and Welford. Thirteen glider pilots from each of the four squadrons of the 437th all eventually left for Italy on 4th August but were assigned to another Group for this operation. Their transportation to Italy was in Air Transport Command C-54 Skymasters staging through Casablanca.

The base of the 437th in Italy was Montalo airfield with a 3,500' dirt runway. Two simulated paratroop drops were carried out, but for the rest of the time personnel relaxed in the summer sun and visited nearby Rome. The invasion commenced on 15th August with the 437th having the role of dropping paratroops over the assault area. Each C-47 carried a stick of 18 paratroopers and slung under the aircraft were 6 parapacks. To the relief of the crews they experienced no flak as they crossed into France. The

paratroops were dropped at the DZ near Le Muy and the aircraft all returned to Italy. The aircraft were quickly turned around for a re-supply mission with take off at 1530 hrs. The same route was flown in the company of fighter and bomber aircraft. The drop was made and once more the aircraft returned to Italy. The glider pilots of the 437th were based at Grosseto near Rome and it was in Rome that their Waco gliders had been assembled. Jack Merrick, one of the glider pilots taking part in the invasion, felt that the landings were a disaster due to poor planning, poor briefing and the gliders being released at too a high an altitude. Over half the gliders were wrecked on landing with complete sticks of troops killed and injured. The 84th TCS lost one of their glider pilots, LeValley, who was killed when his glider struck a glider trap on landing. Overall the operation turned into a success when the US 7th Army linked with the 3rd in the north during early September. The 437th detachment returned to Ramsbury on 23rd August via Gibraltar. One C-47 crew who had loaded up with duty-free 'booze' at Gibraltar, unfortunately ran out of fuel on the return flight to the U.K. and had to ditch in the English Channel. Capt Thompson and Capt Patterson of the 85th TCS, together with their crew, spent a few hours in the water before being rescued. The glider pilots returned in ATC C-54s to St.Mawgan where vehicles were sent from Ramsbury to collect them. In the mean time they hitched a lift in some C-47s going to Welford.

Four aircraft from each squadron of the 437th was left behind when the detachment left for Italy. These were used to carry out re-supply missions to the advancing forces in France. They were joined at Ramsbury by a number of West Country based TCSs. The 93rd TCS from Station 462 Upottery operated from 7th-22nd August. The 98th TCS from Station 463 Exeter operated from 7th 23rd August. Three days after arriving the 98th dropped parapacks to an American infantry battalion which had become encircled at Mortain by the German Army who were attempting to launch a counter-offensive. The 301st TCS arrived from Station 464 Merryfield and flew shuttle flights in and out of France from 7th- 24th August. The 306th TCS from Station 447 Weston Zoyland also carried out transport supplies to France operating

out of Ramsbury from 7th- 24th August.

The US 17th Airborne Division based at nearby Chiseldon Camp, commenced training at Ramsbury airfield from the beginning of September 1944.

The next major operation involving the 437th TCG was Operation *Market*, the airborne invasion of Holland commencing on Sunday 17th September. Five days before this, units of the 101st Airborne Division had moved from their base near Hungerford to a tented camp at Ramsbury.

The task for the Airborne Forces, who were to be dropped first, was to seize a number of towns, canal and river bridges. They were followed by the glider borne forces who took-off on a bright clear morning at 1000 hrs with 70 Waco gliders in two serials, each towed by a C-47. On this operation the gliders only had one pilot as opposed to the two used for previous invasions. The gliders were carrying 311 troops of the US 101st Airborne Division's Signals Company, 326th Medical Company, Recce Platoon, British Phantom Signals Unit, 43 jeeps and 18 trailers. The destination was LZ'W' near Zon, north of Eindhoven. Some gliders failed to reach the LZ for various reasons but 53 successfully landed with 252 troops, 13 trailers and 32 jeeps. A number of C-47s received flak damage and 5 were shot down. This was the blackest day in the history of the 437th TCG. Some of those killed that day were Lt Col Ralph Lehr, CO of the 86th TCS, Calvin Gifford of the 84th, William Yaeger of the 85th, glider pilot Lloyd Shufflelberger, Bill Williams, John Burke, Charles Gilmore of the 83rd and Herman Dedloff. One of the seriously injured was Capt Hutchinson of the 83rd TCG.

On D+1 a re-supply mission was flown again to LZ'W' with take-off at 1120 hrs. The 437th were one of 6 TCGs in the 53rd TCW carrying 2,656 troops of the 327th Glider Infantry Regiment, the 326th Airborne Engineer Battalion and the 326th Airborne Medical Company in 450 Waco gliders. Also transported were 156 jeeps, 111 loaded trailers and a couple of bulldozers. The 437th provided a serial of 40 and 30 aircraft. One of the gliders ditched in the sea and four others aborted. Two C-47s received flak damage but all returned safely.

From this large re-supply mission over 50 lives were lost and there were a number of injuries. Only 5 jeeps and 2 trailers were lost. The operation was determined to be almost 100% successful.

Re-supply missions to provide reinforcements continued for a few more days. The 437th TCG was not involved in all of them and some were cancelled or restricted because of bad weather over England and Holland. Other TCGs operated from Ramsbury during this period. Two were near neighbours, the 435th from Station 474 Welford and the 436th from Station 466 Membury. The damage sustained by many of the aircraft of the 437th during the invasion of Holland was extensive. It took time for repairs to be completed and it became necessary to borrow aircraft from the Group at Exeter, so that a full complement could be used for the re-supply flights. Some of the British troops who fought their way back from the disaster that was Arnhem, arrived at Ramsbury on C-47s flown from Brussels.

After the Dutch operations the business of Ramsbury consisted of everyday flights by the C-47s, hauling tons of essential supplies to hastily constructed airstrips close behind the ever-advancing front line. On the return flights the aircraft, converted to flying ambulances, brought back wounded allied soldiers who had been evacuated from the battle zone. At Ramsbury with the 437th TCG was the 814th Air Evacuation Sqn who would provide flight nurses on each of these 'casevac' flights. They tended to the wounded during the flights back to Wiltshire. Having landed, a fleet of ambulances took the wounded to military hospitals. The closest to Ramsbury was the U.S 347th Station Hospital operating on Marlborough Common. On the Roll of Honour in Ramsbury Church is the name of 2nd Lt Jean V. Herco. She was a Flight Nurse with the 814th Air Evacuation Sqn who was killed in a C-47 crash in the 12th AF Area of Italy on 2nd February 1945. These operations really became a race against time in December 1944 during the period known as the 'Battle of the Bulge' when German forces began their surprise offensive through the Belgium Ardennes. C-47s were leaving Ramsbury loaded with fuel cans for Normandy where they landed on make-shift airstrips or on former Luftwaffe

One of the four C-109 tankers allocated to 437 TCG at Ramsbury, this one with 85th Sqn.
Photo: Don Bolce/Cty Neil Stevens Wilts & Berks ETO Research Group.

airfields which the Allies utilised after the Germans had earlier been pushed back. From there the fuel would be taken up to the front line by land transport. On return from these fuel drops these aircraft also brought back Army casualties. Towards the end of 1944 each squadron in the Group was assigned a C109 tanker (converted B-24 Liberators) for bulk carriage of fuel. Two crews from each of the TCSs were checked out on these gasoline carriers. It was not a popular assignment, as the likelihood of surviving an attack by enemy aircraft was obviously low. Although training with the C-109s was begun, they were never used operationally.

The glider pilots of the 437th who were not operating in the winter of 1944 attended advanced training at the 17th Airborne Camp at nearby Ogbourne St. George.

Security was reinforced by the USAAF at the airfield on 18th/19th November 1944 after receiving reports of a breakout from the German PoW camp in Devizes. Similar precautions were taken on Christmas Eve when it was suspected that the Germans might attempt a mass breakout and make their way to military establishments where they could inflict as much damage as possible before recapture.

One extremely foggy night in December an ATC C-47 arrived over Ramsbury. It had left France en route to an airfield near London. That airfield was closed because of fog which closed in most of the country. Short on fuel, the pilot was forced to land at Ramsbury. He gave his crew the option of jumping but they decided to stick with him. All possible aids to the pilot

were given at Ramsbury. He made several approaches on instruments but each time the engines were heard to power him back up to safety. After half an hour of this, the pilot made his last desperate attempt to land but off line of the runway the aircraft struck trees on the airfield perimeter and crashed. There was no fire but all the crew were killed.

The heavy blanket of fog had lifted by 23rd December 1944 and the 437th were able to take off on Operation Repulse. On the 16th December Hitler ordered a large counter-attack in the Ardennes in which his troops planned to break through the Allied lines and reach their supply port at Antwerp. The German Army initially made rapid gains before reaching Bastogne where by the 20th December they had it completely encircled. Holed up there was US 101st Airborne Division. Heavy fighting took place but the Germans could not break the defence. The Americans however suffered many casualties and were in need of medical teams and all forms of supplies. On the 22nd December the Germans sent two officers to Bastogne under a white flag and they called upon the American General McAuliffe to surrender. He told them 'Nuts' which they didn't understand but the explanation 'Go to Hell' conveyed adequately his reply. At around noon the following day the first of the 437th TCG C-47s were dropping supplies at Bastogne. They received a warm reception from the Germans who subjected them to flak and small arms fire. The 85th Sqn lost one plane which was shot down. The fate of the crew is not known, other than that of Elgan Davis who became a PoW.

On Christmas Eve the planes again

took off from the snow covered Ramsbury airfield bound for Bastogne with more supplies. The weather deteriorated on the way back from Belgium and some aircraft had to land at French airfields. The remainder of the Flight arrived back at Ramsbury in the evening and were turned around in preparation for operations the following day. The crews woke up to thick fog again on Christmas morning. This held throughout the day and prevented all flying. Visibility improved on Boxing Day and by 1000 hrs the C-47s were lifting off from Ramsbury's runway 026 and heading out to Bastogne for the last time before the tanks of the US 4th Armoured Division broke through to relieve Bastogne that evening. Supplies continued to be ferried in by C-47s and gliders of the US 9th Troop Carrier Command up until the Battle of the Bulge ended on 18th January 1945.

Radio Operator Lew Shank had been moved over to Europe following the Normandy landings and was pleased when he was returned to Ramsbury just in time to enjoy a 1944 English Christmas dinner with 'Queenie' Paul of Clifton Street, Swindon. He met her at a dance and they were married five days after the war ended. She was one of the very first G.I. Brides to arrive in America, having sailed in the *Queen Mary*. Her arrival in the U.S. was many weeks after Lew's own homecoming. He recalls the flight made in a clapped-out C-47 that struggled to stay in the air. During the flight the crew had to throw out anything they could to reduce weight and assist the aircraft to maintain height. Unfortunately the COs tunic jacket with his dollar stuffed wallet was accidentally included. Line Mechanic Forrester 'Bud' Quick was another of the 437th who returned to the States after the war with an English bride. 'Bud' had met her when riding a bike to the neighbouring village of Chilton Foliat.

By February 1945 the front line in Europe had extended to such an extent that to be effective in a re-supply role, it was necessary for the 437th TCG to move to the continent in its entirety. On the first day on which the weather was suitable for flying, the advanced echelon of the 437th left Ramsbury for

Sgt Don Bolce with an 85th Sqn ship, probably 42-100806, displaying its mission symbols. Photo: Don Bolce/Cty Neil Stevens Wilts & Berks ETO Research Group.

A-58 Coulommiers/Voisins in France. The new base was made up of tented accommodation and the responsibility of the advance echelon had been to erect these, arrange catering needs and tend to all the other services that would be necessary. It took over a week to transfer everything on the 437th's inventory at Ramsbury. By 25th February the move had been completed, with the entire Group established in France. There were occasions when the C-47s were taken away from the transfer runs to carry out re-supply operations.

The airfield at Ramsbury was not entirely vacated by USAAF. It was retained in reserve with a number of Americans still attached. During the occupancy by the USAAF a number of visiting aircraft seen at the airfield included B-25 Mitchells, B-26 Martin Marauders, P-51B Mustangs and P-47 Thunderbolts.

With the end of the war in Europe the airfield again came under the control of RAF Andover although the Americans were still on site. They actually moved out on 11th June 1945, Ramsbury having transferred to No.4 Group Transport Command on the 8th June. No.1336 Conversion Unit in No.4 Group, formed at nearby Welford on 20th June and ten days later was using Ramsbury as a satellite. The Unit had the brief to train crews in glider towing, paratroop and supply dropping as part

of *Tiger Force*, the invasion of Japan. The aircraft used were Dakotas with Horsa gliders. On 15th September, 'F' Sqn of No.1 Wing, Glider Pilot Regiment moved in and occupied one of the dispersed sites. On the same day Wg Cdr Meharg AFC was appointed Stn Cdr. Another arrival on 29th October was No.22 Glider Pick-up Training Unit from Ibsley. This Unit, which had earlier operated from Zeals, was equipped with 5 Dakota C3s and 5 Hadrian gliders. It was training pilots to pick up stationary gliders using a hook and snatch wire. Training commenced but, as a result of VJ Day, this unit disbanded on 15th November 1945. The redesignated No.1336 Transport Conversion Unit at Welford, stopped using Ramsbury from 20th December 1945.

Post War Years

The airfield was briefly placed on C&M until the 22nd January 1946 when it was transferred to No.23 Group Flying Training Command. 'F' Flt of No.7 Flying Instructors School, Upavon, under the command of Flt Lt Green, moved in equipped with Oxfords for night flying training.

No.1537 Beam Approach Training Flt affiliated to No.7 FIS (A) also used the facility at this time. 'F' Flt returned to Upavon on 29th March and the airfield allocation ceased on 2nd May when it again reverting to C&M.

The last Stn Cdr at Ramsbury was Sqn Ldr Couzens AFC appointed on 24th February 1946.

Closure

Ramsbury remained as an inactive site for a period of time, parented to Welford and Yatesbury. It was then returned to agriculture with Darrell's Farm buildings constructed at the intersection of the two short runways.

A section of the main runway survives as does a large part of the perimeter track which is now in use for farm roads. When the airfield was built, the Ramsbury to Great Bedwyn road was closed when part of it was used to form the perimeter track in the south corner of the airfield. After final closure the road was reinstated. Other visible signs of the airfield are the Operations Block in a private garden, the fire tender shed

The Fire Tender Shed and Romney type huts still in use for farming at Ramsbury.

2) 174/SU274716

The 437th Troop Carrier Group in conjunction with The Wilts & Berks E.T.O. Research Group staged a service of dedication and unveiling of a Roll of Honour at Holy Cross Church, Ramsbury on Sunday 7th May 2000. The Roll of Honour made of Nabresina stone is positioned immediately beneath the above memorial on the north west wall and commemorates personnel who gave their lives during World War 2 whilst serving with the 437th TCG, 53rd TCW, 9th USAAF. Canon Henry Pearson, Rural Dean, St. Mary's Marlborough conducted the service. The Roll of Honour names was read by Forrester A. 'Bud' Quick of the 86th Sqn, 437th TCG Association and the Commemorative Address was given by Col Dennis Kaan 437th Air Wing, USAF, Charleston SC, USA. Former Ramsbury based G.Is and members of the Parachute Regiment attended the ceremony which culminated in a fly past by the RAF Battle of Britain Memorial Flight's C-47 Dakota. The Roll of Honour reads:-

which would have been near to the Control Tower and three Romney type huts on the former Technical Site. The two T2 Type hangars were taken down in 1954 and the Control Tower, although having signs of dereliction, was still standing in 1963 but is thought to have been demolished not long afterwards.

Memorials

1) 174/SU274716 - 5 miles East of Marlborough

In the village church of Holy Cross on the C6. On the north west wall, a memorial tablet of Nabresina stone, unveiled on 20th May 1978 and dedicated to the 437th Troop Carrier Group, United States 9th Air Force. It was at a 1977 reunion of the Group held in St. Louis, that the idea of the memorial was promoted. It was code named 'Operation Kennetside' with its aim being a lasting memorial to their fallen comrades and to record the friendship shown by the people of Ramsbury during the period from January 1944 to February 1945 when the Americans occupied Ramsbury Airfield. The project was co-ordinated by Forrester A. "Bud" Quick of the 86th

Sqn, 437th TCG Association/ Superintendent of Maintenance for National Airlines, Heathrow and the Vicar of Ramsbury, Canon John T. Davies. "Bud" Quick had served as a Line Mechanic with the 437th during its wartime deployment at Ramsbury. The dedication of the memorial tablet was conducted by the Right Reverend John Neale, Bishop of Ramsbury and was attended by some 40 veterans of the 437th together with local dignitaries and parishioners. The memorial tablet bears the crest of the Group at the head and the inscription beneath reads:

DEDICATED TO THE MEMORY OF THOSE
MEMBERS OF THE 437TH TROOP
CARRIER GROUP
9TH AIR FORCE UNITED STATES AIR
FORCE
WHO GAVE THEIR LIVES IN WORLD
WAR 11

ERECTED AS A TOKEN OF THANKS
FOR THE FRIENDSHIP OF THE PEOPLE
OF THE RAMSBURY AREA
JANUARY 1944 TO FEBRUARY 1945

```
THE MEMBERS OF THE 437th TROOP CARRIER GROUP
       WHO LOST THEIR LIVES IN WORLD WAR 11

   HERMAN ALEXANDER            HORACE F. LEAMAN
   RICHARD V. BOLAN            RALPH E. LEHR
   DONALD E. BRADLEY           CHARLES J. LEVANDOSKI
   ROBERT BREWER               ADRIAN R. LOVING
   HOWARD C. BREWSTER          FERDINAND W. LUICK
   FREDERICK V. BROSSARD       HENRY S. MARANZ
   JOHN E. BURKE               GEORGE F. McELHANEY
   WILLIAM J. BURNS            JOSEPH MELEKY
   SAUL BUSH                   RICHARD C. MERCER
   EARL W. CLARK               WARREN R. MILLER
   HERMAN H. DEDLOFF           EARL C. NORDGREN
   VIC DEERE                   FRANCIS J. PAUL
   GUY L. DIFALCO              NICK PEHOTE
   THOMAS G. DOWNS             EDWARD J. PETERSON, JR.
   EDWARD C. FAMBROUGH         MARSHALL H. PITTMAN
   JACOB FASSE                 HAROLD T. POPE
   FORREST C. FISHER           ROBERT J. POWERS
   SAMUEL FLEMING              ROBERT C. REGAN
   WILLIAM S. FROLLI, JR.      JAMES B. RICE
   FRANK W, GIANNOBULE         AGAPIT ROSADA-RIVERA
   BRYCE C. GIBSON, JR.        LLOYD R. SHUFFELBERGER
   CALVIN A. GIFFORD           BENJAMIN SIANO
   CHARLES GILMORE             LLOYD L. SLOAN
   WILLIAM F. GOLDEN           THOMAS E. STEWART
   DONALD W. HANDIGARD         GAYLORD W. STRONG
   ROBERT T. HATCHER           CARSON SYRUSS, JR.
   JEAN V. HERKO               HARVEY THACKER
   FRITZ P. HRANILOVICH        ROBERT THOMAS
   WILLIS R. HUCKLEBERRY       ELDRED TRACHTA
   CEDRIC E. HUDGENS           PHILLIP F. UHLENBROCK
   WILLIAM C. JENN             ALEXANDER WARDEN
   ELMER J. KIEL               SAMUEL C. WELCH
   JAMES A. KINTNER            RAYMOND P. WISNIEWSKI
   CHARLES R. KITTLE           WILLIAM B. WILLIAMS
   FLOYD K. KULLER             FRANCIS J. WOLFE
   RALPH E. LAVALLE            WILLIAM C. YAEGER
   JACK A. LAWSON
```

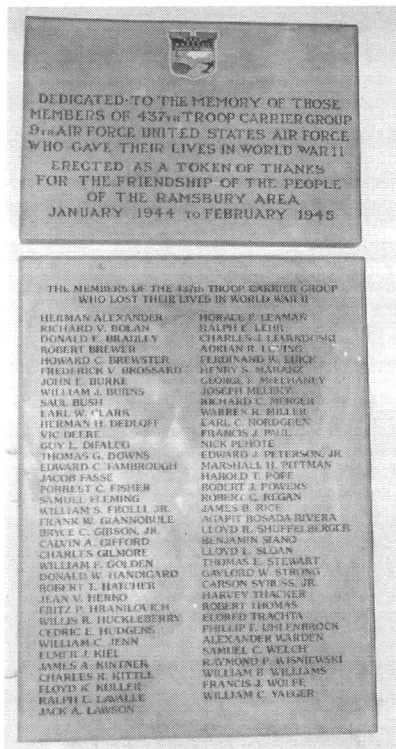

The 437th Troop Carrier Group Memorial Tablet and Roll of Honour in Holy Cross Church, Ramsbury.

3) 174/SU277716   5 miles East of Marlborough

On the C6, in the centre of the village square two benches are positioned beneath a tree. On the rear of each bench is a brass plaque with the inscription:-

```
        DONATED BY THE YANKS
   OF 437TH TROOP CARRIER GROUP
  STATIONED ON THE HILL  1944 - 1945
```

The two benches in the square in Ramsbury.

ROLLESTONE CAMP

Location 184/SU095450 4 miles North West of Amesbury

On the north side of the B3086 (London Road) Shrewton to Larkhill road with the main entrance on the west side of an unclassified road (originally the Salisbury to Devizes coach road).

World War 1 Years

Rollestone had a World War 1 association with flying when the RFC took over an initial 50 acres of land west of Rollestone Bake Farm on which to establish a balloon school. No.1 Balloon School moved there from Manston in July 1916 to train personnel in the use of observation balloons. The Army's Rollestone Camp (Larkhill) was then on the east side of the unclassified road leading to the Bustard Hotel and eventually to Devizes. The army camp was served by the Larkhill Military Railway, a branch of which went south from the camp to Stonehenge and Lake Down aerodromes. In 1916 the Balloon School also had an 'outstation' at Tilshead.

By the end of the war the Balloon School was using 180 acres of land at Rollestone. There were 155 Instructional Staff, with students averaging 25 officers and 120 men. The School came under the RAF as from its formation on 1st April 1918.

Inter War Years

In 1919 the Balloon School was re-designated No.1 Balloon Training Centre. On 16th March 1920 it became the School of Balloon Training and from 12th April was in No.22 Group. The balloons generally used were 2 Type 'R' of 35,000ft capacity. They were housed in two Bessoneaux hangars which were not very stable on windy Salisbury Plain. The hangars were eventually replaced in 1932 by a coupled balloon shed of metal construction. Each shed measured approximately 40'x 105' x 40' in height to the top of the roof ridge. Next to the sheds was a small wood known as Rollestone Clump. Part of the eastern perimeter was planted in the form of the letter 'E'. It is believed that this was laid out so that balloons could be moored in

The Gamma II on the Ranges at Larkhill and close to Rollestone.
Photo: Rex Reynolds Coll.

A balloon launch in front of the Bessoneaux hangars at Rollestone c.1930.
Photo: Sqn Ldr 'Peggy' Gordon/Cty Dr. H.F. Thomas.

the spaces between the trees forming the horizontal bars of the letter. This gave some protection from the winds and additionally iron rings were sunk into concrete bases to which mooring cables could be attached. A smaller Kite Balloon Shed (Nissen Hangar) was built towards the rear and north of the main sheds.

From 1925 the RAF School of Balloon Training was mainly concerned with the observation of artillery fire which was practised in conjunction with the School of Artillery at Larkhill. Training was given to Battery Commanders, Gunners and young officers of the Army. The artillery consisted of two batteries of 9.2" and two of 8" howitzers known as the Hamilton Battery firing from

permanently fixed position and served by a tramway carrying ammunition. Observation was from balloons or aircraft. When balloons were in use, communication between the basket and the ground was by telephone, the line running down the balloon cable. The balloons were raised and lowered using a winch mounted on a lorry. The lorry used was a Peerless in 1933. When aeroplanes were used, and these were generally Bristol Bulldogs or Westland Wallaces, communication was by radio. The machines would fly a figure of eight, passing over the target area and the batteries were positioned at the top and bottom of the loops. The order to fire was given when the aircraft were approaching the intersection of the figure of eight and flying at around 90 m.p.h.

In this picture, in front of the new balloon sheds at Rollestone, a Kite Balloon is being prepared for launch and is being steadied by three guy cables on one side. The lorry which appears to be a Leyland CMM 110, provides hydrogen gas from the high pressure gas bottles it is carrying, with which to inflate the 19,000 cu.ft. capacity balloon. Photo: Rex Reynolds Coll.

The RAF Balloon Centre was formed at Rollestone on 3rd November 1931 from the School of Balloon Training. Until 1931 the former military hospital at nearby Fargo had been in use as married quarters for officers. The RAF Station was another of those in Wiltshire opened to the general public on 30th June 1934 for Empire Air Day. Visitors were able to see balloon handling from the ground, training methods and the transferring of kite balloons across country. A Research Department Flight had been formed within the RAE at Farnborough to conduct impact experiments with Barrage Balloon cables. Kite Balloons were made at Cardington and after trials there in May 1935, three were shipped to Rollestone for use by a Balloon Barrage Flt which had been formed there. A Wellington bomber was used at Rollestone to carry out tests with wing mounted balloon cable cutting apparatus. On 1st November 1936 No.2 Balloon Training Unit (BTU) was formed at Rollestone, ex RAF Balloon Centre, in No.24 Group, Training Command. The CO was Sqn Ldr E.G.C. Stokes. The training courses were of six months duration and involved inflating and handling of balloons, cable maintenance and driving.

Increasing emphasis was placed on the use of barrage balloons therefor a Balloon Command was formed in London on 1st November 1938, under the command of AVM O. T. Boyd OBE, MC, AFC. Until that time all balloon operations had been under the control of Fighter Command.

No.2 BTU remained at Rollestone until

it moved to Cardington on 1st February 1939. Rollestone Camp was then further developed in the area of the coupled balloon sheds on the west side of the unclassified road to Tilshead, and occupied by the RAF Anti-Gas School.

The camp buildings were a mixture of timber, galvanised-iron, concrete, temporary brick and Nissen construction. The provision was similar to most RAF establishments with a Station Headquarters, messing facilities, quarters and barrack blocks for officers, sergeants, airmen and WAAFs, plus the usual support buildings and facilities. In addition, because of the specialist training, there was a gas defence centre, decontamination enclosures, gas equipment store, gas chambers and a decontamination boiling plant.

ROLLESTONE LANDING GROUND

Location - 184/SU088439 4 miles North West of Amesbury

On the south side of the B3086 (London Road) from the village of Shrewton to Larkhill.

Airfield Development

Southwest of Rollestone Camp, this 2500 x 500 yd LG at Middle Farm had a NE/SW 1800 yd. grass landing strip. The two-letter station identification code for Rollestone was RZ. The land was requisitioned in September 1939 following the arrival of the RAF Anti-

Gas School at Rollestone Camp in June 1939. It was in use by aircraft involved in simulated gas attacks. The site was not provided with any buildings and the 'Manby Screen' was the only structural development.

The 'Manby Screen' was assembled on the landing ground at Rollestone in late 1939. The site became known locally as 'Screen Field'. The screen was transferred from RAF Manby where it had been used for trials. The object had been to ascertain whether or not a pilot could land and take-off a fully laden aircraft in the lee of the screen in a steady crosswind of up to approximately 30 mph. It was thought the screen would solve the problem of providing an all weather landing ground in places where only a strip of land was available for a single runway. In particular it was thought an adaptation of the screen may, if the principle was found to be successful, make it possible to improve the situation at Gibraltar where such a condition existed.

The 500yard long screen consisted of a steel framework with a 50' high vertical screen. The screen had a steel frame covered with expanding metal sheeting. The trials were conducted by the CFS and it was thought a few landings and take-offs using a fighter, medium and heavy bomber would be sufficient to prove the object of the exercise. A Westland Wallace, Harrow, Battle, Blenheim and Whitley were used at Manby. The experiments however were incomplete when war broke out and with Manby needed for operational use, the screen was moved to Rollestone where it was extended to 1000 yds. in length and the landing surface was upgraded. The aircraft types used to continue the trials were a Tutor, Miles Master and Hurricane. The trials were successfully completed in June 1940 by which time it had been decided that a provision at Gibraltar would not go ahead but it would go to Scatsta in Shetland, or Newquay where facilities for operational fighter squadrons were required. This did not materialise however, and the entire scheme was dropped. It appears it was not required by any Command and by November 1941 demolition of the screen at Rollestone was complete. The post positions were still visible in 1946.

The screen at Manby on 18th February 1938 where trials were initially carried out before continuing at Rollestone LG after the outbreak of World War 2. Photo: PRO

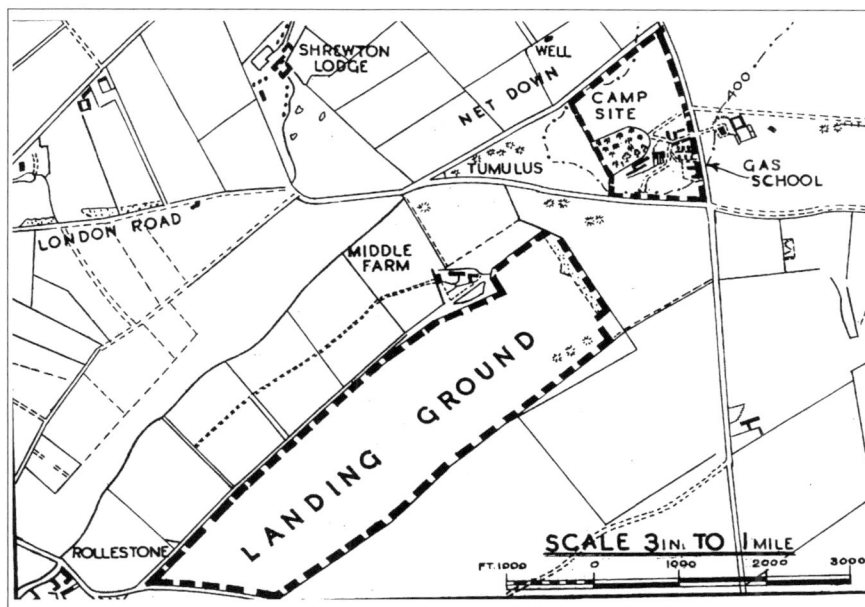

World War 2 Years

On 13th June 1939 the RAF Anti-Gas School in No.24 (T) Group moved to Rollestone Camp from No.1 RAF Depot, Uxbridge. Training was provided throughout wartime and was given to specialist RAF personnel. The School opened with 2 officers, 1 WO and 4 airmen. Sqn Ldr D.V. Irvins took command of the station with Flt Lt A.T. Hughes as Chief Instructor. It is assumed that the need for a LG on site was necessary following commencement of the early courses.

The first three-week course was titled 'No.5 Anti-Gas Course' and commenced on 4th July. It culminated in a series of low level bombing and spray attacks from SDF Boscombe Down based aircraft. Following the declaration of war courses were reduced to 10 days and re-titled with

the current course becoming 'No.1 Anti-Gas (War) Course'. Aircraft used for the low-level exercises were from the SDF Boscombe Down, C.D.E.S. Porton, No.1 S of AC Old Sarum, and No.1 FTS Netheravon. The latter also used the Rollestone LG for night flying.

Flt Lt T.C. Chamberlain with an A/Sqn Ldr rank was appointed CO of the School on 13th May 1940. A number of WAAFs joined the School when it opened and they were inspected in March 1941 by HRH The Duchess of Gloucester. At 0040hrs on 12th May a German aircraft dropped incendiary and H.E. bombs on the Landing Ground with a stick of 8 bombs falling near the perimeter of the camp itself. No serious damage resulted. The enemy was engaged by No.2 machine gun post which reported hits on the aircraft.

On 8th January 1942, the Station was visited by HRH Air Commodore The Duke of Kent. The Station CO was promoted to Wg Cdr rank on 23rd February. From July Rollestone Camp was used for various other training and maintenance courses i.e. Officers Refresher, Junior Instructors, RAF Regiment and Short USAAF Instructors Courses. US Liaison aircraft are believed to have used Rollestone LG and it was possibly at the time of these courses.

On 23rd October 1943 a tragic accident occurred during an exercise involving, in this instance, the Army School of Chemical Warfare. A Westland Lysander I R2613 of 'C' Flt Armament Testing Sqn at Boscombe Down, flown by Fg Off D. Grundy, was carrying out a low-level spray attack exercise over the troops on Porton Ranges when an electrical fault developed. This resulting in the apparatus, which dispensed the spray, falling from the mountings of the aircraft killing 2 soldiers Bdr H.Wood, Bdr M.McCann and 5 women of the Auxiliary Territorial Service (ATS) CSM D.I. Morrhall, Sgt J. Marshall, Cpl C.M. Reynolds, L/Cpl M. Croft and L/Cpl L.J. Kulke. There were also injuries to 5 ATS women, 1 soldier and 2 Canadian Women's Army Corps (WAC) personnel. The spraying of troops with simulated gas continues on Porton Ranges to this day.

The Glider Pilot Exercise Unit based at Thruxton disbanded into an Operational and Refresher Training Unit from 9th December 1943. The Unit used Rollestone as one of its LGs for light glider flights until at least the autumn of 1944. It enabled trained glider pilots to maintain efficiency and provided flying training on Tiger Moths for glider pilots, based at nearby Fargo Camp, who were waiting to attend Heavy Glider Conversion Unit courses.

From 17th February 1944 No.43 OTU at Oatlands Hill used the Rollestone Camp accommodation to augment their own inadequate facilities.

Post War Years

The RAF Anti-Gas School operated from Rollestone throughout the war but moved out to Sutton-on-Hull on 12th October 1945. No.657 (AOP) Sqn arrived four days later ex- B.A.O.R.

A view of Rollestone Camp from the air on 25th September 1945. The balloon sheds can be seen close to the small wood. At the rear of these is an unidentified aircraft which presumably arrived there having passed through the restricted space between the hangars. Photo: NMRO

Defence and Field Services. An internal floor has been added to provide an upper-storey and the sheds have been reclad externally, but the original internal framework remains. A large roller-shutter door has been added in the north side. The new opening was provided in 1983 when the original sliding doors on the front of the sheds were removed and replaced by fixed panels. The aircraft hangar has also been modified to include an upper floor of offices. A number of iron rings from the balloon days can still be seen in the ground near the buildings.

and was accommodated as a Lodger Unit. The squadron equipped with Austers, remained until 25th January 1946 when it moved to Andover. Rollestone was then put on C&M.

used as a civilian prison for most of the period between November 1980 and December 1981. Its use as such was again mooted in 1996 but was not implemented. From the late 1970s until 1984 Short Brothers Air Services Ltd

The renovated former balloon sheds and aircraft hangar at Rollestone. One of the camp buildings is just visible at the front left.

Closure

RAF Rollestone was closed on 25th July 1946 and transferred to the Army. Postwar, flying by fixed wing army aircraft has taken place at Rollestone. This was from a landing strip (184/SU096454) opposite the camp buildings on the eastern side of the old coach road to Devizes.

Rollestone Camp has had a number of uses since its time as a RAF Station. During 1967/68 army ammunition was stored there whilst Fargo Ammunition Compound was being rebuilt on the south side of the road to Larkhill. It was

operated at Rollestone Camp repairing, servicing and storing MATS-B target drones. Some of the drones were used on nearby Larkhill Ranges.

The camp is now called Rollestone Army Training Centre and continues to be used by the Army, providing useful accommodation for units visiting the Plain for training purposes. The huts are in good condition, the camp looking much as it did when the war ended in 1945. The original LG has long since returned to farmland. The balloon sheds have been sold by the MoD and are now used by SERCO

1) In Salisbury Cathedral, west of the A354 Salisbury By-Pass. On the north wall, a stained glass memorial window dedicated to the 551 men of the Glider Pilot Regiment, the RAF and the RAAF lost on glider operations during World War 2. The window, created by Henry Stammers, was unveiled by Field Marshal Lord Alanbrooke on 9th December 1950. Beneath the window is a brass plaque with the inscription: -

> THE STAINED GLASS WINDOW ABOVE
> IS THE MEMORIAL TO
> THE MEN OF THE GLIDER PILOT
> REGIMENT WHO DIED
> BETWEEN 1943 - 45. THE REGIMENT WAS
> THE FORERUNNER
> OF THE ARMY AIR CORPS WHICH WAS
> FORMED IN 1957.

At the foot of the memorial window is the following epitaph: -

See that ye hold fast the heritage that we leave you -
Yea, and teach your children that never in the coming centuries may their hearts fail or their hands grow weak.

The names of the dead are listed in a Book of Remembrance.

The Glider Pilot Regiment stained glass window with the brass plaque on the wall above a wreath.

2) On the same wall of the Cathedral is another stained glass window dedicated to the people of Salisbury who were killed during World War 2 and among the figures depicted on the window is an airman in flying kit. The inscription in glass on the base of the window reads: -

> To the
> memory of those from this city
> who gave their lives in the World
> War of 1939-1945 and whose names
> are recorded in the Chapel of St Michael
> in this Cathedral, this window is
> placed here by the citizens of Salisbury
> A.D. 1949.

The stained glass window dedicated to the people of Salisbury.

184/SU145302 Salisbury City Centre

3) In Salisbury's Royal British Legion Club, Endless Street. A memorial gallery to Wiltshire's Victoria Cross recipients. This particular memorial was instigated by Francis Rynn ex - Royal Navy. He felt that insufficient recognition had been given in the county to these men and decided to re-dress the balance. The memorial was unveiled on 10th July 1996 by Mrs Sara Jones CBE, widow of Lieutenant Colonel 'H' Jones VC, OBE who was killed in action at Darwin in the Falkland Islands, 28th May 1982. The Reverend Wg Cdr Jack Leeming conducted the dedication which was also attended by Lt Gen Sir Maurice Johnston KCB, OBE, Lord Lieutenant of Wiltshire. Two of the twelve named on the memorial are RAF men, Sgt Thomas Gray VC of No.12 Sqn and Flt Lt James Brindley Nicolson VC of No.249 Sqn.

Thomas Gray was born in Urchfont, near Devizes on 17th May 1914. He was the fourth of seven sons, five of whom served with the RAF, four as aircraft apprentices at Halton and of the five three died whilst on flying duties. Following education at Warminster County Secondary School, he enlisted in the RAF as an aircraft apprentice (563627) of the 20th (Halton) Entry on 27th August 1929 and trained for the next three years to become an aero engine fitter (F.A.E). On qualifying from Halton in August 1932 he joined No.40 Sqn servicing the unit's Fairey Gordon bombers at Upper Heyford and Abingdon. During this time he volunteered for 'part-time' flying duties as an airgunner. This was an aircrew category usually filled at that time by ground tradesmen on a volunteer basis additional to their normal duties and which carried with it the attraction of extra 'flying' pay for those who qualified as gunners. Tom became totally absorbed with his aim of becoming full time aircrew and this dedication soon obtained him the qualified air gunner's sleeve badge of a brass 'winged' bullet. In 1933 he passed his qualifying trade tests for upgrading to Leading Aircraftman and in June 1934 joined the re-formed No.15 Sqn at Abingdon, on promotion to Leading Aircraftman. He returned to Halton for a conversion course to Fitter 1 before joining No.58 Sqn at Driffield, where he was able to fly as a 'part-time' gunner in Vickers Virginia heavy bombers. He later transferred to No.51 Sqn at Driffield, when on the 15th March 1937, it was reformed from 'B' Flt. of No.58 Sqn. On 24th March 1937, No.51 Sqn moved to Boscombe Down where Tom and his younger brother Reg both served with the squadron, Tom in 'A' Flight on Ansons and Reg in 'B' Flight on Virginias. In February 1938 Tom joined No.12 Sqn at Andover on promotion to Corporal. That year he trained at No.1 Air Observer's School at North Coates Fitties qualifying as an aircrew Observer and was promoted to Sgt in January 1939. No.12 Sqn was equipped with Fairey Battles at the outbreak of war and the squadron left for Berry-au-Bac in France on 2nd September with Tom serving in 'B' Flt. For the first eight months, a period referred to as the 'Phoney War', the squadron received little operational experience but then with the German's rapid thrust into France, the situation changed overnight. On 10th May 1940 No.12 Sqn, stationed then at Amifontaine, carried out a low-level raid and from this four of the five Fairey Battles deployed failed to return. On 12th May No.12 Sqn's CO asked for volunteers to take part in action against the two bridges at Vroenhoven and Veldwezelt which spanned the Albert Canal. Both were heavily fortified. Five crews were selected by drawing lots and split into two sections, one to each target. Tom Gray was the Observer/Navigator with pilot Fg Off Donald Edward Garland and reargunner LAC Lawrence Royston Reynolds in Fairey Battle P2204. PH-K. They were detailed to lead 'B' Section in attacking the Veldwezelt bridge over the Albert Canal. This was Tom Gray's first bombing sortie. Hurricanes of No.1 Sqn based at Berry-au-Bac, were sent ahead to provide protection for the bomber force but they became fully committed when engaged by Messerschmitts over the target and so little help was afforded the Battles. The three aircraft of 'B' Section, led by Garland, approached the bridge at the lowest practicable altitude where they were confronted with extremely heavy anti-aircraft fire and attack from a large number of enemy aircraft. Fairey Battle L5439 PH-N, flown by Plt Off I.A. McIntosh was hit in the main petrol tank and caught fire. The bomb load was jettisoned before making a force landing and the crew captured. Fg Off Garland released his bombs onto the bridge but his aircraft was hit and crashed. The aircraft of Sgt pilot Fred Marland L5227 PH-J was damaged by heavy enemy fire but managed to drop his bombs on the target before plunging into the ground. There were no survivors from either aircraft.

The memorial gallery to Wiltshire's VC recipients.
Photo: Francis Rynn

The bodies of Fg Off Garland and his crew were recovered by local civilians and buried in a secret grave to prevent them being claimed by the enemy. After the war they were re-interred in the cemetery at Haverlee. Fg Off Donald Garland and Sgt Tom Gray were posthumously awarded the Victoria Cross but unreasonably the third member of the crew LAC Lawrence Reynolds failed to receive any type of recognition. These VCs were the first awarded to RAF personnel during World War 2. The two awards appeared in the London Gazette dated 11th June 1940 and the citation read in part: -

'Much of the success of this vital operation must be attributed to... the coolness and resource of Sergeant Gray who navigated Flying Officer Garland's aircraft under most difficult conditions in such a manner that the whole formation was able to successfully attack the target in spite of subsequent heavy losses.'

The Victoria Cross was presented to Sergeant Gray's parents at an investiture in Buckingham Palace held on 24th June 1941.

Sgt. Thomas Gray being one of the 'Trenchard Brats' of RAF Halton and the only one from thousands who passed out to receive the VC, is commemorated on that Station by the Thomas Gray Centre. On 12th May 1990, fifty years to the day and hour of their deaths, a ceremony took place at the present Veldwezelt bridge in Belgium to mark the event and a memorial was dedicated to the three man crew. The RAF Ensign flew above the stone and the ceremony was attended by former members of No.12 Sqn.

James Brindley Nicolson - (refer to) - **BOSCOMBE DOWN**

SHREWTON RLG

Location - 184/SU084464 - 1 mile North of Shrewton

This RLG was reached from an unclassified road between Tilshead and Rollestone Camp at the junction of the B3086. The main entrance was ½ mile west of the Bustard Hotel at the junction of the road and a straight unmade road leading to Shrewton village. The Bustard Hotel is the former Officers' Mess of No.3 Sqn formed in May 1912 from No. 2 (Aeroplane) Company Air Battalian RE based on Larkhill Airfield.

Airfield Development

The original intention was for No.3 School of Army Co-operation to form at Shrewton in 1940. This did not materialise, therefore the airfield came into operation on 27th July 1940 as an RLG for No.1 SFTS Netheravon, which was operating the Hawker Hind, Hart, Audax, Battle and Harvard. The grass landing strips in this large field were N/S 1200yds, NE/SW 1400yds, E/W 1000yds and SE/NW 650yds. Night-time landing facilities were provided by a permanent flare path party for training and emergency landings. Gooseneck flares were used for this purpose and a Chance light at the touch-down end of the flare-path. The two-letter station identification code was RE.

On 21st December 1942 Shrewton was handed over to the Air Ministry Works Directorate and the following day work commenced at Shrewton to develop the site. Laing's constructed some timber barracks and a mess block in a field outside the north end of the airfield. Three standard blister hangars were built on the airfield on the north eastern boundary. The airfield reopened as an ELG on 24th March 1943.

World War 2 Years

When Shrewton opened for use by No.1 SFTS many of the pupils on the training courses at the time were naval personnel of the FAA. A fair number of these were to lose their lives flying from this field.

During night flying on 19th August 1940, a 'Purple' air raid warning was received and flying ceased. At 2350 hrs

13 bombs were dropped approximately 500yds to the left and parallel to the flare path. At 0032 hrs 5 bombs were dropped approximately 450yds behind the flare path. No damage was done to the landing ground. A similar incident occurred a week later when two salvos of incendiary bombs were dropped 450yds from the flare path and again no damage was sustained.

Shrewton RLG was obviously a popular target as, during night flying training on 7th April 1941, 31 bombs were dropped 200yds from the flare path by a German bomber. It also attacked with machine gun fire, injuring flying instructor Fg Off T.F. Byrne. Seven nights later the enemy visited again, dropping 5 bombs. No serious damage was inflicted from either raid but the same was not the case on 12th May when, during night flying, an HE 111K attacked from around 1000' dropping a stick of 250lb and 500lb HE and numerous incendiary bombs. The same machine made a second pass along the flare path dropping further bombs of the same type. A taxiing Battle was hit and burnt out and the occupant of the front cockpit, pupil W.K. Stewart received injuries from bomb fragments. The landing ground was unserviceable until the bomb craters were filled in the following day.

No.1 SFTS Fairy Battles were using the circuit at Shrewton regularly in 1941 for night flying. Battle I P6673 crashed there on approach at night on 1st January, crew details unknown. On 12th April, Hind I K6644 of No.1 FTS crashed on landing. Acting LA Grant Ryalls RN and Acting LA Frederick Andrew RN both of HMS *Daedalus* were killed in Hind L7205 when it spun into the ground near Shrewton LG on Saturday 26th July when returning to Netheravon from night flying. Acting LA Douglas C. Stewart RN of HMS *Daedalus* was killed when, flying solo in a Master III W8500, it crashed on the boundary of the LG on Wednesday 27th August. Plt Off Arthur J. T. Boddam-Whetham RAFVR 'C' Flt. Instructor, who had been posted to the School from CFS five days previously, was killed on Saturday 25th October together with Acting LA Ronald K.

Brooks RN of HMS *Daedalus*. Their Battle struck a tree when coming into land, turned onto its back and caught fire. Plt Off Boddam-Whetham was buried in Netheravon All Saints Churchyard. Acting LA R.G. Hallas was seriously injured and Acting LA Sydney H. Tyson RN of HMS *Daedalus* was killed when their respective Battles collided in the air during night flying from Shrewton on Wednesday 12th November. Acting LA Desmond Henshaw RN of HMS *Daedalus* was killed on Monday 15th December when he lost control of his machine whilst night flying. Sub Lt Douglas G. Tompkins RNR of HMS *Daedalus* was killed during night flying when he crashed with a suspected engine fault on Wednesday 14th January 1942. Flt Lt Norman Stone AFC, RAuxAF was killed when his Master W8777 crashed with cause unknown on Wednesday 25th February 1942.

Army Co-operation units were also using the field during 1941 and Lysanders of No.16 Sqn detached at Tilshead from Weston Zoyland and those of No.225 Sqn also based at Tilshead, frequently exercised with the Army at Shrewton. In July 1941 No.225 Sqn were required to operate from Shrewton whilst work was carried out at their Tilshead base.

The Army Air Corps was formed on 21st December 1941. The Glider Regiment, to become the Glider Pilot Regiment, was formally established in Army orders on 24th February 1942, having formed the previous month. Lt Col John F. Rock was appointed Commanding Officer of the 1st Battalion of the GPR but, not being a pilot himself, on 2nd January 1942 he joined the first party of 40 officers and men attending No.16 EFTS where he gained his Army 'wings'. The 1st Battalion was based in huts on the airfield at Shrewton. Lt Col Rock was killed as a result of a night flying accident in a Hotspur glider at Shrewton in October 1942. The glider towrope broke in flight and Lt Col Rock tried to land in total darkness. In doing so the glider struck a pole and its ballast load of sandbags broke loose on impact, crushing him and his co-pilot.

The Colonel died of his injuries in a military hospital on Thursday 8th October and is buried at Tidworth Military Cemetery. Major Chatterton, CO of the 2nd Battalion of the GPR at Tilshead, was then appointed, and he was followed later by Lt Col Iain Murray.

Following the formation of the Glider Pilot Regiment and the expansion of the airborne forces, Shrewton became a landing practice ground for the gliders. The Glider Exercise Sqn formed at Ringway and was re-designated as No.296 Sqn on 25th January 1942, moving to Netheravon on 1st February. The squadron was equipped with Hector and Hart tug aircraft and Hotspur gliders and was the main user of Shrewton after No.1 SFTS disbanded in March 1942. The Heavy Glider Conversion Unit in No.70 Group formed at Shrewton on 1st July from a nucleus supplied by Nos. 2, 3, & 6 (P) AFUs. It transferred to No.23 Group Flying Training Command as from 10th July. The unit was equipped with Whitley tugs and Horsa gliders but before these aircraft arrived, it was transferred to Brize Norton on 15th July when it was realised that Shrewton was not suitable. On 12th August 1942 the Glider Pilot Exercise Unit formed at Netheravon to provide periodic refresher training and flying practice for pilots of the Army Glider Pilot Regiment. From 8th October to 16th December 1942, when the Unit left for Chilbolton, Shrewton was used as a satellite by the GPEU. Hectors and Hotspurs carried out night flying. Two RAF pilots, Sgt's David I. M. Allan RAFVR and Robert G.B. Harrison RAFVR were killed on Saturday 5th December when Tiger Moth DE527 in which they were flying crashed. Sgt Allan is buried at Netheravon Cemetery, Figheldean.

No.43 OTU formed on 1st October 1942 in No.70 Group, Army Co-operation Command at Larkhill, its brief was to train air observation post pilots and observers using the ranges on Salisbury Plain. Shrewton was used by 'A' Flt. for a short period from 15th - 19th November and then left for Old Sarum. The site was then closed. Following its redevelopment, it was used by the Army for practising with Horsa gliders. The Army Co-operation Command was disbanded on 1st June 1943 with the airfield being transferred first to Fighter Command and then as

An aerial view of Shrewton taken by the Americans on 24th December 1943. The Domestic Site, Blister hangars and some aircraft are seen bottom left.   Photo: NMRO

an RLG to No.38 Group HQ - Marks Hall. The GPEU based at Thruxton started using Shrewton again as a satellite with their Tiger Moths from 29th September to November 1943. The Tiger Moth Flt moved into Shrewton from Thruxton on 15th October 1943.

The Operational & Refresher Training Unit (ORTU) was formed on 9th December 1943 absorbing the GPEU. The Unit enabled trained glider pilots to maintain flying efficiency and to provide flying training on Tiger Moths for glider pilots waiting for HGCU courses. These pilots were based at Fargo Camp, which was located between Larkhill and Shrewton. The Unit used Shrewton for light glider flights using Masters and Hotspurs.
A&AEE used the airfield in January 1944 for ground firing of rocket projectiles. The tailplane and elevator of Firebrand TF.1 DK367 was damaged by the rocket blast during one of the tests late in the month.

The ORTU transferred to Hampstead Norris on 1st March 1944, with a detachment of the Tiger Moth Flt posted at Shrewton from 1st April until 1st November, when the Flt was disbanded.

Post War Years

When the war ended Shrewton was placed on Care & Maintenance and controlled briefly by Netheravon until closure of the site in April 1946. The

field itself was kept as an ELG for a number of years and during that time was also used as an ALG by A&AEE Boscombe Down for armament trials. The field was soon returned to agricultural use and the only sign of its former role is some foundations and the concrete at the main entrance gate in the NE corner. Outside the entrance gate on the opposite side of the lane a pill-box remains in the area close to the original domestic site.

SOUTH MARSTON AERODROME

Location - 173/SU181888 3 miles North East of Swindon

East of the A361 Swindon to Highworth road between Stratton St. Margaret and South Marston village.

Land at South Marston was chosen to be one of a number of places in the country for locating a 'shadow factory'. The Miles Master training aircraft was being built in large numbers at the factory of Phillips & Powis Aircraft Ltd, Woodley near Reading. When the factory was unable to keep up with demand, the decision was taken by the Air Ministry to aid production by opening a 'shadow factory' near Swindon. It had the advantages of being reasonably close to the Woodley Plant, and the Swindon GWR Works was able to supply some of the skilled labour that was necessary to produce aircraft components. These in the main were from the Carriage & Wagon Works and they became aircraft fitters who were also able to utilise their skills as carpenters.

This c. 1952/53 scene shows the camouflaged Vickers buildings and bottom right, one end of the railway station, with the path from the works leading to it. Two Hillman Minx, a Ford V8 Pilot and an Austin Cambridge are amongst the cars parked in front of the offices.

Aerodrome/Factory Development

The contract to construct the factory and airfield was awarded to Spears of London & Glasgow who commenced the work in early 1940. The GWR had a branch line from the railway station in Swindon to Highworth, a village some two and half miles north of the proposed factory. Whilst the airfield site was being levelled, a cutting was made in which a 1,750' spur was laid from the Highworth Branch line so that materials and subsequently factory workers, could be brought by train direct to the site. The short length of line was officially the South Marston Factory Siding but later was commonly known as the 'Vickers Branch'. The line opened on 29th June 1941 and it is thought to have received Government funding. At its junction with the Highworth Branch a signal box opened on 17th February 1942 to replace the ground frame. The line passed under a bridge carrying the A361 road and a station was built near the terminus end of the 'Vickers Branch'. This comprised a 250' platform with a flat roofed building forming a Waiting Room and Booking Office. It is believed that the Office was never used. Just before the

platform, the single line divided into three parallel sidings which served the passenger station, the weighbridge, the loading bay and boiler house. A private path from the factory was used by the workers catching the train.

Early construction concentrated on the main assembly shop which was to be considerable in size but was reduced when the Air Ministry decided that it would present too much of a target for enemy bombers. By the time this decision was taken much of the assembly shop framework was in position. Two thirds of the steelwork was dismantled, divided into two sections and used for building an aircraft assembly shop two miles away at Blunsdon. The other half went one mile north of the airfield to Sevenhampton, where another assembly shop was built. It was later at Blunsdon that the dispersed production of Stirling bomber fuselages took place and at Sevenhampton where they were fitted out.

Phillips & Powis staff from the Woodley works were drafted to South Marston whilst construction of the factory was still in progress. They were to ensure that production of the Miles Master Mk.I could begin as soon as was practicable. Towards the end of 1940 this had become reality and from

a moving assembly line, the first aircraft was rolled-out for delivery to the RAF on 13th March 1941. Later in the year, when the supply of Bristol Mercury engines improved, production of the Mk.II commenced with delivery of the first of these on 6th October. Production of the Mk.I ceased in 1942 with the last one being delivered on 25th September. At this time the first employees began to be taken over by Vickers Armstrong Supermarine, and were transferred to work on the Mk.IIs which were now being assembled in the main flight shed. The last Mk.II was delivered on 26th March 1943. Phillips & Powis had a test pilot based at South Marston, this was Ken Waller who was later superceded by Hugh Kennedy. He would fly to Swindon from Woodley in the works 'hack', a Miles Sparrowhawk U-0223, to test fly the new aircraft as and when required. ATA pilots were used to deliver the Masters to MUs or Training Schools around the country. Ann Welch did this on 1st and 7th September 1941 when she delivered N8626 to Brize Norton and W8568 to Ternhill respectively. These pilots were flown to factories in an assortment of different aircraft. One such, Puss Moth AX870 of Temporary Ferry Pilots's Pool, crashed on landing at South Marston on 18th June 1941.

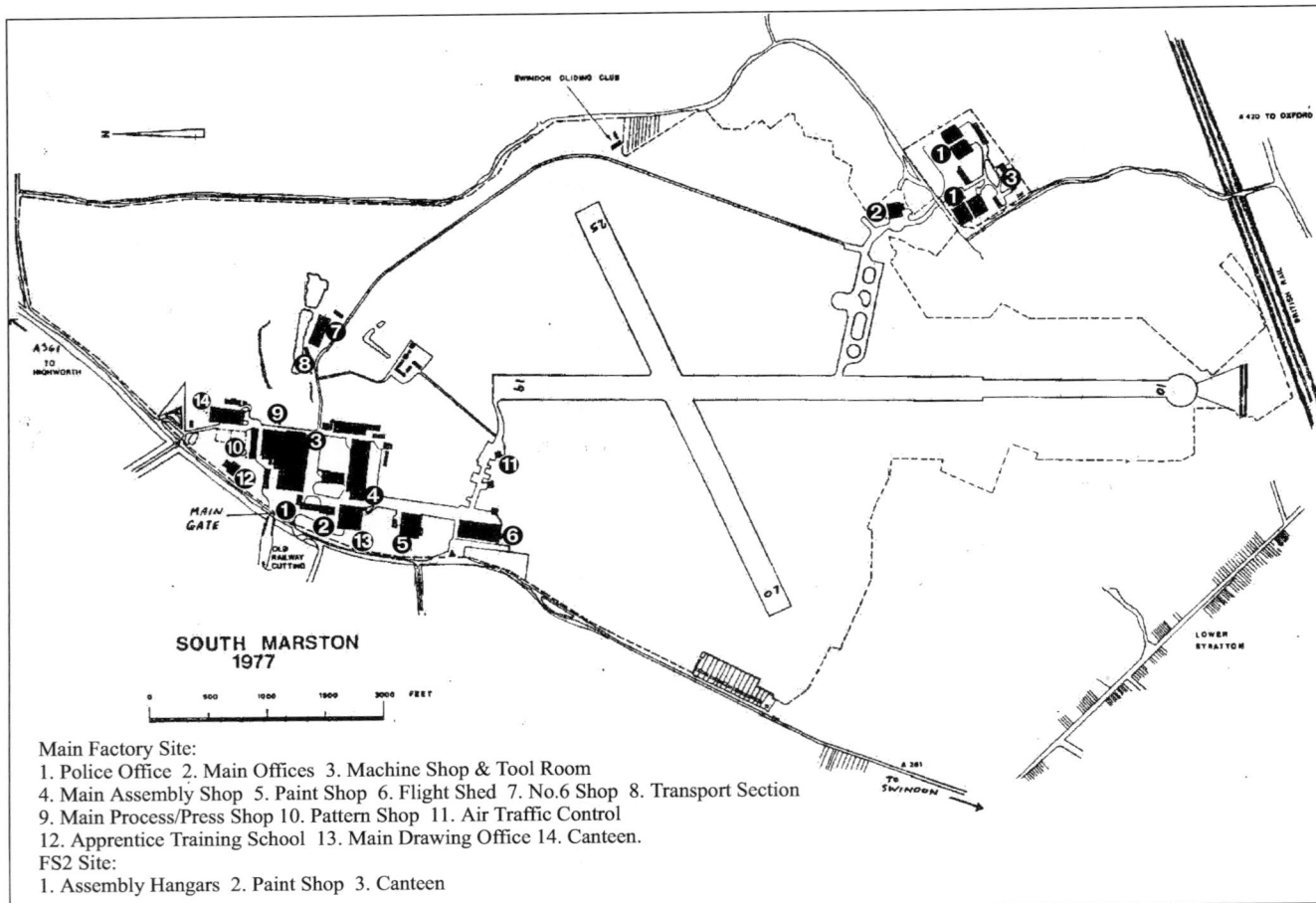

SOUTH MARSTON
1977

Main Factory Site:
1. Police Office 2. Main Offices 3. Machine Shop & Tool Room
4. Main Assembly Shop 5. Paint Shop 6. Flight Shed 7. No.6 Shop 8. Transport Section
9. Main Process/Press Shop 10. Pattern Shop 11. Air Traffic Control
12. Apprentice Training School 13. Main Drawing Office 14. Canteen.
FS2 Site:
1. Assembly Hangars 2. Paint Shop 3. Canteen

In addition to the reduced in size Main Assembly Shop, the largest building on the Phillips & Powis site was the Machine Shop and Tool Room which incorporated the Press and Process Shops. Other buildings comprised Pattern Shop, Paint Shop, Main Offices, Drawing Office and a large canteen which had a wing at each end. It catered for all the staff ranging from management to the workers and held regular dances and concerts. On the edge of the airfield and connected to the north end of the north/south runway by a taxi track and dispersals, was the flight shed. This was a large structure through which all aircraft passed for pre-flight checks prior to test flights. A good size Watch Office with a cupola, added post war, stood beside the taxi track. Numerous other service buildings, fire station etc formed part of the development and others were built later as the emphasis of the site changed. The Apprentice Training School was one such example. Sometime before the latter part of 1943 a small site was formed in the south west corner of the airfield incorporating two small hangars. The site had a taxi-track that connected at the south end of the north/south

The camouflage effect at South Marston taken from a USAAF photographic aircraft on 8th September 1943. The camouflaged runways are seen right of centre. Just below and to the left of these are the main factory buildings. The Stirling assembly sheds are above and to the right of the runways . Photo: NMRO

runway, with the one to the Stirling assembly sheds.

When a decision was taken in 1940 to produce Stirlings at South Marston, the building of two runways commenced.

These were laid N/S 1000yds x 70yds 01/19, and NE/SW 1000yds x 70yds 07/25. At a later date both runways were extended, the N/S by initially 400yds and later again by 600yds with a 50yd width at the south end, and the

The Alan Williams anti-aircraft gun turrets in position north of South Marston airfield. The entrance to the one on the right is seen minus the two sliding doors. One of the turrets is now preserved in the Cobbaton Combat Collection at Barnstaple, Devon. Photo: Jim Winchcombe

FS2 on 4ᵗʰ December 1943 sees the Paint Shop now camouflaged, 2 Stirlings outside of the Flight Sheds and 5 Stirlings dispersed on the side of the taxi-way. Photo: NMRO

NE/SW by 280yds at the south west end. The long runway was tarmac covered and the short one remained with a concrete surface.

In 1942 the camouflaging of South Marston was undertaken for experimental purposes. All of the buildings were first painted appropriately and then covered with camouflage netting. Both runways were tarred over before being covered with wood chips. Camouflage paint was then applied over the surface. A further aid to the effect was the use of portable hedges which, during periods when there was no flying, would be hauled onto the runways. The experiment was deemed a success and the photograph on the previous page shows how it appeared from over-flying aircraft.

Twin Vickers anti-aircraft guns were installed for airfield defence. There were a number of these with one set

FS2 on 29ᵗʰ June 1943, showing the new Paint Shop, without camouflage, and to the left the two pairs of camouflaged Flight Sheds, with a completed Stirling outside. Photo: NMRO

next to the railway bridge and the other in a field close to the north boundary. Each emplacement comprised a pair of Allan Williams steel gun turrets, traversing on rings and connected by a

tunnel. The rings remain in place by the bridge.

The move by Short Brothers (Rochester & Bedford) Ltd from their Stirling production factory at Rochester Airport to Swindon resulted from the severe damage sustained when the factory was bombed around 1530 hours on 15ᵗʰ August 1940. The Ministry of Aircraft Production determined that South Marston could, in addition to building training aircraft, accommodate on the same site the final assembly of these heavy bombers. The building of the sheds for Stirling assembly commenced in the autumn of 1940 on the opposite side of the airfield from that of the Phillips & Powis factory and very close to South Marston village. The Stirling assembly works were known as FS2 (Flight Shed 2, with presumably the Phillips & Powis Main Assembly Shop being FS1). FS2 initially comprised two pairs of double sheds built at right angles to each other and sharing a common apron. This allowed for the assembly of four aircraft at the same time. The Blunsdon, Sevenhampton and South Marston works were completed in 1941 and production commenced on 1ˢᵗ July. At this time the work force was approximately 500 but increased to 5000 by 1943.

Another shed known as the 'Paint Shop' was built and completed by the summer of 1943. The new shed 117' 6' x 120', was slightly smaller than the other four, and was positioned on a taxiway between the south end of the north/south runway and the assembly site. The shed had four sliding doors on the front and none at the rear. Sometime between September and December 1943 it had camouflage paint applied in keeping with the others. The site had other small service huts, including a canteen for the workers. Production control and a drawing office were established by Short Brothers Ltd in a large property at Stratton St. Margaret.

Stirling fuselages in the finishing and test bay at Sevenhampton in December 1942.
Photo: Norman Parker Coll.

Completed fuselage N3679 en route from Sevenhampton to FS2 at South Marston.
Photo: Norman Parker Coll.

Completed wing component en route for FS2. Photo: Norman Parker Coll.

Production

When the Stirling fuselages had been completed at Sevenhampton they were moved to the assembly sheds at South Marston and local people recall these being towed along the narrow lanes. The 3½ mile journey over this tortuous route with fuselages 87ft long must have required considerable control. In the early days of production in Swindon wing components were made in the Phillips & Powis shop on the main site. The GWR works were also used for making Stirling parts which later included wing assemblies and some fuselages. Plessey's in Swindon were then storing undercarriages and flaps. These would be used at the railway works to complete the wings. No.24 Shop at the railway works was used for this. On leaving school at 14, local boy Ken Head went to work in the Machine Shop Assembly at the railway works where he assisted the skilled labour in the production of undercarriage assemblies. Whilst there he witnessed the tragedy involving Emlyn Williams, a young man from South Wales who was working on the Stirling wings and was killed by one. The fuselage end of the wings would be stood upright and secured on a trolley to be moved around the shop. On this occasion the wing was balanced without being secured. Although the sunken railway tracks had been filled in when the shop was taken over for aircraft production work, the trolley wheel went into a section that had been missed. The wing fell off and crushed Emlyn Williams who had been guiding it from that side. Security at this shop was higher than in other parts of the railway site, to the extent that patrols were carried out by its own unit of the Home Guard. At 0640 hrs on 27th July 1942 a lone He.111 dropped five bombs on the northern part of the railway works. This caused extensive damage to the roof and windows of No.24 Shop.

The first Stirlings started to roll off the assembly lines at South Marston by the back end of 1941 with numbers developing the following year to an average of sixteen per month. 96 bombers were built and flown from Swindon during the first twelve months. The A.T.A. pilots of No.1 Ferry Pool White Waltham were used to clear the Stirlings from the South Marston production line.

A Stirling fuselage having its wings attached, having been towed into one of the South Marston Flight Sheds. Photo: Norman Parker Coll.

In the Phillips & Powis works in November 1941, Stirling wing final assembly, showing the attachment of leading edge components. The notice suspended from the roof reads 'Damage Through Carelessness will be Severely Dealt With'
Photo: Norman Parker Coll.

With the increase in pilot training courses under the Commonwealth Air Training Schemes, the requirement for training aircraft such as the Master diminished. A total of 602 Master Mk.Is and 498 Mk.IIs were built at South Marston. It was planned for the Phillips & Powis factory to be turned over to Mosquito production in March 1942 but in September 1942, with the final Masters leaving South Marston, Phillips & Powis moved out to be replaced by the Aircraft Section of Vickers Armstrong Ltd from Castle Bromwich Works. Initially Vickers used the plant to carry out modifications to Spitfire Mk.Vs and to produce Spitfire Mk.21s. Also at this time, Short Brothers Ltd were preparing to relocate in their entirety to Belfast, where after the war, it became Short Brothers & Harland Ltd. By mid 1943 the company had left Swindon and from 1st September, Armstrong Whitworth Aircraft Ltd had replaced it.

The Armstrong move into the former Stirling assembly sheds at South Marston, was intended to aid production of Lancaster bombers. For a twelve month period from February 1943, the manufacturing sites at

This Stirling outside of the assembly sheds is undergoing engine and turret tests.
Photo: Norman Parker Coll.

Blunsdon, Plessey's in Kembrey Street and the GWR No.24 Shop, had jigs and fixtures installed for the production of a range of components, sub-assemblies and details for Lancaster and Lincoln aircraft. With the Allies returning to Europe during 1944 and indications of the war drawing to a close, the need to escalate production ceased. The Company however adopted the kind of role undertaken at some MUs, in that they carried out the conversion of U.S Lend/Lease aircraft, to British specifications. This involved for

example, changing the radios and instruments on American aircraft types such as the Mitchell and Boston for the 2nd Tactical Air Force, and conversion of the American Vultee's Vengeance dive bomber for target towing purposes.

In 1943 the Seafire appeared, and the Mk.45 and 46 were produced in Birmingham and Swindon. The prototype was PS944. The F.45 was a navalised Spitfire F.21 with a Griffon 61 engine and a five bladed propeller. Fifty of the type was built. The F.46 was an improvement having a bubble hood and a contra-prop which at least kept it on a straight line when flying from a carrier, something the F.45 was not capable of. The Mk.47 with a Griffon 88 engine, was an entirely South Marston built aircraft and came with folding wings. This was a true fleet fighter and was the last Mk of Seafire built for the Royal Navy. It bore little resemblance to its predecessors which had basically been Spitfires fitted with a hook. 90 F.47s were built at South Marston with the first entering service with the Fleet Air Arm in early 1948. Some were equipped with an F.24 camera which made them FR.47s. The F.47 fire power was 4 x 20mm cannon and it could carry 8 x 60lb under-wing rockets or 3 x 500lb bombs. It was used operationally by the Navy in Malaya and Korea.

The Vickers Spitfire Mk.21 programme was initiated at their Castle Bromwich plant and was supplemented at South Marston when

Canadian and American Vengeance and Mitchells outside the South Marston Assembly Sheds.
Photo: Norman Parker Coll.

Construction of Spitfire Mk. 24s, possibly in No.4 Shop at South Marston C.1946. The workers in the foreground are mainly female and the aircraft continue to have camouflage applied.
Photo: Graham Tanner

the production lines and staff training came on line. The first aircraft to be completed at the Swindon factory was test flown by Alex Henshaw, Vickers Chief Test Pilot at Castle Bromwich. It is believed that the test was carried out in August 1944. Jeffrey Quill who was CTP for Vickers at Highpost also helped out with test flying when required. Another test pilot was Leslie Colquhoun DFC, GM, DFM, who joined Vickers in February 1945. As a Sgt pilot he had served with No.69 Sqn carrying out photo-reconnaissance duties from Luqa in Malta and was later commissioned. On 23rd May 1950 when taking-off from South Marston in Attacker WA469, the starboard outer wing tip folded to the vertical position. The folding arrangement was for the

benefit of aircraft-carrier stowage. With ailerons locked and the controls almost useless, he managed to keep the aircraft airborne and to make a safe landing, although swinging off the runway due to a burst tyre. In achieving this and being able to provide first hand knowledge of the fault, the problem could easily be resolved, Leslie Colquhoun was awarded the George Medal. Les was also responsible for testing some of the Hovercraft built at South Marston by Vickers-Armstrong following the departure of the Scimitars.

Spitfire F.21 LA198 came off the production line during August 1944 time, and was flown over to No.33 MU Lyneham on 2nd October. The

following May it was issued to No.1 Sqn. then based at Coltishall and went on to serve with No.602 (City of Glasgow) Sqn. This aircraft survives under restoration and on completion will be displayed in the Kelvington Art Gallery, Glasgow.

After the war had ended Vickers took over the entire facility at South Marston. Contracts were now for the modification of Wellington bombers as Mk.10 training aircraft for the RAF. Various Spitfire Mk.IXs passed through South Marston either for trainer conversion or in many cases, in preparation following sales to foreign Air Forces. Lancasters TW870, 873, 883 and 885 were flown in from Coventry by ATA pilots during August 1945. Many other types received similar attention. When the Castle Bromwich works closed in 1946, Spitfire Mk.22 and Mk.24 production was switched to South Marston.

The Government was now promoting the need for high-speed jets as replacements for the Meteor. The Supermarine Attacker was an early type to come off the production line at South Marston. The first order for 63 South Marston built Attacker F.1s was dated 29th October 1948. These were WA469 to WA498 and WA505 to WA537 but with WA536 and 537 being cancelled. The south end of the north/south runway received its extension at the beginning of 1950 to accommodate jets. The first production Attacker WA469 to be completed did not, however, use the facility. It was taken instead, by road to Chilbolton, Supermarines Divisional Flight Test airfield, where it was test flown for the first time on 4th April 1950.

Two of the first batch of production Attackers were lost during testing. On 5th February 1951 WA477, 14 minutes after take-off from South Marston, was seen trailing smoke and went out of control when the spoiler mechanism became damaged by a loose spanner. The aircraft crashed 1¾ miles SW of Marlborough, killing Sqn Ldr Peter G. Robarts. A similarity had occurred in that, a spanner was found in the wreckage of prototype Attacker TS413 which had crashed on 22nd June 1948. On 5th February 1952, WA485 took-off from Chilbolton and climbed to check new flat sided elevators. On returning to the vicinity of Chilbolton and letting down to about 1000' in the circuit, the

A line up of Supermarine Attackers in front of the South Marston control tower. A DH Rapide of the Company Comms Flt is seen in the background. Photo: Graham Tanner

Supermarine Swifts prepared for test flying from South Marston.
Photo: Graham Tanner

aircraft suddenly nosed over into a vertical dive and crashed in water meadows between Leckford village and Fullerton Junction railway station, eleven miles west of the airfield. A&AEE test pilot Lt Cdr Malcolm R. Orr-Ewing RN was killed.

182 Attackers were built, the last 36 destined for the Pakistan Air Force. These were flown to Pakistan from South Marston by company test pilots.

Supermarine Swifts were the next jets to start rolling off the assembly line. The F.1 (Type 541) was the early type although the first two had been built at the company's experimental works at Hursley Park near Winchester. The first

was WK194, making its maiden flight on 25th August 1952. Six different Mks were assembled at South Marston and 170 had been produced by the time the last one left the works in May 1957. The Swift was not a successful aircraft and the production programme was terminated in February 1955. The FR Mk.5 did, however, serve with the RAF in Germany for a good period of time before being replaced by the Hawker Hunter.

The Scimitar was the next and final jet aircraft to be built at the factory. There had been three prototypes of the Scimitar to specification N.9/47, all built at Hursley Park. These were VX133 a Type 508, VX136 a Type 529

and VX138 a Type 525. The former was first flown on 31st August 1951. Three Supermarine Type 544 prototypes were produced in Swindon to Specification N.113D, with the first of these WT854, flown from A&AEE Boscombe Down on 19th January 1956. The other two WT859 and WW134 (with blown flap) were first flown from South Marston on 26th June and 10th October 1956 respectively. 100 Scimitar F1s were ordered in 1956 under contract No.6/A/8812/CB.5(a) from Vickers Armstrong at South Marston. These were numbered XD212-XD250, XD264 XD282 and XD316 XD357. Only 76 were built however. The order was cancelled after XD333. The aircraft were all for the Royal Navy to be used for Fleet Defence, Strike Escort and Offensive Task, i.e. bombing following a low approach, prior to pulling up to release the bomb load. The final production aircraft was delivered to the Navy on 10th January 1961. Although production of aircraft parts continued at the plant, the Scimitar was the last type of aircraft to be built there in its entirety.

The South Marston site continued with aircraft work, mainly sub-contracts from Vickers-Weybridge on VC 10 and BAC 111 components, but this was gradually phased out during the 1960s.

In 1971 the RAF returned Spitfire Mk.21 LA226 in poor condition to South Marston for restoration to static condition for display purposes and for use as a gate guardian at the Swindon works. It had been built at South Marston by Vickers Ltd in 1944. A restoration team of nine men from the company, headed by Section Inspector Des Bowles worked on the project in their own time and completed it the same year. Des Bowles had served as an apprentice in the Great Western Railway Works at Swindon. In 1938, with other ex-apprentices he moved to Phillips & Powis at Woodley, working on aircraft fuselage assembly. When Phillips & Powis transferred to the South Marston works in 1940, Des returned with the company. At this time he was carrying out inspection work. When Phillips & Powis closed down at South Marston at the end of 1942 and Vickers took over, Des continued with the new company, working in various departments, including inspection of components, final inspection of aircraft in the Flight Shed and Design

Spitfire LA226 arriving at Vickers South Marston works on an RAF 'Queen Mary' in 1971.
Photo: Des Bowles

South Marston airfield on 19th May 1976. The north end of the main runway is seen in the foreground. In the centre a fuel bowser can be seen parked by the Comms Flt Shed with the control tower behind. Right of centre on the far side of the field, the Paint Shop on the FS2 Site can just be seen with a pair of the Stirling Assembly Sheds to the left and rear.
Photo:Des Bowles

suitable equipment. For many years the company operated a Merryweather fire engine at South Marston but in 1973 it was replaced by a Land Rover. The Merryweather went to Portsmouth City Museum.

Airfield lighting was British CAA approved sidelighting, threshold lighting and visual slope indicators.

Closure

After Vickers left Swindon the airfield itself continued to be used for private flying. This included the Swindon Gliding Club, which used a site at the N/E end of the short runway. Flying terminated in April 1985 when the airfield and factory site was sold for the development of the South Marston Park Industrial Estate. The largest occupier is the Honda Car Company, positioned on the west side of the N/S runway, which is still used for car tests. Construction and landscaping around the complex prevents casual viewing, so maintaining privacy for the testing of pre-production models. Part of the former NE/SW runway is used for car storage.

The former Drawing Office of Vickers was used for many years by Salamandre plc, a firm of cable trunking specialists. In 2002 it was purchased by Business Space Services,

and Production. When Vickers started using South Marston as one of the bases for their Communications Flight, Des was employed as Air Traffic Controller (ATC), first in a part-time capacity combined with his inspection duties. When aircraft were expected to land or take-off, he would be called from his works duties to the Control Tower. In 1976 he transferred to Vickers London office as full time ATC officer for South Marston.

The Communications Flight maintained by Vickers was for flying sales, engineering staff and customers around Britain and Europe. One of the aircraft based at South Marston which was used for this purpose was Piper Navajo G-AWOW. Another delivered in 1982 was a Cessna Citation 1, G-BIZZ. The Chief Pilot was ex-RAF Wing Comm. T.C. Murray DSO, DFC.

Because it was an active airfield, Vickers was required to have a Fire Section with trained personnel and

Three of the Spitfire restoration team working on the wing assembly
LtoR R.Foot (Quality Assurance Engineer), Des Bowles (Section Inspector) and Jim Reynolds (Paint Shop Sprayer). Photo: Des Bowles

Displaying the markings in which it was originally delivered, Spitfire Mk.21 LA226, the gate guardian at the South Marston works where it was built. Seen here in 1971 following its restoration. It had previously served with No.91 and No.122 Squadrons and with No.3 C.A.A.C.U. The aircraft was first flown on 9th January 1945.

Unoccupied in 2002 is the original Paint Shop.

One of the two pairs of Flight Sheds seen in 2002.

An unearthed air raid shelter with connection to the Flight Shed. This shelter is immediately below the left side windows of the above pair of sheds.

South Marston's Air Traffic Control building and Comms. Flt. aircraft. The developing industrial estate has considerably altered the airfield appearance. Following closure, the ATC building was transported by lorry to the Badminton Estate. Photo: Des Bowles.

who converted it into modern offices with the name Berkeley House. Former Vickers employees attended an opening ceremony in September 2002, when the Battle of Britain Memorial Flight Spitfire Mk XIX PS853 was flown over the site by Sqn Ldr Paul Day OBE., OC the B of B Flt.

The road leading into the industrial estate is named Stirling Road and others on the estate include appropriately Wellington Road and Viscount Way. Although now filled in the rail bridge for the 'Vickers Branch' is still evident but the railway station site has returned to agriculture.

The Paint Shop, the last of the original Stirling Sheds built, remains as the Crown Trading Estate in South Marston village but is unused and on the market for sale. The other two pairs of sheds are used as a furniture storage warehouse and by Leggett Freightways.

STONEHENGE AERODROME

Location - 184/SU115418 - 3 miles West of Amesbury

The aerodrome was located mainly in a triangle formed by the A303, A344 and A360. It was approximately a quarter of a mile west of the prehistoric site of Stonehenge.

crews was in a separate camp created close to Fargo Plantation. Away from the noise of the aerodrome, it allowed them uninterrupted sleep during the daytime

A range of aeroplane hangars was provided for the Royal Naval Air Service when it arrived in 1918. The hangars stretched east along the A344 on the south side from its junction with the A360 at *Airman's Cross* as far as Fargo Plantation on the north side of the road. The hangars consisted of the canvas Bessoneaux type and 4 Handley Page designs. These Handley Page hangars were designed by the aircraft manufacturers to house their HP 0/100 and 0/400 heavy bombers. The Domestic Site was on the north side of the road and provided messing accommodation for officers and ratings. When first arriving at Stonehenge RN personnel had to use tented accommodation. The facilities were constructed on what had been an Australian prison compound.

An aerial view of Stonehenge airfield on 21st May 1921 at 1030hrs, taken from 5000ft, from an aircraft of No.1 FTS Netheravon. Photo: NMRO

World War 1 Years

Stonehenge had the role of day-bomber and heavy night-bomber pilot training. The aerodrome came under the control

Aerodrome Development

As with other new aerodromes in the area, construction of the 360 acre aerodrome was started in early 1917. The main Technical Site was located on the north side of the A303 and the Domestic Site on the south side. Fargo Cottages, the living accommodation provided for the Stonehenge Custodians, were demolished as part of the aerodrome construction.

The grass landing ground was between the Technical Site and the A344 road to Shrewton, which formed the northern boundary of the aerodrome. Branches of the Larkhill Military Railway served both the Handley Page hangars and the Technical Site, the track to the latter curving along close to the A303. The Technical Site was equipped with 6 coupled GS Aeroplane Sheds, Aeroplane Repair Shed and MT Sheds, workshops and numerous stores, huts and offices. The Domestic Site consisted of an Officers' Mess and Quarters, Sergeants' Mess, barrack rooms and other service buildings. Accommodation for the night bomber

The external and internal views of one of the coupled GS Aeroplane Sheds.

The Aeroplane Repair Shed surrounded by various service buildings.

The workshop buildings seen from either side of the partially submerged fuel storage tank.

outdated fighter design. The principle differences between the HP 0/400 and 0/100 were the substitution of the 360 hp Rolls-Royce VIII engines for 285 hp Eagle IVs, the use of identical engines rotating the same way instead of right and left handed, a change to the fuel system and an increased strength and bomb load.

The Handley Page Training Flight of the Royal Naval Air Service, which had formed at Manston in September 1916, transferred to Stonehenge in January 1918. Known as the Handley Page Flying School, the move was made in anticipation, from its formation on 1st April, of the RAF taking over the role of heavy bombing from the RNAS, who had undertaken it throughout the war. The move was also of benefit to the air defences of south east England who were prone to confusion because of the similarity of the HP 0/100s with the German Gotha. On arrival from Manston the RNAS occupied the north-west corner of the aerodrome. At this stage Stonehenge had a RFC CO and a RN CO, the latter was Sqn Cdr G. L. Thomson DSC. He had received his appointment on 5th December 1917.

No.97 Sqn arrived from Waddington on 21st January 1918. It was equipped with various aircraft. Its stay was short and it moved to nearby Netheravon on 31st March 1918.

The syllabus for courses at the No.1 S of N&BD being staged from 12th-18th April 1918, at which DH4s and DH9s were flown, included navigation, cloud penetration, cross country flights, circuits of Salisbury Plain, formation flying, air to air fighting, aerial photography and bombing. Practice in bombing entailed releasing projectiles from heights of 2000', 4000' and 6000' onto a bulls-eye target on the ground. Three points were awarded for a bulls-eye, two for an inner and one for an outer.

Inter War Years

The numbers passing through the school reduced following the Armistice in November 1918 but training did continue until 23rd September 1919 when No.1 School moved to Andover where it disbanded with the resident No.2 School, into the School of Air Pilotage.

of No.33 (Training) Wing RFC with HQ at 2A Winchester Street, Salisbury in Southern Training Brigade. The first unit to occupy Stonehenge when it opened was No.107 Sqn, arriving from Catterick on 18th October 1917. No.108 & No.109 Sqns arrived from Montrose and South Carlton respectively on 12th November 1917. The three squadrons moved along the road to Lake Down on 2nd December 1917, changing places with No.2 TDS,

which was equipped with the DH4, BE2e, RE8 and FK8. No.2 TDS was re-designated No.1 School of (Aerial) Navigation & Bomb-Dropping when it formed at Stonehenge on 5th January 1918. The Chief Instructor was Maj Harold Hemming. The crews were trained on the Avro 504K, Maurice Farman, DH.4 and DH.9, with the twin engine Handley Page 0/400, 0/100 and FE2b used by the night bomber crews. The FE2b had been modified from the

Handley Page 0/400 C.9689 allocated to No.1 S of N&BD at Stonehenge in 1918.
Photo: Mrs D. Locke

Sopwith 7F.1. Snipe E7385 having suffered a damaged wheel strut.
Photo: S. Bradley/Cty Tony West

BE2e C6922 outside one of the GS Aeroplane Sheds.
Photo: S. Bradley/Cty Tony West

AW FK8 B3306 equipped with an early form of undercarriage. This machine served with the
Artillery Co-operation Sqn. Photo: S. Bradley/Cty Tony West

Seen at Stonehenge, this Nieuport 24 is believed to be N5878 which was on charge with CFS Upavon in 1918.
Photo: S. Bradley/Cty Tony West.

The Artillery Co-operation Sqn had moved into Stonehenge during August 1919 but most of its flying was carried out on detachment at Worthy Down. On 8th March 1920 the School was absorbed by the School of Army Co-operation which reformed at Stonehenge on that date in No.7 Group. At the time it was equipped with Bristol Fighters, on which crews were trained during detachments at Worthy Down, before joining army co-operation squadrons. The training responsibility was to develop air to ground co-operation between the Army and the RAF.

During April 1920 'C' Flt. No.4 Sqn moved in from Farnborough with its Bristol F2b Fighters. One of its roles was to subject army troops training on Salisbury Plain to bombing and strafing experience.

Closure

Stonehenge was intended to continue in service as a permanent station after the Armistice, with Old Sarum closing. The plan was reversed and Stonehenge closed with the School of Army Co-operation transferring to Old Sarum in January 1921.

On closure the Domestic Site became the Stonehenge Pedigree Stock Farm and was used as such for approximately 10 years. In 1927 the Technical Sites were purchased by the Devizes building company W.E. Chivers & Sons. Some of the buildings were auctioned but the majority were demolished by the company in 1929 because the Council for the Protection of Rural England had considered them unsuited to the site of Stonehenge monument. This is in direct contrast to a tale frequently told locally whereby the CO of Stonehenge Aerodrome once requested that Stonehenge itself be removed as it was a hazard to flying. Although sheep often grazed on the landing area, another story relates to a pilot from Boscombe Down killing one during a landing and severely

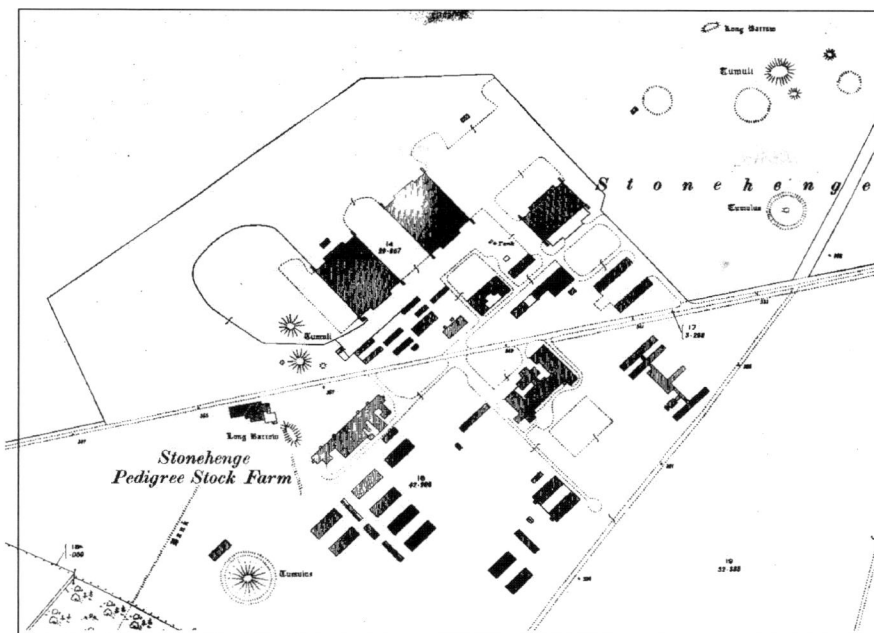

OS map showing the site of Stonehenge Aerodrome following closure. The main London to Exeter road divides the Technical and Domestic sites.

damaging his aircraft. On contacting his CO, he reported with considerable trepidation, the damage caused to the aircraft but the CO was not concerned about this, he said "never mind the aeroplane, but get the sheep back here for the mess".

The Handley-Page hangars survived until they were dismantled. One hangar, reduced by half its height, was transported by Jack Coles of Shrewton and re-erected by the newly established flying club based at High Post Aerodrome which opened in 1931. Other sections went to the Miles Aircraft factory at Woodley and to the Shuttleworth Collection at Old Warden airfield, where it still resides today. The site of Stonehenge Aerodrome has returned completely to agriculture and it is hard to imagine that there was ever a large air force presence there.

World War 2 Years

On Sunday 17th October 1943 a No.23 OTU Wellington X HE824 took-off from Stratford-upon-Avon at 1830hrs for a night cross-country. It is thought to have iced up causing it to crash at 1909hrs on the part of Stonehenge aerodrome, occupied in 1918, by the RNAS Handley Page Training Flt. The five crew killed were Flt Sgt Joseph G. A. Meilleur RCAF (pilot), Fg Off Joseph A. L. Morissette RCAF (nav), Sgt Joseph J. M. P. Marchessault RCAF (B/A), WO2 George Smith RCAF (WOP/AG) and Sgt Joseph A. J. Duhamel RCAF (A/G). Boscombe Down's crash and rescue vehicles attended the scene. All five were buried at Haycombe Cemetery, Bath.

The L-4s of various US Army 9th Air Force units were stationed in the county during 1944. Among them was the 29th Infantry Division based at Tidworth, and this unit is known to have used a strip in the vicinity of the historic stones but whether it was on the site of the original aerodrome is not known for certain.

Memorial

184/SU114426 - 3 miles West of Amesbury.

On the north side of the A344, in the south-east corner of Fargo Plantation, 500 yards west of Stonehenge, stands a Celtic Cross erected in memory of Major A.W. Hewetson. The stonemasons who carved the memorial were the brothers Jack and Arthur Green, quarrymen of Tisbury. The lead lettering on the face of the memorial stone became eroded over the years but following representation by Christopher Green, a former RAF officer and in conjunction with the School of Artillery at Larkhill, the National Trust being the keepers of the stone, carried out renovation work during 1997. A rectangular piece of Welsh Slate, 'V' cut and sized, was fixed to the front of the memorial covering the remains of the original lead letters. The inscription once again clearly reads: -

IN MEMORY
OF
MAJOR ALEXANDER WILLIAM
HEWETSON
66TH BATTERY ROYAL FIELD
ARTILLERY
WHO WAS KILLED WHILST
FLYING
ON THE 17TH JULY 1913 NEAR
THIS SPOT

Maj Hewetson RFA was killed on 17th July 1913 when he crashed in a Bristol Prier-Dickson monoplane, modified by Coanda, on Larkhill Aerodrome during the test for his aviator's certificate. He was one of the earliest members of the Royal Aero Club. The crash site is marked by a stone slab with identical wording beneath a Celtic Cross and surrounded by six wooden posts, railings and a gated entry.

The Technical Site of Stonehenge Aerodrome seen on the right of the A303 with Stonehenge itself to the left of the A344 C.1925. The open ground in between was the landing area. The semi-detached houses in the foreground were built in 1917 for the Custodians of Stonehenge. They were demolished in 1937, having been purchased by public subscription, as they were not considered conducive to the surroundings. The café on the right of the A344 was demolished shortly afterwards.

The Celtic Cross at Fargo Plantation commemorating Maj Alexander William Hewetson.

The original unveiling and dedication ceremony of the Maj Hewetson Memorial.
Photo: Terry Heffernan

1) 183/ST792348 - 1½ miles north east of Zeals

On top of Beech Knoll east of the B3092 on a former grass road leading from Stourhead House to White Sheet Hill. A car parking area at the base of White Sheet Hill can be accessed from Long Lane which leads there from the Red Lion public house on the B3092. Beech Knoll is National Trust land and can be reached on foot from the car parking area.

Set amongst the trees on the site of a Dakota crash, a memorial cairn of local Chilmark Stone with a Crown Stone plaque inset and bearing the following inscription beneath the RAF Crest: -

This memorial is dedicated to
the airmen who lost their lives in
Dakota TS436,
of No.107 OTU Leicester East
which crashed here after taking off from
RAF Zeals on 19th February 1945

F/Sgt. J.O. Allen RAAF	Sgt. R.E. Jelfs RAF
Cpl. K.S. Anderson RAF	F/O F.J. Plant RAF
A.C.2 W.J.E. Colby RAF	F/Lt. A.J. Roberts RAF
F/Lt. T.A. Evans RAF	F/Sgt. J. Ross RAF
Sgt. M.V. Gilder RAF	F/O M.E.L. Scovell RCAF
Sgt. D. Grant RAF	F/Sgt. A.G. Shaddick RAAF
F/O G.J. Guay RCAF	F/Sgt. L.D. Slipper RAF
F/Lt. J.C. Howden RCAF	A.C.2 R.E. Suggars RAF
F/Lt. J. Heywood RAF	F/Lt. D.E. Turnbull RAF
F/Lt. R.T. Hyde RCAF	F/O S.G. Williams RAF

and the pilot F/Lt. M.R.S. Mackay DFC. RAF
who sustained severe injuries and subsequently died.

The dedication service conducted
by the Rev Canon Davey RAF retd.

The memorial cairn on Beech Knoll.

The provision of the commemorative memorial stone was undertaken by the Wiltshire Historical Military Society, with the assistance of the local community and the co-operation of the National Trust. A dedication and unveiling ceremony was staged on Saturday 14th August 1999. It was attended by relatives of the airmen, colleagues, personnel serving at Zeals during the war and local residents. The memorial stone was unveiled by ACM Sir John Gingell, GBE, KCB, KCVO, RAF and the service conducted by The Rev. Canon F. Davey RAF rtd, himself a World War 2 pilot with Coastal Command. Representatives from the three Air Forces were Wg Cdr John Barras RAF, OC No.30 Sqn RAF Lyneham, Sqn Ldr Greg Shaw RAAF and Capt Kirk Bennett RCAF. The ceremony concluded with the playing of the Last Post and Reveille by a bugler from RAF Brize Norton. The Dakota Clubs' 1943 built C47A N47FK then carried out a low-level fly past, using the same flight path as TS436.

2) 183/ST776339 - 1½ miles North of Zeals

In the National Trust village on the C278, west of the B3092. Outside the entrance porch of St. Peter's Church, a memorial seat and plaque with the inscription: -

PRESENTED BY FRIENDS IN MEMORY OF
ROBIN A. BOWES 1944 - 1995
ADMIRED AND RESPECTED DISPLAY PILOT
WHO SADLY MADE HIS FINAL LANDING CLOSE BY

Robin Bowes was killed on 20th July 1995 when his Fokker Triplane replica 425/17 (G-BEFR) crashed at nearby Stourhead. His plane, painted in the all red scheme worn by World War 1 German ace Baron Manfred Von Richthofen, crashed shortly after taking off for his display. Robin Bowes was a well known and respected pilot on the air display circuits in this country and in Europe.

The Robin Bowes memorial seat at St. Peter's Church.

1) 173/SU146845 - West of Swindon Town Centre

At the Milton Workingmen's Club and Institute in Milton Road. In the Fat Albert Lounge, a framed inscription enclosed by curtains: -

---

Fat Albert Association

was opened on 11th. April 1995 by

Mr Richard Wyatt

---

beneath the inscription is a Hercules in silhouette encircled with ' Fat Albert Association' wording.

This Hercules appreciation club was formed by supporters of the aircraft which regularly fly over Swindon from the nearby base at Lyneham. The Fat Albert Association takes its name from the aircrew's affectionate name for the aircraft. HTV personality Richard Wyatt performed the official opening of the Fat Albert Lounge.

2) 173/SU157839 - on the A361 in Old Town

In Christ Church & St Mary, the Roll of Honour transferred there from Swindon High School following its closure in 1979. One of the former pupils, whose name appears, is Fg Off Michael Smith RAFVR, a pilot of No.524 Sqn, who failed to return from an anti-shipping patrol in a Wellington on 2nd October 1944. His name and those of the rest of the crew appear on the Runnymede Memorial. The name of Michael Smith is also recorded on the war memorial at Daunsey's School, West Lavington, where he continued his education after attended Swindon High School.

The Roll of Honour at Christ Church & St Mary in Swindon.

Tilshead had an early connection with flying when in 1916 an outstation of the RFC No.1 Balloon School at nearby Rollestone was set up.

G.H. Griffiths, who lived in the village at the time, recalled that the main equipment site was located in a field on the right hand side of the road leading from the A360 to West Down Camp. It was immediately above the last house in the road on the north side of where the Tilshead Pipe Factory is located today.

World War 1 Years

The balloons were flown from various sites in the location and would be navigated through the village fully inflated by men hanging firmly on to the guy ropes. There was an occasion when a balloon had to be deflated in the village so that it could pass under telegraph wires. Open fires in surrounding properties had to be dowsed to prevent a possible explosion. Two balloons were normally at Tilshead. Each was complete with a basket and a parachute in an attached container. The gas was in containers similar to present day cylinders. German PoW were used for maintaining the balloons

TILSHEAD LANDING GROUND

Location 184/SU025490 - three quarters of a mile north west of the village

Situated some 800yds east of the A360 this temporary landing ground was used during the First World War by No.105 Sqn RFC, following its formation at Andover on 14th September 1917. The squadron, commanded by Capt H.G. Bowen, was equipped at this time with the DH.6, BE.2b, BE2d and the DH.9 with Puma engines. For approximately six months, the squadron was engaged entirely in training its pilots on type. The squadron re-equipped with the RE.8 in April 1918 and Major Joy took command. In May the squadron was mobilised to Omagh in County Tyrone. The Artillery Co-operation Sqn, with

its HQ at 61 New Street, Salisbury, operated at Tilshead during October/November 1918. This was possibly the Sqn's 'A' Flt. which at the time was based at Netheravon.

TILSHEAD LANDING GROUND

Location - 184/SU021478 Half a mile West of Tilshead Village

Tilsheads second landing ground was laid out on Horse Down, west of the C22 Tilshead to Chitterne road.

Inter War Years

It was first used in 1925 by Army Co-operation squadrons involved in exercises. There was never any permanent building construction but tented accommodation was erected as necessary.

One of the squadrons which operated from the ALG was No.13 Sqn, equipped with the Atlas, whilst it was based at Andover and Netheravon in 1929/30. 'B' Flt, from a detachment at Odiham, arrived at Tilshead Practice Camp on 4th May 1929 for artillery co-operation live-shoot exercises with 11th Field Brigade and 5th Light Brigade. On 25th May 'A' Flt replaced 'B' Flt on arrival from Odiham, and carried out live-shoots with 6th & 7th Field Brigades. 'A' Flt returned to Odiham on 14th June and the next day 'C' Flt arrived at Tilshead for live-shoots with the 3rd Medium Brigade, returning to Andover two days later. No.13 Sqn moved from Andover to Netheravon on 23rd September 1929 and the following year continued to use Tilshead. 'A' Flt were there for two weeks in August on Army co-operation exercise with 6th Medium Brigade and 'B' Flt spent a week carrying out the same duties in co-operation with the 58th & 59th Field Brigades RA.

During the 1920s and 30s No.16 Sqn, from nearby Old Sarum, carried out its operations with the Army from ALGs such as Tilshead and Imber. Between the wars the squadron aircraft flying

from Tilshead were the Bristol F2b, Atlas and Audax. In May 1931, the squadron was at Tilshead for a Southern Command Royal Artillery exercise and followed this with a detachment there during the whole of the next month. 'A' Flt. carried out a similar detachment during the summer of 1932 for co-operation with the 1st Medical Brigade RA.

World War 2 Years

There was a period early in the Second World War when the Tilshead LG was not used but in June 1940 it was re-activated and on 1st July No.225 Sqn moved in from Old Sarum with 28 officers, 355 airmen and equipped with 12 Lysander IIs coded 'WU'. The squadron was used for anti-invasion patrols. A tented camp was set up adjoining the airfield. This was known as Tilshead Lodge Camp but later, when the weather deteriorated, nearby Tilshead Lodge was requisitioned for accommodation. On the first day the squadron carried out dusk and dawn patrols but no enemy aircraft were seen. Its role was to patrol the coastline from St Albans Head to Selsey Bill and Bognor Regis to Lizard Point on reconnaissance for infiltration. The Lysanders were often operated out of St.Eval airfield where they would also land to refuel before returning to Tilshead at the end of the daylight hours. An early accident occurred there on 12th July 1940, when L4787 was badly damaged in a crash landing. Fortunately Plt Off Conran (pilot) and LAC Parr (AG) were uninjured. On 29th July one of the Lysanders was carrying out photographic reconnaissance when the crew spotted what they felt was possibly a He111 over Weymouth. Later in the flight the Lysander was attacked by a Me110 but it managed to escape into cloud.

The 13th August 1940 saw some excitement on this remote LG when, at 1630 hrs, an He111 was seen flying north to south at 3000' but only visible at intervals owing to low cloud. The aircraft returned on the same course and then made a wide sweep over the ranges. It approached the LG flying east/west. Ground fire from No.1 and No.2 gun posts and from the rear guns of two

Lysanders on the ground was directed at the enemy. 5 bombs were dropped, with a 250lb bomb appearing to be the larger type of incendiary filled with creosote. One bomb fell on the eastern edge of the LG where two unoccupied tents were destroyed and officers' and airmens' kits badly damaged. One fell in the centre of the LG and the incendiary fell on the western edge of the field, setting fire to the grass. The remaining two fell in a nearby partly built hutted army camp, where one hut was destroyed and four severely damaged. Two Lysanders and a Tiger Moth suffered superficial damage when the enemy aircraft opened fire with its machine guns. Personnel took cover in slit trenches and there were no injuries. The Germans returned again the following day when a He111 and a Dornier 17 passed over the LG, the latter dropping bombs on a tank camp to the south west. The ground defences opened fire on the two enemy aircraft but without results.

'A' Flt. with 6 officers and 77 airmen were posted to No.239 Sqn which reformed at Hatfield on 18th September 1940. They were probably pleased to be leaving their tented camp in Tilshead which had started to become untenable owing to heavy rain. On the 24th September, No.225 Sqn personnel moved into nearby Tilshead Lodge because conditions at the camp had become so bad. Five days later the squadron started to re-equip with the Lysander III. Additional aircraft arrived in the weeks following and the squadron was also using a Miles Master R1858 and a Moth Minor W7975.

During October a detachment on No.16 Sqn arrived with Lysander IIIs from Weston Zoyland to carry out Army co-operation exercises.

Fg Off Daniel P. Crittall (pilot) and Sgt William M. Batson (WOP/AG) of No.225 Sqn were killed on Monday 21st October 1940 when their Lysander III R9128 crashed taking off from Old Sarum. Fg Off Crittall is buried at St. Thomas A Becket churchyard in Tilshead. Plt Off Conran forced landed at Tiverton, Devon on 9th November 1940. He and the AG were injured, the aircraft written off. A similar occurrence later in the month resulted in the write-off of T1530 which forced landed at Chedleigh. This happened during a cross-country flight to Okehampton by Plt Off Judd, who lost his bearings.

'B' Flt. of No.239 Sqn arrived at Tilshead from Gatwick on 29th March 1941 and for two days carried out air-firing practice. During detachment at Pembrey, Plt Off Sargent and his AG of No.225 Sqn were rescued from the sea when they ditched on 29th April 1941. A month later on Wednesday 21st May, also while on detachment at Pembrey, Fg Off Peter W. Lochnan RCAF of No.400 Sqn and Sgt Cave (AG) of No.225 Sqn crashed in Lysander V9361 during bad visibility. The pilot was killed and the AG seriously injured. The No.225 Sqn aircraft was destroyed. Tilshead LG received another detachment for Army co-operation work when on 24th May 'A' and 'B' Flts. of No.239 Sqn, commanded by Sqn Ldr York, with 8 Lysanders and a Gloucester Gladiator, arrived from Garwick to carry out air-firing and bombing practice on the ranges. During the month the squadron flew tactical and photo-reconnaissance sorties as part of a large-scale exercise held to simulate an invasion along the Weymouth coastal area. A station visit was made by Air Marshal Barret on 9th June 1941, he arrived in a DH Rapide X1850. During June and July the squadron carried out night flying from the LG at Shrewton. A No.16 Sqn detachment arrived again from Weston Zoyland in July and took part in exercises. No.225 Sqn was pleased to receive notice of posting to Thruxton in Hampshire, moving there from Tilshead over the first few days of August 1941. The LG continued in use for a while by detachments on exercise, but was released to the Army by the end of the year.

No.225 Sqns Lysander IIIs

R9033	R9064
R9065	R9074
R9121	R9122
R9123	R9125
R9126	R9127
R9128	R9129
R9130	R9133

AIRBORNE CAMP TILSHEAD

Location 184/SU036487 quarter of a mile North of village

The use of airborne troops by the German Army led to the formation, in January 1942, of the Army Air Corps in Britain. The Corps comprised the Glider Pilot Regiment and the Parachute Regiment. A training centre and depot were established as Airborne Camp, Tilshead during January. It consisted of 20 Nissen huts set out on either side of a parade ground with at one end the Administration block, and the NAFFI, the largest building on the camp, at the opposite end. A white flag pole was also provided. The 2nd Battalion GPR moved in that month and was joined by 'C' Company 2nd Battalion Parachute Regiment later in the month. On 27th February 1942 the Parachute Regiment took part in a successful raid to capture a German radar installation from its station at Bruneval in northern France. The Glider Pilot Regiment was not involved in this. After Bruneval the Parachute Regiment returned briefly to Tilshead before moving to its barracks in Derbyshire. In June the 21st Independent Parachute Company moved to Tilshead, remaining until October when it transferred to Newcome Lines, Larkhill.

The Glider Pilot Regiment CO at Tilshead was Major George Chatterton, second in command to Lt Col Rock who was based at Shrewton Camp. Maj Chatterton had been a RAF fighter pilot with No.1 Sqn but having sustained injuries in an air crash during 1935 had been taken off of flying duties and transferred to the Army's Queen's Royal Regiment. Maj Chatterton had two Company Sergeant-Majors from the Guards who were responsible for 'hardening up' the men under training at Tilshead. The two were Jim Cowley (Coldstream Guards) and Mick Briody (Irish Guards).

The trainee glider pilots came from various units of the Army from the Pay Corps to the Guards. One such recruit arriving at Tilshead in September 1942 was Fred Ponsford of the 2nd Oxfordshire and Buckinghamshire Light Infantry. He detrained at Lavington Railway Station and continued his journey to Airborne Camp by Army transport. On the opposite station platform were personnel who had failed their initial glider pilot training at Tilshead and were returning to their former units. They shouted over to the new arrivals that they also would be on the opposite platform the following week.

The discipline at Tilshead was so extreme that men were being rejected for the smallest of misdemeanours.

Dropping out of a 'run march' was a more serious offence that would warrant dismissal. Men would find themselves in the guardroom for leaving a speck of polish on the buckle of their gaiters. Fred Ponsford recalls his time at Tilshead as having been a humiliating experience. One of the things that must have constantly gone through the minds of these men, was the fact that they were all volunteers and were being treated worse than a PoW.

Fred recalls the occasion when the Army, training at Larkhill, were firing 25lb shells over the top of Airborne Camp and onto the Range. One of the shells fell short and struck the Nissen hut used for the MO's Waiting Room. This was full of personnel at the time and resulted in the death of four or five of them and injuries to several others. Tommy Christian lost his nose but was able to have it rebuilt and later rejoined his unit. One of those killed had only an uncle and aunt as nearest relations and they requested a full military service. This resulted in the Glider Pilots being drilled constantly from 0800 to 2000 hours in preparation for the ceremony.

There was, however, a certain degree of respite shortly after Fred's first few weeks on the camp. One of the rejected men, who had left Salisbury Plain on a west-bound train from Lavington Station, wrote of his experiences at Tilshead and submitted it to the magazine *John Bull*. The feature appeared under the title 'Straight from the Shoulder'and pulled no punches in expressing the dictatorial regime operating at Tilshead. The CO and the Instructors were not impressed when they learnt of this but neither was Winston Churchill who ordered a toning down of the discipline and rejection procedures.

The hardship was interspersed with recreational periods. Fred played in a rugby match for the Glider Pilot Regiment. It was played at Tilshead and the other team was RAF Boscombe Down. The GPs were losing 0-3 with 2 minutes left to play, when, from a scrum, the ball was picked up by an Irishman who ran all the way with it to the line. Not knowing the rules, instead of making a touch down, he bounced the ball over the line. The GPs consequently lost the match and their CO who was watching the game was so wild that he threatened to have the Irishman shot.

Airborne Camp became notorious but those who came through it were guaranteed to carry out their dual task of piloting their gliders and after landing them, fighting alongside the ground troops with equal ability. Those who survived Airborne Camp would say they deserved the award of a 'Tilshead Medal'. Having successfully come through the gruelling training at Tilshead, pilots went to EFTSs where flying training, mainly on Magisters, was undertaken before progressing to the gliders themselves. In September 1943 the Glider Pilot Regiment moved from Tilshead to Fargo Camp near Stonehenge. Staff Sgt Fred Ponsford left Tilshead in early 1943 for further flying training at Booker, Kidlington, Brize Norton and Hurn. He flew on the D-Day landings from Harwell, to Arnham from Tarrant Rushton and the Rhine Crossing from Rivenhall. His landing in Normandy on 6th June was not without incident. The Horsa struck a line of 'Rommels Asparagus' (wooden posts in the ground connected by lengths of wire from which mines were suspended) and ripped off the wings. On its approach it also came under heavy machine gun fire. The troops in the glider were from the South Staffs Regiment and one of them in the tail was killed when he was hit in the back by flak.

Before departing England each man was issued with a white blanket which they all thought was for wrapping themselves in to keep warm. They were in fact body blankets which you were wrapped in if killed. It was said that bereaved relatives were charged 7s.6d by the government if the blankets were used. Again it was believed that Churchill quashed the charge when he learnt of it.

Staff Sgt Ponsford holed up for the night and the following day, with other troops, stormed and took a church being held by a German unit. He later made his way back to the coast, was shipped across the channel and returned to Fargo Camp near Stonehenge.

Glider Pilots were recognised as being one of the finest disciplined and efficient bodies of men in the British Army. Their prowess was second to none. The training they endured most certainly influenced this. Fred Ponsford recalls a time in Europe when they were at the rear of a queue for food, were recognised as glider pilots and were all ushered to the front so they could be the first to eat. This is just one small example of the high esteem in which they were held.

It is not surprising that Fred Ponsford in later civilian life was appointed Chief Fire Officer in Bristol and that during the riots in the St. Paul's district of the city in April 1980, without police protection, led his men into the area to fight the fires raging out of control.

The 8th (Midland Counties) Parachute Battalion arrived at Airborne Camp from Bulford Camp at the end of June 1942. The Battalion were in 3 Parachute Brigade commanded by Brigadier James Hill. Lt Col Alistair Pearson was appointed as CO of the Battalion with the remit to prepare them for D-Day. This he did by marching and exercising them continually on a nine-day fortnight and on limited rations. Flying on parachute drops was undertaken from Netheravon in Dakota aircraft. Lives were lost when one of these crashed soon after take-off. He had the men in shape by early March. They worked hard and on their long weekend off duty, they played hard. Time off was spent in towns such as Devizes and Frome and Captain Hunter tells of the various forms of transport that were 'borrowed' by the men returning to Tilshead. These could be found the following day lined up on the road to the camp, but with no damage done to them as would be the case with today's 'joy-riders'. There was just one occasion when damaged was sustained by some 'borrowed' transport. This was a lorry with a trailer load of potatoes. On its journey along the A360 from Devizes, the trailer and contents became detached as it rounded the sharp corner in Potterne village and ended up in the house at the side of the road. The Battalion left Tilshead about 10 days before D-Day, moving into a tented transit camp alongside the airfield at Blakehill Farm.

When the US Forces arrived on the Plain in the autumn of 1943 they were allocated Lodge Camp to the west of the village and 'C' Camp (184/SU039467) a mile to the south. The US First Army, 188th FA Group attached to VII Corps was based at Tilshead, arriving there towards the end of the year. It was equipped with two L-4 Piper Grasshoppers carrying out a communications role and these are thought to have used the former RAF landing ground adjoining Lodge Camp. The unit is recorded as being at Tilshead on 31st May 1944 and left there a few days later in preparation for crossing the Channel in support of the D-Day landings of the 6th June. The parent VII Corps were at Utah Beach on this day.

No.2 Radio School training radio and radar mechanics at Yatesbury used Tilshead as a RLG at this time.

Memorials

1) 184/SU036487 half a mile north of village.

Beside a track onto the Plain leading north from the junction of the road to Westdown Camp. At the site of the former Airborne Camp, a granite memorial was unveiled on 27th July 1996 by Brigadier James Hill DSO, MC and Brigadier Bob Flood MC 8th (Midland Counties) Parachute Battalion. Beneath the winged emblem of the Parachute Regiment, the inscription reads:

The 8th (Midland Counties) Parachute Battalion Memorial Stone at Tilshead.

2) 184/SU035479 in the village

On the side of the A360 near the church entrance, a wooden bench with the inscription on a brass plate:

> Presented to Tilshead
> By
> The 8th (Midland Counties) Battalion
> The Parachute Regiment

> This stone is placed by the people of Tilshead
> In memory of the 8th (Midland Counties)
> Battalion
> The Parachute Regiment.
> The Battalion was formed in 1942 and was stationed
> here until 1946 before moving to Palestine where it
> was disbanded in 1948 on amalgamation.
> The Battalion took part in the following operations:
> D Day 6 June 1944
> The Battle of the Bulge (Ardennes) 1944
> The Rhine Crossing 1945
>
> 'UTRINQUE PARATUS'

The bench presented to Tilshead by the 8th (Midland Counties) Battalion The Parachute Regiment.

In High Street, near the library, a wrought-iron gate can be seen, set in the wall of Gaston Manor. The gate was designed by Bernard Hebblethwaite in memory of his son Fg Off Edwin Charles Long "Peter" Hebblethwaite RAFVR, following his death whilst serving with Bomber Command during World War 2. The family lived at Gaston Manor where Peter grew up, receiving his secondary education at Winchester School.

Peter was observer in the seven man crew of a No.78 Sqn Halifax II R9391 which took off from Croft in County Durham at 2305hrs on Sunday 3rd May 1942, on an operation to bomb Hamburg. Of the 81 aircraft which took part in the raid, No.78 Sqn provided 4, and only 54 managed to bomb on target owing to heavy cloud cover. Despite this, severe damage was inflicted on property in the city centre. After take-off nothing was heard of Peter's aircraft again, it and the crew were presumed to have been shot down. All of the crew of R9391 were killed when the aircraft crashed into the North Sea. 3 Halifaxes (2 of No.78 Sqn) and 2 Wellingtons were lost on this operation. Fg Off Hebblethwaite was initially buried on the island of Sylt, Germany but after the war was reinterred at Kiel War Cemetery, Keil, Schleswig-Holstein, Germany.

The memorial gate is adorned with Peter's initials 'P' and 'H' in gold, the blue Fleur de lys of the Boy Scouts movement, a light blue dove of the RAF, a red rose, the white shield of his school in Winchester and gold crosses for his faith. Over the years the gate became well weathered, so in the summer of 2002 members of Tisbury Youth Club volunteered to carry out renovation. With permission of the present owners, the gate was removed, stripped down and repainted it in its original colours. The renovation followed a visit made to the grave of Fg Off Hebblethwaite, by Wg Cdr Jeff Scholefield RAF (rtd) of Tisbury Royal British Legion.

Photograph of the Gaston Manor Memorial Gate.

TOWNSEND SATELLITE LANDING GROUND
Location - 173/SU064725 - 8 miles West of Marlborough.

This former landing ground is located immediately north of Yatesbury village at the end of an unclassified road leading from the A4 London to Bath road.

Airfield Development

Initially the SLG had one grass landing strip but a second was added in July 1942. One of the two was laid out to 1200yds and the other 1100yds. No hangars were ever built but the site was provided with a Nissen hut for 72 men having ablutions and messing facilities. Also small Maycrete service buildings were provided and sited on the edge of the landing ground, close to Yatesbury village. One of these was used as a Flying Control. Improved access between the landing ground and the four dispersal fields was undertaken by laying hard surfaces. Aircraft storage capacity was increased to 76. Each dispersal area was provided with a guard hut and flying equipment store.

Inter War Years

Pre World War 2, the ground was used for forced landing practice by the Tiger Moths of No.10 E&RFTS in No.26 Group which formed on the 1st February 1938 and was based close by at Yatesbury aerodrome. Use continued until the unit, re-designated No.10 EFTS, moved to Weston-Super-Mare on 7th September 1940.

World War 2 Years

When the German bombing raids started in 1940 it was realised that aircraft storage at Maintenance Units would need to be dispersed, so attention was given to locating suitable Satellite Landing Grounds where aircraft could land and take off but which also provided natural concealment. Townsend was used by No.10 MU Hullavington for almost a year from 10th October 1940 to September 1941. A Wellington and 3 Botha aircraft were flown from the MU to Townsend for storage on 3rd November 1940.

On 26th May 1941, some 15 operational aircraft were dispersed on the field. These were guarded by two patrolling airmen, who were based at Hullavington. A machine gun post was manned, during day-light hours only, by three men from the Bristol Flying School at Yatesbury. A searchlight was sited in a field to the northwest of the landing ground.

Townsend opened as No.45 SLG in No.41 Group on 1st August 1941 and was used by No.33 MU Lyneham. Immediately it received from there, two Wellington IIs, Z8350 and Z8351. They were not sent for storage but to be prepared for service in Egypt with No.104 Sqn. Both Wellingtons left Townsend during September. A detachment from the Wiltshire Regiment relieved the No.10 MU personnel of their guard duties at Townsend from 20th September 1941.

Waterlogging resulted in the site being reduced from storage use as of 27th October 1941 but it was capable of being used for forced landing practice. It was re-opened for storage purposes again the following March when various Mks. of Spitfire arrived from Lyneham and were dispersed amongst the trees on the airfield periphery. Wellingtons also started arriving. Plt Off G. L. Birch became CO and took up his appointment on 13th April 1942. A total of 11 aeroplanes were stored during the month. During May, 15 were received and 10 were issued out. The following month a further 15 arrived with 14 issued.

On 3rd June 1942, Sqn Ldr Maynard of No.33 MU visited Townsend to inspect a Wellington, following a report of unauthorised entry by a Yatesbury based airman. Nothing was found amiss. Plt Off Lucarotti landed in a Spitfire en-route to Mount Farm during bad weather on 2nd August. On 12th August 1942 the RAF Police Dog School at Staverton, Gloucester sent a team of Alsatian dogs and handlers to Townsend to guard dispersed aeroplanes.

Closure

Despite the improvements, a decision was taken to close the SLG as from 1st October 1942, with No.31 SLG at Everleigh being utilised instead. During the first two weeks of September, 31 aeroplanes in storage were flown out, leaving 2. On 12th September one of the 2 was flown out and the police dogs and handlers left for Wroughton. An Army guard remained until the last aeroplane departed. Transport allocated to the RLG was returned to No.33 MU Lyneham who relinquished control of the site.

Townsend was retained by MAP until November 1944 but not used again for aircraft storage. It was, however, in use from 1943 to the summer of 1944 as a satellite for No.2 Radio School, Yatesbury, with its Proctors. In the spring of 1944, the Royal Navy were looking at possible locations for aircraft storage, in particular for that of Seamews. Their representatives inspected Townsend on 5th June 1944 when they were informed that use by the RAF at Yatesbury was about to cease.

The site was considered acceptable for daylight flying of RN aircraft with use being made of the existing Flying Control building for that purpose. Additional requirements were a wind indicator, crash tender, ambulance, radio, medical facilities, petrol and oil bowsers. It was considered that each of the four dispersal areas would be capable of storing between 60-100 aircraft. The site was inspected again on 30th June 1944 at which time a medical officer determined the living quarters were unsuitable on hygiene grounds. Presumably by that time, it had been decided that storage of Corsairs was also required, and because Townsend's winter conditions would be unsuited to this aircraft, coupled with the poor living quarters, the Royal Navy found a facility elsewhere.

The only sign of military occupation remaining, is that of a partially collapsed building on land which was returned to farming many years ago.

UPAVON AERODROME
Location -184/SU157548 8 miles North of Amesbury

On a hill above and about 1 mile east of the village of Upavon on the A342, stands the former RAF Upavon, now occupied by the Army and named Trenchard Lines. Although never a large station, it was destined to achieve a reputation second to none in Military Aviation the world over, through a Unit formed there; the Central Flying School (CFS).

Aerodrome Development

The formation of the Central Flying School was authorised by a Special Army Order on 23rd April 1912. The School, which formed on 13th May 1912, was to be maintained at the joint expense of the Admiralty and the War Office and administered by the latter. The object of the School was to carry out advanced training in flying and instruction in technical and military subjects. The aim was to produce professional war pilots for the Military and Naval Wings of the RFC. In general, pupils were required to obtain the Royal Aero Club's certificate privately before joining the School where they received only advanced instruction.

Brigadier-General D. Henderson Director of Military Training and Capt Frederick Sykes who was to command the Military Wing, visited Salisbury Plain in April 1912. Here they selected 2,400 acres of land used for horse-gallops, located between 550' and 625' above sea level, as the site for the School. The cost of the land was £40,000, and was chosen for three basic reasons:
1) It was an isolated spot, 6 miles from the nearest railway station and this was calculated to minimise sightseers, and reduce danger to the public.
2) The open nature of the surrounding country made it eminently suitable for the purposes.
3) A good road running through the camp for transport.
The choice of the site, 600' above and to the east of the village of Upavon, was subject to some criticism in view of its exposed position. It was also felt that the main airfield left much to be desired, since it sloped to the south-west from around 580' to 480', while a depression ran across the area which

The first aerial photograph of CFS Upavon in 1913. The Aeroplane Sheds on the South Aerodrome are in the foreground separated from the station buildings and North Aerodrome by the public road.

Slightly later C.1913 aerial east to west view with the North Aerodrome and Sheds in the foreground.   Photo: Flt Lt J.O'Donnell

although shallow at first, became more pronounced as it approached the Avon Valley.

Following authorisation of the Special Army Order on 23rd April 1912, work started almost immediately to erect temporary wooden buildings weather proofed with tar, including a two-bed hospital, and aeroplane sheds, at a cost of £25,000. The Advance Party under Lt Col H.R. Cook RA arrived on 14th June. The buildings which had been completed were taken over on 19th June when the first course began to assemble and the Central Flying School opened within Southern Training Brigade. At that stage only accommodation for 20 officers and 60 men was available for occupation. The

officers huts were sited on the slope bordering the northern edge of the site and the men's quarters were below these. Living conditions at Upavon were somewhat spartan in the early months. Those allocated the new huts found them cold, as was the water for washing. Some staff members were better off, having found accommodation in Upavon village. When the Commandant moved to Upavon from the War Office on 25th July 1912 he lived close to the aerodrome at Littlecott House in the village of East Chisenbury. This was the first official residence ever purchased for the use of an RFC officer, and continues in use today by the Adjutant General. Other temporary wooden structures completed by 19th June were a Mess building, engine house, stores, workshops, erecting sheds on the north side of the road and eight aeroplane sheds on the south side of the road. A short time later on the north site, came additional Aeroplane Sheds, a Sergeants' Mess, Regimental Institution, Y.M.C.A, two lecture rooms, one for officers and one for the men and garages for the fleet cars and motor-cycles.

side of the present York Road, four of which would be located to the north of the Officers' Mess and one to the south. By the end of 1913 sporting facilities for officers had been addressed with the provision of two tennis courts and a golf course. The sergeants had a tennis court as did the men who also had cricket and football pitches. It was strictly forbidden to land machines on the golf course. There was an occasion when a

During 1914 considerable progress was made and fourteen permanent buildings were completed. Of these, eight comprised the Sergeants' Mess, Regimental Institute, five small barrack blocks and a building for NCO's quarters situated between the Sergeants' Mess and the Institute. The remaining six buildings consisted of three houses for Warrant Officers in what was later named Devon Road, a squash court near the Officers' Mess, an observatory which in later years was used as a post office and bank, and the Regimental Office. The building of the Officers' Mess was not completed until 1915. The first married quarters for airmen at Upavon were not built until 1932 in what was to be named Beverley Crescent. The temporary wooden Mess was still in use in February 1915 when Rex Warnford of later VC fame, arrived for training. He is reported to have fired 6 shots cowboy fashion, from a revolver, into the roof of the building serving as the Officers' Mess.

With the exception of eleven Aeroplane Sheds, all the buildings were located on the north side of the A342 Upavon to Ludgershall road. The eleven wooden sheds on the south side of the road stood beside the main landing ground separated from it by a tarmac apron. Three sheds were each 140' x 70' and the eight coupled sheds were each 70' x 65'. An original 'U' shaped farm building, Rowden's Bake Barn, used as a garage for the officer's cars, separated the two sheds at the west end.

A further six coupled sheds the same size, were built along the eastern perimeter of the other landing ground on the north side of road, these also had a tarmac apron. A single shed had been added at the west end of the line by December 1917, these seven sheds were occupied by the 'Experimental Flt.' All of the sheds had a zinc trough on the floor to catch waste petrol and oil from the aeroplanes. The Devizes building company of W.E. Chivers & Sons were engaged in providing accommodation for the CFS from 1912-16. The site, as with other early aerodromes built on Salisbury Plain, was not popular with those engaged in the building work. They referred to the area as *Siberia* and those who have experienced Salisbury Plain during bad weather will appreciate the sentiment.

The CFS Fitters' Shop and the workshop with staff C.1913.
Photo: Don Neate & Norman Parker Colls.

The considerable costs involved in construction of the station were justified by virtue of the urgency for the courses to commence at the School. Because of its exposed position, permanent buildings were to be started as soon as possible, the earliest were five concrete block bungalows used as quarters for single officers of the staff. These were built in 1913 on the east

Sopwith Pup half rolled, stayed inverted, and as it approached the golf course it flipped upright and landed. The pilot alighted, swung the propeller and took-off again. It appears he was unconscious when his machine was inverted and he knew nothing until coming to in the cockpit having landed without serious damage to himself, his Pup or the golf course!

Upavon by 1917 had grown from its original size of 2,400 acres to 3,324 acres with many additional buildings including a General Service Aeroplane Repair Shed/Dope Store, workshops and stores on the north aerodrome. The General Service Aeroplane Shed was built on the north end of the original row of timber Aeroplane Sheds. It was provided with end opening doors. The exact construction date has not been determined. This is thought to be the shed referred to in some previous reference as a Tunnel hangar. With the doors open at both ends it was comparable with a tunnel so hence its nick-name. From March 1944 the hangar was known to have been used by the Servicing Sqn. It survived until July 1964 when fire destroyed it.

To assist pilots in locating the aerodrome the Station name of 'UPAVON' was marked in chalk letters around 8' in height on the edge of the south landing ground as per Air Ministry Order No.197 of 1921. The position was approximately 150 yards out from the tarmac apron. It is not known whether this was done on both the landing grounds.

Upavon was one of the stations for which money was made available to upgrade facilities under the 1923/24 RAF Expansion Scheme. Two 'A' Type hangars replaced the line of wooden aeroplane sheds on the south aerodrome in 1926, the same period as the two at Netheravon. The wooden aeroplane sheds on the north aerodrome were possibly demolished at the same time. Also in 1926 a Watch Office/Chief Flying Instructors Office was positioned on the flight line between the two 'A' Type hangars. The position of any original Watch Office has not been determined.

With war clouds gathering, steps were taken to improve and develop facilities at Upavon and the work began on 1st January 1938. The living accommodation for airmen was still the original timber huts and these were replaced with three purpose built barrack blocks. A cookhouse and dining hall for airmen, and new officers' and airmen's married quarters were built. The latter were in roads later to be named Pembroke Road and Oxford Road. The officers' married quarters were increased in number, up until the 1950's. These were built in the later named Comet Avenue, Hastings

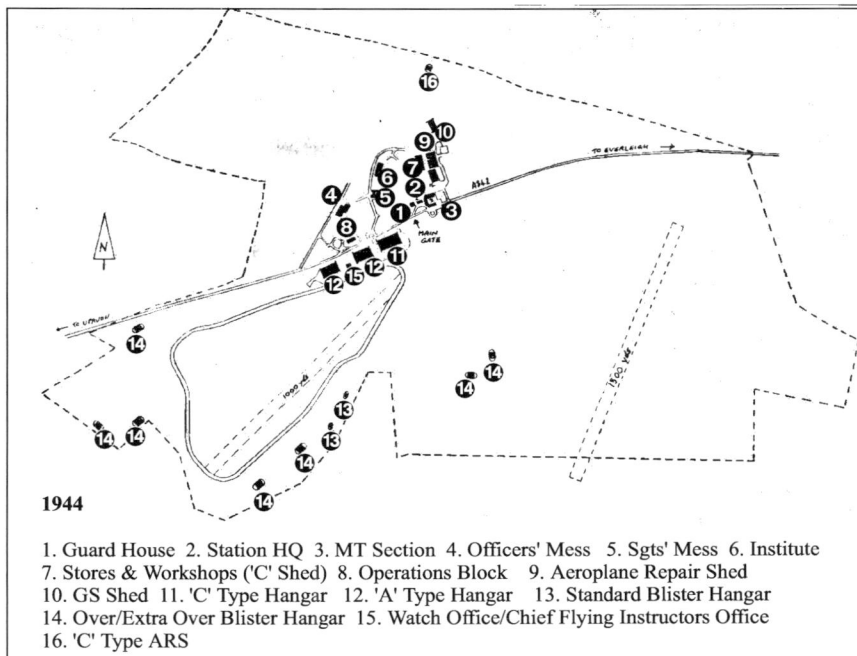

1. Guard House 2. Station HQ 3. MT Section 4. Officers' Mess 5. Sgts' Mess 6. Institute
7. Stores & Workshops ('C' Shed) 8. Operations Block 9. Aeroplane Repair Shed
10. GS Shed 11. 'C' Type Hangar 12. 'A' Type Hangar 13. Standard Blister Hangar
14. Over/Extra Over Blister Hangar 15. Watch Office/Chief Flying Instructors Office
16. 'C' Type ARS

Avenue and Britannia Avenue. A Guard House and workshop buildings were added. One 'C' Type hangar built next to the two 'A' Type on the south aerodrome was completed in April 1939. A 'C' Type hipped roof ARS was added on the edge of the north aerodrome. This was a smaller version of the standard 'C' Type hangar with four steel sliding doors at both ends instead of the normal six. The CFS was now directed to increase the output of trained pupils. From August 1938 course numbers were increased from 40 to 50 and the duration reduced from 11 to 9 weeks.

Ten Blister hangars were erected at Upavon during World War 2, of these, three were standard and the others possibly Over and, or Extra Over Types. It is believed a Type 'L' hangar was intended for Upavon but this was never built. The SW/NE 05/23 grass runway on the south aerodrome was 3000' x 150' and in February 1942 No.5 Works Sqn. started laying a surface of Sommerfeld tracking. This was extended to 3500' on 8th July 1942. With the grass facility aircraft landings were made on other strips of the field. The south landing ground was encircled by a 50' wide concrete perimeter track laid and completed during September 1942. Night landing facilities on the runway were gooseneck flares, which were set out to a pattern known as the 'Upavon Flarepath,' this had been devised at the Station by a WO Turnbull. The

daytime identification was by two letters UA (large white) on the ground by the control tower. At night a red flashing aerodrome beacon (pundit) displaying the letter 'U' in Morse, guided in pilots. Runway detail of the north aerodrome is uncertain other than it was grass.

The Lorenz Blind Approach 1300yds x 50yds NE/SW grass runway was laid out three quarters of a mile to the east of the main runway at Jenner's Firs on the site of the original horse gallops. Construction had been completed by August 1939 but before training with it could start, it was shut down for the early months of the war. BAT was introduced soon afterwards. No.26 Signals Group fitted a code sender on the Beam Approach System on 22nd October 1943. It transmitted the Morse letters VA each two and half minutes for identification purposes.

A new Control Tower was built in 1961 directly opposite the 1926 built Watch Office/CFIs Office. In 1962 new administrative offices were being built at Upavon for use as Transport Command Headquarters. An extension was added in 1968 providing in the main, the new Transport Command Operations Centre.

Pre World War 1 Period

Capt F.H. Sykes 15th Hussars was originally proposed as Commandant, but was ultimately given command of the Military Wing at Farnborough, as it was deemed advisable to appoint an officer of the Royal Navy to command the CFS. Thus the first Commandant of the CFS was Capt Godfrey M. Paine MVO, RN, appointed on 15th May 1912. Winston Churchill, at the time First Lord of the Admiralty, gave him two weeks to become a pilot before assuming command. The Assistant Commandant was Lt Col H.R. Cooke RA. who also instructed in Theory and Construction. The Secretary/Assistant Paymaster was Lt J.H. Lidderdale RN and Quartermaster Lt F.H. Kirby VC, DCM. The Medical Officer was Capt E.G.R. Lithgow RAMC and the Inspector of Engines was Eng.Lt. C.R.J. Randall RN. The flying instructors were Capt J.D.B. Fulton RA, Capt P.W. L. Broke-Smith RE, Capt E.L. Gerrard RMLI and Lt A.M. Longmore RN, all of these were appointed during 15th-20th May.

For the Staff Officers it was a busy time preparing lectures, arranging course programmes and ensuring the workshops were completed before the first course started.

The Commandant was known as Captain *Bloody* Paine because of his colourful language. Capt Fulton had served in the 8th (Howitzer) Brigade, RFA stationed at Bulford, before transferring to the Air Battalion, RE in 1911. By June 1915 he had been appointed Chief Inspector of the Aeronautical Inspection Department, but died at an early age in November of that year. Before they left Eastchurch, the Admiralty offered Lt Longmore and Capt Gerrard any machine they liked. They chose respectively a Deperdussin and the Gordon Bennett Cup winning Nieuport, which they took with them to Upavon.

The organisation of the CFS provided for three courses yearly, each of four months duration. Provision was made for 90 Military, 40 Naval and 15 civilian pilots to pass through the School each year. Half the Army and Navy pilots were to be NCOs, although on arrival at the CFS, some of the officers with their certificates could do little more than keep their machines in the air.

Students and Instructors of No.1 Course CFS with *centre row 4th from left* Lt Smith-Barry and *right end* Maj Trenchard. *Back Row 2nd from right* Capt Salmond.

Prior to, and at the outbreak of war, most of the pilots serving with flying squadrons had passed through the Central Flying School, some became well known, particularly during and after the war. Lt Robert Smith-Barry who was to set down the basic rules of flying, Capt John Salmond, later Chief of the Air Staff and Maj Hugh M. Trenchard DSO who served as the CFS Assistant Commandant between 1st October 1912 and 7th August 1914 and later became the first RAF Chief of the Air Staff. All three were students of the first course, which began on 17th August 1912. At the start of the course it comprised 5 Royal Navy, 10 Military and 4 Special Reserve Officers, Subsequently, 1 Royal Navy and 6 Military Officers joined to make up the complete course.

No.3 Sqn was temporarily based at Upavon from 1st- 25th August 1912, as the Military Aeroplane Trials were being staged at Larkhill Aerodrome.

The Military and Naval officers under training at the CFS were allocated equally to four Flights, each commanded by a Flying Instructor:

'A' Flt Capt Fulton Avro 500s
'B' Flt Lt Longmore Maurice Farmans/BE2s
'C' Flt Capt Gerrard Henri Farman/Short biplanes
'D' Flt Capt Broke-Smith Maurice Farmans
There was also a Staff Flt for the benefit of CFS personnel.

The course syllabus covered practical flying training, maintenance of machines and engines, signalling,

photography and map and compass reading. Instruction began at sunrise and continued until sunset, and was progressive according to ability. Pupils started flying in Maurice Farman aeroplanes, after going solo on this type they progressed to one of the advanced Flights and were given dual training on either the Avro or the BE, finally going solo with these.

Although the Government had placed an initial order for 25 aeroplanes for use at the CFS, the first course suffered from a shortage of machines. Although 8 arrived from Farnborough in time to allow the course to start, only 4 were airworthy. When the second course commenced in January 1913, there were 12 machines allocated to the School and 8 more arrived during the course. Machines known to have been used for the first course were Maurice Farman S.7 (403), (415), Henri Farman (412), Avro 500 (404), (406), BE4 (204) and Short tractor (413). Just as the first course ended, Henri Farman (209) arrived at Upavon having been transferred from No.2 Sqn, BE4 (417) also arrived.

There were only two major accidents during the initial course with neither resulting in injury to the pilots. Capt Alson in an Avro 500 turned it over wrecking the fuselage, when landing on soft ground near Andover, and Lt Hubbard when diving a Short biplane, had no response from the controls and crashed on the aerodrome, writing-off the machine.

The first course ended on 31st December 1912, having over-run by a few weeks, and each student was

Training aeroplanes at CFS in January 1913 *LtoR*: Avro 500, two BE4s, Henri Farman, Short S.27 and two Maurice Farmans.
Photo: The Trenchard Museum

Maj Gerrard in an Avro 500 at Upavon in January 1913. Photo: Norman Parker Coll.

Henri Farman 209 was taken on charge by the Military Wing on 9th July 1912. It was briefly with No.2 Sqn before transfer to CFS and renumbered 420 on 7th December 1912. It is seen here on 6th February 1913 preparing for take-off with Maj Gerrard at the controls. It was later damaged during a landing in strong winds by Capt F. St.G. Tucker and was not flown again.

awarded his flying badge and a RFC Flying Certificate dated 5th December. The initial course had been a success with only two of the 36 pupils failing to show the necessary ability and as a result they were returned to their units.

Before the second course began, it was decided to reduce the length from four months to thirteen weeks to allow more

time for the overhaul of aircraft. This course starting on 13th January 1913 had one unsuccessful pupil. All of No.3 Course, which ran from 17th May, passed out. The establishment of the station in May was 83 officers and 692 other ranks. The 18 aeroplane allocation comprised, 2 BE2s, 6 Maurice Farmans, 3 Henri Farmans (80 hp.Gnome), 3 Henri Farmans (70

hp. Gnome), 3 Avro 500s and a BE7. In 1913 it was considered dangerous to fly in winds stronger than 15 mph, but following experiments at Upavon the Secretary of State for War advised Parliament that a CFS pilot had flown into a 56mph gale. "He has covered 400 yds over the ground" he said with much pride, "and it has taken him 16 minutes". Lt Cholmondely achieved in the same year, the first night landing ever made in England at Upavon.

In the early days of the CFS, the word 'crash' was used whenever a machine had an accident and this description was perpetuated. The first fatal crash at the CFS did not occur until the fourth course when Maj George C. Merrick DSO was killed on 3rd October 1913 (details in memorials at end). Capt Fulton who instructed on the Avro 500, invented and fitted what he called a 'crashometer' to the machines. This enabled him to judge the kind of landings his students made on the occasions he did not witness them.

The First Lord of the Admiralty, The Rt Hon Winston Leonard Spencer Churchill MP visited the CFS on 6th November 1913. He took a twenty-minute flight as a passenger in a Henri Farman biplane No.455, piloted by Maj C.L. Gerrard RMLI.

Two more fatal flying accidents occurred in March 1914. Capt Cyril P. Downer was killed on 10th March and Lt Hugh F. Treeby on 19th March (details in memorials at end).

The BE2b and BE8 biplanes were introduced at CFS when the sixth course started on 12th May 1914. The former was a simple development of the BE2 and 2A, having an improved fuselage giving more protection to the crew. The BE8 was an entirely new development.

The Royal Naval Air Service (RNAS) came into being on 26th June 1914. Previously the Naval Wing of the RFC, it ceased to be part of the Military Wing, which was administered by the War Office, and the Admiralty then administered its own aeroplanes and personnel. The role of the RNAS in conjunction with the Navy, was the defence of Britain and its coast from both sea and air attack. The role of the RFC was in support of the Army.

World War 1 Period

With the outbreak of World War 1 in August 1914 and during the period the 6th course was being held, the CFS became severely denuded of instructors and aircraft, as these were required to bring service squadrons up to a fighting strength. A small instructional staff was sent to Netheravon to instruct officers, not in possession of pilot's certificates, in elementary training preparatory to their being sent to the CFS or Brooklands to receive advanced training. Pilots who were on the 6th course when war was declared and who were considered good enough, were immediately drafted to active service squadrons. Over 100 pilots had been trained by the CFS up to this time.

Because of the war footing in the summer of 1914, security was increased and the Upavon to Everleigh road running through the Station was closed to the public for some of time. Upavon provided facilities for an internment camp and prisoners are thought to have been there until at least 1916, probably used for labour at surrounding farms. To release more male ground staff for active service overseas, girls of the W.A.A.C. and W.R.A.F. were drafted to Upavon on a weekly basis. It would appear a change of the Station cooks took place. A mechanic in the CFS Transport Section, writing to a Daisy Scott in Twickenham told her *We have had our man cooks replaced by women and well we know it. The cooking was not up to much then but now we are suffering their inexperience. It's, as the Australians would say, "kid they can't cook water".*

CFS Staff in January 1913: *rear* Capt E. Lithgow, Lt J. Lidderdale RN, Maj H. Trenchard DSO, Capt G. Paine MVO, RN, Lt Kirby VC, Lt C. Randall RN, *front* Capt J. Fulton, Lt A. Longmore RN, Capt J. Salmond, Maj E. Gerrard.

A CFS programme of Concert and Dance provided some off-duty relief in the midst of war. Tony Mellor-Ellis Coll.

The RFC Upavon Ragtime Band made-up of Navy and Army personnel
Photo: Tony Mellor-Ellis Coll.

With the development of the war, the CFS now became just one of a number of centres for advanced training. There was a number of Reserve Sqns at which students received preliminary pilot training and with qualification they were sent either to the CFS or to a Service Sqn, where their training was completed. Very soon however the CFS could no longer cope with the numbers requiring training, so Reserve Sqns were formed to cope with the increased intake of pilots. The CFS then became a Flying Instructors School and was used for the advanced training of student pilots who showed exceptional promise or who were suitable candidates as instructors. To meet the increased training needs, volunteer civilian pilots were also utilised.

Gwilym Hugh Lewis was a pilot sent to the CFS for advanced training before Upavon became a Flying Instructor's School. Educated at nearby Marlborough College, he paid a £100 and enrolled in the London Provincial School at Hendon, a civilian flying school, where he obtained his flying certificate on 27th November 1915. He joined the RFC and was posted to South Farnborough on 3rd January 1916 attending a course on basic flying instruction. He arrived at Upavon on 7th February where he gained his Wings on 23rd April. His Flt at that time was equipped with the BE8 'Bloater' and the Martinsyde Scout. Other types used then by the School, was the BE2a, BE2b, BE2c, BE8a, DH2 Scout, Vickers Gunbus and FE8. The Sopwith one and a half Strutter followed soon after. Lt Lewis was posted to No.32 Sqn at Netheravon where it had formed that January and was preparing to depart for France. At 18 years of age he was one of the youngest pilots on the squadron, but he learned quickly and in combat disposed of a Fokker E and a Roland C11 before returning to England. In June 1917 he was back at Upavon as an Assistant Instructor teaching pupils arriving from elementary flying training. The BE2e and the BE12 were the types he was instructing on.

The best pilots progressed to Scouts, the less capable went on to fast two-seaters and those left over got artillery machines. During this spell at Upavon, Lt Lewis flew a fellow Old Marlburian in a BE2c to the College at Marlborough where they took lunch with younger brother Emery Lewis. Take-off later from the College Grounds was a little 'hairy' when contact was made with some treetops. Lt Lewis had two officers of the Norwegian Flying Corps for training but was thankful that he had none of the Russians who were attending the School at the time. Lt Lewis was promoted to Capt on 10th September. Given command of the SE Flt he trained pilots for France using for instruction the 150 hp and 200 hp SE5. He went back to France himself in December as a Flt Cdr with No.40 Sqn. This time he accounted for 10 enemy machines, (some were shared kills) and was awarded the DFC. He was posted back to the UK and from 23rd August 1918, was again at CFS Upavon as the senior instructor of the SE5 Sqn. Shortly after the Armistice, Gwilym's sister visited him at the aerodrome and he gave her the flight of a lifetime in a SE5. Capt G.H. Lewis was demobilised on 28th January 1919. During World War 2 he was commissioned into the RAFVR as a Wg Cdr serving as Directorate of Plans in the underground rooms of the War Cabinet in London. His duties included waking the Prime Minister at all hours with good or bad news.

K.B. Bourdillon, a pre-war Oxford don who had entered the Army when war broke out, joined these two the following month. He devised an elementary bombsight whilst serving in France with the Intelligence Corps. The bomb sight was subsequently developed by Experimental Flight CFS and was first used operationally by Nos. 5 and 7 Sqns in September 1915 during a raid on locomotive sheds in Valencienne. The Experimental Flight CFS was equipped with two BE2c machines during the early months of 1915 and shared the Aeroplane Sheds on the south aerodrome.

A comprehensive list of aeroplane types tested by the Flight appears not to have survived, but machines

Gwilym Lewis in the cockpit of a SE5A in 1918.
Photo: The Daily Telegraph

In a War Office memo dated 18th June 1913 it was agreed to establish an 'experimental flight' of the RFC within the CFS at Upavon. This was the start and early roots of the famous Aircraft & Armament Experimental Establishment. The Experimental Flight CFS formed in November 1914 with terms of reference to conduct trials on aeroplanes, devise methods of mounting and firing guns on aeroplanes, develop visual signalling, bomb dropping apparatus and bomb sights. Capt A.H.I. Soames, a pilot formerly of the 3rd Hussars and a scientist Lt Gordon Robson RFC, formerly the civilian meteorologist at Upavon initially staffed the unit. Lt

known to have passed through Upavon in those early years are: - BE2e, BE12, FE2b, FE4, FE8, Sopwith Triplane, Morane-Saulnier BB, Fokker monoplane (German capture) and probably a DH1, DH2 and RE7.

Several other University dons arrived on the staff, one of whom Lt Tizard, would play a particularly prominent part in defence research in later years. The Experimental Flight, as it grew, launched into the scientific assessment of aircraft performance in conjunction with its work on armament development. Capt Soames was killed in June 1915 by a

500lb bomb exploding while he was undertaking ground experiments in Wig Wood near Figheldean. A wire 100yds in length connected the bomb with a switch but when it was operated, a fragment of the exploding bomb hit Capt Soames. He was taken to Netheravon military hospital with appalling injuries from which he died. As a result a decision was taken to transfer armament testing to Orfordness. Experimental Flight CFS then became Testing Flight on 18th July 1916 but was re-designated Testing Sqn by 25th September 1916. Its role now was the comprehensive trials of all new military aeroplanes and captured German ones.

Continuing building work forms the back-cloth to this group of mainly NCOs in 1917.
Photo: Tony Mellor-Ellis

At the Filton Works of the Bristol Aeroplane Company Capt Barnwell their designer addressed the need for a two-seat fighter by creating the S2A. It had a wide fuselage capable of seating the crew side by side but except for this, it was based on the Scout D110 Clerget. Two prototypes 1377 and 1378 were built in May and June 1916. Both were assessed at Filton and Upavon.

The Testing Squadron grew to the extent that it could no longer be accommodated at Upavon, where the capacity of the CFS was stretched by its training function. The Squadron left Upavon for Martlesham Heath on 16th January 1917, remaining there until 3rd/4th September 1939, when it returned to Wiltshire (see **Boscombe Down**).

Upavon saw the formation of several new units in 1917: -

No.72 Sqn on 28th June 1917 from the nucleus of 'A' Flt CFS. Before receiving any aircraft the squadron moved to Netheravon on 8th July 1917.

No.73 Sqn on 2nd July 1917 from the nucleus of 'B' Flt CFS moving to

Lilbourne eight days later.

No.85 Sqn on 1st August 1917 from the nucleus of 'C' Flt CFS moving to Norwich nine days later.

On 8th October 1917 No.36 Wing formed as 36th (Training) Wing RFC at Upper Croft, Thruxton to control Andover, Boscombe Down and Upavon, the two Wiltshire aerodromes sharing an Aeroplane Repair Section.

The CFS in Southern Training Brigade came within Training Division from 5th January 1918. No.7 Group formed on 1st April in No.2 Area, from Southern Training Brigade at 'Rokeby', Waine-a-Long Road, Salisbury and absorbing No.36 Wing. When the RAF was formed on 1st April its units in Britain were divided into five geographical areas. The CFS came within South-Western Area which formed from No.2 Area on 8th May at Chafyn Grove, Salisbury and controlled Nos.7, 8, 9, and 10 Groups. The CFS was part of No.7 Group following its formation and its change to No.7 (Training) Group on 8th August. The Group disbanded at 'Delapre', Manor Road, Salisbury and was absorbed by South-Western Area on 16th August moving there from Chafyn Grove. SW Area disbanded there and reformed as No.7 Group on 20th September. A further change took place on 16th September 1918 when No.8 Group parented CFS.

In the spring of 1918, CFS had four squadrons. 'A' Sqn was equipped with SE5s (D3554) and 'B' Sqn. with Sopwith Camels (C42 *The White Feather*). Sopwith Dolphines and Snipes were added later in the year. These two squadrons carried out advanced training. 'C' and 'D' Sqns were equipped with the Avro 504 for

"Speedy" was the CFS Magazine.
Cty: Tony Mellor-Ellis

ab initio training. During 1918 the School produced an average of 50 pilots each month for single-seat fighter squadrons. This tailed off following the Armistice when the only concern then was to demobilise personnel.

On the night of 4th/5th November 1918, a fierce gale destroyed seventeen aeroplanes and two hangars.

Inter War Period

After the Armistice on 11th November 1918, Upavon suffered from a lack of direction with no firm training policy. This changed when the CFS was redesignated the Flying Instructors School in No.7 Group on 23rd December 1919. The name change did not last long, and on 26th April 1920 training for all of the RAF's flying instructors recommenced under the umbrella of a reformed CFS. The Schools previous pre-war reputation for quality training was

The Avro 504K which struck the barn during the 'Spot Landing Competition'. Photo: Chrysalis Books

quickly reinstated and is justly regarded as the fountain-head of all flying training between the wars. The aircraft allocated for basic training was the Avro 504K, and for advanced flying the Sopwith Snipe.

The pilots attending CFS were encouraged to work hard, play hard and be happy individualists, their escapades were many and various. One light-hearted exploit of the early 1920s period involved the *Cornish Riviera* express, which steamed west along the Berks & Hants railway line daily at noon. Having passed through Pewsey station, its speed was about the same as the cruising speed of the Avro 504K, the pilots would formate on the engine just a few feet from its cab. On one occasion the engine driver and his fireman, who apparently did not appreciate the display, started throwing lumps of coal at their tormentors. It had not previously occurred to the Upavon pilots that the railwaymen did not appreciate their game. Being the gentlemen that they were, a group of the pilots ordered a large hamper of food and drink from Harrods Store which they had sent 'to the crew of the *Cornish Riviera* c/o Paddington Station, with compliments of the CFS'. The next time the Upavon airmen rendezvoused with the train, they were greeted with much waving and smiles from the footplate.

Also in the 1920s, the pilots of No.1 FTS Netheravon were in the habit of flying their DH9As over the CFS at low level in the early hours of the morning and waking up the pilots, much to their annoyance. The time came when the CFS pilots decided on retribution. A mass night raid was decided upon which was fully supported by the then Commandant 'Topsey' Holt. The scheme was hatched by Fg Off D. D'Arcy Greig who accompanied by a pupil, led the line of 504s off the south runway lit by the headlights of every car on the Station. Large packages extracted from the Officers' and Sergeants' Messes filled each cockpit. Although the Upavon men had no prior knowledge of it, their arrival at around 150' over No.1 FTS coincided with the turn out of Netheravon officers and their families from a concert in the Station Theatre. Out from the cockpit went the 'missiles' as each of the 504s roared over the rooftops and not understanding what was happening the fire and ambulance appliances were turned out for the 'emergency'. In the light of the following morning the CO was not amused to observe all the Station buildings festooned like Christmas trees with reams of toilet paper.

Probably the most famous and entertaining exploit dreamed up was the 'CFS Spot Landing Competition', held towards the end of the 13th Course in the summer of 1924. The competition involved two teams made up of instructors and pupils. The engines of the 504s had to be switched off at a height of 1,500' above the 'UPAVON' chalk letters on the south aerodrome, and an engine-off landing made with the intention of stopping with the central landing skid as close as possible to the letter 'U'. The wind on the day was from the south so approach was from the north between the sheds and across the apron. The excitement built up as each pilot made his attempt and it was not long before 504Ks with various degrees of damage littered the aerodrome.

'Topsey' Holt was having the time of his life and called for more machines to replace those unable to fly.

The most serious damage came when a pupil crashed into a telegraph pole but was unhurt. Then another 504K approached far too low, missed the Padre's married quarters by a few feet, took out some telephone wires, hit the roof of the old barn, and bounced clear over it before coming to rest in a cloud of slates and dust beside the barn, the pilot was also unhurt. Fg Off 'Nobby' Clarke an Australian, had watched the incident and was red in the face with laughter until he discovered the pilot was his pupil, flying his 504K and that it had ended up on the roof of his car. When there was no machines left in a flyable condition it was determined the pupils had won the competition with Fg Off Rex Stocken's 504K with its twisted undercarriage ending up just 9" from the 'U'. Most of the machines were repaired within 24 hrs, but the escapade resulted in an Air Ministry Order which banned 'forced landing practice' on the south aerodrome when the wind was from the south.

Despite the fun, courses at CFS were hard work, so official sporting amenities were plentiful. In addition to tennis, golf, squash, a rifle range etc, for an extra 10 shillings (50p) a month, officers were able to join a shoot, fish in the River Avon and go hunting in winter on horses borrowed from the Remount Depot at Tidworth. After a snowfall in the winter of 1924/25, some officers tried skiing on the slopes outside the Mess. This resulted in some bruising and broken skis.

During 1924 CFS was allocated some DH53 Humming Birds for evaluation. These were powered by a 750cc Blackburne Tomtit engine of the kind used in motor-bikes. They had a poor performance and a top speed of just 76 mph and ended up as playthings for the instructors. Fg Off H.R.D. Waghorn modified one to fly upside down. It appears that one day seeing a hangar with the doors open at both ends he flew straight through nearly decapitating the CFI Sqn Ldr Reggie Smart. Another type sent to Upavon for evaluation in October 1925 was the prototype DH Cirrus Moth G-EBKT. Yet another from the same family seen at the School was the DH Genet Moth which was loaned in 1926 for the use of pupils from Greece, whose Air Force was equipped with the type.

A Boulton Paul Bugle bomber J7235 was at Upavon in 1925. The four-seater with two 436hp Jupiter IV engines had been issued to No.58 Sqn at Worthy Down that year where it was used for Service trials, and comparisons with the Vickers Virginia. Sqn Ldr Walter Longton, the CO, arranged to fly the machine at the 1925 Hendon Air Display in a mock fight with two Gloster Grebes, flown by two instructors from the CFS, Flt Lt H. A. Hamersley and Fg Off J. Boothman. The display practice was carried out over Upavon with Sqn Ldr Longton putting the Bugle through violent aerobatic manoeuvres. Flt Lt Christopher Clarkson, who flew as observer in the Bugle had the job of manually maintaining the pressure in its fuel tanks. The combination of this arduous task and the violent manoeuvres so disconcerted him that upon landing he temporarily forgot that he was not in a Virginia. He walked straight into the turning propeller, was hit, luckily by the flat of the blade, and hurled backwards. Fg Off Boothman grabbed him and just prevented him rebounding back into the propeller. Flt Lt Clarkson later organised the first annual reunion dinner for past and present staff held at the CFS in November 1930. This led to the formation of the CFS Association. Sqn Ldr Longton was killed in 1927 in a flying accident at Bournemouth.

Until 1926 the Avro 504K had remained the standard trainer at the CFS. The 504N superseded it although this was not as popular. The single seat Sopwith Snipe fighter and the two-seat

Bristol Fighter were used for advanced flying.

Upavon came under No.3 Group on 1st April 1926, but this was reformed as No.23 Group on 12th April 1926 to control all UK training establishments. Shortly after this it was decided to transfer the CFS from Upavon to Wittering and on 7th October the School took up residence there.

The CFS was granted its own coat of arms on 9th December 1931. The pelican, which surmounts the bearings, was chosen because of its heraldic representation of a seat of learning. Its attitude is a reminder that traditionally the pelican will peck at its breast and suckle its young with its own lifeblood, rather than let them die in times of need. The original Naval and Military origin of the School is signified by the Naval Crown around the bird's neck and by the military (mural) crown above the helmet. The coat of arms consists of a pilot's brevet, a series of wavy lines representing the River Avon, which flows through Upavon close to the site of the School, and a Naval anchor crossed with a military sabre. The motto *Imprimis Praecepta* means 'Our teaching is everlasting'.

The Headquarters and one Flight of No.9 (Bomber) Sqn reformed at Upavon on 1st April 1924, for night flying duties in connection with Home Defence. The squadron was formed by Flt Lt V.R. Gibbs DSC but shortly afterwards Sqn Ldr J.C. Quinnell DFC was posted in as CO. During the month two Vickers Vimy aeroplanes were allocated and on 30th April the squadron left for Manston in an exchange with No.3 Sqn.

On 30th April 1924 No.3 (Fighter) Sqn returned to Upavon from Manston where it had reformed at the beginning of the month. The move this time was on a permanent basis and the squadron under the command of Sqn Ldr John C. Russell DSO, arrived equipped with the Snipe. The squadron was initially accommodated on the north aerodrome but the three Flts 'AA', 'BB' and 'C' took over part of the south aerodrome from the CFS on 1st March 1925. Later the same month the squadron was moved from No.6 to No.7 Group for command purposes but was also under orders of the CFS

Commandant.

The squadron commenced night flying from the south aerodrome in early April and the following month the Woodcock II began replacing the Snipe. The 6 arriving from Brooklands up until August were J7513, J7514, J7515, J7516, J7517 and J7726.

A spell of flying accidents began when in September Plt Off A.T. Studdert crashed whilst ground straffing troops on Army manoeuvres and was admitted to hospital. In January 1926, Plt Off H.C. Kelly crashed an Avro 504N on the aerodrome during heavy fog and was admitted to Tidworth Hospital with serious injuries. On 26th November a far more serious accident occurred resulting in two fatalities. Flt Lt J.A. Slater MC, DFC was the pilot of a dual Snipe with Plt Off J.R. Early under instruction. After take-off and at around one and half miles from the aerodrome, the machine nose-dived straight into the ground. Both men, who were dead on arrival of the ambulance, were buried at Upavon Cemetery.

The Air Ministry designated No.3 (Fighter) Sqn as the RAF's first Night Fighting Sqn on 1st March 1926, at which point it commenced those duties with its Woodcocks. On 23rd April Sqn Ldr J.M. Robb DFC was appointed CO. He received the DSO in May in recognition of his distinguished service in connection with operations in Kurdistan (Choarts Region) during June/July 1925.

The squadron gave a formation display over a number of days in May 1926 at the Birmingham Torchlight Tattoo and repeated it the following month at the Aldershot Torchlight Tattoo. In December, Comparative Trials were carried out by the squadron at Upavon between a SiskinIIIA Supercharged Jaguar IV, Gamecock Jupiter IV and Woodcock Jupiter IV. These were then flown to other aerodromes where they were similarly trialled by other squadrons.

Two accidents occurred early in 1927, one fatal and one amusing. On Wednesday 2nd February Plt Off G.F. Lewis took-off in Woodcock J7736 as target machine for Camera Gun practice. At around 400' the machine

320

appeared to stall and dived into the ground killing the pilot. Whilst on bombing practice, Plt Off R. Kellett dropped a practice bomb on 'B' Flt hangar narrowly missing two civilians who were working on the skylight. As the bomb went by them, it passed straight through the hangar roof, hit an Avro 504K and buried itself in the hangar floor, causing a heavy amount of smoke and dust. The opinions of the two workers were not recorded.

In May the squadron had an annual inspection over two days. The first day was by the AOC-in-C AM Sir John Salmond KCB, CMG, CVO, DSO who arrived by air with his Staff Officers, and the next day by the Air Officer Commanding Fighting Area Sir Robert Brooke-Popham KCB, CMG, DSO, AFC and his Staff Officers.

Plt Off H.C. Kelly who had just completed his 'Ab Initio' training course in the squadron was killed on 26th August in a flying accident on the aerodrome.

Two private flights of interest departed from Upavon in 1927. On the last day of August the Fokker monoplane *St Raphael* with Capt Hamilton (pilot), Col Minchin (av) and Princess Lowenstein-Wortheim (passenger), left Upavon in an attempt to cross the Atlantic Ocean. Nothing was ever heard of the monoplane or its occupants after its departure from Upavon. Three months later on 15th November the Fokker monoplane *Princess Xenia* with Capt MacKintosh (pilot) and Mr Bert Hinckler (nav), left Upavon in an attempt on the non-stop flight to Karachi in India.

On 19th September 1927 Sqn Ldr Robb DSO, DFC was appointed CFI of the CFS, his replacement as No.3 Sqn CO was Sqn Ldr E. Digby-Johnson AFC.

On 5th June 1928 when practising for the RAF Hendon Air Display, Fg Off P. Cranswick and Fg Off D.J.F. McMillan were killed when their two Woodcock machines collided in the air during a combined attack on a Hawker Horsley of No.11 (B) Sqn. Both were buried at Upavon Cemetery. Two months later on 2nd August, whilst carrying out air firing, Flt Lt L.H. Browning was killed at Holbeach Ranges when a wing failure on his Woodcock caused it to crash. All Woodcocks were grounded after this accident. During August and

September the type was replaced on the squadron by the Gloster Gamecock I flown to Upavon from Kenley and Tangmere.

Fg Off H.F. Gower was sentenced to dismissal by general court martial at Upavon on 19th October, for low flying at Paignton. He had carried out a series of aerobatics at low altitude over the sea, turned inland, struck a flag-staff, which was forced through the front spar of the port lower wing, and forced landed in a field on the rise of a hill.

Flt Lt H.W. Taylor collected the first Bristol Bulldog II from Filton on 22nd May 1929. The type re-equipped the squadron with others arriving through the summer and by September it had twelve.

Plt Off J.E. Jorgenson and Sgt C.B. Groom took-off in a dual Siskin J9196 on 17th June. After completing several aerobatics, the machine was seen to dive vertically and with its wings folded back it crashed near Netheravon, killing the two men.

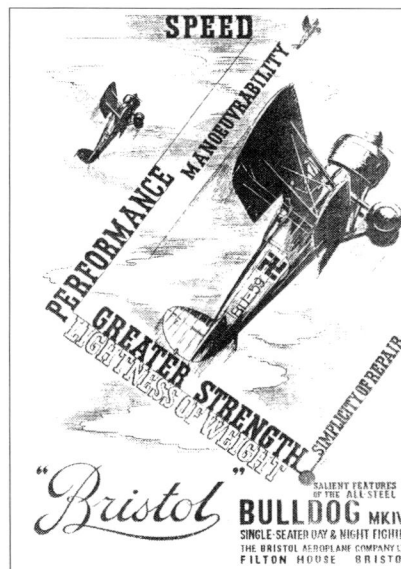

As happened in 1928, practice for the RAF Hendon Air Display claimed another squadron pilot when on 12th June 1930 Plt Off Lord Douglas-Hamilton collided with a Hawker Horsley over the aerodrome causing it to crash and killing its pilot Sgt O'Mears.

Sqn Ldr C.A. Stevens MC was appointed CO of No.3 Sqn on 6th August 1930, replacing Sqn Ldr E. Digby-Johnson AFC.

Cockpit heating was fitted to 'A' Flt machines towards the end of January 1931. A smell of heated enamel made it rather unpleasant. Early the following month oxygen equipment was fitted to all squadron machines.

Bulldog K1079 was destroyed in a flying accident on 9th March 1931. Whilst carrying out spinning practice, Sgt pilot P.C. Ginn was unable to get the machine out of a spin. He made a parachute descent from 2000' but was injured leaving the machine and whilst being dragged across the ground after landing.

In October of the following year, BAC Filton invited the squadron officers to Bristol to visit their works and to take lunch, followed by a golf match at Filton Golf Club. The squadron won the golf and was presented with a trophy. In December the squadron crest design and motto *Tertius Primus Erit* was submitted to HQ Fighting Area and approved. Also in December the squadron re-equipped with Mk.IIA airframes and Jupiter VIIF & VIIF/P engines.

The annual air display practice claimed another life on 17th May 1933 when Fg Off W.I. Clarke was killed when he lost control near the ground and crashed.

After 10 years at Upavon, No.3 Sqn moved to Kenley on 10th May 1934.

A pilot flying from Upavon on 12th December 1925 made an interesting discovery. The pilot was Sqn Ldr Gilbert Insall VC, MC who in 1915 had served at Netheravon, and was an outstanding pioneer of aerial photography. From his aeroplane he observed on the ground below, a ring of black dots within a circular earthen enclosure. This discovery was Woodhenge, the prehistoric circle, which was something of a proto-type for nearby Stonehenge. The site, north of Amesbury on the A345 is close to the original Larkhill aerodrome.

On 14th October 1926, No.17 (Fighter) Sqn moved to Upavon from Hawkinge. The squadron was equipped with the Woodcock II and together with No.3 Sqn operated as the only night fighter units in the RAF. During their eight years at Upavon, the two squadrons, besides giving

Photo: Joe Cox/Cty. Martyn Ford-Jones

46th Flying Instructors' Course, Central Flying School September December, 1935

Top row:
Sgts J.N. Ogle, J.G. Barr, J.S. Bignal, C.A. Robinson, H.G. Sherwood, H.R. Lawson, J.C. Wheeler, T.M. Scott, E.J. Irish, E.E. Sweet,

4th row:
J.G. Priest, G.H. Wright, A.H. Tompkins, H.A.C. Stratton, L.F. Humphrey, S.J. Mansell, L. Lake, R.W. Jawad, A.W. Hall, L. Gregory, B.E. Arnold,

3rd row:
Fg Offs E.F. Porter, B.s Nicholl, D. Sloan, Flt Lt R.B. Wardman, Fg Offs J.O.W. Oliver, D. Adenbrooke, K.F. Ferguson, A.D. Grace, W.H.N. Turner, W.R. Cox, S.E. Mackenzie, J.W. Donaldson,

2nd row
D.W. Reid, S.F. Godden, W.W. Stainthorpe, T.C. Chambers, G.A. Bartlett, F.H. Tyson, G.H. Denholm, R.N. McKern, P.G. Lovell-Gregg, N.J. Tindal, J.L.H. Fletcher, Gp Capt H.G. Smart OBE, DFC, AFC,

1st row
Flt Lts R.C. Jonas, J.W. Gillan, G.R.A. Elsmie, E.C. Lewis, H.R. Dale, A.P. Bett, Fg Off J.G. Glen, Flt Lts L.W.C. Bower, R. B. Councell, F/O P.A. Cooper, F/L J. Cox, F/O H.W.A. Chesterman,

Front row
Flt Lts P. R. Barwell, G. D. Harvey DFC, F. E. Watts, Sqn Ldrs A. R. Thomas, H. H. Down AFC, Wg Cdrs C.Turner AFC, J.T.T. Forbes, Sqn Ldr R. B. Sutherland, Flt Lts F. H. Woolliams, W.M.C. Kennedy, E. A. Slater.

many spectacular displays in various air shows all over the country, did valuable work in evolving a night flying and fighting technique. No.17 Sqn commanded by Sqn Ldr J. Leacroft MC, on arrival at Upavon, took over the hangars and quarters vacated by the CFS.

In June 1927 No.17 Sqn was directed to provide a Woodcock for the use of Col Lindbergh of New York, to enable him to fly from London to Paris. With the armament removed the machine was flown by Fg Off S.A. Thorn to Croyden via Northolt and handed over to the Colonel. Fg Off Thorn left for Paris by Imperial Airways. He was there for two days before returning with the Woodcock to Upavon.

No.17 Sqn suffered a number of casualties Sgt F.T. Pennicott was killed in a flying accident at Upavon on 5th July. Twenty days later Fg Off I.A. Anderson was killed while flying at Northolt when taking part in Air Defence of Great Britain (A.D.G. B.)

exercises. Plt Off Guy Stevenson was killed flying at Tidworth on 17th January 1928.

Sqn Ldr A.R. Arnold DSC, DFC was appointed as CO of No.17 Sqn on 1st April. The squadron took part in the annual RAF Hendon Air Display in June and the following month, the Blackpool Air Display.

In September 1928 No.17 Sqn re-equipped with the Siskin IIIA. One of the type J8880, crashed in flames at

Hawkinge in June 1929, but the pilot, Fg Off E.D. Turner landed by parachute but broke his arm. For five evenings during August, a squadron Flight gave night displays at the Tidworth Tattoo. Plt Off L.E.J. Lucas was killed when his machine crashed at Upavon on 10th September. On 1st October the squadron started to re-equip with the Bulldog II and IIA.

Sqn Ldr Harrison DFC was appointed CO of No.17 Sqn on 1st May 1930.

The squadron lost two pilots on 30th September when Flt Lt C.G.A. Armstrong and Sgt W. Birkinshaw were killed in a crash at Arundel Park, Sussex.

There was a further change of CO when Flt Lt L.M. Elworthy was posted in from No.56 Sqn on 25th May 1932.

Over the years, Oare Hill, between Marlborough and Pewsey, has been the site of numerous aircraft crashes which were often fatal. Plt Off P.S. Gomez crashed on the hill on 29th November, but luckier than most, he escaped with just a broken ankle.

In July 1933 the squadron collected from Martlesham Heath for Service Trials, a Bristol Bulldog R7, a Gloster Experimental Fighter and an A.W.A.2. On completion of the trials, all three were sent to Biggin Hill. In September the squadron took part in Southern Command Exercises, operating from a temporary landing ground at Imber Clump on Salisbury Plain. During the exercises Sgt R.H. Little was killed during a take-off from the landing ground on 22nd September. In November the squadron gave a low-level display at Porton Ranges for the Senior Army Officers' Course at Old Sarum. Further squadron fatalities occurred on 4th December resulting from a mid-air collision in which the two pilots Plt Off G.O. Llewellyn and Sgt J.C. Hopkins were killed. The year ended with the squadron pilots completing an Instrument Flying Course.

No.17 Sqn finally left Upavon for Kenley on 10th May 1934.

In 1934 four FAA squadrons Nos.800, 801, 820 and 821 were stationed at Upavon, which was in use as a shore base. They moved to Gosport on 1st September 1935 which was the day

One of the instructors at the CFS was Flt Lt Joe Cox seen here in the Link Trainer cockpit prior to going under the hood for 'Blind Flying' practice in 1935/36.
Photo: Joe Cox/Cty. Martyn Ford-Jones

Flt Lt Cox explaining 'Blind Flying' to pupils of the CFS prior to putting one under the hood and taking him 'up' in Tutor K3275 in 1935/36. Photo: Joe Cox/Cty. Martyn Ford-Jones

before the CFS in No.23 Group, completed its move back to Upavon from Wittering after an absence of nearly nine years. The Commandant was now Gp Capt H.G. 'Reggie' Smart CBE, DFC, AFC who had been the CFI at the CFS during a period of the 1920s.

Not all of the local residents welcomed the return of the CFS. There were those who could recall the dare-devil antics from 10 years earlier. A letter appeared in *The Times* in January 1936 complaining of the noise and nuisance caused by low-flying aeroplanes over parts of East Wiltshire. In a lengthy

response from the Air Ministry, one point made was the need for forced landing practice and the difficulty in finding suitable landing grounds enclosed by hedges etc, where this could be carried out. Suitable fields were invariably close to inhabited areas. Forced landing practices in the wide-open spaces of Salisbury Plain would be of no benefit to the pilot. The writer then explained that as a temporary measure, one of the forced landing grounds in the area was being transferred to a site one mile west of Marlborough College for a trial period of one month in order to determine the interference to the

Here the pupil is seen under the hood and Flt Lt Cox is about to enter the front cockpit from where he will taxi the machine to the take-off position. The pupil will then take-off 'blind'.
Photo: Joe Cox/Cty. Martyn Ford-Jones

Flt Lt Jonas instructing pupils of the CFS on 'Blind Flying' in 1935/36
Photo: Joe Cox/Cty. Martyn Ford-Jones

College. It is thought the one mile west should have been one mile south. What is known, is that from 15th September the CFS had the use of a landing ground at Manor Farm, Alton Barnes and from January 1936 another, one mile south of Marlborough on the A346.

The next six years saw the CFS concerned mainly with supplying instructors for the increasing number of flying schools. A development was the addition to its syllabus of instruction on twin-engined aeroplanes, as well as the use of link ground trainers, the first of which arrived on 8th September 1937.

The eleven-week duration main courses began in January, May and mid September, each course having 40 pupils of whom one quarter were SNCOs. Some pupils were RN or overseas officers and all were required to have a minimum of 1,000 hrs flying experience. On arrival pupils were divided into the four Flts with two Flts accommodated in each one of the two 'A' Type hangars on the south aerodrome. The training day commenced at 0845 hrs. Each Flt formed two units with one under ground instruction whilst the other received flying instruction. The two

units changed around after lunch. Wednesday afternoons were traditionally used for sporting activities. In the late 1930s, under the RAF Expansion Schemes, there had been a rapid development in the number of civil flying schools in the country, many became Elementary & Refresher Flying Training Schools (E & RFTS), the Bristol School of Flying at Yatesbury being one example. To maintain a uniform standard, all pilots trained as instructors for the civil schools had to be tested and approved by the CFS, having taken their private course. From November 1937 they attended three-week duration Civil Instructors' Categorisation Courses, conducted by the CFS Refresher Flt.

By the time the CFS returned to Upavon, the Avro Tutor (K3214), (K3239), (K3240), (K3241), (K3255), (K3275), (K3294), (K3310), (K3410) was used for basic training. Stan Vigor a resident of nearby Woodborough recalls the Tutors arriving in sections at Woodborough railway station from where they were transported to the aerodrome at Upavon for assembly.

The Fury, Hart (K5864), (K5857), (K5858), (K6452), (K6453) and Anson (K6180) were used for twin-engined training until the Oxford (L4535) started arriving in November 1937. Hector (K9764) was known to be attached with the CFS in August 1938 as was Miles M.16 Mentor (L4394) in October 1938. This was a military communications version of the Miles Nighthawk. Harvards (N7002), (N7015), (N7186) were in use by the School by the time war broke out.

On 9th May 1938, King George VI flew to Upavon in an Airspeed Envoy to visit the CFS. He was welcomed by the Chief of the Air Staff, ACM Sir Cyril Newall KCB, CMG, CBE, AM. He toured the station and inspected a line-up of aeroplanes before taking lunch in the Officers' Mess, after which he returned to Northolt.

The Handling Flight as part of the CFS, was formed at Upavon on 8th December 1938 to prepare Pilot's Notes for new types of aeroplane entering service, one aircraft of each type being sent to Upavon for evaluation. CFS had been carrying out this function on a reduced scale

A line up of Harts, Furies and Anson K6163, for inspection by King George VI on 9th May 1938 when he visited Upavon. Photo: PRO

King George VI with Air Marshal Sir Charles S. Burnett, KCB, CBE, DSO, AOC No.23 Group and Gp Capt J.M Robb DSO, AFC, CFS Commandant, during a 1938 Station Visit.
Photo: Mary Jarvis

since September 1937. The Senior Officer was Wg Cdr D. F.W. Bonham-Carter with 7 former CFS instructors of Sqn Ldr rank as Examining Officers. From this Examiners Pool an Examining Officer prepared the Pilot's Notes following his particular aeroplane evaluation. After a time it was decided, following the large increase in personnel and aircraft brought about by the Examining Officer Scheme, to absorb the Examiners Pool and "E" (Refresher) Flight into a squadron to be known as the Refresher Sqn. The squadron, commanded by Wg Cdr Bonham-Carter, took over the new 'C' Type hangar on the south aerodrome as soon as it had been completed in April 1939. The squadron office accommodation was completed later. The Refresher Sqn was disbanded and transferred to the Flying Squadron on 1st October 1940 as 'E'Flt, and the duties of the Examining Officers were transferred to the A&AEE at Boscombe Down from 8th November 1940.

The Handling Flt expanded to form the Handling Sqn on 11th June 1941, and moved to Hullavington as part of ECFS on 22nd August 1942. On 3rd September 1939, Blackburn Botha I L6106 was delivered for compilation of handling manuals, it was the first production model of the twin-engined reconnaissance bomber, L6104 and L6105 were prototypes. On 29th May 1940 Stirling N3637 was flown in for preparation of Pilot's Notes. The pilot was John L. Parker and the 2nd pilot Hugh Gordon, both Short Bros test pilots. They landed the aircraft successfully up the slope of Upavon's south aerodrome but it was realised that the landing-ground was too small for an aeroplane of this size and so it was flown out to Boscombe Down the following day.

Some of the aircraft types, in addition to the CFS trainers, which could be seen at Upavon in the two years leading up to the war included the Defiant (L6951), Demon, Gladiator,

Hurricane I (L1873) and Spitfire fighters; Battle (N2085), Blenheim, Hampden (L4123), Harrow, Hereford (L6004), Hind, Hudson (N7209), Wellesley and Wellington (L4285) bombers; Hector and Lysander Army Co-operation machines; Don, Harvard, Magister (L8168), Mentor, Miles Kestrel (Master prototype), Nighthawk and Tiger Moth trainers; Cadet, Drone, Swallow, Vega Gull and Whitney Straight lightplanes.

World War 2 Period

With the outbreak of war aircraft were dispersed around the perimeter of the aerodrome and guarded by RAF personnel. Later on, one officer and three men of the 4th Battalion Wiltshire Regiment covered the aerodrome security. They had the task of erecting coils of barbed wire around the perimeter and guarding vulnerable parts of the Station. Aerodrome defence improved as the war developed, and later eight gun posts (pill boxes) were manned by the Anti-Aircraft Machine Gun Section of the RAF Defence Company. All pill-boxes were equipped with two Vickers guns. Camouflaging of the station was not started until the end of June 1940 when the Stucco Company arrived to paint the buildings. A decoy site was prepared to the northwest of the aerodrome at All Cannings (173/SU075615). A Mk.I Spitfire was allocated as the Station Defence Flight. Everleigh was used by the School as a practice forced landing ground and for circuit training during 1940/41, and land at Manor Farm, Alton Barnes became a Relief Landing Ground (RLG) as did land at Mullen's Farm, Manningford.

Once the war started, it became obvious that the CFS could not cope with the vastly increased demand for instructors, and Air Commodore Robb left for Canada on 2ⁿᵈ October 1939 to help plan the highly successful Commonwealth Air Training Scheme. Wg Cdr Bonham-Carter was Acting Commandant until 6ᵗʰ January 1940 when he also went to Canada. A/Wg Cdr George Stainforth then held the post until Robb returned on 26ᵗʰ January. Stainforth was then CO of the Refresher Sqn and Examiners Pool known as 'X' (examiners) Flt.

From November 1939 CFS Upavon was parented in No.23 (Training) Group with Headquarters at South Cerney.

Upavon and its neighbour at Netheravon, suffered from periods of non-flying during the first winter of war when aeroplanes and equipment were heavily covered over with snow and ice.

Pupils of No.63 (4ᵗʰ War) Qualified Flying Instructors Course in the Officers' Mess at Upavon in January 1940. *Standing 3ʳᵈ from left* Fg Off Eric Bradley with Fg Offs M.J. Suett, D.N. Fearson, C.W. Lindsey, W.R.L. Beaumont, Ian W. Brown, J.L. Shaw, D. Hewart, R.A. Land, Molin and two unknown. Photo: Susan Cole

Pilot H.A. Hughes was at Upavon in September 1939 with around 350 hours of light aircraft flying in his logbook. He was given one hour dual instruction in a Harvard and was then sent off solo. The very next day he was sent off in a Battle, alone except for some ballast in the shape of an AC2, to do an hour's circuit flying. He was not even familiar with all of the cockpit controls as he commenced his take-off from the smaller north airfield and he was soon too busy keeping the Battle straight whilst watching the approaching, and already all-too-near, boundary to do anything about it. He learnt the finer details once airborne. It is perhaps easy to see why so many pilots were to lose their lives in wartime flying training accidents due to insufficient and hurried initial instruction.

On 18ᵗʰ September 1939 the 60ᵗʰ Flying Instructors Course, the first to commence after war was declared, became No.1 War Course with a much-reduced duration from nine weeks to four. Conversion training for a number of Rumanian pilots was carried on until the course was completed as Rumania had purchased some Blenheims, but no further courses commenced. Two early war casualties from No.1 War Course were Sgt Charley L.W. Mason RAFVR and Sgt J.H. Hargreaves RAFVR both of whom were killed when their Harvard I N7181 crashed when taking-off at night on 8ᵗʰ October 1939. Sgt Mason was buried at Upavon cemetery.

During the next course South African Sqn Ldr Michael A. Aylmer RAF a CFS instructor, and his pupil Fg Off E.K. Rayson RAFO were also killed during night flying, when their Harvard I N7182 flew into the ground near Puckshipton House between Beechingstoke and Marden (SU173/095584), four miles northwest of the aerodrome on 1ˢᵗ November. Sqn Ldr Aylmer was buried at Upavon cemetery. One of the School's Hart aeroplanes crashed at Harepath Farm near Devizes on 21ˢᵗ February 1940 killing Fg Off Basil A. Mortimer RAF, he was buried at Upavon cemetery. On 11ᵗʰ March the aerodrome at Upavon was suddenly blanketed by fog at 1015 hrs and the School aeroplanes still airborne had to divert. Unfortunately a No.1 FTS Battle from Netheravon crashed at Upavon between the Lorenz beacon and the eastern boundary but details of any casualties were not recorded.

Refresher Sqn was given the role of testing volunteer pilots of the Air Transport Auxiliary (ATA). These were pilots to be used for ferrying single, twin and four-engined aeroplanes from factory or MUs to squadrons. Upavon had not seen anything like them before, all volunteers, some were old, young, unfit and even incapacitated. ATA was unkindly known as 'Ancient and Tattered Airmen'. However the majority rose to the challenge and

passed their tests, even a pilot who had one arm! Later young girls of the ATA appeared, the aviatrix Amy Johnson was one of these and another, Joan Hughes, was only 17 years old.

The legendary Douglas Bader was an early wartime pupil, attending a refresher course at Upavon between November 1939 and February 1940. In this period he flew eight different types of aircraft in 41 flying hours. His instructors were Sqn Ldr Joe Cox and Sqn Ldr Christoper Clarkson. Within a few hours he was allowed to go solo in a Tutor, the first solo since he lost both legs in a flying accident eight years before. He celebrated by flying inverted at 600'. He left Upavon with his ability as a pilot recorded as 'Exceptional'.

Sqn Ldr Cox had first met Douglas Bader at Duxford in 1933. Douglas having by then been fitted with artificial legs, had asked Joe to take him 'up'. Bader was determined to fly again and he had to prove this to the RAF. Joe Cox agreed to his request and flew with him twice in Atlas K-2540 on 7ᵗʰ and 10ᵗʰ March 1933. Bader managed to take-off, perform aerobatics and land the aircraft with such precision it was difficult for Joe to believe the man in the rear cockpit was disabled. On landing the first time, fellow pilots had refused to believe Bader had been at the controls. Joe Cox then took him aloft

Plt Off Douglas Badar at Upavon with his instructor Sqn Ldr Joe Cox to his right.
Photo: Joe Cox/Cty. Martyn Ford-Jones

Atlas K-2540 in which Douglas Bader and Joe Cox flew at Duxford.
Photo: Joe Cox/Cty. Martyn Ford-Jones

again and sat with his hands on his head to prove who was flying the machine. However despite passing the most exacting tests in the air, Bader was rejected as a pilot by higher authority. As he was not allowed to fly he did not wish to remain in the RAF and was invalided out later in the year.

Another well known former officer, 55 year old Lt Col Robert Smith-Barry AFC, of Gosport fame, reported at Upavon on 23rd May 1940 and was appointed to an emergency commission in the General Duties branch of the RAFVR. The appointment was for the duration of hostilities as a Pilot Officer, the most junior of RAF officer ranks. He was attached to the CFS supernumerary pending the start of No.66 (No.7 War) Flying Instructors Course. He shaved off his beard and moustache and had his grey hair cut short. In June he made 41 flights, dual and solo, on Tiger Moths and Tutors; his instructors were Flt Lt Donaldson and Sqn Ldr Bitmead. In July he made 26 flights, dual and solo, on Masters and Oxfords; his instructor

was Flt Lt Stratton. In August he made 20 flights, advanced dual and solo, including aerobatics, on Tutors, Masters, Harvards, Oxfords, Blenheims, Beauforts and a Hurricane; his instructor was Wg Cdr Stainforth. On 14th August he was posted to No.4 Ferry Pilots' Pool at Kemble.

During the three months Smith-Barry was at Upavon, the founding father of the RAF, Lord Trenchard GCB, GCVO, DSO also paid a visit there. He and Smith-Barry were students from the first CFS course in 1912. Those who witnessed the incident were open-mouthed to see a Marshal of the RAF and a Pilot Officer walking arm-in-arm to the mess.

David Carmichael was a wartime flying instructor at Upavon and he recalls the sterling work of the WAAF groundcrew who looked after the training aircraft. Their duties in the winter months were particularly unpleasant and arduous. When the pilots arrived for morning take-off, the cockpit windscreens would have been scraped free of ice. The girls then had to crawl along the cold wing, open a panel, crank the engine using a hand crank and remain there until the engine started or, if it failed, start all over again. Once the engine started they would be in the slipstream of the propeller and would have to remove the crank and secure the panel before sliding back along the wing to drop onto the ground. When run-up was complete, they would crawl under the wing to remove the chocks. Finally their tasks complete, a thumbs up would be given before they returned to the flight shack to warm themselves.

At the end of flying they were again at dispersal in preparation for shutting down aircraft.

Fatalities from training accidents continued to mount. Sgt Edgar F.J. L'Estrange RAFVR was killed when flying a Master I N7539, which dived into the ground on Monday 8th July 1940. Plt Off Brian H. Black RAF and Plt Off Geoffrey E. Moon RAFVR of (No.8 War) Course were killed on 29th July 1940 when their Tutor I K3287 flew into the ground at Manor Farm, Chilmark. Harvard N7174 flew into the ground at Casterley Camp near Upavon on 13th September. Plt Off C.T. Bell survived with a fractured leg but Plt Off John W. Hind-Smith RAFVR was killed. All of the men who died were buried at Upavon cemetery.

In August 1940 an Air Ministry conference decided there was a need to increase the output of the CFS. A 40-pupil intake every fortnight instead of 50 every fourth week commenced, but within three months this became 90 pupils in each five-week period. On 6th September six American pilots, commissioned in the RAFVR, reported for training, 19 Polish pilots arrived on 19th October and many more foreign pupils followed these, by now the numbers passing through was overwhelming the instructors.

The end of May 1940 saw the arrival at Upavon of soldiers returned from Dunkirk. They came by lorry from local railway stations and were billeted in empty huts. Later in the year the Parliamentary Under-Secretary of State for Air, Capt Harold Balfour MC, MP paid a visit to the CFS on 28th September 1940.

From 9th October 1940 the CFS started using New Zealand Farm Relief Landing Ground (RLG) for night flying training and from April 1941, Overton Heath RLG near Marlborough also opened for night flying training. At which time the School ceased using Marlborough LG. Both the north and south aerodromes at Upavon were in constant daytime use until 1941 when possibly flying from the northern field was restricted to the occasional practice flight. George Buckland a LAC 1. CG (Fleet Mechanic) at Upavon from April 1941 to February

1944 indicates that part of the landing-ground was used at that time for storage of 40/50 Oxfords.

Flt Lt R.M.G. Zambra on (No.11 War) Course was killed on 2nd October 1940 when Master I N7749 dived into ground when night flying one mile north of Shrewton LG. Flt Sgt W.A. Sutcliffe was killed on 17th December 1940 when Oxford II P6814 crashed at Upavon. A Belgian pilot Plt Off Saint-Mard was killed when his Master I T8409 crashed on 22nd July 1941. Tutor K3400 crashed on 2nd January 1942 killing Polish pilot Sgt Chodzicki. Master III W8452 crashed and burnt out on 14th January 1942 killing Plt Off Augustice H.D.H. Firman RAFVR and Sgt John Donaldson RAAF, both were buried at Upavon cemetery. This was a South Marston built Master.

The CFS ceased to exist as such from 1st April 1942 when one element formed the Empire Central Flying School at Hullavington and the other remained at Upavon becoming No.7 Flying Instructors School (FIS) in No.23 Group with the function of taking pupils for OTU Instructor courses. The School was commanded by Gp Capt A. J. Holmes AFC. Apart from it s nine years at Wittering, thirty years of CFS at Upavon ended.

No.7 FIS was equipped with 31 + 14 Oxfords, 26 + 13 Masters, 14 + 7 Magister and 1 + 1 Dominie. As from 7th April 1942 the School became No.7 FIS (Advanced), taking eight-week duration Flying Instructors Courses.

The OTU Instructor courses were transferred to No.3 FIS (A) when it formed at Hullavington on 1st August 1942, at the same time it received 21 Oxfords and all the Master aircraft from the Upavon allocation. No.7 FIS (A) received Magisters as replacements. The aircraft allocation for No.7 FIS (A) changed again in February 1944 and comprised 38 + 13 Oxfords and 3 + 1 Ansons.

Marshal of the RAF, Viscount Trenchard, GCB, GCVO, DSO visited his former station on 29th September 1942.

Plt Off William E. Nilsson RNZAF and Plt Off Peter R.C. Mars RAFVR, two pupil instructors with No.7 FIS (A) were involved in a fatal flying accident on 19th October 1942. They landed first

The RAF Boxing Team 1942-43 with coach Freddie Mills, the British Light-Heavyweight boxer, who was also the Station Librarian. Photo: Len Brewster

in a field at Chirton four and a half miles north west of Upavon, their Magister P6413 was seen to take-off again but before gaining height, it smashed into a tree in another field on the edge of the village. The two men were released from the wreckage by villagers and carried into a nearby cottage but it was some time before the ambulance arrived from Upavon by which time Plt Off Nilsson had died. Plt Off Mars was taken to Devizes Hospital where he died eight hours later. Both men were buried at Upavon cemetery. William Nilsson had joined the RNZAF in October 1941, carried out his flying training and was commissioned as a Plt Off in New Zealand, before arriving in England on 28th June 1942. He was at No.3 Personnel Reception Centre (PRC) Bournemouth until posted on 21st July to No.6 (P) AFU Little Rissington. Whilst there he attended an instrument flying course with No.1523 Beam Approach Training Flt. before proceeding to Upavon on 2nd September.

A No.295 Sqn Whitley based at Netheravon crashed with fatalities at Upavon on 9th January 1943 (see **Netheravon**). Two Oxfords collided in mid air near Porton on 29th January. Sgt. Bryan successfully crash-landed one aircraft but Plt Off Perry and Sgt Leonard J. Hughes RAAF died in the crash of the other. The latter was buried at Upavon cemetery. Mustang 2 AG485, believed to be from No.170 Sqn, crashed on making a forced landing at Upavon on 11th April. The pilot Sgt Lawson suffered minor injuries.

No.1537 Beam Approach Training Flt formed at Upavon on 4th May 1943 from 'E' Flt of No.7 FIS (A) in No.23 Group. The establishment was 10 flying instructors with Acting Sqn Ldr H.D. Bisley AFC as CO. The Flt was equipped with 7 + 3 Oxfords for multi-engined instructor training. The aircraft displayed a yellow triangle on the fuselages. Pupils were drawn from the Long F.I. Courses at No.7 FIS. The BAT Courses had a duration of 10 days. An early accident was recorded two days after the Flt formed when during night beam training Fg Off Thorne with two pupils crashed short of the flarepath. The Oxford, which was being flown by a pupil was Cat.'B' damaged and only the instructor received slight injuries. On 2nd July two aircraft flying on the beam collided in mid-air but landed safely. The beam was powered by electricity from the station's main supply and failed numerous times due to excessive demand placed on the system. Beam training was cancelled during these periods.

Fg Off Robert Tomlinson RAFVR and Fg Off John Ahearn RAAF of No.7 FIS (A) were killed on Friday 4th June 1943 when their Magister I L8052 stalled on a gliding turn at about 500' and crashed at Etchilhampton near Devizes. The Australian was buried at Upavon cemetery. Pilot Sgt Stanley A. Snow RAFVR was killed and Sgt H. Bamhill was injured when their Magister I L8069 slipped in whilst turning during a low flying exercise at Collingbourne Kingston on Thursday 15th July. Another fatal crash occurred the following day in the adjoining village of Collingbourne Ducis. Plt Off George E. Holmes RAFVR and Sgt Clifford E. Blanchette RNZAF were killed when their Oxford II X7255, whilst carrying out a steep turn exercise at about 3000', flicked to the right resulting in a spin, and then crashed. Both pilots tried to leave the aircraft but were unsuccessful. Sgt Blanchette was buried at Upavon cemetery. He had joined the RNZAF in March 1942 and carried out his flying training in New Zealand and Canada. He arrived in England in May 1943 and was posted to No.11 AFU Shawbury where he spent two months flying the Airspeed Oxford before proceeding to No.7 FIS (A) Upavon in July 1943 for further training on the Oxford and Magister. Flt Lt Reginald H.P. Thomas RAFVR (Instructor) and South African Plt Off Jacobus A.J. Baard RAFVR (pupil) were killed on Monday 18th October when their Magister R1844 crashed near Woodborough 3 miles north west of Upavon. The crash was attributed to 'a stable yawing dive to which Magisters were prone when the elevators are blanked by rudder when recovering from a stall or spin.' The South African was buried at Upavon cemetery. On Thursday 23rd December 1943 Oxford I LX595 attempting to land at night in bad visibility, struck a flagstaff and crashed into the small 'C' Type maintenance hangar, which caught fire on the north airfield. The pilot Flt Lt Kenneth Holland RAFVR, Fg Off William Bradley RAFVR and LAC Harold J. Brailsford RAFVR (WOP) were killed. Fg Off Bradley is buried at Upavon cemetery. Fg Off Peter Milner RAFVR and Plt Off Ronald W.J. Towle RAFVR were killed on Tuesday 7th March 1944 when Magister I N5397 crashed at Littlecote near Hungerford following an engine failure. Fg Off Charles R. Dodwell RAFVR and Fg Off John A. Wyatt RAFVR were killed on Tuesday 4th July when Oxford II V3532, due to the pilot's inexperience of formation flying, crashed at Kimpton on the north side of Thruxton airfield in Hampshire. Fg Off Dodwell was buried at Bath (Haycombe) cemetery.

Sqn Ldr Mansell was appointed as BAT Flt CO in April 1944 and the establishment of aircraft changed to 5 Oxfords and 4 Harvards from November 1945. The BAT Flt was affiliated to No.7 FIS (A) and used Overton Heath RLG as a satellite from

the time of its formation until August 1945. The BATF moved to Little Rissington on 1st May 1946.

On 18th July 1945 No.7 FIS (A) took over 8 Harvards from No.3 FIS (A). A number of satellite airfields were used by No.7 FIS (A), these were Manningford ELG, New Zealand Farm, Overton Heath RLG and Ramsbury where 'F' Flt Oxfords carried out night flying for two months during 1946. The Harvards of 'A' to 'D' Flts of No.7 FIS (A) used Lulsgate Bottom in Somerset as a RLG after No.3 FIS disbanded there on 18th July 1945.

Upavon had some unexpected visitors in the summer of 1945 when a BOAC York flown by Pilot Captain Taggart landed during a severe rainstorm on 8th August. He took-off again for his base at Hurn after the storm had subsided. Three Meteors on a cross-country flight from Colerne landed short of fuel on 6th September and took off again later.

Post War Period

'A' to 'D' Flts of No.7 FIS (A) left Lulsgate for Little Rissington on 26th April 1946. The main party left Upavon for Little Rissington on 2nd May 1946 where the CFS had reformed. Gp Capt E. A. C. Britton DFC moved there with his staff from Upavon as Commandant and nucleus of the CFS staff.

For over 30 years, Upavon had been synonymous with CFS and flying training of the highest standard, and for a similar number of years it would be synonymous with RAF world-wide Transport. After World War 2, No.38 Group Headquarters, Transport Command, specialising in tactical army co-operation, arrived at Upavon on 31st May 1946, disbanding on 1st February 1950. Transport Command Headquarters was next to arrive on 21st April 1950. The latter was redesignated Air Support Command on 1st August 1967 and reduced on 1st September 1972 to No.46 Group the air support element of Strike Command. The Group was disbanded into No.38 Group on 1st January 1976.

No.38 Group reformed at Upavon on 1st January 1960 as No.38 (Air Support) Group. It was soon realised that the Station was not large enough

to accommodate this Group as well as Transport Command. The problem was overcome by transferring No.38 Group to Odiham on 17th May 1960. It moved to Benson in 1972 in Strike Command and moved to Upavon on 10th November 1975. It disbanded on 17th November 1983 merging into No.1 Group with Headquarters at Upavon, which in turn left for Benson on 30th July 1993.

No.38 Group Communications Flt was in tandem with its Group Headquarters until 1972 at Benson, where it operated as a detachment of No.21 Sqn. The squadron disbanded in early 1976. The Transport Command Communications Flt. arrived from Hendon, likewise in May 1946 but as an independent unit. In the late 50s, early 60s, it was elevated to squadron status. One of its aircraft was Anson T.21 VV981 which is thought to have been struck off-charge in 1963, before being sold for scrap on 20th December 1965. The Sqn disbanded into Western Communications Squadron on 1st April 1964. Based at Andover it provided an Air Support Command detachment of 1 Devon and 1 Pembroke at Upavon from 1st August 1967 to 3rd February 1969, at which time the squadron was redesignated No.21 Sqn at Andover. One of its aircraft remained at Upavon, as AOC-in-C's aircraft, until Air Support Command reduced to Group status on 1st September 1972.

No.1310 Flt reformed at Upavon on 31st March 1953 as No.1310 (Transport) Flt. It was equipped with the York C1 (MW162) and provided support for guided weapon trials. The Flt left Upavon for Mallala near Adelaide, Australia in May 1953.

No.230 Sqn arrived from Dishforth on 30th April 1959 equipped with the Pioneer CC 1 and additionally from February 1960 the Twin Pioneer CC 2. Pioneer CC.1 XL555, a short take-off and landing aircraft (STOL) was written off after it stalled and dived into the ground when taking-off from Upavon on 29th April 1960. There were no fatalities but probably a few bruises. The squadron left for Odiham on 30th May 1960.

A number of Joint Service Trials Units formed at Upavon in Transport Command during 1959/60. No.13

JSTU on 1st June 1959, moving to Boscombe Down on 1st February 1962 for 'Red Top' Air to Air Missile (AAM) evaluation. No.14 JSTU on 2nd November 1959, No.15 JSTU on 1st December 1959 and No.17 JSTU on 1st October 1960. The latter for trials with the Mk.2 Bloodhound. This Unit had moved to North Coates by 1st April 1964.

1962 marked the 50th anniversary of the establishment of the CFS on 19th June 1912 and a special display of flying and static exhibits was staged on 16th June

building (details in memorials at the end). At the final flypast by aircraft of No.1 Sqn, the salute was taken by Marshal of the RAF Sir John Salmond who had been on the first course to be held at the CFS in 1912.

No.46 Group Air Transport Examining Unit moved in from Abingdon on 31st October 1973 to be redesignated No.38 Group Air Transport Examining Unit on 10th November 1975. It was further redesignated as No.38 Group Examining Unit in 1976.

Closure

The RAF ceased using Upavon and handed it over to the Army in 1993. Now called Trenchard Lines it houses the Headquarters Adjutant General's Dept., Headquarters Provost Marshal's Office and Headquarters of the Army Training and Recruiting Agency. Lyneham's Hercules continue to use the maintained reinforced grass runway for Strip Landings. The runway with metal underlay is currently 3,600' x 150'. Chinooks on exercise and helicopters with visiting officials land and take off from the former airfield. The RAF supplies the ATC personnel for these movements. In addition to the RAF's No.622 (Volunteer) Gliding School, the Army Gliding Association Wyvern Club is based at Upavon with their ATC operating from a mobile bus. The club has a number of different gliders such as the ASK13 and 21, PZL (Junior), LS4a and LS4b plus a number of privately owned types.

Upavon is still recognisable as a former RAF Station. Some of the early CFS buildings are now Grade 2 listed, such as the Officers' Mess which remains in use. Internally and externally this is a grand building with its colonnaded entrance. The Sergeants' Mess is used as offices and the Institute is now the Sergeants' Mess. Building works conducive to its listed status were carried out on this building during 2001. The original CFS Regimental Office reopened on 9th September 1983 by Marshal of the RAF Lord Trenchard as the Trenchard Museum and can be viewed by appointment only. This provides a very interesting collection together with the reconstructed Commandant's Office, which was used by Capt G.M. Paine, including a number of personal items such as his binoculars. Displays in other rooms cover the early days of the CFS, some aspects of the work of Trenchard and the development of Upavon throughout its use by the RAF. Other buildings of the pre World War 1 era include the, Operations Block, now used as the HQ of the Provost Marshal and Single Officer's Quarters, one of which was used by Trenchard as his personal accommodation. St. Peter's Station Church it appears did not become a church until 28th October 1956 but the 1925 OS map shows the

HRH Prince Philip inspecting the 1915 Avro 504K in a line up of vintage aircraft at Upavon on a sunny 16th June 1962.   Photo: The Trenchard Museum

FLYING   PROGRAMME

Item					Item			
1.	Ascent of " R " Type Observation Balloon			2.45 p.m.	5.	Fly Past	Shackleton	3.25 p.m.
							Argosy	
							Britannia	
							Comet 4	
2.	Vintage Aircraft	Avro 504K	— 1915	2.45 p.m.			Comet 2	
		Sopwith Pup	— 1916				Canberra	
		Bristol Fighter F.2b	— 1917				Valiant	
		S.E.5A	— 1917				Victor	
		Avro Tutor	— 1931				Vulcan	
		Bristol Bulldog	— 1929				Javelin	
		Gloster Gladiator	— 1934				Lightning	
		Swordfish	— 1936				Sea Vixen	
		Hawker Hart	— 1928				Scimitar	
					6.	Aerobatic Display by Sea Vixens of the Fleet Air Arm		3.35 p.m.
3.	World War II Aircraft	Fulmar		3.10 p.m.	7.	No. 38 Group Set Piece		3.40 p.m.
		Spitfire						
		Hurricane			8.	Demonstration of the P.1127 Vertical Take-Off and Landing Aircraft		4.05 p.m.
		Mosquito						
		Lincoln			9.	Aerobatic Display by the Royal Air Force Aerobatic Team (Lightning Aircraft)		4.10 p.m.
					10.	Fly Past by No. 1 Squadron		4.20 p.m.
4.	Aerobatic Display by five Jet Provosts of the Central Flying School, Royal Air Force			3.20 p.m.		The Salute will be taken by Marshal of the Royal Air Force Sir John Salmond.		

1962 to commemorate the event. The display at Upavon was visited by HRH The Duke of Edinburgh who unveiled a stone memorial plaque at the entrance to the new Transport Command

No.622 (Volunteer) Gliding School transferred from Old Sarum to Upavon in November 1978 and continues to fly from there with Viking T Mk.1s.

The Upavon Officers' Mess seen in 1985.   Photo: The Trenchard Museum

Trenchard's office and the original CFS Headquarters Offices at Upavon, now the Trenchard Museum.

The Watch Office/CFI's Offices.

building used at the time as a Church Hall. The same map shows a Roman Catholic Church but the former was used by all denominations after 1985. The church bell was originally a ship's bell in HMS *Centaur*, an aircraft carrier of 22,000 tons which was completed in 1953, placed in reserve in 1966 and scrapped in 1971.

From the between the wars period the two 'A' Type and the 'C' Type hangar remain on the original south airfield and the small 'C' Type ARS on the north side of the road is now a gymnasium. This has been re-skinned and a false ceiling added. During the 2001 camp building works, asbestos was removed from this former hangar. The Watch Office/CFI's Offices stands between the two 'A' Type hangars facing the 1961 built Control Tower, which is seen in poor condition in the picture on the next page.

CFS Commandants & Senior Staff

Lt Col D. Le G. Pitcher who had been a pupil of the first course became the second Commandant in 1915 when he replaced Capt. Paine. Then in 1916 Lt Col C.J. Burke DSO, who had taken No.2 Sqn to France from Netheravon in August 1914, replaced Lt Col Pitcher. Lt Col A.C.H. MacLean who had been a Flt. Cdr. at Upavon before the war succeeded him the same year, holding the post until 1917. He insisted personnel on the station ate plain food and plenty of milk pudding. The CFS Commandant in the latter months of the war was Lt Col A. J. L. 'Jack' Scott MC until he left for France in September 1918, when 21 year old Major Jack Slessor the Assistant Commandant was left in command. 'Jack' Scott returned when the war ended but died in the influenza epidemic of 1919. Lt Col P.H.L. Playfair MC became Commandant until later in the year when Lt Cdr Charles Breese AFC, RN took over the post as a Wg Cdr until 1920.

Wg Cdr N.D.K. MacKwen CMG, DSO, succeeded him until 1922 when Wg Cdr E.A.D. Masterman CMG, AFC was appointed. In 1923 the popular Gp Capt F.V. "Topsey" Holt CMG, DSO, a strict disciplinarian when required but with a capacity for enjoying life, was the 1920s

The post war built Control Tower looks in bad shape, in the winter of 2002.

Commandant whose regime at the CFS guaranteed an ever-increasing standard of trained personnel. Gp Capt W.R. Freeman DSO, MC became the next Commandant in 1925 and was the man in post when the CFS transferred to Wittering in 1926.

Capt G.M. Paine the Commandant when the CFS was formed became the first Commandant of RAF Cranwell in 1916 (known then as HMS Daedalus) with the rank of Commodore.

During its 1935 to 1942 period at Upavon, the CFS would have just three different Commandants. Gp Capt J.M. Robb DSO, AFC replaced 'Reggie' Smart in December 1936 and held the post until 17th March 1940 by which time he was an Air Commodore. Gp Capt H.H. Down AFC was the final Commandant who left Upavon for Hullavington on 12th March 1942 to form the Empire Central Flying School.

Victoria Cross Recipiants

1) Sgt Thomas Mottershead

The only non-commissioned airman to be awarded a VC during World War 1 volunteered for the RFC on 10th August 1914 and was posted to CFS Upavon as an Air Mechanic, 2nd Class. Such was the calibre of Thomas Mottershead and his work, that by April 1916 he held the rank of Sergeant. He then applied for pilot training, was accepted and within a month his instruction at Upavon began. On 6th July he joined No.25 Sqn at Auchel in France. This was a reconnaissance squadron equipped with the FE2b two-seat pusher biplane.

The squadron engaged in other roles as required and Sgt Mottershead carried out bombing raids, some of which were at low-level. On 22nd September the target was Samain railway station where an ammunition train was bombed from 1500', and was followed by a low-level strike where the gunner Lt Street raked the entire length of another train. A Fokker then attacked from behind the FE2b but it was out-manoeuvred by Mottershead and shot down by his gunner. For this action Sgt Mottershead, soon to be promoted to Flt Sgt, was awarded the DCM on 14th November. On another occasion whilst on reconnaissance accompanied by another FE2b, Tom signalled to the other pilot to follow him in to land at an enemy aerodrome. There they stopped and opened fire into the aeroplane sheds with Tom signalling to his colleague when he felt it was prudent they should leave. Soon after this he was posted to No.20 Sqn equipped with FE2ds at Clairmarais.

On 7th January 1917 Tom with his gunner Lt W.E. Gower and one other squadron machine, engaged a pair of enemy Albatros Scouts. Lt Gower's accurate gunfire sent one Albatros steeply down and out of control but the other enemy machine closed on Tom's FE2d A39 and at close range from the rear, opened fire causing the fuel tank to burst into flames. The fire spread rapidly around the pilot and height was quickly lost. Lt Gower used a fire extinguisher on his pilot whose clothing was alight. Despite the fire and his injuries, Tom took time to locate a suitable place to land so that the life of his gunner would be saved. He made a text book approach and

with fire and smoke emitting from his machine and parts of it breaking off, landed but nosed in when the undercarriage collapsed. Gower was thrown out as the tail raised but landed safely away from the burning machine. He was then helped by soldiers to release Tom who was despatched for treatment of his horrendous burns. He was visited on by a colleague on 11th January who found him cheerful and uncomplaining. He was even able to get on and off his bed unaided. He died however the following day. The announcement of a posthumous award of the VC appeared in the *London Gazette* on 12th February 1917.

2) Sub Lt Rex Warnford

A pupil pilot of the RNAS who arrived at CFS from basic training at Hendon in February 1915 was Sub Lt Rex Warnford. He obtained his Wings and was posted to 2 Sqn RNAS Eastchurch. On 7th June 1915 he shot down an enemy Zeppelin over Belgium for which he was awarded the VC (refer to **Highworth** for details).

3) Lt William Leefe Robinson

Another of the new pilots passing through Upavon for advanced training at this time was Lt. William Leefe Robinson. He had qualified for his Royal Aero Club Pilot's Certificate at South Farnborough in July 1915. He arrived at Upavon on 14th August and flew solo in BE8 693 the following day. He went on to serve with No.10 Reserve Aeroplane Company based at Joyce Green in Kent whose task it was to defend London against aerial attacks. On 3rd September 1916 flying BE2c 2693 he became the first pilot to shoot down an airship (SL11) over Britain when it crashed in flames at Cuffley north of Enfield. For this act he received an immediate award of the VC.

4) Captain Albert Ball

Albert Ball arrived at Upavon having obtained his Royal Aero Club Flying Certificate at Hendon on 15th October1915. He had served in the Army as a 2nd Lt before transferring to the RFC. He was awarded his Wings on 22nd January 1916, eventually joining No.13 Sqn in France on 18th

February and then No.11 Sqn on 7th May. Flying mainly a Nieuport he was credited with 10 enemy machines and an observation kite balloon, which he brought down with phosphor bombs. He was awarded an MC at the end of June for this achievement. In August he joined No.60 Sqn also equipped with the Nieuport. With this squadron he dispatched another 20 enemy machines and was awarded a DSO and Bar before returning to England at the end of September. After a period instructing, he returned to France as a Flight Commander with No.56 Sqn on 7th April 1917. In the next month he destroyed 12 of the enemy and sent one down out of control. Most of the victories were claimed when flying an SE5. He was awarded a second Bar to his DSO. Capt Albert Ball died on 7th May 1917. His SE5 was seen entering a large cloud in pursuit of a red Albatros DIII. This crashed and shortly afterwards was followed by Ball's SE5 in a shallow inverted dive which ended with it striking the ground. It is not thought Ball was shot down, his injuries were those sustained in the crash. He was buried by the Germans with full military honours and the following month the award of a posthumous Victoria Cross was announced.

5) Captain Lionel Rees

In November 1915 Capt Lionel W.B. Rees MC returned to England from France where he had fought aggressively with No.11 Sqn. During a short posting at Upavon he was promoted to Major on 1st December before taking command of No.32 Sqn formed at Netheravon on 12th January 1916. It was whilst fighting with this squadron in France later in the year that he was awarded the VC (refer to **Netheravon**).

6) Captain Anthony Beauchamp Proctor

The South African A. F. E. Beauchamp Proctor arrived in England in March 1917 and over the spring period carried out flying training at Castle Bromwich, Netheravon and at the CFS Upavon where he obtained his Wings. In July he joined No.84 Sqn equipped with the SE5a and left for France on 21st September. Between 3rd January and 8th October 1918 he had destroyed 22 enemy machines, 16 balloons with 16 machines driven down out of control.

In recognition he was awarded the VC and the citation stated that his war record was 'almost unsurpassed in its brilliance'. During the nine months of combat, in addition to the VC, he was awarded the MC and Bar, DFC and DSO. In 1921 he was posted back to Upavon in order to train for that year's display at Hendon. He was to be a part of a formation aerobatics team. During a rehearsal at Hendon on 21st June, the day before the event, his Sopwith Snipe crashed at Enford and the 24 year old Beauchamp was killed. He was initially buried at Upavon cemetery where his headstone still stands but his body was later returned to South Africa for burial.

7) Lt Alan Jerrard

Another eventual VC recipient passed through Upavon for advanced flying training and gained his Wings in June 1917. This was Lt Alan Jerrard who had served with the 5th South Staffordshire Regiment prior to transferring to the RFC. He eventually joined No.19 Sqn but was seriously injured in a forced landing in France on 5th August. Following hospitalisation in England he joined No.66 Sqn in Italy on 22nd February 1918. Flying a Sopwith Camel he sent one enemy down out of control, and destroyed two more plus a balloon in his first three weeks. On 30th March he took-off in Camel B5648 together with two others. It appears they were engaged by a formidable number of enemy machines taking off from an aerodrome, and during the encounter Jerrard shot down three of them before being shot down himself and taken prisoner. The report given by Jerrard to his captors indicated he had only shot down one of their pilots but the report filed by his two colleagues who escaped back to base indicated the three kills. The variance of the reports remains somewhat of a mystery, but the *London Gazette* announced on 1st May 1918 the award of a VC to Lt Alan Jerrard.

Memorials

UPAVON AIRFIELD

1) 184/SU158549

In the porch outside of the main entrance doors to the Headquarters building is a stone plaque inscribed:-

THIS PLAQUE WAS UNVEILED BY MARSHAL OF THE ROYAL AIR FORCE HIS ROYAL HIGHNESS THE PRINCE PHILIP, DUKE OF EDINBURGH KG, K.T., G.B.E. ON 16TH JUNE 1962 TO MARK THE 5OTH ANNIVERSARY OF THE ROYAL FLYING CORPS AND OF UPAVON

2) 184/SU155550

In the entrance hall of the Officers' Mess set into an alcove, is a marble bust of Lord Trenchard. The wooden plaque beneath the bust records in gold lettering:-

MARSHAL OT THE ROYAL AIR FORCE THE VISCOUNT TRENCHARD GCB., OM., GCVO., DSO., DCL., LL.D.

Bust of Viscount Trenchard in the Officers' Mess at Upavon.

3) 184/SU156549

Inside St. Peter's Church on the south wall a brass plaque inscribed:-

> TO THE MEMORY OF
> AIR VICE MARSHAL
> H.G. (REGGIE) SMART CBE DFC AFC
> DIED CAPE TOWN 1963 AGED 72
> SERVED AT UPAVON
> 1915 ROYAL FLYING CORPS
> 1923-27 CHIEF FLYING INSTRUCTOR
> CENTRAL FLYING SCHOOL
> 1935-36 COMMANDANT
> CENTRAL FLYING SCHOOL

4) Inside St. Peter's Church on the north wall, a wooden propeller blade with a metallic boss displaying laurel leaves around the rim and beneath a pair of RAF wings, the following inscription: -

> TO THE GLORY OF GOD AND IN
> PROUD AND LOVING MEMORY OF
> 2. L. STANLEY - CECIL - PAICE RAF
> K. JUNE 4 - 1918 - AGE 30
> R.I.P.

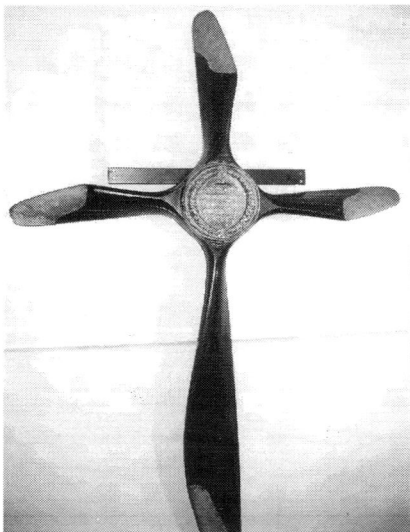

Wooden propeller in memory of 2nd Lt S.C. Paice RAF.

5) Inside St. Peter's Church, in an anti room at the rear of the alter, a free standing bronze memorial plaque, circular in shape, edged with laurel leaves and supported on three legs. The inscription reads: -

> IN MEMORY OF THE
> R.A.F
> 40TH SQUADRON,
> FRANCE, 1918.
> LT LOUIS BENNETT,
> WEST VIRGINIA
> U.S.A
> AUG: 24TH 1918
>
> PER ARDUA AD ASTRA

Bronze memorial plaque to Lt Louis Bennett RAF.

Louis Bennett Jnr. was born in Weston, West Virginia. On leaving Yale University he enlisted in the RFC in Toronto on 9th October 1917. Following initial training he arrived in England on 25th February 1918, joining No.90 (Home Defence) Sqn on completion of training in May. He left for France in July and on the 21st was posted to No.40 Sqn 'C' Flt. His first victory was claimed on 15th August when flying a SE 5A E3947 he shot down a Fokker DVII over Brebieres. On 17th he shot down an LVG.C. and a balloon, four more balloons on the 19th, two on 22nd, another LVG.C. on 23rd and two further balloons on 24th. Whilst attempting a third on this date, his SE 5A E3947 was hit by machine gun fire from the ground and burst into flames. At around 100' he jumped and broke both legs. The enemy, who had shot him down, took him to hospital but he died receiving treatment. He carried out only 25 sorties during his brief time with the Squadron but his twelve victories in 10 days were an incredible record. It was unfortunate that because of the short period, he was unable to be awarded a rightly deserved decoration before his death.

UPAVON

6) 173/SU136551 - 8 miles North of Amesbury

In the centre of the village on the east side of the A345 in St. Mary's Church. On the north wall are four brass plaques erected by the colleagues of those whose names are inscribed:-

> TO THE MEMORY OF
> MAJOR GEORGE CHARLETON
> MERRICK. D.S.O.
> ROYAL GARRISON ARTILLERY.
> KILLED AT UPAVON WHILE FLYING ON DUTY
> ON 3RD OCTOBER. 1913.
> ERECTED BY THE OFFICERS OF THE
> CENTRAL FLYING SCHOOL.

Brass plaque for Major G.C. Merrick DSO.

Maj G.C. Merrick had qualified for his R.Ae.C. flying certificate (No.484) on 17th May 1913. He took off in perfect weather for a practice flight in a Gnome-engined Short biplane on 3rd October and was later seen gliding steeply at around 300', appearing to be making an approach for landing. The angle of descent increased and the machine went into a dive. Not all pilots at that time bothered to strap themselves in and there seemed little doubt that the Major had neglected to do so and slipped forward from his seat during descent onto the control column, pushing it further forward. This resulted in the aeroplane plunging violently down and performing a bunt on its back. As it proceeded to pass over the vertical, the Major fell out of the cockpit and was killed instantly as he struck the ground on the aerodrome.

The funeral cortege of Major George C. Merrick DSO passing through Upavon village Photo: Rex Reynolds Coll.

7)

> TO THE MEMORY OF
> CAPTAIN CYRIL PERCY DOWNER.
> THE NORTHAMPTONSHIRE REGIMENT.
> KILLED AT UPAVON WHILE FLYING ON
> DUTY
> ON 10TH MARCH. 1914
> ERECTED BY THE OFFICERS OF THE
> CENTRAL FLYING SCHOOL.

Brass plaque to Capt. C. P. Downer.

Capt C.P. Downer had qualified for his R.Ae.C. flying certificate (No.608) on 29th August 1913. He took off from Upavon in a BE.2 tractor biplane on 10th March 1914, intending to practice gliding turns. The aircraft was flying at around 2000' when it commenced to descend in a rotating dive, which was practically vertical. At about 500' from the ground, the right hand pair of wings collapsed and it dived into the ground with Capt Downer being killed instantly. When the wreckage was examined both elevator planes were found to be bent down by several inches and the control column was bent back. It is probable that the pilot pushed the latter forward to start his glide and the elevators jammed down which would account for the extremely steep dive and bent column which he was desperately trying to pull back on. The elevators probably freed themselves and came up with a violent jerk. This reversal would have thrown considerable strain on the wing structure causing the collapse. The findings of the R.Ae.C. Accident Committee however was that the inexperience of the pilot attempting to flatten out suddenly from the steep dive caused the wings to collapse.

8)

> TO THE MEMORY OF
> LIEUTENANT HUGH FREDERICK
> TREEBY.
> THE DUKE OF WELLINGTON'S (WEST
> RIDING) REGIMENT.
> KILLED AT UPAVON WHILE
> FLYING ON DUTY
> ON 19TH MARCH. 1914.
> ERECTED BY THE OFFICERS OF THE
> CENTRAL FLYING SCHOOL.

Brass plaque to Lt H. F. Treeby.

Lt H.F. Treeby qualified for his R.Ae.C. flying certificate (No.687) on 16th November 1913. He took off from Upavon in a Maurice Farman pusher biplane on 19th March 1914 and flew around the circuit for 20 minutes. He then made his approach at 350' apparently to land but as he throttled back his engine, he failed to lower the nose sufficiently, stalled and dived into the ground. Lt Treeby died instantly when he was crushed under the engine. He had learnt to fly in a Bristol biplane and it is probable that the unfamiliarity of the Maurice Farman caused him to make an error.

9) On a plaque with the RAF badge at the top and beneath the inscription:-

> IN MEMORY OF SQUADRON LEADER
> WALTER HUNT LONGTON. D.F.C., A.F.C.
> ROYAL AIR FORCE.
> KILLED IN A FLYING ACCIDENT AT
> BOURNEMOUTH
> JUNE 6TH 1927.
> +
> ERECTED BY THE OFFICERS AND
> AIRMEN OF NETHERAVON,
> AND 58 BOMBING SQUADRON,
> WORTHY DOWN,
> IN GRATEFUL REMEMBRANCE.
> R.I.P.

Brass plaque to Sqn Ldr W. H.
Longton DFC, AFC.

Before World War 1 'Scruffy' Longton was a renowned motorcyclist. He joined the RFC and became a test pilot and for his valuable work in this field, he was awarded the AFC in June 1918. With the rank of Lieutenant he then went to France with No.85 Sqn where he claimed 6 enemy aircraft destroyed during July and August and was awarded the DFC. On 27th September he joined No.24 Sqn as 'B'

The funeral cortege of Lt H.F. Treeby passing through Upavon village.
Photo: Terry Crawford Coll.

Flt Commander gaining the rank of Acting Captain. During October he destroyed a balloon and 4 more enemy aircraft with one of the claims shared. All of his victories had been achieved flying a SE 5A and he was one of the few pilots to be awarded two Bars to his DFC (not indicated on the brass memorial plaque). These were awarded for his air combat and ground attack successes. Having attained the rank of Captain, he remained with the RAF after the war and on 1st April 1920 was posted as a Flt Lt to Area Command (U.K.) at Hillingdon House, Uxbridge. In January 1924 he was promoted to Sqn Ldr. Later in the year he was appointed as CO of No.58 Sqn which had reformed at Worthy Down on 1st April, equipped at first with the Vimy and then the Virginia. He was transferred to No.1 FTS at Netheravon on 18th October 1926 and was killed taking part in an air race at Bournemouth on 6th June 1927. On this day he was taking part in a medium power handicap race at a Flying Meeting being held at Ensbury Racecourse. Twelve aircraft were bunched together and having completed the second circuit of the race, the aircraft of Sqn Ldr Longton and that of a Mr L.P. Openshaw, collided at around 300'. The collision occurred when the wings met and interlocked during a crossing of one aircraft above the other. Longton's aircraft was a Blackburn 'Bluebird' (Armstrong Siddeley Genet) biplane G-EBKD, Airframe No.L19303/1 and Openshaws was a Westland Widgeon III (Cirrus Mk.II) G-EBPW, Airframe No.WA1677. The two aircraft crashed at West Parley where Openshaw was pulled from the wreckage with serious injuries. He was lifted into a private car but died on the way to hospital. Longton was trapped beneath the burning wreckage and his remains could not be recovered until after the fire had burnt itself out.

The Blackburn Bluebird had a reputation for providing poor visibility for the pilot. It was difficult to see upwards or sideways while in flight, it was probably not the kind of aircraft in which to attempt a cross over. Possibly in trying this manoeuvre, Longton sadly proved the visibility theory to be all too correct.

Sqn Ldr Longton had won the Grosvenor Cup the previous year and at the Easter Meeting in 1927 at Ensbury

The funeral cortege passing through Netheravon on its journey to Upavon Cemetery with the body of Sqn Ldr Walter H. Longton DFC, AFC. The RAF Crossley car tows the hearse. Photo: Tony Mellor-Ellis Coll.

Although stationed at Netheravon Aerodrome, Sqn Ldr Longton was buried at Upavon Cemetery where the burial party, a large contingent of RAF Personnel and the mourners are seen paying their respects. Photo: Tony Mellor-Ellis Coll.

Park, his same 'Bluebird' was the object of a shooting incident from the ground. He found on landing that both wings and left-hand side fuselage had been punctured by shot gun pellets.

UPAVON CEMETERY

10) 173/SU132552

On the north side of the village in Chapel Lane off the A342. This is a beautiful and well-kept cemetery on the fringe of the village and with over a hundred military graves. Most, as would be expected, are of RFC and RAF personnel but others are of the RNZAF, RAAF, RCAF and U.S. Air Service. One of the RAF gravestones is that of Flt Lt A.W. Beauchamp-Proctor VC, DSO, MC, DFC. He was killed on 21st June 1921, age 24. There is also one WAAF grave, Assistant Section Officer Josephine Pipon who died on 8th July 1941, Age 20. She was the daughter of Captain H.C.B. Pipon RN and Marjorie Pipon of Yelverton, Devon.

The headstone for
Flt Lt A.W. Beauchamp-Proctor
VC, DSO, MC, DFC.

11) After World War 2 a memorial was placed in the cemetery dedicated to all women of the British Isles who had contributed to the victory achieved in two World Wars. The idea for the memorial came from Mrs Amy Walker who was the wife of Dr. Ainley Walker, the family living in Upavon at that time. The stone and bronze memorial depicts Joan of Arc on horseback overlooked by Christ. The inscription on the base reads: -

A Maiden Knight To Me Is Given
Such Hope I Know Not Fear

A second inscription at the rear head of the stone reads:

In Gratitude For The Work
Of British Women In The
Two World Wars

The memorial to the women of two World Wars.

In the village church of St. Leonards in Upper Minety on the C101 road north of the B4040. On the north wall, a stone memorial plaque displaying the coat of arms of the Ludlow-Hewitt family with the inscription: -

REMEMBER Sir EDGAR
RAINEY LUDLOW-HEWITT
9th June 1886 - 15th August 1973
GCB GBE CMG DSO MC DL
Air Chief Marshal RAF
Son of the Revd. T.A. Ludlow-Hewitt
Vicar of Minety from 1901 until 1936

Photograph of memorial plaque.

1918 he was awarded the DSO and given command of the 10th Brigade RAF. Later that year he was appointed Chief Staff Officer for RAF Headquarters, France. With the end of the war and at the age of thirty-one, he had attained the rank of Brigadier. In 1919 he was appointed Companion (of the Order) of St. Michael and St. George. From 1921-23 he was Air ADC to King George V.

'Ludlow', as he was referred to by colleagues, served as Commandant of the RAF Staff College, Andover from 1926-30, Air Officer Commanding in

Iraq from 1930-32, Director of Operations & Intelligence from 1933-35 at the Air Ministry, and as AOC RAF India from 1935-37. In 1933 he was made a Knight Commander (of the Order) of the Bath.

He was recalled from India to take up the post of Commander-in-Chief of Bomber Command with the rank of Air Chief Marshal. He soon realised on the eve of war that his new command was inadequately prepared for the task which it faced. He stated in reports that the medium and heavy bombers would be destroyed within weeks of the commencement of war, and that navigation needed improving, as did the training of airgunners. His continuous submission of reports to the Air Ministry brought accusations of pessimism and even defeatism but later his views were confirmed in the light of operational experiences.

Following some of the disastrous early results where lives were lost, Ludlow-Hewitt visited the squadrons at their stations and his sensitivity was apparent to those he met. His superiors soon realised that his humanitarian instincts were not suited to a man in his position and in addition he was too realistic in promoting the short-comings of his own forces. In 1940 he was replaced as C-in-C Bomber Command by Charles Portal and was appointed to the post of Inspector-General of the RAF, a position he served with distinction until his retirement from the service in 1945. In 1943 he received the Knight Grand Cross (of the Order) of the British Empire and in 1946 the Knight Grand Cross (of the Order) of the Bath. From 1943 to 1945 he acted as principal Air ADC to King George VI.

Following retirement in 1945, he held the position of Chairman of the Board of Governors at the new College of Aeronautics until 1953. Sir Edgar lived with his wife at Westbrook House, Bromham near Chippenham, serving the county of Wiltshire in 1953 as Deputy Lieutenant. He died at Princess Alexandra's RAF Hospital at Wroughton on 15th August 1973.

Sir Edgar Ludlow-Hewitt attended Sandhurst and in 1905 was commissioned into the Royal Irish Rifles. In 1914 he learnt to fly at the Central Flying School at Upavon and in August became a pilot with the Royal Flying Corps. On 7th March 1915 he was posted with No.1 Sqn to St. Omer in France and became a Brevet Major with the Royal Irish Guards. This Squadron had been working-up at Netheravon since 13th November 1914 and left there for France with 8 Avro 504s and 4 BE8s. Action after arrival consisted of flights over the front for artillery spotting, attempted bombing raids and fighter engagements. Edgar Ludlow-Hewitt quickly gained a reputation as an exceptionally able and courageous pilot. He was mentioned six times in dispatches, awarded an MC in 1916 and rapidly promoted to command No.3 Sqn. In February 1916 he was promoted to Wg Cdr, taking over No.3 Wing at Bertangles. In 1917 he became a Chevalier of the Legion of Honour. In

WANBOROUGH RLG

Location - 173/SU225820 5 miles South East of Swindon

In the village of Wanborough on the south side of the long straight C29 Roman Road named *Ermin Way.*

Aerodrome Development

This small grass airfield was developed as a Relief Landing ground (RLG) in 1940 by Flying Training Command and was used during the war as a training establishment for a number of units.

In November 1942 a domestic site was built in the eastern corner of the field where King Edwards' Place Estate adjoins the Roman Road. Around five wooden huts were erected here and three more to the south of the field. Some were barrack huts for airmen and there was a combined Officers' and SNCOs' Mess. The establishment was for 8 Officers and 117 other ranks. Four Extra Over Blister hangars were provided, two on the west side of the airfield and two on the eastern boundary. These two were close to the domestic buildings and served by a hard surface road. There were two designated grass runways N/S 900yds and NE/SW 750yds. Goose-neck flares provided runway lighting.

Aerial view of Wanborough RLG taken on the 14th April 1946 from an aircraft of No.540 Sqn, and showing clearly the blister hangars and centre left, the domestic buildings.
Photo: NMRO

World War 2 Years

To relieve the pressure at its Lyneham base, Wanborough was allocated for use by No.14 FTS from 16th August 1941. This unit was carrying out twin engine training with the Oxford but it never used the facility. Instead No.3 SFTS South Cerney used Wanborough as an SLG with its Oxford Trainers from September 1941 to 1st March 1942 when it was redesignated No.3 (Pilot) Advanced Flying Unit. Wanborough then passed to No.3 EFTS Shellingford in No.50 Group. It was used by the School as an RLG for its Tiger Moths until 9th November 1942 when it was decided to develop the site.

Before the development had been completed, the airfield was occupied on 14th June 1943 by the School of Flying Control from Watchfield in No.50 Group. The School was formed to provide air traffic control training facilities and was equipped with 8 + 4 Ansons. Wanborough was used for the preliminary instruction before pupils continued training at the parent Watchfield. The School had barely settled down to the benefits of purpose built accommodation, when the RLG was required by No.3 Glider Training School, Stoke Orchard. The Flying Control unit moved out and the GTS arrived from Stoke Orchard on 5th December 1943 with Miles Master IIs, Hotspur gliders and Tiger Moths. The first accident soon occurred on 28th December when a glider struck a hedge on approach before making a heavy landing resulting in the death of a passenger. Other crashes followed and were mainly associated with the night flying involvement. The Glider School remained until 22nd May 1944 when it officially returned to Stoke Orchard. It did however continue using Wanborough until October 1944. In May 1944 the School of Flying Control resumed training air traffic controllers and operated alongside the Glider School.

No.1547 Beam Approach Training Flight formed at Watchfield on 1st June 1945, equipped with Oxfords. It was affiliated to No.6 (P) AFU, using the aircraft of No.1 Beam Approach School (BAS) to which it was attached. Wanborough was allocated to the unit as a SLG.

Closure

By the end of August 1945 the RAF had ceased using the field and it was finally closed on 21st May 1946 and subsequently returned at agriculture.

339

At Dauntsey's School in the village of West Lavington on the A360. On the outside west facing wall of the Memorial Hall in the grounds of the school, five Portland stone memorial panels form the school war memorial dedicated to the Old Dauntseians who fell in the two World Wars and the Korean War. This replaced the original mural tablet of teak in the school entrance hall, unveiled on Saturday 26th June 1920, on which were listed the 37 names of those killed in World War 1.

The stone panels were initially set into a curved brick wall forming the main feature of a memorial garden. The panels were unveiled by Mr R. Marrs and dedicated by the Rev. F.R. Gillespy on Saturday 24th June 1950. The school Memorial Hall was later built on the site of this garden and so the five stone memorial panels were incorporated into the structure. The building was unveiled on Thursday 11th July 1974 by the then Lord Lieutenant of Wiltshire, The Lord Margadale, T.P, J.P. with the chapel being dedicated by The Bishop of Sherborne. Of the 112 names on the memorial 36 served with the RFC, RAF and FAA.

The following are service details of just a few of these 'Old Dauntseians': -

Capt Thorold Perkins RFC - Served as a Flt Cdr with No.41 Sqn flying the FE 8. He was killed in the Ypres Salient on 31st March 1917.

Lt Harold Johnston Browne RAF of Hyde Park, London served with No.15 Sqn. Together with 2nd Lt Leslie J. Derrick of Brislington, Bristol, Lt Browne was the pilot of RE 8 C2361, engaged on an army co-operation mission, when they were attacked and shot down by three enemy aircraft. Both men were killed when the RE 8 crashed in flames near Buire-sur-Ancre on Friday 3rd May 1918. Lt Browne was buried at Querrieu British Cemetery Somme, France.

Wg Cdr J.R. Baldwin DSO*, DFC*, AFC is probably one of the most well known airman to have attended the school. "Johnny " Baldwin joined the

Photograph of Dauntsey's War Memorial

RAF at 21, and was posted to No.609 Sqn in 1942. Between August and November the squadron flew from Bourn, Duxford, Biggin Hill and Manston, equipped with Typhoons. He logged just four hours of operational flying on type before claiming his first enemy aircraft destroyed, and by the end of the war had claimed 16 enemy aircraft. On 17th July 1944 he was leading the Typhoons of No.146 Wing (Fighter Bomber) when they happened upon Rommel's staff car which they attacked seriously injuring him. A month later on 27th August Baldwin was involved in one of the worst 'friendly fire' incidents of the war when RAF Typhoons sank two Royal Navy minesweepers off the Normandy coast killing 117 sailors. He was leading 16 aircraft of No.263 Sqn based at B3/Ste-Croix-sur-Mer and No.266 Sqn at B8/Sommervieu. They had taken off at 1305 and 1306 hours respectively, following a request from the Royal Navy Area Headquarters known as Flag Officer, British Assault Area (FOBAA), to make a strike on German shipping in the area off Cap d' Antifer. British minesweepers had been operating in this same area for twelve days up to 25th August but were then moved to another part of the coast by the RN officer commanding minesweeping operations. This information was circulated to all other authorities by signal. On the evening of the 26th August, the deputy of the above RN officer changed the orders and sent the flotilla back to the grounds off Cap d' Antifer. The change of orders was sent also by signal but with the error of

failing to notify (FOBAA). Consequently the attack on what the Navy thought were German ships was in fact on British minesweepers. On his approach to the flotilla Baldwin was immediately suspicious as he thought the ships were in the wrong formation to be German. Before opening his attack he sought confirmation but was directed to continue. On this clear day the aircraft dropped out of the sun at 1330 hours and although not experienced as shipping strike specialists the rockets fired by the Typhoon pilots were accurate and deadly and in less than fifteen minutes the 230 feet long/875 ton HMS Britomart and HMS Hussar had been sunk. Baldwin had queried his orders again between the first and second wave of attacks and again on two further occasions, each time receiving orders to continue his attack. Baldwin and his crews were mortified when later their fears were confirmed but they knew that the alternative to carrying out the attack was to face court-martial themselves. The true facts of course were not made known at the time but the subsequent Court of Enquiry completely exonerated the RAF and its crews whilst a number of naval officers were variously disciplined. 'Johnny' Baldwin was one of the really outstanding fighter wing leaders of the RAF in North-West Europe in the latter part of the war reaching the acting rank of Group Captain.

After the war, as a Sqn Ldr, he was seconded to work with the Egyptian Air Force. He was subsequently promoted again to Wing Commander and was one of the first four RAF pilots sent on exchange with a U.S Air Force fighter squadron in the Korean War, flying the new F-86 Sabre jet fighter. It was in 1952, while flying in dense cloud on a reconnaissance flight over Communist held territory that his Sabre disappeared. The MoD informed his wife that he was presumed dead. However, documents released in later years indicated that the government of the day believed that he had been captured by the Chinese. It is thought that the Chinese handed over a number of western pilots to the Russians. Although investigations into the disappearance of Baldwin have been conducted at the very highest level of government in this country, Russia and America, confirmation of his fate remains unknown.

Fg Off Arthur R.B. Tedder RAF was the son of MRAF Sir Arthur Tedder GCB who served as Chief of the Air Staff 1946-49. Fg Off Tedder, who had served in the No.128 Cambridge University Air Squadron, was a pilot with No.139 Sqn based at Horsham St. Faith. He was killed when his Blenheim IV L9239 XD failed to return from a raid on the airfields of Abbeville (France) and Haamstede Hardyck (Holland) on 3rd August 1940. The aircraft was presumed lost over the English Channel with the other two crew members Sgt D. J. Spencer and Sgt O.R. Evans. Fg Off Tedder was buried at Bayeux War Cemetery, Calvados, France.

Fg Off Gavin J. Lynes DFC, RAF entered the RAF as a pupil pilot in 1939 and was granted a Short Service Commission the same year. He was confirmed in his appointment in March 1940, commencing operations with No.304 (Polish) Sqn on 20th April. On 27th August he took part in a raid on the transformer station at Kelsterbach. While passing over the Dutch coast the aircraft communications became unserviceable but he decided to continue. He reached and passed over the target at 7000 feet, finding it obscured by cloud. As he was unable to pin point the objective he descended below the clouds. He made several attempts to approach the objective but had to carry out such violent evasive action because of the intense anti-aircraft fire that he was unable to make a satisfactory run in. Eventually however, he managed to pass directly

over the target at 2000 feet and released his bombs. He dived to 100 feet at high speed to avoid being hit and whilst escaping from the target area his bomb blasts were observed on the buildings below.

By his persistent determination and his outstanding skill as a pilot, Lynes was able to destroy the primary objective in the face of heavy opposition. His DFC was awarded in September 1940 and by that month he had taken part in thirty-two major bombing raids over Norway, Holland, Belgium, France, Germany and Italy. On 8th May 1941 Fg Off Lynes took-off at 2308hrs from Syerston in Wellington IC R1473 for an operation to Bremen. His aircraft was hit by flak and crashed at Plantlunne on the north bank of the Gr Aa, 12km SSE of Lingen-Ems, Germany where the crew members who were killed were buried. One of the crew, Flt Sgt T.E. Wady, survived to become a POW. In 1945 those who died were reburied at Reichswald Forest War Cemetery, Kleve, Nordrhein-West Falen, Germany.

Fg Off Eric S. Marrs DFC, RAF was educated at Dauntsey's School from 1934-1939. He joined the RAF in 1940 and undertook training as a pilot at Cranwell where he flew Hinds. On passing out at Cranwell he joined No.152 (Hyderabad) Sqn at Acklington in March 1940. The squadron had reformed there on 2nd October 1939 equipped with the Gladiator I & II. It became operational in November and started converting to the Spitfire I by the end of the year. 'Boy' Marrs as he became known in the squadron, initially flew Gladiators as a prelude to the Spitfire which he flew for the first time on the last Sunday in March. He built up to operational standard through April, and in May was at readiness with the rest of the squadron to add his contribution to the Battle of Britain. Both day and night flying were undertaken but Marrs made no contact with the enemy. The squadron crews knew it was only a matter of time before they relieved one of the hard pressed South of England squadrons and so it was on 12th July they moved to Warmwell.

Marrs was on leave for four days during August but was recalled early on 13th following two casualties in the squadron. On return the squadron

were fully involved and he found himself at permanent readiness with no stand-down periods. His first enemy contact was the following day with a Dornier 17 but this escaped into clouds. Thursday 15th August was a day when the full might of the German airforce was thrown against the squadrons of the RAF's Fighter Command and 'Boy' Marrs and his colleagues of No.152 Sqn were fully involved. On his first scramble of the day Marrs observed what he estimated to be some 100 enemy aircraft. These were Junkers 87s escorted by Me 110s. The 87s were in vics of three, in tight formation and more or less surrounded by 110s. Behind, to the right of, and above these 87s was another formation of 110s. The sight of all these aircraft made his heart sink as he felt the chance of stopping such an armada with just nine Spitfires would be impossible. However he was ordered into line astern formation and they dropped out of the sun onto the bombers. He attacked one of the Ju 87s and then put several short bursts into a Me110 during a dog-fight. He next found himself head on to three bombers which he sprayed with shots as they converged. He dived beneath them and found another Me 110 and they circled each other until Marrs noticed a Me 110 providing an easier target and coming up beneath it, gave it a long burst into its belly. He was then involved with yet another Me 110 but on opening fire found himself out of ammunition. He dived for base, was refuelled and within twenty minutes was back in the air. Although he had seen considerable action that day he was unable to confirm any success.

For Marrs the following day was similar. At lunch-time they were sent up to 20,000 ft. east of the Isle of Wight where they were surrounded by enemy fighters. Marrs was fully occupied with trying to keep them off his tail and was unable to fire at them. In the avoiding action he found himself alone with no sight of any other aircraft. He climbed again towards the sun and looked around. He saw what he thought were six Spitfires bearing down on him from his left but on approach saw that they were Me 109s. He did a steep turn, went into a spin and on coming out headed for land, as he was low on fuel and about 20 miles out over sea. He felt guilty returning to base without firing his guns.

That evening he was on patrol with the Flt when suddenly he spotted two Heinkel 111s below them. He called up the leader on the R.T. and they dived on the enemy as they were about to enter cloud. Marrs fired on the rear one as it left the cloud and smoke came from both engines. His own Spitfire was covered in oil from the enemy and Marrs felt confident that it would not have got home.

He was involved in no further shows until Sunday 18th August when a large-scale raid by Ju 87s escorted by Me 109s took place on Southampton and Gosport. No.152 Sqn arrived on the scene off the east end of the Isle of Wight at about 1430 hours just as the Ju 87s had dropped their bombs and about 30 of them were making for France. The Me 109 fighters were at that time being engaged by Hurricanes of No.601 Sqn and Spitfires of No.234 Sqn, which allowed Marrs and No.152 Sqn to dive on to the fleeing bombers as they dropped to 100 ft above the sea. A running chase ensued with the bombers taking evasive action by throttling back and doing steep turns to right and left in an attempt to make the fighters overshoot. Not all were successful and Marrs got in bursts on six of them with one catching fire in the port wing petrol tank before hitting the sea. This was his first confirmed enemy aircraft shot down and with other successes the squadron had that day, was duly celebrated that evening.

His next success on Thursday 22nd August was a Dornier 17 which was shared with another Spitfire of his squadron. On Sunday 25th at around 1600 hours a 100 plus raid was plotted approaching Weymouth Bay and the squadrons of Warmwell, Middle Wallop, Exeter and Tangmere were scrambled in good time to gain all possible height in preparation for interception. The targets for the Ju 88s with their Me 110 escorts was Weymouth, Portland and Warmwell airfield. The British fighters became embroiled with those of the Germans allowing the enemy bombers to drop their loads relatively unhindered, although over Warmwell they were confronted by Hurricanes of No.17 Sqn. Seven bombers did reach the airfield but surprisingly little damage was sustained. Two hangars were hit

and the hospital quarters demolished but no one was there at the time. Marrs became involved in a dog-fight with a Me 110 at about 5000 ft and five miles out to sea. His first burst put his port engine on fire but with his speed he overshot, which left the German on his tail. The German lined up on him and leaving it until the last possible moment, Marrs went in to a steep climbing turn as the tracer passed below. He came out of this behind the enemy and gave a long burst into his starboard engine which caught fire with pieces flying off. Marrs felt it prudent to leave the scene then as another enemy fighter was diving on him out of the sun. At this stage the fight had taken him about 20 miles from the English coast. He returned to Warmwell where he found a bullet through his oil tank had almost drained it so his decision to return probably saved his life.

For Marrs life became less hectic over the next few weeks as the Germans concentrated more on the south-east and London and less on Portsmouth and Southampton. The No.10 Group stations were able to enjoy some respite. Sunday 15th September was the day when Luftwaffe losses at the hands of the RAF must have made it obvious to the German Command that the invasion of Britain was not going to be the certainty they had anticipated. At 11.55 hrs the Duxford Wing, with two Spitfire and three Hurricane squadrons, led by Sqn Ldr Douglas Bader tore into the invaders over London. The bombers ran for the coast dropping their bombs at random. In doing so they lost their fighter protection and made it easy for the defending fighters to attack them. The South played its part later in the day when at approximately 1500 hrs a raid was mounted by 27 unescorted Heinkel Mk.111s. Their target appeared to be Southampton but they turned away west to bomb Portland. They were intercepted by six Spitfires of 'B' Flight, No.152 Sqn, led by 'Boy' Marrs. They shot down one of the bombers and damaged another. Five bombs were dropped on the naval installations at Portland but very little damage resulted.

On Tuesday 17th September, Marrs was leading a section of three Spitfires when they were ordered on to a Ju 88 near Bath. All three aircraft made their attacks shooting down the II.

Gruppen/LG1 enemy aircraft (3188:L1 + XC) which crashed near Imber on Salisbury Plain at 1350 hrs. Marrs received a bullet through his oil cooler and his engine seized so he was forced to land at Colerne, an airfield which was still under construction and covered in concrete blocks to prevent German planes from landing. Marrs however was able to put down without further damage. He had been flying this same Spitfire since joining the squadron. It was then the longest serving one and whilst the damage was only Category 1, he regretted that he would not get it back as it would probably be sent to a training unit after repair.

The following day Marrs with the other two pilots Fg Off O'Brian and Sgt K. C. Holland, drove to the crash site near Imber, on Salisbury Plain at the rear of Dauntsey's School. On arrival they found the Ju 88 in quite good condition. Members of the public were also there but were kept back behind a rope barrier. The three pilots spent a couple of hours climbing over the enemy aircraft which had flown with a four-man crew. Of these two had been killed, one seriously injured and the uninjured pilot was taken into captivity.

On Thursday 19th September, Marrs was leading a section of two when they observed a Ju 88 off Lulworth Cove. It dived for sea level and they pursued it at wave top height towards France firing when they could, but after 10 miles it disappeared into a fog bank. Marrs was given a four-day sentence as Duty Pilot for beating up the airfield at Warmwell on returning.

On Wednesday 25th with another one of his squadron he attacked a formation of Heinkel 111s south of Bristol. These were returning from a raid on the Filton Aircraft Works. The Spitfires had to defend themselves from the escorting Me 110s, and although Marrs used all his ammunition on both bombers and fighters, he was unable to claim any destroyed. The following day Southampton was raided but Warmwell's Spitfires were sent off too late and the bombers with their Me 109 escorts were over the south coast of the Isle of Wight on their way home when the Spitfires arrived.

Friday 27th was a good day for Marrs, who brought down Ju 88 (0393: 4U + 4L) after making strikes on both of its engines. At approximately 0900 hrs, the enemy aircraft landed on the beach at Porlock and Marrs, circling overhead, watched the crew get out. They waved to him and he waved back and then a group of civilians ran up and apprehended them. Marrs beat up the beach and went home where later that day he received a message of congratulations on a very fine fight from the German pilot, who also asked if they could meet.

The weekend was fairly quiet for No.152 Sqn although they were scrambled on Saturday afternoon to combat German offensive patrols. On Monday 30th September the squadron was sent off to patrol Portland where at approximately 1630 hours it made contact with a formation of 40 He 111s and Me 110s of I/KG 55 and II/KG 55 which were en route to attack the Westland Aircraft factory at Yeovil. Hurricanes of Nos.56 and 504 Sqns joined the attack. The Heinkels turned back when they could not locate the target because of cloud. Marrs had just opened fire on a He 111 when bullets smashed into his own cockpit. He pushed the stick hard forward and went into a dive, holding it until he was below cloud. He then took stock of the situation, deciding his chief concern was the petrol gushing into the cockpit at a steady flow over his feet. His leg and knee were tingling, a bullet had smashed away the starter button from the control panel and another had knocked away one of the petrol taps putting splinters in his leg and a hole in the petrol tank. He made for Warmwell but with five miles to go he noticed smoke coming from the control panel. He cut the engine to prevent a possible explosion, the smoke stopped and he glided towards the airfield. Only one of the two wheels came down and on trying to retract it he found it would not respond. He switched the engine back on to get nearer the field but smoke re-appeared so he cut the engine again and drifted over the perimeter fence to make a one wheel landing. This he achieved in some style with only minor damage to the wing tip, which hit the ground when his speed dropped off and the Spitfire slewed around. His injuries turned out to be light and after the M.O had removed some metal splinters from his wrist and leg, he was declared fit for duty.

Not until Monday 7th October was Marrs involved in serious confrontation again. This was to combat a raid on the Westland Aircraft factory by twenty-five Ju 88s of II/KG 51 escorted by around fifty Me 110s of II and III *Gruppen* ZG 26. The German planes crossed the Dorset coast flying north and to the east of Warmwell. As they turned north-west heading for Yeovil, the British aircraft attacked. In the first dive Marrs was unable to get in a shot at the bombers and on regaining height he found himself out of position to try again. He decided to go for the Me 110s and opened up on the last one in a formation, in between the times when the leading aircraft dropped back to take up the rear position. Having no success with this ploy he drew away to take stock of his position. In doing so he noticed a straggler and swooped on it from the starboard rear quarter. He opened fire on the Me 110s starboard engine which instantly streamed glycol. He switched to the fuselage and then over to the port engine. Suddenly the back half of the cockpit flew off and out jumped two men. The aircraft went into the sea and the two men parachuted from 15,000 ft onto land where Marrs watched them being taken away by army personnel. Marrs, who the day before had been made Acting Flight Commander, returned to Warmwell and went on leave. Very little happened while he was away, and his operations after return were uneventful. This then brought to an end Marrs involvement in the period later to be recognised as the Battle of Britain.

On 14th November 1940 he was leading a section of two with Sgt Kearsey when they shot down a Ju 88 which crashed onto a street corner in Parkstone, Dorset. The bombs it was carrying caused a large explosion which set fire to three houses, but fortunately no civilians were killed. Marr's aircraft was hit by enemy fire, a bullet hitting his windscreen, making it opaque and impossible to see through. On 28th November he chased a yellow nosed Me 109 towards France and dispatched it into the sea with 440 rounds from his guns. The pilot parachuted into the sea but was never found. The award of the DFC was announced in "The Times" on Tuesday 31st December 1940: - "Pilot Officer E.S. Marrs has led his Flight with great skill and coolness. He has

destroyed at least six hostile aircraft".

1941 started off well for him when on 4th January he was vectored onto a lone intruder, which turned out to be a Do 17. He attacked it over Weymouth Bay and smoke was seen coming from its engines as it entered cloud. Marrs was unable to find it again but on return to Warmwell was pleased to be told that it had been seen hitting the sea five miles south east of Portland Bill by the Naval Air Liaison Officer (Portland). No bodies were found. On 9th April 1941 Fg Off Marrs and No.152 Sqn transferred with their Spitfire IIAs to Portreath in Cornwall. The airfield construction at this time was only halfway completed. Here the squadron flew on convoy patrols, generally six, seven and sometimes eight hours a day. This left little time for Marrs as Flight Commander to carry out his other routine duties. At the end of the day the officers went to a large house in Portreath which they used as a Mess and the men were billeted in local farmhouses. The airfield under construction was frequently bombed at night, and arrival at the field the following morning would present damaged Spitfires. These aircraft also tended to receive damage from stones being thrown up onto the underside of the wings during take off and landings. The area of patrol covered by the squadron stretched from Lundy Island to the Scilly Isles to Plymouth. While on patrol with Sgt Marsh, his number two, on 18th July they came across a lone He 111 about twenty miles south west of the Scilly Isles and, shooting its tail off, despatched it below the waves with no survivors. On 24th July 1941 a major daylight operation was arranged against the German warships berthed at Brest. This was scaled down at the last minute when the *Scharnhorst* departed for La Pallice. The force despatched to Brest comprised 79 Wellingtons from Nos.1 and 3 Groups, 18 Hampdens with 3 squadrons of Spitfire escorts and 3 B.17s. As a diversion for the Brest raid, 36 Blenheims escorted by Spitfires attacked Cherbourg Docks. Fg Off Marrs was one of these escorts and in carrying out the duty of sticking with the Blenheims his Spitfire P7881 was hit by flak and he was killed in the crash. A couple of his pilots were so incensed at the loss of the 'B' Flight Commander that they broke formation and proceeded to attack every gun position they could find. 'Boy' Marrs was well liked and had been a good Flight Commander. His loss was a sad blow to the squadron and keenly felt by those who had known him. His death came 15 days after his 20th birthday. Fg Off E. S. Marrs DFC was buried at Brest (Kerfautras) Cemetery, Finistere, France.

Fg Off Michael S.C. Smith RAFVR - served with No.524 Sqn at Bircham Newton flying Wellington XIIIs. At 2053 hrs on 2nd October 1944, Wellington MF319 'D' took off on a anti-shipping patrol covering, out and back, an enemy convoy route between 5250N to 0380E. The crew comprised Fg Off Robert H. Ridgway RCAF (Capt), Fg Off Smith (2nd pilot), Fg Off John R. Murray RCAF, Fg Off Gordon E. Pratt RCAF, Plt Off Robert McCloy RCAF (WOP/AG), Plt Off Floyd A. Steels RCAF and Plt Off George A. Slater RCAF. Their aircraft had an estimated time of return at 0125 hrs but was reported missing. The names of the crew appear on the Runnymede Memorial.

The name of Michael Smith appears on the Swindon High School memorial, which is displayed in Christ Church & St. Mary's, Old Town, Swindon. He was educated at the High School before attending Dauntsey's School. The memorial was transferred to the church in 1979 when the former school in Bath Road closed.

Aircraftman Paul Sangster Rivington RAFVR - refer to **WORTON**

L.A.C. Christopher John Street RAFVR – While attending pilot training at No.39 S.F.T.S. Swift Current, Saskatchewan in Canada, he was killed on 13th February 1943 when the Oxford II X6967 trainer in which he was flying with L.A.C. W.H. Lloyd, crashed in bad weather conditions near Rosetown. He was the son of P.H.J. Street who, with his brother A.G. Street, farmed at Middle Wallop until the late 1930s when the Air Ministry acquired the land for use as Middle Wallop Aerodrome.

WINTERBOURNE EARLS

Memorials 184/SU 175345 - 4 miles North East of Salisbury

In the Parish Church of St Michael & All Angels on the A338. A wooden cross is mounted on the wall displaying, at the head, a crown and beneath it the letters IWG encircled by a letter C, (Imperial War Graves Commission). The cross, which was the temporary marker used on the grave at the time of death, bears the inscription: -

> Sgt. Pilot G.W. JEFFERYS RAF.VR.
> Aged 20 years   killed in action.
>
> 18 : 9 : 40.

Sergeant pilot George William Jefferys RAFVR, No.754867 of Winterbourne joined No.43 Squadron based at Tangmere in August 1940. The Squadron was equipped with Hurricane Is. This Sector Station was in No.11 Fighter Group and during July had been heavily involved in the defence of this country, in what was to become known as the Battle of Britain. Sgt. Jefferys was soon in action and claimed his first success over Ashford in Kent at approximately 13.10 hrs. on 2nd September when he shot down a Messerschmitt Bf 109E of I *Gruppe* Jagdgeschwader 53 (II/JG 53) which was based at Rennes. Two days later on the 4th, at approximately 13.35 hrs, he was able to claim a Bf. 110 near Midhurst and on the 6th another Bf 109. He was transferred on the 15th September to No.46 Squadron at Stapleford Tawney, a squadron which was also in No.11 Fighter Group and equipped with Hurricane Is. On the same day he shot down a Dornier DO 215. This was to be his last victory. On the 18th September 1940 at 12.45 hrs he was attacked by a Bf 109 over North Kent. He baled out of his damaged aircraft V7442 over Chatham but was killed when his parachute failed to open.

Sgt. George Jefferys RAFVR is buried in the churchyard at Winterbourne Earls.

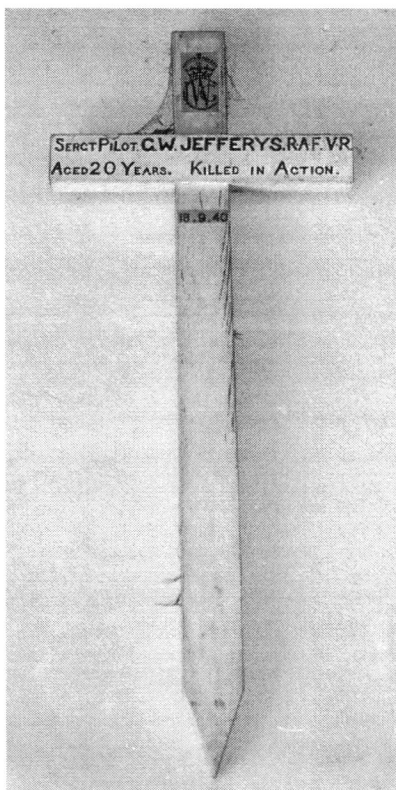

The cross on the wall in the church entrance porch.

WINTERBOURNE STOKE
Memorials 184/SU099429 - 2 miles East of Shrewton

On a grass island in the centre of the A360/A344 and B3086 crossroads on Winterbourne Stoke Down, 2 miles west of Stonehenge and known locally as 'Airman's Cross', stands a Cornish granite Celtic cross bearing the following inscription: -

TO THE MEMORY
OF
CAPTAIN LORAINE
AND STAFF SERGEANT WILSON
WHO WHILST FLYING ON DUTY,
MET WITH A FATAL ACCIDENT
NEAR THIS SPOT
ON JULY 5TH 1912.
ERECTED BY THEIR COMRADES.

A canvas sheet covers the wreckage of the Nieuport on 5th July 1912
Photo: © J.T.Fuller/Terry Crawford Coll.

Capt E.B. Loraine and Staff Sgt R.H.V. Wilson of No.3 Sqn based at Larkhill were killed when the Nieuport monoplane in which they were flying crashed close to the crossroads. They were the first members of the Royal Flying Corps to lose their lives while flying on duty.

Capt Eustace Loraine was commissioned into the Grenadier Guards in 1899 and served with distinction in the South African War. He was promoted to Captain a few years later and was posted to the West African Frontier Force under the command of Hugh Trenchard. Later still Loraine learnt to fly and became one of the well known aviators of the time. Staff Sgt Richard (Bert) Wilson joined the Royal Engineers after completing an engineering apprenticeship. He later transferred to the RFC where his qualities as a leader and his skill with aero-engines were recognised with a promotion to Staff Sgt and by appointment as Senior Technician in No.3 Sqn. In June 1912 he became the second non-commissioned officer in the British Army to qualify as a pilot.

Capt Loraine and Staff Sgt Wilson were both stationed at Larkhill Airfield with No.3 Sqn. On 5th July 1912 Capt Loraine took off at 0430 hrs. with Corporal Ridd in a Nieuport aircraft. Cpl Ridd was the first non-commissioned officer to qualify as a pilot. At around 1000' over Rollestone he engaged a steep left-hand turn which resulted in a stall and a rapid loss of height. He managed to recover control, although the engine was misfiring. He was able to return to the airfield at Larkhill where he had the aircraft checked. Loraine took off again in the same aircraft at approximately 0530 hrs., this time with Staff Sgt Wilson on board. Flying again towards Rollestone he climbed to around 400' and once more engaged a steep left-hand turn. As before the aircraft stalled and lost height but this time there was insufficient height to recover and the Nieuport crashed in a field close to the site on which the memorial now stands. Fox, another pilot from No.3 Sqn at Larkhill, who was flying in the area witnessed the crash and landed close by to render assistance. He found both men still alive but with very serious injuries. He left them to summon help but on returning ten minutes later, found that Staff Sgt Wilson had died. Capt Loraine was taken in a horse-drawn ambulance to hospital at Bulford Camp but died shortly after arrival.

On Monday of the following week, Capt Loraine was taken the short distance from Bulford Camp to the railway station at Bulford Village on a gun-carriage accompanied by 400 officers and men who were led by the full band of the Duke of Cornwall's

The funeral procession of Capt Loraine approaching the railway station in Bulford Village from where he was returned to his home in Bramford, near Ipswich for burial.

added at the base of the cross, mounted with the badges of the Royal Engineers, Royal Flying Corp and Grenadier Guards. It bears the following inscription: -

AIRMAN'S CROSS
RE-DEDICATED 5 JULY 1996
TO THE MEMORY

OF

CAPTAIN
EUSTACE BROKE LORAINE
GRENADIER GUARDS

AND

STAFF SERGEANT
RICHARD HUBERT VICTOR WILSON
ROYAL ENGINEERS

THE FIRST MEMBERS OF THE ROYAL
FLYING CORPS
TO LOSE THEIR LIVES WHILST FLYING
ON DUTY

PLAQUE LAID BY THE FRIENDS
OF
THE MUSEUM OF ARMY FLYING,
MIDDLE WALLOP

Two photographs of the original memorial unveiling of 5th July 1913, one year after the fatal crash. Photo: T.L.Fuller © J.T.Fuller.

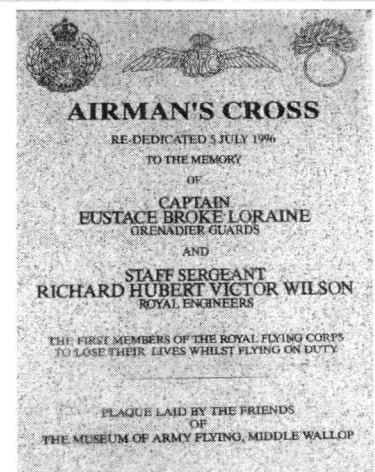

Two photographs of the re-dedicated 'Airman's Cross'.

Light Infantry. The train journey took him to his home near Ipswich where, on 10th July, his funeral was held and attended not only by relatives and friends but by over 200 Grenadier Guards and by the King's representative.

Staff Sgt Wilson was buried in his home town of Andover where the roads were closed to allow the passing of the mile long cortege comprising relatives, military personnel and townspeople.

The memorial stone near Shrewton was first dedicated exactly one year after the crash. The ceremony attracted enormous crowds who joined the families of the aviators and many high ranking officers to witness the unveiling by General Sir Horace Smith-Dorrien who later in World War 1 was to command the Second British Army at Ypres. The Last Post was sounded by the Coldstream Guards.

Over the years the inscription of the memorial became eroded and a campaign began to have it renovated,

led by AVM Barry Newton CB, CVO, OBE. This resulted in it being scheduled in May 1995 as a Grade 2 Listed Building and in the December it was removed for restoration work. On 5th July 1996 a re-dedication service was conducted at Airman's Cross by the RAF Chaplain-in-Chief with the memorial being unveiled by Joy Brockington, a niece and the only surviving relative of Staff Sgt Wilson. The service was attended by the Lord Lieutenant of Wiltshire, Lt Gen Sir Maurice Johnston, Viscount Ridley, Viscount Trenchard (grandson of MRAF Viscount Hugh Trenchard), Lord de Saumarez (relative of Capt Loraine) plus officers of the Grenadier Guards, Royal Engineers and the RAF. Trumpeters of the three units sounded the Last Post and Reveille with the service including a flypast by a RAF Harrier T10 of No.3 Sqn.

As part of the renovation work, the cross now stands on an area of crazy paving set into the grassed area. A horizontal stone plaque has been

In Worton and Marston's Christ Church, Church Lane, Worton off the C20. A brass service book stand, inscribed around the base: -

TO THE GLORY OF GOD
AND IN PROUD AND LOVING
MEMORY OF PAUL SANGSTER
RIVINGTON RAF
10TH JULY 1941.
"O WHAT THE JOY AND THE
GLORY MUST BE"

Note: In this unlocked church the bible stand is not on display. However, it is regularly used during services at the church.

Paul Rivington and the memorial book stand. Photo: Kate Anstie

Paul Rivington was born in Devizes and together with his twin brother Peter was educated at nearby Dauntsey's School in West Lavington. They both attended services at the church in Worton. On leaving school in 1938 Paul obtained a place at the Royal Academy of Dramatic Art in London.

He had just finished his first year when war broke out and he immediately volunteered as a pilot with the RAF (VR). He was called up soon after Christmas 1939. He failed his pilot's course at RAF White Waltham so re-mustered as a Wireless Operator/Air Gunner. While still under training at RAF Cranwell he was killed on 10th July 1941, when the Proctor in which he was flying crashed. The aircraft was being flown by a Polish pilot, when low cloud rolled in over the airfield at Cranwell. In trying to get beneath the cloud, the aircraft struck some trees and both men were killed.

Aircraftman Paul Sangster Rivington is buried at the Church of St. Andrew, Cranwell. His name appears on the war memorial at Dauntsey's School, West Lavington. The bible stand was donated to Christ Church, Worton by his sister after his death.

Photograph of gravestone.

Paul's brother Peter served with the RAF throughout the war years as a pilot with Coastal and Ferry Commands. As a civilian pilot he flew Lancasters during the Berlin Air Lift.

WROUGHTON AERODROME

Location - 173/SU146782 - 4 miles South of Swindon

The first 'air strip' in Wroughton, used between the Wars, was on 'Black Horse' field, north of Artis Farm on the A361. It took its name from the public house that stands in nearby Woodland View, now renamed 'The Check Inn'. The triangular field was primarily a sports field. It had no military use but was ideal for the air circuses that operated during the 1920s and 30s. The type of aircraft seen there were DH60 Moths, Avro 504s and DH9s. Some well known pilots appearing were Alan Cobham and Capt W.E. Jordan, a World War 1 fighter pilot, who during World War 2 ferried aircraft from America to Britain. His visits to Wroughton were made in a three-seat Blackburn biplane. 'Black Horse' field is today covered by the M4 motorway.

Wroughton Airfield itself, is to be found high on the northern edge of the Marlborough Downs, above and to the south of the village of Wroughton on the A361 Swindon to Devizes road. It is close to the site of the Battle of Beranburh (AD556) and the Neolithic Hill Fort known as Barbury Castle. In 1917 the site was planned as an Aircraft Acceptance Park and some preliminary work was done before it was decided to abandon the scheme. Just over twenty years later the site was surveyed for use as an Aircraft Storage Unit. The land required by the Air Ministry was used for farming and gallops to train racehorses that produced winners of the Derby, Grand National and other race meetings. The land was obtained by a compulsory purchase order issue in December 1938. Ernest Manners of Rectory Farm lost his entire land and Fred White of Overtown Farm lost sixty acres. The Swindon branch of the National Farmers Union made a strong protest to the Air Ministry over the loss of almost 1000 acres of good corn growing land. The point was also made that one million pounds had already been spent at nearby Yatesbury in setting up a training school. With war imminent, the protests were, of course, dismissed. As a result, Ernest Manners held a sale on 28th February 1939, where he disposed of his entire livestock and farm machinery.

Aerodrome Development

The estimated cost of the new aerodrome was £800,000 and work on it commenced in May 1939. Holloway Brothers of Millbank, London won the contract for the construction. The buildings of Rectory Farm were demolished and a disused chalk quarry in the planned landing area was filled in to make way for the airfield. The main administration and technical site was located on the opposite side of the airfield from the main A361, in the South East corner, on a lane leading to Barbury Castle. The threat of enemy bombing made it imperative to avoid keeping large formations of aircraft in storage parked close together so ASUs were constructed to provide a number of hangar sites giving maximum dispersal. These would generally be positioned around the perimeter track but this format caused considerable inconvenience with communication, security etc. At Wroughton there were 6 such sites with 7 hangars of the 'L' type, but others in use were 'B1' type 2, built for the glider assembly work of 1942, 'C' type 3, 'D' type 4 and 24 Robin type hangars. Ten of the latter were located away from the main airfield. Three are still in use by local farmers on the west side of the A361 and four to the SE of the airfield. Not all of the hangars had been constructed when the airfield

officially opened in April 1940, but fourteen of them were well on their way to completion by the summer. The first to be erected were the 'C' and 'D' Type on the Main Headquarters Site, No.1 and No.2 Sites. The steel-work and large end sliding doors were constructed by the Cleveland Bridge and Engineering Co. Both types had windows along their length immediately below roof level. The idea was that, should the hangars be hit by bombing, the windows would be blown out first and reduce the risk of blast damage to the walls. The windows were blacked out during war time. The 300' x 150' 'L' Type hangars on Site Nos. 3, 4 and 5 had curved concrete roofs covered with soil and turfed over to provide a good camouflage. This was done by a gang of Irish workmen who were billeted at Site No.4. The final hangars to be erected were the two 230' x 123' 'B' Type at Site No.6. These also had windows along their length immediately below the roofing. The civilian employees tended to refer to the size of hangars by the length of a Lancaster, consequently the 'B' Type was known as 'two Lancs long'. Only 24 of the intended 27 63' x 50' Robin Type hangars were completed.

By the end of April 1940 the civilian staff had built up to over 200 and a temporary canteen had been provided for them, together with a NAAFI for

The two buildings beside this 'D' Type hangar on the HQ Site are the Pilots' Dispersal in the fore-ground and at the rear with the raised roof is the Parachute Packing building.

The 'C' Type hangar on the HQ Site viewed from the airfield.

the servicemen. Only one of the hangars, which had flooded after completion, was operational and the administration offices and domestic accommodation was in wooden huts. As the site developed, corrugated-iron Nissen type huts were erected. The workforce formed a Home Guard Unit, carrying out these duties at the end of their working day. Pill-boxes were constructed in strategic positions, most being on the high ground to the north of the landing strip. Some of these were equipped with sleeping quarters where off duty personnel could rest. Airfield defences included a line of Bofors guns on the northern perimeter, with a gun emplacement on the high ground at the western side of the aerodrome.

The runways are seen in this aerial view with an 'L' Type hangar on Site No.4 to the left, opposite the two 'B' Type hangars on Site No.6 and in the fore-ground the three 'L' Type on Site No.5.   Photo: Des Blake

The Station HQ building appears in the centre and to the right the main gate by the road. Top left can be seen the two 'C' Type hangars on Site No.2.   Photo: Des Blake

Viewed from the perimeter track, the two 'B' Type hangars used currently by the Department of Naval Recruiting.

One of the two 'L' Type hangars on Site No.3.

Wroughton had four dispersal fields at Burderop Park, below Barbury Castle, near Uffcott and Upper Salthrop Farm and two other dispersal areas east of the main station buildings at Overtown Hackpen. These areas were well outside the boundary of the airfield and their provision was necessary for the vast numbers of aircraft which would be stored. Aircraft were towed by Maintenance Unit tractors to the airfield along country lanes or tracks and a journey of two miles was necessary in the case of Burderop Park. Establishments such as Wroughton, in addition to dispersal areas, were allocated Satellite Landing Grounds for storage use. These were generally some distance from the home base and although only used by one MU at a time, Unit allocation changes took place during the war. No.15 MU for example used No.31 SLG Everleigh from November 1941 to 17th September 1942, No.1 SLG Slade Farm, Oxfordshire from 1st October 1942 to February 1943 and No.12 SLG Beechwood Park, Bedfordshire from 17th March 1943 to 1945. It was the

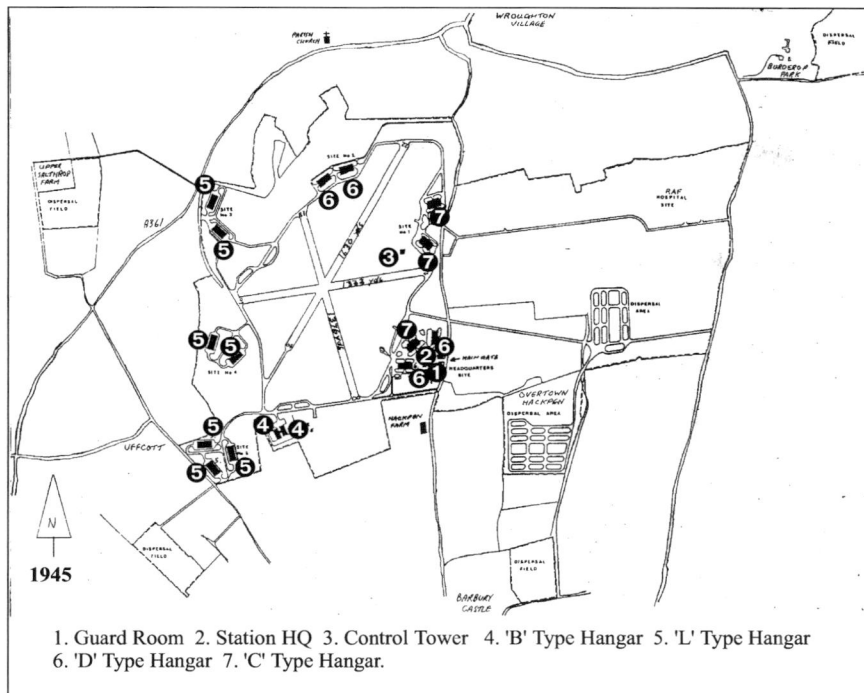

1. Guard Room 2. Station HQ 3. Control Tower 4. 'B' Type Hangar 5. 'L' Type Hangar
6. 'D' Type Hangar 7. 'C' Type Hangar.

Because of the compact site and the hangar configuration, the layout of the runways was unusual, in that they had a common point of intersection. The first and main runway NE/SW 04/22 had a length and width of 1533 x 50yds, later extended to 1630yds. The second, E/W 09/27, 1333 x 50yds, was completed in 1943. The third, NW/SE 00/18, 1376 x 50yds. This runway is now disused. At the time of the first runway construction, a perimeter track of almost 4 miles was laid, together with concrete taxiways from the various dispersed Robin type hangars. The small control tower, of a non-standard pattern, is sited near the eastern end of runway 09/27.

By the late 1960s many of the war time temporary timber huts on the airfield were demolished and the redundant outlying dispersal areas, once scrapping had ceased, were sold back to the local farmers. The Robin type hangars were also given over to those farmers on whose land they stood.

Wroughton's small non-standard Control Tower.

World War 2 Years

No.15 MU occupied the airfield when it opened on 1st April 1940 in No.41 Group (Andover) Maintenance Command with Wg Cdr W.C. Farley as CO. A few days later, the first 30 civilian employees arrived, as did the first aircraft flown by a Staff Officer from Group HQ. Later the same week a detachment of the 8th Battalion Royal Welsh Fusiliers moved in to provide anti-aircraft defence for the airfield. On 10th April a female pilot of the Air Transport Auxiliary landed the second aircraft, a Fox Moth. The aircraft sustained minor damage when she landed on the future permanent landing area instead of the temporary one then in use east of the site. Even this temporary runway was, however, prone to water logging.

intention that No.15 MU would use No.47 SLG Southgrove between Burbage and Collingbourne Kingston on the A346 Marlborough to Salisbury road. This should have been operational from 30th August 1941 but was never used. The aerodrome at Bicester, occupied by No.13 OTU, was also used as a temporary dispersal by No.15 MU for the twelve months between November 1940 and 1941.

While initial airfield construction at Wroughton was being undertaken another area east of the main site was being used as a landing ground, with aircraft flown in and out by Ferry Pilots. This field (173/SU153786) had a steep slope at the north end therefore some of the Air Transport Auxillary pilots would fly parallel to the Marlborough Downs before turning at right angles on to the approach from the south for a landing up the slope. Others preferred an east/west landing, presumably depending on wind direction, at the south end of the LG below the rise of the slope. A wooden hut was provided in the SW corner of the field where pilots arriving with aircraft would have their delivery notes signed. ATA pilot Ann Welch made several deliveries to this field during 1941/42 and her Log Book records five occasions during February 1942: - 2 Oxfords from Portsmouth, 2 from Christchurch and a Walrus W3034 from Eastleigh on the 10th. Following delivery she was collected by the Ferry Pool Anson. There were times when a

pilot would deliver an aircraft in the morning, be flown back to the factory and return later in the day with another one. A number of aircraft landing in this field tipped on to their noses due to the uneven surface. A second temporary landing ground was later brought into use running from East to West at (173/SU1627830). Wroughton's decoy airfield was prepared to the west of Barbury Castle.

By 1941 most of the permanent buildings at Wroughton had been completed. Three hangars, the Headquarters with Unit Operations Control Room, workshops, civilian canteen, mechanical transport section and supply centre formed the Main Site. The 6 storage sites around the aerodrome perimeter each had two or three permanent hangars, supported by its own canteen and guardroom. In addition there were numerous temporary wooden huts interspersed with the permanent structures on each site, giving accommodation for service personnel and additional office facilities. With the development of the airfield and the problems caused by the water-logging of the grass landing and taxiing areas, it became imperative that hard surface runways were constructed as a matter of some urgency. Although work commenced on the first of these in the Spring of 1941, it turned out to be a protracted affair, with the third not completed until 13th March 1944.

At the end of the first month 13 Westland Lysanders and 10 Tiger Moths had arrived from the factories for storage. These caused an immediate problem, as there were insufficient aircraft towing vehicles and the hard surface link tracks between the widely dispersed facilities were incomplete.

The first Bristol Blenheims arrived on 3rd May 1940 with three of them being delivered to No.107 Sqn at Wattisham on 19th May. Conditions in Europe were looking bad when Wroughton received its first Hurricanes on 25th May and the workers were asked to work extra hours in preparing them for operational use. This involved the fitting of self-sealing fuel tanks and machine guns. Gun butts had hastily been constructed at the base of the north side of Barbury Castle, which was a considerable distance from the aerodrome. It was necessary to tow the aircraft there with a man on each wing during windy weather. During darkness hand torches provided the only means of illumination during movements. A gantry was used to lift the tail of the aircraft with a trestle placed underneath when in the horizontal position. The guns were then harmonised before being fired into the earth embankment. By 10th June, 42 Hurricanes were available for release to the squadrons. A more convenient set of butts built with walls of concrete blocks filled with a bank of sand were later constructed near the hangars of No.6 Site. The No.15 MU test pilots formed a 'Defence Flight' with a sole available Hurricane maintained, armed and fuelled to protect the aerodrome. Test Pilot Sgt Jeff Malton did not arrive at Wroughton until June 1941 and he remembers only one occasion when the Hurricane took off in pursuit of an enemy aircraft which was 'stooging' about in the vicinity of the aerodrome. No contact was made. The offices of the four test pilots were on No.6 Site. The Chief Test Pilot was Flt Lt Dickie Dawes. The main flight testing work of these pilots was the satisfactory operation of all airframe/engine controls, performance checks at full throttle plus climb and maximum cruise conditions. Any faults would be corrected and a retest carried out. Occasionally, where Spitfires and Fireflys were equipped with 20mm cannon, the pilots would conduct live firing tests at a range in the Bristol Channel. Barracuda torpedo bombers required radar performance checks and

during these flights a Royal Navy technician would accompany the test pilot.

Wg Cdr C. J. Barrington was appointed as CO in August 1940. Wroughton soon attracted the attention of enemy aircraft were probably aware that it was a source of fighter aircraft supplies. On 13th August 1940, 2 Blenheims on dispersel were damaged when four bombs were dropped from a Heinkel He111. A raid the next day inflicted no damage but on the 19th August four bombs dropped on the main site slightly damaged a 'D' type hangar, which was still under construction, and some of the temporary hutted accommodation. With the Battle of Britain raging, this was a very busy time for No.15 MU which was striving to prepare sufficient aircraft to keep the Fighter Command squadrons supplied. Of the 94 aircraft issued through September 1940, 61 were Hurricanes. In December the CO of Wroughton changed again with the appointment of Wg Cdr G.N. Warrington.

In early 1941 American built Curtiss Tomahawk and Mohawk aircraft started arriving. These were from a French order but were diverted to the UK following the fall of France. On Thursday 2nd January 1941 one of these, Mohawk AR658 crashed at Elcombe Pass Farm shortly after take-off and the pilot Capt H.J. Horsey ATA of No.3 FPP based at Whitchurch Airfield, Bristol sustained head, leg and arm injuries. He was taken to Victoria Hospital Swindon where he died four days later. This was the first major aircraft accident at Wroughton and the arctic conditions of that winter may have contributed to it. Aircraft with the French Air Force were fitted with reverse action throttles, pulled out to increase power and pushed in for reduced, this was the opposite to RAF aircraft. Therefore this may have contributed to the accident if the pilot pushed the throttle forward in error.

The increasing throughput of aircraft resulted in a larger workforce which at this time had swelled to 600 civilians and 150 uniformed personnel. With the entry of America into the war in 1941, following Pearl Harbor, larger quantities of American aircraft arrived and by early 1942 were

concentrated at seven ASUs around the country. Although Wroughton was initially not one of the seven, No.15 MU was added later, as was No.33 MU at Lyneham. Sgt Jeff Malton, one of the four No.15 MU test pilots at Wroughton remembers the Vought V-156-B1 Chesapeakes arriving. The U.K. had ordered 50 of the type and they started arriving in England in 1941 for assembly at Burtonwood Repair Depot. The first ones were allocated to the FAAs 728 Sqn based at Arbroath, but 811 Sqn was the first to deploy them operationally and to discover that they were not suitable for use from escort carriers. Jeff Malton had already decided the Chesapeake I was useless.

No.15 MU was controlled by No.52 Wing when it was reformed at Gatcombe Park near Stroud on 21st May 1941. No.76 MU Packing Depot arrived from Cosford on 26th May, with the responsibility of stripping down aircraft and boxing them for shipment abroad. On arrival this MU used No.1 Site, occupying two 'C' Type hangars following their completion. Later they also occupied 2 'D' type hangars at No.2 Site. Aircraft on arrival were stripped down in one hangar and the sectional packing cases, which were delivered by road, were assembled in the second hangar of the site. Carpenters and labourers would crate the aircraft and seal the already battle-ship grey/blue painted packing cases. These would then be numbered, coded, loaded on lorries and taken to the docks for shipment abroad. If defects were reported by the ATA pilots on delivery to the MU, these would be dealt with at Wroughton and the aircraft test flown by a MU pilot before dismantling. Aircraft to be packaged first had the fuel tanks drained into 50gallon drums outside the hangar. Those with cannon or machine guns installed were checked by armourers to ensure any live ammunition was removed. Electricians disconnected batteries and took out radio sets. When completed, the aircraft would be taken into the hangar for work to commence on dismantling. For the greater part of the war the RAF ASUs were responsible for all the Royal Navy aircraft and in this respect, Wroughton played a particularly prominent role despatching to the main fleet bases in various parts of the world. Throughout the summer months of 1941 aircraft types arriving were the Lysander, Spitfire, Fairey Fulmar, Swordfish, Gladiator, Supermarine Walrus and Tempest but with the Blenheim and Hurricane still predominant. From this it can be seen that some were destined for FAA requirements. Others were for foreign Air Forces in which case RAF roundels were replaced by the appropriate markings. Other aircraft stored at this time were the Bermuda, Bombay, Mosquito, Seafire, Sea Otter, Firefly, U.S. Curtiss Seamew, Oxfords, Tiger Moths and the rare Hafner Gyroplane. The U.K. received 100 lend/lease Seamew SO3C-2Cs. These were allocated to the FAAs 754 and 755 Sqns. They were never used operationally but for training WOP/AGs. As with the Chesapeake, sometimes used as target-tugs, the Seamew was not a popular aircraft with the crews. The Unit averaged an output of between 25 and 30 aircraft per month and by the end of the year had despatched no fewer than 126. The service to the FAA developed considerably after 1943 when it rapidly expanded before the Navy had its own Receipt and Despatch Units at Culham and Anthorn.

In October 1941 Wg Cdr J.H. Maguire became the Wroughton CO and one of his early duties on 7th November was to host a visit to the station by H.R.H. The Duke of Kent. The Duke was then Air Commodore on the staff of the Inspector General of the RAF. Accompanied by senior officers of Maintenance Command, he inspected No.15 MU. Within a few months he was to lose his life when the Coastal Command Short Sunderland, in which he was flying, crashed.

In 1942 men and women were drafted to Wroughton from all over the country, with the number of those employed reaching a peak of nearly 700. Wroughton's second fatal accident occurred on 15th October 1942 when an Airspeed Horsa glider taking off on tow by a Whitley, in strong gusty cross wind conditions, cart-wheeled and disintegrated killing the crew of two Army Sergeant Glider Pilots. This had been one of a series of takeoffs from aerodromes in the locality of Brize Norton where the aircraft were based.

In April 1943 No.76 MU moved from No.2 to No.3 Site when work commenced on the assembly of the Horsa Gliders needed to prepare for the eventual invasion of Europe. The responsibility fell to No.9 MU at Cosford, No.5 MU Kemble, No.6 MU Brize Norton and No.15 MU Wroughton each to produce fifty per month. By the beginning of 1944 however the monthly total output was reduced to a figure of 70 - 90 with No.5 MU being withdrawn from the equation. Glider production at Wroughton did increase with the build up to D-Day on 6th June 1944. Around 100 Hotspur gliders were also assembled by No.15 MU.

For a time in 1943 a batch of Tiger Moths were stored and to save hangar space were stood on their noses, with their tails in the air. This was the normal practice with this type of aircraft, especially in Lamella Type hangars at MUs. No.76 MU did not stay at No.3 Site for very long and was soon moved back to its original No.1 Site. A Glider Test and Ferry Flight (No.15 MU) formed at Wroughton on 20th February 1943 with four Whitley V tug aircraft and an Albemarle I. The purpose of the Flt was to test and deliver the Horsa gliders. Some of these were sent to various southern area ASUs and others to airfields in eastern England. The Flight's Whitleys were later replaced with 14 Albemarles, 1 Anson and a Hudson.

On Friday 19th February a Westland Whirlwind P7062 of No.263 Sqn from Warmwell, crashed at Brimble Hill on the north-east side of the aerodrome. It was one of four taking part in an exercise, Operation Longford. This involved pilots practising the 'shooting up' of enemy convoys. P7062 hit trees on the brow of the hill and spun into Wanshot field. The pilot Flt Sgt Francis L. Hicks RAAF was killed and is buried in St. John the Baptist and St. Helen churchyard, Wroughton.

In September 1943 Wg Cdr C. Duncan was appointed as CO at Wroughton.

With the policy of forming Parent Preparation Units in 1944, during May of that year, Wroughton held its largest volume of wartime aircraft. This policy determined that No.15 MU would be responsible for the preparation of the Blenheim and the Royal Navy's Fairey Albacore, Barracuda, Firefly, Fulmar and Supermarine Seamew, Sea Otter and Walrus. Mosquitos and Spitfires in large numbers also occupied the hangars and dispersals. Wroughton was selected as the main centre for the large scale radio and radar modification programme of Fairey Barracudas. Top priority was afforded to this task by No.15 MU, which was given a target of 90 aircraft per month. This target was not reached, however, due to a shortage of modification kits. A number of Barracudas passing through Wroughton took part in the successful attack on the German battleship *Tirpitz*.

On 5th February 1944 a USAAF P-38 Lockheed Lightning F5B crashed on the NW side of the airfield at Elcombe. The aircraft, of the 13th Photographic Reconnaissance Group

A Fairey Barracuda prepared for the Fleet Air Arm by No.15 MU's civilian personnel.
Photo: Wroughton History Group

353

at Mount Farm, Oxfordshire, was on a test flight when an engine fire developed. The pilot Lt Arthur Waldron USAAF was killed in the crash. In April 2002 the author was invited to attend the recovery of a large amount of the aircraft, including the engines. This was carried out by the Wroughton History Group in conjunction with the East Surrey Aviation Group.

No.88 Gliding School had formed at Wroughton by July 1944, it was equipped with Cadet I & IIs. The school remained until 28th September 1947 when it moved to Hullavington.

With the war drawing to an end, Wg Cdr R.H. Stocken was appointed as CO in January 1945. The Glider Test and Ferry Flight disbanded in August and all Navy aircraft left the Unit. The role of No.15 MU changed to that of aircraft storage over an indefinite time and to the scrapping and disposal of surplus and war worn aircraft. The Lancaster was one of the many types which made their last flight into Wroughton. Two at least were aircraft which had carried out in excess of 100 operations. As bomber squadrons disbanded, these aircraft, which had carried the war into the heart of Germany, poured into Wroughton and by the late autumn around 200 were on site. A few were renovated and later used by Coastal Command, but the majority were scrapped.

Less civilian labour was now needed and by the end of the year it had reduced to approximately 500. Although strictly against regulations, many of the civilian workers were treated to (unauthorised) flights in various types of aircraft during the war years.

One of these was Harold Grey who accidentally released his parachute on leaving a Barracuda following a test flight. He was required to pay to have it repacked.

Post War Years

On 3rd December 1945 a No.15 MU Spitfire F18 TP281 belly-landed in error and was not repaired.

At the end of the month Wroughton had a change of CO with the arrival of Wg Cdr H.R. Barden.

A former No.115 Sqn Lancaster being broken up at No.15 MU.
Photo: Wroughton History Group

The still useful Mosquitos, and then the jet-propelled Meteors, were the predominant type of active aircraft in storage in the early post war years. The older Mosquitos were broken up.

The rest were prepared for issue to night fighter and light bomber squadrons. No.76 MU remained, but its role gradually decreased and it was disbanded on 30th September 1946. This meant further reduction in the civilian labour force.

Come 1947 the MoD was still disposing of some stored aircraft by offering them for sale by tender. These were referred to as a 'sealed bid' and required the purchaser to submit a form stating the amount he or she was prepared to pay for a particular lot. In February British Aviation Services of Blackbushe were successful with bids to obtain three Vickers-Supermarine Sea Otters which were in store with No.15 MU. These were JM747, JM757 and JM759, which on the civil register became respectively G-AJFU, G-AJFW and G-AJFV.

Wg Cdr H.L. Millward MBE became the CO in July 1947 followed by Wg Cdr Parish in November. The station had yet another CO in February 1950 when Wg Cdr P.W.J. Dawes took over the post.

In this aerial view, 70 Lancaster bombers can be seen in late 1945 at the dispersal on the eastern side of the airfield. 2 of the Robin hangars appear bottom right.
Photo: Wroughton History Group

The same aircraft viewed from the ground beneath a cloudy winter sky.
Photo: Wroughton History Group

AVM Sir Basil Embry, Director General of Training, visited Wroughton on 23rd October 1947 and personally air tested the first batch of Mosquitos destined for the Rhodesian Air Force. At this time Rhodesia returned the Harvard trainers which were used there during the war for pilot training under the Empire Air Training Scheme. These went into storage at Wroughton until issued to RAF training units, the Italian Air Force and to the recreated Belgian and Dutch Air Forces.

On 24th March 1950, a Tempest FB6 NX129 of No.1 Ferry Pool, White Waltham was written off when its engine cut out during approach to Wroughton and it belly-landed half a mile west of the airfield. The same happened, but this time on take-off, to Mosquito NF30, MV524 of No.15 MU, when it belly-landed half a mile south of the airfield on 5th February 1951. The unit was at this time engaged in servicing aircraft and carrying out major inspections on Lancasters, Lincolns and Mosquitos. In 1952 the Horsa gliders which had remained in storage were finally scrapped. This was also the year that the Queen granted the Unit an official badge. The badge depicted a warrior's helmet on a grass mound with the motto *Fervet Opus*, the former representing the battles of the past fought locally. The translation of the motto is 'To work with spirit', this epitomising the consistent enthusiasm of the work force over the years. The jet age came to Wroughton with the Meteors, which arrived at an average of ten a month, some of these being the night fighter version. They were issued as replacements for RAF squadrons equipped with the now ageing Mosquito and to the French and Dutch Air Forces. The end of the year saw Wg Cdr F.B. Bristow appointed as CO.

During 1953 the Canberra bombers started to arrive at Wroughton for what was to be a nineteen-year association. Twelve months later a Flight of Vampires was formed there. The CO from May 1955 was Wg Cdr C.A. Mills. Early in 1956 twenty-two Supermarine Swifts arrived by road from the Vickers Armstrong factory at South Marston. These were stored at No.15 MU pending a decision as to their future. Later in the year they were returned to the factory by road. In July 1956 the Nash collection, comprising three World War 1 aircraft, Maurice Farman, Fokker Triplane and Sopwith

Camel, arrived for renovation and storage by the Unit. These would later form part of the RAF Museum collection at Hendon as would Lancaster B.1 R5868 which was also in storage at Wroughton. A Communication Sqn from No.41

The last operational Lancasters in RAF service. On 15ᵗʰ October 1956 Lancaster MR3 RF325 was flown into Wroughton from St. Mawgan where it had served with Coastal Command.
Photo: Wroughton History Group

Group Maintenance Command HQ at Andover arrived at Wroughton in July with Vampire T.11s, remaining there until December 1959. The last Lancaster in RAF Service, MR.3 RF325, flew into Wroughton on 15th October 1956 from the School of Maritime Reconnaissance St Mawgan, following a farewell ceremony. At Wroughton it was broken up and sold as scrap, a regrettable action taken at a time when little thought was given to the conservation of aircraft. This same year the Mosquito was finally

Pilots' Pool formed with Meteor T.7s attached to No.15 MU. It moved to Lyneham in May 1959 attached to No.33 MU. The last Lincoln held by No.15 MU was scrapped in 1958 and the servicing of Canberras for RAF Bomber Command, the Royal New

Zealand and Rhodesian Air Forces continued to keep the Unit staff busy.

The end of the decade saw the arrival of the first Bristol Sycamore helicopter in October 1959 with the Saro Skeeter following the year after. These were followed by the Westland Dragonfly, Whirlwind and Scout.

In July 1960 Wg Cdr E. Stephenson was appointed CO. He was in post until June 1963 when Wg Cdr E. Evans OBE was appointed to succeed him.

A DH Vampire entering a hangar for servicing at No.1 Site.
Photo: Wroughton History Group

declared obsolete and by 1957 all those in storage at Wroughton had been scrapped, including many new ones which had been delivered but never issued for operational use.

In April 1958 Wg Cdr M.C. S. Shepherd OBE became the CO and the same month No.41 Group Test

Westland Wessex and American Bell Sioux helicopters started to arrive at the MU in 1960. Three years later the unit was presented with the task of refurbishing the last airworthy Lancaster PA474, which had been superseded by the Lincoln. It was intended as an exhibition in the then yet to be built RAF Museum at

Hendon. The refurbishment involved a complete airframe overhaul, the fitting of four Rolls Royce Merlin engines with low-hours, and a repaint in wartime camouflage. The work was completed in 1964 whereupon the aircraft was moved to RAF Henlow for temporary storage in the open, as it was too large for the hangars. As the proposed opening of the RAF Museum was some years away, a decision was later taken to transfer PA474 to Waddington where at least it could be given hangar storage. It flew there on 18th August 1965 and went on to become the star attraction of the now famous Battle of Britain Memorial Flight. By 1964 the Meteors and Vampires had gone from the unit and the Canberra was left as the main fixed-wing servicing element. Other service expired Canberras were flown in for storage and eventual scrapping. In August 1966 Wg Cdr H.W. Harrison was CO followed in December 1968 by

Engine fitters working on one of the Canberras at Wroughton.
Photo: Norman Parker Coll.

Wg Cdr Des Blake who was destined to be the last appointee to the post.

By the late 1960s No.15 MU was mainly involved in the modification of rotary winged aircraft with some Canberras still being handled.

In May 1971, with closure imminent,

Wg Cdr Des Blake, the last CO of RAF Wroughton, with his staff car, Sioux (Station Hack), an Army Scout and Wessex Whirlwind helicopters, in 1972.
Photo: Wg Cdr Des Blake

A Sycamore being prepared for one of the Air Forces of the Middle East.
Photo: Norman Parker

Wg Cdr Blake organised a No.15 MU Open Day for the personnel and their families. This involved a static display and flying programme which included a VC10, Britannia and a Belfast from Brize Norton, Spitfire Mk.8 and a display by the 'Red Arrows' Gnats. No.15 MU continued in operation until 31st March 1972 when it was disbanded.

Closure

A ceremony was held on 5th April 1972 when the RAF officially handed over occupation to the Royal Navy. The RAF had been employing some 400 personnel most of who were civilian, but with a uniformed CO and associated officers. Under the Navy this number reduced to 80, again mainly civilian but with a uniformed presence. With the RAF departure the Headquarters site of the airfield was commissioned by the Admiralty as a

Wg Cdr Des Blake (front centre) with No.15 MU personnel in 1972.
Photo: Wg Cdr Des Blake

Westland Whirlwind XK986 ouside one of the 'D' Type hangars at HQ Site.
Photo: Wroughton History Group

A Canberra with modified nose cone housing radar equipment
Photo: Wroughton History Group

Royal Naval Aircraft Yard. Work was carried out on Gazelles, Scouts and Wasps, with the storage of Sioux, and later Sea King and Lynx helicopters. Rundown of the Naval Yard commenced in March 1976 with the intention of closure in 1979. However a reprieve took place when it was realised that the centralisation of military helicopter modification at Fleetlands, Gosport was beyond the Depot's capabilities and the intended storage in the salty air of Culdrose was unsuitable.

In 1978 the Science Museum took over the occupancy of a number of hangars for the storage of some of their larger exhibits, mostly road vehicles but including aircraft from their civil aviation collection. Seven hangars on Sites 1-4 are currently being used with an additional purpose built hangar sized store erected in 1993 at the north end of the disused runway and adjoining the original hangars on Site 2. The Science Museum's Aeronautical Collection was started in 1912 and is one of the oldest collections in the world. Over 20 full size aircraft are displayed in London together with aero-engines and associated material. The core of the Air Transport Collection at Wroughton is a group of full sized airliners, acquired to extend the coverage of the main historic collection into modern times and to illustrate the major technical developments in this form of transportation. The first aircraft purchased for the Air Transport Collection was a 1936 Douglas DC-3 E1-AYO which was flown into Wroughton on 25th October 1978. A Dan-Air De-Havilland D.H.106 Comet 4B, G-APYD was the next to arrive on 1st November 1979 when it was brought in by Captain Joe Wright for its 18,586th landing having completed 32,728 hours flying time. On 21st June 1982 Lockheed L.10A Electra N5171N/G-L10A flew from Florida to Wroughton across the Atlantic via Greenland and Iceland. This aircraft was dismantled and moved to London during 1999. The same 6000 mile delivery flight was made by Boeing 247D N.18E touching down on 3rd August. Lockheed L.749 Constellation N7777G/G-CONI was moved by sea and road from Dublin to Wroughton in August 1983. British Airways Hawker-Siddeley H.S.121 Trident 3B G-AWZM was a further large airliner flown into Wroughton. This arrived on 28th February 1986 and replaced the non-standard Trident 1E G-AVYE which had been purchased by the Science Museum in April 1981. Other aircraft in the collection include the De Havilland D.H.84 Dragon Orcadian, D.H.89 Dragon Rapide, D.H.104 Dove 6 (Devon), once based at Boscombe Down, Handley Page H.P.39 Gugnune and the Italian built Piaggio P.166.

The late 1970s also saw the arrival at Wroughton of the Department of Naval Recruiting (DNR) who took up residence in the two hangars on Site No.6. Here at their Central Work Shops various demonstration units are made up for attendance at exhibitions, recruiting campaigns etc in various locations.

The Royal Navy Aircraft Yard finally closed in 1989 as a naval unit. Maintenance continued to be undertaken at Wroughton by Field Aircraft Ltd with a staff of 80 before it

Official handing over of RAF Wroughton by Wg Cdr Des Blake RAF to Commander
Cryer RN of the Royal Navy on 5th April 1972. Photo: Wg Cdr D. Blake

DH84 Dragon Orcadian G-ACIT and at the rear DH89 Dragon Rapide G-ALXT.   Photo: Don Neate

ended on 3rd September 1992. This did not bring an end to flying at Wroughton as the final three very successful 'Great War Birds' air displays were staged there. The last of these was held over the hot summer weekend of 11th/12th June 1994.

R.N.A.Y Wroughton crest.

Aircraft of a smaller type were on show at Wroughton during the first week of September 1997 when the second World Model Jet Championships were staged. Known as the World Jet Masters, the previous championship had been held in Germany in 1995.

The future for the airfield looks promising with the Science Museum's continuing occupation and expansion. A number of open days and displays with a transport theme are held each year and are well supported. The BBC have used the runways for filming motorway scenes for programmes such as *Casualty*, so earning revenue for the Imperial War Museum and hopefully

Photographs of the "Great War Birds"

Lancaster PA474 taxiing past the B-17 *Sally B*.

With Marlborough Downs as a back-drop, Spitfire MkVc AR501 taxies out to take off for its display over Wroughton airfield.

benefitting the maintenance and promotion of the site. The Naval Yard was sold by the MoD to a Wiltshire based property developer who applied for planning permission to refurbish the three hangers for possible use as film studios. This failed to materialise and the Imperial War Museum is now negotiating to buy the former Naval Yard and with the extra space is hoping to be able to create a national

collection centre where the Museum will be able to work alongside some of Britain's other museums, providing storage and conservation facilities.

Some demolition of original buildings took place during 1997 with the former fire station and generator building being casualties. The World War 2 underground control centre has also been demolished.

WROUGHTON

Memorials

173/SU138803 - 4 miles South of Swindon

In the Parish Church of St. John the Baptist & St. Helen on the A361.

1) On the east side of the main isle stands a Prayer Desk displaying the badge of RAF Wroughton together with a Kneeler embroidered with the RAF Crest.

Prayer Desk & Kneeler.

2) In an alcove on the west wall is a Memorial Book on a wooden stand inscribed: -

Presented by
PA RAF (H) WROUGHTON
16 JULY 1941 - 31 MARCH 1996

Memorial Book & Stand.

The churchyard contains the graves of service personnel of the RAF, RAAF and Polish Forces.

Princess Alexandra's RAF Hospital

One mile east of the airfield, on an unclassified road leading towards the Marlborough Downs, stands the buildings of the former Princess Alexandra's RAF Hospital (173/SU163791). Now boarded up and isolated behind a high wire fence, this former RAF establishment stands as a memorial to the quality of service it rendered primarily to military personnel but also to civilians. Wroughton was chosen to be the largest Casualty Clearing Station in the UK due to its proximity to Lyneham and to Swindon railway station with its connections to London, the Midlands and the West of England. It was envisaged that war casualties would be flown from Europe to Lyneham, taken to Wroughton for treatment and dispersed by rail and ambulance within twenty-four hours. The site chosen for the hospital, known then as the Royal Air Force General Hospital, was on the Burderop Estate. The land was used for farming at the time of the compulsory purchase order issue by the Air Ministry. As with the aerodrome, Holloway Bros. of London received the construction contract for the hospital and work commenced on the foundations in June 1939. The estimated cost for the work was £230,000. The building of

this permanent hospital provided beds for 260 patients together with various modern departments, staff accommodation and blocks for housing single and married personnel. The building was of a two-storey design, built in a letter 'H' configeration. Large windows were installed to provide maximum light to the wards, each having a solarium at one end. During construction a German aircraft dropped four bombs and sprayed the roof with machine gun fire. No damage was sustained when three of the bombs exploded in a sewage trench at the northern end of the building and a fourth failed to go off. The hospital opened on 14th June 1941 in preparation for receiving military casualties. An opening up party of 14 under the command of Gp Capt E.C. Foreman arrived to prepare the buildings for use and, for 260 patients together with various modern departments, staff accommodation and blocks for on 21st August. The first ten convalescent patients arrived from Yatesbury and were put in Ward 6. Patient numbers quickly started to increase with the arrival of aircrew suffering from burns and requiring amputations. The first death in the hospital occurred on 1st November 1941 following the admission of a Sgt Pilot with multiple head wounds received when his aircraft crashed at Cricklade. The hospital also dealt with routine non-emergency operations as in the case of Plt Off LeRoy Grover an American serving in the RAF with No.66 Sqn at Ibsley in June 1942. He was admitted to have

The medical and administrative staff of RAF Hospital Wroughton in the summer of 1942.
Front Row Centre is seen the CO Gp Capt E.C. Foreman with on his left, the Australian Senior Surgeon, Wg Cdr E. Cato and on his right Gp Capt Puwy-Evans who later succeeded Gp Capt Foreman as CO when he was posted to Middle East Command later in the year.
Photo: Dr. Anthony Foreman

his tonsils removed and with the recovery period, spent almost a month at Wroughton.

By October 1943 eight additional wards had been constructed, barrack blocks had been extended and additional storage facilities provided. At the end of March 1944, the hospital was required to increase the bed capacity to one thousand. Extra wards were erected at the rear of the main building extending the bed capacity by 350. These were of the SECO type hutting which had inter-linking corridors which in turn joined to the main hospital corridor system. The busiest period would be the D-Day landings of 1944, stretching the hospital and staff to the limits. Nursing staff from the hospital at RAF Melksham were seconded to assist the permanent Wroughton personnel. One of these was WAAF Cpl Kathleen Lowe, a radiographer, who recalls a tented encampment being erected in the hospital grounds to accommodate the extra staff. The first in-take from the fighting in France came on 13th June. The casualties were not flown into Wroughton airfield but arrived at Lyneham from where they were transported in a fleet of ambulances to the RAF Hospital at Wroughton. A siren operated at the hospital to prepare staff for in-coming casualties and when the all clear was sounded, they knew then that the last flights had arrived at Lyneham. The injured would only have received first aid treatment before leaving Normandy and on arrival at the hospital a team of eight medical officers made an initial diagnosis of the injuries and tied each with a label explaining the treatment they required. Many of the casualties would arrive with the letter 'M' or 'T' marked on their foreheads with lipstick. This indicated to the medical staff that the patient had been treated with morphine or had a tourniquet. The hospital had eight X-Ray units in use and squads of Italian PoW were on hand to take stretcher cases to the various departments for treatment. They also delivered food to the troops and to the hospital staff, who would eat as they worked. Some days the treatment was continuously administered for over twelve hours. Following treatment a casualty would spend the night in one of the wards and the next day would be moved on to a hospital in another part of the country, so freeing Wroughton for the next

The RAF hospital showing the huts built at the rear of the main building complex, to accommodate the D-Day casualties. Towards the top left corner can be seen the Canberra gate guardian. Photo: Wroughton History Group

intake. In the six months following D-Day four thousand eight hundred and eleven casualties passed through the hospital.

During the years following the war the hospital treated both military personnel and from 1958, civilian NHS patients. The facility considerably assisted the Local Health Authority in reducing waiting times for certain operations. It was a general hospital serving RAF stations in a wide catchment area of central, southern and western England and South Wales. It provided inpatient and outpatient facilities in most of the major specialities. It also acted as the Reception hospital for U.K. bound aeromedical flights which came into Brize Norton and provided trained aeromedical teams for escort missions to any part of the world.

Following a visit to RAF Hospital Wroughton by Princess Alexandra on 4th July 1967, the Queen conferred the prefix "Princess Alexandra's" on the hospital on 4th October 1967. As with RAF stations, the hospital had a gate guardian, this was an English Electric Canberra B2 WJ676.

On 9th September 1983 No.4626 (County of Wiltshire) Royal Auxilary Air Force Aeromedical Evacuation Squadron formed at the hospital before moving to Hullavington in 1986.

When the hostages from Beirut began to be released in August 1991, it was Wg Cdr Gordon Turnbull, a psychiatrist based at the Princess

Alexandra Hospital, who with his team de-briefed the three men, John McCarthy, Terry Waite and former fighter pilot Jackie Mann. During the weeks that followed the medical staff provided the counselling necessary to ease them slowly back into freedom.

Since the 31st March 1996 the buildings of the Princess Alexandra's RAF Hospital have stood empty, victims of a Government defence cut. The valuable equipment and contents have gradually been disposed of from one of the airfield hangars where storage was concentrated after the hospital closure. Not only did the Air Force lose a hospital but so did the local community in and around Swindon.

154th American General Hospital, Burderop

The RAF hospital was not the only military hospital in Wroughton. The 154th American Hospital had been built at Burderop by 1942 to receive and treat wounded military personnel from the European Theatre of Operations. This closed at the end of 1945. The 7505th USAF Hospital, Burderop later operated on the same site from 1951- 29th June 1965. The Americans returned on this occasion owing to the escalation of the 'Cold War' between Russia and the West.

YATESBURY AERODROME

The two original aerodromes were established south west of the village of Yatesbury and on the north side of the A4 Bath to London road. The landing areas were laid out on the east and west sides of the C139 road leading from the A4 to the village.

Aerodrome Development

The two aerodromes were built in 1916, each to accommodate two Training Reserve Squadrons of the Royal Flying Corps. Initially, Yatesbury came under the command of Southern Training Brigade, No.21 (Training) Wing and then South Western Area, No.28 (Training) Wing which formed there on 15th May 1917. The HQ of 28th Wing had 47 staff and its offices were on Camp No.1 West. Their role was to train Corps Reconnaissance pilots for Army co-operation with the British Expeditionary Force in France.

Two Training Depot Stations (TDS) were formed in July 1918 absorbing the various training reserve units. They had an establishment of 1,184 personnel of which 240 were officers under instruction.

The Western aerodrome No.1 was formed on part of Cherhill Field which was land that had been requisitioned (post World War 2, it was renamed RAF Cherhill). It comprised an area of 260 acres of which approximately 30 acres were occupied by the station buildings. These were erected at the north end of the grass landing area in two groups, No.1 Camp East and No.1 Camp West. The former initially had 3 RFC 1917 pattern 17 bay timber hangars with curved Belfast Trussed roofs, comprising 1 ARS 170' x 80' and 2 GS Sheds 170' x 80'. In addition there were 3 Bessoneau hangars, 1 MT Shed, stores, workshops, offices, and the Guard Room at the main entrance by the public road. A YMCA timber building was located on the eastern aerodrome side of the public road. The larger West camp included 2 GS Sheds, 1 Bessoneau hangar, 1 MT Shed, Reception Centre, Officers' Mess with tennis court, Sergeants' Mess, Men's Dining Hall, Male and Female Quarters, Regimental Institute, Medical Reception Station, stores,

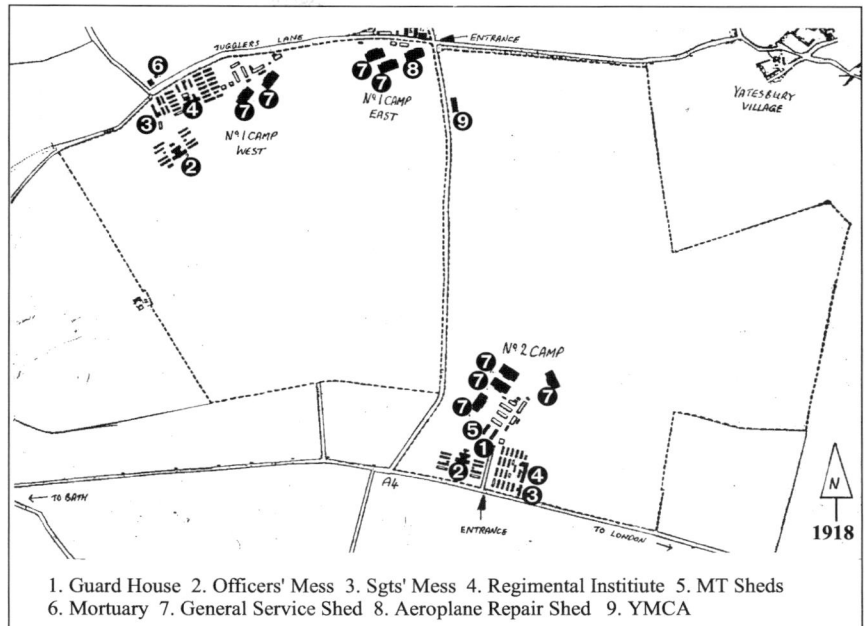

1. Guard House 2. Officers' Mess 3. Sgts' Mess 4. Regimental Institiute 5. MT Sheds
6. Mortuary 7. General Service Shed 8. Aeroplane Repair Shed 9. YMCA

1. Entrance to No.1 Camp

workshops, offices and mortuary. Yatesbury also had the provision of a camera obscura. Surprisingly in 1917 Tomkins & Barrett of Swindon, published a series of captioned postcards showing the buildings.

3. Interior of No.28 Sqn hut, No.1 Camp

2. No.59 TS Sqn huts No.1 Camp

4. Officers' Mess & Medical Reception Station No.1 Camp

5. YMCA hut

6. Entrance to No.2 Camp

7. An RE8 outside a GS Shed No.2 Camp

8. 3 GS Sheds and a number of un-identified aircraft No.2 Camp
Photos: Donald Lovelock Coll.

The Eastern aerodrome No.2 was formed on the requisitioned land of Yatesbury Field. It comprised an area of 278 acres of which approximately 30 acres were occupied by the station buildings. These were erected to the south side of the grass landing area and close to the Bath to London main road. It was known as No.2 Camp and included 4 GS Sheds, 3 Bessoneau hangars, 2 MT Sheds, Officers' Mess, Sergeants' Mess, Men's Dining Hall, Male and Female Quarters, Regimental Institute, stores, workshops, offices and Guard Room part way up the main entrance track from the Bath to London road.

The grass landing areas of both aerodromes were marked by a large grid which was a training aid for the reconnaissance pilots. The western

aerodrome had a rectangular grid of 30 boxes marked in chalk and the eastern one a rectangular grid of 28 boxes. In addition each box was marked with a bulls-eye landing circle.

On the north end of the Eastern aerodrome landing ground, a German PoW camp was built close to the road leading to Yatesbury Village.

World War 1 Years

Yatesbury opened in November 1916 with No.55 Reserve Sqn arriving on 22nd November from Filton. The squadron was equipped with the Avro 504A and the Bristol Scout D. No.59 Reserve Sqn was the next to move in on 30th April 1917 from Gosport, equipped with the DH1, DH6 and FE2b. No.62 Reserve Sqn also from Gosport arrived on 10th May equipped with the Camel. On the same day No.66 Reserve Sqn arrived from Wye with the DH6, FE2b (B1862) and the Sopwith Pup. No.66 Sqn had a number of Russian Army cadet pilots under training during these early days.

Five days later these squadrons came under the command of No.28 Wing which formed at Yatesbury under the command of Lt Col R.A. Cooper. He was succeeded the following year by Lt Col R.P. Mills MC. The squadrons were renamed as Training Squadrons from 1st June 1917.

Lt Jones (centre) and fellow pilots outside the No.1 Camp Officers' Mess.
Photo: Don Neate Coll.

Lts Ashbrook and Chalmers either side of RFC officer Burnet whose rank is not known. Photo: Don Neate Coll.

No.32 TS Australian Flying Corps formed at Yatesbury in June 1917 and was re-designated No.7 (T) Sqn AFC on 14th January 1918 under the command of Maj R.C. Phillips AFC. The squadron in No.28 Wing was equipped with the RE8, Avro 504A and DH6. On 23rd February 1918 the Sqn moved to Leighterton. Shortly after arriving at Yatesbury, Australian Flt Lt Alfred S. Hunt RFC was killed on 20th August 1917 and buried in Yatesbury All Saints churchyard.

No.62 TS moved to Dover on Friday 1st June 1917, and was replaced by No.13 TS from Dover, equipped with the BE2, DH6 and 504A. 2nd Lt Nathaniel F. Clarke RFC took off from Dover on this day in BE2e A1362 accompanied by Air Mech 1st Class W.Fozard RFC. The pilot became lost near Farnborough so landed at Wokingham to find out where he was. Sadly, the aircraft stalled on take off and crashed. AM Fozard was killed out right and Lt Clarke died shortly afterwards.

No.55 TS moved to Gosport on 23rd July 1917. 'C' Flt. of No.59 TS, formed on 1st October 1917 and moved to Red House Farm (Boscombe Down) where No.6 TDS was forming. The Sqn moved to Beaulieu on 30th October 1917. On the day No.55 TS moved out, No.28 Sqn moved in from Gosport (Fort Grange). It was equipped with the Sopwith Pup, DH5, Avro 504 and the Bristol Scout. On Yatesbury's Western Aerodrome and under the command of Maj H.F. Glanville, it re-equipped and worked-up with the

Sopwith Camel before leaving for St. Omer on 8th October 1917. 'B' Flt of No.28 Sqn formed on 22nd August and moved to Lopcombe Corner where No.3 TDS was in the process of forming.

No.99 Sqn formed at Yatesbury on 15th August 1917 from the nucleus of No.13 TS. It was equipped with the BE2 and moved to Ford Farm (Old Sarum) on 30th August. Thirty years later it was to re-form at Lyneham as a transport squadron. The CO of No.13 TS received a letter from the bailiff of

(E2221). The two TDSs and No.28 Wing disbanded on 15th May 1919 to form No.1 Wing. Renamed No.1 (Yatesbury) Wing it disbanded on 25th October 1919.

One of the early pilots who trained to fly at Yatesbury was Billy Cotton who later became famous as a bandleader and racing driver. Sir Francis Chichester the yachtsman was another trainee pilot and the author Arthur C. Clarke Kt. CBE also served here.

Whilst the officers at Yatesbury had their tennis court for recreation the men had to organise their own sport. One of the summer activities of August 1917 was a sports meeting where one of the events was a greasy pole pillow fighting competition. The winner is not known but first prize was 10/- and second prize 5/-.

Aircraft training accidents were fairly commonplace during this period at Yatesbury. A FE2b A873 crashed on the airfield during the latter half of 1917 and despite fire fighting attempts by the mechanics, was completely burnt out. A fully laden FE2b carrying 33 gallons of petrol would soon be destroyed once fire had taken hold. The fate of the crew of this crash is unknown. Sometime in 1918 an RE8 landed on top of an Avro 504, which was completely wrecked. The pilot of the RE8 survived to become ACM Sir John Whitworth Jones. A flight of four aircraft, led by the Sqn Cdr of the No.36 TDS, took-off from Yatesbury at 1435 hrs on Saturday 27th July 1918. Sometime between 1500 and 1600 hrs they were flying over Devizes in an easterly direction before making a turn towards Marlborough. The Flt was at 2500' flying in diamond formation when, in the course of executing the turn, two of the aircraft collided and with their wings locked together dived into the ground. The accident site was a wet and marshy field beside a pond in Stert. Two police officers attending at a hayrick fire which had broken out during the morning at Crookwood Farm, raced across the fields to reach the crash site. They

Pilot and ground crew of a RE8 at Yatesbury in 1917. Photo: Don Neate Coll.

Manor Farm, Codford St. Peter during August claiming £15 for damage by an aeroplane to 32 acres of barley.

As No.28 Sqn moved out on 8th October 1917, No.17 TS moved in from Port Meadow equipped with the RE8, BE2d and DH6. As with No.66 TS, it also had a number of Russian soldiers attached. These, however, were ground crew members under training. No.16 TS arrived from Beaulieu on 30th October 1917 equipped with the RE8, BE2d and DH6, the serial number of one being (A9580).

No.28 Wing came within No.7 Group from 1st April 1918, when the RAF was formed.

On 15th July 1918 No.36 and No.37 Training Depot Stations formed at Yatesbury in No.28 Wing and absorbed Nos 13, 66, 16 and 17 TSs respectively. No.36 TDS used Aerodrome No.2 (Eastern) and was equipped with the RE8 and Avro 504K. No.37 TDS used Aerodrome No.1 (Western) and was equipped with the RE8, Avro 504K, BE2a and F2b, one being serial number

American personnel were based at Yatesbury during the war just as they were at other training aerodromes like Boscombe Down. As was expected of the Americans, their welfare was well catered for but, unlike Boscombe Down, there does not appear to have been a baseball pitch at Yatesbury.

Four un-named American Lts pose in the sunshine outside the Officers' Mess on No.1 Camp.
Photo: Don Neate Coll.

freed the bodies of 2nd Lt Reuben J. Davidson and 2nd Lt R.E. Gorman, who had been killed on impact. Death was confirmed by Dr. Mare from the nearby Devizes Asylum and by Dr. Carter a locum-tenens, both of whom attended the scene. The two RAF pilots are buried at Yatesbury All Saints Church. Coincidentally a Blenheim IV of No.13 OTU Bicester crashed in Stert at almost the same place in 1942, killing the three-man crew.

One of the many trainee pilots at Yatesbury with No.37 TDS was Lt Henry Goodier from 19th October 1918 to 3rd April 1919. He had served as a 2nd Lt with the 5th Battalion Liverpool Regiment and was seconded for service with the RAF from 17th October 1918. He must have taken to flying quite easily, as by 6th November 1918 he was entitled to wear his 'Wings'.

Airco DH9A E8409 at Yatesbury in 1918. This aircraft was called _Liberty_ and was built by the Aircraft Manufacturing Co. Ltd. Photo: Gordon Goodier

An FE2 on the Western Aerodrome at Yatesbury in 1918. This aircraft was called _The Birdcage_. Photo: Gordon Goodier

A tied down HP 0/400 bomber on the Western Aerodrome at Yatesbury in 1918. The MT shed, which still exists, is seen in the background to the left. Photo: Gordon Goodier

Captain Vivsen's Bleriot Type XI following his crash at Yatesbury. Photo: Don Neate Coll.

Lt Henry Goodier at Yatesbury on 22nd January 1919 in a dual Bristol Fighter 'H' with a 200 hp Sunbeam Arab I engine. Photo: Gordon Goodier

Inter War Years

A number of operational squadrons returned from the war to Yatesbury as cadres.

10th Feb 1919 - No.73 Sqn - from Baizieux disbanded 2nd July 1919

12th Feb 1919 - No.65 Sqn - from Bisseghem disbanded 25th October 1919

17th Feb 1919 - No.54 Sqn - from Merchin disbanded 25th October 1919

10th Mar 1919 - No.28 Sqn - from Sarcedo to Leighterton 29th March 1919

10th Mar 1919 No.66 Sqn - from San Pietro-in-Gu to Leighterton 29th March 1919

All five squadrons had been equipped with the Sopwith Camel.

Lt Parkhouse 'Parkus' RN who trained as a pilot at Yatesbury in 1918/19. In the 1930s he became manager of Exeter Airport. Photo: Gordon Goodier.

Neatly decorated RE8 262E of No. 37TDS seen in 1918 minus its gun-ring. This particular aircraft was named _The Coffin_ and was built by the Siddeley-Deasy Motor Car Co. Ltd. Photo: Gordon Goodier

Closure

When RAF Yatesbury closed at the end of 1919, no longer required for military use, the land was returned to the original owners. The Co-operative Wholesale Society then purchased much of the site. The hangars were sold and removed from the Eastern Aerodrome with many of the other buildings being used as a Milk Depot. From the Western Aerodrome one of the hangars was bought by Harris of Calne, the local bacon factory. It was re-assembled near Calne railway station during 1921 and used for food processing. One other hangar was lost to fire not long afterwards. The YMCA building became Cherhill's village hall.

A game of billiards in progress before the initial closure of Yatesbury.
Photo: Don Neate Coll.

Aerodrome Re-development

Western Aerodrome

In August 1935 the Bristol Aeroplane Company was given a contract for a second Reserve Flying Training School to be formed at Yatesbury. They had been operating a civilian school at Filton, Bristol from 1923. Partially funded by the Government, the Bristol Company purchased 290 acres of the original Western Aerodrome and issued a contract to their developers En-tout-cas Ltd to construct in the first phase, a school of flying, the necessary support buildings and to renovate two of the surviving GS Sheds. In building

the new school some of the original 1916 built structures such as the Officers' Mess were demolished.

The new buildings were pleasing to the eye and not out of place in this scenic part of the county, they comprised the Officers' Mess/Offices, Pupil Officers' Accommodation, Instruction Block, power-house and guardroom. Sports facilities were not overlooked with a tennis-court and squash-court provided.

The Bristol Flying School new buildings shortly after occupancy. The Officers' Mess and the Instruction Block with two 1916 GS Sheds to the rear and the tennis court at the front. On the left elevation is the Accommodation Block with squash court behind and a power-house and garage beside the roadway. The semi-detached house is also beside the roadway and close to the GS Sheds. Photo: Yatesbury Association

The second phase of the building works commenced in 1937 with an extension to the Officers' Mess/Offices and to the Instruction Block. Accommodation was built for Airmen and NCOs, who until this time had been billeted at Yatesbury Manor. Garages and a workshop were also erected. With another war imminent, the final building phase commenced in 1938 to provide a gas chamber, rifle range (not for recreation but aerodrome defence training), a second guardroom on the site of the original 1916 structure and some other ancillary buildings. The World War 1 ARS was renovated, and close to it and on the side of the public road, the building of a new north-light steel-framed side-opening hangar was started. The hangar 321' x 121' had 12 west elevation sliding doors each 27' 3". On the rear of the hangar parallel with the public road, single story brick offices 276' x 12' spanned the length of the structure. The building was not completed until after war broke out. The hangar was used to house Dominie aircraft of No.2 E&WS.

Expansion work to up-grade the original Western Aerodrome progressed through the early years of the war with the erection of a Bellman hangar alongside one of the original GS Sheds and the concrete apron in this area was extended. A concrete apron was laid in front of the new side-opening hangar and a concrete perimeter track was laid from the main apron around the west side boundary. Camouflaging was carried out, which included tarmacing the concrete surfaces. Pill-boxes and air-raid shelters were installed. In 1943 the two runways were laid with Sommerfeld tracking: 26/08 NE/SW 946yds x 50yds and 30/12 NW/SE 972 x 50yds. The perimeter track was completed around the field at this time also using Sommerfeld tracking. This linked with a concrete apron and dispersal with 2 single and 2 double Extra Over Blister hangars built at the bottom south east corner of the airfield. On the western boundary the perimeter track connected with another double and a treble Extra Over Blister Hangar.

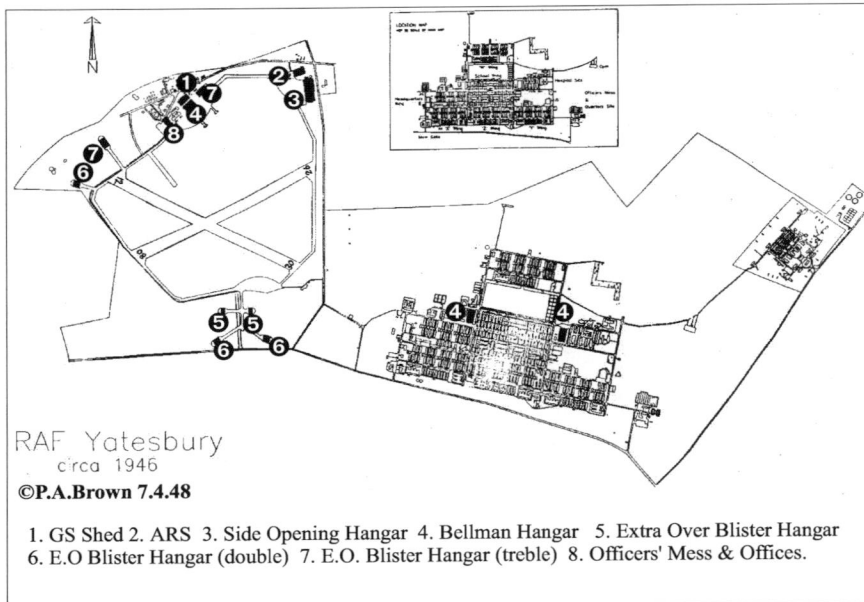

RAF Yatesbury
circa 1946
©P.A.Brown 7.4.48

1. GS Shed 2. ARS 3. Side Opening Hangar 4. Bellman Hangar 5. Extra Over Blister Hangar
6. E.O Blister Hangar (double) 7. E.O. Blister Hangar (treble) 8. Officers' Mess & Offices.

Eastern Aerodome

Yatesbury was chosen by RAF Training Command as the site for a large wireless training school which was to be built on the former 1916 Eastern Aerodrome. Thousands of wireless operators, both RAF and WAAF, did their trade training in this vast camp. The land was repurchased by the Air Ministry early in 1938 and building work began. Much of the materials and sectional timber buildings were brought to nearby Calne by freight train. The main buildings comprised a canvas Bessoneau hangar used as a 500/600 seat station theatre and 2 Bellman hangars, Station HQ and offices, Institute, Officers' Mess and quarters, hospital with 5 wards, a well equipped operating theatre and a mortuary. A prefabricated concrete gymnasium, workshops, cinema, garages, lecture and laboratory huts, male, female, civilian and students quarters, dining rooms, gas centre and guardroom at the camp main entrance on the Bath to London road. The vast majority of the buildings on the camp were of wooden construction. Not all of the buildings formed part of the initial building project. The gymnasium, for example, was put up around 1942. All NCOs and lower ranks were required to attend P.T. there once a week at 0600 hrs unless they were over the age of 35 and were then exempt. Yatesbury had a very large parade-ground but the oblong square was not used to any great extent for that purpose during the war years, and was, in fact, more of a vehicle park or a place where Signallers waved flags at each other. After the war, when No.1 Recruits Centre was formed, the parade ground was used for square-bashing as were the small squares associated with each set of huts allocated to training flights.

Colin Latham, an instructor with No.9 Radio School, recalls the occasion when the parade-ground was in use for a very large wartime parade when, much to the consternation and amazement of all present, a light American aircraft, possibly a L-4 or L-5, buzzed the parade while it was in progress. It came in over the tennis courts at the east-end and flew a foot or two above the ground along most of the length of the square before pulling up sharply and clearing the huts at the western end.

The water tower for the camp stood on the top of Cherhill Down, not far from the White Horse. During the war the tower was guarded by camp personnel, who did two hours on duty and four off. The chalk White Horse was covered over with turf for the duration of the war.

Inter War Years (continued)

Western Aerodrome

The civilian operated Bristol School of Flying opened on the Western aerodrome at Yatesbury on 6th January 1936 even though construction had not been completed. In addition the severe weather conditions prevented flying so students commenced their training at Filton. Conditions later improved and on 2nd February staff and students transferred from Bristol. It was still necessary though for students to be billeted out until April when the station accommodation was finished. The numbers of instructional staff varied between 10 and 12 and Mr T.W Campbell was Chief Instructor. Mr W.L. Palmer superseded him sometime between July and September 1937. Tiger Moths were the aircraft used for basic training.

A trainee pilot who would later be awarded the Victoria Cross, arrived to

Trainee pilots and the Tiger Moths of the Bristol School of Flying at Yatesbury.
Photo: Yatesbury Association

join Flying Training Course No.6 on 16th November 1936. This was 18 year old Guy Penrose Gibson who was to become immortal in the annals of the RAF. He did not show any exceptional abilities when under training at Yatesbury and, like so many others, passed out with a flying rating of 'average'. The weather at the end of the year was as bad as it had been at the beginning with the result that this particular course had to be extended until the end of January 1937. Gibson then moved down the road to No.6 FTS Netheravon where he continued his training until September 1937.

Hugh George joined the RAF on a Short Service Commission in 1937 and, with the rank of Acting Pilot Officer, commenced his pilot training course with the Bristol Flying School on 13th July 1937. There were 29 students on the course, one of whom was David Tomlinson who was later to become a well known actor. The course instructor was Mr E.G. Stevenson. Hugh went solo on 24th July after 8 hours dual. Students kept their own aircraft during initial training; Hugh was allocated Tiger Moth G-AESN. All cross-country flights were localised and were generally kept to Upavon, Whitchurch (Bristol) and the recently opened Hullavington. Course No.10 was completed on 3rd September 1937 with all but 3 passing out. Hugh went on to fly Battles and Blenheims and was in France from 2nd September 1939 with No.XV Sqn on Battles.

Townsend SLG, for forced landing practice.

On 26th September 1938 No.2 Civil Air Navigation School (CANS) was formed out of No.10 E&RFTS at Yatesbury in No.50 Group. Operated by the Bristol Aeroplane Company the school was tasked with training RAF Observers to the same standard of navigation as pilots. Ansons were used for training. No.2 CANS was redesignated No.2 Air Observer & Navigation School on 1st November 1939, carrying out basically the same functions using 12 Ansons. The School was disbanded on 14th December 1940.

Eastern Aerodrome

The first occupant of the camp on the re-developed Eastern aerodrome was No.2 Electrical & Wireless School forming on 1st December 1938 under the command of Gp Capt H.I. Hanmer DFC with Wg Cdr C. S. Richardson MBE as Chief instructor. The school formed to train airmen enlisting as WOPs in aspects of the T1085 transmitters and R1082 receivers.

The civilians were told to find accommodation in Swindon and the police guarding the site had to cater for themselves as best they could. During the first three months of the year the School was formed into 3 Wings, and with further expansion No. 4 Wing formed on 19th August 1939. On 1st February 1939 3 officers and 1087 airmen arrived by rail from Cranwell and formed No.1 Wing. 3 officers and 950 airmen formed No.2 Wing. It was twenty days later when 2 officers and 140 men arrived to form No.3 Wing. Each Wing had a Wg Cdr as CO.

World War 2 Years

Western Aerodrome

When war was declared in September 1939, No.10 E&RFTS was redesignated as No.10 EFTS, which formed in No.50 Group with its HQ in Bristol. Initially it continued with civilian instructors until 1942 when RAF personnel replaced them. The Audax and Hart variants were withdrawn leaving an allocation of 18 Tiger Moths which were soon supplemented by 36 received from disbanded EFTSs and from MUs such as Hullavington, which provided 10.

A Tiger Moth of No. 10 EFTS piloted by Sgt Denton crashed near Yatesbury in January 1940.
Photo: F. Twitchett Cty. Andy Thomas

Tiger Moth No.29 of the Bristol School of Flying preparing to exit one of Yatesbury's GS Sheds.
Photo: Yatesbury Association

On 1st February 1938 the Bristol School was re-designated No.10 E&RFTS under the control of No.26 (Training) Group. Tiger Moths were used for primary training and the Audax and Hart variant for the advanced aspect of the course. The Audax and Hart aircraft were used when night flying was introduced on No.17 Course in May 1939. Strong winds on 1st February damaged 7 of the aircraft and these had to be returned to Filton for repair.

The first Royal Navy flying training course commenced on 6th October 1938 with 41 students from HMS Pembroke and HMS Chatham. During its time at Yatesbury the School Tiger Moths used

These were the standard sets used in the early part of the war. The school absorbed No.1 (Electrical & Wireless) School, Cranwell. The initial opening was something of a disaster owing to the failure of the electrical supply during a spell of severe frost. The heating system froze, pipes burst and considerable damage resulted. The Ration Stores and cookhouse required fly-proofing and the ambulance and fire tender garages had to be widened as they were too narrow for the vehicles. The first batch of 300 students was sent home on extended Christmas leave, to return on 17th January 1939.

Wartime flying accidents at Yatesbury were soon being recorded when, on 3rd March 1940, Sgt Robert H.I. Scott-Kerr RAFVR (pilot) became the first pupil of No.10 EFTS to lose his life when Tiger Moth G-AESO dived into the ground 2 miles northeast of Avebury. On 30th May Sgt Harold R. Birch RAFVR, when carrying out gun post duties, was killed by the wheel of a Tiger Moth taking-off and the same day Moth G-AESM flew into the ground. Both of these casualties were buried at Yatesbury (All Saints) Church.

DH82A Tiger Moth G-ADNX 28 of No.10 EFTS at Yatesbury in January 1940. This aircraft was first registered on 4th October 1935 and was sold to India in February 1941 as VT-ANW.
Photo: Andy Thomas

From spring 1940 Advanced Elementary Flying Training and Pre-Fighter Courses were being conducted. The latter included aerobatics in the syllabus for the prospective fighter pilots. On 29th July 1940 at 0300 hrs the aerodrome was bombed for the first time when 13 H.E. bombs landed close to the HQ of No.10 EFTS. There were no injuries and no serious damage was done. On 7th September 1940 the School moved to the aerodrome at Weston-Super-Mare where the Bristol Aeroplane Company had a factory.

The Bristol Wireless Flt operated by the Bristol Aeroplane Company, was formed on 14th May 1940 to provide aircraft to give flying experience to WOPs under training with No.2 Signals School, later No.2 Radio School. Due to aircraft shortages, from October 1940 the very unpopular Blackburn Botha I, twin-engined reconnaissance bomber was on charge and was endured for almost a year. Botha L6175, 6195, 6270, 6279 & 6281 were delivered prior to March 1941 and L6398, 6456, 6457, 6458, 6467, 6469, 6477, 6478 & 6480 were delivered prior to June 1941. The full establishment of Proctors and Dominies was not achieved until 1942. The Dominies used as flying classrooms usually carried the pilot, instructor and 4-6 students. Cpl Don Clarke who served as a wireless instructor on Dominies at Yatesbury during 1941, reports that it was usual to fly twice in a day taking the students to practice air to ground Morse transmitting. For most of them who were destined to fly as WOP/AGs in Bomber Command, it was their first experience of flying and this frequently showed. Pilots were not required to fly

a set course and could in general please themselves where they went, providing they stayed aloft for around two hours. As Cpl Clarke's home was in the Midlands, some flights took in its location. Most flights went out and returned over the Lansdowne Monument on Cherhill Down, which in time became a familiar landmark and a welcome sight. The adjacent white horse cut into the chalk hill and covered over during the war, was not uncovered again until afterwards. One morning, in the summer of 1949, it was found to resemble a zebra, painted with red stripes. Almost certainly personnel from the camp carried out the deed but it is thought that they were never identified despite concerted enquiries. On another occasion an appendage was added identifying it as a stallion. This was thought to have been carried out by Compton Bassett personnel.

On 16th May 1942, Sgt Edward R. Crosier RAAF was killed when the Proctor he was flying crashed on landing at Yatesbury. He is buried at Yatesbury All Saints churchyard.

A Yatesbury Proctor crashed near Oare on Saturday 10th April 1943 killing the pilot Sgt Robert J. Bennett RAFVR and his pupil LAC Harold Maycock RAFVR. On 31st October 1944 Proctor T LZ629 collided with Tiger Moth N9406 of No.29 EFTS Clyffe Pypard and crashed half a mile north of the Bell Inn at Lydeway near Devizes. Both crews were killed. There was an occasion during the war (date unknown) when a Whitley bomber made an emergency landing on the airfield at Yatesbury but had to be stripped down for removal by road

because of insufficient runway length to allow it to take-off. It is also said that a Manchester landed on the sports field before clearing the road and coming to rest on the airfield.

Devizes in Wiltshire had a German PoW camp located in the town during World War 2. It housed some ruthless Nazi's and led by a hard core of SS troops, a mass breakout was planned towards the end of 1944. Their plan however was thwarted and the SS were moved to a harsh PoW camp at Comrie in Scotland. There they extracted revenge on one of their own whom they had decided had leaked details of the planned breakout to the Allied camp authorities. The prisoner, who was not a Nazi, was severely beaten and hung. Five of the Nazi's involved were convicted of murder and hung at Pentonville Prison in October 1945.

A break-out from the Devizes PoW camp on a small scale did occur, involving German prisoners, who then made their way to Yatesbury in an effort to escape by aircraft. A number of versions of this incident have been put forward but no one has of yet managed to find very much in the way of written evidence from RAF records. Roderick De Normann in his 1996 publication *For Fuhrer and Fatherland* writes of a prison report recording a breakout by 4 Germans on 18th November 1944. They reached an aerodrome on 19th/20th about 8 miles from the camp (Yatesbury). They hid in bushes whilst observing operations, and came to the conclusion it was used only by training aircraft. On the night of the 21st they got into two aircraft but could not start the engines. Cold and wet they gave themselves up the next morning (22nd), in a nearby village.

Flt Sgt Alf Daltry, a young pilot with the Radio School from June 1944 to January 1945, recalls this incident when at breakfast one morning he was told flying was cancelled for the day. This was because during the night escaped PoW from Devizes had tried to steal two Percival Proctors, although they failed to get them started. The Yatesbury pilots welcomed the excitement as a relief from the monotonous daily grind of piloting planes while the cadets carried out wireless operating, air-to-ground exercises. Whilst an influx of military security personnel searched around for the PoW, and for any evidence of sabotage, the pilots retired to the mess to discuss the incident between hands of Poker or Bridge the normal pastime when unable to fly. They thought themselves that the escapees would have been pilots and that their failure to start the planes' engines was understandable because engine starting was a disciplined, but simple, procedure carried out by the pilot and ground staff, and needed a mobile heavy-duty power supply. They disagreed however, as to whether the Germans were capable of comprehending the planes' controls in the dark, and taking off into the night. They were told the next day that three Germans had given themselves up in the nearby village of Cherhill and that no sabotage had been discovered. Alf never heard any more of the incident.

Alice Grant a WAAF teleprinter operator at Yatesbury heard at the time of the break-out of 4 PoW who she says were captured by Sqn Ldr 'Spud' Murphy on his way to camp at 0730 hrs. This took place by the Black Horse public house at Cherhill. Sqn Ldr William H.G. Murphy RAF was to die from exposure on 4th March 1947 after crashing his car at Beckhampton, whilst on his way to the camp. He was buried at St. James The Great Church, Cherill.

Two other PoW left the camp at Devizes on the night of 19th November 1944 and made their way north. They wanted to go to America and hoped to stow away on a ship or an aircraft. On the night of the 20th November, having decided the aircraft which they had been observing during the day at Yatesbury were unsuited to reaching America, they returned to Devizes disillusioned and hungry and were captured trying to re-enter the camp.

ACW Joan Elizabeth Trodd was doing her training with No.3 Radio School at Compton Bassett in 1944. The following is her story. "Whiling away our last few days at Compton Bassett preparatory to taking up our duties as WOPs with Bomber Command, we all felt a bit aimless. One afternoon (I believe 21st November 1944) my colleague Anna and I walked along the country lane to nearby Calne, hoping to enjoy some toast and jam at a WVS or other service canteen. Later in the afternoon we were about midway back

to camp when we were startled by the emergence from a field entrance of three men in RAF uniform. We knew that RAF Yatesbury, where aircrews were under training, was not far away. The first thing we noticed about them was that they were all deeply suntanned, and that was unusual.

In wartime being 'chatted up' by servicemen though, was an unremarkable occurrence which happened all the time. One of the airmen in particular talked easily enough, and told us they had just arrived and didn't know much about the area. The other two didn't say

Tiger Moth EM754 having landed on the hangar roof during take-off.
Photo: Yatesbury Association

much at all but they smiled and were friendly enough but then something was said by one of them that did not seem right. He said "And where is your air station?" Now service personnel wouldn't have spoken that way. It would have been "Where are you stationed?" There was also no mention of where they were stationed. We both took in their unremarkable RAF uniforms. They bore no badges of any sort, not trade, rank or shoulder flashes as worn by those from the Dominions, and they had no recognisable accents.

Warning bells were now ringing in my head as they were with Anna. We were very conscious of security 'Careless talk costs lives' etc. We were now very nervous and wanted to get away but we waffled on about going to a farm to get eggs, to take home and Anna advised them to go into Calne for toast and jam. "Ah! Yes, toast and jam" one of them said, amused "We'll go there". With that we made our get away.

We raced back to camp and arriving at the Guardhouse breathless and excited, explaining to the duty staff about our strange encounter. RAF Security was very attentive and within seconds were chasing off in their utility vehicles back down the lane in the Calne direction. We were not questioned further and appeared to be of little interest from that moment on, which was very demoralising. We kept quiet about our experience feeling sure all would be revealed to us in time and probably our initiative would be mentioned or acknowledged sometime in the future. As the days passed we still heard nothing, so we called at the Guardhouse and asked about it. Those on duty denied knowing anything about escaped PoW and advised us to "see the 'Sarge' when he comes back". No reference was made to the Day Book and it was clear we were being fobbed off.

After my posting to a bomber station, I wrote to Compton Bassett with a stamped addressed envelope asking for information regarding our liaison that afternoon but I never did hear back."

It is strange that there is no mention in the Yatesbury Station Log of the attempt by the Germans to steal the aircraft. Nor is there any mention in the Compton Bassett Radio School Log. Even the Devizes Police Station Radio Log makes no reference to escaping PoW. At the time of the breakouts it is reasonable to assume that military installations in the county were made aware of any incidents. The records of the USAAF 437th Troop Carrier Group based at Ramsbury near Marlborough indicate extra security being arranged on 18th/19th November because of a reported breakout of Germans from the Devizes Camp. Again on Christmas Eve security was increased at Ramsbury on receipt of a report that a possible mass breakout was to be attempted.

Another unusual incident occurred around the same time in 1944 when, Tiger Moth EM754, taking-off at the side of another flown by Flt Sgt Alf Daltrey, embedding itself into the roof of one of the hangars. The aircraft were taking off during severe crosswinds. The pilot didn't allow for this and lost control before hitting the roof.

With the war drawing to a close the Bristol Wireless Flt was disbanded in July 1945 and No.2 EFTS in No.50 Group moved in from Worcester on 9th July equipped with Tiger Moths.

Eastern Aerodrome

With the declaration of war No.2 E&WS came under No.21 (Training) Group with HQ at Cranwell. At the time 3,564 personnel were under instruction at Yatesbury of which 2934 passed out by the end of the year. The instructors had the use of Magister N3892. Six DH89A Dominies were collected during October 1939 to be used as flying classrooms and Dominie R5921 was flown in from Hatfield by Plt Off Bentley. Cyril Hine was on the December 1939 intake of trainee WOPs arriving at Yatesbury from Cardington, where he did his square-bashing. He passed out in June 1940 and was posted to Upavon as an AC1 before returning to Yatesbury in September 1941 with the job of maintaining and servicing the radios on the Dominies and Proctors. Promoted to Corporal in 1942, he was de-mobbed in 1946. During the war Cyril lived at Moreton-in-Marsh. Whilst on leave at home on one occasion, he recalls that a bomb was dropped nearby and he felt quite relieved to return to Yatesbury where he felt much safer.

The eventual allocation of Dominies was 30 and Proctors 60. Those known: - Dominies R5921 to R5934, R9545 to R9548 and Proctor P6273.

In May 1940 No.2 E&WS operated in

No.26 (Signals) Group in Technical Training Command which had formed at Cranwell on 12th February 1940 under the control of No.21 (T) Group, initially to administer Nos.1-5 E&WS and the Special Wireless School. From 26th August 1940 No.2 Signals School formed from No.2 E&WS. No.2 Signals School syllabus included all the technicalities of radio, Morse code sending and receiving at 18 words per minute, aircraft recognition, beam approach, navigation, armament and meteorology. This was all crammed into six months but would have been considerably longer in peacetime. For personnel passing the end of course exam and then accepted for aircrew training, a further three weeks training would be undertaken on a air-gunner's course at somewhere like Jurby on the Isle of Man.

Harold Hames an Electrician, and Cpl Cyril Hine beside a Proctor at Yatesbury in 1944. Photo: Cyril Hine

No.2 Radio School formed at Yatesbury with Wg Cdr R. Thompson as CO and Sqn Ldr E.J. Tippett as Chief Instructor on 18th January 1940. The Special Signals School formed the same day but was absorbed by No.2 RS on 1st March 1941. The first classes at No.2 RS consisted of civilian radio mechanics plus some serving airmen of the same trade, already part trained at Bawdsey. Yatesbury was under the Directorate of Signals until 2nd February 1940 when it was handed over to the Directorate of Training. The training was for Radio Officers, Radio Mechanics ground and air, Radio

Wireless Operator/Mechanic WO Spencer "Black Prince" of the Proctor Workshop Section, with a Proctor at Yatesbury in 1944. Photo: Cyril Hine

Group photograph of No.1 Air Crew Wing in September 1943. The white flashes in the caps of the Cadets indicating they were Aircrew under training. Eric Rock on the far left of the third row trained at Yatesbury first as a WOP/Ground and then as a WOP/Air.

Operators WAAF and Airmen, W.E.Ms, Signal Officers plus a small intake of Radio Mechanic specialists for maintenance of airborne equipment. At this stage timber aerial towers 90' high were built for training on the station.

Training of WAAF operators ceased at Bawdsey on 12th June 1940 and transferred to Yatesbury. What was initially meant to be a lodger unit became permanent at an intake of 108 every 4 weeks. Joan Ellacott was one of the first WAAFs at Yatesbury where she trained as a RDF Operator. On completion of her three-week course she was posted to a radar station at Canewdon in Essex and later went to Cranwell as a WAAF RDF Operator Instructor. She was subsequently selected for a

Commission as a Signals Officer and the eight-month course she attended included flying experience training. This training was undertaken at Yatesbury where she flew as a wireless operator in Dominies and concluded the course by flying solo as the WOP in a Proctor. Joan and three other WAAFs were the first to be given flying training.

Joan Ellacott far right with a colleague and two students by a Dominie at Yatesbury.

No.6 Air Stores Park, arriving back in the UK from France via Plymouth and Falmouth, was at Yatesbury from 18th June 1940 for two days before moving on to Halton, where it disbanded.

Two mobile W/T sections were formed at Yatesbury in October 1940 for the British Expeditionary Force in France.

During the month 88 Czechoslovakian airmen arrived for training on the Station.

Wg Cdr Thompson was replaced as CO of No.2 RS on 13th January 1941 by Wg Cdr Kidd and on 16th April Sqn Ldr George L. Danielson was appointed as Chief Instructor. The first intake of Canadian personnel for training as mechanics arrived on 20th January 1941 and the first intake of New Zealanders arrived on 24th February. Kazik Czajkowski was one of 14 Polish airmen attending a WOP course from April to June 1941. Most of them went on to serve as WOP/AGs or just AGs with Nos.301 and 302 (Polish) Sqns of Bomber Command. Kazik completed more than his one tour of Ops, but only he and two others from the Yatesbury course survived the war.

The majority of personnel posted to Yatesbury travelled there by train, affectionately termed the 'Calne Bunk' or the 'Calne Flyer'. Even in the 1950s the coaches still had wooden seats. There were occasions when, in addition to the passengers, the train carried pigs

The pass used by Geoff Hunt when travelling to Yatesbury or Compton Bassett to issue train tickets. Photo: Donald Lovelock

in trucks at the rear, en route to the Harris Bacon Factory in Calne. On arrival at the railhead in Calne, RAF personnel would be transported to the camp in a Gharry (RAF lorry). This was not the case however on a freezing Christmas Eve in 1940, when Ted Williams, a Technical Instructor, together with other RAF personnel, arriving on a direct 'special' from Blackpool to Calne, were marched the four miles from the railway to the RAF station. The trainees arriving at Yatesbury would be met by the Receiving Officer who categorised them for billetting in one of the Wings.

The rail station became so busy that in 1942 it was necessary to increase the length of the platform and add an extra booking office. These improvements were funded by the Government. Numerous special troop trains were run, many of them being of up to 12 coaches and double headed. These trains were normally operated to Bristol or Paddington. Despite the platform extension, the cattle dock was often used by the troop trains, as the main platform was occupied by the Calne to Chippenham scheduled service. The RAF sent posting lists to Calne Station on Mondays so that tickets could be made up in advance for camp transfers. These normally took place on a Wednesday when trainees left and were replaced by new pupils. In an effort to prevent long queues when personnel left Calne Station with 36 hour weekend passes, two of the booking office staff would travel by railway lorry to the camps at

Selection of railway tickets used by Air Force personnel travelling to Calne Railway Station. Photo: Donald Lovelock

Yatesbury and Compton Bassett on Thursday evenings to dispense tickets. Geoff Hunt carried out this service between 1949 - 61 and recalls the ticket issues being made from the Guardroom. During that period around 50 tickets were issued at each camp but some RAF personnel were using Card's coaches, which operated from the two RAF establishments to London. Douglas Lovelock, the porter in-charge of Black Dog Halt, one of the stations on the Calne branch line, was often employed on overtime of a Sunday night travelling on the trains between Chippenham and Calne to assist the ticket collector with the tickets of the airmen returning to camp. The Bristol Omnibus Company ran services from Calne Station to Compton Bassett and Yatesbury on Sunday nights and Geoff Hunt indicates that three buses would be parked in Station Road awaiting the trains arriving from Chippenham. As late as 1963 Calne Station dealt with 6,132 RAF travel warrants during the year. The last RAF troop train of 8 coaches left Calne Station at 1815 hrs on 28th May 1963.

Much freight, including coal and supplies for the NAAFI, came in by train and damaged aircraft were taken away for repair. The sight of aircraft in the goods yard was quite common. Most, of course were, from the MU at Lyneham. Thomas's of Calne transported much of the freight to the camps from the railway station.

Horrendous weather interrupted training during the first two months of 1940 and again the camp services froze. Frozen rain brought down all the telephone/teleprinter lines, roads were impassable and the electricity failed. This was a constant problem and, as a contrast, during the summer dust storms swirled around the huts in the seemingly interminable wind of the Downs. During some of the very cold spells even the cooking facilities packed up and personnel were then issued with cold pork pies from Harris's of Calne, swilled down with tepid tea from tureens also brought in from off the camp.

In the early days of the war the entertainment facilities on the camp were a little sparse. The cinema and NAAFI provided the main indoor source. Wednesday afternoons, of course was, reserved for sporting activities as is generally the case on military bases. Some took advantage at the weekends to visit London. The lorries travelling along the A4 generally would stop to pick-up service personnel 'thumbing' lifts, dropping them conveniently at Marble Arch. From there they could catch the tube train to Waterloo where accommodation at the Union Jack Club was available for a 1/- (10p) per night. The Windmill Theatre and Mooney's Irish Bar on the Strand were favourite places of entertainment. Personnel would arrive back at Yatesbury in time for parade on Monday morning. Some returned by train from Paddington to Swindon where they were met by Mr Rawlings who ran a taxi service from Avebury village on the northeast side of the camp. His service would have been pre-arranged and his Standard 9 four seater often lurched back to Yatesbury carrying eight airmen, luggage and the driver. As with most RAF camps, there was the inevitable hole in the hedge for use by those late back from leave or who could not remember the password of the day. During the war it was usually the name of a flower.

A troop train leaving Calne in the early 1950s double headed by a 0-6-0 Pannier Tank 9771 and a 2-6-2 Prairie. Photo: Donald Lovelock

Calne Railway Station showing clearly the Government funded platform extension from the water tower to the signal box and the wooden ticket office. The cattle dock is seen on the left, used on occasions by troop trains. Photo: David Hyde

Calne Railway Station with a notice board advising arriving RAF Yatesbury personnel that transport meets all trains between 0600-1800 hrs on Wednesdays. Airmen arriving with heavy baggage at between times should ring the camp for transport but airmen without heavy baggage should travel by bus from The Strand 5 minutes walk from the station.
Photo: © The Lens of Sutton Col.

Lorry drivers were not the only ones prepared to offer lifts. Queen Mary spent some of the war at the Badminton Estate and she also was known to stop her Daimler to give lifts to Yatesbury service personnel. She also handed out special medallions to those receiving lifts. Those who remained on camp on a weekend often walked to the monument at the top of Cherhill Down, stopping off on return for a snack in the café at the bottom of the hill. Close by was a photographic studio in a timber building where those on the camp would have photographs taken of themselves, to send home to relations or to boyfriends and girlfriends. For 2/6d personnel could be photographed in a Spitfire cockpit and wearing a flying helmet. Another popular Sunday afternoon walk was to Calne where the church near Harris's bacon factory would hold a short hymn singing session followed by free refreshments. These consisted of sausage sandwiches from the factory and home made cakes from volunteers. The cinema in Calne always showed a main and 'B' film on Sunday evenings.

Entertainment in the camp did develop. The 'Mikado' was produced in the autumn of 1942 and featured a cast including Wg Cdr W. Kidd and three pre-war professional entertainers. These were Flt Lt John Wright from the 'Sadler's Wells' where he was Stage Manager before the war, Sgt Fred Verity and Cpl Ross Jones a Yorkshire comedian. He later was selected for 'aircrew' but was killed on his first Op. over Germany. The BBC staged a variety broadcast from Yatesbury in April 1943. Colin Latham recalls a chamber music concert attended by all ranks. The players were a couple of mere radar operators of aircraftman rank, who received a standing ovation at the end. Both in civilian life had been a professional pianist and violinist. Talks in the station theatre were given by well known people, such as the Archbishop of Canterbury, Sir Stafford Cripps and Clement Attlee.

At the end of January 1941 there were 3608 pupils under training of which 75 were Polish. Yatesbury had a number of the excitable Polish pilots (WO Radziminski) to fly the training aircraft from which the trainee wireless operators sent and received messages. One of these pilots and a trainee WOP LAC Peter M. Gregory RAFVR were killed when the Proctor in which they

were flying crashed on Friday 28th February 1941. LAC Gregory is buried in Yatesbury All Saints Church. On 21st April 1941, Proctor I P6307 of No.2 Signals School spun into the ground one mile south east of Avebury and on the following day, Dominie I R5923 crashed during take-off.

No.2 Signals School suffered a tragic accident on 27th May 1941 when Dominie R5929 dived into the ground on Easton Hill, Bishops Cannings whilst low flying and killed 7 men on board. Of these, AC2 Frank Billingham RAFVR, AC2 Arthur S. Butcher RAFVR and Cpl Victor C. Chittock RAF are buried at Yatesbury Church.

On 1st May 1941 230 Canadian WOP/AGs, all Sergeants, arrived to receive instruction. One evening

Dominies X7390 205 and X7398 209 of No.2 Radio School, Yatesbury.   Photo: Don Neate Coll.

during their stay, a number of the men caused considerable damage to property in Calne which resulted in confinement to camp for a month. Their additional punishment was to lay-out gardens around each individual barrack hut. The gardens proved popular with the residents who took a pride in their upkeep.

HRH The Duke of Kent visited the school on 6th June 1941, followed 10 days later by Queen Mary who was accompanied by the Yatesbury CO Gp Capt C.W. Attwood. The Queen saw WAAF and Dominion personnel in the Radio Mechanics sub-school under instruction. Officers of the US Navy were now attending short courses on RDF. King George VI was

the third royal visitor in 1941, when he made a station visit to Yatesbury on 23rd October. The year ended with work starting on the erection of a Ground Controlled Interception (GCI) installation.

In February 1942 the staff of the Provost Marshal arrived on the station to carry out an investigation into the disappearance of a secret notebook. The result of the enquiry is not recorded. On 19th March the Radio Mechanics (G) airmen's courses increased from 8 weeks to 14 weeks and the following month the intake for the courses changed from 24 to 48 per fortnight.

No.2 Radio School was re-designated No.2 Radio Direction Finding School on 21st May 1942, reforming as No.9 Radio School on 1st January 1943, having the role of training ground

radar operators. On the same date No.2 Signals School was re-designated as No.2 Radio School. This unit formed to train radio and radar mechanics. It had an establishment of 104 Proctors until July 1945 when it became a ground radio operator's school without aircraft. No.9 Radio School was sited in a separately guarded compound some distance from the main camp to the north-east. Those at the school had to walk some distance along the concrete path from their accommodation on the main camp. Although it was called a 'radio' school this was a deliberate misnomer to aid secrecy. It specialised in radar and later radio-navigational aids. All was so secret that personnel were forbidden to discuss any aspect of their work once leaving the school.

Kathleen Lowe served at Yatesbury during 1942/43. She was posted to the hospital X-Ray Department from Princess Mary RAF Hospital at Halton. For six months she had been there with the Tropical School of Medicine as part of her training as a Radiographer. Yatesbury provided the second half of her training before she became fully qualified. Patients were admitted from a large area of the country suffering from a very varied number of illnesses and accidents. Penicillin was only administered to officers and aircrew, not to ordinary ranks. Kathleen found living conditions at Yatesbury quite luxurious compared with other RAF camps where she had been. Although billeted in wooden huts, these were joined by built in corridors leading from one to the other and to the ablutions. In addition they had central heating and hot water. Each Wing Mess had a monthly dance which meant that there would be one every week on the camp. Invitations were also received to

bully beef, jacket potato and pickles followed by trifle. Tea was usually macaroni cheese and a Lyons 6d square fruit pie. Meals had to be consumed sitting on long wooden benches (no tables) with the food balanced on laps. She remembers an unsavoury situation she found herself in when a fellow WAAF in her Hut 16 asked Kathleen if she would accompany her to the airfield where her Corporal boyfriend was holding a meeting. This she did and on arrival found ten others listening to the Corporal. It soon became evident he was expounding the virtues of Communism. Kate was of the opinion that the meeting contravened the King's Regulations and left. It appears the gatherings were being held weekly but they soon came to the attention of the authorities resulting in arrest of the Corporal by the SPs. He was Court Martialled and discharged from the Air Force, leaving one very distressed WAAF in Hut 16.

A large ambulance section was maintained, serviced and driven by

The wreckage of Tiger Moth N6659 on Cherill Down. Photo: Norman Parker

Halifax RG364 outside one of the Bellman Hangars on the site of the original Eastern Aerodrome. Photo: Norman Parker

Horse and without injury to the crew. No.2 EFTS operated for just over two years, closing on 30th September 1947.

Aircraft used for ground instructional purposes at this time were Lancaster PD428, Halifax RG364, Mosquitos HK241 and HK301.

Norman Parker was a recruit on No.1 Course and recalls his journey to Yatesbury in December 1946 following a period of heavy snow. After leaving the train at Marlborough he managed to hitch a lift to Beckhampton on the A4. From there it was another 2 miles to the camp. Only the telegraph polls gave any indication of the road direction. Fighting his way through the deep snow he eventually arrived at Yatesbury, only to be told that he was the only recruit there, as none of the others had attempted their respective journeys.

On 30th January 1946, No.9 Radio School was absorbed by No.2 Radio School. It covered training in wireless and radio. The Wireless Mechanics course had a duration of 26 weeks and 52 weeks for Wireless Fitters. Individuals were required to take a qualifying course to determine their suitability for the relevant course.

No.2 Radio School became an Advanced Ground Radar School in 1949. At this time Sgt Colin Latham

The hospital staff of RAF Yatesbury in 1943. Photo: Kathleen Ball

attend dances at Prince Maurice Barracks in Devizes where the US 141st General Hospital Unit were based. The Yatesbury camp band was of a good standard and the Entertainment Officer was a peacetime theatre producer so each month there was a new play or opera, with a pantomime at Christmas. Frequent visitors to see the productions were Queen Mary, and Gordon Richards from the stables half a mile up the A4 at Beckhampton.

Kathleen believes Yatesbury was probably unique in holding what was called 'A Field Day' each Wednesday. For this the mess staff had to prepare all the meals in the open air where they were also eaten whatever the weather conditions, and by all ranks. This sometimes involved having to queue in snow, rain and strong winds, draped in a groundsheet or gas-cape for a serving of what for dinner was always soup,

WAAFs at Yatesbury. The vehicles were on the road continually, particularly after the D-Day landings of June 1944. Most journeys were to the south coast port of Southampton from where wounded personnel had to be transported to various hospitals all over the country.

Post War Years

In the early months of 1946 the German PoW were still on the camp awaiting repatriation.

Manningford landing ground near Upavon was transferred to Yatesbury as a satellite in May 1946 and was immediately in use as a RLG by the Tiger Moths of No.2 EFTS. One of the school's Tiger Moths N6659, took off on 11th April 1947 and spun into the hill off a turn, by the Cherill White became a civilian instructor of Foreign Officer Courses employed by the MoD. From 15th September 1958 it operated in No.24 Group, Rudloe Manor, Box. The training of radar operators, fitters and mechanics had come under No.27

No.215 Wing in Technical Training Command formed at Yatesbury in August 1956. The personnel were part of the task force awaiting mobilisation to Egypt for the 'Suez Campaign'. The Wing disbanded on

No.1 Wing, No.1 Recruit Course Dec 1946 to Mar 1947.   Photo: Norman Parker

A billet used by No.1 Recruit Course in 1946/47.   Photo: Norman Parker

Group from 20th July 1953 but the Group disbanded on 1st October 1958.

SAC Rex Wagstaff, serving at Compton Bassett and Yatesbury as a clerk from 1953, indicates that training courses were being held at Yatesbury for RAF recruits and personnel working with Bloodhound missiles. On the recreational side he remembers that some servicemen on the Station were footballers who played to a very good standard and that Bert Head the Swindon Town Football Club manager would ring the Station to ask if he could play them. Rex also recalls the evenings when around 10 buses would leave the camp filled with personnel attending dances in Bath.

15th January 1957. Also for 'Suez' the Casualty Evacuation Flt in No.27 Group was re-formed on 14th August 1956 but disbanded on 23rd December. During the late 1950s anyone passing along the A4 would have seen on the western airfield site (RAF Cherhill from 1st May 1954), half a dozen Lincoln bombers and a Lancaster. These were used for radio training having arrived and later departed by road in the back of Queen Mary trailers.

A gate-guardian, at the main gate to the eastern airfield, was also visible from the A4 and this was the prototype Gloster Meteor F9/40 DG202/G which first flew in May 1943. The aircraft is preserved at RAF Cosford.

Closure

Yatesbury came within the proposed North Wessex Downs Area of Outstanding Natural Beauty and, after the closure of Yatesbury, the MoD was persuaded to remove the whole of the hutted camp on the eastern airfield. All the remaining buildings and 72 acres of land were sold by the Chippenham auctioneers of Thompson, Noad & Phipp on the instruction of the Secretary of State for Defence. The sale was held at the Lansdowne Arms Hotel, Calne on Wednesday 27th July 1966. The land was sold in lots but Wiltshire County Council found that the only way to get the unsightly foundations removed was to purchase it from the new owners and dispose of the concrete itself. This was completed and the camp area returned to farmland, except for one section whose owner refused to sell.

Flying returned to the former east airfield site in January 1995 when the Wiltshire Microlight Centre was given temporary planning permission to form a grass runway and site a temporary building.

On the same site the only original building remaining is the former gymnasium and this is occupied by the Meteor Flight which formed in 1991. Here renovation work on Gloster Meteors takes place. The aim is to return three aircraft to flying condition. A tragic accident occurred on Friday 8th August 1997 when club founder and Chief Engineer Colin Rhodes working alone under Meteor T7 WA591 (G-BWMF) was crushed to death. The framework supporting the aircraft moved and the undercarriage fell on top of him. The two other Meteors of the Flight, which are both with the Bristol Aero Collection, are Meteor T7 WL360 and former Kemble gate-guard Meteor F8 WH364.

Other than the Second World War built gymnasium in use by the Meteor Flight, all the other surviving buildings are on the west airfield site and with the exception of the World War 2 hangar, are in the ownership of Jamal Khanfer, a Jordanian business consultant and air enthusiast. Some of the buildings are Grade 2 listed but have been allowed to deteriorate by the previous owners, who were a

Leeds based property developer. The main buildings comprise two 1917 pattern GS Sheds, and what is left standing of an ARS and the station mortuary. The two GS Sheds had their roofs re-felted in early 1993. The buildings of the 1935 Bristol Flying School also remain and these include the Officers' Mess & Offices with extensions, Officers' Quarters, Airmen & NCOs Quarters, training block, medical quarters, power house, 7 bay MT workshops, various stores and garages, semi-detached house for engineer and foreman, squash and tennis courts. Most of these are in derelict and semi-derelict condition except for the houses which are occupied. One building in good condition and in use by Dalgety Arable is the World War 2 hangar. On the site of what was the boiler house, a two storey extension was added to the south end of the hangar in 2001 for uses as additional offices.

When ownership of the site changed hands in the late 1990s, the new owner had hoped to renovate the buildings and create a museum and flying facilities for vintage aircraft, but unfortunately the necessary planning permission was not forthcoming.

Victory Cross Recipiants

1) Major William George Barker

One of Yatesbury's flying instructors with No.59 TS joined No.28 Sqn as a Flight Commander on 8th October 1917, the day the squadron departed for France. This was William George Barker a Canadian who had been posted to Yatesbury much to his regret, having been wounded by 'Archie' when serving in France with No.15 Sqn. During this time he had won the MC and Bar for Artillery Observation. At Yatesbury he broke every rule in the book in his endeavour to return to an operational squadron. Low flying was his speciality. His score of enemy aircraft whilst with No.28 Sqn was 22. He then joined No.66 Sqn where his tally rose to 38. He was subsequently posted to command No.139 Sqn and was allowed to take with him his faithful Camel B6313, which he had first flown at Yatesbury on 30th September 1917, and from which he had despatched all of his enemy aircraft. His total 'kills' increased by another 8 before the aircraft was dismantled on 2nd October 1918. He

went on to destroy 4 more enemy aircraft when serving with No.201 Sqn and this brought his total to 50 of which 46 were destroyed. Along the way he was awarded the VC, DSO*, MC**, Croix de Guerre and Medagliod'Argento. The VC was awarded for his actions when, alone, he was attacked by 15 Fokker DVIIs and in the resulting combat was twice wounded. He managed to shoot down three and drive down two others before his badly damaged aircraft crash-landed behind the Allied lines. He left the RAF in April 1919. Sadly, he was killed in a flying accident on 12th March 1930 in Ottawa.

'Archie' was the British nickname for German anti-aircraft fire. The saying was originated by 'Biffy' Borton and his observer R.E.G. Small when they were first shot at over Soissons. After each burst they altered course to put the enemy off its aim. As each shot missed them, they sang the words of a music-hall song 'Archibald, certainly not!'

2) Wing Commander Guy Penrose Gibson

Guy Gibson's first squadron posting was on 4th September 1937 to No.83 Sqn at Turnhouse flying the Hind and Hampden. His war began with this squadron on the evening of the first day when he flew an operation to the Kiel Canal. He completed 27 missions and was awarded a DFC on 9th July 1940. He was then due a rest and spent it with a posting to No.29 (Night Fighter) Sqn at Wellingore commencing on 13th November 1940. The squadron was equipped with the Blenheim IF and Beaufighter IF. In carrying out just one short of a hundred night operations he shot down four enemy aircraft and claimed two probables. For this he gained a bar to his DFC on 16th September 1941. His next operational posting was to command No.106 Sqn at Coningsby on 13th April 1942. Between each of his squadron postings he had carried out short periods as an instructor at OTUs. With No.106 Sqn he flew Manchesters and Lancasters and chalked up another 46 bombing operations and was awarded the DSO on 20th November 1942 and the Bar on 2nd April 1943. With the forming of No.617 Sqn at Scampton on 23rd March 1943, the AOC Bomber Command didn't have a problem in finding the ideal officer to command

it. Formed for the special operation of attacking Germany's dams with the bouncing bomb developed by Barnes Wallis, the bomber and ground crews had to be the best of the best and Wing Commander Guy Gibson was the obvious choice to lead the squadron.

Guy Gibson recorded the story of the raid in his book *Enemy Coast Ahead*. It has been told many times since in books and in the film *The Dambusters*. It is without doubt the most famous flying operation of World War 2 and it was for this precision bombing operation that Guy Gibson was awarded the VC on 28th May 1943, and for which he became a household name. Taken off operations and flying a desk, the following year he persuaded authority that he should fly one more mission. Against their better judgement they agreed and on 19th September 1944 he took off from Woodhall Spa flying a No.627 Sqn Mosquito XX KB267 AZ-E to act as 'Master Bomber' for a raid on the heavily defended rail centre at Rheydt. He successfully directed the operation over the target for the Lancasters making their bombing runs. The crews heard his last calm and precise messages. The Mosquito crashed near the East Scheldt estuary. Guy Gibson the legend, and his navigator Sqn Ldr J.B. Warwick DFC were killed and are buried in Steenbergen-en-Kruisland Roman Catholic Cemetery.

3) Sergeant John Hannah

Yatesbury's third VC recipient trained at the station as a WOP during September 1939 and became the youngest VC at 18 years of age. Following his training at Yatesbury, West Freugh and OTU at Upper Heyford, John Hannah joined No.106 Sqn on Hampdens. He was posted to Scampton on 11th August 1940 with No.83 Sqn also equipped with Hampdens. On the night of 15th/16th November 1940 the squadron was tasked with attacking the invasion barges massed in Antwerp. Sgt Hannah was the WOP/AG in Hampden P1355 OL-W, piloted by a Canadian, Plt Off Connor. Having made the attack, their aircraft received a direct hit from flak. It immediately caused a serious fire in the fuselage and quickly enveloped the WOPs cockpit. The fuel tanks were also ruptured by the flak. John

Hannah fought his way through the flames and returned with two fire extinguishers to attack the flames. With these exhausted and the fire still out of control he started beating the flames out with his log-book. During all of this time ammunition was going off all around him and he could see the aircraft structure disappearing beneath his feet. The rear-gunner had left the aircraft after the initial strike and John Hannah could have done the same. The stage came when this was no longer an option as his parachute burnt in the fire. The pilot during all this time kept the aircraft flying and on course for Scampton and Hannah continued to beat the flames, his face and hands blackened and burnt. Eventually he won the battle and extinguished the fire. The badly burnt aircraft made a safe landing at its base. Without doubt John Hannah's actions saved the aircraft and the lives of himself and the pilot. For this he was awarded the VC and the pilot the DSO. Sgt John Hannah VC was posted back to Yatesbury on 4th September 1941 as an instructor with No.2 Signals School. He will be known to a great number of personnel who subsequently passed through the station for his application to halt the practice of saluting when on Pay Parade. It is believed that Yatesbury was the only RAF establishment where this privilege was allowed. On 10th December 1942 whilst still at Yatesbury, he was discharged from the service suffering from tuberculosis. He tragically died on 7th June 1947.

Memorials

173/SU073697- 4 miles East of Calne

On the A4, almost half a mile east of the turning to the village of Yatesbury and next to a farm gate, formerly the main gate of RAF Yatesbury, stand two memorials.

1) A large irregular shaped Sarsen stone displaying a stainless steel plaque set into a recess and inscribed: -

> R.F.C. - R.A. F. YATESBURY
>
> IN MEMORY OF
> THOSE WHO SERVED
> 20th August 1995

The idea of commemorating the site and the memorial provision, was that of Eddie Brown of Malmesbury. He funded the plaque with the stone given by a local lady, Mrs Jean Gantlett and erected by Roger Partridge and Gordon Brown. The ground on which the stone is placed was donated by Cumber & Son (Theale) Ltd. The unveiling of the stone on 20th August 1995 was carried out by Don Scotman RAF, who had served at Yatesbury. Resulting from this initial act of commemoration, the Yatesbury Association was formed by Eddie Brown and his son Paul, with a view to preserving and developing the use of the remaining RFC/RAF buildings. In addition, former personnel who had served at Yatesbury were encouraged to join and this has developed into a membership exceeding 500, of which some members are from the Commonwealth.

2) A memorial built of Cotswold stone mounted with a stainless steel plaque inscribed with a plan of the airfield prepared by Paul A. Brown, plus the camp buildings of No.2 Radio School and the words: -

> RAF Yatesbury
> circa 1946

The provision of this memorial was arranged by the Yatesbury Association to commemorate the former airfield and radio school. The plaque was manufactured and supplied by Hanman Split Ltd., Gloucester and was donated by the site owners Cumber & Son (Theale) Ltd who also funded the wooden rail fencing behind the memorials. The Cotswold stone memorial was designed and erected by John Beresford, a builder from Brinkworth. The unveiling took place on Sunday 18th August 1996 following a service at All Saints Church, Yatesbury. The ceremony was attended by some 200 ex-service men and women who had served at the camps in the past. The memorial was unveiled by Pam Sydney whose husband Sqn Ldr Jim Sydney had been a Senior Instructor at Yatesbury, and she a WAAF adjutant.

3) 173/SU063715 - In All Saints Church on the C139 road in Yatesbury village is a brass plaque on the South wall inscribed: -

> The repairs in this corner
> of the Church are dedicated to
> Squadron Leader JIM SYDNEY
> by his family and friends.
> 1920 - 1982

In one of the pews a Kneeler embroidered with the wings and crown of the RAF has been provided and dedicated to Sqn Ldr Sydney.

In the churchyard there are 3 RFC, 27 RAF, 1 RAAF and 3 Polish Forces graves. In addition is the gravestone of William Bernard Furie marked 'Servant at Yatesbury Officers Mess' died 11/11/42 age 51.

The two Yatesbury memorials at the site of the former station's main gate

ZEALS AERODROME

Location - 183/ST788321 - 5 miles East of Wincanton (Somerset)

The former airfield is located on the north side of Zeals village and the A303 trunk road to the West Country.

Airfield Development

Work on converting the pasture land of part of St Martin's Farm and part of Manor Farm to an aerodrome began during 1941. Bells Lane, a minor road from Stourton to Zeals, was closed as it ran directly through the centre of the site. A pair of cottages on the airfield's southern boundary were blown up so as not to impede low flying aircraft. Col Troyte-Bullock objected to the airfield on the grounds that 'the shooting would naturally be destroyed, the two farms very detrimentally affected on which the tenants interest would be considerable and it would deprive the occupants of quiet enjoyment'. Irish labourers were drafted in to assist with the construction work. They lodged in the area and were fed from a canteen operated by a local lady, Mrs Portnell, whose daughter was later the only Zeals girl to become a GI bride. One of the Irish labourers remembered in the village was Charlie Kidd from Liverpool who each day drove a bus around the various lodgings to collect the other workers.

The 530 acre aerodrome had three grass runways N/S 1600yds, E/W 1417yds and SE/NW 1417yds. A 50ft wide concrete perimeter track encircled the landing area, with 30 hardstandings, 12 of Sommerfeld Track and 6 double pen aircraft standings. A T1 hangar was built on the boundary close to the A303 road. There were 8 Over Blister hangars and a Control Tower with wind-sock, close to the perimeter track. A transmitter building, masts and antenna were sited close to the airfield off of a lane leading to Pen Selwood. Cpl Harold Fudge, a wireless mechanic, remembers giving two aircraft in the circuit permission to land from this building shortly after the aerodrome became operational, and on an occasion when the Flying Control was inoperative. The two-letter station identification code was ZL. The main entrance and technical buildings were in the south east corner with the Administration Site dispersed on the

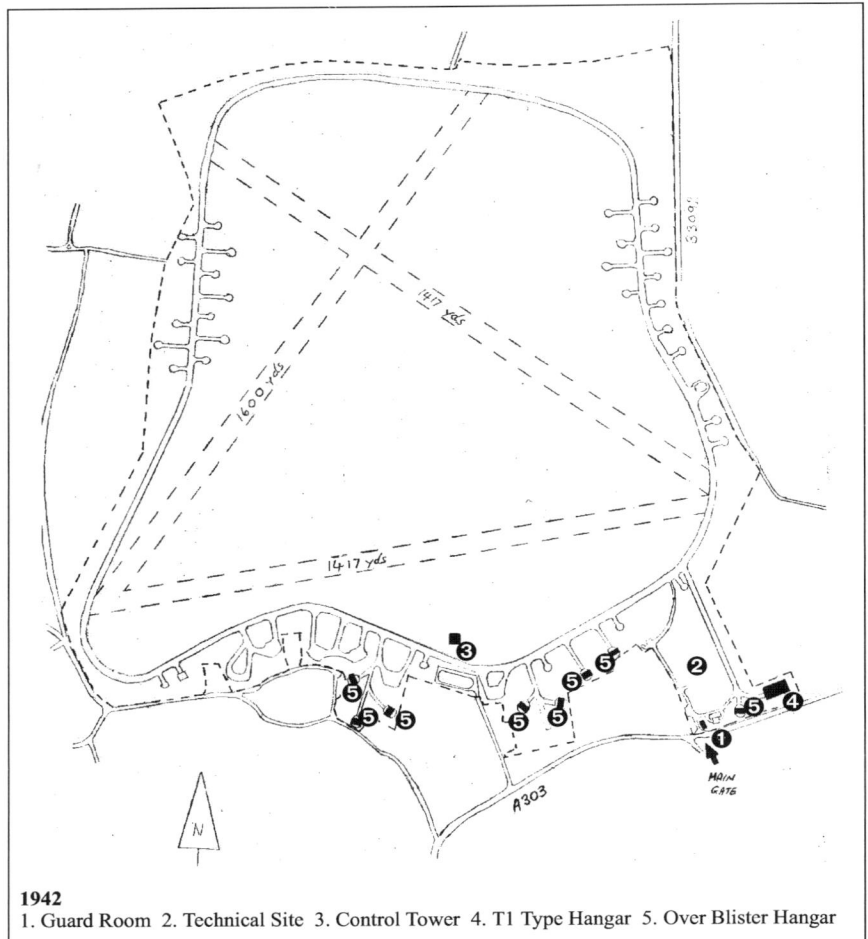

1942
1. Guard Room 2. Technical Site 3. Control Tower 4. T1 Type Hangar 5. Over Blister Hangar

opposite side of the main road. The majority of the domestic quarters were likewise dispersed off of the airfield. There were eleven different sites, with one including a purpose built hospital. Accommodation was provided for a permanent staffing level of 26 Officers, 186 SNCOs and 1914 other ranks including WAAF personnel. The domestic buildings were constructed by Staverton Builders. Night time landing facilities were Glim Lamp and gooseneck flares to Drem Type 1 layout. A Drem Mk II flarepath and off- field lead lights were installed by Alpha Electrical Co.

A well was sunk to provide the base with the vast amount of water it required and water towers were erected at various locations. For a considerable amount of its service occupation, the aerodrome suffered from serious water logging following

continuous heavy rains. This resulted in periods when it was out of commission.

World War 2 Years

Zeals opened as a forward operating airfield in the Colerne Sector of No.10 Group Fighter Command on 21st May 1942. On that day Sqn Ldr T.E. Hubbard arrived on posting from HQ for duty as Station Commander.

The first unit to occupy Zeals was No.286 Sqn which arrived from Lulsgate Bottom on 26th May 1942 under the command of Sqn Ldr M.C. Boddington DFM. The squadron was equipped with 5 Hurricane IICs, 4 Oxfords, 8 Master IIIs and 15 Defiant Is. During June the squadron carried out practice night flying, dusk landings, ferrying and exchanging aircraft with various detachments. Detachments involved Middle

378

Wallop, Fairwood Common, Exeter, Warmwell, Harrowbeer, Colerne, Portreath, Kemble and Rhoose. During July and August it engaged in Army Co-operation exercises. On 31st August 1942 No.286 Sqn left Zeals for Colerne.

The Sqn's 15 Defiant Is on charge were: N1537, N1730, N1735, N1740, N1756, N1771, N3336, N3370, N3373, N3403, N3477, N3489, N3494, N3497 and V1115.

Zeals would see a considerable amount of glider activity during the war and the first landed as part of exercise 'Omega' on 13th August 1942. The purpose of the exercise was to gain experience in landing a complete Infantry Company, with full arms and equipment, from gliders towed in formation. This was with a view to capturing and destroying a vital position, then to enplane before taking off on conclusion of the operation. 14 Whitleys of No.296 Sqn based at Hurn were used as tugs, each towing a Hotspur glider. 83 troops of the 1st Border Regiment were carried in the gliders flown by pilots of 1st Glider Pilot Regiment. The exercise at Zeals was determined as being a success.

On 24th August 1942 No.66 Sqn arrived from Ibsley under the command of New Zealander Sqn Ldr R.D. Yule DFC. He had fought in the Battle of Britain with No.145 Sqn. No.118 Sqn also arrived from Ibsley on 24th August with 34 aircraft and commanded by Flt Lt Newhery. Although it was summer time, a first day entry in the No.118 Sqn Operations Record Book indicated the Station was 'lacking accommodation and being a seething mass of mud'. Plt Off Andrew Deytrikh of No.66 Sqn recalls the Officers' Mess being at Zeals House, much to the annoyance of the owners, the Troyte-Bullock family. They had an Irish Wolfhound which, he remembers, scared the living daylights out of all the officers. Both squadrons were equipped with the Spitfire Vb/Vc and Vb respectively and they operated *Circus*, *Rhubarbs*, wing sweeps, convoy patrols and bomber escort duties. From the time it arrived on the morning of 24th August until last light, No.118 Sqn was placed on readiness. This state was in order to ensure the safety of the Prime Minister who was returning to Lyneham from Russia. On 28th August, 12 of the squadron aircraft took part in a No.11 Group *Circus* in

which 10 Fw 190s were observed but not engaged.

No.118 Sqn used the following Spitfire VBs at Zeals: AR443, AR447, AR448, AR450, AR451, AR452, AR453, AR456, BM574, EN926, EN929, EN953, EN956, EN959, EN966, EN969, EP119, EP124, EP126, EP129, EP130, EP133, EP191, EP202, EP206, EP240, EP328, EP388, EP413, EP459, EP549 and EP646.

On 9th September 1942 No.66 Sqn took off from Warmwell and No.118 Sqn from Zeals to give escort to four No.263 Sqn Whirlwinds attacking four flak ships off Alderney. On this patrol 2 ships were sunk with bombs and cannon fire. No.118 Sqn Spitfire Vb EP202 flown by Plt Off Brown was damaged by flak during the attack. It was not unusual for the Zeals squadrons to start their operations from Warmwell, Hawkinge or Tangmere. On 15th September the two Zeals squadrons, both taking-off from their home base on this occasion, each put up 12 Spitfires to provide bomber escort duties. They were joined by 9 Spitfires of No.501 Sqn from Middle Wallop and accompanied 13 Bostons IIIs of No.107 Sqn, detached at Charmy Down, to Cherbourg. The docks were bombed and the 12,000 ton whaling factory ship *Solglint* was set on fire and gutted. All bomber and fighter escort aircraft returned safely. LAC Charlie West, Airframe Flt Mech with No.66 Sqn during the whole of its deployment at Zeals, recalls that the Bostons, having taken off from their home bases, would land at Zeals to refuel before proceeding across the Channel with the squadron's Spitfires. Sgt Pilot Gilbert W. Slack RAFVR of No.118 Sqn whilst carrying out a cine-gun attack practice in Spitfire Vb AR456 on Tuesday 22nd September, broke away from the attack, executed a half roll and failed to pull out in time. The aircraft crashed near Wilton, killing the pilot. It was determined that the accident was due to an error of judgement by an inexperienced pilot. Ten days after the Cherbourg raid, Air Marshal Sholto Douglas A.O.C. in C. visited Zeals to carry out a station inspection. He was accompanied by AVM A.H. Orlebar. They arrived by road and left by air later in the day. On 26th September, No.66 and No.118 Sqns left temporarily for Predannack

to carry out major operations. They were replaced by No.611 Sqn arriving from Biggin Hill with Spitfire IXs, No.402 (Winnipeg Bear) Sqn RCAF from Kenley with Spitfire IXs and the Defiant Flight from Northolt as relief. Their stay was brief with No.611 Sqn departing the next day for Bolt Head. No.402 Sqn returned to Kenley and the Defiant Flight to Northolt on 29th September, when No.66 and No.118 Sqns reported back at Zeals. Alex Lugg, who as a young boy lived in a cottage on the edge of the airfield, recalls watching from a shed at the bottom of the garden whilst the returning Spitfires were refuelled from mobile petrol bowsers.

A receipt for the laundry of Sgt McSpedden of No.66 Sqn. The washing and ironing was undertaken by one of the ladies in Zeals.

A game of rugby was staged on 9th October 1942 when No.118 Sqn personnel took on the station personnel and won 8-3.

Plt Off Andrew Deytrikh No.66 Sqn behind the Squadron Intelligence Officer Fg Off Sam Lucas after a rugby match at Zeals. Photo: Andrew Deytrikh.

No.2835 Sqn RAF Regiment arrived on permanent location from 10th October.

Returning from an exercise on 16th October, No.118 Sqn was vectored onto an unidentified aircraft over Poole Harbour. This turned out to be a Spitfire IX with floats. Although ground defences had opened up, the squadron pilots recognised the aircraft for what it was and as they broke off, it was seen to make a successful landing in the harbour. Flying from Zeals was difficult for most of October due to heavy rain and fog. One 'wag' suggested that perhaps their aircraft should be fitted with floats as seen on the Spitfire landing in Poole Harbour.

On 21st October 1942 Sqn Ldr Willis took No.421 (Red Indian) Sqn RCAF, with its Spitfire VBs, from Fairwood Common to Zeals. Together with No.66 and No.118 Sqns, under the command of Wg Cdr Morgan, they escorted 12 B-17s to bomb Maupertus aerodrome. All aircraft returned safely. Later the same day No.421 Sqn again provided cover for B-17s flying back from Lorient. Bad weather prevented the squadron from returning to their home base until three days later. They were not there for long and returned to Zeals on 1st November 1942. On Sunday 8th November, No.421 Sqn was engaged on a No.10 Group *Circus* providing top cover for B-17s, when they lost their CO, Sqn Ldr Frank C. Willis RAF in Spitfire Vb EN779 and Flt Sgt Clifford A. Davis RCAF in Spitfire Vb BL896. The names of both appear on the Runnymede Memorial. No.421 Sqn led by acting CO Flt Lt Robertson, together with No.118 and Middle Wallop's No.504 Sqn, took part in another No.10 Group *Circus* two days later with Maupertus again the target. On 14th November No.421 Sqn returned to Angle. The same day No.118 Sqn together with Spitfire VCs of No.504 Sqn took-off from Exeter to support B-17s returning from 'Ops' but pancaked back at Zeals having failed to make contact. An unfortunate incident involving a No.118 Sqn Spitfire Vb BM574 occurred on 29th November when Sgt A.W. Smith was delivering it to General Aircraft Ltd for overhaul. During the landing at Hamworth, the aircraft overshot and collided with a vehicle on the peri-track and at the same time ran into a column of marching ATC cadets, killing one and injuring several.

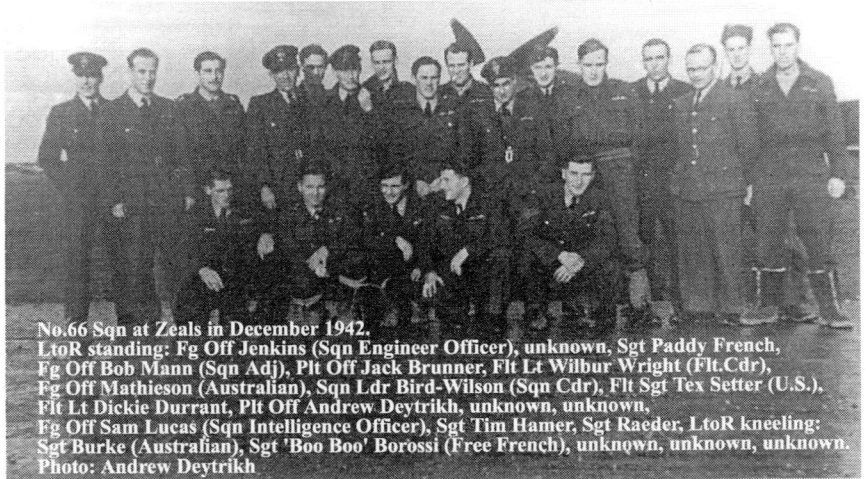

No.66 Sqn at Zeals in December 1942.
LtoR standing: Fg Off Jenkins (Sqn Engineer Officer), unknown, Sgt Paddy French, Fg Off Bob Mann (Sqn Adj), Plt Off Jack Brunner, Flt Lt Wilbur Wright (Flt.Cdr), Fg Off Mathieson (Australian), Sqn Ldr Bird-Wilson (Sqn Cdr), Flt Sgt Tex Setter (U.S.), Flt Lt Dickie Durrant, Plt Off Andrew Deytrikh, unknown, unknown, Fg Off Sam Lucas (Sqn Intelligence Officer), Sgt Tim Hamer, Sgt Raeder, LtoR kneeling: Sgt Burke (Australian), Sgt 'Boo Boo' Borossi (Free French), unknown, unknown, unknown.
Photo: Andrew Deytrikh

No.66 Sqn left Zeals for Warmwell on 1st November 1942 and returned again on 14th. Sqn Ldr Harold A.C. Bird-Wilson DFC replaced Sqn Ldr Bob Yule DFC as No.66 Sqn CO during November when the latter was posted to No.10 Group HQ on staff duties. This coincided with the award of a bar to his DFC. He was awarded a DSO in March 1944. Appointed Wg Cdr in 1951, he was killed in a flying accident on 11th September 1953 whilst rehearsing for the Battle of Britain flypast. Meteor WF695, which he was flying at the time, collided over London with Meteor WK938 which was trying to avoid a Hurricane. He attempted to crash-land between the rows of buildings at Woolwich Arsenal but died in the attempt.

Sqn Ldr Bird-Wilson had joined the RAF in September 1937 and exactly a year later crashed whilst flying a BA Swallow on a navigation course in Yorkshire. He sustained serious facial injuries, requiring four plastic surgery operations carried out by Archie McIndoe of 'guinea pig' fame. Harold Bird-Wilson served with No.17 Sqn, which was equipped with the Hurricane, and was based in France for six days from 17th May 1940, before returning and operating throughout the summer in the Battle of Britain. He was awarded the DFC on 24th September 1940. The same day he was shot down off Chatham in P3878 by Maj. Adolf Galland of JG26, and baled out with severe burns. By this time he had claimed 8 victories, six of which were shared. Following another period in hospital he served as an instructor with No.52 OTU and then as a Flt Cdr with No.234 Sqn. A further period was served with No.52 OTU before being

given command of No.152 Sqn. He was then supernumary with No.118 Sqn until taking command of No.66 Sqn at Zeals. Following a distinguished career he retired from the RAF in 1974 with the rank of AVM.

Nos.66 Sqn and 118 Sqn Spitfires carried out *Ramrod 45* on Monday 7th December 1942, escorting eight No.263 Sqn Whirlwinds, all taking off from Warmwell. During an attack on a 1,300 ton coaster and a 500 ton trawler off Jersey, two Whirlwinds were lost in the sea. P7105, flown by the Sqn Cdr, Sqn Ldr Robert S. Woodward DFC, RAFVR, was hit by flak and ditched 400yds from the ships. The other P6987 flown by WO Donald B. McPhail RCAF was seen to fly through heavy flak on the run up and then hit the sea. The names of both pilots appear on the Runnymede Memorial.

Following more heavy rain during the month and the subsequent waterlogging, the airfield was abandoned to flying when No.66 and No.118 Sqns transferred to Ibsley two days before Christmas, leaving the RAF Regiment as sole occupants. The aircraft took off singly in the mud and with great difficulty.

Although it had no squadron aircraft of its own, Zeals was not entirely without incident when, on 24th January 1943, a No.257 Sqn Typhoon IB R8637 from Warmwell overshot whilst trying to land. Its pilot Plt Off Clift (Burmese) had taken off to carry out routine flying practice but after several unsuccessful attempts to land at Warmwell owing to a hail storm, he was vectored to Zeals. The pilot was uninjured but the aircraft was Cat 'AC' damaged. Poor conditions at Zeals at the time made the airfield unserviceable to all but light aircraft and visibility was bad.

The weather and the conditions at Zeals improved sufficiently to allow it to be included in a 13-day close support exercise with the Army, code name *Spartan*, commencing on 1st March 1943. This was an early rehearsal for what was later to become the 1944 invasion force. No.122 Airfield HQ formed at Zeals on 15th February to control three of the participating squadrons. The first of these, No.132 Sqn arrived at Zeals

Hawker Hurricane IIBs of No.174 Sqn based at Zeals in March/April 1943.
Photo: RAF Museum P019142

from Martlesham Heath on 28th February. The pilots, with their Spitfire VBs, arrived the following day. No.174 and No.184 Sqns arrived on 12th March from Grove with Hurricane IIBs and IIDs respectively. The 14 No.174 Sqn Hurricanes had left their base at Odiham for Chilbolton on 1st March before moving to Grove on 11th. Also on 1st March, the 14 No.184 Sqn Hurricanes had left their base at Colerne for Chilbolton. The Sqn CO, Sqn Ldr Jack 'Bunny' Rose, confirms that their role at Chilbolton was to make camera gun attacks on armoured fighting vehicles (AFVs). He flew 7 sorties against tanks between 4th-10th March. The squadron likewise moved on to Grove on 11th March. *Spartan* ended on 13th March. Whilst at Zeals the Hurricanes of No.184 Sqn flew to a number of different airfields in Southern England for a variety of purposes, taking part in low flying, camera gun exercises and air to ground firing with their 40mm guns at Sand Bay. All of this training formed part of the build up to the invasion of Europe.

Spartan was aptly named as it involved the crews being under canvas whilst rotating airfields. Sqn Ldr Rose recalls them being strictly controlled by umpires. They were permitted only the

rations issued and were not allowed to use local public houses or even to make small purchases from the mobile canteen operated by the WVS and used by the station personnel. Rations were delivered by the Army who had been briefed to cater for one tenth of the number of RAF personnel who actually took part in *Spartan*. Until it was sorted out, the aircrew and the handful of key ground personnel No.184 Sqn were permitted to take with them from Colerne, one small tin of bully beef between two and a few hard tack biscuits. During this period they supplemented their starvation rations by shooting a few hares and stealing some potatoes from a clamp in the corner of a field.

Sir Albert Thomas 'Archie' Lamb DFC, a resident of Zeals, was a Plt Off with No.184 Sqn flying from Zeals at the time. He remembers that on one of the days Sqn Ldr Jack Rose was called to a meeting in London. In spite of all personnel being confined to camp as the airfield was 'closed up', four of his squadron pilots took themselves to London that same night to meet some girls in the Coach & Horses at Kensington. Unfortunately for them, the CO called there after his meeting with the result that the pilots were instructed to report to him in his office first thing in the morning where they were 'carpeted'. Plt Off Lamb joined the squadron from an OTU on 9th March. He was given the name 'Archie' by Sqn Ldr Rose and this nickname stuck, as even in retirement he is known as Sir 'Archie' Lamb. Sgt Len Sharpe joined the squadron on the same day and both pilots caught up with the squadron at Zeals three days later, but too late to participate in *Spartan*. One of Sgt Sharpe's recollections of his time at Zeals was of his Flt Cdr, a man in his thirties and much older than the rest of the squadron pilots, insisting on landing his Hurricane with the wheels up despite a volley of red flares being shot at him. Although well thought of, the

incident nevertheless resulted in his posting to India. The other memory was of a night off of the base, spent in a public house playing the 'locals' at darts and drinking 'scrumpy', which they were warned about but which was the only drink available. A glorious evening was had by all but the after effects were disastrous.

After *Spartan* had ended, the Inspector-General RAF, ACM Sir Edgar Ludlow-Hewitt with Wg Cdr Dennison, flew into Zeals to inspect the station conditions. On 5th April 1943 No.132 and No.184 Sqns left for Eastchurch on the Isle of Sheppey with some of No.184 Sqns aircraft being detached to Milfield in Northumberland for their first experience of rocket firing. No.174 Sqn moved to Gravesend. No.122 Airfield HQ had moved to Eastchurch on 4th April.

After their departure, No.14 Works Area was drafted in to try to improve the airfield's drainage sufficiently to prevent further periods when the airfield would be non-operational. With the extensive works completed, No.263 (Fellowship of the Bellows) Sqn was transported to Zeals from Warmwell on 19th June 1943. The ground staff and equipment were collected by the Zeals RAF Commando Units, using twenty-four 3 ton lorries. 10 Westland Whirlwind Is and a Magister were flown, in with one Whirlwind remaining at Warmwell with a defective radiator. Zeals had been without a resident flying unit since 1942 and No.263 Sqn, under the command of Sqn Ldr Baker DFC and with a depletion of pilots, was to be non-operational. The squadron was to stay for three weeks of intensive flying. It consisted of mainly new pilots carrying out their first Whirlwind solo flights. During the three weeks 20 pilots carried out flying training which included formation flying, dive bombing practice and dummy attacks on the airfield gun-posts. Sgt Wood made 5 dummy attacks on a destroyer off the Needles. One accident occurred at Zeals when Sgt R. J. Hughes selected wheels up instead of flaps up resulting in Cat 'B' aircraft damage. At the end of the month the squadron received additional Whirlwinds from No.137 Sqn, which had re-equipped with the Hurricane IV. At this point No.263 Sqn reverted to being the only RAF

Whirlwind equipped unit. This aircraft was the first of the four cannon fighters and when modified in the summer of 1942 with the Mk.III universal under-wing bomb racks, it was often referred to as the "Whirlibomber" when operated this way. The system included a bomb release button on the throttle lever for the starboard engine, and a jettison switch. On 12th July the squadron moved back to Warmwell.

Lt Stratton, officer-in-charge of an American deployment flew into Zeals in a Cessna C.78 on 27th July 1943 to inspect the station prior to it being handed over to the USAAF on 1st August 1943 when it became Station 450. He returned three days later with 9 men forming the advanced party and the remainder followed four days later. They were allocated dispersal A34 for their use. They had their own workshops, offices and sleeping accommodation. Initially the site was occupied by the 66th Aerodrome Squadron prior to the establishment of the US 8th Air Force No.1 Tactical Air Depot which was set up to support modifications and major maintenance on C-47 aircraft. All RAF personnel remaining on the station after the departure of No.263 Sqn, were moved into Zeals House. From 23rd August 1943 the station was placed on Care & Maintenance and a C&M party was attached to Zeals throughout the occupancy by the USAAF. Sqn Ldr R.G. Rolfe-Rogers arrived to take over as CO from Wg Cdr J. Butterworth.

Soon after the Americans made themselves at home, the heavy rain once more reduced the airfield to a mud bath and they, like many of the units before them, soon became disillusioned with the site. One Flt of Airfield Construction Flight moved in to try and make runway improvements. Sommerfeld tracking was laid and hard-standings constructed. The rain continued and the Americans were still prevented from working up as intended. Other than a Wellington landing with engine trouble on 1st October 1943, two L-4Bs on 6th and a couple of B-17s arriving with stores, very little flying took place. Alex Lugg and his family who lived at the end of the main landing area, recalls being evacuated from the house on the occasions of B-17 landings because of the short landing strip and the possibility of an over-shoot. Zeals was transferred to

the 9th Air Force during October and the uncomfortable conditions didn't prevent an increase in establishment when on 27th October, 11 officers and 262 men of the 81st Aerodrome Sqn & 21st Weather School USAAF arrived. Their stay was also short and they moved out in November. On 1st November the station received a warning of enemy aircraft in the area. Conditions were foggy and one of the aircraft, a Ju.188A 260198, 3E + CL 3/KG6, having carried out a raid on Bath, crashed nearby at Grange Farm, Kilmington. The four crew members were killed, one body being found close to the aerodrome. They were Uffz Walter B. Overhoff, Karl Heinz Siegler, Uffz Karl H. Weisskamp and Ltn Kurt Reckin. Their coffins were conveyed from Zeals to Wincanton railway station on 5th November. Full service honours were accorded the cortege by 50 senior NCOs of the USAAF. The Germans were buried with full military honours by the USAAF at the military cemetery in Bath. On 11th November a further B-17 arrived but in the middle of the night on this occasion and the pilot made an excellent landing.

It was apparent by this time that the grass airfield which remained prone to water logging, would not support the wear and tear to which it would be subjected from the operation of heavy transport aircraft. Plans were therefore changed and the US 9th Air Force, 5th Tactical Air Depot was established with the arrival on 17th November of 56 officers and 1000 enlisted men. Two days later the 81st Aerodrome Sqn moved out. The new arrival resulted in the station coming to life again just before Christmas. On 23rd December 1943, 26 P-47 Thunderbolts of the USAAF 9th Air Force flew in and a further 34 the next day. Christmas was not one of great celebration for the Americans, who witnessed a crash landing of a P-51B Mustang on the airfield on 25th December and slightly east of the field, a B-17 crashed at Zeals Knoll on 29th December. The P-51B No.416456 was on a ferrying mission from Speke to Zeals with pilot 2nd Lt Earle W. Briggs. Nearing his destination, he was forced to descend below low cloud and fog in an attempt to locate the airfield. It appears that his vision was impaired by oil on the windshield so he made a series of 'S' turns to see ahead. While doing this,

the aircraft struck some tree-tops, badly damaging the port wing near the fuselage, propeller, starboard wing tip and the leading edge of the port horizontal stabiliser. The pilot immediately pulled up through the fog and shortly after arrived at his destination, where visibility was improved. He tried to lower his wheels for landing and found that one would not extend, and the other, which did, would then not retract due to loss of hydraulic pressure. This also prevented the use of flaps. In this condition the pilot crashed landed at Zeals with no injury to himself but with additional damage to the aircraft. The board of enquiry determined that 75% of the blame be attributed to weather conditions and 25% to the pilot for flying with a dirty windshield.

The crash on 29th December at Zeals Knoll was a US 8th AF B-17F No.42-30765 from the 381st Bomb Group based at Station 167 Ridgewell in

P-51B No. 416456 after crash landing on the airfield at Zeals.
Photo: AAIR

Essex. Its crew was 1st Lt Bill Ridley (Pilot), 2nd Lt George A. Heffman (Co-Pilot), 2nd Lt Eugene Arning (Navigator), 2nd Lt Carl W. Dittus (Bombardier), T/Sgt James R. Stewart and M/Sgt Edward D. Davis. The pilot made a descent through overcast cloud to confirm their position. Radio contact was made with Flying Control and a course given for Shatesbury. On reaching this and flying low over Coombe House, the pilot climbed into the overcast cloud and, on attempting to turn, made the bank too steep and came back out of the cloud in a diving turn. While attempting to recover the aircraft, it struck some treetops and the starboard wing was damaged sufficiently to cause excessive vibrations. The pilot instructed the crew to prepare for a crashed landing, which was made at Zeals Knoll. There were no injuries to personnel but the fuselage and propellers were damaged. The aircraft was stripped down and removed over the next few days. The board of enquiry determined the cause as 100% pilot error.

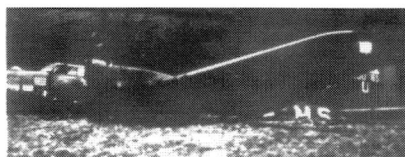

B-17F No. 42-30765 after crash landing at Zeals Knoll. Photo: AAIR

The 43rd Mobile Reclamation & Repair Sqn had been activated at Trowbridge on 5th December 1943 and attached to the U.S Third Army. It moved to Zeals on 4th January 1944 but was non-operational because of a lack of personnel and equipment. Five days later No.1 T.A.D. moved out. Col Harris USAAF arrived to take command at Zeals on 11th January. It was soon obvious that the condition of the airfield would not even sustain the use which it was being given by the P-47s. It was decided to transfer to Chilbolton, so the new year brought the start of the American withdrawal from Zeals when, on the 9th January 1944, the first units moved out followed on 11th March by the last of the P-47s.

From the 20th April 1944, the station was re-established as a forward operational night fighter base in A.D.G.B. No.11 Group, but under the operational control of No.10 Group. Wg Cdr A.L. Mortimer arrived as CO. Two 2nd TAF Mosquito squadrons were installed with the intention of operating against the enemy nuisance (Tip and Run) raids which were occurring at the time. These were No.488 (New Zealand) Sqn and No.410 Sqn. The first of the resident night fighter units to move in was No.488 Sqn with Wg Cdr R.C. Haine DFC as CO. 'B' Flt arrived from Bradwell Bay on 4th May equipped with Mosquito XIIIs. On arrival, however, the station was unfit for the squadron to operate so 'B' Flt moved temporarily to Colerne. 'A' Flt remained at Bradwell Bay before joining 'B' Flt at Colerne on 6th May. 'A' Flt finally moved into Zeals on the 11th May together with most of the ground personnel and 'B' Flt arrived the following day. The squadron pilots commenced their duties by flying Sector reconnaissance. No.147 Airfield HQ arrived from Acklington on 11th May to control No.488 Sqn and No.604 Sqn. The latter was to have a brief posting to Zeals in July. On 12th

An aerial view of Zeals taken on 24th March 1944 by an aircraft of No.544 Sqn. Most of the pans are covered by P-47 Thunderblots of the US 9th Air Force. The vertical dark line running through the centre of the landing ground, shows clearly the road closed when the airfield was constructed. Photo: NMRO

May No.147 (Night Fighter) Wing in No.85 Group formed from No.147 Airfield HQ.

No.183 Sqns Typhoon IBs arrived at Zeals from Thorney Island on 10th May 1944 and carried out dusk flying before departing again. Within a couple of days of returning, No.488 Sqns Adjutant Flt Lt Westcott MBE, a former World War 1 pilot, was transferred to No.85 Group Headquarters at Uxbridge and the Intelligence Officer to the newly formed No.142 Wing at Horne. The squadron also lost its mascot a Great Dane named Bruce. The officers all paid a monthly allowance for its food and they were sorry to lose him, but he left with his keeper, the Adjutant. The squadron was soon in action against the enemy when on the night of 14th/15th May, 6 aircraft were scrambled for *Searchlight Orbits*. They were able to intercept a force of 60 German bombers, which had crossed the coast near Portland, with Bristol as the target. A Ju.188 was

shot down by Flt Sgt Johnny A.S. Hall (pilot) and Fg Off Jock Cairns (nav/rad) in MM551. They obtained a freelance contact on the enemy aircraft and flew up beneath it to obtain visual identification. They then dropped back a hundred yards dead astern before giving it a two-second burst. A fire on the aircraft quickly took hold and two bombs under the wings could be seen. The aircraft then dropped like a stone and exploded on striking the ground. This was Johnny Hall's fifth success. The German pilot was shot in the head and died instantly and the other 3 crew became POWs. They confirmed the fighter was not seen by them, and on being attacked they jettisoned the two 2000 lb bombs they were carrying.

New Zealander Fg Off Ray G. Jeffs and Fg Off Ted Spedding, in HK381, call sign "Dorval 36", shot down a Ju.88 and a Dornier 217K. The Ju.88 was caught in the searchlights 3000' above them; they closed to 700' and gave the enemy aircraft two bursts from their cannon, causing an explosion at the port wing root. The starboard engine also caught fire and the aircraft broke up completely. The Germans took to their parachutes but the pilot was killed when his failed to open. The three survivors reported that they were not shot down by the fighter, which they had seen, but in taking avoiding action had got into spin trying to avoid the searchlights and then baled out. The Dornier had also been caught in the searchlight defences and ten minutes after disposing of the Ju.88, Ray Jeffs closed on the second target from the rear before opening fire at close range. Immediate strikes were observed and it veered off to the left with its starboard engine ablaze. As the stricken aircraft plunged down through the clouds, the crew baled out. The pilot, 20 year-old Leutnant Johannes Domschke was so badly injured that he died from his wounds. The observer, 21 year old Emil Chmillewski, the wireless operator, 22 year old Waldemar Jungke and the air gunner, 23 year old Otto Schott who was injured, became PoW. Ray Jeffs lost sight of the Dornier as it went into cloud so, on return to Zeals, only claimed it as a 'probable'. It was 'confirmed' by a fellow pilot who saw it crash on fire at West Camel. On the same night Flt Sgt Mitchell and Sgt Ron Ballard in HK427, call sign "Dorval 20", attacked and damaged a Ju.88 but lost sight of it before regaining contact and eventually finishing it off. An unfortunate incident occurred on 28th May when Fg Off H.C.D. Webbe on patrol in HK420, shot down two Wellington trainers with Canadian crews. At the time he thought he was engaging a Ju.88 and a Heinkel 217.

William Rumbold an AC.1 with No.488 Sqn recalls driving a lorry load of Mosquito spares from No.210 MU Romsey to Colerne during May but finding the squadron no longer there, returned them to Romsey. On arrival he was sent to Zeals which he reached in the early evening. He remained there over the very busy D-Day period and recalls the great cameraderie evident on the station. It was so good that he recalls a Flt Sgt Mitchell loaning him his uniform jacket, which allowed him to drink in the mess and nobody complained.

On 6th June the CO informed the squadron of the more aggressive duties

AC.1 William Rumbold of the M.T. Section with the RAF lorry used for carrying aircraft spares.
Photo: W. Rumbold

they were now to undertake as part of the D-Day invasion. Their primary role was to carry out patrols to protect the stream of gliders and tugs which would fly all night to and from the American Sector of the beachhead. On the 6th/7th June the squadron carried out seven patrols over the beachhead and during the next week the squadron flew constant sorties. On 12th/13th June, Sqn Ldr Nigel Bunting DFC* and Flt Lt Phil Reed DFC* shot down the squadron's first enemy aircraft over foreign soil. The navigator, using specially adapted night binoculars, identified a Ju.88 with two bombs under its wings flying straight and level over an area of Caen in France. They closed to 100 yards of its tail before opening fire. The first burst of cannon set the port engine alight, the second burst blew up the starboard engine and the third struck at the fuselage. The aircraft fell away and dived straight into the ground.

No.410 *'Cougar'* Sqn, with Wg Cdr G.A. Hiltz as CO, arrived from Hunsdon on 18th June 1944, also equipped with Mosquito XIIIs. Together with No.488 Sqn they were then operating some eight sorties a night each and claiming good results. On the first night of their arrival at Zeals, Fg Off Edwards and Flt Sgt Georges of No.410 Sqn, claimed a Ju.88 as did Lt Harrington and Sgt Tongue. The second of these enemy aircraft was reported as carrying two large bombs on outboard racks,

inboard of the engines. Lt Harrington made an approach from beneath the enemy aircraft and opened fire from 75'. He attacked again from slightly above and the Ju.88 exploded. Debris holed the starboard wing of the Mosquito in two places but it returned safely to base. On Saturday 24th June WO Jones and Flt Sgt Gregory, carrying out a beachhead patrol, attacked a Ju188 which then exploded and hit the sea. The same day Fg Off John R. Steep RCAF and Fg Off Douglas H. Baker RCAF, who were also on a beachhead patrol, were lost when their aircraft was shot down by flak. Fg Off Steep is commemorated on the Runnymede Memorial and Fg Off Baker is buried at the Bayeux War Cemetery, Calvados in France. On Monday 3rd July Flt Lt Edinger and Fg Off Vaessen destroyed a Ju188 off of Raz de la Percee. They approached from below before opening fire. The aircraft exploded and spun into the sea. Five days later Flt Lt Eyolfson destroyed a Me 410 over the outskirts of Paris. The same day Flt Lt Stanley B. Huppert RCAF and Fg Off Christie RCAF shot down a Ju 88 15 miles north of Raz de la Percee. When the enemy aircraft exploded, debris put the starboard engine of the Mosquito out of use. The port engine then overheated and the two men had to bale out over the sea. Fg Off Christie survived but the pilot drowned and is commemorated on the Runnymede Memorial. On 10th July Mosquito HK500 overshot the airfield and crashed at Pen Selwood. Both of the crew escaped.

During June and July 1944, the pilots of No.488 Sqn destroyed four Ju88s, three Fw 190s and a Me110. Both Mosquito squadrons operated as No.147 Wing until 29th June when this Wing moved to Hunsdon and they came under No.149 Wing which had formed at Deanland the previous month. No.488 Sqn lost a crew on Saturday 15th July 1944, when having completed their patrol and returning via Hurn, Flt Sgt Howard G. Scott RNAF and Fg Off Colin C. Duncan RNAF were killed when their aircraft crashed into a wood north east of Holmsley South. Both men were buried at Brookwood Military Cemetery.

In the summer of 1944 RAF Zeals was under the command of Wg Cdr J.G. Sanders DFC, who records that Zeals

House was still being used for the Officers' Mess. The stables housed the Equipment Section where some of the WAAF personnel worked. They cycled there each day from their nearby Nissen huts.

On 10th July 1944 a Norseman UC-64A, 43-5344, tail no.35344 assigned to the 320th Air Transport Squadron, 27th Air Transport Group USAAF, was tasked to transport a Lockheed Hudson V wheel and tyre required to repair an aircraft of the type at Prestwick. On approaching the Somerset/Wiltshire border in thick fog, the pilot requested permission to land at Zeals. Flying Control on the airfield refused permission because of the bad weather conditions and shortly afterwards the aircraft struck the pinnacle of Alfred's Tower positioned on the hill just north of the airfield. It crashed on Hillcombe Farm, South Brewham killing the pilot, 1st Lt Winfred H. Malone and the two NCOs, Master Sgt Lloyd F. Cheek and Cpl Henry A. Mazzie. The two NCOs were passengers who were to install the replacement wheel on arrival at Prestwick. All three were buried at Brookwood Cemetery on 18th July although Cpl Mazzie was later taken back to the States. The 6cwt finial, knocked from the top of King Alfred's Tower by the Norseman, was eventually replaced on 25th June 1986, by the RN who lifted it into position with a helicopter from RNAS Yeovilton.

A.C.2 Eddie Clarke who was with Station Workshops at Zeals between May and September 1944, recalls the occasion when a Lancaster returning from an 'Op', landed at Zeals still carrying a bomb. The Lancaster was left overnight on one of the dispersals on the far side of the airfield, away from the main station buildings, and took off again for its home base the following morning.

A brief visit was paid by 'A' Flt of No.604 (County of Middlesex) Sqn, with Wg Cdr D.F. Hughes DFC** as CO, when it arrived from Colerne on 25th July 1944 with Mosquito VIIs. The day after arriving, 6 aircraft were deployed on defensive patrols. Fg Off J.C. Truscott and Fg Off J. Howarth took off at 2225 hrs in Mosquito MM528 and destroyed a Ju88 off Granville before landing back at Zeals at 0030 hrs. The squadron returned to Colerne on 28th July at the same time

The tow rope being fixed to a Hadrian glider.   Photo: Cty Bernard Pike

as No.410 and No.488 Sqns in No.149 Wing. This was an exchange of base with 'A' and 'C' Flts of No.286 (AAC) Sqn, with Sqn Ldr Joyce as CO, arriving for night flying with Hurricane IICs. During this spell of duty at Zeals flying was restricted because of changeable weather conditions. On the last day of the month the aircraft strength was

Seen here on 30th August 1944, left to right Mrs Francis and Betty Fricker with the NAAFI van used for serving Zeals airfield. Photo: A. J. Gray

recorded as being 17 Oxfords, 9 Hurricane IICs, 3 Martinets and a Tiger Moth. The squadron had been the first to occupy Zeals in May 1942. On its second deployment, it spent two months on the base and in that time helped to promote good liaison in the area. As it was harvest time the local farmers asked the CO for volunteer labour. On 7th August, and following their normal duty hours, a party of 15 officers and men were taken to various farms where they helped to bring in the harvest. This continued for several evenings, the farmers grateful for the assistance. The Sqn moved out to Weston Zoyland on 28th August.

On 21st October 1944 No.3 Glider Training School detachment at Northleach arrived at Zeals for glider instructor training. This involved the towing of Hotspur gliders by Miles Master II tugs. Following a relatively short stay, the unit moved out on 9th December to Culmhead on the Blackdown Hills.

The Glider School was replaced by No.46 Group Transport Command, Glider Pick-up Training Flt (GPTF) of No.107 OTU Leicester East on 20th January 1945. On the same day 26 ground crew arrived from Leicester and by the beginning of February were joined by the instructors, all under the command of Sqn Ldr Philip W.'Pete' Peters, DFC, AFC, who transferred from Netheravon. The unit was equipped with 5 Dakotas and 7 Hadrian gliders. Pilots were under training to snatch gliders from the ground without landing the towing aircraft. The glider would be turned into the wind, the towing rope connected and made into a large loop before being suspended between two vertical poles. The Dakota towing aircraft were suitably strengthened, adapted with a winch, a number of clutches to take the snatch and a 1000' of cable with a hook on the end. The aircraft would make a shallow dive to hook the looped towing rope between the poles. The method provided for the recovery of gliders from positions unsuited to aircraft landings. The idea originated from America where, for some years, mail had been collected from outlying townships by this means. It was intended that the GPTF crews would form part of 'Tiger Force' to be used against the Japanese forces.

The training courses ran over a ten-day period with five crews of fifteen men to a course. On completion of the first course, the five crews together with

GPU Dakota TS435 having approached too low on this occasion to make a successful pick-up. These scenes are probably at Ibsley in 1945, after the unit left Zeals. Photo: Bernard Pike

some ground staff going on leave, took-off on Monday 19th February 1945 for their base at Leicester East in Dakota TS436 crewed by Flt Lt *Bonzo* MacKay DFC (pilot) and Fg Off Frank Plant (nav). Shortly after clearing the airfield the aircraft crashed into a hill and 20 airmen on board were killed, with only the pilot surviving, but suffering serious injuries. Further details of this incident and the memorial stone placed on the crash site, can be seen respectively at the end of this Zeals airfield detail, and see **Stourton**.

The courses continued at Zeals until 21st March when Sqn Ldr Peters and the unit moved to Ibsley with 5 Dakotas and 7 gliders. A replacement Dakota TP187 had arrived from Netheravon on the previous day to replace TS436 lost in the crash. This ended the RAF's operations at Zeals.

Interestingly Sqn Ldr Peters, the last RAF CO at Zeals had, during the early days of his RAF service, carried out one of the most improbable air combat feats of World War 2. Taking off at 0834 hrs on 1st June 1940 Plt Off Peters, stationed at Detling, was ordered to lead a section of three Anson Is of No.500 (County of Kent) Sqn to Dunkirk, and then to patrol the beaches from which the British Expeditionary Force was evacuating. The aircraft were patrolling 50' over the sea, when

at 1040 hrs, Peter's mid-upper gunner reported that nine Me.109s were diving onto the three aircraft. They dropped as a section to wave top height, but the two wing aircraft were severely damaged in the attack so Peters instructed them to make for home. The Anson general reconnaissance aircraft was fitted with nose and mid upper guns as standard but these three aircraft, had an additionally pair of Vickers gas operated guns fitted either side of the fuselage, firing through the rear windows. The co-pilot and wireless operator were sent to man the additional guns and to provide extra eyes for the incoming attack aircraft. By throttling back and executing skid turns, Plt Off Peters allowed his crew to direct fire into the first attacking aircraft. This proceeded to do a stall turn in front of the Anson's nose at which point Peters shot it down using the nose gun. A second Me109 was shot down in similar fashion and a third one, having received direct hits from the Anson, broke off its attack. It was also thought to have been fatally damaged. After returning to Detling at 1237 hrs, Peters found only one bullet hole in the Anson, but months later, when his parachute was being checked, an armour-piercing bullet was found amongst the silk. For his impressive exploit on that summer day in 1940, Plt Off Philip Walford Peters was awarded an immediate DFC. His fellow crew were Sgt Spencer, AC Pepper and AC Smith.

As from the 14th April 1945 the airfield at Zeals was officially taken over by the Admiralty as a replacement for Charlton Horethorne

near Wincanton in Somerset. It was commissioned as HMS *Humming Bird* from 18th May and was one of three RNAS Yeovilton satellites engaged in training aircraft-carrier flight crews for the Japanese conflict. 790 Sqn (Fighter Direction School) had arrived from Charlton Horethorne on 1st April with the Firefly and Oxford. The Corsair Modification Unit was also posted in. 760 Sqn re-formed at Zeals on 10th April as a Familiarisation Unit equipped with the Corsair, Harvard and Hellcat and 704 Sqn formed there on 11th April as a Mosquito OTU equipped with FB.VIs.

On 25th July 1945, 771 Sqn (FCU) moved in from Twatt in Orkney (HMS Tern), with mainly target and glider towing Martinets and the odd Corsair. American built Grumman Wildcats, Hellcats and additional Corsairs arrived for the squadron's use shortly afterwards. The squadron also had use of two Mosquitos and a Reliant. The latter was the squadron communication aircraft. The squadron had been providing Fleet co-operation exercises with the Home Fleet at Scapa Flow until July 1945 when the Fleet moved south to Portland moorings, using Weymouth Bay and the Channel in that area, for its working up exercises. It was for this reason that 771 Sqn was moved to Zeals. Whilst at Twatt, Sea Hurricanes and Bostons were additional aircraft types in use, but they were returned to MUs before the move south.

Flt Lt Denmark was a RAF pilot seconded to the FAA in November 1944 because of his twin engine experience. He was the first member of 771 Sqn to arrive at Zeals when he flew in from Twatt on 24th July 1945 in a Martinet, bringing with him some engineering and servicing equipment in the rear cockpit. The remainder of the squadron flew in over the next few days with the ground crews, stores and equipment arriving by road. The squadron was not immediately operational and it was some time before the Fleet requested exercises. Flt Lt Denmark was one of about six RAF pilots serving with 771 Sqn. He was pleased with the move to Zeals as it allowed him to live off Station with his wife. They moved into the Phoenix Hotel in nearby Gillingham where various other military personnel were also living. From there he was able to cycle daily to Zeals for flying duties. It would seem that a number of Wiltshire's airfields were renowned for their mushrooms growing qualities, proof presumably of wet and warm conditions, and Zeals was no exception. Flt Lt Denmark was able to pick sufficient to allow the Phoenix Hotel to add them to the breakfast menu and this made him a popular resident.

A New Zealand pilot, Alan Malcolm, also recalls flying Corsairs from Zeals and remembers being bussed there from RNAS Yeovilton. On the evening of VJ-Day, the station personnel celebrated into the morning at the local public houses having first toured the surrounding villages in the Station fire tender whilst ringing its bell furiously.

Post War Years

At 1040 hrs on 15th September 1945, 771 Sqn lost an aircraft and its pilot was killed when Martinet Mk.I RG985 crashed on the airfield and was totally wrecked. The Navy now had no further use for their RAF seconded officers and those at Zeals returned to their nominally responsible unit at Thorney Island. Although the Navy was at home on water, they were equally as disillusioned as the RAF and USAAF

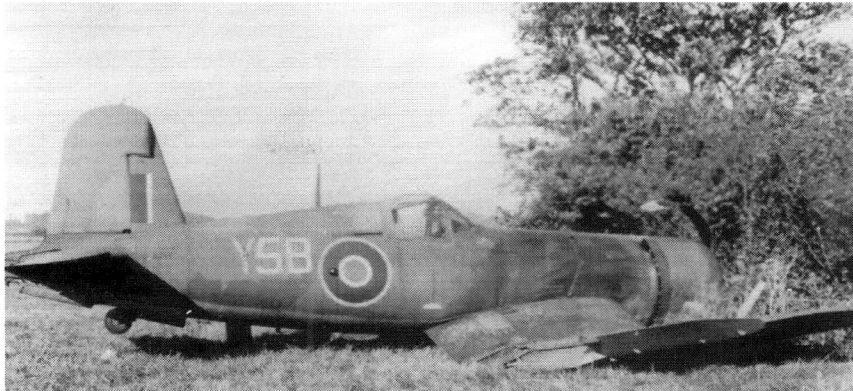

Two 760 Sqn aircraft crash pictures at Zeals airfield. Corsair Y5B on 14th November 1945 and Corsair YIV on 8th December 1945. The Navy man on the far left by the crane is Harry Scott who was part of the recovery team. Both accidents occurred after the squadron had officially moved to Lee-on-Solent in September 1945. Photos: Fleet Air Arm Museum

before them, with the amount they were experiencing at Zeals. With the end of the war and the approach of winter, the resident squadrons started to move out. 790 Sqn left for Dale on 30th August. On 4th September 704 Sqn left for Thorney Island, on 12th 760 Sqn moved to Lee-on-Solent and 771 Sqn moved to Gosport. On 19th September 759 Sqn arrived with Corsair 222s & 2Vs, Seafire 222s, Harvard 222s and Oxfords. The squadron remained until 7th January 1946 when it left for Yeovilton. Although the squadron received Hellcats during January this was probably after their arrival at Yeovilton.

Closure

Just the closing down party was left after 795 Sqn moved out. HMS *Humming Bird* was paid off in January 1946 and the Station reduced to Care & Maintenance. The RN Care & Maintenance Party was withdrawn on 7th June 1946.

Aerial view of Zeals airfield on 8th October 1945, during its occupation by the Royal Navy.
Photo: Fleet Air Arm Museum

Eventually the airfield was returned to agriculture, at first under the War Agricultural Committee, then later the local farmers. German PoW continued to work on the farms after the war. The airfield site remains in use for farming today, with much of it under the ownership of the National Trust. The feeder lane from Stourton to Zeals was re-opened after the closure of the airfield. The most striking feature of the airfield infrastructure, which remains in use as a private dwelling, is the original Flying Control, which stands on the side of Bells Lane. For a number of years it was used to store straw but was converted into living accommodation during 1968 and named 'Tower House'. It has had a number of owners and was last on the market for only a short time in 1998. Many of the Nissen huts were used for housing after the war and the former Armoury building is still in use as a private dwelling. Close by are the gun butts and small Maycrete buildings used for storage. Areas of the perimeter track remain as farm roads and hardstandings for chicken houses. Numerous underground air raid shelters on the base survive. Following the war, the T1 hangar became a Ministry Supply Depot before passing to Unigate who used it for the storage of powdered milk. It was demolished during the 1950s.

The children and young people of Zeals enjoyed a good social life during the time the airfield was in commission. They were invited to parties and films at the NAAFI and dances held in the 'Thunderbolt Club' by the Americans. Alex Lugg recalls the occasion as a young lad, when with a friend, they went to the main gate to talk to the Americans on duty in the sentry box.

The original Flying Control now used as a private dwelling.

The sergeant phoned up the guardroom and shortly afterwards a jeep arrived at the main gate and took them to the guardroom on the pretence of them being too cheeky. After being kept there for a while they were loaded up with chocolates and driven back to the main gate.

During 1941, when the airfield was under construction, it appears that the actor David Niven spent time at Zeals in his role as an Army officer with the GHQ Liaison Regiment. It has not been possible to determine what

American servicemen and local girls doing the Palais Glide at the 'Thunderbolt Club' on the base at Zeals in 1943. Photo: Cty Gwyneth F. Jackson

duties he was undertaking. Visitors to the nearby 'Spread Eagle Inn at Stourhead', will be able to see the signatures of him and his wife Primula, etched by them with a diamond ring, on one of the window panes.

Donald Hutchins was a young boy living at Bourton, near Zeals, during the war years and, as a cadet in 1945, with No.932 Sqn ATC based at Gillingham, flew from Zeals in Stinson Reliants. He recalls watching the Bostons land, Westland Whirlwinds parked beside the main A303 road, the matt black Defiants during their short stay, assembled on the dispersals by the houses at the west end of the airfield and later the Hadrian gliders being snatched using Dakotas. The aircraft crashes which he remembers include a Spitfire in the woods between the Gasper turning and Rocky Arch, a Mosquito in the River Stour near Fords Water, a Miles Master on the Administration Site, on the opposite side of the A303 from the T1 hangar, and the Dakota on Beech Knoll above Search Farm.

Accident involving Dakota III TS436, No.107 OTU on 19/2/45

On 20th January 1945 No.107 OTU based at Leicester East sent a detachment to Zeals to form the

Glider Pick-up Training Flight. Courses were run to teach crews the skills needed to retrieve gliders on the ground without landing the aircraft tug. This involved the glider on the ground being turned into the wind, the towing rope connected, then made into a large loop which was suspended between two poles. The tug aircraft, suitably strengthened, was adapted with a winch, 1000' of cable with a hook on the end and a number of clutches to take care of the snatch.

The Unit at Zeals was in No.46 Group Transport Command with Sqn Ldr Philip W. Peters DFC, AFC as CO. He was transferred there from Netheravon. 26 groundcrew were posted from Leicester East in January and the following month the instructors arrived. The aircraft on charge comprised Hadrian gliders and 5 Dakotas. The duration of each course was 10 days, depending on weather conditions, with 5 crews under instruction at one time.

15 men formed the 5 crews for No.1 Course commencing in February with a crew made up of a Pilot, Navigator and a Wireless Operator or Flight Engineer. Four of the men, who were slightly older than the rest, were RCAF personnel. Flt Lt R.T. Hyde, a 33 year-old American, who had been mentioned in despatches, was the most experienced of the four. Both he and Flt Lt J. Howden from Toronto were qualified pilots. The other two were Fg Off M. Scovell (nav) from Ontario and Fg Off Gerard Guay (WOP) from Winnipeg. There were

two RAAF personnel, 20 year old Flt Sgt A. Shaddick (pilot) from Western Australia and 21 year old Flt Sgt J. Allen (WOP/AG) from Queensland. The remainder were RAF personnel. Flt Sgt L. Slipper from Willesdon, Flt Lt T. Evans from Wales and Flt Lt A. Roberts from Purley were pilots. Fg Off S. Williams from Wales and Flt Sgt D. Grant from Chichester were navigators. Flt Sgt M. Gilder believed from Essex, Flt Sgt J.Ross from Newcastle-on-Tyne and Flt Sgt R. Jelfs from Bristol were Flt Engs. The 15th member of the course was 23 year old Flt Lt D. Turnball (WOP/AG) whose parents lived in Mexico City.

No.1 Course was completed by 19th February and plans were made for the course members to return to Leicester East. They were to travel in Dakota III TS436. Four ground staff going on leave joined the flight north. These were Flt Lt J. Heywood of Rochdale who was the Station Equipment Officer for Zeals, Cpl K. Anderson from Cambridge, AC2 R. E. Suggars and

Fg Off Sidney G. Williams

Flt Sgt James Ross

Flt Sgt Donald Grant

Sgt Ronald E. Jelfs

Front Row Centre - Sgt Thomas A. Evans RAF at No.31 ANS Port Albert, Ontario, Canada on 25th April 1942.

AC2 W. J. E. Colby from Northampton. The pilot of TS436 was Flt Lt M.R.S. *Bonzo* Mackay DFC, an instructor on the course with over 700 hours in his log book, which included

nearly 450 on Dakotas. Born in Kingston, Jamaica, he was a gifted sportsman and had a public school education. His father was an Army doctor and his grandfather a Presbyterian minister. The DFC was awarded for bravery at Arnhem when his No.48 Sqn aircraft came under intense fire with one engine damaged when attempting to drop supplies to ground forces. This necessitated a second run over the DZ, when he successfully dropped the containers, before flying his damaged aircraft back to base.

The navigator for the flight to Leicester East was Fg Off F. J. Plant from East Anglia who was normally the CO's navigator and was the only regular RAF man on board.

The low cloud which covered Zeals airfield that day was no doubt associated with showers and poor visibility and it was not until mid afternoon that the weather improved enough for Sqn Ldr Peters to authorise the flight. At 1523hrs the loaded Dakota, with Flt Lt Mackay at the controls took off from the grass runway. After making a quarter circuit of the airfield, the aircraft flew over the Watch Office at about 200' on a northerly course and after saying "goodbye" over the R/T, in a calm voice, the pilot altered course to N.E. This took it over the buildings at Search Farm and on the correct heading for Leicester East. At 1526hrs the aircraft flew in a laterally level attitude into a clump of 60' beech trees situated on top of a knoll, cutting 10' off of the port wing. The aircraft rolled to port, hit two more trees and finally impaled itself on a cluster of four large trees and caught

Flt Lt M.R.S. Mackay DFC.
Photo: Dr Anthony Foreman

A memorial service was held in St. Martins Church, Zeals on 25th February 1945, following which the four RCAF officers were buried at Brookwood in Surrey, the two Australians and four RAF men at Haycombe Military Cemetery in Bath, whilst the remainder were returned to their home towns.

Flt Lt Mackay recovered from his injuries and returned to flying duties with the GPTF by then based at Ibsley. He left the RAF during 1945 but, as a result of the 1947 Defence White Paper in which the University Air Squadron Scheme was reintroduced, he rejoined as an instructor teaching pupil pilots of the Oxford, Southampton and London University Air Squadrons.

fire. The airframe disintegrated and parts of the aircraft, including the engines, were catapulted forward, wreckage being spread over a distance of approximately 300yds down one slope on the north side of the knoll. All the occupants were killed except the pilot who, was amazingly thrown clear, and later taken to the military hospital at Guys Marsh, Shaftesbury with serious head and leg injuries and classified as "dangerously ill". Gp Capt J.A. Sadler the Chief Investigator of Accidents assembled a Court of Enquiry at Zeals airfield.

The Court of Enquiry Report states: "the cause of the accident cannot be definitely determined, but the evidence strongly suggests that it was due to pilot error..." Flt Lt Mackay found considerable difficulty in settling down after the accident. Understandably he was unable to come to terms with the fact that he had been the sole survivor from the aircraft of which he was the Captain. In 1948 he joined the Colonial Service and the following year was posted to Kenya to serve as a District Officer. Here on 23rd June 1949 at the lonely hill station of Glarissa he took his own life. Without doubt he was yet another casualty of war.

Beech Knoll and the missing trees above Search Farm, as seen today.

ABBREVIATIONS

AA	:	Anti-aircraft
AA	:	Automobile Association
AAR	:	Air to Air Refueling
A & A.E.E.	:	Aeroplane & Armament Experimental Establishment
AAIR	:	Aviation Archaeological Investigation & Research
AASF	:	Advanced Air Striking Force
AAC	:	Anti-aircraft Co-operation
AAC	:	Army Air Corps
AAI	:	Angle of Approach Indicator
AAR	:	Air to Air Refuelling
AAU	:	Aircraft Assembly Unit
AC	:	Army Co-operation
ACC	:	Army Co-operation Command
ACM	:	Air Chief Marshal
ACR	:	Airfield Control Radar
ADC	:	Aide-de-Camp
ADF	:	Aircraft Delivery Flight
ADGB	:	Air Defence of Great Britain
a/c	:	Aircraft
ADC	:	Aide-de-Camp
AE	:	Air Engineer
AEF	:	Air Experience Flight
AEO	:	Air Electronics Officer
AFB	:	Air Force Base
AFC	:	Air Force Cross
AFC	:	Australian Flying Corps
AFEE	:	Airborne Forces Experimental Establishment
AFEO	:	Air Force Experimental Officer
A/Flt.Lt.	:	Acting Flight Lieutenant
AFM	:	Air Force Medal
AFU	:	Advanced Flying Unit
A/G	:	Air Gunner
AI	:	Air Interception
Air Cdre	:	Air Commodore
A/LA	:	Acting Leading Airman
ALG	:	Advanced Landing Ground
AM	:	Albert Medal
AMWD	:	Air Ministry Works Department
AMSL	:	Above Mean Sea Level
ANS	:	Air Navigation School
AOC	:	Air Officer Commanding
AOC in C	:	Air Officer Commanding Chief
AOP	:	Artillery Observation Post
AQM	:	Air Quartermaster
APO	:	Acting Pilot Officer
ARCA	:	Associate of Royal College of Arts
ARS	:	Aeroplane Repair Shed
ASF	:	Aircraft Service Flight
ASI	:	Air Speed Indicator
AST	:	Air Services Training
ASU	:	Aircraft Storage Unit
ATA	:	Air Transport Auxiliary
ATC	:	Air Transport Command
ATC	:	Air Traffic Control
ATC	:	Air Training Corps
ATS	:	Auxiliary Territorial Service
ATSU	:	Air Transportable Signals Unit
AUW	:	All up weight
AVM	:	Air Vice Marshal
AVRO	:	Alliott Verdon-Roe
AWC	:	Asbestos Water-Proofing Compound
AW USAF	:	Air Lift Wing United States Air Force
B	:	Bomber (a/c role)
B/A	:	Bomb Aimer
BABS	:	Blind Approach Beacon System
BADU	:	Beam Approach Development Unit
BAe	:	British Aerospace
Balbos	:	Code name for large formations of fighter aircraft operating together. (Marshal Balbo was an Italian, who before the war had pioneered long-range flights by aircraft in formation).
BAOR	:	British Army of the Rhine
BATDU	:	Beam Approach Training Development Unit
BBC	:	British Broadcasting Corporation
BDP	:	Biological Department Porton
Bdr	:	Bombardier
BDU	:	Bomber Development Unit
BE	:	Bleriot Experimental
BEA	:	British European Airways
BLC	:	Boundary Layer Control
BOAC	:	British Overseas Airways Corporation
BOS	:	Balloon Operations Squadron
Bt	:	Baronet
BTU	:	Balloon Training Unit
BSc	:	Bachelor of Science
BUAS	:	Bristol University Air Squadron
Bullseye	:	Code name for a training exercise involving many aircraft, which also exercised ground crews and radar defence systems.
CAA	:	Civil Aviation Authority
CAACU	:	Civilian Anti-aircraft Co-operation Unit
CAEC	:	Casualty Air Evacuation Centre
CAPT	:	Captain
CATS	:	Civil Aviation Test Section
C&M	:	Care & Maintenance
CB	:	Companion (of the Order) of the Bath
CBDE	:	Chemical & Biological Defence Establishment
CBE	:	Commander (of the Order) of the British Empire
CDE	:	Chemical Defence Establishment

CDEE	:	Chemical Defence Experimental Establishment
CDES	:	Chemical Defence Experimental Station
Cdr	:	Commander
CE	:	Church of England
CFI	:	Chief Flying Instructor
CFS	:	Central Flying School
CGI	:	Chief Ground Instructor
CGM	:	Conspicuous Gallantry Medal
CH	:	Companion of Honour
C in C	:	Commander-in-Chief
Circus	:	Code name for bomber/fighter-bomber operation heavily escorted by fighters
Civ. Obs.	:	Civilian Observer
CND	:	Campaign for Nuclear Disarmament
CMG	:	Companion (of the Order) of St. Michael & St. George
CO	:	Commanding Officer
COB	:	Co-located Operating Base
COL	:	Colonel
COY	:	Company
Cpl	:	Corporal
CRO	:	Community Relations Officer
CSM	:	Company Sergeant Major
CTP	:	Chief Test Pilot
CU	:	Conversion Unit
CWES	:	Chemical Warfare Experimental Station
DAPM	:	Deputy Assistant Provost Marshal
DCM	:	Distinguished Conduct Medal
DERA	:	Defence Evaluation & Research Agency
DFC	:	Distinguished Flying Cross
DH	:	de Havilland
DL	:	Deputy Lieutenant
DNR	:	Department of Naval Recruiting
DSC	:	Distinguished Service Cross
DSO	:	Distinguished Service Order
DTEO	:	Defence Test Evaluation Organisation
DZ	:	Dropping Zone
E&RFTS	:	Elementary & Reserve Flying Training School
ECFS	:	Empire Central Flying School
EFTS	:	Elementary Flying Training School
EFS	:	Empire Flying School
ELG	:	Emergency Landing Ground
Eng.	:	Engineer
ETO	:	European Theatre of Operations
ETPS	:	Empire Test Pilots School
FA	:	Field Artillery
FAA	:	Fleet Air Arm
FAAM	:	Fleet Air Arm Museum
FAE	:	Fitter Aero Engine
FCU	:	Fleet Co-operation Unit
FEAF	:	Far East Air Force
Fg Off	:	Flying Officer
FI	:	Flying Instructor
FIS	:	Flying Instructors School
FIS(A)	:	Flying Instructors School (Advanced)
Flak	:	Fliegerabwehrkanone - enemy anti-aircraft gun
Flt	:	Flight
Flt Cdr	:	Flight Commander
Flt Eng	:	Flight Engineer
Flt Tech	:	Flight Technician
Flt Lt	:	Flight Lieutenant
Flt Sgt	:	Flight Sergeant
Flt Sub Lt	:	Flight Sub Lieutenant
FRAeS	:	Fellow of Royal Aeronautical Society
FRADU	:	Fleet Requirements Air Direction Unit
FSP	:	(Forward) Staging Post
FSTA	:	Future Strategic Tanker Aircraft
FTO	:	Flight Test Observer
FTS	:	Flying Training School
FTU	:	Ferry Training Unit
FUSAG	:	First US Army Group
Gardening	:	Code name for aircraft operating to lay mines in enemy waters
GBE	:	Knight Grand Cross (of the Order) of the British Empire
GCA	:	Ground Controlled Approach
GCB	:	Knight Grand Cross (of the Order) of the Bath
GCHQ	:	Government Communications Headquarters
GCI	:	Ground Controlled Interception
GCIE	:	Knight Grand Commander (of the Order) of the Indian Empire
GCSI	:	Knight Grand Commander (of the Order) of the Star of India
Gee	:	A radio navigational aid
GI	:	General Infantry
GOC	:	General Officer Commanding
Gp Capt	:	Group Captain
GPEU	:	Glider Pilot Exercise Unit
GPR	:	Glider Pilot Regiment
GPTF	:	Glider Pilot Training Flight
GR	:	General Reconnaissance (a/c role)
GS	:	General Service
GTS	:	Glider Training School
GWR	:	Great Western Railway
HAD	:	Home Aircraft Depot
HAF	:	High Altitude Flight
HAS	:	Hardened Aircraft Shelter
HDF	:	Halifax Development Flight
HDU	:	Helicopter Development Unit
HE	:	High Explosive
HGCU	:	Heavy Glider Conversion Unit
HMS	:	His Majesty's Ship
HQ	:	Headquarters
HRH	:	His Royal Highness
H2S	:	An air to ground radar navigation and target identification aid
IFF	:	Identification, Friend or Foe
ILS	:	Instrument Landing System
Instep	:	Code name for fighter interception of German aircraft attacking shipping in the South Western approaches

Intruder	:	Code name for offensive night operations to a fixed point or specific target.
ITW	:	Initial Training Wing
JWE	:	Joint Warfare Establishment
K	:	One Thousand
KBE	:	Knight Commander (of the Order) of the British Empire
KCB	:	Knight Commander (of the Order) of the Bath
LAC	:	Leading Aircraftsman
LACW	:	Leading Aircraftwomen
LDV	:	Local Defence Volunteer
L/Cpl	:	Lance Corporal
Lt	:	Lieutenant
Lt Col	:	Lieutenant Colonel
Lt Cdr	:	Lieutenant Commander
Lt Cmd	:	Lieutenant Commander
LZ	:	Landing Zone
MAP	:	Ministry of Aircraft Production
MBE	:	Member (of the Order) of the British Empire
M/Eng	:	Master Engineer
M/Sgt	:	Master Sergeant
Maj	:	Major
Maj Gen	:	Major General
MC	:	Military Cross
MCSU	:	Mobile Catering Support Unit
MI	:	Medical Inspection
MIMgt	:	Member of the Institute of Management
MN	:	Merchant Navy
MoD	:	Ministry of Defence
Monica	:	A radar aid to detect approach of hostile aircraft from astern
MO	:	Medical Orderly/Medical Officer
MP	:	Member of Parliament
mph	:	Miles Per Hour
MRAeS	:	Member of the Royal Aeronautical Society
MRAF	:	Marshal of the Royal Air Force
MRD	:	Microbiological Research Department
MRE	:	Microbiological Research Establishment
MRF	:	Meteorological Research Flight
M.Sig.	:	Master Signaller
MT	:	Motor Transport
MTRS	:	Mechanical Transport Reception Section
MU	:	Maintenance Unit
MVO	:	Member of the Royal Victorian Order
NAAFI	:	Navy, Army & Air Force Institutes
NASA	:	North American Space Agency
NATO	:	North Atlantic Treaty Organisation
NAV	:	Navigator
NCO	:	Non Commissioned Officer
NFS	:	Night Fighter Squadron
NFS	:	National Fire Service
NFT	:	Night Flying Test

Nickelling	:	Code name for aircraft dropping generally propaganda leaflets
nm	:	Nautical Miles
NMRO	:	National Monument Record Office
NWFP	:	North West Frontier Province
NZEF	:	New Zealand Expeditionary Force
OBE	:	Officer (of the Order) of the British Empire
OC	:	Officer Commanding
OCU	:	Operational Conversion Unit
ORB	:	Operational Record Book
ORTU	:	Operational & Refresher Training Unit
OTU	:	Operational Training Unit
(P)	:	Proto-type
(P)AFU	:	(Pilot) Advanced Flying Unit
PAF	:	Polish Air Force
PC	:	Police Constable
PC	:	Privy Councillor
PE	:	Pressure Errors
PE	:	Procurement Executive
Pfc	:	Private First Class
Plt Off	:	Pilot Officer
PO	:	Petty Officer
POL	:	Packed Oil and Greases
PoW	:	Prisoner of War
PP	:	Permanent Pass
PR	:	Photographic Reconnaissance
PRC	:	Personnel Reception Centre
PSF	:	Parachute Servicing Flight
PSP	:	Pierced Steel Planking
PT	:	Physical Training
Pvt	:	Private
QC	:	Queen's Councel
QFI	:	Qualified Flying Instructor
RA	:	Royal Artillery
RAF	:	Royal Air Force
RAAF	:	Royal Australian Air Force
RAFVR	:	Royal Airforce Volunteer Reserve
Ranger	:	Code name for deep penetration flights to engage targets of opportunity
Ramrod	:	Code name for 'Circus' type operation but with a specific target
RAeC	:	Royal Aero Club
RAOC	:	Royal Army Ordnance Corps
RASC	:	Royal Army Service Corps
RAT	:	Radio Aids Training
RATF	:	Radar Aids Training Flight
RAuxAF	:	Royal Auxiliary Air Force
RCAF	:	Royal Canadian Air Force
RDF	:	Radio Direction Finding
RE	:	Royal Engineers
Rev/Revd	:	Reverend
RFA	:	Royal Field Artillery
RFC	:	Royal Flying Corps.
RFS	:	Reserve Flying School
R/G	:	Rear Gunner
Rgt	:	Regiment

R & I	:	Repairs & Inspections
RLG	:	Relief Landing Ground
RM	:	Royal Marine
RMLI	:	Royal Marine Light Infantry
RN	:	Royal Navy
RNAS	:	Royal Naval Air Service
RNR	:	Royal Naval Reserve
RNVR	:	Royal Naval Volunteer Reserve
RNZAF	:	Royal New Zealand Air Force
RPC	:	Royal Pioneer Corps
RRAF	:	Royal Rhodesian Air Force
R/T	:	Radio Transmitter
Rodeo	:	Code name for fighter sweep
Rhubarb	:	Code name for small-scale raids by fighter or fighter-bombers against targets of opportunity
RSM	:	Regimental Sergeant Major
RTM	:	Rotary Transmission Mode
S of AC	:	School of Army Co-operation
S of AS	:	School of Air Support
SAAF	:	South African Air Force
SAC	:	Strategic Air Command
SAOEU	:	Strike Attack Operational Evacuation Unit
SAS	:	Scandinavian Air Services
SAS	:	Special Air Services
SASO	:	Senior Air Staff Officer
SC11	:	Schutte-Lanz
SDF	:	Special Duties Flight
SCI	:	Smoke Curtain Installation
SFTS	:	Service Flying Training School
Sgt	:	Sergeant
SHQ	:	Squadron Headquarters
SLG	:	Satellite Landing Ground
SN & BD	:	School of Navigation and Bomb Dropping
SOC	:	Squadron Operations Centre
SOC	:	Struck Off Charge
SOE	:	Special Operations Executive
Sqn	:	Squadron
Sqn Cdr	:	Squadron Commander
Sqn Ldr	:	Squadron Leader
SP	:	Service Police
SR	:	Southern Region
S/Sgt	:	Staff Sergeant
SS	:	Steamship
SS	:	Sub Stratosphere
SSQ	:	Station Sick Quarters
ST	:	Saddle Tank
Stn Cdr	:	Station Commander
SUAS	:	Southampton University Air Squadron
Sub Lt	:	Sub Lieutenant
Sweep	:	Terminology for an offensive flight over sea or enemy territory
TA	:	Territorial Army
TAC	:	Tactical Air Command
TAD	:	Tactical Air Depot
TAF	:	Tactical Air Force
TB	:	Torpedo Bomber (a/c role)
TCG	:	Troop Carrier Group
TDS	:	Training Depot Station
TEU	:	Tactical Exercise Unit

TFS	:	Tactical Fighter Squadron
TFW	:	Tactical Fighter Wing
TNT	:	trinitrotoluene
TP	:	Test Pilot
TS	:	Training Squadron
TSR	:	Torpedo Spotter Reconnaissance
UAS	:	University Air Squadron
UDI	:	Unilateral Declaration of Independence
UK	:	United Kingdom
UN	:	United Nations
US	:	United States
USAF	:	United States Air Force
USAAF	:	United States Army Air Force
USN	:	United States Navy
USS	:	United States Ship
VC	:	Victoria Cross
VIP's	:	Very Important Persons
VISTRE	:	Visual Inter-Service Training & Research Establishment
VOR	:	Very High Frequency Omni-directional Range
WAC	:	Women's Army Corps
WACO	:	Weaver Aircraft Company
WAAF	:	Women's Auxiliary Air Force
WAECO	:	Wessex Aircraft Engineering Company
Wg Cdr	:	Wing Commander
WIDU	:	Wireless Interception Development Unit
W/O	:	Warrant Officer
WOC	:	Wing Operations Centre
W/Op	:	Wireless Operator
WOP	:	Wireless Operator
WT	:	Wireless Telegraphy
WVS	:	Women's Voluntary Service
YMCA	:	Young Men's Christian Association
*	:	Bar to a decoration

BIBLIOGRAPHY

Air-Britain, *Aeromilitaria* (various).

Airfield Research Group, *Airfield Review* (various).

Ashworth, Chris, *Action Stations 5 & 9* (Patrick Stevens Ltd, 1982/85).

Berry, David, *The Whispering Giant in Uniform* (Keyham Books, 1996).

Beslievre, June, *Still The Candle Burns* Jersey Cheshire Home Foundation, 1997

Blake, Lord, & Nicholls C.S, *The Dictionary of National Biography 1971-1980* (Oxford University Press, 1986).

Bowyer, Chaz, *For Valour-Thomas Gray VC* (Halton Magazine, Summer 1983).

Bowyer, Chaz, *Mosquito at War* (Ian Allan Ltd, 1974).

Broke-Smith, P.W.L., *History of Early British Military Aeronautics* (Library Association, 1968).

Brookes, Andrew, *Crash; Military Aircraft Disasters, Accidents and Incidents* (Ian Allan, 1991).

Bryan, Tim, *The Great Western at War 1939-1945* (Patrick Stephens Ltd, 1995).

Caine, Philip D, *Spitfires, Thunderbolts, and Warm Beer* (Brassey's 1995).

Campbell, Len, *Netheravon Airfield Camp 1913* (Self Published).

Cedric, Marquis of Ailesbury, *Setting My Watch By The Sundial*

Clifford, Nigel, *RAF Hullavington 1935-45.*

Chorley, Bill, *RAF Bomber Command Losses of the Second World War Vol 1-7* (Midland Counties Publications, 1992-2002).

Colerne History Group, *The Village on the Hill* (Self Published, 1995.

Congdon, Philip, *Per Ardua Ad Astra* (Airlife Publishing Ltd, 1994).

Crawford, Terry S. *Wiltshire and the Great War* (DPF Publishing, 1999).

Crosley, R.M. Comm. DSC*,RN. *Up In Harm's Way* (Airlife Publishing Ltd, 1995).

Dallas Brett, R. *History of British Aviation 1908-1914* Vol.1&11 (The Aviation Book Club).

Delve, Ken. *The Source Book Of The RAF* (Airlife Publishing Ltd, 1994).

De Normann, Roderick, *For Fuhrer and Fatherland* (Sutton Publishing Ltd, 1996).

Drew, P.R, *A Short History of Colerne Airfield* (Self Published, 1990).

Files from the Public Record Office, Kew (various).

Files from the Wiltshire County Record Office (various).

Ford-Jones, Martyn & Valerie, *Oxford's Own* (Schiffer Publishing Ltd, 1999).

Francis, Paul, *British Military Airfield Architecture* (Patrick Stephens Ltd, 1996).

Freeman, Roger A, *U.K. Airfields of the Ninth Then and Now*, (After The Battle).

Gibson, Mary, *Warneford, VC* (The Fleet Air Arm Museum, 1979).

Green, Geoff, *Bristol Aerospace* (Geoff Green, 1990).

Guild, Frank Jr. *Action of the Tiger* (The Battery Press, Inc., 1980).

Halley MBE, James J, *Broken Wings* (Air Britain, 1999).

Haycock, Lorna, *The History of W.E. Chivers & Sons: A Century of Building 1884-1985* (Pipers Publications).

Jackson, G.F., *A Tale of Two Manors, Zeals-A Wiltshire Village*, (Dickins Printers-1997)

James N.D.G, *Plain Soldiering* (The Hobnob Press, 1987).

Jefford MBE, C.G, *RAF Squadrons* (Airlife Publishing Ltd, 1988).

Johnson, Brian, *Test Pilot* (BBC Publications, 1986).

Johnson, Brian & Heffernan Terry, *A Most Secret Place* (Jane's Publishing Co. Ltd, 1982).

Lewis, Gwilym H, *Wings over the Somme 1916-1918* (William Kimber & Co. Ltd, 1976).

Lyall, Andrew, Major DFC, *Memoirs of An Air Observation Post Officer* (Picton Publishing (Chippenham) Ltd, 1985)

Marshall, Sir Arthur, *The Marshall Story* (Patrick Stephens Ltd, 1994).

Mason Francis K, *Battle Over Britain* (McWhirter Twins Ltd, 1969).

Mason, Peter D, *Nicolson VC* (Geerings of Ashford Ltd, 1991).

McCudden, VC, James, *Flying Fury* (Greenhill Books, 2000).

Middlebrook, Martin & Everitt Chris, *The Bomber Command War Diaries* (Midland Publishing Ltd, 1996).

No.16 Sqn Association, *Newsbrief* No.16 Squadron 1939-45.

No.437 Sqn Members, *437 Squadron History*, Hangar Books, 1985).

Priddle, Rod & Hyde, David, *GWR to Devizes* (Millstream Books, 1996).

Robertson, Bruce, *British Military Aircraft Serials 1911-1979* (Patrick Stephens Ltd, 1979).

Russell C.R, *Spitfire Postscript* (C.R. Russell, 1994).

Shores, Christopher, Franks, Norman & Guest, Russell, *Above the Trenches* (Grub Street, 1996).

Smith, David J, *Britain's Military Airfields* (Patrick Stephens Ltd, 1989).

Smith T.M & Heathcliffe G.S, *The Highworth Branch* (Wild Swan Pubs.Ltd, 1979).

Sturtivant Ray, Hamlin John, Halley James. J, *RAF Flying Training & Support Units* (Air-Britain Historians Ltd, 1997).

Sykes, Sir Frederick, *From Many Angles* (George G Harrop & Co. Ltd, 1942).

Taylor, John W.R., *CFS Birthplace of Air Power* (Putnam, 1958).

Tredrey, F.D, *Pioneer Pilot* (Peter Davies Ltd, 1976).

The Keevil Society, *A Book of Keevil*, (The Keevil Society, 1998).

Van Hees, Arie-Jan, *Tugs and Gliders to Arnhem* (Self Published, 2001).

Wakefield Ken, *The Fighting Grasshoppers* (Midland Counties Publications, 1990).

Wakefield Ken, *Operation Bolero* (Crecy Books Ltd, 1994.)

Warneford, Francis E, *The Warnefords* (Alan Sutton Publishing Ltd, 1991).

Williams E.T. & Palmer, Helen M, *The Dictionary of National Biography 1951-1960* (Oxford University Press, 1971).

Willis Steve & Holliss Barry, *Military Airfields in the British Isles 1939-1945* (Enthusiasts Publications, 1990).

Wood Alan, *History of the World's Glider Forces* (Patrick Stephens Ltd, (1990).

Woosnam, Maxwell, *Eilmer* (Friends of Malmesbury Abbey, 1986).

Wroughton History Group, *Wroughton Through to the 60's* (1997).

Fg Off Peter Ernest Nolan RAFVR (pilot) was killed on Thursday 30th August 1945. When the engine of his Mosquito caught fire, he held the aircraft steady to allow his navigator to bale out at 200ft. The pilot then followed but his parachute failed to fully open before he struck the ground and was killed. Peter Nolan was buried on Wednesday 5th September at All Saints Church, East Harnham, Salisbury. It was there on this date that this 21 year old airman was due to have been married.

> My brief sweet life is over, my eyes no longer see,
> No summer walks, no Christmas Trees, no pretty girls for me.
> I've got the 'chop', I've had it. My nightly ops. are done,
> Yet in a hundred years from now…. I'll still be twenty one.

These words form the epitaph of a poem, *Requiem For A Rear Gunner* written by Sgt Ralph W. Gilbert RAF, who was a mid-upper gunner on Halifaxes with No.158 Sqn. It is reproduced with the kind permission of his widow Mary, a former WAAF.

Location Map

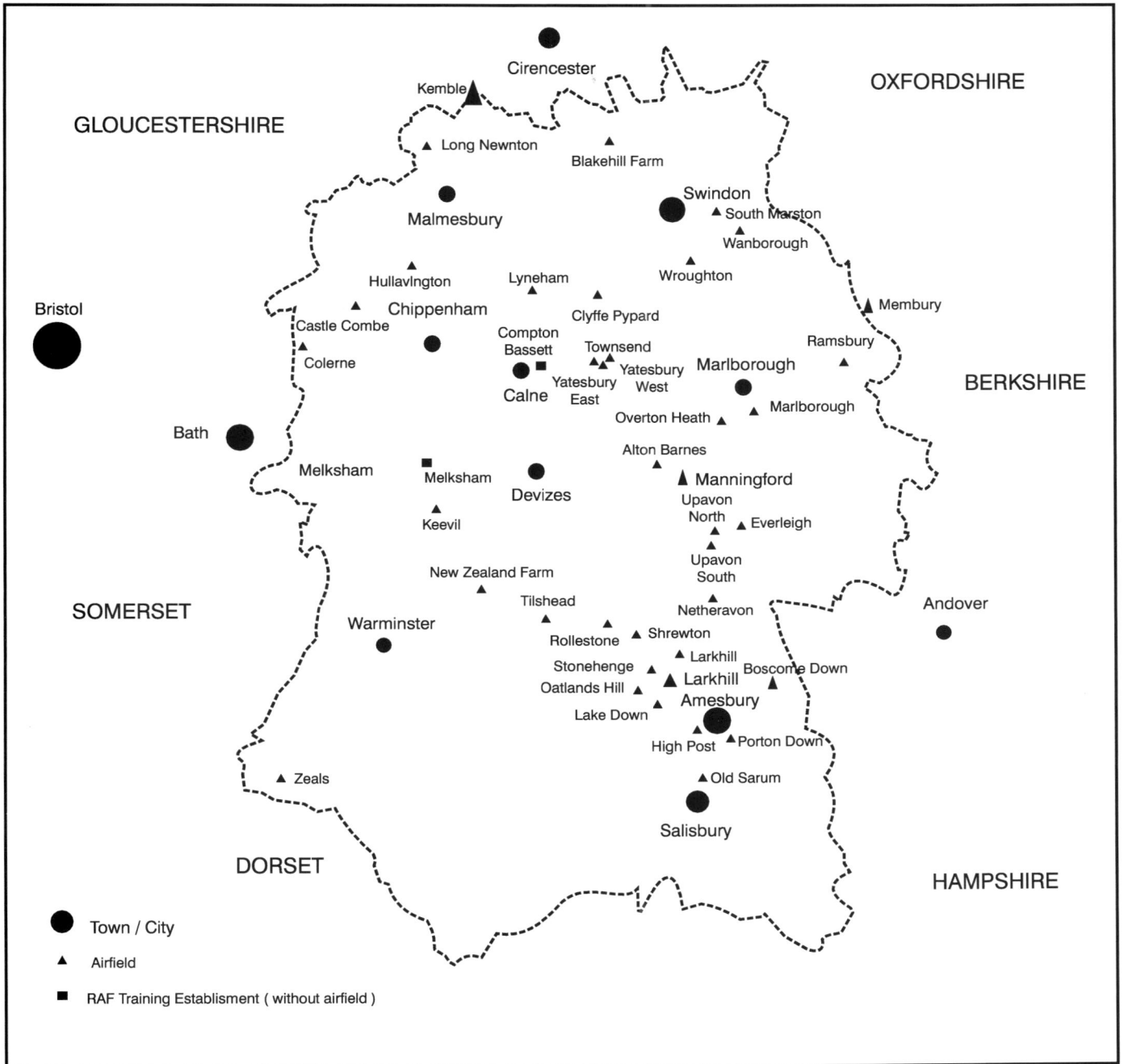

Cirencester

Kemble

OXFORDSHIRE

GLOUCESTERSHIRE

Long Newnton

Blakehill Farm

Swindon

Malmesbury

South Marston

Wanborough

Hullavington

Lyneham

Wroughton

Bristol

Chippenham

Clyffe Pypard

Membury

Castle Combe

Compton Bassett

Townsend

Ramsbury

Colerne

Calne

Yatesbury West

Marlborough

BERKSHIRE

Yatesbury East

Marlborough

Overton Heath

Bath

Alton Barnes

Melksham

Melksham

Devizes

Manningford

Keevil

Upavon North

Everleigh

New Zealand Farm

Upavon South

SOMERSET

Tilshead

Netheravon

Andover

Warminster

Rollestone

Shrewton

Larkhill

Stonehenge

Larkhill

Boscombe Down

Oatlands Hill

Amesbury

Lake Down

High Post

Porton Down

Zeals

Old Sarum

Salisbury

DORSET

HAMPSHIRE

● Town / City

▲ Airfield

■ RAF Training Establisment (without airfield)

397